GS 4.113:983/bk.2

CO-AUT-911

GOVERNMENT DOCUMENTS
RAMAKER LIBRARY

SEP 3   1986

NORTHWESTERN COLLEGE
ORANGE CITY, IOWA 51041

DATE DUE

PUBLIC PAPERS OF THE PRESIDENTS
OF THE
UNITED STATES

PUBLIC PAPERS OF THE PRESIDENTS
OF THE
UNITED STATES

Ronald Reagan

1983

(IN TWO BOOKS)

BOOK II—JULY 2 TO DECEMBER 31, 1983

UNITED STATES GOVERNMENT PRINTING OFFICE
WASHINGTON : 1985

RAMAKER LIBRARY
NORTHWESTERN COLLEGE
ORANGE CITY, IOWA 51041

Published by the
Office of the Federal Register
National Archives and Records Administration

For sale by the
Superintendent of Documents
U.S. Government Printing Office
Washington, D.C. 20402

Foreword

The last half of 1983 was a time when America's role in the world was tested and strengthened.

At home, our economy continued to improve. The rate of inflation remained on a downward trend. Housing starts were up and new jobs—the most important and encouraging sign of economic recovery—were on the rise. The prosperity we had so earnestly sought was finally becoming a reality.

Our attention was largely focused, however, on events away from our shores. The perilous situation in the Middle East continued to present a challenge to all of us who seek a genuine and lasting peace. In Central America, the courage and determination of those dedicated to democracy served as an inspiration to all of us. And in the Pacific, the tragic incident of KAL flight 007 was a poignant and painful reminder to all of us that there is a difference between our values and those of the Soviet Union.

My travels to Japan and Korea were important parts of our efforts to strengthen our relations with two of our most valued allies. In Tokyo and Seoul, we reaffirmed our shared commitment to the ideals of freedom and showed the world that we stand together. Perhaps the most meaningful moment of 1983 came at the demilitarized zone between South and North Korea. There, where our young men and women put their lives on the line every day, the greatness of America can be found—greatness which comes from our willingness to continue the fight for liberty for people we may never meet.

Ronald Reagan

Preface

This book contains the papers and speeches of the 40th President of the United States that were issued by the Office of the Press Secretary during the period July 2-December 31, 1983. The material has been compiled and published by the Office of the Federal Register, National Archives and Records Administration.

The material is presented in chronological order, and the dates shown in the headings are the dates of the documents or events. In instances when the release date differs from the date of the document itself, that fact is shown in the textnote. Every effort has been made to ensure accuracy. Tape recordings of Presidential remarks are used to protect against errors in transcription, and signed documents are checked against the original to verify the correct printing. Textnotes, footnotes, and cross references have been provided by the editors for purposes of identification or clarity. Speeches were delivered in Washington, D.C., unless indicated. The times noted are local times. All materials that are printed full-text in the book have been indexed in the subject and name indexes.

The Public Papers series was begun in 1957 in response to a recommendation of the National Historical Publications Commission. An extensive compilation of messages and papers of the Presidents covering the period 1789 to 1897 was assembled by James D. Richardson and published under congressional authority between 1896 and 1899. Since then, various private compilations have been issued, but there was no uniform publication comparable to the Congressional Record or the United States Supreme Court Reports. Many Presidential papers could be found only in the form of mimeographed White House releases or as reported in the press. The Commission therefore recommended the establishment of an official series in which Presidential writings, addresses, and remarks of a public nature could be made available.

The Commission's recommendation was incorporated in regulations of the Administrative Committee of the Federal Register, issued under section 6 of the Federal Register Act (44 U.S.C. 1506), which may be found in Title I, Part 10, of the Code of Federal Regulations.

A companion publication to the Public Papers series, the Weekly Compilation of Presidential Documents, was begun in 1965 to provide a broader range of Presidential materials on a more timely basis to meet the needs of the contemporary reader. Beginning with the administration of Jimmy Carter, the Public Papers series expanded its coverage to include all material as printed in the Weekly Compilation. That coverage provides a listing of the President's daily schedule and meetings, when announced, and other items of general interest issued by the Office of the Press Secretary. Also included are lists of the President's nominations submitted to the Senate, materials released by the Office of the Press Secretary that are not printed full-text in the book, and acts approved by the President. This information appears in the appendixes at the end of the book.

Volumes covering the administrations of Presidents Hoover, Truman, Eisenhower, Kennedy, Johnson, Nixon, Ford, and Carter are also available.

The Chief Editor of this book was Thomas D. Kevan.

White House liaison was provided by Larry M. Speakes, Assistant to the President and Deputy Press Secretary. The frontispiece and photographs used in the portfolio were supplied by the White House Photo Office.

John E. Byrne
Director of the Federal Register

Frank G. Burke
Acting Archivist of the United States

Contents

Administration of Ronald Reagan

1983

Radio Address to the Nation on the Observance of Independence Day
July 2, 1983

My fellow Americans:

On Monday, America will celebrate her 207th birthday. I love the Fourth of July. I enjoy picnics and fireworks and long summer days, and I get excited with the thought that millions of our people all across our great country will, on this Fourth of July weekend, join together in thinking about freedom and the men and women who sacrificed to make it our inheritance.

It's easy to forget just what a revolution these Americans made. It's easy to forget how they amazed the world and how many hopes they raised. President George Washington, in the very first Inaugural Address, warned Americans that they had a new responsibility. He said, ". . . the preservation of the sacred fire of liberty and the destiny of the republican model of government are justly considered, perhaps, as *deeply,* as *finally,* staked on the experiment intrusted to the hands of the American people."

Now, you may not think of yourself or our democracy as an experiment, but look around. All over the world, millions and millions of people still live under tyranny. Their leaders claim that they're the wave of the future, that history is on their side. And yet, their people look to us for hope. Their people look to America as the cradle of freedom, the place where the great civilized ideas of individual liberty, representative government, and the rule of law under God are realities.

Yes, these people see America as the experiment that works. And democracy works because of the physical and moral courage of individuals—some famous, others deserving of recognition.

I think of a group of women we honored in Washington this past April, an honor long overdue. They were nurses who'd been captured in the Philippines during World War II and then spent nearly 3 years in prison camps. Lieutenant Colonel Madeline Ullom, who was captured at Corregidor, has described tending wounded soldiers during the long months of siege: "Our atmosphere was one of dusty pall, ever present, in which we moved, worked, tried to eat, tried to breathe in an endless nightmare," she said.

In Santa Tomas Prison Camp, Colonel Ullom and her fellow nurses quickly organized into shifts and began to care for other prisoners. They fought against diseases and starvation. They lacked medicine and equipment and food. But miraculously, every one of the 81 American women POW's had survived.

These women would not describe themselves as extraordinary Americans; they simply volunteered to serve their country, and they chose to serve it with courage and hope. Their patriotism, as they gathered in Washington 40 years after their capture and imprisonment, remained strong and vibrant.

Of course, we're accustomed to thinking of courage during a time of war, but democracy requires political courage as well. In 1954, when he was convalescing from a painful back operation, Senator John F. Kennedy had time to think about political courage. The result was a book entitled "Profiles in Courage," in which he wrote, "In the days ahead, only the very courageous will be able to take the hard and unpopular decisions necessary for our survival in the struggle with a powerful enemy. And only the very courageous will be able to keep alive the spirit of individualism and dissent which gave birth to this nation, nourished it as an infant, and carried it through its severest tests upon the attainment of its maturity."

We've seen a great example of this kind

of political courage just recently when a majority, made up of both Republicans and Democrats in the Congress, set aside narrow political considerations and embraced a bipartisan program for enhancing America's security and stability through meaningful arms reductions and modernization of our defenses.

It was not easy for many of these men and women to vote for the MX missile. Some have been harshly criticized by other Members in their own party. Indeed, they faced considerable pressure and corresponding political risks. While accepting such risks, the only benefit they've received is the knowledge that they placed foremost their hopes for successful arms reductions and greater security of their nation.

Together with the Congress, we're doing everything possible to achieve genuine arms reductions. Our negotiators have been given instructions that provide greater flexibility in our negotiations with the Soviet Union. The proposals are fair, realistic, and would bring a much greater degree of stability for all the peoples of the world. There's absolutely no doubt that the prospects for success in our negotiations have been significantly improved because of the political courage shown by the Congress.

The task now is to be patient and to sustain our resolve. On this Fourth of July weekend, I salute those Members of the Congress who are putting the interests of America first. They're part of a long American tradition of proving democracy's critics wrong—of showing that we have the courage to stand up for what is right and what is necessary.

Our democratic experiment is alive and well at year 207. And with the help of the kind of political leadership and vision that we've seen in recent weeks, we can count on many happy returns.

Until next week, God bless you, and God bless America.

Note: The President spoke at 9:06 a.m. from Rancho del Cielo, his ranch near Santa Barbara, Calif.

Message to the Nation on the Observance of Independence Day
July 3, 1983

My fellow Americans:

Today we join together to celebrate freedom's birthday. America is 207 years old. That makes us the oldest living democracy on Earth. I think there's a good reason for that.

It's always been my belief that by a Divine plan this nation was placed between the two oceans to be sought out and found by those with a special brand of courage and love of freedom. Can we imagine the courage it took back in 1620 to pick up family, bid goodby to friends, board those small ships, and set sail across a mighty ocean toward a new future in an unknown world?

Can we appreciate what the patriots endured in that bone-cold snow at Valley Forge when they spent a winter without enough food or medicine or even boots to cover their feet? Maybe we can't. Maybe we look around our more comfortable world of 1983 and say, "That's more than we've known or could endure."

But look closer. Look in our own neighborhoods and families, and you will see America is still a land of heroes with all the courage and love of freedom that ever was before. And that's our best hope for the future.

We've seen our heroes at Normandy, Bastogne, Guadalcanal, and Pork Chop Hill. We saw the agony of our POW's inside prison camps in North Vietnam. We held our breath, then rejoiced and cried when they finally came home, kissed the ground, and thanked God they were free.

We're a melting pot. And our body and spirit have never been stronger or richer, thanks to hundreds of thousands of new heroes—the brave men, women, and children who risked death to escape their communist prisons in Asia and Cuba. They arrived less than 10 years ago. Most were not able to speak a word of English. But with their courage and faith, they brought unbounded determination to work, produce, succeed, and excel. Now, more and more of them are becoming leaders in their communities—small businessowners, hard-working taxpayers, even valedictorians in their high school graduating class. We can be proud and thankful that they're joining us today in parades and ballgames and backyard barbecues as young members of an old family.

We can salute the heroes of our technological age, like the four-man, one-woman crew of the *Challenger*. They dazzled America and the world with another perfect mission into the new frontier of space.

And how can we ignore the countless other examples of courage and love of neighbor from everyday Americans—people like that grandmother in New York who collared a robber and gave him the back of her hand until the police arrived; people all across the country who've been battling angry spring floods and rising rivers so they could save the property and maybe the lives of their families and friends.

Don't let anyone tell us that America's best days are behind her, that the American spirit has been lost. I've never felt stronger than I do now that our people are coming together and that America is moving forward again. I've never been more convinced that fundamental problems of the economy, education, and national defense—neglected for too many years—are now being addressed and can be solved.

They will be solved if we believe in each other and in those values that make us a great and loving people. Think about it. We work and educate for freedom, for service of the ideal of liberty, not for subservience to the state.

Our notion of education is the most revolutionary idea conceived by mankind. When our scholars and teachers learn something

new, they can't wait to teach it to our children. But in a totalitarian country, you're not allowed to read books or discuss ideas that aren't approved by censors. You're not allowed to have a computer in your home, because you might obtain information or knowledge that would make you a threat to the state.

Let us remember this July 4th that America's Revolution remains unique because it's changed the very concept of government. We are the Nation which proudly announced to the world: We are conceived in liberty. Each of us is created equal, with God-given rights, and power ultimately resides in "We the people."

We, the people, have only begun to write a great story that will be passed down through time—the story of America. I'm reminded of a verse I once read about Old Glory. The Red, White, and Blue is a testament to the unity and patriotism of our people and to the deep love and commitment we have for our country, our freedom, and our way of life. The verse was written as if the flag was speaking to us, now and for generations to come.

It said:

> I am whatever you make me, nothing more.
> I am your belief in yourself, your dream of what a people may become.
> I am a day's work of the weakest man and the largest dream of the most daring.
> I am the clutch of an idea and the reasoned purpose of resolution.
> I am no more than you believe me to be and I am all that you believe I can be.
> I am whatever you make me, nothing more.

Happy Fourth of July, and may God bless America.

Note: The President's remarks were taped on June 27 at the White House.

Remarks at the Annual Convention of the American Federation of Teachers in Los Angeles, California
July 5, 1983

I can't think of a more appropriate place to be on July 5th, the morning after our 207th national birthday, than at a gathering of the men and women responsible for America's future.

Yours is a sacred mission. In the words of Henry Adams, "A teacher affects eternity." Each of you, as tiring and routine as your daily duties may sometimes seem, is a keeper of the American dream, the American future. By informing and exercising young minds, by transmitting learning and values, you are the vital link between all that is most precious in our national heritage and our children and grandchildren, who will some day take up the burdens of guiding the greatest, freest society on Earth.

I'm also particularly happy to be addressing a gathering of the American Federation of Teachers. Oh, I know there's a pretty big education organization out there, but it's been my experience that dedication, open-mindedness, and initiative count for just as much as size. It seems to me that in all three categories the AFT, like Avis, tries a lot harder. For this, you have my sincere admiration and my pledge to work with you in building a creative, lasting dialog on a subject close to all our hearts: the renewal of excellence in American education.

Of course, we have our differences, and both this administration and the AFT believe in the benefits of vigorous debate. And that's what living in an open, free society is all about. We've both made our positions well known. And I'm not here today as a salesman trying to peddle a prepackaged, all-purpose, off-the-rack education program. I am fully aware that there are some major areas where we disagree—matters like tuition tax credits and vouchers. But it's the very genius of our democratic, pluralistic system, our society, the key to its unequaled success over more than two centuries, that individuals who sincerely disagree on some matters can still work together in mutual respect and understanding

to serve a higher goal. And I defy anyone to name a higher common goal of domestic policy than working for a renaissance in American education.

Not that long ago, American public education was one of the marvels of the world. Wave after wave of immigrants from the far corners of the Earth came to our shores with little more than the clothes on their backs and hope in their hearts. Many were illiterate, victims of grinding poverty here as well as in the old country. But the public school system, often within a single generation, provided a magic ladder to full participation in American life. And it taught their children more than just the skills they needed for a more abundant life; it taught them the solid values of good citizenship.

To a very large extent, America's schools provided the social bond that gave meaning to the word "America"—that made us, in the midst of our ethnic diversity, "one nation under God, indivisible, with liberty and justice for all."

And, you know, speaking of that, I don't know whether—I just came across this little item the other day about a teacher at a very, very beginning level of elementary education, who was having a little trouble at that tender age—his students, in telling them about how you, where you put your hand when you recited the Pledge and all. They didn't really know the location of the internal organs, and putting their hand on their heart didn't mean too much to them. And finally he showed the ingenuity that is typical of good teaching. He told them to put their hands on the alligators. [*Laughter*]

But, yes, to a very great extent, it was our schools where most Americans heard and spoke the Pledge of Allegiance for the first time that transformed those heart-stirring words into a living ideal, an ideal each generation has come closer to attaining.

Our public schools have played a great historic role in shaping our democracy, and they have a crucial role to play today. You in the AFT can help lead the way, and that's why I'm less deterred by the differences between us than I am encouraged by the important areas of agreement that we share.

The AFT wants to upgrade standards— including emphasis on testing both students and beginning teachers, changing curriculum to strengthen academic requirements, and increasing homework assignments. Well, so do I.

The AFT believes in stricter discipline codes in schools—including provisions to remove students who have histories of repeated disruptive behavior. So do I.

The AFT supports many aspects of this administration's bilingual education legislation, which favors local autonomy in deciding what method will be most effective to teach children who are limited in their ability to speak English. We both agree that children who are truly in need and cannot function in English in a regular classroom environment deserve help. But we also recognize that bilingual programs should serve as a bridge to full participation in the American mainstream. They should never permanently segregate non-English-speaking students in a way that will make it harder, not easier, for them to succeed in life.

There are so many other values and beliefs that we share. The AFT understands the importance of a strong national defense, not just for our own sake but for the sake of our friends and allies in the Americas, Europe, Asia, and the Middle East. Only a strong, credible America can preserve our freedom at home, deter aggression, pursue the cause of meaningful arms reductions, and stand by our friends in time of need.

I also want to commend the AFT for its recognition of the need to upgrade math and science education and for its ringing condemnation of those organizations, one of which I referred to earlier, who would exploit teaching positions and manipulate curriculum for propaganda purposes. On this last issue, you stand in bright contrast to those who have promoted curriculum guides that seem to be more aimed at frightening and brainwashing American schoolchildren, than at fostering learning and stimulating balanced, intelligent debate.

Working together, we can accomplish so much. And we know there is so much to do. When I ran for President in 1980, I said that this country must recognize the problems in our educational system and start doing something about them.

For one thing, many teachers were facing a virtual mission impossible. I noted at the time that you'd been forced to deal with negative, often destructive trends from outside your classrooms. We can only admire the dedication with which the great majority of teachers has tried to meet these problems, because, let's face it, it wasn't you, the teachers, who created and condoned the drug culture, sexual license, and violence in our society. It wasn't you, the teachers, who encouraged the banality of TV over the beauty of the written word. And it wasn't teachers who asked for a Washington-knows-best attitude that too often showered you with rules, regulations, and uniformity, while discouraging the rich variety and excellence of our heritage. For too long you've been fighting a lonely war, and it's about time you got some reinforcement from the rest of us.

And that was one of the main reasons I moved early in this administration to do something never tried before. We wanted a thorough, no-holds-barred study that would stimulate debate and action. So, we set up a bipartisan group, the National Commission on Excellence in Education.

As you know, the Commission recently came out with its report card, and it was pretty tough. The Commission found that about 13 percent of our 17-year-olds are functional illiterates, and the rate was much higher than that for minority youth. About four-fifths of our highschoolers can't write a decent essay. And most of them do less than an hour of homework a night.

In many schools, the hours spent learning how to cook and drive count as much toward a high school diploma as those spent studying mathematics, English, chemistry, U.S. history, or biology. Maybe that helps explain why verbal and math college board scores fell 50 and 40 points, respectively, between 1963 and 1980.

Well, predictably, some people are already wringing their hands at this bad news and casting about for scapegoats. But I deeply believe that this cloud has a silver lining. I believe it can mobilize, energize, and unify this country in a way that we haven't seen for years. Instead of worrying about whether we put together a Republican plan or a Democratic plan, can't we join together on a course of common sense for an American plan? Let us stand together—parents, teachers, concerned citizens—and let us say yes to the challenge of a national agenda for excellence that will uplift every child in our land.

America's not a defeatist nation. We came back from Pearl Harbor to win the greatest military victory in history. We came back from the shock of sputnik to send our astronauts to the Moon and bring them safely home. I believe the nation that met those great challenges can surely meet another. Let us resolve today: The United States will not only reverse its decline in college board scores, we will raise verbal and math scores at least 50 points and do it within the next decade.

At the heart of the Commission's report and our agenda are two themes I've long advocated. First, true excellence in education will require much greater emphasis on the basics—basic skills of learning and teaching with discipline, basic standards and rewards for excellence, and basic values of parental involvement and community control. Second, to meet the demands of this fast-changing world, we need also to broaden our vision of education. Education must become more than just the province and responsibility of our schools. It's also an integral part of our homes, churches, synagogues, communities, and workplaces. And we must recognize that.

To advance our agenda for excellence, I strongly endorse the Commission's fundamental recommendations. The Commission seeks to require 4 years of English in high school, 3 solid years of math, science, and social studies, and one-half year of computer science. It calls for more and longer school days, tighter discipline, higher goals and tougher standards for matriculation and graduation, also, for improved preparation for teachers and better rewards for teachers who excel . . . And I say, "Amen."

The Commission recognizes that school officials must take the lead in developing community support and that States and localities have the primary responsibility for school finance. We're already seeing strong evidence that the Commission's report touched a nerve. All over America, it's stimulating debate and sparking action.

The board in Ypsilanti, Michigan, has voted to extend their elementary school day and raise high school graduation requirements. In Illinois, high school graduation requirements are also being increased. Ditto for Washington State and also Virginia where the school board of education plans to overhaul their public school curriculum this summer.

As President, I intend to do everything I can to promote and enhance these reforms and to broaden the scope of education throughout our society. For example, to help reform the education system, there are areas where the Federal Government can make a direct contribution. Being prepared for the new era in high technology will require improved teaching of math and science. So, we've proposed legislation to stimulate training of more math and science teachers. We're also beginning a new program, one I'm participating in myself, to honor some of America's best math and science teachers.

And our efforts go beyond math and science. Bill Bennett, our Chairman of the National Endowment for the Humanities, is offering summer seminars so high school teachers can increase their teaching competence in history, literature, and the other humanities. We recognize, as most of you, as most teachers always have, that good teaching also means a life-long commitment to learning.

Now, many, if not all of these concepts are supported by the AFT, and we welcome your support. It's going to take the best efforts of all of us to achieve our goal of making American education great again.

I also want to commend the AFT for its fair, openminded approach to other potential means of encouraging good teaching and good teachers. I'm thinking of things like new approaches to differential pay, such as the proposal of Governor Lamar Alexander of Tennessee, which would include peer review. By engaging in free and open discussion and by demonstrating a willingness to examine new ideas even when they may require thinking, or re-thinking long-held views, the AFT is once again providing an example of positive leadership and winning respect for the teaching community. Working with you, with State and local leaders, and with parents and concerned citizens across the country, we can and we will climb the lofty peak to excellence in education.

Clark Mollenhoff, a tough-minded journalist who also understands the crucial importance of parents and teachers, said it very well in a poem he wrote called "Teacher":

> You are the moulders of their dreams—
> Heroes who build or crush their young beliefs in right or wrong.
> You are the spark that sets afire a poet's hand,
> Or lights the flame in some great singer's song.
>
> You are the idols of the young—the very young.
> You are their models, by profession set apart.

You are the guardians of a million dreams.
Your every smile or frown can heal or pierce a heart.

Yours are one hundred lives—one thousand lives.
Yours is the pride of loving them, the sorrow, too.
Your patient work, your touch, make you the source of hope
That fills their souls with dreams, and make those dreams come true.

I appreciate this opportunity to meet with you today. I hope it'll prove to be the first chapter in a long and productive relationship. We won't always agree. Life would be pretty dull if we did. But with a spirit of positive, candid cooperation, we can do much for the country we love and for the young people we serve.

Thank you, and God bless you.

Note: The President spoke at 10:25 a.m. in the California Room at the Bonaventure Hotel.

Following his appearance at the convention, the President returned to Washington, D.C.

Memorandum on Import Relief for the Specialty Steel Industry
July 5, 1983

Memorandum for the United States Trade Representative

Subject: Specialty Steel Import Relief Determination

Pursuant to Section 202(b)(1) of the Trade Act of 1974 (P.L. 93–618), I have determined the action I will take with respect to the report of the U.S. International Trade Commission (USITC), transmitted to me on May 6, concerning the results of its investigation, which was requested at my direction, on the merits of providing import relief to the specialty steel industry. I have determined that the granting of relief is consistent with our national economic interest and is necessitated by the pervasive nature of unfair trading practices in special-

ty steel.

I will, therefore, proclaim import relief but in a modified form and duration from that recommended by the USITC. I will impose relief for four years rather than three, as recommended by the USITC, to provide time for the industry to complete important investment projects, improve productivity, and regain profitability. I have decided to provide relief in a form consistent with my belief in minimal government interference in the marketplace, and which will facilitate the orderly adjustment of the industry while recognizing the substantial differences in the competitive conditions of the various segments of the industry.

For flat rolled products (55 percent of

imports), I will proclaim four years of digressive tariffs. For stainless steel sheet and strip, (excluding razor blade strip and type 434 cladding grade stainless sheet), the tariffs will be increased by 10 percent ad valorem in the first year, declining to 8, 6 and 4 percent in subsequent years. For stainless steel plate, the tariff will be increased by 8 percent in the first year, declining to 6, 5 and 4 percent in subsequent years.

In recognition of the weaker competitive position of the stainless steel rod, bar and alloy tool steel sectors, I will proclaim 4 year global quotas that will expand at an annual rate of three percent. For rod, imports will be limited in the first year to 19,100 tons, increasing to 19,700 tons, 20,300 tons and 20,900 tons in subsequent years. For bar, imports will be limited to 27,000 tons the first year, increasing to 27,800 tons, 28,600 tons and 29,500 tons in subsequent years. For tool steel (excluding

band saw steel and chipper knife), imports will be limited to 22,400 tons the first year, increasing to 23,100 tons, 23,800 tons and 24,500 tons. This global quota may be allocated on a country basis, or orderly marketing agreements may be negotiated with countries that request such negotiations.

I also direct you to undertake an annual review of the necessity for and effectiveness of import relief. Should conditions change or inadequate adjustment efforts be undertaken, you may, in consultation with the Trade Policy Committee, obtain USITC advice and propose changes in the terms of relief.

This determination shall be published in the *Federal Register*.

RONALD REAGAN

[*Filed with the Office of the Federal Register, 2:46 p.m., July 5, 1983*]

SCHEDULE OF RELIEF

Year	I	II	III	IV
Additional tariffs (percentage ad valorem):				
Sheet and strip	10	8	6	4
Plate	8	6	5	4
Quantitative limit (tons):				
Bar	27,000	27,800	28,600	29,500
Rod	19,100	19,700	20,300	20,900
Alloy tool steel	22,400	23,100	23,800	24,500

Letter to the Speaker of the House and the President of the Senate on Import Relief for the Specialty Steel Industry
July 5, 1983

Dear Mr. Speaker: (Dear Mr. President:)

In accordance with Section 203(b)(1) of the Trade Act of 1974, I am writing to inform you of my decision today to grant import relief to the specialty steel industry. My serious concerns last November about the health of the industry led me to direct the United States Trade Representative to ask the United States International Trade Commission to initiate this investigation. The USITC found specialty steel imports to be a substantial cause of serious injury to

the industry. Imports have depressed U.S. prices and captured market share from U.S. producers. This has had the effect of reducing domestic production and capacity utilization, resulting in major losses by most producers. Employment has also fallen significantly.

The relief program I am implementing is tailored to the needs of the industry as well as the objective of trade liberalization as expressed at the Williamsburg summit. It is part of a comprehensive and coordinated approach to this industry's trade problems. In addition to applying import relief under Section 201, I have directed USTR to continue its efforts to achieve the multilateral elimination of trade barriers.

The relief to be implemented is a combination of tariffs and quotas:

(1) For the flat-rolled products which comprise 55 percent of U.S. imports, a four year digressive tariff will be applied in addition to other tariffs due. Beginning in year one, a 10 percent tariff will apply to stainless steel sheet and strip, declining uniformly until year four when the tariff will be 4 percent. With regard to plate, the duty will decline from 8 percent in the first year to 4 percent in the fourth year.

(2) Imports of stainless rod, bar, and tool steel will be subject to a global four year quota. This quota will be expanded at a rate of 3 percent annually, outpacing the historic annual growth of consumption of 1–2 percent. This relief will incorporate the USITC's proposed minimum quantities in year one. (For additional details see attached table.) I am prepared to negotiate orderly market agreements with willing countries on rod, bar, and tool steel.

My decision differs in some respects from the USITC proposal. I have recommended relief for four years instead of three to give the industry sufficient time to complete investment projects, improve productivity, and restore profitability. This relief package has been adopted in order to reflect the substantial differences in the competitive conditions of the various parts of the industry. Tariffs applied to the flat-rolled products will be at levels less restrictive than the relief suggested by the USITC. Producers of flat-rolled stainless steel are on the whole more efficient, progressive, and competitive than their counterparts in the non-flat-rolled industry who have faced greater import competition. They have also recently succeeded in using our antidumping and countervailing duty statutes to obtain special duties on unfairly traded imports from three of their principal foreign competitors. These duties will be added to the normal tariff and the additional tariffs to be imposed under Section 203. Consequently, greater relief is needed for producers of non-flat-rolled products to enable them to make necessary investments.

In closing, I would like to state that I am implementing this relief package so as to achieve two complementary objectives:

(1) to provide help to a domestic industry seriously injured by imports, and

(2) to take steps to further our ultimate goal of trade liberalization.

I have instructed the USTR to form an interagency task force to pursue these dual objectives, and to report to me annually on progress toward them.

Sincerely,

RONALD REAGAN

Note: This is the text of identical letters addressed to Thomas P. O'Neill, Jr., Speaker of the House of Representatives, and George Bush, President of the Senate.

The Schedule of Relief, attached to the President's memorandum to the United States Trade Representative, also was attached to the letters.

Nomination of Clarence J. Brown To Be Deputy Secretary of Commerce
July 6, 1983

The President today announced his intention to nominate Clarence J. Brown to be Deputy Secretary of Commerce. He would succeed Guy W. Fiske.

Mr. Brown served as a Member of the United States House of Representatives from the 7th District of Ohio in 1965–1983. He served on the Joint Economic Committee in 1969–1983 (ranking Republican, 1975–1983); Energy and Commerce Committee in 1967–1983 (ranking Republican on Energy Subcommittee in 1975–1983 and on the Communications Subcommittee in 1971–1975); and Government Operations Committee in 1966–1983 (ranking Republican, Intergovernmental Relations Subcommittee, in 1969–1983).

Since 1965 Mr. Brown has been chairman of the board of Brown Publishing Co., with newspaper and printing operations in Urbana, Lebanon, Miamisburg, Springboro, Eaton, and Ada, Ohio. Since 1978 he has served on the advisory board, Georgetown University Center for Strategic and International Studies, and the advisory council of the American Enterprise Institute Study of Government Regulation.

He graduated from Duke University (B.A., 1947) and Harvard University (M.B.A., 1949). He is married, has three children, and resides in Washington, D.C. He was born June 18, 1927, in Columbus, Ohio.

Executive Order 12430—Reports of Identical Bids
July 6, 1983

By the authority vested in me as President by the Constitution and statutes of the United States of America, and in order to eliminate an agency reporting requirement which has proved ineffective and which consumes resources that could be employed in a more effective manner to prevent antitrust violations, Executive Order No. 10936, of April 24, 1961, is hereby revoked.

RONALD REAGAN

The White House,
July 6, 1983.

[*Filed with the Office of the Federal Register, 11:47 p.m., July 7, 1983*]

Statement on the Supreme Court Decision on Employer-Sponsored Retirement Pension Plans for Women
July 6, 1983

As one who is firmly committed to the cause of fair treatment for American women under the law, I welcome the Supreme Court's decision, announced today, in the *Norris* case.

Last January, in my State of the Union address, I declared this administration's commitment to achieve greater equity for women in the pension field. Today's court ruling has largely achieved this goal and marks a major step forward in making America an even more fair and just society.

Earlier this year, in a closely related case, my administration filed a brief before the Supreme Court in support of equal benefits for women and men under employer-sponsored pension benefit plans. In its decision today, the court decided that such equal benefits must be paid to women and men for pension credits they accrue from this day forward. This decision is a milestone for working women and represents the kind of real legal equity between men and women which I believe we can achieve through existing statutory and legal processes.

In the months ahead, in cooperation with the Congress, we will work for legislative changes consistent with the court's decision and will continue to seek other ways of guaranteeing fair treatment under the law for the women of America.

Message to the Congress Reporting a Budget Rescission and Deferrals
July 7, 1983

To the Congress of the United States:

In accordance with the Impoundment Control Act of 1974, I herewith report a proposal to rescind $15,000,000 in budget authority previously provided by the Congress. In addition, I am reporting four new deferrals of budget authority totaling $34,795,142.

The rescission proposal is for the Department of State's migration and refugee assistance account. The deferrals affect energy activities, the Department of Health and Human Services and the Board for International Broadcasting.

The details of the rescission proposal and deferral are contained in the attached reports.

RONALD REAGAN

The White House,
July 7, 1983.

Note: The attachments detailing the proposed rescission and deferrals are printed in the Federal Register *of July 13, 1983.*

Nomination of Charles C. Cox To Be a Member of the Securities and Exchange Commission
July 7, 1983

The President today announced his intention to nominate Charles C. Cox to be a member of the Securities and Exchange Commission for the term expiring June 5, 1988. He would succeed John R. Evans.

Since 1982 Dr. Cox has been serving as Chief Economist at the Securities and Exchange Commission. Previously he was assistant professor of management at Texas A. & M. University in 1980–1982; assistant professor of economics at Ohio State University in 1972–1980; national fellow at the Hoover Institution at Stanford University in 1977–1978; and a practicing attorney in 1978–1980.

He graduated from the University of Washington (B.A., 1967) and the University of Chicago (A.M., 1970; Ph. D., 1975). He resides in Washington, D.C. He was born May 8, 1945, in Missoula, Mont.

Appointment of Two Special Assistants to the President for National Security Affairs
July 8, 1983

The President today announced the designation of two members of the National Security Council staff as Special Assistants to the President, reporting to the Assistant to the President for National Security Affairs, William P. Clark. They are as follows:

Jack F. Matlock, Jr., Senior Director of European and Soviet Affairs and Special Assistant to the President. Mr. Matlock is currently U.S. Ambassador to Czechoslovakia and a Career Foreign Service officer. He has served three tours of duty at the American Embassy in Moscow, most recently as chargé d'affaires in 1981. He has also been Director of Soviet Union Affairs at the Department of State, Deputy Director of the Foreign Service Institute, and has served at American Embassies in Austria, Ghana, and

Tanzania. Ambassador Matlock received his A.B. from Duke University and an M.A. and certificate of the Russian Institute from Columbia University. Before entering the Foreign Service in 1956, he taught Russian language and literature at Dartmouth College, and from 1978 to 1979, he was a visiting professor of political science and diplomat in residence at Vanderbilt University. He is married, has five children and one grandchild, and resides in Washington, D.C. He was born in North Carolina in 1929.

Christopher M. Lehman, Senior Director of Legislative Affairs and Special Assistant to the President. Prior to joining the National Security Council staff, Mr. Lehman served as Director of the Office of Strategic Nuclear Policy, Department of State. He was special assistant for national security affairs to Senator John W. Warner from 1979 to 1981, and to Senator Harry F. Byrd, Jr., from 1976 to 1978. He has also served as an associate staff member of the Senate Armed Services Committee. Mr. Lehman is a graduate of St. Joseph's College, Philadelphia (A.B.), and holds an M.A. in international relations and an M.A. in law and diplomacy from the Fletcher School of Law and Diplomacy. He is also a Ph. D. candidate at the Fletcher School. He is the author or coauthor of several works on strategic policy and defense issues. Mr. Lehman served in the U.S. Naval Reserve from 1969 to 1971. He is married, has two children, and resides in Vienna, Va. He was born in Pennsylvania in 1948.

Statement on the Employment Situation
July 8, 1983

I am heartened by the news this morning that more Americans found jobs again last month—345,000 between May and June alone. The number of employees on payrolls is up 1.1 million from last December.

Day by day, month by month, America is gathering strength and moving forward. We still have a long way to go, but the recovery is spreading. Our most pressing task is to keep it rolling while holding down inflation, and that means holding down Federal spending. I urge the Members of the Congress—both Republicans and Democrats—to work with us and exercise the discipline we need to continue building a new era of lasting growth for the American people.

Question-and-Answer Session With Reporters on the Carter Administration Campaign Materials
July 8, 1983

Q. Sir, what did you tell your staff this morning?

The President. I told my staff that I wanted everyone there to hear directly from me that they were to make themselves available; if they had any information whatsoever to take it and tell it to the FBI, to the Justice Department, in the investigation which I had ordered of this entire incident. And I further said that this message will be conveyed to the rest of the administration, to the Cabinet officers and others who weren't present there. And I told Mr. Fielding[1] to tell the FBI that everyone in our administration, including myself, is available for questioning, because there's only one thing: We must get to the truth——

Q. Mr. President——

The President. ——the answer to this.

Q. Why was it necessary to say that to them? They were given those orders last week, and it's—every day last week. Why did you have to emphasize it in person this

---

[1] *Fred F. Fielding, Counsel to the President.*

morning?

The President. Well, in view of all that's been going on, I thought they should hear it directly from me.

Q. Do you regret saying that this was "much ado about nothing," when you first were asked about it, Mr. President?

The President. No. If, when the investigation is over and the truth is known, it is necessary to correct that statement, I'll correct it.

Q. Were you aware that ex-Army officers were organized to watch American airbases at home and abroad in case there would be an October surprise?

The President. No, Helen [Helen Thomas, United Press International], I have no knowledge of that at all.

Q. Mr. President, will you fire people if you have to?

The President. I said we want the truth. If there is any evidence of wrongdoing, we'll take whatever action that should be taken at that time.

Q. Including firing people?

The President. Yes.

Q. Thank you.

Note: The exchange began at 3:04 p.m. at the South Portico of the White House as the President was departing for a weekend stay at Camp David, Md.

Statement on the Death of Herman Kahn
July 8, 1983

Herman Kahn was a futurist who welcomed the future. He brought the lessons of science, history, and humanity to the study of the future and remained confident of mankind's potential for good. All who value independent thinking will mourn the loss of a man whose intellect and enthusiasm embraced so much.

I convey my deepest sympathy to Mr. Kahn's family and to all those who believe tomorrow can be better than today.

Executive Order 12431—Level IV of the Executive Schedule
July 8, 1983

By the authority vested in me as President of the United States of America by Section 5317 of Title 5 of the United States Code, in order to place an additional position in level IV of the Executive Schedule, Section 1-101 of Executive Order No. 12154, as amended, is further amended by adding thereto the following new subsection:

"(j) Administrator, Office of Juvenile Justice and Delinquency Prevention, Department of Justice.".

RONALD REAGAN

The White House,
July 8, 1983.

[*Filed with the Office of the Federal Register, 10:16 a.m., July 11, 1983*]

Radio Address to the Nation on Economic and Fair Housing Issues
July 9, 1983

My fellow Americans:

In recent weeks, even the gloomiest critics have had trouble denying that things are getting better for you and your families. The number of people working is up 1.1 million from last December. Unemployment remains too high, but it's coming down—9.8 percent in June, as announced yesterday.

We're seeing strong economic growth, and we're seeing it while inflation is at its lowest level in a decade—3½ percent over the last year. This sharply lower inflation and the first decent tax cut since the 1960's are allowing families to keep more of their own earnings to spend or save.

Contrary to propaganda blasts you hear, America is heading in a better direction today than before. For example, thanks to the tax cuts and our progress against inflation, a medium-income family earning $25,000 has nearly $600 more in purchasing power today than in 1980. Low-income families are being helped, too. Nothing was more cruel for them than those back-to-back years of double-digit inflation—before we got here, I hasten to add. If your family was on a fixed income of $10,000 at the start of 1979, that income was worth less than $8,000 by the end of 1980. In other words, inflation, which for years had been part of deliberate government economic planning, robbed you of $2,000. Now, that's not my idea of fairness, and I doubt if it's yours. If you tried to save a dollar at your bank during that same period, it would have lost 20 cents in value.

Well, we haven't abolished inflation or high taxes, but we're gaining on them. Your after-tax purchasing power helps determine your economic well-being. But this fact is ignored by the big spenders who claim to carry the banner of fairness and compassion. According to them, the whole issue of fairness revolves around government spending programs. And even on government spending, some of them have been misleading you. You've been led to believe that any budget savings in these programs would

hurt the needy, and that's not true.

The problem we set out to solve back when we inherited those record inflation and interest rates was not government doing too much for the needy, but government doing too much for the nonneedy. Before our budget reforms were passed, surveys indicated that 2 out of every 5 dollars in benefits went to those with total incomes and benefits well above the poverty line. Also, some of the programs to help the poor had the effect of keeping them poor and dependent, robbing them of their self-respect.

America is a wealthy nation, but our wealth is not unlimited. So, we've tried to face up to the reality too many have ignored. Unless we prune nonessential programs, unless we end benefits for those who should not be subsidized by their fellow taxpayers, we won't have enough resources to meet the requirements of those who must have our help. And helping those who truly need assistance is what fairness in government spending should be all about. We're trying to do this. Let me give you one statistic I doubt you've ever heard.

Our budget request for 1984 would have the Federal Government spend, after inflation, two-and-a-half times what it spent in 1970 on assistance to the poor. So while, yes, there have been some cuts, they've been nowhere near as draconian as critics charge. Why haven't you had this information? Well, maybe one reason is the drumbeat of gloom and doom from misery merchants in some of the media.

One major newspaper recently ran an editorial entitled, "Poorer, Hungrier." In 1979, according to this editorial, a team of doctors declared Federal food programs had eliminated most of the malnutrition in America. The editorial asked, "What would they find today?" Their answer, of course, was to say that under this administration things had worsened.

The truth is low-income Americans are receiving more food assistance in 1983 than ever before in history. During our administration, food assistance has grown by 34 percent. More people are being served and the grants for the neediest have been increased. We subsidize in whole or in part 95 million meals a day.

The average food stamp benefit, per person, has grown faster than the increase in food prices through inflation. The infant mortality rate has continued to decline. A greater percentage of school-lunch-program dollars are dedicated to providing meals for children of low-income families. Subsidies for meals served to children from low-income families have also increased in this administration.

Our administration is also distributing surplus cheese, butter, powdered milk, rice, flour, honey, and cornmeal to the needy and elderly. This is in addition to commodities regularly provided to schools and charitable institutions. The total comes to $1.7 billion so far.

Those budget reductions you've heard so much about have been achieved by improving efficiency, reducing dependency, cutting waste and abuse, and targeting on the neediest families. And that's as it should be. We're committed to fairness, and we'll continue to take actions needed to bring it about throughout our society.

Next week we'll be taking a new initiative to keep a pledge I made in my State of the Union address—the pledge to strengthen enforcement of fair housing laws for all Americans. We believe in the bold promise that no person in the United States should be denied full freedom of choice in the selection of housing because of race, color, religion, sex, or national origin. We're proposing a series of amendments that will put real teeth into the Fair Housing Act.

For example, the Justice Department can now act on complaints only when there's reason to believe there exists a practice of discrimination. Under our proposal, if conciliation fails, Secretary Pierce at HUD could forward individual complaints to the Attorney General for litigation. We're also proposing to extend the current law to prohibit discrimination on the basis of handicap or size of family. And our proposal will create substantial civil penalties for landlords and others found violating the law. This will include stiff fines up to $50,000 for a first offense and $100,000 for a second offense.

We believe this is an important step for civil rights. For a family deprived of its freedom of choice in choosing a home, our proposal will mean swift action and strong civil penalties to prevent discrimination in the first place. As I said, we're committed to fairness and we're committed to use the full power of the Federal Government whenever and wherever even one person's constitutional rights are being unjustly denied.

Till next week, thanks for listening, and God bless you.

Note: The President spoke at 12:06 p.m. from Camp David, Md.

Message to the Congress Transmitting the Annual Report on United States International Activities in Science and Technology
July 11, 1983

To the Congress of the United States:

In accordance with Title V of the Foreign Relations Authorization Act for Fiscal Year 1979 (Public Law 95–426), I am pleased to transmit the 1982 annual report on the United States Government's international activities in the field of science and technology. This report, as were its predecessors, has been prepared by the Department of State in collaboration with other concerned Federal agencies.

In the past year, there have been several important developments in our international science relationships, all of them reflecting one of our principal foreign policy goals—to give science and technology a more prominent position in our relations with other countries. This is important not only to the conduct of our foreign relations, but to the successful fulfillment of many of our own science and technology objectives. As I have indicated in my Annual Science and Technology Report to the Congress, international collaboration can help advance many of our own national interests. Thus, I have asked my science advisor, Dr. George Keyworth, to pay special attention to international affairs and, throughout the Federal Government, concerted action has been taken to demonstrate our commitment to using the advances in science to overcome both national and international challenges.

There has been substantial progress. For the first time, international science cooperation was a subject for discussion among the leaders of the principal industrial democracies at the Versailles Summit. Those discussions led to a study by the Summit countries of the relationship between technology, employment, and growth, and to the establishment of eighteen new projects for cooperation among us. Although these projects will, in the first instance, be led by one or another of the Summit countries, they could eventually involve other countries and international organizations and lead, in time, to advances for countries of the Third World. These projects for enhanced cooperation were endorsed by the heads of state at the Williamsburg Summit and it was agreed that we would discuss them again at our next meeting.

Last July, Prime Minister Gandhi and I initiated a new program for enhanced scientific collaboration between the United States and India. A group of some of the most distinguished scientists from both our countries met in India in January and prepared a far-reaching program in medicine, agriculture, meteorology, and energy. Work began in April 1983, and we expect to see the first results within the next twenty-four months.

Similarly, when I visited Brazil late last year, President Figueiredo and I reaffirmed our desire to strengthen science and technology collaboration. We have developed a program for joint work in five significant areas and, as part of our projected joint efforts in space, I proposed that a Brazilian payload specialist train with American astronauts for participation in a future space shuttle mission. When President Zia of Pakistan came to Washington in December, we agreed to establish a new Joint Commission to coordinate several bilateral activities, including common undertakings in science and technology.

In May, Dr. Keyworth led a highly successful mission to China for the third meeting of the U.S.-PRC Joint Commission for Scientific and Technological Cooperation. At the conclusion of the meeting, three new protocols on cooperation in nuclear physics and magnetic fusion, aeronautical science and technology, and transportation science and technology were signed. These supplement seventeen existing protocols that already include agriculture, students and scholars, space technology, high energy physics and hydropower. In addition to the new protocols a memorandum of understanding on cooperation in the basic biomedical sciences was also signed. It is in our fundamental interest to advance our relations with China. Science and technology are an essential part of that relationship and I have taken steps recently to ensure that China has improved access to the U.S. technology it needs for its economic modernization goals. We will continue to assist China through mutually beneficial cooperative efforts in science and technology.

We are continuing our cooperation with the U.S.S.R. in science and technology. This is a complex matter made more difficult because of Soviet behavior regarding Afghanistan and Poland, as well as their efforts to acquire sensitive Western technology. Decisions to renew agreements are being made on a case-by-case basis taking these concerns into account along with the benefits to the U.S. through participation. For example, I have recently approved the renewal of an agreement for cooperation with the Soviets on atomic energy, with appropriate limitations to protect our interests while letting the work proceed.

These examples suggest the range of our international effort in science and technology, but they are hardly exclusive. We have programs with more than three dozen countries, in every part of the world, at every level of sophistication. Science, as we know, has always had a special international character, and the advancement of science can make profound contributions to freedom and prosperity around the world. These tasks are formidable, for our scale of measurement must be decades, even generations. For this reason alone, our govern-

ment, in a cooperative spirit, will continue to work closely with others prepared to join with us.

RONALD REAGAN

The White House,
July 11, 1983.

Message to the Senate Transmitting Protocols for Extension of the International Wheat Agreement, 1971
July 11, 1983

To the Senate of the United States:

With a view to receiving the advice and consent of the Senate to ratification, I transmit herewith the Protocols for the Extension of the Wheat Trade Convention, 1971, and the Food Aid Convention, 1980, which Conventions constitute the International Wheat Agreement, 1971. The Protocols were adopted by the International Wheat Council which met in London in December 1982 and were open for signature in Washington from April 4 through May 10, 1983. They were signed by the Secretary of Agriculture for the United States on April 25, 1983.

I transmit also, for the information of the Senate, the report of the Secretary of State with respect to the Protocols.

The Protocols extend both Conventions

through June 30, 1986. They maintain the framework for international cooperation in wheat trade matters, continue the existence of the International Wheat Council, and extend the parties' commitments to provide minimum annual quantities of cereals food aid to developing countries.

I ask that the Senate give early and favorable consideration to the two Protocols so that ratification by the United States can be effected at an early date. Doing so will demonstrate our continued commitment to cooperation on international wheat trade matters and to providing food aid to needy developing nations.

RONALD REAGAN

The White House,
July 11, 1983.

Nomination of Peter Jon de Vos To Be United States Ambassador to Mozambique
July 11, 1983

The President today announced his intention to nominate Peter Jon de Vos, of Florida, a career member of the Senior Foreign Service, Class of Counselor, as Ambassador to the People's Republic of Mozambique. He would succeed Willard A. De Pree.

In 1962 Mr. de Vos entered the Foreign Service as Foreign Service officer for Brazil, in the Department. He was political officer

in Naples (1966–1968), deputy principal officer in Luanda (1968–1970), political officer in São Paulo (1970–1971) and in Brasilia (1971–1973). In the Department he was Special Assistant in the Bureau of Inter-American Affairs in 1973–1975. He was political officer in Athens in 1975–1978 and attended the National War College in 1978–1979. In 1979–1980 he was Deputy Director of Southern African Affairs in the Department. In 1980–1983 he was Ambassador to the Republic of Guinea-Bissau and to the Republic of Cape Verde.

Mr. de Vos graduated from Princeton University (B.A., 1960) and Johns Hopkins University (M.A., 1962). His foreign languages are Portuguese, Spanish, Italian, and Greek. He was born December 24, 1938, in San Diego, Calif.

Appointment of Bruce Chapman as Deputy Assistant to the President and Director of the White House Office of Planning and Evaluation
July 11, 1983

The President today announced the appointment of Bruce Chapman as Deputy Assistant to the President and Director of the Office of Planning and Evaluation (OPE) in the White House. Mr. Chapman will report to Edwin Meese III, Counsellor to the President, and will be responsible for long-range issues identification, statistical analysis, and program evaluation.

Mr. Chapman has been serving as Director of the Bureau of the Census since October 1981. Previously he was secretary of state for the State of Washington in 1975–1981; a member of the Seattle City Council in 1971–1975; a public affairs consultant in 1966–1971; and an editorial writer for the New York Herald Tribune in 1965–1966.

Under Mr. Chapman, the reconstituted Office of Planning and Evaluation will serve as a catalyst for increasing long-range research support from Federal offices outside the White House and for seeking similar assistance from persons and groups outside the Government. The Office also will help stimulate the climate for public discussion of long-range issues of importance to the President's goals. Within the White House, the Office will participate in strategic planning and program analysis. In addition, Mr. Chapman will report on demographic developments and will suggest improvements in the Government's statistical system.

Mr. Chapman graduated from Harvard University (B.A., 1962). He is married and has one child. He was born December 1, 1940, in Evanston, Ill.

Appointment of Five Members of the President's Advisory Council on Private Sector Initiatives
July 11, 1983

The President today announced his intention to appoint the following individuals to be members of the President's Advisory Council on Private Sector Initiatives. These are initial appointments.

Osborne Atwater Day is a consultant to nonprofit organizations in Washington, D.C. He was born October 12, 1920, in New Haven, Conn.

William Lyon is chairman and chief executive officer of the William Lyon Co. in Newport Beach, Calif. He was born March 9, 1923, in Los Angeles, Calif.

William G. Milliken is a former Governor of Michigan. He was born March 26, 1922, in Traverse City, Mich.

Robert T. Monagan is president of the California Manufacturers Association in Sacramento, Calif. He was born July 5, 1920, in Ogden, Utah.

R. William Taylor is president of the American Society of Association Executives in Washington, D.C. He was born July 28, 1929, in Brownsville, Tenn.

Message to the Congress Transmitting Proposed Fair Housing Legislation
July 12, 1983

To the Congress of the United States:

I am transmitting herewith the "Fair Housing Amendments Act of 1983."

The Federal Fair Housing Act was enacted by the Congress 15 years ago. It stands as a bold promise that no person in the United States should be denied full freedom of choice in the selection of housing because of race, color, religion, sex, or national origin. Since its passage, however, a consensus has developed that the Fair Housing Act has delivered short of its promise because of a gap in its enforcement mechanism.

The principal means of redressing violations under the Act is resolution of complaints by the Secretary of Housing and Urban Development through informal methods of conference, conciliation, or persuasion. This informal process is the best and most effective procedure that can be devised for speedy and non-burdensome relief for individual victims of discrimination. It has worked well when it has been approached in good faith by all parties to the dispute. The Secretary achieves conciliation in roughly three-fourths of the cases in which a determination to resolve through conciliation is made, and the success rate of conciliation by State and local agencies to which complaints are referred is comparable. But as few as the cases may be where conciliation is unsuccessful, they are too many.

The gap in enforcement is the lack of a forceful back-up mechanism which provides an incentive to bring the parties to the conciliation table with serious intent to resolve the dispute then and there. When conciliation fails, the Secretary has no place else to go. In those few cases where good will is absent, the exclusive reliance upon voluntary resolution is, in the words of former Secretary Carla Hills, an "invitation to intransigence."

I referred to this widely acknowledged gap in the law in my recent State of the Union message when I said:

Effective enforcement of our Nation's fair housing laws is . . . essential to ensuring equal opportunity. In the year ahead, we will work to strengthen enforcement of fair housing laws for all Americans.

The central objective of the proposed legislation which I am transmitting today is to supply the missing ingredient to effective enforcement. I propose that when conciliation fails, the Secretary may refer the complaint to the Attorney General with the recommendation that an action be commenced on behalf of the United States in Federal District Court. This expands the current jurisdiction of the Justice Department, now limited to cases of discriminatory patterns or practices, to include cases involving individual victims of discrimination. It thus places the leadership in enforcement where it belongs, with the Federal Government rather than with the individual victim. And in order to emphasize the clear public interest in the prevention of discriminatory housing practices as well as to add teeth to the enforcement arsenal, it authorizes the Attorney General to seek substantial civil penalties in addition to equitable relief. While the maximum penalties are severe—as they ought to be in cases of violation of the basic right to be free from illegal discrimination—the tribunal with power to impose these remedies is that one which has earned and enjoyed the confidence of the American people over our history for its impartiality, independence, and fairness.

I also propose several other important improvements to the enforcement process, including:

—Authorization for the Attorney General to seek specific performance of a conciliation agreement.

—Confirmation that a conciliation may contain an agreement to submit to binding arbitration.

—Authorization of temporary equitable relief through the courts while conciliation attempts are proceeding.

—Conforming the attorneys' fee award provisions to those of the Civil Rights Attorneys Fee Award Act.

—Extension of the statute of limitations for private actions from 180 days to two years.

—Removal of the ceiling on punitive damages obtainable in private enforcement actions.

The proposed legislation also will extend coverage of the Fair Housing Act to prohibit discrimination on the basis of handicap. The need to extend the protection of this statute to the handicapped is a subject on which a clear consensus of the Congress emerged during the unsuccessful attempt to adopt amendments in the 96th Congress.

Reform of the Fair Housing Act is a necessity that is acknowledged by all. I urge that the Congress give these legislative proposals its immediate attention so that early enactment may be achieved.

RONALD REAGAN

The White House,
July 12, 1983.

Nomination of Helen M. Witt To Be a Member of the National Mediation Board
July 12, 1983

The President today announced his intention to nominate Helen M. Witt to be a member of the National Mediation Board for the term expiring July 1, 1985. She would succeed Robert Joseph Brown.

Mrs. Witt is a private arbitrator. Previously she was assistant to the chairman, board of arbitration, USS/USWA, in 1975–1982; special arbitrator, U.S. Steel Corp. and United Steelworkers of America, in 1974; appointed to the first expedited arbitration panel formulated by Coordinating Committee Steel Companies and the United Steelworkers under the 1971 basic agreements in 1972; and was in the private practice of law with the firms of Cleland, Hurtt & Witt and Witt & Witt in 1970–1974.

Mrs. Witt graduated from Dickinson College (B.A., 1955) and the University of Pittsburgh School of Law (J.D., 1969). She is married, has five children, and resides in Pittsburgh, Pa. She was born July 13, 1933, in Atlantic City, N.J.

Appointment of Two Members of the National Advisory Committee on Juvenile Justice and Delinquency Prevention
July 12, 1983

The President today announced his intention to appoint the following individuals to be members of the National Advisory Committee on Juvenile Justice and Delinquency Prevention, Department of Justice, for the remainder of terms expiring January 17, 1984, and to be reappointed for the terms expiring January 17, 1987.

Keith T. Koppenhoefer will succeed Mary Anne B. Stewart. He is presently a senior at Elder High School in Cincinnati, Ohio. He was born January 29, 1965, in Cincinnati.

John Leonard Rouse, Jr., will succeed Barbara T. Sylvester. He is a student at Prince Georges Community College. He was born September 28, 1964, in Edinburgh, Scotland.

Remarks at a White House Luncheon Honoring the State Teachers of the Year
July 13, 1983

Ladies and gentlemen, you go right ahead, and everyone can serve dessert and so forth. I just want to make a few remarks here, but I precede with a special bulletin.

I understand there's been some conversation about whether you would have an opportunity to see more of the White House than just this room. And so I've been told that that Diplomatic Reception Room downstairs that you came in, that oval room downstairs, when we depart here, if you will gather there, the guides will be there and conduct you on a tour of the White House, for those of you who—[*applause*]——

And now, just, welcome to the White House. And I think that Ted Bell [Secretary of Education] will agree when I say there isn't a group who belongs here more than you, America's finest educators. I'm very proud and happy to have you here.

Seeing you here today I'm filled with confidence about the preparation of our children and the future of our nation. If I may improvise on a line from one of my predecessors, he said, in this room, "There has not been so much brain power, commitment, and dedication concentrated in this one room since Thomas Jefferson dined here alone." [*Laughter*] But, you know, I've given toasts to Kings and Queens in this room, as well as to Prime Ministers and Presidents, but you're the only group for whom I've ever felt obliged to diagram my sentences. [*Laughter*]

I'd like to congratulate all of you for being recognized as Teachers of the Year in your own States, and I know you'll join me in a special salute to the 1983 National Teacher of the Year, Dr. LeRoy E. Hay. [*Applause*] I was a little disturbed; I had two names for him. One was Lee Hay, but then he told me that this one was the correct one, that his mother really would like it if I used the whole name. [*Laughter*]

Behind each of your awards, of course, are countless individual children whose lives you've touched, whose minds you've broadened, and whose character you've helped shape. The knowledge, the judgment, and the love that you've shared will follow them through their lives, and that will enrich all of us. On behalf of a grateful nation, I thank you.

I also want to thank the Council of Chief State School Officers, the Encyclopaedia Britannica Companies, and Good Housekeeping magazine. Together they've sponsored the National Teacher of the Year competition for more than three decades, promoting and rewarding excellence in our classrooms. And that's just the kind of cooperation and initiative that we need more of if we're to get our education system and our country back on track.

Someone once said that a school is a building that has four walls and tomorrow inside. Our history has been a testament of the fact that our education system, the key that unlocked the golden door of opportunity for our people, has been in those buildings. When our forebears were throwing up makeshift towns across our wilderness continent, among the first structures that they built were the churches, and then came the schoolhouses.

And as a matter of fact, the tradition of the little church-related college—where I went to college in Illinois, Eureka College, the tradition there has—it was reversed when Ben Major, in command of the wagon train, and they stopped in a walnut grove of trees and decided that this was where they would settle, he sank an ax in a tree and said, "Here we will build our school." And they built their school before they built anything, or their own homes.

The recent report of our Commission on Excellence in Education exposed what it labeled as a "rising tide of mediocrity" in education. According to that report, about 13 percent of our 17-year-olds are functional illiterates. More than two-thirds of our high-schoolers can't write a decent essay. The study indicates the quality of learning in our classrooms has been declining for the last quarter of a century—a fact that I'm sure won't surprise many of you.

There's nothing the matter with our children, and I'd like to make it plain once and for all: There's nothing the matter with America's teachers. You are people who savor the sound of a well-turned phrase and delight in introducing youth to Shakespeare, knowing that it was youth that Shakespeare loved. You best understand how a mastery of math can help master life, how science can open endless worlds of the imagination, and how history teaches judgment and perspective.

Many of you have been waving a red warning flag for years now, calling for more stress on basics and pointing out how society has discouraged some of our most capable people from choosing teaching careers. It's time America listened to you again, respected you again, and rewarded your effort and excellence with salaries that will encourage our best young people to follow in your footsteps.

That's why Secretary Bell and I have been pushing hard for a national agenda for excellence in education. And one of the first items on it is the concept of merit pay for teachers. If we want to achieve excellence, we must reward it. It's a simple American philosophy that dominates many other professions, so why not this one? There are plenty of outstanding teachers outside of this room. They're teaching in classrooms all across America. What we must do is find them, promote them, and hold them up as role models not just for other teachers but for our children.

There are many important jobs in American life, but I can't think of any that are more important than teaching. As I told a group of journalists recently, I remember the high school teacher who changed my life: B. J. Fraser—Dixon, Illinois. He taught English and drama. But most important, he channeled my imagination in ways that set it free. I owe him a great deal.

William Ellery Channing, an early American clergyman, once said that "it is a greater work to educate a child than to rule a state." What he said was right then, as America set her first minorities—or priorities, I should say. And it is still true today as we return to them.

America's parents, administrators, and officeholders must join with you in a new campaign for educational excellence. With your continued help and dedication and our renewed commitment, we can and will restore America's ability to educate all our children to the highest standards we know.

So, thank you very much—not only for coming here today but for dedicating your lives to our children and to our future. And just let me know how I can be of help to you. Good luck, and God bless you all.

Note: The President spoke at 12:40 p.m. in the State Dining Room at the White House.

Letter Accepting the Resignation of Edwin L. Harper as Assistant to the President for Policy Development
July 13, 1983

Dear Ed:

I was personally and professionally saddened to receive your resignation from my staff as my Assistant for Policy Development.

You have consistently over the years provided policy and strategic options and alternatives to the Cabinet and to me which were sound in theory, firmly grounded in experience and have at all times been politically and technically feasible.

I will sorely miss your wise counsel and sharp judgment in the difficult and complex times ahead.

Although you have already stayed the course with me far beyond your original intention (and, I'm afraid, at considerable sacrifice to your own private business career), I want you to know how grateful I am for all your help, advice and innovative assistance.

Therefore, please take warning that I fully intend to call on you frequently in the future whenever the need for your incomparable help arises.

Your long and illustrious career of service to your country should be a source of great pride to you.

Nancy joins me in extending to Lucy, and to you and your family, our very best wishes for all that the future may bring.

Sincerely,

RONALD REAGAN

[The Honorable Edwin L. Harper, Assistant to the President for Policy Development, The White House, Washington, D.C. 20500]

July 12, 1983

Dear Mr. President:

In 1980 I joined the majority of Americans feeling that this country was going in the wrong direction. You brought the nation hope that we did not have to be a victim of economic forces but that by trying some new ideas we could master the problems we faced.

Through your leadership our hopes have been realized. The turnaround has been tougher than we had originally hoped, but it has not been the calamity that was inevitable had you not taken the helm. You have made a real difference.

The opportunity you gave me to help you make that difference is indeed a precious gift. I hope my work has justified your giving me that gift.

Your gift of opportunity caused me to abandon the commitment I made at the beginning of the 1980 transition to myself and my family to stay with my private sector career. The opportunities to initiate and lead your program against fraud and waste in government, to help put together your first two budgets, to help develop your mid-term strategic policy plan and to work with the many outstanding people you have attracted to government have been the most exciting and personally satisfying way one could have to serve one's country. Whatever my accomplishments have been they would not have been possible without the excellent career staff and your outstanding appointees at the Office of Management and Budget, the Office of Policy Development and the Inspectors General corps.

As you and I have discussed, it is now time for me to return to the private sector; therefore, with this letter I tender my resignation effective July 31, 1983. As I leave I am asking you for one more opportunity— the opportunity to help you be re-elected for a second term. Lucy joins me in leaving you and Nancy with our every good wish.

Sincerely,

ED
Edwin L. Harper
Assistant to the President for Policy
Development

[The President, The White House, Washington, D.C. 20500]

Nomination of David John Markey To Be an Assistant Secretary of Commerce
July 13, 1983

The President today announced his intention to nominate David John Markey to be Assistant Secretary of Commerce for Communications and Information. He would succeed Bernard J. Wunder, Jr.

Mr. Markey is currently legal assistant to the Chairman of the Federal Communications Commission. Previously he served as chief of staff and legislative director in the office of Senator Frank Murkowski (1981– 1983); legislative counsel and then vice president, congressional relations, for the National Association of Broadcasters (1974– 1981); and administrative assistant in the office of Senator J. Glenn Beall, Jr. (1969– 1974).

Mr. Markey graduated from Western Maryland College (B.S., 1963) and the University of Maryland School of Law (J.D., 1967). He is married and resides in Washington, D.C. He was born July 25, 1940, in Frederick, Md.

Nomination of A. Wayne Roberts To Be a Deputy Under Secretary of Education
July 13, 1983

The President today announced his intention to nominate A. Wayne Roberts to be Deputy Under Secretary for Intergovernmental and Interagency Affairs, Department of Education. He would succeed John H. Rodriguez.

Mr. Roberts is currently the Secretary of Education's Regional Representative (Region I). Previously he was Acting Projects Director for the U.S. Synthetic Fuels Corporation (June 1981–October 1981); Deputy Director of White House Personnel (January 1981–June 1981); and assistant professor of economics and management at Johnson State College (1974–1980). He was with the IBM Corp. from 1965–1973.

Mr. Roberts graduated from Babson College (B.S., 1964) and the University of Massachusetts (M.B.A., 1965). He currently resides in Lexington, Mass., and was born February 25, 1944, in Boston, Mass.

Statement on Signing a Minority Business Enterprise Development Bill
July 13, 1983

I am today signing S. 273, a bill that would amend section 8(a) of the Small Business Act to extend two pilot programs designed to assist minority business development. My approval of this bill demonstrates this administration's continuing commitment to minority business.

S. 273 authorizes the President to select a Federal nondefense agency for a pilot program with the Small Business Administration (SBA) that will direct procurement contracts to minority businesses and thus assist their development. Under the program, SBA will have final authority in selecting the procurements that would best assist the growth of particular minority enterprises.

In addition, S. 273 revives an expired surety bond waiver pilot program and extends it through September 30, 1985. Under this program, SBA would assume the functions and obligations ordinarily performed by a commercial surety company.

The concept behind the 8(a) procurement pilot program is to test whether minority-owned businesses can be advanced through the use of more technically sophisticated, higher volume, and longer term contracts. I believe that this program can be an effective business development tool for small minority enterprises. I will direct SBA and the designated agency to work cooperatively so that this pilot program has a fair and adequate test.

This administration is dedicated to increasing the share of Federal procurement dollars which is placed with minority business. This program can assist us in meeting our minority business development goals as well as assist minority businesses in industries where minorities traditionally have not participated.

Note: As enacted, S. 273 is Public Law 98–47, approved July 13.

Announcement on Awarding the Presidential Citizens Medal to Joe Delaney
July 13, 1983

The President today awarded the Presidential Citizens Medal to Joseph Alton (Joe) Delaney, of Haughton, La., who lost his life while attempting to save three children in a drowning incident at Monroe, La., on June 29, 1983.

Mr. Delaney, a football player for the Kansas City Chiefs, was given the award for making "the ultimate sacrifice by placing the lives of three children above regard for his own safety."

The medal will be presented on the President's behalf by Vice President Bush in ceremonies at the Haughton High School gymnasium at 9:30 a.m., Friday, July 15.

Following is the text of the President's award citation:

Born with God-given physical talent, Joe Delaney brought distinction to himself and pride to his family and friends by exemplifying the best in sportsmanship as an outstanding high school, college and professional football player. Even more important, he set an example of citizenship off the playing field, as a caring, involved member of his community of Haughton, Louisiana.

On June 29, 1983, Joe Delaney, at age 24, made the ultimate sacrifice by placing the lives of three children above regard for his own safety.

By this supreme example of courage and compassion, this brilliantly-gifted young man left a spiritual legacy for his fellow Americans, in recognition of which I, Ronald Reagan, President of the United States, do hereby award Joe Delaney the Presidential Citizens Medal.

Statement by Deputy Press Secretary Speakes on the Economic Recovery
July 13, 1983

The advance retail sales for June, announced today by the Department of Commerce, show continuing good news about the strength of the economic recovery. The President is encouraged by growing consumer confidence, which is reflected by this third consecutive monthly increase in consumer buying. The sales of big-ticket items such as automobiles are a key sign of consumers' expectations for the future. The President's policies have placed the recovery on firm footing and hold the promise of a robust economy in the years ahead.

Remarks on Signing an Executive Order on Minority Business Enterprise Development
July 14, 1983

One item of business we'll be taking care of before we get underway in the Cabinet meeting, and that is the signing of this Executive order today. It's a symbol of the commitment of this administration to do everything it can to keep alive the American dream for all of our citizens. And this is an Executive order that has to do with more Federal involvement in Federal contracts for minority-owned businesses.

Now, while our program for minority business development is important, it's by no means the most important of our efforts to promote this American dream for all our citizens. But beginning in the late sixties, on the very heels of the breakdown of legal racial barriers, the economy entered a period of contraction. And what it amounted to was that just when they achieved the rights to buy a ticket on the train—the economic train that they'd seen going by—got on the train, it started going backward.

So, this has been a problem. The actions taken, the proposals that have been made by this administration are designed to get the train moving again. And the signs are clear now that our program is working. And in addition, because of the progress of the

1960's and this administration's firm commitment to protect the human rights and the economic freedom of all Americans, the passenger list is going to look a little different when the train starts rolling ahead this time.

So, without any further ado, I am delighted to sign this Executive order.

Note: The President spoke at 1:12 p.m. in the Cabinet Room at the White House. Cabinet members and reporters were present to observe the signing ceremony. The President then met with the Cabinet.

Executive Order 12432—Minority Business Enterprise Development
July 14, 1983

By virtue of the authority vested in me as President by the Constitution and laws of the United States of America, including Section 205(a) of the Federal Property and Administrative Services Act of 1949 (40 U.S.C. 486(a)), in order to provide guidance and oversight for programs for the development of minority business enterprise pursuant to my statement of December 17, 1982 concerning Minority Business Development; and to implement the commitment of the Federal government to the goal of encouraging greater economic opportunity for minority entrepreneurs, it is hereby ordered as follows:

Section 1. Minority Business Development Plans. (a) Minority business enterprise development plans shall be developed by each Federal agency having substantial procurement or grantmaking authority. Such agencies shall submit these plans to the Cabinet Council on Commerce and Trade on an annual basis.

(b) These annual plans shall establish minority enterprise development objectives for the participating agencies and methods for encouraging both prime contractors and grantees to utilize minority business enterprises. The plans shall, to the extent possible, build upon the programs administered by the Minority Business Development

Agency and the Small Business Administration, including the goals established pursuant to Public Law 95–507.

(c) The Secretary of Commerce and the Administrator of the Small Business Administration, in consultation with the Cabinet Council on Commerce and Trade, shall establish uniform guidelines for all Federal agencies to be utilized in establishing the minority business programs set forth in Section 2 of this Order.

(d) The participating agencies shall furnish an annual report regarding the implementation of their programs in such form as the Cabinet Council on Commerce and Trade may request, and at such time as the Secretary of Commerce shall designate.

(e) The Secretary of Commerce shall provide an annual report to the President, through the Cabinet Council on Commerce and Trade, on activities under this Order and agency implementation of minority business development programs.

Sec. 2. Minority Business Development Responsibilities of Federal Agencies. (a) To the extent permitted by law and consistent with its primary mission, each Federal agency which is required to develop a minority business development plan under Section 1 of this Order shall, to accomplish the objectives set forth in its plan, establish programs concerning provision of direct assistance, procurement assistance, and management and technical assistance to minority business enterprises.

(b) Each Federal agency shall, to the extent permitted by law and consistent with its primary mission, establish minority business development programs, consistent with Section 211 of Public Law 95–507, to develop and implement incentive techniques to encourage greater minority business subcontracting by Federal prime contractors.

(c) Each Federal agency shall encourage recipients of Federal grants and cooperative agreements to achieve a reasonable minority business participation in contracts let as a result of its grants and agreements. In cases where State and local governments are the recipients, such encouragement shall be consistent with principles of federalism.

(d) Each Federal agency shall provide the Cabinet Council on Commerce and Trade such information as it shall request from time to time concerning the agency's progress in implementing these programs.

RONALD REAGAN

The White House,
July 14, 1983.

[*Filed with the Office of the Federal Register, 10:42 a.m., July 15, 1983*]

Statement on United States Participation in the International Monetary Fund
July 14, 1983

In meetings here today, I have once again asked for congressional approval of the American share of an increase in lending resources for the International Monetary Fund (IMF). The Senate has already approved the request, and the House will take up the measure next week.

The IMF has been a cornerstone of U.S. foreign economic policy under Republican and Democratic administrations for nearly 40 years, and it remains a cornerstone of the foreign economic policy of this administration.

In the past decade the economy has witnessed soaring inflation and interest rates, plunging commodity prices, and worldwide recession. While the international economic outlook is now improving, the experience of past years has contributed to a major international debt problem that poses grave risks for the U.S. and world economies. We have formulated a strategy for dealing with this problem, and IMF plays a key role in it. IMF resources, however, are running low and unless action is taken to increase them, IMF may no longer be able to play that role.

Some argue that increasing IMF resources is simply a way to bail out big bankers who made imprudent loans. This is wrong. In fact, IMF involvement has brought more, not less, participation by private banks. It is important to remember that IMF makes no gifts, that it lends money to governments, and that it charges interest on its loan and assures that proper economic policies are in place to correct the problems and to assure that the loans are repaid.

All of this is very important to the American economy. In 1980 U.S. exports accounted for 19 percent of the total production of goods and, during the decade of the seventies, export-related jobs rose 75 percent to over 5 million. The ability of IMF to deal with the current strains in the international financial system will have a powerful impact on American exports and on American jobs. If IMF is not in a position to help countries help themselves, our economic recovery could be aborted and unemployment start rising again.

Therefore, I urge the House of Representatives to act favorably on this legislation. No legislation now before the Congress is more important to a healthy world economy and to a continuing economic recovery here in the United States.

Appointment of Albert Lee Smith, Jr., as a Member of the Federal Council on the Aging
July 14, 1983

The President today announced his intention to appoint Albert Lee Smith, Jr., to be a member of the Federal Council on the Aging for a term expiring December 19, 1985. He would succeed Jacob Clayman.

Mr. Smith has been special representative for the Jefferson Standard Life Insurance Co. since 1956 and served as a Member of the United States House of Representatives from 1980–1982. He currently serves as a member of the advisory board of the Retired Senior Volunteer Program and as a member of the Arm of Positive Maturity Program.

Mr. Smith graduated from Auburn University (B.S., 1954). He is married, has three children, and resides in Birmingham, Ala. He was born August 31, 1931, in Birmingham.

Appointment of Four Members of the Advisory Committee to the Pension Benefit Guaranty Corporation, and Designation of Chairman
July 14, 1983

The President today announced his intention to appoint the following individuals to be members of the Advisory Committee to the Pension Benefit Guaranty Corporation for terms expiring February 19, 1984. The President intends to designate Roger F. Martin, who has been serving as a member since August 10, 1982, as Chairman.

Joseph Geronimo would succeed Charles Christopher Tharp. He currently serves as vice president, pension products division, employee benefit program, at the Bankers Trust Co. Previously he was with the Chase Manhattan Bank, N.A. (1972–1981). Mr. Geronimo graduated from Villanova University (B.A., 1972). He is married, has one child, and resides in Maplewood, N.J. He was born June 23, 1950, in Jersey City, N.J.

Murray P. Hayutin would succeed Deene Goodlaw Solomon. He has been with the insurance firm of Reichart-Silversmith, Inc., since 1970, first as vice president (1970–1981) and currently as president. Mr. Hayutin graduated from the University of Pennsylvania, Wharton School (B.S., 1959), and the University of Denver (M.B.A., 1963). He is married, has two children, and resides in Littleton, Colo. He was born October 17, 1937, in Denver, Colo.

John F. Hotchkis would succeed Robert Tilove. He is currently a general partner in the investment firm of Hotchkis and Wiley, which he co-founded in 1980. Previously he was an officer, portfolio manager, and director of Everett Harris & Co. (1975–1980); an officer and director of Trust Company of the West (1971–1974); and a general partner and a vice president of Dean Witter & Co. (1951–1971). Mr. Hotchkis graduated from the University of California at Berkeley (A.B., 1954) and UCLA (M.B.A., 1958). He is married, has four children, and resides in Pasadena, Calif. He was born August 3, 1931, in Los Angeles, Calif.

Ralph J. Wood, Jr., has been a personal producing agent in insurance since 1950. In 1959 he established Garwood, Inc., a pension service organization that operates and serves some 150 pension plans in the Chicago area. He is a member of the Illinois Association of Life Underwriters and the Chartered Life Underwriters Million Dollar Roundtable. He graduated from the University of Chicago (B.S., 1948). He is married, has five children, and resides in Flossmoor, Ill. He was born December 27, 1923, in Chicago, Ill. This is a reappointment.

Nomination of Charles G. Wells To Be a Member of the Board of Directors of the African Development Foundation
July 14, 1983

The President today announced his intention to nominate Charles G. Wells to be a member of the Board of Directors of the African Development Foundation for a term of 4 years. This is a new position.

Mr. Wells is currently president and chief executive officer for Sunbelt National Bank in Dallas, Tex. Previously he served as a personal financial consultant (1982–1983); president of the Union Bank of Chicago (1980–1982); vice president and regional manager of the Commercial Credit Co. (1976–1980); director of marketing administration (1975) and then director of human resources (1976) for the Commercial Credit Equipment Corp.; and senior associate with Hay Associates, a private consulting firm.

Mr. Wells graduated from Pace University (B.S., 1961; M.B.A., 1971). He is married, has two children, and resides in Olympia Fields, Ill. He was born August 25, 1936, in Abington, Pa.

Statement on House of Representatives Action on the Caribbean Basin Initiative Legislation
July 14, 1983

I am delighted by today's action by the House of Representatives on the trade and tax provisions of the Caribbean Basin Initiative. Although it took longer than I had hoped to secure passage, the vote today is a giant step forward. I congratulate the chairman of the Ways and Means Committee, Dan Rostenkowski, and Members of the House for the bipartisan cooperation they demonstrated in working for the stability and progress of some of our closest neighbors.

The security and well-being of the people of the Caribbean are very much in the interest of the United States. The region, in reality, represents the third border of our country, and for far too long it has not been given the attention it deserves. Today's vote by the House is a signal to all concerned that we recognize the vital importance of the Caribbean and are willing to meet our responsibilities.

There have been a number of changes in the legislation since its inception, but the heart of the proposal remains intact. Through tax and trade incentives the energy and creativity of the private sector will be put to work on the economic challenges that confront our friends and neighbors in the Caribbean. The Caribbean Basin Initiative will serve as a catalyst for progress and will offer broad new opportunities to the people of the region.

I hope the Congress will move promptly through the remaining legislative steps toward enactment of this vital piece of legislation.

Letter Accepting the Resignation of Lyndon K. Allin as Deputy Press Secretary to the President
July 15, 1983

Dear Mort:

It was with deep personal regret that I learned of your decision to return to your duties at the United States Information Agency. I am, however, deeply grateful for your service on the White House staff and I take satisfaction in knowing that your service to our country will continue as you accept a new assignment overseas.

Throughout your career, and especially here at the White House, you have served with dedication and distinction and with a truly inspirational sense of public duty. I know well of the many long hours you have devoted and of your tireless efforts to serve many constituencies. And through it all, you have maintained the highest standards of personal integrity and loyalty and you have even maintained a sense of humor. I am proud to have had you as my Deputy Press Secretary and I am proud to have you as one of our nation's representatives abroad.

Nancy joins me in wishing you, Mary Ann, Stephanie and Lyndon all of life's blessings.

Sincerely,

RONALD REAGAN

[The Honorable Lyndon K. Allin, Deputy Press Secretary to the President, The White House, Washington, D.C. 20500]

Note: Deputy Press Secretary Larry M. Speakes announced Mr. Allin's resignation and read the text of the President's letter during his daily press briefing, which began at 12:30 p.m. in the Briefing Room at the White House.

Statement on the Economic Recovery
July 15, 1983

The report this morning of the 1.1-percent June rise in industrial production brings welcome news for the summer: America's recovery is strong and continues to build. This seventh straight month of improvement in the Nation's mines and factories saw widespread gains in the production of materials and products. It strongly suggests more Americans will find more jobs in the months ahead.

Our goal is an economic recovery that leads us to a new era—strong and steady growth with greater opportunities for all Americans. The latest news on inflation indicates economic growth can continue without triggering an outburst of new inflation.

We must not permit the specter of towering inflation and interest rates to reappear in America and destroy the progress we've made. So, I appeal to the Members of the Congress—both Republicans and Democrats—to work with us to hold down Federal spending and resist raising taxes on the people.

Proclamation 5072—National Atomic Veterans' Day, 1983
July 15, 1983

By the President of the United States of America

A Proclamation

Between 1945 and 1963 the United States conducted some 235 atmospheric nuclear weapons tests in the Pacific and the American Southwest. At least 220,000 American service men and women witnessed and participated in these tests, or served in forces occupying Hiroshima and Nagasaki immediately following World War II. It is only fitting that their dedication to duty be afforded proper recognition and brought to the attention of the American people.

Many of these American service men and women witnessed the awesome potential of nuclear weapons. In honoring these veterans, let us rededicate ourselves once more to our national goal of a world at peace in which nuclear war is unthinkable.

The Congress, by Senate Joint Resolution 68, has authorized and requested the President to issue a proclamation designating July 16, 1983, as "National Atomic Veterans' Day."

Now, Therefore, I, Ronald Reagan, President of the United States of America, do hereby designate Saturday, July 16, 1983, as National Atomic Veterans' Day, a day dedicated to those patriotic Americans who through their participation in these tests helped lead the United States to the forefront of technology in defense of our great Nation and the freedoms we as Americans hold so dear. I urge my fellow citizens to join with me in appreciation of their service to their country.

In Witness Whereof, I have hereunto set my hand this 15th day of July, in the year of our Lord nineteen hundred and eighty-three, and of the Independence of the United States of America, the two hundred and eighth.

RONALD REAGAN

[*Filed with the Office of the Federal Register, 4:13 p.m., July 15, 1983*]

Appointment of Five Members of the Board for International Food and Agricultural Development, and Designation of Chairman
July 15, 1983

The President today announced his intention to appoint the following individuals to be members of the Board for International Food and Agricultural Development for terms of 3 years. The President also intends to designate E. T. York as Chairman.

Duane Acker will succeed Daryl Arnold. Dr. Acker is president of Kansas State University in Manhattan, Kans. He has served as a director of the U.S. Council on Agricultural Science and Technology and as chairman of U.S. Deans of Agriculture. He is married, has two children, and resides in Manhattan, Kans. He was born March 13, 1931, in Atlantic, Iowa.

Warren J. Baker will succeed C. Peter McGrath. He is president of California Polytechnic State University in San Luis Obispo, Calif. He is also a registered civil engineer and has practiced in the field of geotechnical engineering. He is married, has four children, and resides in San Luis Obispo, Calif. He was born September 5, 1938, in Fitchburg, Miss.

Paul Findley will succeed Harold Frank Robinson. He is a former U.S. Representative from Illinois. He is adjunct professor at Western Illinois University. While serving as a Member of Congress, he was a member of the Foreign Affairs and Agriculture Committees. He is married, has two children, and resides in Falls Church, Va. He was born June 23, 1921, in Jacksonville, Ill.

Benjamin F. Payton will succeed Clifton R. Wharton, Jr. He is president of the Kresge Center at the Tuskegee Institute in Alabama. He is married, has two children, and resides in

Tuskegee Institute, Ala. He was born December 27, 1932, in Orangeburg, S.C.

E. T. York is a reappointment. He is chancellor emeritus of the State University System of Florida. He was provost for agriculture at the University of Florida in 1963–1973. Dr. York is a charter member and on the board of directors of Action for World Development and is a member of the technical advisory committee of the Consultative Group for International Research. He is married, has two children, and resides in Gainesville, Fla. He was born July 4, 1922, in Mentone, Ala.

Appointment of Four Members of the President's Committee on the National Medal of Science
July 15, 1983

The President today announced his intention to appoint the following individuals to be members of the President's Committee on the National Medal of Science for terms expiring December 31, 1985.

Katherine S. Bao will succeed David Baltimore. Dr. Bao is a pediatric cardiologist in Los Angeles, Calif. She also serves as a district medical consultant, Los Angeles Department of Rehabilitation, State of California, and as clinical assistant professor in pediatrics and cardiology, attending physician, University of California at Los Angeles. Dr. Bao is married, has two children, and resides in Los Angeles. She was born September 7, 1920.

Thomas B. Day will succeed Mary Jane Osborn. He is president of San Diego State University. He also serves as a visiting physicist at Brookhaven National Laboratory and Argonne National Laboratory. He is a fellow of the American Physical Society and a member of the American Association for the Advancement of Science. Dr. Day is married, has nine children, and resides in San Diego. He was born March 7, 1932.

Ryal R. Poppa will succeed Chien-Shiung Wu. He is chairman, president, and chief executive officer of BMC Industries, Inc., in St. Paul, Minn. Previously he was chairman and chief executive officer of Los Angeles based Pertec, manufacturer of computers. Mr. Poppa is past chairman and currently a director and member of the executive committee of the Computer and Communications Industry Association. He is married, has two children, and resides in White Bear Lake, Minn. He was born November 7, 1933.

Allan Spitz will succeed Steven Weinberg. Dr. Spitz is vice president for academic affairs and professor of political science at the University of Wyoming. Previously he was dean of the College of Liberal Arts and professor of political science at the University of New Hampshire. He currently serves as a member of the executive council of the National Association of State Universities and Land Grant Colleges. He is married, has two children, and resides in Laramie, Wyo. He was born October 9, 1928.

Statement on the Final Document Negotiated at the Madrid Review Meeting of the Conference on Security and Cooperation in Europe
July 15, 1983

After nearly 3 years of negotiation, the 35 states participating in the Madrid review meeting of the Conference on Security and Cooperation in Europe are approaching agreement on a concluding document—one that will strengthen and extend the undertakings contained in the Helsinki Final Act. It is a call on all 35 CSCE states—particularly those who have so tragically failed to live up to promises made in Helsinki—to give life to these commitments and to rededicate themselves to advancing the freedom and justice on which security in Europe ultimately depends.

We have agreed to this concluding document, as we did in 1975 to the Helsinki Final Act itself, with no illusions about the nature of the Soviet Union or about the system which it seeks to impose over much of Europe. In an ideal world, agreements such as this would not be necessary. But we believe it is the best agreement attainable, one which significantly improves on the Helsinki Final Act and advances the efforts of the West to hold out a beacon of hope for those in the East who seek a more free, just, and secure life.

Together with the Helsinki accords, this agreement sets forth a clearer code of conduct for all 35 CSCE states—a set of standards to which we and the other Atlantic democracies will continue to hold all those who will have pledged their word at Madrid. We will sign it with the hope that it will serve as a step toward achieving our objective of a more stable and constructive relationship with the Soviet Union.

The Madrid accord will add important new commitments to the Helsinki process, including provisions dealing with human rights, the trade union freedoms so tragically violated in Poland, terrorism, religious liberties, reunification of families, free flow of information, and more. It will provide for two important meetings of experts in the humanitarian field and for a security conference which will attempt to negotiate measures reducing the danger of surprise attack in Europe. Another full, followup meeting will take place in Vienna in 1986, where we will review the conduct of the participating states and seek to build on accomplishments at Madrid.

The unity and resolve of the Western democracies at Madrid have made this achievement possible. Ambassador Kampelman and his NATO colleagues deserve the highest praise for bringing this long and often difficult conference to a successful conclusion. We also owe a special vote of thanks to Prime Minister González of Spain, whose thoughtful proposal set the stage for final agreement.

In concluding the Madrid meeting, we reaffirm our commitment to the Helsinki process. We will not flag in our continued determination to work with all governments and peoples whose goal is the strengthening of peace in freedom. As Madrid has shown, dialog, when based on realistic expectations and conducted with patience, can produce results. These results are often gradual and hard-won, but they are the necessary building blocks for a more secure and stable world. The challenge remains. We must all consolidate and build on these gains; we must ensure that good words are transformed into good deeds and that the ideals which they embody are given concrete expression. Giving substance to the promises of Madrid and Helsinki will remain one of our prime objectives.

Radio Address to the Nation on Arms Control and Reduction
July 16, 1983

My fellow Americans:

Today I want to talk to you about peace. Back in June of 1963, President John F. Kennedy delivered an arms control speech that is still remembered for its eloquence and vision. He told the graduating seniors at American University: "I speak of peace, therefore, as the necessary, rational end of rational men. I realize that the pursuit of peace is not as dramatic as the pursuit of war and, frequently, the words of the pursuer fall on deaf ears. But we have no more urgent task."

Twenty years have passed since those words were spoken, and they've been a troubled era, overshadowed by the dangers of nuclear weapons. We've seen the world's inventory of nuclear weapons steadily expand. Despite many sincere attempts to control the growth of nuclear arsenals, those arsenals have continued to grow. That's the bad news.

The good news is that now, at last, there is hope that we can finally begin to reverse this trend. Americans have joined together—Republicans and Democrats, liberals and conservatives—to face the greatest challenge of our time: the urgent task of pursuing a lasting peace in the nuclear era. Our political process has forged a consensus, a bipartisan consensus that has united us in our common search for ways to protect our country, reduce the risk of war and, ultimately, dramatically reduce the level of nuclear weapons—the foundation we need for successful negotiations.

Remember, our MX Peacekeeper missile program calls for the deployment of 100 missiles. The level ultimately deployed, however, will clearly be influenced by the outcome in Geneva. If an agreement is reached which calls for deep reductions— which is, of course, our goal—the number of missiles could certainly be adjusted downward.

As the Scowcroft commission rightly pointed out, the MX Peacekeeper missile is an essential part of a comprehensive modernization and arms control program to ensure deterrence today and in the future. We're building the MX Peacekeeper to strengthen deterrence. But it also provides vital negotiating incentives and leverage in Geneva.

Andrei Sakharov, the distinguished Soviet physicist and Nobel Prize laureate, recently published an eloquent article which forcefully makes the same point. He notes that, given the Soviet advantage in land-based, strategic missiles, talks about limitation and reduction of these systems could become easier if the United States were to have MX missiles, albeit only potentially. Andrei Sakharov is a hard man for anyone to ignore.

When the Congress reaffirms its support for this program and authorizes the funds to modernize our strategic deterrent, our agenda for peace will be strengthened even further. In NATO, as in our other alliances, there's a renewed feeling of solidarity. Last May at Williamsburg, the leaders of the major industrialized nations demonstrated their commitment to vigorously pursue the twin objectives of arms reductions and deterrence in the Williamsburg communique. This solidarity is a source of much strength.

For the graduates of June 1983, this a time of opportunity and hope—a hope that they and their children will enjoy a safer, more secure world. That's why we must sustain our consensus. And that's why I've spent hundreds of hours meeting with members of this administration, with the bipartisan commission on strategic forces, with our arms negotiators, with Members of the Congress, and with concerned citizens.

My message to them and to you is that I have no higher priority than reducing and ultimately removing the threat of nuclear war and seeking the stability necessary for true peace. To achieve that objective, we must reduce the nuclear arsenals of both the United States and the Soviet Union. We must achieve greater stability; that is, we must be sure that we obtain genuine arms reductions, not merely agreements that permit a growth in nuclear arsenals or agreements that proclaim good intentions without the teeth necessary to verify and enforce compliance.

Our current goal must be the reduction of nuclear arsenals. And I for one believe we must never depart from the ultimate goal of banning them from the face of the Earth. That's why we presented ambitious but realistic proposals, and that's why I have been and continue to be willing to consider any serious Soviet counteroffer. And that's why I've made our original proposal more flexible and why I continue to seek new ideas for achieving an arms reduction breakthrough.

Indeed, the draft treaty our negotiators recently introduced in Geneva documents our flexibility. As opportunities permit, the U.S. position will continue to evolve. The United States will negotiate patiently but urgently and always in good faith.

But we cannot and we must not settle for less than genuine, mutual, and verifiable arms reductions. America's postwar generation has preserved world peace in its lifetime, but it's been an uneasy peace. Today's young Americans—indeed, all members of the human family—desire more and deserve more. And you deserve to know that your government is doing everything possible to meet your expectations.

Time and again our nation has proved that there are no limits to what we Americans can achieve when we work together.

Well, today we are working together to do what is right. And as a result, we can look forward to a more secure tomorrow.

Till next week, thanks for listening, and

God bless you.

Note: The President spoke at 12:06 p.m. from Camp David, Md.

Remarks at the Quadrennial Convention of the International Longshoremen's Association in Hollywood, Florida
July 18, 1983

Members of the Cabinet, Senator Hawkins, Members of the House of Representatives who are here, the distinguished people here on the podium, and you ladies and gentlemen:

I want you to know that I thank you for that very warm welcome. If I'd gotten this good a reception in that other Hollywood, I wouldn't have left. [*Laughter*]

But it's a pleasure to be here at this gathering of the International Longshoremen's Association. And it's always a pleasure to be with Teddy Gleason. I'll tell you what I've always liked about Teddy, he sticks by his union. He sticks by his friends, and he sticks by his country—the kind of integrity and loyalty that is hard to come by today. And one reason that I wanted to come here was to thank Teddy and you members of the ILA for your generous support and encouragement. Having the support of union members like yourselves has meant a great deal to me.

I hope I've returned that support. One of the things that I'm trying to do for union members and for all Americans is to fix things so that you can keep more of your hard-earned money in your pocket where it belongs. Not long ago, inflation was public enemy number one. We were told it could be a decade or more before we could ever hope to conquer it. Well, we've brought inflation down from double digit to 3½ percent for the last year and less than 2 percent for the last 6 months. And that has helped the working men and women of this nation.

You hear a lot about compassion in Washington from those who want us to return to the policies of the past. But their compassion is not for people; it's for programs.

Now, maybe there's a little compassion for people, for the people who make careers out of running those programs. What would have happened if we had permitted inflation caused by some of those programs to remain double digit? A family of four on a fixed income of $20,000 a year would be $1,700 poorer in purchasing power today. On top of that, they would have been made even poorer by much higher taxes.

High inflation, of course, drove up interest rates and virtually shut down the automobile industry and the housing industry. The prime rate was 21½ percent when we took office. It is less than half that now. Housing starts are up; auto sales are up; consumer spending is up; personal income is up; productivity is up. Our factories are beginning to hum, and people are being called back to work. Since last December, 1.1 million more people are working.

Let me just pause, if I could, for a second and interject something else about the unemployment picture. There's no question that in every recession unemployment is the last of the economic indicators to improve. And that's tragic. I wish it could be otherwise. I know a little bit about that subject. I was job hunting for my first job in the job market in 1932, in the depths of the Great Depression. But we have to understand that there's more than just people who have lost jobs, who are out of work. Thirty percent of today's unemployed are new entrants into the job market. It is not a static pool of people who, throughout the entire recession have been there unemployed.

Seventy percent of the unemployed today have been unemployed for 7 weeks or less. And of all the weeks of unemployment, 50 percent of them are accounted for by 3½ percent of the total unemployed. But that doesn't mean that we don't think there are things that can be done about it, and that's why we advanced spending for the next several years in public projects—to advance it to the present so that we could stimulate more jobs in that way. And that's why we are dwelling on job training for the changes that have occurred in the job market.

The recession that we're emerging from has been very difficult for many union members, especially those in auto and steel, as I mentioned before. But what we're doing is something that Washington has never had the self-discipline to do in the past. We're building a recovery that won't lapse back into inflation as soon as we turn around. We're building a recovery that is based on economic growth, that is based on government—not based on government temporarily pumping more money into the economy.

The recovery that we're experiencing is an honest one. And we're building it to last. Just look back at the recessions since World War II. I've heard a figure seven before this present one—maybe give or take one or two, that's about right. Again and again the quick fix was applied and inflation rose higher than it had been, and they laid a foundation for the next recession which usually followed in just 2 or 3 years.

You know, one of the things that I'm proudest of from my days in Hollywood is that I served six terms as my union's president. Now, six terms—I'll let you in on something. I don't think I could take six terms in Washington. [*Laughter*] But I'm very proud of my union service. And let me join your union leaders here today in saying, be proud of your service and of your union. Be proud of what unions symbolize. Free unions represent free people. And someday let us hope that the members of a union called Solidarity will be able to assemble like this and enjoy what ILA members enjoy every day—the freedom to organize.

Our democracy encompasses many freedoms—freedom of speech, of religion, of assembly, and so many other liberties that we often take for granted. These are rights that should be shared by all mankind. This union has always patriotically stood up for those freedoms. And that's why I want to talk to you today about freedom not in the United States, but in a part of the world that's very close and very important to us: Central America.

We all know that Central America suffers from decades of poverty, social deprivation, and political instability. And because these problems weren't dealt with positively, they're now being exploited by the enemies of freedom. We cannot afford the luxury of turning away from our neighbors' struggle as if they didn't matter. If we do turn away, we'll pay a terrible price for our neglect.

In April I reported to the Congress that the problems in Central America have the potential to affect our national security. This is still the case, and I want to reinforce it. Many of our citizens don't fully understand the seriousness of the situation, so let me put it bluntly: There is a war in Central America that is being fueled by the Soviets and the Cubans. They are arming, training, supplying, and encouraging a war to subjugate another nation to communism, and that nation is El Salvador. The Soviets and the Cubans are operating from a base called Nicaragua. And this is the first real Communist aggression on the American mainland. And we must never forget that here in the Western Hemisphere we are Americans in every country from pole to pole.

This Florida community where we meet today is closer to Nicaragua than it is to Washington, D.C. Two-thirds of our foreign trade and nearly half of our petroleum pass through the Caribbean. It's well to remember that in early 1942, a handful of Hitler's submarines sank more tonnage in that area than in all of the Atlantic Ocean, and they did this without a single naval base anywhere nearby. Today, Cuba is home to a Soviet combat brigade, a submarine base capable of servicing Soviet subs, and military air bases visited regularly by Soviet military aircraft that control our shores. If the Nazis during World War II and the Soviets today have recognized that the Caribbean and Central America is vital to our interests, don't you think it's about time that we recognize that, too?

Some people throw up their hands and

say, well, there's not much we can do down there. They say poverty and violence, repression in Central America are just the way of life, that democracy can't work. Well, I say "baloney." And I think we'd all say something stronger if we were down on the docks. [*Laughter*]

Costa Rica is as strong a democracy as you will find anywhere with a long history of peace, free elections, and stability. They don't even have an army. If democracy can work in Costa Rica and Honduras, if it can work in El Salvador and Nicaragua and Guatemala, there is still time for the people of Latin America to build a prosperous, peaceful, and free future. And we have an obligation to help them for our own sake as well as theirs.

People throughout Latin America are waiting to see if Republicans and Democrats in this country can work together to make the United States what it should be: a loyal friend and reliable defender of democracy and human decency. I believe that we must exercise that leadership, and the time is now.

Since I spoke to the Congress in April, Cuba has sent one of its best known combat generals to Nicaragua. More Cuban soldiers and Soviet supplies have arrived in Nicaragua. This cannot be allowed to continue.

Tomorrow, July 19th, is the fourth anniversary of the Sandinista revolution. This was a revolution that promised to bring freedom to the Nicaraguan people. History will call it the revolution of broken promises. Tomorrow, the nine military commanders who rule Nicaragua with Cuban and Soviet power will indulge in boastful revolutionary rhetoric. But there are few left who will believe them. This consensus throughout the hemisphere is that while the Sandinistas promise their people freedom, all they've done is replace the former dictatorship with their own, a dictatorship of counterfeit revolutionaries who wear fatigues and drive around in Mercedes sedans and Soviet tanks and whose current promise is to spread their brand of revolution throughout Central America.

What kind of freedom have the Sandinistas established? Just ask the 1,300 stevedores at the Nicaraguan port of Corinto. Last month, their union assembly was packed with Sandinistas, and six union leaders were arrested. Their presumed crime was trying to develop ties with independent trade unions, including some here affiliated with the AFL–CIO. I can tell you one thing, if all the longshoremen in Corinto are like Teddy Gleason, the Sandinistas have got a real fight on their hands.

Matter of fact, if they've got one like you, Teddy, they may be like those two fellows that were up sawing on a limb and one of them fell off. And there was a wildcat down below, and there were sounds of struggle coming up. And the one still up on the limb called down and said, "Hold on." And he said, "Hold on?" He said, "Come down and tell me how to let him go." [*Laughter*]

What kind of democracy is it? Ask the Nicaraguan refugees who've risked starvation and attack to escape to Honduras. Let me read to you directly from a newspaper article: ". . . one Nicaraguan man—still filthy, ragged and, above all, hungry after an odyssey that began 5 weeks ago— breathed a note of thanks: 'God has smiled on us.'" Imagine, with barely clothes on his back and nothing in his stomach, he believed that God had smiled on him because he'd arrived in free, democratic Honduras.

This man fled Nicaragua in May with many others when they learned the Sandinistas planned to relocate their villages. Let me quote again what one of the many others—what they had learned and what they had to say. They said, "We left everything. We left the pigs, the corn, the animals. . . . This year they wouldn't let us plant, because they wanted us to move closer to the military bases, they wanted us to be in the militia, and we did not want to be executioners."

Well, when the Sandinistas first took power, all their neighbors hoped that they would embrace democracy as they promised. In the first year and a half after the revolution, the United States sent $118 million worth of emergency relief and recovery aid to Nicaragua, more than provided by any other country in the world. But the Sandinistas had lied. They rejected their pledges to their own people, to the Organization of American States, and to the world.

Let me say a few more words about those

specific promises. The Sandinistas had promised the Organization of American States that they would hold elections and grant all human rights that go with a democracy. In short, they literally made a contract to establish a true democracy. The dictator Somoza was then persuaded by the OAS to resign and the government was turned over to the revolutionaries and recognized officially by the Organization of American States.

So far so good. But then, one faction of the revolutionaries, backed by Cuba and the Soviet Union, seized total power and ousted their revolutionary comrades who had been fighting to establish a real democracy. Nicaragua today is a nation abusing its own people and its neighbors. The guerrilla bands fighting in Nicaragua are trying to restore the true revolution and keep the promises made to the OAS. Isn't it time that all of us in the Americas worked together to hold Nicaragua accountable for the promises made and broken 4 years ago?

There's a vital link between what's happening in Nicaragua and what's happening in El Salvador. And the link is very simple: The dictators of Nicaragua are actively trying to destroy the budding democracy in neighboring El Salvador.

El Salvador is moving toward a more open society and government in the midst of a foreign-supported guerrilla war. National Presidential elections are planned. Through their Peace Commission, they've offered to talk even to the violent opposition about participating in these forthcoming elections They've implemented an effective land reform program which has provided land for over half a million Salvadorans, and they've given amnesty to former guerrillas.

This is El Salvador's revolution—it is one that is building democracy. Contrast this with the corrupted revolution in Nicaragua, one which has repressed human liberties, denied free unions and free elections, censored the press, and threatened its neighbors and violated a public pledge.

It's time El Salvador's recognized for what they're trying to do. And it's true that their path has been a hard one. Peaceful change has not always been easy or quick. We realize the human rights are not all in

El Salvador that we would like them to be. The killing must stop. But you have to realize much of the violence there—whether from the extreme right or left—is beyond the control of the government. El Salvador is moving in the right direction. Its elected government is committed to further improvement. They need and they deserve our help.

Just remember that scene last year after months of campaigning by a variety of candidates, the people of El Salvador were offered a chance to vote, to choose the kind of government they wanted. The guerrillas threatened death to anyone who voted. They destroyed hundreds of buses and trucks to keep the people from getting to the polling places. Their slogan was brutal: "Vote today and die tonight." But on election day, an unprecedented 80 percent of the electorate braved ambush and gunfire, and many of them trudged for miles to vote for freedom.

Members of our Congress who went there as observers told me of a woman who was wounded by rifle fire on the way to the polls. She refused to leave the line to have her wound treated until after she'd voted. Another woman had been told by the guerrillas that she would be killed when she returned from the polls. She was a grandmother. And she told the guerrillas, "You can kill me. You can kill my family. You can kill my neighbors. You can't kill us all." The real freedom fighters of El Salvador turned out to be the people of that country. The world should respect this courage and not allow it to be belittled or forgotten. And I say that we can never turn our backs on that.

The United States has only recently attempted to correct past neglect so that we could help Central America's struggle for freedom. We're working for political and economic development. Most of our aid is not military at all. Seventy-seven cents out of every dollar that we will spend this year will go for economic assistance—food, fertilizers, and other essentials to help break the vicious cycle of poverty. And make no mistake about this, of all the words that I've spoken today, let me underline these especially: America's emphasis in Central America is on economic and social progress, not on a purely military solution. But to give democracy and development a chance to work in the face of increasing attacks, we're providing a shield of military training and assistance to help our neighbors protect themselves.

Meanwhile, the trade provisions of the Caribbean Basin Initiative will stimulate production and employment. Last week's congressional vote on the CBI is a step toward more work for their longshoremen and ours. Nor is that all. We are actively supporting the search for political solution and dialog among and within these nations.

We know that peace ultimately can come only if people talk to each other and learn to accommodate in an atmosphere of freedom. To this end, I dispatched my special emissary to the region. Despite the fact that the guerrillas rejected our offer, we remain ready to facilitate free and open elections. We also support the process started at Contadora for a multilateral approach to peace.

In my speech to the Joint Session, I asked the Congress to join me in a bold, generous, bipartisan approach to the problems of peace and poverty, democracy and dictatorship in this region. Many Members of the Congress have responded in a genuine spirit of cooperation, despite divergent views on specific strategy. Senators Jackson and Mathias, Congressmen Barnes and Kemp have suggested the formation of a national commission to build on our bipartisan concern for these key issues.

I agree with them that this is a good idea. So, today, I am announcing a bipartisan national commission on Central America. The commission will lay the foundation for a long-term, unified, national approach to the freedom and independence of the countries of Central America. The commission will be honored by a very distinguished American, outstanding in the field of diplomacy, virtually a legend in that field. It will be headed by Dr. Henry Kissinger, who will present recommendations to me later this year. Their focus will be on long term, looking to what it is that we want and what we must do in the years ahead to meet the underlying problems of the region.

In the meantime, we must not allow totalitarian communism to win by default.

But we cannot succeed unless the Congress approves the necessary resources. All that our neighbors ask is for the tools to do the job themselves. And I ask you and every American, regardless of political party, to join in a common effort to promote freedom for all the people of this hemisphere.

Just as you work so your children will have a better future, the United States must work so that the fledgling democracies of this hemisphere will have a better future and so that our own future can be more secure. The legislative branch must bear its share of responsibility for ensuring this promise.

You know, I was down in that area on a trip, I met with the heads of several of the states of Central and South America. And I pointed something out to them that very often we tend to forget. This Western Hemisphere is unique. We are, as I said before, 30 countries down there, the three here in the northern continent—but we are all Americans. We cross a line into another country; it is still North and South and Central America. And we haven't gotten together the way we should. We don't know enough about that area, and we need to do more.

Can you imagine what a power for good in the world these two continents, linked by the Isthmus of Central America—we worship from South Pole to North Pole the same God. We have the same heritage of coming here as pioneers to these virtually undiscovered continents. And what a power for good we could be with all the resources available in these continents if we help them in achieving what we have achieved here in this land—in freedom, in economic progress, in standard of living.

Human rights means working at problems, not walking away from them. Without the necessary funds, there's no way for us to prevent the light of freedom from being extinguished in Central America, and then it will move on from there. A truly bipartisan approach to these problems can produce the kind of progress that will help the people of the region help themselves.

You know, I've heard, already and before—knowing Teddy Gleason, you know I've heard that ILA stands for I Love America. And that's true. I don't think America has a more patriotic union than this one. This union is great for the same reason America is great—because so many different groups are working together, pulling together toward a common goal. The cultural diversity of this union and this country make us both strong and free.

President Harrison once said, "In America, a glorious fire has been lighted upon the altar of liberty. Keep it burning; and let the sparks that continually go up from it fall on other altars, and light up in distant lands the fire of freedom."

Today I ask you to join me in an effort to keep the light of liberty alive in Central America. We must never let freedom fade where there's a chance to save it. We must never let the enemies of human dignity die out simply because it's—the embers, I should say, not the enemies, the embers of human dignity die out because it's easier to turn the other way. With a timely investment now, we can save freedom in Central America. And I believe we must make that investment. I believe we have a moral responsibility to do so. And I believe with the help of organizations like the ILA, we will succeed in expanding freedom for the people of Central America.

Thank you, and God bless you.

Note: The President spoke at 12:52 p.m. in the convention center at the Diplomat Resort and Country Club. He was introduced by Thomas W. (Teddy) Gleason, president of the association. Prior to his remarks, the President met with the association's leadership.

Following his appearance at the convention, the President held separate meetings with the executive council of the International Longshoremen's Association and south Florida Jewish leaders at the resort. He then returned to Washington, D.C.

Nomination of Edmund DeJarnette To Be United States Ambassador to the Central African Republic
July 18, 1983

The President today announced his intention to nominate Edmund DeJarnette, of Virginia, a career member of the Senior Foreign Service, Class of Minister-Counselor, as Ambassador to the Central African Republic. He would succeed Arthur H. Woodruff.

Mr. DeJarnette served in the United States Coast Guard in 1960. In 1964 he was appointed to the Foreign Service and was Foreign Service officer general in Niamey in 1965–1967. In 1968 he resigned to become State campaign coordinator of the Pollard for Governor campaign in Richmond, Va., and was fundraiser in the Capital Development Office of Randolph-Macon College in Richmond in 1969–1970. In 1970 he was reappointed to the Foreign Service as Peace Corps Deputy Director for Ecuador in Quito (1970–1972), for Latin America in Washington (1972–1973), and in Quito, Ecuador (1973–1975). In 1975–1977 he was Deputy Chief of Mission in Libreville. He attended the Industrial College of the Armed Forces in 1977–1978. In the Department he was personnel officer of the Office of Performance Evaluation in the Bureau of Personnel in 1978–1980. Since 1980 he has been Deputy Chief of Mission in Dakar.

Mr. DeJarnette graduated from the University of Virginia (B.A., 1959; LL.B., 1963) and George Washington University (M.S., 1978). His foreign languages are French, Spanish, and Portuguese. He was born January 15, 1938, in Richmond, Va.

Remarks at the Welcoming Ceremony for Amir Isa bin Sulman Al Khalifa of Bahrain
July 19, 1983

The President. Your Highness, it is a pleasure for Nancy and me to welcome you to the United States as a guest of the American people. Your concern for your people is well known, particularly your commitment to the education and economic well-being of your citizens. Your personal involvement in the problems of even the humblest of your countrymen is legendary. For these reasons and others, I've looked forward to the day when we could meet.

Your Highness, you've guided Bahrain through a difficult first decade of independence with admirable skill, bringing economic progress with imaginative leadership. With far fewer oil resources than some of your neighbors, you've transformed Bahrain into a financial and industrial center with one of the most diversified economies in the region. Just as important, because of your progressive leadership, Bahrain also leads the area in health care and education. As it has been since ancient times, Bahrain continues to be a place where people of different cultures and religions live together in tolerance and peace. Your efforts to build a humane and diverse society provide an effective link in the exchange of technical skills and cultural values between East and West.

Under your leadership, Bahrain continues to be an inspiring example for all of the Middle East and the world. The American people are pleased to have been counted as supportive friends as you built this record of achievement. Our two peoples have been partners for progress and peace since the beginning of this century. We have found this relationship to be of great mutual benefit. Many of the 70 United States companies in Bahrain today continue to train Bahrainis in technology and other skills, whether they be modern banking techniques, setting up new industries, or preparing coaches and athletes for Bahrain's Olympic teams. Our long history of private sector cooperation is a shining example of what can be achieved in a partnership based on mutual trust and respect.

Your Highness, as you're keenly aware, continued prosperity for your people and those of the Gulf region depend on peace and security. It is no secret that the United States has a vital national interest in the Middle East. We and our allies depend on oil originating there, much of it produced in and nearby your country. Yet we also recognize the value of partnership and respect for the culture and aspirations of states like your own—unlike another world power which seeks to impose its system by encouraging and exploiting conflict and unrest. But the United States seeks peace and stability.

Together with other peace-loving nations in the Gulf region, we've made rapid progress in recent years, not only by helping our friends meet their own defense requirements but also by developing our own ability to come to their assistance should the need ever arise.

Many Americans who work in the region have experienced hospitality of the Bahraini people, and for this I am most appreciative. During his recent visit, Crown Prince Hamad deepened his friendship between our two countries.

Your Highness, I want to assure you that I share your concern about the conflict between Iraq and Iran. The loss of tens of thousands of young men on both sides and the destruction borne by both countries is tragic. I look forward to consulting with you about what more our countries might do to encourage a negotiated end to this conflict, which threatens the security and even the marine ecology of the entire area.

We've appreciated your government's understanding as we pursue our goal of seeking the withdrawal of all foreign forces from Lebanon and securing a settlement for the Palestinian people that is firmly rooted in the principles of security and justice embodied in the United Nations Security Council Resolutions 242 and 338.

As you know, Secretary Shultz returned

recently from the Middle East. We remain undaunted in our effort to prevent the forces of violence from exercising a veto over the rights of the Lebanese people. The people of Lebanon must have restored their basic human right to pursue their own destiny in an atmosphere of peace, security, and mutual trust.

I look forward to discussing our many common concerns with you today. I know our shared goals of peace and prosperity for the region can be met in the same spirit of good will and partnership that has characterized our friendship thus far.

On behalf of the American people it is my privilege to welcome you to the United States.

The Amir. Mr. President, I would like to offer my appreciation and thanks for the kind thoughts expressed in your address towards the State of Bahrain and for the welcome and hospitalities extended to us from the very beginning of our official visit to your friendly country. This indicates the strength of the friendly ties existing between our two countries. I offer my genuine good wishes to the friendly people of the United States of America for their well-being and prosperity.

I believe that this visit will succeed in developing the relations between our two countries, open up a new chapter in our fruitful cooperation, and support our efforts to help maintain peace, security, and justice for the world community. As you have referred, Mr. President, in your address, to some of the most important economic and political issues in the world, I should commend in this respect the positive role you play for the prosperity and security of the world. We, no doubt, support and uphold the great effort you make in this field; as we firmly believe that such issues are very important for the progress of the individual in the modern world and that without them clashes and war will break out. Clashes and war will break out and destroy all of the progress made over the years.

In the light of many common views we share in the political field, we believe, as you do, that the Middle East problem comes in the forefront of political issues in the world. It is one of the burning and explosive problems in the world, which passes now through a very dangerous stage that poses a serious threat to the world peace and security. This imposes upon us the duty to make every effort to save the region from this disastrous situation.

We hope that the sincere and good effort you make to find a suitable solution to this problem will result in establishing just and durable peace in the region, which has been exposed to five major wars within 35 years with disastrous effects to its people. The tragic events in Lebanon and the damage it has suffered are but some of many inevitable results of the explosive situation in the region. Lebanon deserves all the help and backing so that its government will exercise full control over its unified territories.

We believe that there will be no hope of stability in the Middle East without the application of the same universal principles upon the people of the region; and concluding, the Palestinian people, when they are dealing with their legitimate right to live in peace within secure national boundaries.

We are prepared to do our best and participate in every sincere, international effort to establish security in the Middle East region, within this framework, in order to put an end to this terrible conflict and enable the people of the region to live in peace.

Finally, it is my pleasure to conclude by wishing you, Mr. President, all the success in your efforts for the progress and advance of the friendly people of the United States of America, and to bring peace, justice, and prosperity to the people of the world.

Thank you.

Note: The President spoke at 10:09 a.m. on the South Lawn of the White House, where the Amir was accorded a formal welcome with full military honors.

Following the ceremony, the President and the Amir, together with U.S. and Bahraini officials, met in the Oval Office.

Appointment of Angela M. Buchanan as a Member of the President's Advisory Committee on Women's Business Ownership, and Designation as Chairperson
July 19, 1983

The President today announced his intention to appoint Angela M. Buchanan to be a member of the President's Advisory Committee on Women's Business Ownership. This is a new position. The President also intends to designate her Chairperson.

Ms. Buchanan served as Treasurer of the United States in 1981–1983. Previously she was national treasurer of the Reagan for President Committee and later the Reagan-Bush Committee. She served as Chairperson of the Interagency Committee on Women's Business Enterprise from May 1983 until her resignation as Treasurer of the United States in July 1983.

She graduated from Rosemont College (B.A.) and McGill University (M. Sc., mathematics). She is married, has one child, and resides in Los Angeles, Calif. She was born December 20, 1948.

Appointment of Frank D. Stella as a Member of the President's Commission on White House Fellowships
July 19, 1983

The President today announced his intention to appoint Frank D. Stella to be a member of the President's Commission on White House Fellowships. This is an initial appointment.

Mr. Stella is president and founder of the F. D. Stella Products Co. in Detroit, Mich. He was a member of the board of trustees (1971–1980) and the executive committee (1971–1977) of the University of Detroit. He served as chairman of the Income Tax Board of Review, city of Detroit, for over 9 years.

He is married, has seven children, and resides in Detroit, Mich. He was born January 21, 1919, in Jessup, Pa.

Nomination of Alvin L. Alm To Be Deputy Administrator of the Environmental Protection Agency
July 19, 1983

The President today announced his intention to nominate Alvin L. Alm to be Deputy Administrator of the Environmental Protection Agency. He would succeed John Whitlock Hernandez, Jr.

Mr. Alm is presently serving as director of the Harvard Energy Security Program and lecturer at the Harvard Kennedy School of Government. Previously he was Assistant Secretary for Policy and Evaluation at the Department of Energy (1977–1979); Assistant Administrator for Planning and Management at the Environmental Protection Agency (1973–1977); and Staff Director at the Council on Environmental Quality in 1970–1973. He serves on the Environmental Studies Board of the National Academy of Sciences and is on the board of editorial advisers of "Environmental Forum."

He graduated from the University of Denver (B.A., 1960) and Syracuse University Maxwell Graduate School (M.P.A., 1961). He is married, has one child, and resides in Cambridge, Mass. He was born January 27, 1937, in Denver, Colo.

Statement by Deputy Press Secretary Speakes on the Situation in the Middle East
July 19, 1983

The President, as you know, spoke this morning with Prime Minister Begin regarding the postponement of the Prime Minister's visit to Washington, which had been scheduled for next week.

While we regret the President and the Prime Minister will not be able to meet next week, we look forward to rescheduling the meeting before the end of the year.

Meanwhile, we anticipate discussions on the Middle East peace process with Israel and other nations in the region will continue. We see this as in no way an impediment to the progress of our peace initiative in Lebanon or in the region as a whole. Secretary Shultz has just completed an extensive round of talks with the leaders of Israel, Syria, Egypt, Lebanon, Saudi Arabia, and Jordan regarding the current situation. In Israel, he had detailed discussions with the Prime Minister, the Foreign Minister, and the Defense Minister. We anticipate our diplomatic discussions will continue at all levels during this critical period.

As far as the President is concerned, we will continue our pursuit of the full withdrawal of all foreign forces from Lebanon, the reestablishment of Lebanon's sovereignty over all its territory, and the security of its borders. We will continue to have discussions with all parties leading toward this objective.

At the same time, we will continue our pursuit of peace as outlined by the President last September 1.

Note: Deputy Press Secretary Larry M. Speakes read the statement to reporters assembled in the Briefing Room at the White House for the daily press briefing, which began at 12:30 p.m.

Earlier in the day, Mr. Speakes announced that Prime Minister Menachem Begin of Israel telephoned the President that morning to say that he would have to postpone his visit to the United States for personal reasons.

Remarks at a Ceremony Marking the Annual Observance of Captive Nations Week
July 19, 1983

Thank you. You know, I have to apologize here for keeping you waiting. And I always wonder if there isn't some way, without making it sound that way, if in that announcement they couldn't say "the late President"—[*laughter*]—"of the United States."

But thank you all very much. And Members of the Congress and Excellencies here, and fellow Americans and, may I add, fellow citizens of the world who yearn to breathe free, we're honored to welcome all of you. I'd like to thank Congressman Jerry Solomon for his strong support of this event.

And today we come to show solidarity with our brothers and sisters who are captives, not because of crimes that they have committed but because of crimes committed against them by dictators and tyrants.

We met here last month with a group of Baltic Americans honoring Baltic Freedom Day. And I said that we gathered to draw attention to the plight of the Baltic people and to affirm to the world that we do not recognize their subjugation as a permanent condition.

Today, we speak to all in Eastern Europe who are separated from neighbors and loved ones by an ugly iron curtain. And to every person trapped in tyranny, whether in the Ukraine, Hungary, Czechoslovakia, Cuba, or Vietnam, we send our love and support and tell them they are not alone. Our message must be: Your struggle is our struggle, your dream is our dream, and someday, you, too, will be free. As Pope John Paul told his beloved Poles, we are blessed by divine heritage. We are children of God and we cannot be slaves.

The prophet Isaiah admonished the world, ". . . Bind up the brokenhearted to proclaim liberty to the captives." Some 25 centuries later, philosophers would declare that "the cause of freedom is the cause of God."

We Americans understand the truth of these words. We were born a nation under God, sought out by people who trusted in Him to work His will in their daily lives, so America would be a land of fairness, morality, justice, and compassion.

Many governments oppress their people and abuse human rights. We must oppose this injustice. But only one so-called revolution puts itself above God, insists on total control over the peoples' lives, and is driven by the desire to seize more and more lands. As we mark this 25th observance of Captive Nations Week, I have one question for those rulers: If communism is the wave of the future, why do you still need walls to keep people in and armies of secret police to keep them quiet?

Democracy may not be perfect, but the brave people who risk death for freedom are not fleeing from democracy—they're fleeing to democracy from communism.

Two visions of the world remain locked in dispute. The first believes all men are created equal by a loving God who has blessed us with freedom. Abraham Lincoln spoke for us: "No man," he said, "is good enough to govern another without the other's consent."

The second vision believes that religion is opium for the masses. It believes that eternal principles like truth, liberty, and democracy have no meaning beyond the whim of the state. And Lenin spoke for them: "It is true, that liberty is precious," he said, "so precious that it must be rationed."

Well, I'll take Lincoln's version over Lenin's—[*laughter*]—and so will citizens of the world if they're given free choice.

Now, some believe we must muffle our voices for the cause of peace. I disagree. Peace is made or broken with deeds, not words. No country has done more or will strive harder for peace than the United States. I will personally embrace any meaningful action by the Soviet Union to help us create a more peaceful, safe, and secure world. I welcome the Soviet pledge of cooperation at the Madrid review Conference on Security and Cooperation in Europe. With every ounce of my being I pray the day will come when nuclear weapons no longer exist anywhere on Earth. And as long as I'm President, we'll work day in and day out to achieve mutual and verifiable reductions in strategic weapons.

When Congress approved the MX Peacekeeper program last May, America demonstrated its bipartisan consensus to implement the recommendations of the Scowcroft commission. This bipartisan step marked progress toward genuine arms reductions. In the next few days, the Congress will vote on the question of supreme importance: Do we continue forward, or do we turn back from the Scowcroft commission's recommendations?

In terms of speaking to the world with one bipartisan voice, of standing up for U.S. vital interests, and of strengthening America's agenda for peace, no question matters more for this country in 1983.

Rather than seek temporary, partisan advantage, let us work together for the future of mankind. We must not waver in our request for genuine peace and cooperation. We must keep our military strong to deter aggression. And we will never shrink from speaking the truth.

Ask yourselves: Was it our words that destroyed peace in Afghanistan, or was it Soviet aggression? Is peace served by sealing our lips while millions are tortured or killed in Vietnam and Cambodia? Or should we not speak out to demand those crimes be stopped? It's not provocative to warn that once a Communist revolution occurs, citizens are not permitted free elections, a free press, free trade, free unions, free speech, freedom to worship, or property, or freedom to travel as we please. Many military regimes have evolved into democracies. But no Communist regime has ever become a democracy, provided freedom or given its people economic prosperity.

We will speak the truth. Aleksandr Herzen, the Russian writer, warned: "To shrink from saying a word in defense of the oppressed is as bad as any crime." That's why we want improved and expanded broadcasts over the Voice of America, Radio Free Europe, and Radio Liberty. And that's why we want, and the Cuban people need, Radio Marti.

Now, many of you here have known the suffering that I've described. You are the conscience of the free world, and I appeal to you to make your voices heard. Tell them: "You may jail your people. You may seize their goods. You may ban their unions. You may bully their rabbis and dissidents. You may forbid the name of Jesus to pass their lips. But you will never destroy the love of God and freedom that burns in their hearts. They will triumph over you."

Help us warn the American people that for the first time in memory we face real dangers on our own borders, that we must protect the safety and security of our people. We must not permit outsiders to threaten the United States. We must not permit dictators to ram communism down the throats of one Central American country after another.

We've seen construction in Cuba of a naval base from which Soviet nuclear submarines can operate. We see Soviet capacity for air reconnaissance over our eastern coast from Cuban bases. And we see the Soviets and Cuba building a war machine in Nicaragua that dwarfs the forces of all their neighbors combined. Let's not fool ourselves: This war machine isn't being built to make Central America safe for democracy. It isn't being built to pursue peace, economic or social reform. It's being built, by their own boast, to impose a revolution without frontiers.

Now, this is not my problem; it's our problem. But if we pull together, we can solve it. As I announced yesterday, I'm appointing a bipartisan commission on Central America. And let us resolve today: There must be no more captive nations in this hemisphere.

With faith as our guide, we can muster the wisdom and will to protect the deepest treasures of the human spirit—the freedom to build a better life in our time and the promise of life everlasting in His kingdom.

Aleksandr Solzhenitsyn told us, "Our entire earthly existence is but a transitional stage in the movement toward something higher, and we must not stumble and fall, nor must we linger . . . on one rung of the ladder."

With your help, we will stand shoulder to shoulder, and we'll keep our sights on the farthest stars.

Thank you very much, and God bless you.

Note: The President spoke at 1:38 p.m. in Room 450 of the Old Executive Office Building.

On June 6, the President signed Proclamation 5067, proclaiming the week beginning July 17 as Captive Nations Week.

Executive Order 12433—National Bipartisan Commission on Central America
July 19, 1983

By the authority vested in me as President by the Constitution and laws of the United States of America, and in order to establish, in accordance with the provisions of the Federal Advisory Committee Act, as amended (5 U.S.C. App. I), the National Bipartisan Commission on Central America, it is hereby ordered as follows:

Section 1. Establishment. (a) There is established the National Bipartisan Commission on Central America. The Commission shall be composed of not more than 12 members appointed or designated by the President. These members shall be drawn from among distinguished leaders of the government, business, labor, education, Hispanic and religious communities. No more than seven members shall be of the same political party.

(b) The President shall designate a Chairman from among the members of the Commission.

Sec. 2. Functions. (a) The Commission shall study the nature of United States interests in the Central American region and the threats now posed to those interests. Based on its findings, the Commission shall provide advice to the President, the Secretary of State and the Congress on elements of a long-term United States policy that will best respond to the challenges of social, economic, and democratic development in the region, and to internal and external threats to its security and stability. The Commission also shall provide advice on means of building a national consensus on a comprehensive United States policy for the region.

(b) The Commission shall report to the President by December 1, 1983.

Sec. 3. Administration. (a) The heads of Executive agencies shall, to the extent permitted by law, provide the Commission such information as it may require for purposes of carrying out its functions.

(b) Members of the Commission shall serve without compensation for their work on the Commission. However, members appointed from among private citizens of the United States may, subject to the availability of funds, be allowed travel expenses, including per diem in lieu of subsistence, as authorized by law for persons serving intermittently in the government service (5 U.S.C. 5701–5707).

(c) The Secretary of State shall, to the extent permitted by law, provide the Commission with such administrative services, funds, facilities, staff and other support services as may be necessary for the performance of its functions.

Sec. 4. General. (a) Notwithstanding any other Executive Order, the functions of the President under the Federal Advisory Committee Act, as amended, which are applicable to the Commission, shall be performed by the Secretary of State, in accordance with guidelines and procedures established by the Administrator of General Services.

(b) The Commission shall, unless otherwise extended, terminate 60 days after submitting its final report.

RONALD REAGAN

The White House,
July 19, 1983.

[*Filed with the Office of the Federal Register, 11:16 a.m., July 20, 1983*]

Appointment of the Membership of the National Bipartisan Commission on Central America
July 19, 1983

The President today announced his intention to appoint the following individuals to be members of the National Bipartisan Commission on Central America:

Dr. Henry Kissinger, Chairman of the Commission, New York, N.Y.

Nicholas F. Brady, managing director, Dillon Read & Co., Inc., Far Hills, N.J.

Henry G. Cisneros, mayor, San Antonio, Tex.

William P. Clements, Jr., former Governor of Texas, Dallas, Tex.

Dr. Carlos F. Diaz-Alejandro, professor of economics, Yale University, New Haven, Conn.

Wilson S. Johnson, president, National Federation of Independent Business, San Mateo, Calif.

Lane Kirkland, president, AFL–CIO, Washington, D.C.

Dr. Richard M. Scammon, political scientist, Chevy Chase, Md.

Dr. John Silber, president, Boston University, Brookline, Mass.

Potter Stewart, Associate Justice, Supreme Court of the United States (Retired), Washington, D.C.

Ambassador Robert S. Strauss, attorney at law, Washington, D.C.

William B. Walsh, president, Project Hope, Bethesda, Md.

The President's Representative to the Commission will be:

Ambassador Jeane J. Kirkpatrick, United States Representative to the United Nations.

The Commission is bipartisan, with no more than 7 of its 12 members from the same political party. In addition to the above, there will be Senior Counselors designated by the President. They will include two Democrats recommended by the Speaker and two Republicans recommended by the minority leader from the House of Representatives, and two Republicans recommended by the majority leader and two Democrats recommended by the minority leader from the United States Senate.

Proclamation 5073—Bicentennial Year of the Birth of Simon Bolivar
July 19, 1983

By the President of the United States of America

A Proclamation

July 24, 1983, marks the bicentennial of the birth of Simon Bolivar, the great Liberator who laid the foundation for the Inter-American System. The Government and people of the United States take pride in joining with the other countries of the Americas in celebrating this historic event. A great soldier and patriot, Simon Bolivar serves as an inspiration to all the peoples of the western hemisphere. Through turbulent and frustrating times, he had the vision to see that the unity of the Americas could be achieved.

Bolivar's military prowess made independence possible for Venezuela, Colombia, Peru, Ecuador, Bolivia, and Panama in a struggle similar to that which had brought the United States its liberty forty years earlier. Although shaken by personal tragedy and disappointed by two unsuccessful attempts to establish an independent republic in his homeland, Bolivar persevered. His burning desire for freedom could not be extinguished, and his subsequent brilliant military victories inspired an entire continent. Likewise, his vision of a united Americas continues to inspire new generations of citizens in every country of this hemisphere.

Bolivar's letter from Jamaica on September 6, 1815, poignantly expressed his dream of a union "with a single bond that unites its parts among themselves and to the whole." With this aim in mind, he convoked the Congress of Panama in 1826, which signalled a decisive step toward the system of cooperation we enjoy today. The Treaty drawn up by that Congress was ratified by only one country, but the idea of forming a coalition of American Republics took root, slowly developed, and finally evolved into a unique and beneficial system of international cooperation.

From the seeds planted by Simon Bolivar, the Organization of American States was born. Bolivar's ideals of Pan Americanism, based on independence, solidarity, sovereignty, as well as the right of all nations to live in peace, find clear expression in the Charter of the Organization of American States.

The debt owed by all Americans to Simon Bolivar is incalculable. Thus, it is fitting that we should pause and reflect upon his great achievements in this bicentennial year of his birth. On this occasion, we in the United States join with our hemispheric friends to remember the great hero whose ideals bind us closer together. Bolivar, more than any other figure in the history of the western hemisphere, understood that, while we are citizens of separate countries, we are members of one family in the new world—we are Americans.

The Congress of the United States, by Senate Concurrent Resolution 14, has authorized and requested the President to issue a proclamation designating the period from July 24, 1983 through July 23, 1984, as the bicentennial year of the birth of Simon Bolivar.

Now, Therefore, I, Ronald Reagan, President of the United States of America, do hereby designate the year beginning July 24, 1983 through July 23, 1984 as the Bi-centennial Year of the Birth of Simon Bolivar, hero of the independence of the Americas.

In Witness Whereof, I have hereunto set my hand this 19th day of July, in the year of our Lord nineteen hundred and eighty-three, and of the Independence of the United States of America the two hundred and eighth.

RONALD REAGAN

[*Filed with the Office of the Federal Register, 11:18 a.m., July 20, 1983*]

Executive Order 12434—Alaska Railroad Rates
July 19, 1983

By the authority vested in me as President by the Constitution and statutes of the United States of America, including the Alaska Railroad Act, as amended (38 Stat. 305, 43 U.S.C. 975–975g), and in order to determine the procedures for establishing rates for the Alaska Railroad, it is hereby ordered as follows:

Section 1. General Responsibility. The Secretary of Transportation is authorized to operate and administer the Alaska Railroad, except that the authority of the Secretary to fix, change, or modify rates for the transportation of passengers and property shall be subject to the authority of the Interstate Commerce Commission, pursuant to Section 3 of this Order.

Sec. 2. Rates—Secretary of Transportation. (a) In exercising the authority granted by this Order to fix, change, or modify rates of the Alaska Railroad, the Secretary of Transportation is authorized to establish rates and enter into rate arrangements, including contracts, with other parties to the same extent as comparable rail carriers subject to the jurisdiction of the Interstate Commerce Commission under subchapter I of chapter 105 of title 49 of the United States Code. Such rates shall be filed with the Interstate Commerce Commission to the same extent as rates are filed by comparable rail carriers subject to its jurisdiction.

(b) Any contract filed with the Commis-sion shall be available to any other shipper for rates and services for transportation of the same type of commodity under similar conditions to the contract on file, if the other shipper is able to enter into such contract at a time essentially contemporaneous with the period during which the contract on file is offered.

(c) Connecting water carriers may participate in Alaska Railroad contract rate agreements.

(d) Alaska Railroad rates, rate arrangements, and contracts entered into pursuant to this Order and Executive Order No. 11107 of April 26, 1963 are subject to the actions of the Interstate Commerce Commission, pursuant to Section 3 of this Order.

Sec. 3. Rates—Interstate Commerce Commission. With respect to rates filed by the Secretary with the Interstate Commerce Commission pursuant to Section 2 of this Order, the Commission may act in the same manner as though the Alaska Railroad were subject to section 10101a; subchapter I of chapter 105; subchapter I of chapter 107; subchapter II of chapter 107, except sections 10723 and 10724; subchapter III of chapter 107, except sections 10746 and 10751; subchapter IV of chapter 107; subchapter I of chapter 111; subchapter II of chapter 111; and chapter 117, except sections 11703 and 11704 of title 49 of the

United States Code: Provided, however, that to the extent Section 2 of this Order may grant additional authority or impose additional limitations, the standards established by Section 2 shall be applicable.

Sec. 4. Conforming Provisions. (a) Executive Order No. 11107 is superseded.

(b) Any existing Alaska Railroad rate entered into under Executive Order No. 11107 shall have the same force and effect as if it had been entered into in accordance with the provisions of this Order.

(c) Any Alaska railroad rate entered into in accordance with this Order shall be deemed to be in compliance with the Alaska Railroad Act, as amended.

RONALD REAGAN

The White House,
July 19, 1983.

[Filed with the Office of the Federal Register, 11:17 a.m., July 20, 1983]

Proclamation 5074—Temporary Duty Increases and Quantitative Limitations on the Importation Into the United States of Certain Stainless Steel and Alloy Tool Steel
July 19, 1983

By the President of the United States of America

A Proclamation

1. Pursuant to section 201(d)(1) of the Trade Act of 1974 (the Trade Act) (19 U.S.C. 2251(d)(1)), the United States International Trade Commission (USITC) on May 6, 1983, reported to the President the results of its Investigation No. TA–201–48 under section 201(b) of the Trade Act (19 U.S.C. 2251(b)). The USITC determined that certain bars; wire rods; and plates, sheets, and strip, not cut, not pressed, and not stamped to nonrectangular shape; all the foregoing of stainless steel or certain alloy tool steel; and round wire of high speed tool steel; provided for in items 606.90, 606.93, 606.94, 606.95, 607.26, 607.28, 607.34, 607.43, 607.46, 607.54, 607.72, 607.76, 607.88, 607.90, 608.26, 608.29, 608.34, 608.43, 608.49, 608.57, 608.64, and 609.45 of the Tariff Schedules of the United States (TSUS) (19 U.S.C. 1202), are being imported into the United States in such increased quantities as to be a substantial cause of serious injury to the domestic industries producing articles like or directly competitive with the imported articles. The USITC recommended the imposition of quantitative restrictions on imports of articles classified in the above TSUS

items with exemptions for certain articles which are not produced in the United States or are produced in such small quantities that their exemption would not have an adverse impact on the domestic industry.

2. On July 5, 1983, pursuant to section 202(b)(1) of the Trade Act (19 U.S.C. 2252(b)(1)), and after taking into account the considerations specified in section 202(c) of the Trade Act (19 U.S.C. 2252(c)), I determined to impose additional tariffs and quantitative restrictions, with exemptions for certain articles which are not produced in the United States or are produced in such small quantities that their exemption would not have an adverse impact on the domestic industry. On July 5, 1983, in accordance with section 203(b)(1) of the Trade Act (19 U.S.C. 2253(b)(1)), I transmitted a report to the Congress setting forth my determination and intention to proclaim these additional tariffs and quotas, and stating the reasons why my decision differed from the action recommended by the USITC.

3. Section 203(e)(1) of the Trade Act (19 U.S.C. 2253(e)(1)) requires that import relief be proclaimed and take effect within 15 days after the import relief determination date.

4. Pursuant to sections 203(a)(1), 203(a)(3), and 203(e)(1) of the Trade Act (19 U.S.C. 2253(a)(1), 2253(a)(3), and 2253(e)(1)), I am

providing import relief through the temporary imposition of increased tariffs and quantitative restrictions on certain stainless steel and alloy tool steel, as hereinafter proclaimed.

5. In accordance with section 203(d)(2) of the Trade Act (19 U.S.C. 2253(d)(2)), I have determined that the level of import relief hereinafter proclaimed pursuant to section 203(a)(3) of the Trade Act (19 U.S.C. 2253(a)(3)) permits the importation into the United States of a quantity of articles which is not less than the average annual quantity of such articles imported into the United States in the 1972–1982 period, exclusive of 1975 and 1982, which I have determined to be the most recent representative period for imports of such articles.

Now, Therefore, I, Ronald Reagan, President of the United States of America, acting under the authority vested in me by the Constitution and the statutes of the United States, including sections 203 and 604 of the Trade Act (19 U.S.C. 2253 and 2483), and in accordance with Article XIX of the General Agreement on Tariffs and Trade (GATT) (61 Stat. (pt. 5) A58; 8 UST (pt. 2) 1786), do proclaim that—

(1) Part I of Schedule XX of the GATT is modified to conform to the action taken in the Annex to this proclamation.

(2) Subpart A, part 2 of the Appendix to the TSUS is modified as set forth in the Annex to this proclamation.

(3) The United States Trade Representative (USTR) is hereby directed to take such actions and perform such functions for the United States as may be necessary to administer and implement the relief set forth in the Annex hereto, including the allocation of quota quantities on a country-by-country basis; to negotiate orderly marketing agreements pursuant to section 203 of the Trade Act (19 U.S.C. 2253); and to modify, pursuant to section 203, the relief set forth in the Annex hereto. In order to carry out said directive, the USTR is hereby authorized to delegate to appropriate officials or agencies of the United States authority to perform any functions necessary

for the implementation and administration of said relief. The USTR is hereby authorized to make any changes in the headnote or TSUS items created in the Annex hereto which may be necessary to implement the foregoing authority, such changes to be effective on or after the date of their publication in the *Federal Register* or such other date as may be specified therein.

(4) The President's authority in sections 203(g) (1) and (2) of the Trade Act (19 U.S.C. 2253(g) (1) and (2)) to prescribe regulations providing for the efficient and fair administration of any restriction herein proclaimed or governing the entry or withdrawal from warehouse of articles covered by any orderly marketing agreement negotiated hereunder or of like articles which are the product of countries not parties to any such agreement, has been delegated to the Secretary of the Treasury pursuant to section 5(b) of Executive Order No. 11846, as amended. Such authority shall be exercised by the Secretary of the Treasury, upon direction by the USTR, in consultation with representatives of the member agencies of the Trade Policy Staff Committee.

(5) The USTR is directed to conduct an annual review of the necessity for and effectiveness of such relief and recommend to the President any appropriate action under section 203(h)(4) of the Trade Act (19 U.S.C. 2253(h)(4)), and to set up such interagency bodies as may be necessary to monitor the progress toward adjustment of the domestic industry.

(6) The Secretary of the Treasury shall take such actions, not otherwise in contravention of law or in derogation of the authority of the Secretary, as the USTR shall determine are necessary to implement any import relief under this proclamation, or modifications thereof.

(7) This proclamation shall be effective with respect to articles entered, or withdrawn from warehouse for consumption, on or after July 20, 1983, and before the close of July 19, 1987, unless the period of its effectiveness is earlier expressly modified or terminated.

In Witness Whereof, I have hereunto set my hand this 19th. day of July, in the year of our Lord nineteen hundred and eighty-three, and of the Independence of the United States of America the two hundred and eighth.

RONALD REAGAN

[*Filed with the Office of the Federal Register, 11:19 a.m., July 20, 1983*]

Note: The annex is printed in the Federal Register *of July 21, 1983.*

Letter to Members of the House of Representatives on Production of the MX Missile
July 19, 1983

This week the House will consider Title III of the Fiscal Year 1984 Defense Authorization Bill which implements the bipartisan recommendations of the Scowcroft Commission. Endorsing these recommendations will give this Nation a very solid chance to secure a balanced, verifiable arms reduction that, through greater stability, can make our Nation, our world, our people safer. In terms of speaking with one bipartisan voice, of standing up for U.S. vital interests, and of strengthening America's agenda for peace, this vote is of special significance.

When I endorsed the entire Scowcroft Commission Report, I did so by recounting a quote from the report's conclusion: "If we can begin to see ourselves in dealing with the issues, not as political partisans or as crusaders for one specific solution to a part of this complex set of problems, but rather as citizens of a great Nation with the humbling obligation to persevere in the long-run task of preserving both peace and liberty for the world, a common perspective may finally be found."

These words, which guided the Commission, were instrumental in forging that bipartisanship which aims for deep reductions in both the U.S. and Soviet strategic arsenals, coupled with necessary modernization of our strategic forces in a way which will enhance stability.

Andrei Sakharov, the distinguished Soviet physicist and Nobel laureate, made a supporting argument to those aims when he stated in a recent letter that "arms control talks with the Soviets would be much easier if the United States were to have the MX albeit only potentially."

The MX Peacekeeper is being built, as an integral part of the bipartisan Scowcroft Commission's package, to strengthen deterrence. It also provides vital negotiating leverage in Geneva. That lever is working.

Although the Commission called for the deployment of 100 missiles, the level ultimately deployed will be influenced by the outcome in Geneva. If an agreement is reached which calls for deep reductions—which is our goal—the number of missiles could certainly be adjusted downward.

We need the MX, not only for force modernization, but to keep the Soviets moving at the negotiation tables. That is why congressional endorsement of the Scowcroft Commission recommendations, as embodied in Title III of the Defense Authorization Bill, is so important.

The American people believe that this should not be a partisan issue. I hope that I can count on your help to implement all elements of the Scowcroft Commission recommendations. Together we can ensure a continuing national consensus that can lead to the eventual elimination of all nuclear weapons.

Sincerely,

RONALD REAGAN

Note: As printed above, this item follows the text of the letter released by the Office of the Press Secretary.

White House Announcement Following a Meeting of the President's National Security Telecommunications Advisory Committee
July 19, 1983

The second meeting of the President's National Security Telecommunications Advisory Committee (NSTAC) was held on July 19–20, 1983, at the Headquarters of the Strategic Air Command (SAC) at Offutt Air Force Base, Nebr.

All 29 NSTAC members are senior executives of major U.S. corporations in the telecommunications industry. During its business session, NSTAC finalized and voted to send recommendations to the President addressing enhancements in telecommunications capabilities to support national security requirements. Those recommendations will now be reviewed by the Secretary of Defense. That review is expected to be completed this summer with the President reviewing and acting upon NSTAC recommendations thereafter.

During the meeting, President Reagan, who addressed the members via videotape, expressed his appreciation for the efforts of NSTAC members and the substantial commitment of corporate resources each had made to the NSTAC process.

Toasts of the President and Amir Isa bin Sulman Al Khalifa of Bahrain at the State Dinner
July 19, 1983

The President. It's been a pleasure for Nancy and me to welcome to Washington today His Highness Shaykh Isa bin Sulman Al Khalifa, the Amir of Bahrain.

Your Highness, in view of the long history of technical cooperation our two countries have enjoyed, I can think of no more appropriate guests tonight than our five astronauts from the space shuttle *Challenger.* The members of that crew typify the highest American accomplishments, both in technical skill and teamwork, which benefit all of mankind. And the teamwork between our two countries, Your Highness, has led to growth, prosperity, and development of human and natural resources. We must draw on our foundation of partnership as we search for stability and peace with justice in the Middle East.

I'd like to restate the commitment of the American people to fulfilling our role as a loyal friend and cooperative partner to Bahrain. As an island country, Bahrain has prospered by reaching outward. You have been especially sensitive to the ebb and flow of international events while others were content to look inward. Your recent economic accomplishments have been the result of hard work and effective government, but they also reflect your personal imagination and leadership. That same vision has made you, Your Highness, a leader in the cooperative effort with your friends to strengthen the security of your region.

We in America understand the importance of maintaining steady economic growth in an uncertain world so that the lives of the Bahraini people can continue to improve. The United States stands ready to consult with you on whatever we can do to participate more fully in your remarkable economic and social progress. I'm particularly pleased that you'll be meeting with Secretary of Treasury Regan to discuss the world economic outlook.

As in the days when it was known as Dilman, Bahrain is a crossroad for the cultures of the globe. As a banking and financial center, an important ship-repair port and site of international petrochemical and metallurgic cooperative ventures, your country is an open and inviting land of growth and opportunity where Arabs and

Westerners can freely share their lives and views. As such, Bahrain contributes immeasurably to peace and mutual understanding.

Americans deeply respect your personal courage and vision, Your Highness. We've seen you guide your people with confidence through a turbulent period in the history of the Gulf, never sacrificing your personal commitment to a humane and just society.

Your Highness, I salute you. The American people are fortunate to have you as a friend and proud to stand side by side with the people of Bahrain in seeking stability, prosperity, and peace for us all. Thank you very much, and on behalf of the American people, it's been my pleasure to welcome you to Washington and to the White House.

The Amir. Mr. President, Mrs. Reagan, ladies and gentlemen:

Our initial delight in visiting this friendly country has been greatly increased during our useful meeting with you, Mr. President, this morning. Our discussions with Senator Charles Percy and his colleagues today were informative and positive. We are sure that two more happy days are awaiting us.

Thank you, Mr. President, for your invitation to us tonight and for the kind words you have spoken about Bahrain and its people. Needless to say, that we have always admired the enterprising spirit of the American people. Today, we in the Gulf are enjoying many of the fruits of their achievement in all field—notably in science and technology.

Mr. President, you will be pleased to know of two similarities between American past and the Gulf present. Firstly, two centuries ago, 13 British colonies succeeded in building a free and strong nucleus of future America. Two years ago, 6 Arab States of the Gulf decided to follow a similar path of cooperation and ultimate unity. If your 13 managed to survive and later increase, surely our 6 must have an equal chance.

Secondly, like your country—that's so an awaking of the American mind during and immediately following the Jacksonian era— the Arab States of the GCC [Gulf Cooperation Council] are the scene of growing activities in the field of economy, industry, social services, education, communication, and culture. We are confident that the help and understanding of our friends will make the aspiration of our people and the process of achieving those aspiration peaceful for all mankind.

However, Mr. President, there is one notable difference so far: We have not been offered to buy a Louisiana or an Alaska. [*Laughter*] The oil money seems unable to match the American gold. [*Laughter*]

We are, indeed, happy and proud that Astronaut Crippen and his colleagues are among us tonight. They surely deserve a decent, earthly meal. [*Laughter*] We hope that, while cruising in outer space, they noted an island that swam in a sea of spilled oil. For their information, that was Bahrain. [*Laughter*] We take this opportunity to salute their daring skill and achievement.

God bless you all. Thank you very much.

Note: The President spoke at 9:34 p.m. in the State Dining Room at the White House.

Statement on the Death of Frank Reynolds of ABC News
July 20, 1983

Frank Reynolds was one of America's foremost broadcast journalists, trusted and respected by millions of his fellow citizens, Nancy and I among them. To us he was also a warm, considerate friend who will be missed for his outstanding human qualities as well as for his many contributions as a newsman. Our prayers and sympathy are with Frank's family in their bereavement.

Appointment of Harry W. Shlaudeman as Executive Director of the National Bipartisan Commission on Central America
July 20, 1983

The President today announced his intention to appoint Harry W. Shlaudeman to be Executive Director of the National Bipartisan Commission on Central America.

Mr. Shlaudeman has been serving since October 1980 as Ambassador to Argentina. Previously he was Ambassador to Peru from 1977 to 1980. Shlaudeman joined the Foreign Service in 1954 and was posted in Barranquilla, Bogotá, Sofia, and Santo Domingo. From 1963 to 1965, he was chief of Dominican affairs at the State Department, and from 1965 to 1966, he was Assistant Director of the Office of Caribbean Affairs. He was in the senior seminar in foreign policy in 1966–1967. From 1967 to 1969, Shlaudeman was Special Assistant to the Secretary of State. He was Deputy Chief of Mission in Santiago from 1969 to 1973 and Deputy Assistant Secretary of State for Inter-American Affairs from 1973 to 1975. From 1975 to 1976, he was Ambassador to Venezuela, and from 1976 to 1977, he was Assistant Secretary of State for Inter-American Affairs.

Shlaudeman was born May 17, 1926, in Los Angeles, Calif., and is a resident of San Marino, Calif. He served in the U.S. Marine Corps from 1944 to 1946. He received a B.A. from Stanford University in 1952.

Statement by Deputy Press Secretary Speakes on the Situation in Central America
July 20, 1983

As you know, yesterday in Managua, Daniel Ortega, the coordinator of the Sandinista Directorate, issued a statement. Our response to that is we welcome any sincere and verifiable proposal to lessen tensions in Central America. Taking Mr. Ortega at his word, we believe the Nicaraguan proposal is a positive step in that it acknowledges the regional nature of the problem and the need to address external support for insurgencies and terrorist groups.

The proposal still contains a number of serious shortcomings. For example, the proposal seeks to put the insurgents in El Salvador on the same level as the democratically elected government. It fails to take into account the need for true democracy as a means to resolve internal problems of the countries of the region. It does not deal with Nicaragua's military buildup, and there are no clearly articulated provisions for effective verification.

Nonetheless, we would hope that the Nicaraguan proposal, along with those put forth by other countries of the region, would be considered, refined, and expanded as necessary at the next meeting of the Contadora nine, scheduled for later this month.

Note: Deputy Press Secretary Larry M. Speakes read the statement during his daily press briefing for reporters, which began at 12:30 p.m. in the Briefing Room at the White House.

Remarks on Providing Additional Federal Funds for the Washington, D.C., Summer Youth Employment Program
July 20, 1983

Thank you, Ray. And Mayor Barry, Secretary Donovan, and ladies and gentlemen, and all of you young guests who are up here and out there, I'm pleased to announce today that $800,000 in additional summer youth employment funds is being allocated to the District of Columbia.

When Secretary Ray Donovan learned that my adopted hometown here was running out of money for its summer jobs program, he called Mayor Barry and offered to help. The result is today's check drawn from available funds at the Department of Labor. These funds will be added to the $8.2 million already transferred to the city and should provide 2,200 more summer jobs for unemployed young people in our Nation's Capital, a city that is very special to all of us as Americans.

This money is part of over $800 million that is being distributed nationally to enable State and local governments, and this will provide an estimated 800,000 summer jobs for young people throughout the United States. Our goal is to offer disadvantaged young people valuable work experience and at the same time provide the community with their services, which, I might add, will be more than welcome by cities and nonprofit agencies which will be receiving their help.

I have to add to what the Secretary said about that first summer job. Mine was when I was 14 years old. And I regret that a lot of rules and regulations have changed some things since then, because at that time I wound up with a construction company that was remodeling houses, and I ended the summer up, at my age even, at laying hardwood floors, shingling roof, painting houses. And I know that some regulations make that impossible today. Maybe we can keep on going till we change some of those back again to help all of you.

This summer youth program is funded by the Department of Labor and operated by State and local governments throughout the country. It'll continue to be an important part of the Job Training Partnership Act, which will replace the old CETA program this October. But this program is only part of an overall effort we've made to help deserving young people get a start.

We've put in place a tax-credit program that gives employers who hire eligible teenagers a tax credit for up to 85 percent of the wages of these new, summertime employees. In some cases, the credit will enable an employer to hire a disadvantaged youth for the entire summer at a cost of only $260. The young person gets not only a paying job but also the valuable experience participating in the private sector. The employer gets a young employee the company may not have been able to afford without the tax break. And everyone's better off because of it.

We've made a special effort this summer to focus business and industry attention on this problem. The White House Office of Private Sector Initiatives and the National Alliance of Business have been in the forefront of this drive to give those young people who want to work this summer the chance they deserve.

My White House Office on Private Sector Initiatives has been doing a tremendous job. I know that because they've enlisted me on a number of occasions on this particular issue. As part of a well-coordinated program, I've written 5,300 chief executive officers of companies across the country asking for their support. I've been making videotapes and phone calls to job-a-thons in order to kick off summer job efforts in cities across the country.

Along with Bill Kolberg and David Roderick and others with the National Alliance of Business, we've reached out, and I'm proud to say that the business community has responded. Companies like McDonald's, which hopes to provide 30,000 additional summer jobs; Mobil Oil, which donated generously to meet the challenge; the New York City Partnership Summer Jobs '83, headed by Philip Morris, has provided over

15,000 jobs for young people. And with us today is Hank Butta from C & P Telephone of Maryland. His Blue Chip-In program in Baltimore has been a tremendous success. All of these private initiatives and many, many more like them presented here today—or represented here today, I should say—deserve our thanks.

All of these efforts, coupled with the tax credit program and, yes, the economic recovery, have had an effect. We're just now emerging from one of the most frustrating times in our country's history. After years of economic uncertainty, of devastating inflation, business stagnation, ever-increasing taxation and a resulting drop in investment, of high interest rates, and declining stock prices, we've begun to turn things around. It wasn't easy, but together, all of us together, we've got the American economy on the move again.

While we've been trying to straighten out the situation, we know it's been a particularly hard time for the unemployed, especially the young. Economists tell us the unemployed are the last ones to feel an economic upsurge. But we all can be happy that last month total employment rose 1.2 million nationwide.

Clearly, the Federal funds that are being allocated to States and local governments are important to the young people they help. But we also want to take this opportunity to highlight the private initiatives that have been taken throughout the country as well.

And now, Mayor Barry, it's my pleasure today to give you the check that will make this summer a lot nicer for so many of our local young people: $800,000. I was tempted to leave for California, but it was made out so that I couldn't. [*Laughter*]

Note: The President spoke at 1:52 p.m. in the Rose Garden at the White House. Also participating in the ceremony were Secretary of Labor Raymond J. Donovan and Mayor Marion Barry of Washington, D.C.

Appointment of Three Members of the Committee for Purchase from the Blind and Other Severely Handicapped
July 20, 1983

The President today announced his intention to appoint the following individuals to be members of the Committee for Purchase from the Blind and Other Severely Handicapped:

Ira L. Kemp, to be the Department of the Air Force member. He will succeed Maj. Gen. Joseph H. Connolly, USAF. He is the Associate Director of Contracting Policy, Deputy Chief of Staff, Research, Development and Acquisition, Headquarters, U.S. Air Force. He is married, has three children, and resides in Rockville, Md. He was born March 31, 1924, in Brooklyn, N.Y.

Maj. Gen. Joseph H. Connolly, to be the Department of Defense member. He will succeed Brig. Gen. Charles F. Drenz. He is director of Contracting and Manufacturing Policy, Office of the Deputy Chief of Staff, Research, Development and Acquisition, Headquarters, U.S. Air Force, Washington, D.C. He is married, has one child, and resides in Falls Church, Va. He was born November 21, 1930, in Paterson, N.J.

Earl H. Cunerd will succeed Diane S. Roupe. He has been executive director of United Cerebral Palsy Associations, Inc., in New York City since 1967. He was vice president of the National Health Council in 1973. He is married, has one child, and resides in Moorestown, N.J. He was born January 26, 1918, in Philadelphia, Pa.

Appointment of Three United States Commissioners of the Council and the Commissions of the North Atlantic Salmon Conservation Organization
July 20, 1983

The President today announced his intention to appoint the following individuals to be United States Commissioners on the Council and the Commissions of the North Atlantic Salmon Conservation Organization. These are new positions.

Richard A. Buck has been chairman of the Restoration of Atlantic Salmon in America, Inc., since 1973. Previously he was chairman of the Committee on the Atlantic Salmon Emergency (CASE) in 1969–1973. He graduated from Yale University in 1932. He is married, has two children, and resides in Dublin, N.H. He was born October 21, 1909.

Frank Eberle Carlton has been serving as president of the National Coalition for Marine Conservation, Inc., since 1973. He was commissioner of the Atlantic States Marine Fisheries Commission in 1973–1980. He graduated from Emory University (A.B., 1958; M.D., 1961). He is married, has four children, and resides in Savannah, Ga. He was born October 31, 1933.

Allen Eric Peterson, Jr., is regional director, Northeast Region, for the National Marine Fisheries Service in Gloucester, Mass. Previously he was director of marine fisheries for the Commonwealth of Massachusetts in 1976–1979. He graduated from the University of Massachusetts at Amherst (B.S., 1962; M.S., 1964). He is married, has two children, and resides in Sandwich, Mass. He was born March 6, 1940.

Remarks and a Question-and-Answer Session With Reporters on Domestic and Foreign Policy Issues
July 21, 1983

Nation's Economy; MX Missile Production

The President. Good morning. I have a brief statement, two very welcome pieces of news. This morning's report of a surge to 8.7 percent in second-quarter real economic growth and last night's bipartisan victory for the MX Peacekeeper program send an important signal to the world. I think that confidence in America's economic recovery and leadership for peace continue to build.

The economy is growing with more vigor than most economists predicted, and this heartens us. Vigorous growth is the surest road to more jobs, declining deficits, and a future filled with opportunity for all our people. We must encourage the roots of confidence to grow strong and deep by protecting the recovery from a new burst of runaway inflation and interest rates. We support the commitment of the Federal Reserve Board to a monetary policy that ensures stable prices, and we urge the Congress to help us make the Fed's job easier, not by taking more money out of the people's pockets, but by exercising discipline to hold down Federal spending.

I want also to thank courageous Republicans and Democrats in the House for giving America the bipartisan unity needed to pursue two vital national goals—strategic modernization and arms control. It's now time for the Senate to act. If the Senate joins the House in approval of funds for production of the Peacekeeper, the United States representatives in Geneva will have increased leverage to negotiate significant mutual and verifiable strategic arms reductions. End of statement.

Helen [Helen Thomas, United Press International]?

Central America

Q. Mr. President, are we trying to overthrow the Government of Nicaragua with a sending of what some people would call a kind of a gunboat diplomacy approach?

The President. No, we're conducting exercises such as we've conducted before here in this hemisphere. We've conducted them in other parts of the world, and there haven't been too many questions about that or suggesting that we're starting——

Q. Well, what is the purpose?

The President. ——to try to start a war in those other areas. We conduct annual maneuvers more than once a year, as a matter of fact.

Q. Are you saying they have no political purpose?

The President. We're conducting exercises there. And I think that there's every reason for us to do so with the responsibility we have in this hemisphere.

Yeah, Bill [Bill Plante, CBS News].

Q. Mr. President, would you say that the pressure the U.S. has put on the Government of Nicaragua, by supporting the rebels against that Government, has helped to bring the Government to a position where they are expressing some willingness to negotiate? Would you attribute that to the pressure that the U.S. has been able to bring to bear? And would you accept a negotiated solution in El Salvador contingent on a solution in Nicaragua?

The President. Well, you're getting very complicated there and getting me deep into the field of things that I don't think are at hand yet. I'd have no way of reading their minds as to why. I think it could be assumed that maybe what is happening there with the *contras,* who are opposing the Sandinista regime, have something to do with this decision. Undoubtedly Contadora did also have something to do with it.

I welcome this first step. I don't think it's far enough. But what really is needed is what the *contras* are asking for, and that is that the Sandinista government is in violation, literally, of a contract that they made with the Organization of American States. That's not just the United States; that's 30 other American States. They made a contract during the revolution that, if they had the help of the OAS in persuading the Somoza regime to step down and let their revolution take over, they made specific promises as to what they would do with regard to freedom of press and freedom of—well, all the freedoms that we enjoy here in this country. They have violated all

of those provisions. And the OAS considers that the violation of a contract. And what the *contras* are really seeking, having been members of the Sandinista revolution for the most part in its effort to bring democracy to Nicaragua, they are trying to restore the original purpose of the revolution.

Q. Well, just to follow, if I may, sir. Would you consider a negotiated settlement in El Salvador if there can be a settlement in Nicaragua?

The President. Well, without even waiting for Nicaragua, we have proposed and the Salvadoran Government has proposed that if the guerrillas will lay down their arms and come in and participate in the democratic process of election, they will be granted amnesty. They have a peace commission that is organized to negotiate such a thing with them. And, so far, the guerrillas in El Salvador have refused any such meeting on that.

Q. Mr. President, Henry Kissinger was someone that you said should resign back in 1976. He's controversial because of his role in overthrowing the Allende regime in Chile, because of his support for covert action. Why did you choose him to head this Commission, considering your past doubts about him? And aren't you, in effect, shortcircuiting the work of the Commission, since the administration is already planning an increase of some $400 million in its aid request for next year for that region?

The President. I don't think any such figure has been advanced by us as yet. We're asking for the $110 million that we had proposed for 1983 and which the Congress has so far refused to give us. We have asked for some increase in that in our request for the 1984 budget, but nothing of that figure.

But, with regard to the first part of your question, as I recall in '76 the entire issue of Henry Kissinger came up in response to questions from the audiences as to whether I would choose him as my Secretary of State. And I said that I had other things in mind and I would make my own choice of a Secretary of State.

I've chosen him for this committee because I believe here is a man with a distinguished record in diplomacy. I believe he is exceptionally well qualified to bring back the information that, I think, we all need and that would help the Congress make the decisions it needs to make about Central America.

Q. Well, to follow up—to ask you whether you think that there is no need, then, for this massive increase, because there are administration officials who have said that there are planning papers already at the budget office for this big increase in economic and military aid. Do you think it will not be necessary?

The President. You know, if I ever find those unnamed individuals that are quoted as administration sources, I'm going to take their White House passes away from them. [*Laughter*]

Q. Right in your office.

The President. I don't know who they are.

Q. Is it true or not?

The President. No——

Q. We can give you a list of names.

The President. ——I have never heard that figure advanced as anything that we're asking for. But I do think that this commission—what I want is to bring back and with the Congress sit down with the idea of an overall program for all of our neighbors here in the hemisphere. It is what I talked to leaders about when I made my one trip to South and Central America—talked to them about all of us becoming equal allies here in the Western Hemisphere, all dedicated to the same thing, to progress, economic reform, what social reforms are needed in some areas and so forth. And this is my goal for Central America.

To achieve it, however, you've got to stop the shooting. You have got to let them proceed with these reforms without getting murdered by terrorists who want a continuation of what we've seen too much of in the past, and that is revolutions that only overthrow one set of rulers in order to establish another set of rulers.

Yes, Larry [Laurence I. Barrett, *Time*].

Q. Mr. President, in view of your frequent criticism of the Sandinista regime, which you repeated here this morning, do you think it's possible to get any kind of regional settlement and regional stability if that regime remains in office? Or do you think that regime would have to go before

there would be any settlement?

The President. Now, we're talking—now, wait a minute, which country, again, are we talking——

Q. I'm talking about in quest of regional stability——

The President. Yes.

Q. ——do you think that's possible in Central America if the Sandinista regime survives in Nicaragua?

The President. Well, if the Sandinista regime remained, but remained true to the original purpose of the revolution—this is a government by one faction of the original revolution. It exiled, it jailed, it threw out of office the other leaders of the revolution because they wanted democracy and the present group wanted Communist totalitarianism. And this is what they presently have there. So, what is being struggled for there is a restoration of the original revolution.

Q. So, you think if this present faction remains in power alone in Nicaragua, there cannot be a satisfactory settlement. Is that your——

The President. I think it would be extremely difficult, because I think they're being subverted, or they're being directed by outside forces.

Gary [Gary F. Schuster, *Detroit News*]?

Q. Mr. President, with the presence of the American ships off the western coast of Central America, is there any plan by the United States to go on the Gulf side of Central America, especially off the coast of Nicaragua, to impose a naval blockade?

The President. Well, a blockade is a very serious thing, and I would hope that there will—that eventuality will not arise. There are going to be maneuvers of various kinds——

Q. In the Gulf?

The President. Yes, just as last year we had some maneuvers in the Caribbean, I prefer to call it. And we will be doing that again because of our interests there and the importance of that to the United States.

Yeah.

Poland

Q. Sir, the Polish Government says it's going to lift martial law, as of tomorrow, and free some, but not all, of the political prisoners. Is this action enough to cause you to lift the remaining sanctions or not?

The President. We just have received the actions of the Parliament there, and what it is they're proposing. And so, I do not have the result of any study of what those proposals are.

What we want to be on guard for is—having a cosmetic change, in which they lift technically martial law, but replace it with equally onerous regulations. If that's true, then the situation has not changed. And so, I can't answer until we know whether there actually has been any improvement.

Then we've always said, if there is, we're going to go by deeds, not words. If there is something that indicates that a reciprocal action by us is desired—us and our allies—then we'll consult on that.

Q. Well, sir, as you know, the Parliament has also approved new laws which people like Lech Walesa say make the government just as onerous from the standpoint of having the ability to control the country as martial law.

The President. Well, that's what we want to find out for ourselves in the study when we analyze what has been done.

Ms. Thomas. Thank you, Mr. President.

Q. Mr. President—may I finish my sentence, Helen?

The President. All right. Helen's just laughing, but I think she's laughing "yes."

Unemployment

Q. Thank you. Within the framework of the economic recovery, what can you say to the 11 million unemployed? Is there any tangible message of hope, or whatever for them?

The President. Oh, yes, there is. Now, we know that the unemployment is the last thing that responds to the economic recovery. But, look, there are 1,100,000, 1,200,000 more people employed than were employed last December; 345,000 more just between May and June, was the increase in the number of people employed. I have been informed by industrial leaders in the automobile industry of their plans in just the next several weeks for the recall of lay-offs.

We do know this: I think sometimes we look at the pool of unemployed—and, remember, the rate is down to 9.8 percent; we're out of that 10-percent bracket now. We look at the unemployed, and we incline to believe that this is the same group of people that have been sitting there helpless and hopeless throughout the entire recession. Seventy percent of the unemployed today have been unemployed 7 weeks or less. Thirty percent of the unemployed today are newcomers to the job market, seeking their first employment. And if you want another rather hard-to-imagine figure, if you take the total weeks of unemployment, more than half of them were accounted for by only 3½ percent of the unemployed.

Now, it's a more complicated picture than just simply transferring one thing to the other—the number of young people that are being put to work this summer in summer jobs, more than in several years and in part due to—as yesterday out in the Rose Garden, our ceremony where we contributed some money here, but that was only part of another $800 million nationwide. We've been working with the private sector on this. The job-a-thons held by television and radio stations throughout the country, particularly television—they've had a remarkable success. And it happens within the time of the program literally that these people get them back.

So, there is reason for encouragement. There's only a very limited number of people who have been unemployed 6 months or longer. And they are the hard core, and they are the real basic problem we want to get to. But we have to deal with it as it is. And I think there is certainly very definite reason for hope of employment.

All right, thank you.

Q. Is that a new tie—1 of your 12?

The President. You're pretty observant. [*Laughter*]

Note: The President spoke at 10:30 a.m. in the Briefing Room at the White House.

Statement by Deputy Press Secretary Speakes on the Release of David Dodge in Beirut, Lebanon
July 21, 1983

The President was informed this morning that David Dodge, who was kidnaped last July 19 from the campus of the American University of Beirut, where he was serving as acting president, has been released. The Government of the United States is grateful to Syrian President Hafiz al-Assad and to Dr. Rifaat al-Assad for the humanitarian efforts they undertook which led to Mr. Dodge's release.

The President is deeply gratified by Mr. Dodge's release and has directed that a U.S. military aircraft be put at Mr. Dodge's disposal for his return to the United States.

The President also expressed his appreciation for the excellent work of the State Department in assisting in Mr. Dodge's release.

Nomination of Henry F. Schickling To Be a Member of the Board of Directors of the Overseas Private Investment Corporation
July 21, 1983

The President today announced his intention to nominate Henry F. Schickling to be a member of the Board of Directors of the Overseas Private Investment Corporation, U.S. International Development Cooperation Agency, for a term expiring December 17, 1985. This is a new position.

Since 1973 he has been international president of the International Union of Tool, Die & Mold Makers, International Society, in Rahway, N.J. He is also president of the International Society of Skilled Trades. He has been Chairman of the National Advisory Council for Career Education and was a member of the Federal Committee on Apprenticeship, U.S. Department of Labor.

Mr. Schickling is married, has five children, and resides in Langhorne, Pa. He was born December 13, 1926, in Philadelphia, Pa.

Appointment of Two Members of the Federal Service Impasses Panel
July 21, 1983

The President today announced his intention to appoint the following individuals to be members of the Federal Service Impasses Panel, Federal Labor Relations Authority:

Roy M. Brewer, for the remainder of the term expiring January 10, 1984. He would succeed Beverly K. Schaffer. He is presently serving as consultant to Local No. 695, Sound Technicians. Previously he was international representative of the International Alliance of Theatrical Stage Employees and was labor relations consultant to Walt Disney Productions, Inc. He is married, has two children, and resides in Tarzana, Calif. He was born August 9, 1909.

Thomas A. Farr, for the remainder of the term expiring January 10, 1985. He would succeed Donald F. Rogers. He is presently serving as law clerk to the Honorable Frank W. Bullock, Jr., United States District Judge for the Middle District of North Carolina. Previously he was with the Office of the General Counsel at the Office of Personnel Management in 1982–1983. He graduated from Hillsdale College (B.A.,

1976), Emory University School of Law (J.D., 1976), and Georgetown University Law Center (LL.M., 1983). He resides in Greensboro, N.C., and was born October 24, 1954.

Appointment of Two Members of the United States Holocaust Memorial Council
July 21, 1983

The President today announced his intention to appoint the following individuals to be members of the United States Holocaust Memorial Council for the remainder of terms expiring January 15, 1986:

Norman Braman would succeed Frank R. Lautenberg. Mr. Braman is president of a car dealership in Miami, Fla. He has served as vice president of the Greater Miami Jewish Federation. He was a founder and serves on the board of the Mount Sinai Medical Center. He graduated from Temple University (B.S., 1955). He is married, has two children, and resides in Miami Beach, Fla. He was born August 22, 1932, in West Chester, Pa.

William J. Lowenberg would succeed Albert A. Spiegel. Mr. Lowenberg is a real estate developer in San Francisco, Calif. He is president-elect of the Jewish Community Federation and is a board member of the Council of Jewish Federations. Mr. Lowenberg is a survivor of the Nazi Holocaust of World War II. He is married, has two children, and resides in San Francisco, Calif. He was born August 14, 1926, in Ochtrup, Germany.

Statement on the Consumer Price Index for June
July 22, 1983

Once again, with today's release of the Consumer Price Index for June, we see evidence that a healthy economic recovery is underway, one that is better than anything most of the experts were predicting just a few months ago. The new CPI figure is especially good news for Americans living on fixed or modest incomes—the people who suffer the most from the ravages of inflation. By keeping inflation down, our economic policy protects those Americans who are most vulnerable—and that, not the inflationary policies of the big spenders, is an important part of fairness and compassion.

Between May and June, consumer prices rose by only .2 percent. Food prices actually declined, and the increase in gasoline prices tapered off considerably from recent months. Most important, the level of the CPI this June was only 2.6 percent higher than a year ago. That represents the lowest 12-month rate of increase in consumer prices in more than 15 years.

Taken together with yesterday's good news of 8.7-percent real economic growth in the second quarter of the year, it is clear that our program, and the American economy, are on the right track—the track to a strong, sustained, noninflationary recovery.

Remarks of President Reagan and President Amin Gemayel of Lebanon Following Their Meetings
July 22, 1983

President Reagan. It is a great pleasure to welcome our friend, President Gemayel, to the White House again. We've had excellent talks today covering many vital concerns of both our countries. During his first visit here 9 months ago, President Gemayel and I discussed the principles upon which United States policy toward Lebanon is based: the full withdrawal of all foreign forces from Lebanon; support for a strong central government capable of asserting its authority over all of Lebanon; and security for Israel's northern border.

Today, I've reaffirmed these principles to President Gemayel. A united, sovereign, and independent Lebanon, free of all foreign forces, is the legitimate aspiration of the Government and the people of Lebanon and a goal shared by the people of the United States. Our talks today focused on the next steps in securing Lebanon's independence. We admire the courage and wisdom demonstrated by the Lebanese Government during its negotiations that resulted in an agreement for the departure of Israeli forces.

The United States remains firmly committed to the earliest possible resolution of the conflict in Lebanon. This morning, President Gemayel and I have gone over the difficult agenda and have agreed on next steps which we should take together to set this process in motion and carry it through.

And I have today designated Robert McFarlane, currently my Deputy Assistant for National Security Affairs, as my Personal Representative in the Middle East. In that role, he will succeed Philip Habib, who must return to his business and academia duties. Phil has set a high standard in bringing us through 8 months of difficult negotiations to the situation we face today, and he will be sorely missed.

After further consultation here in Washington next week, Bud McFarlane and his team will depart for the Middle East within 10 days.

I'm happy to have had this opportunity to confer with President Gemayel once again. I'm impressed with the progress that he and the Government and people of Lebanon have made in rebuilding their country. It's my belief that energy and perseverance will triumph in the end. And as I told President Gemayel, we do not lack for either. Lebanon can count on our support.

Mr. President, pleased to have you here.

President Gemayel. My second visit to the White House in the course of the year is a further confirmation of our appreciation for the consistent support President Reagan has given Lebanon and the Lebanese objective, which is the withdrawal of all foreign forces and the reconstruction of a sovereign, democratic, and united Lebanon.

I'm very happy to have with me this time the Prime Minister, Mr. Shafiq Wazzan. This should emphasize the importance we attach to the visit. Indeed, conditions in Lebanon have changed immensely since my visit last October. And you are going through dramatic developments, highlighted in particular by today's events in Lebanon. During our meeting this morning and the talks held by my delegation with the State Department and the Pentagon, we have amply covered the various practical ways and means available to the Government of Lebanon and the United States in order to fulfill our common goals.

I continue to be confident that the major problems still confronting us in Lebanon and the Middle East can best be addressed and resolved by full cooperation with our Arab community and our American friends. President Reagan has reassured us of his continuing concern and determination to pursue his initiative in Lebanon with the same strength and commitment. Our two governments will intensify their consultations until the expected results are achieved.

I would like, finally, to thank Philip Habib. I'll tell him, he is always welcome in Lebanon. He is a friend of Lebanon. He was with us during the difficult time. And, also, I'll say in advance, welcome to Mr. McFarlane.

Note: President Reagan spoke at 1:18 p.m. to reporters assembled on the South Grounds of the White House.

Earlier, the two Presidents met in the Oval Office and then held a working luncheon, together with U.S. and Lebanese officials, in the State Dining Room.

Appointment of Robert C. McFarlane as the President's Personal Representative in the Middle East
July 22, 1983

The President announced today his intention to appoint Robert C. McFarlane as his Personal Representative in the Middle East with the personal rank of Ambassador. Mr. McFarlane is the Deputy Assistant to the President for National Security Affairs, a position he has held since January 1982. He will continue to serve in that position.

In January 1981, Mr. McFarlane was nominated as Counselor, Department of State, where he served until becoming Deputy Assistant to the President. In 1979–1981 he was a member of the professional staff of the Senate Committee on Armed Services. He was a senior research fellow at the National Defense University in Washington, D.C., in 1977–1978. In 1976–1977 he was Special Assistant to the President for National Security Affairs. Mr. McFarlane

was Executive Assistant to the Assistant to the President for National Security Affairs in 1975–1976. From 1973 to 1975, he was military assistant to Dr. Henry Kissinger at the White House. In 1971–1972 he was a White House fellow and Executive Assistant to the Counsel to the President for Legislative Affairs.

Mr. McFarlane was a U.S. Marine officer. He is a graduate of the U.S. Naval Academy and studied in international relations at the Institut des Hautes Études in Geneva, Switzerland. He is a recipient of the Distinguished Service Medal, the Nation's highest peacetime military decoration. Mr. McFarlane is married and has three children. He resides with his family in Bethesda, Md. He is 46 years old.

Radio Address to the Nation on the International Monetary Fund and on Organ Donorship
July 23, 1983

My fellow Americans:

Before I get to the heart of my remarks today, I want to mention some important legislation currently before the Congress. I'm sure you're all aware of the difficulties some countries are having in meeting payments on their debts. Their problem touches all of us in a very real way and, indeed, poses a threat to the stability of the world financial order. For that reason, something called the International Monetary Fund was created some years ago. It's better known as

the IMF, and that's how I'll refer to it.

Nations, including our own, contribute to IMF, and countries with temporary balance-of-payment problems borrow from it on a short-term basis. In order to get a loan, they have to agree to terms the Fund managers lay down with regard to correcting the practices and policies that contribute to their financial difficulties.

I've asked the Congress to approve an $8½ billion contribution to the Fund. Some in the Congress and a great many citizens think this is a giveaway which will increase our deficit. The IMF is not foreign aid, and the $8½ billion is not being given away. We will have additional drawing rights in that amount from the IMF. In fact, in its entire history, the two countries that have borrowed the greatest amounts from the Fund have been the United Kingdom and the United States. The sum we're asking Congress to approve does not increase our budget and is returned with interest as loans are repaid.

In addition, it creates jobs, because it keeps the wheels of world commerce turning. Exports account for one out of five manufacturing jobs in the United States. The IMF and its programs help keep Americans at work. This is important legislation for international economic stability, and I hope you'll support it.

But today, I want to speak only of—or not speak, I should say, of great national issues. Instead I'm taking to the airwaves in hopes we can save one little 11-month-old girl from Texas and many others like her. The young girl from Texas is Ashley Bailey, and all 11 pounds of her are in critical condition at the University of Minnesota Hospital in Minneapolis. She is now fed intravenously and has but 2 or 3 weeks to live unless she receives a liver transplant.

Back in May, Congressman Charlie Stenholm of Texas wrote me of the plight of this baby girl who must receive a transplant to survive. The surgery was estimated to cost $140,000. The Congressman said there'd been a tremendous outpouring of community and business support in the Abilene, Texas, area and about $75,000 already had been raised. A week or so after I received the letter, the Texas and Federal Medicaid programs contributed $82,000 toward the operation and medical expenses were no longer a problem for little Ashley. What she needed then, and needs now, is a donor. Time is running out. I'm issuing a plea to the Nation to find Ashley a donor.

Once one is found, an Air Force jet is standing ready in case immediate, commercial transportation is not available. Have a pencil ready; I'll give you a phone number in just a few seconds.

Right now, somewhere in America, there might be a pair of stunned and grief-stricken parents whose own baby has died in an accident or is sadly near death. I know if these parents were aware their baby could make it possible for Ashley to live, they would have no hesitation in saying, "Save that little girl."

I urge any of you who know of a possible liver donor for Ashley to call The Living Bank in Houston. The number is 800–528–2971. I'll repeat the number: 800–528–2971. Please call.

There are many other children like Ashley. We're looking for donors for them, as well. Right here in the White House we have an electrician, Stuart Thomas, whose daughter Candi—another 11-month-old girl—is waiting for a transplant. The helicopter squadron at Andrews Air Force Base is alerted to transport Candi and her mother to Pittsburgh as soon as a suitable liver is found.

In the last few days we lost little Courtney Davis from Beaumont, Texas, and Michelle Heckard from Shenandoah Heights, Pennsylvania, because we couldn't find livers to save their lives.

Nancy and I receive so many requests from families in need of organ donors that I directed the Surgeon General to conduct a conference on organ transplants. The major recommendation was to develop a public awareness program on organ donorship. This is underway, and I hope my broadcast today adds to the momentum. The project will stress education for doctors, State highway police, hospital officials, and others on the need to consider organ donorship when accidental death occurs.

America has faced shortage in the past of everything from nylons during World War II to oil in the 1970's. But modern medical science has provided us with a new shortage—a shortage of living organs: livers, hearts, lungs, eyes, kidneys. I urge all Americans to fill out donor cards, little cards you carry in your wallet or purse that, in the event of your death, offer the hope of life to others. You can obtain these cards by simply calling your local kidney, heart, or lung associations.

Americans are giving people. In many of the cases where these very expensive operations are essential, local citizens have raised money to help the families in need. I've already mentioned the community support given to Ashley. Well, not far from Washington, Morningside, Maryland, raised over $100,000 for the Goode family, whose little Nicky needs a transplant.

That kind of caring should make us all proud to be American. We can save more of our children and adults through organ donorship. Organ donors offer the greatest gift of all—the gift of life. Right now Ashley Bailey, as well as other desperately ill children, are waiting for that gift. Please help us find donors for these children.

Until next week, thanks for listening, and God bless you.

Note: The President's remarks were taped at 10:30 a.m. at the White House for broadcast at 12:06 p.m.

Remarks on Presenting the J. Paul Getty Wildlife Conservation Prize
July 25, 1983

The President. Well, first let me welcome you all to the White House. I don't need to welcome Russell Train of the Wildlife Fund. Russell's more at home here than I am. [*Laughter*] He served in two administrations, and this is my first. [*Laughter*] I'm pleased that we have representatives of other conservation groups here today, as well.

But let me say how proud I am to present the J. Paul Getty Wildlife Conservation Prize. This is the largest award given specifically for outstanding service to wildlife conservation. This honor is so distinguished it's often been likened to a Nobel Prize for conservation. And our award winners today deserve that distinction: Alvaro Ugalde, Director of the National Park Service of Costa Rica, and Mario Boza, who is Costa Rica's first Park Service Director. They have contributed greatly to building their country's park system. And you gentlemen have my warmest congratulations.

They have a genuine treasure to protect. Someone has told me that Costa Rica's wildlife includes more than 850 bird species, 205 mammals, 150 amphibians, 210 reptiles, and 700 species of butterflies.

Well, I'm always using Costa Rica as a positive example for Central America. It's more than that, however. Costa Rica is a positive example for the entire world—a model of democracy and political stability that all nations could do well to emulate. Costa Rica's strength flows from the fact that the people choose their own leadership through the ballot box. And this is what we wish for Costa Rica's neighbors and for all nations. This is why we're helping countries in Central America defend themselves against those who would see them under the authoritarian rule of communism.

Costa Rica exemplifies what democracy is all about. It's no surprise that Costa Rica, throughout several political administrations, has demonstrated great leadership in the conservation and wise management of natural resources.

I'm especially pleased that the strong conservation leadership demonstrated by Costa Rica has earned the continuing support of private, voluntary organizations in the United States, such as the World Wildlife Fund, the Nature Conservancy, and the New York Zoological Society. I could talk to you all morning about the role that private initiative can play in solving so many of the problems that face us. And I think the World Wildlife Fund—U.S. embodies to the fullest what the private sector can accomplish. I want to recognize its sponsorship of the prize that we're handing out here today.

So, again, congratulations to our award winners for their fine public service not only to Costa Rica but to all of us who place the importance on wildlife conservation that we do. And we thank you all.

And now, Mario Andres Boza.

[*At this point, the President presented the award to Mr. Boza.*]

Mr. Boza. Thank you, Mr. President.

The President. Alvaro Ugalde.

[*The President presented Mr. Ugalde with his award.*]

Mr. Ugalde. Thank you.

The President. It's a pleasure to have you here.

Mr. Train. Mr. President, can I put our Panda pin on you?

The President. Yes.

[*At this point, Mr. Train pinned the Panda pin on the President's lapel.*]

Mr. Train. That makes you a member of the World Wildlife Fund.

The President. Thank you very much.

Mr. Train. Thank you, Mr. President.

The President. I appreciate this very much, and I'm very honored and pleased to have it. On our own ranch out in California, we have an awful lot of wildlife. And it's still there. And, as a matter of fact, if the Treasury agents won't object to my telling this experience, one day, one of them hung duty up on a hill up above the ranch house, came down, and he looked a little wild-eyed—or wide-eyed, I should say. And finally he spoke, because he wasn't quite sure that what had just happened to him was something that you just normally expect around the ranch or whether it was a little unusual.

He'd been sitting there doing his duty and looking out over the place. And he still sat there very quietly when a mountain lion just strolled by. [*Laughter*] And I told him we knew that they were around, but what had happened was a little unusual, and he probably had done exactly the right thing. [*Laughter*]

Well, thank you very much.

Mr. Train. Thank you again, Mr. President.

The President. Thank you all.

Note: The President spoke at 11:30 a.m. in the Rose Garden at the White House, where he presented the seventh annual Getty Prize to the 1983 winners.

Russell E. Train is president of the World Wildlife Fund—U.S.

Statement by Deputy Press Secretary Speakes on the Situation in Central America
July 25, 1983

There has been planning for a combined U.S.-Honduran military exercise to take place this year, but since planning is still underway, we cannot provide specifics at this time. The U.S. has conducted combined military exercises with Honduras and other nations in the world before and will do so again. This series of combined exercises involving U.S. and Latin American forces began in 1965. Such exercises pose no threat to any nation. They play a crucial role in training of troops and support personnel of our own forces and those of the host country.

The recent deployment of the U.S.S. *Ranger* carrier group in the Pacific is for training purposes and to demonstrate our interest in the Central American region. As plans for the joint exercise are developed, we will consult with Members of Congress.

We have consistently expressed our support for a political solution to the problems in Central America, not a military one. We fully support the proposals for a lessening of tensions in the region expressed in the Final Act of the San José Conference of last October. We support the Contadora process and other regional initiatives to ease tensions in the area. Ambassador [Richard B.] Stone, the President's special envoy, is currently on his third trip to the area and is conveying to the Governments of the Contadora Four countries of Colombia, Mexico, Venezuela, and Panama a Presidential message which conveys our continuing support to the Contadora process. The recent Presidential appointment of a National Bipartisan Commission on Central America is an additional indication of this government's long-term interest in that part of the world.

Our commitment to a political solution and to the strengthening of democracy and economic development in Central America is clear. Democracy and economic development, however, must have a basis in security, and our military aid to our allies, as well as our efforts to help them strengthen their own defensive capabilities, are designed to increase their security and thus shield the growth of democratic processes, economic development, dialog, and negotiations.

Our policy toward Central America is based on the four principles outlined by the President in his April 27 speech to the joint session of Congress: support for democracy, development, dialog, and the necessary military assistance to provide a shield for the first three. As a practical manner, all four aspects are interdependent, and we are continuing to evolve practical steps to implement all the facets of that policy.

Proclamation 5075—Helsinki Human Rights Day
July 25, 1983

By the President of the United States of America

A Proclamation

When the Final Act of the Conference on Security and Cooperation in Europe, widely referred to as "Helsinki accords," was concluded in Helsinki on August 1, 1975, thirty-three governments of Eastern and Western Europe, as well as the United States and Canada, committed themselves to "respect human rights and fundamental freedoms, including the freedom of thought, conscience, religion or belief, for all without distinction as to race, sex, language, or religion." The participating governments further committed themselves to foster "freer movement and contacts," improved access to information, and cultural and educational exchanges.

The Helsinki accords are a major achievement in the development of universal standards of international conduct and fundamental human rights. These standards go back to the earliest days of the American Republic. In a letter from Paris written to James Madison in 1787, Thomas Jefferson said that "a bill of rights is what the people are entitled to against every government on earth." The Helsinki accords are, in effect, a bill of rights for all the people of Europe.

The Government of the United States is firmly committed to the full implementation of the human rights and humanitarian provisions of the Helsinki accords. The American people are unalterably dedicated to the preservation and promotion of fundamental human rights throughout the world. The Helsinki accords are a powerful diplomatic instrument to advance the cause of human dignity and liberty.

At the Helsinki follow-up meeting in Madrid, the United States along with other Western countries has pointed out the failures of the Soviet Union and East European states to comply with their obligations under the humanitarian and human rights provisions of the Helsinki accords. The suppression of the trade union *Solidarity* in Poland, the continuing acts of repression directed against the Helsinki monitors, the drastic decrease in the level of emigration from the Soviet Union, and the harassment and persecution throughout the Soviet Union and Eastern Europe of citizens attempting to express their religious and political freedoms flagrantly denies the principles of Helsinki agreed to by the respective governments. These repressive actions not only threaten the achievement of genuine security and cooperation in Europe, but have a chilling effect on the human spirit of the brave peoples enduring this tyranny.

The Congress, by Senate Joint Resolution 96, has designated August 1, 1983 as "Helsinki Human Rights Day" and has authorized and requested the President to issue a proclamation in observance of that day. On this occasion, Americans are afforded the opportunity to reaffirm their commitment to the human rights principles embodied in the Final Act of the Conference on Security and Cooperation in Europe and to demonstrate their solidarity with the peoples of the Soviet Union and Eastern Europe, whose basic human rights are being violated by their governments on a continuing and regular basis.

In Witness Whereof, I have hereunto set my hand this 25th day of July, in the year of our Lord nineteen hundred and eighty-three, and of the Independence of the United States of America the two hundred and eighth.

RONALD REAGAN

[*Filed with the Office of the Federal Register, 4:48 p.m., July 25, 1983*]

Remarks at Ceremonies Marking the 75th Anniversary of the Federal Bureau of Investigation
July 26, 1983

Attorney General Smith, Judge Webster, the special agents and staff, and the distinguished guests of the FBI:

The proclamation that I am about to sign outlines the history and accomplishments of the Federal Bureau of Investigation. Believe me, it makes for impressive reading. But I couldn't help thinking this morning that no document or official history of the exploits of the men and women of the FBI could ever really capture what the Bureau, what the letters "FBI" themselves mean to the people whose way of life you are sworn to serve and protect.

To the American people you're a legend, and that is rightfully so. FBI agents have always been thought of as a cut above the ordinary, as law enforcement agents whose dedication and professionalism make them a first line of defense against mobsters, spies, corrupt officials, and other professional wrongdoers who prey on the innocent and undermine the moral foundations of our society. The personal qualities of the special agents of the FBI have made the Bureau the most corruption-free institution in the history of law enforcement and one of the most modern and advanced agencies of its kind in the world.

Recently, we've passed through a painful era in American history when it seemed that many of our proudest values and most important institutions were called into question. It's my personal belief that as mindless and destructive as some of the criticism was, its final result has been not only a reaffirmation of those institutions and those values but a new and greater understanding and appreciation for their usefulness and their meaning. The FBI will continue to look to the future, to use the latest and most sophisticated techniques to fight organized crime, white-collar crime, terrorism—in short, to do what needs to be done to protect the law-abiding people of the United States.

Today, under Judge Webster's leadership, the FBI takes on great new challenges. For the first time you are involved in the investigation of narcotics and dangerous drugs trade, and already you have brought to this endeavor the kind of expertise and skill that we've come to expect of you. You also face the threat of increased KGB and other hostile intelligence activities.

The challenge of crime today in America is a grave one. As you know, upon entering office this administration addressed itself immediately to the economic crisis that we were facing at that time as well as to the dangerous decline that had taken place in our Nation's national security and military strength. Yet even while we worked on these difficult problems we still kept work on the Nation's crime problem foremost in our minds.

Last year, when I announced at the Justice Department our eight-point program for attacking this problem, I was pleased to be able to announce a very sizable expansion of Justice Department personnel, including for the first time in many years additional agents for the FBI. We're now moving forward with other elements of the crime program, and we're doing so methodically and carefully but with one goal in mind. The recent increase in the drug trade, which has led to your new role in this battle, is really a reflection of an even deeper problem: the criminal networks and syndicates that have been tolerated in America for too long. I can only repeat to you that we're going after organized crime, root and branch. Our goal is to break the power of the mob in America and nothing short of it. We mean to end their profits, imprison their members, and cripple their organization.

The FBI has been, and is today, in the forefront of this battle. In recent years you scored admirable successes against professional criminals and their organizations. What is called for now is a renewed national strategy and a unified effort to achieve this objective.

You stand at the forefront of our efforts to detect and counter the increasing hostile intelligence threat to our country. Espionage, theft, and diversion of our technology, and Soviet "active measures" threaten us as never before. This part of your duty, about which I can say little in detail here, is vital to our national security, and I ask that you continue to devote the special attention which this difficult task requires.

On this, your 75th anniversary, I ask you to redouble your efforts to break apart and ultimately cripple the criminal syndicates in America. I also ask that you continue to give the highest priority to deterring and countering hostile intelligence activities within the United States. The FBI's record of fidelity, bravery, and integrity is a long and distinguished one. At each turn in your history, when criminals have engaged in new or advanced forms of criminal activity, you have led the law enforcement community in responding to these threats.

Once again, you're being asked by the American people for that kind of leadership, that kind of selfless dedication. I want to say to you that I know that you will respond as you always have—with excellence and with fervor.

Let me say to all the agents and staff of the Federal Bureau of Investigation the American people are proud of your past and your present, and we're grateful that you will be there for all of the challenges that lie in our future.

And now I will sign the proclamation designating today, July 26th, 1983, as FBI Day. It's nice to recognize something in Washington that's older than I am. [*Laughter*]

Thank you.

Note: The President spoke at 11:12 a.m. in the courtyard of the J. Edgar Hoover F.B.I. Building.

Proclamation 5076—FBI Day, 1983
July 26, 1983

By the President of the United States of America

A Proclamation

"Fidelity, Bravery, Integrity." As the motto of the Federal Bureau of Investigation, these words serve as a reminder of the vital part this institution plays in maintaining order and justice in our free society. From its inception under President Theo-dore Roosevelt to the present, the FBI has worked diligently to enforce our laws, ensure the Nation's security, and further the pursuit of justice across our land. Under the strong and dedicated leadership of its Directors, the FBI has been shaped into the modern, efficient, and highly regarded crime-fighting agency it is today.

During the past three-quarters of a century, the FBI has fought against gangsters, foiled Axis-inspired espionage and sabotage, dealt serious blows to organized crime, worked to stem racial violence, and undertook the responsibility of safeguarding America against threats of hostile intelligence agents and efforts to subvert our form of government. Beyond this, today's FBI is not only preeminent in scientific investigative support, but has demonstrated great vision and distinction in the performance of its duties and the training of its Special Agents.

In a world tested by terrorism and turmoil, the FBI faces new, complex, and difficult challenges. In dealing with these problems, the Nation can be confident that the agency will continue to protect the rights of our citizens while vigorously addressing the ravages of crime.

By designating July 26, 1983, as FBI Day, we mark the seventy-fifth anniversary of the creation of the Federal Bureau of Investigation. In celebrating this event, law enforcement agencies throughout the Nation join the American people in expressing their debt of gratitude to the men and women who have made the FBI the world's foremost criminal investigative organization. This major milestone provides an opportunity for all our citizens to join in honoring those whose dedicated efforts have made the FBI a formidable foe of criminals and a stalwart defender of America's freedom and security.

Now, Therefore, I, Ronald Reagan, President of the United States of America, do hereby designate July 26, 1983, as FBI Day.

In Witness Whereof, I have hereunto set my hand this 26th day of July, in the year of our Lord nineteen hundred and eighty-three, and of the Independence of the United States of America the two hundred and eighth.

RONALD REAGAN

[*Filed with the Office of the Federal Register, 4:07 p.m., July 26, 1983*]

Nomination of Frederick M. Bernthal To Be a Member of the Nuclear Regulatory Commission
July 26, 1983

The President today announced his intention to nominate Frederick M. Bernthal to be a member of the Nuclear Regulatory Commission for a term of 5 years expiring June 30, 1988. He would succeed John Francis Ahearne.

Since 1978 Mr. Bernthal has been serving on the staff of Senator Howard Baker as legislative assistant (1978–1979) and then as chief legislative assistant (1980–present). Previously he was associate professor of chemistry and physics (1975–1977) and assistant professor (1970–1975) at Michigan State University; visiting scientist, Niels Bohr Institute, University of Copenhagen, in 1976–1977; and staff postdoctoral scientist at Yale University in 1969–1970.

Mr. Bernthal is a member of the American Physical Society and the American Chemical Society. He is the author of more than 40 scientific publications in professional scientific journals including Physical Review, Physical Review Letters, and Nuclear Physics.

He graduated from Valparaiso (Indiana) University (B.S., 1964) and the University of California at Berkeley (Ph. D., 1969). He resides in Washington, D.C., and was born January 10, 1943.

Letter to President Ricardo de la Espriella of Panama on the Situation in Central America
July 26, 1983

Thank you for the letter which you and the presidents of Colombia, Mexico, and Venezuela have sent to me concerning the meeting held in Cancun on July 17, to review the current situation in Central America.

I would like to congratulate you on the efforts which the Contadora Four are making to promote dialog among the countries of Central America. My government has consistently expressed strong support for the Contadora process. The Cancun Declaration, by articulating the crucial issues which must be treated to reach an effective and enduring resolution of the Central American conflict, is an important contribution to advancing that process.

I continue to believe that a solution to the crisis in Central America must encompass four basic principles:

First, it is essential that democratic institutions be established and strengthened as a means to resolve political differences within the Central American states. Only by ensuring free and open participation in the democratic process can the peoples of Central America achieve reconciliation within their societies.

Second, there must be respect for the principle of non-intervention, including a ban on support for subversive elements that seek to destabilize other countries.

Third, the conflict in Central America must be removed from the context of an East-West confrontation, through such measures as the verifiable withdrawal of all foreign military and security advisers and a certifiable freeze on the acquisition of offensive armaments.

And finally, the countries of Central America must work among themselves and with their neighbors to achieve and sustain a level of economic growth that will guarantee the basic needs of their people.

I am pleased that the Cancun Declaration recognizes the importance of these fundamental principles. These issues are inextricably inter-related, and must be addressed on a comprehensive, regional basis which treats simultaneously the concerns of all the states affected by the Central American conflict. An attempt to resolve these issues sequentially, or on a piecemeal basis, will not achieve the goal we all share of a lasting peace for all of Central America.

Equally important is the need to ensure that all undertakings assumed by the Central American states be fully reciprocal and subject to comprehensive, fully adequate verification. Clearly, no initiative can bring true peace to Central America if one state is permitted to take unjust advantage of its neighbors through failure to abide by peace conditions which bind the others. The Charter of the Organization of American States makes clear that it should be the purpose of the OAS to either prevent unjust acts committed by one state against another, or to provide for common action on the part of the members in the event of difficulties. I believe the OAS, as this Hemisphere's regional forum, is the appropriate mechanism to ensure that those who make commitments, comply with them.

The problems of Central America are complex, and their solution demands untiring efforts. The activities which you and your colleagues in the Contadora group have undertaken are proof of your sincere dedication to the goal of a genuine and lasting peace throughout the region. My own efforts in this regard have been to dispatch my Special Emissary to the region and establish a bipartisan commission to examine the problems of Central America and to propose solutions. You have my prayers and those of my countrymen as you continue your work.

Sincerely,

RONALD REAGAN

Note: The White House announced that similar letters were addressed to Presidents Belisario Betancur Cuartas of Colombia,

Miguel de la Madrid Hurtado of Mexico, and Luis Herrera Campins of Venezuela. As printed above, this item follows the text of the letter released by the Office of the Press Secretary.

Nomination of W. Tapley Bennett, Jr., To Be an Assistant Secretary of State
July 26, 1983

The President today announced his intention to nominate W. Tapley Bennett, Jr., to be an Assistant Secretary of State (Legislative and Intergovernmental Affairs). He will succeed Powell Allen Moore.

Since 1977 Mr. Bennett has been serving as the United States Permanent Representative on the Council of the North Atlantic Treaty Organization with the rank of Ambassador. From 1973 to 1977, he was Deputy Representative to the United Nations with the rank of Ambassador. Previously, from 1971 to 1973, he served as Deputy Representative of the United States in the Security Council of the United Nations with the rank of Ambassador.

Prior to his entry into the Foreign Service in 1941, Mr. Bennett was an instructor at the University of Georgia and a trainee at the National Institute of Public Affairs in Washington. He served in the Department of Latin American Affairs, becoming officer in charge of Central America and Panama Affairs in 1950. He became Deputy Director of the Office of South American Affairs

in 1951. In 1954 Mr. Bennett attended the National War College.

He served as foreign affairs officer in the Office of the Deputy Under Secretary in 1955 and as Special Assistant to the Deputy Under Secretary in 1956. He was assigned to Vienna as a political counselor in 1957 and to Athens as counselor of the Embassy in 1961.

Mr. Bennett served as Ambassador to the Dominican Republic from 1964 to 1966 and as Ambassador to Portugal from 1966 to 1969. From 1969 to 1971, he was a faculty adviser at Air University, Maxwell Air Force Base.

He was born April 1, 1917, in Griffin, Ga. He received an A.B. degree from the University of Georgia in 1937 and an LL.B. from George Washington University in 1948. He took graduate studies at the University of Freiburg, Germany, in 1937 and 1938.

Mr. Bennett speaks German, Spanish, and French. He served in the U.S. Army from 1944 to 1946.

The President's News Conference
July 26, 1983

Central America

The President. I have an opening statement here.

A while back I got a letter from a 13-year-old, and I apologize for not having answered her as yet. She wrote, "Don't you wish sometimes you could just stamp your feet and shout at the press or Senators to be quiet, sit down, and listen to what you're saying?" Well, yes, Gretchen, I sometimes

do feel that way and particularly over the past week.

On April 27th I went to Capitol Hill, addressed a Joint Session of the Congress on a subject of vital importance to all Americans. I talked about our goals in Central America, and I asked for congressional understanding and support.

In Central America, as elsewhere, we support democracy, reform, and human freedom. We support economic development. We support dialog and negotiations among and within the countries of the region. And, yes, we support a security shield for the region's threatened nations in order to protect these other goals.

In my view, there's been entirely too much attention to the efforts that we're making to provide that security shield and not nearly enough to the other elements of our policy. Yet in each of the four elements of the policy, we find they reinforce each other and that they are being pursued simultaneously in a carefully balanced manner.

I dispatched Ambassador Dick Stone to the region to facilitate the process of dialog and negotiations. He's there now with a personal message from me to leaders of countries in the region, the text of which I'm making public tonight. I'm heartened by the efforts of the Contadora countries—led by Colombia, Mexico, Panama, and Venezuela—to reach a peaceful regional solution. I'm encouraged by some recent statements from Nicaragua and Cuba that seem to indicate that they, too, now recognize the merit to regional negotiations. I trust their words will be followed by positive actions to ease tension and to stop the fighting in the region.

Here at home I've appointed a bipartisan commission to make recommendations on the long-term measures, including economic assistance, that we should undertake to help these struggling nations. And I hope soon to be signing the legislation on the Caribbean Basin Initiative, passed by an overwhelming bipartisan majority of both Houses. The program will bolster the economic independence of the region.

We continue to promote elections as the best way to guarantee peace, human freedom, and responsive government. The greatest portion of our aid goes toward humanitarian and economic assistance. For every $1 we provide for security assistance to that region, we provide $3 for economic and human development.

But we recognize that democracy and development can hardly flourish when threatened by violence. Dialog and negotiations can best succeed when the parties are convinced that their goals cannot be achieved

through the barrel of a gun. It's especially important in our own hemisphere that the United States continue to be the foremost protector of peace. As part of this mission, as a way to provide a shield for democracy and development, we, together with our friends, are now planning joint training exercises in the Caribbean and Central America. And let me set the record straight on what these exercises are and what they are not.

Essentially, there will be two sets of practice training in coming months—one, a series of ground exercises in Honduras with the combined forces of Honduras and the United States; second, a series of ocean exercises with our own fleet. We have conducted joint exercises with Latin American countries on a regular basis since 1965. The latest exercises with Honduras took place earlier this year. Much larger scale exercises have taken place in Europe, Asia, and Latin America. Moreover, these training exercises are limited in purpose.

Yes, we want to underscore once and for all that the United States, along with our friends, seriously opposes the use of force by one neighbor against another in Central America, but we're not seeking a larger presence in that region, and U.S. forces have not been requested there. The United States stands firmly on the side of peace. As a nation, we remain steadfast in policy and purpose. We want to see an end to violence and bloodshed, to the export of revolution. We want to help our neighbors lift themselves up to prosperity. We want to usher in a new era of peace and social justice. Now, these are great goals, worthy of a great and generous people. And we shall continue to keep faith with ourselves in the days ahead.

Now, Helen [Helen Thomas, United Press International].

Central America

Q. Mr. President, you complain of too much attention. How can the people ignore two battleship groups, thousands of combat troops going to Honduras, it is said the covert funding of 10,000 rebels, Nicaraguan rebels? My question—and all these things have happened since April 27th—my question, sir, is, in seeking solutions, how far will you go militarily, and I'd like to follow up.

The President. Well, I have told you, we have no military plans for intervention of that kind. We have 55, mainly noncommissioned officers helping to train the Salvadoran Army. We know that Cuba has somewhere in the neighborhood—well, it has thousands of military personnel in Nicaragua. It does seem a little overbalanced with regard to the attention that's being paid to 55 as against attention that's being paid to the thousands. I suppose what my question is, Helen, to answer with a question, is why are maneuvers that we have performed before, and regularly, suddenly treated with such suspicion when only—well, within this year, last spring, we had military maneuvers in Honduras, and last year we had naval maneuvers in the Caribbean, and no one seemed to be excited about them at all. So, is it just that there's no confidence in the fact that when I say these are maneuvers of the kind we've been holding regularly and for years?

Q. But they're unprecedented—to last 6 months. The polls show the American people are not for them, and they fear it may lead to war. And my question is, remembering the lessons in Vietnam, does this bother you? And do they have any say?

The President. First of all, there is no comparison with Vietnam, and there's not going to be anything of that kind in this. And maybe the people are disturbed because of the confused pattern that has been presented to them and the constant drumbeat with regard to the fact of suspicion that somehow there is an ulterior purpose in this.

It hardly seems to me that those ships are going there—and I don't know that they're going to be there 6 months. I don't know what the length of time for the training is. I don't know the number of ships involved. But I didn't know the number that were involved in the Caribbean exercises. But if they were there for some kind of a hostile purpose—we happen to know that right now a Soviet freighter, the *Ul'Yanov,* is approaching the Port of Corinto in the vicinity of Nicaragua—that port is in Nicaragua—and it is carrying a load of military equipment, helicopters, transport helicopters for military purposes, and so forth. And no one

shot at them.

Jim [Jim Gerstenzang, Associated Press]?

Q. Mr. President, you've mentioned your interest in easing the tensions, and you've said that you hope the Nicaraguan proposals will have that effect. Now, your spokesman has said that the 4,000 troops that you're planning to send down there will——

The President. Between three and four.

Q. ——between 3- and 4,000 troops that you're planning to send down there will have standing orders to defend themselves if they're fired upon. How does that help to ease tensions?

The President. Well, wait a minute. That is something that has been true for a long time, as far as I'm concerned, with our troops and our forces anywhere they may be.

We went through a period some years ago when American forces were pretty much fair game. Look back at some of our aircraft that were shot down on the charge that they had ventured out over international waters—or out of international waters, into the airspace of a Communist bloc country and shot down, and we protested diplomatically.

It seems to me that young men and women who are going to defend this country of ours and who join the military should know that they have the right to defend themselves if we have placed them in a position where they could come under fire. And this is just a standard order. We don't want war. But I don't think that you prevent war by letting your personnel out there become the victims.

Q. But doesn't this simply increase the chances of war?

The President. No, I don't think so. All of the ships that are down in that area and that are going there are outside the 12-mile limit. They're out in international waters where they have a right to be.

Now, wait a minute before all of your hands go up here. You change personnel every once in a while, and new people come into the White House press corps. And it's only been recently that an effort has been made to see that I have an opportunity to meet them and get acquainted. And so recently, I met five newcomers to the press corps, but only three of them are here tonight. And when I met them I told them that in this, the first press conference that I knew they were here, that I was going to call on them if they had a question.

Candy [Candy Crowley, Associated Press Radio], do you have a question?

Q. How can I turn that down? [*Laughter*]

A little earlier you said, yes, that the military exercises—that you did want to underscore that the U.S. is opposed to the use of force——

The President. Yes.

Q. ——in the region. Is sending down our military might to the region a way to show that we oppose force? Isn't there some sort of contradiction there? Wouldn't it be better to say—if we do these things regularly—isn't this the time now not to do it, not to heighten the tensions, and to say we oppose the use of force? How can you oppose it by sending down all these ships and men?

The President. Well, since the trouble that is going on down there comes from outside the area, is revolution exported from the Soviet Union and from Cuba and from others of their allies, then wouldn't there perhaps be a risk if we changed our pattern and withdrew? Wouldn't we be sending some kind of a signal that might be the wrong kind of signal to send if we want peace in that area?

The simple truth is no one has asked for American forces to come to their aid; in fact, they've gone quite the contrary and said the reverse—that they don't. And yet, they do acknowledge that they need the material assistance that we're giving them, both economic and to provide a shield, or help them provide their own shield against the attacks that are preventing them from making the economic progress that they want to make, now that they have installed a democratic type of government there.

But, as I say, we've done this regularly. I don't think that it's destabilizing, nor should it be.

Q. You know, you've said in your letter to the four Contadora nations that you want to take this out of the realm of an East-West confrontation. But doesn't somebody have to begin to take it out of that realm? And couldn't the U.S. be the leader in that way

and not make it that kind of an atmosphere of confrontation?

The President. Well, we think we are. We have tried to make contact with the guerrillas in El Salvador to see if they would not meet with the peace commission that was created by the El Salvadoran Government to discuss participating in the democratic process, in the elections that are coming up before the year is out. In the entire area, I have just sent letters—which have been made public now—but letters to the Contadora Four of our approval of what they're doing and our recognition of what they are, and that we stand ready to support them in what they're trying to accomplish. We want a political and peaceful solution.

Now wait a minute. There are two more here that—Bob Rowley [Storer H. Rowley, Chicago Tribune].

Q. Thank you. Mr. President, military leaders in the Pentagon have stated recently that they never want to be involved in another war without the support of the American people. Do you have any sense or feeling now for whether the American people are ready to support a war to defend our interests in Central America?

The President. Well, in the first place, I don't think the American people have ever wanted a war. I think we're probably the most peace-loving people in the world. And maybe this has been part of what has lured us into wars in the past, because we haven't been ready for them.

No, I don't think the American people—and I don't think that they, frankly, I don't think that they're as aware as perhaps they should be. We've tried to make them aware that this does constitute something of a threat in this hemisphere, to peace in the entire hemisphere, if those who are exporting the revolution here are successful.

But no, we're not planning a war, and we don't think that that's going to happen at all. I've seen four wars in my lifetime. I have sons, and I have a grandson. And I agree with General Eisenhower that war is man's greatest stupidity. I don't want to see such a thing. We want peace.

But we also must recognize that you've got to do more than just want peace. You have got to prevent what is happening down there to people who want peace, also, but are not allowed to have it because of outside forces that are seizing upon their situation and hoping to further their own ideological aims.

Q. Sir, do you feel the people support your policies in Central America?

The President. Those that have been informed and understand it do. I just met with some today who made it evident that they did. Now, if we all get together and explain what's happening down there, perhaps that'll resolve the situation in that regard.

Now, Ben Taylor [Boston Globe].

Q. Mr. President, if there is an incident where the American forces down there engaging in the military exercises are fired upon and they are forced to fire back, do you see any contingency where such an incident might lead to deeper American involvement in Central America?

The President. No, I don't really, because I don't foresee—first of all, those maneuvers that are going to be held in Honduras are not going to put Americans in any reasonable proximity to the border. It would have to be something in the nature of a terrorist attack, something of that kind, and I think that any of us—that could happen in a base here in America. And again, I believe that those people who have taken it upon themselves to be our defenders and protectors have a right to defend and protect their own lives.

Q. I have a followup, sir. If Nicaragua attacks Honduras, would the United States assist Honduras militarily under the terms of the Rio Mutual Defense Pact Treaty?

The President. Well, we haven't considered that. But a great many people should know that since 1947—and so, obviously, our administration didn't have anything to do with it—there is a pact, the Rio Pact, that says that any attack, or an attack on any American State shall be considered as an attack on all American States. Now, that would require, of course, actual outside visible attack on a state and, I suppose, by a country flying under its own flag instead of under surrogate troops.

So, we would have to deal with that problem when it arose and deal with it with all of our neighbors and friends in the Organization of American States.

Q. Thank you, Mr. President. I'd like to give you a chance to silence this drumbeat of confusion that you were talking about. Why not say categorically that Central America will not be another Vietnam, that under no circumstances will you impose U.S. troops in a combat situation in Central America?

The President. Well, I said the last time we gathered that there are some things—I can make every assurance in the world that we have no such plans, we have no desire, nor do the countries down there want us involved in that way. But I used an expression that has been used by Presidents like Franklin Delano Roosevelt and others, and that is that a President should never say "never," because that's a hypothetical question that then asks you to try to predict what could possibly take place in the future. And I just don't believe you can answer a hypothetical question, unless it's——

Q. May I follow up?

The President. What?

Q. Could I follow up?

The President. All right.

Q. What about increasing the number of U.S. advisers in El Salvador? Are you planning to at all?

The President. No one has presented a proposal to me about increasing the number. There's no question that 55 of them—if there was an increase, probably we could train the Salvadoran Army and its new recruits—that are coming in actually requiring basic training—a little faster than we're doing it. But there's been no proposal for such an increase.

Now, Bill [Bill Plante, CBS News].

Q. Mr. President, since you yourself have identified massive social problems as one of the root causes——

The President. Yes.

Q. ——of the troubles in Central America, are you prepared to make a commitment to substantial U.S. aid on the order of the Marshall plan if the hostilities down there can be calmed?

The President. Well, what we've appointed the Commission for, the Kissinger-chaired Commission, is for the purpose of coming up and recommending a long-range plan that would particularly deal with the things that you mention. There's no question that our neighbors to the south have, for too many years, suffered revolutions in which one set of rulers simply were exchanged for another set of rulers. And there's no question but their economic and social policies have left much to be desired as far as the opportunity for the great mass of their people.

And what we want is a long-range policy—and this is what I discussed when I visited there and in South America and discussed with them—of how we can have the kind of development that will make these countries economically self-sufficient, that will give them a standard of living in which there isn't the fertile soil that is presently there for subversion, for people offering promises of pie in the sky and then arousing to revolution, and to, in other words, have a program that makes all of the nations here in the Americas equal partners in the development of this Western Hemisphere. And what a great power for good that we could be if we were so organized. And we want—this is my dream, and it's what I hope that the Commission will come back with.

Q. Sir, is the United States prepared to make the kind of massive dollar commitment that that would undoubtedly entail?

The President. It does not follow that it has to undoubtedly entail that. For example, many of those countries are considered too high a risk for private investment. If, together, we could agree upon guarantees that investment would not be confiscated, taken over by governments and in changes of government, and so forth, there is far more in the private investment pool, far more there than any government could possibly do.

And it is to find out what is practical and what can be done. And we're not completely alone in this, because our allies, the other industrial nations in the world, have made it plain to us—and again, at Williamsburg—that not only here in our hemisphere but in their own, we want to come up and find ways that we can help the developing part of the world and help them to faster development and a better way of life.

Sam [Sam Donaldson, ABC News]?

Lebanon

Q. Sir, the Lebanese President said this past week that the Israeli partial withdrawal in Lebanon amounted to de facto partition of that country. Do you agree?

The President. No, I am very hopeful that if this partial withdrawal takes place that it will be recognized and admitted to be, by the Israelis, as one phase of their agreement to withdraw. If they withdraw in a phased withdrawal, it certainly will give us a better case for breaking the roadblock that has been established by Syria and persuading them to keep their original promise that when others withdrew they would withdraw.

I can't answer as to whether that is the way that this is going to be perceived or whether the Israelis will admit to it or not, but I will be talking in a couple of days with the two ministers who are here from Israel, and about this very thing.

But if this is a phased withdrawal, I think there is fear if there's simply a withdrawal to another line and then a digging in and fortifying along that line, that this would be what it looks like Syria is doing, and that is simply trying to partition Lebanon, reduce Lebanon, and grab off some territory for themselves. But with the agreement that's been signed between Lebanon and Israel, I don't think Israel has that in mind.

Q. Sir, what would happen if Lebanon is partitioned? Would it be that awful?

The President. Well, I just believe that the people of a country have a right to determine their own destiny, choose their own government, and if it was partitioned, it would be occupation by other countries and, yes, I think that is awful. We set out to help Lebanon, after all these years of strife, regain sovereignty of its own land, protection of its own borders. And we're helping in every way we can to bring that about.

I have to turn in some other direction here.

Chris [Chris Wallace, NBC News]?

Dr. Henry A. Kissinger

Q. Mr. President, I'd like to ask you about the Chairman of your new commission on Central America, Dr. Henry Kissinger. There have been, as you know, a number of charges over the years that Mr. Kissinger during the Nixon years tried to destabilize the duly elected Government of Chile and that he also once told a Chilean official that whatever happens in the south is of no importance. Did you check into Mr. Kissinger's record on Latin America before you appointed him?

The President. I know what his position was prior to my taking over this Office and how seriously he considered the problems that are going on. Remember, Salvador didn't start with us. It was already in turmoil before we got here. And I know how he feels about that. And I know, also, that there is no hard and fast—well, let me put it this way: I think there are some stereotypes about Mr. Kissinger that a little actual reading and re-reading of the history would indicate that those stereotypes are not necessarily valid.

The Gender Gap

Q. Mr. President, if I may follow up with another question about the Commission, you talk a lot here, and your aides do, about the gender gap. And yet that Commission was appointed—12 men, no women. Doesn't that add to the perception that you're insensitive to women?

The President. It might add to the perception, and that's all it is is a perception, because if anyone wants to really dig into the facts, I will match our record against any other administration that has ever been here with regard to what we have accomplished for women—in the field of economics, our tax policies that reduced and hopefully will in the near future eliminate the marriage penalty tax; the measures that we passed in the IRA's that not only working women but housewives can have these tax-free savings accounts. We have almost doubled the tax credit for child care.

But in addition to that, I noticed the other night that someone on the air was comparing our record to that of the previous administration. And we came out a little behind with regard to the appointment of women to positions in government, except that it turned out that without their acknowledging it, they were comparing the 4-year record of the previous administration with our first 2 years. And when you compare our first 2 years with their first 2 years, well, we're quite a ways out ahead.

Q. Why no women on this Commission?

The President. On this particular Commission, maybe it's because we're doing so much and appointing so many that we're no longer seeking a token or something. It just came out that these were the 12 we selected. We wanted six opponents; we wanted six on our side.

But we've appointed over 1,000 women in executive positions here in government—three members of the Cabinet—never before in history—and one member of the Supreme Court. So, I think our record—it's just a case of our record isn't known.

Jerry [Jeremiah O'Leary, Washington Times]?

Central America

Q. Mr. President, since Cuba has repeatedly been labeled as the fountainhead of most of the violence in Central America, why has your administration elected to go to the recipients of the arms and the equipment that comes in instead of going to the source?

The President. Well, we have interdicted some of the supplies that are going from Nicaragua over to El Salvador. If you go to the source, I think you're talking about the Soviet Union. They know, and we have communicated to them, how we feel about this, and we have also to our friends in Cuba—told them how we feel about it.

We're trying to bring about the very thing that all of you seem to think that we're shying away from, and that is not broadening a war but trying to limit it and trying to bring about a peaceful and political settlement in Central America.

George [George E. Condon, Jr., Copley News Service]?

Q. Mr. President, in reply to Helen's question you spoke of confusion. But isn't this administration to blame for much of that confusion? Some of our own ambassadors in Central America were taken by surprise by the maneuvers. Some of the friendly governments, expecially in the Contadora group, were puzzled by your latest actions. My question is, why was there not more prior consultation, and what can you do now to reassure any of those friendly governments that we're not today closer to war down there than we were last week?

The President. Well, as I've told you, I sent four—I've sent letters to all four leaders of the Contadora countries. And I don't think that there's that much disturbance among our friends and allies about this.

Sometimes there's a slip up, and an ambassador doesn't find out something they should find out soon enough in advance. As a matter of fact, I received a cable from one about that—my most recent appointee as the Ambassador of Austria. And Helene [von Damm] let me know that something had taken place, and she hadn't been told about it in advance. And when Helene speaks, I listen.

Q. Mr. President, who do you think is to blame for this confusion you spoke of then?

The President. I don't think there is as much confusion as they're trying to point out about this. The training feature with Honduras—this has been well advertised and known for a long, long time that it's going to take place. And as I say, we regularly conduct, and conduct joint maneuvers with, very often not only on land but with the navies of our friends and allies in Central and South America. And so I just don't think that there's great confusion about this.

Q. Mr. President, is it true that you're planning a vast expansion of covert aid to the anti-Sandinista rebels in Nicaragua? And what would congressional action to cut off such aid mean to your efforts in Central America?

The President. Well, I think it would be a very grave mistake if the legislature interfered with what we're trying to do, and we're trying to keep them apprised of our actions.

I can't answer your question about covert aid. I think this is like discussing intelligence matters. If you discuss covert aid, it's no longer covert.

So, I can only tell you that we're continuing on a policy that we believe is aimed at, first of all, bringing about peace in El Salvador, hopefully through negotiations with those who are presently radicals and fighting as guerrillas, and in Nicaragua, hoping that we can persuade the Nicaraguan, the Sandinista government to return to the

principles of the revolution and which they, in writing, guaranteed to the Organization of American States was going to be the policy of their government.

Q. Let me follow up on covert aid, Mr. President. Given the fact that this covert operation is not so covert any more, haven't we reached a point where it really might make more sense to do things on an overt basis? In other words, hasn't the thing really become counterproductive?

The President. No. No, I don't think so. And I think what we're doing is well within the limits of common sense. And those who are attempting to make it impossible for us to bring aid down in that area, I think are the ones who are building up—if they have their way—to a giant headache down the road a ways. And we're trying to prevent such a headache from coming about.

Carter Briefing Materials

Q. Mr. President, could you tell us what possible crime could be involved in the Carter briefing book caper to justify calling out the FBI?

The President. There you go again. [*Laughter*] No, I——

Q. And I have a followup.

The President. ——I just couldn't help that.

Q. That's all right.

The President. I thought we were going to set a record, and I was going to go upstairs and be able to say, "How about that? Not a single question on it."

This is why, when this charge was made—the allegation was made—this is why I said there's only one answer to this. Certainly, the best investigative force in the United States is the Federal Bureau of Investigation. And I have told them to go completely to the bottom of this to see if there was any wrongdoing, to see if there was anything unethical in what had taken place. And I have told all of our people to make themselves available, anyone who knows anything about this, and that includes me—and I didn't know anything about it until I read it in the paper—to get to the bottom of this, so that everyone in this country can be reassured that we know the truth.

Q. Yes, sir, but my question was what crime? Or would you deny the possibility that all of this is little more than Washington Post-National Enquirer-style summer theater?

The President. Oh, you're tempting me. [*Laughter*]

Q. That's what I intended to do.

The President. We'll find out when the investigation is completed.

Q. What's the crime, Mr. President?

The President. All right, there are any number of things contained in the allegations and the wild flurry that immediately followed this. There could have been a break-in. And when you're——

Q. In the White House?

The President. Well, that's what was al-leged. That was what some of them said that they suspected. I would have to tell you, having lived here for awhile, that I don't think it's possible, either. But, also, there could be the element of were these things actually stolen by someone in the White House? Was there involvement of White House staff in campaign activities who were supposed to be performing other government positions? There are any number of things that should be looked at.

Ms. Thomas. Thank you, Mr. President.

The President. Helen, thank you. Good night.

Note: The President's 19th news conference began at 8:02 p.m. in the East Room at the White House. It was broadcast live on nationwide radio and television.

Nomination of Charles Franklin Dunbar To Be United States Ambassador to Qatar
July 27, 1983

The President today announced his intention to nominate Charles Franklin Dunbar, of Maine, a career member of the Senior Foreign Service, Class of Counselor, to be Ambassador to the State of Qatar. He would succeed Charles E. Marthinsen.

Mr. Dunbar was a statistical coding clerk with the District of Columbia Department of Transportation in 1961–1962 and a clerk in the Office of Communications with the Department of State in 1962. He entered the Foreign Service in 1962 and attended consular and Persian language training at the Foreign Service Institute. He was Foreign Service officer general in Tehran (1963–1964), vice consul in Isfahan (1964–1967), and political officer in Kabul (1967–1970). In the Department he was associate watch officer, then staff officer in the Executive Secretariat in 1970–1972. In 1972–1973 he attended Arabic language training at the Foreign Service Institute. He was political officer in Rabat (1973–1975), in Algiers (1975–1978), and Deputy Chief of Mission in Nouakchott (1978–1980). In 1980–1981 he attended senior training at the Woodrow Wilson School, Princeton University. He was Acting Deputy Chief of Mission (1981–1982) and Acting Chargé d'Affaires (1982–1983) in Kabul.

Mr. Dunbar graduated from Harvard College (A.B., 1959) and the School of International Affairs at Columbia University (M.I.A., 1961). His foreign languages are Persian, French, and Arabic. He was born April 1, 1937, in Cambridge, Mass.

Statement on Production of the MX Missile
July 27, 1983

It is good news for all Americans that the House and Senate have again demonstrated bipartisan unity in pursuit of two vital national goals—strategic modernization and arms control. Their authorization of production of the Peacekeeper missile reaffirms the fact that, as a nation, we are united in our approach to arms reductions and protecting peace.

In May the Congress established a new bipartisan unity endorsing the Scowcroft commission recommendations. In the past 2 weeks, that unity was tested and sustained.

Thanks to this bipartisan support, we are now in a stronger position to continue making progress at the START negotiations. If we can maintain our stable, bipartisan, consistent approach here at home, we have a great opportunity to achieve what we all want—lasting stability in the nuclear balance and significant reductions of nuclear arsenals on both sides.

Proclamation 5077—National Animal Agriculture Week, 1983
July 27, 1983

By the President of the United States of America

A Proclamation

Foods from animal origin supply 70 percent of the protein, 35 percent of the energy, 80 percent of the calcium, 60 percent of the phosphorous, and important quantities of the "B" vitamins and trace minerals in the average American's diet. The application of scientific methods has markedly improved the efficiency of meat production in recent years and enhanced the desirability of these foods to consumers.

During July 1983, the American Society of Animal Science is celebrating its seventy-fifth anniversary. Its 7,500 members provide research, extension and educational services to all segments of animal agriculture in both the United States and other countries.

In recognition of the great progress which has been made in the past seventy-five years in applying scientific principles to animal agriculture production and the role

of animal products in our daily life, the Congress of the United States, by Senate Joint Resolution 77, has authorized and requested the President to designate the week of July 24 to July 31, 1983, as "National Animal Agriculture Week."

Now, Therefore, I, Ronald Reagan, President of the United States of America, do hereby designate the week beginning July 24, 1983, as National Animal Agriculture Week. I call upon the people of the United States and interested organizations to mark this week with appropriate observances to honor the contributions made by animal agriculture production to our economy.

In Witness Whereof, I have hereunto set my hand this 27th day of July, in the year of our Lord nineteen hundred and eighty-three, and of the Independence of the United States of America the two hundred and eighth.

RONALD REAGAN

[*Filed with the Office of the Federal Register, 4:44 p.m., July 27, 1983*]

Appointment of J. Joseph Lydon as a Member of the Advisory Committee of the Pension Benefit Guaranty Corporation
July 27, 1983

The President today announced his intention to appoint J. Joseph Lydon to be a member of the Advisory Committee to the Pension Benefit Guaranty Corporation for the remainder of the term expiring February 19, 1985. He will succeed L. R. Hubbard, Jr.

Since 1963 Mr. Lydon has been in the general practice of law, specializing in labor relations and pension law. In addition, he served as labor counsel to the commissioner, Massachusetts State Police, in 1970–1976; assistant corporation counsel, city of Boston, in 1969–1971; and chief legislative counsel to the Massachusetts Port Authority in 1968–1970.

Mr. Lydon graduated from Suffolk University (A.B., 1957), Boston College Law School (LL.B., 1961), and Burdett College (A.A., 1964). He is married, has three children, and resides in Dover, Mass. He was born May 18, 1930, in Boston, Mass.

Remarks on Establishing the President's Commission on Organized Crime
July 28, 1983

Judge Kaufman and Attorney General Smith, Judge Webster[1], Chairmen Thurmond and Rodino, other distinguished members of this Commission, and ladies and gentlemen:

We're here today to redeem this administration's promise to do all in our power to break apart and cripple the organized criminal syndicates that for too long have been tolerated in America.

The power of these syndicates infects every part of our society. The cost in human and fiscal terms is incalculable. The climate of lawlessness that their very existence fosters makes this confederation of career criminals a costly and tragic part of our history.

The reasons for the mob's success are clear. Its tactics and techniques are well known: organizational cohesion and discipline, vows of secrecy and loyalty, insulation for its leaders from direct criminal involvement, bribery and corruption of law enforcement and public officials, violence and threats against those who would testify or resist this criminal conspiracy—all of these have contributed to the curtain of silence that surrounds the mob.

Through the years, a few dedicated Americans have broken this curtain of silence and fought this menace. Their names are familiar—prosecutor Thomas Dewey and Judge Samuel Seabury, Federal agent

---

[1] *William H. Webster, Director of the Federal Bureau of Investigation.*

Eliot Ness, Senators Kefauver and McClellan, Attorney General Kennedy, investigative reporter Don Bolles. But for too long this fight has been left to a few dedicated policemen, prosecutors, journalists, or public officials, and too often their efforts have resulted in only temporary gains against this menace. The time has come to make these gains more permanent, to fully redeem the contributions of those who have waged a lonely battle against difficult odds. And the time has come for all of us to assist in the fight to break the power of the mob in America.

It's often been said that no government can eliminate or end the illegal activities that provide much of the revenue and support for organized crime. Well, that is only true as far as it goes. I agree that government cannot stop or abolish the human impulses that make racketeering profitable. But I also believe we'd have the capacity to break apart and ultimately destroy the tightly knit regional and national networks of career criminals who live off these activities.

Late last year, I announced a national strategy to expose, prosecute, and ultimately cripple organized crime in America. We're proceeding carefully with the elements of that strategy. Its final goal is the removal of a blot on American history that has lasted nearly a hundred years.

As I've said before, few weapons against organized crime have proven more effective or more important to law enforcement

than the investigations of the Kefauver committee in the early fifties, the labor racketeering hearings of the McClellan committee in the midfifties, and the testimony of Federal informant Joseph Valachi before a Senate committee in the 1960's. While some other commissions on crime have been appointed since then, each has been of short duration and had neither the time nor the resources to fully investigate the syndicate and lay out a national program for its elimination.

I'm pleased to announce today that one of America's most distinguished jurists, Judge Irving Kaufman, from the U.S. Court of Appeals for the Second Circuit, has agreed to lead a panel of 15 [20] distinguished Americans from diverse backgrounds and professions in this pursuit.

The purpose of this Commission, which will last for nearly 3 years, will be to undertake through public hearings a region-by-region exposure and analysis of organized crime, to measure its influence and impact on American society, and make judicial and legislative recommendations.

Judge Kaufman has won widespread praise for his leadership of a number of important commissions on judicial and law enforcement problems. After I expressed my gratitude to him today in the Oval Office for taking this assignment, we were joined by the rest of the Commission members, including Senator Thurmond and Congressman Rodino, the chairmen of the Senate and House Judiciary Committees, whom, I am especially pleased to announce, have agreed to serve on this Commission. And I want, also, to acknowledge the generous assistance of Justice Potter Stewart, who, in addition to his other responsibilities, has agreed to play a vital role in this endeavor.

The membership of this Commission shows strong geographical balance, and it includes representatives of the judiciary, the Congress, the academic community, the private sector, and most important, law enforcement at all levels. We've been especially careful to include—and I believe this will be one of the Commission's greatest strengths—a number of individuals who, though not widely known, have had extensive, frontline experience with organized

crime and are among the acknowledged experts in this field.

I know that some will wonder why another commission is needed. They'll ask, "Aren't the Justice Department and the FBI and other law enforcement agencies damaging organized crime with their prosecutions? Don't congressional committees have the resources to conduct investigations?" The answer to these questions is simply, yes. Recent prosecutions have done the mob considerable damage. And, yes, the Congress has, as I said before, done highly effective work with its investigations.

But prosecutions by themselves can never dig out the roots of a problem that reaches so deeply into our society. Nor is the Congress, which has many other matters on its agenda, in a position to take responsibility for the business of exposing organized crime, its latest techniques and inroads. That's why this Commission is so vitally important, one of the centerpieces in our strategy for a frontal assault on the mob in America.

I believe this Commission can expose to the American people the small group of career criminals who run the rackets, push drugs, corrupt policemen and public officials, and, ultimately, undermine the very basis of our democratic society itself. I believe this Commission can mobilize the American people against organized crime by triggering the kind of public support that is vital for its final isolation and elimination.

One reason we sought to include a broad cross section of America in the membership of this Commission stems from our firm belief that this battle can never be fully won at the Federal level. Only when we work in our States and communities to put out of business the racketeering that fills the coffers of organized crime, only when we fully expose and isolate those groups or individuals who work or do business with organized crime can we expect a final victory.

More than 23 years ago, as he sentenced defendants in a trial following the notorious Apalachin Conference in upstate New York, a Federal judge noted that the defendants before him had not stumbled into criminal activity thoughtlessly or because of under-privileged backgrounds. He referred to them as hardened, sophisticated criminals who thought of themselves as a group above the law, men who placed loyalty to each other above loyalty to their country and its law-abiding citizens. He noted that these men "wear two faces," that they cloaked themselves in the respectability of charitable or civic organizations, even as they work to prey on innocent people and undermine the very moral foundations of our society.

Judge Kaufman, your words were true then, and unfortunately, they are true today. I want you and the members of the Commission here to know, as you seek sub-pena power from the Congress and go about the difficult tasks ahead of you, that you have my full support, the support of the Attorney General, who was instrumental in the formation of this Commission, and the support of this entire administration.

And I thank all of you here, and God bless you. And I am now going to sign the document that is necessary.

Still writing with these one-word pens. [*Laughter*]

Note: The President spoke at 11:40 a.m. in the Rose Garden at the White House.

Executive Order 12435—President's Commission on Organized Crime
July 28, 1983

By the authority vested in me as President by the Constitution and laws of the United States of America, and in order to establish, in accordance with the provisions of the Federal Advisory Committee Act, as amended (5 U.S.C. App. I), an advisory committee on organized crime, it is hereby ordered as follows:

Section 1. (a) There is established the President's Commission on Organized Crime. The Commission shall be composed of not more than twenty members appointed or designated by the President.

(b) The President shall designate a Chairman from among the members of the Commission.

Sec. 2. (a) The Commission shall make a full and complete national and region-by-region analysis of organized crime; define the nature of traditional organized crime as well as emerging organized crime groups, the sources and amounts of organized crime's income, and the uses to which organized crime puts its income; develop in-depth information on the participants in organized crime networks; and evaluate Federal laws pertinent to the effort to combat organized crime. The Commission shall advise the President and the Attorney General with respect to its findings and actions which can be undertaken to improve law enforcement efforts directed against organized crime, and make recommendations concerning appropriate administrative and legislative improvements and improvements in the administration of justice.

(b) The Commission shall report to the President from time to time as requested and shall submit its final report by March 1, 1986.

Sec. 3. Administration. (a) The heads of Executive agencies shall, to the extent permitted by law, provide the Commission such information as it may require for purposes of carrying out its functions.

(b) Members of the Commission shall serve without compensation for their work on the Commission. However, members appointed from among private citizens of the United States or who are Members of Congress or Federal Judges may, subject to the availability of funds, be allowed travel expenses, including per diem in lieu of subsistence, as authorized by law for persons serving intermittently in the government service (5 U.S.C. 5701–5707).

(c) The Attorney General shall, to the extent permitted by law, provide the Commission with such administrative services, funds, facilities, staff and other support services as may be necessary for the performance of its functions.

Sec. 4. General. (a) Notwithstanding any other Executive Order, the functions of the President under the Federal Advisory Committee Act, as amended, except that of reporting to the Congress, which are applicable to the Commission, shall be performed by the Attorney General, in accordance with guidelines and procedures established

by the Administrator of General Services.

(b) The Commission shall, unless otherwise extended, terminate two years from the date of this Order.

RONALD REAGAN

The White House,
July 28, 1983.

[*Filed with the Office of the Federal Register, 4:26 p.m., July 28, 1983*]

Appointment of the Membership of the President's Commission on Organized Crime
July 28, 1983

The President today announced his intention to appoint the following individuals to be members of the President's Commission on Organized Crime. The President also announced his intention to designate Irving R. Kaufman to be Chairman.

Irving R. Kaufman, of New York, N.Y., has been serving as Circuit Judge for the U.S. Court of Appeals for the Second Circuit since 1961 and served as chief judge in 1973–1980. He was judge on the Southern District Court of New York in 1949–1961. He was born June 24, 1910.

Phyllis Teresa Aranza, of Houston, Tex., is a lieutenant with the homicide division of the Houston Police Department. She is pursuing a masters degree in criminal justice at Sam Houston State University. She was born September 23, 1945.

Jesse A. Brewer, Jr., of Los Angeles, Calif., has been a member of the Los Angeles Police Department since 1947 and its deputy chief since 1981, with responsibility for supervision of numerous major crimes investigations. He was a member of the Task Force on Disorders and Terrorism of the National Advisory Committee on Criminal Justice Standards and Goals, named by the Law Enforcement Assistance Administration (1976). He was born October 11, 1921.

Carol Corrigan, of Oakland, Calif., is a deputy district attorney assigned to the senior felony staff for Alameda County and an assistant professor of law at the University of California Hastings College of Law. She served as special consultant and staff editor to the Presidential

Task Force on Victims of Violent Crime in 1982 and has authored a number of publications relating to criminal law issues. She was born August 16, 1948.

Justin J. Dintino, of Hilltop, N.J., is executive officer of the New Jersey State Police Department. He is general chairman of the law enforcement intelligence unit and serves on the Organized Crime Committee of the International Association of Chiefs of Police and the policy board of the Middle Atlantic-Great Lakes State Organized Crime Law Enforcement Network. He was born October 30, 1928.

John F. Duffy, of San Diego, Calif., has been sheriff of San Diego County since 1970, having previously held various positions in the Sheriff's Department since 1953. He is president of the Police Executive Research Forum and serves on the board of directors of the National Sheriffs Association and on the board of directors of the National Institute of Justice. He was born June 10, 1930.

William J. Guste, Jr., of New Orleans, La., is attorney general of Louisiana. He has been a member of the Governor's Commission on Law Enforcement and the Administration of Justice since 1974. He served as a member and president of the New Orleans Metropolitan Crime Commission in 1956–1957 and as a member and chairman of the Juvenile Court Advisory Committee of Orleans Parish in 1961–1963. He was born May 26, 1922.

Judith Richards Hope, of the District of Columbia, is a partner in the law firm of Paul, Hastings, Janofsky, and Walker. She was associate director of the White House Domestic Council

1095

in 1975–1977. She was born November 30, 1940.

Phillip Manuel, of Alexandria, Va., is president of the Phillip Manuel Resource Group, a consulting firm that assists corporate clients and law firms with investigations involving economic crimes. He was chief investigator of the Senate Subcommittee on Investigations in 1968–1979. He was born November 9, 1936.

Thomas McBride, of California, is associate dean of the Stanford University Law School. He was an Associate Watergate Special Prosecutor in 1973–1975 and later served as Inspector General of the Departments of Labor and Agriculture. He was born February 8, 1929.

Eugene Methvin, of McLean, Va., is a senior editor of Readers Digest. He has written about crime and the law for more than 30 years and contributed to the passage of the Organized Crime Control Act of 1970. He was born September 19, 1934.

Edwin L. Miller, Jr., of La Jolla, Calif., is a district attorney for San Diego County and will assume the presidency of the National Association for District Attorneys in August. He is past president of the California Association of District Attorneys and was U.S. attorney for the Southern District of California in 1966–1969. He was born January 17, 1926.

Manuel J. Reyes, of Miami, Fla., is an attorney and executive vice president of the board of directors of Miami International Hospital. He also served as chairman of the Hispanic branch of the Miami Organized Crime Commission, and as a leader of the Hispanic community, he mobilized citizen groups to press for crackdowns on the influx of illegal drugs into the Miami area. He was born July 29, 1924.

Representative Peter W. Rodino, Jr., of New Jersey, is chairman of the House Judiciary Committee. He was born June 7, 1909.

Charles H. Rogovin, of Philadelphia, Pa., is a professor of law at Temple University. He was president of the Criminal Justice Associates in 1974–1977 and president of the Police Foundation in 1970–1972. In 1974–1976 he was a member of the Massachusetts Organized Crime Control Council. He headed the Organized Crime Committee of the Criminal Law Section of the American Bar Association in 1971–1972 and was Administrator of the Law Enforcement Assistance Administration in 1969–1970. He was born January 24, 1931.

Barbara Ann Rowan, of Manassas, Va., is a lawyer with Rowan Associates and was formerly an Assistant Director with the Federal Trade Commission. She served as staff attorney for the House Ethics Committee's Korean influence-buying investigation in 1977–1978 and was a staff attorney with the Legal Services Corporation and an assistant U.S. attorney for the Southern District of New York in 1971–1974. She was born September 6, 1938.

Frances A. Sclafani, of West Islip, N.Y., is presently deputy chief of the major offense bureau of the Suffolk County District Attorney's Office and the first woman to hold this position. She is also associate director of the National District Attorney's Association. She was born August 25, 1949.

Samuel K. Skinner, of Lake Forest, Ill., is a partner in the Chicago law firm of Sidley and Austin. He was chairman of the Governor's Fraud Prevention Commission in 1977–1979. He was U.S. attorney for the Northern District of Illinois, overseeing major organized crime investigations in the area. He was assistant U.S. attorney in the Northern District in 1968–1975. He was born June 10, 1938.

Potter Stewart, of the District of Columbia. Justice Stewart was an associate justice of the Supreme Court from 1958 until his retirement in 1981. He was born January 23, 1915.

Senator Strom Thurmond of South Carolina. Senator Thurmond is chairman of the Senate Judiciary Committee. He was born December 5, 1902.

Message to the Congress Reporting Budget Deferrals
July 28, 1983

To the Congress of the United States:

In accordance with the Impoundment Control Act of 1974, I herewith report three new deferrals of budget authority totaling $16,118,000.

The deferrals affect Energy Activities and the Department of Justice.

The details of the deferrals are contained in the attached reports.

RONALD REAGAN

The White House,
July 28, 1983.

Note: The attachments detailing the deferrals are printed in the Federal Register *of August 15, 1983.*

Nomination of Danny J. Boggs To Be Deputy Secretary of Energy
July 28, 1983

The President today announced his intention to nominate Danny J. Boggs to be Deputy Secretary of Energy. He would succeed W. Kenneth Davis.

Mr. Boggs has served in the Office of Policy Development at the White House since 1981, serving as Senior Policy Adviser (1981–1982) and currently as Assistant Director and Special Assistant to the President. Previously he was of counsel with the law firm of Bushnell, Gage, Reizen & Byington (1979–1980); deputy minority counsel, Senate Committee on Energy and Natural Resources (1977–1979); assistant to the Chairman, Federal Power Commission (1975–1977); and assistant to the Solicitor General of the United States (1973–1975).

Mr. Boggs graduated cum laude from Harvard University (A.B., 1965) and the University of Chicago Law School (J.D., 1968). He is married and has three children. Mr. Boggs is a permanent resident of Kentucky and now resides in Arlington, Va. He was born October 23, 1944, in Havana, Cuba.

Statement on Worldwide Terrorist Attacks Against Turkish Diplomats
July 28, 1983

Yesterday's attack in Lisbon on the residence of the Turkish Ambassador to Portugal was only the latest in a series of brutal and increasingly indiscriminate terrorist attacks against Turkish diplomats and other innocent civilians. In yesterday's attack, for which the Revolutionary Armenian Army claims responsibility, the wife of a senior Turkish diplomat was killed and a young child was seriously wounded. Only 2 weeks earlier, a Turkish diplomat was murdered outside his home in Brussels, and 1 day later 7 other individuals were killed as they waited to board a Turkish airliner in Paris.

No real or imagined grievance could possibly justify these modern-day horrors.

On behalf of the people and Government of the United States, I extend the deepest sympathy to the Turkish Government and to the families of the victims of this attack. But more than sympathy is required. This senseless violence must cease. To that end, I will be speaking to other heads of state in the days ahead regarding urgent and more effective cooperative measures to eliminate from the civilized community such barbaric and inhuman acts.

Statement by Deputy Press Secretary Speakes on a United States-Soviet Union Grain Sales Agreement
July 28, 1983

Ambassador William E. Brock, U.S. Trade Representative, and Secretary of Agriculture John R. Block announced today that the United States and the U.S.S.R. have reached agreement in principle on a new Long-Term Grain Agreement (LTA). The agreement will commence October 1, 1983, and will cover 5 years.

Under its terms, the U.S.S.R. will purchase from the United States 9 million metric tons of grain annually in approximately equal quantities of wheat and corn. Up to 1 million metric tons of the minimum could be satisfied by Soviet purchases of 500,000 metric tons of soybean and/or soybean meal. If this soybean/soybean meal option is exercised in any year, the minimum of wheat and corn for that year will be 8 million metric tons. During any year of the agreement, the Soviet Union may purchase 3 million metric tons of wheat and corn in addition to the minimum of 9 million metric tons without prior consultation.

The general framework of the new agreement follows that of the original LTA that was signed in 1975. The agreement was reached on July 28 in Vienna during the third round of negotiations regarding a new LTA. The U.S. negotiating team was lead by Ambassador Robert E. Lighthizer, Deputy U.S. Trade Representative. Daniel G. Amstutz, Under Secretary of the Department of Agriculture, was the senior official for the USDA on the team. Formal signing of the agreement will take place in late August.

The current agreement that expires on September 30, 1983, called for a minimum annual purchase of 6 million metric tons of wheat and corn by the U.S.S.R., and provided an option for the Soviet Union to purchase an additional 2 million metric tons per year. The original agreement covered a 5-year period beginning in 1975. It was extended for a 1-year period on two occasions.

Remarks at a White House Reception for the National Council of Negro Women
July 28, 1983

Thank you, Dorothy, very much, and thank all of you. And I'm grateful to our Faith Whittlesey [1] for bringing us all together here.

Nancy and I are delighted to welcome Dorothy Height and the National Council of Negro Women to the White House. I can think of no group that better represents what is good and right and hopeful about America. You have been an important force for progress and opportunity, not just in America but around the world. On behalf of the thousands you've helped and a nation that you've made proud, I thank you. And I

---

[1] *Assistant to the President for Public Liaison.*

especially would like to recognize the superb leadership of your president, Dorothy Height.

Dorothy, you've been quoted as saying, "We have common problems, common desires and common goals, it's time for us to begin to work on the problems of the world, together." Your words have never been more true than they are today. Our country and our people face serious challenges, and our values and families are bearing considerable strain. We need unity, not divisiveness to see us through. If we're to remain strong and free and good, we must not waste the talents of one mind, the muscle of one body, or the potential of a single soul. We need all our people—men and women, young and old, individuals of every race—to be healthy, happy, and whole. Our young people must grow up free of drugs; our families must stay together; our people must have jobs; and our elderly must live out their days secure from want and from fear. I know these are your goals, and I share them.

Your Alliance for Volunteerism, as you mentioned, Operation Cope, and the National Collaboration for Children and Youth, to name just a few of your efforts, testify to your commitment. Your willingness to give of yourselves should lift the hearts of all who are tired and discouraged. Dorothy's words, which I know have been an inspiration to you, must become a rallying cry for all Americans who love freedom. We are one family of humankind, and together we can make our dreams real. Obstacles of inequality and discrimination are still great, but our combined determination to overcome them is greater. If we persevere together, we can and we will succeed together.

As women and as blacks, you know better than almost anyone else the difficult problems of discrimination. And through your volunteer work, you are keenly sensitive to the needs of our underpriviledged and disadvantaged. I want to help in your cause. The door to the Oval Office will always be open to Dorothy Height and the members of the National Council of Negro Women.

I have to tell you, though, I'm more than a little self-conscious facing you here and saying these things. There's been such a case made that I am prejudiced, if not an outright bigot, that I find myself wondering if maybe you're thinking that I don't mean what I'm saying, and this is just another dose of political hot air. Well, believe me, it is not. Nothing has frustrated me more than the totally false image that has been created of me.

I've lived a long time, but I can't remember a time in my life when I didn't believe that prejudice and bigotry were the worse of sins. My mother was the kindest person I've ever known and truly believed that we are all brothers and sisters—children of God. My father was a rough, tough Irishman. He might not have expressed himself the way my mother did—[*laughter*]—but

when that great motion picture classic "The Birth of a Nation" came to our small town, the two kids in town who didn't get to see it were me and my brother.

That picture, as you know was a classic—not so much for the subject matter—it had charted a whole new course in the method of making pictures, and therefore, is still considered today a kind of historic monument. But our father said it was about the Klu Klux Klan, and no one in his family was going to see that picture. And to this day, after more than 25 years in the motion picture industry, I haven't seen it, and I don't intend to.

From boyhood on, the way we were raised, my brother and I challenged every time we ran across it—the, sometime, the customs of the times, customs that we're doing away with—may not have succeeded entirely; but, oh, what changes we've made since those days when I was a boy.

As a radio sports announcer almost 50 years ago, I used to speak out on the air against the then ban on blacks in organized baseball. And before that, playing college football, a little school in the Midwest, my closest teammate and buddy down there in the center of the line—he was center and I was right guard—was a man named Franklin Burghardt. Burky was black. He went on to become the athletic director of Morgan State University in Baltimore. And I have thanked the Lord many times that we were reunited after many years of being apart—although we kept in correspondence—but back here, shortly before he was to end his life, and that Nancy and I could have he and his wife as guests here in this house that belongs to all the people.

I have to tell you just one little thing about how much Burky meant to us. In those days, not very many got to college, and if you did it was because you could play football or something, which is how I got there. [*Laughter*] But we were playing a game one day and—with the score 14 to nothing against us and only 2 minutes left in the first half. The other team, who wasn't blessed with having someone like Burky on their team, began to pick on him for the reasons that were more obvious then than they are today. And to give you an indication of what we all thought of Burky, we ended the half 14 to 14 and ended the game 43 to 14. [*Laughter*] He was quite a man.

As Governor in California, I broke a subtle barrier that had made it virtually impossible for blacks to rise above the very lowest civil service positions in State government. We increased by 60 percent the number who held supervisory positions and appointed to executive and policymaking positions more minority members than all the previous Governors of California put together.

I intended and am going to tell just some of the things that—well, forgive me for taking the time to say this; but, as I said, I've been frustrated by all the demagogic image-making of the last couple of years. Now, let me tell you just some of the things we're doing in this administration and some of the things that we hope to do.

It's no secret that we're trying to reduce the cost of government, but not, as some have charged, at the expense of government's real responsibilities. Our budget calls for spending $632.2 million for Federal civil rights activities in 1984. And that is more than a 24-percent increase over the last year of the previous administration.

As evidence of our commitment to equal employment opportunity, we are fighting well over a hundred ongoing cases throughout the country against public employers charged with discriminating against minorities. In fiscal year 1982 alone, the Equal Employment Opportunity Commission obtained more than $134 million in back pay for victims of employee discrimination, a 74-percent increase over the last year of the previous administration.

But there are two sides to government's responsibility to provide opportunity. One is a fairminded and vigorous enforcement of antidiscrimination laws, and that's what we're doing. But enforcement alone will not create the jobs our people need so badly. What will create jobs is a healthy and growing economy. We can all find hope in the strength of the economic recovery that has begun, and I assure you this: We intend to see that every American, regardless of race, religion, or gender, benefits from that recovery.

Our minority youth, as you're only too painfully aware, are suffering nearly a 40-percent unemployment rate. To combat that, the Department of Housing and Urban Development last month launched the Minority Youth Training Initiative, a nationwide demonstration involving partnerships between city government, local private industry councils, and public housing authorities. This project will train minority youths in 20 cities for entry-level jobs in the public and private housing field. As many as 14,000 disadvantaged young people will be taught housing management and maintenance skills.

Also, our summer youth employment program has a budget of more than $800 million—an increase of a hundred million dollars over last year—to provide more than 800,000 summer jobs for young people throughout the United States. In fact, just last week here in the Rose Garden we found another $800,000—well, we didn't find it in the Rose Garden. [*Laughter*] We're not that careless! We found it over at the Labor Department—[*laughter*]—and in the Rose Garden we gave it to Mayor Barry for more youth jobs here in the District of Columbia. We've put in place a tax credit program that gives employers who hire eligible teenagers a credit for up to 85 percent of their wages. And we've made a special effort this summer to focus the attention of business and industry on the difficulties of minority youth. The White House Office of Private Sector Initiatives and the National Alliance of Business have worked hard to give these young people the chance they deserve. And I have been told that so far this summer nationwide summertime employment for young people is up 20 percent.

With Nancy's prodding and assistance, we've run up a battleflag on drug abuse. Drugs are a scourge of inner-city life, as you know so well. They can snuff out the bright prospects of a young person before he or she gets a chance to become an adult. We're implementing a tough, new enforcement strategy for the first time, coordinating the efforts of nine departments and 33 government agencies. There'll be no excuses. Drugs are bad, and we're going after them, and we're going to win.

To fight housing discrimination, we've put real teeth into the fair housing law by introducing legislation to give the Federal Government, for the first time, legal authority to protect people from housing discrimination. We believe that all Americans should be free to choose where to make their homes. If our proposed amendments are passed by the Congress, heavy financial penalties will be levied for the first time against those who practice bigotry and discrimination in housing.

We also believe that a good, solid education is the right of every child in our land. It is a vital, first step to opportunity, the means by which Amercian families traditionally have made life better for themselves and for generations who followed. And that's why we've launched a national campaign to improve the quality of America's classrooms and have begun to outline an agenda for excellence in education that will leave no child behind. We are also aggressively combating segregation in schools. The Justice Department, for example, has recently taken legal action against one State, charging discrimination in its higher education system.

And, again, speaking of my frustration, I've seen the news stories that, well, this is all a grandstand stunt by us, because next year is an election year. Well, we have authorized for filing three school desegregation cases, more than was authorized by the previous administration during its first 30 months in office.

I'm also proud to note that our administration recognized the educational significance of Meharry Medical College in Nashville, Tennessee, an institution that has trained more than 40 percent of all the black physicians in America. Earlier this year we authorized the expenditure of more than $30 million so that Meharry Medical College can continue its historic service to the Nation. This commitment of resources by government will help to ensure that Meharry Medical College can continue as a major educational resource for primary-care physicians. It was in deep trouble, and we were very proud and happy to be able to set it on its course.

We've also proposed the longest extension of the life of the Civil Rights Commission in its history—20 years—and nominated individuals to serve on that body whose strong credentials will assure its independence.

I could go on and on, but I don't think you want me to—or need me to read a long laundry list of accomplishments. If you like, I can provide more details for you later. [*Laughter*] But let me assure you, I hear your call. With your help, this administration will continue to respond not just with words but with action.

Now, you may not have heard much about our commitment, but take it from an informed White House source—[*laughter*]—who doesn't have to be nameless that we will continue to build a record that proves it.

Your founder, Mary McLeod Bethune, once said that black people in America only want what other Americans want—an opportunity to make real what the Declaration of Independence and the Constitution and the Bill of Rights say, what the Four Freedoms establish. She said black people only want an equal chance to realize those ideals. And that's why we're eager to work with you, the organization that she founded on the premise that while government can assure equal treatment, government alone cannot provide that equal chance. That's the important work of families and communities and of organizations such as your own.

Let me say again, my door is open, and so is Faith Whittlesey's. Let's make this meeting the beginning of a lasting, positive relationship. We may not always agree on every detail, but together we can make this land we all love a better, freer place for our children and our children's children.

Now, I've used up more than my share of the schedule, so I'll just thank you for being here with us today, and I do look forward to working with you. And God bless you all.

Note: The President spoke at 5:09 p.m. in the East Room at the White House.

Letter on the Withdrawal of the Nomination of Thomas F. Ellis To Be a Member of the Board for International Broadcasting
July 28, 1983

Dear Tom:

I have received your letter withdrawing yourself from further consideration as my nominee for the Board for International Broadcasting.

I regret the circumstances that have led to your decision, but I want to add that during this affair, you have acted in a manner consistent with the reputation for honor that you have always possessed. I know that reputation among your friends and associates will continue to be strong.

Please accept my best wishes for future success.

Sincerely,

RONALD REAGAN

[Mr. Thomas F. Ellis, Maupin, Taylor and Ellis, P. A., Raleigh, North Carolina 27602]

Dear Mr. President:

I appeared on Tuesday before the Senate Foreign Relations Committee for consideration of my appointment to the Board for International Broadcasting. It became obvious to me from the outset of the questioning by Senators Tsongas and Biden that they would use that occasion to attempt to divert the hearing away from broadcasting the U.S. views of freedom behind the Iron Curtain into a personal attack on me by my political enemies.

As a matter of fact, Senator Tsongas had issued a press release prior to the hearing criticizing you and prejudging my qualifications. It was an obvious partisan political effort to drive a wedge between you and the black community using me as the instrumentality. I have attached a copy of my letter to Senators Tsongas and Biden.

Frankly, I do not mind taking whatever heat these two ultra-liberal senators want to generate in my direction. However, I believe it is vital to America that they and their ilk be denied the opportunity to use me to hinder your struggle to return economic stability and provide an adequate national defense to our nation. Therefore, I am respectfully requesting that you withdraw my name from consideration for appointment to the Board for International Broadcasting.

Let me say in closing that I appreciate your appointing me to the Board. I did not seek the appointment but was most anxious to serve as I believe our only hope to survive the spread of Soviet slavery across the free world and to free the hostage people of the USSR is to broadcast the tenets of Christian belief through mass communication. I trust that the Board of International Broadcasting will carry out this task without fear of interference from some of those in public office who do not recognize the threat of Communist world domination.

God bless you and Nancy,

Sincerely,

TOM

[President Ronald Reagan, White House, 1600 Pennsylvania Avenue, Washington, D.C. 20500]

Note: Mr. Ellis' nomination was submitted to the Senate on February 8.

Nomination of Thomas J. Healey To Be an Assistant Secretary of the Treasury
July 29, 1983

The President today announced his intention to nominate Thomas J. Healey to be an Assistant Secretary of the Treasury (Domestic Finance). He would succeed Roger William Mehle, Jr.

Since 1982 he has been managing director of Dean Witter Reynolds Capital Markets and manager of its corporate finance department. Previously he was manager, Project Finance Group, at Dean Witter in 1975–1982; vice president of finance at Instrumentation Engineering, Inc., in 1971–1975; and managing partner of Camargo Associates in 1967–1971.

Mr. Healey graduated from Georgetown University (A.B., 1964) and received his master of business administration from Harvard University in 1966. He is married, has two children, and resides in Chatham, N.J. He was born September 14, 1942, in Baltimore, Md.

Nomination of Richard L. McElheny To Be an Assistant Secretary of Commerce
July 29, 1983

The President today announced his intention to nominate Richard L. McElheny to be an Assistant Secretary of Commerce (Trade Development). He would succeed William H. Morris, Jr.

Since 1982 Mr. McElheny has been Director General of the Commercial Services, International Trade Administration, Department of Commerce. Previously he was Director General of the Foreign Commercial Service of the International Trade Administration in 1981–1982; president and chief executive officer of Econo Therm Energy Systems in 1979–1981; senior vice president/corporate development, Victorio Co., Phoenix, in 1978–1979; and vice president

of marketing, then executive vice president and chief operating officer and president, beginning in 1971, of Farmhand, Inc., Hopkins, Minn. (1969–1978).

In 1977 he served as chairman of the Minnesota Association of Commerce and Industry and as president of the National Farm Industry Association. He was a member of the District Export Council, U.S. Department of Commerce, in 1974–1977.

Mr. McElheny graduated from Stanford University (B.S. 1958; M.B.A., 1960). He is married, has two children, and resides in Washington, D.C. He was born May 24, 1936.

Remarks to Representatives of the Future Farmers of America
July 29, 1983

The President. Thank you very much, and good afternoon. I understand that we've got youth leaders with us from every State and also from Puerto Rico, Canada, and the United Kingdom. Well, welcome to the White House. And I know it's a little warm, isn't it—*[laughter]*—so, I'd better get on with it and let you get toward the shade.

I'd like to take this opportunity, however, to offer special congratulations to Jan Eberly from my home State of California— the first woman to be national president of

your organization.

Ms. Eberly. Thank you.

The President. I always get a kick out of meeting with the Future Farmers of America. And I think my ties go back quite a long way. Many of my friends when I was growing up back in Illinois were Future Farmers. And I wasn't too far away from them, because I lived in the kind of a town that even in the center of town, you weren't too far from plowed ground. [*Laughter*]

But what was then true then is still true today. And that was the Future Farmers of America does more than give a good start to some fine young people. By cultivating leadership skills and patriotism, it ensures the strength and vitality of our country.

This generation of American farmers has astounded the world with its productivity. Farm output since 1950 has jumped 89 percent, with agricultural productivity rising more than four times faster than industrial productivity per hour worked. Last year, with less than three-tenths of 1 percent of the world's farmworkers, our country produced 65 percent of the world's soybeans, 48 percent of the corn, 33 percent of the sorghum, 25 percent of the oranges, 32 percent of the poultry, 26 percent of the beef. And the list goes on and on.

Today, one of our farmworkers produces enough food to feed himself plus 50 other Americans and 20 people in other countries in the world. So, it doesn't take a Harvard-trained economist to see what this means to our economy and the well-being of our people.

American agriculture has been so efficient that we often tend to take the abundance of food for granted. We can be very proud that we live in one of the few countries of the world that will not tolerate hunger and that your profession could take a lion's share of the credit for our ability to live up to that goal.

Agricultural productivity has permitted us to develop human values and to put those values into practice. And this just didn't happen by accident. Our abundance is a product of the hard work of our farmers, the skill and technological know-how that we put into agriculture and, most important, the freedom of which we're so proud here in America.

By the way, you might be interested to know that in some of the efforts to help the Third World, the developing countries—and when we met in Cancún, Mexico, the industrial nations on this subject, I spoke to them of some of the things that we could do other than just handing out grants-in-aid and told them what it could be like if we could send teams of agriculturalists, of farmers from our country to some of those countries to help them become more self-

sustaining in their food. And you might be happy to know that we have called a number of times already, and every time American farmers have volunteered and sent task forces to these undeveloped countries to tell them how they can better feed themselves.

There's another country with resources just every bit as much as our own, a major power. Its citizens are decent, hard-working people, but they have no freedom. And that lack of freedom is matched by a lack of productivity. There's no better proof that freedom and material progress can only survive together. And a story that I like to tell about that—as a matter of fact, it's a story these people in that country tell about their own country. I'm kind of making a collection of jokes that the Russian people tell about their own country. [*Laughter*]

And this is one in which the commissar went out to one of their collective farms, stopped one of the workers there, and asked him how things were, any complaints. "Oh, no, sir," he said. "I've never heard anyone around here complain about anything." "Well," he said, "what about the crops?" "Oh," he said, "the crops, just greater than ever." He said, "And the potato harvest?" He said, "If we piled all the potatoes we've harvested up in one pile, they'd reach the foot of God." And the commissar said, "This is the Soviet Union. There is no God." He said, "That's all right. There aren't any potatoes either." [*Laughter*]

Well, I know that the Future Farmers of America is doing its part to build character and to keep our country in the forefront of the production of food and fiber. I'd like to congratulate you for FFA's theme this year, which I understand is "Keeping America on the Grow." You're now just emerging from some hard times that have been a long time in the making. I know things have been rough and still are for many farmers. But I hope when you go back to your homes, you'll tell your families and your friends of our confidence that things are getting better. And while you're at it, tell them that a White House source—[*laughter*]—told you personally that America's farmers are not going to be left out of the good times that lie ahead.

I hope all of you are enjoying yourselves and learning a lot while you're here in the Nation's Capital. And I think that one general—we owe General Motors a thank-you for sponsoring this leadership conference and making it possible. This kind of enlightened support from the private sector speaks well of American business.

And let me leave you with this thought: When you go home and remember all the sights you've seen in Washington, the shrines of American liberty, remember that back at the time the ideals of our nation emerged, it was composed overwhelmingly of men and women who made their living from the land. Today, we rely on you to maintain our ties to the land and to live up to our ideals. And I know you won't let us down.

Thank you for coming over here to visit, and God bless you all.

Note: The President spoke at 12:58 p.m. in the Rose Garden at the White House.

Remarks at a White House Reception for the National Association of Elementary School Principals and the National Association of Secondary School Principals
July 29, 1983

Well, thank you all, and let me welcome you all to the White House.

You know, I've been out of school for a little over 50 years now, but I still get nervous around so many principals. [*Laughter*] And I don't know why I should think of this story except that it has to do with school, and I know that—and teachers, and I know also that it's very dangerous to ever try to tell stories to people of one profession about their profession. But I'll take a chance anyway.

It was the teacher that was trying to impress on her students, the children—winter had come along and the cold season and all. And she was trying to tell them how to— the need to avoid catching colds. And so, she told a very heart-rending tale which she said was about her one-time little brother. And she said that—told her little brother that—or the class that she had this little brother and that he was a fun-loving little boy, and he went out with his sled. And he stayed out too long, and he caught cold. And that was pneumonia, and three days later he was dead. And when she'd finished with the tale, the way she told it, there was just dead silence in the room. And she thought she had really gotten to them. And then a voice in the back said, "Where's his sled?" [*Laughter*]

Well, that isn't the attitude that I wanted our Committee on Excellence in Education to take, but I did want them to approach their task with some hard-eyed realism. And you're, by now, well acquainted with the Commission's findings.

Two of our Commission members are school principals, because we wanted the important perspective that you here represent. You know the problems that our educational system faces. So many things have changed in our society from the structure of family life to drug abuse among our young that, over time, it's begun affecting education. The principals and the teachers alone cannot correct these social ills any more than any single level of government can, by itself, improve the schools. But we can and we must build a new consensus among parents, teachers, and students, principals, and elected officials to bring about a renaissance in American education.

Most of the attention is focused on the need to reward excellence. Now, I can't imagine anything more discouraging for young teachers than to see a rigid salary scale laid out for the rest of their lives that ignores their efforts no matter how good they might be.

I saw something interesting in the Washington Post several weeks ago. It was a story on how the Soviet leadership is considering ways to get the Soviet economy moving again. Well, one proposal is to depart from the practice of paying Soviet citizens relatively equal wages irrespective of job performance. Now, if even Yuriy Andropov and the Soviet bureaucracy are beginning to realize the need for merit pay, why can't certain segments of our own educational establishment?

And there are many other things that we can do to improve our educational system that don't cost money. Secretary Bell tells me that research on what makes one school more effective than another has shown that challenging students through high standards and high expectations results in increased achievement. In other words, if we don't expect anything from our kids, why should they expect anything of themselves? And here, of course, I'm talking about adopting more rigorous academic standards. I'm talking about strengthening graduation requirements in terms of curriculum and reducing discipline problems by enforcing codes of student conduct.

Before I go on, I just have to tell—I made a phone call just a couple of weeks ago to a young man out in the Midwest—a great basketball star. He had suffered a knee injury, and that knee injury led to a lot of reassessment for him. And he'd gone to Marva Collins in Chicago. And he'd gone there to learn to read and write.

He had been a basketball star for a couple of years in one of our fine universities. He was six feet five when he was in junior high, and the coach suggested he start shooting some baskets. But he got all the way through high school, and there he was then in the university, and he couldn't read or write.

And when I spoke to him—he wanted an education. He wasn't satisfied just being an athlete. And he thought that—and was trying to get one. And so, he went to this school, and he sat there with fourth grade students, and he told me, he said, "Yes, it was embarrassing." "But," he said, "I have to hand it to them," he said, "the kids were wonderful." And he said, "They helped me a great deal." And I asked him what he was going to do, and now he's going to try to get a college diploma, now that he can read

and write.

But I'm also reading some interesting things about new textbooks that can do wonders with increasing math skills. I'm sure you've probably heard about that new math textbook. It's by a fellow named John Saxon, that has average I.Q. students scoring above high I.Q. students and has Algebra I students who use this textbook doing better on tests than Algebra II students who use the traditional text. I believe some principals in Oklahoma and some other States have been involved in this experiment. So, here's another area we could look into. All we'd have to do is simply replace the old books as they wear out with new books of this kind.

But we simply can't tell the taxpayer that more funds are needed to improve quality when, during the 20-year period between 1960 and 1980, spending on education was shooting up while the college board scores were going down. If a 600-percent increase, which is what we had in spending in those 20 years, couldn't make America smarter, how much more do we need? What we do need is a commitment to education and not just more money. Now that I have the Commission's findings in hand, I've been going around the country trying to keep the dialog alive, and I think we're making progress.

In its report, the Commission calls upon you, the principals, to play a crucial leadership role in developing school and community support for its reforms. You're deeply dedicated to our children's education, or you wouldn't be in the field that you are. And I have confidence that working together, we can make the U.S. educational system what you want it to be. I believe we can make it meet your standards. And I wanted to meet with you today to tell you personally how much I respect what you're doing for the Nation and to ask you to help me further in the debate.

And I just can't leave—I told some of the type of students that you deal with, many of you, the Future Farmers of America from all over the United States are in Washington right now. And I was talking to them about their particular trade—farming. But it also has to do with that previous story I told about the Soviet Union. And I think I'm going to repeat it here. Maybe there's a little meat in it.

The commissar went out to the farm, their state farm, and stopped one of the workers and asked him how things were, any complaints. And he said, "Oh, no, sir. No, never heard anyone complain." "Well," he said, "how are the crops?" "Oh, the crops are wonderful." "What about the potato harvest?" "Oh," he said, "the pota-

toes." He says, "Comrad," he said, "if we piled the potatoes up in one pile, they would reach the foot of God." And the commissar said, "This is the Soviet Union. There is no God." He said, "That's all right. There are no potatoes." [*Laughter*]

Thank you. Thank you for coming, and God bless you.

Note: The President spoke at 2:45 p.m. in the East Room at the White House.

Executive Order 12436—Payment of Certain Benefits to Survivors of Persons Who Died in or as a Result of Military Service
July 29, 1983

By the authority vested in me as President by the Constitution and laws of the United States of America, including Section 156 of Public Law 97–377 (96 Stat. 1920; 42 U.S.C. 402 note), in order to provide certain benefits to the surviving spouses and children of certain persons who died in or as a result of military service, it is hereby ordered as follows:

Section 1. The Administrator of Veterans' Affairs is designated to administer the provisions of Section 156 of Public Law 97–377.

Sec. 2. The Secretary of Health and Human Services shall provide to the Administrator of Veterans' Affairs such information and such technical assistance as the Administrator may reasonably require to discharge his responsibilities under Section 156. The Administrator of Veterans' Affairs shall reimburse the Department of Health and Human Services for all expenses it incurs in providing such information and technical assistance to the Veterans' Administration. Such expenses shall be paid from the Veterans' Administration account de-

scribed in Section 3 of this Order.

Sec. 3. During fiscal year 1983 and each succeeding fiscal year, the Secretary of Defense shall transfer, from time to time, from the "Retired Pay, Defense" account of the Department of Defense to an account established in the Veterans' Administration, such amounts as the Administrator of Veterans' Affairs determines to be necessary to pay the benefits authorized by Section 156 during fiscal year 1983 and each succeeding fiscal year, and the expenses incurred by the Veterans' Administration in paying such benefits during fiscal year 1983 and each succeeding fiscal year. Such transfers shall, to the extent feasible, be made in advance of the payment of benefits and expenses by the Veterans' Administration.

Sec. 4. This Order shall be effective as of January 1, 1983.

RONALD REAGAN

The White House,
July 29, 1983.

[*Filed with the Office of the Federal Register, 10:07 a.m., August 1, 1983*]

Proclamation 5078—National Paralyzed Veterans Recognition Day, 1983
July 29, 1983

By the President of the United States of America

A Proclamation

The people of this great Nation owe a tremendous debt of gratitude to the brave men and women of our Armed Forces who have fought to preserve America's freedom and independence. National Paralyzed Veterans Recognition Day offers us an opportunity to express our appreciation to a very special group of our veterans—those who suffer the disability of paralysis.

On this day of tribute to these dedicated citizens, we honor them for the great sacrifice they made for their country, and praise them for the courage, determination, and perseverance they demonstrate daily in facing the difficult challenges of their disabilities. The strong will and spirit which they exhibit in overcoming the limitations of their paralysis serve as an inspiring display of the American drive to achieve, build, and advance which has kept this country strong for the past two centuries. Each of us is heartened by the knowledge that this Nation's paralyzed veterans lead active, productive lives which enrich us all. It is indeed appropriate that we set aside a special day upon which to thank them for their past and continuing contributions to this country.

In recognition of the sacrifices and contributions that these veterans have made and the service rendered by the many veterans who later suffered paralysis from nonservice related causes, the Congress of the United States, by House Joint Resolution 258, has designated August 3, 1983, as "National Paralyzed Veterans Recognition Day," and has authorized and requested the President to issue a proclamation in observance of that day.

Now, Therefore, I, Ronald Reagan, President of the United States of America, do hereby proclaim August 3, 1983, as National Paralyzed Veterans Recognition Day. I call upon the people of the United States and interested organizations to mark this day with appropriate observances to honor the sacrifices and service of paralyzed veterans.

In Witness Whereof, I have hereunto set my hand this 29th day of July, in the year of our Lord nineteen hundred and eighty-three, and of the Independence of the United States of America the two hundred and eighth.

RONALD REAGAN

[*Filed with the Office of the Federal Register, 10:06 a.m., August 1, 1983*]

Nomination of Two Members of the Board of Directors of the National Institute of Building Sciences
July 29, 1983

The President today announced his intention to nominate the following individuals to be members of the Board of Directors of the National Institute of Building Sciences for terms expiring September 7, 1984.

MacDonald G. Becket would succeed Warner Howe. He is chairman of the board of the Becket Group of companies including Welton Becket Associates, an architectural/engineering firm. He is a founding contributor to the Architectural and Design Endowment for the Museum of Contemporary Art in Los Angeles and a fellow of the American Institute of Architects. He also served on the U.S. Capitol Architect's Long-Range Planning Committee and has been admitted to the National Council of Architectural Registration Boards. He is married, has four children, and resides in Los Angeles, Calif. He was born November 2, 1928.

Kyle Clayton Boone would succeed Blanca C. Cedeno. He has been proprietor of Boone: Hunton Associates (architects, planners, interior designers) since 1968. Previously he was an architect with Six Associates architectural firm in Asheville, N.C., in 1963–1968; and architect with Echols-Sparger architectural firm in Marion, Va., in 1962–1963. He received the Reynolds Aluminum prize for architectural students in 1962. He is married, has four children, and resides in Weaverville, N.C. He was born December 16, 1932.

Radio Address to the Nation on Organ Donorship and on Reform 88
July 30, 1983

My fellow Americans:

Last Saturday, I told you about little Ashley Bailey and her desperate need for a liver transplant. I expressed the hope that someone listening might know of a possible donor who could assure 11-month-old Ashley of a chance to live. I listed several others who, like Ashley, are waiting for transplants if donors can only be found. I gave a phone number where possible donors could respond. Well, God bless you all, the response was overwhelming. Over 5,000 calls were received from people in 47 States. Many callers asked for donor cards so they could help others even after they're gone. Six liver transplants have already taken place. Six children, including Candi Thomas, one of the little girls I mentioned last week, have been given a new lease on life. And two people have received cornea transplants. They were given the gift of sight by one of our neighbors who heard about a chance to help.

I'm sorry to say, Ashley's situation remains the same. None of the available livers was suitable. She still needs a transplant soon, in order to live. Time is short. But your response has been so generous, I have to believe there will be a donor found. I'm going to keep on praying. One thing I know: We live in a country where people truly care for one another.

Today, I'd like to take you behind the headlines and talk about an issue that affects every U.S. taxpayer—efficient management of the Federal Government. Government has grown like a patchwork quilt. Whenever a new need was identified, a new program was patched on regardless of what it cost. The door was wide open for fraud, waste, and abuse. Is it any wonder that we hear so many infuriating stories about government throwing money away, about food stamp rings that illegally obtain aid meant for the poor and needy, or about illegal aliens receiving government loans?

Already, we've cut the volume of new Federal regulations by one-quarter, reducing paperwork on the American people by 300 million hours a year. We've reduced the rapid rate of growth in government spending. And the Inspector General program has helped save or put to better use over $22 billion that was being improperly spent.

In the Defense Department alone, our efforts have saved or put to better use $16.1 billion. And the Department's 18,000 auditors and investigators have my full backing in their continuing fight against the fraud and waste typified by the recent $916 plastic cap purchase. Would you pay that much for a plastic cap? Well, the Government shouldn't either. And Secretary Weinberger is cracking down, seeing to it that negligent employees will be fired and irresponsible government contractors taken to court. Those horror stories you've been seeing and hearing about scandalous prices that we're paying for spare parts are the result of our own investigations and represent the findings of more than a score of Defense Department Inspector Generals.

We've saved $50 million in government-wide travel costs by using airline discount fares. We've also discontinued one out of every five government publications, eliminating 73 million copies of such vital reports as "A Moment in the Life of a Lizard" and "Growing Ornamental Bamboo". And we're ahead of schedule in our efforts to reduce Federal civilian employment by the equivalent of 75,000 full-time workers.

This coming week I'll bring my senior appointees together at the White House to continue an ambitious program to upgrade management of the Federal Government. Our long-range goal is to overhaul the entire administrative system. I call this effort Reform 88. It's a big job. Our government has over 2.8 million civilian and 2 million active military personnel in over 22,000 buildings, using 19,000 computers, 330 differing financial systems, and 200 payroll systems, and there's never been an effective effort to manage this growing administrative monster.

Each year we've fallen behind the private sector in management techniques. Well, we're bringing this to an end now. Reform 88 is geared to get results. Over a 6-year period, it'll save the taxpayers or result in a better use of tens of billions of dollars that could mean as much as the equivalent of nearly $2,000 for the average American family. And these savings won't be obtained by cutting help to the deserving but by eliminating waste and inefficiency.

For example, in debt collection, where the Government is owed over $280 billion, we'll be using modern methods to ensure that Federal loans are paid back. You may have heard about the individual who obtained 10 Housing and Urban Development loans and defaulted on all 10. Well, in the future, deadbeats like that will be headed off at the pass. We'll do it by using credit bureaus and prescreening to determine the credit worthiness of applicants for loans and grants. And to help reduce the $40 billion in delinquent debt, we'll be automating our collection techniques just like private industry.

It's about time the notion that government is the servant, not the master, came back into fashion. One of our highest priorities is to restore to the American people a government well managed and responsive to your needs and respectful of your tax dollars. The greatest nation in the world deserves the best government, and with your support, we'll have it.

Until next week, thanks for listening, and God bless you.

Note: The President spoke at 12:06 p.m. from Camp David, Md.

Remarks at the Annual Meeting of the American Bar Association in Atlanta, Georgia
August 1, 1983

Thank you very much, Morris Harrell, members and officers of the ABA, and ladies and gentlemen. I'm delighted to be back in beautiful Atlanta. And it's with a happy heart that I share with you the honor of this special occasion, the 105th annual meeting of the great American Bar Association. It isn't true that I attended the first meeting. [*Laughter*]

You know, a speaker always hopes that he can identify some way, and that there's some relationship between himself and his audience. And I was just reading something the other day that maybe made it—that I can do that. It said that to be a great trial lawyer you have to have some histrionic ability and a little bit of ham. [*Laughter*]

Now, you had to remember back a ways for that. [*Laughter*]

Well, we respect the gentleman who has led your organization with vision and skill—Morris Harrell. As you all know, there are a lot of jokes—as I just tried one—with lawyers as the target. Thomas Jefferson reportedly blamed his problems with the Congress on a hundred lawyers whose trade it is, as he said, "to question everything, yield nothing, and talk by the hour." [*Laughter*] Well, I'd like to say something else, and say it for the record today. Under Morris Harrell's leadership, the ABA has not sought to control America; you have sought to serve America.

And now, I didn't remember enough

whether the figures are going to be correct that I'm giving, but I understand that you have some 30,000 lawyers and 300 law firms contributing toward the $10½ million raised for your Second Century Fund. These contributions are the centerpiece of the ABA's public service work for America: hundreds of programs addressing public concerns ranging from child abuse to the problems of the elderly, from government waste to the high cost of justice, from juvenile crime to the energy challenge. We need your idealism and compassion in our families, neighborhoods, businesses, and government. We need you to carry on this fine tradition of public service.

May I also congratulate Morris Harrell's successor, Wallace Riley. And, Wally, I want you to know that the door to the Oval Office will always be open to you and your members.

Much like Sam Johnson said about the man to be hanged, it concentrates my mind—[laughter]—to stand before so many of America's finest attorneys. I'm reminded of a challenge that one of America's foremost lawyers had to face. I'm speaking about Abraham Lincoln. As a young lawyer, he once had to plead two cases in the same day before the same judge. Both involved the same principle of law. But in one Lincoln appeared for the defendant and in the other for the plaintiff. Now, you can see how this makes anything above a 50-percent success rate very difficult. [Laughter]

Well, in the morning, Lincoln made an eloquent plea and won his case. Later, he took the opposite side and was arguing just as earnestly. And puzzled, the judge asked why the change in attitude. "Your Honor," said Honest Abe, "I may have been wrong this morning—[laughter]—but I know"—[laughter]. He knew he was right in the afternoon.

Well, I haven't come today to plead two cases, but to plead one. I've not come to tell you what I'm against, but what I know all of us are for. We must preserve the noble promise of the American dream for every man, woman, and child in this land. And, make no mistake, we can preserve it, and we will. That promise was not created by America. It was given to America as a gift from a loving God—a gift proudly recog-

nized by the language of liberty in the world's greatest charters of freedom, our Declaration of Independence, the Constitution, and the Bill of Rights.

Seventy-seven years after it was adopted, Lord Acton said of the men who had written the Constitution that "they had solved with astonishing and unexampled success two problems which had hitherto baffled the capacity of the most enlightened nations: they had contrived a system of Federal Government which . . . increased the National power, and yet respected local liberties and authorities; they had founded it on the principle of equality, without surrendering the securities for property and freedom." Well, here, for the first time in the history of the world was a system in which man would not be beholden to government; government would be beholden to man.

The explicit promise in the Declaration that we're endowed by our Creator with certain inalienable rights was meant for all of us. It wasn't meant to be limited or perverted by special privilege or by double standards that favor one group over another. It is a principle for eternity, America's deepest treasure. Father Hesburgh reminded us, our rights are "corollaries of the great proposition, at the heart of Western civilization, that every . . . person is a *res sacra*, a sacred reality, and as such is entitled to the opportunity of fulfilling those great human potentials with which God has endowed man."

The promise of America, the character of our people, the thrust of our history, and the challenge of our future all point toward a higher mission: to build together a society of opportunity, a society that rewards excellence, bound by a body of laws nourished with the spirit of faith, equity, responsibility, and compassion. The streets of America would not be paved with gold; they would be paved with opportunity. Success would depend upon personal initiative and merit.

Thomas Jefferson said his criteria for honor and status was not wealth, but virtue and talent. In "Abraham Lincoln: The Prairie Years," Carl Sandburg wrote that Lincoln believed "the accent and stress was to be on opportunity, on equal chance, equal access to the resources of life, liberty, and the pursuit of happiness. To give man this equal chance in life was the aim, the hope, the flair of glory, spoken by the Declaration of Independence."

Through the years, this promise was made real, thanks to the hard work, the dedication, and commitment to freedom of the American people. Our commitment to freedom has meant commitment to the rule of law, and commitment to the law has created opportunity: for example, historic legislation like the Homestead Act; passage of the 14th amendment to strengthen the guarantee of civil rights for every citizen, regardless of race, creed, or color; and, more recently, *Brown* vs. *Board of Education*, which emphatically decreed that race can never be used to deny any person equal educational opportunity. No future will outshine ours if we hold tight to the torch of freedom, if we remain true to the rule of law, and if we meet the challenge of providing opportunity to all our people.

One of my dreams is to help Americans rise above pessimism by renewing their belief in themselves. And I'm glad to say we are seeing a renewal of confidence in America. We're determined to build an agenda for opportunity on three pillars: excellence, equality, and growth—economic growth.

This must be an agenda that opens the gates of freedom so all people can go as far as their God-given talents will take them. For every legal and economic action we consider, I ask: Will this serve to liberate and empower the individual; will it encourage us to reach for the stars, or will it weaken us and drag us down into submission and dependence?

Law is the handmaiden of liberty, essential to preserving order in freedom. And we cannot have order unless people are certain of their full scope of their rights and legal protections. Vague or excessive laws, or inconsistent judicial decisions, threaten our freedom. As organizers, negotiators, and protectors of our civil liberties, your role is crucial. You can help us correct laws which are barriers to opportunity. You can insist on fairness and consistency in the administration of justice. You can help us create America's agenda for opportunity.

We believe that agenda begins with a

search for excellence—men and women of excellence—to serve as leaders of our government. It's people, after all, who must operate a government that is based upon law.

With your counsel, we've sought judicial nominees who support the limited policy-making role for the Federal courts envisioned by the Constitution. The Founding Fathers did not want our judiciary system to be first among equals. They wanted it to be one of three coequal branches of government.

We aim for a cross section of appointments that fully reflects the rich diversity and talent of our people. But we do not and will never select individuals just because they are men or women, whites or blacks, Jews, Catholics, or whatever. I don't look at people as members of groups; I look at them as individuals and as Americans. I believe you rob people of their dignity and confidence when you impose quotas. The implicit but false message of quotas is that some people can't make it under the same rules that apply to everyone else.

When an opening appeared on this nation's highest court, I selected the person I believed the most outstanding candidate. I'm proud that for the first time in our history, a woman, named Sandra Day O'Connor, now sits on the Supreme Court of the United States. But I'm proudest of this appointment not because Justice O'Connor is a woman, but because she is so well qualified.

We're committed to appointing outstanding blacks, Hispanics, and women to judicial and top-level policymaking positions in our administration. Three women are members of my Cabinet, more than ever before in history. In our first 2 years, we appointed more women to top-policy posts than any administration before us. And I think that's a pretty good start.

Now, permit me to speak, too, on behalf of our nominees to the Civil Rights Commission: Morris Abram, John Bunzel, Robert Destro, and our nominee for Staff Director, Linda Chavez. They are people of distinction and integrity—all Democrats—whose talent, independence, and commitment to civil rights are beyond question. They are champions of opportunity. But these fine Americans are under fire. My nominating them supposedly compromises the independence of the Commission. Well, forgive me, but that's hogwash.

Historian Carl Brauer wrote that John Kennedy sought, through appointments, to liberalize the Commission. And officials of his administration, and even a representative of the Democratic National Committee, met regularly with the Staff Director of the Civil Rights Commission to plan strategy. Presidents Johnson and Carter also sought to appoint individuals who reflected their ideas on how to achieve our common goal of civil rights for all Americans. So, isn't it strange that we never heard in the past this charge about compromising the independence of the Commission? Let's be fair and recognize the attack upon our nominees for what it is.

The plain truth is, our nominees are independent, independent from every voice but their own conscience. They don't worship at the altar of forced busing and mandatory quotas. They don't believe you can remedy past discrimination by mandating new discrimination. They are committed activists for genuine civil and human rights, wise and courageous citizens. And I think they deserve your strong support.

If excellence is one pillar of the agenda for opportunity, equality is another, and it's just as important—equality of rights, treatment, and protection under the law. We want every American to participate fully in society on the basis of individual merit, regardless of race, sex, or national origin. I reaffirm today our unshakable commitment to eliminate discrimination against blacks, women, the handicapped, and other minorities. And let me add, this is not just our legal commitment; it is also our moral commitment.

Racial violence and other criminal violations of civil rights laws are among the most heinous intrusions upon individual liberty. We do not shy from prosecution or punishment. The Department of Justice has filed more than a hundred new cases charging criminal violations of civil rights laws. We have tried 80 cases. That's not just a respectable number; it's substantially more than any prior administration during a comparable period.

In the area of fair housing, we're keeping our pledge to strengthen enforcement of the Fair Housing Act. We introduced legislation to significantly amend the law for the first time since its enactment so we can put real teeth into the principle of equal protection from discrimination.

In a democracy, there is no greater expression of equal opportunity than the right to vote. And I am proud to have supported and signed into law the longest extension ever of the Voting Rights Act. Under this administration, the Department of Justice has reviewed approximately 25,000 proposed electoral changes under the Voting Rights Act. They have objected to 165 on the grounds of racial discrimination. The Department has been active in litigation, participating in a total of 52 cases, 25 of which were initiated under this administration.

We're also committed to eliminating all traces of discrimination in the law against women. At the same time, we're doing our best to restore respect for the family and the homemakers who do so much to hold our society together.

Take a look at America, 1983. Things are changing—and for the better. The income tax marriage penalty has been greatly reduced; the maximum child care tax credit for working mothers has been increased—almost doubled; we've eliminated the estate tax for surviving spouses. We've authorized larger I.R.A. contributions for working women. We're strengthening child support enforcement to make absent fathers meet their obligations; and we've moved in the courts to remedy inequities in pensions. As I've mentioned, we've appointed more women to top policy posts than any administration before us. And we've increased the purchasing power of all Americans by knocking down inflation.

Those who specialize in partisan rhetoric and the politics of accusation may close their eyes to progress, but Americans are fairminded. They don't look at the world with blinders. If given the facts, I'm confident they'll agree that much has and is being done to assure that every woman has an equal opportunity to achieve the American dream.

All these reforms are important. We're committed to them and to doing more. But we need another reform, assurance that the American people can walk the streets and sleep in their homes without being afraid. The rule of law represents the civil discourse of a free people. Crime is the uncivilized shout that threatens to drown out and ultimately silence the language of liberty. I believe the scales of criminal justice have tilted too far toward protecting criminals. And more must be done to protect the rights of law-abiding citizens.

Crime is an issue of social justice. Its elimination is essential to full freedom and opportunity for all Americans. To cite just one example, in 1980, blacks were victimized by crimes against persons at a 25-percent higher rate than whites. So, we've introduced the Comprehensive Crime Control Act of 1983—to deny bail to a defendant posing a threat to the community; to make prison sentencing more certain; to end abuses of parole; and to modify the exclusionary rule, so that evidence obtained in good faith can be used in a criminal trial.

Over 50 percent of violent crime goes unreported. I have appointed a Presidential Task Force on Victims of Crime, and it has made 68 recommendations. Many of them are being acted upon. We're also carrying out many enforcement initiatives. We now have law enforcement coordinating committees in over 90 judicial districts. Last Thursday, I had the honor of appointing a commission to conduct a region-by-region analysis of organized crime infiltration—a commission headed by one of the most distinguished members of your profession, Judge Irving R. Kaufman. And we've set up 12 regional drug enforcement task forces. They're modeled on the successful South Florida Task Force, which stemmed the heavy flow of drugs into Florida. They're working on 260 cases. We think it's time, also, to crack down on the peddlers of filth and smut. The Justice Department has a program to do this, and we've notified U.S. attorneys that enforcement of pornography laws is a prime concern.

Finally, I submit to you, it's not good enough to have equal access to our law; we must also have equal access to the higher law—the law of God. George Washington warned that morality could not prevail in exclusion of religious principles. And Jefferson asked, ". . . can the liberties of a nation be thought secure, when we've removed their only firm basis, a conviction in the minds of people that these liberties are the gifts of God."

The first amendment was not written to protect the people from religious freedom. The first amendment was written to protect people's religious beliefs from government tyranny. The American people support a constitutional amendment permitting their children to begin their days as the Members of Congress do: with prayer. Prayer would be voluntary. It could not be state composed, and I hope the ABA will support it. And I'm not going to add that if the children start out the same way as the Congressmen, I hope they'll turn out more—[*inaudible*]. [*Laughter*]

Our last great pillar of our agenda is opportunity—or for opportunity is for economic growth. Franklin Roosevelt told us that ". . . freedom is no half-and-half affair. If the average citizen is guaranteed equal opportunity in the polling place, he must have equal opportunity in the market place."

A sparkling economy is the best hope for all who strive to pull themselves up. And we have a program to do that. It's called economic recovery. One of the best signs that that program is working is that they don't call it Reaganomics anymore. [*Laughter*] What bothers many in Washington is our belief that you can only build a durable recovery with more freedom, not more government. But I think Justice Brandeis was right when he said, "Experience teaches us to be most on our guard in protecting liberty when Government's purposes are beneficent."

As attorneys you understand the importance of evidence and experience. Oliver Wendell Holmes said a page of history is worth of volume of logic. If we look at recent history, I believe one conclusion is inescapable: No overall improvement occurred in reducing poverty in America during the very period when government spending in the name of the poor was exploding. The decline in the percentage of people in poverty began leveling off in the late sixties, reversing almost two decades of dramatic improvement. Then, and even worse, between 1971 and 1980, the percentage of American households dependent on welfare rose by 20 percent.

This tragedy was accompanied by the increasing breakdown of families. Nearly half of all poor families in 1980 were headed by women, and the number of single teenage mothers is estimated to have grown by 50 percent in the decade of the seventies. The dramatic increase in dependence was clearly associated with a change in the nature of public assistance. The emphasis shifted from F. D. R.'s model of direct payments to the needy. We began supporting a growing army of professionals. I don't question their good intentions, but their economic self-interest lay in extending dependency, not in ending it. And that's exactly what happened. Eligibility standards were also relaxed, and the tradition that public assistance should be shunned was replaced with an income transfer ethic.

Encouraging dependency had a clear impact on reducing economic growth. Irresponsible spending added to the ranks of poverty by generating higher inflation. This triggered a sharp increase in the tax burden, destroying incentives for savings and investment, crippling real earnings. The Joint Economic Committee estimated the drop in productivity growth in the 1970's cost the average household nearly $3,000 in income. America wasn't going forward. We were going backward. Let us have the courage to speak the truth: Policies that increase dependency and break up families are not progressive; they're reactionary, even though they are invariably promoted, passed, and carried out in the name of fairness, generosity, and compassion.

The good news is we're beginning to turn incentive structures and the economic situation around. Poverty is far from solved. Problems which had been neglected for more than a decade were made worse by the recent recession. But the conditions for meaningful and lasting improvement are clearly being established. Spending growth has been cut. Public assistance is being re-targeted to the truly needy. And over 85 percent of those who have left the welfare rolls have not returned. They're out there independent. Just as important, we've reduced tax rates and restored incentives for growth.

The United States is leading the world into economic recovery with strong growth and low inflation. The experts said it couldn't be done. Who will benefit most from an inflation rate below 3 percent—it's been 2.6 percent for the last 12 months, the lowest rate in more than 15 years—and a growth rate which approached 9 percent in the second quarter? Well, the answer is those with the lowest incomes. Inflation hurts them most, and our success against inflation will help them most. And let's remember, when the economy was strong and healthy during the fifties and sixties, poverty rapidly declined.

I think we need a new dialog in America. It might begin with an intellectual housecleaning in Washington, D.C. It's time to bury the myth that bigger government brings more opportunity and compassion. In the words of Morris Abram, our nominee to the Civil Rights Commission, it's time for some people, he said, to "stop shouting slogans of the past and begin dealing with facts, figures and conditions of the present."

In the name of fairness, let's stop trying to plunder family budgets with higher taxes, and start controlling the real problem—Federal spending. In the name of growth, let's stop talking about billions for more dependency and start creating enterprise zones and new incentives for opportunity—so we can keep the dream alive for millions of aspiring whites, blacks, and Hispanics. In the name of America, let's stop spreading bondage and start spreading freedom.

Let's remember what we're all about. All of us, as Americans, are joined in a common enterprise to write the story of freedom—the greatest adventure mankind has ever known, and one we must pass on to our children and our children's children—remembering that freedom is never more than one generation away from extinction.

The warning, more than a century ago, attributed to Daniel Webster, remains as timeless as the document he revered when he asked, "Who shall reconstruct the fabric of demolished government? Who shall raise again the well proportioned columns of Constitutional liberty? Who shall frame together the skillful architecture which unites national sovereignty with states rights, individual security, and public prosperity?" And then he said, "Hold onto the Constitution of the United States of America and to the Republic for which it stands. Miracles do not cluster—what has happened once in 6,000 years may never happen again. Hold onto your Constitution, for if the American Constitution shall fall there will be anarchy throughout the world."

Trusting in God and helping each other, we can and will preserve the dream of America, the last best hope of man on Earth.

Thank you very much, and God bless you all.

Note: The President spoke at 11:12 a.m. in the Robert F. Maddox Auditorium at the Atlanta Civic Center.

Following his remarks, the President met with Georgia Republican leaders in the Exhibit Hall at the civic center. He then returned to Washington, D.C.

Remarks at a White House Briefing for Administration Officials on Federal Management Reform
August 2, 1983

Thank you all for coming this afternoon. Seeing you here reminds me that we've put together a team of pros, of top-notch professionals. And your talents and energies are getting the business of government back on track.

We haven't been in Washington a long time, but I think we've accomplished a great deal. Nowhere is this more true than here at home. America's economic pulse is getting stronger and steadier every day.

Inflation, which had hit double digits when we took office, is running at the lowest annual rate in more than 15 years—2.6 percent for the last 12 months. And that translates into real savings: A medium-income family—income of $25,000—has about $600 more in purchasing power today than it had in 1980. And there's even good news at the supermarket. Food prices not only have stopped rising—they stopped that last month—but they actually have declined. You know, for a time there when you went to the market to buy food, it looked as if it might be cheaper to eat money. [*Laughter*]

The prime interest rate is less than half what it was. The GNP is growing faster than most economists dreamed it would. Personal income is up; production is up; fac-

tory orders are up; retail sales are up; and, as we've heard once again today, housing sales are still going up. In the months ahead, I think we'll see more evidence and that even that last dragon—unemployment—has started to wilt.

Now, I have a feeling that a lot of you are just as familiar with all these things that I've just said as I am. But the plain truth is, I just like the sound of them so much, that I wanted to say it out loud again. [*Laughter*]

I have a story about that. I don't know whether Jimmy Stewart would object to my repeating his remarks when we were campaigning together. And he would introduce me at the various banquets out there on the campaign trail, and every time they'd talk about—the emcee in introducing him, he would talk about his great stardom in pictures and all. And then each time I would get up and think it was only fair—apologize to the emcee for correcting him, but say in addition to that—his war record and that Jimmy Stewart not only flew the Hamburg run, but he's a major general in the Air Corps Reserve. And one time, after several of these situations, the master of ceremonies did refer to his military record and then said "Brigadier General Jimmy Stewart." So, when I got up I apologized to the emcee again and said, "It's 'Major General Jimmy Stewart.' " And I'm thinking about this when I think about saying these things over again.

That night when we got back to the hotel, Jimmy said, "Ron," he said, "that fellow tonight was right." [*Laughter*] He said, "It is brigadier general." He said, "I just never corrected you before because it sounded so good." [*Laughter*]

So, I think the statistics sound good, and we can all talk about them some more. We've done good teamwork, and I think we can all be proud.

With the cornerstones of our economic program in place, it's time to shine the limelight on another mammoth challenge that we also undertook in the early days of the administration. Our attack was on waste and fraud in the Federal Government. We came here vowing to rein in the unwieldy Federal bureaucracy and get this government running as honestly and efficiently as any successful American business. We've been making some pretty good progress on that, and I've invited you here today to enlist your further help in expanding our reach and making our improvements permanent.

I'm proud to report that through the strike force efforts of our departmental I.G. offices, 29.3 billion tax dollars have been saved or put to better use so far. The Government has collected $3½ billion in debts that otherwise wouldn't have been collected. The paperwork burden has been cut by 20 percent. Our plan to reduce nondefense Federal employment is ahead of schedule. We've cut the cost of Federal publications by a fifth, travel by 16 percent, and audiovisual projects by 15 percent.

Over at the Veterans Administration, as Harry Walters and Everett Alvarez can tell us, we've set up a computer matching system that stopped a phony benefits check scheme and saved some $70,000 in VA benefits just in that.

At the GSA, Jerry Carmen has really turned things around. He's got work-in-progress time down from 30 days to 7 days, while absorbing budget cuts of 20 percent and the attrition of 7,000 employees.

And over at the Pentagon, Cap Weinberger and our service Secretaries along with many others, have identified nearly $16.1 billion in savings or cost avoidances on waste and fraud. And during the next 7 years, multiyear procurement and other acquisition initiatives will save us almost $30 billion.

There's much more that we've done, but there's still much more to do. Another major initiative undertaken by this administration is our Private Sector Survey on Cost Control, which was established a year and a half ago to identify waste and inefficiency in the Federal Government. Under the chairmanship of Peter Grace, the Survey already has issued 37 reports containing over 2,000 recommendations which could result in cost savings and revenue opportunities totaling as much as $300 billion over the next 3 years. The Survey will issue more reports during the next several months, which should point out even more opportunities to cut corners and save. I expect to receive their final, summary report early this fall.

But as important as whistleblowers, investigators, and surveyors are, what our government needs most are good managers on the frontline. And that's why I need you. And that's why I'm calling on you—on all program managers in every agency of the Government—to find more efficient ways of carrying out their programs.

Last fall, I asked Joe Wright to head up the Reform 88 program. And he's coordinating our effort to achieve lasting savings by changing financial and information management systems in every department and agency. Our management improvement initiatives will expand the goals of our earlier efforts to streamline and reorganize the processes that control the money, information, personnel, and property of the Federal Government. These new initiatives will bring us closer to fulfilling a promise that we made to the American people: to limit government to its proper role and make it the servant, not the master, of the people.

There's not a lot of glory in our task, but I'm determined that, when this administration leaves the stage, the American people will have a Federal Government that operates in a businesslike manner. Now, that means providing high-quality, essential public services as efficiently as possible. And it means that, by reducing the money lost to boondoggles, more money will be available for legitimate government programs. By cutting waste and abuse and through better targeting of aid, we can ensure that those Americans who need and deserve our help can get it.

I know we share the same goals, and that I can continue to depend on you for your help. We have a chance to leave our permanent stamp on the executive branch. To-gether, we can do it. And if we succeed, we'll leave behind a better government and a better nation.

I thank you all for what you've done already, and for all you're about to do for the good of our country and the generations who will follow us. And, again, good luck, and God bless you.

Note: The President spoke at 1:34 p.m. in the East Room at the White House.

Nomination of Robert Hopkins Miller To Be United States Ambassador to Ivory Coast
August 2, 1983

The President today announced his intention to nominate Robert Hopkins Miller, of Washington, a career member of the Senior Foreign Service, Class of Career Minister, as Ambassador to the Republic of Ivory Coast. He would succeed Nancy V. Rawls.

Mr. Miller served in the United States Army in 1945–1947. In the Department he was junior management intern (1951–1952) and international relations officer in the Office of European Regional Affairs (1952–1954). In 1954–1957 he was political officer in Paris NATO. In the Department he was international relations officer in the Executive Secretariat (1957–1960) and Belgium-Luxembourg desk officer (1960–1962). In 1962–1965 he was deputy chief of the political section in Saigon. In the Department he was Director of the Vietnam Working Group in 1965–1968 and attended the Im-perial Defense College in London in 1968. In 1968–1971 he was senior adviser, United States Delegation to the Paris Meetings on Vietnam, in Paris. In 1971–1973 he was Deputy Executive Secretary in the Department and was on detail as Assistant Director for International Affairs at the United States Arms Control and Disarmament Agency in 1973–1974. In 1974–1977 he was Deputy Assistant Secretary of State for East Asian and Pacific Affairs in the Department. He was Ambassador to Malaysia in 1977–1980 and has been Director for Management Operations in the Department (1980–1983).

Mr. Miller graduated from Stanford University (A.B., 1949) and Harvard University (M.A., 1951). His foreign language is French. He was born September 8, 1927, in Port Angeles, Wash.

Memorandum on Establishing a Task Force on Food Assistance
August 2, 1983

Memorandum for Edwin Meese III

Subject: Task Force on Food Assistance

I am deeply concerned about the extent to which we have a problem that should not exist in this great and wealthy country. That is the problem of hunger. America is literally the breadbasket of the world. We produce and export more food than any other nation. Our farms are the envy of the world.

Yet, I have seen reports in the press in

past weeks of Americans going hungry. I am deeply concerned by these stories, because I know the suffering that each of these incidents represents.

At the same time, I admit to being perplexed by these accounts because, the fact is, federal law guarantees that *every* poor person with an income at or below 130% of the poverty level is eligible to receive *free* food stamps. Additional federal aid includes free school lunches, free school breakfasts; the Women, Infants and Childrens program, and numerous other federal programs. If the poor, who are eligible by law for this help, are not receiving it, then something is wrong.

In addition, our Administration has been distributing free surplus dairy products to the needy, including cheese and butter. Since we began this distribution program in December 1981, the federal government has given away nearly 700 million pounds of dairy products worth more than a billion dollars. If this assistance is not reaching those for whom it is intended, then again something is grievously wrong.

Unfortunately, we in government cannot respond effectively to this problem unless we know the nature of the difficultuies we seek to remedy. It may be that some people are not aware that federal aid is available to them. It may be that these programs are not administered well enough to serve all those who are eligible. Or some people may have just decided not to take advantage of the available aid programs. We simply do not know enough to say.

But I intend to find out. As you know, I am fully committed to feeding the poor people of this Nation. No child, senior citizen, deserted mother or invalid should have to go hungry in America—not only because we are a land of plenty, but because federal law guarantees that our plenty is to be shared with those in true need.

To ensure that this promise is realized, I have decided to create a Task Force on Food Assistance to examine the extent of America's hunger problem, to determine its causes, and to recommend specific solutions. This Task Force should be composed of leading experts in poverty research, economics and government administration— men and women from academia, the private sector, and with experience at all levels of government.

I want the Task Force to bring me a no-holds-barred study. If the food assistance programs are being mismanaged, I want to know that. If certain aspects of our food assistance programs require more funding, I want to know that, too.

Realizing the importance of this problem, I want the Task Force to complete its work and report to me within 90 days.

Please take whatever final steps are necessary so that I may form this Task Force as soon as possible.

If even one American child is forced to go to bed hungry at night, or if one senior citizen is denied the dignity of proper nutrition, that is a national tragedy. We are too generous a people to allow this to happen. I hope that the work of this Task Force will help solve the problem of hunger in America once and for all.

RONALD REAGAN

Appointment of Nine Members of the Presidential Commission on Indian Reservation Economies, and Designation of Cochairmen
August 2, 1983

The President today announced his intention to appoint the following individuals to be members of the Presidential Commission on Indian Reservation Economies. These are new positions:

Robert Robertson, of McLean, Va., is vice president of Occidental International Corp., in Washington, D.C. In 1969–1974 he was Executive Director of the National Council on Indian Opportunity in the Office of the Vice President. He is married and has six children. He was born March 5, 1929, in Bayonne, N.J.

Ross O. Swimmer, of Tahlequah, Okla., has been Chief of the Cherokee Nation (Oklahoma) since 1975. He served as general counsel to the Cherokee Nation in 1972–1975. He is married and has two children. He was born October 26, 1943, in Oklahoma City, Okla.

Daniel Alex, of Anchorage, Alaska, is president of Ekultna, Inc. He is president of the Alaska Native Land Managers Association and a member of the Citizens Advisory Commission on Federal Management Areas in Alaska. He has one child. Mr. Alex was born March 9, 1941, in Ekluna, Alaska.

Ted Bryant, of Greenwood Village, Colo., is director of the Native American programs in Denver, Colo. He is also president of the National American Indian Republican Federation. He was assistant to the Director, Office of Indian Programs, Department of Housing and Urban Development, in 1977. He is married and has four children. He was born April 21, 1929, in Hortschorne, Okla.

Manuel H. Johnson, Jr., of Fairfax, Va., is Assistant Secretary for Economic Policy at the Department of Treasury. Previously he was associate professor of economics in the graduate school of George Mason University. He is married and has two children. He was born February 10, 1949, in Troy, Ala.

David J. Matheson, of Plummer, Idaho, is chairman, tribal government, for the Couer d'Alene Tribe. Previously he was director, Division of Planning and Natural Resources (1981) and economic development planner (1980) for the Couer d'Alene Tribe in Plummer. He is married and has three children. He was born November 5, 1951, in Plummer, Idaho.

Neal A. McCaleb, of Edmond, Okla., is president and chief executive officer of McCaleb Associates and has advised numerous tribes on design and construction of public works projects and development of real estate resources. He served on the Oklahoma Indian Affairs Commission (1968–1970) and the National Council on Indian Opportunity in 1972. He is married and has four children. He was born June 30, 1935, in Oklahoma City, Okla.

B. Z. Kastler, of Salt Lake City, Utah, is chairman of the board of Mountain Fuel Supply Co. He is a member of the Salt Lake Area Chamber of Commerce and served as president in 1977–1978. He is a director of the Mountain States Legal Foundation. He is married and has two daughters. He was born October 30, 1920, in Billings, Mont.

Walter B. McKay, of Paradise Valley, Ariz., is president and chairman of Agricultural Chemical Services, Inc. He also serves as secretary-treasurer of International Chemical Traders and as a general partner in the Picacho Farming Co. He is married and has two children. He was born October 21, 1944, in Harlingen, Tex.

The President intends to designate Robert Robertson and Ross O. Swimmer as Cochairmen.

Remarks at the Annual Convention of the National Federation of Business and Professional Women's Clubs
August 3, 1983

Thank you very much. Maxine Hays, I thank you for, let me say, a very graceful and gracious introduction. [*Laughter*] If I wore a hat, I would have thrown it in first before I came in. [*Laughter*]

But before I say what I came here to say, may I just tell you how very proud all of us in our land are of your president, Maxine Hays, and these 3 years that she has served you and, in serving you, has served the Nation and the world. And she has proven many of the things that most people need to understand about women, because not only is she the very epitome of our free enterprise system as a small business-

woman, as the president of your worldwide organization; but, also, her State of Oregon has chosen her Mother of the Year.

And now to the business at hand. [*Laughter*] I know how hard Polly Madenwald [1] worked to set up the tour of the White House—the people's house. And when I found out yesterday what had happened I picked up the telephone, and she very graciously answered—[*laughter*]—and I told her that I was standing on the third floor

---

[1] *President of the National Federation of Business and Professional Women's Clubs.*

window ledge of the White House, prepared to jump.[2] [*Laughter*] And when I asked if I couldn't come here and apologize to all of you, and she said that I could, I have now decided—of course, I didn't jump—[*laughter*]—I'm going back to the White House, find out who was responsible, put them on the window ledge, and shove. [*Laughter*]

As Maxine said a little earlier coming in here, yesterday was one of those examples—to those of you from all the other countries of the world, welcome here to the United States and, honestly, we don't act that way all the time. [*Laughter*] We hope we'll have another opportunity to make good on what should have happened yesterday. But we have an old saying in America; it's called Murphy's Law. [*Laughter*] And Murphy's Law is, "If anything can go wrong, it will go wrong." And Murphy's Law was very much in effect yesterday at 1600 Pennsylvania Avenue. So please just know how very sorry we all are. Evidently, it only confirms some of the criticisms I've made over past years about what can happen at certain bureaucratic levels of government.

And let me just say, also, that I believe it's not enough just to say "I'm sorry," so I intend to do penance. And we have been doing a number of things here with regard to the thing of great interest to you, and that is the recognition of women's place. I want you to know I've always recognized it, because I happen to be one who believes if it wasn't for women, us men would still be walking around in skin suits carrying clubs.

But we have been doing a number of things in this administration, and some things that are carrying on where I began as Governor of California. And we now have—I won't go into great detail; I know that your leadership has been briefed by Faith Whittlesey [Assistant to the President for Public Liaison] of my staff on some of the things that we are doing here to being about more equality—and I will just men-

---

[2]*Because of a scheduling error, members of the federation were precluded from attending a White House tour on the previous day.*

tion this one, and this is where I'll do penance. We have, since we've been here, been having our Justice Department comb all the laws and all the regulations—and they're vast in number—here at our national level.

And I say this, that perhaps many of you from other lands might, if it is necessary in your land, take this as a suggestion for future activity there. They have been combing them to find any law or regulation in our land that has a vestige of discrimination in it on the basis of sex. And they have just delivered the results of that study. It is a packet of computer readouts about that thick. And we are now combing through this to find out what can we do administratively, simply by Executive order, to eliminate these matters of discrimination that might be embodied in these laws and those that will require legislation, and then to frame the legislation and send it to Congress to have those laws and those regulations changed.

And in view of what happened yesterday, my penance is going to be that I think that I, personally, am going to read that stack of readouts. I'm not going to take a chance on bureaucracy. [*Laughter*]

But I know I've taken too much of your time already. I know that you've very kindly let me come into the midst of your business meeting here, so I will make my departure now. And incidentally, to show you contact with the opposite sex, a letter that I've referred to a number of times here in our own country that I received shortly after I got here was from an 11-year-old girl. And this 11-year-old girl told me in some detail in the letter about the matters that I would have to deal with. And I must say, I was greatly impressed. I don't think at 11 years old I could have written someone and told them about the international affairs that I would be faced with, the economic situation that I would be faced with. But she told me, and gave me some solid suggestions as to what to do, and then wound up with a P.S., a postscript, at the end of her letter. She said, "Now, get over to the Oval Office and go to work." [*Laughter*]

So, I'll go over to the Oval Office and get

to work, beginning with "How did yesterday happen?"

Thank you very much.

*Note: The President spoke at 10:08 a.m. in
the main ballroom at the Sheraton Washington Hotel.*

Remarks of President Reagan and President Mobutu Sese Seko of Zaire Following Their Meeting
August 4, 1983

President Reagan. President Mobutu and
I have just had a warm and useful discussion. And I am pleased to have been able to
meet again with President Mobutu, who's
been a faithful friend to the United States
for some 20 years. The President and I took
this opportunity to review the state of U.S.-
Zairian relations, and we found a large area
of agreement on the major points we discussed.

I expressed our admiration for President
Mobutu's courageous action in sending
troops to assist the Government of Chad in
its struggle against Libyan-backed rebels.
On the home front, the President has informed me of progress on his government's
economic stabilization plan. Zaire is taking
the difficult but necessary steps to ensure
sustained economic progress, and it's important that we and Zaire's other friends do
what we can to help.

President Mobutu and I also discussed his
country's political situation, and I told him
of the positive reaction in the United States
to his recent decision to offer amnesty to
his political opponents.

This visit has permitted the President and
me to reaffirm our common desire for
peace and stability in Africa. And I am confident that the close relations between our
two countries, based on shared interests and
perceptions, will advance the cause of
peace and development in Africa. And
we're very pleased to have him visit us

once again as he did a year and a half ago.

Mr. President?

President Mobutu. I have expressed to
President Reagan during our meeting, first
of all, my thanks for the wonderful and
warm welcome extended to us in the atmosphere of great friendship that we have
experienced throughout our stay in Washington.

We surveyed world events. We talked
about the economic situation in Zaire, about
the program for financial and economic recovery which is being worked out with the
IMF. We talked of Chad, of the aggression
against that country, a founder of the OAU
and a member of the United Nations. We
talked also of Namibia, South Africa, and
Central America. In brief, we surveyed
world events. Some decisions have been
made for economic aid to Zaire, and some
more decisions will be made in that context.

I extended to President Reagan and to his
associates my congratulations and thanks for
all they have done to facilitate our stay in
every way during our visit here.

Thank you.

*Note: President Reagan spoke at 12:02 p.m.
to reporters assembled on the South
Grounds of the White House. President
Mobutu spoke in French, and his remarks
were translated by an interpreter. The two
Presidents and U.S. and Zairian officials
had met in the Oval Office.*

Nomination of Richard W. Murphy To Be an Assistant Secretary of State
August 4, 1983

The President today announced his intention to nominate Richard W. Murphy to be an Assistant Secretary of State (Near Eastern and South Asian Affairs). He would succeed Nicholas A. Veliotes.

He has been serving as Ambassador to Saudi Arabia since 1981. Ambassador Murphy, a career Foreign Service officer, served as Ambassador to the Philippines (1978–1980), to the Syrian Arab Republic (1974–1978), and to Mauritania (1971–1974). In the Department of State he served as country director, Office of Arab Peninsula Affairs (1970–1971), and as personnel placement officer and Assistant Executive Director for Personnel in the Bureau of Near Eastern and South Asian Affairs (1968–1970). His other assignments included Aleppo, Jidda, and Amman.

Ambassador Murphy graduated from Harvard University (B.A. 1951) and Cambridge University (B.A. 1953). He is married and has three children. He was born July 29, 1929, in Boston, Mass.

Nomination of Robert E. Lamb To Be an Assistant Secretary of State
August 4, 1983

The President today announced his intention to nominate Robert E. Lamb to be an Assistant Secretary of State (Administration). He would succeed Thomas M. Tracy.

Since 1979 Mr. Lamb has been serving as administrative officer in Bonn, Germany. Previously he was Deputy Director (1977–1979) and Director (1979) of the Passport Office in the Bureau of Consular Affairs. He served as special assistant to the Assistant Secretary for Administration in 1974–1976 and as Director of Personnel/Career Management in 1976–1977. His other assignments include executive assistant to the Ambassador in Monrovia, administrative officer in Kathmandu, and deputy director of the regional finance center in Bangkok.

He graduated from the University of Pennsylvania (A.B., 1962). He is married and has three children. He was born November 17, 1936, in Atlanta, Ga.

Nomination of William C. Harrop To Be Inspector General of the Department of State and the Foreign Service
August 4, 1983

The President today announced his intention to nominate William C. Harrop to be Inspector General of the Department of State and the Foreign Service. He would succeed Robert L. Brown.

Since 1980 he has been serving as Ambassador to Kenya. Previously Ambassador Harrop served as Deputy Assistant Secretary for African Affairs at the Department of State in 1977–1980; Ambassador to Guinea in 1975–1977; Deputy Chief of Mission, Canberra, in 1973–1975; and at the Department of State as international relations officer, policy planning (1971–1973), and Office Director, African Research, Bureau of Intelligence and Research (1969–

1971). His other assignments included Lumbumbashi and Brussels.

Ambassador Harrop graduated from Harvard University (A.B., 1950). He is married and has one child. He was born February 19, 1929, in Baltimore, Md.

Nomination of Ronald I. Spiers To Be an Under Secretary of State
August 4, 1983

The President today announced his intention to nominate Ronald I. Spiers to be Under Secretary of State for Management. He would succeed Jerome W. Van Gorkom.

Since 1981 he has been serving as Ambassador to Pakistan. Ambassador Spiers joined the State Department in 1955 as foreign affairs officer in the Bureau of International Organization Affairs. In 1957–1961 he was officer in charge of disarmament affairs in the Office of the Special Assistant to the Secretary of State. He was Director of the Office of Political Affairs with the Arms Control and Disarmament Agency in 1961–1962. In the Department in 1962–1966, he was Deputy Director, then Director of NATO Affairs, in the Bureau of European Affairs. He was counselor for political affairs in London in 1966–1969 and Director of the Bureau of Politico-Military Affairs in the Department in 1969–1973. In 1973–1974 he was Ambassador to the Commonwealth of the Bahamas. He was Deputy Chief of Mission (Minister) in London in 1974–1977 and served as Ambassador to the Republic of Turkey in 1977–1980. Since 1980 he has been Director of Intelligence and Research in the Department.

Ambassador Spiers graduated from Dartmouth College (A.B., 1948) and Princeton University (M.P.A., 1950). He served in the United States Navy in 1943–1946. He is married, has four children, and resides in South Londonderry, Vt. He was born July 9, 1925, in Orange, N.J.

Nomination of Nicholas A. Veliotes To Be United States Ambassador to Egypt
August 4, 1983

The President today announced his intention to nominate Nicholas A. Veliotes to be Ambassador to the Arab Republic of Egypt. He would succeed Alfred L. Atherton, Jr.

Mr. Veliotes has been serving as Assistant Secretary of State (Near Eastern and South Asian Affairs) since May 1981. He was Deputy Assistant for Near East and South Asian Affairs, Department of State, in 1977–1978. In 1976–1977 he was Deputy Director, Policy Planning Staff, and Special Assistant for Employee-Management Relations, Bureau of Personnel, in 1975–1976.

Mr. Veliotes was Deputy Chief of Mission in Tel Aviv in 1973–1975; Special Assistant to the Under Secretary of State in 1970–1973; international relations officer, African regional affairs; chief, political section in Vientiane, in 1966–1969; political officer in New Delhi in 1964–1966; foreign affairs officer, Bureau of Cultural and Educational Affairs, in 1962–1964; international relations officer, Executive Secretariat staff; economic/general services officer in Rome in 1957–1960; and consular/administrative officer in Naples in 1955–1957.

Mr. Veliotes graduated from the University of California (B.A., 1952; M.A., 1954). He was born October 28, 1928, in Oakland, Calif.

Statement on Establishment of the President's Commission on Industrial Competitiveness
August 4, 1983

On June 28 I signed an Executive order establishing a Commission on Industrial Competitiveness. I charged the Commission with advising me and my administration on ways to strengthen the competitiveness of U.S. industry.

This nation's greatest competitive advantage in the past were ideas that helped America grow. We need to put the power of ideas to use again, for the good of our future. America needs her best minds to create technologies that will enhance America's economic leadership in the 1980's. To sustain high rates of real economic growth, we must continue to create new "miracles" of high technology—miracles both for innovation and for modernization of the major areas of our economy in manufacturing, agriculture, and services.

The Commission members I am appointing today are distinguished leaders from large and small businesses, from labor, and from academia. They are ideally suited to lead us in a national dialog—a discussion of the kinds of actions required by the public and private sectors to make U.S. industries more competitive in domestic and foreign markets. The Commission will be chaired by John A. Young, president of the Hewlett-Packard Co.

The Commission will focus its attention on government and private sector actions, specifically:

—Identifying the problems and opportunities for the private sector to transform new knowledge and innovations into commercial products, services, and manufacturing processes.

—Recommending policy changes at all levels of government to improve the private sector's ability to compete in the international marketplace and to maintain and create opportunities for American workers.

The Commission will report to me and work closely with the Department of Commerce, the Office of Policy Development, and the Office of Science and Technology Policy.

The increasingly rapid pace of technological advancement assures us that our economy will change constantly in the future. New developments in information processing, biology, and materials science are spawning sunrise industries. They are improving our quality of life and standard of living in ways few could have foreseen. These technologies are transforming all sectors of our economy and even our livestyles. Not only can information processing capabilities improve the way farmers manage their livestock, provide the "brains" in a flexible manufacturing system, and keep track of the paper flow in an office; they will also change the way we live.

Now some believe that the Government should try to read these trends to determine which products, services, and industries have a place in our future and which do not. They would have government planners divert resources away from traditional industries and channel them into new fields. But the history of progress in America proves that millions of individuals making decisions in their own legitimate self-interest cannot be outperformed by any bureaucratic planners.

Government's legitimate role is not to dictate detailed plans or solutions to problems for particular companies or industries. No, government serves us best by protecting and maintaining the marketplace, by ensuring that the rules of free and fair trade, both at home and abroad, are properly observed, and by safeguarding the freedoms of individual participants.

In carrying out this role, the Government must maintain fiscal policies which encourage personal initiative, and monetary policies which ensure stable prices. The lasting, noninflationary growth we are now building will facilitate the movement of capital toward promising economic activities. Stable economic growth will provide markets for new products and employment opportunities for workers displaced by changes in the way things are produced.

By establishing this Commission, we reaffirm this administration's commitment to making sure that this government will be a help, not a stumbling block, as U.S. industries compete in domestic and international markets, opening up new opportunities for all Americans.

Appointment of 20 Members of the President's Commission on Industrial Competitiveness
August 4, 1983

The President today announced his intention to appoint the following individuals to be members of the President's Commission on Industrial Competitiveness. As announced on June 28, 1983, the Commission will be chaired by John Young.

Robert Anderson is chief executive officer of Rockwell International Corp. in Pittsburgh, Pa.

Dimitri V. D'Arbeloff is chief executive officer of the Millipore Corp. in Bedford, Mass.

Frederick B. Dent is president and treasurer of Mayfair Mills, Inc, in Arcadia, S.C.

Rimmer De Vries is senior vice president of Morgan Guaranty Trust Co. in New York, N.Y.

Edwin D. Dodd is chairman and chief executive officer of Owens-Illinois, Inc., in Toledo, Ohio.

B. Kipling Hagopian is a general partner in Brentwood Associates in Los Angeles, Calif.

Robert A. Hanson is president and chief executive officer of Deere and Co. in Moline, Ill.

Edwin L. Harper is executive vice president of Overhead Door Corp. in Dallas, Tex.

George A. Keyworth II is Science Adviser to the President in the Executive Office of the President, Washington, D.C.

Gerald D. Laubach is president of Pfizer, Inc., in New York, N.Y.

George M. Low is president of Rensselaer Polytechnic Institute in Troy, N.Y.

Bruno J. Mauer is president of Rickert Industrial Supply Co. in Milwaukee, Wis.

Rachel McCulloch is professor of economics at the University of Wisconsin in Madison.

Sybil C. Mobley is dean of the School of Business, Florida A & M University, Tallahassee, Fla.

Thomas J. Murrin is president of Westinghouse Electric Corp. in Pittsburgh, Pa.

John Doyle Ong is chairman, president, and chief executive officer of B. F. Goodrich Co. in Akron, Ohio.

Michael E. Porter is professor of business administration at Harvard University in Boston, Mass.

Ian M. Ross, is president of Bell Laboratories in Murray Hill, N.J.

Stephen I. Schlossberg is former director of government and public affairs, United Auto Workers; partner, Zwerdling, Schlossberg, Leibig and Kahn, Washington, D.C.

Mark Shepherd, Jr., is chief executive officer of Texas Instruments in Dallas, Tex.

Remarks at a Meeting of the Cabinet Council on Management and Administration
August 4, 1983

Interest on the public debt will cost the American taxpayer over $103 billion in fiscal 1984. One of the major efforts initiated by my administration to reduce this drain is the improvement of the Government's cash management. Cash management has become a highly specialized art practiced by most major corporations and small businesses in America. In fact, most individuals have learned to manage their checkbooks to even out the flow of expenses and income. The Federal Government is just beginning to learn this lesson.

Better cash management is one of our key priorities under Reform 88. It also has been highlighted by the President's Private

Sector Survey, the Department of the Treasury, and the Office of Management and Budget. The Department of the Treasury fiscal service is spearheading initiatives to speed the collection process, to time our payments properly, and to improve cash processing and financial management practices.

We are currently putting a great deal of effort into this area. From January 1981 to May 1983, the Government realized $4.6 billion in savings, resulting from more efficient cash management practices. This has been accomplished by using modern technology, such as electronic transfer of funds, as well as improved management techniques. Nevertheless, we are only just getting started. Twenty agencies and departments have developed detailed cash management improvement plans. These plans have been approved by the Secretary of the Treasury and the Director of the Office of Management and Budget. Potential savings of $5.3 billion in interest expense have been identified by these agencies through fiscal '88, as well as an average annual cash acceleration savings of $4 billion during the same period.

Efficient cash management is not a one-time issue which will fade away. It must be part of a continuous effort to better manage our resources. The active cooperation of every governmental organization is required. Government executives must be made aware of how they can improve cash management practices within their areas of responsibility, supported, if necessary, by developmental training and performance-based incentives. Efficient cash management has to be a joint, cooperative effort to manage better this most critical part of the public trust.

I am therefore today directing you to take advantage of each opportunity to protect our cash resources and to continue to review your cash management programs to ensure they meet that end. You should be prepared to work closely with the Treasury Department and the Office of Management and Budget to implement measurable savings and to give cash management projects a high priority.

Note: The President met in the Cabinet Room at the White House with the Cabinet Council at 2 p.m.

As printed above, this item follows the text of the President's prepared remarks as released by the Office of the Press Secretary.

Proclamation 5079—Women's Equality Day, 1983
August 4, 1983

By the President of the United States of America

A Proclamation

The 19th Amendment to the Constitution, which gave women the right to vote, became law sixty-three years ago on August 26, 1920.

Since that important milestone in the history of the United States, women have used the ballot just as they have always used their energies and talents—to affect and improve our national life.

When the great philosopher and historian Alexis DeTocqueville visited America, he took a long look at our way of life and wrote, "If I were asked. . . . to what the singular prosperity and growing strength of that people ought mainly to be attributed, I should reply: To the superiority of their women."

Women have every reason to be proud of their contributions to every aspect of our society—science, space, government, business, medicine, education, health, and the family. And their contributions are growing.

We continue, as a Nation, to pursue equal opportunity and rights for all of our citizens, granting each person the chance to reach his or her goals.

On this occasion, it is appropriate that we recognize the accomplishments of the women of America and renew our efforts to ensure equal opportunity for all people in this great land.

Now, Therefore, I, Ronald Reagan, President of the United States of America, do hereby proclaim August 26, 1983, as Women's Equality Day. I call upon all Americans and interested organizations to mark this occasion with appropriate observances.

In Witness Whereof, I have hereunto set my hand this 4th day of August, in the year of our Lord nineteen hundred and eighty-three, and of the Independence of the United States of America the two hundred and eighth.

RONALD REAGAN

[*Filed with the Office of the Federal Register, 4:12 p.m., August 4, 1983*]

Remarks on Signing the National Child Support Enforcement Month Proclamation
August 5, 1983

Margaret, thank you very much.

It's a shocking fact that over half of all women who receive child support orders receive less than what they're due. In fact, 28 percent of these women and their children receive no payments at all. There are children in this country who are owed $4 billion from delinquent parents. This is an absolutely unacceptable situation.

Secretary Heckler has called it a growing national disgrace, and I agree completely. A parent's obligation to a child is one which must not be abrogated. And this is not only a financial debt; it's a moral one.

As Governor of California, I made sure that our State had tough child support enforcement laws. I even came before the Congress to lobby for an effective national system to protect the welfare of our nation's children.

Today, in proclaiming August as Child Support Enforcement Month, I hope to focus the Nation's attention on these children who are at the mercy of thoughtless parents. Let's make it our national goal to achieve 100 percent collection from the absent, neglectful parents.

August will kick off this drive, but let me say slack enforcement of child support payments will never be tolerated. The Federal child support enforcement program itself can stand improvement, and I want to thank Secretary Heckler and the composers of our proposal for their diligent and compassionate work. We must reform the Federal child support enforcement system so that it can effectively serve the cheated children of America. I urge the Congress to pass the legislation that we've introduced. We want parents who are deadbeats to pay up and deliver on their responsibilities. And I hope signing this resolution will draw attention not only to the problem but to the solution.

And now, thank you for being here. And I will sign the resolution, and, hopefully, one day we'll sign the legislation.

[*At this point, the President signed S.J. Res. 56 and the proclamation.*]

That does it.

Note: The President spoke at 10:50 a.m. at the signing ceremony in the Cabinet Room at the White House. Also participating in the ceremony were Secretary of Health and Human Services Margaret M. Heckler, Members of Congress, and leaders of child support enforcement organizations.

Proclamation 5080—National Child Support Enforcement Month, 1983
August 5, 1983

By the President of the United States of America

A Proclamation

More than 15 million children are living in families where the father is absent, and nearly one-third of those are living in poverty. More than half the families who should receive court-ordered child support to not receive full payment, thus depriving children of billions of dollars in support each year. In some cases, these unfortunate children are left without the necessities of life.

The American people willingly extend help to children in need, including those whose parents are failing to meet their responsibilities. However, it is our obligation to make every effort to place the financial responsibility where it rightly belongs—on the parent who has been legally ordered to support his child.

For several years, the Federal government has worked with the States to recover child support payments from non-custodial parents. Collections for these children have improved dramatically in recent years, enabling thousands of families to leave the public assistance rolls. Nonetheless, we must work even harder to ensure that all American children are provided the financial support they deserve and to support enforcement personnel, judicial officials, and the legal community in alleviating this problem.

The Congress, by Senate Joint Resolution 56, has designated the month of August 1983 as National Child Support Enforcement Month and has authorized and requested the President to issue a proclamation in observance of that month.

Now, Therefore, I, Ronald Reagan, President of the United States of America, do hereby proclaim the month of August 1983 as National Child Support Enforcement Month, and I call upon all government agencies and the people of the United States to observe the month with appropriate programs, ceremonies, and activities.

In Witness Whereof, I have hereunto set my hand this 5th day of August, in the year of our Lord nineteen hundred and eighty-three, and of the Independence of the United States of America the two hundred and eighth.

RONALD REAGAN

[Filed with the Office of the Federal Register, 10:43 a.m., August 8, 1983]

Appointment of Larry M. Speakes as Assistant to the President
August 5, 1983

The President today appointed Larry M. Speakes to be Assistant to the President. Mr. Speakes will be the President's chief spokesman and will continue to serve as Principal Deputy Press Secretary to the President.

Prior to joining the White House staff as Deputy Press Secretary to the President on January 20, 1981, Mr. Speakes was vice president of the international public relations firm of Hill and Knowlton in 1977–1981. He served as deputy spokesman in the office of the President-elect during transition and was on the communications staff of the Reagan-Bush committee during the 1980 campaign.

Mr. Speakes started his newspaper career in 1961 as editor of the Oxford (Mississippi) Eagle and was managing editor of The Bolivar Commercial in Cleveland, Miss., in 1962–1966. He was general manager and editor of Progress Publishers of Leland, Miss., publishing weekly newspapers in four cities, in 1966–1968. His newspapers won top awards from the Mississippi Press Association for 6 straight years.

Mr. Speakes came to Washington in 1968 as press secretary to Senator James O. Eastland (D-Miss.), serving as spokesman for the Committee on the Judiciary and a coordinator for Senator Eastland's 1972 reelection campaign. During his service with Senator Eastland, Mr. Speakes directed press relations for major Judiciary Committee hearings, including the confirmation of four Supreme Court Justices.

In 1974 Mr. Speakes joined the Nixon administration as a staff assistant to the President and was later appointed press secretary to the Special Counsel to the President. In August 1974, he became Assistant Press Secretary to the President in the Ford administration. During the 1976 Presidential campaign, he was press secretary to Senator Bob Dole (R-Kans.), the Republican candidate for Vice President. When President Ford left office in 1977, Mr. Speakes became his press secretary, serving until June 1, 1977.

Mr. Speakes attended the University of Mississippi, where he majored in journalism. He has received honors and awards, including the Distinguished Journalism Alumni Award from the University of Mississippi in 1981; Kappa Sigma Fraternity National Man of the Year Award in 1982; honorary doctor of letters degree from Indiana Central University in 1982; and the Special Achievement Award for 1983 from the National Association of Government Communicators.

He is married to the former Laura Crawford, has three children, and resides in Annandale, Va.

Appointment of Leslie A. Janka as Special Assistant to the President and Deputy Press Secretary for Foreign Affairs
August 5, 1983

The President today announced his intention to appoint Leslie A. Janka to be Special Assistant to the President and Deputy Press Secretary for Foreign Affairs. He will assume his duties on September 1, 1983.

Mr. Janka has extensive experience in foreign policy and public affairs, having previously served three Presidents. Since 1978 Mr. Janka has been a consultant and lecturer specializing in Middle Eastern defense and international economic issues. He has been associated with the government relations firm of Neill and Co. in Washington, D.C.

He served as Deputy Assistant Secretary of Defense (International Security Affairs) for Near Eastern, African and South Asian Affairs in 1976–1978. Mr. Janka was senior staff member of the National Security Council for legislative and public affairs in 1975–1976. He was staff assistant to Henry Kissinger, then Assistant to the President for National Security Affairs, in 1971–1975. He was assistant dean of the School of Advanced International Studies, The Johns Hopkins University, in 1968–1971, and was a management specialist at the United States Information Agency in 1964–1968.

Mr. Janka graduated from the University of Redlands (California) (B.A., 1962) and the School of Advanced International Studies, The Johns Hopkins University (M.A., 1964). He is a recipient of the Department of Defense Outstanding Performance Award (1977) and the Secretary of Defense Meritorious Civilian's Service Medal (1978).

He was born June 9, 1940, in San Bernardino, Calif. He is married to the former Michele Reichelt and resides in Washington, D.C.

Appointment of Marlin Fitzwater as Special Assistant to the President and Deputy Press Secretary for Domestic Affairs
August 5, 1983

The President today announced his intention to appoint Marlin Fitzwater to be Special Assistant to the President and Deputy Press Secretary for Domestic Affairs. He will assume his duties on September 1, 1983.

Mr. Fitzwater has extensive government public affairs experience, serving as key spokesman in various departments over a period of 13 years. Since 1981 Mr. Fitzwater has served as Deputy Assistant Secretary for Public Affairs at the Department of the Treasury. In that position he served as press spokesman for Secretary Donald T. Regan and the Department of the Treasury. In recognition of his service, he was awarded the Meritorious Executive Award by President Reagan in 1982. Previously he served in the Office of Public Affairs at the Environmental Protection Agency in 1972–1981. During that time he served as spokesman for three Administrators. He served in the Office of the Secretary of Transportation in 1970–1972, as speechwriter for Secretary John Volpe.

Mr. Fitzwater was an advertising executive with the Manhattan (Kansas) Mercury and correspondent for the Topeka (Kansas) Capitol-Journal in 1962–1965.

He graduated from Kansas State University (B.A., journalism, 1965). He was born November 24, 1942, in Salina, Kans. He has two children and resides in Arlington, Va.

Nomination of George E. Moose To Be United States Ambassador to Benin
August 5, 1983

The President today announced his intention to nominate George E. Moose, of Maryland, a Foreign Service officer of Class one, to be Ambassador to the People's Republic of Benin. He would succeed James B. Engle.

Mr. Moose served as an intern with the Department of State in Mexico City in 1966–1967. He was area development officer on detail to the Agency for International Development in Vietnam in 1967–1970 and was political officer in DaNang, Vietnam, in 1970–1971. In 1971–1972 he was personnel officer, Board of Examiners, for the Foreign Service in the Department and political officer in Bridgetown in 1972–1974. In the Department he was foreign affairs analyst in the Bureau of Intelligence and Research (1974–1976), international relations officer (1976–1977), Deputy Director (1978–1979) in the Office of Southern African Affairs, and special assistant in the Office of the Under Secretary of State for Political Affairs (1977–1978). He was foreign affairs fellow on the Council on Foreign Relations in New York City in 1979–1980. In 1980–1983 he was Deputy Counselor for Political and Security Affairs at the United States Mission to the United Nations in New York City.

Mr. Moose received his B.A. degree in 1966 from Grinnell College and attended Syracuse University in 1966–1967. His foreign languages are Vietnamese and some knowledge of French and Spanish. He was born June 23, 1944, in New York, N.Y.

Statement by Deputy Press Secretary Speakes on the Situation in Northern Africa
August 5, 1983

The U.S. has a strong strategic interest in assuring that Qadhafi is not able to upset governments or to intervene militarily in other countries as is currently happening in Chad. Qadhafi has considerable resources, both military and financial, which makes Libya particularly threatening. If Libya or Libyan-supported forces were to gain control of Chad, close U.S. allies such as Egypt and Sudan would be seriously concerned about their own security. Other states in the region would also be deeply worried. It is important to the United States that its allies and friends be able to count upon its assistance to defend themselves against Libyan aggression.

Note: Deputy Press Secretary Larry M. Speakes read the statement during his daily press briefing for reporters, which began at 12:30 p.m. in the Briefing Room at the White House.

Remarks at a White House Luncheon for Hispanic Leaders
August 5, 1983

Ladies and gentlemen, welcome to the White House. It's a pleasure for me to have old friends here, and I know there are some new ones, also. I hope they will be friends. I look out and see so many of you, however, who've been with me in campaigns over the past years, and to each and all of you for all you've done, *muchas gracias*. And for you who played such an important role in getting here, I think at this occasion it's appropriate for me to add, *mi casa es su casa*.

I have to tell you, I remember the first time when I understood the real meaning of that expression. It was during the time I was Governor of California, and we had experienced one of those natural disasters that we have there when it rains a little bit more than usual. So, I visited an area down in the Santa Barbara part of our State where there had been great mudslides. And I was in there to see what the damage does and what we could do and to be of help and perhaps to forestall this happening in the future. And an elderly gentleman of Mexican descent motioned to me and invited me to come into his home. And I did. And there we stood in the wreckage of what had been his living room, both of us knee-deep in the muddy water that was still there in that room. And with the greatest of dignity, he said to me, *"Mi casa es su casa."* [*Laughter*]

Right now, we're just emerging from a time of great economic adversity and national uncertainty. Unlike the old gentleman I just mentioned, what we suffered didn't result from a natural catastrophe or something beyond our control. It wasn't even the result of bad people doing something out of malice or on purpose. Our economic problems were a predictable result of decades of irresponsible government spending and taxing policies. And with your support, we've changed those taxing and spending patterns. And I'm proud to tell you today, it's working.

In fact, just this morning we received new and dramatic evidence of the ongoing economic recovery—great news for all Americans. Unemployment for July is down to 9.3 percent, total unemployment, from 10 percent last month. The number of unemployed declined by 556,000, and the number of employees on payrolls rose by 487,000. And that means that the economic recovery has added 1.7 million new jobs to the economy since last December. Now, the number of long-term unemployed also fell sharply—a decline of 365,000.

And the good news is that jobs spread across the board. The unemployment rate went down in every major category, from every group that you could name, and spread evenly across men and women employees.

You know better than anyone, the unemployment rate for Americans of Hispanic descent has been much higher than the national average—14 percent in June. Well, it's still too high, no question about that. But we've got it down to 12.3 percent.

Now I also understand that many of you come from districts in the country where the national average is not the story in those districts. Unemployment is not evenly distributed according to a national average. Sometimes when we use these figures, it's a little like the man that drowned trying to wade across a river whose average depth was only 3 feet. [*Laughter*]

We know that there are places in this country—and it isn't inclined to any one segment of our society, but due to the kind of employment—where there are still pockets of great and heavy employment [unemployment], and we know this is particularly true along our Southern border, many communities down there. So, we're going to keep on with what we've been doing until we can eliminate those pockets as well.

We know that our economic policies are working, and they are getting Americans back on the job. It hasn't been easy, but we've laid the foundation for a strong, noninflationary recovery that is benefiting all our people. When we got here, inflation was running at double-digit levels and had been doing so for 2 straight years. It was the first time that we'd had back-to-back, double-digit inflation in 60 years in this country. But we've brought it down to where, for the last 12 months, it's been running at 2.6 percent. That's the lowest 12-month rate in nearly 16 years.

When we got here the prime interest rate had hit 21½ percent. Carefully and slowly we brought that down to half that amount. And after years of almost no growth and declining real wages, last quarter the annual growth rate hit 8.7 percent, and real wages are on the rise. Productivity is up. Factory orders are up. Retail sales are up, housing starts and auto sales have turned around. And let me say, this isn't just happening—as some would have us believe—by accident.

We're restoring opportunity to hardworking people like yourselves to get America moving again. There's one way you can tell our program is beginning to work: They don't call it Reaganomics anymore. [*Laughter*] Well, we've managed to give the people a tax rate reduction and to start—because this is a continuing struggle—to get spending under control. And this is no time to let up.

There are those who constantly are pushing to return to the disastrous taxing and spending patterns of the past, and I hope I can count on you to stand with us to make sure that doesn't happen. We can't let the people forget what it was like just 3 years ago. You can remember: Our people seemed to have lost the optimism that is so characteristic of Americans. Some people were saying America's best days were behind us. Well, together we've turned the situation around and given the American people hope for the first time in years.

And before we have a dialog, instead of me just standing up here making a speech, I'd like to mention one other area which is vital to all of us as Americans. You, as Americans of Hispanic descent, know well that our country had ignored Central and South America for too long. If we're to prevent the people of this important area from falling under the heel of Marxist dictators and spreading instability to our own borders, it's going to take a determined commitment. It'll require economic and military aid and national resolve.

Let there be no question in your minds: We're dealing with an issue that affects our national interests. Moreover, alien philosophies are being forced on countries that are ill-equipped to reject them. And so we're standing by our friends. We're using American economic and security assistance in the best tradition of President Truman to protect the forces for democracy, economic opportunity, and peace against the expansion of communism. The difference is President Truman was helping countries thousands of miles away when he had to do this. We're trying to assist nearby neighbors who are only a few hundred miles away. And if we run away from our responsibilities so close to home, it won't be our grandchildren, but our children, who will pay the price. So, I just hope that I have your support in what we're trying to do. It affects us all.

You, as leaders in the Hispanic community, can serve as a bridge to our understanding our neighbors to the South. I hope to work closely with you on this and on other challenges that we face. My representative, Cathy Villalpando,[1] a young woman from Texas, will be keeping me up to date on your ideas and areas of concern.

We have many fine Americans of Hispanic descent, like Cathy, who are playing major roles in this administration. The number stands at 125 right now. And don't let anyone tell you these people are being brought on board because of their ethnic background. They are hard-working, competent people, first and foremost professionals. And that's why they're in those positions, because they were the best available for the job. So, we may like to point out that Hispanics are playing a significant role—Hispanics like Joe Salgado,[2] who comes from California and has been brought to the White House to make personnel decisions—and we're glad to have them. They're fine individuals.

And now we're going to have dessert and coffee, and then we'll have some more communication. And I will get to say, individually, hello to all of you in the other room as we leave here, and I'll get to shake your hands, which I'm looking forward to.

Note: The President spoke at 12:51 p.m. in the State Dining Room at the White House.

Radio Address to the Nation on International Trade
August 6, 1983

My fellow Americans:

I'd like to talk to you today about trade— a powerful force for progress and peace, as you well know. The winds and waters of commerce carry opportunities that help nations grow and bring citizens of the world closer together. Put simply, increased trade spells more jobs, higher earnings, better products, less inflation, and cooperation over confrontation. The freer the flow of world trade, the stronger the tides for economic progress and peace among nations.

I've seen in my lifetime what happens when leaders forget these timeless principles. They seek to protect industries and jobs, but they end up doing the opposite. One economic lesson of the 1930's is protectionism increases international tensions. We bought less from our trading partners, but then they bought less from us. Economic growth dried up. World trade contracted by over 60 percent, and we had the Great Depression. Young Americans soon followed the American flag into World War II.

No one wants to relive that nightmare, and we don't have to. The 1980's can be a time when our economies grow together, and more jobs will be created for all. This was the spirit of the Williamsburg summit in May. The leaders of the industrialized countries pledged to continue working for a more open trading system. But sometimes that's easier said than done.

Take the case of our own economy. Things are looking up for America. Inflation has been knocked down to 2.6 percent. Economic growth in the second quarter reached 8.7 percent, and 1,700,000 Americans have been hired since last December. Yesterday we learned that total unemployment has dropped to 9.3 percent. Nearly 500,000 of our fellow citizens found jobs in July. More Americans are working than any time in this nation's history. This good news restores confidence in our economy and our currency.

---

[1] *Special Assistant to the President for Public Liaison.*

[2] *Associate Director of Presidential Personnel.*

Some people dislike our strong dollar and blame it on our interest rates. Well, we do not want disorderly currency markets, and we've intervened to bring back order to otherwise disorderly markets. But let's remember something. Other countries have higher interest rates than we do, yet their currencies have fallen in relation to ours. One good reason is inflation. It's not the interest you earn from holding a currency that matters most; it's the confidence you have that the value of your money won't depreciate from higher inflation.

America's inflation rate has declined dramatically. Now a strong dollar makes our purchases from abroad less expensive, and that's good.

Winning the war against inflation is probably the best economic legacy we could leave to the next generation. Remember what life was like only a few years ago when the value of the dollar was being talked down and inflation was going through the roof?

But a strong dollar also brings problems. It makes the goods our exporters are trying to sell more expensive. Still, we're tough competitors. Some $200 billion worth of goods were sold by Americans last year. So, do we listen to those who would go back to dead end protectionism and to sabotaging the value of our currency, or do we go forward, keeping our faith in the American people who made this nation the greatest success story the world has ever known?

I believe our challenge is to marshal the power of this country's best minds and create the technology that will restore America's economic leadership. I have appointed a Presidential Commission on Industrial Competitiveness, asking distinguished leaders from business, labor, and academia to advise us on how best to strengthen our ability to compete in world markets.

We believe the U.S. trade position would be strengthened by uniting many of this government's trade responsibilities under one roof, so we proposed legislation to create a department of international trade and industry. We're also taking action to create opportunities for trade.

Ten days ago, our negotiators reached a new, long-term grain agreement with the Soviet Union. Since 1981 we've ended the unfair embargo that had been slapped on American farmers. And now we have an agreement that obligates the Soviets to increase their minimum purchase of wheat— or grain, I should say—by 50 percent.

This, along with the likelihood of substantial purchases from China, represents a major step forward for our farmers. It symbolizes our determination to help them regain the markets they lost. It also proves that while we oppose Soviet aggression, we seek to promote progress and peace between our peoples.

Yesterday I signed legislation to stimulate more trade and opportunity—the Caribbean Basin Initiative. This package of incentives will establish new commercial relationships between the people of the Caribbean and the United States. Stimulating trade will mean new jobs for their citizens as well as ours. It underscores our belief that economic development based on free market principles is the key to helping our neighbors build a future of freedom, democracy, and peace.

Finally, let me mention an important agreement on textiles we've just reached with the People's Republic of China. No free market currently exists in textiles, and only what is called the multifiber arrangement, signed by 46 countries. We're a party to that arrangement, but China is not, and our bilateral agreement with them expired last December. To prevent a flood of imports from harming our struggling textile industry, we imposed unilateral quotas on China's products. They responded with large reductions in their purchases of American farm products.

We faced three options: option 1, end our restrictions on Chinese textiles, which would help our farmers but risk further damage to our textile workers; option 2, cut back Chinese exports even further, which would cost our farmers billions more in lost sales; or option 3, negotiate a tough but fair 5-year agreement with China to permit controlled, moderate growth of Chinese exports. We chose option 3.

Our textile producers can be assured there will be no flood of imports, and they can get on with the task of modernizing their industry, which is the best long-term assurance of jobs for our own people. This new agreement will mean more business for our farmers, and it promises China the opportunity to sell its products here. That's important for good relations between our two countries.

Bit by bit, we're restoring America's reputation as a reliable supplier and as a supporter of free and fair trade for progress and for peace.

Till next week, thanks for listening, and God bless you.

Note: The President spoke at 12:06 p.m. from Camp David, Md.

Nomination of Matthew V. Scocozza To Be an Assistant Secretary of Transportation
August 8, 1983

The President today announced his intention to nominate Matthew V. Scocozza to be an Assistant Secretary of Transportation (Policy and International Affairs). He would succeed Judith T. Connor.

Since 1982 Mr. Scocozza has been serving as Deputy Assistant Secretary of State for Transportation and Telecommunications. Previously he was senior counsel, U.S. Senate Committee on Commerce, Science, and Transportation, in 1977–1982; senior attorney for the Interstate Commerce Commission in 1976–1977; minority counsel for the U.S. House of Representatives, Committee on Appropriations, Subcommittee on Transportation, in 1975–1976; legislative director for Congressman Silvio O. Conte in 1975–1976; and trial attorney for the Interstate Commerce Commission in 1974–1975.

Mr. Scocozza graduated from Murray State University (B.S., 1970) and the University of Tennessee, College of Law (J.D., 1973). He resides in Washington, D.C., and was born October 13, 1948.

Proclamation 5081—Child Health Day, 1983
August 8, 1983

By the President of the United States of America

A Proclamation

More than anything else, we seek the blessing of good health for our children. We hope for the sound minds in sound bodies that lead to lives of strength and achievement.

Through the resources of a health care system second to none, this Nation strives to protect all of our children from preventable diseases, to encourage behavior that fosters good health, and to treat their episodic illnesses.

Unfortunately, some children are burdened with disabilities and chronic illnesses and need long-term healing and care. Their ability to thrive and to contribute to society depends on their receiving the kinds of treatment and health care that are available in this country as in few other places on earth.

Our task on this Child Health Day, 1983, is to fuse our efforts as parents, volunteers, health professionals, and educators to help all children—particularly those with special health needs—take advantage of opportunities that enable them to heal, to grow, and to achieve everything of which they are capable.

Now, Therefore, I, Ronald Reagan, President of the United States of America, pursuant to a joint resolution of May 18, 1928, as amended (36 U.S.C. 143), do hereby proclaim Monday, October 3, 1983, as Child

Health Day, 1983.

I urge all Americans to join me in encouraging good health habits and attitudes in our children and invite all citizens and all agencies and organizations interested in child welfare to unite on Child Health Day with appropriate observances and activities directed toward establishing such practices in the youth of our country.

In Witness Whereof, I have hereunto set my hand this 8th day of Aug., in the year of our Lord nineteen hundred and eighty-three, and of the Independence of the United States of America the two hundred and eighth.

RONALD REAGAN

[Filed with the Office of the Federal Register, 10:43 a.m., August 9, 1983]

Memorandum on the Combined Federal Campaign
August 8, 1983

Memorandum for the Heads of Departments and Agencies

This Administration is committed to helping people help themselves by strengthening private sector initiatives. We have supported the many efforts made by corporations, civic and religious groups, and other voluntary organizations to increase their involvement in meeting the needs of the people in their communities.

As leaders of the Federal government we have a great opportunity to practice what we preach through the Combined Federal Campaign.

Secretary of the Air Force Verne Orr has agreed to serve as the 1984 Combined Federal Campaign Chairman for the National Capital Area. I hope that you will agree to serve as Chairman of the Campaign in your organization and appoint a top official as your Vice-Chairman. Please advise Secretary Orr of the person you designate. Your visible support and active participation in this important program is vital to our success.

I am counting on you to take a personal interest in this year's Campaign, to make a special effort to encourage your employees to achieve greater levels of support than ever before for the programs of the Combined Federal Campaign. This is our chance to serve as an example of American volunteerism and concern.

Our neighbors in need are counting on us. The private voluntary agencies are counting on us. Let our increased giving through the Combined Federal Campaign clearly demonstrate our commitment.

RONALD REAGAN

Memorandum on the Combined Federal Campaign
August 8, 1983

Memorandum for All Federal Employees and Military Personnel

Each year we have an opportunity to show our concern for those in need through participation in the Combined Federal Campaign. The Campaign combines the annual fund-raising efforts of a number of charitable organizations working in the fields of health and social welfare both in the United States and abroad.

Through voluntary giving, we can provide services and programs for our neighbors and countrymen without making them dependent on government. We can help relieve pain and health problems now and support research to help eliminate them in the future. The Campaign also makes it possible to help the less fortunate in other

1137

countries, extending a helping hand to friends around the world.

Federal employees and members of the Armed Services have a proud record of generosity and concern for others. I am confident that record will continue this year. While the amount you give is a personal, voluntary decision, I hope that each of you will join me in supporting the Fall 1983 Combined Federal Campaign.

RONALD REAGAN

Letter to the Speaker of the House and the President Pro Tempore of the Senate on United States Assistance to Chad
August 8, 1983

Dear Mr. Speaker: (Dear Mr. President:)

In recent weeks, the Government of Chad has requested the Governments of France and the United States to assist in its self defense against armed aggression by Libyan forces and Libyan-supported insurgents in Chad. As you have been informed, in response to these requests I have directed that various forms of material assistance be provided to the Government of Chad and other friendly governments assisting it in dealing with this Libyan aggression. In further response to the urgent requirements of these governments to counter this aggression, I have now directed the deployment of certain United States aircraft to the region to be available for the purpose of collecting and providing essential information, including surveillance data and early warning. In accordance with my desire that the Congress be kept informed on this matter, and consistent with Section 4 of the War Powers Resolution, I am hereby providing a report on the deployment and mission of these United States Armed Forces.

On August 7, 1983, two Airborne Warning and Control Systems (AWACS) E3A and eight F-15 (Eagle) all-weather fighter aircraft with air and ground logistical support forces began to arrive in Sudan. These forces will be available to operate in close coordination with the Government of Chad and other friendly governments assisting it. The mission of the F-15 aircraft, which are equipped for combat, is to be prepared to provide protection to the other United States aircraft, if necessary.

It is not possible at this time to predict the precise duration of this deployment of United States Armed Forces in the region. They will remain for only a limited period to meet the urgent requirements posed by the present situation. I will keep the Congress informed as to further developments with respect to this situation.

This deployment of the United States Armed Forces is being undertaken pursuant to my constitutional authority with respect to the conduct of foreign relations and as Commander-in-Chief of the United States Armed Forces. I believe that this action will support the objective of helping to preserve the territorial integrity, sovereignty, and political independence of Chad.

Sincerely,

RONALD REAGAN

Note: This is the text of identical letters addressed to Thomas P. O'Neill, Jr., Speaker of the House of Representatives, and Strom Thurmond, President pro tempore of the Senate.

Statement by Deputy Press Secretary Speakes on the Situation in Chad
August 9, 1983

Libya's forces are centrally involved in the fighting in Chad. In fact, if it were not for Libya's forces—both through advisers and combat elements and air power—there wouldn't be the kind of fighting that we are seeing in Chad.

The precise numbers in a situation like this are hard to come by, but our estimate is that there are 1,500-2,000 Libyan troops in Chad and that this represents a significant increase over the number present in the weeks before the rebel attack on Faya Largeau. There is no question that the Libyan troops are there, including mechanized units; nor is there any question of repeated Libyan air attacks against various northern centers, including Faya Largeau. We have reports that the Libyan troops and Libyan-supported rebels besieging Faya Largeau have a substantial number of Libyan armored vehicles and heavy artillery for bombardment and that their air attacks have included both bombs and napalm.

We consider the situation at Faya Largeau serious and threatening. The Libyan Government seems to be seeking to portray what's happening in Chad as a civil conflict and to portray the Government of Chad as not having legitimacy. The fact of the matter is that the Organization of African Unity has recognized the legitimacy of the Habre government. The most recent OAU statement was one issued in mid-July by the OAU summit bureau calling for an end to foreign interference and appealing for a cease-fire. There is no question in the eyes of the OAU and the majority of African States that Habre's is the legitimate government. Libya would like to have it otherwise. Libya would like to overturn that government and substitute its surrogate as the government of Chad. Were this to happen—if Qadhafi were able to set up an established government simply by using its overwhelming military might to do so—that this would have consequences beyond the borders of Chad.

Our view is that we have provided limited materiel support for the Government of Chad. We have done so in the context of other African support for that government and in a far larger French effort. In all of our contacts, we have no information to suggest that in fact France has changed its position on support of Chad. A French statement over the weekend was subsequently clarified in Paris, and we understand the French position to be that they will make appropriate decisions in light of the situation in Chad. We are operating in the context of African and French support for the Government of Chad.

Remarks of President Reagan and President Abdou Diouf of Senegal Following Their Meetings
August 10, 1983

President Reagan. It's been an honor and a pleasure to welcome President Abdou Diouf to the White House today. And it is especially fitting that our meeting takes place on the 100th anniversary of our American Consulate on the Senegalese island of Goree.

President Diouf is one of Africa's most impressive leaders. He's a peacemaker and problemsolver, whose fine reputation preceded him to Washington. After meeting with him, working with him, and talking to him, I can only say it is a reputation well deserved.

In our conversations this morning and at

lunch, we discussed many important international problems, particularly those of Africa, the Third World, and the Middle East. On many of the issues our views converge; on others we've agreed to differ. We've always done so, however, in the spirit of mutual respect and in the context of a valued bilateral relationship. I have formed a high personal regard for President Diouf's wisdom and integrity, and I value both his views and his counsel.

Senegal and the United States are relative rarities in this troubled world, democratic nations living under the rule of law and devoted to human rights, committed to the search for peaceful solutions for international problems. I've assured President Diouf of America's support for him and for Senegal. I've also expressed our admiration for his accomplishments at home and abroad. In the months ahead, I look forward to both building our personal friendship and stengthening the important ties that bind our two peoples, knowing our relationship can only further the cause of world peace.

President Diouf. I should like, first of all, to thank President Ronald Reagan, to thank the American Government and the American people for the particularly warm welcome that they have extended to me and to my delegation on this my first official visit to the United States. The fact that my visit coincides, as President Reagan so appropriately recalled, with the centennial of the first American Consulate in Goree bears witness to the longstanding relations of friendship and cooperation between Senegal and the United States, two democratic nations attached to respecting human rights and basic freedoms.

The fruitful meetings we had this morning and during the lunch were the occasion for thoroughgoing exchanges of views on strengthening and furthering our bilateral cooperation. I should like to rejoice here, reflecting upon both its quality and its effectiveness. We also discussed major international issues confronting the world of today in Africa, the Middle East, and the Third World. We are agreed, in the spirit of the relationship based on confidence that has been established between our two countries, to pursue and intensify our consultation in order to find the most effective solutions in the interests of peace and international security.

To that end we rely upon the wisdom of President Reagan, a leader whom we admire for his candor and his pragmatism. He has already proved, by his actions inside the United States as well as outside of the United States, that he is a major statesman, fully consistent with the full measure of American people. And I should like to avail myself of this opportunity to renew the assurance that we, the people of the Third World, are following with great interest and comprehension the untiring efforts that he is constantly undertaking in order to secure the triumph of the ideals of peace, democracy, and justice in the world.

Note: President Reagan spoke at 1:17 p.m. to reporters assembled at the South Portico of the White House. President Diouf spoke in French, and his remarks were translated by an interpreter.

Earlier, the two Presidents met in the Oval Office and then held a working luncheon, together with U.S. and Senegalese officials, in the Residence.

Appointment of Gabriele Murdock as a Member of the President's Committee on the Arts and the Humanities
August 10, 1983

The President today announced his intention to appoint Gabriele Murdock to be a member of the President's Committee on the Arts and the Humanities. This is a new position.

Mrs. Murdock is a trustee of the Los Angeles County Museum of Art and serves as a member of the acquisitions and exhibitions committee and the budget and finance committee. She is a member of the board of the Music Center Dance Corp. (Joffrey Ballet).

She is married, has three children, and resides in Los Angeles, Calif. Mrs. Murdock was born November 3, 1941, in Munich, Germany.

Announcement on Measures To Strengthen the United States Arms Control and Disarmament Agency
August 10, 1983

President Reagan this week advised Congress of a number of steps to strengthen the Arms Control and Disarmament Agency (ACDA) and reiterated his determination to pursue effective reductions in nuclear arms. ACDA has key roles in advising the President, the Secretary of State, and the National Security Council on arms control matters and in negotiating arms control agreements with the Soviet Union and other nations. The decisions today follow on the President's announced intentions earlier this year to invigorate the Agency.

The President has asked the Congress to consider an amendment to ACDA's 1984 budget in the amount of $2,095,000. This represents a 10-percent increase over the administration's previously approved request. He has also approved an increase of 25 people in the Agency's personnel level over the next 2 years or an increase of 12 percent.

These additional resources will be used primarily to strengthen the Agency's support for the negotiations to reduce strategic nuclear arms and intermediate nuclear forces and in the verification area. The resources will also provide the Agency with a modern state-of-the-art secure computing capability.

Praising the work of the Agency, the negotiators, and advisers, the President also announced that he would seek legislation to upgrade the Agency's executive positions. The Deputy Director, the START negotiator, and the INF negotiator would be upgraded to Executive Level III, while the Agency's four Assistant Directors would be upgraded to Executive Level IV. This reflects the important role of the Agency's leadership and negotiators. This change will put them on the same level as their counterparts in other U.S. Government agencies.

Together these measures will help the Arms Control and Disarmament Agency fulfill its critical missions.

Designation of 11 Senior Counselors of the National Bipartisan Commission on Central America
August 10, 1983

The President today designated the following individuals to be Senior Counselors to the National Bipartisan Commission on Central America:

Ambassador Jeane J. Kirkpatrick, of Maryland, Representative of the United States of America to the United Nations, who in this capacity will serve as the President's Representative to the Commission

Upon recommendation of the Senate Majority Leader:

Sen. Pete V. Domenici of New Mexico

Sen. Charles McC. Mathias, Jr., of Maryland

Upon recommendation of the Senate Minority Leader:

Sen. Lloyd Bentsen of Texas

Sen. Henry M. Jackson of Washington

Upon recommendation of the Speaker of the House of Representatives:

Repr. Michael D. Barnes of Maryland

Repr. Jim Wright of Texas

Upon recommendation of the House Minority Leader:

Repr. William S. Broomfield of Michigan

Repr. Jack F. Kemp of New York

William D. Rogers, of Virginia, partner, Arnold and Porter

Winston Lord, of New York, executive director, Council of Foreign Relations.

Announcement on the Naming of Two Naval Aircraft Carriers
August 11, 1983

The President has approved Secretary of the Navy John Lehman's recommendation to name the Navy's two new carriers *Abraham Lincoln* (CVN–72) and *George Washington* (CVN–73).

Recalling the enormous contributions the two former Presidents made to our nation's history during difficult periods of war, President Reagan said, "In naming our two carriers after Abraham Lincoln and George Washington we honor their memory, reflect upon their understanding of sea power, and dedicate ourselves to achieving the requisite naval superiority we need today, by building a 15-carrier, 600-ship navy."

When completed, these ships will bring the Navy's deployable carrier strength to 15.

Proclamation 5082—200th Anniversary of the Signing of the Treaty of Paris
August 11, 1983

By the President of the United States of America

A Proclamation

On September 3, 1983, we celebrate the 200th anniversary of the signing of the Treaty of Paris, which brought our War of Independence from Great Britain to a successful and formal conclusion.

When our Founding Fathers boldly declared our independence in 1776, our fledgling Nation began a seven-year struggle for its freedom and survival; at no other time in our history has our security and existance been so severely threatened. Yet we emerged from the Revolutionary War a united and sovereign Nation.

In the Treaty of Paris, Britain formally acknowledged the independence of the United States of America. This "American Birth Certificate" inaugurated an era of peace for the new Nation which led to the adoption of the Constitution of the United States of America on September 17, 1787.

It is only fitting that this Treaty was signed in Paris, the capital of our oldest ally, thereby recognizing the extraordinary role France played in securing the independence of the United States in fulfillment of the obligations it assumed in the Franco-American Alliance of 1778.

The American Peace Commissioners who negotiated the Treaty—John Adams, Benjamin Franklin, and John Jay—carried to Paris the aspirations of a peaceful Nation willing and able to defend its sovereignty. The brave Americans who fought for our Nation's independence ensured that Adams, Franklin, and Jay could negotiate from a position of strength to achieve an agreement with just and equitable provisions. Their efforts gained respect for the United States among nations of Europe and the world—an achievement considered the greatest triumph in the history of American diplomacy.

The Treaty of Paris was the first step toward an alliance with Great Britain which has grown stronger through two centuries to become one of our most important alliance relationships. Political, cultural, economic, and defense ties between our two nations are firm and lasting. The solidarity we and all our allies demonstrated at the recent Williamsburg Summit is the heritage of the Treaty of Paris and confirms again our Nation's willingness to pursue peaceful relations and our desire to befriend those others who share our commitment to democracy and liberty.

In tribute to the remarkable accomplishments of the Treaty of Paris, the Congress of the United States, by House Joint Resolution 321, has authorized and requested the President to issue a proclamation which would designate September 3, 1983, as a day of national celebration of this monumental document.

Now, Therefore, I, Ronald Reagan, President of the United States of America, do hereby designate September 3, 1983, as a day to celebrate the signing of the Treaty of Paris, and I invite the people of this Nation to observe that day with appropriate ceremonies to honor the spirit of peace and liberty which the Treaty represents.

In Witness Whereof, I have hereunto set my hand this eleventh day of August, in the year of our Lord nineteen hundred and eighty-three, and of the Independence of the United States of America the two hundred and eighth.

RONALD REAGAN

[*Filed with the Office of the Federal Register, 10:27 a.m., August 12, 1983*]

Note: The President signed the proclamation at a ceremony in the Roosevelt Room at the White House. Attending the ceremony were Members of Congress, Bernard Vernier-Palliez and Sir Oliver Wright, French and British Ambassadors to the United States, and Joan Challinor, chairman of the National Committee for the Bicentennial of the Treaty of Paris.

Remarks and a Question-and-Answer Session With Reporters on Foreign Policy Issues
August 11, 1983

National Bipartisan Commission on Central America

The President. I've been so used to seeing your tear-stained faces as I pass you by out on the South Lawn.

I have held the first meeting with the—— [*laughter*]. It took a little while, didn't it? [*Laughter*]

I just attended the first meeting with the Commission chaired by Dr. Kissinger, the Commission on Central America, and have explained to them—if any explanation was needed—what it is that we have in mind for that Commission: that I've believed for a long time that this country in the past, even though it has suggested plans for better neighborly relations with the countries in the rest of the Americas, and while the intentions were good, somehow maybe

there was an insensitivity about our size and our suggesting something as a plan that everyone should adopt; that I have been looking for a way in which we could get their cooperation, their ideas, and bring all of the nations of the Americas closer together as equal partners and allies; and that this is the kind of long-range plan to bring this about—to alleviate some of the conditions that have made many of those countries subject to recurring revolutions, because the revolutions have always been—or for the most part have been revolutions that simply changed one set of rulers for another set of rulers.

And I began this before I'd even taken office with regard to our nearest neighbor, Mexico, and to see if we can't make the borders meeting places instead of lines for confrontation or separation. And the very fact that we're all Americans from South Pole to North Pole here in these two continents, with a common pioneer heritage, with a common desire for individual freedom, is such that I just hope that we can begin to bring this about and bring together the more than 600 million people in our two continents and the Isthmus, and that their job would be to start with Central America and see how we could have economic and social reforms that would help bring this about.

Situation in Chad

Q. Mr. President, how far are you willing to go militarily to save Chad from falling into the hands of the rebels backed by Libya?

The President. Well, Helen [Helen Thomas, United Press International], Chad, actually, you might say, is in a sphere of interest of the French. France, because of its historic relationship with that area, has made it plain that they consider this their principal place. We're in consultation with them and we have, in answer to request, provided weapons and some trainers in the use of those weapons.

We are, at the same time now, because of the concern of all the northern African States there, or the central African States about the Libyan intervention—Qadhafi and his adventuring down there have them all concerned, and for that reason, many of the African States are providing troops. We have volunteered to some of them to aid in the transportation of those troops, but we're not in any way in line for participating militarily other than that.

Q. What do you think are the chances, in view of the fall today of Faya Largeau, that Chad will survive under the present regime?

The President. Well, it's a very volatile situation, and I don't know that I could— I'm not going to hazard a guess. But Chad looks so small on the map when you see it pictured so often there. We forget the size of Africa, because if Chad is superimposed on a map of the United States, you find that it's a country that extends virtually from the Mexican to the Canadian border and is a few States wide when it's looked at in that way.

So, Faya Largeau is a city, of course, but it's our understanding, as well as we can get information out of there, that the Habre forces have been withdrawn, that they came out not dispersed or captured or overrun. But again, I have to caution you that any reports we're getting—there are conflicting reports of all kinds coming from there.

But, no, I don't think that this is such a key spot that this marks the imminent end of the war. The reason I gave you the geographical description is that's a long way from the capital, N'Djamena, where the French paratroop forces have gone in and things of that kind.

I'm going to start, as I said before, I'm going to try to start with some back there a little further, because I never get beyond about the first two lines.

Q. Mr. President, would the United States allow Chad to fall to Qadhafi and the Libyans rather than intervene?

The President. As I've said before, it's not our primary sphere of influence; it is that of France. We remain in constant consultation with them, but I don't see any situation that would call for military intervention by the United States there.

National Bipartisan Commission on Central America

Q. Mr. President, I wanted to ask you a question on the Commission. Have you decided whether to retain or remove the Cuban-American member of the Commission while the allegations remain against him?

The President. There is, as you know, a clearance that has to be done for everyone that is appointed to any group of that kind or to any position. And pending such a clearance, which is going on, why, I'm not going to comment about any. I think it is a fine Commission and represents a variety of viewpoints, and I hope that it will be passed intact.

Situation in Chad

Q. Mr. President, you've described Chad as lying within the French sphere of influence. Do you feel the French are, at the moment, doing enough to counter Libyan adventurism?

The President. I have to tell you that I'm not aware of what their plans might be or what it is that they're prepared to do. I know they have introduced ground forces in there, but I'm just not privy to their military planning, and I think that's explainable. I think that they know that the more something is talked about, the more chance there is of leaks, and the leaks in this case could benefit the wrong people.

Q. Mr. President, you have said, though, that you're in consultation, close consultation, with the French. Do you think that it would be helpful if they provided air support to Chad? And should they be providing more than the limited ground forces and the trainers that they've sent already?

The President. Well, as I say, I don't know what their plans are. Frankly, we had believed at first that there was going to be some aerial activity there. Now, I don't know whether they're negotiating at the same time with Libya or not. But I know that we had thought that because part of Libya's forces, and key forces in their first advance, not only have been motorized troops on the ground but have been aerial attacks.

Q. To follow up, sir, why are we so concerned about that part of the world? If it is the French sphere of influence, what is it about Qadhafi and perhaps the Sudan or Egypt, why is this an American concern?

The President. Well, I think the whole attitude of Qadhafi and his empire-building is of concern to anyone, but the main concern is to the surrounding African States. They are all very much alarmed and disturbed because they believe that Qadhafi is intent on adventuring far beyond his own borders, and they believe that they're all under a threat.

U.S. Forces Around the World

Q. Mr. President, are you worried that the United States forces are being stretched too thin around the globe, as I believe the Army Chief of Staff put it recently?

The President. Well, I think what he was pointing out is that in training the military and in planning your own security, you have to consider what are all of the contingencies that could require, for our security, some action by us. And then this is why you have war games in various parts of the world and joint training exercises.

And what he was pointing out, I think, was that today, unlike a previous day when weapons weren't quite of the kind they are now—the world has grown more interdependent—that at one time, and within my lifetime, our principal protection was shore batteries of artillery along our coasts. And I think he was pointing out that our military requirements are different. And in considering the possible contingencies and where we would feel that our security was actually involved is so much more widespread than it has ever been, that our peacetime forces, yes, if they had to be called into action—but I think, also, that's considering that they could be called into action in all those places at once.

Q. Mr. President, the United States now has marines in Lebanon. We have AWACS planes in North Africa. We have a military training mission going on with Egypt. And we have a show of military force in Latin America. And there's an impression now that you are responding to troublespots always in a military fashion. Has there been a change in your approach to problems around the world? Is there a shift in our policy?

The President. I don't think so at all. Under a previous President, a few Presidents back, there was an entire division in Lebanon. This was part of our peace program there. They're not there in a combat state; they're there to help while the Libyan Government—or the Lebanese Government tries to regain control over its own territory. The war games in Egypt that are going on or the practice maneuvers, joint maneuvers, that's an annual thing that we've done for a long time.

Now, I noticed that you changed the tone and said that it was a show of force in Central America. Well, we have held joint maneuvers, both naval and on land, repeatedly with our friends and allies here in the Americas. As a matter of fact, many of you have referred to the one in Honduras as the biggest. It's only about half as big as the one we held within the year in Panama, where there were 10,000 troops involved.

Q. To follow up on that, are you saying that it's not the American role to play policeman around the world?

The President. No, it is not. It is to recognize that the threats can be that widespread, and the threats to our security, because we know, for example, that a great percentage of the strategic minerals that are needed for our industrial might come from various places in the world. The oil that we import—we can't stand by and say that we have no consideration of what might happen in closing off the sealanes that are used by the tankers supplying us with the oil that we must import. So, this is all based on what could be, what could involve our own security.

Ms. Thomas. Thank you, Mr. President.

The President. I was just going to get back into the middle there again.

Q. Are you going to China?

The President. What?

Q. Are you going to China?

Deputy Press Secretary Speakes. Andrea [Andrea Mitchell, NBC News], how many times do I have tell you?

Q. Give us a hint, a hint.

The President. Do you expect me to defy Larry? [*Laughter*]

Q. Sure.

Q. Yes, we do all the time. [*Laughter*]

Note: The President spoke at 2:30 p.m. in the Briefing Room at the White House. Earlier in the afternoon, he met for the first time with members of the National Bipartisan Commission on Central America and several of the Senior Counselors of the Commission.

Proclamation 5083—Minority Enterprise Development Week, 1983
August 11, 1983

By the President of the United States of America

A Proclamation

The entrepreneurial spirit underlies our free enterprise system and is one of the principal sources of America's strength.

Ownership of one's own business is an aspiration held by many Americans. Minority Americans share fully in this aspiration. The success of minority business enterprise demonstrates that hard work and individual determination can serve as a powerful engine for social mobility and economic progress.

As a Nation, we are indebted to minority entrepreneurs for their contributions to our economic well-being. They bring innovative products and services to the marketplace, create jobs, and provide training to thousands of workers.

Our challenge today is to enhance the ability of minority Americans to participate more fully in the market economy and to achieve greater economic independence.

In my December 17, 1982, statement, I promised to designate the first full week in October each year to honor the many valuable contributions minority businessmen and businesswomen make to our society.

Now, Therefore, I, Ronald Reagan, President of the United States of America, do hereby proclaim the week of October 2 through October 8, 1983, as Minority Enterprise Development Week, and I call upon all Americans to join together with minority business enterprises across the country in appropriate observances.

In Witness Whereof, I have hereunto set my hand this 11th day of August, in the year of our Lord nineteen hundred and eighty-three, and of the Independence of the United States of America the two hundred and eighth.

RONALD REAGAN

[*Filed with the Office of the Federal Register, 10:28 a.m., August 12, 1983*]

Executive Order 12437—Fuel Use Prohibitions
August 11, 1983

By the authority vested in me as President by the Constitution and statutes of the United States of America, and in order to eliminate unnecessary administrative burdens and costs associated with the conversion of certain Federal powerplants to alternative sources of fuel, as required by the Powerplant and Industrial Fuel Use Act of 1978 (92 Stat. 3289), it is hereby ordered that Executive Order No. 12217 is revoked.

RONALD REAGAN

The White House,
August 11, 1983.

[*Filed with the Office of the Federal Register, 10:29 a.m., August 12, 1983*]

Memorandum on Competition in Federal Procurement
August 11, 1983

Memorandum for the Heads of Departments and Agencies

Subject: Competition in Federal Procurement

Competition is fundamental to our free enterprise system. It is the single most important source of innovation, efficiency, and growth in our economy.

Yet, far too often the benefits of competition are excluded from the Federal procurement process—a process which now results in expenditures of over $160 billion annually. Numerous examples of waste and exorbitant costs due to the lack of competition have been detailed by the Congress and the press during recent months.

Although efforts have been initiated by this Administration through the Reform '88 Management Improvement Program to correct this longstanding problem, I am convinced that more needs to be done. Consequently, I have directed Don Sowle, the Administrator for Federal Procurement Policy in the Office of Management and Budget, to issue a policy directive on noncompetitive procurement to all departments and agencies. That policy directive will establish government-wide restrictions on the use of noncompetitive procurement and will be reflected in the government's procurement regulations. While such congressionally mandated programs as contracting with minority firms and handicapped persons will not be affected, the unwarranted use of noncompetitive practices must and will be curtailed.

Pending the formal issuance of this new policy by the Administrator, I call upon each of you to assure that competition is the preferred method of procurement in your department or agency.

RONALD REAGAN

Announcement on Actions To Restrict Noncompetitive Procurement Practices in the Federal Government
August 11, 1983

The President today directed that Federal procurement policies be changed to curtail noncompetitive contracting practices, stating that "Competition is fundamental to our free enterprise system."

The President urged that competitive

procurement practices be given preference in agency buying programs. He directed the Administrator for Federal Procurement Policy in the Office of Management and Budget to issue a formal policy directive restricting use of noncompetitive procurement practices. That directive will be issued later this week.

The Presidential action followed a discussion of the nature and extent of noncompetitive procurement practices by the Cabinet Council on Management and Administration on August 4. In his memorandum to the departments and agencies, the President characterized free competition as ". . . the single most important source of innovation, efficiency, and growth in our economy."

He pointed out that "far too often the benefits of competition have been excluded from the Federal procurement process—a process which now results in expenditures of over $160 billion annually." "While such congressionally mandated programs as contracting with minority firms and handicapped persons will not be affected, the unwarranted use of noncompetitive practices must and will be curtailed." At least a third

of all Federal contract dollars are spent without benefit of competition. Under the new policies being proposed, it is estimated that up to $10 billion can be saved annually.

On March 17, 1982, the President issued Executive Order 12352, directing agencies to develop criteria to enhance competition and limit noncompetitive actions. Noting that while the administration had made efforts to correct the longstanding problem of too little competition, the President stated that he was ". . . convinced that more needs to be done."

The action announced today is part of the President's Management Improvement Initiative: Reform 88—a 6-year program to modernize the management practices and administrative systems of government, reducing costs of doing business while maintaining essential public services. Procurement is one of the primary areas targeted for simplification and cost reduction, as reflected in the administration's intention to reduce the number of government procurement regulations by half, through issuance of a single, comprehensive Federal acquisition regulation, expected to be issued next month.

Nomination of Gwyneth Gayman To Be a Member of the National Council on Educational Research
August 12, 1983

The President today announced his intention to nominate Gwyneth Gayman to be a member of the National Council on Educational Research for a term expiring September 30, 1984. She would succeed Bernard C. Watson.

Mrs. Gayman is a former teacher, counselor, and department head at Sun Valley Junior High School in Sun Valley, Calif. She is also a former member of the Los Angeles

Board of Education. She coauthored a text, "Plotting Your Course," for graduating students. She has also been a newspaper columnist.

Mrs. Gayman graduated from the University of California at Los Angeles (B.A.) and received a secondary teaching degree from Los Angeles State College. She resides in La Canada, Calif., and was born March 24, 1914.

Remarks on Signing the Railroad Retirement Solvency Act of 1983
August 12, 1983

Just a few months ago, there was legitimate alarm that the Railroad Pension System would soon run out of money. Without legislative action, rail industry pensions would have been reduced by 40 percent beginning this October. In addition, a second crisis has arisen. The Railroad Unemployment and Sickness Insurance System was so insolvent that the interest on its debt to the Rail Pension Fund would exceed its income. It was time to act and act in a spirit of bipartisan cooperation.

This bill will prevent the drastic rail pension reductions that would otherwise have been necessary to save the system from insolvency. According to the Railroad Retirement Board's actuary, it'll assure the solvency of the Railroad Pension System, at least until the end of the decade. This will be accomplished through real contributions and sacrifices on the part of all parties involved and through Federal participation.

In February, railroad labor and management requested financing changes that provided a sound starting point for designing a solution to the problem. The process of negotiation and compromise needed to devise legislation that would be acceptable to all parties involved railroad employees, railroad management, railroad retirees, and the American taxpayer, and it was long and arduous.

While recognizing the real contributions proposed by the rail-sector participants, Congressman Broyhill, Senator Hatch, and others joined the administration in pointing to the need for further improvements to make the bill fair and equitable to all involved. The Ways and Means Committee recognized the need for additional rail-sector contributions and for measures to address the Rail Unemployment and Sickness Program funding crisis. With the strong leadership of Chairman Rostenkowski, subcommittee chairmen Pickle and Ford, and the active cooperation of Representative

Florio, major improvements were made in the bill. Without their important work and Senator Dole's prompt action in the Senate, we wouldn't be signing this bill today.

None of us would pretend that this bill is perfect. It is a compromise, a reconciliation of differences with a common concern for the need to assure timely payment of full rail pensions to 1 million railroad retirees, the majority of whom are elderly. But given the need for prompt action, it is acceptable to the administration.

While I would have preferred a bill that also resolves the long-term financing problems of the Railroad Unemployment and Sickness Program, this bill will at least put us on the road to real reform of that troubled system.

In the interest of all railroad retirees, I want to thank the people who played such an important role in the development of the legislation. There are so many people who deserve credit for this effort—the members of the Energy and Commerce Committee, the Ways and Means Committee, the Senate Finance Committee, the Labor and Human Resources Committee; and the leadership of the Senate and the House and railroad labor and management were all instrumental. As was the case with the Social Security Commission, the spirit of bipartisanship displayed by all who were involved was the key to developing an acceptable solution.

And now I am pleased to sign the Railroad Retirement Solvency Act of 1983 into law.

Note: The President spoke at 10:15 a.m. in the Rose Garden at the White House. Attending the ceremony were Members of Congress and railroad management and union leaders.

As enacted, H.R. 1646 is Public Law 98–76, approved August 12.

Statement on Signing the Railroad Retirement Solvency Act of 1983
August 12, 1983

I have today signed H.R. 1646, which will prevent drastic railroad pension reductions that would otherwise have been necessary to save the system from insolvency. According to the Railroad Retirement Board's actuary, this bill will assure the solvency of the railroad pension system at least until the end of the decade.

In signing this bill, I wish to note that section 416 of the bill requires the Board concurrently to submit to the Congress any "budgetary estimate, budget request, supplemental budget estimate, or other budget information, legislative recommendation, prepared testimony for congressional hearings, or comment on legislation" whenever it transmits such information to the President or the Office of Management and Budget. The section also specifically prohibits any agency of the United States from requiring the Board to submit this material to any officer or agency of the United States for approval or review prior to transmission to the Congress.

The Attorney General has advised me that such concurrent reporting provisions raise serious issues with respect to the separation of powers under the United States Constitution. Such a provision would be an impermissible violation of the constitutionally required separation of powers if applied to a purely executive agency. However, because it applies to the Railroad Retirement Board, which is an independent agency with quasi-judicial functions, the constitutional issues are less formidable.

Note: As enacted, H.R. 1646 is Public Law 98–76, approved August 12.

Remarks at the Annual Convention of the United States Hispanic Chamber of Commerce in Tampa, Florida
August 12, 1983

The President. Thank you very much, and thank you, Hector. I appreciate the chance to be with you all here today.

Over the last 2½ years, your president, Hector Barreto, and others in the leadership of the Hispanic Chamber have been a tremendous source of advice and inspiration to me. So let me begin by saying to you, Hector, and to all of you for what you stand and for what you've done, *"Muchas gracias."* I can't do too much more in your language—*[laughter]*—than that.

But without you in the business community, where would we be? It's your decisions, investments, and risk-taking that make our country a miracle of efficiency and the envy of the world.

There's a story, you know, about a fellow whose friend was so successful in business that he was opening up a new branch office. And he decided to send a floral arrangement, some nice flowers there for the grand opening. When he got there, he was shocked to find that the wreath that was delivered bore the inscription, "Rest in peace." *[Laughter]* He was angry, and on the way home he stopped in at the flower shop to complain. And he was going at it, and the florist said, "Wait a minute. Just look at it this way: Somewhere in the land today a man was buried under a wreath that said, 'Good luck in your new location.'" *[Laughter]*

But you business men and women of Hispanic descent, you stand for much more than efficiency. I feel very much at home with you. There are people in this blessed land who feel that expressions of love for country and family are old-fashioned. They squirm and get uneasy when we talk about pride in neighborhood and work or speak of religious values. There are people like that.

But you know something? You won't find them in the United States Hispanic Chamber of Commerce.

To every cynic who says the American dream is dead, I say, "Come to the Hispanic business community; come see how entrepreneurs of Hispanic descent are not just building new corporations, they're building America's future for all of us."

Inspirational examples of individual accomplishment abound. Your own president and my friend, Hector Barreto, has an inspiring story that I wish every schoolchild in America could hear. Twenty-five years ago, as a struggling immigrant, he dug potatoes for 80 cents an hour. Today, he owns a piece of the dream. In fact, he owns several businesses, including a successful tile distribution company.

And then there is Lourdes Miranda, born in Puerto Rico, into a family in which neither parent had a formal education. Yet, with persistence and uncompromising desire for excellence, she went to college and then on to doctoral studies at the University of Madrid. She is now president of a highly successful media consulting firm in Bethesda, Maryland.

There's another story of hard work and triumph about a junior high school dropout named Manuel Caldera, a veteran, who later earned his G.E.D. degree. He went on to be an electronic technician and an engineer. And with money he saved and with help from a minority loan program during the Nixon administration, he started AMEX Systems, a company specializing in the development and manufacture of electronic equipment. And today, his company does more than support his family; his company supports 700 employees and earns some $62 million a year in sales.

These few that I've mentioned and others of you right in this room offer us a vision of progress and hope. You prove that with freedom of enterprise comes values that make America more than a rich country— they make us a good country.

I don't have to tell you that when Hector Barreto is not running his own business, he's overseeing a host of community service projects. If I could find out where he gets his energy, I'd package it and bring it back to Washington. [*Laughter*]

Nor has Lourdes Miranda's success dampened her concern for others. Her company provides specialized training for young Hispanic women. Last year she helped train 40 women to qualify for job opportunities in today's market.

In a fine example of a private sector initiative, Manuel Caldera's company contributes $500 a month to an orphanage in Tijuana, Mexico. And each year, he personally gives to Whittier College for scholarships that enable students of Hispanic descent to study science and engineering.

These are not unusual stories. They are, instead examples of a byproduct of freedom that is always present but often unnoticed— respect and concern for others. Business men and women realize that success depends on fulfilling the needs of others and doing it courteously and efficiently. And by doing for others, you are also achieving for yourself.

This system of ours has produced the most material abundance, the greatest freedom, and the most compassionate country in the history of mankind. Our people came here from every corner of the world, from every ethnic background, and every race and religion seeking freedom and opportunity. Our history isn't perfect, but we can be proud of our country. And Americans of Hispanic descent can be particularly proud of the contributions they have made and are making to the well-being of this nation.

Today it's my special honor to present your award to the Hispanic business man and woman of the year. So, if Hector will join me, I'd like to ask—I *would* like to ask Manuel Caldera, but I can't; his plane was delayed and so, instead, Sergio Banuelos is going to accept in his behalf—and ask Lourdes to stand up here with us and receive these awards.

I have been mispronouncing it, haven't I? Lourdes.

Ms. Miranda. Yes, you have, Mr. President. [*Laughter*]

The President. It's Lourdes. Thank you, Hector. I told you I wasn't too good in your language. [*Laughter*]

Ms. Miranda. You're doing very well. Thank you.

The President. Well, congratulations.

Ms. Miranda. Thank you very much.

The President. You know, maybe I've told this to some of you before, but this whole matter of language difficulties—some years ago when I was Governor, I was speaking in Mexico City. And I sat down to rather unenthusiastic and not very impressive applause, and I was a little embarrassed. Then a gentleman—it was worse when a gentleman followed me and started speaking in Spanish—which I didn't understand—but he was being applauded about every paragraph. So to hide my embarrassment, I started clapping before everyone else and longer than anyone else until our Ambassador leaned over to me and said, "I wouldn't do that if I were you. He's interpreting your speech." [*Laughter*]

But I believe that all of us share a sacred responsibility to maintain the opportunity and the freedom that we've enjoyed and to pass it on to future generations. Our task hasn't been easy. We're just now emerging from an economic crisis so severe that it would have robbed our children of the America that we all know and love.

Three years ago the ominous signs were everywhere. The world seemed to be counting us out, saying America's best days were past. Even our leaders were throwing up their hands, suggesting we were in a malaise, was the word they used, and our problems were unsolvable.

Well, it's taken patience and hard work. Entrenched policies were squeezing the life out of our economy, and basic change was essential. But I'm pleased to report to you today, America has made a new beginning. This great nation is moving forward again, and we're not turning back.

When we got to Washington 2½ years ago inflation was running at double-digit levels and had been doing so for 2 straight years—the worst performance in 60 years. Well, we've knocked that inflation from double digits down to 2.6 percent for the last 12 months, the lowest it has been for 12 months in 16 years. And for all their talk about compassion, those who call themselves liberal gave us a terrible inflation that would have devastated millions had we permitted it to continue. And today, a family of four earning $25,000 has $600 more in purchasing power than in 1980.

But let me just interject here that there is another figure that has just come out today that I think you should hear. One of the things that I tried to stress in those things we were doing, laying the groundwork for the economic recovery, was that this time we had to do the job right—a solid, sustained, noninflationary recovery that would last. Well, today, this other piece of news is we are on the right track. The Bureau of Labor Statistics announced the Producer Price Index—Consumer Price Index for 12 months: 2.6—the Producer Price Index of finished goods has risen only 1.4 percent over the last 12 months, and that's the lowest for a 12-month period in 16 years.

We are launched into a solid recovery. Just before I took office, the prime rate hit 21½ percent, and there were loud cries for a quick fix. Well, we didn't heed the hysteria. We followed common sense. Today the prime interest rate stands at 11 percent. There will be slight fluctuations like we experienced this week, but if the Congress acts responsibly with regard to spending, interest rates will come down more.

When we took office, America was suffering from years of wasteful, uncontrolled spending and taxing. Federal spending was growing at a rate of 17 percent. We've cut that increase by 40 percent.

Paying for all that spending had doubled the Federal tax in just 5 years, between 1976 and 1981. Average working people were being taxed at rates that were once reserved for the wealthy, only a short time before. In these last few years, we have cut personal income tax rates by 25 percent, and soon they will be indexed so that the Federal Government will never again profit from inflation at your expense.

And I don't have to tell you business people about the burden of excessive Federal regulation. Under the direction of Vice President Bush, we have cut 300 million man-hours off the processing of needless redtape and paperwork that was demanded by government.

The cumulative effect of our efforts is just now being felt, and the signs are good. Consumer spending is up. Productivity is up. Industrial production, retail sales, auto sales, housing and construction are all up since the beginning of the year. Last quarter, the economy grew by 8.7 percent, a much bigger jump than any of us had expected or predicted.

One of the last indicators to turn around is unemployment. I feel deeply about the suffering of the unemployed, and don't let anyone tell you differently. I went through looking for a job in the Great Depression of the thirties. Do you think that going back to the policies that dragged our economy down and set fire to inflation will really help the unemployed? Or would you agree that the best way to help all Americans is to continue the reforms that have brought down inflation, interest rates, taxes, and that last month gave us the biggest monthly drop in unemployment in almost 24 years?

In these 2½ years, we have fundamentally changed the direction of government in America. We were headed toward ever-increasing government control, toward a society where power and decisions would be controlled not by you the people, but by a faceless central authority. Permit me to ask you one more question. Is that the America you want to live in and leave to your children? Or do we want to live in a society where all people have the right to make decisions for themselves?

Here again, the Hispanic Chamber is playing a significant role. You have provided a valuable resource to your community, bridging the gap between major corporations and government, making certain that your enterprises and business people have the technical assistance and the contracts they need to compete. In only 5 years, the number of Hispanic-owned firms has jumped 65 percent to some 363,000 businesses, generating about $18 billion in sales per year.

My administration remains firm in its commitment to expanding minority-owned business. And through the strong efforts of the Small Business Administration, which has as its Deputy Administrator, Eddie Herrera, and through our commitment to minority procurement, we've put our money where our mouth is.

Let me answer some of the criticisms that are being hoisted and thrown around, and let's make one thing plain. Our goal isn't welfare or handouts, it's jobs and opportunity. [*Applause*]

Thank you very much. You have just sent a message to some people that need to hear it in Washington, D.C.

If we can prevent our country from being drawn back to the policies of tax, spend, and inflate—policies that knocked the wind out of our economy in the first place—we'll be on our way to a new era of growth and expansion that will better the life of every American. With the energy and enthusiasm I sense in this room, I predict Americans of Hispanic descent will be leading the way. Let us join together today to accept a great challenge. And the challenge is to double the number of businesses owned by Americans of Hispanic descent and to do it in the next 4 years.

What we are struggling to build, however, is much more than a society of wealth. You need only to look around the world to see the relationship between economic freedom and political and social freedom. Nations with government-controlled economies usually have government-controlled speech, religion, and press, as well. Some of you here know that from personal experience.

And of course, some people believe that governments should dominate human action and that individuals must live like sheep. Such people don't believe in the political and social freedoms that we hold dear. They are contemptuous of the worship of God. That philosophy is alien to this hemisphere and has brought deprivation and tyranny wherever it's gained a foothold.

No better example exists than Cuba. Under Castro's rule, Cuba has become the economic basket case of the hemisphere. The Cuban Government sells its young men as Soviet cannon fodder in exchange for a massive subsidy without which it couldn't survive. The Cuban people have been betrayed. They have neither freedom nor material goods. The only things abundant there today are slogans, weapons, repression, and shortages. Food and the necessities of life are severely rationed.

You know, I have to interrupt and tell you something, 'cause I just heard a little joke that I think some people in Cuba are telling. [*Laughter*] Castro was making a speech to a large audience, and he said, "They say that I am—accuse me of intervening in Angola." And a man going through the audience said, "Peanuts, popcorn!" He said, "They say that I'm intervening in Mozambique," and the same voice said, "Peanuts and popcorn!" And he said, "They say I'm intervening in Nicaragua." "Peanuts and popcorn!" And by this time he's boiling mad, and he said, "Bring that man who's shouting 'peanuts and popcorn' to me, and I'm going to kick him all the way to Miami." [*Laughter*] And everybody in the audience started shouting, "Peanuts and popcorn!" [*Laughter and applause*]

Thank you.

Cuba's repression and economic failure, seriously, are consistent with what has happened in every Communist country. Jamaica flirted with radical socialism, and it turned a tranquil, peace-loving country with great economic potential into a bitterly divided, impoverished society. It's a tribute to the freedom-loving Jamaicans that they withstood the totalitarian temptation and are now rebuilding their country's prosperity with the tools of freedom and democracy.

Today, our nation is confronted with a challenge of supreme importance. A far-away totalitarian power has set its sights on our friends and neighbors in Central America and the Caribbean. If we don't meet our responsibilities there, we'll pay dearly for it.

The security aspect of this challenge must be addressed. Those who suggest otherwise are courting disaster. So, we're helping our friends to defend themselves, and we will continue to help them, showing them we'll stand by them in their hour of need.

But let's get one thing straight. Those who claim our support is only of a military nature are building a huge strawman. Security assistance is not the essence of our approach to Central America and the Caribbean. I don't know how many times it must be repeated before the message gets through: Three out of every four dollars we send to the region are in the form of economic aid. From the early days of this administration, we've been promoting democracy, dialog, and economic progress in Central America and the Caribbean.

When I got to Washington, one of the first heads of state to visit the White House was Jamaica's Prime Minister Seaga. He was anxious to build his economy and, together, we worked out a program to encourage private sector investment. By turning his country away from socialism, Prime Minister Seaga has ended 7 years of economic decline that plagued his people. One hundred sixty-two new investments have been made to date, providing the potential for thousands of new jobs.

Our Caribbean Basin Initiative is designed to bring the power of private enterprise—America's most potent weapon—to help build Central America and the Caribbean. I was finally able to sign this important legislation just 1 week ago, after too long a wait.

As far as I'm concerned, too much politics has been played with what should be our role in Central America. When it comes to keeping our country safe, there must be no Republicans, no Democrats, just Americans. [*Applause*]

Thank you.

Our AID [Agency for International Development] program continues to do some great work in developing the potential of the region's private sector. In Honduras, a team of private sector experts sent by AID helped that country reorganize its forest management, permitting it to protect its resources while reaping the benefits of valuable timberland. I had the honor of personally handing the report of the task force to President Suazo of Honduras.

In the Dominican Republic and Haiti, where swine fever disease threatened their entire pork production, AID helped them eradicate the dreaded disease.

In Jamaica, AID helped finance an aquaculture project that when fully implemented will provide a new cash crop from fish ponds, just as it's providing loans, capital, to numerous small business enterprises in other developing Latin American countries.

In Guatemala, AID teams with scientific know-how showed farmers how to use less fertilizer and still double their crops.

Similar efforts are being made in El Salvador, where AID-financed technical assistance is helping tens of thousands of new landowners under the agrarian reform program to learn how to manage their land and increase their income.

And there in El Salvador, as is true in other countries in the region, the AFL–CIO's American Institute for Free Labor is playing an admirable role, both in assisting the land reform process and in providing guidance in the creation of a free union movement.

I'm also aware of what the Hispanic Chamber is doing to strengthen our ties with your business counterparts to the South. I applaud you for your international trade conference, held in Guadalajara, and the initiative that you are demonstrating in the Western Hemispheric Congress of Latin Chambers of Commerce and Industry.

But much more of this information should be given to the American public. We're in the midst of a long overdue awakening. The time has come when all us in the Americas, in the Western Hemisphere, can and must recognize our common bonds. Most of us are descended from pioneers, people with the courage to leave the familiar and start again in a new world. We came here in search of a dream, looking for freedom and a better life. We worship the same God. From the tip of Tierra del Fuego to the north slopes of Alaska, we are all Ameri-

cans, a new breed of people.

And what a mighty force we can be for good if we work together and use our combined potential. There have been mistakes made in the past, but we can overcome those mistakes because what binds us together is far stronger than what divides us.

I have a vision of a united hemisphere, united not by the arbitrary bonds of state but by the voluntary bonds of free ideals. Today you, our citizens of Hispanic descent, can be a bridge to our neighbors in the south. We have much to do together as Americans and as citizens of the hemisphere. And with God's help, there is nothing that we cannot accomplish.

Thank you for having me with you, and *vaya con Dios* [God be with you].

Note: The President spoke at 2:31 p.m. in the Regency Ballroom at the Tampa Hyatt Regency Hotel. The convention and International Business Exchange was attended by approximately 5,000 representatives from government, the corporate sector, and the Hispanic business community in the United States, Mexico, and other Latin American countries.

Following his remarks, the President went to the Marriott Hotel in El Paso, Tex., where he remained overnight.

Message to the House of Representatives Returning Without Approval a 1984 and 1985 Feed Grain Programs Bill
August 12, 1983

To the House of Representatives:

I am returning herewith without my approval H.R. 3564, "To require the Secretary of Agriculture to make an earlier announcement of the 1984 crop feed grain program and of the 1985 crop wheat and feed grain programs."

H.R. 3564 directs the Secretary of Agriculture to announce the 1984 and 1985 feed grain programs no later than September 30 of the preceding year and to announce the 1985 wheat program no later than July 1, 1984. Current law sets Novem-

ber 15 as the announcement date for feed grains; the wheat program announcement date in current law is August 15. Thus, in each case the announcements would have to be made approximately six weeks earlier than the current law now requires.

The main purpose of acreage adjustment programs is to assist producers in adjusting supplies to meet demand. When projecting the supply/demand situation for the next crop year, it is essential to have the best possible information about the current crop year, while giving due consideration to producers' planning needs. Sound estimates of production as well as timely announcements are a vital component for designing successful programs. Good program design ultimately serves the best interests of producers, consumers, and taxpayers.

The Administration is sympathetic to the need for making acreage adjustment program announcements as early as possible. When conditions warrant, the Secretary of Agriculture will continue the ongoing practice of announcing commodity programs before the statutory deadlines. However, when the appropriate program decision is not obvious, it is essential that the Secretary retain the discretion to announce wheat as late as August 15 and feed grains as late as November 15.

This flexibility will enable the Secretary to respond quickly to unforeseen circumstances, such as drought or early frost. Without this flexibility, the mandate in H.R. 3564 could either exacerbate a surplus supply situation and needlessly increase budget outlays by substantial amounts or unnecessarily create a grain shortage and cause food prices to increase sharply.

RONALD REAGAN

The White House,
August 12, 1983.

Note: For the President's statement on signing a feed grain programs bill, see page 1390.

Radio Address to the Nation on the Situation in Central America
August 13, 1983

My fellow Americans:

I'm speaking to you from El Paso, Texas. Tomorrow, I'll be in Mexico, meeting with President de la Madrid.

Earlier this week I met with the new national, bipartisan Commission on Central America. The Commission will look at long-range issues and recommend a truly national approach to them.

One thing especially impressed me. The Commission members are all distinguished, well-educated people, but they've made their first task a concentrated study of Central America. Professor Kissinger has promised to make their learning program a tough one. I mention this because the polls say many Americans are confused about what we're supporting in Central America and about why that region, so close to home and to our strategic trading arteries, is important to us.

The mail I receive tells the same story. Well, my staff recently put together a composite letter that combines the most widespread misconceptions. It goes like this:

"Dear Mr. President: The United States has not learned any lessons from history. We refuse to understand the root causes of violence and revolution. El Salvador proves that we continue to support ruthless dictators who oppose change and abuse human

freedom. And by refusing to deal decently with the Sandinista government in Nicaragua, we have forced it into the arms of Cuba and the Soviet Union. Military measures will just make things worse. Anyway, democracy can't work in Central America." End of composite letter.

Sound familiar? I'm sure you've heard it all before. But let's look at what is really happening.

We have learned from history. Years of poverty and injustice in Central America are a root cause of the violence. That's why our economic assistance there is greater, three times greater than our military aid.

We are on the side of peaceful, democratic change in Central America, and our actions prove it daily. But we aren't the only ones interested in Central America. The Soviet Union and Cuba are intervening there, because they believe they can exploit the problems so as to install ruthless Communist dictatorships, such as we see in Cuba.

We are not supporting dictators either of the far right or the far left. We're working hard with Costa Rica and Honduras, which are true democracies, and we're helping El Salvador to become one. Only democracy can guarantee that a government will not turn against its own people, because in a democracy, people are the masters of government, not the servants.

Now, it's true that some members of El Salvador's security forces still misuse their public trust. You can't instantly erase something that's been going on for a century or more. But we deplore even passive acceptance of such actions, and I can assure you great progress is being made. Can anyone really believe that the situation would improve if our influence for moderation were removed?

Commitment to human rights means working at problems, not walking away from them. And there are many brave Central Americans who, at great personal risk, are working to end these abuses. President Magaña of El Salvador is such a man.

That brings me to Nicaragua. We have dealt decently with Nicaragua, more decently than the Sandinista government there has treated its own citizens and neighbors. The Sandinistas were not elected. They seized power through a revolution that, true enough, overthrew a dictatorship, but then the Sandinistas betrayed their repeated promises of democracy and free elections. They betrayed many who fought beside them in the revolution, and they've set up a Communist dictatorship. Having seized power, the Sandinista bosses revealed they had chosen sides with Cuba and the Soviet Union a long time ago. We did not push them into that camp.

Unfortunately, there have been such distortions about U.S. policy in Central America that the great majority of Americans don't know which side we're on. No wonder a great many sincere people write angrily that we should support regional dialog, emphasize economic assistance, or take any number of other actions, all of which we're already doing and have been doing for more than 2 years.

Well, it's time to get away from fairy tales and get back to reality. We support the elected Government of El Salvador against Communist-backed guerrillas who would take over the country by force. And we oppose the unelected Government of Nicaragua, which supports those guerrillas with weapons and ammunition. Now, that, of course, puts us in sympathy with those Nicaraguans who are trying to restore the democratic promises made during the revolution, the so-called *contras*.

Our neighbors in the Americas are important to us, and they need our help. We're working hard to provide economic and political support for development so that ballots will replace bullets in that troubled region. That's the reason for the Caribbean Basin Initiative and all our economic assistance. At the same time, we're helping our neighbors create a defensive shield to protect themselves from Communist intervention while they go forward with economic reform. We do this by providing training, assistance, and firm demonstrations of our resolve to deter Communist aggression. And that's the reason for the bipartisan commission, which has now begun its work.

If we all look calmly at the facts, we can unite to protect our national interests and give our neighbors the help they need without spooking ourselves in the process.

Till next week, thanks for listening, and God bless you.

Note: The President spoke at 10:06 a.m. from the Marriott Hotel in El Paso, Tex.

Remarks at the Annual Convention of the American G.I. Forum in El Paso, Texas
August 13, 1983

Thank you very much, Ernie, for those kind words.

Our chairman, Mr. Ambassador, reverend clergy, your national head, Jose Cano, Senator Tower, the very distinguished guests here at the headtable, and you ladies and gentlemen:

Let me say right off that our administration knows how responsive the man you've honored here, John Tower, is to the concerns of the G.I. Forum. John is easily one of the most experienced and powerful Members of the Senate. He's been a great friend to you. He's one of the major reasons America is moving toward strength and prosperity. And I join you in saluting Senator John Tower today.

But seeing John and all of you is a great pleasure. You know, it's an odd thing, but the farther we get from Washington, the better I feel. As a westerner, of course, I feel at home here in Texas. For one thing there is the food. You know about my inclinations in this area. After all, we served enchiladas to the Queen of England. And sometimes when a Cabinet meeting starts to drag, I wonder what would happen if the jellybean jar there and the Cabinet table was filled with jalapeño jellybeans. [*Laughter*] I'm thinking of trying it one of these days.

But I relish every stop we make while we're on the road. But I have to tell you that this gathering today is one I've especially looked forward to. Speaking to the G.I. Forum gives me a chance to do something that not many American Presidents have done: to say something important to all Americans of Hispanic descent, something that should have been said a long time ago.

The G.I. Forum was founded by Hispanic Americans who wore our country's uniform, who fought in our wars, who account for some of the most astonishing acts of valor and personal sacrifice in the great and long history of our nation's Armed Forces. I don't think I have to recount those deeds to you. I know you're proud of them, and I know they are part of the proud heritage that you pass on to your children. And that's why I thought you might like to know about something that happened recently in Washington—something that says a lot about the courage and contributions of Hispanic Americans to our freedom.

The Pentagon has a wonderful tradition of dedicating their hallways to some of our greatest military figures. Now, like myself, most of you who were in the military probably didn't spend much time in the Pentagon during your careers. But, as President,

I've had a chance to see some of the exhibits and memorabilia in those corridors dedicated to great men like Generals MacArthur and Eisenhower.

Every citizen should know Americans of Hispanic descent have an impressively high, if not the highest honor recipient for their representation in the military. There is a permanent exhibit at the Pentagon, not to a single person, but to these 37 men of valor—names like Lucian Adams, Jose Lopez, Cleto Rodriguez, Rodolfo Hernandez, Joseph Rodriguez, Louis Rocco, and Roy Benavidez. And I'm proud to tell you today that just last week, Secretary Weinberger opened a new exhibit near the Hall of Heroes with a portrait depicting each of these American heroes of Hispanic descent. It is a real crowd-pleaser. I hope many of you have a chance to visit it. But whether you get there or not, remember one thing: That exhibit—your exhibit—is an inspiration to all the American people.

The exhibit is only a small sign of what I see when I visit our military installations or ships throughout the world—Hispanic names and faces everywhere. For me, those names are a sign of all you've given and continue to give to America. America has always been blessed by the diversity of our people and the rich heritages they brought to our shores. But the contribution of Hispanic Americans—your devotion to country, your belief in the values of family, work, neighborhood, and religion—these are among our most precious gifts.

And so today, as perhaps the first President who's had the chance to say it, and on behalf of every American—I want to thank Hispanic Americans who have served so valiantly in our Armed Forces, and who serve today. Yours is a record of honor and devotion that makes not just you but every American proud.

And maybe we should be reminded that these gentlemen up here, holders of the Congressional Medal of Honor, it is given for service above and beyond the call of duty. But you know better than most that Hispanic Americans have not always been remembered for their service or valor, have not always been treated with the dignity, respect, and fairness they deserve. This was particularly true at the end of World War II, when those who had fought for their country returned home to confront discrimination in education, health care, housing, employment, and other areas. But true to your tradition, you responded with character and courage.

One of your number, Dr. Hector Perez Garcia, a physician and surgeon in Corpus Christi, founded this forum, and under his leadership, veterans gathered to fight for the rights of Americans of Mexican descent. Within a year's time, there were over 100 chapters in Texas alone. Word of your courage and success spread throughout neighboring States, and then the entire Nation. And today you have 500 chapters in approximately 200 cities in 33 States upholding the rights of Hispanic Americans.

As you fought for your rights everywhere, you helped preserve the dream that began this country: the dream of government that worked for the people, and not the other way around; the dream of equal justice under the law; of the right of every man, woman, and child to enjoy the blessings of liberty, not as a function of their class or background, but only because they bore the simple title—that proudest of all boasts: "I am an American." Your fight against discrimination was every American's fight. Your efforts made America better for all of us, and today, on behalf of all your countrymen, I thank you for that too.

As Americans of Hispanic descent take their rightful place in the front ranks of our nation's leadership, I know you will always remember those who began so much in Texas 35 years ago. Dr. Garcia, all of us pay tribute to you today. I speak for everyone here when I say to you, sir—and I hope I can get this right—*Usted es un gran líder de su pueblo* [You are a great leader of your people].

With my inability at languages, you may not have to translate that for the Anglos; you may have to translate it for the Hispanics. [*Laughter*]

Now, I don't need to tell you the struggle against discrimination is never over, and this administration will stand beside you as you continue the struggle. We have appointed more than 125 Hispanics to key positions in this administration. And our Justice Department is ever alert to safeguard your civil rights and those of all Americans.

Let me just say a word about our excellent relations with the G.I. Forum. They begin with the efforts of one outstanding individual, your chairman, Jose Cano. Now, he and I may not always agree, but we've worked well together to accomplish a great deal and my pledge to him is my pledge to you: You have a friend in Washington. As long as I am there, the Oval Office will be a place of warmth and hospitality for Hispanic Americans.

Ladies and gentlemen, the concern that you've shown for justice for your own people is the best tradition of America. You should be especially proud that even in the seventies, when the demands of special interest politicians were in full cry, you always advanced your own cause within the framework of advancing your country's interest first.

Now, we've just emerged from the era of special interests, a sad time when coalitions were built with an eye toward the next election, not what's good for the country. Some would have us forget what that kind of politics did to us, especially to those at the bottom of the socioeconomic ladder. It was those Americans—many of them of Hispanic descent—who suffered most from the economic mess that was left to us in 1980. It was they who were deprived of the only chance they ever really wanted: the chance to show how far their faith, dreams, and talents could take them in a free society.

Today, many who still practice the politics of the past would take you back to the days of lost opportunities, special interest politics, tax and tax, spend and spend. Well, let me remind you what those days were like. In the 1970's, it was special interest politics that tripled Federal spending and special interest politics that doubled Federal taxes in just 5 years, between 1976 and 1981. All that big spending and taxing drained life and energy from the economy. Opportunities dried up, and lower income Americans found it harder to make ends meet.

Think back to those desperate days when paychecks grew smaller and the grocery bills grew higher and higher. In 1980 we had the worst inflation since the Second World War, the highest prime interest rate—21½ percent—in more than a century, soaring taxes, and rising unemployment. But what had you heard from those in Washington: that you suffered from a malaise, that it was your fault, that you wanted too much, that you had to give up your hopes and tell your children not to dream as you once dreamed.

The bureaucratic profiteers were in full control. Even as the economy was collapsing around them, they could only come up with more and more schemes to superintend their disasters and run our lives—even down to restricting credit cards and supervising thermostats.

But there's a strain of pride, independence, and common sense that runs through this country which no fast-talking, chicken-in-every-pot politician has ever really escaped for long. From the very beginning of this country, our people have had an uncanny knack for reminding politicians who's really in charge here, who it is under the American Constitution that has the final say. And so the people spoke. They spoke for the future and their children's future. They spoke for change.

And that's when we went to work, even as the special interest politicians predicted doom and disaster. They said we couldn't do it—indeed, they fought us all the way—but we cut the growth in Federal spending by 40 percent. They said we couldn't do it—they fought us all the way—but we cut every American's tax rates by 25 percent. They said we couldn't do it—they fought us all the way—but we came up with the most important reform of them all. In 1985 your income tax rates will be indexed, so that never again will you be pushed into higher tax brackets just by inflation, by which government profits.

In a little over 2½ years we've moved from economic disaster to economic growth. Sure we have a long way to go, but look at the results coming in: The prime rate is down by nearly half; inflation is down by 80 percent; the economy grew last quarter at an annual rate of 8.7 percent; purchasing power is going up; and more Americans are now working than ever before in the history of the United States.

But you know there's an easier way that you can tell that our program is working. Our critics don't call it Reaganomics anymore.

But let me touch on one more important area where we're moving forward, trying to make things better. When I visited San Antonio in May I expressed my concern about the impact of the peso devaluation on the people of southern Texas and the border areas of other States. I said this is not just your problem; it's our problem, and we'll meet it together. Well, that's exactly what we're doing.

I designated a southwestern border States working group to study the problems and give me recommendations. They have done that just a few days ago. And I am pleased to announce that today we are ready to move.

I have just asked the Vice President to oversee the establishment of an interagency action group. We are determined to coordinate every government program we can tap to mitigate economic hardship in your border regions. We will work with your State and local leaders to help stimulate jobs and diversify your economies, and we'll start doing it not next year or next week—today.

I believe that we're beginning to restore hope and confidence in America. And it doesn't stop with the economy. Remember a few years ago when American prestige seemed to decline with every new crisis, when Soviet intervention on four continents was going unchecked, even unnoticed? Remember when American Embassies were sacked, when our hostages were taken, when our government seemed to be intimidated by every two-bit dictator in this hemisphere and elsewhere? Remember how our national defenses were crumbling?

Well, today our defenses are being rebuilt. The Soviet Union's attempts to dominate the world are being checked, and we have begun hard bargaining that can result in realistic and verifiable arms control treaties.

Let me say something here about a foreign policy area I know you have a special interest in. Our policy in Central America can be very simply put and clearly understood: We want to see the peoples of those nations escape the poverty and oppression of their pasts; we want to see them move toward societies where democratic and human rights are protected and where a decent standard of living is assured. We will bend every effort through economic and technical assistance to help them accomplish this goal. But I know that you'll agree with me that they'll never have a chance to build their future of freedom and prosperity if they're surrendered to the tender mercies of Fidel Castro, Colonel Qadhafi, and their superintendents in Moscow. We can't let that happen; we won't let it happen.

The goal of our policy south of the border is plain: The Americas belong to the peoples of the Americas and nobody else. And we're all Americans. From the South Pole to the North Pole—and no other place on Earth can say this—all of us in the more than 30 countries of this Western Hemisphere are Americans.

Yes, we respect and we honor our national sovereignty and we're loyal, each to our own countries, but where else in the world do you cross a border as you can here into another nation and still be among Americans?

Now, I realize the naysayers and doomcriers are not tripping over each other to give us credit for a stronger foreign policy, updated defenses, or economic recovery, and I can sympathize with them—just think of all those campaign speeches that would have to be rewritten. The special interest politicians may forget that the record is clear. Because Americans didn't take no for an answer, they believed in their future, rejected counsels of retreat and supported this administration's efforts to get our measures through the Congress, America is growing in pride and strength at home and abroad.

It seems to me that those naysayers have some explaining to do. They are the ones who said we couldn't do it, but we did it. They're the ones who said it wouldn't work, but it's working. And always remember, they are the ones who fought us all the way and are still fighting us today.

The theme of your convention is the Hispanic American renaissance. During your meetings, I hope you'll keep in mind the real message I have goes far beyond the statistics I've recited or the economic growth that we're enjoying. The fundamental question before us today is not just the Hispanic American renaissance; it is our country's renaissance. Do we keep our country upward-bound and on the move again? Or do we go back to big government and economic decline? Will we hold fast to the values of work and family, or will we return to never-ending government intrusions into how we spend our paychecks and how we raise our children?

There isn't time to outline all that we're trying to do to give back to you, the American people, control over your own lives and destinies. Even as we fight to restore prosperity at home and our prestige abroad, we're dealing firmly and imaginatively with the menace of crime and drugs that has cost us so dearly, especially here in Texas. We've expanded the success of the South Florida Task Force by establishing 12 similar task forces throughout the Nation, including one in Houston. That means more than 1,200 new investigators and prosecutors will be cracking down on the drug racketeers.

We're launching a frontal assault on organized crime with the recent appointment of a Kefauver-style commission, headed by a distinguished jurist, that will hold regional hearings throughout the country.

And we're moving in another area: to end the politicizing of education, bring excellence back to our schools, better opportunity for our schoolchildren, including effective bilingual programs so important for Hispanic children. And I hope you'll join me in persuading the Congress to accede to the overwhelming desire of the American people for a constitutional amendment permitting prayer in our schools.

Here then are the questions before you and before every American in the years ahead: Will we be better off with a future aimed at growth and opportunity, or one bogged down in lowered expectations and economic decline? Will we choose a future with a sparkling economy where young men and women can climb as far as their talents take them, or will Americans of Hispanic descent face a future with more government, more taxes, and more bureaucracy which suffocate enterprise and initiative?

Will we be better off relying on our pride, respect, and accomplishments as a people, or must we sink into dependency through government busing and quotas and all the other elaborate social schemes dreamed up in Washington during the past 40 years?

And what about our national security? Which road will we take there? Will we be better off with a future where America's interests are firmly protected and defended, or will we choose a future where the only clear goal seems to be a deal cut at almost any price with America's adversaries in the world?

Hispanic Americans are at the threshold—I think you can sense your own power, your ability to influence America in the future. The decisions you make in the next few years will have an enormous impact on our society. As we move toward the 21st century, you'll be increasingly in positions of power, and your fellow citizens will look up to you for leadership and guidance.

I urge you today remain true to the values—the devotion to God, family, and country—that have made you the proud people you are today. Hold fast to the dreams you've always had for your children. Reject those who say that your dreams cannot fashion your future, that your destiny is in the hands of unelected bureaucrats and social engineers in Washington. Cherish your dreams, cherish them because they are what brought you or your fathers or their fathers to this country and have contributed so much to America's growth and vitality.

America is "a willingness of the heart," F. Scott Fitzgerald once said. Well, the hearts of Hispanic Americans have always been willing. You've defended America on countless battlefields; you've strengthened our economy, enriched our culture, broadened our perspectives.

"A man wouldn't sell his life to you," William Manchester wrote of his days as a marine in the South Pacific, "but he will give it to you for a piece of colored ribbon." You have always understood this better than most. You've known that the values, faith, and dreams of a people mean far more than a thousand promises of an easy life or a comfortable existence. You have reminded us that independence, honor, and devotion to country and family are more than just words. You have stood by those values, you've lived them, and you've been an inspiration to your children and your countrymen.

As I said when I began, I've come here today to thank you for all that. But I came here today, too, to speak of the future and to challenge you to the role that you must play in it. Because the people have spoken for change, America is better off because of that than she was a few years ago. Now it is in your hands to continue that progress—through this century and the next. Don't let America sink back into the boredom and mediocrity of collectivism, into the politics of envy, protest, and special interests.

Keep America upward bound, on the move; keep her always that shining city, that inspiration, that "last best hope" to all the oppressed and helpless of the world.

God bless you, and God bless America. Thank you.

Note: The President spoke at 1:38 p.m. in the El Paso Civic Center. He was introduced by Ernest Angelo, the forum's national committeeman from Texas.

On Friday evening, August 12, the President met at the Marriott Hotel with the leadership of the forum. The following morning, he met at the hotel with Senator John Tower.

Following his appearance at the civic center, the President met with representatives of the National Narcotics Border Interdiction System and the El Paso Intelligence Center at the Marriott Hotel. He remained at the hotel overnight.

Message to the House of Representatives Returning Without Approval a Bill Providing Funds for Desegregation of the Chicago School System
August 13, 1983

To the House of Representatives:

I am returning herewith without my approval H.J. Res. 338. This bill was originally included in the 1983 Supplemental Appropriation bill, which I recently signed (P.L. 98–63), but was separately passed because it was inadvertently omitted from the enrolled version of that bill. Normally such bills passed as a result of enrollment errors are signed as a matter of course. I am taking this unusual action because of the extraordinarily important constitutional principles raised by this particular measure.

H.J. Res. 338 appropriates $20 million for the purpose of providing a source of funds from which the Secretary of Education could comply with the June 30, 1983 order issued in *United States* v. *Board of Education of the City of Chicago*, No. 80C5124 (N.D. Ill.), if the order is upheld on appeal. The case was brought by the United States to desegregate the Chicago school system. The court ordered the United States to provide a minimum of $14.6 million and froze more than $250 million appropriated by Congress for other educational programs in order to meet expenses incurred by the Chicago Board of Education in carrying out its constitutional responsibilities to desegregate its school system. The court enjoined the Department of Education from providing grants to hundreds of other worthy grantees under several programs of national significance, including grants intended to facilitate local desegregation efforts and others intended to follow up on the report of the National Commission on Excellence in Education.

I well understand the reasons motivating the Congress to pass this legislation. Under the order of the court in Chicago, other education programs throughout the country were denied the funding they rightfully expected to receive. The Chicago court's ostensible purpose in issuing this order was to provide a source of funds for the implementation of its decree. Congress hoped by the passage of this legislation to induce the court to release the funds that were impounded by the court. But I believe that the better course is to seek swift reversal of the district court's order.

This veto is not premised on a desire to protect the Federal budget. It is based upon my conviction that the Constitution and its process of separated powers and checks and balances does not permit the judiciary to determine spending priorities or to reallocate funds appropriated by Congress. Those are exclusively the functions of the Legislative and Executive branches, and the use of judicial decrees to assume such power raises problems of profound constitutional significance.

If finally ordered to pay additional funds to the Board of Education of the City of Chicago, the Federal government will of course do so. It is inappropriate, however, for a court to withhold millions of dollars worth of unrelated and necessary education programs to enforce its orders.

Under these circumstances, I must reluctantly veto this bill.

RONALD REAGAN

The White House,
August 13, 1983.

Remarks on Arrival in La Paz, Mexico, for Meetings With President Miguel de la Madrid Hurtado
August 14, 1983

President de la Madrid. Your Excellency, Mr. Ronald Reagan, President of the United States of America, ladies and gentlemen:

It is my great pleasure to welcome you and the distinguished members of your party to Mexican territory. I am sure that our meeting, although brief, will contribute to the further strengthening of the loyal, dignified, and fruitful friendship of our peoples.

This part of Mexico has been the scene of many facets of our history. It was here on the shores of Cortez' Vermillion Sea that dreams of discovering new worlds began to come true, and here today we find the scene of a new search and affirmation, a search for economic and social progress and the assertion of a convinced and unwavering determination to strengthen our territorial integrity, our will to sovereignty, our national identity, and our commitment to the ideals of freedom, development, and justice that define the historical force of the Mexican people.

Mr. President, you have arrived in a Mexico that trusts in the firmness of its destiny, a Mexico shaped by its own effort, a Mexico that has shown its ability to cast seed on fertile soil and to convert adversity into challenge and trust. Our people are proud of their heritage and of what is theirs today. We are committed to their values and to the development of our nation. However, we are not a self-absorbed people, nor are we engrossed in our immediate circumstances.

History and perception open Mexico to the world and thus the solidarity and constructive contact with other peoples and nations. We know that peace and progress are now, more than ever, shared ideals as well as interlinked realities and that their attainment by all can only come from shared and equal effort based on dignified and respectful relations.

The momentum of history cannot in itself remove the obstacles that states encounter in their course. It is men and peoples who through their will and their action determine the outlines of history, hence the unquestionable value of solidarity, sustained international cooperation, of negotiation and understanding as premises for a concord in these times of redefinition and crisis that are threatening plural and peaceful coexistence and the harmonious development of nations.

Today, as never before, whatever happens in any part of the planet affects the peoples of all countries. In the case of Mexico and the United States, our proximity gives rise to many and complex relations. Despite our different viewpoints and interests, the inescapable consequence of our diverse social, economic, and cultural backgrounds, the border itself creates ample opportunities for cooperation and exchange that can benefit our two peoples.

The maturity of a political relationship which bears witness to our intention of achieving coexistence based on respect, dignity, and mutual benefit rises to oppose the many barriers and new problems brought about by the unique development of the two nations and those created by a frankly deteriorating world. The maturity is the reflection of long and consistent efforts and has not been attained without difficulty. At the same time it is the sound foundation of our desire to comprehend, to understand, and to cooperate. We trust that it will continue to permeate the actions of our governments and our societies for the good of equitable, respectful, and productive bilateral relations.

President Reagan, today as you enter Mexico you cross the threshold of Latin America. The border between the United States and Mexico is also the boundary between two different components of our continent and two different expressions of development and culture—both a national and a regional boundary, its two faces simultaneously express uniqueness and reciprocal influence.

The worlds of North and South America,

the industrialized and the developing worlds, are linked today by their complementary potential and their manifold contradictions. In Latin America, the need for social changes is confronted today with the dramatic impacts of a troubled world that limit its long, unsatisfied urge for development, freedom, democracy, and justice.

In the face of social underdevelopment now aggravated by a profound economic crisis and by shows of force which threaten to touch off a conflagration, we must urgently respond with a firm vocation for peace and solidarity by showing respect for the law and for the institutions of the parties involved and by furthering the development and full predominance of a balanced, realistic, and constructive political dialog.

Mr. President, allow me to express my most fervent hope that at the conclusion of our meeting we may look forward for the good of our two great peoples and of the region to an effective contribution toward the achievement of that peace and solidarity so deeply desired in our times.

May your stay in Mexico be a pleasant one, Mr. President.

President Reagan. Good morning. It's a pleasure to return to your proud and beautiful country.

This will be my first visit with President de la Madrid as President. At our initial meeting last October in San Diego and Tijuana, President de la Madrid observed that

personal and friendly contact encourages a free and open exchange of ideas. That meeting was very constructive, and I look forward to today's discussion.

We are neighbors, and as such, we are concerned for one another. Our sessions today should open new avenues to put that concern to good use. It's my hope that President de la Madrid and I will continue to meet periodically. Our countries share a host of common objectives and hopes. Open and friendly communication between us will benefit us both.

Last October President de la Madrid and I had the opportunity to get to know each other better and to strengthen the cooperation between our two countries. Today we will be able to build on our relationship and openly discuss our differences as well as our many areas of agreement. I'm sure that our meeting will further strengthen the mutual respect and understanding which is the cornerstone of relations between the United States and Mexico.

Note: The exchange of remarks began at 9:50 a.m. at the Palace of Government, where President Reagan was accorded a formal welcome. Following the ceremony, President Reagan participated in a wreath-laying ceremony at the Benito Juárez Monument.

President de la Madrid spoke in Spanish, and his remarks were translated by an interpreter.

Remarks Following Meetings With President Miguel de la Madrid Hurtado of Mexico in La Paz
August 14, 1983

President de la Madrid, members of the official party, and ladies and gentlemen:

I'm delighted to be here in La Paz in Baja California Sur on the Bay of Peace. This is a particularly appropriate place for us to meet as we work to ensure peace in our hemisphere and in other areas of the world. Your cordiality and hospitality, Mr. President, are deeply appreciated.

Mr. President, you and I have spent a

good bit of our time this morning discussing the future and how we can make sure that it's good for both our peoples. Relations between our countries are excellent. Last October we got off to a good start when we met in Tijuana and San Diego prior to your inauguration.

Our sessions have given us a further chance to get to know each other as individuals. I can tell you that you are a man whom I respect and admire. It's a pleasure to work with you. I pledge to you, Mr. President, my best efforts to strengthen and broaden our personal and professional relations to the benefit of both our peoples.

Mexico and the United States share a continent together. We share many traditions and values, as well. Coming from one of the Southwestern States, I greatly appreciate the magnitude of our common bonds and of the strong Hispanic traditions that we have—something of which I've been reminded these past few weeks when I met with various Hispanic groups in the United States. They are keenly aware of our relations with Mexico and stressed to me the importance of strengthening our ties. These citizens of Hispanic descent are a permanent link for us to the Hispanic world.

I do not minimize the differences between our two countries. We have every reason to be proud of the distinct cultural traditions of our two peoples. Yet our differences need never diminish our good will and our respect for one another, because good will and mutual respect always should be the hallmark of relations between the United States and Mexico.

We have a 2,000-mile common border. I prefer not to look on it as a border, but instead as a meeting place. It provides enormous potential for cooperation that we can tap.

Cooperation between our two governments has already accomplished much.

Increasingly effective narcotics control activities by Mexican authorities have made a major contribution to my government's efforts to attack this problem. We're deeply grateful for your help.

Over the years, our two governments have established a wide spectrum of arrangements concerning science and technology, educational and cultural exchanges, housing and urban development, and coordinated responses to natural disasters.

In a series of treaties and other agreements stretching down through this century, the United States and Mexico have established effective mechanisms for an equitable division of the border water resources. The International Boundary and Water Commission has been exceptionally successful in defusing problems and developing equitable solutions to difficulties involving our precious water resources.

As one would expect of a friend, during Mexico's financial crisis of last summer the United States took the lead in arranging international support for Mexico's recovery efforts.

Mr. President, I think that we can be pleased with the successes that we've had. And the businesslike atmosphere of today's meeting suggests that much more will be accomplished in the future.

Yes, mistakes have been made in the past by our governments in their dealings with one another. Human beings err, and that's to be expected. But friendship can overcome mistakes, and that, too, should be understood.

I came primarily to listen, to try to understand the concerns of the Mexican people and, as our actions have shown, to be responsive.

In the United States, we're just now emerging from a long period of economic turmoil, and we fully appreciate the tough job you face in restoring economic health. We're impressed with the efforts being taken by you, Mr. President, and the citizens of your country to resolve Mexico's economic problems. As you've said on a number of occasions, the solution to Mexico's economic difficulties will come from Mexico itself. That, clearly, is as it should be, and we applaud your determination.

Our role is to support your efforts as best we can. We appreciate that droughts and other factors during the past 3 years have severely affected agricultural production in Mexico, compounding Mexico's economic problems. Therefore, I have approved the extension this fiscal year of additional commodity credits to help finance the purchase of agricultural commodities in the United States. We hope that these agricultural credits will be useful to Mexico in buying the food it needs without impeding your economic recovery efforts. We also hope to negotiate a further purchase of Mexican petroleum for our Strategic Petroleum Reserve.

Mr. President, we've demonstrated on several occasions that we intend to shape our future as equal partners. I am pleased that our meetings today have been productive and that we've laid the groundwork for future action along these lines.

In our discussions today, we dealt with a number of significant trade matters. Mexico is one of our largest markets and a vital source of supply. We are Mexico's largest market and supplier. Despite the current difficulties, Mexico rightly looks to our market as fundamental to the strength and vitality of its own, and I can assure you that we consider Mexico's economic health of great importance to our prosperity and well-being.

Mr. President, you and I are determined to continue working out our trade problems and to reduce impediments to commerce that prevent our people from enjoying its maximum benefits.

We also see investment as an avenue for Mexico to obtain the capital it needs to expand its industry and increase efficiency. I know that you, Mr. President, understand this and are determined to work out arrangements that will attract investors. We agree that the Maquiladora and the Twin Plants program make a contribution to the economies of both our nations by increasing jobs and promoting economic activity, especially at the border.

Much of our discussion today related to the border. We are looking into ways we can work together to foster economic stability and prosperity there. We're also concerned about protecting the environment in the border region, especially with respect to pollution of the air, water, and land.

President de la Madrid, you and I will sign an agreement today which establishes a framework for environmental action in the border region. We expect this agreement to strengthen cooperation between our two countries by addressing serious pollution problems. Our joint International Boundary and Water Commission has discussed the problem of sewage which affects the communities of Tijuana, San Diego, Mexicali, and Calexico, and other locations. We need to solve these problems quickly, as they affect people in both countries. President de la Madrid, I know you and I are both committed to this task.

Finally, Mr. President, we've discussed the situation in Central America and, while we have differences, there are substantial areas of potential cooperation. I continue to believe that a solution to the crisis in Central America must encompass four basic principles: one, establishment and strengthening of democratic institutions in order to resolve political differences within each state; two, respect for nonintervention, including ending support for subversive elements seeking to destabilize other countries; three, removal of the conflict from East-West confrontation through such measures as the verifiable withdrawal of all foreign military and security advisers and a freeze on the acquisition of offensive weapons; and four, cooperation to sustain a level of economic growth that guarantees the basic needs of the people of this area.

The principle of self-determination is as important to citizens of the United States as anyone. Our history proves it. We've fought wars for that very principle. We believe that people should be able to determine their own solutions, and that's why we've responded to calls for help from certain of our Latin American neighbors. We will consider it a beautiful day in the history of that region when all foreign elements, including our own, may be safely withdrawn.

Mr. President, I hope that God, who made us neighbors, will look favorably upon us as we work closely together to find solutions to our mutual problems.

Thank you.

Note: The President spoke at 1:45 p.m. to reporters assembled in the Baja California Sur Legislative Chambers. Earlier, the two Presidents met privately in the Governor's Office at the Palace of Government. They then moved to the Governor's Conference Room, where they were joined by U.S. and Mexican officials, for further discussions.

United States-Mexico Agreement on the Environment in the Border Area
August 14, 1983

Agreement Between the United States of America and the United Mexican States on Cooperation for the Protection and Improvement of the Environment in the Border Area

The United States of America and the United Mexican States,

Recognizing the importance of a healthful environment to the long-term economic and social well-being of present and future generations of each country as well as of the global community;

Recalling that the Declaration of the United Nations Conference on the Human Environment, proclaimed in Stockholm in 1972, called upon nations to collaborate to resolve environmental problems of common concern;

Noting previous agreements and programs providing for environmental cooperation between the two countries;

Believing that such cooperation is of mutual benefit in coping with similar environmental problems in each country;

Acknowledging the important work of the International Boundary and Water Commission and the contribution of the agreements concluded between the two countries relating to environmental affairs;

Reaffirming their political will to further strengthen and demonstrate the importance attached by both Governments to cooperation on environmental protection and in furtherance of the principle of good neighborliness;

Have agreed as follows:

Article 1

The United States of America and the United Mexican States, hereinafter referred to as the Parties, agree to cooperate in the field of environmental protection in the border area on the basis of equality, reciprocity and mutual benefit. The objectives of the present Agreement are to establish the basis for cooperation between the Parties for the protection, improvement and conservation of the environment and the problems which affect it, as well as to agree on necessary measures to prevent and control pollution in the border area, and to provide the framework for development of a system of notification for emergency situations. Such objectives shall be pursued without prejudice to the cooperation which the Parties may agree to undertake outside the border area.

Article 2

The Parties undertake, to the fullest extent practical, to adopt the appropriate measures to prevent, reduce and eliminate sources of pollution in their respective territory which affect the border area of the other.

Additionally, the Parties shall cooperate in the solution of the environmental problems of mutual concern in the border area, in accordance with the provisions of this Agreement.

Article 3

Pursuant to this Agreement, the Parties may conclude specific arrangements for the solution of common problems in the border area, which may be annexed thereto. Similarly, the Parties may also agree upon annexes to this Agreement on technical matters.

Article 4

For the purposes of this Agreement, it shall be understood that the "border area" refers to the area situated 100 kilometers on either side of the inland and maritime boundaries between the Parties.

Article 5

The Parties agree to coordinate their efforts, in conformity with their own national legislation and existing bilateral agreements to address problems of air, land and water pollution in the border area.

Article 6

To implement this Agreement, the Parties shall consider and, as appropriate, pursue in a coordinated manner practical, legal, institutional and technical measures for protecting the quality of the environmental in the border area. Forms of cooperation may include: coordination of national programs; scientific and educational exchanges; environmental monitoring; environmental impact assessment; and periodic exchanges of information and data on likely sources of pollution in their respective territory which may produce environmentally polluting incidents, as defined in an annex to this Agreement.

Article 7

The Parties shall assess, as appropriate, in accordance with their respective national laws, regulations and policies, projects that may have significant impacts on the environment of the border area, so that appropriate measures may be considered to avoid or mitigate adverse environmental effects.

Article 8

Each Party designates a national coordinator whose principal functions will be to coordinate and monitor implementation of this Agreement, make recommendations to the Parties, and organize the annual meetings referred to in Article 10, and the meetings of the experts referred to in Article 11. Additional responsibilities of the national coordinators may be agreed to in an annex to this Agreement.

In the case of the United States of America the national coordinator shall be the Environmental Protection Agency, and in the case of Mexico it shall be the Secretaría de Desarrollo Urbano y Ecología, through the Subsecretaría de Ecología.

Article 9

Taking into account the subjects to be examined jointly, the national coordinators may invite, as appropriate, representatives of federal, state and municipal governments to participate in the meetings provided for in this Agreement. By mutual agreement they may also invite representatives of international governmental or non-governmental organizations who may be able to contribute some element of expertise on problems to be solved.

The national coordinators will determine by mutual agreement the form and manner of participation of non-governmental entities.

Article 10

The Parties shall hold at a minimum an annual high level meeting to review the manner in which this Agreement is being implemented. These meetings shall take place alternately in the border area of Mexico and the United States of America.

The composition of the delegations which represent each Party, both in these annual meetings as well as in the meetings of experts referred to in Article 11, will be communicated to the other Party through diplomatic channels.

Article 11

The Parties may, as they deem necessary, convoke meetings of experts for the purposes of coordinating their national programs referred to in Article 6, and of preparing the drafts of the specific arrangements and technical annexes referred to in Article 3.

These meetings of experts may review technical subjects. The opinions of the experts in such meetings shall be communicated by them to the national coordinators, and will serve to advise the Parties on technical matters.

Article 12

Each Party shall ensure that its national coordinator is informed of activities of its cooperating agencies carried out under this Agreement. Each Party shall also ensure that its national coordinator is informed of the implementation of other agreements concluded between the two Governments concerning matters related to this Agreement. The national coordinators of both Parties will present to the annual meetings a report on the environmental aspects of all joint work conducted under this Agreement and on implementation of other relevant agreements between the Parties, both bilateral and multilateral.

Nothing in this Agreement shall prejudice or otherwise affect the functions entrusted to the International Boundary and Water Commission, in accordance with the Water Treaty of 1944.

Article 13

Each Party shall be responsible for informing its border states and for consulting them in accordance with their respective constitutional systems, in relation to matters covered by this Agreement.

Article 14

Unless otherwise agreed, each Party shall bear the cost of its participation in the implementation of this Agreement, including the expenses of personnel who participate in any activitiy undertaken on the basis of it.

For the training of personnel, the transfer of equipment and the construction of installations related to the implementation of this Agreement, the Parties may agree on a special modality of financing, taking into account the objectives defined in this Agreement.

Article 15

The Parties shall facilitate the entry of equipment and personnel related to this Agreement, subject to the laws and regulations of the receiving country.

In order to undertake the monitoring of polluting activities in the border area, the Parties shall undertake consultations relating to the measurement and analysis of polluting elements in the border area.

Article 16

All technical information obtained through the implementation of this Agreement will be available to both Parties. Such information may be made available to third parties by the mutual agreement of the Parties to this Agreement.

Article 17

Nothing in this Agreement shall be construed to prejudice other existing or future agreements concluded between the two Parties, or affect the rights and obligations of the Parties under international agreements to which they are a party.

Article 18

Activities under this Agreement shall be subject to the availability of funds and other resources to each Party and to the applicable laws and regulations in each country.

Article 19

The present Agreement shall enter into force upon an exchange of Notes stating that each Party has completed its necessary internal procedures.

Article 20

The present Agreement shall remain in force indefinitely unless one of the Parties notifies the other, through diplomatic channels, of its desire to denounce it, in which case the Agreement will terminate six months after the date of such written notification. Unless otherwise agreed, such termination shall not affect the validity of any arrangements made under this Agreement.

Article 21

This Agreement may be amended by the agreement of the Parties.

Article 22

The adoption of the annexes and of the specific arrangements provided for in Article 3, and the amendments thereto, will be effected by an exchange of Notes.

Article 23

This Agreement supersedes the exchange of Notes, concluded on June 19, 1978 with the attached Memorandum of Understanding between the Environmental Protection Agency of the United States and the Subsecretariat for Environmental Improvement of Mexico for Cooperation on Environmental Programs and Transboundary Problems.

Done, in duplicate, in the city of La Paz, Baja California, Mexico, on the 14th of August of 1983, in the English and Spanish languages, both texts being equally authentic.

Note: President Reagan and President de la Madrid of Mexico signed the agreement during their appearance before reporters in the Baja California Sur Legislative Chambers in La Paz, Mexico.

Toast at a Luncheon Hosted by President Miguel de la Madrid Hurtado of Mexico in La Paz
August 14, 1983

President de la Madrid, Secretaries Sepúlveda and Shultz, Your Excellencies, our Ambassadors Espinosa de los Reyes and Gavin, members of the delegations, and friends:

There have been many words said today. Agreements have been reached, understandings have been reached, but perhaps the most significant aspect of our talks was our spirit of cooperation. And through meetings like this, where we treat each other as partners with respect and courtesy and, yes, with honest good will, we define the mature relationship of our two countries.

President de la Madrid, this spirit of cooperation and businesslike approach to the issues of concern to us both have been deeply appreciated on our side. We all have an important responsibility, and that is to represent the interest of our peoples as best we can.

As President, I understand the economic challenges that you face. As a matter of fact, they sound very familiar. We've had a little economic trouble ourselves, and I have every confidence that you will succeed.

Last year when I visited South and Central America—I always have believed, and even more so after that trip, that while we are citizens of our individual countries, and no one would suggest that we in any way forsake the culture, the tradition, the differences that make us different countries, we should also remember that in this most unique double continent, hemisphere that we're in—no one else in the world could say anything like this—even when we cross the borders into one another's country, we're still among Americans, from the North Pole to the South Pole.

And this morning, earlier, I told the President of a dream that I have long cherished. And that is—that in this North and South America and Central America—that all of us as Americans might one day find a way as equal partners, neighbors, to set out to develop these two great continents, to erase the injustices that exist here and there, to bring about economic reform to the point that one day we can stand there as a shining example to all the world, from South Pole to North Pole, that we are united in our determination to be free, to respect each individual in our two countries because individual freedom, I think, is the thing that sets us apart from so many parts of the world in so many areas today. And that if this dream—I won't say "if;" *when* this dream comes true—'cause we're going to work to make it come true—when it does, more than 600 million Americans here in the Western Hemisphere will be such a force for good throughout the world that the world will never have seen anything like it.

And I'm more encouraged than I've been in a long time about the fulfillment of that dream in the meetings that we've had, particularly this one, and we're going to have more of them. I also told the President that the only time people get in trouble is when they're talking about each other, not when they're talking to each other. And we're going to on a regular basis continue to talk to each other.

And I'm not going to say any more because I know that I've confused the interpreter very much by not sticking to the script. But, to the President of Mexico, Miguel de la Madrid, to the people of Mexico, and to the friendship between our two peoples.

Note: The President spoke at 3:50 p.m. at the Governor's Residence in response to a toast by President de la Madrid.

Following the luncheon, the President participated in a departure ceremony at the Governor's Residence. He then traveled to the Hilton Hotel in New Orleans, La., where he remained overnight.

Joint Communique Following Discussions With President Miguel de la Madrid Hurtado of Mexico
August 14, 1983

President Ronald Reagan of the United States of America and President Miguel de la Madrid of Mexico met in La Paz, Baja California, Mexico, on August 14, 1983. This meeting was one of a continuing series between the Presidents of the United States and Mexico that is traditional for the two countries.

Arranged at the invitation of President de la Madrid, the current meeting offered both Presidents an opportunity to discuss important bilateral issues of common concern and to strengthen the ties they established during their previous meetings. They discussed economic, trade and financial matters, as well as border issues, narcotics control, immigration, fisheries, ecological and scientific and technical cooperation.

The Presidents also had a useful discussion on the situation in Central America.

The two Presidents reaffirmed their determination to strengthen still further the spirit of cooperation, understanding and friendship which exists between their two countries.

The Presidents reviewed recent economic developments which have taken place in their countries. President de la Madrid stated that the economic policies of his administration are aimed at restoring the necessary conditions for rapid, just, balanced and independent national economic development. President Reagan stated that his government recognized Mexico's efforts to adjust and reorder its economy and reaffirmed United States support of and assistance to the Mexican government in its efforts to resolve its current economic problems.

The two heads of state also discussed negotiations on subsidies and countervailing duties and have committed their administrations to resolving these issues as expeditiously as possible. They discussed problems related to tuna fisheries and stated their hope that the issue could be resolved as soon as possible. While expressing understanding of Mexico's needs to resolve its balance of payments problems, President Reagan conveyed his hope that Mexico would soon return to normal trade patterns. On this subject President de la Madrid stated that the dynamics of trade between the two countries would benefit from greater Mexican exports which would generate foreign exchange revenue and thus help to finance the imports needed for the development of Mexico's economy.

In view of the need for continuing discussion of bilateral trade issues, they recognized the useful role played by the Joint Commission on Commerce and Trade, the consultative body established by both governments in strengthening commercial exchange between the two countries.

Both Presidents recognized the importance of trade along the border and agreed to continue efforts directed toward solving the problems being confronted by border communities of both countries. To that end, they considered a proposal to establish a working group for economic and trade matters in the border region within the Binational Commission. They also discussed sanitation problems along the border, a matter which adversely affects citizens of both countries.

The two heads of State gave special attention to cultural exchange as well as scientific and technical cooperation between Mexico and the United States. They agreed on the need to continue the promotion of such exchange and cooperation and strengthening existing programs and mechanisms in these areas.

The Presidents expressed their satisfaction with the excellent results of the campaign carried out by the Mexican Government in cooperation with the Government of the United States to combat illegal drug production and trafficking. They agreed on the need to continue such cooperation for the benefit and the well-being of both their people.

In this same spirit, they decided to intensify cooperation between the two governments with a view to finding more suitable responses to the problems of environmental pollution along the border. They noted that a cooperation agreement was signed today that establishes the framework for bilateral action on pollution of water, air and land.

In the discussion on the situation in Central America the two Presidents agreed on the need to contribute to the restoration of peace and to the prevention of an even greater conflict in the area by promoting fast processes of political dialogue and negotiation. President Reagan reiterated his strong support for the Contadora initiative. President de la Madrid and President Reagan agreed also on the importance of helping Central American countries to settle their conflicts peacefully. The Presidents furthermore reiterated their strong support of non-intervention and the self-de-

termination of people. Finally the Presidents recognized the necessity for equitable social and economic development in the region.

The Presidents ended their talks fully convinced that strengthening the friendship and cooperation between Mexico and the United States remains a common objective of their governments. They reaffirmed their desire to hold periodic working meetings between themselves and other high officials of their governments.

President Reagan expressed his pleasure and appreciation for the hospitable welcome accorded to him by the Mexican Government and by the authorities of the State of Baja California Sur. He also extended a cordial invitation to President Miguel de la Madrid to visit the United States in the near future.

Remarks at the Annual Convention of the Veterans of Foreign Wars in New Orleans, Louisiana
August 15, 1983

Thank you for that warm greeting and that applause, and since that applause is coming from veterans, I have to ask: Is it for how I'm doing my job, or how I'm doing on the late late show in "Hellcats of the Navy?" [*Laughter*]

Whenever I meet with the members of the Veterans of Foreign Wars, I remember what the poet Yeats said: "Think where man's glory most begins and ends and say my glory was I had such friends." It's great to be among you once again. As you know, someone in my shop originally turned down this invitation without my knowledge. Now it seems there were some logistic problems about flying from the tip of Baja, Mexico, to Louisiana, and then back to California this afternoon. Well, let me say—and I want them to keep their ears open and hear this—I would fly halfway around the world for the honor of meeting with the Veterans of Foreign Wars.

I haven't forgotten your support in 1980 and all you've done since. And as a demonstration of our common goals, after my re-

marks today I'm going to sit down here in front of this audience and sign the Emergency Veterans' Job Training Act of 1983.

Three years ago this week, I stood before your convention and said nothing would mean more to me as President than to live up to your trust. I've tried to maintain the faith that our men and women in uniform must have in their Commander in Chief. The greatest privilege of this office has been to lead those who wear America's uniform.

And while Ann Griffiths[1] is sitting here, let me just say: We are determined to account for every serviceman who wore America's uniform in Southeast Asia. This administration will not forget their sacrifice, and we will not rest until their families can rest.

Three years ago when I spoke to you, I

---

[1] *Executive director of the National League of Families of American Prisoners and Missing in Southeast Asia.*

pledged that peace—a peace in which freedom could flourish and justice could prevail—would be our highest priority. I also spoke of the need to provide a stronger defense for the American people. At the time, those were words of hope. Today, those words are the national security policy of this country.

I'd like to report to you on the progress we've made in these areas, because there is no more appropriate forum for such a report. No organization has devoted more energy to America's well-being and security than the VFW. Your uniforms may be in mothballs, but your readiness to assist your country is spit and polished.

In 1980 the people made it clear they wanted a new direction in foreign affairs. Yet, changing America's foreign policy is a little like towing an iceberg. You can only pick up speed as the frozen attitudes and mistakes of the past melt away.

We began by letting the world know what we stood for once again. Winston Churchill said of his service in World War II, the nation "had the lion's heart. I had the luck to give the roar." Well, America is the lion's heart of democracy. We have an obligation to give that democracy a voice, even an occasional roar.

For too long our nation had been moot to the injustices of totalitarianism. So we began speaking out against chemical warfare; inflicted on the people of Afghanistan and Southeast Asia, against broken treaties, against the denial of human liberties. We began speaking out for freedom and democracy and the values that all of us share in our hearts.

Now some critics said that this was a return to the rhetoric of the past. Well, if that's the case, then Sakharov and Solzhenitsyn and all those who've suffered to speak the truth are my compatriots, and I'm honored to be counted among them. This nation cannot simply ignore the suffering of oppressed peoples and remain true to our basic strengths and principles. We cannot follow a foreign policy based on the self-delusion that problems would not exist if we did not mention them. We cannot abdicate our obligation to speak out for those who cannot speak for themselves.

And, you know, it's amazing. In my meetings with foreign leaders and their ministers, they've told me how good it is to know what the United States stands for once again. They may not always agree with us, but they respect us. And there's a growing recognition abroad that America once again will stand up for her democratic ideals. Our country is the leader of the free world, and today it is providing that leadership.

But our responsibilities are not only moral, they're practical. One of our most crucial national security objectives was to turn America's economic decline around. Yes, that's a national security objective, and it remains a key one. A country that is weak internally cannot meet its obligations externally.

I'm pleased to report we're economically stronger today than we were at your last convention. We have a growth strategy for America. We called it economic recovery; some who didn't think it would work dubbed it Reaganomics Well, inflation is down from double digits to 2.6 percent for the last 12 months, the lowest rate in 16 years. The prime interest rate was 21½ percent when we took office; it's about half that now. Taxes have been reduced, and with our indexing reform inflation will never again push families into higher and higher tax brackets. We don't need tax increases; we need spending restraint. And as I've said a few times lately, I know our program is working, because they're not calling it Reaganomics any more. [*Laughter*]

Basic industries like housing, construction, and autos are getting back to business. In fact, Lee Iacocca[2] has even paid back that billion-dollar loan 7 years early.

Unemployment is still too high, but it's heading down. Last month's drop was the biggest in 23 years. More Americans are on the job than at any time in the U.S. history. Economists can argue about the semantics—strong recovery, steady recovery, robust recovery—but what matters most is that Americans have regained confidence in the economy, and we're going to make sure they keep that confidence.

Another of our objectives has been to re-

---

[2] *Chairman of Chrysler Corp.*

store America's defense strength. I don't need to educate this audience on how strength keeps peace, but it can be explained in one word—deterrence. When I spoke to you last, the United States had planes that couldn't fly, ships that couldn't leave port, and military personnel who couldn't wait to get into civilian clothes.

Well today, America's military is back on its feet and prouder than ever. We're acquiring and keeping very good people. Today, more of our new recruits are high school graduates than ever before in the history of our military. Retention is also way up. So far this year, 70 percent of those we hoped to retain have reenlisted. In 1980 the figure was only 55 percent.

Yes, the hard-hit economy accounted for a portion of these increases, but the economy didn't raise the dignity and morale of our service men and women or restore their pride in military service. I've heard it from generals and I've heard it from privates that morale, discipline, and unit cohesion have all improved dramatically. Once again, it's an honor to wear the uniform, and our service men and women know it. And I hope that makes you as proud as it does me.

New equipment is now entering the inventory, training is way up, maintenance backlogs are being reduced, and combat readiness rates have surged. We've made real progress. And I'm delighted to report it's across the board. America is safer and more secure today than 3 years ago.

There's something I want to get off my chest, and it deals with the headlines about the Pentagon paying $100 for a 4 cent diode or $900 for a plastic cap. Now what is missing or buried in all these stories about waste is that this administration is the one that found these abuses, the abuses that have been going on for years.

It was Cap Weinberger's people—Defense Department auditors and inspectors—who ordered the audits in the first place and conducted the investigations. We're the ones who formed a special unit to prosecute Department of Defense fraud cases. And in just an 18-month period, the Department has obtained 650 convictions. And this doesn't count the number of settlements that have been made.

Our task is to sustain our defense effort. Some would have us slow down just when we're about to achieve what our security requires. Remember the 1970's, when there were those who argued that we should forgo a wide range of modern weapons systems—airplanes, missiles, a variety of equipment—because there was something better on the drawing boards for the future? Well, look where that got us. It got us where we were 3 years ago. You can't protect America and her people with drawing boards.

But look out, some people are still talking about drawingboards. They would have us forget the MX missile and wait for a small, mobile missile which wouldn't be operational until the 1990's. That small missile will provide better long-term stability and deterrence. I'm for it, and we need it. But drawingboards for tomorrow won't give the Soviets incentive to negotiate reductions in nuclear arms today. So, I'm asking you, give us your strong support as we approach the next round of the MX this autumn, and together we'll help keep America secure and free.

Another of our goals has been to strengthen our Western alliances economically and militarily. We've significantly improved our economic relations with the industrial democracies. And I'm certain the recent Williamsburg summit will become known as the recovery summit. At Williamsburg we established a unified strategy for pursuing our common economic interests [from combatting][3] protectionism to fighting inflation, and we agreed on security concerns, as well. We agreed to cut the flow of military-relevant technology to those who would use it against us and reduce dependence on any one energy source. We agreed to end the practice of giving subsidized interest rates to the Soviet Union. The minimum loan rate is now set 4 full percentage points higher than it was before. And at home, we're working to bring interest rates down. But we've pushed them up for the Soviets.

By the way, did you hear that the Com-

---

[3] *From the advance text of the President's remarks.*

munists now have a million-dollar lottery for their people? The winners get a dollar a year for a million years. [*Laughter*]

You know, there's a story I'd like to tell you. I've became a collector of stories that the Russians are telling among themselves which reveal a great cynicism about their system. And this one has to do with a commissar, they're telling, who went out to a collective farm, grabbed the first worker there that he saw, and he asked him about life on the farm and all. And the fellow said, "It's wonderful, comrade." "Well," he said, "any complaints?" "Oh, no, sir; no complaints at all." "What about the crops?" "Oh, the crops? Never been better." "The potatoes?" "Commissar, comrade, if we piled all the potatoes up in one pile they would reach the foot of God." And the commissar said, "Just a minute. This is the Soviet Union; there is no God." And he said, "That's all right; there are no potatoes." [*Laughter*]

Our Western military alliances are stronger than they've been in years. In Europe, despite pressure and propaganda, NATO has stood firm in pursuing the dual objectives of arms reduction and deterrence. NATO today is more confident in its ability to preserve its strength and promote the peace. We in the industrial democracies have forged a clear sense of purpose for our economic and military safety. We still have disagreements, but for the first time in a long time we have unity on where we're going, and I call that real progress.

Of course, another of our objectives is arms control. We've launched the most sweeping proposals for arms control since nuclear weapons became a threat. In our search for peace, we have more negotiations currently under way with the Soviets than any administration in history.

At the strategic arms reduction talks in Geneva, we've proposed deep cuts as well as extensive confidence-building measures to reduce the possibility of any accidental misunderstandings. In contrast to previous agreements which simply dealt in ceilings, the Soviet Union now, for the first time, is willing to talk about actual reductions. The same hard work is proceeding on intermediate-range nuclear forces in Geneva. And in Vienna, the Soviets have shown some

movement on the verification needed to reduce conventional forces.

However, we must recognize that the search for real arms reductions involves complex, time-consuming negotiations. This is the occupational hazard of diplomats, and especially those who deal with the Soviet Union. But if I can assure you, we'll keep chipping away and inching along. We're deeply committed to arms reductions. As we remain firm in our objectives, we'll be flexible in our approach. And with the support of the VFW and the support of the Congress, we'll achieve what we all want—a reduction in nuclear weapons.

Our next objective concerns the United States responsibility as peacemaker. This commitment currently is most visible in Central America. In spite of the discouraging hype and hoopla that you often hear, quiet, solid progress is being made in Central America. Bob Currieo recently returned from a trip there, and I believe he's reported to you on that trip. I know he's referred to news accounts, saying he thinks we're all getting a distorted view of what's actually taking place.

Well, Bob is absolutely right. You wouldn't know from some of the coverage that the greatest portion of our aid to Central America is humanitarian and economic. You wouldn't know that democracy is taking root there. And I don't blame the media alone, because in many cases they're just reporting the disinformation and demagoguery that they hear coming from people who put politics ahead of national interests.

The countries of Central America are working hard to develop and defend their democracies. I'm sure you recall the March '82 Constituent Assembly elections in El Salvador. Eighty percent of those eligible to vote took part in the elections, despite incredible intimidation and threats from the guerrillas. In neighboring Honduras, an elected government took office last year. Costa Rica, of course, already is the democratic jewel of Central America.

We support democracy, reform, and human freedom. We support economic development. We support negotiations. We support any avenue that will give the people of that region a more free and prosperous future.

"The problem in Central America is not the United States or United States policy." Now you see, there I go again borrowing from your national commander, because that's what Bob said. We're doing everything we can to build peace and prosperity. Our Caribbean Basin Initiative is designed to help the nations there help themselves through trade and private investment. The Soviet and Cuban Caribbean Basin initiative, on the other hand, is to brutally impose Communist rule and deny individual freedom. Do you have any doubt which initiative the people in Central America would choose?

Because of this aggression, we also support a security shield for the area. The security shield is very much like a program that's springing up all over the United States—the Neighborhood Watch. The Neighborhood Watch is where neighbors keep an eye on each other's homes so outside troublemakers and bullies will think twice. Well, our policy in Central America is like a neighborhood watch. But this watch doesn't protect someone's silverware; it protects something more valuable—freedom.

Our policy is to help people toward a better life—to help them toward liberty, to help them reverse centuries of inequities, to help them toward peace. And let me say with all the conviction I can muster, America would not be America if we abandoned the struggling neighbors here in our own hemisphere.

Elsewhere in the world, we also search for peace. The tragic conflict in the Middle East has one bright spot: Peace between Israel and Egypt was finally concluded in April of 1982, thanks to the American diplomacy that went to work in the Camp David talks. Today our peacekeeping forces in the Sinai, along with those of our allies, are rarely mentioned because they're doing their job in keeping this once volatile area quiet. Unfortunately, the same is not yet so for Lebanon. But whatever progress toward peace we've made in that country is largely due to our marines, who along with peacekeeping troops from France and Italy are striving to give Lebanon a chance to pull itself together. Our diplomats continue to search for agreement among bitter, divided opponents. Yes, America has an active national security program, and it's working.

May I just interject here that there have been some charges made that we're building weapons and spending money on defense, but we don't have any plan, so we're just building weapons like you'd go in and shop for something off the counter and say, "Let's buy that or buy that." That isn't true. We have carefully worked out a strategy that is based on what we think are all the possible contingencies that could affect our national security, and then our military planning and our weapons purchases are based on that strategy.

But to secure the peace and prosperity we all seek, we cannot sit back and hope that somehow it'll just happen. We can't be apologetic when we're acting in our own and the free world's interests. We must pursue our goals with strong leadership and a clear sense of direction.

Let me explain by way of a true story what guides this administration in its conduct of foreign affairs. Most of you fought in the Second World War or Korea or Vietnam. You fought in places like Anzio and Pork Chop Hill and Danang. A thousand painful stories emerge from war. One tale of British POW's who built a Japanese railway in Thailand was made famous as "The Bridge on the River Kwai."

Well, there really is a River Kwai. Near its banks is a cemetery, the final resting place for those who died building that bridge and that railway. Many of the grave markers are inscribed with nothing more than a name and a service number. Yet now and then there's a small monument, built by a mother or father or a widow who trekked half way around the world searching for a marker with a very special service number. On one of these monuments, erected by a woman named Irene, are the following words: "To the world, you were only one; but to me you were all the world."

My fellow citizens, my friends, let us always remember when we speak of America's security, [we speak of the sacrifice][4] of individuals. When we speak of freedom, we speak of the freedom of individuals. I feel a sacred trust to America's soldiers and citizens alike. I feel a sacred trust to protect their lives and their liberty.

Our nation also has a sacred trust—to defend and develop democracy. And as long as this administration is responsible for the Nation's foreign policy, we will protect the freedom of our own citizens and we will pursue liberty for all people.

Now, before I thank you for inviting me here, I'm going over and I'm going to sit down at this table that you've probably wondered about. And I'm going to hope that this microphone is turned on.

This bill which I am about to sign, the Emergency Veterans' Job Training Act of 1983, will provide targeted job training for unemployed veterans of the Korean and Vietnam conflicts. The legislation is above and beyond the partisan jobs bill that I signed earlier this year and other administration programs to promote opportunities for our veterans. This bill provides incentives to employers to train veterans by defraying part of the costs of training. But this is not just a training program. The employer who participates must employ the veteran on a permanent basis after the training is completed.

As I said earlier, the Nation has a special commitment to those who've served in the military. And that commitment includes not only our continuing respect but practical assistance, as well. This program will aid veterans at the same time it aids the many small businesses that will participate.

You've already heard one speech by me, so I won't give you another. But a couple of days ago I was at Fort Bliss in El Paso. As I drove through the base on the way into town, the road was lined with service men and women and their families. I felt a great pride in them and in what they're sacrificing for America. And I feel the same way about the veterans that we're about to help today. They did their best for us, now we must do our best for them.

Now you can see that they're guaranteeing I'm going to sign this. [*Laughter*]

[*At this point, the President signed into law H.R. 2355, the Emergency Veterans' Job Training Act of 1983, which is Public Law 98–77.*]

God bless all of you. Thank you very much for letting me be here, and God bless America.

Note: The President spoke at 9:55 a.m. in the South Hall of the Rivergate Exhibition and Convention Center. He was introduced by James Currieo, national commander of the VFW.

Following his remarks, the President met at the center with VFW leaders and then with Louisiana Republican leaders. He then left New Orleans and went to Rancho del Cielo, his ranch near Santa Barbara, Calif.

Statement on Signing the Student Loan Consolidation and Technical Amendments Act of 1983
August 16, 1983

I have signed H.R. 3394, a bill entitled the Student Loan Consolidation and Technical Amendments Act of 1983.

A major provision in this bill is the extension of temporary authority of the Student

---

[4] *From the advance text of the President's remarks.*

Loan Marketing Association to consolidate various outstanding student loans into new Guaranteed Student Loans with longer repayment periods. This authority has been used in the past year on an experimental basis to see how it could address concerns about student debt burden and capability to repay loans.

Any lengthy extension and expansion of

loan consolidation authority must be carefully studied and the costs fully understood before any final action is taken in legislation. Such a change in the current law would affect significantly how college costs would be financed, and under several options it could add hundreds of millions of dollars annually to the Federal budget. The Congress has been considering a variety of approaches to loan consolidation in recent months, but because of the uncertainty about long-term costs has wisely chosen to provide in H.R. 3394 only an interim extension of the current consolidation authority to November 1, 1983. This will provide an opportunity for the Congress and the administration to review loan consolidation options and costs over the coming weeks, so that the future of the consolidation approach can be carefully and fairly assessed.

It is primarily because of the responsible manner in which the loan consolidation issue has been handled that I am signing H.R. 3394. I find certain other provisions of this bill troublesome.

The Congress continues to reject our efforts to ensure that Federal spending on student aid, especially in the Pell Grants and subsidized Guaranteed Student Loan programs, is better targeted on those who need it most. Recent regulations published by the Secretary of Education relating to family contributions to the cost of education, to the amounts allowed for certain commuting students, and to the definition of independent student are all overridden by this bill.

The cost of education is primarily the responsibility of the family. The Federal Government has a role to play in helping needy students get a chance to receive a college education. This year we are spending over $6 billion on student aid, and the administration has sought to assure that these funds are used most effectively. The relatively modest rule changes promulgated by the Secretary and nullified by the bill would have helped concentrate available funds more on those who most need them to secure higher education.

I want to make clear that my approval of H.R. 3394 does not indicate endorsement of the provisions that would benefit the least needy participants in the student aid programs. Our Federal student assistance dollars are not unlimited, and we will continue to seek legislative and regulatory changes aimed at ensuring that they are spent where they are most needed.

Note: As enacted, H.R. 3394 is Public Law 98–79, approved August 15.

Nomination of Donald Charles Leidel To Be United States Ambassador to Bahrain
August 17, 1983

The President today announced his intention to nominate Donald Charles Leidel, a career member of the Senior Foreign Service, Class of Minister-Counselor, to be Ambassador to the State of Bahrain. He would succeed Peter A. Sutherland.

Mr. Leidel served in the United States Air Force in 1951–1954 as first lieutenant. In 1951 and from 1954 to 1962, he was employed with the Central Intelligence Agency serving on administrative duties in Washington, D.C., Vienna, and Frankfurt. From 1962 to 1965, he was chief of the training staff in the Bureau of Personnel in the Department of State. He was personnel officer in Buenos Aires in 1965–1968 and administrative officer in Mexico City in 1968–1972. From 1972 to 1973, he attended the executive seminar in national and international affairs at the Foreign Service Institute. In the Department he was Executive Director in the Bureau of Educational and Cultural Affairs in 1973–1977, in the Bureau of European Affairs in 1977–1980, and since 1980 he has been Deputy Director of Management Operations.

Mr. Leidel graduated from the University of Wisconsin (B.A., 1949; LL.B., 1951; J.D.,

1966). He is married, has three children, and resides in Washington, D.C. He was born August 31, 1927, in Madison, Wis.

Nomination of John C. McGraw To Be Assayer of the United States Mint at Philadelphia, Pennsylvania
August 17, 1983

The President today announced his intention to nominate John C. McGraw to be Assayer of the Mint of the United States at Philadelphia, Pa., Department of the Treasury. He would succeed Jack Herbert Keller.

Mr. McGraw has served as Acting Assayer at the Philadelphia Mint since January 1983. Previously he was plant metallurgist in 1982; manufacturing engineer in 1980–1982; general engineer in 1980; production supervisor in 1974–1980; and quality control metallurgist in 1973–1974.

Mr. McGraw graduated from Drexel University (B.S., 1971). He is married, has two children, and resides in Springfield, Pa. He was born May 28, 1948, in Philadelphia, Pa.

Nomination of Robert Oberndoerfer Harris To Be a Member of the National Mediation Board
August 17, 1983

The President today announced his intention to nominate Robert Oberndoerfer Harris to be a member of the National Mediation Board for the term expiring July 1, 1986. This is a reappointment.

Mr. Harris has served on the National Mediation Board since 1977. He has been Chairman since 1982 and also served in that position in 1979–1980. He is adjunct professor at Washington College of Law at the American University. Previously he was staff director and counsel, Committee on the District of Columbia, United States Senate, in 1971–1977; staff director and counsel, Committee on Labor and Public Welfare, United States Senate, in 1969–1971; counsel, Labor Subcommittee of the Committee on Labor and Public Welfare, United States Senate, in 1967–1969; and assistant to the Chairman of the National Labor Relations Board in 1961–1967.

Mr. Harris graduated from Columbia College (A.B., 1951), Yale Law School (LL.B., 1954), Georgetown Law School (LL.M., 1961), and attended the Harvard Business School advanced management program in 1972–1973.

He is married, has two children, and resides in Washington, D.C. He was born November 11, 1929, in New York, N.Y.

Statement by Deputy Press Secretary Speakes on Hurricane Damage in Texas
August 18, 1983

Following reports of extensive property damage and the loss of life in the wake of Hurricane Alicia, the President this morning telephoned Senator John Tower and Governor Mark White of Texas. The President told the Senator and the Governor he had directed all appropriate resources of the Federal Government to be made available to the people of Texas.

Initial reports indicate that damage in south Texas is widespread, with heavy property losses in Houston, Galveston, and the six-county surrounding area. There are also reports of some loss of life. The President says he is directing the Federal Emergency Management Administration to move expeditiously to provide relief to the citizens of south Texas. "The Federal Government stands ready to move quickly and is doing so. Our teams are ready to go into the area immediately, and I have impressed upon them the urgency of the situation. We deeply sympathize with the people of Galveston and south Texas who face this massive storm and stand to lose their homes and possessions."

The President paid tribute to emergency workers of civil defense, police, fire, and volunteer emergency services for their role in the evacuation of citizens from the area. "We are confident the actions of these individuals saved lives, and they are to be commended."

As a result of the President's instructions, FEMA Administrator Louis O. Giuffrida has said that the President has instructed him to "do all the law will allow." The FEMA regional office was in contact with the Governor's office yesterday and again today. Governor White has announced in a press conference within the hour that he has sent a telegram to the President requesting Federal assistance. FEMA before noon Pacific time will be airlifting via the Air Force an emergency communications van to provide communications in the affected areas.

FEMA will open a series of offices to have flood insurance claims and start processing those claims immediately. Fifty to seventy thousand people in the area have flood insurance. Six FEMA field teams will be dispatching to the area to coordinate Federal services. They will be en route as soon as their aircraft is able to land following the winds subsiding in the area.

As soon as we receive the request in Washington from Governor White and if the requirements of the Disaster Relief Act are met, which we are confident they are by the severity of the storm, we will make a judgment as to what services are beyond the capability of State and local governments, and then the President will move to issue a Federal disaster declaration.

FEMA has a number of people on standby and will be mustering representatives of more than 20 Federal agencies to be of assistance. These include the Small Business Administration, Department of Agriculture, Army Corps of Engineers, Federal Aviation Administration, and the Department of Transportation.

Note: Deputy Press Secretary Larry M. Speakes read the statement during his daily press briefing for reporters in the briefing facility in the Sheraton Santa Barbara Hotel in Santa Barbara, Calif.

Letter to the Speaker of the House and the Chairman of the Senate Foreign Relations Committee Reporting on the Cyprus Conflict
August 18, 1983

Dear Mr. Speaker: (Dear Mr. Chairman:)

In accordance with Public Law 95–384, I am herewith submitting a report on progress made in the past sixty days toward a negotiated settlement of the Cyprus problem.

Since my last report to you there has been little progress toward settlement. It has been a period of reevaluation by both sides and the intercommunal talks have not resumed.

On June 15 the United Nations Security Council renewed the mandate of the UN Forces in Cyprus (UNFICYP). The report issued at that time by the Secretary General on UNFICYP's activities and on general Cypriot developments is attached.

On July 4 UN Secretary General Perez de Cuellar met in Geneva with Turkish Cypriot leader Denktash. Two days later the Secretary General's Special Representative, Ambassador Gobbi, returned to Nicosia where he remained until August 10 attempting to reconvene the intercommunal talks.

Our position continues to be one of full support for the Secretary General and his Special Representative. We support their efforts to reconvene the intercommunal talks as the best vehicle for an eventual settlement of the Cyprus problem.

Sincerely,

RONALD REAGAN

Note: This is the text of identical letters addressed to Thomas P. O'Neill, Jr., Speaker of the House of Representatives, and Charles H. Percy, chairman of the Senate Foreign Relations Committee.

Message to the Congress Reporting a Budget Deferral
August 18, 1983

To the Congress of the United States:

In accordance with the Impoundment Control Act of 1974, I herewith report a new deferral of budget authority for the Railroad Retirement Board, totaling $165,000.

The details of the deferral are contained in the attached report.

RONALD REAGAN

The White House,
August 18, 1983.

Note: The attachment detailing the deferral is printed in the Federal Register *of August 23, 1983.*

Appointment of John A. Svahn as Assistant to the President for Policy Development
August 19, 1983

The President today announced the appointment of John A. (Jack) Svahn, of Maryland, to be Assistant to the President for Policy Development. The appointment will be effective September 12, 1983.

Mr. Svahn, who has served since March as Under Secretary of Health and Human Services and, concurrently since May 1981, as Commissioner of Social Security, will be responsible to Edwin Meese III, Counsellor to the President, for issue analysis and policy development in all areas of domestic policy. He succeeds Edwin L. Harper.

Mr. Svahn, 40, also served as Director of the U.S. Office of Child Support Enforcement during his service as Social Security Commissioner until his appointment as HHS Under Secretary. In these positions, as well as in his concurrent capacity as Chief Administrator of Disability Insurance, Supplemental Security Income (SSI), and Aid to Families with Dependent Children (AFDC), he played a central policy and management role in income maintenance, health, and social services programs serving 51 million recipients and indirectly affecting nearly every American. Programs under his concurrent supervision account for more than one-third of the annual Federal budget.

Mr. Svahn served on the Reagan administration transition team in 1980 as head of the task force on the Health Care Financing Administration.

Before joining the administration, he was a consultant specializing in public policy management problems. From 1976 to 1979, he was manager of government services for the accounting/management consulting firm of Deloitte Haskins and Sells, Inc.

Mr. Svahn was born in New London, Conn., May 13, 1943. He received a B.A. degree in political science from the University of Washington in 1966. In 1966–1968 he served with the U.S. Air Force.

Beginning in 1968, Mr. Svahn held positions with the State of California and the Federal Government. In California he served first in the State Highway Department and later as chief deputy director and as acting director of social welfare. During then-Governor Reagan's administration in California, he was a principal member of the Governor's welfare reform task force.

From 1973 to 1976, Mr. Svahn held a succession of major Federal positions in the Social and Rehabilitation Service of the then-Department of Health, Education, and Welfare. He was Administrator of the SRS and Director of the U.S. Office of Child Support Enforcement, positions he held concurrently in 1975–1976. While heading SRS, Mr. Svahn was credited with developing and implementing the title XX social services program and the child support enforcement program.

Mr. Svahn is married, has two children, and lives in Severna Park, Md.

Nomination of Philip Abrams To Be Under Secretary of Housing and Urban Development
August 19, 1983

The President today announced his intention to nominate Philip Abrams to be Under Secretary of Housing and Urban Development. He would succeed Donald I. Hovde.

Since 1982 Mr. Abrams has been Assistant Secretary for Housing and Federal Housing Commissioner at the Department of Housing and Urban Development. Previously he was Deputy Assistant Secretary for Housing in 1981–1982. Prior to his position in the administration, he was a developer and builder in the general contracting business for 16 years. He is a member and past president of the Associated Builders and Contractors of America since 1967.

Mr. Abrams graduated from Williams College (B.A., 1961). He served in the United States Navy in 1961–1965 and the U.S. Naval Reserve in 1961–1969. He is married, has three children, and resides in Washington, D.C. He was born November 13, 1939, in Boston, Mass.

Appointment of Harrison H. Schmitt as a Member of the President's Foreign Intelligence Advisory Board
August 19, 1983

The President today announced his intention to appoint Harrison H. Schmitt to be a member of the President's Foreign Intelligence Advisory Board.

Mr. Schmitt served in the United States Senate (R-N. Mex.) in 1976–1982. He was a Senate leader on issues dealing with intelligence activities and served as chairman of the Subcommittee on Legislation and Rights of Americans of the Senate Select Committee on Intelligence and a member of the Subcommittee on Collections and Foreign Operations. During the last 2 years of his term in office, Mr. Schmitt was chairman of the Senate Commerce Committee's Subcommittee on Science, Technology, and

Space and of the Senate Appropriations Committee's Subcommittee on Labor, Health and Human Services, and Education. He was also a leader of the Appropriations subcommittees dealing with defense, energy, and natural resource matters.

Previously Mr. Schmitt was Assistant Administrator for Energy Programs, NASA, in 1974–1975; Chief, Scientist Astronaut Office, NASA, in 1973; and was scientist-astronaut in 1965–1973. He was the Apollo 17 lunar module pilot in 1972.

He graduated from the California Institute of Technology (B.S., 1957) and Harvard University (Ph. D., 1964). He is the recipient of many awards and honors including the NASA Distinguished Service Medal in 1973.

Mr. Schmitt resides in Albuquerque, N. Mex. He was born July 3, 1935, in Santa Rita, N. Mex.

Appointment of Albert D. Wheelon as a Member of the President's Foreign Intelligence Advisory Board
August 19, 1983

The President today announced his intention to appoint Albert D. Wheelon to be a member of the President's Foreign Intelligence Advisory Board.

Since 1966 Dr. Wheelon has been with the Hughes Aircraft Co., joining as corporate vice president (engineering). In July 1970, he was named senior vice president and group president (space and communications). This group is responsible for all the development and production of communications satellites and other space vehicles, spacecraft instrumentation, earth terminals, and terrestrial communications equipment. Previously he was with the Central Intelligence Agency in 1962–1966.

Dr. Wheelon graduated from Stanford University (B.S., 1949) and the Massachusetts Institute of Technology (Ph. D., 1952). He was a teaching fellow in physics at MIT, a research associate in the research laboratories for electronics at MIT, and a visiting professor of engineering at the University of California at Los Angeles in 1957–1961. He is a member of the National Academy of Engineering and a fellow of the Institute of Electrical and Electronics Engineers.

Dr. Wheelon has two children and resides in Los Angeles, Calif. He was born January 18, 1929, in Moline, Ill.

Statement by Deputy Press Secretary Speakes on the Situation in Lebanon
August 19, 1983

Four weeks ago President Reagan reaffirmed his commitment to three fundamental goals in Lebanon—the earliest possible withdrawal of all foreign forces, the extension of Lebanese sovereignty throughout its territory, and that Lebanon shall not again become a source of hostile actions against Israel. The agreement concluded between Israel and Lebanon on May 17 is an important step toward achievement of these goals. The President directed that U.S. efforts be renewed in a mission to the Middle East headed by Ambassadors Robert McFarlane and Richard Fairbanks.

Since that time Ambassadors McFarlane and Fairbanks have traveled extensively throughout the region, undertaking intensive talks with Arab and Israeli leaders. Several conclusions have emerged from these talks.

First and foremost is the solid foundation

of support in the Arab world and in Israel for the principles of full withdrawal and full authority for the Lebanese Government. Equally clear is the enormity of the task the Lebanese Government faces in seeking to strengthen the consensus among the diverse confessional groups in Lebanon which is so essential to the reconstruction and revitalization of the Lebanese economy and the establishment of political stability. It is clear that President Gemayel is committed to these goals.

In its efforts the Government of Lebanon will soon face an opportunity to restore stability and extend the process of reconstruction and consensus building to the districts of Alayh and Shuf as the Government of Israel withdraws its forces from these areas. This move by Israel is the first in a process of withdrawal envisaged in the May 17 agreement. In recent weeks some have questioned the motives underlying this withdrawal by Israel, saying that it presages a permanent partition of Lebanon. We are convinced that the Israeli Government is committed to the full withdrawal of its forces in Lebanon. In this regard it is instructive to note official Israeli statements such as the following:

"It is the policy and the intention of the Government of Israel to withdraw from the whole of Lebanon and that the redeployment of our forces along the Awwali line is only part of that total withdrawal.

"It is our firm desire to see a strong central government restoring its authority over the whole of Lebanon and maintaining security throughout its 10,452 square kilometers; thus, all allegations regarding Israeli intentions of bringing about a partition or division of Lebanon are completely baseless and totally without foundation."

We are confident that further Israeli withdrawal will take place as efforts continue to secure the concurrent withdrawal of PLO and Syrian forces.

The United States pledges its best efforts to help create conditions which will allow these withdrawals to take place at the earliest possible moment. Within this context, the Governments of Israel and Lebanon will coordinate the smooth and orderly return of responsibility in the Alayh-Shuf areas. Concurrently, efforts by the Government of Lebanon to strengthen the consensus will continue so that stability and reconstruction can take hold.

We call upon Syria and the PLO for a corresponding process of withdrawal so that Lebanon can be restored as a unified, sovereign, independent country.

Note: Deputy Press Secretary Larry M. Speakes read the statement to reporters assembled in the briefing facility at the Sheraton Santa Barbara Hotel in Santa Barbara, Calif., at 10:07 a.m.

Radio Address to the Nation on Federal Civilian Employment
August 20, 1983

My fellow Americans:

Before getting into the main subject of today's broadcast, I have what I think is a newsworthy item.

Just about a year ago the Security and Loan Association of Milwaukee, Wisconsin, made a sizable sum—millions of dollars—available for home mortgage loans at an 11.9-percent interest rate. The going rate at the time was about 16 percent. I'm happy to say a number of banks throughout the country followed suit. I'm even happier to

say that Milwaukee Security Savings and Loan has done it again. One hundred million dollars has been made available for home mortgages at a 9.9-percent interest rate. The president of the savings and loan says it's their way of trying to help the economic recovery that is now under way. Well, they deserve a big "thank you" from all of us.

Last month, on one of these talks, I told you about a few of the things we've been doing to cut down on waste and fraud, unnecessary paperwork, redtape, and on abuses of Federal loan programs, all adding up to current and future savings to you, the taxpayer, of billions of dollars. Well, I didn't have any illusions about making the front page with that information, and we didn't. But I thought you had a right to know we've been making progress in restoring government to its rightful role as the servant of the people.

Today, I'd like to share with you some of the other things we're doing to protect your tax dollars and make government more efficient and responsive to your needs.

One important area in which we've made real progress is the employment figure for nondefense Federal agencies. There are a number of vital functions that the Federal Government has to perform, as we all know. But the Federal Government should perform those functions in an efficient, economical manner. It shouldn't cost you, the taxpayer, a penny more than is needed to get the job done.

With that in mind, we made a department-by-department, agency-by-agency review of government operations, looking for needless fat. As a result, by last January, there were 112,000 fewer people working in nondefense Federal agencies. Fifteen departments, agencies, and commissions have been able to reduce their payroll numbers by 20 percent or more. And we've accomplished 90 percent of these savings not by layoffs, but by just not replacing those who retired or left government service. And guess what? The Government is actually doing things more efficiently than it was before.

We're still providing the needed services, and we're doing it with fewer people. The savings to the taxpayer is nearly a billion and a half dollars a year in salaries alone. As you know, most civilian government jobs are not particularly hazardous. Yet we found that one out of every four retirements from government service was a disability retirement. The government didn't require much evidence of disability and this led to considerable abuse of the system.

Today, just by requiring adequate evidence before allowing that kind of retirement, the figure is down nearly 40 percent since 1979 with a savings to the taxpayer of

more than a billion dollars by 1985. And to help prevent accidents and disabilities, we have initiated a new health and safety program for Federal employees to reduce the number of injury claims by 3 percent per year over the next 5 years.

The civil service retirement system is one of the most generous in the world. And of course, we all want dedicated government employees to be rewarded for their efforts, just as the overwhelming majority of Americans who work in the private sector deserve to be. But sometimes civil servants have received preferred treatment.

When we came to office, the civil service retirement system was indexing benefits to inflation twice a year, an advantage enjoyed by virtually no one in the private sector. By going to a once-a-year cost-of-living adjustment for Federal retirees and by making other fair adjustments, we have continued to protect them from inflation while saving the taxpayer some 2½ billion by 1985.

In recent weeks, there's been a lot of talk about my call for merit pay to reward outstanding teachers in America's schools. Well, I think the same principle should apply to the Federal Government itself. Earlier this year, we announced a proposal to require Federal employees to earn, not just automatically inherit, their pay raises. We're still working with Members of the Congress to refine this merit plan to reward good work and good workers so that you, the people, are better served by your government.

Finally, there's something I'd like to get off my chest. It deals with all those headlines about the Pentagon paying $100 for a 4-cent diode or $900 for a plastic cap. What is missing or buried in all those stories about waste is who provided those figures for all the horror stories. This administration exposed those abuses—abuses that had been going on for years. It was Defense Secretary Cap Weinberger's people, his auditors and inspectors, who ordered the audits in the first place, conducted the investigations, and formed a special unit to prosecute defense-related fraud. In just an 18-month period, the Defense Department has obtained 650 convictions, and we're going to keep on exposing these abuses where we find them. I thought you deserved to know that.

Well, till next week, thanks for listening. God bless you.

Note: The President spoke at 9:06 a.m. from Rancho del Cielo, his ranch near Santa Barbara, Calif.

Statement by Deputy Press Secretary Speakes on the Assassination of Benigno S. Aquino, Jr.
August 21, 1983

We regret the murder of Senator Benigno S. Aquino, Jr., in Manila, on August 21st. It is a cowardly and despicable act which the United States Government condemns in the strongest terms.

The U.S. Government trusts that the Government of the Philippines will swiftly and vigorously track down the perpetrators of this political assassination, bring them to justice, and punish them to the fullest extent of the law.

The U.S. Government extends our sympathy to his wife and children in Massachusetts and to the family and friends and supporters in the Philippines.

Note: Deputy Press Secretary Larry M. Speakes read the statement to reporters assembled in the briefing facility at the Sheraton Santa Barbara Hotel in Santa Barbara, Calif., at 10:30 a.m.

Nomination of Alan Lee Keyes To Be United States Representative on the United Nations Economic and Social Council
August 22, 1983

The President today announced his intention to nominate Alan Lee Keyes, of California, to be the Representative of the United States of America on the Economic and Social Council of the United Nations, with the rank of Ambassador. He would succeed Jose S. Sorzano, who is Deputy Representative of the United States to the United Nations.

Mr. Keyes was a teaching fellow at Harvard University in 1974–1978. In 1978 he was TV-radio news secretary with the Bell for Senate Committee in New Jersey and that same year entered the Foreign Service. In 1979–1980 he was consular officer in Bombay. In the Department he was Zimbabwe desk officer in 1980–1981 and a member of the policy planning staff in 1981–1983. In 1983 he resigned from the Foreign Service.

Mr. Keyes received his B.A. (1972) from Harvard College and his Ph. D. (1979) from Harvard University. His foreign languages are French and Spanish, and some knowledge of Italian and Classical Greek. He was born August 7, 1950, in New York, N.Y.

Nomination of Brigadier General Jerome Bernard Hilmes To Be a Member of the Mississippi River Commission
August 22, 1983

The President today announced his intention to nominate Brig. Gen. Jerome Bernard Hilmes to be a member of the Mississippi River Commission. He would succeed Maj. Gen. Hugh Granville Robinson.

He is currently serving as Commander of the United States Army Engineer Division, North Central, in Chicago, Ill. Previously he was Deputy Assistant Chief of Engineers for Facilities and Housing, Office of the Chief of Engineers in Washington, D.C., in 1981–1983; Director of Facilities and Engineering, United States Army Garrison, Fort Bragg, N.C., in 1980–1981; Commander, 7th Engineer Brigade, United States Army Europe, in 1978–1980; and Chief, Engineering and Housing Division, later Assistant Deputy Chief of Staff, Engineer, Office, Deputy Chief of Staff, Engineer, United States Army Europe and Seventh Army, in 1976–1978.

He graduated from the United States Military Academy (B.S.) and Iowa State University (M.S., Ph. D.). He was born December 21, 1935, in Carlyle, Ill.

Appointment of Flora Laney Thornton as a Member of the Library of Congress Trust Fund Board
August 22, 1983

The President today announced his intention to appoint Flora Laney Thornton to be a member of the Library of Congress Trust Fund Board, Library of Congress, for the term of 5 years from March 9, 1983. She will succeed Milton A. Wolf.

Mrs. Thornton serves as a member of the board of regents of Pepperdine University. She also serves as a member of the associates of the University of Southern California and of the board of directors of the Los Angeles World Affairs Council. In 1981 she served as commissioner of the California Commission on Food and Nutrition. Mrs. Thornton is a benefactor of the Music Center and Los Angeles County Museum of Art.

She has two children and resides in Los Angeles, Calif. She was born November 1, 1913, in Independence, Kans.

Informal Exchange With Reporters in Los Angeles, California
August 22, 1983

Q. Mr. President.

Q. How was the check-up?

Q. Are you going to the Philippines?

Q. Are you worried about going to the Philippines, Mr. President?

The President. What's this?

Q. Are you worried about going to the Philippines?

The President. No.

Q. Are you going to go?

The President. What?

Q. Are you going?

The President. Well, I haven't had an opportunity to talk or know the details of this or talk to the State Department, but I am sure that we'll be making a decision on that sort of thing.

Q. Are you going to be talking about re-election this week, about politics and so on?

Are you going to meet with any of your political types?

The President. No.

Q. No?

Q. How is your hearing?

The President. What? [*Laughter*]

Q. How is your hearing?

The President. They said that there has been in that bad ear just very slight deterioration, just about the same as it was last year. Just keeping tabs.

Q. Thank you, Mr. President.

Note: The exchange began at 9:40 a.m. as the President was departing from the office of Dr. John William House, where he had a regular ear examination.

As printed above, this item follows the text of the White House press release.

Statement by Deputy Press Secretary Speakes on the President's Meeting With Senator John Tower of Texas
August 23, 1983

The President certainly respects [Senator Tower's] decision but also regrets it. He has the utmost respect for [Senator] Tower as an outstanding chairman of the Armed Services Committee and also as a Republican leader and strong supporter of the President's policies. The President understands his reasons and respects his reasons, but regrets it.

Note: Deputy Press Secretary Larry M. Speakes made the statement to reporters onboard Air Force One, en route to Seattle, Wash., from Los Angeles, Calif. He also stated that the President met with Senator Tower on August 13 in El Paso, Tex., and that the Senator had then informed the President of his decision not to seek reelection.

Remarks at the Annual Convention of the American Legion in Seattle, Washington
August 23, 1983

Thank you very much, Commander Keller, Governor Spellman, Secretary Donovan, Senator Gorton, Members of Congress who are here, and all of you, my fellow legionnaires:

I thank you for that warm greeting, and the feeling is mutual.

It's always a special pleasure to address the Legion, and today is no exception. So, Legionnaire Ronald Reagan, Pacific Palisades Post—as you've been told—283, reporting for duty. My uniforms are long since in mothballs, but one of the major responsibilities that goes with my present job is being the chief advocate for America's Armed Forces and veterans, and I take that responsibility seriously.

One of the great lessons of life is that if you set high standards and do your best to live up to them, you won't go wrong. The Legion has set high standards for itself and for our country. And as long as America lives up to your standards, America will not go wrong.

At home and abroad, our country is on the right track again. As a nation, we've closed the books on a long, dark period of failure and self-doubt and set a new course. With your continuing support and the support of millions of other patriotic, God-fearing Americans, we've come a long way. But the task we face is still a challenging one, and a lot of hard work remains to be done. But let's be sure we know what needs to be done.

We've got a few people in Washington who don't want to hear when we tell of our arms control and strategic modernization program and America's responsibility to protect peace and freedom. My own concern with these issues is nothing new, as many of you know. Three years ago at your Boston convention, I pledged to restore America's military posture so that we could promote peace while safeguarding our freedom and security. With the help of groups like the Legion, we've kept that pledge.

Our military forces are back on their feet and standing tall. Modern equipment is being delivered to the troops, training is way up, and combat readiness rates have really soared. And once again, young Americans wear their uniforms and serve their flag with pride. We're getting and keeping very good people in all of the services. We've made great progress, and we're going to make more. And I hope that makes you as proud as it does me.

I have to interrupt and tell you a little thing—and I don't mean this that these young men and women in our armed services are hostile or warlike; they know that they're the peacekeepers. But an ambassador wrote me a letter—our Ambassador to Luxembourg—and he said that he'd been up on the East German frontier and visiting the 2d Armored Cavalry Regiment. And as he went back to his helicopter, he was followed by a young 19-year-old trooper, and the young man asked him if he thought he could get a message to me. Well, being an ambassador, he allowed as how he could. And the kid says, "Well, will you tell him we're proud to be here, and we ain't scared of nothing."

But while I'm on the subject of our military forces, I want to reaffirm our determination to account for every brave American who served in Southeast Asia. This administration has not forgotten and will never forget the sacrifices that they and their families have made. And we will not rest until the fullest possible accounting has been made.

The other half of restoring our military posture concerns our strategic forces. In the past, we paid a grim price for indecision and neglect—for a one-way restraint that was never returned by the other side. The resulting imbalance weakened the credibility of our nuclear deterrent, the deterrent that has been the single greatest bulwark for peace in the postwar era. While past American leaders hesitated or naively hoped for the best, the Soviet Union was left free to pile up new nuclear arsenals without any real incentives to seriously negotiate reductions.

Well, history doesn't offer many crystal-clear lessons for those who manage our nation's affairs. But there are a few, and one of them is surely the lesson that weakness on the part of those who cherish freedom inevitably leads to trouble—that it only encourages the enemies of both peace and freedom. On the other hand, history teaches us that by being strong and resolute we can keep the peace—and even reduce the threats to peace.

And that was why, at your Boston convention in 1980, I pledged to strive for arms reduction agreements—not so-called arms control agreements that permitted further growth, but real arms reductions.

We've kept that pledge, too. For the past 2½ years, this administration has steadfastly followed a dual track of deterrence through modernization and the search for a more stable peace through arms reduction negotiations. There is no contradiction in this dual approach, despite what some of the critics in Washington might have you believe. The restoration of a credible deterrent and the search for real arms reductions and stability are two sides of the same coin—a coin that is inscribed with the words "peace" and "security."

Now, our efforts are designed to sustain peace, plain and simple. We don't seek an arms race; indeed, we seek to reverse the trends that cause it by beginning to lower the levels of the nuclear arms. But we will not, and we cannot, accept anything that would be detrimental to our security and to the freedom and safety of our children and our grandchildren.

And that's what is so important about the MX. The MX Peacekeeper missile and our program to develop a new, small, single-warhead missile are critical to our country's present and future safety. They will maintain state-of-the-art readiness against the Soviets' already modernized systems. They will also ensure stability and deterrence, making it clear that aggression by the Soviet Union would never pay. And they're an essential incentive for the Soviets to negotiate seriously for genuine arms reduction so that we can move to a more stable world in which the risk of war is reduced.

Modernization goes hand in hand with deterrence. Both are necessary incentives for successful negotiations. Many of our critics willfully ignore this interrelationship. Instead, they focus their attention and their criticism on some single point which doesn't address the central issue. Often, it's based on wishful thinking or downright misinformation.

For example, one argument contends that the MX Peacekeeper would pose a first-strike threat to the Soviet Union. Well, in the most fundamental sense, this argument runs counter to the whole history of America. Our country has never started a war, and we've never sought nor will we ever develop a strategic first-strike capability. Our sole objective is deterrence, the strength and credibility it takes to prevent war.

And in any case, there is no way that the MX, even with the remaining Minuteman force, could knock out the entire Soviet ICBM force, so the argument is a false one, both philosophically and technically. What we really want and what we would have with the MX in place is enough force that tells the enemy we'd do them a lot of damage.

But the example that I've given is typical of the twisted logic of the anti-MX lobby. It reminds me of that tale told of an armed services poker game which took place a few years back on a western military base. The MP's were tipped off, raided the barracks. The four poker players just managed to hide the cards and poker chips in time. When the police got there, they were sitting at an empty table, staring innocently at each other, and the MP sergeant asked each one in turn if he'd been gambling. And the soldier bit his lip and replied, "No, sarge, I haven't been gambling." And the sailor paused, silently asked the Lord's forgiveness, and also said he wasn't gambling. And

the airman answered the same way. And that finally brought them to the marine. And they said, "Have you been gambling?" And the MP looked the cop right dead in the eye and asked, "Who with?" [*Laughter*] That was quick thinking, but the marine sure avoided a real issue, and the real issue's what counts.

The real national defense issue of our time is maintaining deterrence while seeking arms reductions. And today I'm pleased to be able to report some good news on the negotiating front. Our fundamental negotiating positions in both the START and INF talks have been strengthened by a number of related developments that have occurred this year. Let me share a few of them with you.

First on the list is that strong, bipartisan support is beginning to surface for our strategic program. Starting with the perceptive recommendations of the Scowcroft commission, and strengthened by the bipartisan congressional support in strategic modernization votes in May and July, America has finally begun to forge a national consensus for peace and security.

The MX Peacekeeper program and the development program for a new, small, single-warhead missile will complement the B–1 bomber and Trident submarine programs, the other legs of the triad. But we aren't over the hump yet. There's still work to be done, and I'm counting on your continuing and active support as we approach the next legislative round on appropriations for the MX this autumn. If we see this mission through, the combined efforts of this administration and the Congress will restore the credibility of America's strategic posture—the essential foundation for deterrence and successful negotiations.

We've learned over and over again that only common resolve in the West can bring responsiveness from the East. And fortunately, Western allied unity today is a firm reality. Our negotiations have been preceded by close consultations with the Congress and with our allies. This process has continued during the negotiations in Geneva, and we've given our negotiators the flexibility to explore all possible avenues with the Soviets.

"Peace" is a beautiful word, but it is also freely used and sometimes even abused. As I've said before, peace is an objective, not a policy. Those who fail to understand this do so at their peril. Neville Chamberlain thought of peace as a vague policy in the thirties, and the result brought us closer to World War II. Today's so-called peace movement—for all its modern hype and theatrics—makes the same old mistake. They would wage peace by weakening the free. And that just doesn't make sense.

My heart is with those who march for peace. I'd be at the head of the parade if I thought it would really serve the cause of peace. But the members of the real peace movement, the real peacekeepers and peacemakers, are people who understand that peace must be built on strength. And for that, the American people and free people everywhere owe all of you a deep debt of gratitude.

Like you, our allies remain united in a common effort to strengthen both deterrence and the prospect for arms reduction through negotiations. They recognize the dangers to allied unity of Soviet propaganda and thinly veiled threats—at causing NATO to abandon its dual-track decision to modernize and negotiate. If we lack the will to provide a credible deterrent, then we could look forward to ever more aggressive Soviet behavior in the futue. Because NATO understands this, NATO will persevere.

When you add it all up, despite the problems, there is strong reason for hope. This administration has worked very hard over the course of many months to refine our own negotiating objectives and positions. We've developed a sound, well-thought-out strategy to achieve them. We stand united with the Congress and our allies. Our strategic triad is being modernized. We're negotiating arms reductions in good faith. And there's been encouraging movement in these negotiations.

For the first time, in the START negotiations, the Soviets are willing to actually talk about actual reductions. In Vienna, at the mutual balanced force reduction talks, the Soviet negotiators have shown movement on the verification issues needed to permit us to negotiate reductions in the conventional force safely. There has also been progress in discussing confidence-building measures. All these indicators, modest though they may seem, point in the same positive direction—new hope for arms reductions and a more secure world.

Let's not kid ourselves. There are lots of ambiguities, and we've still got a long way to go, a long way from agreement. Plenty of tough, hard bargaining remains to be done at the negotiating table. But I can assure you that our highest priority is focused on this, the most challenging and important issue of our lifetime, and we're making headway for peace.

Another issue of critical importance to all Americans—and one I view as the centerpiece of American foreign policy—concerns our responsibility as peacemaker.

We can't build a safer world with honorable intentions and good will alone. Achieving the fundamental goals our nation seeks in world affairs—peace, human rights, economic progress, national independence, and international stability—means supporting our friends and defending our interests. Our commitment as peacemaker is focused on these goals. Right now this commitment is most visible in Central America, the Middle East, and Africa.

Our policy in Central America is to help the people of that troubled region help themselves—help them to build a better life, to help them toward liberty, and to help them reverse centuries of poverty and inequity. And that's what they want, too. In Costa Rica, democracy and respect for human rights are a long and proud tradition. In Honduras, democratic institutions are taking root. In El Salvador, democracy is beginning to work even in the face of externally supported terrorism and guerrilla warfare.

We know that democracy in Central America will not be built overnight. But step by step, with humanitarian, economic, and private sector assistance from the United States, it can and will be achieved.

And that's why we established the Caribbean Basin Initiative, a program designed to help the people in that region help themselves. The Caribbean Basin Initiative is based on a combination of trade and private investment incentives. We decided to listen and learn from what our neighbors have been saying for a long time—that the best thing we could do is to help them build a better, freer life for themselves. We agree, and though you wouldn't know it from some of the coverage, by far the greatest portion of our aid to Central America is humanitarian and economic.

Now, there are some—in Moscow and Havana—who don't want to let our Caribbean neighbors solve their problems peacefully. They seek to impose their alien form of totalitarianism with bullets instead of ballots. And that's why we're supporting a security shield for those nations that are threatened.

Unless that shield is there, democracy, reform, economic development, and constructive dialog and negotiations cannot survive and grow. Other than training our own troops, this is the only purpose behind our military exercises—to demonstrate our commitment to the free aspirations and sovereign integrity of our neighbors.

I've said it before, and I'll say it again: Human rights means working at problems, not walking away from them. Would America be America if, in their hour of need, we abandoned our nearest neighbors? From the tip of Tierra del Fuego to Alaska's Point Barrow, we're all Americans. We worship the same God, cherish the same freedom. Can we stand idly by and allow a totalitarian minority to destroy our common heritage?

Our concern is justice. Has communism ever provided that? Our concern is poverty. Has a Communist economic system ever brought prosperity? No. If the United States were to let down the people of Central America—people who are struggling for the democratic values that we share—we would have let ourselves down, too. We could never be certain of ourselves, much less of the future, if we turned our back on our nearest neighbors' struggle for peace, freedom, and evolving democracy.

In the Middle East, the pursuit of peace between Israel and its Arab neighbors remains another fundamental objective of this administration. Yes, it's a thorny problem, and our negotiators have faced serious difficulties over the past 2½ years. But there's been real progress.

The Sinai Peninsula was returned to Egypt in April of 1982. This essential step in the establishment of peace between Egypt and Israel wouldn't have been possible without our decision to contribute to the multinational force and observers that are currently operating in the Sinai.

In Lebanon, our marines continue to serve alongside their French, British, and Italian comrades as we work for the withdrawal of all foreign forces from that troubled land. Our joint presence strengthens the resolve of the Lebanese Government to assume the tough task of maintaining order.

We Americans covet no foreign territory, and we have no intention of becoming policeman to the world. But as the most powerful country in the West, we have a responsibility to help our friends keep the peace. And we should be proud of our achievements and especially proud of the fine men and women of our Armed Forces who undertake these tough yet vital tasks.

In Africa, we're engaged in a parallel commitment—economic development, the growth of democracies, and the peaceful resolution of conflict. And here, too, our emphasis is on developmental and economic assistance.

We maintain only a handful of military advisers on the whole African continent. Our economic aid is four times larger than what we spend on security assistance. Contrast this with what the Soviet Union is doing. The record shows that since the Soviets began their aid program to Africa in 1954, military aid has outpaced all other Soviet aid by 7 to 1. Then add more than 40,000 Soviet and surrogate military personnel stationed in Africa, and it's no wonder that Africa is rife with conflict and tension.

For our part, we're actively working to defuse the tensions and conflict in Namibia and Angola while we help fight poverty in the region. In Chad, the United States is a partner in a multinational economic assistance package designed to get this tragically poor and strife-torn country on its feet. But without protection from external aggression, there can be no economic progress. And naked, external aggression is what is taking place in Chad today.

Drawing upon the nearly $10 billion

worth of Soviet military equipment and munitions now in Libya, Colonel Qadhafi has been using Soviet-built fighter bombers, T–55 tanks, and artillery in a blatant attempt to destroy a legitimate government. President Habre and the people of his country are truly beleaguered as they struggle to preserve their independence. It is in this context that we have joined a number of other countries in providing emergency security assistance to Chad.

Yes, in Africa there is real reason for concern. But there are also harbingers of hope. Less than 2 weeks ago, I had the pleasure of meeting with President Diouf of Senegal. He's a great man doing a great job. His outstanding leadership has brought Senegal fully into the community of truly democratic states. And a similar democratic success story has just taken place in Nigeria, Africa's most populous nation, where free Presidential elections were successfully completed last week.

That's right, there's a democratic revolution going on in this world. It may not grab the headlines, but it's there, and it's growing. The tide of history is with the forces of freedom—and so are we.

That's the real message, and that's the overwhelming news story of our time, even though it seldom makes the front page. The light of the democratic ideal is not slowly fading away. It gains in brightness with every passing day, but it needs our care and cultivation.

You know, Mark Twain once remarked that he spent $25 to research his family tree, and then he had to spend $50 to cover it up. [*Laughter*] Well, America is more fortunate. We can be proud of our heritage,

and we need never hide from our roots. The world we live in is not an easy one, but we've inherited a noble mission, a mission that casts a beacon of hope for all the Earth's people.

America, more than anything, wants lasting peace—peace with liberty, with justice, and with the freedom to follow the dictates of God and conscience. To succeed, we will need wisdom, strength, and imagination. We'll need patience and vigor. But to seek anything less would be to deny our heritage and the real meaning of our great nation.

You know, our national anthem is probably the only one that asks a question: Does that banner still wave o'er the land of the free and the home of the brave? When Francis Scott Key wrote that, he was asking if our flag was still flying. Well, today we know the flag still flies. But what we continue to answer is that it does wave over a people that are still free and still brave and determined to preserve this land for generations to come.

Thank you for all that you and the Legion are doing to help America stay true to this quest, and God bless you all.

Thank you.

Note: The President spoke at 12 noon in the Seattle Center Mercer Forum Arena. He was introduced by Albert Keller, Jr., national commander of the American Legion.

Following his remarks, the President met with Republican Party donors and attended a fundraising reception for the Republican Party at the Seattle Center. He then returned to Los Angeles, Calif., and the Century Plaza Hotel, where he remained overnight.

Message to the Senate Returning Without Approval a Bill To Suspend Temporarily a Deduction Under the Milk Support Program
August 23, 1983

To the Senate of the United States:

I am returning herewith without my approval S.J. Res. 149, "To temporarily suspend the authority of the Secretary of Agri-

culture, under the milk price support program, to impose a second 50 cents per hundredweight deduction from the proceeds of sale of all milk marketed commercially in the United States."

Current law allows the Secretary to deduct 50 cents per hundredweight from the proceeds of sale of all milk marketed, if the Commodity Credit Corporation (CCC) purchases of surplus milk are expected to exceed 5 billion pounds. This deduction program became effective April 16, 1983. Current law also authorizes the Secretary to deduct another 50 cents per hundredweight if CCC purchases of surplus milk are expected to exceed 7.5 billion pounds. Dairy farmers who reduce their milk production according to Department of Agriculture guidelines will be entitled to refunds of this second 50 cents.

This second deduction and the refund program are scheduled to go into effect on September 1 and are expected to produce net receipts by CCC of about $60 million during September. Even with both deductions in effect, the Department of Agriculture projects that CCC purchases of milk will still exceed 16 billion pounds for the current marketing year at a net cost to taxpayers of $2.4 billion.

I cannot support S.J. Res. 149, as it would reduce by $60 million the amount of funds available to be used to defray the cost of the milk price support program and would reduce the desired downward effect upon milk production. Without the added downward pressure of the second 50-cent deduction there will be less incentive to decrease milk production.

In addition, if I signed S.J. Res. 149, there would be even greater confusion on the part of milk producers. The first deduction has been the subject of extensive litigation. Since Secretary Block has announced that the second deduction and the refund program will begin on September 1, a delay of one month would only add to the confusion and make planning by producers even more difficult.

Implementation of the deduction has already been delayed considerably. As a result, the cost savings contemplated when this provision was enacted have not materialized, further worsening the Federal deficit.

The annual cost of the dairy price support program is now over $2 billion and will continue to grow unless something is done. We cannot continue to absorb these enormous costs. The Administration's position last year, which the Congress failed to accept, called for increased flexibility to set support levels that would facilitate a more favorable supply and demand balance and reduce Federal outlays. We remain committed to an economically sound dairy industry with adequate supplies of milk and dairy products for consumers, and we will continue to work with the Congress to achieve that end. However, until Congress can act on a mutually acceptable dairy program that accomplishes the objectives stated above, we must continue to exercise without further delay what authority we have to deal with our dairy problem.

RONALD REAGAN

The White House,
August 23, 1983.

Executive Order 12438—Review of Increases in Rates of Basic Pay for Employees of the Veterans' Administration
August 23, 1983

By the authority vested in me as President by the Constitution and laws of the United States of America, including Section 4107(g)(4) of title 38 of the United States Code, in order to establish procedures for review of proposed increases in the rates of basic pay of certain employees of the Veterans' Administration, it is hereby ordered as follows:

Section 1. The Director of the Office of Personnel Management is designated to exercise the authority vested in the President by Section 112 of Public Law 96–330 (94 Stat. 1037) to review and disapprove increases in the rates of basic pay proposed by the Administrator of Veterans' Affairs and to provide the appropriate Committees of the Congress with a written statement of the reasons for any such disapprovals.

Sec. 2. In exercising this authority, the Director of the Office of Personnel Management shall assure that any increases in basic pay proposed by the Administrator of Veterans' Affairs are in the best interest of the Federal government; do not exceed the amounts authorized by Section 112; and are made only to:

(1) Provide pay in an amount competitive with, but not exceeding, the amount of the same type of pay paid to the same category of health-care personnel at non-Federal health-care facilities in the same labor market;

(2) Achieve adequate staffing at particular facilities; or

(3) Recruit personnel with specialized skills, especially those with skills which are especially difficult or demanding.

Sec. 3. The Administrator of Veterans' Af-

fairs shall provide to the Director of the Office of Personnel Management such information as the Director may request in order to carry out the responsibilities delegated by this Order.

Sec. 4. The Director shall provide the Administrator of Veterans' Affairs with a copy of any written statement, provided to the appropriate committees of the Congress, which sets forth the reasons for disapproval of any proposed increase in rates of basic pay under this Order.

RONALD REAGAN

The White House,
August 23, 1983.

[*Filed with the Office of the Federal Register, 11:11 a.m., August 29, 1983*]

Note: The text of the Executive order was released by the Office of the Press Secretary on August 24.

Excerpt From an Interview With Ann Devroy of the Gannett News Service on Women's Issues
August 24, 1983

Ms. Devroy. I promised not to ask you any nonranch questions. Can I ask you one question about women?

The President. Yes.

Ms. Devroy. Why are you so misunderstood on this issue?

The President. I don't know.

Ms. Devroy. Do you think you are misunderstood?

The President. Yes, I do. But I think part of it is very deliberate and political. I think, very frankly, in the 1982 election, it was made apparent that some of those who are most active in this are most active if it's in behalf of the Democratic candidates. Let me just point out: We had some fine Republican women candidates, and they didn't get any help or support, even though they were in—well, Millicent Fenwick is an example. So, I think this is part of it.

But if they look back, the California record, I don't know of anyone else in the

country that did this. Yes, it's true that I happen to disagree about the equal rights amendment, but not because I think it would give women something of value to them.

I'm surprised that more of them have not looked at how much mischief could be done, brought about by men, that could take advantage of that and then say, "Hey, you can't make me do this because, labor regulations and so forth," that are definitely there for the benefit of women. I could see some troublemaking men, mischiefmakers just saying, "Well, look, I don't have to do that." The same would be true militarily. But mainly, the main thing is, as I see it, it would put—it isn't an instant solution. It would put things in the hands of the courts that belong in the hands of the legislature. If you thought it was discrimination, you would have to take—you would have to file a suit.

Now, what I set out in California, when I was faced with this, and I finally came to the decision about that, I said, but there should be equality. And so we started combing the statutes to find out where in the State law might be based discriminations. We found 14 laws that deliberately discriminated against women. For example, a wife with her own money could not invest that money without her husband's permission. Well, that's ridiculous. And so, we got all these 14 changed.

Then when I got to Washington, I'd been dreaming about this—and one other State had done it—and I said let us in this whole federalism talk, let us go to the States, to the Governors, the State legislatures, and see if they won't set up the same kind of operation. Well, all 50 States did. Now, I understand, if what Miss [Barbara] Honegger said is right, that maybe some of them have dallied and so forth. There's a limit. Once I persuade them to do this, you can't force them. The States are sovereign in our system here. But maybe there is more we could do to encourage them.

Ms. Devroy. Well, Larry's getting mad at me.

Deputy Press Secretary Speakes. What he is saying is what I said about 15 minutes ago.

Ms. Devroy. I know.

The President. This was true. But we also started the Justice Department on this combing of the Federal laws. Well, that's quite a sizable undertaking. And she's absolutely wrong in what she said about what we're doing there, and the pace. It has come in, as I understand it, in three very voluminous packets.

Well, out of the first one we have already submitted recommendations to Senator Dole, who is following through now legislatively. These things have to be done by legislation. And there has been a kind of a full plate there for the legislature. And you can't just get on the phone and say, "Pass this."

So, we're doing this, and, believe me, I'm sincere about it and want to correct it and want it done. And I wasn't joking when I said that women actually were the civilizers of humanity.

Ms. Devroy. I guess people didn't understand that.

The President. No. And I think a great many scholars have said that in the past before I ever thought of it, that women have been the civilizing influence. You are kind of the superior people.

Ms. Devroy. Maureen and I talked about this just 2 days ago.

The President. Golly, I think we've talked all there is about the ranch.

Mr. Speakes. What's amazing about your answer is I just gave about a 30-minute lecture to the press that you'd say I got from the horse's mouth.

Ms. Devroy. You sure did. The same points, very similar points.

Thank you, Mr. President. I appreciate it.

The President. Thank you.

Note: The interview began at 11:20 a.m. at the Century Plaza Hotel in Los Angeles, Calif.

As printed above, this item follows the text of the White House press release.

Nomination of Saundra Brown Armstrong To Be a Commissioner of the Consumer Product Safety Commission
August 24, 1983

The President today announced his intention to nominate Saundra Brown Armstrong to be a Commissioner of the Consumer Product Safety Commission for a term of 7 years from October 27, 1983. She would succeed Edith Barksdale Sloan.

Since 1982 she has been serving as a trial attorney for the Public Integrity Section of the Criminal Division at the Department of Justice. Previously she was deputy district attorney for Alameda County in 1980–1982; senior consultant to the California Assembly

Committee on Criminal Justice in 1979–1980; deputy district attorney of Alameda County in 1977–1978; and a policewoman with the City of Oakland Police Department in 1970–1977.

Mrs. Armstrong is a member of the Alameda County Bar Association, the California District Attorneys' Association, and the National Council of Negro Women.

She graduated from California State University (B.A., 1969) and the University of San Francisco (J.D., 1977). She is married and resides in Arlington, Va. She was born March 23, 1947, in Oakland, Calif.

Announcement of the Vice President's Trip to Africa and Europe
August 24, 1983

At the request of the President, the Vice President, accompanied by Mrs. Bush, will visit Morocco, Algeria, Tunisia, Yugoslavia, Romania, Hungary, and Austria between September 11 and September 21.

The Vice President's visit to the countries of north Africa will reaffirm our long friendships with Tunisia and Morocco and will strengthen our relations with Algeria, an important nonaligned country. The Vice President's visits to Yugoslavia and Austria underscore the important international role of these countries and U.S. support for Austria's neutrality and respect for Yugoslavia's independence and nonalignment. Finally, the Vice President's visits to two important Eastern European countries underscore the United States continued willingness to maintain dialog with the East and the continuing U.S. policy of differentiation toward the countries of Eastern Europe.

Proclamation 5084—National Hispanic Heritage Week, 1983
August 25, 1983

By the President of the United States of America

A Proclamation

National Hispanic Heritage Week pays tribute to a rich part of America's cultural tradition, offering all Americans a welcome opportunity to recognize the qualities and contributions of Hispanic Americans from earliest colonial times to the present. The dedication to principles of loyalty, patriotism, strong religious faith and devotion to family displayed by Hispanic Americans is basic to the American way of life.

Hispanic Americans have played an important role in the development of our rich cultural heritage and every State has benefitted from their influence. They have distinguished themselves in the arts and sciences, education, industry, government and many other areas of productive endeavor. Indeed, they are a part of all that makes America great.

Just as their forefathers sought a dream in the New World, Hispanic Americans have realized their dreams in our great Nation and will continue to do so. Their dedication to higher purposes reflects what is best in the American spirit.

Through the years, Hispanic American citizens have risen to the call of duty in defense of liberty and freedom. Their bravery is well-known and has been demonstrated time and again, dating back to the aid rendered by General Bernardo de Galvez during the American Revolution.

In recognition of the many achievements of the Hispanic American Community, the Congress, by joint resolution approved September 17, 1968 (82 Stat. 848), authorized and requested the President to issue annually a proclamation designating the week which includes September 15 and 16 as National Hispanic Heritage Week.

Now, Therefore, I, Ronald Reagan, President of the United States of America, do hereby proclaim the week beginning September 11, 1983, as National Hispanic Heritage Week in honor of the Hispanic peoples who have enriched our daily lives, our traditions and our national strength. In this spirit, I ask all of our citizens to reflect on the sense of brotherhood that binds us together as one people.

In Witness Whereof, I have hereunto set my hand this 25th day of Aug., in the year of our Lord nineteen hundred and eighty-three, and of the Independence of the United States of America the two hundred and seventh.

RONALD REAGAN

[*Filed with the Office of the Federal Register, 11:10 a.m., August 29, 1983*]

Remarks at the Hispanic Economic Outlook Preview Luncheon in Los Angeles, California
August 25, 1983

Thank you, Tony, Mr. Chairman, Mr. Toastmaster, presidents and officials of the organizations represented here, and you ladies and gentlemen. I'm a little handicapped right now with your remarks about the three essential languages. I only know one of them. [*Laughter*]

I had an occasion to regret that once. I was in Mexico, speaking to an audience there, and then sat down to very scattered and unenthusiastic applause. And I was embarrassed, of course, and more so when the next speaker started speaking in Spanish, which I didn't understand, but was being interrupted almost every other sentence with applause. So, to hide my embarrassment, I started clapping before anyone else, and clapped longer than anyone and louder until our Ambassador leaned over to me and said, "I wouldn't do that if I were you. He's interpreting your speech." [*Laughter*]

But it's great to be back in California speaking to business men and women who are on the front lines of economic progress in America. If our country is to move forward, if our people are to improve their standard of living, if we're to meet the challenges of world competition, it will depend in large measure on you, your skill, your faith, and your dedication.

Business men and women make decisions every day that direct the resources and energies of our country, making investments and taking risks and putting in that extra effort that makes all the difference between success and failure. This is what made our country a miracle of efficiency and the envy of the world.

Now, of course, it's possible to have too much of a good thing. There was a small town on a lake, and a young man there named Elmer, who went into business for himself selling fish to the local restaurant. But no one could figure out how Elmer managed to catch so many fish every day and deliver them on time to the restaurant. And so, the game warden asked his cousin, who happened to be the sheriff, Elmer's cousin, to look into the matter. So, the sheriff just, one day, asked Elmer, he says, "Why don't you take me out with you when you go fishing," figured he'd find out where this fabulous fishing hole was, and they rowed out to the middle of the lake. The sheriff cast in his line; Elmer reached down in the tackle box and came up with a stick of dynamite, lit the fuse, threw it into the water. And after the explosion, of course, the fish, by the hundreds, belly up, came floating to the surface. [*Laughter*] Well, the sheriff looked at his cousin and said, "Elmer, do you realize you just committed a felony?" Elmer reached into the tackle box, came up with another stick of dynamite, lit it, handed it to the sheriff, and said, "Did you come here to talk or to fish?" [*Laughter*]

You business men and women of Hispanic

descent stand for much more than efficiency. Being back here in California, I feel very much at home, but there's something else that makes me feel comfortable, and that is being among men and women like you who exemplify the values I admire.

There are people in America today who feel that expressions of love for country and family are old-fashioned. They squirm and get uneasy when we talk about pride in our neighborhood or our work or speak of religious values. Yes, there are people like that. But you won't find them in the Hispanic business community.

To every cynic who says the American dream is dead, I say look at the Americans of Hispanic descent who are making it in the business world. With hard work and no one to rely on but themselves, entrepreneurs of Hispanic descent are not just building corporations, they're building a better America for all of us.

Inspirational examples of individual accomplishment abound. Recently, the Hispanic Business Magazine and the Los Angeles Times featured stories about a junior high school dropout named Manuel Caldera, a veteran who later earned his G.E.D. degree. He went on to become an electronic technician and then an engineer. And with money he saved and with help from a minority loan program during the Nixon administration, he started AMEX Systems, a company specializing in the development and manufacture of electronic equipment. Today his company does more than support his family. His company supports 700 employees and earns some $62 million a year in sales.

And then there is Xochitl Galvan, born in Mexico. Coming to a new country without a word of English, she and her husband Ramon worked as laborers. And in 1960 the family pooled their savings, and with a private loan, they started a small restaurant in Santa Monica. With hard work and an eye on quality, their business expanded and eventually they opened nine restaurants in the Los Angeles area. In 1980 they moved to San Diego, and today they've opened four Casa Bonita restaurants there.

This is the success story of a husband and wife business team, but it's also a warm, human story. While making her mark in the business world, Xochitl raised eight fine children. Her seven lovely daughters take after their mother. All of them, along with their brother, are deeply involved in the family business.

The strength and dignity of Hispanic women cannot be underestimated and are characteristic of all of which you should be very proud.

I know Robert Alvarez agrees with that. He and his wife Marguerite are another husband and wife team with a dream. In 1949 Robert saved $700 he earned as a laborer, bought some produce, and started selling it from the back of a truck in San Diego. He operated that way for several years till he figured out his paperwork wouldn't be that much greater if he expanded his operation. So, he set up an office and started to deliver to stores. In 1962 his wife joined in and so did the children. By 1972 Marguerite was elected president of a growing concern. Today, Coast Citrus Corporation is a multimillion-dollar business, and the whole family plays a part.

Success didn't come easily for any of these people. Sometimes there were failures along the way. Julio Rivera, who immigrated from Colombia 18 years ago, began as a repairman and then tried to start his own mail-sorting business. He wasn't successful in that first try, but it was just a first try. He reorganized, brought in some partners, worked hard, and operated with no frills, and today has an up-and-coming bulk-mail company that employs 84 people.

Now, these few that I've mentioned, and others of you right in this room, offer us a vision of progress and hope. You prove that freedom of enterprise, with it come values that make America more than a rich country—they make us a good country.

I don't have to tell you that the Mexican and American Foundation named Robert Alvarez man of the year for 1983. And, Robert, congratulations. But Robert was honored for more than his business accomplishment. He and Marguerite have used their success to help others, providing scholarships for young Americans of Hispanic descent and giving generously to religious and humanitarian efforts. Through the Mexican and American Foundation, they've given over $10,000 in the last few years to a home for orphaned girls in Tecate, Mexico.

Manuel Caldera provides scholarships so students of Hispanic descent can study engineering and science at Whittier College. The Galvan family contributes to a school for retarded children in Tijuana. In Washington, we call these things private sector initiatives. I hope I get this right, my pronunciation. Americans of Hispanic descent call it *corazon.* To any Anglos who didn't understand that, it means "heart." [*Laughter*]

These are not unusual stories. They are, instead, a byproduct of our freedom that is always present but often unnoticed—respect and concern for others. Business professionals realize that success depends on fulfilling the needs of others and doing it courteously and efficiently. And by doing for others, you're also achieving for yourself.

This system of ours in the United States, based on that principle, has produced a better quality of life and more freedom than any other country has ever known. We're a people blessed with abundance. And we're a compassionate people. We came here from every corner of the world, from every ethnic background and every race and religion, seeking a better way of life. Our history isn't perfect, but we can be proud of our country. And our citizens of Hispanic descent can be particularly proud of the contributions that they have made and are making to the health and vitality of this nation.

All of us share a sacred responsibility—to maintain the opportunity and freedom we've been given and to pass it on to future generations. In a free society, the future is in the hands of the people, and that means us.

In recent years, our task has not been easy. We're now emerging from an economic crisis so severe that had we not taken the necessary steps to correct it, it would have robbed our children of the America that we know and love.

Three years ago, pessimism totally inconsistent with our national character had spread across this land. I think you'll remember. The world seemed to be counting us out, suggesting that America's best days were past, that even our leaders were throwing up their hands, talking of national malaise, and saying that our problems were unsolvable.

Well, at first, the challenge seemed overwhelming. It's taken patience and hard work, just as it does for any enterprise. What was needed was not slight alterations, but basic change. I'm pleased to report to you today that after a long period of stagnation and decline, this great nation is moving forward again, and we're not turning back.

When we got to Washington, inflation was running at double-digit levels and had been doing so for 2 years straight. Long-range investment and planning were useless. Capital flowed into nonproductive inflation hedges instead of job-producing investment. Our senior citizens helplessly watched as the value of their savings eroded. Poor and middle-class working people saw their real wages and their standard of living begin to shrink. Well, together, we've licked inflation, and we're never going back to the policies that unleashed this monster on the American people.

Inflation was only part of the picture. Two-and-a-half years ago the prime interest rate hit 21½ percent. Today the prime stands at 11 percent. There will be slight fluctuations, but if the Congress acts responsibly, interest rates will come down some more, and soon.

And here again there are individuals that don't wait. In fact, the Security Savings and Loan Association in Milwaukee, Wisconsin, has just made a hundred million dollars available for home mortgages at a 9.9-percent interest rate. I like to talk about that 'cause I hope some others'll get the same idea. [*Laughter*]

The basic reason for our economic troubles, troubles from which we're now just emerging, is that for years, government was spending too much and taxing too much. And I don't have to tell you in the business community; if more and more resources are channeled into the government bureaucracy, consumers will have less and less to spend and business will have less to invest and create new jobs.

Getting control of spending and taxes was

priority number one. When we got to Washington, government spending was growing at an annual rate of 17 percent. We have cut that by nearly 40 percent.

Paying for all that spending doubled the Federal tax take in just 5 years between 1976 and 1981. You know, there's an old saying that in levying taxes, as in shearing sheep, it's best to stop when you get to the skin. [*Laughter*] Well, by the end of the 1980's, the tax rates were—or the seventies, I should say—the tax rates were making a lot of us bleed. Average working people were being taxed at rates that, only a short time before, had been reserved for the wealthy.

We've managed to put in place a tax program that cut personal income tax rates across the board, 25 percent, and soon they will be indexed so the Federal Government will never again profit from inflation at your expense.

And under the direction of Vice President Bush, we've freed the business community as well as State and local government from 300 million man-hours of needless paperwork. This will save Americans billions of dollars.

Now, it's taken time for our program to take hold, but the cumulative effect of our efforts is just beginning to be felt, and the signs are good. Consumer spending is up; productivity is up; industrial production, retail sales, auto sales, housing and construction are all up since the beginning of the year. Last quarter, the economy grew by 9.2 percent. They first reported that as 8.7 percent and then had to make a correction; it was really 9.2, a much bigger jump than anyone had expected. The leading economic indicators have been on the rise for a full year now.

One of the last indicators to turn around, of course, has been unemployment. The suffering of the unemployed is a deep concern to me, and don't let anyone tell you differently. But let me ask you: Do you think that going back to the policies that dragged our economy down and set fire to inflation will really help the unemployed? Or would you agree that the best way to help all Americans is to continue the reforms that have brought down inflation, interest rates, taxes, and unemployment, which last month

dropped by a half percent, the biggest monthly decline in almost 24 years.

Our economy got into trouble because past leadership permitted our country to drift away from some of the fundamentals that were the basis of our progress and freedom. We were headed toward a society where the power and decisions would be in the hands not of you the people, but of a faceless central authority. Well, giving such power to the government and blindly hoping that it will benevolently watch over our interests is not the American way, and besides, it just doesn't work.

We believe in the dignity of work. We believe in rewarding it. We want everyone to succeed. Your four organizations prove that by working as independent forces in the community and working together, you can help others succeed. I know, for example, of the Latin Business Association's sponsorship of the Silesian Boys Clubs in East Los Angeles, helping promote skills and healthy self-images at an early age in order to open new horizons for tomorrow.

I know of the trade fairs and the training seminars conducted by the Hispanic Business and Professional Association of Orange County and the Inland Empire. And Ray Najera has told me of the professional guidance of the scholarship and loan fund of the Hispanic Business and Professional Association of Orange County and the Mexican and American Foundation.

All of this activity is aimed at building strong and independent people, individuals who can contribute and earn their own way in doing so. Your organizations are providing technical assistance and contacts so Hispanic businesses can compete. With this kind of effort going on all over the country, no wonder in 5 years the number of Hispanic-owned firms has leaped 65 percent to some 363,000 businesses, generating about $18 billion in sales per year. I want to take this opportunity to applaud those in the American corporate world who've seen the potential of the Hispanic community and invested in it. You can count on me to encourage them to do that more.

This administration remains firm in its commitment to expanding minority-owned businesses. Through the strong efforts of the

Small Business Administration, which has as its Deputy Administrator, Eddie Herrera, and through our commitment to minority procurement, we put our money where our mouth is.

Let's make one thing clear: Our goal is not welfare or handouts; it is jobs and opportunity. And if we keep on course and not be maneuvered back into the policies of tax, spend, and inflate, policies that are the root cause for the economic turmoil we've been through, we'll be on our way to a new era of growth and expansion that will better the life of every American. And looking around me today, I predict Americans of Hispanic descent will be leading the way.

What we're working for is much more than wealth. One need only look at a map to see the relationship between economic freedom and the other freedoms that we hold so dear. Nations with centralized, government-controlled economies usually have government-controlled speech, religion, and press, as well. They are countries with neither freedom nor material well-being, na-tions that erect walls and barbed wire to keep their people inside.

Much of the world is in turmoil, with the mass of humanity living in wretched conditions, suffering deprivation and tyranny. I know that you agree with me that all of us can be so grateful for this blessed land. God has placed in our hands the responsibility of watching over it. I thank you for all that you have done. Together we will keep America the land of the free and the home of the brave, a land that still offers that last, best hope of mankind.

Vaya con Dios [God be with you].

Note: The President spoke at 12:55 p.m. in the Biltmore Bowl at the Los Angeles Biltmore Hotel. Prior to his remarks, he met at the hotel with the leaders of the Hispanic Business and Professional Association of Orange County, the Hispanic Business and Professional Association of Greater Inland Empire, the Latin Business Association, and the Mexican and American Business Association.

Remarks at the Republican Women's Leadership Forum in San Diego, California
August 26, 1983

Thank you, Betty, for those very kind and generous words. And I thank all of you for that warm welcome. And I don't mean to be critical, but 84?—I'm not that old. [*Laughter*]

I'm especially delighted to be here today, Women's Equality Day, the 63d anniversary of women's suffrage and the date on which, in 1920, the 19th amendment was finally added to the Constitution. That was a great milestone for individual rights, but there is so much more. Republican women have a great deal to celebrate. Our party was at the forefront in seeing to it that women got the right to vote and has, our party has a great history of fighting for the rights of all Americans. We want to continue those traditions. And that's why today I want to urge women not only to vote, but to run for public office.

I know that many of you are interested in doing just that. In fact, many of you here hold office. I know women have felt excluded in the past. We're changing that. Now, more than ever, we need women like you—Republican women—to run for office, to serve in local, State, and Federal appointments, to work for the party. We need your leadership, your perspective, and your experience. We need your participation. And that's why I believe wholeheartedly in what you're doing at this forum. I applaud your efforts to recruit, train, finance, and elect Republican women. Nothing would make me happier than to hear that many of you have returned home ready to run.

And we do belong to a party that has pioneered women's rights. Republicans were the party that was primarily responsible for suffrage for women, as I said. Republicans were the first to elect a woman to the Congress. The GOP is the only party to elect women to the Senate who had not first filled unexpired terms. And today, the two women in the United States Senate are both Republicans—Nancy Kassebaum and Paula Hawkins.

I'm still disappointed that Millicent Fenwick didn't make it to the Senate, and I regret that some who supposedly are women's advocates didn't support that distinguished legislator. Indeed, in last year's election, it was apparent that some who talk the loudest in behalf of women's equality only extend their advocacy to women candidates if they're Democrats. Now, we have outstanding Republican women serving in the House, including our own Bobbi Fiedler, who's with us here today. And all across the country in statehouses and city halls, Republican women are making significant contributions to our democracy.

Republicans have a proud history of supporting women in public office. And I'm proud that this administration has continued the tradition of political opportunity for women. And just look at the record: For the first time in history, three women serve in the Cabinet of the United States—Secretary Dole, Secretary Heckler, and Ambassador Kirkpatrick. They bring a depth of experience with them.

And I think you should know that just as we did in California, the Cabinet isn't something that just gathers a few weeks for a kind of ceremonial visit, as has been rather traditional in the past. We operate the Cabinet like a board of directors. We meet regularly and often, and the problems that come up, we believe aren't really limited to one Cabinet office or agency. They do cross lines. And therefore it is a meeting of give and take, and I can tell you that in that Cabinet system the three women who are there are not observers, they are active participants, and their opinions carry great weight.

The only thing that I haven't been able to get done is, the Cabinet doesn't vote on issues like they would in a board of directors. I finally have to make the decision. [*Laughter*]

We've also appointed more women to top policymaking positions in our first 2 years than any previous administration has in a similar period. We've appointed more than 1,200 women to executive positions throughout the government. And while that record is better than our predecessors, it's only a beginning.

And of course in another beginning, I'm proud to say we appointed the first woman to the Supreme Court. There have been a few decisions in which I've been very happy that she was there. [*Laughter*] Well, what all this adds up to is clear: The greatest political opportunity for women in this country, real progress rather than words and promises, rests with the Republican Party.

What some cannot accept is that women are not a monolithic group. Women in the 1980's are a diverse majority with varied interests and varied futures. Some seek to start their own businesses. Some seek to advance in their chosen careers. Some seek to focus on the home and family. Some seek political office. And some women seek to do all of these things.

We must meet these needs, but we must meet these needs in different ways:

For women whose husbands are delinquent in child support payments, we have proposed strengthening the Federal child support enforcement system.

For women receiving Aid to Families with Dependent Children, we've increased training opportunities that will help them secure permanent productive jobs. Our Job Training Partnership Act, which replaces the discredited CETA program, specifically targets these women as a group that must be served.

For women and men working in the Federal Government, I signed into law the bill extending flexible work hours, but this especially helps women who are holding down a job and raising a family.

For all women, we've provided various forms of tax relief. We've greatly reduced the income tax marriage penalty and increased, almost doubled, the maximum child care tax credit for working mothers. We've expanded participation in IRA accounts, benefiting women whether they work at home or in paid jobs, and we're acting to remedy the inequity some women suffer in pension programs. And of course, we have also virtually eliminated, and eventually will, what was known as the widow's tax—the estate taxes levied on a surviving spouse. This has special benefit to those with family farms and small businesses, where women have been hardworking partners.

But I know that your interests range far beyond what are narrowly called "women's issues." Women are interested in the very same issues that interest men—those that affect the peace and prosperity of this nation. And I believe our record on these issues is an excellent one for women candidates to run on in 1984.

Just consider where the Nation was 3 years ago. Our leaders were throwing up their hands and throwing in the towel, suggesting that we were in a malaise—that was their word—and our problems were unsolvable. But the American people didn't buy the argument that America's best days were behind her, and they were right. It's taken patience and hard work, but I'm pleased to report to you today that America is moving forward again, and we're not turning back.

When we got to Washington, inflation was running at double-digit levels, and America had been living under that burden for 2 straight years. That was the worst such performance, with regard to inflation, in 60 years. Inflation was taking an especially serious toll on those on fixed incomes, a disproportionate number of whom are women. In the 2 years before we took office, inflation robbed the purchasing power of low-income men and women on a fixed income of $10,000 by over $2,000.

Well, we've reduced that inflation to 2.4 percent for the last 12 months, the lowest 12-month inflation rate in 17 years. You know, they had told us that it would take years, possibly decades, before we could bring down inflation; that it had become institutionalized. But they forgot about something that we brought with us to Washington: It's sometimes called determination. Or maybe it was just that we didn't know it couldn't be done, so we did it. [*Laughter*]

Today, a family of four on a fixed income of $20,000 has nearly $2,000 more in purchasing power this year alone than it would

have had if we hadn't taken action against inflation. Now, if food prices had risen these last 2 years, as they did in the 2 years before we took office, a loaf of bread would cost 7 cents more, a half gallon of milk would cost 18 cents more, and a pound of hamburger would cost 60 cents more.

We cut the prime interest rate from 21½ percent to 11 percent. There will be a little jiggling up and down as we've just seen in the last week or two, but if the Congress acts responsibly, the rates will continue to decline. And I know that the three Representatives who are with us today from the Congress are going to act responsibly. [*Laughter*]

Incidentally, interest rates aren't all that fixed either, what someone says is the official rate. I got a call just a few days before I came on this trip. It was from the chairman of the board of directors of the Milwaukee, Wisconsin, Security Savings and Loan. And they told me, or he told me, that their financial institution has just made $100 million available for home mortgages at a 9.9-percent interest rate. Now they did something like this a year ago, a higher interest rate, but still several points below the going rate. And I made that public, as I'm doing now, because a number of other banks around the country got the idea and followed suit. So, spread the word.

When we took office, America was suffering from years of uncontrolled spending and taxing. Federal spending was growing at a rate of 17 percent a year. We've cut that by nearly 40 percent. And following 5 years in which the Federal tax take doubled, we came in and reduced personal income tax rates by 25 percent across the board. And soon they'll be indexed so that beginning in 1985, the Federal Government will never again profit from inflation at the people's expense.

The cumulative effect of all our economic efforts is now being felt. That's why they don't call it Reaganomics anymore. [*Laughter*] As they say down at Cape Canaveral, we have a lift-off. [*Laughter*] Our economy is lifting off, and it's because of the policies that we've been pursuing over the past 2½ years. Consumer confidence and spending are up. Productivity is up. Industrial production, retail sales, auto sales, housing and construction are all up since the beginning of the year.

Last quarter, the economy grew at an annual rate of 9.2 percent. It was a much bigger jump than anyone had predicted or expected. It was first announced as 8.7, and then they had to go back and correct themselves. It was 9.2.

You know, statistics are usually boring, but I kind of like these. [*Laughter*] And here are some later ones. As a matter of fact, they're so late, they were just made public at 10 a.m. this morning. The output for all businesses in the second quarter rose by 12½ percent. Now, that means that productivity is increasing at a rate of 5.7 percent and the unit labor cost, the cost of labor per unit of production, fell by 2.1 percent, which is a further pledge that we've got inflation under control.

Well, unemployment, of course, I should say, is the last of the major indicators to show improvement. The rate is still too high. But last month we achieved the biggest monthly drop in almost 24 years. Nearly 2 million jobs have been added to the economy since the first of the year. And I don't know why I included this one in here: The unemployment rate for adult women—[*laughter*]—has dropped from 9.2 percent in December to 7.9 percent today.

But what we're seeking for women is what we're seeking for all Americans: economic opportunity and economic security associated with a sustained recovery, the security to plan for the future. If we can prevent our country from being drawn back to tax, spend, and inflate policies of the past, we'll be on our way to a new era of growth and expansion, and women will share in this.

It's estimated that in the next decade, two out of three new workers will be women. And I'm very optimistic about women's business ownership. There are almost 3 million women-owned businesses in the United States, and their number is growing dramatically, several times the rate of man-owned businesses in recent years. These are businesswomen who share our philosophy. They know how tough it is to meet a payroll. They understand the importance of a sound economy. They appreciate

the battle that we've been waging to reduce spending and regulation.

But a growing economy not only will help these women, it will help all women—those who are looking for work, those who seek to advance up the career ladder and, yes, those who have families to feed. At this point in the pursuit of equality, economic opportunity provides the greatest, most immediate advance for women. It's economic recovery that will move women forward the fastest. It's economic recovery that will produce more options for women than anything else.

I believe the greatest contribution this administration can make to women is to get the economy moving and keep it moving. This will provide more opportunities for women than if all the promises of the Democratic Presidential candidates were enacted into law. You know, the truth of it is not any one of them could get all of them enacted, because they've made so many differing promises to differing groups that they conflict with each other.

But economic opportunity doesn't guarantee equal opportunity. There are laws already on the books to safeguard the rights of women. Those laws must be enforced; some must be strengthened. I think it's time to cut through the fog of demagoguery that surrounds this whole issue. All of us are interested in one goal—ensuring legal equity for women.

At my direction, by Executive order, our administration is making a comprehensive review of Federal laws and regulations that unfairly differentiate on the basis of sex, and I initiated this because I believe it's important. And contrary to what you might have heard or read, that process is going forward. After receiving a preliminary report, we worked with Senator Dole on legislation that will make many of the necessary corrections recommended by the report. Recently, the third quarterly report was submitted for review to the Cabinet Council on Legal Policy. I have directed the Justice Department and the Cabinet Council to accelerate their review of Federal laws and to have specific recommendations on my desk for discussion immediately upon my return to Washington.

In addition to the review of Federal laws, I initiated a project to encourage the States to review their own laws. Now, I did it based on our successful experience here in California when I was Governor. And of course, the Federal Government could not and should not tell the States what they have to do or should do. But if the States are not moving fast enough, you who live in some of those States can help, because they did, every one of the 50 Governors appointed a representative to start that process in their own States. I understand that some of them are not moving as fast as others in that regard.

Americans, of course, are interested not only in the economy, they're interested in the safety and security of the Nation. They want peace. You want peace, lasting peace. And here, again, is a record that Republican women can run on. I know you'll recall when only a few years ago the United States had war planes that couldn't fly, ships that couldn't leave port, and military personnel that couldn't wait to get into civilian clothes. This was a situation that endangered America's security and the peace. And there was serious talk at the time that the volunteer military was a failure, and that we must return to the draft.

Well, we didn't return to the draft, and today our volunteer military is back on its feet and prouder than ever. We have a backlog of applicants. We have a higher intelligence and educational average than we've ever had in the history of the military. Maintenance backlogs are being reduced; training and retention are up; combat readiness rates have surged. We're recruiting very good men and women. Morale, discipline, and unit cohesion have improved dramatically. I've heard it from generals and I've heard it from privates that once again it's an honor to serve in our military. I'm sure that makes you as proud as it does me. And what this means is that all those sons and daughters who wear America's uniform are safer today than they were 3 years ago, and so are the people of this country.

Contrary to what some think, our men and women in uniform serve the cause of peace. Today, American marines serve in Lebanon, increasing the chances for a peaceful settlement there in that very troubled area. No one should think that our current efforts there mean that we're any less concerned about solving the broader problems of the Arab-Israeli conflict, particularly the search to reach a fair and practical resolution to the Palestinian problem.

The Middle East peace initiative which we announced just almost a year ago is definitely alive and available to those parties willing to sit down and talk. It's unfortunate that neither Israel nor its Arab neighbors have yet grasped the opportunities afforded. We remain committed to the positions we set forth, positions that remain sound, positions that thus far are the only realistic basis for a solution. We'll continue the pursuit for peace in the Middle East.

We're also pursuing arms control. We've undertaken the most sweeping proposals for arms reductions since nuclear weapons became a threat. In our search for peace, we have more negotiations underway with the Soviets than any administration in history. In strategic nuclear forces, in intermediate-range nuclear forces, in conventional forces, we want to lessen the danger to ourselves and our children. We remain flexible in our bargaining, but as Commander in Chief I have an obligation to protect this country, and I will not let political expediency influence these crucial negotiations.

The issues I've been discussing today and our solutions to them are the basis for a solid record on which all Republicans can run in 1984 with pride. The path we've followed is one that leads to prosperity and peace.

I came here today to urge Republican women to run for public office and to participate more actively in State and national Republican conventions, beginning with our Republican convention in 1984. You embody the goals that guide the Republican Party. You share the values that have made America the great nation she is. And you represent the future, a future of opportunity and equality.

Now is the time to become active. America's women have the right to the economic, political, and social power of this country. Exercise that right. And with the greatest encouragement I can summon, I urge you to declare your candidacy. I urge you to campaign on the issues that face us. I urge you to run, and run as Republicans, and win.

And now, for a very high spot in my vacation, I thank you. God bless all of you.

Note: The President spoke at 11:25 a.m. in the Mission Bay Room at the Bahia Hotel. He was introduced by Betty Heitman, co-chairman of the Republican National Committee.

Remarks at a Fundraising Reception for Representative Robert J. Lagomarsino in Santa Barbara, California
August 26, 1983

Bob, thank you very much, and thank all of you for letting us join you today.

I can think of no better reason for us to get together than to support the reelection of a close friend, a man on whom I have relied so heavily, both as Governor and now in my present job—Congressman Bob Lagomarsino. And I'd like also to offer my words of thanks, too, for some other friends, Barney and Diane, for all of their hospitality today.

You know, it's no secret that in the last few years, Nancy and I have grown to view this area as home. The Santa Ynez Mountains and the beautiful coastline are as precious to us as I know they are to you. One of the nice things about living here is that we're represented in the Congress, as he told you, by Bob Lagomarsino, a man whose roots go very deep, a good and decent man who reflects the values and traditions of this unique part of California.

Bob was born and educated here. He was first elected mayor of Ojai when he was just 33 years old, and then 2 years later, 1961, he was elected to the State Senate. That ancient history wouldn't be so important, except that the elected Governor of California in 1966 was anxious for advice and guidance of a seasoned pro like Bob. [*Laughter*] Well, Bob was with me during those things—the welfare reform and the tough days and the other battles that we had here. And, Bob, wherever Nancy and I go, it seems that you and Norma Jean all get there a few years ahead to scout the territory. [*Laughter*]

In '74 Bob won his seat in the Congress. And by the time I arrived, 2½ years ago, he was already well accustomed to fighting the growth of Federal taxes and spending. In fact, when it comes to responsible government, to keeping control of the budget and taxes, few in the Congress can boast a record that is equal to Bob's.

Now, I may have to fish around in my notes here for what I'm going to say next, because—well, you get the idea when I tell you that what I was going to say, with his help, we've managed to turn around an economic situation that was destroying much of what we know and love about this blessed land. And when I say "with his help," though, I mean he was instrumental to the whole game plan.

Bob is a member of the House Republican leadership group, and that's why we meet frequently, because they come down and we get together there on the problems and how we as a minority are going to have our way. And we've done pretty well at it. Some of those problems Bob talked about, we were told, were unsolvable. I've just come from speaking to a group of Republican women in San Diego, and I explained to them why maybe some of them turned out to be solvable.

You know, inflation was supposed to be institutionalized, couldn't get rid of it in less than decades. Well, we just didn't know that, so we did it. [*Laughter*] And it's been, as he told you, running at those double digits, and now down to the 2.4 percent. Government spending—he left that out—was running at 17 percent a year—increasing at 17 percent a year, and we've cut that by 40 percent. Taxes were rising faster than people's incomes, pushing working people into tax brackets that had been reserved for the wealthy only a short time before.

The Federal tax take doubled in just the 5 years of 1976 to 1981. But that's been turned around, too, with the 25-percent cut across the board. And beginning in 1985, your taxes—and it's already been passed, so it will go into effect automatically—your taxes will be indexed to inflation so that never again can government make a profit on inflation off the people of this country.

And you were told by Bob about the growth, the increase in housing and in construction and in retail sales and auto sales and all of those things. Last quarter, the economy grew by 9.2 percent, and that was a much bigger jump than had been expected. As a matter of fact, they had to announce it twice, because the first time they had it at 8.7, and then they had to correct themselves. It was 9.2. The leading economic indicators have been on the rise. Even unemployment has begun to drop. Last month gave us the biggest single monthly decline in unemployment in almost 24 years.

But, Bob, I've got some new ones for you that just came out as of 10 o'clock this morning—*[laughter]*—and that is that the growth of all business output in the second quarter was up 12½ percent. Now, that means an annual productivity rate of increase of 5.7 percent. And, at the same time, unit labor cost, the labor cost per unit of productivity in the country, was down 2.1 percent, which means we do have control of inflation.

But Bob recognized early on the threat confronting America from the south. It's our sacred responsibility to see that Central America does not become a string of anti-American, Marxist dictatorships. And I pledge to you right now, we don't intend to let that happen. We will stick by our friends, helping them develop their democratic institutions and to strengthen their economies, while at the same time we will provide them what they need to defend themselves. We don't intend to let Soviet-supported Marxists shoot their way into power in those countries of the Americas. To do that would be to gamble with our country's security and with our children's future.

You know, it's strange that the last few days I've been reading that because I have spoken to some groups of our fine Hispanic Americans that, well, I'm doing this all now just in the interest of trying to fence build and because there's an election year coming and so forth. How many remember that within 24 hours after I announced my candidacy in 1979, I made a speech outlining my dream for the Americas?—that these borders that separate us here in the Americas are separating us, even though we're all Americans from the South Pole to the North Pole. We all worship the same God; we all have the same pioneer heritage. And my dream has been—and that's why I have continued and why I went to South and Central America a year ago to talk to the leaders there.

Yes, we've proposed plans before of what we could do. But always it was the big colossus of the north coming down with our idea and saying, "Hey, here's what everyone should do." Well, I went down there and asked them what we should do. I said, "How can we recognize that we are, even when we cross a border into another country here in this hemisphere, we're among Americans. And I said, "Maybe you think that we've taken that name for ourselves because we call ourselves Americans. But," I said, "that's just because of the name we picked for our country. We can't walk around calling ourselves a united state." *[Laughter]* But they were very pleased to hear that we felt that way and recognized they, too, were Americans.

And so this isn't any last-minute thing. And the other day, speaking to an Hispanic group in Los Angeles, the man who introduced me, chairman of one of those business groups, gave me a line that I think we should all adopt. He said, "We talk about the international boundaries here in the Americas." "Well," he said, "a boundary kind of sounds like something that separates us." He said, "Why don't we start calling them the international seams, because seams bring you together and hold you together." So, I've just been waiting to be among some friends where I could explain that I'm not a Johnny-come-lately on this whole idea of the Americas getting together. [*Laughter*]

But now——

Audience member. You're among friends with Hispanics, too.

The President. What?

Audience member. You're among friends with Hispanics, and don't listen to those few that are against you.

The President. God bless you, and thank you very much. Thank you. I'm very proud to be friends; they have been good citizens in our land here.

Audience member. And the women are for you, too. [*Laughter*]

The President. And that's very nice to hear. [*Laughter*]

Well, I must conclude, but I just want to say due to the disgraceful redistricting that we've gone through here in California, redistricting that hit even new lows in the annals of power politics, Bob is in the fight of his political life. And we need him, and therefore, he needs all of us.

So I hope that as election day draws near, you'll redouble your efforts on his behalf.

Bob Lagomarsino is a man whom I respect, and I'm proud to be here helping any way that I can in supporting him today, because he has been of great support to all that we've accomplished and all that we're trying to do there in Washington.

I used to say when I was here in California that if they'd only listened to us—as a matter of fact, I had the presumption when Her Majesty was here on that wonderful visit—[*laughter*]—to point out to her that if those first settlers to this country had only come across the Pacific instead of the Atlantic, the Capital would be in California. [*Laughter*] Of course, maybe it's just as well, because the rest of the country never would have become developed. [*Laughter*]

Well, God bless you all, and thank you very much. Thank you.

Note: The President spoke at 1:30 p.m. at the residence of Barney and Diane Klinger. Following the reception, the President and Mrs. Reagan went to Rancho del Cielo, their ranch near Santa Barbara.

Nomination of George Roberts Andrews To Be United States Ambassador to Mauritius
August 26, 1983

The President today announced his intention to nominate George Roberts Andrews, of Maryland, a career member of the Senior Foreign Service, Class of Minister-Counselor, as Ambassador to Mauritius. He would succeed Robert C. F. Gordon.

Mr. Andrews entered the Foreign Service in 1954 as consular officer in Hamburg. He served in Paris as consular officer (1956–1958) and political officer (1958–1959). In the Department he was personnel officer (1959–1962) and desk officer for Belgium and Luxembourg (1962–1964). He was political officer in Stockholm (1964–1967), chief of the political section in Dakar (1967–1970), chargé d'affaires in Conakry (1970),

and consul general in Strasbourg (1970–1971). In 1971–1974 he was Deputy Assistant and Deputy Chief of Mission in Guatemala in 1974–1978. He attended the executive seminar in national and international affairs at the Foreign Service Institute in 1978–1979. In 1979–1983 he was chief of senior officers personnel in the Bureau of Personnel in the Department.

Mr. Andrews graduated from Princeton University (B.A., 1953) and the Université de Strasbourg in France (M.A., 1954). His foreign languages are French, Spanish, German, and Swedish. He was born February 26, 1932, in Havana, Cuba, of American parents.

Nomination of Richard H. Francis To Be President of the Solar Energy and Energy Conservation Bank
August 26, 1983

The President today announced his intention to nominate Richard H. Francis to be President of the Solar Energy and Energy Conservation Bank, Department of Housing and Urban Development. He would succeed Joseph S. Bracewell.

Since 1982 he has been serving as Manager of the Solar Energy and Energy Conservation Bank at the Department of Housing and Urban Development. Previously he was Special Assistant to the Secretary for Policy Development and Research, Department of Housing and Urban Development, in 1981–1982; executive vice president, National Multi-Housing Council, in 1978–1981; director, government relations, National Association of Independent Colleges and Universities, in 1976–1978; and associate director, federal relations, Association of American Colleges, in 1974–1976.

He graduated from the U.S. Naval Academy (B.S., 1949), Yale University (M.A., 1959), and the University of Maryland (Ph. D., 1977). He is married, has three children, and resides in Fairfax Station, Va. He was born March 8, 1925, in Boston, Mass.

Nomination of Barbara E. McConnell To Be a Member of the Civil Aeronautics Board
August 26, 1983

The President today announced his intention to nominate Barbara E. McConnell to be a member of the Civil Aeronautics Board for the term expiring December 31, 1983, vice Elizabeth E. Bailey, and for the term of 6 years expiring December 31, 1989, reappointment.

Since 1982 she has been serving as Executive Assistant to the Chairman of the Civil Aeronautics Board. Previously she was associate general counsel and assistant secretary of Southwest Forest Industries, Inc., in Phoenix, Ariz., in 1980–1982; corporate attorney for the Greyhound Corp. in Phoenix, Ariz., in 1976–1980; and personnel director of the Yavapai Community Hospital in Phoenix in 1974–1975.

She graduated from Arizona State University (B.S., 1972; M.P.A., 1975; J.D., 1978). She resides in Washington, D.C. She was born December 26, 1950, in Indiana Community, Pa.

Statement on the 20th Anniversary of the March on Washington for Jobs and Freedom
August 27, 1983

Twenty years ago today, a quarter of a million Americans peacefully and prayerfully assembled in the shadow of the Lincoln Memorial for a noble cause. They asked only what all of us ask of our country: that it live up to its high ideals, those cherished ideals of freedom, human dignity, opportunity, and brotherhood that gave birth to the United States. It was a moving moment in American history, and those of us who witnessed it will never forget it.

Although the emphasis of the 1963 March on Washington was on the rights of black Americans, the values that were appealed to are shared by us all—the goal of a more just, more abundant, more free society that

Dr. Martin Luther King, Jr., so eloquently spoke of on that day. In the last 20 years, great progress has been made. It is fitting that on this anniversary we should give thanks for that progress, and to those who sacrificed so much to bring it about. But much remains to be done.

America, mankind's last, best hope for freedom, is a special place, a place where so many dreams have come true. Today, let us resolve anew to do everything we can, in our time, to continue to fulfill Dr. King's dream—a dream that all men and women of good will, black and white alike, share with all their hearts.

Statement on Signing a Marine Safety and Seamen's Welfare Bill
August 27, 1983

Senate bill 46, which I have signed into law, is a major step forward in this administration's efforts to revitalize the United States merchant marine and shipping industry. The bill modernizes and simplifies the marine safety and seamen's welfare laws administered by the Coast Guard. This legislation is remarkable in that it culminates more than 50 years of effort to make these laws more understandable by the regulated public and by the administering agency.

The marine safety and seamen's welfare laws are currently compiled in title 46 of the United States Code. Title 46 is a confusing collection of statutes that have been enacted throughout the history of this nation. Some of the provisions date back to 1790 and were among the first laws passed by the Congress. Many of the provisions have outlived their usefulness. Those that are still relevant are poorly organized and confusing. Because of their complexity, these laws are difficult for the Coast Guard to administer. Individuals subject to the requirements are often unsure of their rights and obligations. Understanding these laws is a difficult task, even for an experienced maritime attorney. The Supreme Court has labeled these laws a "maze of regulations." S. 46 eliminates this maze.

S. 46 represents a truly nonpartisan effort. Without the cooperation of both Houses of Congress, industry, labor, and the maritime bar, I would not be signing this bill today. This is an important step, but much still needs to be done to help the United States merchant marine and shipping industry revitalize itself. This is a priority goal of the Department of Transportation and of my administration. Therefore, I look forward to rapid enactment of the administration's maritime promotional, deregulatory, and reauthorization legislation.

I urge all elements of the maritime community to continue to work with my administration to develop creative solutions to the problems that affect this vital industry.

It is with great pleasure that I have signed this bill.

Note: As enacted, S. 46 is Public Law 98–89, approved August 26.

Radio Address to the Nation on the Situation in the Middle East
August 27, 1983

My fellow Americans:

Last June, the 19th of June to be exact, a well-known TV network producer was the commencement speaker at the high school where he had graduated on that same day, June 19th, 43 years ago. In speaking to this year's graduates, he pointed out some things that should be of concern to them regarding the state of the world. They were items taken from the front page of a June

19th issue of the New York Times, their graduation day.

He said, "In Washington, the administration is asking for more money, not to fight cancer or educate young people, but more money to build some of the most destructive weapons the world has ever seen." Not very reassuring for a high school graduate hoping to live to an old age, and not very reassuring, either, to have a President who is called a warmonger.

He went on to say, "In Latin America, the Times tells us, the United States is prepared to go to war to keep unfriendly powers out of this hemisphere. If push comes to shove, a young high school graduate could end up fighting there."

"In Europe," he told them, "a people not much different from you is being crushed in what the Times reports is being called an uncompromising and unrelenting fashion. And in Detroit, the Japanese threat, among other things, is forcing the Ford Motor Company out of the car business."

He pointed out that it didn't seem like much of a world to look forward to, but there it was on page 1, graduation day, June 19th. Yes, *his* graduation day, June 19th, 1940. And as he went on to say, "We're all still here," although he wouldn't have bet on it back in 1940.

The President being called a warmonger was Franklin Delano Roosevelt, who kept increasing the defense budget. The Japanese threat was military, not economic, and Ford was going into the fighter plane business. And, oh, yes, the European country that was being crushed was France, not Poland.

Well, here it is 43 years later, and as he told that class of '83, "A good case can be made that the world is better, not worse." And the class of 1940 had something to do with that, just as the class of '83 can have a hand in making things better for graduating classes yet to be, even a class 43 years from now.

Young Americans are already doing their share to build a better world. Today our servicemen are participating in multinational peacekeeping forces in Lebanon and the Sinai Peninsula.

In the agreement between Lebanon and Israel, Israel agreed to withdraw its military forces totally. The responsibility now rests on others to negotiate in good faith on their own arrangements for withdrawal. Until this happens, Lebanon will remain a potential trouble spot.

But our current efforts in Lebanon are only a small part of our search for peace in the Middle East, including a compassionate, fair, and practical resolution to the Palestinian problem.

The Middle East peace initiative which we announced almost a year ago is definitely alive and available to those parties willing to sit down together and talk peace. We remain committed to the positions we set forth, and we stand ready to pursue them in the context of the Camp David accords. Those positions are in the best long-term interests of all parties. Most importantly, they're the only realistic basis for a solution that has thus far been presented.

The United States continues to support UN Security Council Resolutions 338 and 242.

The establishment of new Israeli settlements in the occupied territories is an obstacle to peace, and we're concerned over the negative effect that this activity has on Arab confidence in Israel's willingness to return territory in exchange for security and a freely and fairly negotiated peace treaty.

The future of these settlements can only be dealt with through direct negotiations between the parties to the conflict. The sooner these negotiations begin, the greater the chance for a solution.

This administration, like those before it, is firmly committed to the security of the State of Israel. We will help Israel defend itself against external aggression. At the same time, the United States believes, as it has always believed, that permanent security for the people of Israel and all the peoples of the region can only come with the achievement of a just and lasting peace, not by sole reliance on increasingly expensive military forces.

Unfortunately, the opportunities afforded by our initiative have yet to be grasped by the parties involved. We know the issues are complex, the risks for all concerned high, and much courageous statesman—

statesmanship, excuse me, will be required. Nevertheless, those complex issues can be resolved by creative and persistent diplomacy. Those risks can be overcome by people who want to end this bitter and tragic conflict. And in the process, the United States will be a full partner, doing everything we can to help create a just and lasting peace.

Until next week, thanks for listening, and God bless you.

Note: The President spoke at 9:06 a.m. from Rancho del Cielo, his ranch near Santa Barbara, Calif.

Statement by Deputy Press Secretary Speakes on the Death of Two United States Marines in Lebanon
August 29, 1983

We are shocked and grieved by the deaths of the U.S. marines in Lebanon. They died while serving the United States in its efforts to help the Lebanese Central Government restore order to the greater Beirut area. We condemn those who are responsible for the continuing violence, which has claimed many victims, including our own marines. Our forces are there at the request of the Government of Lebanon in helping to provide security for the Lebanese people. Once more we call on all elements to end this senseless violence and unite behind the Lebanese Government to restore national harmony.

The President was informed this morning at 1:55 a.m. Pacific time at the ranch by national security adviser Bill Clark. This notification took place 1 hour and 6 minutes after the incident occurred in Beirut. The President expressed profound sorrow, terming the death of two U.S. marines as tragic. The President paid tribute to the courage of the marines in their role as peacekeepers. The President will shortly speak by telephone to the families of the two marines, expressing his and Mrs. Reagan's personal condolences and sorrow.

The President this morning has conferred by telephone with Secretary of State George Shultz and Secretary of Defense Caspar Weinberger, as well as Bill Clark. At the President's direction, a national security group, composed of representatives of the departments and agencies most involved in this matter, was convened in Washington this morning. The purpose was to review the current situation in Beirut and to make additional recommendations on the U.S. role in continuing to pursue the peaceful withdrawal of all foreign forces from Lebanon.

The President directed a meeting of the administration's most senior officials be convened this afternoon in Washington to continue the review. I would anticipate the President will confer with the Vice President following that meeting.

In the Middle East, Ambassador McFarlane continues his mission. He is in Beirut today. His goal is to negotiate with all groups in Lebanon to facilitate a peaceful withdrawal of all foreign forces. The President has directed his staff to inform the congressional leadership and the chairmen and ranking members of the Armed Services Committees and the Foreign Relations Committee members on the situation.

Note: Deputy Press Secretary Larry M. Speakes read the statement concerning the death of S/Sgt. Alexander M. Ortega and 2d Lt. Donald G. Losey at his daily press briefing in the briefing facility in the Sheraton Santa Barbara Hotel in Santa Barbara, Calif.

Proclamation 5085—Citizenship Day and Constitution Week, 1983
August 29, 1983

By the President of the United States of America

A Proclamation

There can be no more precious possession than United States citizenship. As the Columbus, Ohio, *Dispatch* so fittingly stated many years ago:

"In the darkness that has settled over so much of the world and which shadows the existence of men in places where individual liberty still struggles to live, the United States of America has become the source of hope and aid to the millions of oppressed who once knew freedom and the hated enemy of the overlords of darkness who would destroy it wherever they can."

The Constitution provides a framework for our continuous striving to make a better America. It provides the basic balance between each branch of government, limits the power of that government, and guarantees to each of us as citizens our most basic rights. The Constitution, however, is only the outline of our system of government. It is through each individual citizen living out the ideals of the Constitution that we reach for a full expression of those ideals. Therefore, while we celebrate Citizenship Day and Constitution Week, let us rededicate ourselves to a full realization of the potential of the great country which the Founding Fathers struggled to create more than two hundred years ago.

Not only during this week, but throughout the year, we should continue to seek that "more perfect union" which will establish justice and insure domestic tranquility for each of us and our future generations through the Constitution.

In recognition of the importance of our Constitution and the role of our citizenry in shaping our government, the Congress, by joint resolution of February 29, 1952 (36 U.S.C. 153), designated September 17th of each year as Citizenship Day and authorized the President to issue annually a proclamation calling upon officials of the government to display the flag on all government buildings on that day. The Congress also, by joint resolution of August 2, 1956 (36 U.S.C. 159), requested the President to proclaim the week beginning September 17th and ending September 23rd of each year as Constitution Week.

Now, Therefore, I, Ronald Reagan, President of the United States of America, call upon appropriate government officials to display the flag of the United States on all government buildings on Citizenship Day, September 17, 1983. I urge Federal, State and local officials, as well as leaders of civic, educational, and religious organizations to conduct ceremonies and programs that day to commemorate the occasion.

I also proclaim the week beginning September 17th and ending September 23rd, 1983 as Constitution Week, and I urge all Americans to observe that week with appropriate ceremonies and activities in their schools, churches and other suitable places.

In Witness Whereof, I have hereunto set my hand this twenty-ninth day of August, in the year of our Lord nineteen hundred and eighty-three, and of the Independence of the United States of America the two hundred and eighth.

RONALD REAGAN

[*Filed with the Office of the Federal Register, 12:40 p.m., August 30, 1983*]

Letter to the Speaker of the House and the President Pro Tempore of the Senate Reporting on United States Participation in the Multinational Force in Lebanon
August 30, 1983

Dear Mr. Speaker: (Dear Mr. President:)

On September 29, 1982, I reported to you concerning the introduction of United States Armed Forces in Lebanon to participate in the Multinational Force (MNF) requested by the Government of Lebanon. The presence of this Force was designed to facilitate the restoration of Lebanese Government sovereignty and authority, and thereby further the efforts of the Government of Lebanon to assure the safety of persons in the area and bring to an end the violence that had tragically recurred. I directed this deployment pursuant to my constitutional authority with respect to the conduct of foreign relations and as Commander-in-Chief of the United States Armed Forces.

We have periodically provided Congress with updated information on the activities of these forces and on the circumstances of their deployment in Lebanon. In light of recent events, I am providing this further report on the deployment, in accordance with my desire that Congress continue to be informed on this matter, and consistent with Section 4 of the War Powers Resolution.

On August 28, sporadic fighting between Lebanese Armed Forces and various armed factions took place in South Beirut; from time to time during the course of this fighting, positions in the vicinity of the Beirut airport manned by U.S. Marines of the MNF came under small-arms fire (without injury to U.S. personnel), and this fire was returned. On August 29, fighting erupted again. Marine positions came under mortar, rocket, and small-arms fire, with the result

that two Marines were killed and fourteen wounded. In addition, several artillery rounds fell near the U.S.S. IWO JIMA (an amphibious support vessel lying offshore), with no resulting damage or injuries. As contemplated by their rules of engagement, U.S. Marines returned fire with artillery, small arms, and, in one instance, rocket fire from a helicopter gunship. There were additional exchanges of fire earlier today, August 30, without injury to U.S. personnel.

Later today, a ceasefire came into effect in the area in which the Marines were deployed, and firing on Marine positions ceased. Diplomatic efforts are underway to extend this ceasefire. In the meantime, U.S. forces will be prepared to exercise their right of self-defense should such attacks recur.

I believe that the continued presence of these U.S. forces in Lebanon is essential to the objective of helping to restore the territorial integrity, sovereignty, and political independence of Lebanon. It is still not possible to predict the duration of the presence of these forces in Lebanon; we will continue to assess this question in the light of progress toward this objective.

I will keep the Congress informed as to further developments with respect to this situation.

Sincerely,

RONALD REAGAN

Note: This is the text of identical letters addressed to Thomas P. O'Neill, Jr., Speaker of the House of Representatives, and Strom Thurmond, President pro tempore of the Senate.

Message to Captain Richard H. Truly and the Crew of the Space Shuttle *Challenger*
August 30, 1983

I wish you and the crew of the *Challenger* Godspeed on your historic journey. Like those other select Americans who at heroic risk to themselves traveled into space before you, you will have the minds and hearts of your fellow countrymen—and of the world—with you.

Nancy joins me in prayer for your historic mission and homecoming. God bless you.

Note: The message was sent by telegram.

Appointment of Five Members of the Intergovernmental Advisory Council on Education
August 30, 1983

The President today announced his intention to appoint the following individuals to be members of the Intergovernmental Advisory Council on Education for terms expiring July 27, 1987:

Alan Cropsey is presently serving as State senator from Michigan. He resides in DeWitt, Mich., and was born June 13, 1952. This is a reappointment.

Ralph Perk served as mayor of Cleveland, Ohio, from 1971 through 1977. He resides in Cleveland, Ohio, and was born January 19, 1914. This is a reappointment.

Betty R. Sepulveda is a former administrator for the Denver Public Schools, where she served as an instructional consultant for language development in the office of curriculum. She resides in Denver, Colo., and was born January 26, 1923. This is a reappointment.

Mary C. Tucker serves as chairman of the Advisory Neighborhood Commission—4B in Washington, D.C., and as president of the Roosevelt High School Parent Teachers Association. She resides in Washington, D.C., and was born January 4, 1942. She will succeed Manuel J. Justiz.

Harriet M. Wieder is supervisor for the second district for the Orange County board of supervisors. She resides in Huntington Beach, Calif., and was born October 7, 1920. This is a reappointment.

Appointment of Nell Kuonen as the Federal Representative on the Klamath River Compact Commission, and Designation as Chairman
August 30, 1983

The President today announced his intention to appoint Nell Kuonen to be the Federal Representative on the Klamath River Compact Commission. She will succeed Samuel S. Johnson. She will also serve as Chairman.

Mrs. Kuonen is currently serving as commissioner of Klamath County in Klamath Falls, Oreg. She was first elected to serve as commissioner in 1976. She serves on the legislative committee for the Association of Oregon Counties and represents Klamath County on the council of State Forest Trust Land Counties. Since 1977 she has been chairman of the Klamath-Lake County Manpower Commission.

She is married, has two children, and resides in Klamath Falls, Oreg. She was born November 10, 1928, in Lubbock, Tex.

Statement on the Third Anniversary of Solidarity
August 31, 1983

Three years have passed since the working class of Poland challenged the whole might of a modern totalitarian state and without shedding one drop of blood won the right to have their own free trade unions. In the 15 months of its legal existence, Solidarity offered a ray of hope that people who had no other weapons but their courage and determination may gain more freedom for themselves and thus bring about a more peaceful and secure world.

It seemed for a moment that such hopes were dashed in December 1981, when the military regime of General Jaruzelski, acting under strong pressure from the Soviet Union, introduced a state of war, and the legal structure of Solidarity was destroyed by force. But such an assessment was wrong. The 13th of December 1981 did not mark the end of the Polish quest for freedom. Solidarity leaders were interned; others were thrown into jail; strikes were broken by police; some people were killed, wounded, or badly beaten; many thousands lost their jobs or were forced to leave their country. Solidarity suffered many setbacks, but its spirit remained unbroken. In spite of all repressive measures, the movement has been longer in existence now than the era of Solidarity itself. The Poles refused to be intimidated. And it is clear today that no force can eradicate the memories of the historical event of August 31, 1980. As a prominent Pole said recently, "Solidarity remains alive in the minds and hearts of Polish people."

One more thing has to be said on this occasion. In spite of the great intensity of hostile feelings generated by repressive measures, there was not one single case of violence against the oppressive regime in Poland. Solidarity has remained a nonviolent, massive popular movement which is renouncing the use of force or any attempts to overthrow the government. In our world tormented by terrorism, this is in itself a remarkable achievement.

Winston Churchill once said that Poland is like a rock. It may from time to time be submerged for a while by a tidal wave, but it will remain a rock.

Throughout their thorny history, the Poles have never lost hope and have never surrendered. Solidarity perseveres in its peaceful struggle in a hope that one day—sooner or later—the Polish Government will have to recognize that Polish problems can be solved not by intimidation, but only on the basis of reconciliation with this proud and courageous people. If the Polish Government makes tangible progress toward this end, we are prepared to reciprocate with concrete steps of our own.

To us Americans, Solidarity should serve as a reminder of the power of ideas born out of peoples' readiness to accept sacrifices and to face risks. The Poles are struggling for the common values which we cherish in our democratic society: for dignity and the rights of man and nations. They can proudly repeat their old motto: for your freedom and ours.

Appointment of Christian A. Herter, Jr., as Deputy United States Commissioner of the International Whaling Commission
August 31, 1983

The President today announced his intention to appoint Christian A. Herter, Jr., to be Deputy United States Commissioner on the International Whaling Commission. He will succeed Thomas Garrett.

Since 1978 Mr. Herter has been a teacher at the Johns Hopkins University School of Advanced International Studies in Washington, D.C. He is an attorney by profession and was a partner in the Boston law firm of

Bingham, Dana and Gould. He is a former Deputy Assistant Secretary of State for Environmental and Population Affairs and former Chairman of the U.S. Section of the International Joint Commission—U.S. and Canada.

Mr. Herter graduated from Harvard College (B.A., 1940) and Harvard Law School (LL.B., 1948). He is married and has three children. He was born January 29, 1919, in Brooklyn, N.Y.

Remarks by Telephone to Crewmembers on Board the Space Shuttle *Challenger*
August 31, 1983

The President. Commander Truly?

Commander Richard H. Truly. Yes, sir, Mr. President.

The President. Well, you know, I can't help but ask, since I'm sitting in California, just about where in the world are you now?

Commander Truly. We're over Hawaii, sir.

The President. Over Hawaii and coming this way.

Commander Truly. Yes, sir, coming your way at about 150 miles up.

The President. In about 20 minutes you should be here.

Well, listen, congratulations on a successful and a spectacular night launch. Every one of these launches of the shuttle is a spectacular and a noteworthy event, but this one has certainly its share of firsts. I know it was touch and go with the weather, but you were launched right on schedule, and I think about 250 million Americans breathed a great sigh of relief.

But you've got a lot of firsts there. And, Guy, congratulations. You, I think, are paving the way for many others, and you're making it plain that we are in an era of brotherhood here in our land. And you will serve as a role model for so many others, and be so inspirational that I can't help but express my gratitude to you. And then Bill, at 54, is the oldest astronaut to ever fly in space. You have an especially warm place in my heart. It makes me think that maybe some day I might be able to go along.

I know this has been a busy day, with the successful deployment early this morning of the Indian National Satellite, which I understand will bring a broad range of communication and weather resources to the people of India and serves as a good example of international cooperation in space. But on behalf of all our people, I want to thank you all for your courage, your commitment to space research. You've set a fine example for all our young people, who represent our hope for the future.

Now, I know that this call came—I caught you on your way to your bunks for some well-deserved sleep, so I better cut this short. I just wanted to let you know that we're all looking forward to another successful mission and to your safe landing here in California on Labor Day. God bless all of you.

Commander Truly. Mr. President, thank you so much. We appreciate your taking the time to call us. And we're very pleased and proud to be here. And thank you for calling, very much.

The President. Well, it's my pleasure, and I know I'm speaking on behalf of all your fellow countrymen when I say good flying and a happy landing on Labor Day here, here in the USA. Again, God bless you. Carry on.

Commander Truly. Thank you, Mr. President.

Note: The President spoke at 8:58 a.m. from Rancho del Cielo, his ranch near Santa Barbara, Calif.

Message to the Congress Transmitting an Alternative Plan on Federal Civilian Pay Increases
August 31, 1983

To the Congress of the United States:

Under the Federal Pay Comparability Act of 1970, an adjustment in Federal white collar pay will be required in October, 1983.

The Act requires that calculations be made annually of the adjustments that would be required in Federal statutory pay systems to achieve comparability with private sector pay for the same levels of work. Using the calculation methods developed in the past, my pay advisers have indicated that an average 21.51 percent increase would be required to achieve comparability as that concept is presently defined.

The Comparability Act gives me the authority to propose an alternative adjustment in lieu of comparability on the basis of "economic conditions affecting the general welfare." Under that authority, in accordance with our economic recovery program, I am submitting to the Congress an Alternative Plan for a 3.5 percent increase in Federal white collar pay effective in January, 1984 in lieu of the 21.51 percent increase indicated under current comparability calculation methods.

Current law governing military pay increases provides that the annual increase in military pay be the same as the average Federal white collar increase. The Congress is currently considering legislation that could affect both military and civilian pay increases. If legislation is enacted, it could supersede the increase that Federal employees would otherwise receive under this Alternative Plan.

RONALD REAGAN

The White House,
August 31, 1983.

Message to the Congress Transmitting a Report on Exclusions From the Merit Pay System
August 31, 1983

To the Congress of the United States:

Supervisors and management officials in GS–13, 14, and 15 positions throughout the Federal Government are covered by the Merit Pay System as required by Chapter 54, Title 5, U.S. Code, unless otherwise excluded by law.

Upon proper application from the heads of affected agencies and upon recommendation of the Director of the Office of Personnel Management, I have, pursuant to 5 U.S.C. 5401(b)(2)(B), excluded three agencies and units of agencies from coverage under the Merit Pay System.

Attached is my report describing the agencies and units of agencies to be excluded and the reasons therefor.

RONALD REAGAN

The White House,
August 31, 1983.

Note: The exclusions affect employees of the Office of the United States Trade Representative, the Defense Intelligence Agency, and the Federal Aviation Administration.

The text of the message was released by the Office of the Press Secretary on September 1.

Accordance of the Personal Rank of Ambassador to Leonard H. Marks While Serving at the World Administrative Radio Conference for Planning Use of the High Frequency Broadcasting Bands
September 1, 1983

The President has accorded the personal rank of Ambassador to Leonard H. Marks in his capacity as Chairman of the United States Delegation to the first session of the World Administrative Radio Conference for Planning Use of the High Frequency Broadcasting Bands of the International Telecommunication Union. This rank would be while he is conducting preliminary bilateral and multilateral consultations as well as the first session of the Conference, which convenes from January 10 through February 10, 1984.

Mr. Marks was an assistant professor of law at the University of Pittsburgh Law School in 1938–1942. He was assistant to the General Counsel of the Federal Communications Commission in Washington, D.C., in 1942–1946. In 1946–1965 and since 1969, he has been a partner in the law firm of Cohn and Marks in Washington, D.C. He was Director of the United States Information Agency in 1965–1969.

Mr. Marks served as the American delegate to the International Broadcasting Conference, Incorporator of the Communications Satellite Corporation, and Chairman of the International Conference on Communications Satellites. He was president of the International Rescue Committee in 1973–1979, and Chairman of the United States Advisory Commission on International Educational and Cultural Affairs in 1974–1978.

Mr. Marks graduated from the University of Pittsburgh (B.A., 1935; LL.B., 1938). He is married, has two children, and resides in Washington, D.C. He was born March 5, 1916, in Pittsburgh, Pa.

Statement on the Soviet Attack on a Korean Civilian Airliner
September 1, 1983

I speak for all Americans and for the people everywhere who cherish civilized values in protesting the Soviet attack on an unarmed civilian passenger plane. Words can scarcely express our revulsion at this horrifying act of violence.

The United States joins with other members of the international community in demanding a full explanation for this appalling and wanton misdeed. The Soviet statements to this moment have totally failed to explain how or why this tragedy has occurred. Indeed, the whole incident appears to be inexplicable to civilized people everywhere.

Mrs. Reagan and I want to express our deepest sympathy to the families of the victims. Our prayers are with them in this time of bereavement, and they have my personal assurance that I will make every effort to get to the bottom of this tragedy.

I have ordered the flags of the United States flown at half staff at all Federal installations and U.S. military bases around the world.

Note: Deputy Press Secretary Larry M. Speakes read the President's statement during a press briefing for reporters, which began at 2:33 p.m. at the Sheraton Santa Barbara Hotel in Santa Barbara, Calif.

Proclamation 5086—Death of American Citizens on Board Korean Airlines Flight
September 1, 1983

By the President of the United States of America

A Proclamation

As a mark of respect for the American citizens and all those who died violently on board the Korean Airlines flight which was ruthlessly shot down by Soviet fighters between Sakhalin and Monoron Islands on September 1, 1983, I hereby order, by virtue of the authority vested in me as President of the United States of America, that the flag of the United States shall be flown at half-staff upon all public buildings and grounds, at all military posts and naval stations, and on all naval vessels of the Federal Government in the District of Columbia and throughout the United States and its Territories and possessions through Sunday, September 4, 1983. I also direct that the flag shall be flown at half-staff for the same length of time at all United States embassies, legations, consular offices, and other facilities abroad, including all military facilities and naval vessels and stations.

In Witness Whereof, I have hereunto set my hand this first day of September, in the year of our Lord nineteen hundred and eighty-three, and of the Independence of the United States of America the two hundred and eighth.

RONALD REAGAN

[*Filed with the Office of the Federal Register, 9:20 a.m., September 2, 1983*]

Note: The text of the proclamation was released by the Office of the Press Secretary on September 2.

Statement by Deputy Press Secretary Speakes on Employment Statistics for August
September 2, 1983

Today the Department of Labor released figures showing that the unemployment rate for August is essentially unchanged from July. The overall unemployment rate increased slightly from 9.3 percent to 9.4 percent, which is not regarded as statistically significant. The old civilian rate remained unchanged at 9.5 percent.

The Labor Department also noted that adjusted payroll employment for August increased about 300,000.

Employment statistics for August are complicated by a very large increase in the number of workers on strike: 710,000 more persons were on strike in August than in July. Striking workers are not counted among the unemployed, but they also are not counted for payroll employment. Actual payroll employment fell 411,000 between July and August, but an adjustment for the increased number of strikers shows that about 300,000 persons were added to payrolls.

This pause in declining unemployment rates comes on the heels of an unusually large drop in July. A downward trend over several months, combined with the increase in payroll employment, point to a steadily improving jobs picture. Economic news continues to be encouraging.

Nomination of Clayton E. McManaway, Jr., To Be United States Ambassador to Haiti
September 2, 1983

The President today announced his intention to nominate Clayton E. McManaway, Jr., of the District of Columbia, a career member of the Senior Foreign Service, class of Minister-Counselor, as Ambassador to Haiti. He would succeed Ernest H. Preeg.

Mr. McManaway served in the United States Navy as lieutenant in 1955–1957. In 1959 he was bond underwriting apprentice with the Fidelity and Casualty Co. of New York in San Francisco, Calif. In 1959–1960 he was flight purser with Trans World Airlines in New York City, and in the foreign advertising department of the Borden Food Co. in 1960–1961.

He was with the Agency for International Development in 1961–1971; successively serving as executive trainee (1961–1962); Assistant Program Officer, then acting Program Officer, USAID Mission on Phnom Penh (1962–1964); Special Assistant to the Director of the Office of Vietnam Affairs (1964–1965); Deputy Program Director, USAID Mission in Saigon (1965–1966); Assistant Director of Plans and Evaluations in the Office of Civil Operations in Saigon

(1966–1967); Director of Plans, Policies and Programs, MACV/CORDS, in Saigon (1967–1970). In 1970–1971 he was on detail as fellow at the Center for International Affairs at Harvard University. In 1971–1973 he was Deputy Assistant Secretary of Defense, Office of Systems and Analysis, Department of Defense. In 1975 he was on detail to the Department of State as Deputy Director of the Presidential Task Force for the Evacuation of Saigon and the Resettlement of Refugees from Indochina.

Mr. McManaway served at the Department of State in 1975 as Deputy Assistant Secretary/Acting Director of the Sinai Support Mission. In the Department he was Director of Management Operations (1976–1978), Senior Inspector of the Office of the Inspector General (1978), Deputy Assistant Secretary for Classification/Declassification Center (1978–1981), and Deputy Executive Secretary (1981–1983).

Mr. McManaway graduated from the University of South Carolina (B.S., 1955) and the American Institute of Foreign Trade (B.A., 1959). He was born March 5, 1933, in Greenville, S.C.

Remarks to Reporters on the Soviet Attack on a Korean Civilian Airliner
September 2, 1983

First, let me just say that Nancy and I were deeply saddened last night to hear of the death of Senator Henry Jackson. He was a friend, a colleague, a true patriot, and a devoted servant of the people. He will be sorely missed, and we both extend our deepest sympathy to his family.

And now, in the wake of the barbaric act committed yesterday by the Soviet regime against a commercial jetliner [Korean Air Lines flight 007], the United States and many other countries of the world made clear and compelling statements that ex-

pressed not only our outrage but also our demand for a truthful accounting of the facts.

Our first emotions are anger, disbelief, and profound sadness. While events in Afghanistan and elsewhere have left few illusions about the willingness of the Soviet Union to advance its interests through violence and intimidation, all of us had hoped that certain irreducible standards of civilized behavior, nonetheless, obtained. But this event shocks the sensibilities of people everywhere. The tradition in a civilized world has always been to offer help to mariners and pilots who are lost or in distress on the sea or in the air. Where human life is valued, extraordinary efforts are extended to preserve and protect it, and it's essential that as civilized societies, we ask searching questions about the nature of regimes where such standards do not apply.

Beyond these emotions the world notes the stark contrast that exists between Soviet words and deeds. What can we think of a regime that so broadly trumpets its vision of peace and global disarmament and yet so callously and quickly commits a terrorist act to sacrifice the lives of innocent human beings? What could be said about Soviet credibility when they so flagrantly lie about such a heinous act? What can be the scope of legitimate and mutual discourse with a state whose values permit such atrocities? And what are we to make of a regime which establishes one set of standards for itself and another for the rest of humankind?

We've joined in the call for an urgent United Nations Security Council meeting today. The brutality of this act should not be compounded through silence or the cynical distortion of the evidence now at hand. And tonight I will be meeting with my advisers to conduct a formal review of this matter, and this weekend I shall be meeting with the congressional leadership.

To the families of all those on the ill-fated aircraft, we send our deepest sympathy, and I hope they know our prayers are with them all.

Note: The President spoke at 12:35 p.m. at Point Mugu Naval Air Station, Calif., where he had helicoptered from Rancho del Cielo, his ranch near Santa Barbara. Following his remarks, he boarded Air Force One *for the return to Washington, D.C.*

Radio Address to the Nation on the Soviet Attack on a Korean Civilian Airliner and on the Observance of Labor Day
September 3, 1983

My fellow Americans:

This weekend marks the 89th observance of Labor Day, a special day for all Americans. Before I get to that topic, however, I'm going to speak to you briefly about the recent act of brutality that continues to horrify us all. I'm referring to the outrageous Soviet attack against the 269 people aboard the unarmed Korean passenger plane.

This murder of innocent civilians is a serious international issue between the Soviet Union and civilized people everywhere who cherish individual rights and value human life. It is up to all of us, leaders and citizens of the world, to deal with the Soviets in a calm, controlled, but absolutely firm manner. We have joined in this call for an urgent U.N. Security Council meeting.

The evidence is clear; it leaves no doubt; it is time for the Soviets to account. The Soviet Union owes the world a fullest possible explanation and apology for their inexcusable act of brutality. So far, they've flunked the test. Even now, they continue to distort and deny the truth.

People everywhere can draw only one conclusion from their violent behavior: There is a glaring gap between Soviet words and deeds. They speak endlessly about their love of brotherhood, disarmament, and peace, but they reserve the right to disregard aviation safety and to sacrifice human lives.

Make no mistake on this last point. This is not the first time the Soviets have shot at and hit a civilian airliner when it flew over Soviet territory. Our government does not shoot down foreign aircraft over U.S. territory, even though commerical aircraft from the Soviet Union and Cuba have overflown sensitive U.S. military facilities. We and other civilized countries follow procedures to prevent a tragedy, rather than to provoke one. But while the Soviets accuse others of wanting to return to the cold war, it's they who have never left it behind.

I met with the National Security Council last night. Tomorrow I will meet with congressional leaders of both parties to discuss this issue, as well as the situation in Lebanon, on which the National Security Council met today. We're determined to move forward and to act in concert both with the Congress and other members of the international community. We must make sure that the fundamental rules of safety of travel are respected by all nations, even the Soviet Union.

Now, let me turn to another subject that's also very much on our minds this weekend—Labor Day. More than any other country in the world, ours was built not by some small, privileged elite, but by the physical, mental, and moral strength of free working men and women; people who asked for nothing but the chance to build a better future in a climate of fairness and freedom. As one of the founding fathers of the American labor movement, Samuel Gompers, put it, our society is based on the right of working people "to be full sharers in the abundance which is the result of their brain and brawn and the civilization of which they are the founders and the mainstay."

Those words have meant a lot to me over the years. I've always believed that America can only be true to itself when its promise is shared by all our people. One of the best ways to make sure that happens is to build a healthy, growing economy that opens up more and more opportunity to our people. We've been working at that for more than 2½ years now. With your help and the help of a bipartisan group in the Congress, our efforts are showing good results.

Just this week, Commerce Secretary Baldrige announced that in July inventories registered their biggest advance in 20 months. That means the economic recovery has boosted the confidence of manufactur-

ers and encouraged business firms to restock. It adds up to more work for people in a wide range of industries and trades and means this recovery will continue to be strong.

Meanwhile, the civilian unemployment rate has dropped by 1.3 percentage points since last December. The number of unemployed has declined by more than 1.3 million, and a healthy, growing economy has added almost 2½ million people to the Nation's payrolls.

Another good way of testing progress is to measure how well the American family, the average family, is doing today. An American family earning $25,000 has $600 more today in purchasing power than it would if inflation were still raging at its 1980 rate. And then there are your tax savings. The typical American family will pay $700 less in Federal income taxes than if the old 1980 rates were still in effect.

Now, I know that for many Americans on this Labor Day, life is still tough. None of us can be fully satisfied until many more of our people find work. And we won't be satisfied until we cut inflation all the way back to zero. But every week, our economy is gaining fresh strength, and that's good news for us all.

Finally, let me say that on this weekend, I hope you'll take a moment to celebrate not only the working people of this nation but something that makes it all possible—our freedom. As I mentioned at the outset, we've watched with horror these past few days as totalitarianism has shown its ghastly face once again. That's why here in America we must remain a bastion of free men and women working together toward a brighter future.

Till next week, thanks for listening, and God bless you.

Note: The President spoke at 12:06 p.m. from the Oval Office at the White House.

Remarks to Reporters Following a Meeting With Ambassador Paul H. Nitze
September 3, 1983

The President. Ladies and gentlemen, this is a photo opportunity. We have been meeting. In fact, all we've been doing for quite some time is meeting. But the Ambassador and I have been meeting with regard to his return tomorrow to the negotiating table in Geneva, by way of some of our allies in NATO, on the intermediate-range nuclear weapons discussions.

This being a photo opportunity, we won't take questions, but he will be briefing you this afternoon and meeting with you at a later moment, as you well know.

Q. Don't you even want to tell us what this Soviet incident is going to do to those arms control talks?

The President. I'm going to take one question, because I meant to say this in my opening remarks and didn't. And the only thing is, yes, we are still meeting, and to-morrow we'll be meeting with Congressmen on that particular problem, that issue. And I don't believe that that should reduce the importance of continuing the talks that we hope will lead to a reduction in the number of nuclear weapons in the world. I think peace is that all-important that we shall continue those talks. But that doesn't lessen our feeling, our anger about that terrible tragedy and the Soviet attitude that they've taken following that. But I think we've agreed the disarmament talks must continue.

Q. But, Mr. President, if you say they're barbarians, how can we negotiate?

Deputy Press Secretary Speakes. Thank you, sir.

Note: The President spoke at 1:15 p.m. in the Rose Garden at the White House.

Message on the Observance of Labor Day
September 4, 1983

Each Labor Day provides us with an opportunity to pay homage to the workers who have helped make America great.

I join with all Americans in saluting the contributions of the nation's working men and women, the most productive workers in the world.

The endeavors of today's workers and their unions assure that our country will have an even brighter future. Yet the bounty we have reaped from these labors is not limited to mere products and services. Our workers have been one of the cornerstones of our democratic system. The values they have passed down from generation to generation have strengthened America as the land of opportunity.

Even though the nature of our labor has changed over the years, Americans still believe that all work is noble. In celebrating the efforts of American workers, past and present, we honor this fundamental truth as well.

On this day we also reflect on our foremost domestic challenge: providing job opportunities for all Americans who want to work. Through my Administration's Economic Recovery Program, we are bringing new hope to Americans. Already this year more than 1.7 million more Americans are employed than last December. The resurgence of our economy is bringing real jobs—jobs with a future—in the private sector.

The improved economic climate we now enjoy promises all Americans a prosperous future. I know that the nation's workforce will play a vital role in helping America realize its full economic potential.

RONALD REAGAN

Address to the Nation on the Soviet Attack on a Korean Civilian Airliner
September 5, 1983

My fellow Americans:

I'm coming before you tonight about the Korean airline massacre, the attack by the Soviet Union against 269 innocent men, women, and children aboard an unarmed Korean passenger plane. This crime against humanity must never be forgotten, here or throughout the world.

Our prayers tonight are with the victims and their families in their time of terrible grief. Our hearts go out to them—to brave people like Kathryn McDonald, the wife of a Congressman whose composure and eloquence on the day of her husband's death moved us all. He will be sorely missed by all of us here in government.

The parents of one slain couple wired me: "Our daughter . . . and her husband . . . died on Korean Airline Flight 007. Their deaths were the result of the Soviet Union violating every concept of human rights." The emotions of these parents—grief, shock, anger—are shared by civilized people everywhere. From around the world press accounts reflect an explosion of condemnation by people everywhere.

Let me state as plainly as I can: There was absolutely no justification, either legal or moral, for what the Soviets did. One newspaper in India said, "If every passenger plane . . . is fair game for home air forces . . . it will be the end to civil aviation as we know it."

This is not the first time the Soviet Union has shot at and hit a civilian airliner when it overflew its territory. In another tragic incident in 1978, the Soviets also shot down an unarmed civilian airliner after having positively identified it as such. In that instance, the Soviet interceptor pilot clearly identified the civilian markings on the side of the aircraft, repeatedly questioned the order to fire on a civilian airliner, and was ordered to shoot it down anyway. The aircraft was hit with a missile and made a crash landing. Several innocent people lost their lives in this attack, killed by shrapnel from the blast of a Soviet missile.

Is this a practice of other countries in the world? The answer is no. Commercial aircraft from the Soviet Union and Cuba on a number of occasions have overflown sensitive United States military facilities. They weren't shot down. We and other civilized countries believe in the tradition of offering help to mariners and pilots who are lost or in distress on the sea or in the air. We believe in following procedures to prevent a tragedy, not to provoke one.

But despite the savagery of their crime, the universal reaction against it, and the evidence of their complicity, the Soviets still refuse to tell the truth. They have persistently refused to admit that their pilot fired on the Korean aircraft. Indeed, they've not even told their own people that a plane was shot down.

They have spun a confused tale of tracking the plane by radar until it just mysteriously disappeared from their radar screens, but no one fired a shot of any kind. But then they coupled this with charges that it was a spy plane sent by us and that their planes fired tracer bullets past the plane as a warning that it was in Soviet airspace.

Let me recap for a moment and present the incontrovertible evidence that we have. The Korean airliner, a Boeing 747, left Anchorage, Alaska, bound for Seoul, Korea, on a course south and west which would take it across Japan. Out over the Pacific, in international waters, it was for a brief time in the vicinity of one of our reconnaissance planes, an RC–135, on a routine mission. At no time was the RC–135 in Soviet airspace. The Korean airliner flew on, and the two planes were soon widely separated.

The 747 is equipped with the most modern computerized navigation facilities, but a computer must respond to input provided by human hands. No one will ever know whether a mistake was made in giving the computer the course or whether there was a malfunction. Whichever, the 747 was flying a course further to the west than it was supposed to fly—a course which took it into Soviet airspace.

The Soviets tracked this plane for 2½ hours while it flew a straight-line course at 30 to 35,000 feet. Only civilian airliners fly in such a manner. At one point, the Korean pilot gave Japanese air control his position as east of Hokkaido, Japan, showing that he was unaware they were off course by as much or more than a hundred miles.

The Soviets scrambled jet interceptors from a base in Sakhalin Island. Japanese ground sites recorded the interceptor planes' radio transmissions—their conversations with their own ground control. We only have the voices from the pilots; the Soviet ground-to-air transmissions were not recorded. It's plain, however, from the pilot's words that he's responding to orders and queries from his own ground control.

Here is a brief segment of the tape which we're going to play in its entirety for the United Nations Security Council tomorrow.

[*At this point, the tape was played.*]

Those were the voices of the Soviet pilots. In this tape, the pilot who fired the missile describes his search for what he calls the target. He reports he has it in sight; indeed, he pulls up to within about a mile of the Korean plane, mentions its flashing strobe light and that its navigation lights are on. He then reports he's reducing speed to get behind the airliner, gives his distance from the plane at various points in this maneuver, and finally announces what can only be called the Korean Airline Massacre. He says he has locked on the radar, which aims his missiles, has launched those missiles, the target has been destroyed, and he is breaking off the attack.

Let me point out something here having to do with his closeup view of the airliner on what we know was a clear night with a half moon. The 747 has a unique and distinctive silhouette, unlike any other plane in the world. There is no way a pilot could mistake this for anything other than a civilian airliner. And if that isn't enough, let me point out our RC–135 that I mentioned earlier had been back at its base in Alaska, on the ground for an hour, when the murderous attack took place over the Sea of Japan.

And make no mistake about it, this attack was not just against ourselves or the Repub-

lic of Korea. This was the Soviet Union against the world and the moral precepts which guide human relations among people everywhere. It was an act of barbarism, born of a society which wantonly disregards individual rights and the value of human life and seeks constantly to expand and dominate other nations.

They deny the deed, but in their conflicting and misleading protestations, the Soviets reveal that, yes, shooting down a plane—even one with hundreds of innocent men, women, children, and babies—is a part of their normal procedure if that plane is in what they claim as their airspace.

They owe the world an apology and an offer to join the rest of the world in working out a system to protect against this ever happening again. Among the rest of us there is one protective measure: an international radio wavelength on which pilots can communicate with planes of other nations if they are in trouble or lost. Soviet military planes are not so equipped, because that would make it easier for pilots who might want to defect.

Our request to send vessels into Soviet waters to search for wreckage and bodies has received no satisfactory answer. Bereaved families of the Japanese victims were harassed by Soviet patrol boats when they tried to get near where the plane is believed to have gone down in order to hold a ceremony for their dead. But we shouldn't be surprised by such inhuman brutality. Memories come back of Czechoslovakia, Hungary, Poland, the gassing of villages in Afghanistan. If the massacre and their subsequent conduct is intended to intimidate, they have failed in their purpose. From every corner of the globe the word is defiance in the face of this unspeakable act and defiance of the system which excuses it and tries to cover it up. With our horror and our sorrow, there is a righteous and terrible anger. It would be easy to think in terms of vengeance, but that is not a proper answer. We want justice and action to see that this never happens again.

Our immediate challenge to this atrocity is to ensure that we make the skies safer and that we seek just compensation for the families of those who were killed.

Since my return to Washington, we've held long meetings, the most recent yesterday with the congressional leadership. There was a feeling of unity in the room, and I received a number of constructive suggestions. We will continue to work with the Congress regarding our response to this massacre.

As you know, we immediately made known to the world the shocking facts as honestly and completely as they came to us.

We have notified the Soviets that we will not renew our bilateral agreement for cooperation in the field of transportation so long as they threaten the security of civil aviation.

Since 1981 the Soviet airline Aeroflot has been denied the right to fly to the United States. We have reaffirmed that order and are examining additional steps we can take with regard to Aeroflot facilities in this country. We're cooperating with other countries to find better means to ensure the safety of civil aviation and to join us in not accepting Aeroflot as a normal member of the international civil air community unless and until the Soviets satisfy the cries of humanity for justice. I am pleased to report that Canada today suspended Aeroflot's landing and refueling privileges for 60 days.

We have joined with other countries to press the International Civil Aviation Organization to investigate this crime at an urgent special session of the Council. At the same time, we're listening most carefully to private groups, both American and international, airline pilots, passenger associations, and others, who have a special interest in civil air safety.

I am asking the Congress to pass a joint resolution of condemnation of this Soviet crime.

We have informed the Soviets that we're suspending negotiations on several bilateral arrangements we had under consideration.

Along with Korea and Japan, we called an emergency meeting of the U.N. Security Council which began on Friday. On that first day, Korea, Japan, Canada, Australia, the Netherlands, Pakistan, France, China, the United Kingdom, Zaire, New Zealand, and West Germany all joined us in denouncing the Soviet action and expressing our horror. We expect to hear from additional countries as debate resumes tomorrow.

We intend to work with the 13 countries who had citizens aboard the Korean airliner to seek reparations for the families of all those who were killed. The United States will be making a claim against the Soviet Union within the next week to obtain compensation for the benefit of the victims' survivors. Such compensation is an absolute moral duty which the Soviets must assume.

In the economic area in general, we're redoubling our efforts with our allies to end the flow of military and strategic items to the Soviet Union.

Secretary Shultz is going to Madrid to meet with representatives of 35 countries who, for 3 years, have been negotiating an agreement having to do with, among other things, human rights. Foreign Minister Gromyko of the Soviet Union is scheduled to attend that meeting. If he does come to the meeting, Secretary Shultz is going to present him with our demands for disclosure of the facts, corrective action, and concrete assurances that such a thing will not happen again and that restitution be made.

As we work with other countries to see that justice is done, the real test of our resolve is whether we have the will to remain strong, steady, and united. I believe more than ever—as evidenced by your thousands and thousands of wires and phone calls in these last few days—that we do.

I have outlined some of the steps we're taking in response to the tragic massacre. There is something I've always believed in, but which now seems more important than ever. The Congress will be facing key national security issues when it returns from recess. There has been legitimate difference of opinion on this subject, I know, but I urge the Members of that distinguished body to ponder long and hard the Soviets' aggression as they consider the security and safety of our people—indeed, all people who believe in freedom.

Senator Henry Jackson, a wise and revered statesman and one who probably understood the Soviets as well as any American in history, warned us, "the greatest threat the United States now faces is posed by the Soviet Union." But Senator Jackson said, "If America maintains a strong deterrent—and only if it does—this nation will continue to be a leader in the crucial quest for enduring peace among nations."

The late Senator made those statements in July on the Senate floor, speaking in behalf of the MX missile program he considered vital to restore America's strategic parity with the Soviets.

When John F. Kennedy was President, defense spending as a share of the Federal budget was 70 percent greater than it is today. Since then, the Soviet Union has carried on the most massive military buildup the world has ever seen. Until they are willing to join the rest of the world community, we must maintain the strength to deter their aggression.

But while we do so, we must not give up our effort to bring them into the world community of nations. Peace through strength as long as necessary, but never giving up our effort to bring peace closer through mutual, verifiable reduction in the weapons of war.

I've told you of negotiations we've suspended as a result of the Korean airline massacre, but we cannot, we must not give up our effort to reduce the arsenals of destructive weapons threatening the world. Ambassador Nitze has returned to Geneva to resume the negotiations on intermediate-range nuclear weapons in Europe. Equally, we will continue to press for arms reductions in the START talks that resume in October. We are more determined than ever to reduce and, if possible, eliminate the threat hanging over mankind.

We know it will be hard to make a nation that rules its own people through force to cease using force against the rest of the world. But we must try.

This is not a role we sought. We preach no manifest destiny. But like Americans who began this country and brought forth this last, best hope of mankind, history has asked much of the Americans of our own time. Much we have already given; much more we must be prepared to give.

Let us have faith, in Abraham Lincoln's words, "that right makes might, and in that faith let us, to the end dare to do our duty as we understand it." If we do, if we stand together and move forward with courage, then history will record that some good did come from this monstrous wrong that we will carry with us and remember for the rest of our lives.

Thank you. God bless you, and good night.

Note: The President spoke at 8 p.m. from the Oval Office at the White House. The address was broadcast live on nationwide radio and television.

Statement by Deputy Press Secretary Speakes on United States Marine Casualties in Lebanon
September 6, 1983

The deaths of the two U.S. marines and wounding of three others in the early morning hours of September 6 saddened us all. We condemn those responsible for the continuing violence that has claimed thousands of innocent victims. We are proud of our own forces and the important role they are playing to achieve security for the Lebanese people.

The Lebanese Government has issued a call to all parties to unite to restore national dialog. We will continue to work with them toward that end. The goal of a newly united Lebanon, free of foreign forces, is a dream of the Lebanese people, regardless of their religious community. Together with our Italian, French, and British partners in the multinational force, we are performing a critical role in support of the effort of the central government. No one should mistake our determination to continue in this just cause.

Note: Deputy Press Secretary Larry M.

Speakes read the statement during his daily press briefing for reporters, which began at 1:30 p.m. in the Briefing Room at the White House.

Proclamation 5087—Fire Prevention Week, 1983
September 6, 1983

By the President of the United States of America

A Proclamation

This great Nation of ours, the richest and most technologically advanced in the world, continues to lead all major industrialized countries in per capita deaths and property loss from fire.

Each year thousands of American lives are lost, billions of dollars in property are needlessly destroyed, and thousands of persons are permanently disfigured or disabled by burn injuries from preventable fires.

Obviously, we must continue to address fire prevention as a national priority, and I strongly urge each citizen to make a personal commitment to aid in the reduction of this senseless and tragic waste of precious lives, property, and natural resources from fire. Through a concentrated effort our Nation can substantially reduce the human suffering and economic losses from fire.

Since most deaths and injuries from fire occur in the home, it is essential that families install and maintain smoke detectors to provide early warning should a fire occur. In addition, each family should establish and practice home fire escape plans. Commercial enterprises and State and local governments should consider installation of fast-response sprinklers to protect lives in residences, hotels, motels, and nursing homes.

An indispensable ingredient of fire pre-vention is our professional firefighter. Firefighting is one of our most hazardous occupations. We are indebted to the brave men and women who serve communities across the Nation so bravely—often at the risk of their own safety and sometimes at the cost of their own lives.

We must also applaud the efforts of our fire chiefs, the National Fire Protection Association, the Fire Marshals Association of North America, the International Association of Fire Chiefs, the International Association of Firefighters, the National Volunteer Fire Council, the International Society of Fire Service Instructors, the Joint Council of National Fire Service Organizations, the National Safety Council, and others for their work to reduce fire losses. These dedicated men and women need and merit our assistance and support.

Now, Therefore, I, Ronald Reagan, President of the United States of America, do hereby designate the week of October 9 through 15, 1983, as Fire Prevention Week, 1983.

In Witness Whereof, I have hereunto set my hand this 6th day of Sept., in the year of our Lord nineteen hundred and eighty-three, and of the Independence of the United States of America the two hundred and eighth.

RONALD REAGAN

[*Filed with the Office of the Federal Register, 11:08 a.m., September 7, 1983*]

Proclamation 5088—National School Lunch Week, 1983
September 6, 1983

By the President of the United States of America

A Proclamation

The National School Lunch Program—now in its 37th year—operates to provide nutritious and well-balanced meals to many young people of our country. The school lunch program is an outstanding example of the partnership between the Federal government and State and local governments to make available the food, funds, and technical support that insures continued nutritional assistance for school students.

The youth of America are our greatest resource. The school lunch program demonstrates the awareness, concern, and willingness to work together that we all share in promoting the health and well-being of our students.

Over 23 million lunches are served daily in some 90,000 schools throughout the country. This effort is being conducted by resourceful and creative food service managers and staff in cooperation with government, parents, teachers, and civic groups.

By joint resolution approved October 9, 1962, the Congress designated the week beginning on the second Sunday of October in each year as National School Lunch Week and requested the President to issue annually a proclamation calling for the observance of that week.

Now, Therefore, I, Ronald Reagan, President of the United States of America, do hereby urge the people of the United States to observe the week of October 9, 1983, as National School Lunch Week and to give special and deserved recognition to those people at the State and local level who, through their innovative efforts, have made it possible to have a successful school lunch program.

In Witness Whereof, I have hereunto set my hand this 6th day of Sept., in the year of our Lord nineteen hundred and eighty-three, and of the Independence of the United States of America the two hundred and eighth.

RONALD REAGAN

[*Filed with the Office of the Federal Register, 11:09 a.m., September 7, 1983*]

Proclamation 5089—Columbus Day, 1983
September 6, 1983

By the President of the United States of America

A Proclamation

It is fitting that Americans honor those individuals who have altered the course of history in this country by exhibiting great moral character and courage—men and women who have contributed to the development of personal liberties we enjoy today. Thus, it is especially appropriate that I urge all Americans to honor one of those individuals, Christopher Columbus.

Columbus was a bold and adventurous navigator who left Europe in 1492 in search of new lands and first recorded the sighting of the North American continent. In this sense he personifies the courage and vision so many explorers exhibited during this period. Yet he is more than this. He represents a spirit, the spirit of the Renaissance which contributed to the development of America. Along with Galileo, Copernicus, and others, Columbus symbolizes a quest for knowledge, a willingness and fortitude to go beyond what is accepted as truth in the name of progress. Columbus did not fall off the face of the earth; rather, through daring, risk, and innovation, he discovered new horizons.

Since Columbus discovered America, numerous families have exhibited that same courage and fortitude in setting sail across the seas to become American citizens. By taking that step into the new and unknown, those same families created an opportunity to realize increased prosperity and greater freedom here in these United States. The accomplishments and contributions of Christopher Columbus provide an example of the rewards that can come from taking initiatives. Today Americans have the opportunity and freedom to make accomplishments and contributions of their own and to enjoy the feelings of accomplishment which follow.

Of course Columbus Day is a day of special importance to Americans of Italian heritage. It is a day when all Americans should join in recognizing the great contributions of Italian-Americans to this country's cultural, scientific, athletic and commercial achievements, and religious vitality.

In tribute to the achievement of Columbus, the Congress of the United States, by joint resolution approved April 30, 1934 (48 Stat. 657), as modified by the Act of June 28, 1968 (82 Stat. 250), has authorized and requested the President to issue a proclamation designating the second Monday in October of each year as Columbus Day.

Now, Therefore, I, Ronald Reagan, President of the United States of America, do hereby designate Monday, October 10, 1983, as Columbus Day. I invite the people of this Nation to observe that day in schools, churches and other suitable places with appropriate ceremonies in honor of this great explorer. I also direct that the flag of the United States be displayed on all public buildings on the appointed day in memory of Christopher Columbus.

In Witness Whereof, I have hereunto set my hand this 6th day of Sept., in the year of our Lord nineteen hundred and eighty-three, and of the Independence of the United States of America the two hundred and eighth.

RONALD REAGAN

[Filed with the Office of the Federal Register, 11:10 a.m., September 7, 1983]

Proclamation 5090—General Pulaski Memorial Day, 1983
September 6, 1983

By the President of the United States of America

A Proclamation

On October 11, 1779, the Polish and American patriot Casimir Pulaski was mortally wounded while leading his troops in battle at Savannah, Georgia. Pulaski died fighting in our American Revolution so that we could live as a free and independent Nation.

It is fitting that we should pay tribute to this martyr for freedom and that free men and women everywhere should take this occasion to rededicate themselves to the principles for which Pulaski gave his life. The power of the ideal of freedom remains vital, both in Pulaski's homeland and in his adopted country. In paying tribute to Casimir Pulaski, we pay tribute as well to all those Poles who have sacrificed themselves over the years for their common goal: the freedom of that heroic nation.

Now, Therefore, I, Ronald Reagan, President of the United States of America, in recognition of the supreme sacrifice General Pulaski made for his adopted country, do hereby designate October 11, 1983, as General Pulaski Memorial Day, and I direct the appropriate Government officials to display the flag of the United States on all Government buildings on that day.

In Witness Whereof, I have hereunto set my hand this 6th day of Sept., in the year of our Lord nineteen hundred and eighty-three, and of the Independence of the United States of America the two hundred and eighth.

RONALD REAGAN

[Filed with the Office of the Federal Register, 11:11 a.m., September 7, 1983]

Proclamation 5091—White Cane Safety Day, 1983
September 6, 1983

By the President of the United States of America

A Proclamation

One of the great blessings of life is to be able to move at will from place to place unhampered by fear for one's personal safety. For those who are blind, the white cane helps to make such freedom of movement possible. It enables the blind to use our streets and public facilities with maximum safety and thereby know the joys of self-reliance and independence and experience a more fulfilling life.

All Americans should be aware of the significance of the white cane and extend every courtesy and consideration to the men and women who carry it. In this way, we respect the privacy of the visually disabled and contribute to enlarging their mobility and independence.

In recognition of the significance of the white cane, the Congress, by a joint resolution approved October 6, 1964 (78 Stat. 1003), has authorized and requested the President to proclaim October 15 of each year as White Cane Safety Day.

Now, Therefore, I, Ronald Reagan, President of the United States of America, do hereby proclaim October 15, 1983, as White Cane Safety Day. I urge all Americans to mark this occasion by giving greater consideration to the special needs of the visually disabled, and, particularly, to observe White Cane Safety Day with activities that contribute to maximum independent use of our streets and public facilities by our visually handicapped.

In Witness Whereof, I have hereunto set my hand this 6th day of Sept., in the year of our Lord nineteen hundred and eighty-three, and of the Independence of the United States of America the two hundred and eighth.

RONALD REAGAN

[*Filed with the Office of the Federal Register, 11:12 a.m., September 7, 1983*]

Proclamation 5092—National Forest Products Week, 1983
September 6, 1983

By the President of the United States of America

A Proclamation

Throughout our history, our Nation's abundant forests have served us in so many vital respects that we sometimes forget this extraordinary renewable natural resource. The growing and harvesting of trees, and the work force that turns them into useful products, make a valuable contribution to the Nation's economic well-being, and to providing homes for our people.

Familiar and useful items ranging from furniture to grocery bags to turpentine were once parts of trees in the forest. Our forest lands also provide water for homes, agriculture, and industry and pastures for grazing animals. Our forests serve us in many other ways. They provide a home for wildlife and are a source of recreational activities ranging from driving through and enjoying the scenery, to mountain climbing and backpacking in our numerous parks and wilderness areas.

We recognize that maintaining a healthy environment and a healthy economy are essential and complementary goals. We can be proud of our success and commitment to effective forest management, which strikes a vital balance between preservation and development of our forests. Through wise and sensitive management, we will maintain this vitally important part of our Nation's heritage, so those who follow will inherit forests that are even more useful and productive.

To promote greater awareness and appreciation for our forest resources, the Congress, by Public Law 86–753, 36 U.S.C. 163, has designated the week beginning on the third Sunday in October as National Forest Products Week.

Now, Therefore, I, Ronald Reagan, President of the United States of America, do hereby proclaim the week beginning on October 16, 1983, as National Forest Products Week and request that all Americans express their appreciation for the Nation's forests through suitable activities.

In Witness Whereof, I have hereunto set my hand this 6th day of Sept., in the year of our Lord nineteen hundred and eighty-three, and of the Independence of the United States of America the two hundred and eighth.

RONALD REAGAN

[*Filed with the Office of the Federal Register, 11:13 a.m., September 7, 1983*]

Recess Appointment of Two Members of the Board of Directors of the Inter-American Foundation
September 6, 1983

The President today recess appointed the following individuals:

J. William Middendorf II, Permanent Representative of the United States of America to the Organization of American States, with the rank of Ambassador, to be a member of the Board of Directors of the Inter-American Foundation, for a term expiring September 20, 1988. He will succeed Marc Leland.

Langhorne A. Motley, an Assistant Secretary of State (Inter-American Affairs), to be a member of the Board of Directors of the Inter-American Foundation, for the remainder of the term expiring September 20, 1984. He will succeed Thomas O. Enders.

Remarks at a White House Ceremony Announcing the Adult Literacy Initiative
September 7, 1983

Thank you very much, and welcome to the White House.

I know that Barbara Bush is very disappointed that she couldn't be here with us today, but she's down in Dallas, if you haven't been told already. That's the penalty of coming in this way after the meeting has started—I don't know who said what. [*Laughter*]

But she's participating in a recognition ceremony for volunteers working in Operation LIFT, a literacy organization supported solely by the private sector. And yesterday, I had the pleasure in my office of meeting Sherman Swenson. He's the chief executive officer of Dalton Booksellers, and that corporation has launched a program nationwide on this very subject.

I know that Barbara would be as encouraged as I am at the broad array of groups and individuals represented here today—leaders from the Congress, from education, business and industry, church and service groups, and State and local government.

This is heartening, because it will take a united effort by all our people to achieve our goal: the elimination of adult functional illiteracy in the United States.

In this decade, America faces serious challenges on many fronts—to our national security, our economic prosperity, and our ability to compete in the international marketplace. If we're to renew our economy, protect our freedom, we must sharpen the skills of every American mind and enlarge the potential of every individual American life. Unfortunately, the hidden problem of adult illiteracy holds back too many of our citizens, and as a nation, we, too, pay a price.

Conservative estimates are that 23 million Americans, one in five, are functionally illiterate—a statistic that includes men and women of every race, religion, and economic status, and every region of the country.

I asked Secretary Bell to explore with you the best ways and means to erase adult illiteracy from our country, and the result is this initiative that we announce today. Some of the key points in the initiative are: to provide initial Federal funding for the Coalition for Literacy and support the National Ad Council in its awareness campaign; to establish a national adult literacy project identifying model literacy programs and developing and testing new programs, materials, and methods.

The Department of Education will work closely with the White House Office of Private Sector Initiatives to enlist more nongovernment support. An additional $310 million has been requested for college work-study programs to include students in our effort, and I have also asked the Department to recruit literacy volunteers on college campuses. Federal employees will also be encouraged to volunteer, and the Department of Education will conduct a series of national meetings and conferences to increase awareness and promote cooperation.

As I'm sure you realize, there are many more items on our agenda, but this sampling should indicate the energy, commitment, and creativity we intend to apply to this problem.

Let us today resolve to roll up our sleeves and get to work, because there's very much to be done. Across this great land, let those of us who can read teach those who cannot. Let the lights burn late in our classrooms, our church basements, our libraries, and around our kitchen tables—wherever we can gather to help others help themselves to the American dream.

I appreciate all that you've already done, but today I'm asking you for more. Together, we can rouse the spirit of our people and apply our enormous national will to the task at hand. If we succeed, we will have come an important step closer to making America great again.

Now, I know that all of the ladies and gentlemen here on the platform are distinguished and are very prominent, and I extend a thanks to them. But I can't help but tell you, also, this has just been a very great moment for me, because I've been a fan of Marva Collins ever since I heard of her, and I at last had the opportunity to meet her. God bless you. As a matter of fact, hearing of some of what you've done, Marva, made me ashamed of the times that I cheated in English literature on Shakespeare. [*Laughter*]

But I thank you all again for being here, and God bless you all. And now, they've told me I've got to get back to the Oval Office. Thank you all again.

Note: The President spoke at 11:33 a.m. in the East Room at the White House following remarks by Secretary of Education Terrel H. Bell.

Message on the Observance of the Jewish High Holy Days
September 7, 1983

It is a pleasure for Nancy and me to extend greetings to Jews in this country and the world over as you join in celebration of the High Holy Days.

We know that Rosh Hashanah, the New Year, is a time for introspection, reflection, and renewal. It is also a time when members of the Jewish Faith reexamine the year past and look to the one ahead in a spirit of prayer and hopefulness.

Ten days later, Yom Kippur, the Day of Atonement, is a solemn period of fasting and penitence which culminates the High Holy Days.

For all of you this is an especially thoughtful season, and we join fellow Americans in sharing your hopes and aspirations for peace and human understanding and for an end to hatred and violence.

As the shofar calls Jews to their places of worship during this period, our thoughts and warm good wishes will be with you. May the year 5744 bring health, prosperity, and peace to you and your families.

RONALD REAGAN

Statement by Deputy Press Secretary Speakes on the Soviet Attack on a Korean Civilian Airliner
September 7, 1983

The Soviet TASS "news analysis" of September 7 on "Larry Speakes' Strange Logic," has come to my attention. In it, their commentator Yuriy Kornilov writes that his country will continue to act "in compliance with Soviet laws" which call for the shooting down of unarmed aircraft which may chance to fly over their airspace. This comes on the heels of the Soviet Government's admission of yesterday that its forces shot down the unarmed airliner of another country on August 31 and killed 269 people from 13 countries. This admission came only after the truth was known everywhere else in the world—and even known to some in the Soviet Union through BBC, VOA and other international broadcast outlets that bring the facts to the truth-starved people under the control of the Soviet regime. The admission, however, was coupled with a flat Soviet statement saying they will take the same action in the future in similar circumstances—in other words, that they will shoot down the next offcourse unarmed aircraft that transgresses the territory prescribed by Soviet law.

As Under Secretary of State Lawrence Eagleburger said yesterday, the international community is being asked to accept that the Soviet Union is not bound by the norms of international behavior and human decency to which all other nations subscribe.

Fortunately, the international community is not accepting this, and continues to ask—at the United Nations in particular—that the Soviets provide a full accounting of what transpired, an unequivocal apology for Soviet actions, restitution for the victims' families, full cooperation with international efforts to investigate this tragedy and recover its victims, and assurances that the Soviet Union will take specific steps to ensure that the massacre of August 31 not occur again. The case is in no way closed by the Soviet admission of yesterday.

Note: Deputy Press Secretary Larry M. Speakes read the statement during his daily briefing for reporters, which began at 12:30 p.m. in the Briefing Room at the White House.

Nomination of Two Members of the Board for International Broadcasting, and Designation of Chairman
September 7, 1983

The President today announced his intention to nominate the following individuals to be members of the Board for International Broadcasting. These are reappointments. The President also intends to redesignate Frank Shakespeare as Chairman.

Frank Shakespeare, to serve for a term expiring May 20, 1986. Mr. Shakespeare is president of RKO General, Inc., in New York, N.Y. He is married, has three children, and resides in Greenwich, Conn. He was born April 9, 1925, in New York City.

Ben J. Wattenberg, to serve for a term expiring April 28, 1986. Mr. Wattenberg is a senior fellow at the American Enterprise Institute in Washington, D.C. He is married, has three children, and resides in Washington, D.C. He was born August 26, 1933, in New York City.

Appointment of Two Members of the President's Commission on White House Fellowships
September 8, 1983

The President today announced his intention to appoint the following individuals to be members of the President's Commission on White House Fellowships. These are initial appointments.

Willa Ann Johnson is senior vice president of The Heritage Foundation in Washington, D.C. She resides in Takoma Park, Md. She was born May 25, 1942, in Whittier, Calif.

John D. Saxon is counsel to the U.S. Senate Select Committee on Ethics. He is married, has one child, and resides in Washington, D.C. He was born July 21, 1950, in Anniston, Ala.

Message to the Senate Transmitting the United States-Denmark Convention on Taxation and Fiscal Evasion
September 8, 1983

To the Senate of the United States:

I transmit herewith, for Senate advice and consent to ratification, the Convention between the Government of the United States of America and the Government of the Kingdom of Denmark for the Avoidance of Double Taxation and the Prevention of Fiscal Evasion with respect to Taxes on Estates, Inheritances, Gifts and Certain Other Transfers, signed at Washington on April 27, 1983.

The Convention is the first of its kind to be negotiated between the United States and Denmark. It will apply, in the United States, to the Federal estate tax, the Federal gift tax, and the Federal tax on generation-skipping transfers and, in Denmark, to the duty on inheritances and gifts.

A principal feature of the Convention is that the country of the transferor's domicile may tax transfers of estates and gifts and generation-skipping transfers on a worldwide basis, but must credit tax paid to the other State on the basis of location or *situs* of specified types of property.

I recommend that the Senate give early and favorable consideration to the Conven-tion and give its advice and consent to rati-fication.

RONALD REAGAN

The White House,
September 8, 1983.

Appointment of Andrew H. Card, Jr., as Special Assistant to the President for Intergovernmental Affairs
September 8, 1983

The President today announced his inten-tion to appoint Andrew H. Card, Jr., to be Special Assistant to the President for Inter-governmental Affairs with primary respon-sibility for liaison with the Nation's Gover-nors. He will succeed James M. Medas, who has been appointed Deputy Assistant Secre-tary of State in the Bureau of European and Canadian Affairs.

Mr. Card is presently serving as vice president of CMIS Corp., a computer soft-ware engineering firm located in Vienna, Va. He served as a representative to the general court of the Commonwealth of Massachusetts in 1975–1982. He was named one of the Nation's outstanding legislators in 1982 by the National Republican Legisla-tors' Association. In 1982 Mr. Card was a candidate for the Republican nomination for Governor of Massachusetts.

Mr. Card received a bachelor of science degree in engineering from the University of South Carolina and attended the United States Merchant Marine Academy. He is a structural design engineer by profession.

He is married, has three children, and resides in Holbrook, Mass. He was born May 10, 1947.

Nomination of Jack E. Ravan To Be an Assistant Administrator of the Environmental Protection Agency
September 8, 1983

The President today announced his inten-tion to nominate Jack E. Ravan to be an Assistant Administrator of the Environmen-tal Protection Agency (Water Programs). He would succeed Frederic A. Eidsness, Jr.

Since 1982 Mr. Ravan has served as direc-tor of Project Development, Clean Water Group, Wheelabrator-Frye in Atlanta, Ga. Previously he was director of the Alabama Department of Energy in 1980–1982; on the executive management committee and a director of business development for Jordan, Jones & Goulding in Atlanta, Ga., in 1977–1980; Chairman of the Southeastern Federal Regional Council in 1973–1977; a member of the Ohio River Basin Commis-sion in 1972–1977; and Regional Adminis-trator, southeastern region, Environmental Protection Agency, in 1971–1977.

He graduated from the United States Military Academy (B.S., 1959). He is mar-ried, has three children, and resides in Dun-woody, Ga. He was born June 18, 1937, in Easley, S.C.

Accordance of the Personal Rank of Ambassador to Alberto M. Piedra While Serving at the Meeting of the Inter-American Economic and Social Council in Paraguay
September 8, 1983

The President today accorded the personal rank of Ambassador to Alberto M. Piedra while serving as Head of the United States Delegation to the meeting of the Inter-American Economic and Social Council to be held September 20–23, 1983, in Asuncion, Paraguay.

Mr. Piedra was a professor at the University of Villanova in Havana, Cuba, in 1958 and 1959. In 1962–1982 he was associate professor at the Catholic University of America in Washington, D.C. He began his government career as economist, Consejo Nacional de Economia, in Havana in 1958 and was director general, Ministry of Commerce, in Havana in 1959. In 1960–1964 he was staff economist at the Organization of American States in Washington, D.C. Since 1982 he has been Alternate United States Representative to the United States Mission to the Organization of American States and also the United States Representative to the Inter-American Economic and Social Council (CIES), in Washington, D.C.

Mr. Piedra was born January 29, 1926, in Havana, Cuba. He graduated from the University of Havana (LL.B., 1951) and Georgetown University (Ph. D., 1962). His foreign languages are Spanish, French, and German.

Statement by Deputy Press Secretary Speakes on the Soviet Attack on a Korean Civilian Airliner
September 8, 1983

In response to the brutal and unprovoked Soviet attack on Korean Air Lines Flight 007 on September 1, 1983, the President has requested the Civil Aeronautics Board to take strong action against the Soviet airline Aeroflot. In a letter sent this morning to CAB Chairman Dan McKinnon, the President asked the Board to take the following action, effective September 12, 1983:

(1) to suspend the right of Aeroflot to sell tickets in the United States;

(2) to prohibit U.S. airlines from selling tickets in the United States for transportation on Aeroflot;

(3) to preclude U.S. airlines from carrying traffic to, from, or within the U.S. where an Aeroflot flight is on the ticket;

(4) to direct U.S. airlines to suspend any interline service arrangements with Aeroflot; and

(5) to prohibit U.S. airlines from accepting any tickets issued by Aeroflot for air travel to, from, or within the United States.

The President has also reaffirmed the suspension of Aeroflot flights to and from this country which has been in effect since January 5, 1982. The impending Board decision would prevent Aeroflot from marketing any of its services through U.S. carriers or their American agents.

The President requests all United States airlines and travel agents to comply with the letter and spirit of these actions.

The duration of these measures in the civil aviation area will be for a period of time, in part dependent upon the extent to which the U.S.S.R. demonstrates its willingness to honor essential standards of civil aviation, makes a full account of its shoot down of the airliner, and issues an apology as well as compensation to aggrieved parties.

In another action, as directed by the

President, Acting Secretary of State Lawrence S. Eagleburger informed Soviet Ambassador Dobrynin today that the Soviet airline Aeroflot must close its offices in the United States by September 15. Aeroflot airline officials must depart this country by that date.

The United States will continue to work with the members of the international community in their efforts to promote air safety and to deter such Soviet actions from happening again.

Note: Deputy Press Secretary Larry M. Speakes read the statement to reporters assembled in the Briefing Room at the White House at 5 p.m.

Executive Order 12439—President's Task Force on Food Assistance
September 8, 1983

By the authority vested in me as President by the Constitution and laws of the United States of America, in order to establish, in accordance with the provisions of the Federal Advisory Committee Act, as amended (5 U.S.C. App. I), an advisory committee to examine programs intended to render food assistance to the needy and to make recommendations on how such programs may be improved, it is hereby ordered as follows:

Section 1. Establishment. (a) There is established the President's Task Force on Food Assistance, which shall be composed of not more than fifteen persons, who shall be appointed by the President from among citizens of the United States who are not full-time officers or employees of the Federal Government.

(b) The President shall designate a Chairman, and may also designate a Vice Chairman, from among the members of the Task Force.

Sec. 2. Functions. The Task Force shall analyze Federal and other programs intended to render food assistance to the needy and shall make recommendations to the President and the Secretary of Agriculture with respect to how such programs may be improved. The Task Force shall submit its report to the President within ninety days of its first meeting.

Sec. 3. Administration. (a) The heads of Executive agencies shall, to the extent permitted by law, provide the Task Force such information as it may require for purposes of carrying out its functions.

(b) Members of the Task Force shall serve without compensation for their work on the Task Force, but may be allowed travel expenses, including per diem in lieu of subsistence, as authorized by law for persons serving intermittently in the Government service (5 U.S.C. 5701–5707), to the extent funds are available therefor.

(c) The Secretary of Agriculture shall, to the extent permitted by law and subject to the availability of funds, provide the Task Force with such administrative services, facilities, staff and other support services as may be necessary for the effective performance of its functions.

Sec. 4. General. (a) Notwithstanding any other Executive Order, the functions of the President under the Federal Advisory Committee Act, as amended, which are applicable to the Task Force, except that of reporting to the Congress, shall be performed by the Secretary of Agriculture in accordance with guidelines and procedures established by the Administrator of General Services.

(b) The Task Force shall, unless sooner extended, terminate thirty days after submission of its report to the President, but in no event later than January 31, 1984.

RONALD REAGAN

The White House,
September 8, 1983.

[*Filed with the Office of the Federal Register, 10:45 a.m., September 9, 1983*]

Appointment of the Membership of the President's Task Force on Food Assistance
September 8, 1983

The President today announced his intention to appoint the following individuals to be members of the President's Task Force on Food Assistance. The President also intends to designate James La Force, Jr., as Chairman.

James Clayburn La Force, Jr., of Los Angeles, Calif., is dean of the Graduate School of Management at the University of California at Los Angeles. He was born December 28, 1928.

Richard L. Berkley is mayor of Kansas City, Mo. He was born June 29, 1931.

Kenneth W. Clarkson, of Miami, Fla., is director of the Law and Economics Center at the University of Miami in Coral Gables, Fla. He was born June 30, 1942.

Erma Davis, of Peoria, Ill., is director of the George Washington Carver Association in Peoria. She was born April 2, 1930.

Midge Decter, of New York, N.Y., is executive director of the Committee for the Free World in New York City. She was born July 25, 1927.

John Douglas Driggs, former mayor of Phoenix, Ariz., is serving as chairman of the board of Western Savings and Loan Association in Phoenix. He was born June 16, 1927.

George Gordon Graham, of Owings Mills, Md., is professor of international health (human nutrition) and of pediatrics at Johns Hopkins University. He was born October 4, 1923.

Edward J. King, former Governor of Massachusetts, is currently serving as a business consultant in Winthrop, Mass. He was born May 11, 1925.

Betsy Brian Rollins, of Durham, N.C., is director of St. Philip's Community Kitchen at St. Philip's Community Church in Durham. She was born March 20, 1937.

John M. Perkins, of Jackson, Miss., is founder and minister at large for the Voice of Calvary Ministries. He was born June 16, 1930.

J. P. Bolduc, of Clarksville, Md., is senior vice president of W. R. Grace & Co. and chief operating officer for the President's Private Sector Survey on Cost Control. He was born July 17, 1939.

Sandra R. Smoley, of Sacramento, Calif., is president of the National Association of Counties. She was born July 8, 1936.

Donna Carlson West, of Mesa, Ariz., is director of government relations for Crafco, Inc., in Chandler, Ariz. She is a former State representative. She was born February 19, 1938.

Executive Order 12440—President's Commission on Industrial Competitiveness
September 8, 1983

By the authority vested in me as President by the Constitution and laws of the United States of America, including the Federal Advisory Committee Act, as amended (5 U.S.C. App. I), and in order to increase the membership of the President's Commission on Industrial Competitiveness, it is hereby ordered that the second sentence of Section 1(a) of Executive Order No. 12428 of June 28, 1983 is hereby amended to provide as follows:

"The Commission shall be composed of no more than thirty members appointed or designated by the President.".

RONALD REAGAN

The White House,
September 8, 1983.

[*Filed with the Office of the Federal Register, 10:46 a.m., September 9, 1983*]

Note: The text of the Executive order was released by the Office of the Press Secretary on September 9.

Appointment of Three Members of the Advisory Council on Historic Preservation
September 9, 1983

The President today announced his intention to appoint the following individuals to be members of the Advisory Council on Historic Preservation:

Virginia Workman Bremberg, to serve for the remainder of the term expiring June 10, 1985. She will succeed Lawrence F. Kramer. She is presently serving as mayor of Glendale, Calif. She is married and has two children. She was born November 27, 1925, in Tracy, Minn.

Clifton Caldwell, to serve for a term expiring June 10, 1987. He will succeed Joseph B. Mahan, Jr. He is a rancher and investor with Caldwell-Cline in Richardson, Tex. He is married and has five children. He was born March 2, 1933, in Abilene, Tex.

Roger Alan DeWeese, to serve for a term expiring June 10, 1987. He will succeed Frances Edmunds. He is president of RDI & Associates, a landscape architectural and planning firm, in Del Mar, Calif. He is married and has two children. He was born June 12, 1939, in Glendale, Calif.

Appointment of Two Members of the International Private Enterprise Task Force
September 9, 1983

The President today announced his intention to appoint the following individuals to be members of the International Private Enterprise Task Force. These are new positions.

George M. Ferris, Jr., is chief executive officer of Ferris & Co., Inc., in Washington, D.C. He is married, has five children, and resides in Chevy Chase, Md. He was born March 11, 1927, in Washington, D.C.

Howard West is associate executive vice president of California Polytechnic State University in San Luis Obispo, Calif. He is married, has four children, and resides in San Luis Obispo. He was born September 16, 1934, in Merced, Calif.

Statement on International Investment Policy
September 9, 1983

I am releasing a major statement on international investment. This statement was developed by my Senior Interdepartmental Group on International Economic Policy, chaired by Treasury Secretary Regan, and encompasses the views of this administration on international investment.

The last time such a policy paper was released was in July of 1977—more than 6 years ago. Since then, we have come to view international investment which responds to market forces as a vital and necessary ingredient in a stable, growing world economy.

A world with strong foreign investment flows is the opposite of a zero-sum game. We believe there are only winners, no losers, and all participants gain from it.

International investment flows significantly affect the United States and world economies. With the current environment of widespread international debt problems, foreign direct investment flows take on increased importance. As the preeminent home and host country for foreign direct investment, we have a substantial interest in the conditions under which those flows occur.

The statement I am releasing enunciates the fundamental premise of our policy—that foreign investment flows which respond to private market forces will lead to more efficient international production and thereby benefit both home and host countries.

It also highlights three other important points. First, our concern with the increasing use of governmental measures to distort or impede international investment flows. Secondly, our strong support for the concept of national treatment which extends to foreign direct investors in the United States. And finally, an enumeration of specific multilateral and bilateral steps the administration has taken, and will take, to help liberalize international investment flows.

A free and open international investment climate will play a key role not only in sustaining our own economic recovery here at home, but also in resolving many of the current international debt problems.

INTERNATIONAL INVESTMENT POLICY STATEMENT

Executive Summary

International direct investment plays a vital and expanding role in the world economy. To ensure its maximum contribution to both global and domestic economic well-being, the United States believes that international direct investment flows should be determined by private market forces and should receive non-discriminatory treatment consistent with the national treatment principle.

The United States welcomes foreign direct investment that flows according to market forces. The United States accords foreign investors the same fair, equitable, and non-discriminatory treatment it believes all governments should accord foreign direct investment under international law.

The United States opposes continued and increasing government intervention that impedes or distorts investment flows or attempts to shift artificially the benefits of these flows. These measures include trade-related or other performance requirements,

fiscal or financial incentives, and discriminatory treatment of foreign investment.

To counter such measures, the United States will pursue an active international investment policy aimed at reducing foreign government actions that impede or distort investment flows and at developing an international system, based on national treatment and most-favored-nation principles, that permits investment flows to respond more freely to market forces. The United States will work to protect U.S. investment abroad from treatment which is discriminatory or otherwise inconsistent with international law standards. Under international law, no U.S. investment should be expropriated unless the taking is done for a public purpose, is accomplished under due process of law, is non-discriminatory, does not violate previous contractual arrangements, and is accompanied by prompt, adequate, and effective compensation.

In carrying out its international investment policy, in multilateral institutions, the United States will continue to:

—encourage OECD member governments to adhere to, strengthen, and extend OECD investment and capital liberalization instruments;

—explore ways of extending the principles embodied in the OECD instruments to non-OECD countries;

—support efforts to increase awareness of the extent and adverse effects of government intervention in order to build a global political consensus to reduce such intervention;

—work toward increased recognition of intellectual property rights;

—work in the OECD to examine investment problems that affect the service industries, recognizing that for these sectors the opportunity to do business in foreign countries is dependent, in many respects, on the ability to establish foreign operations that are governed by discriminatory investment rules;

—work in the OECD for a "data pledge" which would assure that no new barriers to data flows will be imposed by developed countries and encourage all countries to join in adopting more open and liberal policies on transborder flows;

—work to ensure that any technology transfers which occur are carried out on a sound commercial basis subject to national security and foreign policy considerations;

—encourage the multilateral banks to explore ways to strengthen the private sector role in facilitating financial flows to the developing world;

—support investor access to third-party arbitration to settle investment disputes.

In its relations with individual countries, the United States will:

—provide services and assistance to American investors abroad and offer the full support necessary to ensure that their investments are treated in accordance with standards of international law;

—seek to ensure that the provisions of U.S. Friendship, Commerce, and Navigation treaties and bilateral investment treaties and agreements are fully observed;

—seek to conclude bilateral investment treaties and agreements with interested countries;

—explore other appropriate ways to support private direct investment in developing countries;

—reserve the right to take action against the use of performance requirements and similar policies, consistent with international obligations. The United States will also exercise its rights under existing international agreements.

The United States believes that a combination of multilateral and bilateral efforts will contribute to a more open global climate for investment and thus enhance the prospects for economic growth in the United States and globally.

U.S. GOVERNMENT POLICY ON INTERNATIONAL INVESTMENT

I. Setting

The United States believes that international direct private investment plays a vital and expanding role in the U.S. and world economies. It can act as a catalyst for growth, introduce new technology and management skills, expand employment and improve productivity. Foreign direct investment can be an important source of capital and can stimulate international trade. Both home and host country econo-

mies benefit from an open international investment system.

International direct investment can provide particular benefits to developing countries. Foreign investment capital can help to expand the domestic resource base, augmenting locally generated investment and foreign concessional flows. Foreign direct investment may be of particular value to developing countries in that it contributes to domestic productive capacity without increasing the debt service burden. Further, developing countries may look to foreign direct investment to create new employment opportunities and to provide needed managerial and technical skills that cannot be gained through foreign trade.

Under present circumstances, however, international direct investment is being prevented from making its full contribution to global economic growth. While the current world trade and monetary systems (as embodied in the GATT and the IMF) developed after World War II remain an important foundation for the long-term growth and prosperity of the world economy, there unfortunately exists no comparable system for international direct investment. There has been inadequate collective restraint on widespread and distortive interventions by both developed and developing governments, attempting to control the flow of foreign direct investment and the benefits associated with it. While the effects of intervention are difficult to quantify, the impact can be negative for home, host, and third countries because intervention distorts international investment and trade flows, thereby preventing the most efficient allocation of resources.

Useful attempts have been made to address this problem, particularly in the OECD, but progress has been slow. The inability to arrive at an international consensus on these issues has created pressures in many countries, including the United States, to abandon more traditional economic policies based on market forces and to move toward still greater government intervention.

In light of these developments, it is important that there be a clear understanding both at home and abroad of U.S. policies with respect to international direct investment issues and how the United States intends to implement these policies.

II. U.S. Policy Precepts

The United States believes that an open international investment system responding to market forces provides the best and most efficient mechanism to promote global economic development. Government intervention in the international allocation of investment resources can retard economic growth.

The United States has consistently welcomed foreign direct investment in this country. Such investment provides substantial benefits to the United States. Therefore, the United States fosters a domestic economic climate which is conducive to investment. We provide foreign investors fair, equitable, and non-discriminatory treatment under our laws and regulations. We maintain exceptions to such treatment only as are necessary to protect our security and related interests and which are consistent with our international legal obligations.

The United States believes that U.S. direct investment abroad should also receive fair, equitable, and non-discriminatory treatment, consistent with international law standards. The basic tenet for treatment of investment is the national treatment principle: foreign investors should be treated no less favorably than domestic investors in like situations. Exceptions should be limited to those required to protect national security and related interests. In these cases, foreign direct investment should be accorded treatment consistent with the most-favored-nation principle.

The United States opposes the use of government practices which distort, restrict, or place unreasonable burdens on direct investment. These include such measures as trade-related or other performance requirements (such as local content, minimum export, and local equity requirements), fiscal or financial incentives. Interference with the market mechanism can cause serious distortions in trade and investment flows, encourage the retaliatory use of similar measures by other governments, and precipitate a downward spiral in global investment flows. The United States intends to continue its efforts to reduce or eliminate measures that restrict, distort, or place undue burdens on international direct investment flows. In this regard, the United States will make a particular effort to prevent the introduction by other countries of new measures of this type. Moreover, the United States will continue to attempt to deal with this issue on a multilateral basis, although non-multilateral approaches may be appropriate on a case-by-case basis.

The United States will continue to work for the reduction or elimination of unreasonable and discriminatory barriers to entry of investment. The United States believes that foreign investors should be able to make the same kinds of investment, under the same conditions, as nationals of the host country. Exceptions should be limited to areas of legitimate national security concern or related interests. Because establishment questions are not adequately covered in existing multilateral instruments relating to investment, the United States will encourage broader exploration, identification, and discussion of these issues in the OECD and elsewhere.

The United States is particularly concerned with foreign investment rules that prohibit service industries from doing business abroad. Service sectors are among the most dynamic in today's economy, but there exists a number of limitations that inhibit export opportunities. For many service sectors, there is a universal requirement of establishment in host countries, with the competitive success of these industries heavily dependent upon the presence of branches to meet peculiar regulatory requirements. Thus, the investment policies of foreign countries have special importance to the service sectors.

The United States recognizes that international direct investment frequently serves as a vehicle for transfer of technology and can benefit the economic development goals of both home and host countries. Technology transfers should be carried out on a sound commercial basis, subject to national security and foreign policy considerations.

The United States places high priority on the protection of U.S. investment abroad from discriminatory treatment, or treatment which is inconsistent with international law standards. Under international law, no U.S. investment should be expropriated unless the taking (a) is done for a public purpose; (b) is accomplished under due process of law; (c) is non-discriminatory; (d) does not violate any previous contractual arrangements between the national or company concerned and the government making the expropriation; (e) is accompanied by prompt, adequate, and effective compensation.

III. General U.S. Objectives

The United States accords foreign investors open access to investment opportunities. What we seek is similar access for United States investors abroad. A major objective of our international investment policy is acceptance of the national treatment principle.

In addition, the United States seeks to:
—strengthen multilateral and bilateral discipline over government actions which affect investment decisions, such as incentives and performance requirements, particularly when such actions distort international trade and investment flows;
—reduce unreasonable and discriminatory barriers to establishment;
—create, through cooperation among developed and developing nations, an international environment in which direct investment can make a greater contribution to the development process;
—foster a domestic economic climate in the United States which is conducive to investment, ensure that foreign investors receive fair and equitable treatment under our statutes and regulations, and maintain only those safeguards on foreign investment which are necessary to protect our security and related interests and which are consistent with our international legal obligations.

IV. Multilateral

The United States will:
—continue to adhere to the OECD Investment Declaration and related Decisions on national treatment, international investment incentives and disincentives, and Guidelines for Multinational Enterprises as adopted in 1976 and reviewed in 1979. We also adhere to the OECD Code of Liberalization of Capital Movements, adopted in 1961, and support its expansion;
—encourage OECD governments to abide by the OECD investment and capital liberalization instruments and to strengthen and extend these instruments through broader extension of the principle of national treatment and the right of establishment;
—explore ways of extending the principles embodied in the OECD instruments to non-OECD countries. To increase the effectiveness of these instruments on a global basis, the developing countries, and in particular the newly industrialized countries, need to be brought into any multilateral understanding on investment;
—support efforts to increase awareness of the extent and adverse effects that government intervention, e.g., through performance requirements, can have on the U.S. and world economies. This is essential in order to reduce the predatory use of such measures, and especially to limit the introduction of new measures and the expansion of existing measures. The United States will encourage and actively participate in continued work in multilateral institutions to address these questions;
—encourage adherence by all countries to the Paris Convention for the Protection of Industrial Property and enactment of effective industrial property laws, guaranteeing recognition of patent, copyright, and other industrial property rights. These are essential for the flow of foreign direct investment into both developed and developing countries. The lack of adequate property rights is a major disincentive to investment in manufacturing facilities and research and development and to the transfer of technologies. The Paris Convention for Industrial Property Protection is currently undergoing revision under the auspices of the World Intellectual Property Organization. The United States will support continued efforts aimed at improving protection of industrial property rights, fight to maintain current protection levels where they are adequate and to upgrade protection where it is inadequate, and work to ensure that such principles are upheld in negotiations of codes relating to transfer of tech-

nology and transnational corporations which are now underway in the U.N.;

—continue to work in the OECD for a "data pledge" which would assure that no new barriers to data flows will be imposed by developed countries and encourage all countries to join in adopting more open and liberal policies on transborder data flows;

—encourage adherence to the Code of Capital Movements and support its expansion;

—support the multilateral development banks in their efforts to foster more rapid economic growth in the developing countries. The United States will continue to encourage the Banks to explore ways to develop new programs to strengthen the private sector role in financial flows to the developing world;

—support investor access to third-party arbitration to settle investment disputes, such as the facilities of the World Bank's International Centre for the Settlement of Investment Disputes. The United States believes that governments should effectively support investor access by adherence to the Convention of the Settlement of Investment Disputes between States and Nationals of Other States or the Inter-American Convention on International Commerical Arbitration, and by evidencing their commitment to be bound by third-country arbitral awards by adhering to the Convention of the Recognition and Enforcement of Foreign Arbitral Awards.

V. In its bilateral relations, the United States:

—in cases of expropriation or nationalization of American investment abroad, will provide full support for American investors to ensure that standards of international law are honored by host governments;

—will provide appropriate facilitative services to assist American investors overseas and, in particular, will assist them in obtaining information on the host country investment climate, economic objectives, and investment opportunities;

—will work to ensure that the relevant provisions of our Friendship, Commerce, and Navigation treaties are fully observed;

—as a means to facilitate and protect American investment, will seek to conclude bilateral investment treaties and agreements with interested countries. The treaties will contain appropriate provisions on, *inter alia,* treatment of existing and new investment (including national treatment and most-favored-nation treatment); transfers; dispute settlement; use of performance requirements; and compensation in the event of expropriation;

—will explore, through our bilateral economic assistance programs with developing countries, appropriate ways to increase nonofficial flows and will seek to ensure that these programs effectively support private direct investment;

—reserves the right to take unilateral action against the use of performance requirements and similar policies, consistent with our international obligations. The United States is now exercising and will continue to exercise its rights under existing international arrangements, including the GATT and OECD.

The United States believes that a combination of multilateral and bilateral efforts will contribute to the achievement of a more open global climate for investment and thus enhance the prospects for economic growth in the United States and globally.

Proclamation 5093—National Day of Mourning, Sunday, September 11, 1983
September 9, 1983

By the President of the United States of America

A Proclamation

To the People of the United States:

September 1, 1983, will be seared in the minds of civilized people everywhere as the night of the Korean Air Lines Massacre. Two hundred sixty-nine innocent men, women and children, from 13 different countries, who were flying aboard KAL flight 007, were stalked, then shot out of the air and sent crashing to their deaths by a missile aimed and fired by the Soviet Union.

Good and decent people everywhere are filled with revulsion by this despicable deed, and by the refusal of the guilty to tell the truth. This was a crime against humanity that must never be forgotten, here or throughout the world.

We open our hearts in prayer to the victims and their families. We earnestly beseech Almighty God to minister to them in their trial of grief, sorrow, and pain.

In their memory, we ask all people who cherish individual rights, and who believe each human life is sacred, to come together in a shared spirit of wisdom, unity, courage, and love, so the world can prevent such an inhuman act from ever happening again.

Now, Therefore, I, Ronald Reagan, President of the United States of America, in tribute to the memory of the slain passengers of Korean Air Lines Flight 007, and as an expression of public sorrow, do hereby appoint Sunday, September 11, 1983, to be a National Day of Mourning throughout the United States. I recommend that the people assemble on that day in their respective places of worship, there to pay homage to the memory of those who died. I invite the people of the world who share our grief to join us in this solemn observance.

In Witness Whereof, I have hereunto set my hand this ninth day of September, in the year of our Lord nineteen hundred and eighty-three, and of the Independence of the United States of America the two hundred and eighth.

RONALD REAGAN

[*Filed with the Office of the Federal Register, 3:04 p.m., September 9, 1983*]

Note: The President signed the proclamation in a ceremony in the Oval Office at the White House.

Announcement of the Naming of the U.S.S. *Henry M. Jackson*
September 9, 1983

The President announced today a nuclear-powered Trident fleet ballistic missile submarine will be named U.S.S *Henry M. Jackson* in honor of the late Senator Henry Martin Jackson of Washington State. Senator Jackson, who died September 1, was elected to the House of Representatives in 1940 and to the Senate in 1952. "During his unique career of national leadership, he was a bipartisan champion of personal freedoms and of a strong national defense. One of his many legislative accomplishments was serv-ing as principal congressional advocate and sponsor of the Trident submarine program," the President said.

The *Henry M. Jackson*, fifth ship of the Ohio class, will be 560 feet long, 42 feet wide, and will displace approximately 18,700 tons when submerged. She will carry 24 Trident I ballistic missiles, along with Mark 48 torpedoes.

SSBN–730 originally was designated U.S.S. *Rhode Island.* The Navy now intends to name the Los Angeles class nuclear attack submarine SSN–719 U.S.S. *Providence*, in honor of the capital city of Rhode Island.

The *Henry M. Jackson* will be launched by the Electric Boat Division of General Dynamics Corp. on October 15, 1983, at Groton, Conn., and will join the Pacific Fleet in 1985, homeported at Bangor in Senator Jackson's home State of Washington.

Radio Address to the Nation on American International Broadcasting
September 10, 1983

My fellow Americans:

During my first press conference 9 days after being sworn in as your President, I was asked a question having to do with Soviet intentions. In my answer I cited their own words—that they have openly and publicly declared the only morality they recognize is what will further world communism; that they reserve unto themselves the right to commit any crime, to lie, to cheat, in order to attain that. And I pointed out that we should keep this in mind when we deal with them.

I was charged with being too harsh in my language. I tried to point out I was only quoting their own words. Well, I hope the Soviets' recent behavior will dispel any lingering doubt about what kind of regime we're dealing with and what our responsibilities are as trustees of freedom and peace. Isn't it time for all of us to see the Soviet rulers as they are, rather than as we would like them to be?

Rather than tell the truth about the Korean Air Lines massacre, rather than immediately and publicly investigate the crash, explain to the world how it happened, punish those guilty of the crime, cooperate in efforts to find the wreckage, recover the bodies, apologize and offer compensation to the families, and work to prevent a repetition, they have done the opposite. They've stonewalled the world, mobilizing their entire government behind a massive coverup, then brazenly threatening to kill more men, women, and children should another civilian airliner make the same mistake as KAL 007.

The Soviets are terrified of the truth. They understand well and they dread the meaning of St. John's words: "You will know the truth, and the truth will set you free." The truth is mankind's best hope for a better world. That's why in times like this, few assets are more important than the Voice of America and Radio Liberty, our primary means of getting the truth to the Russian people.

Within minutes of the report of the Soviet destruction of the Korean jet, the Voice of America aired the story in its news programs around the globe. We made sure people in Africa, Asia, the Middle East, Europe and, most important, the people in the Soviet bloc itself knew the truth. That includes every Soviet misstatement, from their initial denials through all the tortured changes and contradictions in their story, including their U.N. representative still denying they shot down the plane even as his own government was finally admitting they did.

Accurate news like this is about as welcome as the plague among the Soviet elite. Censorship is as natural and necessary to the survival of their dictatorship as free speech is to our democracy. That's why they devote such enormous resources to block our broadcasts inside Soviet-controlled countries. The Soviets spend more to block Western broadcasts coming into those countries than the entire worldwide budget of the Voice of America.

To get the news across to the Russian people about the Korean Air Lines massacre, the Voice of America added new frequencies and new broadcast times. But within minutes of those changes, new Soviet jamming began. Luckily, jamming is more like a sieve than a wall. International radio broadcasts can still get through to many people with the news. But we still face enormous difficulties.

One of the Voice of America's listeners in the Middle East wrote, "If you do not strengthen your broadcasting frequencies, no one can get anything from your program." Our radio equipment is just plain old, some of it World War II vintage. I don't mind people getting older; it's just not so good for machines.

More than 35 percent of the Voice of America's transmitters are over 30 years old. We have a similar problem at Radio Free Europe and Radio Liberty. We have 6 antiquated 500-kilowatt shortwave transmitters. The Soviets have 37, and theirs are neither old nor outdated. We regularly receive complaints that Soviet broadcasts are clearer than ours. One person wrote and asked why it's not possible for a nation that can send ships into space to have its own voice heard here on Earth.

The answer is simple. We're as far behind the Soviets and their allies in international broadcasting today as we were in space when they launched sputnik in 1957.

We've repeatedly urged the Congress to support our long-term modernization program and our proposal for a new radio station, Radio Marti, for broadcasting to Cuba. The sums involved are modest, but for whatever reason this critical program has not been enacted.

Today I'm appealing to the Congress: Help us get the truth through. Help us strengthen our international broadcasting effort by supporting increased funding for the Voice of America, Radio Free Europe, Radio Liberty, and by authorizing the establishment of Radio Marti.

And I appeal to you, especially those of you who came from Eastern Europe, Russia, and Soviet-dominated countries, who understand how crucial this issue is, let your Representatives hear from you. Tell them you want Soviet rulers held accountable for their actions even by their own people. The truth is still our strongest weapon; we just have to use it.

Finally, let us come together as a nation tomorrow in a National Day of Mourning to share the sorrow of the families and let us resolve that this crime against humanity will never be forgotten anywhere in the world.

Until next week, thank you for listening, and God bless you.

Note: The President spoke at 12:06 p.m. from the Oval Office at the White House.

Message on the Observance of Grandparents Day
September 10, 1983

America's grandparents are truly a national treasure and a living resource. Most of us can remember having long talks with our grandparents and hearing stories of days gone by. They form a link to the past that is far more colorful and personal than what we read in history books. Their knowledge and wisdom come from experience— they are an invaluable source of advice to us.

The special attachment between grandparent and grandchild is one of love spanning two generations. A grandchild looks up to his grandparents with respect and admiration while grandparents view their grandchildren with great pride and rejoice at their every accomplishment.

Our grandparents encourage us in every way to have faith in ourselves, to work hard, and to achieve all that we can. We learn from their example, and we gain inspirations from their success.

In this modern, fast-paced society, it is important that we be mindful of the many contributions of our grandparents. They built our families, and they've helped build America. Because of their persistence and belief in themselves, our country has weathered the bad times as well as the good. Let us rededicate ourselves to preserving their legacy so that we can bequeath to our grandchildren an America blessed with the opportunities and freedoms we enjoy.

Congress has designated the first Sunday after Labor Day as National Grandparents Day. Nancy and I urge all Americans to take the time to honor our grandparents on September 11.

RONALD REAGAN

Remarks at the Annual Meeting of the National Association of Towns and Townships
September 12, 1983

Thank you all very much. Well, thank you, George Miller. Senator Percy, Congressman Horton, and ladies and gentlemen, as I recall, back in World War II, that's what we fought the war for—mom's apple pie. [*Laughter*] [1]

Well, it's a pleasure for me to be here with you today. Growing up as I did, as you were told, in Dixon Township, I know well the role that towns and townships play in America. Incidentally, between Tampico and Dixon there were two other small towns in Illinois in which I lived before I was about 8 years old. Those towns are the cradle of democracy. And if anyone has any doubts about the vitality of American liberty, I would suggest that they visit some of your town meetings. I'm sure that Patrick Henry and Thomas Jefferson would feel right at home.

One aspect of town government is that people know each other. Some are even related. [*Laughter*] There's a story about townfolk. You know, usually if you're going to tell a joke, you try to tie it into something that has to do with what you're talking about. The closest I can come is that this story is kind of typical of the humor and the flavor of smalltown America. It's about a fellow named Elmer. In his town, he fished, and he made a living selling fish to the local restaurant. But he was able to

provide so many fish every day that the game warden got a little suspicious. And the sheriff, being Elmer's cousin, he went to him and said, "Why don't you go fishing with him and find out how he's doing this?" So they did. And they got out in the middle of the lake in a rowboat, and the sheriff threw his line in and Elmer reached down in the tackle box and pulled out a stick of dynamite, lit the fuse, tossed it overboard, and with the explosion up came the fish, belly up. And the sheriff said, "Elmer, do you realize you've just committed a felony?" Elmer reached down into the tackle box, took out another stick of dynamite, lit it, handed it to the sheriff, and said, "Did you come here to fish or talk?" [*Laughter*]

But this gathering here today is testimony to the fundamental change that's taking place in our country, change for which many are unaware—or of which many are unaware, and yet it's altering the face of America. What we're experiencing is nothing less than a renaissance of smalltown life. I'm here to tell you that this administration recognizes it and that the days when your role in our country was taken for granted are over.

Small towns and townships have always played a vital part in American life, and yet about the time of the Civil War, urban areas began to grow at a faster clip. I wasn't around at the time—[*laughter*]—but a little later I was witness to that move to the urban areas. Now, I'm certain that all of you are aware that that trend has reversed itself. In the 1970's some rural areas continued to—or grew at a rate that was far above the growth—50 percent faster than the

---

[1] *Prior to the President's remarks, George Miller, president of the association, presented the President with an apple pie, which he said was symbolic of the fact that "small towns and local townships believe in local control" and "look forward to their fair share of the Federal pie."*

growth in urban centers. Now, today, one out of four of our citizens lives in nonmetropolitan areas, and some polls indicate that 60 percent of the American people would join them if they could find work in those smaller towns.

The influx of people into small towns and rural areas reflects not just the material well-being or desire of that, but the desire for a better, different quality of life. During the 1960's, there were those who scoffed at smalltown values—at family, the talk of family and God and neighborhood. And they said those things in which we believe are old-fashioned and corny. Well, there's been some growing up in this country in the last few years, and people are discovering that those basic values we hold so dear are stronger than the fads that make a big splash one day and evaporate the next.

Many of the problems we face today are the results of drifting away from principles that kept our country on a sound footing through most of its history. Our Forefathers believed that government should be limited and power should be decentralized. Calvin Coolidge, a President I deeply admire, put it well. "Our country," he said, "was conceived in the theory of local self-government. It has been dedicated by long practice to that wise and beneficent policy. It is the foundation principle of our system of liberty."

There are people that down through the years have not expressed much admiration for Cal Coolidge, but I remember something that I think would strike all of you as typical of him. It was the summer, and his son had a job working on the farm up in New Hampshire. It was hard and hot work, and one day another kid that was working there at lunch time said to him, as they were sitting there eating out of their brown paper bags, he said, "Boy, if my father were President, I wouldn't be doing this." And Cal's son said, "If your father were my father, you would." [*Laughter*]

The American system, decentralized and based on guaranteed individual rights, served our country well. And yet, in the last two decades or more something went haywire. The people began turning to Washington with greater and greater frequency. Every problem became something of Fed-

eral concern. Worst of all, we were to believe that Federal money came free, and it's taken quite a while for us to realize that Federal money came out of the same pockets as did local and State taxes—our pockets.

On the other end, well-intentioned individuals thought if they were only given the power they could right every wrong. As I said, they were well-intentioned, but there's a well-known road paved with good intentions. No one likes to go where it takes you.

There's a story about a young fellow riding a motorcycle. He had good intentions, too. The wind was kind of chilly and coming through the buttonholes on his jacket, and so he got this idea. He stopped and put his jacket on backward and that eliminated the chill factor through the buttonholes, but it kind of restricted his arm movement. And down the road, his motorcycle hit a patch of ice. He skidded into a tree. When the police got there, a crowd had gathered. And they elbowed their way through and they said, "What happened?" And one of them said, "Well, we don't know. When we got here he seemed to be all right, but by the time we got his head turned around straight, he was dead." [*Laughter*]

I think that has a tie-in with some of the things that the government does. [*Laughter*] But in the last two decades, government expanded with the best of intentions, but we paid a steep price. By the end of the 1970's, average citizens trying to solve even the simplest problems were frustrated by a conglomeration of interlocking jurisdictions and an absence of accountability. Unelected Washington officials were making decisions that rightfully should be made by local people working and talking together. Americans felt that they'd lost control of essential services like schools, welfare, and roads.

The idealistic goals of those who centralized American government didn't change the nature of what we confronted. Supreme Court Justice Louis Brandeis once said that "Men born to freedom are naturally alert to repel invasion of their liberty by evil-minded rulers. The greatest dangers to liberty lurk in insidious encroachment by men of zeal, well-meaning but without understanding."

In the end, the growth of Federal power complicated our problems and threatened our freedom. Nowhere was that clearer than the grants-in-aid program. In 1950 the Federal Government had 132 categorical grant programs costing $7 billion. Twenty years later, by 1970, the number had tripled to more than 400, costing $90 billion. And it took 166 congressional committees just to keep track of this mishmash of programs, including 13 programs for energy, 36 for pollution control, 66 for social services, and 90 for education.

The frustration of dealing with faraway bureaucracy wasn't the only price that we were paying. Between 1976 and 1981, the Federal tax doubled, draining the private sector of money it needed for investment and the creation of jobs. And by the time the Federal tax vacuum was done, there was little left for local and State government.

The growth of Federal power was stagnating our economy and destroying our hopes for a better future. By 1980 inflation was running at double-digit levels for the second year in a row, robbing our senior citizens of the value of their savings. The poor and middle-class working people saw their real wages and their standard of living begin to shrink.

The spirit of optimism, long the hallmark of our people, turned to pessimism and cynicism. Even our leaders were throwing up their hands, claiming that we were in a malaise and that our problems were unsolvable.

Well, one should never sell the American people short. Once we put our minds to it, there's nothing Americans cannot accomplish if the Federal Government will just get out of the way.

When I got to Washington, we faced the awesome responsibility of changing the direction of government. And that's not easy, and it's not painless. I'd like to take this opportunity to thank George Miller and all of you in the National Association of Towns and Townships for the support that you've given over these 2½ years. I remember meeting George and your officers in the White House. And believe me, it was expressions of support like the ones I heard

that day that kept me going. After our meeting, I told my staff they just had a dose of good old-fashioned grassroots Americanism, and I sense that same spirit in this room today.

It's taken time, but I'm proud to tell you that together we've turned around a desperate situation, and we're never going back to the policies of tax, spend, and inflate that brought our country to the edge of disaster.

Together we've brought inflation from double digits down to 2.4 percent over the last 12 months, and that's the best 12-month record in nearly 17 years. I don't have to tell you what this means to the cost of doing business for our towns and townships.

There's also been progress with interest rates, which are as important to you as they are to business. Just before I took office, they were going through the roof. The prime at the time was 21½ percent, and today it stands at 11 percent. There will be slight fluctuations in this recovery, but if the Congress acts responsibly interest rates are going to come down even more, and not too far in the future.

We're getting the Federal spending and taxing juggernaut under control. Spending was growing at a rate of 17 percent a year when we got here. We've cut that by nearly 40 percent. And let me say that still isn't good enough.

There's an old saying that in levying taxes, as in shearing sheep, it's best to stop when you get to the skin. [*Laughter*] Well, by 1980, taxes were making our economy bleed. We've cut the income tax rate of the American people 25 percent across the board. And in 1985 they'll be indexed so that never again will the Federal Government profit from inflation at the people's expense.

There's one part of our tax reform program of which I'm particularly proud, and that is that by raising the exemption on the inheritance tax and by eliminating it altogether for surviving spouses, we've restored the right to American people of passing on their family farm or small business to their children.

From the start, we recognized that excessive Federal regulation was not only strangling American enterprise but preventing you folks at the local level from doing your job. Since we took office, we've freed the business community as well as State and local government of 300 million man-hours—man- and woman-hours—[*laughter*]—of needless paperwork. And this will save Americans billions of dollars and free you to handle local problems as you see best.

Returning power to levels of government closer to the people has been one of the guiding principles of this administration. Decentralizing remains one of our utmost goals, as George told you, and don't let anyone tell you that we're satisfied with what has been done so far. Phase one of our Federalism program may be accomplished, but that's just phase one.

Again, with your help, we managed to get through the Congress a block grant package that consolidated 57 programs into nine block grants that in 1982 eliminated some 5.4 million hours of work for State and local officials and, in subsequent years, will eliminate some 5.9 million hours a year. We continued this effort with the enactment of the Job Training Partnership Act and the urban mass transportation grants program. This year we've proposed legislation that will consolidate over $22 billion of spending in 34 programs into four block grants. Included among these is the Rural Housing Block Grant, which will give you more control and flexibility over programs costing $850 million annually.

The significance of the block grant, as most of you well know, is that it isn't tied with all the rules and regulations and specifics as to how the program must be managed, as is true in the individual or specific grants. It gives you the flexibility to set the priorities and determine how best that money can be spent.

The biggest resistance to our efforts has been from politicians who simply don't believe that local government is competent to do the job. Their opposition seems to be based on the notion that the Federal bureaucracy has a monopoly on compassion and efficiency, which I think you'd find mighty strange. It's been said that "A man's intelligence does not increase as he acquires

power. What does increase is the difficulty in telling him that." [*Laughter*]

If it was ever true that Federal employees had greater capabilities than their local counterparts, those days are rapidly coming to an end. Today, modern technology is opening up greater and greater opportunities for State and local government. Even small towns have computer services available to them that were out of reach only a decade ago. I know your own organization is moving forward with great training and communications programs that will open up broad new horizons at the local level.

Today, local government across the country is proving itself efficient and responsive to the will of the people. I'd like to see some of the politicians here in Washington who don't think you can do the job try to handle some of your responsibilities. Bart Russell tells me that as head of a local township, you've got to be a parliamentarian, bookkeeper, business manager, ombudsman, and government liaison expert—all at the same time. And plus, you've got to do all that while keeping the hometown folks happy. [*Laughter*] And I thought dealing with Capitol Hill was hard. [*Laughter*]

Well, I can assure you that this administration knows and appreciates the job you are doing. We're taking every care so that in transferring programs back to levels of government closer to the people, you also receive the resources necessary to get the job done.

I have a dream that some day we can provide you with the revenue sources that have been co-opted by the Federal Government, so that local money no longer has to make a round trip through Washington before you can use it back in your local area—minus a certain carrying charge. [*Laughter*] In the meantime, you can count on us to be sensitive to current obligations. I continue to support general revenue sharing and will oppose any changes—[*applause*]—I will oppose any changes in the general revenue sharing formula that unduly impact on towns and townships. And if I remembered all the lessons of my previous occupation, I'd quit right there after that response. [*Laughter*]

Of course, transferring revenues is not

going to bring lasting change. Real progress will come as a result of creative approaches that harness the power of the marketplace. With this in mind, we've proposed legislation to create enterprise zones to encourage private business to locate in disadvantaged areas. And one-third of the 75 zones in the bill that we've suggested would be in rural areas.

There's enormous support for this concept. Already, 20 States have passed State enterprise zone legislation. The Senate has already passed this bill once, and although it was dropped in conference, we're confident they'll support it again. And in the House we have 181 Members, nearly a majority, who have cosponsored the legislation this time. So far, of course, the House has failed to act, and only recently has the House leadership even agreed to hold hearings. I'd like to take this opportunity to ask you to join us in escalating efforts to pry this legislation out of the House. Just remember, we don't have to make them see the light, just make them feel the heat. [*Laughter*]

I'll square that with present company later. [*Laughter*]

It's about time that you had a fair say in the Federal policies that affect you. I want to assure you that I continue to support strongly, legislation that would provide for a member nominated by your organization to be placed on the Advisory Commission on Intergovernmental Relations.

Over the last 2½ years, we've had to make some tough decisions. And I fully appreciate that the townships you represent have felt the pain of reducing the growth of Federal spending. We couldn't have gone on the way things were, and you've done

more than your share. As we move forward, I've instructed my staff to be diligent that your good citizenship is not taken advantage of and when it comes to budget control, towns and townships are treated equally with other segments of American society.

We must always remember that on our shoulders rests the responsibility of our country's future. In less free societies, the burden rests only on the head of state. The freedom to enjoy places a heavy burden on all of us, in and out of government. Together we've overcome an economic threat that could well have destroyed the America that we know and love. The signs suggest that we're over the hump, but as is engraved on our National Archives building, "Eternal vigilance is the price of liberty."

There is every reason for us to be confident. We are still the same people who conquered a wilderness and turned it into a dynamo of freedom and abundance. I think that today there is a greater understanding of the miracle of America, of what made her great and kept her free.

John Foster Dulles once said that, "If we are faithful to our past, we shall not have to fear our future." Well, together we've proven that we can do what is necessary to keep faith with those who came before.

I thank you for all that you've done, and I thank you for having me here with you today. Thank you all, and God bless you all.

Note: The President spoke at 10:13 a.m. in the Presidential Ballroom at the Capital Hilton Hotel.

The National Association of Towns and Townships is a local government membership organization that represents more than 13,000 local entities nationwide.

Remarks at a White House Ceremony Commemorating National Hispanic Heritage Week and Announcing the Nomination of Katherine D. Ortega To Be Treasurer of the United States
September 12, 1983

Thank you, and welcome to the White House. I am delighted to have this opportunity to kick off National Hispanic Heritage Week. Americans of Hispanic descent are rightfully proud of their heritage, and I hope this ceremony will draw the entire Nation's attention to the contributions of our Hispanic citizens.

For too long, the contributions of our Hispanic citizens have gone unnoticed, and I thought perhaps the best way I could note this occasion would be by reading the proclamation designating this special week, which I signed on August 25th. And let me read directly from it.

"National Hispanic Heritage Week pays tribute to a rich part of America's cultural tradition, offering all Americans a welcome opportunity to recognize the qualities and contributions of Hispanic Americans from earliest colonial times to the present. The dedication to principles of loyalty, patriotism, strong religious faith and devotion to family displayed by Hispanic Americans is basic to the American way of life.

"Hispanic Americans have played an important role in the development of our rich cultural heritage and every State has benefitted from their influence. They have distinguished themselves in the arts and sciences, education, industry, government and many other areas of productive endeavor. Indeed, they are a part of all that makes America great.

"Just as their forefathers sought a dream in the New World, Hispanic Americans have realized their dreams in our great Nation and will continue to do so. Their dedication to higher purposes reflects what is best in the American spirit.

"Through the years, Hispanic American citizens have risen to the call of duty in defense of liberty and freedom. Their bravery is well-known and has been demonstrated time and again, dating back to the aid rendered by General Bernardo Galvez during the American Revolution.

"Now, therefore, I"—and I say my name and so forth and the slogan or the proclamation—"President of the United States of America, do hereby proclaim the week beginning September 11, 1983, as National Hispanic Heritage Week in honor of the Hispanic peoples who have enriched our daily lives, our traditions and our national strength."

The concluding line is, "In this spirit, I ask all of our citizens to reflect on the sense of brotherhood that binds us together as one people." This was a proclamation I was very happy to set my hand to.

All over this great land, Hispanic Americans are contributing to our democracy, our economy, and our culture. And today, I'm very pleased to announce another contribution that an American of Hispanic descent will be making to this country.

Katherine Ortega, the youngest of nine children, is from New Mexico and the descendant of pioneer families who settled in that State during the 1800's. She is symbolic of the values the Hispanic community represents, and I am honored that she is to become a part of this administration. I intend to nominate Katherine Ortega to the post of Treasurer of the United States.

Katherine is currently serving as Commissioner of the Copyright Royalty Tribunal and was a member of the President's Advisory Committee on Small and Minority Business. She's a certified public accountant, served in a number of important capacities in the financial services industry. Of her many achievements, I might mention one in particular. As past president and director of the Santa Ana Bank, she was the first woman president of a California bank. So, you can see that she's being nominated not just because she is Hispanic, but because she is highly qualified.

As Treasurer of the United States, she will supervise over 5,000 employees, manage a budget of some $220 million, and serve as one of the key people of our management team, as Buchanan did before her.

I'm delighted by the increased participation of Hispanic Americans in all phases of the political process. Congressman Lujan here is a wonderful model for Hispanic people seeking to become involved in politics. And I'm very proud that my own administration has over 125 Hispanics already in positions and another 20 or 25 who soon will be. We've appointed them to positions that are not just traditionally Hispanic positions. Today, you will find Hispanics at the FCC and the CAB and all over government. They offer professionalism, and we intend to take advantage of that talent. And I look forward to the Hispanic community's sound values influencing the course of government and our nation.

And let me say wholeheartedly, nothing is a better influence on America than the strength and decency of the Hispanic family.

We need your participation and your beliefs to guide this nation, because the hopes and dreams of Hispanic Americans are the same hopes and dreams that founded this country. Become involved and help America become what we all want her to be.

I thank you for coming. God bless all of you. And now, Katherine?

Ms. Ortega. Mr. President, Mr. Secretary, distinguished guests, it is with a deep sense of joy, pride, and gratitude to my President, to my country, and my family that I am honored to be selected for nomination as Treasurer of the United States.

The Hispanic tradition of strong devotion to family is evident here today. I called my brothers and sisters 3 or 4 days ago to tell them about the event here this morning. There was no doubt in my mind they would be here to share this occasion with me, for our parents taught us, and we learned well, not only to work together but to help each other and to share and support each other. And so, I was very confident that they would be here to share this occasion with me.

Since 1928, when my father opened a blacksmith's shop in New Mexico, the family has been working together. For at that time my older brothers, who were then 8 and 10 years of age, were already helping my father.

I have often said I was born a Republican. I am the product of a heritage that teaches strong family devotion, a commitment to earning a livelihood by hard work, patience, determination, and perseverance. And in this great country of ours, it is still possible to achieve upward mobility and success through our economic, social, and political system. And our greatest American treasure is that as a people, we recognize the inherent dignity and worth of the individual human being.

Through his strong leadership and sound economic policies, President Reagan has ensured that this national treasure will flourish, that individual women and men can continue to succeed and progress through initiative, resourcefulness, and equal economic opportunity. And besides building economic stability, the policies of the Reagan administration have strengthened the family values, belief in each other and in God, which makes us the greatest nation in the world.

Over the years, I have been blessed with many opportunities and challenges. Today President Reagan and Secretary Regan are presenting the greatest opportunity to prove myself. I accept this challenge and look forward to working with Secretary Regan and the other fine men and women at the Department of the Treasury.

It is an honor and a privilege to be part of President Reagan's administration.

Note: The President spoke at 11:33 a.m. in the East Room at the White House.

Nomination of Katherine D. Ortega To Be Treasurer of the United States
September 12, 1983

The President today announced his intention to nominate Katherine D. Ortega, of New Mexico, to be Treasurer of the United States. She would succeed Angela M. Buchanan.

Ms. Ortega is currently a Commissioner of the Copyright Royalty Tribunal, a position to which she was appointed on Decem-

ber 10, 1982. Previously Ms. Ortega served as a member of the Presidential Advisory Committee on Small and Minority Business Ownership.

Before joining the Reagan administration, Ms. Ortega acquired extensive experience in the banking and savings and loan industries. She became the first woman to serve as a bank president in California, when she was elected president of the Santa Ana State Bank in 1975.

In 1977–1982 she was a consultant to Otero Savings and Loan Association in Alamagordo, N. Mex. In 1972–1975 she was vice president and cashier of the Pan American National Bank in Los Angeles. In 1969–1972 Ms. Ortega, who is a certified public accountant, was tax supervisor for Peat, Marwick, Mitchell & Co. in Los Angeles.

Ms. Ortega was the 1977 recipient of the Outstanding Alumni Award from Eastern New Mexico University, where she received her B.A. in 1957. She has also received the California Businesswomen's Achievement Award and the Damas de Commercio Outstanding Woman of the Year Award in Los Angeles.

She was born in New Mexico on July 16, 1934, and currently resides in Washington, D.C.

Nomination of Terry Calvani To Be a Commissioner of the Federal Trade Commission
September 12, 1983

The President today announced his intention to nominate Terry Calvani to be a Federal Trade Commissioner for the term of 7 years from September 26, 1983. He would succeed David A. Clanton.

Since 1980 he has served as professor of law at Vanderbilt University Law School. In addition, he has been of counsel to the firm of North, Haskell, Slaughter, Young & Lewis in Birmingham, Ala. Previously he served as associate professor of law (1977–

1980) and assistant professor of law (1974–1977) at Vanderbilt University School of Law. He was an associate attorney with the firm of Pillsbury, Madison & Sutro in San Francisco, Calif., in 1973–1974.

He graduated from the University of New Mexico (B.A., 1969) and Cornell University (J.D., 1972). He is married, has two children, and resides in Nashville, Tenn. He was born January 29, 1947.

Nomination of Daniel Anthony O'Donohue To Be United States Ambassador to Burma
September 12, 1983

The President today announced his intention to nominate Daniel Anthony O'Donohue, of Virginia, a career member of the Senior Foreign Service, Class of Minister-Counselor, as Ambassador to the Socialist Republic of the Union of Burma. He would succeed Patricia M. Byrne.

Mr. O'Donohue served in the United States Army in 1953–1955. In 1956–1957 he was a budget examiner for the Michigan State government in Lansing. In 1957 he entered the Foreign Service as consular officer in Genoa. He was political officer in Seoul in 1960–1964. In the Department he was international relations officer in 1964–

1968. He was political officer in Accra in 1968–1971 and attended the Army War College in 1971–1972. In 1972–1974 he was counselor for political affairs in Seoul. In the Department he was Director of Korean Affairs (1974–1975) and Executive Assistant to the Under Secretary of State for Political Affairs (1976–1977). In 1977–1978 he was Deputy Chief of Mission in Bangkok. In the Department he was Deputy Director of the Bureau of Political-Military Affairs in 1978–1981, and since 1981 he has been Deputy Assistant Secretary of State for East Asian and Pacific Affairs.

Mr. O'Donohue graduated from the University of Detroit (B.S., 1953) and Wayne State University (M.P.A., 1958). His foreign language is Korean. He was born October 27, 1931, in Detroit, Mich.

Appointment of William Lee Hanley, Jr., as a Member of the Board of Directors of the Corporation for Public Broadcasting
September 12, 1983

The President today recess appointed William Lee Hanley, Jr., to be a member of the Board of Directors of the Corporation for Public Broadcasting for a term expiring March 1, 1984. He would succeed Gillian Martin Sorensen.

Mr. Hanley is presently serving as president, chairman of the board, and chief executive officer of Hanley, Inc., in New York, N.Y. He graduated from Yale University (B.A., 1964).

He is married, has five children, and resides in Greenwich, Conn. He was born January 27, 1940, in New York, N.Y.

Nomination of Susan E. Phillips To Be Director of the Institute of Museum Services
September 12, 1983

The President today announced his intention to nominate Susan E. Phillips to be Director of the Institute of Museum Services, National Foundation on the Arts and the Humanities. She would succeed Lilla Burt Cummings Tower.

Since 1982 Miss Phillips has been serving as Director of Intergovernmental and Interagency Services at the Department of Education. Previously she was expert consultant, grants and contracts, Department of Education, in 1982. She served as director of research and publications for the Conservative Caucus and the Conservative Caucus Research in 1976–1982.

She graduated from the University of Massachusetts (B.A., 1967). Miss Phillips was born June 23, 1945, in Cambridge, Mass., and currently resides in McLean, Va.

Statement on Proposed Legislation To Improve Industrial Productivity and Competitiveness
September 12, 1983

Today I am proposing legislation entitled the "National Productivity and Innovation Act of 1983." When enacted, the bill will modify antitrust, patent, and copyright laws in a way that will greatly enhance this country's productivity and the ability of U.S. industry to compete in world markets.

Improving domestic industrial productivity and competitiveness will depend largely on our ability to create and develop new technologies. Technological advances provide our economy with the means to produce new or improved goods and services at lower cost than those already on the market. Over the last 80 years, the development of new technologies accounted for almost half of the growth in our real per capita income. New technology creates jobs and gives this country a competitive edge. The U.S. computer industry, for example, directly provides jobs for about 830,000 people and is a leader in world markets.

New technologies are seldom created by luck; they are instead the result of private and public sector investments of time, money, and effort. With this in mind, we propose to increase Federal funding of research and development (R. & D.) by 17 percent to $47 billion in 1984 and to encourage private sector R. & D. by improving the economic and legal climate for such efforts.

A number of things have already been done to encourage private sector efforts. The Economic Recovery Tax Act of 1981, for example, provides a 25-percent tax credit to firms which invest in additional R. & D. And by reducing inflation and interest rates, our economic program has lowered substantially the cost of conducting research.

When enacted, the National Productivity and Innovation Act will improve the legal climate for technological advancement by clarifying and modifying the Federal antitrust and intellectual property laws. Those laws have a substantial effect on private investment in R. & D. The antitrust laws are designed to protect consumers from anticompetitive conduct. Yet we must recognize that while vigorous competition among independent businesses generally serves the economy best, in some areas, like the creation and development of technology, cooperation is necessary if American industry is to compete internationally. Similarly, the intellectual property laws, such as those dealing with patents and copyrights, encourage competition by providing individuals with exclusive rights to their technology.

My proposed legislation will ensure that the antitrust and intellectual property laws are fully compatible with efficient creation and development of technology, while, at the same time, maintaining strong safeguards against anticompetitive behavior.

Title II of the bill will ensure that antitrust laws do not unnecessarily inhibit the formation of joint R. & D. ventures. Joint ventures often may be necessary to lower the risk and cost associated with R. & D. So long as these ventures do not facilitate price fixing or reduce innovation, such ventures should not be considered a violation of antitrust laws. Nevertheless, the risk remains that some courts may overlook the beneficial aspects of joint R. & D. This risk is unnecessarily magnified by the triple damages awarded to an injured private party who wins an antitrust damage suit.

Title II will reduce the adverse deterrent effect that triple damages have on procompetitive joint R. & D. ventures. The title mandates that the courts may not find a joint R. & D. venture in violation of the antitrust laws without first considering its procompetitive benefits. In addition, title II provides that a joint R. & D. venture that has been fully disclosed to the Department of Justice and the Federal Trade Commission found in violation of antitrust laws may be sued only for the actual damage, plus prejudgment interest, caused by its conduct.

Title III will ensure that antitrust laws encourage procompetitive intellectual property licensing, which greatly enhances our economy's ability to create and develop technology. Intellectual property owners often cannot obtain their legitimate reward from R. & D. unless they license their technology to others. Such licensing enables intellectual property owners to use the superior ability of other enterprises in the marketing of their technology. This can be particularly important for small businesses that do not have sufficient resources to develop the full range of applications of a new technology discovered through their research efforts.

Recognizing the significance of licensing, we have designed title III to ensure intellectual property owners the fruits of their ingenuity. First, the title prohibits courts from condemning an intellectual property licensing arrangement without first considering its procompetitive benefits. Second, the title eliminates the potential of triple damage liability under the antitrust laws for intellectual property licensing. Although those who suffer antitrust injury as a result of licensing could still sue, title III would minimize the deterrence that antitrust laws currently have on beneficial licensing.

Similarly, title IV encourages the procompetitive use of intellectual property. Courts will be able to refuse to enforce a valid patent or copyright because of misuse only after considering the economic ramifications.

Title V of the act increases Federal protection for process patents. Currently, if someone violates a process patent outside the country and then imports the resulting product into the United States, the importer is not guilty of violating patent law. Our bill closes this loophole, permitting the owners of process patents to obtain their rightful reward by preventing such unauthorized use of their technology.

This legislation will, if enacted, stimulate the creation and development of new technology, increase this country's productivity, and enable our industries to compete more effectively in world markets, while continuing to protect the interests of American consumers. I strongly urge Congress to move forward on this proposed legislation and, by doing so, encourage innovation and increase the employment opportunities and standard of living for all Americans.

Message to the Congress Transmitting Proposed Legislation To Improve Industrial Productivity and Competitiveness
September 12, 1983

To the Congress of the United States:

I am transmitting to the Congress today a legislative proposal entitled, the "National Productivity and Innovation Act of 1983." The bill would modify the Federal antitrust and intellectual property laws in ways that will enhance this country's productivity and the competitiveness of U.S. industries in international markets.

As you know, one of the most important goals of my Administration has been to revitalize the competitiveness and productivity of American industry. Tax cuts proposed by my Administration and enacted during the 97th Congress have greatly stimulated economic activity. In addition, our efforts to rationalize Federal rules and regulations have significantly enhanced the efficiency of our economy. For the first time in over a decade, there exists the foundation for a period of strong and sustained economic growth.

The ability of the United States to improve productivity and industrial competitiveness will also depend largely on our ability to create and develop new technologies. Advances in technology provide our economy with the means to produce new or improved goods and services and to produce at lower cost those goods and services already on the market. It is difficult to overstate the importance of technological development to a strong and healthy United States economy. It has been estimated that advances in scientific and technological knowledge have been responsible for almost half of the increase in this country's labor productivity over the last 50 years. New technology also creates new jobs and gives us an advantage in world markets. For example, the U.S. computer industry, which was in its infancy just a short time ago, directly provides jobs for about 830,000 Americans and is a leader in world markets.

The private and public sectors must spend a great deal of time, money, and effort to discover and develop new technologies. My Administration has moved to bolster research and development (R&D) in the public sector by proposing in our 1984 budget to increase Federal funding of R&D by 17 percent, to $47 billion. However, it is vital that our laws affecting the creation and development of new technologies properly encourage private sector R&D as well.

The Economic Recovery Tax Act of 1981 provides a 25 percent tax credit to encourage firms to invest in additional R&D. Our economic program has helped reduce inflation and interest rates and thus has lowered substantially the cost of conducting research.

The antitrust and intellectual property laws also have a very significant effect on private investment in R&D. The antitrust laws are designed to protect consumers from anti-competitive conduct. While the economy generally benefits most from vigorous competition among independent businesses, the antitrust laws recognize that in some areas, like the creation and development of technology, cooperation among producers, even competitors, can actually serve to maximize the well-being of consumers.

The intellectual property laws, for example, those dealing with patents and copyrights, also serve to promote the interests of consumers. The promise of the financial reward provided by exclusive rights to intellectual property induces individuals to compete to create and develop new and useful technologies.

After reviewing the effect of the antitrust and intellectual property laws on the creation and development of new technologies and after consultations with key members of Congress, I have concluded that the antitrust laws can be clarified in some respects and modified in other respects to stimulate significantly private sector R&D. This can be done while maintaining strong safeguards to protect the economy against collusive actions that would improperly restrict competition. The National Productivity and Innovation Act of 1983, which embodies those changes, is a package of four substantive proposals that deals with all phases of the innovation process.

Title II of the bill would ensure that the antitrust laws do not unnecessarily inhibit United States firms from pooling their resources to engage jointly in procompetitive R&D projects. Joint ventures often may be necessary to reduce the risk and cost associated with R&D. So long as the venture does not threaten to facilitate price fixing or to reduce innovation, such ventures do not violate the antitrust laws. Nevertheless, the risk remains that some courts may not fully appreciate the beneficial aspects of joint R&D. This risk is unnecessarily magnified by the fact that a successful antitrust claimant is automatically entitled to three times

the damages actually suffered.

Title II would alleviate the adverse deterrent effect that this risk may have on procompetitive joint R&D ventures. This title provides that the courts may not find that a joint R&D venture violates the antitrust laws without first considering its procompetitive benefits. In addition, Title II provides that a joint R&D venture that has been fully disclosed to the Department of Justice and the Federal Trade Commission may be sued only for the actual damage caused by its conduct plus prejudgment interest. This combination of changes will encourage the formation of procompetitive joint R&D ventures. And unlike some other proposals currently before Congress, it will do so with the minimal amount of bureaucratic interference in the functioning of those ventures.

If we are to assure that our laws stimulate investment in new technologies, however, it is not enough merely to correct the adverse deterrent effect the antitrust laws may have on procompetitive joint R&D. Rather, we must also assure that the antitrust and intellectual property laws allow—indeed encourage—those who create new technologies to bring their technology to market in the most efficient manner. Only in this way can those who invest their time, money, and effort in R&D be assured of earning the maximum legitimate reward.

Titles III and IV recognize that very frequently the most efficient way to develop new technology is to license that technology to others. Licensing can enable intellectual property owners to employ the superior ability of other enterprises to market technology more quickly and at lower cost. This can be particularly important for small businesses that do not have the ability to develop all possible applications of new technologies by themselves. However, the courts have not always been sympathetic to these procompetitive benefits of licensing.

Title III would prohibit courts from finding that an intellectual property licensing arrangement violates the antitrust laws without first considering its procompetitive benefits. In addition, the title would eliminate the potential of treble damage liability under the antitrust laws for intellectual property licensing. Although those who suffer antitrust injury as a result of licensing would still be able to sue for their actual damages plus prejudgment interest, Title III would minimize the deterrence that the antitrust laws currently may have on potentially beneficial licensing of technology.

Title IV would also encourage the pro-competitive licensing of intellectual property. Pursuant to this title, the courts may refuse to enforce a valid patent or copyright on the ground of misuse only after considering meaningful economic analysis.

Finally, Title V will close a loophole in the patent laws that has discouraged investment in efficiency-enhancing technologies. Creation of and improvements in the process of making products can be just as important as creating and improving the product itself. Currently, if someone uses a United States process patent outside this country without the owner's consent and then imports the resulting product into the United States, the importer is not guilty of infringement. Title V of the bill would close this loophole so that owners of process patents can earn their rightful reward by preventing the unauthorized use of their technology.

We must not delay making the necessary changes in the law to encourage the creation and development of new technology, to increase this country's productivity, and to enable our industries to compete more effectively in international markets. We must act now. I therefore urge prompt consideration and passage of this legislative proposal.

RONALD REAGAN

The White House,
September 12, 1983.

Statement by Deputy Press Secretary Speakes on the Intermediate-Range Nuclear Force Negotiations
September 12, 1983

The United States is constantly reviewing the progress of the negotiations to see how best to move the talks forward, and we are continuing intensive consultations with our allies on the INF talks. The sixth round of these talks has just begun, and the United States is engaged in serious negotiating efforts to obtain an agreement that meets alliance security concerns. Both sides are bound to respect the confidentiality of the negotiations. Press speculation about the substance of the talks is not helpful.

As in the previous round, U.S. negotiators have great flexibility to consider any serious Soviet proposal according to criteria set forth by the President earlier this year.

These five criteria remain the basis of our position: equal rights and limits for the United States and U.S.S.R., no compensation for third country systems, global limits with no shifting of the threat from Europe to Asia, no adverse effect on NATO's conventional deterrent, and effective measures to ensure verifiability.

We and the allies remain convinced that the best long-term results of the negotiations would be the elimination of all land-based U.S. and Soviet LRINF missiles, and that as long as the Soviets remain unwilling to accept this outcome, the President's interim agreement proposal provides a flexible framework for progress.

Accordance of the Personal Rank of Ambassador to Thomas J. Dunnigan While Serving at the Annual Meeting of the Inter-American Council for Education, Science, and Culture
September 13, 1983

The President today accorded the personal rank of Ambassador to Thomas J. Dunnigan, a career member of the Senior Foreign Service, Class of Minister-Counselor, while serving as Head of the United States Delegation to this year's annual meeting of the Inter-American Council for Education, Science, and Culture to be held in Kingston, Jamaica, September 19–23, 1983.

Mr. Dunnigan served in the United States Army in 1943–1946. In 1946 he entered the Foreign Service as Foreign Service officer general, then political reporting officer in Berlin. He was political officer in London (1950–1954), in Manila (1954–1956), and Hong Kong (1956–1957). In 1957–1961 he was foreign affairs officer in the Department, and attended the National War College in 1961–1962. In 1962–1965 he was political officer in Bonn. In the Department he was supervisory personnel management specialist, the personnel officer in 1965–

1969. He was political officer in The Hague (1969–1972), Deputy Chief of Mission in Copenhagen (1972–1975), and in Tel Aviv (1975–1977). In 1977–1978 he was diplomat in residence at Centre College in Kentucky. In 1978–1981 he was Deputy Chief of Mission in The Hague. Since 1981 he has been in the Department as group director of the Iranian Small Claims Group (1981–1982), State Department Representative to the National Intelligence Emergency Support Office (1982–1983), and from 1983 to the present, he has been Deputy United States Permanent Representative to the United States Mission to the Organization of American States, and also as United States Representative to the Inter-American Council for Education, Science, and Culture.

Mr. Dunnigan graduated from John Carroll University (A.B., 1943) and George Washington University (M.A., 1967). His foreign languages are Dutch and German. He was born May 22, 1921, in Canton, Ohio.

Announcement of the First Presidential Awards for Excellence in Science and Mathematics Teaching
September 13, 1983

The President today announced the selection of 104 secondary schoolteachers to receive the first Presidential Awards for Excellence in Science and Mathematics Teaching. The awards will be formally presented by the President at the White House on Wednesday, October 19.

The awards program was first announced by the President's Science Adviser last January as a way to provide national recognition to outstanding teachers of science and mathematics in the country's secondary schools. The awards carry with them $5,000 grants to each of the teachers' schools for use in science or mathematics instructional

programs.

Teachers receiving awards are:

Alabama

Peggy Mullins Coulter, Central High School, Tuscaloosa

Mary Nell Gonce, Bradshaw High School, Florence

Alaska

Mildred Janice Heinrich, Robert Service High School, Anchorage

Sondra Dexter, Wendler Junior High School, Anchorage

Arizona

C. Diane Bishop, University High School, Tucson

David T. Smith, Townsend Junior High School, Tucson

Arkansas

Rudy B. Beede, Forrest City Middle School, Forrest City

Jo Anne Rife, Harrison High School, Harrison

California

Clyde L. Corcoran, California High School, Whittier

Arthur Vernon Farmer, Gunn High School, Palo Alto

Colorado

Vaughan Aandahl, George Washington High School, Denver

Irwin J. Hoffman, George Washington High School, Denver

Connecticut

Nancy De Simone Cetorelli, Stratford High School, Stratford

Ronald I. Perkins, Greenwich High School, Greenwich

Delaware

Denise I. Griffiths, Concord High School, Wilmington

Verna M. Price, Central Middle School, Dover

District of Columbia

Doris Broome DeBoe, Banneker Senior High School

Katie Walker, Howard D. Woodson Senior High School

Florida

Frances L. Stivers, Terry Parker High School, Jacksonville

Jo Anne Stephens Taber, Gulliver Academy Middle School, Coral Gables

Georgia

Richard R. Bell, Turner Middle School, Lithia Springs

James Earl Pettigrew, Central High School, Macon

Hawaii

Barbara Kagan, Moanalua High School, Honolulu

Arthur I. Kimura, McKinley High School, Honolulu

Idaho

Jerry Hong, Blackfoot High School, Blackfoot

Charles Robert Humphries, Buhl High School #412, Buhl

Illinois

Charles L. Hamberg, Adlai E. Stevenson High School, Prairie View

Henry Rosenbaum, Von Steuben Metropolitan Science Center, Chicago

Indiana

Robert Dale Lovell, North Side High School, Fort Wayne

Cheryl L. Mason, Highland High School, Highland

Iowa

Roger D. Fuerstenberg, Sudlow Junior High School, Davenport

Karen Murphy, Nathan Weeks Transitional, Des Moines

Kansas

Sharon Kay Carnes, Olpe High School, Olpe

Wendell G. Mohling, Shawnee Mission Northwest High School, Shawnee Mission

Kentucky

Joanne H. Greaver, J. M. Atherton High School, Louisville

Douglas C. Jenkins, Warren Central High School, Bowling Green

Louisiana

Gayle M. Ater, University Laboratory School, Baton Rouge

Jacque P. Treese, Green Oaks High School, Shreveport

Maine

Wesley H. Hedlund, Bangor High School, Bangor

Neil Tame, Oxford Hills High School, South Paris

Maryland

Andrea R. Bowden, Forest Park Senior High School, Baltimore

Ronald Lee Culbertson, Gilman Middle School, Baltimore

Massachusetts

Margaret B. Andersen, Westfield High School, Westfield

Margaret M. Bondorew, Medway Junior-Senior High School, Medway

Michigan

Patricia R. Fraze, Huron High School, Ann Arbor

Walter Scheider, Huron High School, Ann Arbor

Minnesota

Bruce J. Bauer, Stillwater High School, Stillwater

Larry Luck, North Community High School, Minneapolis

Mississippi

Catherine Perry Cotten, Columbia High School, Columbia

Bess Moffatt, Pascagoula High School, Pascagoula

Missouri

Bill M. Brent, Rolla Senior High School, Rolla

Akehiko Takahashi, Wentzville High School, Wentzville

Montana

Glenda M. Tinsley, North Junior High School, Great Falls

Herbert J. York, St. Ignatius High School, St. Ignatius

Nebraska

John J. Skrocky, Jr., Northwest Senior High School, Omaha

Buren G. Thomas, Lincoln Northeast High School, Lincoln

Nevada

Steven W. Pellegrini, Yerington Intermediate School, Yerington

Larry D. Wilson, Valley High School, Las Vegas

New Hampshire

Herwood W. Curtiss, Kearsarge Regional High School, North Sutton

Eleanor T. Milliken, Oyster River High School, Durham

New Jersey

George R. Hague, Jr., Bernards High School, Bernardsville

Mary Dell Morrison, Columbia High School, Maplewood

New Mexico

Helen M. Foster, Santa Fe High School, Santa Fe

Jimmie Fern Lees, Portales High School, Portales

New York

Alfred Kalfus, Babylon Junior-Senior High School, Babylon

Annette Miele Saturnelli, Marlboro Central High School, Marlboro

North Carolina

Anne F. Barefoot, Whiteville High School, Whiteville

Burton W. Stuart, Jr., Chapel Hill Senior High School, Chapel Hill

North Dakota

Gary W. Froelich, Bismarck High School, Bismarck

Marcia Steinwand, Robinson Public School, Robinson

Ohio

Carolyn H. Farnsworth, Jones Middle School, Columbus

William J. Hunt, Mayfield High School, Mayfield

Oklahoma

Charles Eugene Hobbs, Byng Public School System, Ada

Jimmie Pigg, Moore High School, Moore

Oregon

Sue Ann McGraw, Lake Oswego Senior High School, Lake Oswego

George Allen Tinker, Marshfield High School, Coos Bay

Pennsylvania

Louis F. DeVicaris, Cheltenham High School, Wyncote

Annalee Henderson, State College Area High School, State College

Puerto Rico

Jose L. Garrido, Collegio San Ignacio de Loyola, Rio Piedras

Luz V. Concepcion de Gaspar, University of Puerto Rico High School, San Juan

Rhode Island

Mary C. Christian, North Providence High School, North Providence

Marcelline Anne Zambuco, John F. Deering Junior High School, West Warwick

South Carolina

Johanna O. Killoy, Dreher High School, Columbia

Elizabeth Lynch Lashley, D.W. Daniel High School, Central

South Dakota

Gerald E. Lommer, Rapid City Central High School, Rapid City

James A. Nelson, Simmons Junior High School, Aberdeen

Tennessee

Josephine A. Bennett, Whitehaven High School, Memphis

Nancy Nelms Gates, Overton High School, Memphis

Texas

Paul A. Foerster, Alamo Heights High School, San Antonio

Janet A. Harris, Cy-Fair High School, Houston

Utah

Carl L. Bruce, Bonneville High School, Ogden

Jacquelyn Marie Igo Stonebraker, Evergreen Junior High School, Salt Lake City

Vermont

Judith L. Allard, Burlington High School, Burlington

Jean Carole Hackett, Hazen Union, Hardwick

Virginia

Edna Hyke Corbett, I. C. Norcom High School, Portsmouth

Joyce Ann Richardson Weeks, Hampton High School, Hampton

Washington

Barbara Schulz, Shorewood High School, Seattle

Thomas F. (Tony) Sedgwick, Lincoln High School, Tacoma

West Virginia

Ava Florence Crum, Winfield High School, Winfield

Robert E. Phipps, Parkersburg South High School, Parkersburg

Wisconsin

David R. Johnson, Nicolet High School, Glendale

Edward M. Mueller, Shattuck Junior High School, Neenah

Wyoming

Bernie Richard Schnorenberg, Sundance Junior-Senior High School, Sundance

Elizabeth B. Shelton, Big Horn Junior-Senior High School, Big Horn

Remarks of the President and Prime Minister Robert Mugabe of Zimbabwe Following Their Meetings
September 13, 1983

The President. I know that the press is very grateful that they're not out in the rain.

It's been a great pleasure to have had the opportunity today to meet with Prime Minister Robert Mugabe of the Republic of Zimbabwe. As the first Prime Minister of Africa's newest independent state, his wise leadership has been a crucial factor in healing the wounds of civil war and developing a new nation with new opportunities. Our discussions today have covered a wide range of topics, including our bilateral relationship and regional issues. We've spoken very frankly and in an atmosphere of mutual respect. We didn't always agree but have all gained much from hearing your views, Mr. Prime Minister.

I believe that our two countries will continue to cooperate on those areas where common concerns are shared and that we will come closer to an understanding on those issues where our views diverge. The United States and Zimbabwe have much in common. We both came to independence through a revolutionary process. We are both multiracial societies. And our constitutions offer protection to all our citizens, black and white, ensuring their political freedoms as well as their individual rights.

I'm glad to say that since Zimbabwe's independence relations between Zimbabwe and the United States have been very good and, strengthened by this exchange of views, will become even better.

We look to Zimbabwe for leadership in southern Africa. Blessed with natural resources, a hard-working, multiracial population, and a spirit of national reconciliation, Zimbabwe can provide a firm foundation of economic viability and political stability and serve as an inspiration in its part of the world.

Mr. Prime Minister, our talks today have confirmed that we also share a desire for peace and stability in southern Africa, and I know that we both look forward to a time when all countries there can achieve a level of amity which will allow them to work toward economic, social, and political development, free from the threat of attack from whatever quarter.

The ultimate responsibility for resolution of their problems, however, rests with the states of the regions themselves. And here, Mr. Prime Minister, you've taken a leading and constructive role. I know that you'll be meeting with a number of leaders in all walks of American life during your stay here in Washington and elsewhere in our land. I'm sure they will benefit as I have from your thoughtful views on our bilateral relationship as well as on regional and global issues.

I'm delighted that you accepted our invitation to visit Washington, and I look forward to meeting you again.

The Prime Minister. Thank you.

Mr. President, ladies and gentlemen, may I on behalf of my delegation, on behalf of the Government and people of Zimbabwe, express to you on this historic occasion of our visit—the first such by the head of government of the Republic of Zimbabwe—express to you our heartfelt thanks and appreciation for that support which the United States has given us all along the way. And this support starts, really, from the time we were still struggling for our independence, as the United States offered itself as party to the negotiations that were underway to bring about a democratic order in Zimbabwe.

We got pledges from your government, from your predecessors, that upon attainment of our independence the United States would not be found wanting in extending to Zimbabwe that amount of aid the United States was capable of extending to it to enable the young state to attend to those problems created by the war which the young country would feel necessary to attend to.

And so here we are, a young state that yesterday was only a toddler but today is able to do a little more than it was able to do yesterday. And this is because of the amount of assistance—I think the United States contributes the largest amount towards our whole program of reconstruction and development. And that input into our own efforts has enabled us to create the necessary base for our socioeconomic transformation.

We have enjoyed excellent relations with your country. There has never been an occasion when we have had to complain to the United States on issues of bilateral relations falling in the political or diplomatic sphere. Yes, as you admit, there have been areas of difference. We are different on the modality of bringing about Namibia's independence, the linkage with the Cuban question. But, sir, generally we have looked at issues through the same glasses, one might say. And our posture regarding international situations of conflict has been identical. We all are opposed—we both are opposed to interference in the domestic affairs of a country by another.

And I'm sure this identity of viewpoint makes for the greater friendship and solidarity that we find between our two countries and our two people. We have enjoyed every minute of our stay in your country. We continue our talks with leaders of your society. But I'm very happy that the discussions we've just had have dwelled on those issues which are of mutual interest to our two sides.

As you have said, we have discussed bilateral relations, the question of economic aid to Zimbabwe, the question of our original relations, and the fact that South Africa continues to destabilize our region. We have discussed Namibia, we have discussed the apartheid system in South Africa, and there is a greater measure of agreement. There might be some difference here and there in respect of the method of bringing about change, positive change to the area.

We are very happy, indeed, that this visit has taken place. And may I thank you and Vice President Bush, who visited us not long ago, for extending this invitation to me and enabling me therefore to come to this wonderful country with a wonderful people and a wonderful tradition and express to them the gratitude of the people of Zimbabwe.

We are a young country. We may make mistakes as we move forward, but we are prepared that where we err we shall correct ourselves and get back to course.

We don't intend to vitiate at all those principles which underline the constitutional order that we have created. We are determined that a nonracial society shall exist in Zimbabwe and that racism, tribalism, regionalism, and whatever other "isms"—these are things of the past. What we would uphold as fundamental is that principle which binds us together and makes us one regardless of our race, color, or creed.

And these are matters on which the United States has long made a decision, matters of principle which make for greater democracy and greater freedom in society. We are prepared that this shall also be our tradition.

May I thank you for the kindness and hospitality which has been showered on me and my delegation since our arrival. We have come as friends; we go back as greater

and closer friends still.

Thank you.

Note: The President spoke at 1:23 p.m. to reporters assembled in the East Room at the White House. The remarks were scheduled to be given outside at the South Portico, but because of inclement weather the event was held in the East Room.

Earlier in the day, the President and the Prime Minister met in the Oval Office and then held a working luncheon, together with U.S. and Zimbabwean officials, in the State Dining Room.

Nomination of Diane K. Steed To Be Administrator of the National Highway Traffic Safety Administration
September 13, 1983

The President today announced his intention to nominate Diane K. Steed to be Administrator of the National Highway Traffic Safety Administration, Department of Transportation. She would succeed Raymond A. Peck, Jr.

Since 1981 Miss Steed has been serving as Deputy Administrator of the National Highway Traffic Safety Administration. Previously she was chief of the regulatory policy branch of the Office of Management and

Budget in 1978–1981; management associate, economics and government, at the Office of Management and Budget in 1973–1978; senior budget analyst for ACTION in 1972–1973; and management analyst, contract administration services, Defense Supply Agency, in 1968–1972.

Miss Steed graduated from the University of Kansas (B.S., 1967). She was born November 29, 1945, in Hutchinson, Kans., and now resides in Washington, D.C.

Nomination of Louis Roman DiSabato To Be a Member of the National Museum Services Board
September 13, 1983

The President today announced his intention to nominate Louis Roman DiSabato to be a member of the National Museum Services Board of the Institute of Museum Services, National Foundation on the Arts and the Humanities, for a term expiring December 6, 1987. He would succeed Lloyd Hezekiah.

Since 1968 Mr. DiSabato has been serving as director of the San Antonio Zoo. Previously he was director of Seneca Park Zoo in

Rochester, N.Y., in 1963–1968 and director of the Columbus Zoo in Columbus, Ohio, in 1961–1963.

He was a director of the American Association of Zoological Parks and Aquariums for 2 terms. He has been a member of the International Union of Directors of Zoological Gardens since 1970.

He is married, has five children, and resides in San Antonio, Tex. He was born October 7, 1931, in Columbus, Ohio.

Appointment of Five Members of the National Advisory Council on Continuing Education
September 14, 1983

The President today announced his intention to appoint the following individuals to be members of the National Advisory Council on Continuing Education:

J. A. Kinder is executive secretary of the Missouri State Teachers Association in Columbia, Mo. He was born April 1, 1933, in Mound City, Mo. This is a reappointment for a term expiring September 30, 1986.

Elsie Frankfurt Pollock is president of Page Boy, Inc., in Beverly Hills, Calif. She was born July 22, 1919, in Dallas, Tex. This is a reappointment for a term expiring September 30, 1986.

John H. Richert is president of the College of

Saint Mary in Omaha, Nebr. He was born March 12, 1941, in Chicago, Ill. This is a reappointment for a term expiring September 30, 1986.

Talmage Eugene Simpkins is executive director of the AFL–CIO Maritime Committee in Washington, D.C. He was born September 27, 1927, in Goreville, Ill. This is a reappointment for a term expiring September 30, 1986.

Hilary Paterson Cleveland is a professor at Colby-Sawyer College in New London, N.H. She was born December 7, 1927, in Orange, N.J. She will succeed Robert C. Angel for the remainder of the term expiring September 30, 1984.

Nomination of Albert James Barnes To Be an Assistant Administrator of the Environmental Protection Agency
September 14, 1983

The President today announced his intention to nominate Albert James Barnes to be an Assistant Administrator of the Environmental Protection Agency (General Counsel). This is a new position.

Since 1981 Mr. Barnes has been serving as General Counsel at the United States Department of Agriculture. Previously he was a partner in the law firm of Beverage, Fairbanks & Diamond in 1973–1981; assistant to the Deputy Attorney General at the Department of Justice in 1973; assistant to the

Administrator of the Environmental Protection Agency in 1970–1973; and trial attorney and special assistant to the Assistant Attorney General, Civil Division, at the Department of Justice in 1969–1970.

He graduated from Michigan State University (B.A., 1964) and Harvard Law School (J.D., 1967). He is married, has one child, and resides in Washington, D.C. He was born August 30, 1942, in Napoleon, Ohio.

Nomination of Josephine S. Cooper To Be an Assistant Administrator of the Environmental Protection Agency
September 14, 1983

The President today announced his intention to nominate Josephine S. Cooper to be an Assistant Administrator of the Environmental Protection Agency (Congressional and External Affairs). This is a new position created by P.L. 98–80 of August 23, 1983.

Since 1981 she has been serving on the professional staff to Senator Howard Baker and on the U.S. Senate Committee on the Environment and Public Works. She served as Special Assistant to the Assistant Administrator for Research and Development at the Environmental Protection Agency in 1980–1981 and in 1979. Previously she was legislative assistant to Senator Howard Baker and to Congressman Dick Cheney and an American Political Science Association congressional fellow in 1979–1980; environmental protection specialist, Environmental Criteria and Assessment Office, EPA Office of Research and Development, at Research Triangle Park in North Carolina, in 1978–1979; and as program analyst in the Office of Air Quality Planning and Standards, EPA, at Research Triangle Park in 1971–1978.

Ms. Cooper graduated from Meredith College (B.A., 1967) and Duke University (M.S., 1977). She resides in Alexandria, Va., and was born August 2, 1945.

Nomination of John C. Martin To Be Inspector General of the Environmental Protection Agency
September 14, 1983

The President today announced his intention to nominate John C. Martin to be Inspector General of the Environmental Protection Agency. He would succeed Matthew Norman Novick.

Since 1981 he has been serving as Assistant Inspector General at the Department of Housing and Urban Development. Previously he was supervisory special agent for the Federal Bureau of Investigation in 1976–1981; special agent, FBI, in 1971– 1976; assistant to the city manager, city of Rockville, Md., in 1968–1971; and deputy city manager, city of Wilkes-Barre, Pa., in 1967–1968.

Mr. Martin graduated from King's College, Wilkes-Barre, Pa. (B.A., 1967), and the University of Maryland (M.A., 1970). He is married, has six children, and resides in Dumfries, Va. He was born March 4, 1945, in Wilkes-Barre, Pa.

Remarks and a Question-and-Answer Session With Writers for Hispanic, Religious, and Labor Publications
September 14, 1983

The President. It's a pleasure to have you here today. I understand that you've been briefed on some domestic and foreign policy issues, and we're concerned that all Americans are fully aware of what we're doing and how it relates to them.

For those of you in the Hispanic press, I want you to know that my concern is not something new or some grand campaign strategy, as some have indicated. Since my days as Governor of California, I've been aware of the rich contributions that Americans of Hispanic descent have made and are making to our country. Within 24 hours of declaring my candidacy for President in 1979, I outlined a program that emphasized the importance of better relations among all of us in this hemisphere. I said then and have echoed since at Cancún, during my trip to Central and South America, and during many consultations with the Presidents of Mexico, that we in this hemisphere are all Americans. We worship the same God. We have enormous potential if we can build on the many things that bind us together here, from North to South Pole, in this hemisphere.

And those of you who are with us today from the religious press understand, perhaps better than most, how faith brings people together. Recently I visited Hispanic business leaders in meetings in Florida and

California, and I was impressed by the enthusiasm and the optimism that I found. Their spirit and energy were reminiscent of Americans of an earlier age when entrepreneurs turned an undeveloped wilderness into a dynamo of freedom and abundance. There's no better proof that the American dream is alive and well than what is happening in the Hispanic community in America today.

Many Americans of Hispanic descent are moving into positions of influence and authority, not because of some quota, but because they are top quality individuals. Earlier this week I appointed Katherine Ortega. She was the first woman to become a bank president in the State of California, and I appointed her to be Treasurer of the United States. She and the many others of Hispanic descent in this administration will continue to play an important role in building our economy.

Now I could recite a list of economic indicators, but by now I hope it's clear—and you probably heard in the briefing earlier by others—that we've turned a graveyard situation around, and the economy's taking off with new strength, confidence, and vigor. It's caught some of our critics by surprise. Only 3 years ago, some of the experts were saying that it would take a decade to squeeze inflation out of the economy. But you see, we didn't know any better, so we just went ahead and did it. [*Laughter*]

There's one word of warning, however. We can't take economic expansion for granted. The growth of government with its taxing and spending gave us double-digit inflation, sky-high interest rates, business stagnation, and unprecedented pessimism—and that was just 3 years ago. We've got our country back on the road to noninflationary economic growth, but if we're lured back into the policies of tax and spend and inflate, policies that caused our problems in the first place, everyone will be worse off.

Strengthening America's economy hasn't been our only challenge. We've accelerated our efforts to rebuild our military strength, and this has permitted, or had been permitted to seriously erode during the last decade. Now, we've done this not because we enjoy spending money—I don't want the Federal Government spending 1 cent

more than is absolutely necessary—but what we've done is for the preservation of our freedom and the maintenance of world peace. Wishful thinking is a threat to peace. There are members of the labor press, I know, here today, and I want you to know that I fully appreciate America's longstanding—or labor's longstanding contribution to our country's security. I should. Maybe some of you aren't old enough to know that I was six times president of my own union, and I think I'm the only fellow that ever held this job as a lifetime member of a union.

The magnitude of our challenge was brought home to many Americans just 2 weeks ago when an unarmed passenger liner was willfully shot down by the Soviet Union, a massacre of 269 innocent people.

That gruesome episode unmasked the Soviet regime for what it is—a dictatorship with none of the respect for human values and individual rights that we in the Western democracies hold so dear. That brutal regime stamps out any dissent that might serve as a moderating influence. Worshiping God is considered a social evil. Well, we can't permit such a regime to militarily dominate this planet. This incident should reaffirm our commitment and that of our allies to rebuild our defensive strength. We must and will continue to reach out for arms reduction agreements to reduce the nuclear and conventional arsenals that threaten humankind. But with a regime that callously shoots down passenger planes, demonstrating that their values are far different than our own, this is a great challenge, one that we must meet with faith, wisdom, unity, and courage.

Perhaps if any good has come out of this tragedy, it is that the Western democracies better appreciate that peace will take more than gestures of good will and sincerity.

We're encouraged that today the Western alliance is more unified than in many years. In this hemisphere we enjoy a healthy dialog with our neighbors, and a new level of respect has developed among us. In contrast, the Soviet Union is becoming increasingly isolated, as the free people of the world become more aware of the nature of the Soviet regime.

I thank you all very much for letting me be a part of this, and now you have some questions.

Offensive Weapons in Cuba

Q. Mr. President—[*inaudible*]—I don't have to tell you how much we like you in Miami. You know about that.

There has always been talk about the Kennedy-Khrushchev understanding of 1962. [*Inaudible*]—and Bill Casey[1] and Secretary Weinberger have said that the Russian—[*inaudible*]—understanding throughout the years on the Cuban—[*inaudible*]—bringing offensive weapons into the islands.

What is your position? What are your feelings on this understanding? Should the United States live up to it?

The President. I have been looking at that, and with all the things that are going on, we haven't been able to talk as much as we should about it. But I have to tell you that as far as I'm concerned, that agreement has been abrogated many times by the Soviet Union and Cuba in the bringing in of what can only be considered offensive weapons, not defensive, there. And we'll get around to that.

We did try to open some talks when there seemed to be an indication coming from Cuba that there was a willingness for that. They got nowhere. So we're going to carry on with what we're doing.

Cuban Refugees

Q. Mr. President, in January of 1982, your Press Secretary said that you were shocked and dismayed when you learned that a Cuban stowaway had been deported back to the island. You were right; that Cuban is now back in jail. Since then about 50 Cubans have come over on small boats fleeing communism. They are at the Chrome Avenue Detention Camp in South Bay. Do you think that's fair?

The President. It is to this extent, that out of the Mariel boatlift we found that there had been deliberately planted among legitimate refugees a great number of Cuban criminals who were released from prisons, some from mental institutions, and they had been responsible for—some of those that

---

[1] *Director of Central Intelligence.*

moved out into our society, before we were aware of this—had been responsible for some very violent and very vicious crimes. And we're holding many more than what you just mentioned here. Those, I'm sure, are being held while we do a little checking on them.

We are holding these others. We have appealed a number of times to Cuba to take them back. They have refused. And we're still trying to deal with this problem and what we do with those who were infiltrated. We cannot deny that there is evidence, also, that in addition to this kind of individual, that they have used this refugee movement to, well, infiltrate subversives into our country. And so we're trying to do a little better job of checking.

President's Decision on Seeking Reelection

Q. Mr. President—[*inaudible*]—could you tell us when you will announce that you will seek or not seek the Presidency again?

The President. At the last possible moment—[*laughter*]—that I can announce a decision, and for a very obvious reason. Number one, if the answer is no, I'm a lameduck and can't get anything done. If the answer is yes, they'll charge that everything I'm doing is political—[*laughter*]—and I can't get anything done. So, I'm going to wait as long as I can.

Let me move over to this side now just a minute.

National Right-to-Work Law

Q. Mr. President, do you support a national right to work law? And if so, why? If not, why not?

The President. Whatever I may personally believe, I will tell you that officially my position is that I believe that this still belongs at the State level for determination, that this is something that the States should determine. Having been a Governor, I'm a great believer that the Federal Government has moved into many areas where the authority properly belonged to the States. We are a federation of 50 sovereign States, and that is one of the greatest guarantees of our freedom. So my position is that's for the States to determine.

Agricultural Programs

Q. Mr. President—[*inaudible*]—there is concern among the agriculture community, because of the drought all over the Nation, that the disaster provision in the 1981 farm bill will not be enacted by the administration. There is also some concern and some requests that the PIK program be extended through 1983. Can you tell us what the status on both of those is?

The President. No, I can't, other than the fact that they're very much on the agenda for us. As a matter of fact, we had a Cabinet meeting yesterday just for a complete report on the economic problems brought about by the drought. But all of these things are, as I say, on the agenda, and I can't give you any answers right now.

Foreign Missionaries and Intelligence Gathering

Q. Mr. President—[*inaudible*]—is there an administration position and has there been an Executive order to prohibit the use of missionaries for gathering of intelligence, or the use of an intelligence officer posing as a foreign missionary? We have 3,000 foreign missionaries in 100 countries.

The President. For heaven's sakes. Have you got an answer on that? I don't. [*Laughter*] As a matter of fact, the question has never been brought to my attention. But all I can tell you is now you having asked it, I'm going back over to the Oval Office and I'm going to say, "Hey, is there?"

I would not be aware and am not aware that anything of that kind has ever been done. I have the greatest respect for those people whose religious calling takes them out into the world, and I wish them well.

Hispanics in the Administration

Q. Mr. President—[*inaudible*]—your appointments of Linda Chavez and Katherine Ortega have been hailed as appointments of both women and Hispanics, and yet there's still concern these aren't policymaking positions. Do you have any plans to appoint Hispanics or women to top-level policymaking positions soon?

The President. Yes. As a matter of fact, we have about 125 in the administration right now, and we are constantly, in our personnel section, on the search for more.

We would have had a member of the Cabinet, except that at the last moment, probably faced with all the reporting and the revelations and the personal affairs and so forth that have to be made, like so many others, this individual turned away and said no, I don't want any part of it, and left us.

I don't mean to say that he did this because of any wrongdoing on his part. You'd be surprised, growing out of some of the past problems of Watergate and so forth, there have been a number of restrictions that have been placed on people who were willing to volunteer and serve for government, restrictions that have prevented many fine, capable people when they just take a look and they say no, that's humiliating, and I'm not going to do it, and they turn away from us.

I wish we could return to some sanity and recognize that people who are willing to give up their personal lives and careers for a period and come in and serve government aren't doing it for any personal gain. As a matter of fact, I don't know of anyone on our Cabinet today who did not make a tremendous sacrifice, personally and economically, to serve in government.

El Salvador

Q. Mr. President—[*inaudible*]—since the ultimate outcome of the struggle going on in El Salvador depends on the improvement of the economic condition of the people, why don't we hear more in America about what that government is doing, with our help, to improve the economic condition of the El Salvadoran people, instead of so much about the warfare that is going on?

The President. You are all members of a profession that could do a lot about that. Now there are some very well-kept secrets in Washington, not because we want them kept secrets but because they just don't seem to be of interest to the media.

Now, we have over and over again said that our help to El Salvador has been three dollars of economic and social help for every dollar of military help. And yet the bulk of the people, according to the polls in the country today, don't even know which side we're on in El Salvador—whether we're on the government's side or the guerrillas' side. We have tried, yes.

The Government of El Salvador has a reversal, over centuries of another form of government there, have been trying to implement these social and economic reforms, the land reform program, but because of what the guerrillas are doing, many of those people who are now landowners through this government program are in refugee camps, driven off their land and unable to farm it, because it would mean death to go out in the fields. The guerrillas would see to it that it would mean death.

Just as when they had the election last year, the guerrillas' slogan was "Vote Today and Die Tonight." And yet, more than 83 percent of the eligible voters in El Salvador made their way to the polls and voted. They are working at instituting democracy. They haven't made a hundred-percent cleanup of some of the past practices that have taken place, but they've made remarkable progress.

And yes, the people should know about that. We have seen plenty of shots about our military games that are going on in Honduras, the joint military exercises. But has anyone shown you some of the hospitals, you know, those balloon-type buildings that you inflate and blow up, that are there? One hospital alone—27 doctors and a full complement of nurses from our country, and not just for military purposes—treating and taking care of the people who have not had proper medical care, the civilians in that area.

There's a great story to be told about what's going on down there and what we're trying to help them in accomplishing. So talk to some of your colleagues out there in the general media.

Q. Talk about it Saturday on the radio. [*Laughter*]

U.S.-Israeli Relations

Q. Mr. President—[*inaudible*]—and mine is in a religious realm. The Bible says in the Old Testament, in Deuteronomy, Genesis, and Joshua, God made a covenant with Abraham with respect to Israel. Now, what I would like to know, Mr. President—and I'm glad you're our President—how do you cope with this and how does this affect your decision on shaping up our foreign policy in Israel?

The President. I would have to tell you that I believe—and this is not just our administration, but since 1948 when Israel became a nation—the policy of the United States Government, under Democrat and Republican Presidents and legislatures, has been one of alliance with Israel and assurance of Israel's continuation as a state. And I don't think that any American administration would ever forsake Israel.

This is one of the reasons for our peace plan. When Sadat did what he did and brought peace between Egypt and Israel, the two that had been actually in combat with each other, it was my belief that what we should do is start working with the Arab nations to see if among them we could not first bring their recognition of the right of Israel to exist and then see if we could not create additional Egypts, nations that would enter into a peace treaty, because no nation can go on having to maintain the military stature that Israel does. When you stop to think that the 500 men that they lost in the fighting in Lebanon, if that was the United States, proportionately, that would have been more than 30,000 dead.

Economically, the strain on them is so great that the answer to their problem must be peace. And peace can only come when all of them recognize, all the other nations recognize the right of this nation to exist. This was one of the reasons why we would never negotiate with the PLO, because they openly said they denied the right of Israel to be a nation. Their dream was of driving them into the sea. And we said how could we talk to someone who believes that way?

Right now, we started with the idea that the Lebanese situation had to be cleared up and the foreign forces all get out of Lebanon before we proceed with these peace talks. I am still optimistic that we're going to be able to bring this about, and we'll continue to try.

I'm sorry I can't take the rest of the hands here. Thank you all very much.

Note: The President spoke at 11:33 a.m. in Room 450 of the Old Executive Office Building.

Proclamation 5094—Youth of America Week, 1983
September 14, 1983

By the President of the United States of America

A Proclamation

More than 50 million American youth are included in the Nation's general population. These young citizens play major roles in our society as they mature into adulthood. They make important contributions to our country by pursuing their educations, working in the economy, upholding the law, and joining the military services.

Our young Americans have every reason to be proud of their contributions to the American way of life. They can look forward to doing more as they complete their educations and move into positions in science, space, education, medicine, business, labor, government, military service, and other fields. The future of America depends on the preparation and dedication of our younger citizens, because one day, it will be their responsibility to ensure the security of our Nation, both at home and abroad. They must be given every opportunity to achieve their goals as they pass through adolescence to full maturity.

Among the American youth population are many in special need. The Federal government works actively with State and local governments and the private sector in important programs responding to the needs of runaway and homeless youth, unemployed youth, and to those who experience physical, emotional, and social handicaps.

To assure our Nation's youth of our commitment to share our knowledge, experience, and wisdom, which will help nurture in them democratic principles, and the development of strong moral and spiritual values so vital to the survival and future betterment of America, the Congress of the United States, by Senate Joint Resolution 116, had designated the week of September 4 through September 10, 1983, as "Youth of America Week" and has authorized and requested the President to issue a proclamation in observance of that week.

Now, Therefore, I, Ronald Reagan, President of the United States of America, do hereby proclaim the week beginning September 4, 1983 as Youth of America Week.

In Witness Whereof, I have hereunto set my hand this fourteenth day of September, in the year of our Lord nineteen hundred and eighty-three, and of the Independence of the United States of America the two hundred and eighth.

RONALD REAGAN

[*Filed with the Office of the Federal Register, 10:09 a.m., September 15, 1983*]

Remarks at the Fundraising Dinner of the Republican National Hispanic Assembly
September 14, 1983

Ambassador Gavin, Tirso del Junco, I thank you both for those magnificent words. Reverend clergy, the Members of the Congress who are here, other members of government, but especially all of you ladies and gentlemen of this Hispanic Assembly:

Let me welcome you to Washington, and I know that Nancy joins me in this. And welcome to the twilight zone. [*Laughter*] I should warn you that things in this city aren't often the way they seem. Where but in Washington would they call the department that's in charge of everything outdoors, everything outside, the Department of Interior. [*Laughter*]

You know, I know I've probably told some of you this little anecdote, but I'm going to tell it, dedicated to Tirso, here tonight again. You know, life not only begins at 40 but so does the tendency to tell stories over and over again to the same people. [*Laughter*] I know I have told some of you. It is said that Castro was making a speech to a large assembly, and he was going on at great length. And then a voice out in the crowd said, "Peanuts, popcorn, cracker-jack!" And he went on speaking, and again the voice said, "Peanuts, popcorn, cracker-jack!" And about the fourth time this happened, he stopped in his regular speech and he said, "The next time he says that, I'm going to find out who he is and kick him all the way to Miami." [*Laughter*] And everybody in the crowd said, "Peanuts, popcorn, crackerjack!" [*Laughter*]

You know, some things in life, however, are exactly as they seem. I know that I can always count on the ideals and the convictions of the Republican National Hispanic Assembly. Each of you should be congratulated for what you've done. But accomplishments also require leadership. And tonight I'd like to take this opportunity to thank Tirso del Junco for the great job that he's doing here with the Republican National Hispanic Assembly.

I'm delighted that we could gather to share our hopes and dreams for America. I've always believed that this blessed land was set apart in a special way, that there was some divine plan that placed the two great continents here between the oceans to be found by people from every corner of the Earth who had a deep love for freedom and the courage to uproot themselves, leave home and friends, and come to a strange land.

You here tonight are part of this tradition. And whether your journey here began in the Caribbean Islands, or North or South or Central America, we came together, all, as Americans. That's the heritage of this Western Hemisphere. Now perhaps you are the first generation citizens of the United States of America, or the second, perhaps, or the third, or perhaps as far back as the United States herself goes. But there are no prouder, more patriotic Americans than are gathered here tonight in this room.

We all believe in America's mission. We believe that in a world wracked by hatred and crisis, America remains mankind's best hope. The eyes of history are upon us, counting on us to protect the peace, promote a new prosperity, and provide for a better tomorrow. This evening I want to talk to you as Republicans and Hispanics, and as Americans foremost of all, about these very values that we cherish so deeply.

In recent years, America's values almost seemed in exile. Just consider where our nation was or where it stood just 3 years ago. Our leaders were struggling and shrugging their shoulders and saying that we were in some kind of a malaise and that our problems were unsolvable. Pessimism, totally inconsistent with our national character, had spread across this land, and our leaders had forgotten the strength and determination that runs deep in our people. They'd forgotten that values, not programs and policies, serve as society's compass. They seemingly had forgotten what a decent, moral nation we are. We need make no apologies to the world. After all, we do not occupy any countries. We don't build walls to keep our people in. And we don't cold-bloodedly open fire on aircraft loaded with innocent passengers.

Americans didn't accept the idea that our best days were behind us, and neither did the Republican Party. And today—it's taken blood, sweat, and tears, and a few legislative victories—but I am pleased to report to you tonight America's star is rising again, and it is the star of the future.

When we got to Washington, inflation was running at double-digit levels, as you remember, and it had been doing so for 2 straight years. It was the worst performance in 60 years in our country. And inflation was taking an especially serious toll on those citizens with low incomes. In the 2 years before we took office, inflation decreased the purchasing power of low-income people on a fixed income of $10,000 by over $2,000. Now, if that's what they call Democratic compassion, then the people can't stand too much of it. [*Laughter*]

But here's the good news. We reduced that inflation to 2.4 percent for the last 12 months, and that's the lowest 12-month rate in 17 years. Now, they told us that it would take years, possibly decades, before we could bring down inflation. But they forgot about something that we'd brought with us to Washington. It's called determination. And besides that, we didn't know that you couldn't do it, so we did it. [*Laughter*]

Today, a family of four on a fixed income of $20,000 has $2,000 more in purchasing power this year alone than it would have had if we hadn't slapped inflation down.

I don't want to dredge up too painful a memory, but do you remember when interest rates were 21½ percent? That was the equivalent of pouring concrete onto the economy. The economy hardened and then began collapsing. Well, we cut the prime interest rate from 21½ percent. It's now 11 percent. And we're going to work so that those rates continue to decline, and I think they're going to start doing that soon, and our economy will become synonymous with economic growth.

When we took office, this America was suffering from years of uncontrolled spending and taxation. Federal spending was growing at a rate that was steep enough to make a mountain goat dizzy. And the problem was that the Democrats genuinely believed—and poor, misguided things, they still believe—[*laughter*]—that money can buy happiness. Well, Federal tax money can't buy happiness. It can't buy our citizens real jobs and real opportunity. Ask the Democrats what it takes to get people back to work, and they won't answer that we need responsible and constant economic policies. No, they'll answer that we need billions of dollars more in Federal job programs.

Well, money alone can't buy our children quality education. I don't know how certain politicians, with a straight face, can tell taxpayers that simply more funds are needed to improve education. During the 20-year period between 1960 and 1980, spending on education was shooting up while college board scores were going down. If a 600-percent increase in 20 years in school spending could not make America smarter, how much more do we need? The Democrats' predictable answer is, "Billions more," of course.

Well, Federal money doesn't buy happiness, except for the bureaucrats and the special interests that luxuriate in those programs. All it buys is a bigger debt. We haven't stopped the growth in Federal spending, but we've slowed it by almost 40 percent. And if the Congress acts responsibly—and those who are present will—we can bring it further under control. I only wish the majority of that illustrious body were as responsible as Manny Lujan.

Taxes were rising right along with spending, and paying for all those special interest programs doubled the Federal tax bite in just 5 years, between 1976 and 1981. You know, there's an old saying that in levying taxes, as in shearing sheep, it's best to stop when you get to the skin. [*Laughter*] By the end of 1980, the tax rates were skinning the American taxpayer, and we were paying with our hides. Average working people were being taxed at rates that only a short time before were reserved for the wealthy.

We've put into place a tax program that cut personal income tax rates across the board by 25 percent. Now that was a commitment we made to the working people of this country, and we have another protection waiting in the wings. Soon, beginning in 1985, America's taxes will be indexed, so that never again will government profit from inflation at the peoples' expense.

The cumulative effect of all our economic efforts is now being felt. That's why they don't call it Reaganomics anymore. [*Laughter*] As they say down at Cape Canaveral, we have liftoff. Our economy is lifting off, and it's because of the policies that we've been passing over the past 2½ years. Consumer confidence and spending are up. Productivity is up. Industrial production, retail sales, auto sales, housing and construction are all up since the beginning of the year. And last quarter, the economy grew at an annual rate of 9.2 percent, a much bigger jump than anyone had predicted.

Although unemployment is still too high, it's coming down rapidly, and we'll continue to chip away and knock that statistic down to size. As a matter of fact, last month it was the biggest single-month drop in unemployment in 23 years. Now, we must help those who, through no fault of their own, are without jobs, but let's be clear: Our goal isn't welfare or handouts, it's jobs and opportunity. And if I didn't believe that, I think you, the people in this room, would tell me that's what we need and what you want.

Just as we've been building a stronger economy, we've been building a stronger defense. I know that you'll recall a few years ago our military personnel were putting their uniforms in mothballs, and we had a lot of ships and planes that belonged there—in mothballs. And this situation endangered our national security and the peace.

As Commander in Chief, I can say to you America is more secure than she was 3 years ago. I've heard it from generals and I've heard it from privates, that once again it's an honor to be in our military. We have an abundance of applicants with more education than ever before. Morale, discipline, and unit cohesion have improved dramatically. Training and retention are up. Maintenance backlogs are being reduced. Combat readiness rates have surged. New equipment is being added to our inventory. Our military is once more becoming shipshape.

In 1980 the people also made it clear that they wanted a new direction in foreign affairs. Well, we began by letting the world know what we stood for once again. For too long, our nation had been mute to the injustice of totalitarianism. So, we began speaking out against chemical warfare inflicted on the people of Afghanistan and Southeast Asia, against broken treaties, and against the denial of human liberties. We began speaking out for freedom and democracy and the values that all of us share in our hearts.

And you know, it's amazing. In my meetings with foreign leaders and their ministers, they've told me how good it is to know what the United States stands for once again. Now, they may not always agree with us, but they respect us. There's a growing recognition abroad that America once again will stand up for her democratic ideals. Our country is the leader of the free world, and we morally cannot shirk that responsibility.

We are providing democratic leadership in Central America. A ruthless power has set its sights on our neighbors in Central America and the Caribbean. The security aspect of this threat must be addressed, so we're helping our friends to defend themselves, and we will continue to stand by them in their hour of need.

But let's get one thing straight, and I don't know how many times we must repeat this before it sinks into the skulls of some in this town—that $3 out of every 4 that we send down there is in the form of humanitarian and economic aid. The people in Central America and the Caribbean are our neighbors. They need our help, and we will not abandon them to indifference.

We're also pursuing peace through arms control. In our search for peace, we have more major negotiations underway with the Soviets than any administration in history. We've undertaken the most sweeping proposals for arms reductions since nuclear weapons became a threat. And for the first time the Soviet Union is willing to talk about actual reductions rather than just ceilings, as in previous administrations. In strategic nuclear forces, in intermediate-range nuclear forces, and in conventional forces, we want to lessen the danger to ourselves and our children. We remain flexible in our bargaining. But as Commander in Chief, I have an obligation to protect this country, and I will not let political expedience influence those crucial negotiations. We will restore equality of strength with the Soviet Union either one way or the other, and the choice is theirs.

I believe that we share a sacred responsibility, all of us, to maintain the opportunity and freedom we've enjoyed and to pass it on to future generations. Americans of Hispanic descent understand completely the traditional values of work, of family, of freedom, and of God. That's why I'm so supportive of VIVA 84, your grassroots Hispanic voter education and registration drive, conceived by Dr. del Junco.

Well, America needs the values of our Hispanic citizens. We need those values to be expressed at the polls and through our political system. And I urge you, the members of the Republican National Hispanic Assembly, to run for public office, so that your values will carry even more influence. And nothing would please me more than to see the Republican National Hispanic Assembly become the voice of millions of Hispanics in our country.

As Republicans, we must work in unity toward 1984. We must pull together for the values we treasure. Hispanic Americans know the real meaning of this country. Those who fled oppression especially cherish America's freedom. Those who fled poverty especially cherish America's opportunity. And all of us deeply love this beautiful ideal that is America.

Every American has the right to dream great dreams. I want to keep the dreams of even the poorest, most powerless American great, because he and she are the hope and future and meaning of this nation. Tonight, my friends, I'm asking for your help, your commitment to preserving the American dream, and I have a hunch I know your answer already. Freedom—*siempre* [always]. Opportunity—*ahora* [now]. America—*fuerte* [strong]. [*Applause*] Thank you all.

You know that this is Hispanic Heritage Week. Do you know that at the Pentagon, those great corridors over there are dedicated to various things that they want to keep before America and want to honor and remember, and one of those corridors is dedicated to those who have won that highest honor that our country can give, the Congressional Medal of Honor, and 37 of those who have won that honor since the Civil War are Hispanic Americans?

Friday—I believe I have the day right—Friday, the Pentagon is going to hold a ceremony there in honor of what Hispanic Americans have meant in arms and in pre-serving the peace in America by way of our military. And I have witnessed a little 12-minute film that was made, perhaps, in connection with that.

Now there's something in that film that I don't think you would know—I didn't know it—but it is something to be so proud of. In a little town in Illinois, there's a short street called Second Street in that town. There are 22 homes and families on that street, and those 22 families are all Hispanic Americans. And when war came, 85 sons of those 22 families went off to war for this country. Now, a number of them did not come back. And the people of that little town, for their Hispanic American neighbors, have taken down the street signs that say Second Street, and it now reads Hero Street. I felt that you would want to know that, and I wanted to share it with you.

But it is a proud record that you have. And I'm sure that you know what the creed is and the slogan is of your sons, your brothers, or your fathers and husbands who have gone and who've served this country in time of war, and that is, "The first in and the last out." God bless you all.

Note: The President spoke at 9:21 p.m. in the Regency Ballroom at the Hyatt Regency Crystal City Hotel in Arlington, Va.

In his opening remarks, the President referred to U.S. Ambassador to Mexico John A. Gavin and Tirso del Junco, national chairman of the Republican National Hispanic Assembly.

Statement by Deputy Press Secretary Speakes on the Resignation of Prime Minister Menachem Begin of Israel
September 15, 1983

The resignation of Prime Minister Begin was formalized today. The President wishes Mr. Begin well and states that the Prime Minister has played a unique and central role in the history of his country. His dedication to peace and his efforts on behalf of the people of Israel are truly commendable. His statesmanship and leadership have been a source of inspiration. Prime Minister Begin has shown the courage and determination to make the kind of difficult decisions for peace, as demonstrated at Camp David, decisions which are so necessary to bring stability to this troubled region of the world.

The President will be sending his personal message to the Prime Minister shortly.

Note: Deputy Press Secretary Larry M.

Speakes read the statement during his daily briefing for reporters, which began at 12:33 p.m. in the Briefing Room at the White House.

Remarks at the Welcoming Ceremony for President António dos Santos Ramalho Eanes of Portugal
September 15, 1983

President Reagan. Mr. President, Nancy and I are honored and delighted to welcome you and Mrs. Eanes to the United States. Ever since President George Washington opened formal diplomatic relations between Portugal and the new American Republic, our history has been one of warm friendship. And, Mr. President, I know I speak for our people when I say a friendship as warm and true as ours is more valuable than the richest treasure. I've looked forward to this opportunity to get to know you personally and to discuss relations between our two countries, as well as international matters of mutual interest.

In the 9 years since the revolution of April 25th, 1974, Portugal has made great strides in building a vigorous democracy. Today, the fundamental institutions of a democratic country—an open press, a free economy, and broadly based political parties—are in place and flourishing. We in the United States recognize, Mr. President, that the establishment of democracy in your country met sharp challenges. Portugal's success in surmounting those challenges demonstrates the courage of your leaders and the love of your people for freedom.

And you, yourself, Mr. President, have played a large and crucial role during these past 9 years. You have stated that Portugal must have an open, clear democracy. And as President, you've labored tirelessly to give Portugal just that. Your efforts have earned you not only a place in your nation's history but a chapter in the noble story of freedom throughout the world.

In foreign relations, our two countries share a number of vital interests, and these will receive due attention during our discussions today. I might note in particular, Mr. President, that your nation's experience in Africa gives Portugal a unique and invaluable perspective on current events on that continent, especially in Angola and Mozambique. Both our nations are actively interested in southern Africa, and your country has always been generous in sharing with us insights drawn from your own wide experience. During your stay here, I would like to discuss southern Africa, and I want you to know that the United States not only values the counsel you've given to us on this matter in the past but intends to remain in close consultation with Portugal about it in the future.

Along with our allies, Portugal and the United States share the responsibility of defending the Western World. Our security relationship is critical to the NATO alliance and to both our nations. We in the United States take pride in our military cooperation with your country. Currently our two governments are negotiating a new security cooperation agreement that will broaden and strengthen our collaboration on common defense objectives. The United States fully supports Portugal's efforts to enlarge its role in Western defense. We recognize that as those efforts proceed, Portugal will need to modernize its armed forces, and we're committed to helping you do so.

We take further pride, Mr. President, in the economic cooperation that we have established with Portugal, particularly in recent years. That cooperation expresses the concern of the American people for the well-being of the Portuguese people and this country's unshakeable support for your country's economy and democracy.

Mr. President, 15 days ago an event took place that sickened people throughout the world. The Korean Air Lines massacre reminds us that although we in the West belong to a community of nations that strives to do good, others in the world do not shrink from doing evil. Let us in the Western alliance join together to retrieve meaning from those scores of innocent deaths, and let us rededicate ourselves to the defense of human freedom.

I am confident, Mr. President, that your visit to the United States will strengthen relations between our two countries and reaffirm our commitments to shared goals. I know that my countrymen are eager to give you a warm reception. Nearly half a million Portuguese have come to America as immigrants, and both they and their descendants have earned the gratitude of all Americans by contributing honorably and diligently to the building of our country.

So, once again, Mr. President, Mrs. Eanes, on behalf of the American people, welcome to the United States.

President Eanes. Mr. President, I wish to thank you for the most generous welcome you have extended to us and for the words addressed to me as the representative of the Portuguese people who, as you know, is a loyal and firm ally of the United States of America. The ties uniting Portugal and the United States are indeed strong. The Portuguese maritime adventure, the Atlantic Ocean and the geopolitical concepts that it imposes, the sharing of the same democratic ideals, and the presence in the United States of a large and significant Portuguese community creates real affinities and require from our countries a mutually advantageous approach.

It is with great pleasure that I pay this official visit to your country, Mr. President, certain as I am that it affords an opportunity for an open and frank exchange of views on political and international developments and, in a very special way, on the most positive means of strengthening the relations between our two countries.

It will thus be possible to reaffirm our loyalty to mutual commitments and to reinforce our longstanding cohesion in the defense of our common interests. This is an objective that is imposed on us by the present and by the future, and it is an aim that it is all the more important to attain inasmuch as your actions, Mr. President, have proved, through your courage and

your consistency in the defense of democratic principles, that the values of freedom have, in you, a committed defender.

Portugal is a small country with a long history and vast political experience. With its eight centuries of independence, Portugal has participated in the long and complex course leading to the Europe we know today. But with its active presence in various regions of the world that it discovered and helped to know and to develop, Portugal has gained practical political knowledge that contributes to our unique way of relating to and understanding other peoples. From our history, we draw the conviction that the assertion of freedom of expression and of pluralist democracy, as well as the permanent guarantee of human rights and firmness in the defense of the essential values of our society, cannot be called into question. For us, the search for negotiated solutions to all conflicts, respecting other positions and different cultural patterns, is also natural, provided that those solutions do not run counter to the autonomy and sovereignty of each people and are expressed in terms of a common concern for safeguarding the peace.

In these last few years, the Portuguese overthrew a dictatorship half a century old and managed to overcome new totalitarian attempts through the rigorous fulfillment of the rules of a pluralist democracy, at a time when some believed that such an objective was already impossible to achieve. The Portuguese showed that when democracy is given an opportunity, a serious, committed opportunity, the totalitarianisms that deny freedom are defeated by the only real and consistent way of ensuring victory—the citizens free choice.

But the superiority of democracy must equally be evidenced in its capacity to guide society, adjusting social expectations to what it is really possible to organize. Societies, or some social groups, when faced with the impossibility of attaining material expectations that they consider legitimate or that have been promised to them, may question the validity of global models of political organization and then nourish radical tendencies.

Only a political power that is democratically legitimate, competent, and efficient and able to ensure the balance of interests, a negotiated consensus, and conscious participation will be able successfully to carry out the tasks of economic reorganization.

In this regard, the greatest concern for the present and the immediate future lies in the economic area, both in respect of Portugal and within the framework of the Atlantic alliance and of international relations in general. And further, it is in that context of global democratic concern that it is justified to expect the demonstration of the solidarity of the democratic countries and, first of all, of the United States. In this way, our security will be reinforced, guaranteeing the present and future substance of the Atlantic alliance and illustrating, in many other areas and in practical realities, that all truly democratic forces and pro-

grams may count on effective support.

I am certain, Mr. President, that our exchange of views on these and other subjects, while confirming our alliance, will justify a future of active and committed cooperation. I look forward to meeting with you, Mr. President, and discussing with you means for us to carry out this fruitful cooperation in the future between the United States and Portugal.

Thank you very much.

Note: President Reagan spoke at 10:09 a.m. on the South Lawn of the White House, where President Eanes was accorded a formal welcome with full military honors. President Eanes spoke in Portuguese, and his remarks were translated by an interpreter.

Following the ceremony, the two Presidents met in the Oval Office.

Proclamation 5096—National Housing Week, 1983
September 15, 1983

By the President of the United States of America

A Proclamation

The provision of a home and a suitable living environment for every American family continues to be a national housing goal. Homeownership and decent housing instill pride in our citizens and contribute to the vitality of communities throughout America.

The resurgence of America's housing industry is both a contribution to and a result of our Nation's economic recovery. The substantial increase in housing starts in 1983, by restoring and creating thousands of jobs in housing and related industries, has been a major factor in the reduction of unemployment.

In recognition of our Nation's commitment to housing and homeownership and the role that housing plays in economic recovery, the Congress, by Senate Joint Resolution 98, has authorized and requested the President to issue a proclamation designat-

ing the week of October 2 through October 9, 1983, as "National Housing Week."

Now, Therefore, I, Ronald Reagan, President of the United States of America, do hereby proclaim the week beginning October 2, 1983, as National Housing Week, and call upon the people of the United States and interested groups and organizations to observe this week with appropriate activities and events.

In Witness Whereof, I have hereunto set my hand this fifteenth day of September, in the year of our Lord nineteen hundred and eighty-three, and of the Independence of the United States of America the two hundred and eighth.

RONALD REAGAN

[Filed with the Office of the Federal Register, 11:19 a.m., September 16, 1983]

Note: The President signed the proclamation during a meeting with representatives of the National Association of Home Builders in the Oval Office at the White House.

Statement on the Joint Congressional Resolution Condemning the Soviet Attack on a Korean Civilian Airliner
September 15, 1983

On behalf of all Americans, I salute the House and Senate for their overwhelming, bipartisan support of a resolution condemning the Soviet Union's murder of 269 innocent people aboard KAL 007. This wanton, barbaric act violated the most basic principle of international law and morality—the sanctity of human life.

The Kremlin is on notice: When it comes to responding to its aggression, there are no Republicans or Democrats—only Americans, united and determined to protect our freedom and secure the peace.

I urge the American people to stand by the families whose loved ones were taken from them. And let us appeal to the conscience of the civilized world: The passengers of KAL 007 must never be forgotten; nor must we rest until the world can prevent such a crime against humanity from ever happening again.

Note: For a statement by the President on signing the resolution, see page 1384.

Toasts of President Reagan and President António dos Santos Ramalho Eanes of Portugal at the State Dinner
September 15, 1983

President Reagan. Mr. President, this morning I mentioned the gratitude that all Americans feel for the part that Portuguese immigrants and their descendants have played in building our nation. And tonight, I must tell you that I owe a personal debt of gratitude to Portugal for another reason: It was in 1542 that a Portuguese explorer, Juan Cabrillo, discovered California, the State that is closest to my heart. [*Laughter*]

But, Mr. President, this morning we had a chance to explore issues that concern us both. Our discussion about relations between our two countries, our common support for the NATO alliance, and our close consultations on southern Africa demonstrate how much our nations share a firm commitment to freedom and peace.

Americans esteem those who rise from humble beginnings to positions of national service. You and Mrs. Eanes have probably seen the Lincoln Memorial, the monument to a President who began life in a simple log cabin. In many ways your own life parallels that of Lincoln, for you, too, began life in modest surroundings, then rose in the service of democracy to your nation's highest office.

And, Mr. President, we honor you for that achievement. You once stated your determination that the Portuguese people will have their democracy. Today, the Portuguese people do indeed have their democracy and Portugal, fully committed to political and economic freedom, has taken its rightful place among the democracies of the West. As a full and active participant in the NATO alliance, Portugal has proven its willingness to help defend the Western community of nations and the values for which that community stands.

Portugal has thus earned a reputation as a staunch and reliable ally. The security relationship between our two countries has for many years been one of full cooperation and complete mutual respect. Our negotiations for a formal renewal of the security relationship are going well, and I have every confidence that the new agreement will strengthen the security of the West and enhance Portugal's already vital role in the Atlantic alliance.

We in the United States understand the benefit of alliances between allies, and we intend to help Portugal meet its military and economic needs. This is a simple matter of *amizade*, of friendship. I didn't place the emphasis on the right syllable, but that's as close as I could get. [*Laughter*]

So, in the spirit of that long and warm friendship between our two nations, Mr. President, I propose a toast to you and to the Republic of Portugal.

President Eanes. President Reagan, Mrs. Reagan, distinguished guests:

Gatherings like this among friends and allies always constitute pleasant social occasions to get to know and to understand each other better. They are also political occasions for affirming our common democratic commitment. And this is, in fact, the strongest reason for our easy and natural mutual understanding.

In the past, when Portugal lived under a dictatorial regime, it might have been considered an uncomfortable ally. Kept for decades apart from democratic life, the Portuguese are well aware of the difference that exists between imposed obligations and freely chosen positions.

Today, we can affirm our presence in the Atlantic alliance and assume within it all the necessary positions with the certainty that these positions are supported by the Portuguese people. For that reason, within the framework of the express will of the Portuguese people, we are a responsible ally of the United States with natural and justified expectations.

The deep historical bonds and existing common interests are now strengthened by the common identity of our pluralist democratic political systems. Peoples understand each other more easily and support each other with greater determination when their political institutions have similar modes of action and similar legitimacy.

In our opinion, the world of today clearly confirms that foreign policy involves societies as a whole. For this reason, the harmony of decisions and the continuity of political action have shown themselves to be of such importance in achieving truly consequential objectives in conditions of security, social support, and the furtherance of democracy.

It is only natural for a Portuguese to cite his recent experience of the establishment of a democratic regime in order to underline the importance of internal social conditions for the security and the permanence of external alliances. And it is for this reason that I should like to stress the concern with which I follow the evolution of economic indicators, which point to the need for a joint and determined effort to reorganize this vital sector of contemporary society.

And this is essential for all those who believe in the superiority of the democratic system. In our view, it is also a necessary condition in order to ensure the security not only of each of the democracies but also of the Atlantic alliance itself, and for achieving useful cooperation with various regions of the world.

As a result of the talks that we have been holding, Mr. President, I am further strengthened in my conviction that your statesmanship, sir, is an essential contribution to our mutual commitment to peace and to the strengthening of democratic societies, for these are the necessary conditions for the continuity of political action and for harmony in the decisionmaking process which will lead to a new era of progress and prosperity.

Mr. President, you have the courage to show firmness in the defense of democratic values and determination in guaranteeing their security, and these are qualities which deserve our sincere admiration.

In this context, it is right that our close friendship should be seen together with our position as a responsible ally which has definite expectations. I am sure that by truly expressing our respective interests, based on democratic legitimacy, we are certain to be able to find ways in which our means and our wills can complement each other in such a way that we will lead to mutual commitments and to joint action.

This is the challenge of our day, when the uncertainties of changing times call for the greatest firmness in the affirmation and defense of democratic values.

Ladies and gentlemen, may I invite you in this spirit of responsibility and friendship to join me in a toast to President and Mrs. Reagan, to whom I wish the greatest happiness and through whom I address to all Americans our best wishes for happiness and prosperity.

Note: President Reagan spoke at 9:40 p.m. in the State Dining Room at the White House. President Eanes spoke in Portuguese, *and his remarks were translated by an interpreter.*

Letter to Former Chancellor Bruno Kreisky of Austria on Arms Control and European Public Opinion
September 12, 1983

Dear Mr. Kreisky:

I appreciated your thoughtful letter concerning the impact of arms control questions on public opinion in Europe. Let me assure you that the points you raise are also of great concern to me. It is especially troublesome that NATO's dual-track decision is not clearly understood by young people in Europe, despite our constant efforts and those of our Allies to articulate and clarify it.

During your appearance before the National Press Club in Washington last February you stated clearly and succinctly the principle behind the Alliance decision. NATO did not, as you noted, decide to station new weapons in Europe on its own initiative. NATO's dual-track decision was necessitated by the rapid proliferation of Soviet nuclear forces, especially the intermediate-range SS–20. The introduction of this highly accurate and lethal missile system threatened to break the security link between the United States and our European Allies. This link has served as the underpinning of European stability for nearly four decades.

In response, the NATO Allies approved the deployment of new intermediate range weapons, while emphasizing their common determination to make every possible effort to limit or make these weapons unnecessary via negotiations with the Soviet Union. We also made it clear that if it proved impossible to achieve a satisfactory arms agreement, we would take the steps necessary to protect our security by proceeding with the missile deployments. Let me underline that we set no deadline to the negotiations; only a small number of the total planned missiles will be deployed at the end of this year and we are prepared to continue negotiations

thereafter. Let me stress as well that any missile that is deployed can always be withdrawn, if negotiations are eventually successful.

In this connection, I wish to reiterate that the United States adamantly opposes an arms race. There are certain facts that receive almost no publicity. For example, the United States has fewer nuclear warheads today than we had fifteen years ago. And over the last three years we withdrew unilaterally 1,000 nuclear weapons from Europe. Moreover, if we are forced to deploy INF missiles, we have agreed with our Allies that for every modern warhead introduced, an existing nuclear warhead will be withdrawn.

We are willing, in the interest of arms reductions, to consider every option. I reaffirmed this to Ambassador Nitze prior to his return to Geneva for the current round of negotiations, which we are earnestly pursuing, despite the Korean airline tragedy. But the USSR's approach to negotiating reductions has been disappointing, particularly in that the Soviets have continuously refused to acknowledge the security interest of the nations on their periphery.

As you will recall, Moscow initially refused to negotiate at all. It was NATO's modernization decision that brought the Soviets to the negotiating table. Since commencement of the Geneva talks in 1981 the Soviet Union, however, has refused to move from its insistence on maintaining a missile monopoly despite flexible proposals we tabled aimed at stimulating progress. Our negotiating positions, which have been developed through extremely close cooperation with our NATO Allies, insist only on U.S.–Soviet equality, a principle that the Soviet Union has so far refused to honor.

When the Soviets made plain their opposition to the zero option, we proposed parity at the lowest possible level. The Soviets have said this is equally unacceptable. It is Soviet intransigence that is blocking progress.

While I know that some young people are opposed to the prospect of new weapons deployments, there are much larger numbers who support our determination to maintain the common defense. If, as you say, we will disappoint many of our citizens by beginning deployments on schedule, how many more will be affected if we go back on our joint decision and postpone implementation of the dual-track decision? A delay in our deployments would only encourage the Soviets to believe that NATO's resolve was faltering and that they could stretch our negotiations endlessly without addressing our legitimate security concerns.

I wholeheartedly agree with your point that solidarity among the democracies is our objective, a bond that can only be strong when it is deeply rooted in people's minds. What a striking contrast presented to us by the Soviet example, where the leadership can commit such a horrible deed as the destruction of the KAL civilian airliner and not feel compelled to answer to its people. The Soviet Union openly professes its desire to impose its totalitarian system throughout the world, an objective we can repulse by maintaining our common defense and resolutely promoting our democratic ideals.

I do not believe that the relationship of European youth to their democratic systems is as tenuous as you suggest. In my travels, I have seen strong evidence that young people in both Europe and the United States, and elsewhere respect both the responsibilities as well as the privileges of democracy. Our joint task is to demonstrate to them, through both words and deeds, the meaning and continued validity of Western principles. Securing the common defense is one of the most important of these responsibilities.

I assure you that I am deeply committed to seeking every possibility for peace, in Europe and throughout the world. I know that I can count on you and other leaders to help Europe's young people find their way among the difficult choices facing them today.

With warm personal regards.

Sincerely,

RONALD REAGAN

[His Excellency, Bruno Kreisky, Vienna, Austria]

August 10, 1983

Dear Mr. President,

When I retired from the Austrian government you wrote me a letter in a spirit of friendship which I highly appreciated. This spirit has encouraged me to turn to you with some of my reflections on the current situation about which I am deeply concerned.

Let me make it very clear that I am not interested in publicity. For three months now, I have refused almost all requests for interviews. You will know that in the democratic countries of Europe there are enormous differences in public opinion. But what I consider much more important is that people in these democracies have come to be divided by a deep gap over the armament issue. I am profoundly convinced of your sincere commitment to the idea of peace, but I should like to add that I am equally convinced that Mr. Andropov does not want war. Yet, the experience of a long political career tells me that such events may occur even against the will of leading personalities in powerful states. And I am afraid that something of the kind might happen some day.

The point in question are the Geneva talks for which a deadline has been set. I am not under the delusion that I can make any contribution to these talks, but I should like to urge you not to be guided by prestige thinking. If no results should be reached by the deadline you have set, do prolong the negotiating period for another few months, and reasonable people throughout the world will understand that you seek to get a result. There is no sense in upholding prestige while letting negotiations founder. Please consider that a prolongation may also induce the other party to continue negotiating; and if it is made, it will be by far easier to explain to people who is responsible for a failure to reach a mutually satisfactory solution.

My particular concern is young people's relationship to democracy, because they are the main force in the peace movement. I am quite simply afraid that democracy may be headed for a crisis similar to the one I lived through in my youth, and that such a crisis might generate developments none of us would welcome. Democratic order is a delicate structure which cannot be maintained by rough interference from the state's law and order forces. What is at stake is the relationship of a major part of Europe's young generation to democracy, and I appeal to you, Mister President, to attribute just value to this stake. It will be of decisive and profound importance to the relations between our democracies, the European and the American one.

I belong to those who know what European democracy owes to American democra-

cy. We are fully aware of the role played by the two big American parties. It is entirely up to the American people to choose their leaders, but the crucial point is solidarity between the democracies, which can only be strong, if democracy is deeply rooted in people's minds.

This is why I ask you to reconsider if you really wish to adhere to that deadline. It might involve the danger of turning it into a "dead line" other than the one implied by Anglo-Saxon usage.

I remain, Mister President, with kind regards,

Sincerely yours,

BRUNO KREISKY

[H.E., Mr. Ronald Reagan, President of the United States of America, Washington]

Note: As printed above, this item follows the text of the letters released by the Office of the Press Secretary on September 16.

Proclamation 5095—National Respiratory Therapy Week, 1983
September 15, 1983

By the President of the United States of America

A Proclamation

Chronic lung diseases constitute an important health problem in the United States. They afflict nearly 18 million Americans and cause nearly 70,000 deaths each year, many of which are the direct result of cigarette smoking. Thousands of other persons annually suffer some degree of permanent disability as a result of these disorders. The economic cost of these diseases has been estimated to exceed $16 billion annually.

For some of these diseases the cause is unknown, and for many there is no cure. The timely initiation of appropriate therapy, however, can usually slow their progress, relieve their symptoms, reduce the extent of permanent lung damage and respiratory disability, and avert or delay the onset of life-threatening complications. Although the lung damage already caused by

these diseases cannot be undone, respiratory therapy may help preserve lung function that might otherwise be irretrievably lost and can also help the patient make the most effective use of that which remains.

Respiratory therapy may take many forms, including drugs to dilate open air passages or protect against respiratory infections; respiratory-assistance techniques to maintain adequate blood oxygen levels; and exercise programs to improve the efficiency of breathing and condition respiratory muscles to bear the increased burden imposed on them. Kicking the smoking habit is also important to all respiratory therapy.

In recognition that chronic lung diseases are an important cause of death, ill health, and disability and that respiratory therapy can do much to lessen their effects, the Congress, by Senate Joint Resolution 67, has authorized and requested the President to proclaim the week of September 25, 1983, through October 1, 1983, as "National Respiratory Therapy Week."

Now, Therefore, I, Ronald Reagan, President of the United States of America, do hereby proclaim the week of September 25 through October 1, 1983, as National Respiratory Therapy Week. I call upon all interested organizations and persons to utilize this opportunity to focus public attention on the national health problem posed by chronic lung diseases and to reaffirm our commitment to bring these diseases under effective control.

In Witness Whereof, I have hereunto set my hand this 15th day of September, in the year of our Lord nineteen hundred and eighty-three, and of the Independence of the United States of America the two hundred and eighth.

RONALD REAGAN

[Filed with the Office of the Federal Register, 11:18 a.m., September 16, 1983]

Note: The text of the proclamation was released by the Office of the Press Secretary on September 16.

Proclamation 5097—Leif Erikson Day, 1983
September 15, 1983

By the President of the United States of America

A Proclamation

In the grand tradition of the Nordic seafarers, Leif Erikson's courageous adventures in the North Atlantic represent an enduring symbol of man's resourceful response to the challenge of exploration and discovery. Medieval sagas describe supplies of timber and wild grapes which he brought back to Greenland from North America. His exploits offer inspiration for our continuing efforts to conquer fear of the unknown and explore new worlds.

Erikson, who was charged by King Olaf I to spread religion among settlers in Greenland, also embodies the tradition of Nordic enrichment of the wider western world. That tradition has been memorably dramatized for Americans during the past year by the *Scandinavia Today* program across this country. This splendid program has given people in all parts of the United States an admiring new appreciation of the rich cultural and intellectual heritage brought to this country by Nordic immigrants and the vitality of contemporary life in the Nordic countries.

As a mark of respect for the courage of Leif Erikson and the valuable continuing contribution which the Nordic people have made to life in the United States, the Congress of the United States, by joint resolution approved September 2, 1964 (78 Stat. 849, 36 U.S.C. 169c), authorized the President to proclaim October 9 in each year as Leif Erikson Day.

Now, Therefore, I, Ronald Reagan, President of the United States of America, do hereby proclaim Sunday, October 9, 1983 as Leif Erikson Day. I direct the appropriate Government officials to display the flag of the United States on all Government buildings that day. I also invite the people of the United States to honor the memory of Leif Erikson on that day by holding appropriate exercises and ceremonies in suitable places throughout the land.

In Witness Whereof, I have hereunto set my hand this 15th day of Sept., in the year of our Lord nineteen hundred and eighty-three, and of the Independence of the United States of America the two hundred and eighth.

RONALD REAGAN

[Filed with the Office of the Federal Register, 12:32 p.m., September 16, 1983]

Note: The text of the proclamation was released by the Office of the Press Secretary on September 16.

Proclamation 5098—Thanksgiving Day, 1983
September 15, 1983

*By the President of the United States
of America*

A Proclamation

Since the Pilgrims observed the initial Thanksgiving holiday in 1621, this occasion has served as a singular expression of the transcending spiritual values that played an instrumental part in the founding of our country.

One hundred and twenty years ago, in the midst of a great and terrible civil conflict, President Lincoln formally proclaimed a national day of Thanksgiving to remind those "insensible to the ever watchful providence of Almighty God" of this Nation's bounty and greatness. Several days after the dedication of the Gettysburg battlefield, the United States celebrated its first national Thanksgiving. Every year since then, our Nation has faithfully continued this tradition. The time has come once again to proclaim a day of thanksgiving, an occasion for Americans to express gratitude to their God and their country.

In his remarks at Gettysburg, President Lincoln referred to ours as a Nation "under God." We rejoice in the fact that, while we have maintained separate institutions of church and state over our 200 years of freedom, we have at the same time preserved reverence for spiritual beliefs. Although we are a pluralistic society, the giving of thanks can be a true bond of unity among our people. We can unite in gratitude for our individual freedoms and individual faiths. We can be united in gratitude for our Nation's peace and prosperity when so many in this world have neither.

As was written in the first Thanksgiving Proclamation 120 years ago, "No human counsel hath devised nor hath any mortal hand worked out these great things. They are the gracious gifts of the Most High God." God has blessed America and her people, and it is appropriate we recognize this bounty.

Now, Therefore, I, Ronald Reagan, President of the United States of America, in the spirit of the Pilgrims, President Lincoln, and all succeeding Presidents, do hereby proclaim Thursday, November 24, 1983, as a National Day of Thanksgiving, and I call upon Americans to affirm this day of thanks by their prayers and their gratitude for the many blessings upon this land and its people.

In Witness Whereof, I have hereunto set my hand this 15th day of Sept., in the year of our Lord nineteen hundred and eighty-three, and of the Independence of the United States of America the two hundred and eighth.

RONALD REAGAN

[*Filed with the Office of the Federal Register, 12:33 p.m., September 16, 1983*]

Note: The text of the proclamation was released by the Office of the Press Secretary on September 16.

The Office of the Press Secretary stated that the word "first" should be deleted from the text where it appears in the second and fourth paragraphs.

Remarks at a White House Ceremony Honoring Hispanic Americans in the United States Armed Forces
September 16, 1983

Thank you. I want to extend to all of you a warm welcome. Many ceremonies are held here in the Rose Garden, all of them for important purposes, all of them—well, I don't mind telling you, never mind that, this moment is special for me, and I think for the American people.

During the Korean war, James Michener wrote about the lonely and sometimes thankless life endured by those who wear their country's uniform. In the final scene of his novel, "The Bridges at Toko Ri," an admiral stands on the darkened bridge of his carrier, watching pilots take off on missions from which he knows some may never return. And as he waits, he asks in the silent darkness, "Where did we get such men?" Almost a generation later, I asked that same question when our POW's were returned from savage captivity in Vietnam: "Where did we find such men?"

Today, as so many proud men and women continue to serve their country in the cause of freedom, millions of Americans wonder with me in awe and gratitude, "How are we so lucky to have them, where did we find them?" Well, the truth is, of course, we find these young Americans where we've always found them—in our villages and towns, on our city streets, in our shops, and on our farms. And always, we've found them when you speak of Americans, any Americans, you always keep in mind, well, the bloodlines of all Americans go back to all the nations of the world, to every corner of the world. And so we have found them. We've found them very proudly among the ranks of Americans of Hispanic descent, and I mention this because this is Hispanic Heritage Week.

A word seems to be said on this point. We're here today in the presence of authentic heroes. Those of you before me have achieved in life, not as a result—we're going to have to do something about that [1]—not as result of any special treatment or artificial quotas or political favoritism, but as talented individuals on your own. Your acts of personal sacrifice and valor, too numerous to relate, are part of the thrilling story of Hispanic heroes in defense of freedom, a story so powerful and moving that it sometimes defies belief.

Since the Civil War, Americans of Hispanic descent have been winning Medals of Honor. To this date, there have been 36

---

[1] *The President was referring to the noise of an airplane flying overhead.*

such winners, an incredible number, all out of proportion to the percentage of the Hispanic population in our country. The stories of these Americans, the stories of many of you here today who were wounded, decorated, and promoted in your country's service, account for some of the most astonishing acts of valor and personal sacrifice in the history of our nation's armed services.

You know, I must tell you I saw a wonderful film recently—believe it or not, the story of a street, a street in an Hispanic neighborhood, what used to be called Second Street in Silvis, Illinois. At the end of it is a monument, the end of that street, to eight heroes from this street who gave their lives in the defense of America. In fact, from 22 families on this block, 84 men served in World War II, Korea, and Vietnam. In World War II and Korea, 57 came from that street. The two Sandoval families sent 13—6 from one family, 7 from the other, and 3 of the Sandoval sons never came back. I think you will agree with one man in the film who says they so willingly defended America because it was for them, as for all of us, a place of opportunity. I think you will agree with his words when he said, "I don't think there's any more to prove than has been proven on this street." And perhaps you will understand why the name on Second Street in Silvis, Illinois, was changed a few years back. The new name is Hero Street.

But Hero Street is only one Hispanic contribution to America's defense. Indeed, "first in, last to leave" seems to be the watchwords of Hispanic American heroism. One of the units to fight the first major battle of the Civil War was Hispanic, and one of the last units of the Confederacy to fight on after Lee's surrender was Hispanic. Hispanic members of the New Mexico National Guard were among the original cadre of Teddy Roosevelt's Rough Riders. Among your number have been the first American flier to be shot down over Vietnam; the first American to escape from captivity in Vietnam and make his way to freedom through Communist-infested territory; the last marine to leave Saigon, a young sergeant who had also fought in the early years of the Vietnam war; and, of course, the last

American to have received the Medal of Honor for conspicuous gallantry. And it's with a special sense of gratitude that we remember the supreme sacrifice of Staff Sergeant Alexander Ortega and Corporal Pedro Valle, gallant marines who recently gave their lives in the service of peace in Beirut, Lebanon.

Hispanic Americans continue to excel in the Department of Defense mission, which is to preserve peace through strength. We have with us today bright and dedicated young men and women from our service academies, our enlisted ranks, and our officers corps. We also find more and more Hispanic general and flag officers, many of whom are here today, providing strong and sensitive leadership in promoting peace within this hemisphere and around the world. Our fine Hispanic women, military women, are equal partners with their male colleagues on the defense team. They're competing successfully in many nontraditional career fields and are advancing rapidly. And the Hispanic heritage of strong family values has particularly enriched our American military community.

Here I would like to pay special tribute to our military spouses and family members whose sacrifices on behalf of this great nation too frequently go unnoticed. America owes all of them and all of you who are here a special thank you.

This record of honor is one that Americans of Hispanic descent take great pride in, and it's part of the proud heritage they pass on to their children. And by the way, in case you haven't heard, at our request the United States Postal Service will be issuing a commemorative stamp in honor of this enormous and awe-inspiring record. And this is a replica of what that stamp will look like. And if you can't read the printing, and if you will forgive my probably incorrect pronunciation, it says, *"Una herencia de valor* [A heritage of valor]!"

But let me assure you this record of valor, all Americans take pride in. And that is the real importance of this ceremony. We celebrate this day just as we've celebrated the events of Hispanic Heritage Week. We pay tribute to Americans of Hispanic descent, but especially to the culture and the values that bred in men and women like your-

selves a respect for family, work, neighborhood, and religion, a belief in duty to God and country and fellow man. More than ever, today America needs these values, these ideals. More than ever, America needs your example. And so we honor you today not just because of our pride in what you've achieved, but because you live by the values and beliefs that account for America's greatness and that keep her strong and free.

We're just now emerging from a time when many people here in Washington thought the business of governing meant only assembling coalitions of special interests, groups that could vote or exert pressure to push government in a certain direction. Well, yes, government must recognize the legitimate rights and concerns of individual Americans and social, ethnic, or racial groups they belong to. But I've always believed that it is ideas, it is hope and idealism that count most with the American people.

When they speak out on the issues of the day, when they go to the polls, most Americans, especially Hispanic Americans, know how high the stakes are. They know their children's future is at stake. They know the future of freedom depends not on "what's in it for me?" but on the ethic of what's good for the country, what will serve and protect freedom, and they pass this precious gift on to future generations. You've dedicated your lives to that proposition. You stand ready to defend America today just as valiantly as you have in the past. You do so because America and all she stands for means more to you than self-interest or personal gain ever could. The calculus of the self-seeking is not for you; duty, honor, and country are.

"A man wouldn't sell his life to you," William Manchester wrote of his days as a marine in the South Pacific. "He wouldn't sell his life to you, but he will give it to you for a piece of colored ribbon." He meant simply that shared values and the hope of freedom have always meant more to the American people, and especially to Americans of Hispanic descent, than private gain or personal interest.

As I said to the G.I. Forum a few weeks

ago in Texas, Americans of Hispanic descent have always understood this better than most. You've known that the ideals, the faith, and the dreams of a people mean far more than a thousand promises of an easy life or a comfortable existence. You've reminded us with the example of your lives that independence, honor, and devotion to country and family are more than just words. "There are those I know," the poet Archibald MacLeish once said, "who will reply that the liberation of humanity, the freedom of man and mind is nothing but a dream." They're right. It is. It is the American dream.

Well, it's your dream and our dream, one that you've given of your lives and talents to protect and preserve. And so today our purpose is simple. On behalf of the American people, I want simply to say something that should have been said a long time ago. I want to thank Americans of Hispanic descent. Thank you for accounting for so

much of our economic and social progress as a nation, for enriching our national culture and heritage, but most of all, for upholding the values that account for America's greatness. That's what made us a beacon to the oppressed and the poor of the world. There's no better symbol of those values and that greatness than those of you here in uniform today. We honor you, we thank you. We want you to know that as you continue to serve your country, our thoughts and our grateful prayers are with you.

God bless you all.

Note: The President spoke at 9:52 a.m. in the Rose Garden at the White House.

Prior to the President's remarks, Secretary of Defense Caspar W. Weinberger addressed the audience and introduced Gen. Richard E. Cavazos, FORSCOM (United States Armed Forces Command), the first Hispanic 4-star general in the U.S. Army.

Nomination of Richard Thomas Montoya To Be an Assistant Secretary of the Interior
September 16, 1983

The President today announced his intention to nominate Richard Thomas Montoya to be an Assistant Secretary of the Department of the Interior (Territorial and International Affairs). He would succeed Pedro A. Sanjuan.

Mr. Montoya is currently serving as Deputy Assistant Secretary at the Department of the Interior for Territorial and International Affairs. Previously he was director of the Governor of Texas Office of

Regional Development in 1979–1983; Deputy Secretarial Representative at the U.S. Department of Commerce in 1976–1979; and Assistant Regional Director for the U.S. Small Business Administration in Dallas, Tex., in 1971–1976.

He attended Southern Methodist University and New Mexico State University. He is married and currently resides in Arlington, Va. He was born May 5, 1947, in Las Cruces, N. Mex.

Statement by Deputy Press Secretary Speakes on the Soviet Attack on a Korean Civilian Airliner
September 16, 1983

In their recent statements on the Korean Air Lines tragedy, senior Soviet officials

have shocked the world by their assertion of the right to shoot down innocent civilian airliners which accidently intrude into Soviet airspace. Despite the murder of 269 innocent victims, the Soviet Union is not prepared to recognize its obligations under international law to refrain from the use of force against civilian airliners. World opinion is united in its determination that this awful tragedy must not be repeated. As a contribution to the achievement of this objective, the President has determined that the United States is prepared to make available to civilian aircraft the facilities of its Global Positioning System when it becomes operational in 1988. This system will provide civilian airliners three-dimensional positional information.

The United States delegation to the ICAO [International Civil Aviation Organization] Council meeting in Montreal, under the leadership of FAA Administrator J. Lynn Helms, is urgently examining all measures which the international community can adopt to enhance the security of international civil aviation. The United States is prepared to do all it can for this noble aim. We hope that the Soviet Union will at last recognize its responsibilities and join the rest of the world in this effort.

Note: Deputy Press Secretary Larry M. Speakes read the statement during his daily briefing for reporters, which began at 12:30 p.m. in the Briefing Room at the White House.

Radio Address to the Nation on the Soviet Attack on a Korean Civilian Airliner
September 17, 1983

My fellow Americans:

Five days after the Soviets shot down KAL 007, I went on nationwide television to urge that all of us in the civilized world make sure such an atrocity never happens again. And I pledged to you that night, we would cooperate with other countries to improve the safety of civil aviation, asking them to join us in not accepting the Soviet airline Aeroflot as a normal member of the international civil air community—not, that is, until the Soviets satisfy the cries of humanity for justice.

On Thursday, an American delegation lead by Lynn Helms, who heads up the Federal Aviation Administration, went to Montreal for an emergency session of the ICAO, the International Civil Aviation Organization. This meeting was called at the request of the Republic of Korea, and 32 countries are attending. The group immediately went to work on a resolution to call for an international investigation, to deplore this atrocity, and to review procedures to prevent civilian aircraft from ever being attacked again. Yesterday, the resolution passed by an overwhelming majority.

The Soviets have not budged. Apparently, their contempt for the truth and for the opinion of the civilized world is equaled only by their disdain for helpless people like the passengers aboard KAL Flight 007. They reserve for themselves the right to live by one set of rules, insisting everyone else live by another. They're supremely confident their crime and coverup will soon be forgotten, and we'll all be back to business as usual. Well, I believe they're badly mistaken. This case is far from closed. The Soviets aggression has provoked a fundamental and long overdue reappraisal in countries all over the globe. The Soviet Union stands virtually alone against the world.

Good and decent people everywhere are coming together, and the world's outrage has not diminished. Repercussions such as that emergency ICAO meeting in Montreal are just beginning. Take the example of aviation. Canada suspended Aeroflot landing rights for 60 days and froze the signing of an agreement for Aeroflot refueling at Gander. The Canadian Air Traffic Controllers Association has withdrawn from a long-standing exchange agreement with its Soviet counterpart organization.

The IFALPA—that's the International Federation of Air Line Pilot Associations—declared the U.S.S.R. an offending state. It called for its member associations to ban all flights to Moscow for 60 days, and it called on related international unions and professional associations to take similar actions. It demanded Soviet guarantees that similar attacks will never be repeated, and what is most encouraging because it underscores this reappraisal I mentioned, the IFALPA promised to consider further actions against the Soviets if no such guarantees are given.

Scandinavian Airlines has suspended flights within Soviet airspace for 60 days. Norwegian pilots and air traffic controllers are boycotting all air service between Norway and the Soviet Union. With the exception of France, Greece, and Turkey, all the NATO nations and Japan have temporarily suspended civil air traffic between their respective nations and the Soviet Union. Even neutral Switzerland and pilots in Finland have joined the general boycott. Australia and New Zealand are also taking strong measures in the area of civil aviation.

In the United Nations, the Security Council voted a resolution deploring the Soviet attack, forcing the Soviets to cast their veto to block its adoption. Here, too, we're seeing evidence that a fundamental reappraisal is in the works. Most countries rebuke the Kremlin. Only a few of Moscow's dependables stood up for its defense. Nonaligned nations are looking to the United States for leadership. I've instructed our Ambassador to the U.N., Jeane Kirkpat-

rick, to sit down with them to seek out new areas of cooperation.

In the Congress, both the House and the Senate mobilized overwhelming bipartisan support for a resolution of condemnation. Some would have us lash out in another way by canceling our grain shipments. But that would punish American farmers, not the Soviet aggressors. The most effective, lasting action against their violence and intimidation—and it's the one action the Soviets would welcome least—will be to go forward with America's program to remain strong.

I'm confident that if enough of you at the grassroots make your voices heard, we can and will do just that. We may not be able to change the Soviets ways, but we can change our attitude toward them. We can stop pretending they share the same dreams and aspirations we do. We can start preparing ourselves for what John F. Kennedy called a long twilight struggle. It won't be quick, it won't make headlines, and it sure won't be easy, but it's what we must do to keep America strong, keep her free, and yes, preserve the peace for our children and for our children's children.

This is the most enduring lesson of the Korean Air Lines massacre. If we grasp it, then history will say this tragedy was a major turning point, because this time the world did not go back to business as usual.

Until next week, thanks for listening, and God bless you.

Note: The President spoke at 12:06 p.m. from Camp David, Md.

Remarks at a White House Ceremony Marking the 10th Anniversary of Executive Women in Government
September 19, 1983

Welcome to the White House.

Ten years ago, during the Nixon administration, Executive Women in Government was organized to bring more women into positions of authority and influence within the Federal Government. And under your first chairman, Air Force General Jeanne

Holm, your organization set out to encourage talented women to enter government and to ensure that women had the opportunity to play significant roles once they got involved.

You started out with 38 members, and today you have 246. I know you're a wonderfully diverse group—scientists, judges, lawyers, managers. You've been activists within the system, serving as a point of contact for professional women and a catalyst for change during four administrations. Now, I don't want to make this a partisan event, but three of the four were Republican administrations. [*Laughter*]

Over the last few months much has been said about women in general and in our administration. I just wish that those who are doing all the talking would focus more on the many top-notch women in the administration instead of talking in generalities. I'm exceptionally proud of the women who are making great contributions to achieving our goals.

Women are in top policy and decision-making positions throughout the executive branch, yet they are by-and-large ignored by those who are claiming our record is not up to par. Well, we've appointed more women to significant positions than any other administration.

We appointed the first woman to the Supreme Court, and I can tell you that there have been a few decisions when I was mighty happy she was there. [*Laughter*] And for the first time in history, we've got three women of Cabinet rank—Secretaries Dole and Heckler and Ambassador Kirkpatrick. I'd just like to add something important here. During this time of tension over the Soviet massacre of 269 airline passengers, Jeane Kirkpatrick has been a tower of strength and dignity, and she's doing a great service to her country.

But these female stars in our administration receive far less personal attention from the public than they deserve. And other women within the administration, individuals who are making decisions that are affecting the lives of tens of millions of people, are getting too little public recognition.

Being intimately involved in government, we know, but how many other citizens are aware, for example, of the tough job Mary Jarratt is doing as Assistant Secretary of Agriculture for Food and Consumer Services? She has responsibility for programs totaling $19 billion.

Or how about Arlene Triplett, the Assistant Secretary for Administration at the Department of Commerce? She oversees 35,000 employees and a budget of about $2 billion. And then there is Dorcas Hardy, Assistant Secretary for Human Development Services at HHS. She's been instrumental in improving services to some of our nation's most vulnerable citizens. And then there is your own chairman, Nancy Harvey Steorts, who heads up the Consumer Product Safety Commission, which has the responsibility of ensuring the safety of some 15,000 generic consumer products.

All of these and so many others that I couldn't possibly take the time to name are in positions of authority not because of some artificial quota, but because they're capable, committed, and responsible individuals.

Now, most of them are in positions that traditionally have nothing to do with their sex, but instead are concerned only with their expertise and skill. You know, it makes me think of a little incident that happened. There was an accident one day, victim lying there, bystanders had gathered around. There was a woman bending over him trying to help, and a man came elbowing his way through the bystanders, shoved the woman aside, and said, "Let me at him. I have first aid training." And she stepped aside, and he knelt down and started doing the prescribed things in his training, and at one point she touched him on the shoulder and said, "When you get to that part about calling the doctor, I'm right here." [*Laughter*]

But we, all of us in this administration, came here to strengthen America. We're part of one team and, frankly, it bothers me that talented women like yourselves get so little public recognition.

I want to encourage all of you to speak out with a louder voice about the job you are doing, and I'm going to suggest at the next Cabinet meeting that this encouragement be passed on throughout the executive branch.

Let me just diverge a moment to make a short announcement on another subject, because it affects that goal I spoke about. Strengthening America begins with strengthening American families by providing new opportunity. We've been working hard to do this from the outset of this administration. Reducing tax rates, estate taxes, and the marriage penalty, increasing the child care credit, and bringing down inflation and interest rates are all important steps of progress. But there is another side, a darker side to family life in America. The problem of family violence, the terrible cost of this violence in emotional grief, shattered lives, and more crimes in the future must be squarely faced. This year the President's Task Force on Victims of Crime recommended, in particular, the creation of a task force to study the problem of violence in families. And today, we're announcing the creation of the Attorney General's Task Force on Family Violence. This task force will be asked to make specific recommendations, and it will be chaired by William Hart, the chief of police of Detroit, Michigan.

All of you have much of which to be proud. I'm tempted to go through a list of accomplishments, but it's sufficient to say that all Americans are better off because of what the women and the men of this administration have done, aided by capable and dedicated career staff, in these last 2½ years. I'm happy to have had this opportunity to thank you for the role that you're playing and to congratulate you on the occasion of your 10th anniversary.

So, I'm not going to end without saying keep up the good work, and God bless you all. Thank you.

Note: The President spoke at 11:34 a.m. in the Rose Garden at the White House.

Appointment of Richard A. Gallun as a Member of the Advisory Committee on the Arts of the John F. Kennedy Center for the Performing Arts
September 19, 1983

The President today announced his intention to appoint Richard A. Gallun to be a member of the Advisory Committee on the Arts of the John F. Kennedy Center for the Performing Arts. This is an initial appointment.

Since 1978 Mr. Gallun has been serving as chairman of the board of Electri-Wire Corp. in Waukesha, Wis. He served as president of Electri-Wire Corp. in 1970–1978.

Mr. Gallun serves as president of the Ballet Foundation of Milwaukee, Inc., and of the Zoological Society of Milwaukee.

He graduated from Williams College (B.A., 1957) and Harvard Graduate School of Business Administration (M.B.A., 1964). He is married, has three children, and resides in Fox Point, Wis. He was born December 28, 1935, in Milwaukee, Wis.

Proclamation 5099—National Historically Black Colleges Day, 1983
September 19, 1983

By the President of the United States of America

A Proclamation

The one hundred and three historically black colleges and universities in the United States have contributed substantially to the growth and enrichment of the Nation. These institutions have a rich heritage and tradition of providing the challenging higher education so essential to an individual's full participation in our complex technological society.

Historically black colleges and universities bestow forty percent of all degrees earned by black students. They have awarded degrees to eighty-five percent of the country's black lawyers and doctors and fifty percent of its black business executives. Throughout the years, these institutions have helped many underprivileged students to attain their full potential through higher education.

In recognition of the fact that the achievements and goals of these historically black colleges and universities deserve national attention, the Congress of the United States, by Senate Joint Resolution 85, has designated and requested the President to proclaim September 26, 1983, as National Historically Black Colleges Day.

Now, Therefore, I, Ronald Reagan, President of the United States of America, do hereby proclaim September 26, 1983, as National Historically Black Colleges Day. I ask all Americans to observe this day with appropriate ceremonies and activities to express our respect and appreciation for the outstanding academic and social accomplishments of the Nation's black institutions of higher learning.

In Witness Whereof, I have hereunto set my hand this 19th day of September, in the year of our Lord nineteen hundred and eighty-three, and of the Independence of the United States of America the two hundred and eighth.

RONALD REAGAN

[*Filed with the Office of the Federal Register, 11:01 a.m., September 20, 1983*]

Proclamation 5100—Veterans Day, 1983
September 19, 1983

By the President of the United States of America

A Proclamation

None among us deserve more respect than the millions of patriotic men and women who have worn our Nation's uniform to preserve America's freedom and world peace.

Our Armed Forces veterans have earned a special day in which you and I may focus on their heroic accomplishments. For their unselfish devotion to duty, Congress established Veterans Day as a national expression of gratitude. On this historic occasion, our hearts and minds should be with our living veterans and their deceased comrades who have contributed so much to the defense of our country's ideals.

From Valley Forge when our Nation was in its infancy, to the Vietnam conflict where our men and women in uniform served and died for the human rights of others, through war and peace, these valiant citizens have answered the call to service with honor and dignity. They are indeed worthy of a formal tribute from a grateful Nation. Special consideration is due to those veterans who are sick and disabled. There is no better tangible expression of our affection than by remembering to visit them at home or in our hospitals.

In order that we pay meaningful tribute to those men and women who proudly served in our Armed Forces, Congress has provided (5 U.S.C. 6103(a)) that November 11 shall be set aside each year as a legal public holiday to honor America's veterans.

Now, Therefore, I, Ronald Reagan, President of the United States of America, do hereby proclaim Friday, November 11, 1983, as Veterans Day. In recognition of their valor, I urge all Americans to join with me in a fitting salute to our veterans, and I call upon Federal, State, and local government officials as well as private citizens to mark Veterans Day by displaying the flag of the United States, and I ask those Government officials to support fully and personally its observance by appropriate ceremonies throughout the country.

In Witness Whereof, I have hereunto set my hand this 19th day of Sept., in the year of our Lord nineteen hundred and eighty-three, and of the Independence of the

United States of America the two hundred and eighth.

RONALD REAGAN

[*Filed with the Office of the Federal Register, 11:21 a.m., September 20, 1983*]

Letter Accepting the Resignation of John J. Louis, Jr., as United States Ambassador to the United Kingdom
September 19, 1983

Dear John:

It is with special gratitude for your contributions to the conduct of foreign policy that I accept with regret your resignation as Ambassador to the United Kingdom of Great Britain and Northern Ireland, effective November 7, 1983.

The remarkable dedication and purpose with which you have carried out your demanding duties as Ambassador have added singular luster to your distinguished career. The alliance today between the United States and Great Britain is adamantine and for that you are in no small part responsible. I know that you leave diplomatic service with the true respect and admiration of your colleagues at Embassy London and in the Foreign Office. To that I may only add my warm personal thanks for a job well done.

Nancy and I extend to you and Jo our heartfelt wishes for prosperity and happiness in the future. We look forward to your continued friendship in the years to come.

Sincerely,

RONALD REAGAN

———

Dear Mr. President:

It is with deep regret that I tender my resignation as United States Ambassador to the Court of St. James effective November 7, 1983. I shall be returning to the United States, and to the business affairs and civic, educational and charitable work which had been my life until you honored me with this appointment in 1981.

I leave with a great sense of accomplishment. Anglo-American relations are excellent. Britain's support for alliance policies, and the effectiveness of our consultations, have allowed the United States and the United Kingdom to work together with renewed strength and enthusiasm for creative diplomacy. There is a refreshing candor in both official and personal contacts with Mrs. Thatcher's government. Our two countries have been effective partners in numerous initiatives all over the world, and our successes together have been important contributions to the search for peace and security. I am very proud of these achievements.

Mr. President, you have paid me the highest compliment, and the highest honor by appointing me as your personal representative at this post. My responsibilities here have been the most demanding, the most thrilling, and the most satisfying of my life; and I shall remain forever grateful to you for your trust.

Sincerely,

JOHN J. LOUIS, JR.,
Ambassador

Note: As printed above, this item follows the text of the White House press release.

Nomination of Joan M. Clark To Be an Assistant Secretary of State
September 20, 1983

The President today announced his intention to nominate Joan M. Clark, a career member of the Senior Foreign Service, Class of Career Minister, to be Assistant

Secretary of State for Consular Affairs. She would succeed Diego C. Asencio.

Since 1981 she has been serving as Director General of the Foreign Service and Director of Personnel. Miss Clark served as Ambassador to the Republic of Malta in 1979–1981. Previously she held various posts at the Department of State, including Director of the Office of Management Operations in 1977–1979; Executive Director of the Bureau of European Affairs in 1972–1977; Deputy Executive Director of the Bureau of European Affairs in 1971–1972; and personnel officer and administrative officer in the Bureau of Inter-American Affairs in 1969–1971.

Her foreign language is French. She was born March 27, 1922, in Ridgefield Park, N.J.

Nomination of Alfred L. Atherton, Jr., To Be Director General of the Foreign Service
September 20, 1983

The President today announced his intention to nominate Alfred L. Atherton, Jr., a career member of the Senior Foreign Service, to be Director General of the Foreign Service, Department of State. He would succeed Joan M. Clark.

Since 1979 Mr. Atherton has been serving as Ambassador to Egypt. Previously he was Ambassador at Large (Near Eastern Affairs) in 1978–1979. He served as Assistant Secretary of State for Near Eastern and South Asian Affairs (1974–1978) and Deputy Assistant Secretary of State for Near Eastern and South Asian Affairs (1969–1974). He served in various positions at the Department of State, including country director for Israel and Arab-Israeli affairs in 1967–1969; country director for Lebanon, Jordan, Syria, and Iraq in 1966–1967; and Director of the Office of Near Eastern Affairs in 1965–1966. He was economic officer in Calcutta in 1962–1965.

Mr. Atherton graduated from Harvard University (B.S., 1944; M.A., 1947). His foreign language is German. He was born November 22, 1921, in Pittsburgh, Pa.

Nomination of Charles H. Price II To Be United States Ambassador to the United Kingdom
September 20, 1983

The President today announced his intention to nominate Charles H. Price II, of Missouri, to be Ambassador to the United Kingdom of Great Britain and Northern Ireland. He would succeed John J. Louis, Jr.

Mr. Price served in the United States Air Force in 1953–1955. In 1955–1981 he was with the Price Candy Co. and also served as president or chairman of the board of American Mortgage Co., Price Bank Building Corp., American Bancorporation, Inc., Linwood Securities Co., and Twenty-one Central United, Inc. In 1969–1981 he was vice chairman, then chairman of the board, of the American Bank and Trust Co. of Kansas City, Mo. In 1976–1981 he was chairman of several businesses in Boise, Idaho. Since 1981 he has been Ambassador to Belgium.

Mr. Price has received the alumni award from the University of Missouri School of Business and Public Administration; award of appreciation, Midwest Research Institute; and the outstanding achievement award, University of Missouri-Kansas City, Perform-

ing Arts Center.
He attended the University of Missouri.

He was born April 1, 1931, in Kansas City, Mo.

Nomination of Reginald Bartholomew To Be United States Ambassador to Lebanon
September 20, 1983

The President today announced his intention to nominate Reginald Bartholomew, of Virginia, a career member of the Senior Foreign Service, Class of Minister-Counselor, to be Ambassador to the Republic of Lebanon. He would succeed Robert Sherwood Dillon.

Mr. Bartholomew was an instructor in social science at the University of Chicago (1961–1964) and in government at Wesleyan University in 1964–1968. He was with the Department of Defense in Washington, D.C., as Assistant Deputy Director of Policy Plans for National Security Council Affairs (1968–1972) and Director of Policy Plans for National Security Council Affairs and Task Force on Mutual and Balanced Force Reductions (1973–1974). He first served at the Department of State in 1974 as Deputy Director of the Policy Planning Staff. He was Deputy Director (1979) and Director (1979–1981) of the Bureau of Politico-Military Affairs. In 1977–1979 he was on detail to the National Security Council at the White House. He was Special Cyprus Coordinator, Bureau of International Organization Affairs, in the Department of State in 1981–1982. Since 1982 he has been United States Special Negotiator for United States-Greek Defense and Economic Cooperation (base) Negotiations in the Department. He was accorded the personal rank of Ambassador on December 17, 1982.

Mr. Bartholomew graduated from Dartmouth College (B.A., 1958) and the University of Chicago (M.A., 1960). His foreign languages are French, German, and Italian. He was born February 17, 1936, in Portland, Maine.

Nomination of Walter Leon Cutler To Be United States Ambassador to Saudi Arabia
September 20, 1983

The President today announced his intention to nominate Walter Leon Cutler, of Maryland, a career member of the Senior Foreign Service, Class of Career Minister, to be Ambassador to the Kingdom of Saudi Arabia. He would succeed Richard W. Murphy.

Mr. Cutler served in the United States Army in 1954–1956, prior to entering the Foreign Service. He was consular officer in Yaounde in 1957–1959. In the Department he was foreign affairs officer in the Executive Secretariat (1959–1961) and staff assistant to the Secretary of State (1961–1962). He was political officer in Algiers (1962– 1965), principal officer in Tabriz (1965–1967), political officer in Seoul (1967–1969) and in Saigon (1969–1971). In 1971–1973 he was international relations officer in the Department. He attended the executive seminar in national and international affairs at the Foreign Service Institute in 1973–1974. He was country director of Central African affairs in the Department in 1974–1975 and served as Ambassador to the Republic of Zaire in 1975–1979. He was Deputy Assistant Secretary of State for Congressional Relations in 1979–1981. Since 1981 he has been Ambassador to the Republic of Tunisia.

Mr. Cutler graduated from Wesleyan University (B.A., 1953) and the Fletcher School of Law and Diplomacy (M.A., 1954). His foreign language is French. He was born November 25, 1931, in Boston, Mass.

Nomination of Geoffrey Swaebe To Be United States Ambassador to Belgium
September 20, 1983

The President today announced his intention to nominate Geoffrey Swaebe, of California, to be Ambassador to Belgium. He would succeed Charles H. Price II.

Mr. Swaebe was executive officer with Florsheim Shoe Co. in Chicago, Ill., in 1936–1938 and divisional merchandise manager with Thalhimers Department Store in Richmond, Va., in 1938–1948. He was general merchandise manager with Pizitz Department Store in Birmingham, Ala., in 1948–1950; general manager, director, and vice president of the Hecht Co. in Baltimore, Md., in 1950–1962; and chairman of the board and president of the May Department Stores of California in Los Angeles, Calif., in 1962–1972. In 1972–1981 he was self-employed as a business and management consultant in Los Angeles. Since 1981 he has been Representative of the United States of America to the European Office of the United Nations, with the rank of Ambassador.

He served in the United States Army in 1942–1946. He was a commissioner of the Community Redevelopment Agency of the city of Los Angeles and a member of the Mayor's Advisory Committee. He attended Boston University. He was born March 23, 1911, in London, England, and became naturalized in 1942.

Nomination of Frank V. Ortiz, Jr., To Be United States Ambassador to Argentina
September 20, 1983

The President today announced his intention to nominate Frank V. Ortiz, Jr., of New Mexico, a career member of the Senior Foreign Service, Class of Minister-Counselor, to be Ambassador to Argentina. He would succeed Harry W. Shlaudeman.

Mr. Ortiz was liaison officer at the United States Senate in 1943–1944 and served in the United States Army Air Force in 1944–1946. In 1951–1953 he was assistant officer in charge of Egypt and Anglo-Egyptian Sudan affairs in the Department of State. He was economic officer in Addis Ababa (1953–1955) and political officer in Mexico City (1955–1957). In the Department he was special assistant to the operations coordinator in the Office of the Under Secretary (1957–1960) and special assistant to the Assistant Secretary of State for Inter-American Affairs (1960–1961). He was special assistant to the Ambassador in Mexico City in 1961–1963. In 1963–1966 he was country desk officer for Spain in the Department. He attended the National War College in 1966–1967. He served as counselor for political affairs in Lima (1967–1970) and Deputy Chief of Mission (Chargé d'Affaires, 1973) in Montevideo (1970–1973).

At the Department of State he was country director of Argentina, Uruguay, and Paraguay (1973–1975) and Deputy Executive Secretary (1975–1977). In 1977–1979 he was Ambassador to Barbados and to Grenada, and United States Special Representative to Dominica and St. Lucia, and to the Associated States. He was Ambassador to

Guatemala (1979–1980) and political adviser to the commander in chief of the United States Southern Command in Panama (1980–1981). Since 1981 he has been Ambassador to Peru.

Mr. Ortiz graduated from Georgetown University (B.S., 1950) and George Washington University (M.S., 1967). He attended the University of Madrid (1950) and the University of Beirut (1952). His foreign languages are Spanish, French, and Italian. He was born March 14, 1926, in Santa Fe, N. Mex.

Nomination of Gerald E. Thomas To Be United States Ambassador to Kenya
September 20, 1983

The President today announced his intention to nominate Gerald E. Thomas, of California, to be Ambassador to the Republic of Kenya. He would succeed William C. Harrop.

In 1951 Mr. Thomas began his career with the United States Navy, serving on the U.S.S. *Newman K. Perry* (1951–1954) and the U.S.S. *Worcester* (1954–1956). He attended naval school in 1956–1957 and was assigned to the National Security Agency in 1957–1960. He was executive officer on the U.S.S. *Lowe* (1960–1962), assistant head of the college training programs section in the Bureau of Naval Personnel in 1963–1965, and attended the Naval War College in 1965–1966. In 1966–1967 he was commanding officer on the U.S.S. *Bausell*. He was executive officer of the NROTC Unit of Prairie View A. & M. College at Prairie View, Tex., in 1967–1969 and professor of naval science in 1969–1970. He attended the NROTC Unit at Yale University in 1970–1973. He was Commander of Destroyer Squadron NINE (1973–1974) and of Cruiser Destroyer Group FIVE (1974–1976). In 1976–1978 he was Director of the Near East and South Asia Region of the Office of the Assistant Secretary of Defense and was Commander of Training Command of the Pacific Fleet in 1978–1981. He retired as rear admiral in 1981. Since 1981 he has been Ambassador to the Cooperative Republic of Guyana.

Mr. Thomas graduated from Harvard University (B.S., 1951), George Washington University (M.S., 1966), and Yale University (Ph. D., 1973). He was born June 23, 1929, in Natick, Mass.

Nomination of Nicolas M. Salgo To Be United States Ambassador to Hungary
September 20, 1983

The President today announced his intention to nominate Nicolas M. Salgo, of Florida, as Ambassador to Hungary. He would succeed Harry E. Bergold, Jr.

Mr. Salgo was a trainee and export manager with Manfred Weiss Co. in Budapest, Hungary, in 1933–1938 and in Geneva, Switzerland, in 1938–1939. He was partner and director of Salvaj and Cie in Geneva in 1939–1948. In 1948–1958 he was owner and president of Indeco Corp., Coal Credit Corp., and Salvaj and Co. in New York City. He was executive vice president of Webb and Knapp, Inc., in New York City (1950–1957) and president and chief executive officer of the Norbute Corp. in Butte, Mont. (1954–1960). He was founder and owner of Nicolas Salgo and Co. in New York City in 1959–1983. In 1960–1974 he was vice chairman and chairman of Bangor Punta Corp. and subsidiaries in Greenwich, Conn. He was co-owner and president of the ZX

Ranch in Paisley, Oreg., in 1966–1980.

Mr. Salgo was founder and limited partner of the Watergate Improvement Associates in Washington, D.C. (1960–1977), and has served as chairman of the Watergate Companies since 1977. He has also been a consultant to the United States Information Agency since 1982 and a member of the International Private Enterprise Task Force since May 1983.

He received his LL.D. and Ph. D. from the University of Budapest (Hungary) in 1937. His foreign languages are fluent Hungarian, French, and German. He was born August 17, 1914, in Budapest, Hungary, and became naturalized in 1953.

Nomination of James E. Goodby for the Rank of Ambassador While Serving at the Conference on Confidence and Security Building Measures and Disarmament in Europe
September 20, 1983

The President today announced his intention to nominate James E. Goodby for the rank of Ambassador in his position as Chief of the United States Delegation to the Conference on Confidence and Security Building Measures and Disarmament in Europe. This a a new position.

Since 1981 Mr. Goodby has been serving as Deputy Chairman of the U.S. Delegation to START. He served as Ambassador to Finland in 1980–1981. Previously he served at the Department of State as Deputy Assistant Secretary of the European Bureau (1977–1980) and as Deputy Director of the Bureau of Politico-Military Affairs (1974–1977). He was political officer, USNATO, Brussels, in 1971–1974 and in 1969–1971 served as international relations officer general in the European Bureau at the Department of State.

Mr. Goodby graduated from Harvard University (A.B., 1951). His foreign languages are French and German. He was born December 20, 1929, in Providence, R.I.

Nomination of Sol Polansky for the Rank of Ambassador While Serving at the Strategic Arms Reduction Talks
September 20, 1983

The President today announced his intention to nominate Sol Polansky for the rank of Ambassador as Vice Chairman of the United States Delegation to the Strategic Arms Reduction Talks and the Department of State Representative. He would succeed James E. Goodby.

From February 1981 until June 1983, Mr. Polansky served as Deputy Chief of Mission in Vienna. He was Deputy Chief of Mission in East Berlin in 1976–1979. Previously he was at the Department of State as officer in charge of Soviet exchange programs in the Bureau of European Affairs in 1974–1976; at the National War College in 1972–1973; political officer in Moscow in 1968–1972; political officer in West Berlin in 1966–1968; and international relations officer general in the Bureau of European Affairs at the Department of State in 1962–1966.

He graduated from the University of California (A.B., 1950). His foreign languages are Polish, Russian, and German. He was born November 7, 1926.

Remarks to Reporters Announcing a Bipartisan Congressional Leadership Agreement on the Continued Role of United States Forces in Lebanon
September 20, 1983

The President. I have a brief statement here. But I won't be able to take any questions, because we're running on a very tight schedule with regard to our arrival in South Carolina.

An agreement has been reached among the bipartisan leadership of the Congress to introduce and seek to enact a resolution authorizing the continued presence and mission of the U.S. peacekeeping forces in Lebanon.

While I have substantial reservations about parts of this resolution—reservations which I made clear to the leadership—I am pleased that this agreement among the congressional leadership supporting our presence and policies in Lebanon has been reached, and I would be willing to sign the proposed resolution, while expressing my reservations, if it is passed in the form that has been presented to me this morning.

I'm especially pleased that this proposed resolution not only supports our policies in Lebanon but now enables us to advance United States peacekeeping interests on the solid bipartisan basis that has been the traditional hallmark of American foreign policy.

Q. Does that mean you don't think that the War Powers Act applies?

The President. It's all explained in the resolution.

Note: The President spoke at 1:25 p.m. at the South Portico of the White House.

Remarks at Convocation Ceremonies at the University of South Carolina in Columbia
September 20, 1983

Dr. Holderman, Judge Russell, Chairman Dennis, Governor Riley, Senator Thurmond, the distinguished Members of Congress, the board of regents, the faculty and administrators of this university, and you the students, and ladies and gentlemen:

I want to offer my heartfelt thanks for this honorary degree. I must confess to you, when Judge Russell presented me as a candidate for the degree I was filled with mixed emotions. It stirred up a guilty feeling that I've nursed for some 50 years. Judge Russell, I thought the first one they gave me was honorary. [*Laughter*]

But it was a particular pleasure to have you present me. And by the way, as I looked at that summary of Judge Russell's career—Assistant Secretary of State, president of this university, Governor of South Carolina, United States Senator, and now Judge in the Court of Appeals—I couldn't help but thinking just what you might have done if you had put your mind to it. [*Laughter*]

But thank you, everyone, for an honor that I will cherish always.

I wish every day could be as happy as this one, but I can't forget a terrible event that took place 21 days ago over the Sea of Japan that revolted the world. The Korean Air Lines massacre reminded us that in dealing with adversaries as brutal as the Soviets, America must remain strong to preserve the peace.

Peace through strength—that's a principle the people of this State have always understood. Today, in this historic place, I believe I understand why. Here, on the grounds where you're sitting, during the War Between the States, soldiers from both sides drilled and trained—soldiers who wanted nothing more than to go home to their families, their mothers and fathers, their wives, their children. Here, in these buildings flanking these grounds, war councils were held by officers who only months before had been running their businesses or working their farms in peace. And here, makeshift hospitals were erected for those wounded in battle. Many of the wounded left the hospitals permanently disabled; many never left them at all.

Perhaps more than any other State, South Carolina has suffered the ravages of war. And because the citizens of this State possess a keen sense of history, one of the marks of a truly civilized people, you and your Representatives in Washington have always urged our nation to avoid war by maintaining a sound defense.

So, on behalf of all Americans, I want to thank Senator Thurmond, Congressmen Spence, Campbell, and Hartnett, and the people of South Carolina for the role you've played in keeping our beloved country at peace.

And now, may I say a word to you students here today? As a new school year begins, many of you probably wonder what kind of world it is that you're preparing for. You wonder whether you'll find jobs in a nation created to offer expanding opportunity to all; whether you'll have the means to raise your own families as well or maybe better than your parents raised you; or whether you won't be able to afford your own homes or give your children the education they deserve. And yes, you have a good reason to ask those questions. In recent years, so many claimed that we live in a world of limits where all nations, even those as bountiful as our own, must learn to live with less. Perhaps you remember a report published a few years back called "The Limits to Growth." That title—limits to growth—said it all.

Well, my college days, if you can stretch your imaginations back that far, happened to fall during the Great Depression of the thirties. The overall unemployment rate was more than a fourth of the work force, almost double—or more than double what it is today. The Federal Government broadcast radio messages in those days telling all

of us not to leave home to look for jobs because there were none; just wait at home for the government to take care of you.

Well, I remember that all my way through high school and college I had a job as a lifeguard on the banks of a river in Illinois. The job didn't pay much, but it was something. And when I left that job at the end of the summer to start classes—incidentally, I went to another job there on the campus. It was not one of the worst jobs I've ever had; I washed dishes in the girls' dormitory. [*Laughter*] But I wondered whether my 4 years in college in those drab Depression days, whether I would have to go right back to being a lifeguard, and that could only be for the summer. Well, I did go back for the summer following my graduation in order to get some money to go job hunting. If ever there was a time to talk about limits to growth, it was then.

But here we are half a century later, and the American people enjoy a standard of living unknown back in the thirties or even before the thirties, before there was a Depression. During the past 50 years, each decade, employment in our country has risen on an average of some 12 million people in each 10 years, and real income per person has increased on the average of nearly 30 percent.

And think of the things that we take for granted today that didn't even exist before—television, computers, space flights. Two big thrills in my life were hearing Charles Lindbergh had landed safely in France, and then some five decades later, watching the space shuttle *Columbia* land safely in California. And it was impressed on me, the great technology, when I was told, as we sat on the platform looking toward the western sky for it to come into view, that it had started its approach over Honolulu.

Well, I know that hunger and sickness in many parts of the world haven't been wiped out. But thanks to breakthroughs in agriculture and medicine, today more people on this Earth eat better and live longer than ever before in history. I've already lived some two decades longer than my life expectancy when I was born. That's a source of annoyance to a number of people. [*Laughter*] But life on Earth is not worse; it is better than it was when I was your age. And life in the United States is better than ever.

Now, what about your generation? Well, we've only seen the beginning of what free and brave people can do. You've all heard, of course, and studied the Industrial Revolution. Well, today our nation is leading another revolution even more sweeping as it touches our lives. It's a revolution ranging from tiny microchips to voyages into the vast, dark reaches of space; from home computers that can put the great music and film and literature at a family's fingertips to new medical devices and methods of healing that could add years to your lives and even enable the halt to walk and the blind to see.

Your generation stands on the verge of greater advances than humankind has ever known. I remember my disbelief when I was told one day of a communications satellite that could deliver the entire Encyclopaedia Britannica in 3 seconds. But for you to take advantage of these staggering advances, and your children, too, we must forge an education system to meet the challenges of change. The Senator spoke eloquently of this.[1] The sad fact is that system doesn't exactly exist today. Of course, there are many fine schools—this university a notable example—and thousands of dedicated schoolteachers and administrators. But overall, lately, American schools have been failing to do the job they should.

For the past 20 years, scholastic aptitude test scores have shown a virtually unbroken decline. Thirty-five of our States require only 1 year of math for a high school diploma, and 36 require only 1 year of science. And we've begun to realize that compared to students in other industrialized countries, many of ours perform badly.

Now, some insist there's only one answer: more money. But that's been tried. Total expenditures in our nation's public schools

this year, according to the National Education Association, will total $116.9 billion. And that's up 7 percent from last year—more than double the rate of inflation, and more than double what we spent just 10 years ago.

Is there an echo in here?[2] [*Laughter*]

If money was the answer, the problem over the last 10 years would have been shrinking, not growing. Despite the loud chorus from big spenders, most Americans understand that to make our schools better we don't need money as much as we need leadership from principals and superintendents, dedication from well-trained teachers, homework, testing, efficient use of time, and good, old-fashioned discipline.

It is we, not the young people of today, that are responsible for this failure. Maybe we thought we were making things nicer or easier for them after our experiences with war and with depression and all. But we have failed them in not bringing them up to the fullest extent and to the limits of their ability.

The Federal Government can do much to help set a national agenda for excellence in education, a commitment to quality that can open new opportunities to you and to our sons and daughters. And I believe the Federal Government can do that without recycling still more tax dollars or imposing still more regulations. Let me cite a few commonsense goals and guiding principles.

To begin with, we have to realize that our young people don't all go to school in Washington, but in thousands of American cities and towns, parishes, and neighborhoods. And that means that we have to restore, as the Senator said, parents and local governments to their rightful place in the educational process.

And then, too, we need to make certain that excellence gets rewarded. Teachers should be paid and promoted on the basis of their competence and merit. Now this may require more money, but responsibility for that should rest with authorities close to

---

[1] *Senator Strom Thurmond addressed the convocation prior to the President's remarks.*

[2] *The President was responding to shouting by a member of the audience.*

the schools themselves, not the Federal Government. Hard-earned tax dollars should encourage the best. They have no business rewarding mediocrity and incompetence.

We can encourage excellence still further by encouraging parental choice and competition, and that's exactly what we want to do through our programs of tuition tax credits and vouchers. Parents should have the right to choose the schools they know would be best for their children. America rose to greatness through the free and vigorous competition of ideas. We can make American education great again by applying these same principles of intellectual freedom and innovation to our schools.

And one more idea which may be laughed and sneered at in some supposedly sophisticated circles, but I just have to believe that the loving God who has blessed this land and thus made us a good and caring people should never have been expelled from America's classrooms. It's time to welcome Him back, because whenever we've opened ourselves and trusted in Him, we've gained not only moral courage but intellectual strength.

I'm convinced that if we can send astronauts to the Moon, we can put these commonsense principles into practice. It'll take hard work, because many special interest groups will resist. But with your support and with help from dedicated public servants like Senator Thurmond and your Members of the House of Representatives, we can give your generation and those that follow the education you'll need for the future—a future more dazzling than any America has ever before known.

If I could leave you with one last thought, it's this: There are no such things as limits to growth, because there are no limits on the human capacity for intelligence, imagination, and wonder. A century ago, oil was nothing more than so much dark, sticky, ill-smelling liquid. It was the invention of the internal combustion engine that turned oil into a resource, and today oil fuels the world's economy. Just 10 years ago, sand was nothing more than the stuff that deserts are made of. Today, we use sand to make the silicon chips that guide satellites through space. So, remember, in this vast and wonderful world that God has given us, it's not what's inside the Earth that counts, but what's inside your minds and hearts, because that's the stuff that dreams are made of, and America's future is in your dreams. Make them come true.

And before I sit down—and I'm not just doing this to be polite—all the time that I've been waiting and that I've been up here, I've been wondering whether I should or not, and I can't sit down without recognizing that magnificent choir. When they sang the National Anthem, they did more than just sing it with their voices. I thought it came from their hearts, and we, therefore, listened with our hearts. And you know, that National Anthem of ours. I don't know all the national anthems in the world, but I don't know of any that end with a question. Yes, the question was the one that Francis Scott Key asked—did we see, could we see that banner through the smoke and the bomb burst when morning came? Well, today, we can ask the same question. When he asked, was it floating o'er the land of the brave and the home of the free? We're asking the question now. We know it's still flying, but it's up to us to see that it continues to fly over a land that is free and brave.

Thank you. God bless you.

Note: The President spoke at 3:51 p.m. in an area of the campus known as the Horseshoe, a quadrangle patterned after English universities.

In his opening remarks, the President referred to Dr. James B. Holderman, who presented the President with an honorary doctor of laws degree, and R. Markley Dennis, chairman of the board of trustees of the university.

Remarks at a Fundraising Dinner for Senator Strom Thurmond in Columbia, South Carolina
September 20, 1983

Senator Thurmond—Strom, thank you very much for a very warm and very flattering introduction. Governor Jim Edwards, Senator Baker, George Graham, Bill Cassels, Members of the Congress who are here, and all of you ladies and gentlemen:

I don't have the words to thank you properly for the welcome that I've had. I'm delighted to be back in your beautiful State—the location that Sir Walter Raleigh described as paradise on Earth. And I'm delighted to be here, speaking for someone who is a true legend in his time. Strom Thurmond is a man of character, wisdom, energy, and leadership, and he's one big reason America is back on the road to greatness again.

He's a man of the people. His heart treasures those values that make us a good and loving people—family, work, neighborhood, peace, and freedom. They say you can't live in South Carolina for long without meeting Strom in person. Not many can match his sense of responsibility to his State.

You know, it's been said that experience is the yeast of success. Well, take a look at the chapters in Strom's life. He's been a teacher, superintendent of schools—he helped start the tech schools that transformed South Carolina from an agrarian to an industrial-based economy—then a judge, major general in the Army Reserve, Governor, and now Senator, not to mention being a patriot, husband, father, and a kind and good man. Strom, I couldn't grab that many roles if I'd spent the rest of my life in Hollywood. [*Laughter*]

Maybe you'll understand why I say Strom is my friend, and I like him by my side giving me counsel and advice. And I trust the good sense of his friends. I'm confident that come November 1984, you'll send him right back to Washington to keep on doing a great job as your Senator.

And Strom, we're grateful to you for giving us one of your most talented and trusted advisers, the man who managed your 1978 campaign, Lee Atwater, from

right here in Columbia.

Strom speaks with a voice of common sense, and common sense is about as common in Washington, D.C., as a Fourth of July blizzard in Columbia, South Carolina. [*Laughter*] There's a great sympathy in Washington for practically any scheme to spend money. But for years, Strom has been one of those lonely voices telling the awful truth: that government can only spend what it borrows or taxes away from the people. And hard-working people in South Carolina need higher taxes like they need a plague of locusts. You don't need to be taxed more; government needs to spend less.

We didn't go to Washington to raise taxes. We went there with a radical idea: to put this economy and the destiny of this great nation back in the hands of you, the people. And that's exactly what I think we've begun to do. With your support and Strom's, we came to the rescue of a nation whose house was on fire. We put out the flames and, brick by brick, we're rebuilding a foundation of strength, safety, security, and prosperity for America, and that's not bad for a new beginning.

Now, it's true, some people don't seem to like anything we do. Our opponents resist our budget savings. They oppose our tax cuts. And they complain that all their special interests have been hurt. Well, pardon me, but let them resist and oppose and complain, because I intend to remind the people the big spenders who saddled America with double-digit inflation, record interest rates—as Strom has told you—huge tax increases, too much regulation, credit controls, farm embargoes, no growth, and phony excuses about malaise are the last people who should be giving sermonettes on fairness and compassion.

I'm a firm believer in the need for bipartisan cooperation, especially in foreign policy where politics should stop at the water's edge. And sometimes we succeed. But there just isn't much sympathy among some there in Washington for reducing the tax burden on hard-working American families. And if the liberals in the Congress had their way, the American people would never have received any tax cut—no first year, no second year, or, as the girl in the TV ad says, "no nothin'." If we had followed their blueprint for compassion, the average family of four would be paying, as Strom told you, nearly $700 in higher taxes this year. And isn't it strange that we never hear a fairness argument that is framed that way?

But never mind, because that average family won't be paying the higher taxes some of those complainers on the Hill tried to pass. Thanks to the help of Strom Thurmond, his Republican colleagues here with us tonight, and a lot of responsible Democrats, we passed the first decent tax cut for every working American since 1964.

Despite all the threats from the other side, we kept our promise to the people. And we still have one more promise that must and will be kept. Indexing, an historic reform, will begin in 1985—it's already been passed—so that never again will government be able to profit from inflation at your expense.

Now, I'll be the first to admit that we still have a long way to go. But take a look around us. America is getting well, and she's getting strong. We've got a recovery train going. And rather than whine and carp and complain, the misery merchants should get on board and help us keep America moving forward. And if they can't do that, then let them get out of the way.

Inflation has plummeted by four-fifths, 80 percent, as Strom told you. And it's been under 2½ percent during the past 12 months, and that's the lowest 12-month rate in more than 15 years. The prime rate is almost half what it was when we took office. Estate taxes on family farms and businesses are being cut sharply. Strom and I happen to believe widows and children shouldn't be forced to sell the family farm or the family business just to pay Uncle Sam, and now they won't have to.

Factory orders, industrial production, auto sales, and housing starts are up since the beginning of the year. Housing starts, we just learned yesterday afternoon, were

up last month to the highest level since December of 1978. The stock market has come back to life and today hit a new record. Workers' real wages are rising for the first time in 3 years—that's real wages, constant dollars. And while unemployment remains too high, we're putting people back to work across the country. Since December, more than 2 million of our fellow citizens have found jobs. More Americans are on the job than any time in United States history. We're moving forward again, and as Al Jolson used to say, "You ain't heard nothin' yet."

You know, you can recite all these facts and figures or you can use an easier way, a kind of a layman's way to tell our economic program is working: Our opponents don't call it Reaganomics anymore. [*Laughter*] You know, I never did call it that. I just called it America getting back on track.

Increasing housing starts, greater automobile production, rising personal income should be music to the ears of one crucial industry in South Carolina—your textile industry. And no one in the United States Congress works harder for the textile industry than your Senator, Strom Thurmond.

Recognizing the importance of that industry to the national economy—an employer of nearly 2 million people—I told Strom our administration would seek to relate imports to growth in the domestic market. We believe progress is built with competition, keeping faith with the magic of the marketplace, but we also know there are times when exceptions must be made due to special circumstances in market conditions. And that's why we've continued to support the Multifiber Arrangement which gives us the ability to protect our domestic textile and apparel manufacturers within the international system.

Reflecting the concerns of Strom Thurmond, we've negotiated a series of bilateral agreements which are far tighter than any existing before we took office. Our new China agreement contains 33 categories of textiles and apparel, as opposed to eight in 1981. Where other threats to our import textile and apparel industry have appeared, we've tried to counter them. And as you know, we have much to do, and I pledge to you tonight, our administration will strive to work toward an ever closer relationship of textile imports and domestic market growth, consistent with our existing international obligations.

Strom, I hope the good people of your State won't mind if I also tell them what a determined and effective advocate you are for South Carolina's farmers.

Senator Thurmond and I share a very profound belief: We must preserve the American system of family farming. Strom has fought to protect the tobacco price support program from those who don't understand it. You know, talking about our family farms and what they can do—every person out there in farming in America, feeding not only himself and his family but feeding more than 50 other people in the world—there's a story that's going the rounds in Russia.

I've kind of become a collector of the stories that the Russian people tell each other which reveals their cynicism about their own government. And this story is just one of my favorites. The commissar goes out to one of their collective state farms, corrals one of the workers and says, "How is everything going? Any complaints?" "Oh," he says, "I've never heard anyone complain, comrade, sir." He says, "No, nothing." "How are the crops?" "Oh," he said, "the crops are wonderful, never been better." "Potatoes?" He said, "If we pile potatoes up in one pile, they'd reach the foot of God." And the commissar said, "This is the Soviet Union; there is no God." The worker says, "That's all right; there are no potatoes." [*Laughter*]

Strom personally traveled to Chicago on September 2d to meet with Secretary Block and discuss drought conditions in South Carolina and request appropriate aid.

And I can't finish these words about Strom without mentioning what I think might be his most important contribution not just to his fellow South Carolinians, but to free people everywhere. Strom Thurmond has been on the frontlines in our struggle to strengthen our foreign policy. He said some nice things about me on this, but he stands up for a strong national defense to make America second to none.

The debate on defense is about protect-ing lives and preserving freedom, because they're the source of all our other blessings. We both believe it's immoral to ask the sons and daughters of America to protect this land with second-rate equipment and weapons that won't work.

The savage Soviet attack against the unarmed Korean airliner reminds us we live in a dangerous world with cruel people who reject our ideals, who don't even understand them, and who disregard individual rights and the value of human life. We can only keep our families safe and our country free and at peace when the enemies of democracy know America has the courage to stay strong. And Strom and I intend to make sure they do. His leadership will be important on key appropriations votes that are coming up on defense and the MX.

And let me just add how much it meant to me when I returned to Washington after the downing of that Korean plane to have Strom over at the White House for advice and support.

But when we talk about defense, I think we should remind people what things were like back in 1980. Remember all those planes that couldn't fly, the ships that couldn't sail for lack of crew or spare parts, troops who couldn't wait to get into civilian clothes? One weapons program after another was being eliminated or delayed. America was falling behind. The free world was losing confidence in our leadership. But what we heard from our leadership was lectures on our inordinate fear of communism.

Well, just as we're turning the economy around, we're also strengthening the Armed Forces and bringing a new sense of purpose and direction to America's foreign policy. In the military, the number of combat-ready units has gone up by a third since 1980. The deployable battle force in the Navy has risen from about 480 ships when we took office to 510 today—well on its way to our goal of 600. The percentage of new recruits with high school diplomas has risen throughout our Armed Forces. And since 1980 the reenlistment rate has gone up by more than a fourth. We're attracting better recruits. We're keeping them longer, because we're giving them better pay and better equipment and because we're giving them the respect and appreciation they've always deserved.

Let me just interject something here, because the last time I gave a speech in Columbia during the 1980 campaign I said one of the most important ways to control Federal spending is to control waste, fraud, and abuse. Perhaps you've seen those headlines and the TV news about the Pentagon paying $100 for a 4-cent diode or $900 for a plastic cap. Now, what is missing or buried in all of those stories is the most important fact of all: It was Cap Weinberger's people—Defense Department auditors and inspectors—who ordered the audits in the first place and who conducted the investigations that revealed those figures. Those are our figures. We're the ones who formed a special unit to prosecute Department of Defense fraud cases. And in just an 18-month period, the Department has obtained 650 convictions, and this doesn't count the number of settlements that have been made not going to court. So despite all the headlines, we are keeping that promise to weed out waste, fraud, and abuse.

In foreign policy, we've let the world know that America stands up for democratic ideals again. And one other thing: Under our administration, this nation is through with hand-wringing and apologizing. We don't have to put up walls to keep our people in. We don't use an army of secret police to keep them quiet. We don't imprison political and religious dissidents in mental hospitals. And we don't coldbloodedly shoot defenseless airliners out of the sky.

What we are doing is working tirelessly for a just peace in the Middle East, promoting human rights in southern Africa, giving firm support to the forces of democracy in Central America, and negotiating for balanced and verifiable arms reductions. In fact, in our search for peace we have more major arms control negotiations underway with the Soviets than any other administration in history. And this is the first time that the Soviets have agreed to go beyond nuclear arms ceilings to negotiate actual reductions in nuclear weapons.

They haven't done it as well as they should; we haven't got them to the point that we think they should be. But at least they're there talking. And I don't think they would be there talking if it wasn't for the buildup in the military strength of the United States, the sort of signal they've gotten.

We can hold our heads high. I believe with all my heart that the United States is safer, stronger, and more secure today—both economically and militarily—than before. And if enough of you would just make your voices heard, we can make two more powerful contributions to the cause of good: We can welcome God back into America's classrooms, and we can finally protect the life of the unborn child.

I believe one word sums up the difference between today and 1980: Hope. Hope is being reborn in America. A better future awaits us, and together, we can make America a nation of winners again. So let us have faith. Let us go forward, remaining true to our vision of progress—the vision Strom Thurmond has worked so hard to achieve. It begins with your families, churches, schools, and neighborhoods. We don't ask the people to trust us; we say trust yourselves, trust your own values, and working together, we'll make America great again.

Too many of our opponents are only comfortable trusting government. Their solutions—higher taxes and more spending—could bring us back full circle to the source of our economic problems, with the Government deciding that it knows better than you what should be done with your earnings and how you should live your life. Their road is timid and appeals to fear and envy. We have a great message. We can keep dreams alive in the hearts of our people. And one sure way to do that is to reelect in 1984 our friend, Strom Thurmond, Senator of South Carolina.

I want to thank all of you. I just have to say this afternoon I had a most thrilling afternoon out on the campus of South Carolina, at the University of South Carolina, and seeing thousands of those wonderful young people. And you looked out at them, and you know I did some of my life in public office back in the riotous days when if I went to a campus, I started a riot. And to see those thousands of young people out there was to see the future of America. To see these young people, also from that campus, and hear them up here tonight is to see the future of America. And I assure you, the future is very bright indeed.

Thank you very much, and God bless you all.

Note: The President spoke at 7:45 p.m. in the Cantey Building at the South Carolina State Fairgrounds. Prior to the dinner, the President attended two Republican Party fundraising receptions at the fairgrounds.

Following the dinner, the President returned to Washington, D.C.

Proclamation 5101—National Cystic Fibrosis Week, 1983
September 20, 1983

By the President of the United States of America

A Proclamation

Cystic fibrosis is one of the most common fatal genetic diseases among children in the United States. In spite of its prevalence, however, the disease remains a mystery in many ways. Its underlying cause is elusive, as is a method for identifying carriers who have no symptoms. Even in victims of cystic fibrosis, the disease manifests itself in many different ways, often masquerading as other conditions, and thus confounds diagnosis.

Through the combined efforts of the Federal government's National Institutes of Health, private voluntary agencies, and researchers at medical centers and universities across the country, we are making inroads toward explaining the mysteries of cystic fibrosis. While the disease once was almost invariably fatal in infancy and early childhood, innovations in diagnosis and treatment over the past 20 years have virtually doubled the average age of survival of its victims. For example, half of the children born with cystic fibrosis can now expect to live to age 21.

But this good news brings with it new hurdles. While people with cystic fibrosis are embarking on careers and assuming societal responsibilities to a greater extent than ever before, they do so in the shadow of a disease that remains progressively debilitating.

Therefore, the challenge remains to identify the cause of this disease and ultimately, we hope, to prevent it. Scientists are uncovering in greater and greater detail the metabolic defects involved in cystic fibrosis. By focusing on the unique physiology of people with the disease, researchers are getting closer to being able to identify its cause. In this effort, public awareness of the hallmarks and treatment of cystic fibrosis and of the importance of continuing scientific research are critical.

To enhance the public's awareness of this disease, the Congress of the United States, by Senate Joint Resolution 131, has designated the week of September 18 through September 24, 1983 as "National Cystic Fibrosis Week" and has authorized and requested the President to issue a proclamation in observance of that week.

Now, Therefore, I, Ronald Reagan, President of the United States of America, do hereby proclaim the week beginning September 18, 1983, as National Cystic Fibrosis Week, and I call upon the people of the United States to observe that week by focusing attention on cystic fibrosis and the continuing efforts to clarify the causes of the disease and improve the treatment of its victims.

In Witness Whereof, I have hereunto set my hand this 20th day of September, in the year of our Lord nineteen hundred and eighty-three, and of the Independence of the United States of America the two hundred and eighth.

RONALD REAGAN

[*Filed with the Office of the Federal Register, 11:07 a.m., September 21, 1983*]

Nomination of United States Representatives and Alternate Representatives to the 38th Session of the United Nations General Assembly
September 20, 1983

The President today announced his intention to nominate the following individuals to be Representatives and Alternate Representatives of the United States of America to the 38th Session of the General Assembly of the United Nations.

Representatives

Jeane J. Kirkpatrick, U.S. Ambassador to the United Nations.

Jose S. Sorzano, U.S. Deputy Representative to the United Nations.

John L. Loeb, Jr., currently serving as U.S. Ambassador to Denmark.

Joel Pritchard, U.S. Representative from the State of Washington.

Stephen J. Solarz, U.S. Representative from the State of New York.

Alternate Representatives

Charles M. Lichenstein, Alternate Representative of the United States of America for Special Political Affairs in the United Nations, with the rank of Ambassador.

William C. Sherman, Deputy Representative of the United States on the Security Council of the United Nations, with the rank of Ambassador.

Constantine N. Dombalis, of Richmond, Va.

Alan L. Keyes, the President's nominee to be Representative of the United States on the Economic and Social Council of the United Nations, with the rank of Ambassador.

Lyn P. Meyerhoff, of Owings Mills, Md.

Executive Order 12441—Amending the Generalized System of Preferences
September 20, 1983

By virtue of the authority vested in me as President by the Constitution and statutes of the United States of America, including Title V of the Trade Act of 1974 (19 U.S.C. 2461 *et seq.*) as amended, and Section 604(a) of the Trade Act of 1974 (19 U.S.C. 2483(a)), in order to modify the limitations on preferential treatment for eligible articles from countries designated as beneficiary developing countries and to make technical corrections to provisions of the Tariff Schedules of the United States (TSUS) (19 U.S.C. 1202), it is hereby ordered as follows:

Section 1. The article description in item 153.05 of the TSUS is modified by deleting therefrom "and blackberry".

Sec. 2. Annex II of Executive Order No. 11888 of November 24, 1975, as amended, listing articles that are eligible for benefits of the GSP when imported from any designated beneficiary developing country is further amended by deleting TSUS item 304.58 and by inserting in numerical sequence TSUS item 544.41.

Sec. 3. Annex III of Executive Order No. 11888, as amended, listing articles that are eligible for benefits of the GSP when imported from all designated beneficiary countries except those specified in General Headnote 3(c)(iii) of the TSUS, is further amended by deleting item 544.41 therefrom.

Sec. 4. General Headnote 3(c)(iii) of the TSUS, listing articles that are eligible for benefits of the GSP except when imported from the beneficiary countries listed opposite those articles, is modified—

(a) by deleting "544.41 . . . Mexico";

(b) by inserting "Hong Kong" in addition to Taiwan and Republic of Korea opposite item 678.50; and

(c) by deleting "Taiwan" opposite TSUS item 688.43 and inserting in lieu thereof "Hong Kong".

Sec. 5. (a) The amendments made by Sections 1 and 4(b) of this Order are effective with respect to articles both: (1) imported on and after January 1, 1976, and (2) entered, or withdrawn from warehouse for consumption, on or after the third day following publication of this Order in the *Federal Register*.

(b) The other amendments made by this Order are effective with respect to articles both: (1) imported on or after January 1, 1976, and (2) entered, or withdrawn from warehouse for consumption, on or after March 31, 1983.

RONALD REAGAN

The White House,
September 20, 1983.

[*Filed with the Office of the Federal Register, 11:08 a.m., September 21, 1983*]

Note: The text of the Executive order was released by the Office of the Press Secretary on September 21.

Message to the Senate Transmitting the United Nations Convention on Contracts for the International Sale of Goods
September 21, 1983

To the Senate of the United States:

With a view to receiving the advice and consent of the Senate to ratification, I transmit herewith the United Nations Convention on Contracts for the International Sale of Goods. This Convention was adopted on April 11, 1980, by the United Nations Conference on Contracts for the International Sale of Goods and was signed on behalf of the United States at United Nations Headquarters on August 31, 1981.

The Convention would unify the law for international sales, as our Uniform Commercial Code in Article 2 unifies the law for domestic sales.

The Convention was prepared, with the active participation of representatives of the United States, by the United Nations Commission on International Trade Law (UNCITRAL) and received the unanimous approval of this worldwide body; the Convention was then adopted, without dissent, by the United Nations Conference of sixty-two States. This unanimity attests to the broadly perceived need for the Convention and the value of its provisions.

The House of Delegates of the American Bar Association recommended in 1981 that the United States ratify the Convention, subject to a declaration permitted under Article 95 as to the grounds for applicability. I concur fully in this recommendation for the reasons set forth in the enclosed report of the Department of State.

The report of the Department of State provides a summary of the Convention and describes its approach. Worthy of emphasis is the international deference that the Convention accords to the contract made by the parties to an international sale. The parties may agree that domestic law rather than the Convention will apply, and their contract may modify or supplant the Convention's rules. The uniform international rules play their significant role when, as often occurs, a problem arises that the parties did not anticipate and solve by contract.

International trade now is subject to serious legal uncertainties. Questions often arise as to whether our law or foreign law governs the transaction, and our traders and their counsel find it difficult to evaluate and answer claims based on one or another of the many unfamiliar foreign legal systems. The Convention's uniform rules offer effective answers to these problems.

Enhancing legal certainty for international sales contracts will serve the interests of all parties engaged in commerce by facilitating international trade. I recommend that the Senate of the United States promptly give its advice and consent to the ratification of this Convention.

RONALD REAGAN

The White House,
September 21, 1983.

Message to the Senate Transmitting a Protocol to the United States-Canada Convention on Taxes
September 21, 1983

To the Senate of the United States:

I transmit herewith, for Senate advice and consent to ratification, a Protocol signed at Ottawa on June 14, 1983, amending the Convention between the United States and Canada with respect to taxes on income and on capital, signed at Washington on September 26, 1980. I also transmit a related exchange of notes and the report of the Department of State with respect to the Protocol.

Senate consideration of the Convention, which was transmitted for advice and consent to ratification by letter dated November 12, 1980, has been delayed pending the correction of certain technical problems in its text. The Protocol resolves these technical problems by clarifying the language of the Convention to assure that its original intent is fulfilled.

In addition, the Protocol makes a neces-sary change regarding pensions, annuities and alimony and amends the Convention to permit the United States to exercise its full taxing right, under the Foreign Investment in Real Property Act, section 897 of the Internal Revenue Code. The Protocol also includes a new rule which affects an athlete resident in one State who is a recipient of a bonus from an employer resident in another State. The new rule protects such a recipient by limiting the rate of tax in the State of the employer.

It is most desirable that this Protocol, together with the Convention, be considered by the Senate as soon as possible and that the Senate give advice and consent to ratification of both instruments.

RONALD REAGAN

The White House,
September 21, 1983.

Message to the Senate Transmitting the United States-Thailand Treaty on Penal Sentences
September 21, 1983

To the Senate of the United States:

With a view to receiving the advice and consent of the Senate to ratification, I transmit herewith the Treaty Between the United States of America and the Kingdom of Thailand on Cooperation in the Execution of Penal Sentences, which was signed at Bangkok on October 29, 1982.

I transmit also, for the information of the Senate, the report of the Department of State with respect to the Treaty.

The Treaty would permit citizens of either nation who had been convicted in the courts of the other country to serve their sentences in their home country; in each case the consent of the offender as well as the approval of the authorities of the two Governments would be required.

This Treaty is significant because it represents an attempt to resolve a situation which has inflicted substantial hardships on a number of citizens of each country and has caused concern to both Governments. The Treaty is similar to those currently in force with Bolivia, Canada, Mexico, Panama, Peru and Turkey. I recommend that the Senate give favorable consideration to this Treaty at an early date.

RONALD REAGAN

The White House,
September 21, 1983.

Nomination of Michael I. Burch To Be an Assistant Secretary of Defense
September 21, 1983

The President today announced his intention to nominate Michael I. Burch to be an Assistant Secretary of Defense (Public Affairs). He would succeed Henry E. Catto, Jr.

He was a full-time military officer from 1963 until his retirement in 1983, serving as a public affairs officer in the U.S. Air Force. He most recently served as military assistant to the Assistant Secretary of Defense for Public Affairs at the Pentagon in 1979–1983. Previously he was Deputy Chief, Operations Branch, Armed Forces News Division, the Pentagon, in 1976–1979; special assistant to the Director of Public Affairs, Office of the Secretary of the Air Force, the Pentagon, in 1974–1976; public affairs officer, Operations Branch, Office of the Secretary of the Air Force, in 1972–1974; and Air Force public affairs officer in the United States and overseas in 1962–1972.

He graduated from the University of Missouri (B.A., 1963) and did graduate work at Boston University and American University. He is married, has one child, and resides in Woodbridge, Va. He was born June 20, 1941, in St. Louis, Mo.

Statement on the Intermediate-Range Nuclear Force Negotiations
September 21, 1983

One of my first decisions in the aftermath of the tragic shooting down of Korean Air Lines Flight 007 was that the United States must continue its efforts in the interest of peace to pursue equitable and verifiable arms control agreements with the Soviet Union.

On September 3, I met with Ambassador Nitze to discuss the INF negotiations in Geneva and to reaffirm my commitment to seeking a successful result in those talks.

Since then, the United States has held extensive consultations with our NATO allies and Japan regarding the U.S. position in the talks. These consultations have included both direct correspondence between myself and allied leaders, meetings of the NATO Special Consultative Group, and bilateral consultations with the Japanese.

In those consultations, suggestions for U.S. initiatives to move the negotiations forward were offered. These suggestions were welcomed by allied leaders, who reaffirmed their strong support for the U.S. negotiating effort. Our NATO allies also reaffirmed their commitment to the NATO double-track decision.

Based on the results of these consultations, Ambassador Nitze has received new instructions to pursue these U.S. initiatives with the Soviet negotiators in Geneva. These initiatives represent significant further development of the U.S. proposal for an interim agreement which the U.S. put forward last March. They address a number of Soviet concerns.

The U.S. action in taking these additional steps is further demonstration of U.S. commitment, and that of our allies, to achieving a positive outcome in the Geneva talks.

We call on the Soviet Union to respond in a constructive manner to these proposals, so that the Geneva negotiations can arrive at a positive result.

Note: Deputy Press Secretary Larry M. Speakes read the President's statement to reporters during his daily press briefing, which began at approximately 12:30 p.m. in the Briefing Room at the White House.

Appointment of 13 Members of the National Highway Safety Advisory Committee
September 21, 1983

The President today announced his intention to appoint the following individuals to be members of the National Highway Safety Advisory Committee.

The following individuals to serve for terms expiring March 15, 1985:

Walter W. Gray, Jr., of Terre Haute, Ind., is professor of health and safety and director of the Indiana State University driver and traffic safety program. He will succeed Francis H. Goodwin.

Henry Edward Hudson, of Arlington, Va., is the Commonwealth's attorney for Arlington County, Va. He will succeed John C. Landen.

Paul R. Meyer, Jr., of Wilmette, Ill., is professor of orthopedic surgery and director of the spinal cord injury program at Northwestern University Medical School. He will succeed Deborah D. Richards.

The following individuals for terms expiring March 15, 1986:

G. Lawrence Keller, of Wichita, Kans., is a consultant and former senior vice president of the Coleman Co. This is a reappointment.

John W. Ruger, of Katonan, N.Y., retired in 1977 after 37 years of service to the General Motors Acceptance Corp. This a reappointment.

Melville P. Windle, of Rancho Palos Verdes, Calif., is vice president and general counsel for the Transamerica Insurance Co. This is a reappointment.

Peter Griskivich, of Washington, D.C., is vice president of the motor truck manufacturers division of the Motor Vehicle Manufacturers Association. This is a reappointment.

Thomas Kallay, of Santa Monica, Calif., is professor of law at Southwestern University School of Law in Los Angeles, Calif. He will succeed J. T. Quigg.

Don MacGillivray, of Santa Barbara, Calif., is former mayor of Santa Barbara and a former State legislator. He will succeed Philip Theodore Abraham.

Alan G. Loofbourrow, of North Key Largo, Fla., is a retired Chrysler Corp. executive, engineer, and inventor. He will succeed Patricia Fossum Waller.

Paul D. Coverdell, of Atlanta, Ga., is a State senator from Georgia. He will succeed Walter W. Gray.

John L. Moriarity, of Calabasas Park, Calif., is a private trial attorney at the Van Nuys Law Center. He will succeed Henry Edward Hudson.

Margaret L. Nordyke, of Santa Barbara, Calif., was developer/coordinator of the Santa Barbara County "Alternate Behavior for the Drinking Driver" program at Santa Barbara City College. She will succeed Paul R. Meyer, Jr.

Appointment of Charles H. Pillard as a Member of the Advisory Committee for Trade Negotiations
September 21, 1983

The President today announced his intention to appoint Charles H. Pillard to be a member of the Advisory Committee for Trade Negotiations .for a term of 2 years. This is a reappointment.

Mr. Pillard has been serving as international president of the International Brotherhood of Electrical Workers since he was first elected in 1970. Previously he served as acting president (1968–1970) and member of the IBEW International Executive Council (1961–1968).

He served in the United States Army in 1941–1945, achieving the rank of captain. He is married, has two children, and resides in Silver Spring, Md. He was born October 26, 1918, in Buffalo, N.Y.

Appointment of Carmen Joseph Blondin as United States Commissioner of the North Pacific Fur Seal Commission
September 21, 1983

The President today announced his intention to appoint Carmen Joseph Blondin to be United States Commissioner on the North Pacific Fur Seal Commission. This is a reappointment.

Mr. Blondin is presently serving as Acting Deputy Assistant Administrator for Fisheries Resource Management at the National Oceanic and Atmospheric Administration. He has been employed with the National Marine Fisheries Service since 1973. He was appointed as U.S. Commissioner to the North Pacific Fur Seal Commission in 1975.

He is also serving as the senior U.S. member of the Fisheries Claims Board with the U.S.S.R., Poland, and Spain.

He served in the Armed Forces in 1948–1973 with service in the U.S. Coast Guard and the Submarine Service of the U.S. Navy, retiring with the rank of commander. He graduated from the U.S. Coast Guard Academy (B.S., 1955) and George Washington University Law School (J.D., 1962). He is married, has five children, and resides in Ft. Washington, Md. He was born May 13, 1930, in Paterson, N.J.

Appointment of Richard Herbert Pierce as a Member of the Commission on Presidential Scholars
September 21, 1983

The President today announced his intention to appoint Richard Herbert Pierce to be a member of the Commission on Presidential Scholars.

He is currently serving as regional vice president for the United Student Aid Fund, Inc., and executive director of the Maine Educational Loan Marketing Corp., in Augusta, Maine. He is a former Maine State senator and served as assistant majority leader.

Mr. Pierce resides in Waterville, Maine. He was born February 3, 1943, in Waterville.

Remarks and a Question-and-Answer Session With Regional Editors and Broadcasters on Domestic and Foreign Policy Issues
September 21, 1983

The President. Good afternoon, and welcome to the White House. I've enjoyed this opportunity to break bread with you once again.

The professional relationship between those of us in public office and members of the press is an important ingredient of American freedom. Senator Moynihan once pointed out that countries which have papers filled with good news usually have jails filled with good people. Earlier this year, I suggested that perhaps—and it was a gentle suggestion—that perhaps the press could focus a bit more on the many wonderful things that Americans are doing for each other, especially during National Volunteer Week. There were a few cries of outrage, but now that the dust has settled, I think there's been a movement in the last few months to show the uplifting side of American life as well as our flaws. Of course, the imperfections need to be brought out; otherwise, they might never be corrected.

One of our greatest national treasures is our right as Americans to criticize government without fear of reprisal. There's a story about a Soviet citizen who was telling an American traveler that people in Russia are free to speak just like they are in the United States. The difference is that in the United States, they're free after they speak.

Journalism is not an easy profession, especially when the events of the day are immersed in theories and schools of thought not familiar to an individual that's trying to meet a deadline. In the first 2 years of this administration, economic issues became the focus of news coverage as never before. We were making fundamental changes in the direction of this country, and it wasn't always easy to understand what was happening and why the changes were being made. Well, these changes take time before they can take hold. As you understand, the suggestion that economic freedom needs time to work isn't good copy after a few weeks, and it's a bit difficult to visualize for a news audience how bad things would be if certain changes hadn't taken place.

For example, thanks to our program against inflation, a middle-income family today has $600 more in purchasing power than in 1980. Now, I think that's an important story, yet it's a hard one to present visually on a newscast. Since the beginning of the year, the expansion of the economy has been robust. America is beginning to move again after years of isolation and—or I should say inflation and stagnation. I think that was a Freudian slip when I said isolation there.

But yesterday, the stock market, as you know, hit a new alltime high. And I'm pleased to report that this morning we received more heartening news about the economy. The figures for second quarter economic growth in gross national product had been revised upward for the second time from 9.2 percent to 9.7 percent, and now it is estimated that economic activity in the third quarter is rising at an annual rate of 7 percent.

Some of the foreign policy challenges we face are just as vexing as those concerning our economy, and they're just as difficult for journalists to cover. When we got to Washington we were faced with an unrelenting buildup of armaments and military equipment in Central America. Much of this material is provided by the Soviets and their Cuban and Libyan allies. The American people and even some journalists are confused about what's happening in Central America. Well, stated succinctly, we're trying, even amid the turmoil, to encourage democracy, to ensure economic development, and to engage in dialog and listen to every idea that might put an end to the bloodshed and bring peace. What we cannot do is permit Soviet-armed and Cuban-trained insurgents to shoot their way into power, simply because we're unwilling to provide those who believe in democratic government with the means to defend themselves.

The Middle East is another area where America's role as peacemaker will require courage and commitment. The agreement reached yesterday with leaders of both parties in the Congress is a welcome step forward in our pursuit of peace in Lebanon. If approved by both Houses, it'll send a signal to the world that America will continue to participate in the multinational force trying to help that nation back on its feet. We've informed the Congress that we have reservations about certain features of the resolution, and our agreement is subject to those reservations. But that should not obscure a fundamental point: This resolution, hammered out in long hours of discussion between the congressional and executive branches, represents a bipartisan commitment that America will continue to play a significant role in the search for peace in the Middle East. And it's on that basis that I urge the Congress to act on this resolution quickly.

Peace is our highest goal. We've been working tirelessly to achieve it through diplomacy, but our participation in the multinational force of U.S., French, Italian, and British troops is absolutely crucial if the fighting is to stop, the Soviet-sponsored aggression against Lebanon is to end, and the diplomats have a chance to succeed. I'm very pleased that many Members of the Congress on both sides of the aisle recognize this reality and are willing to work with us in this pursuit.

Three years ago, America was being counted out by friend and adversary alike. It was being said that our best days were behind us. Well, today we can be proud that where freedom is on the line the United States is living up to its responsibilities, and we must not permit domestic politics to get in the way of these responsibilities.

Ultimately, the answer to many of these problems will be found in better relations between the Soviet Union and the rest of the world. The massacre of 269 airline passengers has brought home to many just how difficult this will be. At an absolute minimum, the Soviets should give the world an apology, an admission of responsibility, pay reparations to the victims' families, and provide assurances that such a crime will never

be repeated. For our part, we stand ready to work with the Soviet Government to see that this kind of tragedy never happens again and to deal on other vital issues such as arms reduction.

After consultation with our allies, I have sent Ambassador Paul Nitze, our INF negotiator, instructions to pursue new U.S. initiatives with the Soviet negotiators in Geneva. On these or any of the other areas of concern, the time has come for the Soviets to show the world that they're serious about peace and good will.

And that's enough of a statement from me. I know that you must have some questions.

Antitrust Laws

Q. Mr. President, we've been asked to identify ourselves. I'm Jared Lynch from WTAE-TV in Pittsburgh. There are many people in the Pittsburgh area, sir, who believe that no matter what you have been able to do so far with the Commerce Department relative to steel imports and restricting imports that the final breakthrough will hinge on whether or not we are able to allow some revision or readjustment or relook at the antitrust laws that will allow some companies to use their best skills in combination with other companies and other expertise to, in effect, merge not the two giant corporations, perhaps, but certain portions of those corporations to take advantage of what they have—[*inaudible*]. Do you agree with that, number one?

The President. Well, let me say this: In theory and in principle, yes, I do, because we ourselves have proposed a change in the antitrust laws with regard to a number of things such as research, things of that kind that industry in America, for its own progress and for our country's progress, should be allowed to do without being in violation of the antitrust laws.

Now, I can't give you all the specifics on that, but we have introduced quite a package for legislation on that subject.

Q. Do you think it might apply to the steel industry?

The President. Yes, because I would think that there, too, innovation and research is very much a part of the problems confronting them today.

Lebanon

Q. Mr. President—[*inaudible*]—your assessment of the—[*inaudible*]—obtaining cease-fires in Lebanon—[*inaudible*]——

The President. Well, we have to continue to try to bring that about. And while there's a great deal of attention spent on whether we're shooting back or not shooting back when our marines are in danger, we are in continuous diplomatic negotiations by way of our Ambassador there and by the two Ambassadors that we sent, Fairbanks and McFarlane. They're back and forth between Damascus and Beirut constantly to help bring this about.

The mission that the multinational force was created for has not changed. At the time the first request came in, you'll remember that the Israelis were in, the Syrians were in, the PLO was in, and the fighting was going on, and hundreds and hundreds of innocent people were being killed in the shelling and bombing that was taking place.

For several years, the Government of Lebanon had been literally set aside by the factions in Lebanon in which each one had its own militia. And the request came, and the multinational force went in with the idea of helping provide stability as the foreign forces withdrew and left Lebanon, then, to establish its government and establish its supremacy or sovereignty over its own territory.

We have helped in the training of the Lebanese Army, and I must say that while the Lebanese Army has not been able to expand to the size to handle all the problems facing it, it is a well-trained and capable force.

Everything was proceeding on schedule, our negotiations in which we helped Lebanon and Israel to come to an agreement. You will remember at the time Syria had promised that when everyone else got out, they, too, would get out. Then they changed their minds. Whatever reason, well, we can take our own guess at that. They've made it pretty apparent that they feel that they have a proprietorship over much of Lebanon. They—and I think under the influence of the Soviet forces that are

there in their own country—are behind much of what is presently going on.

But the fact still remains, the multinational force is there to help in this achieving of stability and control by Lebanon, and I think the mission still goes on. But from the very first, I said we will never send our men any place where they will not be allowed to defend themselves if they come under attack, and that recently has happened, and they have been defending themselves.

But the efforts toward a cease-fire still go on. And the opposition to that is coming from Syrians and now from PLO who have reinfiltrated after they were once taken out of the country and have moved into the fighting. And if this fails, the peace plan for the whole Middle East that we had proposed and offered our help in bringing about, based on Camp David and the United Nations resolutions that they had passed, I think also goes. All of us must ask ourselves, if we're not aware, that the reason we were trying to promote a peace plan is that the Middle East is vital to the Western World, the United States, and to our allies.

Q. Mr. President—[*inaudible*]—how far will you back the Gemayel government and the Lebanese Army, and is American prestige now completely tied up in their success?

The President. Well, we can't, obviously, can't guarantee victory. But such things as this recent shelling and the controversy about whether that was in defense of the marines was based on the commanders on the ground recognizing that if that particular vantage point in the hills was taken, it would make the position held by our marines untenable, because those who had been shooting at them will be looking right down their throats from those heights, very close.

And so we're convinced, and I hold, that this was part of them defending themselves. But we're continuing, as I say, with the negotiations. And I think there is—well, we still have reason to believe that we can attain that cease-fire.

Q. Mr. President—[*inaudible*]—some of your advisers, in fact, have said that this was a defense of the Lebanese Army and that there is great concern that the Gemayel government will fall.

The President. Well, the idea was that the multinational force was there to try and preserve order while the army then proceeded to take over and take over from those militia factions in their own country. So I think that the mission that we're on is still operative.

Cuba

Q. Mr. President—[*inaudible*]—today that you commented to a Cuban American colleague of mine in Miami regarding a secret—[*inaudible*]—agreement and how you felt that the shipment of Soviet—[*inaudible*]—offensive arms might mean that the U.S. is not bound by its promise not to invade Cuba. It stirred a lot of commotion in south Florida's Cuban American community. They want to know more—if, in fact, this secret agreement is under review; if so, what are the implications, and are we going to get tougher with Castro now that the Soviets are—[*inaudible*]—around the world?

The President. Well, the statement that I made was based—that agreement is not, you know, in the form of some formal treaty or agreement. This was a series of letters exchanged between President Kennedy and the Castro regime.

To our knowledge, they have not brought back in nuclear weapons, which was part of it. We have felt, in a number of instances, the so-called agreement in this letter form is rather ambiguous on many points. I think what I was trying to say was that we believe that in spirit, certainly, that has been abrogated, and yet, it's very hard to pin it down as you would with a treaty and say, "You've broken the treaty."

We tried to establish communications with Mr. Castro quite some time ago when he had indicated that perhaps this should be done, and we got no place. And as far as we're concerned, we are going to continue there, and the Soviet efforts to establish another Cuba on our mainland in Central America, and we're going to do that as we have been doing it in Central America.

Central America

Q. Mr. President, also, now that the Soviet regime is—[*inaudible*]—around the world, is it time for—[*inaudible*]—have on our doorstep, you know, violations of international rules with Cuba. Can we get tougher? And regarding Central America, are we getting into a war to avoid a Communist takeover in Central America?

The President. Now, you've asked a question that I really shouldn't answer. I don't see the necessity for the United States going to war in any place where we are. But as I once said in a press conference here—and some of the regular White House press corps tried to hang me out to dry on it—there are some things about which a President should never say never, and I just think things of this kind.

But there is nothing in our plans that envisions a war for the United States. Our job is trying to prevent war wherever it may come in the world. And this is the reason for our military buildup, and it's the reason for our meeting in disarmament talks—more than any other administration has ever had going at one time in our history.

So, I can just say that we're going to continue on this line, and that any time that Castro—whose country is in dire straits, is an economic basket case—any time that he wants to make the moves to return to the community of American nations here in the Western Hemisphere, we'd be happy to sit down with him and work that out. But it begins with him coming out from under the wing of the Soviet Union.

Q. Mr. President?

The President. Now, wait a minute. I've got to go to the back of the room.

Lebanon

Q. [*Inaudible*]—as you know, sir, Jacksonville—[*inaudible*]—navy base. There are many navy families in Jacksonville that are concerned about their—[*inaudible*]—on the *Eisenhower* off the coast of Lebanon. What are the chances, sir, that that situation might widen U.S. involvement in a direct attack on artillery battery or whatever, on the U.S. fleet to protect the aircraft carrier?

The President. So far, we see no indication of anything of the kind there. You can't rule anything out when you're dealing with some of the kind of people that we're having to deal with in that episode. But I would think that they would do thinking two or three times more before they would attempt anything of that kind.

Q. What would we do, sir, if they did shell the American fleet or our people—[*inaudible*]——

The President. Well, I asked at my table here a while ago if anyone has ever heard a 16-inch gun go off. The *New Jersey* should be arriving very shortly. The same thing would apply to the fleet that applies to the marines: They will defend themselves if attacked.

Q. What specific purpose does the battleship have there when there are 1,200 marines on the ground?

The President. Well, we just thought that with all of the hotspots around the world and all, and the *New Jersey* is newly in service—it's been down off the Central American coast, as you know, and we just thought that it ought to get a look at joining up with the Sixth Fleet for a while in the Mediterranean.

Q. Sir, could I just ask you one quick last one? [*Inaudible*] Concerning the length of the resolution, the congressional resolution, Senator Kennedy is calling that "a blank check for far too long a period". What do you think about the length of the resolution, and also that puts it past the election?

The President. I think that the agreement has worked out; both sides have some reservations. I'll be voicing mine, probably at the time of signing, if it passes. I think the Senator is absolutely wrong. And I think those people that have advocated such things as invoking the 60-day clause are very shortsighted, because if you did that, aren't you simply saying to the people who are causing the trouble now, step up the trouble for 60 days and your problems will be over, the multinational force will go home?

Eighteen months gives us a long enough period of time that that doesn't hold true. And I would point out that the first person who ever voiced 18 months as a reasonable

time was Speaker of the House Tip O'Neill, and——

Q. [*Inaudible*]—the political considerations——

The President. ——I was happy to agree with him.

Q. [*Inaudible*]—in terms of the election timing and bringing it beyond that, is that a plus for everyone?

The President. Oh, I think he was thinking out also the same thing that I just mentioned—that makes it a long enough time that that does not become a factor in the strategizing of the people who are causing the trouble.

President's Visit to the Philippines

Q. [*Inaudible*]

Q. Can I just ask you one more question? Yesterday, the Philippine President, President Marcos, said that if you canceled your trip to the Philippines that would be a "slap in the face" to his country. And I was wondering if you made any decision yet as to whether you would be going or not and whether that might happen?

The President. Well, I can understand his saying that if we deliberately bypassed the Philippines at this point as part of the planned trip. There are no plans to change the trip as of now. The whole Southeast Asian trip is planned, and as far as we're concerned is going ahead on schedule.

Location of United Nations Headquarters

Q. What about the U.N.? We have been hearing a lot about the U.N., that it would move for—[*inaudible*]. What are your thoughts?

The President. Well, I think that the gentleman who spoke for us the other day—I'm three questions past that last question here. [*Laughter*] I think the gentleman who spoke the other day had the hearty approval of most people in America in his suggestion that we weren't asking anyone to leave, but if they chose to leave, goodby. Jeane Kirkpatrick has made an interesting suggestion, also, that should be thought about. But maybe all of those delegates should have 6 months in the United Nations meetings in Moscow and then 6 months in New York, and it would give them an opportunity to see two ways of life.

Q. Thank you, Mr. President.

The President. And we'd permit them.

Note: The President spoke at 1 p.m. in the East Room at the White House.

Executive Order 12442—Presidential Commission on Indian Reservation Economies
September 21, 1983

By the authority vested in me as President by the Constitution and laws of the United States of America, including the Federal Advisory Committee Act, as amended (5 U.S.C. App. I), it is hereby ordered as follows:

Section 1. Section 2(d) of Executive Order No. 12401 is hereby amended to provide as follows:

"The Commission shall submit its final report to the President and the Secretary of the Interior by November 30, 1984.".

Sec. 2. Section 4(b) of Executive Order No. 12401 is hereby amended to provide as follows:

"The Commission shall, unless sooner extended, terminate 30 days after it transmits its final report to the President.".

RONALD REAGAN

The White House,
September 21, 1983.

[Filed with the Office of the Federal Register, 11:26 a.m., September 22, 1983]

Memorandum on Federal Spending
September 21, 1983

Memorandum for the Heads of Executive Departments and Agencies

Subject: Reducing and Controlling Wasteful Year-End Spending

Prevention of waste and inefficiency in Federal programs is a top priority of this Administration at any time of year. It has a special priority now. The end of the fiscal year is approaching and the temptation is great to obligate funds simply so that they will not lapse and be unavailable for obligation after September 30.

In a memorandum dated June 21, 1983, the Director of the Office of Management and Budget provided guidance to you on ways to prevent wasteful year-end spending. I ask you now, in the remaining days of this fiscal year, to redouble your efforts to prevent this form of waste.

It is absolutely essential that we do everything in our power to restrain the growth of Federal spending. Avoiding wasteful year-end spending is an obvious way to help do that, one that the taxpayers have every right to expect of us.

I know that I can count on your continued personal attention to this effort.

RONALD REAGAN

Proclamation 5102—National Sickle-Cell Anemia Awareness Month, 1983
September 21, 1983

By the President of the United States of America

A Proclamation

Sickle-cell disease affects the health of some 50,000 to 60,000 Americans, most of whom are blacks. An additional two million blacks are carriers of the sickle-cell trait. Though the trait usually does not have clinical symptoms, it is very important in the genetic transmission of sickle-cell disease.

Since the early 1970's, the Federal government has conducted a National Sickle-Cell Disease Program. Coordinated by the National Heart, Lung, and Blood Institute, it promotes efforts toward prevention, diagnosis, and treatment of this disease. In addition, the National Institutes of Health have supported ten Comprehensive Sickle-Cell Centers throughout the United States. These facilities have been successful in developing unified programs of basic and clinical research, training, and community service directed at sickle-cell disease.

In the past decade, there has been substantial progress in research on sickle-cell disease. Diagnostic procedures have been greatly improved. Measures to ameliorate the excruciatingly painful sickle-cell crises

have been introduced for those afflicted with the disease. Our ability to combat life-threatening complications also has improved. Although much has been accomplished through this comprehensive national effort, more remains to be done to conquer this serious health problem.

Now, Therefore, I, Ronald Reagan, President of the United States of America, do hereby proclaim the month of September 1983, as National Sickle-Cell Anemia Awareness Month. I invite all Americans to join with me in reaffirming our commitment to reduce the burden of illness, disability, and premature death imposed by this disease.

In Witness Whereof, I have hereunto set my hand this 21st day of September, in the year of our Lord nineteen hundred and eighty-three, and of the Independence of the United States of America the two hundred and eighth.

RONALD REAGAN

[*Filed with the Office of the Federal Register, 4:11 p.m., September 22, 1983*]

Note: The text of the proclamation was released by the Office of the Press Secretary on September 22.

Statement by Deputy Press Secretary Speakes on the Soviet Attack on a Korean Civilian Airliner
September 22, 1983

I would like, on behalf of the President, to thank the OAS member countries for their extraordinary support regarding the Korean Air Lines tragedy, which they expressed at the OAS Permanent Council meeting yesterday. As the President has often said, there is far more that unites us in this hemisphere than could ever divide us, and the demonstration of this was never plainer than at yesterday's OAS Permanent Council meeting.

The unanimous messages of condolence, and the deploring of this act by all 24 OAS Permanent Representatives present at the meeting, reconfirms our belief that terror and indiscriminate use of force will not go unchallenged by the nations of the Western Hemisphere. This unanimous sign of compassion by the OAS members makes us confident that the world has learned a bitter lesson from this tragedy.

Appointment of Four Members of the Advisory Commission on Intergovernmental Relations
September 22, 1983

The President today appointed the following individuals to be members of the Advisory Commission on Intergovernmental Relations for terms of 2 years:

Robert Boone Hawkins, Jr., of Loomis, Calif., is president of Sequoia Institute in Sacramento, Calif. He was a program coordinator for the State and local government program at the Woodrow Wilson International Center for Scholars. He was born September 6, 1941, in Berkeley, Calif. This is a reappointment.

Sandra R. Smoley, of Sacramento, Calif., is supervisor (third district), Sacramento County. She is also serving as president of the National Association of Counties. She was born July 8, 1936, in Spirit Lake, Iowa. She will succeed Peter F. Schabarum.

Mary Kathleen Teague, of Springfield, Va., is executive director of the American Legislative Exchange Council in Washington, D.C. She was born February 29, 1948, in St. Louis, Mo. She will succeed Wyatt Durette.

Lee L. Verstandig, of Washington, D.C., is Assistant to the President for Intergovernmental Affairs at the White House. He was born September 11, 1937, in Memphis, Tenn. He will succeed Richard Salisbury Williamson.

Remarks at the White House Conference on Productivity
September 22, 1983

Well, good morning, and I'm delighted to welcome all of you, even though I'm a bit of a visitor here myself. Before I begin, let me thank Bill Simon and Bill Seidman[1] for their strong leadership in shepherding this idea forward. I know so many of you have given your time and talents during the preparations preceding this conference. We're impressed with the broad diversity of your group—leaders from management, labor, academia, and government at all levels. Another important point that I think will help us down the road in body and spirit: Your group is bipartisan. We're pleased that the conference steering committee included both Senator Bill Roth and Congressman John LaFalce.

We come together today in shared appreciation of a basic truth: The challenge of greater productivity growth is of supreme importance to America's future. When we arrived in Washington almost 3 years ago, we faced a situation unprecedented in postwar history. From 1948 to 1968, productivity in the private economy had risen at an average rate of about 3 percent a year, providing the American people with one of the highest standards of living in the world. But after 1968, that rate began dropping. By 1979 and 1980, it had actually turned negative, as inflation and interest rates reached new thresholds of pain.

We know the productivity problem was a paramount concern. We also know what productivity is and why it's so important. I think correspondent Lloyd Dobbins stated it simply and clearly in a documentary he did for NBC in 1980. "Productivity," he said, "is not some esoteric economic subject. It is how much we produce and how much it takes to produce it. The object is to make more for less; if you do, everyone benefits."

Well, as Bill Simon points out, "Only through productivity gains can real living

---

[1] *Chairman and vice chairman, respectively, of the White House Conference on Productivity.*

standards be improved." And certainly there are plenty of areas in our economy where this is still happening. We think of the American farmer who a century ago toiled all year to feed himself, his family, and a few others. Today a farmer feeds himself and 77 other people. Being the breadbasket for the world—that's productivity. And we think of those first computers which could cost up to a million dollars and were so big they filled a room, a big room. Today a computer chip that performs the same functions can fit in the palm of your hand and costs under $10. That's productivity, too.

There's no denying that greater productivity growth is the cornerstone of price stability and sustained economic growth. It's vital to regaining our competitive position in world markets and creating job opportunities for an expanding American labor force.

If we can agree on what productivity is and why it's so important, we can also identify certain principles that are present in productive societies. For example, productive societies reward saving, investing, building, and creating, rather than consuming. Productive societies do not selfishly tax and spend the product of today's labor without a thought toward tomorrow's needs. Thomas Jefferson, a man of the people in his day, understood this well when he said, "A wise and frugal government . . . shall not take from the mouth of labor the bread it has earned."

Productive societies also nourish the spirit of adventure, innovation, and entrepreneurship. And productive societies share common objectives, and their leading institutions work together. Business, government, labor, and academia view each other as partners, not adversaries. The late Samuel Gompers, founder of the American Federation of Labor, spoke often for a partnership between labor and management, viewing them as trustees for the preservation of the American free enterprise system.

From this, we should agree that there is no single, all-encompassing solution for increased productivity. I realize that among some a perception exists that we need only to work harder and the problem will disap-

pear. And I don't deny there are some sluffers out there. You remember that comment that Pope John allegedly made when he was asked how many people work in the Vatican? And his answer was, "About half." [*Laughter*] Well, there's nothing wrong with admonishing people to have a positive and dedicated attitude toward their jobs. But it's just as important to give them the tools, the training, and the proper economic environment to work better and more productively.

We need to move on many fronts. We must spur capital formation by encouraging savings, investment, and modernization. We must stimulate adequate research, development, and technological innovation by appropriate incentives. We must improve our work force by providing training for solid jobs and encouraging greater cooperation between labor and management. We must sharpen the skills of tomorrow's leaders by improving America's educational system. And, yes, we must prevent government from suffocating initiative, innovation, and risk-taking through overregulation.

In sum, we must free enterprise. And make no mistake, I believe we can. America is no second-best nation. Our people come from sturdy stock. Their energies have always carried them past their highest dreams. And that's why immediately upon arriving in Washington, we moved to unlock the power and drive of our people. We identified four areas where broad-based reforms were necessary.

First, we cut by nearly 40 percent the rate of growth of Federal spending. It had been rising at a 17-percent annual rate in 1980.

Second, we passed sweeping incentives for individuals and businesses by cutting personal tax rates 25 percent across the board, by providing new incentives for IRA and Keogh plans, and by accelerating depreciation schedules for businesses, large and small.

Third, under the able leadership of Vice President Bush, we curbed the growth of Federal regulations and redtape. The number of proposed new regulations has been reduced by one-third in the past 2 years. By the end of 1983, the time our citizens spend filling out Federal forms and reports will have been cut by over 300 million man-hours annually.

Fourth, we have urged the Federal Reserve Board to promote monetary policies that ensure the price stability needed for lasting economic growth.

How are we doing? Well, the one statistic that interests us most—productivity—is headed in the right direction again. Productivity has gone up the last four consecutive quarters. This week has been a messenger for very good economic news. The recovery is strong, broad-based, and maintaining its momentum without unleashing a deadly new wave of record inflation and interest rates. Housing starts in August were at their highest level since December of 1978. The demand for automobiles is outstripping supply. The stock market has set a new closing high. Unemployment is going down. And yesterday, we learned the gross national product rose 9.7 percent in the second quarter and is rising by 7 percent—in the first estimate—in the third quarter.

I'll be the first to say we have a long way to go. We face unacceptably large deficits. But let's make one thing very plain: We didn't get those deficits because Americans are undertaxed; we got those deficits because government has overspent. Rather than moan and weep about my stubborn refusal to raise taxes, I urge all those of good will to work with me. Together, let us summon the courage to roll up our sleeves and do the right and proper thing for our country by getting control of Federal spending once and for all. This would free more resources for the private sector to invest in productive capital projects.

America is moving forward. And we're supplementing our general recovery program with legislation to meet the needs of a more productive society. America needs her best minds to create new miracles of high technology, miracles both for innovation and for modernization of the major areas of our economy—in manufacturing, agriculture, and services.

We have enacted the first tax incentive program for research and development. We seek to improve the instruction of science and math in secondary schools. We want to encourage greater and more creative cooperation between university and industry scientists and engineers. And we're attempting to remove legal impediments that prevent inventors from reaping the rewards of their discoveries.

Partnership, training, incentives, responsibility—these are the building blocks for a stronger economy, renewed world leadership, and a better life for all Americans. Two landmark programs will help lead us there.

The Job Training Partnership Act, which is set to begin October 1st, will train more than a million Americans a year for productive, self-sustaining jobs in the private sector. Unlike the old CETA program which was run primarily by government officials and which often provided little training or trained people for a job that didn't exist, this program will be run primarily by business and labor people at the grassroots—those who know best what training is needed for existing jobs. They will be part of organizations called PIC's—Private Industry Councils—designed to provide training needed right there on Main Street America.

Another positive program that we've introduced is the National Innovation and Productivity Act of 1983. This bill would encourage companies to work together on complex and expensive research and development, stimulating new technologies, new products, more exports, and higher employment. Current antitrust laws often discourage joint research and development efforts. Well, we can't afford to sleepwalk into the 21st century, permitting our competitors to seize the advantage and overtake us. I am confident the Congress will work with us to pass this legislation.

We've also proposed to consolidate all U.S. trade functions in one department so we can help them sell their products abroad. Large projected trade deficits underscore the importance of enhancing our producers' ability to compete. American business, labor, and farmers deserve the strongest possible Federal representation on trade.

As we move in all these areas, we'll eagerly await your own recommendations. As you remember, I appointed the National

Productivity Advisory Committee in 1981, assembling a cross section of distinguished American leaders. Of that committee's 46 recommendations, we have already adopted a significant number. This White House Conference on Productivity provides a window of opportunity to build on that first committee's work.

Many of you attended important preparatory conferences this summer, and we followed them with interest. You discussed how capital, human resources, government, and private sector initiatives all contribute to productivity. Well, we look to you now for new guidance.

I have every confidence that this great nation, built by pioneers with courage and vision to persevere in the face of great adversity, is ready to charge forward again. As one of your fellow citizens, Bill Mellberg, recently wrote, "Opportunities do exist for those who dream, who believe, who work hard, and who willingly take risks. The Constitution does not guarantee success. It guarantees the opportunity to succeed. As Will Rogers put it, 'America is a great country but you can't live in it for nothing.' Today's generation must remember that success demands commitment. Thank God

we have the freedom to choose."

Well, we do, and together we'll choose hope and progress, passing the torch of freedom to our children and our children's children.

I just have to say, just as a reminder of harking back to our continued effort with regard to nonsensical regulations—I had once, back out on the mashed-potato circuit, a government example, true and confirmed, and I used it as an example of what needed to be done. I'll tell it to you. This was of a fellow here in government who sat at a desk, and documents came to his desk, and then he forwarded them on to the proper destination, initialed them, and passed them on. And one day a classified document came to his desk. But it came there, so he read it, decided where it should go, initialed it, and passed it on. And a day later it came back to him with an attached memo that said, "You weren't supposed to see this. Erase your initials and initial the erasure." [*Laughter*]

Thank you very much. God bless you all, and God bless America.

Note: The President spoke at 11:12 a.m. at the State Department Auditorium.

Remarks at a White House Luncheon Marking the Observance of American Business Women's Day
September 22, 1983

Well, good afternoon, and since American Business Women's Day is your day, a heartfelt congratulations. Our thanks, as well, to Senator Jepsen and Congressman Tom Tauke who introduced the resolution calling for an American Business Women's Day and to the other Members of the Congress here today who supported their efforts. Connie Aden, president of the American Business Women's Association; Nancy Bruner, chairman of the Task Force for Business Women's Day; Mary Jo Jacobi, the first woman to be White House business liaison; and all of you who worked so hard to give us American Business Women's Day—you deserve our gratitude.

In recent decades more and more American women have entered the work force until today, more than half of all women over 16 work outside the home. Workmen work in all sectors of the economy, at all kinds of jobs. And I would like to have you listen, for example, to the names of just a few of the organizations that were invited to send representatives here today: the American Council of Railroad Women, the Association of Women in Architecture, the Association for Women Veterinarians, the Society of Women Engineers, the International Association of Women Police, the National Association of Women in Construction, and American Women in Radio and

TV.

Women entrepreneurs make up the fastest growing segment of the small business community. They own 22 percent of all sole proprietorships and take in gross receipts of over $40 billion a year. They own businesses from construction companies to clothing stores to coal mines. And today our nation honors you, American businesswomen, for your achievements in business, for your contributions to our nation's economic vitality, and for paving the way for future generations.

Besides extending my congratulations, I want you to know that our administration is supporting American businesswomen in the most important possible way—by working to revive our economy so that all American business can prosper.

The economy was pretty sick when we came into office, and as the doctor on the case I'm pleased to report that the patient is not only out of bed but back on the job. [*Laughter*] And we couldn't do it just by saying take two aspirins and get a good night's sleep.

Inflation, which was running in double digits when George Bush and I were inaugurated, has dropped to 2.4 percent for the last 12 months, and that's the lowest annual 12-month rate in more than a decade and a half. And that translates into renewed consumer confidence and strong demand for your products and services. The prime interest rate is about half what it was. Businesses have easier access to funds for new investments, leading economic indicators have been on the rise for the past 11 months, and our gross national product is growing faster than most economists expected—by a whopping 9.7 percent last quarter and at an estimated 7-percent rate this quarter.

You know sometimes—having a degree in economics myself I can kid about them because I'm talking about our own group—but I sometimes remind economists that they have a watch chain with a Phi Beta Kappa key on one end and no watch on the other. [*Laughter*]

Personal income is up, and so are auto sales, factory orders, retail sales, and housing starts. Since August a year ago, the stock market has gone up over 400 points, providing business with a rich flow of capital. You may remember Will Rogers' advice about the stock market. "Don't gamble," he said. "Buy some good stock and hold it till it goes up; then sell it. If it don't go up, don't buy it." [*Laughter*]

Well, these days people are having a lot less trouble with stocks that don't go up. Unemployment is still too high, but it's begun to drop and, as business continues to expand, it'll drop still further. You and other businesswomen helped create and shape this recovery. The number of self-employed women has been growing about five times faster than the number of self-employed men in recent years.

And many of those self-employed women have started small entrepreneurial businesses—the kind that create the most new jobs. You know, if America already had the national industrial policy planned and supervised by the Federal Government, which some of our critics want, I have to wonder. Would the plan have allowed businesses owned by women to grow five times faster than businesses owned by men? It would probably have underestimated your potential. Women are doing far better in the marketplace than all the so-called experts could have predicted. I just have to believe that government intervention would never offer the same opportunity as economic freedom.

And if you women here who are members of the Women Executives in Government would permit me, I want to tell a little story that I told you the other day, and if you don't mind, to repeat it. I like it; it explains a lot of things. There was an accident. The victim stretched out; crowd had gathered around; a man elbowed his way through. There was a woman bending down over the victim, and the man shoved her aside and said, "I have had training in first aid. Let me take care." She stepped meekly back, and he started. And he started doing all the things he had learned about. And then she tapped him on the shoulder and said, "When you get to that part about calling the doctor, I'm right here." [*Laughter*]

Now, many Americans still face discrimination, and I want you to know that our administration is committed to making sure that all Americans, women and men, have opportunities to live their lives as they want. We're determined to rid our country of unjust discriminatory laws and to guarantee vigorous enforcement of codes that are now on the books.

Some of the contributions that I'm proudest of in this administration have been aimed at removing barriers to economic freedom. We've increased, almost doubled, the maximum child care credit for working parents. We've authorized larger IRA contributions for working women, and we're working to remedy discrimination in pension programs. We've also virtually eliminated estate taxes levied on surviving spouses, a tax that because of the longer life expectancy of women used to strike widows especially hard.

And our administration is moving to provide assistance to women entrepreneurs. The Small Business Administration has created a national initiatives program to conduct conferences across the country to advise and encourage women in business. In addition, we recently announced the formation of the first-ever President's Advisory Committee on Women's Business Ownership and of the Interagency Committee on Women's Business Enterprise.

The Advisory Committee will be made up of 15 outstanding business leaders, chaired by the former Treasurer of the United States, Angela Buchanan. It'll advise me and the Small Business Administration on the needs of women entrepreneurs. The

Interagency Committee, chaired by Becky Norton Dunlop, will spur and coordinate Federal efforts to assist women business owners. These and other initiatives will help American women find the business opportunities they seek.

Today our nation faces a great transition, a time when new technology is working a dazzling revolution, a time when we can strengthen our economy and set for the world an economy of what free people are—or an example, I should say, of what free people can do. Yet we can only find the strength we need by drawing on the energies and talents of all our people—young and old, women and men. And I'm proud that today our nation is honoring the role of American businesswomen, women like you who are working to make American dreams come true.

I thank you, and God bless you. And now, if Senator Jepsen and Congressman Tauke would join me, I'm going to sign a proclamation, the proclamation that I mentioned.

[At this point, the President signed the proclamation.]

I think, now, that two of us in here are supposed to get ahead of all of you and get in the next room. And then we're going to have a chance to meet each one of you individually, and we'll have our pictures taken.

So, George? Let's go to the Red Room.

Note: The President spoke at 1:02 p.m. in the East Room at the White House.

Proclamation 5103—American Business Women's Day, 1983
September 22, 1983

By the President of the United States of America

A Proclamation

The activities of American businesswomen have experienced a dramatic transition and expansion in recent years. More and more women are participating in every aspect of business—as owners, executives,

professionals, support staff and production workers.

Women play an increasingly important role in the Nation's economy and in determining and implementing the direction of both the private and public sectors of our Nation. Women entrepreneurs currently are the fastest growing segment of the small business community, owning twenty-two percent of all sole proprietorships and realizing gross receipts of over $40 billion. Women own businesses as diverse as coal mining, construction, manufacturing, and wholesale and retail trade.

With more options and choices available to them, women are realizing their potential as a vital force in the American economy.

In recognition that businesswomen are increasingly influencing the growth of our economy and the direction of our Nation, the Congress, by Senate Joint Resolution 18 (Public Law 98–55), has designated September 22, 1983, as "American Business Women's Day" and has authorized and requested the President to issue a proclamation in observance of that day.

Now, Therefore, I, Ronald Reagan, President of the United States of America, do hereby proclaim September 22, 1983, as American Business Women's Day. I call upon every American to join me in observing this day with appropriate ceremonies and activities.

In Witness Whereof, I have hereunto set my hand this 22nd day of September, in the year of our Lord nineteen hundred and eighty-three, and of the Independence of the United States of America the two hundred and eighth.

RONALD REAGAN

[*Filed with the Office of the Federal Register, 4:12 p.m., September 22, 1983*]

Statement by Deputy Press Secretary Speakes on the Situation in Kampuchea
September 22, 1983

The United States supports ASEAN's [Association for Southeast Asian Nations] efforts to achieve a comprehensive political settlement of the problem in Kampuchea based on the complete withdrawal of Vietnamese forces and internationally supervised elections. These principles have been adopted by the great majority of the world's nations in the declaration of the U.N.-sponsored International Conference on Kampuchea (ICK) and successive resolutions of the U.N. General Assembly.

The Khmer resistance coalition is an important element of ASEAN's strategy. The U.S. was not directly involved in the coalition's formation, but we have welcomed it as a vehicle formed to achieve a political settlement in Kampuchea. We give moral, diplomatic, and political support to the coalition's non-Communist elements, led by Prince Sihanouk and former Prime Minister Son Sann. We provide no assistance to and have no contact with the Khmer Rouge.

Last year Prince Sihanouk and Son Sann met with Vice President Bush in Washington during the U.N. General Assembly. The President will meet with Prince Sihanouk and Mr. Son Sann, not as representatives of the Government of Democratic Kampuchea, which we have never recognized, but as respected Khmer nationalists and leaders of non-Communist groups struggling to free their country from Vietnamese occupation.

The President will reaffirm our opposition to the Vietnamese occupation of Kampuchea and our support for ASEAN's efforts to achieve a settlement which will restore Kampuchea's independence. He will also seek their views on the present situation in Kampuchea and prospects for the current U.N. General Assembly. We have no plans to provide military assistance to the coalition or any of its members.

Note: Deputy Press Secretary Larry M. Speakes read the statement during his daily press briefing for reporters, which began at 1:20 p.m. in the Briefing Room at the White House.

Remarks and a Question-and-Answer Session During a Teleconference With Members of the Republican Northeast Regional Leadership Conference
September 23, 1983

The President. Well, good morning, and my greetings to you all. I'm delighted to speak with you about our challenge for '84 and how I know we can and will work together for victory. I wish I could see your faces beyond this little red light, because maybe you've gotten the same feeling I have from around the country. I believe things are looking up for our economy, for our Grand Old Party, and for America.

As I said this week in South Carolina, one word captures the difference between today and 1980: Hope. Hope is being reborn in America. We've been through some mighty rough waters during these first 2½ years, no doubt about that. But confidence is making a comeback. America is getting stronger. We're on a new road, a far better road, and we're not going back to the mess from before. And let's make sure that people remember that.

Indeed, a real mess was dumped in our laps. When we arrived in Washington, we felt a little like Noah must have felt the morning he left the Ark to begin all over again. And we've been fighting an uphill battle ever since to reduce Washington's hammerlock on our economy and our people. But we're making progress.

You know, I asked two questions during the last campaign, and you'll probably be hearing them thrown back at you in the months ahead. Are you better off today than you were before? Do you feel America is more secure today than it was? Well, I welcome those questions, and I hope you do too, because as I said this week in South Carolina, I think it's now time we held our heads high and made our case to the people. Yes, we're better off than before and, yes, America is more secure today than in 1980.

We've got a recovery train going, and rather than whine and complain, our critics should get on board and help us keep America moving forward. Why are we better off? Because 2.6-percent inflation over the last 12 months is one heck of a lot better than the 12.4 percent that we inherited; because an 11-percent prime interest rate is a big improvement over a 21½-percent prime rate; and because permitting the middle-income family to keep $700 more of the money it earns is better than the big, built-in tax increases condoned by the last administration.

Do you remember what the experts warned? They warned that if our plan passed, double-digit inflation was here to stay for the rest of the decade. They told us interest rates were sure to rise to 25 or 30 percent, and they said by decontrolling oil we would send the price of gas at the pump soaring. Well, they were dead wrong. Just as they have been so often in the past.

The truth is, America's future is looking better every day. For the first time in many years, America has the opportunity for a lasting, noninflationary economic expansion, and that's a lot better prospect than we faced in 1980.

Let's tell the truth about our critics. They sob enough about deficits to fill an ocean. But it's an ocean of crocodile tears. What they're after is a blank check for higher taxes, more spending, and greater control over the people's lives. They say they plan to talk about fairness. Well, fine, let them. Because those who gave America runaway spending, double-digit inflation, record interest rates, huge tax increases, too much regulation, credit controls, no growth, and excuses about malaise, are the last people who should be giving sermonettes about fairness and compassion. Families living on a fixed income of $10,000 at the start of 1979 saw the worth of that income drop to less than $8,000 by the end of 1980. In other words, inflation, which for years had been part of deliberate government planning, robbed them of $2,000.

That's not my idea of fairness. Perhaps that worst poverty is the poverty of their arguments. Thanks to the progress of our economic recovery program, real wages for the American worker have increased for the first time in 3 years. But you know, there's an easier way you can tell our critics are wrong and that our plan is working: They don't call it Reaganomics anymore.

That brings me to another point. We're making America safer for your families by rebuilding a military force that will bring peace through strength. Here, too, we have something important to remind the people. Our military forces had been dangerously neglected before we came in. In 1980 we had planes that couldn't fly, ships that couldn't sail, and troops that couldn't wait to get into civilian clothes. Our major weapons programs were being eliminated or delayed, and America was falling behind. But in Washington, the leadership lectured us on our inordinate fear of communism. Well, the savage Soviet attack against the unarmed Korean airliner is a reminder. We live in a dangerous world with cruel people who reject our ideals and who disregard individual rights and the value of human life. It is my duty as President, and all of our duties as citizens, to keep this nation's defenses second to none so America can remain strong, free, and at peace.

We are also pursuing arms control, and for the first time in history the Soviets are negotiating reductions of nuclear weapons, not just limits on their growth. We've undertaken the most sweeping proposals for mutual and verifiable arms reductions since nuclear weapons became a threat. In our search for peace, we have more major negotiations underway with the Soviets than any administration in history. In strategic nuclear forces and in measures to build confidence and trust, in intermediate-range nuclear forces and in conventional forces, we want to lessen the danger to ourselves and our children. We remain flexible in our bargaining. But as Commander in Chief, I have an obligation to protect this country, and I will not let political expediency influence these crucial negotiations.

I'll be the first to acknowledge that we still have a long way to go. Unemployment is still much too high, but that, too, is headed in the right direction. Two million jobs have been created since last December, and all indications point to more strength developing in the job market. In the meantime, we're doing everything we can to stimulate jobs.

Come October 1st, the Job Training Partnership Act will be in full force. It's designed to train more than a million Americans a year for productive, self-sustaining jobs in the private sector. We've also introduced another pro-jobs bill, the National Innovation and Productivity Act of 1983. This bill would encourage companies to work together on joint research and development projects to stimulate new products, new technology, and more jobs.

In that same spirit, we gave approval to a New England group of eight firms—it's known as Small Business Technology Groups, Inc.—to join forces to scout for high-tech government contracts, primarily in defense.

So, as I said, I think we can hold our heads high. You're the people who can spread that message, because no one has worked harder and given more from the heart for the cause that unites us than you. Our greatest challenges are to maintain control of the Senate and increase our numbers in the House. If we can do that, we can check the big spenders, keep America strong, and keep her moving forward on a road that's bold and filled with opportunity.

Let us remain united and true to the Republican vision of progress, a vision that begins with the people and their families, churches, synagogues, schools, and neighborhoods. We don't ask them to trust us. We say trust yourselves, trust the values that made us a good and loving people.

You are the key. So, I just want to thank you with all my heart for all your support. And I urge you as strongly as I can, keep doing what you do best so we can preserve freedom, prosperity, and hope in America.

Thank you so much, and God bless you all. And now I believe I'm supposed to take some questions.

Mr. Rollins. Yes, you are, Mr. President. I think there's nobody more fitting than George Clark, who is our 1976 Reagan chairman, who led the GOP delegation with 20 delegates that were pledged to you in 1976. He's been the party chairman in

New York since 1981. He was the Brooklyn County chairman for 10 years prior to that, and he's a dear friend of both of ours.

George?

U.S. Marines in Lebanon

Q. Thanks, Ed. Hi, Mr. President. It's nice to see you, and please give our best regards to Nancy.

Mr. President, I have a two-part question. Number one, what is the role of our marines in Lebanon, and is there a time limit as to when they'll be home?

The President. Well, George, first of all, hello, and I'm delighted to have a chance even in this way to talk to you for a little bit.

Our role is what it was when we first sent them in as a part of the multinational force. As you recall, Lebanon, beginning back several years ago, had kind of come apart. The Syrians had moved in on one side. And then with the northern border of Israel violated by PLO attacks that were shelling and sending rockets across the border and killing innocent civilians, they had moved into Lebanon.

We, as you know, a year ago submitted a plan for peace in all of the Middle East and we set out with an effort to persuade the more moderate Arab States to recognize Israel's right to exist and then to come together and, in effect, create more Egypts, more nations that would sign peace treaties with Israel.

But first we had to restore the order in Lebanon or see it restored. You will recall that Israel, in its own defense, had moved all the way up to Beirut; the shelling was going on; Syrians were coming in from the other side; and there were several factions that over these several years in Lebanon had created militias, armies of their own, and were fighting each other. Well, the idea was that the multinational force would move in to be a stabilizing force as we persuaded the other nations to get out—the PLO, the Syrians, the Israelis to get out of Lebanon. And then as a new government of Lebanon would attempt to regain control over its own borders and its own land, the multinational force would be there, as I say, as a kind of stabilizing force to help maintain order.

This is still the mission. Now, what happened was that Israel announced its intention to withdraw. The PLO, as you know, was ushered out of Lebanon. Then the Syrians—who had said that when everyone would withdraw, they'd be a part of it, they would withdraw—they reneged. And the Syrians stayed in. And there's no question but that they're influenced by the Soviet Union, which has put people in there, and weapons systems, and is urging them to support, and they are supporting, some of those internal Lebanese factions.

But we're there with the idea of maintaining order while the Lebanese Army—which we in this same interim period have helped train, and it is an excellent force—tries to restore the order, the internal order. Now they've been reinfiltrated by PLO that have come back in. The Syrians, as I say, are encouraging these groups and even supporting them with supplies and, we believe, sometimes manpower.

The one thing that has changed is the violence has struck at all of the multinational force. There have been casualties among all the nations that are involved there, including four marines killed and a number wounded. And we've given orders, and our allies in that force have given orders to their people, to defend themselves. And so we've been doing that. Now, as to a time certain for getting out, I don't know that anyone knows that. But at the same time, we do have very heavy diplomatic efforts going forward, with our representatives there trying to bring about a cease-fire in the internal conflict and then turn our attention to the Syrians and the others getting out of Lebanon.

There is some reason—we have seemed several times to be on the verge of a cease-fire which would be the beginning of success in those diplomatic efforts. And I believe it is essential for the entire Middle East situation that we continue there. We've asked the Congress, or negotiated with the Congress for, I think, we have a bipartisan agreement on a longer period of time that is guaranteed if needed that they will be there, but they will be taken out the first minute that there is no longer a need for them to be there.

Mr. Rollins. Mr. President, our next question comes from the national committeewoman from Pennsylvania, Elsie Hillman. Elsie was very active in your 1980 campaign, and she was also the first woman county chairman of Allegheny County in Pennsylvania.

Elsie?

Allied Response to the Soviet Attack on a Korean Civilian Airliner

Q. Good afternoon. How do you do, Mr. President? We want to know how you feel about the frustration or the lack of willingness on the part of some of the member nations of the Atlantic alliance to support strong sanctions against the Soviets as a result of the tragic downing of the Korean airliner and, further, if there is further action planned by our government?

The President. Well, Elsie, I have to answer the first part of that question with mixed emotions, because never have the bulk of our allies in NATO been more united than they are today. And they have been in full support. Some of the things that people have suggested we should be doing about the Soviet Union are already agreed upon and have been done long before this tragic shootdown of all those innocent people; that is, with regard to high technology, we obtained last July agreement with our allies that we are all united in not delivering any high technology to the Soviet Union.

Last spring, we reached agreement with them on ending any more favored treatment with regard to interest rates in their trade with the Western World. So those things that some people are talking about today have already been done.

We are going to watch for, and continue in every effort that we can think of that might be effective in bringing them to the realization that this must never happen again, and bringing them to the admission of the wrong they've done and that compensation should be provided for the families of those who were victims.

So, we are in a measured way looking for every opportunity to do things. The mixed emotions come about because a few of our allies did not go along with us on some of the things that we're doing, particularly

right now with regard to cutting off air traffic to the Soviet Union.

Mr. Rollins. Unfortunately, Mr. President, this will have to be our last question because Sandra Day O'Connor, your appointment to the Supreme Court, is waiting to have lunch with you.

The next questioner is Ed DiPrete. Ed is the mayor of Cranston in Rhode Island. He is the only Republican mayor in the State. He was first elected in 1978, and the last time he got 83 percent of the vote in 1982.

Administration Policies Toward the Poor

Q. Mr. President, what is your response to those who would say that this administration has been unfair to the poor?

The President. Mr. Mayor, thank you for asking that question. I'm sorry that I went so long on George's answer that I'm afraid I shut some of you off.

I think that whole talk about fairness with regard to our administration was begun and founded in or based in political demagoguery. Certainly, there are no facts to substantiate it. What could be worse for the people of lower income, what could be worse, as I pointed out in my remarks, that, say, someone who had $5,000 fixed income in 1979, at the beginning of the year of '79, and by the end of the year 1980, in just 2 years, that was only worth $4,000 in purchasing power? That's a pretty big blow.

We have set out and, as I have pointed out in my remarks, been pretty successful in reducing that double-digit inflation and bringing it down to where it is. For the first time, people's real income is actually increasing. Now, this has to benefit the people at the lower income level more than anyone else, because they were the ones that were suffering the most from this continued depreciation of the dollars that they had. And we're going to continue with that kind of a recovery.

Our tax program, they've said, "Oh, this benefited the rich." They can't substantiate that. It was across the board, the same percentage cut. Had it not been across the board and the same percentage cut, then that tax cut would have further increased the progressivity of the tax structure. My belief is that those on the other side of the aisle who want to increase progressivity of, say, the income tax, should have the courage to stand up and propose that. They shouldn't try to sneak it in by an unbalanced reduction. We wanted it to be fair, across the board.

But many other things have been done. I know that some of this is based on our budget cuts, and we've never gotten all that we asked in that regard, and we're still going to try for more. They're necessary if we are to reduce the deficits that are looming on the horizon. But what they fail to mention is that we are feeding more people who need help in nutrition than ever before in history. We're feeding more school children with free school lunches—some 10 million of them. We're buying meals for about 50 million people. We're supporting housing for 10 million people.

In all of these, the figures are up to the highest point they've ever been in our nation's history. What they are distorting is the fact that in all of these areas of help, we discovered that the way the programs were being administered, there were many people who were receiving help from their fellow citizens who didn't deserve it because their incomes were as high, and in some instances higher, than many of their fellow citizens who were supporting them through their tax dollars.

So, we redirected the effort toward the truly needy. This was even true in our education programs, in providing grants and loans for students to get college educations. We found there were people getting those loans who could well afford to send their sons and daughters to college and who were reinvesting that loan at a low interest rate in government paper paying a higher interest rate and making a profit on the whole deal.

We changed that. And as I say, we redirected all of this aid, including food stamps. We found more than 800,000 people getting food stamps who had no legitimate or moral reason to be getting them. But we have increased the total number of people that are getting food stamps and the total number of dollars that we're spending on those food stamps—all redirected to people at the lower earning level.

So, they don't have a leg to stand on on any charge of fairness. What they should be defending is, how could they call it fair to have gone along with their deliberate, planned inflation and their deficit spending? You know, with their sobbing about the prospective deficits now, are we to forget how they used to tell us that the national debt didn't matter because we owed it to ourselves and that deficit spending was necessary to maintain prosperity? Well, by the time we got here there wasn't much prosperity. Now I campaigned in cities in this country where the unemployment rate then was 20 percent, and the present recession was just a worsening of the recession that was already underway. And that was hurting people unfairly.

Mr. Rollins. Thank you, Mr. President.

Q. Mr. President, we are thankful that you have spent a few moments with us today. And as I discussed with you when I chatted with you from Scottsdale in the Western States Conference about a week ago, the message here from the Northeast Republicans is the same, and that is, "Four More in '84," Mr. President.

The President. You understand why I don't respond to that answer right now, but we'll be talking about that before too long.

Note: The President spoke at 12:10 p.m. from the Diplomatic Reception Room at the White House to participants in the conference, which was held at the Mayflower Hotel.

Edward J. Rollins is Assistant to the President for Political Affairs.

Nomination of Courtney M. Price To Be an Assistant Administrator of the Environmental Protection Agency
September 23, 1983

The President today announced his intention to nominate Courtney M. Price to be an Assistant Administrator of the Environmental Protection Agency (Enforcement). This is a new position.

Mrs. Price is currently serving as Acting General Counsel at the Environmental Protection Agency. Previously she was Associate Administrator for Rulemaking at the National Highway Traffic Safety Administration in 1982–1983; Deputy Chief Counsel at the National Highway Traffic Safety Administration in 1981; staff attorney in the Office of the General Counsel at the Department of Energy in 1979–1981; and an associate attorney with the law firm of Haite, Dickson, Brown & Bonesteel in Los Angeles in 1975–1978.

She graduated from the University of Alabama (A.B., 1963) and the University of Southern California (J.D., 1975). She is married, has two children, and resides in Washington, D.C. She was born September 12, 1942, in Jackson, Miss.

Proclamation 5104—Modification of Country Allocations of Quotas on Certain Sugars, Sirups and Molasses
September 23, 1983

By the President of the United States of America

A Proclamation

1. Headnote 2 of subpart A, part 10, schedule 1 of the Tariff Schedules of the United States (19 U.S.C. 1202), hereinafter referred to as the "TSUS", provides in relevant part as follows:

"(i) . . . if the President finds that a particular rate not lower than such January 1, 1968, rate, limited by a particular quota, may be established for any articles provided for in items 155.20 or 155.30, which will give due consideration to the interests in the United States sugar market of domestic producers and materially affected contracting parties to the General Agreement on Tariffs and Trade, he shall proclaim such particular rate and such quota limitation, . . ."

"(ii) . . . any rate and quota limitation so established shall be modified if the President finds and proclaims that such modification is required or appropriate to give effect to the above considerations; . . ."

2. Headnote 2 was added to the TSUS by Proclamation 3822 of December 16, 1967 (82 Stat. 1455) to carry out a provision in the Geneva (1967) Protocol of the General Agreement on Tariffs and Trade (Note 1 of Unit A, Chapter 10, Part I of Schedule XX; 19 U.S.T., Part II, 1282). The Geneva Protocol is a trade agreement that was entered into and proclaimed pursuant to section 201(a) of the Trade Expansion Act of 1962 (19 U.S.C. 1821(a)). Section 201(a) of the Trade Expansion Act authorizes the President to proclaim the modification or continuance of any existing duty or other import restriction or such additional import restrictions as he determines to be required or appropriate to carry out any trade agreement entered into under the authority of that Act.

3. By Proclamation 4941 of May 5, 1982 (47 F.R. 19661), I modified the quantitative limitations on the importation into the United States of certain sugars, sirups and molasses established in headnote 3 pursuant to the authority in headnote 2 and provided for a country-by-country allocation of the quota quantity established therein.

4. I find the additional modifications of the quantitative limitations which are here-

inafter proclaimed are appropriate to carry out the trade agreement described in paragraph 2 of this Proclamation and the International Sugar Agreement, 1977 (31 U.S.T. 5135), and give due consideration to the interests in the United States sugar market of domestic producers and materially affected contracting parties to the General Agreement on Tariffs and Trade.

Now, Therefore, I, Ronald Reagan, President of the United States of America, by the authority vested in me by the Constitution and Statutes of the United States, including section 201 of the Trade Expansion Act of 1962, Section 301 of Title 3 of the United States Code, the International Sugar Agreement, 1977, Implementation Act (7 U.S.C. 3601 *et seq.*), and notwithstanding Executive Order 12224, and in conformity with headnote 2 of subpart A, part 10, schedule 1 of the TSUS, do hereby proclaim until otherwise superseded:

A. Notwithstanding the provisions of Proclamation 4941, as amended, paragraph (c)(i) of headnote 3 of subpart A, part 10, schedule 1 of the TSUS is modified by designating the note at the end of the table "NOTE 1" and by adding the following new note:

"NOTE 2: Beginning with the quota year beginning September 26, 1983, the quota allocations for Nicaragua, Costa Rica, El Salvador and Honduras shall be as follows:

Nicaragua.—6,000 short tons, raw value;

El Salvador.—2.6 percent of the total base quota amount permitted to be imported under paragraphs (a) and (b) of this headnote plus 18 percent of the difference between 2.1 percent of the total base quota amount and 6,000 short tons, raw value;

Honduras.—1.0 percent of the total base quota amount plus 52 percent of the difference between 2.1 percent of the total base quota amount and 6,000 short tons, raw value;

Costa Rica.—1.5 percent of the total base quota amount plus 30 percent of the difference between 2.1 percent of the total base quota amount and 6,000 short tons, raw value".

B. The provisions of this Proclamation shall be effective for sugars, sirups, and molasses, entered or withdrawn from warehouse for consumption, on or after September 26, 1983.

In Witness Whereof, I have hereunto set my hand this twenty-third day of September, in the year of our Lord nineteen hundred and eighty-three, and of the Independence of the United States of America the two hundred and eighth.

RONALD REAGAN

[*Filed with the Office of the Federal Register, 11 a.m., September 26, 1983*]

Remarks at the Swearing-in Ceremony for Barbara E. McConnell as a Member of the Civil Aeronautics Board
September 23, 1983

Our honoree, who is here today, Justice O'Connor, Secretary Dole:

Dan, with your words, you've kind of aroused a lot of deja vu and so forth. I didn't know about the horse background here—[*laughter*]—and now winding up with things to do with airplanes makes me think. I was a Reserve officer in the horse cavalry and wound up in World War II flying a desk for the Air Force. [*Laughter*]

And the whole administration is touched. Tomorrow we'll have a Cabinet Secretary

out riding in the rodeo. And when I called him to ask Mac Baldrige to be Secretary of Commerce, I got his wife instead. And she said he couldn't come to the phone; he was in a calf roping contest. [*Laughter*]

Well, I'd say welcome to the team, but as Dan has indicated, Barbara, you're already a member of the team. As Dan's executive assistant, as he told you, she's been immersed in the work of the Civil Aeronautics Board for over a year.

Barbara, the Board is getting a new

member and an experienced hand at the same time, and that's the best kind of appointment to make.

Barbara's appointment brings this CAB back to strength, but it also brings the Board back up to a three-member majority of women. Earlier this week I met with the Executive Women in Government and mentioned that the many talented women in this administration are not getting the public attention they deserve. Some women's groups simply ignore those individuals who are playing important roles throughout the administration. Barbara, as one would expect of an appointment at this level, brings to her job impressive expertise and credentials. And she reflects the large number of women in this administration who are in positions of responsibility because they're highly qualified individuals, not because of some quota system. Much of the negativity we face has less to do with the number of women appointees than it does with the fact that we have a different political philosophy than those who are doing the complaining.

Well, in addition to being professionally qualified, Barbara has been an active Republican for many years and amply reflects the ideals and philosophy of our team. I understand she's been working precincts since she could walk. The outcome of the 1980 election was determined by a basic agreement of the people with the goals that we expressed. And it's important that those filling executive level posts in the departments and agencies agree with why the people sent us here. I know I can count on Barbara to represent us well in the Civil Aeronautics Board and ensure the airline deregulation process is completed and the

CAB sunsetted by at least January 1, 1985.

Now, I know that Justice O'Connor is here to do the swearing in, so I know we should move on to the main event—Justice O'Connor and Barbara. But before we do, I just can't resist. The other day out in the Rose Garden I met with the Women Executives in Government, told them a story, and then I met down here in the State Dining Room for a lunch the other day with some American businesswomen, and I told them the same story. And I'm going to tell it to you, just because the occasion gives me an excuse, and I like to tell the story. [*Laughter*]

Seems there was an accident. The victim was lying out there. A crowd had gathered around. A woman was bending over him, and a man rushed in, pushed her aside and said, "I've had training in first aid; let me at him." And he got down, and she stepped back meekly and stood there. And he did those things that he'd been taught to do. And at one point she tapped him on the shoulder and said, "When you come to the part about sending for the doctor, I'm right here." [*Laughter*]

Justice O'Connor. Barbara.

Note: The President spoke at 4:52 p.m. in the East Room at the White House. He was introduced by Dan McKinnon, Chairman of the Board.

Following the President's remarks, Associate Justice Sandra Day O'Connor of the Supreme Court made brief remarks and administered the oath of office, while Secretary of Transportation Elizabeth H. Dole held the Bible for Ms. McConnell.

At the conclusion of the ceremony, a reception was held in the East Room for invited guests.

Radio Address to the Nation and Peoples of Other Countries on Peace
September 24, 1983

My fellow Americans and fellow citizens of the world:

This is Ronald Reagan, President of the United States, speaking to you live from the broadcast studios of the Voice of America in Washington, D.C.

In 2 days I will be going to the United Nations General Assembly to speak for a cause that people everywhere carry close to their hearts—the cause of peace. This subject is so important I wanted to share our message with a larger audience than I usually address each Saturday afternoon in the United States. So today I'm speaking directly to people everywhere, from Los Angeles to New Delhi, Cairo, Bangkok, and I'm attempting to speak directly to the people of the Soviet Union. I'd like to talk about ideas and feelings all of us share which I intend to communicate to the United Nations on Monday.

Let me begin by bringing you greetings from the American people and our heartfelt wishes for peace. In these times of stress, I believe that the people of the world must know and understand how each other feel, their fears as well as their dreams. We Americans are a peace-loving people. We seek friendship not only with our traditional allies but with our adversaries, too. We've had serious differences with the Soviet Government, but we should remember that our sons and daughters have never fought each other in war and, if we Americans have our way, we never will.

People don't make wars; governments do. And too many Soviet and American citizens have already shed too much blood because of violence by governments. The American people want less confrontation and more communication and cooperation, more opportunity to correspond, to speak freely with all people over our respective radio and television programs and, most important, to visit each other in our homes so we could better understand your countries and you could know the truth about America.

The treasure we Americans cherish most is our freedom—freedom to lead our lives the way we choose, freedon to worship God, to think for ourselves, and freedom to speak our minds even to the point of criticizing our own government. We do not believe in censorship. When another government criticizes us, we know about it. And if they ever say something good, you can bet we'll know that, too. The trouble is, we don't always have that same freedom to speak to others, especially those who live in the Soviet Union. And one-way communication prevents us from better understanding each other.

For example, the Soviet Government has taken extraordinary steps to justify its firing on a Korean civilian airliner, killing 269 helpless people from 14 countries. But I ask those who have been told the United States is responsible: If you're hearing the truth, why has the outcry been so intense from members of the United Nations, the International Civil Aviation Organization, and why are pilots all over the world boycotting flights to Moscow? We have no quarrel with you, the Soviet people. But please understand, the world believes no government has a right to shoot civilian airliners out of the sky. Your airline, Aeroflot, has violated sensitive U.S. airspace scores of times, yet we would never fire on your planes and risk killing one of your friends or your loved ones.

Now, I guess the picture painted of me by the officials in some countries is pretty grim. May I just say—and I speak not only as the President of the United States but also as a husband, a father, a grandfather, and as a person who loves God and whose heart yearns deeply for a better future—my dream is for our peoples to come together in a spirit of faith and friendship, to help build and leave behind a far safer world. But dreams for the future cannot be realized by words alone. Words must be matched by deeds, by an honest, tireless effort to reduce the risks of war and the loss of life. In this era of nuclear weapons, no achievement could be more meaningful than a verifiable agreement that would dramatically reduce the level of nuclear armaments.

American negotiators in Geneva are offering fairminded, equitable proposals in the interests of both our countries. In the strategic arms reduction talks, we propose deep cuts in both the number of warheads carried by intercontinental ballistic missiles and in the number of missiles themselves. This proposal offered cuts to far below current United States levels. The Soviet Government declined to consider them. We tried again. Last June we proposed a more flexible approach. Then, during the last round of talks in Geneva, we presented a draft treaty responding to concerns expressed by the Soviet Government.

Also, from the outset of the intermediate-range nuclear force talks 2 years ago, I made clear that the United States was ready to join with the Soviet Union in the total elimination of an entire class of intermediate-range, land-based nuclear missiles. That offer still stands. I regret that the Soviet Government continues to reject this proposal. What could possibly be better than to rid the world of an entire class of nuclear weapons?

But in the effort to move the negotiations forward, we proposed an interim solution—some number on both sides below current levels. Again, the Soviet Government refused. I'm deeply aware of people's feelings and frustrations. I share them. And I intend to keep trying. On Monday, I will go to the United Nations to propose another package of steps designed to advance the negotiations. All we seek are agreements to reduce substantially the number and destructive power of nuclear forces.

Yes, we insist on balanced agreements that protect our security, that provide greater stability, and that are truly verifiable, but these requirements are the essence of fairness. They would provide greater security for all nations.

We, the American people, deeply yearn for peace. If our dreams and hopes are to mean anything, we must sit down together and in good faith let honest negotiations bring us a safer world. But I must speak plainly. Just as government censorship is a barrier to understanding, the inflexibility of the Soviet Government on arms control is holding back successful negotiations.

I have said to my own people, you have the right to expect a better world and to demand that your government work for it. This Monday I will have the honor to carry that message to the 38th General Session of the United Nations. It will be a commitment from the heart and one that I know all people share. For the sake of our children and our children's children, I pray that the Soviet Government will not censor my words, but will let their people listen to them and then negotiate with us in good faith.

Thank you for listening, and God bless you all.

Note: The President spoke at 12:06 p.m. from the broadcast studios of the Voice of America (VOA). The address was broadcast over VOA's worldwide network and carried live, with simultaneous translation in Russian, Ukrainian, Romanian, Lithuanian, Urdu, Bengali, and Hausa. The address was rebroadcast to Europe 1 hour later when VOA's English service to Europe began its regular broadcast cycle. VOA's 34 other language services broadcast the address as they began their programs throughout the remainder of the day.

Remarks at a Rodeo of the Professional Rodeo Cowboy Association in Landover, Maryland
September 24, 1983

I think I'd be speaking for all of you if I said a heartfelt thank you to all these people who have entertained us so royally here today. There aren't too many activities in this land of ours, with all the many things we do, that are as purely American as what we have seen here. We're very proud of all of you and grateful to you.

You know, a rodeo here on the east coast, I think, establishes the fact that rodeos are now a national sport, not just a kind of a Western pastime. Madison Avenue, the advertising business—they found that out a long time ago. They found out Americans still love cowboys and cowgirls. And, of course, there's been one advertisement that I've never quite understood, and that is that one—the picture, and there's a cowboy out there in the middle of a herd of cattle and the caption on the picture is, "Come where the flavor is." [*Laughter*]

But again, I just want to thank you. And what a bit of West you brought here. You know, we have a ranch in California, and tomorrow I'm getting on an airplane and going to—New York. [*Laughter*]

But God bless all of you. It's been a won-derful day, and all of this has been wonderful. Thank you.

Note: The President spoke at 4 p.m. at the conclusion of the rodeo, which was held at the Capital Centre.

Remarks at a White House Barbecue for the Professional Rodeo Cowboy Association
September 24, 1983

Don't let these few pieces of paper scare you. I once had a lesson in the importance of brevity in a speech. I had made a speech, and in the audience was the late Bill Alexander, a preacher from Oklahoma. And he took it upon himself to tell me the story of his first sermon. And I thought there was a connection.

He said that his first appearance in the pulpit, he'd worked for weeks on this first sermon, and then he was to preach at an evening service in a little country church in Oklahoma. He stood up in the pulpit that night and looked out at a church that was empty, except for one lone little fellow sitting down there in all the empty pews. So after the music, he went down and he said, "Look, my friend, I'm just a young preacher getting started. You seem to be the only member of the congregation that showed up. What about it, should I go through with it?" The fellow said, "Well, I'm a little old cowpoke out here in Oklahoma. I don't know much about that sort of thing, but I do know this: If I loaded up a truckload of hay, took it out on the prairie, and only one cow showed up, I'd feed her." [*Laughter*]

And, Bill took that as a cue, got back up in the pulpit, and an hour-and-a-half later said, "Amen." And he went back down, and he said, "My friend, you seem to have stuck with me. And like I told you, I was a young preacher getting started, what did you think?" "Well," he says, "like I told you, I don't know about that sort of thing, but I do know this: If I loaded up a truckload of hay, took it out on the prairie, and only one cow showed up, I sure wouldn't give her the whole load." [*Laughter*]

Secretary Baldrige, Ken Stemler, and all of you, welcome to the White House, and congratulations to all of you winners.

This has been a very special day. Watching you out there riding those bulls, I knew that I was among a group that understands what it's like to get a legislative program through Congress. [*Laughter*] Secretary Baldrige has proven himself a multitalented Cabinet member. Every time we come up to a real problem, he has the same solution: "I'll rope 'em; you tie 'em." [*Laughter*] After watching all of you in action, I think Mac and I could put you all to work up here.

When I was about the age of some of you, I joined the horse cavalry. In those days, they still had horses in the Army, and I've enjoyed them ever since. It was heartwarming today to see the children out there from the Therapeutic Riding Association. I think we can all be happy that the National Therapeutic Riding Center provides these very special kids this kind of experience. And I know the results have proven that something I learned back in the cavalry is true, and that is, that there's nothing so good for the inside of a person as the outside of a horse.

The American cowboy remains a figure that is dear to the hearts of American people. The men and women of the Old West may not have been as slick as they were sometimes portrayed by Hollywood, but there was a certain integrity of character that shines through as we look back at them from the vantage place of history.

Now today, we have an author with us, an author who has made enormous contributions to Western folklore and our frontier heritage. Louis L'Amour's storytelling ability has made him one of the most widely read novelists in American history. One hundred and forty million copies of his books have been sold. He's written 87 books, many of which have been adapted for motion pictures and television. He's a man who, like the rodeo—[*different pronunciation:*]—rodeo—[*laughter*]—see, I've been back East too long—brought the West to the people of the East and to people everywhere.

Former Senator Milton Young, Senators Andrews and Armstrong, along with Congressman Carlos Moorhead, have spearheaded an effort that I'm proud to participate in today. If Louis will step forward.

There you are, you sneaked up on me just like Bowdrie.[1]

Mr. L'Amour. That's right.

The President. Well, I have the honor to present to you a very special Congressional Gold Medal. It is for your literary contribu-

tions, your contributions to the appreciation of the West. And you are the first novelist who has ever been honored by Congress with this medal.

Mr. L'Amour. Thank you, Mr. President.

The President. Well today, Louis L'Amour and those of you from the rodeo, you represent this great tradition of the American West, and I know America means a lot to you. I just want you to know that you mean much more to America. I wish you success and good health. Thanks for the fine exhibition today. And now, because of the business that I used to be in, I've saved the applause line for last: Let's eat. [*Laughter and applause*]

Note: The President spoke at 6:06 p.m. on the South Grounds of the White House, where he and Mrs. Reagan hosted a barbecue for members of the association. The association's rodeo was held earlier in the day at the Capital Centre in Landover, Md. At the barbecue, the President assisted in the presentation of awards to six rodeo winners, along with Ken Stemler, president of the association.

Question-and-Answer Session With Reporters on the Cease-fire in Lebanon
September 25, 1983

Q. Mr. President, what can you tell us about the cease-fire in the Middle East?

The President. Well, I was just waiting till everyone got in place to tell you that Secretary-General de Cuellar and myself, we have just called President Gemayel to congratulate him on what has taken place. It is a first step, and you see my fingers crossed. It is the beginning, of course. And the cease-fire will be announced, or has been announced, and now they can get down to the real business of settling the issues and,

we hope, bringing about peace and the solution to the Lebanese problems.

We all are very happy for this first step that has come about, and I'm not going to make any projections or predictions. There is still a long road to go in settling many of the issues there. But as President Gemayel himself said, now with this first step they can have the beginning of that process.

Q. What roles will the Syrians play in the cease-fire and in the negotiations?

The President. Well, we commended President Gemayel for what he has done, but also we have to say the Syrians are evidently cooperating in this, and the Saudi Arabians. We must recognize that Saudi Arabia had a very definite hand in bringing

---

[1] *Chick Bowdrie, Texas Ranger, the main character in Mr. L'Amour's collection of short stories entitled* Bowdrie.

about this first step, this cease-fire.

Q. And will the marines stay in while this cease-fire is——

The President. Well, I'll tell you, all questions like that will be answered for you at 5 o'clock this afternoon. Secretary Shultz is going to have a briefing on the subject.

Q. When did you first hear of it?

The President. I imagine about the same time that you did, although we learned earlier today that it looked like this agreement had been arrived at.

Q. Thank you, Mr. President.

Note: The President spoke at 2:10 p.m. in the Presidential Suite at the Waldorf-Astoria Hotel, where he had met, upon his arrival in New York, N.Y., with Javier Perez de Cuellar de la Guerra, Secretary-General of the United Nations.

Following the meeting, the President and Mrs. Reagan went to the Archdiocese residence behind St. Patrick's Cathedral, where they met with Terence Cardinal Cooke.

Upon his return to the Waldorf-Astoria, the President met in the Presidential Suite with Prince Sihanouk of Kampuchea and Son Sann, President of the Khmer People's National Liberation Front. He then held another meeting in the suite with Samuel K. Doe, Head of State and Chairman of the People's Redemption Council of Liberia.

Remarks at a Reception for the Heads of Delegation to the 38th Session of the United Nations General Assembly in New York, New York
September 25, 1983

George, thank you very much. Ambassador Kirkpatrick, Mr. Mayor, and distinguished guests and friends:

Thank you for coming this evening. And on behalf of all my fellow citizens, let me welcome you to the United States as we gather for the 38th Session of the U.N. General Assembly. The United States is proud to be the home of this organization whose purpose is to bring peace to all the people of the planet, and your presence honors our nation.

I'm looking forward to addressing the General Assembly tomorrow because I bring a message that's very important to me personally, to my country, and I believe to all the members of the U.N. I've come to speak before the General Assembly because, like so many others, I'm disturbed by the drift of world events in recent weeks. I still believe the United Nations is an effective forum for not only discussing our problems but doing something about them.

As much as the Korean airline tragedy has been on my mind over the past few weeks, tonight I want to say just a few words about another tragedy that has been troubling me greatly—the one that is occurring in Lebanon, that beautiful, prosperous land which was once a model of coexistence among peoples and faiths. It has been shattered by violence for reasons which are especially complex.

Our goal, as well as the United Nations, is the territorial integrity, the sovereignty, and the political independence of Lebanon within its internationally recognized boundaries. It's long been clear that we can best fulfill this role by working to strengthen the legitimate Government of Lebanon, by negotiating the withdrawal of all external forces, and by promoting a cease-fire and national reconciliation among Lebanese communities.

At the request of the Lebanese Government, my nation, as you know, joined with France, Italy, and the United Kingdom in sending peacekeeping troops to give Lebanon a chance to pull itself together while our diplomats continue to search for internal agreement and an end to external intervention.

Well, just a short while ago, today, welcome news flashed across the Middle East that a cease-fire has officially been declared.

Within a few hours, it is hoped that guns will finally be stilled. No one can underestimate the challenges that still lie ahead. Lebanon has been racked by so many conflicting forces for so long that the building of peace and national reconciliation will be very formidable tasks. But this is the critical first step. We hope it marks a new beginning in Lebanon, a period of calm when Lebanon can begin to reclaim its nationhood free of outside forces and the threat of new bloodshed.

The coming days must be a time for restraint and reconciliation by all parties. We in the United States will continue to be as helpful as we can in this process, and I hope and pray there will be U.N. observers on hand to help in that process.

Let me say that President Gemayel of Lebanon has shown true statesmanship during this period. The Secretary-General and I spoke with him by telephone earlier today to congratulate him on this cease-fire and to wish him well. The assistance of Saudi Arabia, the cooperation of Syria have also been indispensable during this process.

Finally, if I may, can I congratulate those who have served in the peacekeeping forces in Lebanon as well as two of our own United States diplomats, Robert McFarlane and Richard Fairbanks. All of them have played an enormously constructive role and they, too, must share in our happiness this evening.

We must all remember that what is at stake in Lebanon is a vital principle of international law and international morality, a principle at the heart of the U.N. Charter. A country's right to decide for itself how best to achieve its sovereign objectives, free of occupation, threat, and blackmail—that is what the goal must be. The people of the United States have no driving desire to become involved in the internal affairs of other nations. Contrary to what some have alleged, we have no objectives of our own in Lebanon beyond peace for its people and freedom from external intervention. We would prefer that everyone just mind their own business and live their lives peacefully, but we recognize that as a major power we have major responsibilities. In good conscience, we can't turn our back on those responsibilities.

The problems of Lebanon, important in their own right, are at the same time a part of the greater question of peace for all of the Middle East. We remain committed to the principles I outlined on September 1st, 1982, which were based on U.N. Security Council Resolution 242, 338, and the Camp David accords. The United States will not let up in its efforts to promote a just and lasting, comprehensive negotiated peace so that the nations and peoples of the Middle East can live together in peace.

In closing, let me say that I've come to New York this year because I want to reaffirm that the United States of America will continue to work constructively in the United Nations and in every other forum to help resolve conflicts, to support the forces of peace and international civility, and to promote economic cooperation and prosperity. We believe arms reductions are of particular importance. The commitment of the United States to the goals of the U.N. Charter is unwavering. In the cause of peace, my country will play its part and carry its share of the burden.

Thank you all.

Note: The President spoke at 7:08 p.m. in the Hilton Room at the Waldorf-Astoria Hotel. Ambassador Jeane J. Kirkpatrick made welcoming remarks and introduced Mayor Edward Koch of New York City and Secretary of State George P. Shultz, who then introduced the President. The reception was hosted by the United States for heads of state, foreign ministers, and heads of delegation to the United Nations session.

Following the reception, the President and Mrs. Reagan returned to the Presidential Suite at the hotel, where they remained overnight.

Remarks at the Annual Pulaski Day Banquet in New York, New York
September 25, 1983

Well, I thank you, President Cieslik. And I don't want to offend anyone, but down at the end of the table, on the way in, I was given another Solidarity button, and I might as well put it on.

Grand Marshal Zagurek, honored guests, ladies and gentlemen, I'm most pleased to have this opportunity to be with you, even though it's only for a few moments because I've got to move on to my duties with the United Nations.

America is a land composed of many cultures, and yet we all have one thing in common: We love freedom. And I'm proud to be here honoring citizens whose passion for liberty is second to none.

Polish Americans have always been head and shoulders above the crowd when it comes to love of country and responsible citizenship. And it's a great pleasure for me to recognize and show appreciation for the great contributions of Polish Americans to this nation. And we begin by what you're doing, honoring General Casimir Pulaski, one of our nation's first Polish American heroes. He gave his life for our country in the Battle of Savannah, Georgia, on October 11, 1779. By making this supreme sacrifice, General Pulaski showed the deep love of freedom that burns in the hearts of those who have come to these shores to start a new life.

The example set by such great men has been continued over the centuries. Polish Americans have shed much blood in the defense of our nation, and you know what sacrifices are sometimes called for to defend that cherished freedom. I know that this same love of freedom is in the hearts of your friends and relatives in Poland today. Tonight, in your presence, I would like to reaffirm my commitment to a free and democratic Poland.

In doing so, I would also like to thank you for your strong support of our policies. To all of us here in America, whether our heritages be Polish or Lithuanian or Chinese or Irish, the struggle of the Polish workers serves as a constant reminder of the power of ideas and the human dignity which comes from the willingness to sacrifice oneself for the freedom of our fellow man. Today, we must face challenges to our freedom with the courage and dedication of men like Pulaski. We can face the future with confidence.

Recently, the Soviet massacre of 269 airline passengers shocked the civilized world. But Polish Americans know all about the brutal nature of the regime that has controlled the Soviet Union since 1917. You know that downing a passenger airliner is totally consistent with a government that murdered 15,000 Polish officers in the Katyn forest. We cannot let the world forget that crime, and we will not.

Poland has suffered so much throughout her history, but she's given so much more to the world. And today, the world is grateful that Poland has given us a man whose courage and faith inspires us all and gives us hope when it would be so easy to despair. I say to your in all sincerity, thank God for Pope John Paul and all that he is doing. And may we all pray that his life be protected.

We Americans of all backgrounds have a tremendous responsibility. If freedom is to survive, it will depend on us. I know that together, we will see to it that America remains a mighty force for good in the world.

May God bless you, and God bless America. Thank you all very much.

Note: The President spoke at 6:29 p.m. in the Grand Ballroom at the Waldorf-Astoria Hotel.

In his remarks, the President referred to Adam J. Cieslik, president of the General Pulaski Memorial Committee, and Michael J. Zagurek, Sr., grand marshal of the General Pulaski Day Parade.

On September 6 the President signed Proclamation 5090, proclaiming October 11 as General Pulaski Memorial Day.

Address Before the 38th Session of the United Nations General Assembly in New York, New York
September 26, 1983

Mr. Secretary-General, Mr. President, distinguished delegates, ladies and gentlemen of the world:

Thank you for granting me the honor of speaking today, on this first day of general debate in the 38th Session of the General Assembly. Once again I come before this body preoccupied with peace. Last year I stood in this chamber to address the Special Session on Disarmament. Well, I've come today to renew my nation's commitment to peace. And I have come to discuss how we can keep faith with the dreams that created this organization.

The United Nations was founded in the aftermath of World War II to protect future generations from the scourge of war, to promote political self-determination and global prosperity, and to strengthen the bonds of civility among nations. The founders sought to replace a world at war with a world of civilized order. They hoped that a world of relentless conflict would give way to a new era, one where freedom from violence prevailed.

Whatever challenges the world was bound to face, the founders intended this body to stand for certain values, even if they could not be enforced, and to condemn violence, even if it could not be stopped. This body was to speak with the voice of moral authority. That was to be its greatest power.

But the awful truth is that the use of violence for political gain has become more, not less, widespread in the last decade. Events of recent weeks have presented new, unwelcome evidence of brutal disregard for life and truth. They have offered unwanted testimony on how divided and dangerous our world is, how quick the recourse to violence. What has happened to the dreams of the U.N.'s founders? What has happened to the spirit which created the United Nations?

The answer is clear: Governments got in the way of the dreams of the people. Dreams became issues of East versus West.

Hopes became political rhetoric. Progress became a search for power and domination. Somewhere the truth was lost that people don't make wars, governments do.

And today in Asia, Africa, Latin America, the Middle East, and the North Pacific, the weapons of war shatter the security of the peoples who live there, endanger the peace of neighbors, and create ever more arenas of confrontation between the great powers. During the past year alone, violent conflicts have occurred in the hills around Beirut, the deserts of Chad and the western Sahara, in the mountains of El Salvador, the streets of Suriname, the cities and countryside of Afghanistan, the borders of Kampuchea, and the battlefields of Iran and Iraq.

We cannot count on the instinct for survival to protect us against war. Despite all the wasted lives and hopes that war produces, it has remained a regular, if horribly costly, means by which nations have sought to settle their disputes or advance their goals. And the progress in weapons technology has far outstripped the progress toward peace. In modern times, a new, more terrifying element has entered into the calculations—nuclear weapons. A nuclear war cannot be won, and it must never be fought. I believe that if governments are determined to deter and prevent war, there will not be war.

Nothing is more in keeping with the spirit of the United Nations Charter than arms control. When I spoke before the Second Special Session on Disarmament, I affirmed the United States Government's commitment, and my personal commitment, to reduce nuclear arms and to negotiate in good faith toward that end. Today, I reaffirm those commitments.

The United States has already reduced the number of its nuclear weapons worldwide, and, while replacement of older weapons is unavoidable, we wish to negotiate arms reductions and to achieve significant, equitable, verifiable arms control agreements. And let me add, we must ensure that world security is not undermined by the further spread of nuclear weapons. Nuclear nonproliferation must not be the forgotten element of the world's arms control agenda.

At the time of my last visit here, I expressed hope that a whole class of weapons systems, the longer range INF—intermediate nuclear forces—could be banned from the face of the Earth. I believe that to relieve the deep concern of peoples in both Europe and Asia, the time was ripe, for the first time in history, to resolve a security threat exclusively through arms control. I still believe the elimination of these weapons—the zero option—is the best, fairest, most practical solution to the problem. Unfortunately, the Soviet Union declined to accept the total elimination of this class of weapons.

When I was here last, I hoped that the critical strategic arms reduction talks would focus, and urgently so, on those systems that carry the greatest risk of nuclear war—the fast-flying, accurate, intercontinental ballistic missiles which pose a first-strike potential. I also hoped the negotiations could reduce by one-half the number of strategic missiles on each side and reduce their warheads by one-third. Again, I was disappointed when the Soviets declined to consider such deep cuts, and refused as well to concentrate on these most dangerous, destabilizing weapons.

Well, despite the rebuffs, the United States has not abandoned and will not abandon the search for meaningful arms control agreements. Last June I proposed a new approach toward the START negotiations. We did not alter our objective of substantial reductions, but we recognized that there are a variety of ways to achieve this end. During the last round of Geneva talks, we presented a draft treaty which responded to a number of concerns raised by the Soviet Union. We will continue to build upon this initiative.

Similarly, in our negotiations on intermediate-range nuclear forces, when the Soviet leaders adamantly refused to consider the total elimination of these weapons, the United States made a new offer. We proposed, as an interim solution, some equal number on both sides between zero and 572. We recommended the lowest possible level. Once again, the Soviets refused an equitable solution and proposed instead what might be called a "half zero option"—zero for us and many hundreds of warheads for them. And that's where things stand today, but I still haven't given up hope that the Soviet Union will enter into serious negotiations.

We are determined to spare no effort to achieve a sound, equitable, and verifiable agreement. And for this reason, I have given new instructions to Ambassador Nitze in Geneva, telling him to put forward a package of steps designed to advance the negotiations as rapidly as possible. These initiatives build on the interim framework the United States advanced last March and address concerns that the Soviets have raised at the bargaining table in the past.

Specifically, first, the United States proposes a new initiative on global limits. If the Soviet Union agrees to reductions and limits on a global basis, the United States for its part will not offset the entire Soviet global missile deployment through U.S. deployments in Europe. We would, of course, retain the right to deploy missiles elsewhere.

Second, the United States is prepared to be more flexible on the content of the current talks. The United States will consider mutually acceptable ways to address the Soviet desire that an agreement should limit aircraft as well as missiles.

Third, the United States will address the mix of missiles that would result from reductions. In the context of reductions to equal levels, we are prepared to reduce the number of Pershing II ballistic missiles as well as ground-launched cruise missiles.

I have decided to put forward these important initiatives after full and extensive consultations with our allies, including personal correspondence I've had with the leaders of the NATO governments and Japan and frequent meetings of the NATO Special Consultative Group. I have also stayed in close touch with other concerned friends and allies. The door to an agreement is open. It is time for the Soviet Union to walk through it.

I want to make an unequivocal pledge to

those gathered today in this world arena. The United States seeks and will accept any equitable, verifiable agreement that stabilizes forces at lower levels than currently exist. We're ready to be flexible in our approach, indeed, willing to compromise. We cannot, however, especially in light of recent events, compromise on the necessity of effective verification.

Reactions to the Korean airliner tragedy are a timely reminder of just how different the Soviets' concept of truth and international cooperation is from that of the rest of the world. Evidence abounds that we cannot simply assume that agreements negotiated with the Soviet Union will be fulfilled. We negotiated the Helsinki Final Act, but the promised freedoms have not been provided, and those in the Soviet Union who sought to monitor their fulfillment languish in prison. We negotiated a biological weapons convention, but deadly yellow rain and other toxic agents fall on Hmong villages and Afghan encampments. We have negotiated arms agreements, but the high level of Soviet encoding hides the information needed for their verification. A newly discovered radar facility and a new ICBM raise serious concerns about Soviet compliance with agreements already negotiated.

Peace cannot be served by pseudo arms control. We need reliable, reciprocal reductions. I call upon the Soviet Union today to reduce the tensions it has heaped on the world in the past few weeks and to show a firm commitment to peace by coming to the bargaining table with a new understanding of its obligations. I urge it to match our flexibility. If the Soviets sit down at the bargaining table seeking genuine arms reductions, there will be arms reductions. The governments of the West and their people will not be diverted by misinformation and threats. The time has come for the Soviet Union to show proof that it wants arms control in reality, not just in rhetoric.

Meaningful arms control agreements between the United States and the Soviet Union would make our world less dangerous; so would a number of confidence-building steps we've already proposed to the Soviet Union.

Arms control requires a spirit beyond narrow national interests. This spirit is a basic pillar on which the U.N. was founded. We seek a return to this spirit. A fundamental step would be a true nonalignment of the United Nations. This would signal a return to the true values of the charter, including the principle of universality. The members of the United Nations must be aligned on the side of justice rather than injustice, peace rather than aggression, human dignity rather than subjugation. Any other alignment is beneath the purpose of this great body and destructive of the harmony that it seeks. What harms the charter harms peace.

The founders of the U.N. expected that member nations would behave and vote as individuals, after they had weighed the merits of an issue—rather like a great, global town meeting. The emergence of blocs and the polarization of the U.N. undermine all that this organization initially valued.

We must remember that the nonaligned movement was founded to counter the development of blocs and to promote détente between them. Its founders spoke of the right of smaller countries not to become involved in others' disagreements. Since then, membership in the nonaligned movement has grown dramatically, but not all the new members have shared the founders' commitment of genuine nonalignment. Indeed, client governments of the Soviet Union, who have long since lost their independence, have flocked into the nonaligned movement, and, once inside, have worked against its true purpose. Pseudo nonalignment is no better than pseudo arms control.

The United States rejects as false and misleading the view of the world as divided between the empires of the East and West. We reject it on factual grounds. The United States does not head any bloc of subservient nations, nor do we desire to. What is called the West is a free alliance of governments, most of whom are democratic and all of whom greatly value their independence. What is called the East is an empire directed from the center which is Moscow.

The United States, today as in the past, is a champion of freedom and self-determination for all people. We welcome diversity; we support the right of all nations to define and pursue their national goals. We respect their decisions and their sovereignty, asking only that they respect the decisions and sovereignty of others. Just look at the world over the last 30 years and then decide for yourself whether the United States or the Soviet Union has pursued an expansionist policy.

Today, the United States contributes to peace by supporting collective efforts by the international community. We give our unwavering support to the peacekeeping efforts of this body, as well as other multilateral peacekeeping efforts around the world. The U.N. has a proud history of promoting conciliation and helping keep the peace. Today, U.N. peacekeeping forces or observers are present in Cyprus and Kashmir, on the Golan Heights and in Lebanon.

In addition to our encouragement of international diplomacy, the United States recognizes its responsibilities to use its own influence for peace. From the days when Theodore Roosevelt mediated the Russo-Japanese War in 1905, we have a long and honorable tradition of mediating or damping conflicts and promoting peaceful solutions. In Lebanon, we, along with France, Italy, and the United Kingdom, have worked for a cease-fire, for the withdrawal of all external forces, and for restoration of Lebanon's sovereignty and territorial integrity. In Chad we have joined others in supporting the recognized government in the face of external aggression. In Central America, as in southern Africa, we are seeking to discourage reliance upon force and to construct a framework for peaceful negotiations. We support a policy to disengage the major powers from Third World conflict.

The U.N. Charter gives an important role to regional organizations in the search for peace. The U.S. efforts in the cause of peace are only one expression of a spirit that also animates others in the world community. The Organization of American States was a pioneer in regional security efforts. In Central America, the members of the Contadora group are striving to lay a foundation for peaceful resolution of that region's problems. In East Asia, the Asian countries have built a framework for peaceful political and economic cooperation that has greatly strengthened the prospects for lasting peace

in their region. In Africa, organizations such as the Economic Community of West African States are being forged to provide practical structures in the struggle to realize Africa's potential.

From the beginning, our hope for the United Nations has been that it would reflect the international community at its best. The U.N. at its best can help us transcend fear and violence and can act as an enormous force for peace and prosperity. Working together, we can combat international lawlessness and promote human dignity. If the governments represented in this chamber want peace as genuinely as their peoples do, we shall find it. We can do so by reasserting the moral authority of the United Nations.

In recent weeks, the moral outrage of the world seems to have reawakened. Out of the billions of people who inhabit this planet, why, some might ask, should the death of several hundred shake the world so profoundly? Why should the death of a mother flying toward a reunion with her family or the death of a scholar heading toward new pursuits of knowledge matter so deeply? Why are nations who lost no citizens in the tragedy so angry?

The reason rests on our assumptions about civilized life and the search for peace. The confidence that allows a mother or a scholar to travel to Asia or Africa or Europe or anywhere else on this planet may be only a small victory in humanity's struggle for peace. Yet what is peace if not the sum of such small victories?

Each stride for peace and every small victory are important for the journey toward a larger and lasting peace. We have made progress. We've avoided another world war. We've seen an end to the traditional colonial era and the birth of a hundred newly sovereign nations. Even though development remains a formidable challenge, we've witnessed remarkable economic growth among the industrialized and the developing nations. The United Nations and its affiliates have made important contributions to the quality of life on this planet, such as directly saving countless lives through its refugee and emergency relief programs. These broad achievements, however, have been overshadowed by the problems that weigh so heavily upon us. The problems are old, but it is not too late to commit ourselves to a new beginning, a beginning fresh with the ideals of the U.N. Charter.

Today, at the beginning of this 38th Session, I solemnly pledge my nation to upholding the original ideals of the United Nations. Our goals are those that guide this very body. Our ends are the same as those of the U.N.'s founders, who sought to replace a world at war with one where the rule of law would prevail, where human rights were honored, where development would blossom, where conflict would give way to freedom from violence.

In 1956 President Dwight Eisenhower made an observation on weaponry and deterrence in a letter to a publisher. He wrote: "When we get to the point, as we one day will, that both sides know that in any outbreak of general hostilities, regardless of the element of surprise, destruction will be both reciprocal and complete, possibly we will have sense enough to meet at the conference table with the understanding that the era of armaments has ended and the human race must conform its actions to this truth or die." He went on to say, ". . . we have already come to a point where safety cannot be assumed by arms alone . . . their usefulness becomes concentrated more and more in their characteristics as deterrents than in instruments with which to obtain victory. . . ."

Distinguished ladies and gentlemen, as we persevere in the search for a more secure world, we must do everything we can to let diplomacy triumph. Diplomacy, the most honorable of professions, can bring the most blessed of gifts, the gift of peace. If we succeed, the world will find an excitement and accomplishment in peace beyond that which could ever be imagined through violence and war.

I want to leave you today with a message I have often spoken about to the citizens of my own country, especially in times when I felt they were discouraged and unsure. I say it to you with as much hope and heart as I've said it to my own people. You have the right to dream great dreams. You have the right to seek a better world for your people. And all of us have the responsibility to work for that better world. And as caring, peaceful peoples, think what a powerful force for good we could be. Distinguished delegates, let us regain the dream the United Nations once dreamed.

Thank you.

Note: The President spoke at 10:34 a.m. in the General Assembly Hall at the United Nations Headquarters Building. Upon arrival at the United Nations, the President met with Secretary-General Javier Perez de Cuellar de la Guerra and then with Jorge Illueca, President of the 38th Session of the General Assembly, who introduced the President to the session.

Following his address, the President returned to the Waldorf-Astoria Hotel.

Remarks at a Reception Sponsored by the Women's Sports Foundation in New York, New York
September 26, 1983

The President. I'm delighted to have this opportunity to be here with you today. I have just come from addressing the United Nations, and I have to tell you, with all due respect to them, I feel more at home here, because—*[laughter]*——

In addition to athletics in school, and when I was in school I started my career as a radio sports announcer, and thought that my life was going to go on connected with sports. Now here I am, and maybe I'm going to get back to it.

Ms. de Varona. We hope so. We welcome you.

The President. Well, I'd be pleased to do it.

You know, the Women's Sports Foundation's annual awards program and Hall of Fame is providing, as you well know, some overdue and well deserved recognition to some very fine athletes. So, before I go any further, let my just say to Donna—and I was going to say de Varona—[*different pronunciation:*]—but it's de Varona——

Ms. de Varona. Very good.

The President. Micki King Hogue, Tenley Albright, Andrea Mead Lawrence, Helen Stephens, Martina Navratilova, Mary Decker, Flo Hyman, Arie Selinger—and I'm afraid that I met more awardees than I had names for down here, so to all of them also I think all can be rightfully proud of their accomplishments.

There was a time—and it wasn't long ago—that people thought that a woman's place in sports was in the grandstand. Old thought patterns are hard to break, and I'd like to congratulate all of you in the Women's Sports Foundation for what you're doing to expand opportunities for participation for half of America's population. Your efforts to open up sporting events and change attitudes toward female sports participation, competition, and fitness is doing a great service.

You should be especially proud of your work to encourage women and girls to get involved in physical fitness programs. You're having a great influence, and it was a result in health and happiness for people who otherwise might have lived less healthy lives.

We can all be grateful for the private sector support that you've been getting from corporations like Kimberly-Clark, Avon, and Milky Way, and I have a feeling that there are more of those present and helping than I was given names for. So, to all of them, you're reaching women and girls that are all over the country with a call for involvement, fitness, and health. This type of support from respected corporations is just the type of initiative that we're encouraging, and I applaud those companies for their good citizenship.

I'm pleased to learn that the United States Olympic Committee and Women's Sports Foundation have teamed up to ensure that there is a bright future for women in sports and fitness. I wish you success for your national conference in November, which will address the ways in which we can improve the status of girls' and women's sports in America. Sports and fitness opportunities are for everyone. And through activities like this one today, you can assure that every individual has an opportunity to participate, to compete, and to reach his or her potential.

So, good luck to you again and congratulations to your award recipients and thanks for letting me play a part in this effort. And let me just say, I can understand your suggestions to me, but I also know, and I just want to say to you in my own behalf, that there has been some misperception about what my attitude might be. And I want you to know that what it really is is probably one of the best kept secrets in Washington, and I've been doing my best to get the truth out.

And I can't leave without telling a little story that has to do with my particular trade today, though, but I think it kind of fits the occasion. I am a fan also of not particularly an athlete but a very wonderful woman, Margaret Thatcher of England. And when we had the summit conference in Williamsburg, Virginia, where it's so—you know, the restored community, restored to exactly what it was at the time of the American Revolution, and the first night I knew our first get-together was going to be around the dinner table, so I was all set. When we sat down, I was going to say, "Margaret, if one of your predecessors had been a little more clever, you'd be hosting this gathering." [*Laughter*] I'd underestimated her because we all got there, sat down, and I said, "Margaret, if one of your predecessors had been a little more clever——" She said, "I know, I would have been hosting this gathering." [*Laughter*]

Well, thank you for letting me spend a few minutes here. I've got to go back to the affairs of state now. But this has been a pleasure, and I assure you, you won't have anything to worry about from me.

Ms. de Varona. Thank you, Mr. President.

Note: The President spoke at 11:39 a.m. in the Empire Room at the Waldorf-Astoria Hotel. He was introduced by Donna de

Varona, president of the Women's Sports Foundation, which sponsored the reception to honor five inductees into the foundation's Hall of Fame.

Exchange With Reporters in New York City on Arms Control and Reduction Negotiations
September 26, 1983

Q. Mr. President, have you put the Soviets on the defensive?

The President. Well, not purposely.

Q. Has Ambassador Nitze had any response, sir, following your new initiatives to the Soviets?

The President. What's that?

Q. Has Ambassador Nitze had any response in Geneva yet on your new initiative?

The President. Not that I know of, no, because this is the first time that we publicly voiced them.

Q. He gave it to them earlier, I think.

The President. I assume that he did. I've heard nothing officially.

Q. Good to see you.

The President. Thank you.

Note: The exchange began at 1:53 p.m. in the Presidential Suite at the Waldorf-Astoria Hotel. The reporters were present to observe the beginning of the President's meeting with Prime Minister Indira Gandhi of India.

Earlier, the President hosted a working luncheon with King Hassan II of Morocco in the Presidential Suite.

Interview With Members of the Editorial Board of the New York Post in New York City
September 26, 1983

Q. Well, Mr. President, first of all our genuine appreciation for sparing us the time. We know your schedule is very busy, and we know that time is limited. So, we'd like to get down to business right away.

The President. All right. Well, let me say I'm appreciating your paper and its upholding of our country and the principles that involved and so forth—very refreshing.

Q. Well, we shall continue to do so.

Lebanon

Mr. President, it would seem that congratulations are in order over your efforts to bring about a Lebanon cease-fire. However, all Mideast cease-fires seem to be fragile at best, and we're wondering what are the contingency plans if the cease-fire breaks down. Secretary Shultz has said there is no timetable to pull out the marines, says that goes for the Navy as well.

The President. Yes. I think right now this is a first step. We know that it's a tenuous one and that it's a very complex problem that has to be worked out. But it is right in line with the mission that took the whole multinational force there to be in a position to help preserve stability as a government of Lebanon reinstitutes its sovereignty over its own territory and the foreign forces get out.

So, we could be hopeful and optimistic, and certainly we have to be grateful that the shelling has stopped. But much yet remains to be done.

Q. Mr. President, you said yesterday that the Saudis played an important part in the helping to bring the cease-fire about. Did they put pressure on Syria by threatening to withhold their bankrolling?

The President. I don't know of any pressure of that kind. But I do know that just as we had two ambassadors there who were back and forth working virtually around the clock, trying to bring the various parties together, they were most helpful in doing the same thing and, I think, have to be recognized for that. So, I wouldn't know what persuasion was used or anything else, but finally we have the cease-fire.

1984 Presidential Campaign

Q. On October the 15th, Paul Laxalt and others will be forming the committee for your reelection. Can you say at this stage if you have made up your mind to run? If not, will you at least endorse Mr. Laxalt's committee?

The President. At least I would endorse what?

Q. Mr. Laxalt's committee.

The President. Oh. Well, no, let me just say I don't think this is a time when I can make an answer of any kind to that question. First of all, I believe that campaigns are too long anyway. But I've said there is no way that I'm going to make or announce a decision until the last possible moment that it could be done, because either way it's going to make things difficult. If you're not a candidate, you're a lameduck, and if you are a candidate, suddenly everything you try to accomplish is viewed as part of the political campaign.

So, I know there's coming a day when I'm going to have to make a statement, but not now.

Q. Have you discussed the possibilities yet with your family?

The President. Well, obviously this has come up in conversation. [*Laughter*]

Q. Will you endorse the committee that's being formed, though? Is it with your blessing?

The President. That would be getting into the area of commenting that I still don't think I should.

Q. When do you think, Mr. President, the day may come when you'll have to make a decision public? Do you see it within the next month or so, perhaps?

The President. Well, I haven't set any specific date, and so I won't hazard one. But, as I say, I know that such a day is coming, that there is—reality alone says that a decision

must be announced.

Terence Cardinal Cooke

Q. You had a rather historic meeting of prayer with Cardinal Cooke yesterday. How did you find that very brave man?

The President. Very brave. And it was just amazing. He expressed his interest in so much that's going on in the world and some of the things that we're trying to do. And it was a moving experience. But also we were so grateful for the opportunity to see him and have this meeting with him. They had arranged a little prayer service in his chapel, but not with him present. But we then went to his room, and he concluded the service before our visit with the final prayer.

James G. Watt

Q. Senator D'Amato of New York and many others have been very forceful in their language calling for Mr. Watt to resign. What are your views about that?

The President. Well, first of all, I think Mr. Watt has done a very capable job as Secretary of Interior. I think we have to point out with all of this that it was an unfortunate remark. It certainly was a mistake, and he has admitted that—both those points. He has apologized not only to me, but he's apologized to the people on the Commission for that. But I think in all fairness we have to recognize that, yes, it was a very improper thing to say, but it certainly was not said in the sense of any bitterness or bigotry or prejudice. If I thought he was bigoted or prejudiced, he wouldn't be a part of our administration. It was an attempt at lightness that, as we all have to admit, fell very flat. And it was unfortunate.

So, I think that we have to recognize that, hope it won't be repeated.

Q. Do you think it'd be possible for him to continue in office?

The President. What's that?

Q. Do you think it would be possible for him to continue in office?

The President. Well, I think that's a decision that he, himself, would have to make, whether he feels that he has made it questionable as to whether he can be effective or not.

Q. You have no plans, Mr. President, to ask him to leave, then?

The President. No. I accepted his apology.

United Nations Address

Q. If we could turn to your speech at the United Nations today, which is very calm and very measured. Had you, while you were preparing the speech, had any indication or signal of any sort that your proposals might be agreeable to the Soviets?

The President. Well, you can always hope. What I said today I've thought for some time the things that needed saying, both with regard to the United Nations and to their approach to these matters. I just feel very deeply that if—and when I remarked about governments starting wars, that if the representatives of the Soviet Union and ourselves sat down at those tables, those negotiating tables, with the conviction in our minds that there must not be a war, then there won't be a war, and there could almost instantly be a reduction in those terrible and dangerous arms, those weapons. I'm certain that the Russian people don't want a war, and I know our people don't. We don't. And I just do—are they willing to come to the table with that idea in mind, instead of an idea as to how they can preserve some margin of superiority for themselves.

Korean Airliner Incident

Q. [*Inaudible*]—heard, Mr. President, has there been the slightest signal of the overall regret expressed by some segments of the Soviet leadership, which there has been, small as it may be. Have you regarded that as any kind of genuine signal?

The President. No, because I don't think it's come from the kind of people that normally would give the signals. But it is an indication there of, certainly, recognition on the part of some, as you say, that this was as terrible a deed as we have said it was. And I just think the world is owed an apology plus a statement to the effect that they're going to join the rest of us in cooperating to see that such a thing can never happen again. And that could be aided and abetted also if they would recognize some responsibility in compensation for the families of the victims.

Q. Mr. President, do you think there may be some sort of a high-level political dispute going on in the Kremlin, that the statements by these lower level officials, which were just referred to, may represent and in fact there isn't unanimity in there on what happened?

The President. I wouldn't hazard a guess on that. But I do say that there is evidence that is a little different than what we usually expect, because usually the official reply comes out with unanimous support over there, and that's it, and that's the story everyone tells. So, this has been a little different, that there have been voices that have begun now. They weren't heard for quite a while.

In fact, there was such a difference in the stories that it just further added to the evidence of how deliberate and despicable this act was. Most people are tending to forget that their first statement was that they just didn't know anything about it. It just disappeared from their radar. And then when the evidence was presented that it had been shot down and that they were responsible for that, suddenly they come up with a new story about spy plane and so forth. No one's mentioned this yet, but isn't that a pretty hard—the idea of error—a pretty hard thing to believe, when that plane is one on a regular schedule, that at least every week is flying that same route and at the same time of day?

Visit to the Philippines

Q. Mr. President, are your plans firm for Manila?

The President. What's that?

Q. Are your plans firm for Manila?

The President. Well, the trip is still planned. If there would be any reason to change it, it would be domestic, because there is a probability—we had planned that trip with the idea that Congress would not be in session, that it would have gone home. And that is questionable now as to whether they're going to go home. And now it makes you wonder, how can you be in two places at once? But don't take that as an indication. So far the trip is still on.

Q. The First Lady had expressed second thoughts, misgivings about that particular trip, given the recent events, the recent, tragic events.

The President. Well, let me just say—and I sympathize with her very deeply, but since a previous experience that we had—I shouldn't use the expression "she's a little gun shy." [*Laughter*] No, but she does feel a legitimate concern and in many places where I have to appear.

Arms Reduction

Q. Mr. President, just to come back to your speech to the U.N. today and your three proposals, I was struck—let me not talk for everyone, because we haven't all talked about it—but it struck me as being rather generous towards the negotiating position, in the view that they've constantly said no, and you say, "Well, all right, now, we'll count the aircraft, and we won't count the missiles in the Far East. So that would reduce the total number to which we are responding in Western Europe."

The President. Ah, but we reserve the right to place in other areas——

Q. Yes.

The President. ——to counter what other threats might be involved in their disposition in other areas of their missiles.

Q. Yes, and you go very far towards meeting the Soviet position over the Pershings, which they've been making the most noise about.

The President. Maybe that was a restatement of something that was always in our mind. The original concept of what was going in NATO in INF was going to be a mix of Pershings and cruise missiles. And at one time, there was a Russian voice raised that, well, they might listen to cruise missiles but not Pershings at all. Well, this in a way today was a restatement that, no, there will still be a mix, but we are willing that if they agree to reductions, that means that our original figure must be reduced. That reduction will be in both Pershings and cruise missiles.

But as I said in the remarks, I'd like to see it on the zero-zero basis. We know that can't be. Well, now we want—any reduction that can be achieved is going to be better than what threatens us now and threatens our allies in Europe. And so,

that's what we're going to continue to strive for, is to the lowest possible point that they will come, and we will meet them on an equal and a verifiable basis.

Q. Mr. President, you've been at the U.N.—[*inaudible*]—and there have been reports out of your administration that you and some of your senior aides feel that there is a double standard operating—[*inaudible*]—for example, being quick to condemn Israel for its invasion of Lebanon but not condemning the Soviet downing of the airliner or the Libyan invasion of Chad. Do you feel after being here that there is a double standard?

The President. Well, no, I've noticed that many times they on many votes have been able to marshal a majority of votes their way and not on ours. What I was trying to point out was again the—something happens to the whole concept of the U.N. if we find the U.N., like the world, beginning to divide up into blocs. The ideal was supposed to be that every nation would be there as an individual and seeking the same thing, the things that are called for in the charter of the U.N. And there has been evidence of the other, of kind of taking sides or bloc voting, and I was just trying to call their attention back to the original purpose.

I'll tell you, may I say something else about that, too? It's time that all of us recognize that maybe we're not as civilized as we were when I was a young man growing up. By that I mean that it was taken for granted for years and years, the days prior to World War II, that all the rules of warfare were aimed at limiting warfare to warriors and providing protection and neutrality for civilians. And without quite realizing it's happened, we're in a world today where not only are the civilians fair game, but the most potent weapons systems, the nuclear weapons, are definitely aimed at the destruction of civilians. And wouldn't it be nice if in a forum of this kind we could get back to being as civilized as we once were?

Jewish Vote

Q. Since we're in New York, could we ask you a question about the Jewish vote? In 1980 you scored a very high proportion of the Jewish vote for a Republican, but since then, it has been suggested that support has dwindled. Do you think it would be possible to recapture that element in your 1984 strategy?

The President. Well, I never conceded that we lost them. I think we have more to offer them than the other side does. And, no, I haven't felt that at all. I know that sometimes in all of this debate with regard to the peace plan and all, there were times when the Israelis and ourselves found ourselves differing on various points. But that never in any way—and they knew this as well; the Israelis knew this—that never slackened in any way or weakened the resolve of this country, which has existed since 1948, of a moral obligation to see that the State of Israel continues to exist as a nation.

Q. Thank you, sir.

1984 Presidential Campaign

Q. Could I ask one last question? Mr. President, I wonder if I could ask you as an astute political observer, not as a President, who you think amongst the Democratic candidates for President might be the toughest candidate?

The President. If I knew the answer to that one, I wouldn't give it to you. [*Laughter*] Why should I help them make their decision? [*Laughter*]

Note: The interview began at 2:35 p.m. in the Presidential Suite at the Waldorf-Astoria Hotel. Among those participating in the interview were Rupert Murdoch, publisher, Roger Wood, executive editor, Bruce Rothwell, editorial page editor, and Steve Dunleavy, George Artz, and Fred Dicker.

Following the interview, the President returned to Washington, D.C.

Remarks on Signing the Challenge Grant Amendments of 1983
September 26, 1983

Secretary Bell, George, Barbara, you ladies and gentlemen, welcome to the White House.

I know we both had a full day, and I'm happy we were able to arrange this gathering where we could meet in a more relaxed atmosphere. As you perhaps are aware, we've just returned from New York, where I addressed the United Nations.

It's clear that our country faces serious challenges in the years ahead, but there are numerous reasons for optimism. If the United States is to remain the leader of the free world, if our freedom and our prosperity to be maintained, we must make certain that every American has the opportunity to live up to his or her potential. Historically black colleges and universities have played and are playing a vital role. And I'm proud that in the last 2 years we've stood shoulder to shoulder with you.

Today is your day, as declared by a joint resolution of the Congress, and I hope that you won't think it presumptuous, but I'd like to think of it as our day.

We remain committed to the proposition that keeping historically black colleges and universities a vibrant force in American education should not be just the goal of black Americans but of all of us.

I'd like to take this opportunity to offer a special thanks to a man with us today who has done so much over the years and continues to be an inspiration to us all. This distinguished gentleman, a former president of Tuskegee Institute, founded the United Negro College Fund in 1944. His hard work and leadership have meant that hundreds of thousands of our citizens are living richer and more meaningful lives. He's a man of deep conviction, yet he knows the value of businesslike approaches to achieving goals. He recognized long ago the significance of a strong endowment system to the viability of black colleges and universities. And I am, of course, referring to Dr. Frederick Douglass Patterson.

Dr. Patterson, congratulations.

Dr. Patterson is named after a great

American and, I might add, a great Republican—[*laughter*]—Frederick Douglass.

Well, since we last met a year ago, much has been accomplished. We set a goal of identifying and eliminating unfair barriers to your participation in federally sponsored programs. We set out to encourage the private sector to get more involved. Well, we also identified the 27 Federal agencies which provide nearly all of the Federal funding for higher education and made sure that they were aware of and shared our commitment to strengthening historically black colleges and universities. And I'm happy to say that preliminary figures suggest that those 27 agencies will be providing 11½ percent more funds to your universities and colleges in '83 than they did in '82.

Now, much of this is in the form of research grants, from which historically black colleges have been shortchanged over the years. Well, we're making sure that doesn't happen any more.

These grants offer colleges and universities a chance to develop new educational capabilities while providing a needed service. There's no reason for them to be concentrated only in the larger institutions that have developed the skill of granstmanship into an art form. I'm especially pleased that many of the projects stimulated by our initiative involve science, mathematics, and engineering.

But Federal research grants and other government subsidies are not an end in themselves. We must continue to work toward the goal of self-sufficiency. In that regard, our administration has strongly supported legislation which passed the Senate last week and the House today. This legislation, which I will sign this afternoon, will amend title III of the Higher Education Act to authorize matching endowment grants to colleges and universities.

These grants will promote independence and self-sufficiency by aiding and encouraging the development of substantial endowment funds and by providing incentives to promote fundraising activities. This program will help guarantee the continued viability of black colleges and universities, fulfilling a longstanding dream of Dr. Patterson.

Attracting better private sector support has also been one of our goals this year. Much has been accomplished in this area as well. Our project—or one project underway provides a computer network in electrical engineering, connecting a number of black colleges and universities, and will improve the training of 1,500 electrical engineering students at these schools. Over $389,000 of private sector contributions are involved in this.

In the White House, our Private Sector Initiative Office is currently working with the National Alliance of Business to link specific black colleges and universities with local businesses and corporations. It's been 2 years since the signing of Executive Order 12320, and I think we can all agree that progress has been made.

We can also agree we've got a long way to go. I hope that over this next year I'll have the opportunity to meet with some of you, perhaps in a smaller group, to hear your views personally. Until then, let me assure you I remain fully convinced of the importance of educational institutions.

You represent a proud part of America's heritage. You're a great national resource we can't afford to see dwindle for lack of care. You offered hope to many of our citizens in a time of despair. You gave faith to many when it was sorely needed.

And I can't help but tell a little story I heard the other day about faith. A fellow fell off a cliff, and as he was falling grabbed a limb sticking out the side of the cliff and looked down 300 feet to the canyon floor below and then looked up and said, "Lord, if there's anyone up there, give me faith. Tell me what to do." And a voice from the heavens said, "If you have faith, let go." [*Laughter*] He looked down at the canyon floor and then took another look up and said, "Is there anyone else up there?" [*Laughter*]

Well, working together, we can have faith that we will succeed and that our country will be a decent place and a land of opportunity for all that we want it to be. So, I thank you all for being here. God bless you.

And now I'm going to sign Senate bill 1872.

And the Senator whose name is on this

bill as President pro tem of the Senate is Strom Thurmond's. I know Tip [O'Neill] isn't here because I would have seen him. [*Laughter*]

[*At this point, the President signed the bill.*]

Dr. Patterson, I think the best idea would be if you got the signing pen.

Note: The President spoke at 4:49 p.m. at the reception for representatives of historically black colleges and universities in the East Room at the White House. Among those attending the reception were Secretary of Education Terrel H. Bell and the Vice President and Mrs. Bush.

As enacted, S. 1872 is Public Law 98–95, approved September 26.

Remarks at the Annual Meeting of the Boards of Governors of the World Bank Group and the International Monetary Fund
September 27, 1983

Good morning. Mr. de Larosière, Governors of the World Bank, and its affiliates, and of the International Monetary Fund, distinguished colleagues and guests:

On behalf of my fellow Americans, I'm delighted to welcome you to the United States and to our Nation's Capital.

And I am honored to have this opportunity to speak again to your distinguished members. I say honored because I believe that your institutions, the World Bank and affiliates and the International Monetary Fund, serve noble purposes. There can be no higher mission than to improve the human condition and to offer opportunities for fulfillment in our individual lives and the life of our national and our world communities.

You are the leaders of the world community in bringing a better life to the diverse and often tragically poor people of our planet. You have worked tirelessly to preserve the framework for international economic cooperation and to generate confidence and competition in the world economy.

The unending quest for economic, social, and human improvement is the basic drive that inspires and unites all of us. In 1945, when your great institutions were established, the civilized world had been brought to its knees by a wave of totalitarian violence that inflicted suffering, sacrifice, and the suppression of human rights on millions of innocent people.

Security, freedom, and prosperity were very much on the minds of the citizens of the world in 1945. They should be on our minds today. The institutions you represent could not have been born, could not have flourished and, may I add, will not survive in a world dominated by a system of cruelty that disregards individual rights and the value of human life in its ruthless drive for power. No state can be regarded as preeminent over the rights of individuals. Individual rights are supreme.

In this civilization we've labored so faithfully to resurrect, preserve, and enhance, let us be ever mindful: It is not just development and prosperity, but ultimately our peace and our freedom that are always at stake. Too often the demands of prosperity and security are viewed as competitors when, in fact, they're complementary, natural, and necessary allies. We cannot prosper unless we're secure, and we cannot be secure unless we're free.

The goals of the great international political and economic institutions—the United Nations where I spoke yesterday, and the World Bank, its affiliates, and the IMF you represent here today—were to be reached by trusting in a shared and enduring truth: The keys to personal fulfillment, national development, human progress, and world peace are freedom and responsibility for individuals and cooperation among nations. When I addressed the delegates of the United Nations yesterday, I reminded them: You have the right to dream great dreams, to seek a better world for your people. And all of us have the responsibility to work for that better world. As caring, peaceful peoples, think what a powerful force for good we could be.

Today I come before your distinguished assembly in that same spirit—a messenger for prosperity and security through the principles of freedom, responsibility, and cooperation.

When our nations trusted in these great principles in the postwar years, the civilized world enjoyed unparalleled economic development and improvement in the human condition. We witnessed a virtual explosion of world output and trade and the arrival of many free, self-determined, independent nation states as new members of the international system.

And, as I said when I last spoke to you, the societies that achieved the most spectacular, broad-based economic progress in the shortest period of time have not been the biggest in size nor the richest in resources and, certainly, not the most rigidly controlled. What has united them all was their belief in the magic of the marketplace. Millions of individuals making their own decisions in the marketplace will always allocate resources better than any centralized government planning process.

Trust the people—this is the crucial lesson of history. Because only when the human spirit is allowed to worship, invent, create, and produce, only when individuals are given a personal stake in deciding their destiny and benefiting from their own risks, only then do societies become dynamic, prosperous, progressive, and free.

In the turbulent decade of the 1970's, too many of us, the United States included, forgot the principles that produced the basis for our mutual economic progress. We permitted our governments to overspend, overtax, and overregulate us toward soaring inflation and record interest rates. Now we see more clearly again. We're working and cooperating to bring our individual economies and the world economy back to more solid foundations of low inflation, personal incentives for saving and investment, higher productivity, and greater opportunities for our people.

Our first task was to get our own financial and economic houses in order. Our coun-

tries are interdependent, but without a foundation of sound domestic policies, the international economic system cannot expand and improve. Merely providing additional official development assistance will not produce progress. This is true for all countries, developed and developing, without exception. As the 1983 development report of the World Bank notes, "International actions can greatly improve the external environment confronting developing countries but cannot supplant the efforts that the developing countries must make themselves."

I believe the United States is making real progress. Since we took office, we've reduced the rate of growth in our Federal Government's spending by nearly 40 percent. We have cut inflation dramatically, from 12.4 percent to 2.6 percent for the last 12 months. The prime interest rate has been cut nearly in half, from 21½ percent to 11 percent. Figures released last week reveal our gross national product grew at an annual rate of almost 10 percent in the second quarter, and about 7 percent is estimated for the third.

In the United States we still face large projected deficits which concern us, because deficit Federal spending and borrowing drain capital that would otherwise be invested for stronger economic growth. But as Secretary Regan correctly pointed out in the Interim Committee, Sunday, the deficit is coming down as a result of economic growth. Revenues are higher than anticipated, and we expect continued improvement. We'll continue to work for greater restraint in Federal spending, but we will not risk sabotaging our economic expansion in a short-sighted attempt to reduce deficits by raising taxes. What tax increases would actually reduce is economic growth, by discouraging savings, investment, and consumption.

One other point about the United States deficit: Let me make clear that it is caused in part by our determination to provide the military strength and political security to ensure peace in the world. Our commitment to military security is matched by our resolve to negotiate a verifiable nuclear arms reduction treaty. Only then can we safely reduce military expenditures and their drain on our resources. As I mentioned at the outset, there can be no lasting prosperity without security and freedom.

Turning more directly to economic development, all signs point to a world economic recovery gaining momentum. As early as last February, the Conference Board predicted that economic growth rates in the United States and six major industrial countries spell economic recovery in any language. Since then, industrial production in the OECD [Organization for Economic Cooperation and Development] countries has been moving up. Your own IMF economists are predicting growth in the world economy of at least 3 percent next year. This is the brightest outlook in several years.

As the U.S. economy picks up steam, our imports rise with it. When you consider that half of all non-OPEC developing country manufactured goods exported to the industrialized countries come to the United States, it's clear what a strong stimulus our imports provide for economic expansion abroad. And as other economies prosper, our exports in turn increase. We all gain.

Many nations are moving steadily forward toward self-sustaining growth. And like us, they're doing it by relying again on the marketplace. This period of adjustment has not been easy for us; in fact, it's been very painful. But it is the one way that does work, and it's beginning to pay dividends.

Economic recovery is spreading its wings and taking flight. We all know those wings have not spread far enough and, I would add, recovery alone is not good enough. Our challenge is far greater: lasting, worldwide economic expansion. Together, we must make the 1980's an historic era of transition toward sustained, noninflationary world growth. I have every confidence that we can, and with our combined leadership and cooperation, we will.

The IMF is the linchpin of the international financial system. Among official institutions it serves as a counselor, coaxing the world economy toward renewed growth and stability. At various times in its history, the IMF has provided important temporary balance of payments assistance to its member nations, including my own. At times it must play the "Dutch uncle," talk-

ing frankly, telling those of us in government things we need to hear but would rather not. We know how significant the IMF's role has been in assisting troubled debtor countries, many of which are making courageous strides to regain financial health. We warmly applaud the efforts of Mr. de Larosière and his staff.

My administration is committed to do what is legitimately needed to help ensure that the IMF continues as the cornerstone of the international financial system. Let me make something very plain: I have an unbreakable commitment to increased funding for the IMF. But the U.S. Congress so far has failed to act to pass the enabling legislation. I urge the Congress to be mindful of its responsibility and to meet the pledge of our government.

The IMF quota legislation has been pending for several months, and I do not appreciate the partisan wrangling and political posturing that have been associated with this issue during recent weeks. I urge members of both political parties to lay aside their differences, to abandon harsh rhetoric and unreasonable demands, and to get on with the task in a spirit of true bipartisanship. The stakes are great. This legislation is not only crucial to the recovery of America's trading partners abroad and to the stability of the entire international financial system, it is also necessary to a sustained recovery in the United States.

The sum we're requesting will not increase our budget deficit, and it will be returned with interest as loans are repaid to the IMF. What's more, it will keep the wheels of world commerce turning and create jobs. Exports account for one out of eight manufacturing jobs in our country, the United States. Forty percent of our agricultural products are exported. I'm afraid that even today, too few in the Congress realize the United States as interdependent with both the developed and the developing world.

Examine the record: The United States has been a dependable partner, reaching out to help developing countries who are laboring under excessive debt burdens. These major debtor countries have already undertaken difficult measures in a concerted effort to get their economic houses in order. Most of them are working closely with the IMF to overcome economic hardships. They continue to demonstrate a commendable willingness to make necessary adjustments. And that's why I can state that our participation in the IMF quota increase is not a government bailout of these debtor countries or of the banks which are sharing the burden. On the contrary, IMF plans to assist financially troubled countries call for the banks to put up more new money than the IMF itself.

This is by nature a cooperative enterprise. If the Congress does not approve our participation, the inevitable consequence would be a withdrawal by other industrialized countries from doing their share. At the end of this road could be a major disruption of the entire world trading and financial systems—an economic nightmare that could plague generations to come. No one can afford to make light of the responsibility we all share.

We strongly support the World Bank; in fact, the United States remains its largest single contributor. We recognize its key role in stimulating world development and the vital assistance it provides to developing nations. Here again, I have proposed legislation to meet our commitment for funding the World Bank and especially the International Development Association. It is important that these funds be available to help the people in the poorest countries raise their standards of living. Tomorrow, Secretary Regan will be discussing both the Fund and the Bank in more detail. Because our investment in the World Bank's operations is so large, we feel a special responsibility to provide constructive suggestions to make it even more effective.

Let me simply underscore again a fundamental point, and I say this as a spokesman for a compassionate, caring people. The heart of America is good, and her heart is true. We've provided more concessional assistance to developing nations than any other country—more than $130 billion in the last three decades. Whether the question at hand be Bank project financing or Fund balance of payments assistance, it must be considered a complement to, not a substitute for, sound policies at home. If

policies are sound, financing can be beneficial. If policies are irresponsible, all the aid in the world will be no more than money down the drain.

As we work together for recovery, we must be on guard against storm clouds of protectionist pressures building on the horizon. At the recent economic summit in Williamsburg, my fellow leaders and I renewed our commitment to an open, expanding world trading system. The Williamsburg Declaration reads, "We commit ourselves to halt protectionism, and as recovery proceeds, to reverse it by dismantling trade barriers."

Whether such words will prove to be empty promises or symbols of a powerful commitment depends on the real day-to-day actions which each of our governments take. Everyone is against protectionism in the abstract. That's easy. It is another matter to make the hard, courageous choices when it is your industry or your business that appears to be hurt by foreign competition. I know; we in the United States deal with the problem of protectionism every day of the year.

We are far from perfect, but the United States offers the most free and open economy in the world. We import far more goods than any nation on Earth. There is more foreign investment here than anywhere else. And access to our commercial and capital markets is relatively free.

Protectionism is not a problem solver; it is a problem creator. Protectionism invites retaliation. It means you will buy less from your trading partners, they will buy less from you, the world economic pie will shrink, and the danger of political turmoil will increase.

You know, I've made this analogy before. But we and our trading partners are in the same boat. If one partner shoots a hole in the bottom of the boat, does it make sense for the other partner to shoot another hole in the boat? Some people say yes and call it getting tough. I call it getting wet—all over. [*Laughter*]

We must plug the holes in the boat of open markets and free trade and set sail again in the direction of prosperity. No one should mistake our determination to use our full power and influence to prevent anyone from destroying the boat and sinking us all.

I firmly believe that we can and must go forward together, hand in hand, not looking for easy villains to explain our problems but resolved to pursue the proven path on which these institutions embarked almost four decades ago—a path of economic progress and political independence for all countries and for all people.

In closing, let me share with you a very deep, personal belief I hold. We are all sovereign nations and therefore free to choose our own way as long as we do not transgress upon the sovereign rights of one another. But we cannot really be free as independent states unless we respect the freedom and independence of each of our own individual citizens. In improving their lot, which is the only reason you and I hold high offices in our lands, we cannot forget

that how we help them progress economically must be consistent with this highest objective of all—their personal dignity, their independence, and ultimately their freedom. That's what this job of ours is all about.

Thank you very much, and God bless you all.

Note: The President spoke at 10:10 a.m. in the main ballroom at the Sheraton Washington Hotel at the annual meeting of the International Monetary Fund, the International Bank for Reconstruction and Development (World Bank), the International Development Association, and the International Finance Corporation.

In his opening remarks, the President referred to J. de Larosière, Managing Director and Chairman of the Board of Executive Directors of the International Monetary Fund.

Message to Prime Minister Robert Hawke of Australia on the Victory of the *Australia II* in the America's Cup Competition
September 27, 1983

Dear Bob:

If the America's Cup had to leave the United States, I am delighted that it's home will be Australia—at least until the next race. All Australians must be justifiably proud of the extraordinary team effort, skill and sportsmanship that brought off this magnificent victory. I hope you will share with all those who had anything to do with *Australia II*'s success my congratulations and those of the American people.

One major consolation for us is that the next race will provide a large number of

Americans the opportunity to enjoy the beauty and hospitality of Perth as they seek to bring home the Cup.

Sincerely,

RONALD REAGAN

Note: The White House announced that the President spoke by telephone with Dennis Conner, captain of the defending yacht Liberty, on September 26 to discuss the races.

As printed above, this item follows the text of the White House press release.

Remarks of President Reagan and President Mauno Koivisto of Finland Following Their Meetings
September 27, 1983

President Reagan. President Koivisto and I have just completed a cordial and fruitful discussion about relations between Finland and the United States and about the current international situation. And it's a pleasure to say that we did not discuss problems in the Finnish-American relationship, because there are no bilateral problems between Finland and the United States. Our relations are excellent and have been for a long time.

The United States supports Finland's position of internationally recognized neutrality, and we value their perspective on world problems.

I welcome this chance to hear President Koivisto's views and expressed our own commitment to international cooperation and world peace. Americans have always had a warm place in their hearts for the Finnish people, and it's been a pleasure to welcome their President to our country today. Thank you, and thank you, sir, for being here.

President Koivisto. I appreciate very much this opportunity to meet with President Reagan here in Washington today. It confirms a longstanding tradition of good relations and personal contacts, both warm and friendly, between our two countries.

Our talks have given me a very ample opportunity to gain insights into the policies of the United States. Naturally, I have also expressed our own views and aspirations with regard to the international situation. Finland's foreign policy is based, in the first place, on good relations and confidence with regard to our neighboring countries. In accordance with our policy on neutrality, we want to have good relations with all nations of the world.

Finland's impact on world affairs is understandably limited. However, we remain determined to make whatever contribution we can to restrain international conflicts and promote peaceful solutions.

Finland recognizes with deep appreciation the friendship she has always received from the people of the United States, for whom we have the greatest respect and affection.

Note: President Reagan spoke at 1:06 p.m. to reporters assembled at the South Portico of the White House.

Earlier, the two Presidents met privately in the Oval Office and held a working luncheon, together with U.S. and Finnish officials, in the State Dining Room.

Letter to Congressional Leaders on United States Participation in the Multinational Force in Lebanon
September 27, 1983

Dear Mr. Speaker:

I know you were as gratified as I with Sunday's announcement of a cease fire in Lebanon. While there were many things that contributed to the cease fire, it is my belief that your agreement to advance the compromise resolution on war powers—and the favorable action by the Foreign Affairs and Foreign Relations Committees—were particularly important. At a crucial point, your agreement and the supporting committee actions expressed a commitment to bipartisanship in U.S. foreign policy. Please accept my thanks.

Let me also take this opportunity to clarify an issue with respect to the interpretation of the compromise resolution. The compromise resolution refers to the requirements of section 4(a) of the Lebanon

Emergency Assistance Act; I gather that a question has arisen as to the Executive Branch's understanding and intention in this regard. My understanding and intent remain exactly as they were when I signed the Lebanon Emergency Assistance Act: It would be my intention to seek Congressional authorization—as contemplated by the Act—if circumstances require any substantial expansion in the number or role of U.S. armed forces in Lebanon.

In addition, regarding the Administration's intentions with respect to the 18-month time period, I can assure you that if our forces are needed in Lebanon beyond the 18-month period, it would be my intention to work together with the Congress with a view toward taking action on mutually acceptable terms.

Again let me thank you for your support for the compromise agreement. I believe its prompt enactment will only further improve the chances for the stable peace we seek in Lebanon.

Sincerely,   RON

Note: This is the text of identical letters addressed to Thomas P. O'Neill, Jr., Speaker of the House of Representatives; Senate Majority Leader Howard H. Baker, Jr.; Charles H. Percy, chairman of the Senate Foreign Relations Committee; and Clement J. Zablocki, chairman of the House Foreign Affairs Committee.

Nomination of Hugh W. Foster To Be Alternate United States Executive Director of the International Bank for Reconstruction and Development
September 27, 1983

The President today announced his intention to nominate Hugh W. Foster to be United States Alternate Executive Director of the International Bank for Reconstruction and Development for a term of 2 years. He would succeed George R. Hoguet.

Since 1982 Mr. Foster has served as United States Alternate Executive Director of the International Bank for Reconstruction and Development. He is currently on leave of absence from the Wells Fargo Bank in San Francisco, Calif., where he last served as vice president and area manager of the bank's Asia Pacific division. Previous-

ly he served as vice president and area manager in Mexico City in 1977–1980; vice president and area manager, China Sea area, in 1975–1977; and assistant vice president and area manager, Australasia area, in 1974–1975. He has held other positions with Wells Fargo Bank since 1969.

Mr. Foster graduated from Colgate University (A.B., 1965) and Stanford University Graduate School of Business (M.B.A., 1969). He is married, has five children, and resides in Washington, D.C. He was born December 13, 1943, in Baltimore, Md.

Nomination of Earl Oliver To Be a Member of the Railroad Retirement Board
September 27, 1983

The President today announced his intention to nominate Earl Oliver to be a member of the Railroad Retirement Board for a term of 5 years. This is a reappointment.

Mr. Oliver has been a member of the Railroad Retirement Board since August 1977. Previously he served as a consultant to the National Railway Labor Conference (1975–77). He was with the Illinois Central Gulf Railroad (1948–75) and retired as senior vice president for personnel and administration in late 1975.

Mr. Oliver graduated from Oklahoma State University (B.A., 1938). He is married, has two sons, and resides in Chicago, Ill. He was born February 25, 1917, in Monticello, Ky.

Appointment of Vincent P. Barabba as United States Representative on the Population Commission of the United Nations Economic and Social Council
September 27, 1983

The President today announced his intention to appoint Vincent P. Barabba to be the Representative of the United States of America on the Population Commission of the Economic and Social Council of the United Nations. He would succeed Maj. Gen. William H. Draper, Jr.

Mr. Barabba is currently director, market intelligence, of the Eastman Kodak Co. Previously he served as Director, Bureau of the Census, U.S. Department of Commerce (1979–1981 and 1973–1976); manager, market research, Xerox Corp. (1976–1979); chairman of the board, Decision Making Information (1969–1973); and president, Datamatics, Inc. (1966–1969).

Mr. Barabba graduated from California State University (B.S., 1962) and University of California, Los Angeles (M.B.A., 1964). He is married, has two children, and resides in Rochester, N.Y. He was born September 6, 1934, in Chicago, Ill.

Appointment of Two Members of the President's National Security Telecommunications Advisory Committee
September 27, 1983

The President today announced his intention to appoint the following individuals to be members of the President's National Security Telecommunications Advisory Committee. These are new positions.

Joseph A. Boyd is currently chairman and chief executive officer of Harris Corp. in Melbourne, Fla. He is married, has two children, and resides in Indiatlantic, Fla. He was born March 25, 1921, in Oscar, Ky.

Monroe M. Rifkin is chairman of the National Cable Television Association and president of Rifkin & Associates, Inc., in Denver, Colo. He is married, has three children, and resides in Englewood, Colo. He was born August 27, 1930, in Brooklyn, N.Y.

Proclamation 5105—United Nations Day, 1983
September 27, 1983

By the President of the United States of America

A Proclamation

The United Nations remains today—38 years after its creation—an institution uniquely endowed to promote international political, economic, social, and technical cooperation. Conceived during a brutal war and nurtured in a troubled peace, the United Nations has seen many of its shining promises realized, but many others have been frustrated. More often than the world community can afford, rivalries and divisions among states prompt abuse or misuse of the powers and machinery of the United Nations. Despite these imperfections, the system and its machinery continue to offer opportunities for mediating differences which threaten to erupt in hostilities; for arranging and overseeing agreements to end tensions or conflicts; for promoting the technical and scientific cooperation essential to meet problems of growth and development; and for coping with international emergencies of all kinds.

The people and the Government of the United States of America take pride in the support—moral, intellectual, political, and financial—which we have rendered to the United Nations, and in the leadership which we have provided to help bring about its foremost achievements. We also take pride in the knowledge that the principles of the United Nations charter are the same ones which underlie our liberty, our progress, and our development as a democratic society.

Now, Therefore, I, Ronald Reagan, President of the United States of America, do hereby designate Monday, October 24, 1983, as United Nations Day, and urge all Americans to better acquaint themselves with the activities and accomplishments of the United Nations.

I have appointed William M. Ellinghaus to serve as 1983 United States Chairman for United Nations Day, and I welcome the role of the United Nations Association of the United States of America in working with him to celebrate this special day.

In Witness Whereof, I have hereunto set my hand this 27th day of Sept., in the year of our Lord nineteen hundred and eighty-three, and of the Independence of the United States of America the two hundred and eighth.

RONALD REAGAN

[*Filed with the Office of the Federal Register, 2:59 p.m., September 27, 1983*]

Proclamation 5106—National Sewing Month, 1983
September 27, 1983

By the President of the United States of America

A Proclamation

Over fifty million Americans sew at home. Their efforts demonstrate the persistence, skill, and self-reliance which are so characteristic of this Nation. The home sewing industry generates over $3,500,000,000 annually for our economy and serves to introduce many younger Americans to activities which lead to careers in such fields as fashion, textile design, interior design and retail merchandising.

In recognition of the importance of home sewing to our economy, the Congress, by House Joint Resolution 218, has designated September 1983 as "National Sewing Month."

Now, Therefore, I, Ronald Reagan, President of the United States of America, do hereby proclaim September 1983 as National Sewing Month. I call upon the people of the United States to observe this month with appropriate ceremonies and activities.

In Witness Whereof, I have hereunto set my hand this twenty-seventh day of September, in the year of our Lord nineteen hundred and eighty-three, and of the Independence of the United States of America

the two hundred and eighth.

RONALD REAGAN

[*Filed with the Office of the Federal Register, 11:22 a.m., September 28, 1983*]

Proclamation 5107—National Adult Day Care Center Week, 1983
September 27, 1983

By the President of the United States of America

A Proclamation

Adult day care centers provide supervised community settings in which partially disabled men and women of all ages can obtain care that may not be available in their own homes. These centers provide opportunities for adults who are socially isolated to find friends and learn skills. Day care centers enable individuals to obtain the care they need without being forced to live in institutions, and they offer needed respite to families whose infirmed relatives live with them.

In recognition that adult day care centers and their dedicated professional staffs serve many health maintenance functions, provide vital medical care, including medication monitoring, therapies, and health education, and provide invaluable opportunities for social interaction to disabled elderly Americans, the Congress of the United States, by House Joint Resolution 132, has

designated the week beginning September 25, 1983, as "National Adult Day Care Center Week" and has authorized and requested the President to issue a proclamation in observance of that week.

Now, Therefore, I, Ronald Reagan, President of the United States of America, do hereby proclaim the week beginning on September 25, 1983, as National Adult Day Care Center Week, and I call upon every American community to consider the value of adult day care centers and to give appropriate recognition to centers offering these important services throughout that week.

In Witness Whereof, I have hereunto set my hand this 27th day of September, in the year of our Lord nineteen hundred and eighty-three, and of the Independence of the United States of America the two hundred and eighth.

RONALD REAGAN

[*Filed with the Office of the Federal Register, 11:23 a.m., September 28, 1983*]

Nomination of Neal B. Freeman To Be a Member of the Board of Directors of the Communications Satellite Corporation
September 27, 1983

The President today announced his intention to nominate Neal B. Freeman to be a member of the Board of Directors of the Communications Satellite Corporation until the date of the annual meeting of the Corporation in 1985. He would succeed Justin

Dart.

Mr. Freeman is president of Jefferson Communications, Inc., in Reston, Va. He is also executive producer of "American Interests" (public television series). He has served as contributing editor for "The Advocates" (public television series) in 1977–1979 and as Washington editor for "National Review" in 1978–1981. Prior to founding Jefferson Communications in 1976, he was with the Hearst Corp. in New York. He was a director of the Corporation for Public Broadcasting in 1972–1975.

He graduated from Yale University (B.S., 1962). He is married, has three children, and resides in Vienna, Va. He was born July 5, 1940, in New York City.

Remarks at a Fundraising Dinner for the Republican Majority Fund
September 27, 1983

Chairman Ted Welch, Senator Baker, Dr. Kissinger, ladies and gentlemen:

Henry, I came here with some lessons that I brought with me that I'd learned in a previous life out on the west coast: Don't get involved in scenes with kids or dogs. [*Laughter*] And tonight I've learned another one. Don't get on the program following Henry Kissinger. [*Laughter*]

But we're here to recognize those Senators who stood with us for 3 years and who are now running for reelection. And we are here also to salute their leader and ours in the United States Senate, a man who means much to all of us, both professionally and personally.

One of the first things I learned when I got my current job was just about how serious Howard Baker really is about photography. [*Laughter*] He's one of the few Members of Congress who would rather take your picture than twist your arm. [*Laughter*] Well, there's a story, and I understand it's true. It's about a newspaper photographer out in Los Angeles, kind of reminds me of Howard.

He was called in by his editor and told of a fire that was raging in Palos Verdes. That's a hilly area in the southern part of Los Angeles County. And the photographer's assignment was to rush down to a small local airport, board a waiting plane, go out and get some pictures of the fire, and be back in time for the afternoon edition. Well, he raced down the freeway, broke all the traffic laws, got to the airport, drove his car to the end of the runway, and sure enough there was a plane revving up its engines, ready to go. He jumped in the plane shouting "Let's go!" and they were

off. At about 5,000 feet he began getting his camera out of the bag, told the fellow flying the plane to get him over the fire so he could get his pictures and get back to the paper. And from the other side of the cockpit there was a deafening silence, and then he heard those words he will always remember: "Aren't you the instructor?" [*Laughter*]

Well, since 1966, Howard has been making the picture as well as taking the picture. Howard, I'll say you'll be missed, but if you make yourself scarce, we're going to come looking for you, and you can count on that.

It is more than fitting that a dinner like this, which is beefing up the Republican Majority Fund, would salute Senator Baker. Under his leadership, the Republicans in the United States Senate served faithfully as the loyal opposition. And for the last 3 years and for the first time in half a century, Republicans have maintained a majority in the upper House for two consecutive sessions—the first and only time in 50 years.

Howard may not remember this, but he did me a tremendous service several years back. It was just before the 1976 election, and I ran into Howard and Joy. He had a new camera, and I was inspecting it. And I asked him if that was really the camera he wanted, and I'll always remember his answer. He said, "We bought it; we paid for it; and we intend to keep it." [*Laughter*]

Seriously, though, with Howard's guidance, we've proven to the American people that there is a difference in the two political parties and that, if given the chance, we can make a sometimes frustrating democratic process work for the betterment of our people.

During the election of 1980, we Republicans stated our case and outlined our program, and we did not, as some now suggest, just run against my predecessor. The opposition, with few exceptions, had control of both Houses of the Congress almost continually for 50 years. In those 50 years, we have held both Houses of the Congress for 4 of the 50 and one House, the Senate, for these last almost 3 years. And for long stretches, our opponents held not only the Congress of the United States but the White House as well, and all the departments and agencies. And now as much as they would like to blame the near crisis we inherited on my immediate predecessor, we know that's not true. It was not one individual who caused all those enormous problems America faced in 1980. It was decades of their liberal policies, their policies with good intentions, but unworkable solutions.

In January of '81, we set out to do what we proposed to do. Together we have fundamentally changed the direction of American Government. We can be proud of what we've accomplished. And when I say "we," I mean a Republican "we". To those who criticize, I say to them, let them clearly state the alternative. Then let them explain how this blueprint would differ from the many years when their party dominated the Federal Government and left us with near disaster.

What has been achieved in the last 3 years has been the result of a team effort. We can be particularly proud of the 1981 tax and spending cut packages, the most significant economic legislation in memory. Without Republican control of the Senate, and without the kind of leadership Howard has been providing, that recovery package would still be bottled up in committee.

It takes time for any program to take hold. The opposition was declaring that our program was a failure the morning after it passed, and did everything to pull the rug out from under our reforms before they had a chance to work. Well, ladies and gentlemen, we've weathered the storm. It is clear now even to our critics that after years of stagnation and inflation, our economy, thanks to the basic changes we've made, is beginning to move again. We're witnessing the first phase of lasting economic growth.

We must work together to keep what Howard has called "that inflation beast locked in its cage." And the most important question we must ask in next year's election is: Do we continue the responsible policies that are giving our economy new vitality and giving our people hope, or do we go back to the failed ideas of tax, spend, and inflate that brought us stagnation and despair?

Each and every Senate race will be crucial. And the Republican Majority Fund we contribute to this evening will give us a fighting chance to protect the gains we've made. But the special interests, groups that profited from big government, from high taxes and high inflation, will be out in force. As for me, I'm confident. When we got here, inflation had been running at double digits for 2 years. The prime interest rate had soared to its highest level, 21½ percent, in more than a hundred years. Taxes had doubled in just the 5 years between 1976 and 1981, siphoning off resources needed for savings, job-creating business investment growth, and economic development.

Our system is based on faith in the people, and I have faith that they will not vote to return to the failed policies of the past. Our biggest job is to remind them what things were like, how we turned that desperate situation around, and just as important, the crucial difference between our efforts and vision for the future and theirs. We offer solid progress and real hope, not fear, envy, and failure. We will not be on the defensive as we move into the 1980 elections—or '84 elections. On the contrary, Republicans will be on the offensive. We're the party that lowered tax rates, reduced inflation, and put the American economy back on the path to real growth.

And something else we're not going to let the people forget: Three years ago our allies and adversaries alike were counting America out. It was being said that our best days were behind us. Morale in our Armed Forces was at a low ebb, and the weapons and equipment they had to use were wearing out. We had planes that couldn't fly and ships that couldn't sail. Well, we've turned that situation around, too. We're ending the Vietnam syndrome that had broken the will of the American people. And today we've established ourselves as a reliable ally, and we're rebuilding our defensive capabilities.

The number of combat-ready units has gone up by a third since 1980, and that means they have improved their chances of never having to be in combat. Our Navy's fleets have risen from 480 ships to 510, that we have today, and it's on the way to 600. And military officers tell me that morale in our services has never been higher.

We strengthened America's capabilities, and we've strengthened America's resolve to meet our responsibilities in the world. The likelihood of peace is not enhanced by weakness or gestures of good will to tyrants. Peace and the preservation of our freedom is not more likely if we put our head in the sand and run away from our responsibilities. The peace of the world and the freedom of the United States instead depend on hard work, courage, and strength.

Now, this is not just my philosophy. This is Republican philosophy. And it's a philosophy that the voters of the United States will back up when they're given the chance.

Howard has told us that one of the reasons he's taking a sabbatical from govern-ment is that he needs time to get reacquainted with the people of the United States. Well, I think he's going to find out they're the same people they always were, the kind of people who took a vast wilderness and turned it into this blessed land of liberty and abundance. They had courage, faith in God, and a willingness to roll up their sleeves and get on with the job at hand.

John Foster Dulles once said, "If only we're faithful to our past, we shall not have to fear for our future." Well, that's our challenge, and I'm certain that like those before us, we'll do the job that has to be done.

What we need to look forward to and dream on is after 50 years, with only a brief interlude, with us there, able to really make the policy that fits our Republican philoso-phy, what it can be and what can happen for the world and this nation if we can one day in the very near future have not just one House but have the Congress and the executive branch and the bureaus and agencies and departments carrying out the philosophy that you and I have believed in for so long.

Note: The President spoke at 8:54 p.m. in the Regency Ballroom at the Hyatt Regency Hotel.

Executive Order 12443—Central Intelligence Agency Retirement and Disability System
September 27, 1983

By the authority vested in me as Presi-dent of the United States of America by Section 292 of the Central Intelligence Agency Retirement Act of 1964 for Certain Employees, as amended (50 U.S.C. 403 note), and in order to conform further the Central Intelligence Agency Retirement and Disability System to certain amend-ments in the Civil Service Retirement and Disability System pursuant to Public Laws 97–253, 97–346, and 97–377, it is hereby ordered as follows:

Section 1. Section 231(b)(2) of the Central Intelligence Agency Retirement Act of 1964 for Certain Employees, as amended, shall be deemed to be amended to read as follows:

"(b)(2) If the annuitant receiving disability retirement annuity is restored to earning capacity, before becoming sixty years of age, payment of the annuity terminates on reemployment by the Government or 180 days after the end of the calendar year in which earning capacity is restored, which-ever is earlier. Earning capacity is restored if in any calendar year the income of the annuitant from wages or self-employment or both equals at least 80 per centum of the current rate of pay of the position occupied at the time of retirement.".

Sec. 2. Section 5 of Executive Order No. 12326 of September 30, 1981, which previously amended the Central Intelligence Agency Retirement Act of 1964 for Certain Employees, as amended, shall be deemed to be amended to read as follows:

"Sec. 5. For the purpose of ensuring the accuracy of information used in the administration of the Central Intelligence Agency Retirement and Disability System, the Director of Central Intelligence may request, from the Secretaries of Defense, Health and Human Services, and Labor, and the Administrator of Veterans Affairs, such information as the Director deems necessary. To the extent permitted by law:

"(a) The Secretary of Defense or the Secretary's designee shall provide information on retired or retainer pay provided under Title 10 of the United States Code;

"(b) The Administrator of Veterans Affairs shall provide information on pensions or compensation provided under Title 38 of the United States Code;

"(c) The Secretary of Health and Human Services or the Secretary's designee shall provide information contained in the records of the Social Security Administration; and

"(d) The Secretary of Labor or the Secretary's designee shall provide information on benefits paid under subchapter I of Chapter 81 of Title 5 of the United States Code.

"The Director, in consultation with the officials from whom information is requested, shall ensure that information made available under this Section is used only for the purposes authorized.".

Sec. 3. Section 281(a) of the Central Intelligence Retirement Act of 1964 for Certain Employees, as amended, shall be deemed to be amended by inserting after "at 3 per centum per annum" the following: "through December 31, 1984, and thereafter at the rate computed under Section 8334(e) of Title 5 of the United States Code."

Sec. 4. Section 221(k) of the Central Intelligence Agency Retirement Act of 1964 for Certain Employees, as amended, shall be deemed to be amended to read as follows:

"(k) For the purpose of an annuity computed under this section, the total service of any participant shall not include any period of civilian service on or after October 1, 1982, for which retirement deductions or deposits have not been made under section 252(b), unless the participant makes a deposit for such period as provided in section 252, or no deposit is required for such service as provided under Section 8334(g) of Title 5 of the United States Code, or under any statute.".

Sec. 5. Section 241(a) of the Central Intelligence Agency Retirement Act of 1964 for Certain Employees, as amended, shall be deemed to be amended to read as follows:

"(a) Whenever a participant becomes separated from the Agency, or is transferred to a position in which he is not subject to this Act, for at least thirty-one consecutive days without becoming eligible for an annuity in accordance with the provisions of this Act, the total amount of contributions from his salary with interest thereon at 4 percent per year to December 31, 1947, and 3 percent per year thereafter compounded annually to December 31, 1956, except as provided in section 281, shall, upon application, be returned to him. The return of contributions shall be made only if the participant is not reemployed in a position in which he is subject to this Act at the time he files the application for refund and will not become eligible for an annuity within thirty-one days after filing such application. The receipt of the payment of the lump-sum credit by the participant voids all annuity rights under the Act based on the service on which the lump-sum credit is based, until the participant is reemployed in the service subject to the Act. The payment of the lump-sum credit shall include amounts deposited by a participant covering earlier service as well as any amounts deposited under section 252(h)".".

Sec. 6. Section 291(f) of the Central Intelligence Agency Retirement Act of 1964 for Certain Employees, as amended, shall be deemed to be amended by striking out "fixed at the nearest" and inserting "rounded to the next lowest" in lieu thereof.

Sec. 7. Section 221(a) of the Central Intelligence Agency Retirement Act of 1964 for Certain Employees, as amended, shall be deemed to be amended by adding the following at the end thereof:

"Each annuity shall be stated as an annual amount, one twelfth of which, rounded to the next lowest dollar, constitutes the monthly rate payable on the first business day of the month after the month or other period for which it has accrued.".

Sec. 8. Section 221(i) of the Central Intelligence Agency Retirement Act of 1964 for Certain Employees, as amended, shall be deemed to be amended to read as follows:

"(i) Except as otherwise provided, the annuity of a participant shall commence on the first day of the month after separation from the service, or on the first day of the month after pay ceases and the service and age requirements for title to an annuity are met. With respect to those participants who serve three days or less in the month of retirement, the annuity will commence on the day after separation or the day after pay ceases and the service and age requirements for title to an annuity are met. The annuity of a participant involuntarily separated from the service, except for removal for cause on charges of misconduct or delinquency, or of a participant retiring due to a disability shall commence on the day after separation from the service or the day after pay ceases and the service and age or disability requirements for title to an annuity are met. Any other annuity payable from the Fund shall commence on the first day of the month after the occurrence of the event on which payment thereof is based.".

Sec. 9. Section 252(e) of the Central Intelligence Agency Retirement Act of 1964 for Certain Employees, as amended, shall be deemed to be amended by inserting "(1)" before the first sentence thereof, by inserting "(2)" before the second sentence thereof and by striking out "chapter 11" and inserting "section 301" in lieu thereof, by deleting the last sentence thereof and by adding the following paragraph (3):

"(3) Except as provided in paragraphs (1) and (2) of this subsection, the service of an individual who first becomes a Federal employee before October 1, 1982 shall include credit for each period of military service performed before the date of the separation on which the entitlement to an annuity under this subsection is based, subject to

section 252(f); and the service of an individual who first becomes a Federal employee on or after October 1, 1982 shall include credit for:

"(i) each period of military service performed before January 1, 1957, and

"(ii) each period of military service performed after December 31, 1956, and before separation on which the entitlement to annuity under this section is based, only if a deposit (with interest, if any) is made with respect to that period as provided in subsection (h) of this section.".

Sec. 10. Section 252(f) of the Central Intelligence Agency Retirement Act of 1964 for Certain Employees, as amended, shall be deemed to be amended by inserting "(1)" after "(f)" and adding new paragraphs (2) and (3) as follows:

"(2) The provisions of paragraph (1) above relating to credit for military service shall not apply to—

"(A) any period of military service of a participant with respect to which he or she has made a deposit with interest, if any, under section 252(e) of this Act; or

"(B) the military service of any participant who has been awarded retired pay on account of a service-connected disability caused by an instrumentality of war and incurred in the line of duty during a period of war as that term is defined in section 301 of Title 38 of the United States Code.".

"(3) The annuity recomputation required by paragraph (1) above shall not apply to any individual who was entitled to an annuity under this section on or before September 8, 1982. Instead of an annuity recomputation, the annuities of such individuals shall be reduced at age 62 by an amount equal to a fraction of their Social Security benefit. This reduction shall be computed by multiplying their monthly Social Security benefit by a fraction, the numerator of which is their total military wages that were subject to Social Security deductions and the denominator of which is their total lifetime wages, including military wages, that were subject to Social Security deductions. The reductions so computed shall not be permitted to be greater than the reductions that will be required by paragraph (1) if that paragraph applied to the individual for that period. The new formula shall be applicable to all annuity payments payable after October 1, 1982, including annuity payments to those individuals who had previously reached age 62 and whose annuities had already been recomputed.".

Sec. 11. Section 252 of the Central Intelligence Agency Retirement Act of 1964 for Certain Employees, as amended, shall be deemed to be amended by adding a new subsection (h) as follows:

"(h)(1) Each participant who has performed military service before the date of separation on which the entitlement to any annuity under this section is based may pay, in accordance with rules issued by the Director, to the Agency an amount equal to 7 percent of the amount of basic pay paid under section 204 of Title 37 of the United States Code to the participant for each period of military service after December 1956. The amount of such payments shall be based on such evidence of basic pay for military service as the participant may provide, or if the Director or his designee determines sufficient evidence has not been provided to adequately determine basic pay for military service, such payment shall be based upon estimates of such basic pay provided to the Director under paragraph (4).".

"(2) Any deposit made under paragraph (1) of this subsection more than two years after the later of—

(A) October 1, 1982; or

(B) the date on which the participant making the deposit first becomes an employee of the Federal government—shall include interest on such amount computed and compounded annually beginning on the date of expiration of the two-year period. The interest rate that is applicable in computing interest in any year under this paragraph shall be equal to the interest rate that is applicable for such year under subsection (b) of this section.".

"(3) Any payment received by the Agency under this subsection shall be immediately remitted to the Office of Finance for deposit in the Treasury of the United States to the Credit of the CIARDS Fund.

"(4) The Secretary of Defense, the Secretary of Transportation, the Secretary of Commerce, or the Secretary of Health and Human Services, as appropriate, shall furnish such information to the Director as the Director may determine to be necessary for the administration of this subsection.".

Sec. 12. Section 261(d)(2) of the Central Intelligence Agency Retirement Act of 1964 for Certain Employees, as amended, shall be deemed to be amended by adding after the words "allowed for military service" the following: ", less an amount determined by the Director to be appropriate to reflect the value of the deposits made to the credit of the Fund under section 252(e), and".

Sec. 13. Section 235(a) of the Central Intelligence Agency Retirement Act of 1964 for Certain Employees, as amended, shall be deemed to be amended by deleting the final sentence thereof and substituting the following wording:

"A participant who is separated involuntarily from service, except by removal for cause on charges of misconduct or delinquency, is entitled to an annuity only if the participant has not declined a reasonable offer of another position for which he or she is qualified, which is not lower than two grades below his or her current position and which is in the same commuting area. Voluntary early retirements will be permitted only if a major reorganization, reduction in force, or transfer of function will result in a significant number of participants being separated or immediately reduced in pay. Participants retired under this subsection shall receive retirement benefits in accordance with the provisions of section 221.".

Sec. 14. Section 291 of the Central Intelligence Agency Retirement Act of 1964 for Certain Employees, as amended, shall be deemed to be amended by adding a new subsection (g) as follows:

"(g)(1) An annuity shall not be increased by reason of an adjustment under this section to an amount which exceeds the greater of—

"(A) the maximum pay payable for GS-15 thirty days before the effective date of the adjustment under this section; or

"(B) the final pay (or average pay, if higher) of the participant with respect to whom the annuity is paid, increased by the overall annual average percentage adjustments (compounded) in rates of pay of the General Schedule under subchapter I of chapter 53 of title 5 of the United States Code during the period—

(i) beginning on the date the annuity commenced (or, in the case of a survivor of the participant, the date of the participant's annuity commenced), and

(ii) ending on the effective date of the adjustment under this section.

"(2) For the purposes of paragraph (1) of this subsection, 'pay' means the rate of salary or basic pay as payable under any provision of law, including any provision of law limiting the expenditure of appropriated funds.".

Sec. 15. Section 252(g) of the Central Intelligence Agency Retirement Act of 1964 for Certain Employees, as amended, shall be deemed to be amended by deleting "paragraph (b)" and inserting "paragraphs (b), (c)(4), and (h)" in lieu thereof.

Sec. 16. The amendments made by this Order shall be effective as follows:

(a) Sections 2, 5, 9, 19 [1], 12 and 13 shall be effective October 1, 1982.

(b) Section 1 shall be effective October 1, 1982 but shall apply only with respect to income earned after December 31, 1982.

(c) Section 3 shall apply with respect to deposits for service performed on or after October 1, 1982, and with respect to funds for which application is received on or after such date. The provisions of section 252, as in effect on September 7, 1982, shall continue to apply with respect to periods of service and refunds for which application was received on or before September 30, 1982.

(d) Section 4 shall apply with respect to deposits for military service performed on or after October 1, 1982 and military service performed on or after January 1, 1957 and with respect to refunds for which applications are received by the Agency on or after October 1, 1982. The provisions of section 221 (k), as in effect on September 7, 1982 shall continue to apply with respect to periods of civilian service occurring before October 1, 1982.

(e) Section 6 and Section 7 shall apply with respect to any annuity commencing on or after October 1, 1982, and with respect to any adjustment or redetermination of any annuity made on or after such date.

(f) Section 8 shall apply to annuities which commence on or after January 1, 1983.

(g) Section 11 shall take effect October 1, 1982 except that any participant who retired after September 8, 1982 and before October 1, 1983, or is entitled to an annuity under the CIA Retirement Act of 1964 for Certain Employees, as amended, based on a separation from service occurring during such period, or a survivor of such individual, may make a payment under section 252(h).

(h) Section 14 shall not cause any annuity to be reduced below the rate that is payable on September 8, 1982 but shall apply to any adjustment occurring on or after this date under section 291, or to any annuity payable from the Central Intelligence Agency Retirement and Disability Fund, whether such annuity has a commencing date before, on, or after September 8, 1982.

(i) Section 15 shall be effective as of September 8, 1982.

RONALD REAGAN

The White House,
September 27, 1983.

[Filed with the Office of the Federal Register, 2:41 p.m., September 28, 1983]

Note: The text of the Executive order was released by the Office of the Press Secretary on September 28.

---

[1] *In Sec. 16(a) the "19" should read "10".*

Proclamation 5108—National Employ the Handicapped Week, 1983
September 27, 1983

By the President of the United States of America

A Proclamation

Our Nation's history is rooted in the struggle to attain independence: the right of free choice by free citizens in a society that honors the efforts of individuals. The movement of disabled people to full participation in our society, with all its benefits and responsibilities, is an ideal whose time has surely come.

All across this Nation, disabled people are striving to obtain more control over their lives through choices that minimize their reliance and dependence on others. They are taking charge of their own lives and becoming responsible for their own affairs. They are participating in the day-to-day life of the community and fulfilling the whole range of social roles possible in our society.

Since World War II, the United States has set aside one week each year to emphasize ways in which more people with disabilities can be assisted in their efforts to become independent through gainful employment. Despite past and present efforts of employers to hire people with disabilities, the unemployment level of disabled people continues to be unnecessarily high. To solve this problem, we must plan and develop strategies to demonstrate that disabled people are a valuable resource to our economy and our society.

The Congress, by joint resolution of August 11, 1945, as amended (36 U.S.C. 155), has called for the designation of the first full week in October of each year as National Employ the Handicapped Week. During this week, let us renew our commitments to expand the opportunities for disabled citizens and help them to attain their personal goals.

Now, Therefore, I, Ronald Reagan, President of the United States of America, do hereby proclaim the week beginning October 2, 1983, as National Employ the Handicapped Week.

I urge all governors, mayors, other public officials, leaders in business and labor, private citizens, and especially the disabled citizens of this great Nation to help meet the challenge of the day. Let us all work together to fulfill the dreams of our disabled citizens: full participation in our expanding economy.

In Witness Whereof, I have hereunto set my hand this 27th day of Sept., in the year of our Lord nineteen hundred and eighty-three, and of the Independence of the United States of America the two hundred and eighth.

RONALD REAGAN

[*Filed with the Office of the Federal Register, 2:39 p.m., September 28, 1983*]

Note: The text of the proclamation was released by the Office of the Press Secretary on September 28.

Proclamation 5109—National High School Activities Week, 1983
September 27, 1983

By the President of the United States of America

A Proclamation

Extracurricular activities in the high schools of this country provide our students with valuable opportunities to discover and develop talents in areas other than those covered within the classroom. Extracurricular activities also build school spirit and demonstrate the importance of promoting common goals.

Through such programs as student government, athletics, music, drama, debate, journalism, community service, and many others, students gain key insights into the roles which competition and cooperation play in our society. Moreover, these experiences help students to learn to set and achieve goals, to organize their time effectively, and to enhance the social skills that are needed to enjoy and succeed in life.

In recognition of the significant place extracurricular opportunities have in the growth of our high school students, the Congress of the United States, by Senate Joint Resolution 101, has authorized and requested the President to proclaim the week of October 17 through October 23, 1983 as National High School Activities Week.

Now, Therefore, I, Ronald Reagan, President of the United States of America, do hereby proclaim the week beginning October 17, 1983 as National High School Activities Week, and I call upon the people of the United States to observe this period with appropriate programs, ceremonies, and activities.

In Witness Whereof, I have hereunto set my hand this 27th day of Sept., in the year of our Lord nineteen hundred and eighty-three, and of the Independence of the United States of America the two hundred and eighth.

RONALD REAGAN

[*Filed with the Office of the Federal Register, 2:40 p.m., September 28, 1983*]

Note: The text of the proclamation was released by the Office of the Press Secretary on September 28.

Message to the Congress Reporting Budget Deferrals
September 28, 1983

To the Congress of the United States:

In accordance with the Impoundment Control Act of 1974, I herewith report increases to amounts previously deferred totaling $64,119,643.

The deferral increases affect the Board for International Broadcasting and the United States Information Agency.

The details of the deferrals are contained in the attached reports.

RONALD REAGAN

The White House,
September 28, 1983.

Note: The attachments detailing the deferral increases are printed in the Federal Register *of October 3, 1983.*

Remarks on Presenting Awards for Excellence in Education
September 28, 1983

I'm pleased to be here, and I hope you've been enjoying our Marine Band. Well, please be seated, and good morning.

I understand that there are some 150 principals with us here today. I'm delighted you're here, but I have to confess to some mixed emotions. I remember on a number of occasions when I was sent to see the principal, and now the principals are coming to see me. [*Laughter*] But I thank you, everyone, principals, superintendents, and school board presidents. Thanks for joining us on this day that has been set aside to honor outstanding American secondary schools.

America has always had a love affair with learning. From polished men of letters like Thomas Jefferson to humble, self-taught people like Abe Lincoln, Americans have put their faith in the profound power of education to enrich individual lives and to make our nation strong. But lately many of our schools haven't been doing their job. Yes, there are many fine schools, dedicated principals, teachers, present company included. But since 1963, we all know that scholastic aptitude tests have shown a virtually unbroken decline. As of the '82–'83 school year, half of our States required only 1 year of math and 1 year of science for a student to graduate. And 14 States impose no requirements for graduation at all.

We've begun to realize that compared to students in other industrialized nations, many of ours perform badly. But let me make one thing clear: that is if we take the overall student body across the Nation, and on the average, we don't compare favorably. On the other hand, when you take our top students, then they compare very favorably with the top students, the best in those other countries.

But I can't help but tell you about an experience that I had for 8 years. Every year, as Governor of California, the exchange students from all over the world used to come for a visit with me at the capital in Sacramento. And every year for 8 years I asked the same question. I would ask these young people from these foreign lands how it compared, our education to theirs; was it harder or more difficult. And there would be silence. And then there would begin to be some smiles, and then they would look at each other, and pretty soon they would break into laughter. And that happened every time. And then they would begin volunteering the difference in what was required of them and what we're requiring of our students.

I think the fact, though, that our top students and those from the schools such as you represent do compare favorably should be an answer to those who wonder whether American education can ever again become first rate. The 152 secondary schools we're honoring today answers that loud and clear. The answer is, "You bet!"

The panel of experts, people who know just what it takes to make a school good, carefully reviewed the records of hundreds of schools under consideration for national honors. After the progress of rigorous selection, the panel recommended that your schools were those that best demonstrate the excellence that our sons and daughters deserve. Your schools provide proof of what the National Commission on Excellence in Education concluded in its report last April: America can do it.

Now, although each of your schools is unique, they all share a number of traits that the rest of us can learn from. Let me cite five that stand out.

First, all of your schools know the meaning of team effort. You have school boards that skillfully translate community educational goals into sound policy. Superintendents, principals, and teachers carry the policy to the students and armies of parents are supportive of your efforts. This summer I visited one of the schools that's represented here today, Pioneer High School from Whittier, California. I met students, faculty, and community representatives. I was impressed with the way they all were pulling together.

Second, all of your schools share a few basic ideas about what goes into a good education. All of you happen to believe in leadership, from superintendents and principals, dedication from teachers, homework, testing, using time efficiently, and firm discipline.

Third, you are resourceful. Whether it's buying new test tubes for the chemistry lab, finding transportation to send the band on tour, all of you've shown ingenuity and skill in meeting your schools' needs. And you not only marshal resources; you share them. Secretary Bell has told me that a number of you have built good will in your communities by giving the public a chance to use the high school swimming pool, gymnasiums, classrooms, after hours.

Fourth, you've placed a strong emphasis on good teaching. You all recognize that good teachers are the heart and soul of any good school. And you promote good teaching. To do that, you've taken measures to reward it. Secretary Bell and I believe that schools across the country should learn this lesson and adopt policies and salary structures to reward outstanding teachers.

And last, your schools have rejected contemporary academic standards in favor of your own much higher standards. You get more from your teachers and students because instead of accepting mediocrity, you demand excellence.

And today we're giving you flags to honor your efforts. By teaching your students the meaning of good education, you're teaching America as well.

You know, I don't normally advocate busing, but right now I wish I could bus this group to every high school in the country that isn't represented here. And with that said, you've probably noticed that we have a problem we haven't been able to solve in Washington yet. It has to do with the local airport. [*Laughter*]

But God bless you all for being here, and thank you very much.

Note: The President spoke at 11:30 a.m. on the South Lawn of the White House. Following the President's remarks, Secretary of Education Terrel H. Bell presented the awards to those representing the 152 secondary schools at the ceremony.

Nomination of Raymond J. O'Connor To Be a Member of the Federal Energy Regulatory Commission, and Designation as Chairman
September 28, 1983

The President today announced his intention to nominate Raymond J. O'Connor to be a member of the Federal Energy Regulatory Commission, Department of Energy, for a term expiring October 20, 1987. He would succeed Charles M. Butler III. The President also intends to designate Mr. O'Connor Chairman.

Since 1975 Mr. O'Connor has been with Prudential-Bache Securities, Inc., in New York, N.Y. He served as senior vice president and manager of the Public Utility Corporate Finance Department in 1975–1981 and is presently serving as executive vice president and director of the Energy Group, Corporate Finance Department. He was vice president, Energy Systems Department, Citibank, N.A., New York City, in 1968–1975 and served as assistant to the vice president of the Southern Co. in New York City in 1965–1968.

Mr. O'Connor graduated from the University of Dayton (B.A., 1954), St. John's University (J.D., 1959), and New York University (LL.M., 1968). He is married, has four children, and resides in White Stone, N.Y. He was born October 16, 1932.

Remarks on Greeting the Australian and American Crewmembers of the America's Cup Competition
September 28, 1983

The President. Well, Ambassador and Lady Cotton, Commodores Stone and Dalziell, crewmembers of both vessels, and ladies and gentlemen:

Two hundred years ago when the British Army surrendered at Yorktown, a song was played as the British troops marched out under a white flag, played by the British band because the colonials didn't have a band. The song they were playing was called "The World Turned Upside Down." Today people must be questioning whether the term "down under" applies to Australia any more.

I want to take this opportunity to congratulate the crews of both vessels. You all did an outstanding job. You captured the imagination of the people the world over.

Skipper John Bertrand, you and the crew of the *Australia II* have shown us the stuff of which Australians are made. I know that your countrymen are proud of you. And I want you to take this message back: that Americans are proud, too; we're proud to have Australians as our very dear friends. We salute you in your hour of triumph.

To the crew of the *Liberty* I say, and I'm certain all Americans feel this way, "Well done." I spoke with Dennis Conner shortly after the race. I'm sorry he couldn't be with us today. We should think of him not as the loser of this race, but as the man who successfully defended the cup in 1980 and a skipper who's had a brilliant yachting career.

A special word of congratulations to Alan Bond. Alan, you represent the kind of tenacity with which Americans and Australians can identify. For 13 years and four challenges and at heavy financial sacrifice, you've been trying to accomplish this feat. You just kept on coming. But don't relax now, because, Alan—and that's the other message to our friends in Australia—the Americans are coming back stronger than ever next time around.

Seriously, the competition that we celebrate today is a tribute to the spirit and peace-loving character of our two nations. During that race 132 years ago, when our yacht, the *America*, competed against a squadron of Britain's best, at one point, with the *America* 7½ miles in the lead, our vessel passed the Royal Yacht. The captain of the *America* and the crew doffed their caps and stood at attention as a salute to the Queen and to their competitors.

A British paper of the day noted "a mark of respect to the Queen, not the less becoming because it was bestowed by Republicans." [*Laughter*] I understand that Commodore Stone and the members of the New York Yacht Club paid the same tribute to the crew of the *Australia II* at the end of this America's Cup. And I join them. I might add that when we won that cup back in 1851, there were numerous comments about the *America*'s unique design. We had every innovation of the day—except a winged keel, of course.

Let me just say that was 132 years ago. If we had to get beat, we're glad it was by the Aussies. But one final bit of advice to the Perth Yacht Club: Don't bolt that cup down too tightly. [*Laughter*]

Congratulations to all of you, both teams, and God bless you both.

Mr. Jewett. Mr. President, on behalf of the crew of *Liberty* and our sponsor, the Fort Skyler Foundation, I want to thank you very much for inviting us to be here today. Dennis Conner regretted that he couldn't be here, but he certainly appreciated your phone call at a moment when he felt rather depressed, and all of us did. But you gave us a very good feeling that evening.

We wanted to show you, however, that in spite of losing the longest winning streak in sports history, that we did put up a good race. We did bring you a little memento which will show you that indeed we were ahead of *Australia* at times. It's a picture of *Liberty* and *Australia* very close, I might add, which is the way it was the entire time. And also on behalf of our syndicate, this is the burgee that we flew all this summer. And we would like to add that to your collection.

And now, I have to say that Alan Bond and I arrived in Newport, Rhode Island, in 1974 for the first America's Cup competition. Our group, with *Freedom*, beat you in 1980, and now here you are back again, and you beat us in '84. But as the President says, watch out for us in '87. Alan, congratulations.

Mr. Bond. Mr. President, it gives me great pleasure on behalf of our syndicate and the crew and the people of Australia that I present you this book which is two decades of the America's Cup. All of our crew and their contingent, and those who could not be here today, have signed this for you. And I hope you will keep this as a memento not just to us winning the cup but to the great friendship that exists between our two nations. *Liberty* and its crew put up a great effort. And we were just the better yacht on the day, but take nothing from them.

Thank you, Mr. President.

The President. Thank you.

Well, I'm very proud to have these mementos. I am very proud to have—I'd call it a flag; you called it something else—[*laughter*]—and this picture. And again, I just want to say that I think the people of Australia and the people of the United States all can be very proud of this event, of all of you who made it what it was. And it's just kind of a shame for those of us who look on that we have to wait all these years now until it's done again.

Thank you all.

Note: The President spoke at 3:38 p.m. in the Rose Garden at the White House.

Statement on Signing the Joint Congressional Resolution Condemning the Soviet Attack on a Korean Civilian Airliner
September 28, 1983

I am grateful to the Congress for its swift response to my request that it pass a joint resolution condemning the Soviet crime of shooting down a Korean airliner with 269 innocent persons on board. The strength of the joint resolution and the unanimity with which it was adopted will make clear to the Soviet Union that the American people are united in their condemnation of this dreadful act and in their demand that the Soviet Union take full responsibility for its action and publicly agree to take necessary meas- ures to ensure this tragedy is not repeated. In its passage of the defense authorization bill the same day as this joint resolution the Congress has backed up its expression of outrage with a firm statement of American resolve.

I am proud to affix my signature to this joint resolution.

Note: As enacted, H.J. Res. 353 is Public Law 98–98, approved September 28.

Statement on House of Representatives Approval of United States Participation in the Multinational Force in Lebanon
September 28, 1983

I want to thank the House of Representatives for its strong, bipartisan vote today supporting our policies in Lebanon and the continued presence of the U.S. peacekeeping force. This vote would not have been possible without the strong leadership of Speaker O'Neill, Majority Leader Wright, Minority Leader Michel, Chairman of the House Foreign Affairs Committee Zablocki, and Ranking Minority Member Broomfield. A spirit of cooperation between members of the two parties, and between the executive and the legislative branches of our Government, has been the traditional hallmark of a successful foreign policy. Today, we continue the process of restoring that bipartisan spirit. Now we look to the Senate for a similar demonstration of responsible leadership.

Nomination of Robert Michael Isaac To Be a Member of the Board of Trustees of the Harry S. Truman Scholarship Foundation
September 29, 1983

The President today announced his intention to nominate Robert Michael Isaac to be a member of the Board of Trustees of the Harry S. Truman Scholarship Foundation for a term expiring December 10, 1987. He would succeed Richard A. King.

Since 1979 Mr. Isaac has been serving as mayor of Colorado Springs, Colo. He is also a partner in the law firm of Isaac, Johnson & Alpern. He was a councilman for the city of Colorado Springs in 1975–1979. He has served as a judge for the Colorado Springs Municipal Court (1966–1969) and as assistant district attorney for the Fourth Judicial District of Colorado (1965–1966).

He graduated from the United States Military Academy (B.S., 1951) and the University of Southern California (J.D., 1962). He is married and has five children. He was born January 27, 1928, in Colorado Springs, Colo.

Statement by Deputy Press Secretary Speakes on Arms Control and Reduction Negotiations and the Soviet Statement on United States Foreign Policy
September 29, 1983

Mr. Andropov's statement is deeply disappointing, for it fails to address concrete steps which would reduce tensions and lead to a more peaceful world.

On Monday, the President put forward a series of concrete proposals, and we shall continue to press for resolution of problems at the negotiating table. But we are still awaiting signs that the Soviet Union is prepared to negotiate differences on a realistic and equitable basis. Deeds, not words, are urgently required.

We do not hide our view of the nature of the Soviet system and of the dangers to the world of many Soviet policies and actions. For their part, the Soviet leaders have never been reticent in expressing their view of us. But while we disagree profoundly on the way human society should be organized to protect human rights, ensure justice, and achieve prosperity, we know that we must live on the same planet and that peace is imperative to mankind if it is to survive.

The door remains open to work in concrete ways to ensure peace. We hope the Soviet Union will enter the room and get down to the task at hand.

Note: Yuriy V. Andropov is Chairman of the Presidium of the Supreme Soviet of the Soviet Union.

Remarks of the President and Prime Minister Margaret Thatcher of the United Kingdom Following Their Meetings
September 29, 1983

The President. I have had the pleasure of cordial and productive discussions with Prime Minister Thatcher on a wide range of mutual interests and concerns. Our conversations reflected the superb relations that exist between our two countries and our determination to broaden our cooperation and consultation.

We reaffirm today our resolve to maintain a strong Western defense to protect freedom and maintain peace. We'll carry out our commitments to the alliance, moving forward in the modernization of NATO's conventional and nuclear deterrent. At the same time, I have pledged America's best efforts to reach acceptable agreements on arms reduction with the Soviet Union.

The Prime Minister informed me of what her government is doing to prepare for the scheduled deployment of cruise missiles should we fail to reach an agreement with the Soviets. I expressed the thanks of the American people to the Prime Minister for Britain's strong and unequivocal support on this vital issue.

We also discussed developments in the Middle East, especially the situation in Lebanon, where both our countries are participating in a peacekeeping force. We agree that the solution to that tragic conflict can only come from the Lebanese themselves, free from all foreign interference. I've reviewed with the Prime Minister U.S. efforts to engage all Lebanese factions in a constructive dialog toward the goal of withdrawing all foreign forces from their country and reestablishing the rule of peace and law.

Prime Minister Thatcher and I also discussed developments in this hemisphere. I explained our energetic efforts to end the violence that plagues Central America and to promote democracy and economic development in that region.

In our discussion of economic matters, we reaffirmed the course set out at the Williamsburg summit as the best blueprint to sustain economic recovery and counter protectionism. We agreed on the need for continued close consultations as a means of resolving any differences between us in matters of trade and commerce.

Prime Minister Thatcher, we're grateful for your visit, your friendship, especially as this month marks the 200th anniversary of the signing of the Treaty of Paris which made us friends instead of countrymen. And when you finish speaking here, we can go over and look at that Treaty of Paris.

The Prime Minister. Thank you very much. Mr. President, ladies and gentlemen, today's visit has been a very important one. I've had just about 2 hours of talks with the President on the many things which he has indicated, all of them which are extremely vital for the future of our peoples in our several countries.

I've also seen, earlier this morning, Secretary Regan, when we discussed economic matters and, in particular, the problems of unitary taxation. I saw, too, Mr. Volcker, because naturally we are all concerned that the great international debt position should find a solution which enables trade to continue and those countries to come out of their grievous debt problems.

The President and I started first, as he has indicated, on East-West relations. I think I can put our position like this: We both believe in defending our way of life, and we must do that to keep that way of life secure. But our purpose in having military strength is entirely defensive—to defend our way of life. We would like to be able to have that security at a lower cost in weaponry and in expenditure and in men. In order to achieve that lower cost, we have seriously and continuously to negotiate with the Soviet Union to try to get a balance in men, materials, weapons, and in nuclear strength. If we can achieve that, we can keep our security at a lower expenditure.

It takes two to negotiate, and the President has constantly put forward detailed proposals to the Soviet Union. Such is the anxiety of the West genuinely to negotiate disarmament reductions. He has put forward the latest proposals. Mr. Andropov has replied. I hope now that the proposals will be seriously discussed by the Soviet Union at the negotiating table. If they are not successful in reaching zero option, the cruise and Pershing missiles will be deployed by the end of this year. Our nerve is being tested; we must not falter now. That should not be the end of the negotiations. I hope and it is my earnest belief that they should continue, so that although we were not able to negotiate zero option, we should be able to negotiate the deployment of a lesser number of weapons than the full total, provided, again, the Soviets will genuinely negotiate on balance.

We have also discussed, as the President indicated, the Middle East, and we're very conscious that although all eyes are focused on Lebanon, the fundamental problem of the Middle East—a secure Israel and a legitimate deal for the Palestinian people— has still to be resolved.

I have pointed out to the President we support his Central American policy and, particularly, the most excellent strategic view he gave of it during his very famous speech in April. And we are constantly pointing out that of the aid which the United States gives to Central America, 75 cents out of every dollar goes to civil aid, and that is a record to be proud of.

We've also had a word about Belize, and I, naturally, as you would understand, have made my views known about arms to Argentina. I discussed with Secretary Regan this morning and again at lunch the wider issues affecting the economy and the impor-

tance of trying to secure lower interest rates so that we can get a full recovery in the world which would be to the benefit of the United States, Europe, and also to the peoples of the underdeveloped countries.

If I may sum up, altogether this has been another chapter in the close discussion, consultation, and similar beliefs in shared ideals between the United States and Britain. Against that background, it's not surprising that we find common views and we pursue them with common purpose in the wider world.

Thank you very much.

Note: The President spoke at 1:33 p.m. to reporters assembled at the South Portico of the White House.

Earlier, the President and the Prime Minister met in the Oval Office and then held a working luncheon, together with American and British officials, in the State Dining Room.

Remarks on Greeting Members of the Washington Capitals and United States Olympic Hockey Teams
September 29, 1983

The President. What's the penalty for delaying the game? [*Laughter*]

Well, a welcome to all the players, the coaches, and the managers, and thank you all for coming. I understand we're going to have a little exhibition right here in the Rose Garden. Just don't let me be caught between the two teams. From the hot rivalry we hear you have going, you may just melt the ice at the Capital Centre Friday evening.

Athletic rivalry is the best spirit of competition, and you've put me in a predicament for Friday's game, because both teams here are in a sense hometown teams. The U.S. Olympic team is America's hometown team, and the Capitals are Washington's hometown team. So, I'm not going to pick a favorite. In politics, they call this fence-sitting. [*Laughter*] We do wish both teams the best of luck for a good game.

Now, a couple of members of the '84 Olympic team also played in the 1980 Lake

Placid games. Before the big game with the Soviet team, the coach told the players, "You were born for this moment. This is your moment." And I don't think we'll ever forget the picture of those young Americans, not favored to win by a long shot, but win they did.

Abe Pollin, the owner of the Capital Centre, is here today, too. I should tell the teams to check the rink pretty carefully before you skate out on it Friday. I was out there last Saturday, and where you'll be skating there was a rodeo going on. [*Laughter*]

But the Capitals give Washington a very much needed team to cheer for. And I want you all to know I follow your progress. Last year you were great. This year we hope you'll be even better. And, again, thank you all for being here. And good luck tomorrow night. And, well, play ball. [*Laughter*]

Mr. Langway. Mr. President, on behalf of the Washington Capitals, we'd like to give you this official Capital jersey on behalf of the whole team.

The President. Well, thank you very much.

Mr. Langway. Also, I'd like to give you a little token from a little slogan on the puck, "The puck stops here in '83 and '84." [*Laughter*]

The President. Thank you very much.

Mr. Langway. And also, Mr. Vice President, we'd like to give you the same thing.

The Vice President. Why, thank you. Beautiful. That's great.

Mr. Verehota.[1] Mr. President, on behalf of the 1984 Olympic team, we also have an official Olympic jersey to go along with that Washington Capital jersey.

Team member. We're a little short on players, so you might have to play tomorrow night.

The President. I just got an offer to play tomorrow night. [*Laughter*]

Thank you.

Mr. Verehota. Mr. Vice President, we'd like to give you our team pendant.

The Vice President. Hey, thank you very much. Thanks a lot. I appreciate it.

Mr. Brooke.[2] Mr. President, on behalf of the U.S. Olympic team in 1984, for our appreciation for having us here and your support, a little token of our gratitude. [*Laughter*]

The President. Thank you very much.

Mr. Langway. Well, Mr. President, we hear that you were a pretty good athlete in *your* day—[*laughter*]—so, I think we're going to try a new sport for you. And I'd like to show you how to shoot a puck, if I can shoot one. [*Laughter*]

___

[1] *Phil Verehota, captain of the Olympic team.*

[2] *Bob Brooke, defenseman on the Olympic team, presented the President with a trophy filled with jellybeans.*

This is Gretsky's stick. He's got a lot of goals with it, so I'm sure you—[*laughter*]——

[*At this point, Rod Langway, team captain of the Washington Capitals, and the President stepped onto a small plexiglass rink, complete with goal, which had been constructed in the Rose Garden. Mr. Langway shot several pucks at the goal, tended by Olympic team member Bob Mason, as he talked.*]

It's like sweeping dust off the ice. That's all you do.

Team member. Between his legs, he's weak. [*Laughter*]

Mr. Langway. It's all yours.

The President. [*Inaudible*]—try and get it by him?

[*The President shot a puck past Mr. Mason and into the goal.*]

You will never see me hit another puck again as long as I live. [*Laughter*]

[*The President walked back onto the rink, pulled a bogus hockey puck from his pocket, and dropped it onto the rink.*]

And for the press that keeps asking questions in photo opportunities—[*laughter*]——

[*The President shot the puck toward the reporters gathered behind the goal.*]

Want to try one, George?

The Vice President. No. [*Laughter*]

The President. Well, listen, thank you all very much.

Mr. Pollin. Are you sure you're busy tomorrow night, Mr. President?

The President. What?

Mr. Pollin. After the way you shot that, you sure you're busy tomorrow night? [*Laughter*]

The President. I think I'd better confess, I was really aiming at him. [*Laughter*]

Mr. Langway. That's what we all do.

The President. Well, good luck to all of you. Thank you.

Reporter. What about Andropov? [*Laughter*]

Note: The President spoke at 3:15 p.m.

Letter to the Speaker of the House Transmitting Proposed Pension Equity Legislation
September 29, 1983

Dear Mr. Speaker:

I enclose for your consideration a draft bill entitled the "Pension Equity Act of 1983." This legislation seeks to amend the Employee Retirement Income Security Act (ERISA) and the Internal Revenue Code to provide greater equity in the provision of retirement income for women.

In my State of the Union Address last January, I underscored my commitment to taking action to end inequities in the provision of pensions to women. This issue is a top priority of my Administration, and I believe passage of legislation is imperative to eliminate difficulties faced by women both in earning their own pensions and receiving retirement income as widows and divorcees.

Many of these provisions are similar to proposals contained in S. 19, the "Retirement Equity Act," which has been introduced in the Senate by Senator Dole. Further, the Administration has testified before the Senate Finance Committee where we stated our strong endorsement of many of these proposals and urged their prompt consideration and enactment. We believe that these and the other amendments contained in our bill are long overdue and will significantly improve the ability of women to realize a fair and equitable retirement income. At my direction, we will continue to work closely with Senator Dole and other members of the Senate to enact pension equity legislation this year.

We are specifically transmitting this legislation to you to focus the attention of the House of Representatives on many of the problems facing women in securing an adequate pension. We look forward to working with the appropriate Committees of the House to provide whatever assistance may be required to achieve enactment of these extremely important statutory provisions.

Sincerely,

RONALD REAGAN

[The Honorable Thomas P. O'Neill, Jr., Speaker of the House of Representatives, Washington, D.C. 20515]

Statement on Senate Approval of United States Participation in the Multinational Force in Lebanon
September 29, 1983

In the last 2 days, Republican and Democratic Members of the Congress have won a great victory for an honorable and all important American tradition—a responsible, bipartisan foreign policy.

Today's vote in the Senate, authorizing, as the House did yesterday, the continued presence of the U.S. peacekeeping force in Lebanon, sends a strong signal to the world: America stands united, we speak with one voice, and we fulfill our responsibilities as a trustee of freedom, peace, and self-determination.

By working together to promote peace in Lebanon, to give Lebanon back to the Lebanese people, and to help them rebuild their democracy, we are strengthening the forces for peace throughout the Middle East. This is neither a Republican nor a Democratic goal. Peace in that troubled region is the cause that unites us all.

Statement on Signing a 1984 and 1985 Feed Grain Programs Bill
September 29, 1983

I have today signed H.R. 3914, a bill "To require the Secretary of Agriculture to make an earlier announcement of the 1984 crop feed grain program and of the 1985 crop wheat and feed grain programs."

I vetoed an earlier bill on this subject, H.R. 3564, because it mandated early and rigid announcement dates. They would not have allowed the Secretary of Agriculture sufficient time to collect and evaluate critical information on the harvest of current crops, before committing to a specific program for the following year.

H.R. 3914 will permit the Secretary of Agriculture a 30-day period to adjust the initial program announcements. H.R. 3564 did not permit such an adjustment.

I am approving H.R. 3914 because I believe that it will meet the needs of farmers, while also allowing the Department of Agriculture to carry out its responsibilities to manage these programs in a timely and efficient manner.

Note: As enacted, H.R. 3914 is Public Law 98–100, approved September 29.

The President's message to the House of Representatives returning without his approval H.R. 3564 is printed on page 1155.

Statement on Signing the Bill Establishing a Commission on the Bicentennial of the United States Constitution
September 29, 1983

I have signed today S. 118, a bill that establishes a commission which will coordinate the commemoration of the bicentennial of the Constitution.

Our nation is approaching the 200th anniversary of the Constitutional Convention's approval of the Constitution, which occurred on September 17, 1787. Our Constitution contains the principles that have formed the basis of our national strength, unity, and prosperity. This bicentennial offers an opportunity to rededicate ourselves to the principles embodied by the Constitution.

I welcome the participation of the Chief Justice, the President pro tempore of the Senate, and the Speaker of the House of Representatives in the activities of the Commission. However, because of the constitutional impediments contained in the doctrine of the separation of powers, I understand that they will be able to participate only in ceremonial or advisory functions of the Commission, and not in matters involving the administration of the act. Also, in view of the incompatibility clause of the Constitution, any Member of Congress appointed by me pursuant to section 4(a)(1) of this act may serve only in a ceremonial or advisory capacity.

I also understand that this act does not purport to restrict my ultimate responsibility as President for the selection and appointment of members of the Commission, under article II, section 2, clause 2, of the Constitution.

Note: As enacted, S. 118 is Public Law 98–101, approved September 29.

Announcement of the Annual President's Volunteer Action Awards Program
September 30, 1983

The President today announced the third annual President's Volunteer Action Awards, a program designed to honor outstanding volunteers and volunteer groups and to focus public attention on the contributions of the Nation's 96 million volunteers.

The President will present the awards at a White House ceremony in early May. Awards are made in 10 categories: arts and humanities, education, the environment, health, human services, international volunteering, jobs, material resources, public safety, and the workplace.

In a unique cooperative effort between the private sector and the Government, VOLUNTEER: The National Center for Citizen Involvement, a private, nonprofit volunteer support organization, and ACTION, the Federal agency for volunteering, are cosponsoring the program for the third year. Funding for the program is provided by corporate and foundation sponsors.

VOLUNTEER is the primary national organization supporting greater citizen involvement in community problem-solving, providing technical assistance to volunteer-involving organizations, public agencies, unions, and corporations. It works closely with a network of over 225 associated Voluntary Action Centers and more than 1,000 other local, State, and national organizations.

ACTION serves to stimulate voluntarism and to demonstrate the effectiveness of volunteers in addressing social problems. Its major programs include the Foster Grandparent, Retired Senior Volunteer, and Senior Companion programs for the elderly and a variety of programs for youth. ACTION also promotes private sector initiatives by providing short-term grants to innovative volunteer projects in such areas as literacy and drug abuse.

Among the supporters of the 1984 awards program are Aid Association for Lutherans, Avon Products, Inc., Keyes Martin Advertising and Public Relations, Mutual Benefit Life. Insurance Co., Rexnord and Tenneco, Inc.

President Reagan presented the second annual awards to 17 individuals and groups, one labor union, and two corporations at a White House ceremony on April 13. Official nomination forms can be obtained by writing P.O. Box 37488, Washington, D.C. 20013. The deadline for submission of nominations for the 1984 awards is January 31, 1984.

Nomination of Susan Meredith Phillips To Be Chairman of the Commodity Futures Trading Commission
September 30, 1983

The President today announced his intention to nominate Susan Meredith Phillips to be Chairman of the Commodity Futures Trading Commission. She has been serving as a Commissioner on the Commission since 1981.

Dr. Phillips was an associate professor with the finance department of the University of Iowa in 1978–1981 and associate vice president of finance and university services in 1980–1981. She also served as interim assistant vice president of finance and university services in 1979–1980. Previously she was an SEC economic fellow in 1977–1978; a Brookings economic fellow in 1976–1977; and directorate of economic and policy research, Securities and Exchange Commission. She was an assistant professor at the University of Iowa in 1974–1978 and at Louisiana State University in 1973–1974.

She graduated from Agnes Scott College (B.A., 1967) and Louisiana State University (M.S., 1971; Ph. D., 1973). She resides in Iowa City, Iowa. She was born December 23, 1944, in Richmond, Va.

Remarks of President Reagan and President Mohammed Hosni Mubarak of Egypt Following Their Meetings
September 30, 1983

President Reagan. President Mubarak and I have concluded another of our regular consultations on regional and bilateral issues. Our discussions were warm and frank, as discussions between good and trusting friends should be. They strengthen our sense of common purpose in working for regional peace and security.

There was basic agreement on the critical issues our nations face in the Middle East and Africa. We discussed the urgent need to achieve a just and comprehensive peace for the Middle East which would permit the nations there, all the states in the region, to live in peace while safeguarding the legitimate rights of the Palestinian people. In that regard, I reiterated my commitment to the peace initiative that we announced a little more than a year ago and my desire to work closely with President Mubarak to bring the parties to negotiation. Our policy remains firmly based on U.N. Security Council Resolutions 242 and 338 and the Camp David accords.

We reviewed the situation in Lebanon, and I thank the President for Egypt's support of Ambassador McFarlane's efforts to produce a settlement there, and assured him of my determination to support the territorial integrity, sovereignty, and independence of Lebanon. To that end, there must be an enduring cease-fire, political reconciliation, and the prompt withdrawal of all foreign forces.

In discussing Africa, we agreed on the need to support nations such as Chad which are subject to external threat.

On bilateral questions, I reiterated the information—or the importance that I attach to our continued assistance to Egypt and to our strategic cooperation. I've assured the President that our assistance will be responsive to Egypt's needs. And I also reviewed steps that we've taken to increase the flexibility of our economic assistance so that it can support President Mubarak's efforts to reform the Egyptian economy. We agree that we should continue our dialog on economic issues.

President Mubarak's visit, the third since he was elected to office, highlights the special nature of our relationship with Egypt and the importance that I attach to his personal friendship and wise counsel. Our two countries share a common dedication to building a Middle East that is peaceful, prosperous, and secure from outside intervention. The Egyptian-American partnership has already produced significant results, and we'll continue to build on our record of accomplishment.

Mr. President, it's a pleasure again, as always, to have you here.

President Mubarak. Thank you. It's a great pleasure for me to meet again with my friend President Reagan and discuss with him several issues of common concern.

As we share the commitment to the cause of peace, we focus on the situation in the Middle East. We both rejoiced in the cease-fire agreement recently reached in Lebanon. The cease-fire must continue so that efforts to bring about national reconciliation in Lebanon be given the chance to succeed, and succeed they must. Lebanon has seen much bloodshed and destruction, and it deserves a lasting peace and stability and the real opportunity to reconstruct the country. The key to our breakthrough is the complete withdrawal of Israeli and other foreign forces. The authority of the Lebanese leadership over the entire country must be consolidated. Short of this, the situation would remain tense and explosive.

At the same time, we must not neglect the Palestinian problem. In this regard, I welcome President Reagan's assurances that he remains committed to the peace initiative of the 1st of September, 1982. The time has come to reactivate this initiative with a view to secure the participation of Jordan and the representatives of the Palestinian people in the negotiations. I am confident that through negotiations Palestinian legitimate rights will be fully recognized, and peace between Israel and all her Arab neighbors will emerge, assuring for each the right to live within secure and recognized borders and thus allowing the region to devote its energies to development and progress.

President Reagan and I have also agreed on the necessity to put an end to the war between Iran and Iraq immediately. The promulgation of the meaningless war is detrimental to the interests of all nations. We call upon Iran to respond positively to Iraq's offer of terminating the war and entering into a peace negotiation without preconditions.

We also discussed current African problems. We fully support the Government of Chad and uphold the presence of foreign occupation forces there. The territorial integrity of Chad must be preserved. We support the efforts of the Organization of African Unity in this regard.

On bilateral matters, President Reagan and I are fully satisfied with our cooperation in all fields. We share the determination to bolster our fraternal ties and cement our friendship each day.

As always, I have found President Reagan most gracious and responsive. I thank him and the American people for their understanding and constructive spirit.

Thank you.

Note: President Reagan spoke at 1:15 p.m. in the East Room at the White House.

Earlier, the two Presidents met in the Oval Office and then held an expanded meeting, together with their advisers, in the Cabinet Room. Following the meetings, the U.S. and Egyptian officials attended a luncheon in the State Dining Room.

Radio Address to the Nation on the Economic Recovery and Employment
October 1, 1983

My fellow Americans:

With autumn here, schools reopened, and people back at work, a question is on everyone's mind: Will the economic recovery last and the job market continue to improve? Well, I believe the answer is yes. I'm bullish on America. I've been called an optimist. But I'm not like the fellow who notices a car has a flat tire, and says, "It's all right; the tire's only flat on the bottom." My optimism springs from solid evidence that America has turned the corner toward long-term economic expansion. If all of us act responsibly we can enjoy a renaissance of growth, progress, and opportunities, free from the ruinous inflation and record interest rates of old.

America's job picture will improve during the next 3 months, and it's likely to get even better after April. That's the good news from a nationwide survey of 11,400 employers in 354 cities, conducted by Manpower, Incorporated. Other recent surveys reflect increases in help wanted ads across the country. Some of the biggest increases were in the areas that need jobs the most—industrial Midwest States like Ohio, Michigan, Illinois, Indiana, and Wisconsin. Georgia, Maryland, Florida, Virginia, North Carolina, Alabama, Tennessee, and Kentucky also saw increases above the national average.

Growth creates more growth. As workers are called back and start receiving paychecks, the economy expands, increasing the need for still more workers. Since last December the number of unemployed has declined by 1.3 million, and economic growth has added nearly 2½ million people to America's work force. But we must not rest till every American who wants a job can find a job. We need the strength of every back and the power of every mind. Still, let's not be swayed by downbeats who never admit anything's right, never acknowledge the huge problems we inherited, and never admit the progress we've made reducing inflation, interest rates, and yes, creating new jobs.

The truth is more Americans are working now than at any time in this nation's history. The rising tide of employment is reaching across America into communities large and small, farms and factories, and it's helping people from all walks of life. Sixty percent of the jobs lost in the construction industry during the last recession have been recovered; add to that 70 percent of the jobs in furniture and fixtures, 90 percent in rubber and plastics, 90 percent in automobiles, and 125 percent in lumber and wood products.

One of the most encouraging trends we're seeing is higher employment for women: 2.3 million more women are working now than before we took office. And the jobs are better, too. Women filled more than half of all new jobs in managerial, professional, and technical fields between 1980 and 1982. Also, did you know that self-employed women are the fastest growing part of our business community—growing, in fact, five times faster than the number of self-employed men? It puzzles me why we hear so little about this progress, this proof that opportunities for all Americans are expanding.

Now, many of the people who remain jobless are part of a category economists call "structural unemployment." They may live in economically depressed areas where firms and factories have become outmoded, or they may lack the skills and training needed to seize opportunities in the new service industries and areas of high technology. One of the most serious problems we still face is youth unemployment. Nearly 40 percent of the unemployed in America are less than 25 years old, and nearly half of that group are teenagers.

But there's hope. To strengthen the skills of young Americans, to provide new opportunities for prospective workers of all ages, we've charted a new approach that looks to the future rather than the past. Beginning today, October 1st, an historic and bold program—the Job Training Partnership Act—will train and retrain more than a million people a year for productive, lasting jobs in the private economy. At the core of my philosophy is the belief that progress begins with trusting people. You at the grassroots can spend your tax dollars far more wisely and productively than any collection of bureaucrats in the Federal Government. That's why this Job Training Partnership Act will be a major step forward from past programs.

Unlike the old CETA program run primarily by government officials and which either didn't provide enough training or else trained people for jobs that didn't exist, this program will be planned by business and labor people in your own communities—those who know best what training is needed for existing jobs. They'll be receiving the block grants that the Federal Government sends to their own State governments. This time, private enterprise will be participating in a very meaningful way. The business and labor people will be working together in organizations called PIC's—Private Industry Councils, designed to provide training skills needed right on Main Street America. At least 70 cents of every Job Training Partnership Act dollar must go to training.

On Monday, the Indianapolis Private Industry Council will start sponsoring training at ITT to place low-income youth and adults in existing jobs. In Wilmington, welfare women will be trained for skilled, entry-level jobs. These are just two examples among many of hope being reborn across America. No civilization can survive and grow if it does not learn the lessons of its own history. The Job Training Partnership Act is an important reform that demonstrates we're not only correcting mistakes from our past, we're moving with wisdom and confidence to shape a brighter future. The outlook for America is good and getting better.

Till next week, thanks for listening, and God bless you.

Note: The President spoke at 12:06 p.m. from the Oval Office at the White House.

Proclamation 5111—Twenty-fifth Anniversary of the National Aeronautics and Space Administration
October 1, 1983

By the President of the United States of America

A Proclamation

America is justifiably proud of its accomplishments in aeronautics and in space research. In the 25 years since the National Aeronautics and Space Administration (NASA) was created by an Act of Congress, our country and the world have witnessed an unsurpassed record of scientific and technical achievements which has established the United States as the world leader in aerospace research and development.

In aeronautics, the National Aeronautics and Space Administration has conducted an effective and productive research and technology program that continues to contribute materially to the enduring preeminence of United States civil and military aviation. Two-thirds of the world's commercial aircraft fleet is American designed and built, accounting for some $10 billion in positive trade balance in 1982. NASA's wind tunnels, laboratories, and such experimental aircraft as the X–15 provide the solid essential research base for technology advancement and leadership.

In space, the National Aeronautics and Space Administration has conducted one of the most dramatic of all human endeavors: the Apollo Project which, 14 years ago, landed men on the Moon for the first time and returned them safely 240,000 miles to Earth. In addition, remotely controlled spacecraft have been dispatched on missions extending from near Earth orbit to the far reaches of the solar system. Through the Viking mission, the winds of Mars have been measured; through the Voyager mission, volcanoes on a moon of Jupiter have been observed and the rings of Saturn have been counted. More information has been gathered about the cosmos in 25 years than had been gleaned in all the preceding centuries. In the Space Shuttle, first launched in 1981, America now has a sophisticated new system for space research—a machine that delivers payloads routinely to orbit; allows humans to work in space; returns crew, experiments, and unrepairable spacecraft to Earth; and is reconditioned within a short period for its next launch. The Shuttle is booked through 1988, an indication of how utilitarian space has become. The government uses it to preserve the national security; the private sector uses it for commercial advantage; NASA uses it in a search for knowledge, not just of the beyond, but applied knowledge which will shed light on conditions and circumstances critical to the Earth and its inhabitants.

Significant benefits have already been derived from space research. For example, communications satellites now provide worldwide communications to well over 100 countries. Communications satellites have profoundly changed modern life, making events immediate, impacts instantaneous, and instruction possible almost anywhere. Future benefits will be even more impressive. The future looks bright, and NASA will be an important part of it.

The government-industry-university partnership, pioneered by NASA, has worked exceedingly well in aerospace research, providing a model to others on how the different sectors of American society can work together. This effort reflects America at its best: peacefully seeking knowledge and enlightenment, advancing technology for mankind's benefit, and organizing resources to accomplish great missions.

In order to recognize the enormous achievements by the National Aeronautics and Space Administration, the Congress has, by House Joint Resolution 284, authorized and requested the President to proclaim October 1, 1983, as the "Twenty-fifth Anniversary of the National Aeronautics and Space Administration."

Now, Therefore, I, Ronald Reagan, President of the United States of America, do hereby proclaim October 1, 1983, as the "Twenty-fifth Anniversary of the National Aeronautics and Space Administration." I call upon the people of the United States to observe that occasion with appropriate ceremonies and activities.

In Witness Whereof, I have hereunto set my hand this first day of October, in the year of our Lord nineteen hundred and eighty-three, and of the Independence of the United States of America the two hundred and eighth.

RONALD REAGAN

[*Filed with the Office of the Federal Register, 10:15 a.m., October 3, 1983*]

Proclamation 5110—National Alzheimer's Disease Month, 1983
September 30, 1983

By the President of the United States of America

A Proclamation

Alzheimer's disease, a devastating disease that affects the cells of the brain, is now regarded as the major form of old age "senility." While experts formerly believed that Alzheimer's occurred only in persons under 65, it now is recognized as the most common cause of severe intellectual impairment in older individuals. Presently, there is no established treatment that can cure, reverse or stop the progression of this disease, which is the cause of serious confusion and forgetfulness in about 1.5–2.5 million elderly persons in the United States.

Because there is an association of dementia with aging and because Americans are living longer, the numbers affected by this disease will continue to grow. As many as half of those in nursing homes suffer from this degenerative brain disease. Also, because of the decrease in life expectancy accompanying the illness, Alzheimer's is thought to be the fourth leading cause of death among adults of age 65 or more. Generally, from the time of onset, the disease reduces a person's remaining life expectancy by about one-half. It also deprives its victims of the opportunity to enjoy life and takes a serious toll on its victims' families and friends.

The emotional, financial and social consequences of Alzheimer's disease are so devastating that it deserves special attention. Science and clinical medicine are striving to improve our understanding of what causes Alzheimer's disease and how to treat it successfully. Right now, research is the only hope for victims and families.

To recognize that progress is being made against this disease and to show understanding and support for the individuals and the families and friends of those who are affected, the Congress of the United States, by Senate Joint Resolution 82, has authorized and requested the President to proclaim November 1983 as National Alzheimer's Disease Month.

Now, Therefore, I, Ronald Reagan, President of the United States of America, do hereby proclaim the month of November 1983 as National Alzheimer's Disease Month. I call upon government agencies and the people of the United States to observe this month with appropriate ceremonies and activities.

In Witness Whereof, I have hereunto set my hand this thirtieth day of September, in the year of our Lord nineteen hundred and eighty-three, and of the Independence of the United States of America the two hundred and eighth.

RONALD REAGAN

[*Filed with the Office of the Federal Register, 10:14 a.m., October 3, 1983*]

Note: The text of the proclamation was released by the Office of the Press Secretary on October 3.

Message to the Congress Transmitting the Annual Science and Technology Report
October 3, 1983

To the Congress of the United States:

I am pleased to submit to the Congress the fifth Annual Science and Technology Report, as required under the National Science and Technology Policy, Organization, and Priorities Act of 1976, as amended.

Today the United States faces major challenges to both our economic well-being and our national security. We turn increasingly to science and technology to help us maintain the competitiveness of our industries in the international marketplace and to ensure the continued technological superiority of our defense capabilities.

The science and technology policies described in this report outline the framework in which our Administration is addressing these challenges. The significant increases in Federal R&D support, especially in basic research—the fount of new technologies and new knowledge—is evidence of our long-term commitment to strengthening the economy and security of America through science and technology. Programs to increase the supply of well trained scientists and engineers will ensure the best possible talent for continued technological advances in industry, universities, and government. The results of these important actions, in conjunction with the vigorous investment in research and development by the private sector, will be greater security and strong economic growth in the years ahead.

RONALD REAGAN

The White House,
October 3, 1983.

Note: The 139-page report is entitled "Annual Science and Technology Report to the Congress: 1982—Office of Science and Technology Policy in Cooperation With the National Science Foundation."

Remarks at the Swearing-in Ceremony for Katherine D. Ortega as Treasurer of the United States
October 3, 1983

The President. Today we're here to welcome Katherine Ortega as our new United States Treasurer. Also with us today are three former Treasurers—Bay Buchanan, Francis Neff, and Ramona Banuelos.

As is the case so often when appointments are made to prominent positions, we're not welcoming a new person on board. Instead, we're congratulating someone already on the team for moving up. Katherine Ortega's been a Commissioner on the Copyright Royalty Tribunal and a member of our Advisory Committee on Small and Minority Business Ownership. She's been one of those invaluable individuals who has shaped the character of our administration—always taking her task seriously, getting her job done, and rarely winning public attention. She's a true professional, a hard worker, and a good American.

And, Katherine, I know your family must be very proud of you today; I certainly am. You've proved to all of us that the American dream is alive and well.

Katherine is the youngest of nine children and comes from a family whose heritage is the stuff of which novels are made. She comes from sturdy pioneer stock, brave people who tackled the wilderness, when it was a wilderness, of New Mexico. And she's demonstrated that same pioneer spirit in her own endeavors.

After a successful career as a certified public accountant, she became the first woman bank president in California history. She brings to her new job experience and credentials.

I was also pleased that when we announced her appointment, she indicated her longtime commitment to Republican principles. In fact, she said she was born a Republican. That's better than me; I'm only a convert. [*Laughter*]

Well, it's important that key positions within an administration be filled by people who reflect the goals and ideals for which the people voted. And this is certainly the case today. As Treasurer of the United States, Katherine will oversee a budget of $340 million and supervise over 5,000 employees. I have faith in her, and I'm pleased and honored that she's a part of the team.

Being Treasurer gives one a certain immortality, because it's the Treasurer's name which appears on all new paper currency. I can't think of a better name to have on our money than Katherine Ortega. So, let's get on to the main event, and then I understand we'll get a chance to see her put her signature to good use.

[*At this point, Ms. Ortega was sworn in by Secretary of the Treasury Donald T. Regan.*]

Ms. Ortega. Mr. President, Mr. Secretary, distinguished guests:

The number of messages I have received since my nomination for Treasurer of the United States from people across the country from all walks of life have been an inspiration to me.

Among the letters I received was one from an 87-year-old Cuban man with the surname of Ortega. And I would like to share with you a poem he wrote for me and which I have translated. "Congratulations, Mrs. Ortega. And thanks to Mr. President for appointing you to such an important position. You now have in your life a marvelous road, an excellent opportunity and future. God has extended you his hand with a prestigious position as Treasurer of the United States."

President Reagan, by appointing me as Treasurer of this wonderful country of ours, you have provided an inspiration to women and to members of the Hispanic community. Many will take encouragement that, yes, it is possible to work and to attain the many opportunities available in our country.

And so it is with a deep sense of honor and pride that I shall serve as our country's 38th Treasurer. And following the Hispanic tradition, I have chosen to have my name appear on our currency as Katherine Davalos Ortega. For in doing so, I will be honoring my father as well as my mother. Thank you.

Secretary Regan. As the three former Treasurers of the United States who are here will recognize, what Katherine Davalos Ortega is doing is putting specimens of her signature that will later be translated to those on the actual bills. What she will do over the next year is to see that name on about 5½ billion separate notes with a value of about $60 billion.

[*At this point, Ms. Ortega completed the signatures.*]

There we go. Now I think Treasury can translate that to the bills.

Note: The President spoke at 11:02 a.m. in the Rose Garden at the White House.

Remarks at a White House Ceremony Marking the Observance of Minority Enterprise Development Week
October 3, 1983

Thank you, and welcome to the White House. We are here today to celebrate the contributions of minority business to American economic life, and we're also here to encourage the development of minority business itself.

Having one's own business is a powerful engine for social and economic progress. Countless of our minority citizens are taking advantage of the opportunity called free enterprise. It's very fitting that today we acknowledge what minority business people are doing, not just for themselves and their families but for our nation. You know, there were some hearings on the Hill the other day on the way minorities, especially black and Hispanic Americans, are portrayed on television. And if you'll bear with me for a moment, it relates to what we're doing here today.

Many who spoke at the hearing believe that television very often stereotypes minorities and ignores their range of talents and interests. Well, let me put on my old actors' union hat for a moment, because there's some truth in that. There are hundreds of thousands of small business men and women in this country who are black or Hispanic, as you well know. Why can't the casting directors more frequently assign parts as shopowners and business people to minorities? After all, there are 600,000 minority businesses in this nation. Now, our minority actors should also get parts as lawyers and doctors, even cowboys—there were a great many black cowboys in our history. You know, this isn't the first time I've said things like this because for six terms I was president of the Screen Actors Guild, my union, and, believe me, we were working on this very problem then as a union.

But minority business people contribute a great deal to our economic well-being, and I think it's time that they are recognized more, including on television and the screen. And recognition is one reason for Minority Enterprise Development Week, and why we're here. We also have some awards, as you've seen, that symbolize what minority business people are doing out there in the American economy. And let me first, if I may, recognize, as you already have, the winners of the Small Business Administration 8(a) Contractors of the Year Award.

As you know, the 8(a) program, you've been told, provides greater access for minorities to government contracts. Since 1968, over $15 billion in Federal procurement contracts have been directed toward minority-owned businesses. Our winners today participated in that program, and I'm very pleased to congratulate our co-win-

ners: Mr. Jaime Torres, of El Paso, Texas, the founder of J. T. Construction, and Mr. Norris Carson, the founder of N. L. Carson Construction of Carthage, Mississippi. And let me also congratulate all the regional winners and say that the Nation is just as proud of your contributions. And we wish you, too, continued success.

The other award is the Entrepreneur of the Year Award from the Minority Business Development Agency at the Department of Commerce. MBDA, as it's called, provides managerial and technical assistance to minority enterprises, and it assisted our winner today. And the winner, as you know, the Entrepreneur of the Year Award is Mr. Liborio Hinojosa from Mercedes, Texas, the president of H & H Meat Products Company. He couldn't be here today, but it's a genuine pleasure to honor his entrepreneurial spirit, as well.

Minority business is contributing to a stronger America, and this administration intends to encourage that. It's one reason we strongly support a bold initiative called Enterprise Zones, to stimulate business activity in some of the most destitute areas of our country. It's tragic that this legislation has been bottled up in the House of Representatives for so long. If the Congress refuses to act, hopes and dreams of millions will be lost in a cloud of indifference.

I've directed the Small Business Administration and the Minority Business Development Agency to assist in creating 60,000 new minority businesses and in expanding an additional 60,000 over the next 10 years. I've established a goal of $15 billion in Federal contract and subcontract awards to minority business over the next 3 years.

An important tool is the 8(a) pilot program which gives a wider range of contracts to minority businesses. And I have designated the Department of Transportation to participate in this program. Federal procurement in the last year of the previous administration was $3.1 billion. Last year Federal procurement to minority business was approximately $4.4 billion. We're doing these things because we believe in minority small business.

But my congratulations again to the winners, and it's especially good that we could honor them during the first annual Minority Enterprise Development Week. And I've signed many proclamations designating days and months and years and weeks particular things. But I was very delighted to be able to sign that particular proclamation. Again, God bless you all.

Note: The President spoke at 1:20 p.m. in the East Room at the White House.

Prior to the President's remarks, Secretary of Commerce Malcolm Baldrige presented the Minority Entrepreneur of the Year Award to Liborio Hinojosa. The plaque was accepted by his brother Rubin Hinojosa. James C. Sanders, Administrator of the Small Business Administration, then presented the SBA's Contractors of the Year Awards to Jaime Torres and Norris Carson.

On August 11 the President signed Proclamation 5083, designating the week of October 2 through October 8, as Minority Enterprise Development Week, 1983.

Nomination of Daniel Oliver To Be General Counsel of the Department of Agriculture
October 3, 1983

The President today announced his intention to nominate Daniel Oliver to be General Counsel of the Department of Agriculture. He would succeed A. J. Barnes.

Mr. Oliver is currently General Counsel of the Department of Education. Previously he was president of Rincon Communications Corp. in New York (1980–1981). He was with the law firm of Alexander & Green (1976–1979 and 1971–1973) and served as editorial assistant (1970–1971) and executive editor (1973–1976) of National Review magazine. He was with the law firm of Hawkins, Delafield & Wood (1967–1970) and was a candidate for the New York State Assembly in 1965, 1966, and 1968.

Mr. Oliver graduated from Harvard University (A.B., 1964) and Fordham Law School (LL.B., 1967). He is married, has five children, and resides in Greenwich, Conn. He was born April 10, 1939, in New York, N.Y.

Nomination of Ralph Leslie Stanley To Be Administrator of the Urban Mass Transportation Administration
October 3, 1983

The President today announced his intention to nominate Ralph Leslie Stanley to be Urban Mass Transportation Administrator, Department of Transportation. He would succeed Arthur E. Teele, Jr.

Mr. Stanley is presently serving as Chief of Staff for the Department of Transportation. Previously he was a Special Assistant to the Secretary, Department of Transportation, in 1981–1983; associate with the law firm of Bracewell and Patterson in 1978–1981; and summer associate with the law firm of Loomis, Owen, Fellman and Howe in 1978.

Mr. Stanley graduated from Princeton University (B.A., 1974) and Georgetown University Law School (J.D., 1979). He is married and resides in Alexandria, Va. He was born September 13, 1951, in Teaneck, N.J.

Appointment of Eight Members of the National Commission for Employment Policy, and Designation of Chairman
October 3, 1983

The President has appointed the following individuals to be members of the National Commission for Employment Policy, effective October 1, 1983. The President has designated Kenneth M. Smith as Chairman.

For a term of 2 years:

Roberto Cambo is sole owner and president of Rocam Produce Co., Inc., in Miami, Fla. He is married, has three children, and resides in Key Biscayne, Fla. He was born April 15, 1937, in Cuba.

Paul R. Locigno is research director, Ohio Conference of Teamsters. He is married, has one child, and resides in Windham, Ohio. He was born September 17, 1948, in Cleveland.

Roderick R. Paige is professor of health and physical education, Texas Southern University. He is married and resides in Houston, Tex. He was born June 17, 1933, in Monticello, Miss.

For a term of 3 years:

Kenneth M. Smith is president and chief executive officer, International Management and Development Group Ltd., a management consulting firm in Washington, D.C. He is married, has one child, and resides in Queenstown, Md. He was born April 5, 1949, in Auburn, N.Y.

Daniel Quinn Mills is professor of business administration, Harvard Graduate School of Business Administration. He is married, has two children, and resides in Winchester, Mass. He was born November 24, 1941, in Houston, Tex.

Norma Pace is senior vice president of the American Paper Institute in New York, N.Y. She is married and resides in Lakeville, Conn. She was born September 20, 1921, in New York, N.Y.

Kenneth O. Stout is self-employed and involved with real estate investment programs. He is married, has two children, and resides in Anchorage, Alaska. He was born October 5, 1929, in Wheatland, Mo.

Jack A. Gertz is public affairs and media relations manager with A.T. & T. (Bell System) in Washington, D.C. He is married, has one child, and resides in Potomac, Md. He was born April 10, 1916, in Chugwater, Wyo.

Statement by Deputy Press Secretary Speakes on the Postponement of the President's Visits to the Philippines, Indonesia, and Thailand
October 3, 1983

President Reagan has most reluctantly and with regret decided to postpone visits planned for this November to the Republic of the Philippines, Indonesia, and Thailand.

On Friday, September 30, Deputy Chief of Staff and Assistant to the President Michael K. Deaver departed Washington to visit each of the countries to express the President's regret and to deliver personal messages from the President to the heads of state of the three countries explaining the need for postponement. These discussions have now been completed.

In view of the fact that Congress will be in session, that key appropriations bills have not yet been enacted, and that a continuing resolution has been enacted but will expire November 10, it is clear that the first 2 weeks in November will be particularly demanding legislative weeks.

The President made the decision to postpone this portion of his planned trip after a careful review of the planned 17-day itinerary and an assessment of legislative issues with which he must deal.

Our relations with the Philippines, Indonesia, and Thailand are excellent, and we expect them to remain so. The President is disappointed that his original plans had to be changed, but this fact does not alter in any way the fundamental, positive relationship between the United States and the

ASEAN countries.

The President still plans to visit Japan and the Republic of Korea in November.

Note: Deputy Press Secretary Larry M.

Speakes read the statement during his daily briefing for reporters, which began at 2:20 p.m. in the Briefing Room at the White House.

Proclamation 5112—National Year of Partnerships in Education 1983–1984
October 3, 1983

By the President of the United States of America

A Proclamation

America's future is dependent upon the health and vitality of her education system. Although thousands of businesses, industries, individuals, organizations, teachers, administrators, and government at all levels have been involved in the education of our youth, there is more work to be done. More people must become active in improving the quality of education in our Nation.

Recently, many schools have developed private sector partnerships in an effort to broaden available resources and reach out to their communities for support. The private sector has much to offer the growing national movement to improve our education system. Some of the most effective methods include helping educators identify the learning needs of our society; encouraging professional exchanges between teachers, educators, and businesses; contributing expertise, financial resources, and equipment; and providing technical assistance in school administration and curriculum devel-

opment. In order to encourage this trend, I call upon businesses, organizations, individuals, and agencies to become involved with their local schools.

Partnerships in Education Year gives us the opportunity to acknowledge the efforts of the private sector and to encourage the creation of new partnerships in education all across this Nation.

Now, Therefore, I, Ronald Reagan, President of the United States of America, do hereby proclaim the period from October 1, 1983, through June 30, 1984, as the National Year of Partnerships in Education. I invite all Americans to join me in my commitment to the excellence and quality of education offered to all Americans.

In Witness Whereof, I have hereunto set my hand this 3rd day of Oct., in the year of our Lord nineteen hundred and eighty-three, and of the Independence of the United States of America the two hundred and eighth.

RONALD REAGAN

[Filed with the Office of the Federal Register, 9:56 a.m., October 4, 1983]

Message to the Congress Reporting Budget Deferrals
October 3, 1983

To the Congress of the United States:

In accordance with the Impoundment Control Act of 1974, I herewith report nineteen new deferrals of budget authority

totaling $1,909,569,000 and one new deferral of outlays totaling $15,209,000.

The deferrals affect programs in the Departments of Agriculture, Commerce, Defense (Civil and Military), Energy, Health and Human Services, Interior, State, Transportation, Treasury, and the Appalachian Regional Commission, Pennsylvania Avenue Development Corporation, Railroad Retirement Board, Tennessee Valley Authority, and the U.S. Railway Association.

The details of the deferrals are contained in the attached reports.

RONALD REAGAN

The White House,
October 3, 1983.

Note: The attachments detailing the deferrals are printed in the Federal Register *of October 6, 1983.*

Appointment of Thomas W. Hannon as a Member of the Presidential Commission for the German-American Tricentennial
October 3, 1983

The President today announced his intention to appoint Thomas W. Hannon to be a member of the Presidential Commission for the German-American Tricentennial. This is a new position.

Mr. Hannon has been with the Hannon Co. of Canton, Ohio, since 1948. He was named plant manager in 1948, general manager in 1950, and in 1953 established the first foreign subsidiary for the Hannon Co. in Holland. Currently he serves as president, chairman, and chief executive officer of the Hannon Co.

Mr. Hannon is married, has four children, and resides in Louisville, Ohio. He was born June 1, 1929, in Canton, Ohio.

Nomination of T. M. Alexander, Sr., To Be a Member of the Board of Directors of the African Development Foundation
October 3, 1983

The President today announced his intention to nominate T. M. Alexander, Sr., to be a member of the Board of Directors of the African Development Foundation for a term of 6 years. This is a new position.

Mr. Alexander presently serves as president of T. M. Alexander & Co., Inc., an insurance agency with major offices in At-lanta, Ga., and Washington, D.C. He is also an adjunct professor of insurance at Howard University, Washington, D.C.

He graduated from Morehouse College (B.S., 1931). He is married and resides in Washington, D.C. He was born March 7, 1909.

Remarks at a Dinner Marking the 10th Anniversary of the Heritage Foundation
October 3, 1983

It's wonderful for Nancy and me to be here tonight and see old friends like Joe Coors. Actually, I was a little surprised by the warmth of Joe's introduction. I'm not sure how many of you know this, but there's a certain coolness between Joe and me tonight. I guess maybe that's my fault. When I arrived at the reception here I said, "Joe, it's been a long, hard day in the Oval Office, but now it's Miller time." [*Laughter*]

That's when he showed me his Mondale button. [*Laughter*]

Seriously, though, where are those Democratic candidates with their grandiose solutions now that we need them? The America's Cup race, for example. Now, there was a problem that could have been solved with more money and a lot of wind. [*Laughter*]

And I'm delighted to be here with Heritage. I remember the days when a conservative intellectual was considered a contradiction in terms—you know, like "thrifty liberal"—[*laughter*]—"modest government," and "pennypinching Congressman." [*Laughter*] But it's a great privilege to be here tonight at an extraordinary moment not only in the history of the Heritage Foundation but, I firmly believe, in the intellectual history of the West.

Historians who seek the real meaning of events in the latter part of the 20th century must look back on gatherings such as this. They will find among your numbers the leaders of an intellectual revolution that recaptured and renewed the great lessons of Western culture, a revolution that is rallying the democracies to the defense of that culture and to the cause of human freedom, a revolution that I believe is also writing the last sad pages of a bizarre chapter in human history known as communism.

Now, we have been living in an age when the cult of overwhelming government was the reigning ideology. It dominated our intellectual thought and claimed some of the best minds of our society and civilization. And now all of that is changing. The evidence is before us in this room and in the astonishing growth of a remarkable institution called the Heritage Foundation.

You know, during the years when I was out on the mashed-potatoes circuit I was sometimes asked to define conservatism, and I must confess that, while I have the cream of the conservative intellectual movement before me, I'm tempted to use Justice Potter Stewart's definition. He gave it for another subject, by the way. He said he couldn't define it exactly, but "I know it when I see it." [*Laughter*] He was talking about pornography. [*Laughter*] Well, I can see conservatism here tonight. There is no better evidence that the time of the conservative idea has come than the growth of the Heritage Foundation.

Back in the midseventies this foundation was begun, as you've been told, by Paul Weyrich and Ed Feulner with only a few staff members, some modest offices, and not very much in the way of funding. And today, of course, you know Heritage has more than a hundred staff members, many more associates and consultants, as you've been told, a brand-new office building—its picture is on the program there—a budget that's gone from 3 million to 10 million in 5 years. But it's not money or numbers of people or size of the offices that measure Heritage's impact. Your frequent publications, timely research, policy papers, seminars, and conferences account for your enormous influence on Capitol Hill and, believe me, I know at the White House. Yes, the Heritage Foundation is an enormous undertaking and achievement.

It's great to see old friends from California that are also Heritage activists, like Frank Walton, but I particularly want to single out here for their enormous efforts some who've already been mentioned: Joe Coors, the Noble family, our master of ceremonies, Frank Shakespeare, and, of course, Heritage's guiding light, Ed Feulner.

Ed likes to say that not too many years ago a phone booth was just about big enough to hold a meeting of conservative intellectuals in Washington; he said it here tonight. I know what he means. Washington has a way of being the last to catch on. [*Laughter*] Just as the growth of Heritage has stunned the pundits, the conservative cause itself—the Goldwater nomination in 1964, the growth of the New Right in the 1970's, the conservative victory in 1980, and the tax-cut victory of 1981—all of these came as huge surprises to the Washington technocrats who pride themselves on knowing what's going on in politics.

Well, the reason is plain. Many people in the power structure of our Capital think that appealing to someone's narrow self-interest is the best way to appeal to the American people as a whole, and that's where they're wrong. When the American people go to the polls, when they speak out on the issues of the day, they know how high the stakes are. They know the future of freedom depends not on "what's in it for me," but on the ethic of what's good for the country, what will serve and protect freedom.

Success in politics is about issues, ideas, and the vision we have for our country and the world—in fact, the very sum and substance of the work of the Heritage Foundation. Don't take my word for it. In a book called "The Real Campaign," a study of the 1980 campaign, commentator Jeff Greenfield argues that gaffes or polls or momentum and all those other issues Washington experts thought were important in the election of 1980 were not. Mr. Greenfield argues that issues and ideas did count, that the electorate voted the way they did in large part because they rejected what liberalism had become, and they agreed with the coherent conservative message they heard from our side.

This point about politics and elections is reflected in what some have been saying about our economic system. As George Gilder points out, it isn't just self-gain or personal profit that drives the free market and accounts for the entrepreneurial spirit. There are larger issues involved: faith, a clear vision of the future, a hidden altruism, that simple human desire to make things better.

One current bestseller, "In Search of Excellence," has caused a great flurry in the business management world, because it argues that intangibles like shared values and a sense of mission are the great overlooked factors in accounting for the success of business institutions. Well, this is true of nations as well. The American electorate seeks from its national leadership this sense of shared values, this reaffirmation of traditional American beliefs. They do not want a President who's a broker of parochial concerns; they do not want a definition of national purpose, a vision of the future. And I believe that we conservatives have provided that vision during the past few years.

When this administration took office, we declined to go with patchwork solutions and quick fixes. We delivered, instead, on the promises we'd made to the American people, promises that were part of a consistent and coherent view of this nation's needs and problems. We had a policy; we put it

into effect. We made our promises, and we kept them. We said we would stop the juggernaut buildup of 40 years of increased Federal spending, and we did.

Despite the momentum accumulating from a host of new social welfare and entitlement programs, we still managed to cut the growth in Federal spending by nearly 40 percent. For the first time since 1964 all personal income tax rates have been cut, and cut by a hefty 25 percent across the board. And we made the most important reform of them all; in 1985, your income taxes will be indexed, so never again will you be pushed into higher tax brackets by inflation.

The story is the same for our efforts to deregulate the American economy. It was only a few years ago that every time you turned around, some government bureau had slapped on more restrictions on our commerce, our trade, and our lives. We were at the point where we could hardly adjust our thermostats or use our credit cards without checking first with Washington. Our regulatory task force has already cut the number of final regulations issued by almost 25 percent and saved American industry some 300 million hours of filling out forms.

And now that inflation has been reduced to 2.6 percent and the economy is on the move again, I'm just wondering where are all those folks who kept insisting that Reaganomics would lead to crippling recession or runaway inflation. In fact, how come no one calls it Reaganomics anymore? I never did call it that. That was their name when they thought it wouldn't work. I just called it common sense. But is it because our program is doing what we said it would, making America prosperous and strong again?

I think the picture on the foreign front is very much the same. You can all remember the days of national malaise and international humiliation. Everywhere in the world freedom was in retreat, and America's prestige and influence were at low ebb. In Afghanistan the liberty of a proud people was crushed by brutal Soviet aggression. In Central America and Africa Soviet-backed attempts to install Marxist dictatorships were successfully underway. In Iran international law and common decency were mocked, as 50 American citizens were held hostage. And in international forums the United States was routinely held up to abuse and ridicule by outlaw regimes and police state dictatorships.

That was an America that once upon a time not too long ago knew that an American in some distant corner of the world could be caught up in revolution or conflict of war of some kind, and all he had to do was pin a little American flag to his lapel, and he could walk through that war and no one would lay a finger on him because they knew this country stood by its people wherever they might be. We're going to have that kind of America again.

Verifiable and equitable arms control agreements were nowhere in sight, and our own military might had sharply declined. Even friendly governments were toning down their pro-American rhetoric, abandoning their anti-Soviet declarations, withdrawing support for our diplomatic initiatives, and beginning to be influenced by Soviet diplomatic and commercial programs they had previously dismissed outright.

All this is changing. While we cannot end decades of decay in only a thousand days, we have fundamentally reversed the ominous trends of a few years ago.

First, our economic program is working, and our recovery sets the pace for the rest of the world. We strengthen the hand of other democracies.

Second, the willingness of the American people to back our program for rebuilding America's defenses has added to the respect, the prestige, and deterrent capability we need to support our foreign policy goals.

Third, we have significantly slowed the transfer of valuable free world technology to the Soviet Union.

Fourth, throughout the world today the aspirations for freedom and democracy are growing. In the Third World, in Afghanistan, in Central America, in Africa and Southeast Asia, opposition to totalitarian regimes is on the rise. It may not grab the headlines, but there is a democratic revolution underway.

Finally, our new willingness to speak out forthrightly about communism has been a critically effective foreign policy step. We're making clear that the free world, far from plunging into irreversible decline, retains the moral energy and spiritual stamina to tell the truth about the Soviets, to state clearly the real issues now before the world. That issue is not, as our adversaries would have us believe, the choice between peace and war, between being dead or Red, but, rather, the choice between freedom and servitude, human dignity and state oppression.

And now let me speak a word for a moment about a matter that needs to be cleared up. There are a number of Congressmen on the Hill, including conservatives, who, while being inclined to vote for our defense policies want to be absolutely sure of our desire for arms control agreements. Well, I hope my recent speech at the United Nations has helped to clarify this. But just let me add a personal note— and this is a matter of conscience.

Any American President, anyone charged with the safety of the American people, any person who sits in the Oval Office and contemplates the horrible dimensions of a nuclear war must, in conscience, do all in his power to seriously pursue and achieve effective arms reduction agreements. The search for genuine, verifiable arms reduction is not a campaign pledge or a sideline item in my national security agenda. Reducing the risk of war and the level of nuclear arms is an imperative, precisely because it enhances our security.

In our relations with the Soviet Union, we're engaged in a comprehensive agenda of major arms control negotiations. And for the first time, the Soviets are now talking about more than nuclear arms ceilings; they're talking about nuclear arms reductions. And tomorrow I will be meeting with Ambassador Ed Rowny to give him the new instructions he will carry back to the START talks in Geneva on Wednesday. In fact, let me take this a step further and explain why it's our willingness to be candid about the Soviet Union, about its nature and expansionist policies. It improves the chances of success in the arms control area.

History shows us what works and doesn't work. Unilateral restraint and good will does not provide similar reactions from the Soviet Union, and it doesn't produce genuine arms control. But history does teach that when the United States has the resolve to remain strong and united, when we stand up for what we believe in, and when we speak out forthrightly about the world as it is, then positive results can be achieved. Weakness does not offer the chance for success; strength does. And that strength is based on military capability, strong alliances, a willingness to speak the truth and to state our hope that someday all peoples of the world will enjoy the right to self-government and personal freedom.

You can remember one administration that tried to minimize the differences between the Soviets and the democracies. They lectured us on our "inordinate fear of communism." Under that administration arms control efforts not only failed, but the hope of improved East-West relations ended in Soviet expansionism on three continents, the invasion of Afghanistan, and an actual discussion by an American President before a joint session of Congress about the use of military force against any attempt to seize control of the Persian Gulf.

We must never be inhibited by those who say telling the truth about the Soviet empire is an act of belligerence on our part. To the contrary, we must continue to remind the world that self-delusion in the face of unpleasant facts is folly, that whatever the imperfections of the democratic nations, the struggle now going on in the world is essentially the struggle between freedom and totalitarianism, between what is right and what is wrong. This is not a simplistic or unsophisticated observation. Rather, it's the beginning of wisdom about the world we live in, the perils we face, and the great opportunity we have in the years ahead to broaden the frontiers of freedom and to build a durable, meaningful peace.

Let us never underestimate the power of truth. Not long ago, Aleksandr Solzhenitsyn reminded us that righteousness, not just revolutionary violence, has such power. Indeed, that's why I believe the struggle in the world will never be decided by arms, but by a test of wills—a test of Western faith and resolve.

And this brings me to a second point: The goal of the free world must no longer be stated in the negative, that is, resistance to Soviet expansionism. The goal of the free world must instead be stated in the affirmative. We must go on the offensive with a forward strategy for freedom. As I told the British Parliament in June of 1982, we must foster the hope of liberty throughout the world and work for the day when the peoples of every land can enjoy the blessings of liberty and the right to self-government.

This, then, is our task. We must present to the world not just an America that's militarily strong, but an America that is morally powerful, an America that has a creed, a cause, a vision of a future time when all peoples have the right to self-government and personal freedom.

I think American conservatives are uniquely equipped to present to the world this vision of the future—a vision worthy of the American past. I've always had a great affection for the words of John Winthrop, delivered to a small band of Pilgrims on the tiny ship *Arabella* off the coast of Massachusetts in 1630: "We shall be a city upon a hill. The eyes of all people are upon us, so that if we shall deal falsely with our God in this work we have undertaken and so cause Him to withdraw His present help from us, we shall be made a story and a byword throughout the world."

Well, America has not been a story or a byword. That small community of Pilgrims prospered and, driven by the dreams and, yes, by the ideas of the Founding Fathers, went on to become a beacon to all the oppressed and poor of the world.

One of those early founders was a man named Joseph Warren, a revolutionary who would have an enormous impact on our early history—would have had, had not his life been cut short by a bullet at Bunker Hill. His words about the perils America faced then are worth hearing today. "Our country is in danger," he said, "but not to be despaired of. On you depends the fortunes of America. You are to decide the important question on which rests the happiness and liberty of millions yet unborn. Act worthy of yourselves." Well, let his idealism guide us as we turn conservative ideas into political realities.

And as I urged in those closing days of the 1980 campaign, let us remember the purpose behind our activities, the real wellspring of the American way of life. Even as we meet here tonight some young American coming up along the Virginia or Maryland shores of the Potomac is looking with awe for the first time at the lights that glow in the great halls of our government and the monuments to the memory of our great men.

We're resolved tonight that young Americans will always see those Potomac lights, that they will always find here a city of hope in a country that's free so that when other generations look back at this conservative era in American politics and our time in power, they'll say of us that we did hold true to that dream of Joseph Winthrop and Joseph Warren, that we did keep faith with our God, that we did act worthy of ourselves, that we did protect and pass on lovingly that shining city on a hill.

Thank you very much, and God bless you all.

Note: The President spoke at 9:30 p.m. in the International Ballroom at the Washington Hilton Hotel.

Message to the Senate Transmitting an Amendment to the Convention on International Trade in Endangered Species of Wild Fauna and Flora
October 4, 1983

To the Senate of the United States:

I transmit herewith, with a view to receiving the advice and consent of the Senate to acceptance, an Amendment to the Convention on International Trade in Endangered Species of Wild Fauna and Flora (CITES), done at Washington, March 3, 1973. The Amendment provides for accession by regional economic integration organizations to CITES and, upon entry into force, would permit the European Community to become Party to the Convention. Accession of the Community would serve to make application of CITES within the Community an internationally binding obligation and thus enhance implementation and enforcement of the Convention, an objective which the United States strongly supports. The report of the Department of State is enclosed for the information of the Senate in connection with its consideration of the Amendment.

CITES was established to facilitate international conservation, providing for the control and monitoring of international trade in specimens of species endangered or threatened with extinction. The Convention, as currently constituted, provides only for accession of States. The European Community seeks to achieve accession through an Amendment which would open the Convention for accession by regional economic integration organizations constituted by sovereign States which have competence for the negotiation, conclusion and implementation of international agreements in matters transferred to them by their Member States and covered by the convention. In such matters, the organizations would exercise the rights and fulfill the obligations attributed to their Member States. The Amendment, with revisions added at United States instance, was adopted by the CITES Parties at an extraordinary meeting in Gaborone, Botswana, April 30, 1983.

I recommend that the Senate act favorably at an early date on this Amendment, and give its advice and consent to acceptance.

RONALD REAGAN

The White House,
October 4, 1983.

Remarks at the Welcoming Ceremony for President Karl Carstens of the Federal Republic of Germany
October 4, 1983

President Reagan. Mr. President and Mrs. Carstens, Mr. Minister and Mrs. Genscher, honored guests, I'm delighted to welcome you and your party to Washington and to the United States.

During my inspiring visit to Bonn in June 1982, we agreed that you would come to this country for an official visit as part of our joint celebration of German-American friendship.

This year has special significance. We celebrate the 300th anniversary of the first German immigration to America. Those first families—or settlers, I should say, were 13 families from the Rhineland. They were followed by millions of their countrymen, men, women, and children who became a strong thread running through the fabric of America. German Americans have meant so much to the development of this nation. And today German-American friendship is vital to the security and freedom of both our peoples.

Nineteen eighty-three is a landmark year for our two countries and for the NATO alliance as a whole. We and the rest of our allies must continue to have the courage and mutual trust to do what is necessary to maintain peace and security in Europe.

We decided in December 1979 that if no agreement with the Soviet Union could be reached, maintaining a balance of force in Europe would require the modernization of NATO's deterrent forces. So far, the Soviet Union has not been willing to negotiate a fair and verifiable arms reduction agreement with us. Let there be no mistake, an agreement will be far better for all concerned. We seek the elimination of these weapons, and we will continue our unflagging efforts to reach an acceptable agreement. But if the Soviet intransigence continues, we must begin deployment and ensure NATO's deterrent.

We're confident that the alliance will meet this challenge and that the strength of the German-American partnership will be a major factor enabling NATO to do so. For our part, we remain convinced that a strong NATO alliance remains the key to European peace, and German-American cooperation and trust are the linchpin of that alliance.

In meeting today and in your visit to many parts of the United States, I believe that you will see that the reservoir of good will our people hold for the Federal Republic of Germany runs just as deep as ever.

By resolution of both our Congress and the German Bundestag and by my proclamation of last January, the year 1983 is the tricentennial year of German settlement in America. Commemoration of this momentous event in the life of our two nations has been and will be vigorous on both sides of the Atlantic. The cities on your itinerary are poised to welcome you. The people of America are waiting to share the high points of their celebrations with you. Your presence here marking this anniversary touches us deeply. We are proud to say— and I hope I can correctly—*Wir heissen Sie willkommen.*

We greet you. We welcome you. We cherish your friendship. And may God bless you and Mrs. Carstens.

President Carstens. Mr. President, thank you very much for your warm words of welcome and thank you for your invitation to visit this country together with the Vice Chancellor and Foreign Minister, Mr. Genscher.

I'm looking forward to my talks with you, Mr. President, with the Vice President, with the Secretary of State, with Members of Congress. And I'm looking forward to meet thousands of American citizens while traveling through this country.

The purpose of my visit is to strengthen the ties of friendship between the Federal Republic of Germany and the United States of America. We commemorate the arrival of the first German settlers in Philadelphia 300 years ago. And you, Mr. President, proclaimed that day as a day which we all should celebrate. We also commemorate the contribution which millions of German emigrants made to the building of the American nation.

But I further want to express the gratitude of us Germans towards the American people for what they did after two World Wars. And I have only to recall millions of CARE parcels which were sent from America to Germans when we were in great need. I have only to recall the Marshall plan, which saved our economy after World War II. And I have only to recall the Berlin Airlift of 1948–49, which saved the freedom of Berlin.

Today, we are partners in the North Atlantic alliance, the most efficient alliance of modern times because it has preserved peace and freedom for its members over a period for more than 30 years. Under the terms of this alliance, 250,000 American soldiers serve in Germany. We greet them as allies, partners, and friends. And in saying this, I speak in the name of the vast majority of the citizens of the Federal Republic of Germany.

But we are not only linked by our alliance, we also have—and I think that is as important—common values underlying our system of government. And by that I mean democracy, personal freedom, human dignity, and rule of law. Looking to the future, I think we must give our peoples the opportunity to understand each other even better. And particularly we must give this opportunity to the young generation.

While I'm here, I shall, together with members of the German parliament—and I'm happy to say that Mrs. Renger, the vice president of the parliament, is here—I shall work for the implementation of different exchange programs under which more than 10,000 young Americans will go to Germany and young Germans will go to America. This is, I think, the best way for nations to become friends, because they will realize that we, the Germans, and you, the Americans, have much more in common than most of them have been aware of.

I am happy to be back in America, a country to which I owe personally a great deal, namely part of my legal education at one of your finest universities.

Thank you very much.

Note: President Reagan spoke at 10:10 a.m. on the South Lawn of the White House, where President Carstens was accorded a formal welcome with full military honors.

Following the ceremony, the two Presidents met in the Oval Office. They then met, together with U.S. and German officials, in the Cabinet Room.

Nomination of David A. Zegeer To Be an Assistant Secretary of Labor
October 4, 1983

The President today announced his intention to nominate David A. Zegeer to be Assistant Secretary of Labor for Mine Safety and Health. He would succeed Ford Barney Ford.

Since 1977 Mr. Zegeer has owned and run a mining consulting business in Lexington, Ky. Previously he was manager and division superintendent, Bethlehem Mines Corp. (1956–1977), and served in various positions at Consolidation Coal Co., including assistant to the president (1946–1956).

Mr. Zegeer graduated from West Virginia University School of Mines (BSEM, 1944). He is married, has three children, and resides in Lexington, Ky. He was born August 27, 1922, in Charleston, W. Va.

Remarks to Reporters Announcing New United States Initiatives in the Strategic Arms Reduction Talks
October 4, 1983

Ladies and gentlemen, later today Ambassador Ed Rowny and the other members of the START delegation will depart for Geneva for the opening of the fifth round of the strategic rrms reduction talks. They'll carry with them a new set of instructions. From the first day of these negotiations our highest goal has been to achieve a stable balance at reduced levels of nuclear arsenals. We want to reduce the weapons of war, pure and simple.

All our efforts in both the START and the INF negotiations continue to be guided by that objective. Just this morning, I repeated this commitment to President Carstens of the Federal Republic of Germany. As I pledged to the United Nations, the United States will accept any equitable, verifiable agreement that stabilizes forces at lower levels than currently exist. We want significant reductions, and that pledge stands.

In the last round of negotiations we proposed a number of new initiatives which where in harmony with the recommendations of the Presidential Commission on Strategic Forces and which provided additional flexibility to our negotiations. Those initiatives supported our basic goals, and they also responded to a number of Soviet concerns.

I deeply regret that the Soviet Union has yet to give any significant response. Throughout the negotiating process it's the United States who's had to push, pull, probe, and prod in an effort to achieve any progress. The heartfelt desire shared by people everywhere for an historic agreement dramatically reducing nuclear weapons could and indeed will be achieved, provided one condition changes: The Soviet Government must start negotiating in good faith.

Now, let me emphasize that the United States has gone the extra mile. We've removed the dividing line between the two phases of our original proposal; everything is on the table. We're still most concerned about limits on the fast-flying, most danger-ous systems, but we're also prepared to negotiate limits on bomber and air-launch cruise missile limits below SALT II levels. We've shown great flexibility in dealing with the destructive capability of ballistic missiles, including their throw-weight. We've also relaxed our limits on the number of ballistic missiles.

We've gone a very long way to address Soviet concerns, but the Soviets have yet to take their first meaningful step to address ours. Particularly in the INF talks, but also in START, they've been stonewalling our proposals. When we proposed confidence-building measures that could be agreed to right now, they said wait. Apparently they believe that time is on their side, that they can exploit one democracy against another, and that their uncompromising attitude and delay will ultimately win out.

Well, we'll prove them wrong. The diversity of our democracies is a source of strength, not weakness. From free discussion among free people comes unity and commitment. The sooner this is understood, the sooner we'll reach an agreement in the interests of both sides. We'll continue to press Moscow for an equitable, fair, and verifiable agreement.

When the START negotiations resume tomorrow, the United States delegation will again have sustained flexibility. Within the framework of the basic principles that have guided us throughout these negotiations, I am directing Ambassador Rowny to offer the following new initiatives. We're incorporating into START a series of build-down proposals. The United States will introduce a proposal for a mutual, guaranteed build-down, designed to encourage stabilizing systems. The proposal will include specific provisions for building down ballistic warheads and, concurrently, for addressing a parallel build-down on bombers.

To discuss these major new initiatives, we will also propose the establishment of a U.S.-Soviet build-down working group in the Geneva talks. On another front, and in our effort, again, to be absolutely as flexible as possible, we will be willing to explore ways to further limit the size and capability of air-launch cruise missile forces in exchange for reciprocal Soviet flexibility on items of concern to us.

We seek limits on the destructive capability of missiles and recognize that the Soviet Union would seek limits on bombers in return. There will have to be tradeoffs, and the United States is prepared to make them, so long as they result in a more stable balance of forces.

The Soviet Union should not doubt the bipartisan support for our efforts. During our review process I looked for ways to broaden America's bipartisan approach to our overall arms control effort. We've consulted with many Members of the Congress and again with the Commission headed by Brent Scowcroft. Their counsel has been invaluable, and I want to thank them for their tireless efforts and helpful advice.

A solid, national, bipartisan consensus, sustained from year to year and from administration to administration, is crucial if we are to keep America safe and secure and if we're to achieve successful arms reductions. Therefore, I've decided to take a number of new steps. Among these are to designate a member of the Scowcroft commission, James Woolsey, as a Member at Large to our START negotiations. These actions reflect America's democratic process at its best.

Ambassador Rowny, as you and your team depart for Geneva, you go with the certain knowledge that you're negotiating with the full support of the American people. Our bipartisan support is stronger than ever before, and you carry with you fair, equitable proposals that are in the interest of both nations and all humankind.

It's fitting today to repeat what I said last week. The door to an agreement is open. All the world is waiting for the Soviet Union to walk through. Should the Soviet leadership decide to join us now in our good faith effort, the fifth round of these negotiations will be the one in which, finally, a breakthrough was made, and finally the world began to breathe a bit easier.

So, to the entire START delegation, Ambassador Rowny, good luck and Godspeed.

Note: The President spoke at 2:22 p.m. in the Rose Garden at the White House. Prior to his announcement, the President met in the Oval Office with Ambassador Edward L. Rowny, Special Representative for Negotiations, U.S. Arms Control and Disarmament Agency.

Appointment of R. James Woolsey as Member at Large of the United States Delegation to the Strategic Arms Reduction Talks
October 4, 1983

The President today announced the appointment of R. James Woolsey to be Member at Large of the United States delegation to the strategic arms reduction talks. Previous Members at Large have been former Secretary of Defense Harold Brown (during SALT I and II) and U.S. Arms Control and Disarmament Agency Director George Seignious (during SALT II).

Mr. Woolsey is currently serving as a member of the President's Commission on Strategic Forces. He served as Under Secretary of the Navy from 1977 to 1979. He is a partner in the Washington law firm of Shea and Gardner.

Mr. Woolsey was graduated from Stanford University, was a Rhodes Scholar at Oxford University, and holds a law degree from Yale University. He was born September 21, 1941. He is married to the former Suzanne Haley, and they have three sons.

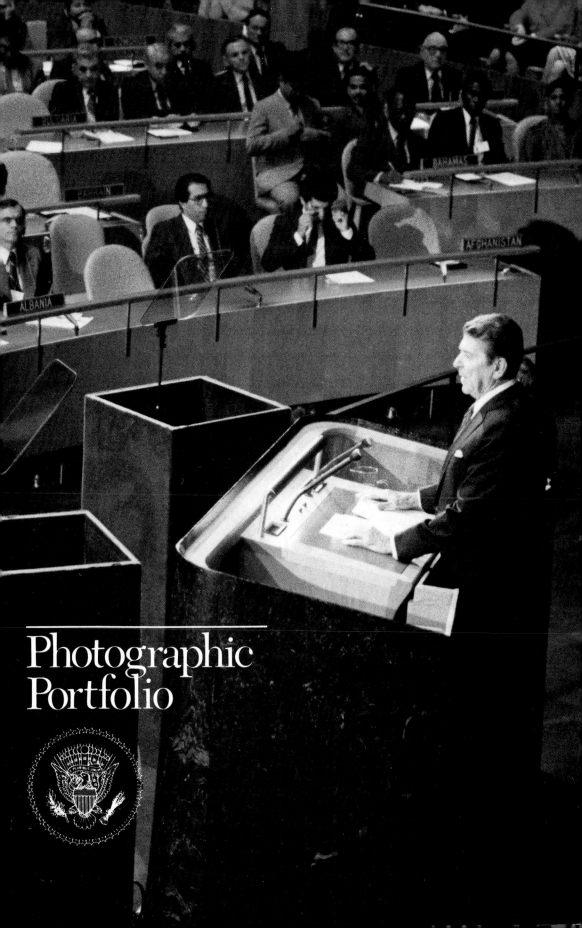

Photographic
Portfolio

Overleaf: Addressing the 38th Session of the United Nations General Assembly in New York City, September 26. *Above left:* Exchanging toasts with Mexican President Miguel de la Madrid Hurtado at the Governor's Residence in La Paz, Mexico, August 14. *Below left:* Barbecue for members of the Professional Rodeo Cowboy Association on the South Grounds of the White House, September 24. *Right:* Greeting members of the Washington Capitals and the U.S. Olympic Hockey Teams in the Rose Garden, September 29. *Below right:* With Secretary of the Treasury Regan at the swearing-in ceremony for Katherine D. Ortega as Treasurer of the United States, in the Rose Garden, October 3.

Left: Signing the bill making the birthday of Martin Luther King, Jr., a legal public holiday, in the Rose Garden, November 2. *Below:* Greeting wounded servicemen from the conflicts in Lebanon and Grenada, at a Camp Lejeune, N.C., memorial service, November 4. *Right:* With Japanese Emperor Hirohito during the formal arrival ceremony at Akasaka Palace in Tokyo, November 9.

Statement on the National Energy Policy Plan Transmitted to the Congress
October 4, 1983

The U.S. energy situation today is significantly better than it was in 1981 when my administration took office.

Total energy efficiency has increased, domestic energy resources are being developed more effectively, oil prices have declined, U.S. dependence on foreign energy sources has diminished, and the Nation's vulnerability to energy supply disruptions has been reduced markedly, especially through additions to our Strategic Petroleum Reserve and through lower levels of oil imports. Only about one-fourth of our oil consumption this year is from imports, and less than half of that from OPEC. The real price of imported oil to the U.S. has fallen almost 40 percent.

A key factor contributing to today's improved U.S. energy situation is the implementation of a national energy policy first described in my 1981 National Energy Policy Plan. This policy includes a goal, strategies for pursuing that goal, and Federal programs and action determined by those strategies.

A hallmark of our national energy policy is to foster an adequate supply of energy at reasonable costs, minimize Federal control and involvement in energy markets, and promote a balanced and mixed energy resource system.

I am proud of the actions we have taken since 1981 which have led to substantial progress and a reinvigorated national energy system.

We have removed price and allocation controls on crude oil and petroleum products. This has resulted in increased production of domestic resources and lower gasoline prices to consumers. Real gasoline prices are about 15 percent below pre-decontrol levels.

Since the end of 1980, the amount of oil stored in the Strategic Petroleum Reserve has tripled, to more than 360 million barrels today. It now holds about 90 days of our average net oil imports and well over a year of our Arab OPEC imports. Together with private petroleum stockpiles, the SPR is an important part of our program for improving international energy security. It can be an invaluable form of insurance against the potentially severe effects of an oil supply interruption.

The world energy scene remains volatile. Even though we now produce about 90 percent as much energy as we consume, we need to press onward with improvements. The National Energy Policy Plan we transmit to Congress today discusses all of our plans and accomplishments, but it emphasizes the need to finish the task of decontrolling natural gas. Today the regulatory system has led to higher prices and lower supplies. Today we have unused capacity that natural gas control is restricting. That capacity could lower prices, reduce oil imports, and set us on a sensible course for the future. I will be working closely with the Senate and House in the weeks ahead to pass sensible natural gas legislation to allow the market to work.

We can face the energy future with confidence, not complacency. We must all continue to use energy prudently and to improve our technology for finding and conserving energy. With the leadership of Secretary Hodel in the Energy Department, and under the guidance of the National Energy Policy Plan, we will continue to improve our energy situation through the efforts and genius of the American people.

Note: The plan is entitled "The National Energy Policy Plan, October 1983—A Report to the Congress Required by Title VIII of the Department of Energy Organization Act (Public Law 95–91)—U.S. Department of Energy" (Government Printing Office, 25 pages).

Appointment of Ruth E. Denk as a Member of the Presidential Commission for the German-American Tricentennial
October 4, 1983

The President today announced his intention to appoint Ruth E. Denk to be a member of the Presidential Commission for the German-American Tricentennial.

Mrs. Denk is currently president of Denk Baking Corp., which she cofounded with her husband in 1971. She is also president of DBC Enterprises of Charleston, S.C. Previously she served on the board of directors of the New York State Easter Seals Society and served as a member of its finance corporation (1970–1974).

Mrs. Denk graduated from New York University (B.S., 1977). She is married, has one child, and resides in New York, N.Y. She was born January 29, 1934, in Wiesbaden, Germany.

Proclamation 5113—National Productivity Improvement Week, 1983
October 4, 1983

By the President of the United States of America

A Proclamation

The challenge of greater productivity growth is of supreme importance to America's future. Only through productivity gains can real living standards be improved. Greater productivity growth is the cornerstone of price stability and sustained economic growth. It is vital to regaining our competitive position in world markets and creating job opportunities for an expanding American labor force.

Productive societies reward saving, investing, building, and creating rather than consuming. A productive society lives within its means and does not pursue a pattern in its spending habits that results in simply shifting its burdens forward to the future. Productive societies also nourish the spirit of adventure, innovation and entrepreneurship. Productive societies share common objectives and their leading institutions work together—business, government, labor, and academia view each other as partners, not adversaries.

We have made much progress in restoring the foundation for a prosperous and productive society. By reducing the rate of growth of government spending, by strengthening the incentives to save and invest, by eliminating many unnecessary and burdensome regulations, and by encouraging monetary policies that ensure the price stability needed for lasting economic growth we have created an environment for sustained increases in productivity.

The improvement of our Nation's productivity depends on all Americans. The recently concluded White House Conference on Productivity brought together an outstanding group of distinguished citizens from all walks of life and sectors of our economy. Their recommendations for actions at all levels in the public and private sectors will help us build on the foundation we have laid.

In order to encourage better understanding of the need for productivity growth and the development of methods to improve productivity in the private and public sectors, the Congress, by Senate Joint Resolution 142, has designated the week of October 3 through October 9, 1983, as National Productivity Improvement Week.

Now, Therefore, I, Ronald Reagan, President of the United States of America, do hereby proclaim the week of October 3 through October 9, 1983, as National Productivity Improvement Week. I call upon the people of the United States to observe such week with appropriate ceremonies and activities.

In Witness Whereof, I have hereunto set my hand this 4th day of Oct., in the year of our Lord nineteen hundred and eighty-three, and of the Independence of the United States of America the two hundred and eighth.

RONALD REAGAN

[*Filed with the Office of the Federal Register, 10:49 a.m., October 5, 1983*]

Statement by Deputy Press Secretary Speakes on Immigration Reform Legislation
October 4, 1983

The President was naturally disappointed today to hear press reports quoting Speaker O'Neill as saying that immigration reform legislation would not be considered by the House this year. The President hopes that the Speaker will reconsider and allow the House to vote on a bill that is essential to the future well-being of this nation.

As we understand it, the Speaker commented that there was no discernible constituency for the bill and that there had been mixed signals from the White House. We respectfully disagree with the Speaker on those points.

The Senate has twice passed immigration legislation—by overwhelming bipartisan margins. And in the Congress immigration legislation has also been considered and approved by four committees in the House, including the Committee on the Judiciary. Administration officials have testified on the reform measures a total of 28 times.

This is not a political issue; it is not a partisan issue; it is an issue that concerns all Americans. And it is in the best interests of all Americans to have the Nation regain control of its borders.

One final point remains to be made. The President sent the original immigration reform legislation to the Congress more than 2 years ago. He supported it then. He supports it today.

Toasts of President Reagan and President Karl Carstens of the Federal Republic of Germany at the State Dinner
October 4, 1983

President Reagan. Well, Mr. President and Mrs. Carstens, Mr. Minister and Mrs. Genscher, honored guests:

I said this morning, and I would like to say it again, how happy and proud that Nancy and I are to welcome you to the United States. Your own ties with our country, including a master of laws degree from Yale University, are longstanding and deep. Your life is a monument to the shared values and interests that have long provided our two peoples with a bounty of good will. And today, all Americans celebrate our ties and are grateful for our solid friendship with the German people.

Three hundred years ago, a small group of hardy pioneers set out from Krefeld, in the Rhineland, to sail into the unknown. In America they found the religious freedom they sought, but hard work was the price they paid for their new-found freedom. And those 13 German families brought with them courage and industry to build new lives. Their talents and those of their descendants helped create the great city of Philadelphia and the great State of Pennsylvania, both of which share our honor in

1415

welcoming you.

This year we commemorate the remarkable odyssey of the Krefelders and of the millions of others who followed them. The virtues of courage, industry, and belief in freedom which they brought helped build our country, contributing to what is best about the United States. The contributions of German Americans have been invaluable to the development of our great country.

The people of the Federal Republic of Germany have proven that they still possess those traits that helped build America. From the rubble of the Second World War the industrious German people constructed a strong, healthy, and free democracy. We stand firmly together in the search for peace and freedom.

Anniversary celebrations tend to look back, but we should not limit our commemoration to reminiscences of the past. A strength of both of our peoples is that we also look to the future. The true meaning of this anniversary week is an enduring partnership that will lead to a more secure peace in the decades ahead.

Many colorful events have been organized throughout the United States to celebrate our ties. I congratulate the sponsors of these undertakings and of the numerous initiatives which have sprung up during this tricentennial year. The tricentennial reinvigorates the cultural, historical, and political ties between our two peoples. It symbolizes something real, tangible, and enduring—German-American friendship.

Mr. President, we're grateful for your visit. We thank you for all that you've personally done in your distinguished career to support close ties between our two nations. And I want to tell you, knowing your background here in America, when I was a boy I read about Frank Merriwell at Yale; I didn't read Brown of Harvard. [*Laughter*]

We raise our glasses to you, Mr. President. To President Carstens and to the friendship that your visit represents.

President Carstens. Mr. President, Mrs. Reagan, ladies and gentlemen:

It gives me great pleasure, Mr. President, to be your guest here in the White House. And I thank you most cordially, also, in the name of my wife and in the name of the Vice Chancellor, Foreign Minister and Mrs.

Genscher, and of our other German guests, for the warm and generous hospitality which you are again extending to us.

I am deeply moved that it has been granted to me, as representative of the German people, to visit the United States and to strengthen the bonds of friendship with your great country. I look forward with eager expectation to the days in Philadelphia, St. Louis, Dallas, Seattle, Madison, New York, and New Haven.

Let us, Germans and Americans, bear in mind our common history, and let us take strength from our common ideals and our common goals. On this visit, personal memories shall be accompanying me. I have been to the United States on numerous occasions in an official capacity. However, my thoughts go back, above all, to the time immediately after the Second World War when I obtained a scholarship from Yale University in 1948.

The year which I spent there added a new dimension to my life. The good will and the cordiality which I encountered are firmly engraved in my memory. At Yale I studied American constitutional law, and I later qualified as a university professor in Germany with a study on this subject. This aroused my interest in public affairs and in politics. I felt more and more called upon to work for the common good.

And it also became clear to me at Yale as to what constitutes the real strengths of the American nation; namely, the conviction of its citizens that there are basic values which precede every and any governmental system. Among these values rank the dignity of man, justice, and freedom, and also something which you, Mr. President, have repeatedly stressed; namely, trust in God. This has been true from the beginning, and the tricentennial of the first German immigration into North America marks an appropriate moment for recalling it.

"Proclaim freedom throughout the land, for all its citizens." These words, from the book of Leviticus, are inscribed on the Freedom Bell in Philadelphia. In the first place, they refer to religious freedom. But they also included the other human rights, the inalienable rights—life, liberty, and the pursuit of happiness, as the Declaration of

Independence expresses them. In these ideals, and in the earnest endeavors to realize them, lay the great attraction of the United States from the very beginning. Millions of Germans felt this attraction and went to America, and they included many of our nation's best sons and daughters—freedom-loving, industrious, adventurous men and women who found a new home here.

They became pioneers in building your country, and they tied the cordial bonds of attachment between America and Germany which have proved their constancy despite several setbacks. Germans played, as you have mentioned, Mr. President, a role in the advance of American civilization and the natural science, the social sciences, the fine arts and music, a civilization which has entered upon an unparalleled, victorious march through the whole world in our epoch and which has profoundly influenced the lifestyle of almost all countries, including ours.

But the United States did not only lay a new foundation for the social life within their own country but also towards other countries. "Observe good faith and justice towards all nations," declared George Washington in his farewell address. "Cultivate peace and harmony with all to give to mankind the magnanimous and noble example of a people always guided by an exalted justice and benevolence."

Clearly it is difficult always to comply with such a high claim. However, the benevolence and magnanimity remained guiding principles for American policy. And we Germans also experienced the charitable assistance of the Americans after the Second World War. The granting of eonomic aid in the shape of the Marshall plan furnish examples of this, as does the airlift to Berlin, a city which owes so much to America and which you visited last June—June of last year—Mr. President.

Safeguarding freedom in Europe—that is the purpose of the North Atlantic alliance in which our two countries are partners. This alliance is a defense community. And I need not stress that it only serves to defend. It is an alliance between free peoples who have joined together because they share the same values, including freedom, which they wish to preserve.

This alliance has granted us security and peace over three decades. During this time, about 9 million American citizens served as soldiers in Germany. Together with our young German conscripts and troops from other member countries of the alliance, they ensured that we can live in the manner desired by the overwhelming majority of our citizens; namely, in a free democracy governed by the rule of law.

Germany is a divided country; yet we Germans adhere to the unity of our people. The policy pursued by the Federal Republic of Germany is directed towards a state of peace in Europe in which the German people will regain their unity through free self-determination. We thank America for always supporting this goal of ours.

As I said, for about 30 years the United States and Germany are members of the alliance. And if the alliance endeavors to obtain a military equilibrium at as low a level as possible, this will guarantee not only freedom but also peace. Both of these, freedom and peace, would be endangered, I think, if the other side were to acquire military superiority. The fate of Afghanistan provides a sad example. We must never tire of pointing out these implications time and again to those among our citizens who champion the cause of unilateral disarmament, even though I respect their motives.

We Germans shall stand by your side as your allies and partners also in the future. And with this thought in mind, may I now raise my glass to drink to your health and success. Mr. President, to your health, Mrs. Reagan, to a happy future for the United States of America, the leading power of the free nations, and to another three centuries of German-American friendship.

Note: President Reagan spoke at 10:50 p.m. in the State Dining Room at the White House.

Remarks at a White House Ceremony Marking the Implementation of the Caribbean Basin Initiative
October 5, 1983

Well, thank you all, and I say that—I think I can say that on behalf of the Vice President and myself. We're delighted to welcome all of you distinguished members from the diplomatic community, the Senators and Representatives and honored guests.

And today we celebrate the passage of legislation that I've held close to my heart for a long time. I know all of us wished it could have come sooner, but as I promised when some of you were here last December, the time is short and the needs are great. We're all Americans. Together we can be a mighty force for good. We can show the world that we conquer fear with faith, we overcome poverty with growth, and we counter violence with opportunity and freedom. And now we're making good on our promise. I'm proud to stand with you for this celebration on the long-awaited first stage of implementation of the Caribbean Basin Economic Recovery Act.

Ours is a collective partnership for peace, prosperity, and democracy in the Caribbean and in Central America—a partnership that's born of our shared vision that democracy is a God-given birthright and that faith, freedom, and respect for the dignity of every citizen are the mainsprings of human progress. From the very outset of our administration, we've never wavered in our long-term goal to foster true stability and democracy. And to do so, we must work together to help improve the underlying conditions for economic development.

Peace and security in the Caribbean Basin are in our vital interest. When our neighbors are in trouble, their troubles inevitably become ours. What these countries need most is the opportunity to produce and export their products at fair prices. That's what the Caribbean Basin Initiative is all about. It offers them open markets in the United States and initiatives to encourage investment and growth. Far from a handout, the proposal will help these countries help themselves. Trade, not aid, will mean more jobs for them and more jobs for us.

The CBI package proposed to the Congress in March of '82 was designed by the governments and private sectors of the region's countries, including those of Puerto Rico and the U.S. Virgin Islands. It had three major elements: a supplemental appropriation of $350 million to provide emergency balance-of-payment support, the elimination for 12 years of nearly all of the remaining tariff barriers on Caribbean Basin country exports to the United States, and tax incentives to promote new investment in the tourist industry.

The $350 million supplemental appropriation received strong bipartisan support and was approved by the Congress in September of 1982. These moneys have now been obligated, allowing the importation of raw materials and capital goods to help get stalled economies in the region moving again.

Aid levels to the Caribbean Basin have doubled since 1980. The other CBI proposals were an innovative and unprecedented plan to integrate trade preferences, investment incentives, and other measures to encourage the economic and social development of the countries of the Caribbean Basin. We seek to help countries implement free market strategies to stimulate their exports and strengthen their economies by expanding growth.

Our original proposals evolved during many months of congressional consideration and the Caribbean Basin economic recovery act was approved on July 28th. And the bill that I signed in August is true to our original intent. I'm convinced that over time it will contribute significantly to the economic stability and social tranquillity of countries in the Caribbean Basin.

The first element of this legislation is a 12-year, one-way, free trade arrangement for all goods produced in the Caribbean Basin except textiles, apparel, canned tuna, leather goods, shoes, and petroleum products. This marks a step our country has never taken before. It's evidence of our commitment to the economic health of our good neighbors.

The second element would allow U.S. citizens attending business conventions in the Caribbean Basin and Bermuda to deduct from their income taxes the reasonable expenses incurred. The Secretary of Treasury is here. He wants me to say "reasonable" again. [*Laughter*]

Now, these benefits will become all the more important as the vigorous expansion of our own economy brings about an increase in our imports and more and more business travel. As a footnote, you should know that we have 125 Peace Corps volunteers trained in small-scale agribusiness. They're helping small farmers increase and diversify food production for their countries' needs and for winter markets in Europe and North America. Fifty more American volunteers will receive this training within the next few weeks.

I was especially gratified that support for the CBI was overwhelming and bipartisan. I offer special recognition to the many Members of Congress who strongly supported our proposals, guided them through the approval process, in particular, Congressman Dan Rostenkowski and Senator Bob Dole.

You know, almost a year ago, Dan Rostenkowski took members of his Ways and Means Committee to visit five countries and meet with the Prime Ministers of more than 10 Caribbean countries. And it was on this trip that Dan coined a saying which was picked up by everyone in the Caribbean. "CBI," he said, "would be friends helping friends."

In that spirit, I extend my appreciation to the governments and peoples of the Caribbean Basin countries themselves. They never tired in explaining why the CBI should be passed. They include the very effective spokesmen for both the region's private sectors and labor unions.

I also want to express my appreciation to David Rockefeller and his associates at the Council of the Americas and Central American Action for their help in providing key business support for passage of this bill. And I pledge to you today that enactment of the landmark Caribbean Basin economic recovery act will be followed by a vigorous implementation effort on the part of this administration.

Ambassador Brock will continue as Chairman of our Senior Interagency Task Force responsible for its policy and program development. I'm calling on the other Cabinet members who've contributed to the CBI's development to give Ambassador Brock by January 1st their proposals on how to make the CBI the most effective means of expanding economic opportunity in the region.

The formal process of designation which the Congress has given me the responsibility to carry out has been with delegations visiting with all the potential beneficiaries. Those discussions have been conducted with the kind of mutual commitment to friendship and good will which has made us all so excited about the future of the region.

I'm optimistic that we will be extending the benefits of the program to virtually all the beneficiaries by the first of next year. The economic and social development of the Caribbean Basin should be part of a collective effort by the international community. Even before my original announcement of the CBI, we held consultations with the Governments of Canada, Mexico, and Venezuela, as well as with our European allies and Japan. Colombia subsequently agreed to become a participant.

Enactment of the CBI should encourage other donor governments and appropriate international organizations to expand their assistance activities in the region. The problems of the Caribbean Basin region are deep-seated, and reducing them will be a great challenge. But we can gain strength from our shared vision.

Nearly a century ago Jose Marti, a great citizen of the Caribbean and the Americas, warned that, "Mankind is composed of two sorts of men: those who love and create, and those who hate and destroy." And Pope John Paul II has told us that, "Only love can build." With faith, wisdom, courage, and love we can overcome injustice, hatred, and oppression and build a better life together for all of the Americas.

I'm confident we will. I think back to an incident during my last trip to Central

America. As I was beginning to speak in Costa Rica, suddenly I was loudly interrupted by a gentleman who was determined to make his own speech out there from the audience. I didn't know exactly what was going on, and I turned to the President of Costa Rica, asked him, and he informed me that this was a Communist, a Marxist member of their congress, their legislature, and that he was determined to denounce us. And that's what he was doing.

He was speaking in Spanish, so I didn't really know what he was saying. And, finally, it reached a point that he seemed to be going on, and I was standing there, and I realized I had a microphone and he didn't. So, I just overrode him and pointed out to the audience what I knew about him, what I'd been told about him, and what a tribute it was to their democracy, of which they're very proud, that he was allowed to say these things in that forum, and yet he would never be allowed to do what he was doing in any of the Communist countries. Well, the audience of more than 1,000 rose in a standing ovation. There was a lump in my throat; must have been one in his, because he sat down. [*Laughter*]

I knew in my heart they weren't applauding me. They weren't even applauding the United States. They were applauding the principles, the ideals, and the dreams that we all share and which they, the brave Costa Rican people, have had the courage to live up to.

I have to tell you a little postscript there,

that later the President told me that that Communist member of the legislature was the only member of the legislature that could afford to drive a Mercedes. [*Laughter*] But if the people of the Americas are given a free choice, they'll all choose to be like Costa Rica, not Castro's Cuba.

Only a counterfeit revolution builds walls to keep people in and employs armies of secret police to keep them quiet. The real revolution lives in the principle that government must rest on the consent of the governed, and this spirit of democracy and freedom of opportunity is the driving force behind the Caribbean Basin Initiative. We're building together a future of new hope and more opportunity. And I pledge the best efforts of our administration to carry this positive program forward, making it worthy of the ideals and dreams that gave it birth.

And now I'd like to ask Bill Brock to make a few remarks. And I thank you very much, and God bless you all. Bill?

Note: The President spoke at 11:32 a.m. in the Rose Garden at the White House. The ceremony was attended by Members of Congress, members of the diplomatic community, U.S. Ambassadors to the Caribbean region and Caribbean Ambassadors to the United States, and representatives of the business community involved in the initiative.

Ambassador William E. Brock, United States Trade Representative, also spoke at the ceremony.

Remarks at a Ceremony Marking the Beginning of the Job Training Partnership Program
October 5, 1983

Well, I thank you all very much for a most warm welcome. Secretary Donovan, Ray, Assistant Secretary Al Angrisani—and I understand that maybe we wouldn't be celebrating this particular event today, Ray tells me, Al, if it hadn't been for your devotion to this cause and all that you've put in—our other guests here on the top shelf—

[*laughter*]—I thank you for inviting me over today to be a part of this ceremony for the Job Training Partnership Act.

You know, so much of what we're trying to do, so much of this depended on real communications. And I can't resist. I've told this story before, and if some of you've heard it before—it illustrates communications—you'll have to forgive me. But life not only begins—or lumbago, I should say, not only begins at 40 but so does the tendency to tell the same story over and over again. [*Laughter*] But I've always thought of the importance of communication and how much a part it plays in what you and I, what all of us are trying to do. And one day a former placekicker with the Los Angeles Rams, who later became a sports announcer, Danny Villanueva told me about communications.

He said he'd been having dinner over at the home of a young ballplayer with the Dodgers. The young wife was bustling about getting the dinner ready. They were talking sports and the baby started to cry. And over her shoulder, his busy wife said to the ballplayer, "Change the baby." And he was a young fellow, and he was embarrassed in front of Danny, and he said, "What do you mean change the baby? I'm a ballplayer. That's not my line of work." And she turned around, put her hands on her hips, and she communicated. [*Laughter*] She said, "Look buster, you lay the diaper out like a diamond. You put second base on home plate. You put the baby's bottom on the pitcher's mound. You hook up first and third, slide home underneath, and if it starts to rain, the game ain't called, you start all over." [*Laughter*]

But we really do have a lot to celebrate, because this act, which went into effect a couple of days ago, initiates a new, more effective way of helping our unemployed, as you've been told. The people up here on the dais, other people in the administration and the Congress, and many of you in the audience, especially you in the Employment and Training Administration, played a role in making this positive program happen.

From a personal perspective, this act represents the change of direction that I hoped to bring to Washington when I came here. I had seen many Federal programs out there from another vantage point as Governor of a State, and I want to thank all of you for bringing this particular program about. I'm very proud of your work. This program will train, as you've been told, more than a million people a year for permanent, self-sustaining employment. And you know what is

different about this program is, the primary goal is real, results-oriented job training, training that leads to jobs people can build lives and futures on.

It represents genuine opportunity, not temporary balm to a liberal conscience. It focuses on the long-term needs of the unemployed, not on short-term political quackery. Its moneys go to real training, not simply to income transfer, welfare-type programs or into administrative overhead. Another thing different about this program is that it meets the local needs, which is where the jobs are and where the unemployed live.

This program, as Secretary Donovan said, is a partnership between Federal, State, and local government and the private sector. The government has trained too many individuals in skills that aren't needed in their communities. Still other unemployed people have been steered into make-work government jobs. This program will make a difference on Main Street. It'll provide help; it'll bring hope and encourage self-reliance.

Private enterprise will be participating in a very meaningful way. Business and labor will be working together in organizations called private industry councils, designed to provide training skills needed right in the community. And unlike a great many other programs in the past, at least 70 cents of every Job Training Partnership Act dollar must go to actual training.

On Monday, the first day of the program that it became effective, the Indianapolis Private Industry Council started sponsoring training at ITT to place low-income youth and adults in existing jobs. In Wilmington, welfare women will soon be trained for skilled, entry-level jobs. Now, these are just two examples, among many, of hope that is being reborn across America. I think this is the start of something big. In fact, it could be much bigger than many people realize.

This act provides the possibility of a fundamental change, not only in job-training practices but in welfare, vocational education, and economic development. State legislatures and Federal agencies are looking into the State and local councils set up as a result of this act as a funnel for other programs. This could be a great step forward for other programs, for federalism, and for meeting the needs of our communities, and that's a pretty exciting prospect.

Now, there are some people who currently have plenty of time to run for office, but they don't seem to have any time for new ideas. Most of them are younger than I am. Everybody is. [*Laughter*] But I just have to call some of those young people I've been describing as the "old men of Washington," because their ideas are so old and threadbare. You'd think they'd been asleep for a hundred years. They're like political Rip Van Winkles, still dozing along on the programs of the past, not realizing we must change with the times and try new ways of solving the problems that face us.

You see them peddling the same old economic nostrums that got us into our economic difficulties in the first place. Well, I can assure you, we're not going backward. We're heading forward toward the future.

Not only in terms of this job training act but in other areas as well, we've begun to turn things around a little bit here in town. Inflation, which had been running at those horrendous double digits, has for the last 12 months been running 2.6 percent. That's the lowest 12-month average in 17 years. Now, of course, they said it couldn't be done. And we said it could. And we did it. It's nice sometimes not to know how many things you can't do—[*laughter*]—because usually you can.

The prime interest rate was 21½ percent. It's now 11 percent. And I think we're going to—it's still too high; it's about half of what is was—but I think we're going very shortly to see interest rates coming down some more.

The tax take doubled in the 5 years before we had a chance to do anything about it. Well, we cut personal tax rates 25 percent across the board. And beginning in 1985 taxes will be indexed so that never again will inflation push you into higher and higher tax brackets just because you got a cost-of-living pay raise.

The economy's been growing at a good clip. There have been increases in housing, construction, retail and auto sales—all those things that show that the economy is recovering nicely. And that brings me to the place where America's nest eggs, billions of dollars, workers' pension funds are invested. The gains in the stock market have met a higher return for all of America's workers and their retirement savings. And that's very good news for retirees and workers.

These are some of the good things that have been happening. Unemployment is going down, but it's usually the last of the major indicators to turn around. And, yet, a month ago we had a drop that was the biggest 1-month drop in unemployment in 24 years.

The turnaround in the economy is what is getting the people back to work. The Job Training Partnership Act is directed toward those who would have trouble in getting jobs even if the unemployment rate was not at the level it is. It's targeted toward those who face significant barriers to employment. These are the people that government can help through training. This money is much more effectively spent than all-purpose, politically motivated jobs bills that you see working their way through the Congress.

So, I'm very proud of the work that you've accomplished with this new legislation. America is regaining her confidence. We're headed in a new and a better direction. I'm very optimistic about the accomplishments to come.

Since I'm here at the Department of Labor, I'd like to take a moment this afternoon to send a message of warmest congratulations to one of the world's greatest labor leaders, Lech Walesa.

Just a few hours ago, the world was thrilled to learn Lech Walesa has been named to receive the 1983 Nobel Peace Prize. Now, this award represents the triumph of moral force over brute force. It's a victory for those who seek to enlarge the human spirit over those who seek to crush it. And surely it's a victory, too, for peace.

For too long, the Polish Government has tried to make Lech Walesa a nonperson and destroy the free trade union movement that he helped to create in Poland. But no government can destroy the hopes that burn in the hearts of a people.

The people of Poland have shown in their support of Solidarity, just as they showed in their support for His Holiness Pope John Paul II during his visit to Poland, that the government of that nation cannot make Lech Walesa a nonperson, and they can't turn his ideas into nonideas.

This award demonstrates that the world will always remember and will honor the commitment to freedom and the commitment to free trade unions that Lech Walesa and millions of brave Polish people share. This award also underlines the need for the Polish Government to turn away from a policy of confrontation toward one of reconciliation with all of the Polish people. And I earnestly hope they will seize this opportunity.

Now, my congratulations are not just for Mr. Walesa but for all of you here today and this new job training and partnership act. And I just wanted to come over and stop by and tell you thanks and, then, unless you think you're going to get off scot-free, keep up the good work. [*Laughter*]

And God bless you all.

Note: The President spoke at 1:29 p.m. in the Great Hall at the Department of Labor.

Proclamation 5114—Myasthenia Gravis Awareness Week, 1983
October 5, 1983

By the President of the United States of America

A Proclamation

Americans with myasthenia gravis cannot move about freely, as most of us can. This chronic neuromuscular disease, which has no known cause, produces progressive muscular weakness and abnormally rapid fatigue of the voluntary muscles. Myasthenia gravis can also result in a life-threatening medical crisis, particularly when a patient's throat muscles are affected.

Myasthenia gravis can strike any person, at any age, at any time. At least 100,000 people have been diagnosed as having this disorder, and scientists estimate that another 100,000 persons with myasthenia gravis have not yet been diagnosed.

In the past, myasthenia gravis patients died or were severely incapacitated by their weakened muscles. Several forms of treatment developed by scientists in private and Federal research institutions have led to improved management of the disease. Research supported by the Myasthenia Gravis Foundation, Inc., in collaboration with the Neurological Institute of the National Institutes of Health, has made important contributions to the management of this neurological disorder. Today, myasthenia gravis patients can expect to lead nearly normal lives.

Although much has been learned about myasthenia gravis, we still do not have the means to prevent this crippling disease. In order that the public should be made aware of the suffering endured by those who have the disease, the Congress, by Senate Joint Resolution 140, has authorized and requested the President to proclaim the week of October 2 through October 8, 1983, as "Myasthenia Gravis Awareness Week."

Now, Therefore, I, Ronald Reagan, President of the United States of America, do hereby proclaim the week beginning October 2, 1983, as Myasthenia Gravis Awareness Week. I call upon all government agencies, health organizations, and the people of the United States to observe this week with appropriate ceremonies and activities.

In Witness Whereof, I have hereunto set my hand this 5th day of October, in the year of our Lord nineteen hundred and eighty-three, and of the Independence of the United States of America the two hundred and eighth.

RONALD REAGAN

[*Filed with the Office of the Federal Register, 4:13 p.m., October 5, 1983*]

Appointment of Richard H. Jones as a Member of the Advisory Board of the National Air and Space Museum
October 5, 1983

The President today announced his intention to appoint Richard H. Jones to be a member of the National Air and Space Museum Advisory Board, Smithsonian Institution. He would succeed James P. Moore, Jr.

Mr. Jones is currently an attorney, specializing in aviation law, with the firm of Lewis, Wilson, Lewis & Jones. He has been a captain with Eastern Airlines since 1959.

Mr. Jones graduated from Virginia Polytechnic Institute (B.S., 1958) and American University (LL.B., 1964). He is married, has three children, and resides in Arlington, Va. He was born September 2, 1930, in Portsmouth, Va.

Statement on the Death of Terence Cardinal Cooke
October 6, 1983

All of America is saddened by the loss of Cardinal Cooke, a saintly man and a great spiritual leader. In life, Terence James Cooke inspired us with his personal holiness, his dedication to his church, his devotion to his flock. But in death as well, he had for us a special gift and a special inspiration. The world has rarely seen a more moving display of the three cardinal virtues than in the faith, hope, and love with which Cardinal Cooke confronted and conquered death. He bore his suffering in imitation of his savior.

Nancy and I consider it one of the great privileges of our lives that in his final months we had the chance to visit and pray with Cardinal Cooke. We join the people of New York and all America in mourning the grievous loss of a wonderful and holy man.

Remarks on Presenting the Young American Medals for Bravery
October 6, 1983

Thank you, Bill. Ladies and gentlemen, Members of the Congress, I think all of us can feel privileged to be here today. We are in the presence of authentic heroes. You know, there's a great tendency in this business of government to get lost in the pursuit of policy and power. We tend to forget in all the hustle and bustle of official Washington the really important things in our lives.

One of those important things is our sense of wonder at the incredible heights of generosity, courage, and magnificence that human beings can rise to. Well, I can think of no better way to renew that sense of wonder than the stories of our two medal winners here today. The accounts of their deeds are simple and straightforward, but they speak volumes about the mobility—the nobility, I should say, of the human spirit and about the nobility of our two medal winners.

In December of 1982 Ben Pionke came upon a struggling 6-year-old boy who had fallen through the ice while playing on a pond in Clarendon Hills, Illinois, where Ben and the young man lived. Without hesitating, Ben went to the rescue. He crashed through the ice himself, into water that was over his head, but somehow managed—Ben was 10 years old at the time—to keep the younger boy's head above water, to get him to shore, finally to safety.

The facts surrounding the story of Karen Hartsock are also simple and brief. In June of 1982 the Russell County, Virginia, home of Karen, who was then 14 years old, was destroyed by fire. But Karen risked her own life to rescue two other members of her family. Karen suffered second- and third-degree burns over 80 percent of her body. This has required months of care in the Burn Unit and, later, the Children's Rehabilitation Center of the University of Virginia Medical Center. Karen was brave that night, and she's been brave ever since.

Ben and Karen, I think I speak for everyone here when I say you honor us with your presence. I know your families are proud of you and proud to be here today. And I know, Karen, that in one sense your father is not with us today. And I want to extend my sympathy to you and to the rest of your family. But in another sense, Karen, I believe with all my heart he is here. And he's very proud. I hope you know you gave him a priceless gift before he died—wonderful moments of love and pride.

Someone once said that heroism is the brilliant triumph of the soul over the flesh—that is to say, fear. Heroism is the dazzling and glorious concentration of courage. Well, it goes without saying that today all of us are dazzled by the deeds of these two medal winners and even more overwhelmed by the fact that they are so young.

"To believe in the heroic makes heroes," Disraeli said. I think what he meant was that only those societies which value the unselfish virtues that make up heroism will ever be lucky enough to have heroes. Ben and Karen are such heroes, and they've taught us again the value of courage and unselfishness and devotion to others.

Ben and Karen, for all of that, we're grateful to you, proud of you. We congratulate you, and God bless you.

Note: The President spoke at 11:30 a.m. at the ceremony in the Rose Garden at the White House. He was introduced by Attorney General William French Smith. At the conclusion of his remarks, the President presented the medals to Carolyn Hartsock, 16, of Castlewood, Va., and Bennitt Pionke, 11, of Clarendon Hills, Ill.

Message on the Observance of National Newspaper Week, October 9–15, 1983
October 6, 1983

Since the founding of this nation, freedom of the press has been a fundamental tenet of American life. The economic freedom that has earned us such great bounty and the precious freedoms of speech and assembly would have little meaning or be totally nullified should freedom of the press ever be ended. There is no more essential ingredient than a free, strong, and independent press to our continued success in what the Founding Fathers called our "noble experiment" in self-government.

Today, as we survey the globe, we find increasing hostility to the principles of open communication. Both the governments of many nations and certain international organizations advocate or enforce policies alien to a free flow of ideas. This promotion of censorship reflects a manifest fear of the truth and depreciation of the great importance of liberty to human advancement.

The theme of this year's observance of National Newspaper Week, "A Free Press—Democracy's First Defense," helps focus attention on the essential role of a free press to the progress and development of democratic institutions. This occasion also serves as a reminder of the singular worth of a free press to the well-being of our country. As Thomas Jefferson wrote, "Our liberty depends on the freedom of the press."

Throughout National Newspaper Week, all Americans are pleased to note the many contributions of the men and women of our nation's press to the preservation of the First Amendment's guarantee of freedom of the press. Of the forces shaping the destiny of our civilization, none is more crucial to our future than the responsible reporting and truthful analysis of the events of our era. I commend your dedicated efforts in pursuit of their goals.

RONALD REAGAN

Message on the Observance of International Newspaper Carrier Day, October 15, 1983
October 6, 1983

I am delighted to extend my warm congratulations and appreciation to those who deliver our newspapers as we observe International Newspaper Carrier Day.

This occasion provides a welcome opportunity for me to express my high regard for your role in keeping Americans informed. Millions of our citizens depend on you to receive the essential and timely in-depth information that only newspapers bring to our daily lives.

As part of the communication industry of our democracy, you play a valuable part in the development of an educated and knowledgeable electorate. I commend your contributions to a strong America.

RONALD REAGAN

Nomination of the United States Representative and Alternate Representatives to the 27th Session of the General Conference of the International Atomic Energy Agency
October 6, 1983

The President today announced his intention to nominate the following individuals:

To be the Representative of the United States of America to the Twenty-seventh Session of the General Conference of the International Atomic Energy Agency:

Donald P. Hodel, Secretary of the Department of Energy, of Arlington, Va.

To be Alternate Representatives of the United States of America to the Twenty-seventh Session of the General Conference of the International Atomic Energy Agency:

Richard T. Kennedy, of Washington, D.C.

Nunzio J. Palladino, of State College, Pa.

Richard S. Williamson, of Vienna, Va.

Appointment of Marion Newbert Jorgensen as a Member of the Board of Trustees of the John F. Kennedy Center for the Performing Arts
October 6, 1983

The President today announced his intention to appoint Marion Newbert Jorgensen to be a member of the Board of Trustees of the John F. Kennedy Center for the Performing Arts, Smithsonian Institution, for the remainder of the term expiring September 1, 1992. She would succeed Donna Tuttle.

Mrs. Jorgensen serves as a trustee of St. Johns Hospital and Health Center and also as a trustee of Loyola Marymount University in Los Angeles. She is a member of the board of Continental Airlines and the Los Angeles World Affairs Council. She was the first woman to serve as chairman of the board of overseers of the Huntington Library Art Gallery and Botanical Gardens.

Additionally Mrs. Jorgensen serves on the President's Blue Ribbon 400 Music Center and is director of the Los Angeles Symphony Association.

Mrs. Jorgensen is married, has six children, and resides in Santa Monica, Calif. She was born March 3, 1915, in Chicago, Ill.

Designation of Anthony G. Sousa as Acting Chairman of the Federal Energy Regulatory Commission
October 7, 1983

The President today announced his intention to designate Anthony G. Sousa to be Acting Chairman of the Federal Energy Regulatory Commission, Department of Energy, effective October 8, 1983. The present Chairman, Charles M. Butler III, is resigning.

Since 1981 Mr. Sousa has been a member of the Federal Energy Regulatory Commission. Previously he was vice president and general counsel of the Hawaiian Telephone Co., a subsidiary of General Telephone & Electronics Corp., in 1973–1981. He was counsel, then senior counsel, and finally administrative law judge with the California Public Utilities Commission in 1968–1973. He was with the U.S. Steel Corp. in 1967. He was in the traffic department and later, western regional distribution manager with Thomas J. Lipton, Inc., of San Francisco, Calif., in 1959–1967.

Mr. Sousa graduated from St. Luiz Gonzaga College (B.A., 1945) and the University of San Francisco Law School (J.D., 1966). He is married, has three children, and resides in Washington, D.C. He was born on August 8, 1927.

Appointment of Ernest B. Hueter as a Member of the Presidential Commission for the German-American Tricentennial
October 7, 1983

The President today announced his intention to appoint Ernest B. Hueter to be a member of the Presidential Commission for the German-American Tricentennial. This is a new position.

Mr. Hueter is presently serving as president of the National Legal Center for the Public Interest in Washington, D.C., and is chairman emeritus of the Interstate Brands Corp. in Kansas City, Mo. He has been with the Interstate Brands Corp. since 1947, serving in various positions including chairman of the board, president, and chief executive officer. He served as chairman of Diamond H. Enterprises, Inc., in Kansas City, Mo., in 1979–1980.

He graduated from the University of New Mexico (B.A., 1942). He is married, has two children, and resides in Washington, D.C. He was born June 15, 1920, in San Francisco, Calif.

Nomination of William H. Luers To Be United States Ambassador to Czechoslovakia
October 7, 1983

The President today announced his intention to nominate William H. Luers, of Illinois, a career member of the Senior Foreign Service, Class of Career Minister, as Ambassador to the Czechoslovak Socialist Republic. He would succeed Jack F. Matlock, Jr.

Mr. Luers served in the United States Navy in 1952–1956 as lieutenant. He entered the Foreign Service in 1957 as consular officer in Naples. In 1959–1962 he was an officer in the Office of Soviet Affairs in the Bureau of European Affairs in the Department. In 1962–1963 he attended Russian language and area studies in Garmisch, Germany, and was political officer in Moscow in 1963–1965. In the Department, he was intelligence research specialist in the Bureau of Intelligence and Research (1965–1967) and international relations officer (1967–1969). In 1969–1973 he was counselor for political affairs in Caracas. In the Department, he was Deputy Executive Secretary (1973–1975), Deputy Assistant Secretary for Inter-American Affairs (1975–1977), and Deputy Assistant Secretary for European Affairs (1977–1978). In 1978–1982 he was Ambassador to Venezuela. Since 1982 he has been Director's Visitor at the Institute for Advanced Study in Princeton, N.J.

Mr. Luers graduated from Hamilton College (B.A., 1951) and Columbia University (M.A., 1958). His foreign languages are Spanish, Russian, and Italian. He was born May 15, 1929, in Springfield, Ill.

Proclamation 5115—National Schoolbus Safety Week, 1983
October 7, 1983

By the President of the United States of America

A Proclamation

Schoolbus transportation serves a very special and important segment of this Nation—our children. More than twenty-two million young Americans use schoolbuses to get to school.

When we consider the millions of young people who are transported and the millions of trips schoolbuses make each year, we can take great pride in our safety record. Nevertheless, we must reaffirm our commitment to providing the safest possible transportation for our children. They are our most important resource, and their safe transport deserves to be one of our highest priorities.

In recognition of the national program which is underway to call public attention to the importance of schoolbus safety, and in recognition of the importance of safe transport of our young students to and from school, the Congress, by House Joint Resolution 137, has authorized and requested the President to issue a proclamation designating the week of October 2 through October 8, 1983, as National Schoolbus Safety Week.

Now, Therefore, I, Ronald Reagan, President of the United States of America, do hereby proclaim the week beginning on October 2, 1983, as National Schoolbus Safety Week. I call upon the people of the United States and interested groups and organizations to observe that week with appropriate activities and ceremonies.

In Witness Whereof, I have hereunto set my hand this seventh day of October, in the year of our Lord nineteen hundred and eighty-three, and of the Independence of the United States of America the two hundred and eighth.

RONALD REAGAN

[*Filed with the Office of the Federal Register, 11:16 a.m., October 11, 1983*]

Appointment of 11 Members of the Board of Directors of the Legal Services Corporation
October 7, 1983

The President today announced his intention to appoint the following individuals to be members of the Board of Directors of the Legal Services Corporation:

For the remainder of the terms expiring July 13, 1984:

Robert A. Valois would succeed William F. Harvey. Mr. Valois is an attorney with the firm of Maupin, Taylor & Ellis. He was born May 13, 1938, in New York, N.Y., and now resides in Raleigh, N.C.

Leaanne Bernstein would succeed David E. Satterfield III. Mrs. Bernstein is Assistant to the President of the Legal Services Corporation. She was born February 22, 1950, in Poplar Bluff, Mo., and now resides in Baltimore, Md.

Claude Galbreath Swafford would succeed Howard H. Dana, Jr. She is in the private practice of law in South Pittsburg, Tenn. She was born December 7, 1925, in Greeneville, Tenn., and now resides in South Pittsburg.

Paul B. Eaglin would succeed Robert Sherwood Stubbs II. Mr. Eaglin is a partner in the law firm of Cooper, Davis, Eaglin & deSilva in Fayetteville, N.C. He was born August 10, 1948, in Baltimore, Md., and now resides in Fayetteville.

Arnie Marie Gordon would succeed George E. Paras. Mrs. Gordon is president of Flatonia Community Club. She was born December 25, 1932, in Flatonia, Tex., where she currently resides.

Henry Chavira would succeed William J. Olson. Mr. Chavira is a sales representative for R. L. Pope & Co., in El Paso, Tex. He was born August 18, 1936, in El Paso, where he currently resides.

For terms expiring July 13, 1986:

Michael B. Wallace would succeed Donald Eugene Santarelli. Mr. Wallace is joining the law firm of Jones, Mockbee and Bass in Jackson, Miss. He was born December 1, 1951, in Biloxi, Miss., and now resides in Jackson.

William Clark Durant III would succeed Frank J. Donatelli. Mr. Durant is in the private practice of law in Detroit, Mich. He was born May 13, 1949, in Detroit and now resides in Grosse Point, Mich.

Robert Francis Kane would succeed Milton M. Masson. Mr. Kane is in the private practice of law in San Mateo, Calif. He was born March 15, 1926, in Denver, Colo., and now resides in San Mateo.

Bernard M. Bloom would succeed Daniel M. Rathbun. Mr. Bloom has served as judge of the Surrogate Court of Kings County (New York) since 1976. He was born August 21, 1926, in Brooklyn, N.Y., where he currently resides.

Pepe J. Mendez would succeed Robert E. McCarthy. Mr. Mendez is in the private practice of law in Denver, Colo. He was born September 4, 1945, in Gunnison, Colo., and now resides in Denver.

Remarks at the Biennial Convention of the National Federation of Republican Women in Louisville, Kentucky
October 7, 1983

I've found out in this job there are some days better than others. [*Laughter*] And I told an interviewer yesterday, with regard to '84, that I believe the people tell you whether you should or not. So, I shall remember what you have said.

Betty Rendel, Betty Heitman,[1] and all those who are here, members of our Cabinet—Secretary Dole and Secretary Heckler—three Congresswomen—Bobbi Fiedler, Lynn Martin, and Claudine Schneider—Director of the Peace Corps, Loret Ruppe, and we have two Cabinet wives here, Mrs. Midge Baldrige and Mrs. Sue Block, and all of you, I'm delighted to be with you, members of America's largest political organization. You are not just the pride and joy, you are the heart and soul of the Republican Party.

Your work and dedication and that of all your members who aren't here today have resulted in the election of thousands of Republicans all across this country—people who have carried our ideas and principles at the Federal, State, and local levels. Thanks to your energy and talent, you've often been called the foot soldiers of our party. But that description is becoming outdated. You've got a good share of generals in your ranks—[*laughter*]—and that share is growing.

We Republicans have always been in the forefront of supporting women's rights and encouraging their participation in all shades of society. It began with our backing of women's suffrage, and it continues today with many able women serving in public and political office.

Republicans have a good, proud history of electing women to public office. I've said it before, and I'm proud to say it again: The Republican Party was the first to elect a woman to the United States Congress. We are the only party to elect women to the United States Senate who were not first filling unexpired terms. And we shouldn't let anyone forget that the only two women in the United States Senate, Nancy Kassebaum and Paula Hawkins, are Republicans. And we've got nine great Republican women in the House, and as I've said, three of them are here with us today. Let me just ask them, "Wouldn't you like a little more company?"

---

[1] *President of the National Federation of Republican Women and Cochairman of the Republican National Committee, respectively.*

I believe we should set a new goal for ourselves. Let us at least double the number of Republican women in the House and Senate, and let's do it in 1984. And, Claudine Schneider, I hope you're listening, because I'd like to think that one of those new Senators will be you.

I want you to know that back in Washington we're appointing top-quality people to responsible positions throughout the Government. And because we're looking for the best, we've appointed many women to key jobs—women like our United Nations Ambassador, Jeane Kirkpatrick; women who come from among your ranks, like Elizabeth Dole, our Secretary of Transportation, Margaret Heckler, our Secretary of Health and Human Services, and another member of whom we're all extremely proud, Supreme Court Justice Sandra Day O'Connor. And on some 5-to-4 decisions since she arrived there, how I have thanked heaven that she is there.

They are the stars. But throughout the administration, women are involved in making the serious decisions that are shaping America's destiny. I'm glad your convention is focusing on the crucial issue that is facing America in the 1980's—the economy. America's society has changed dramatically during the last decade, and American women have been a major force behind those changes. Fifty-three percent of you are working outside the home, up from 38 percent just 20 years ago. And that's one reason why the key to your, or anybody else's, progress is a strong, growing economy. And believe me, our goal is not just economic recovery. We seek to build a new era of lasting economic expansion filled with opportunities for all our people that will be a dramatic improvement from what we inherited.

In 1981 we were faced with an economic crisis that was destroying opportunity. Back-to-back years of double-digit inflation had undermined every American family's financial security. Families living on a fixed income of $10,000 at the start of 1979 saw the purchasing power of that income drop to less than $8,000 by the end of 1980. Yet, our opponents preach to us like apostles of fairness. Well, maybe they are fair in at least one way: Their policies don't discriminate; they bring misery to everybody. [*Laughter*]

Let us remind our fellow Americans what our opponents want everyone to forget: They had their chance, and they failed. For 4 straight years they exercised total control over the Federal Government. They controlled both Houses of the Congress, the White House, and every department, bureau, and agency.

We must have the courage to speak out and to challenge their credibility. Those who saddled America with double-digit inflation, record interest rates, huge tax increases, too much regulation, credit controls, farm embargoes, and phony excuses about malaise are the last people who should be giving sermonettes about fairness and compassion.

We're doing things a little differently. We're providing true fairness by increasing real wages for the first time in 3 years. We've reduced inflation to 2.6 percent over the last 12 months. Sometimes people buying their groceries and other items don't realize how much inflation is down, because the prices are still going up. The difference is they're not going up much—or they are going up much more slowly than before. For example, if food prices had continued rising the last 2 years at the same rate as in the 2 years before we took office, a loaf of bread would cost 7 cents more today; a half gallon of milk would cost 18 cents more; a pound of hamburger would cost 60 cents more; and a gallon of gas would cost 97 cents more. But I'm not going to be satisfied—and I don't think you are—until inflation is zero. And that's where we're going to get it.

In 1980 the prime interest rate hit 21½ percent, the highest level in more than 100 years. Now it's about half what it was. The cost of doing business, mortgage, education, and car loans have come down. Parents, students, entrepreneurs, workers, and consumers—all are benefiting. And if the Congress would just act responsibly, we can knock those interest rates down even more.

On another front, we've cut 300 million hours of Federal paperwork. This will save consumers, business, and State and local officials billions of dollars. It's taken time, but

virtually every sector of the economy—from housing to the auto industry to high technology—is expanding, creating greater opportunities and new hope for a better and more secure future. The gross national product, the GNP, is growing faster than even we expected—growing by a whopping 9.7 percent in the second quarter of this year and an estimated 7 percent for the next quarter.

But you know that the best clue that our program is working is our critics don't call it Reaganomics anymore. [*Laughter*]

Unemployment, which, tragically, is often the last indicator to turn around in a recovery, is on a downward path. Just this morning we received the more welcome news; at 8:30 they released the statistics. Total unemployment in September dropped to 9.1 percent. As you'll remember, in August it dropped the biggest single monthly drop in 24 years. The number of people holding jobs in September increased by 382,000 to a total number of people working in this country of 101.9 million and that is an all-time high in the history of the United States.

Now you might be interested to know that the unemployment rate for adult women dropped from 8 to 7.8 percent. More women are working now than ever before we took office—since before we took office over 2.3 million more are working. Your opportunities are expanding, and your jobs are better. Women filled more than half of all the new jobs in managerial, professional, and technical fields between 1980 and 1982. The number of women-owned businesses is growing five times faster than it is among men.

The trouble is some people just won't open their eyes. Our opponents refuse to see any progress. They refuse to admit that America is getting well, refuse to recognize the recovery that is getting stronger all the time. These critics seem prepared to drown recovery in pessimism. Their specialty isn't solutions, it's scare tactics about deficits. Well, make no mistake, no one should minimize the danger of those budget deficits. But I feel compelled to ask an unpleasant question: Aren't these the same people who left us with government spending soaring at

17.4-percent annual rate in 1980, the same people who opposed every effort of ours to slow the rate of increase in government spending? Where have these born-again budget balancers been? [*Laughter*]

I'll tell you where they've been. They've been using every trick in the book to sabotage what the American people truly want—a balanced Federal budget.

Now one of the ways to get there is by a constitutional amendment. Now, I recognize that that idea would not be a cure-all; it wouldn't even go into effect right away. But in the interim period, the Congress and the President would have to sit down together to agree on a budget of real discipline and one that would not penalize those dependent on government for help.

Now I still believe this idea is right for America. Our goal was and remains to bring the Federal budget into balance by bringing spending down in line with revenues. And this is the only true course toward fiscal sanity.

Barely a year ago, 236 responsible Republicans and Democrats, a clear majority in the House, joined us in an historic attempt to pass that constitutional amendment. But that amendment required a two-thirds majority. Incredibly, the liberal House leadership—the same people who now take the well of the House each morning to decry deficits—claimed, believe it or not, that a balanced budget would wreck our economy. That's a little like saying that good exercise, three square meals a day, and plenty of sleep at night will destroy your health. [*Laughter*]

This upside-down logic is at the core of their so-called deficit solutions. Well, hold on to your seatbelts, because I warn you, the day the liberal leadership regains control of the government—if it ever does—Americans are on their way to being taxed into the poorhouse.

Several months ago we had to beat back their plan to raise taxes by $315 billion over the next 5 years. Nor did they have any intention to spend less, not on your life. Along with the tax increase they planned a $181 billion increase in domestic spending. Just imagine how quickly this would have decimated savings and investment, sunk the recovery, and raised unemployment—all of which would have made the deficit much bigger, not smaller.

The unfair Democratic tax increases would have cost a typical median-income family $3,550 over 5 years. Now, how does such punishment help parents, students, entrepreneurs, and working people to get ahead? How do you help an economy grow by draining away its life, energy, and spirit?

Our idea of fairness is not tax increases, it's tax reductions and indexing. Our tax cut is already saving the average working family $700 a year. Our idea of opportunity is not to destroy hope, but to work with responsible Republicans and Democrats to reward initiative and help all Americans achieve economic equality. We've been doing it by reducing the marriage tax penalty, increasing the maximum child care credit—almost doubling it—increasing the limits for IRA and Keogh contributions, and by virtually eliminating estate taxes on family farms and businesses for a surviving spouse. Now, this is real progress for America.

The liberal thesis—that we can whack the deficit by soaking the rich and cutting defense spending—is just plain wrong. Let's take the case of taxpayers earning $75,000 a year or more, and let's presume that we'll not only raise their taxes, we'll confiscate every single penny they earn above $75,000. This would be a marginal tax rate of 100 percent.

Question: How much money would we raise? Answer: Approximately $33 billion, enough to run the government for 14 days and cover about 18 percent of the deficit, less than one-fifth of the deficit. Well, sorry, that won't quite do it. And remember, the government would only confiscate that $33 billion one time. Raising taxes sets off an alarm. It tells people don't take risks, don't invest more, don't produce or save, because government is waiting to take it away from you next year. Thirty-three billion would not be there to tax and the deficit would grow.

Now, what was their other idea for reducing the deficit? Oh, yes, cut military spending and, as a few urge, cut it to the bone. After their proposed tax increase the deficit, according to their estimate, would still be around $150 billion. Now remember we have already reduced our planned defense increase by $66 billion. We did that ourselves. Forget that defense spending as a share of the Federal budget is nearly 40 percent less today than it was under John F. Kennedy 20 years ago. Forget that the Russians have been out-investing us in defense by about 2 to 1. We have a deficit left of about $150 billion, which our opponents say can be eliminated by reduced defense spending. So, let's start by eliminating—for an entire year—spending on the Pershing missile, the B–1 bomber, the MX missile, the cruise missile, the Trident submarine and its missiles, the M–1 tank, and then cancel the orders for all the ammunition for all our weapons, including even the bullets for our soldiers' rifles. And that will reduce the deficit of $150 billion by $13.2 billion in 1984.

What else would they have us do—ask the soldiers, sailors, marines, and airmen to work free and give up eating? The path to lower deficits is not paved with tax increases and unilateral disarmament. We will reduce deficits by encouraging growth and handcuffing the big spenders. Yes, the President is a Republican, and there's much talk in Democratic circles that the budget and the deficit are the President's; they come full-blown from the White House. But the Constitution doesn't give the President power to appropriate or spend money. That power belongs only to the Congress, and the Congress has only been Republican in both Houses for 4 of the last 50 years.

When we protested over those years the size of the growing debt, how many remember they told us the debt didn't mean anything because we owed it to ourselves? Indeed, we can recall them saying that deficit spending and its accompanying inflation were essential to continued prosperity. Now, that can only be called hypocrisy. These people who sabotaged the balanced budget amendment, who resisted tooth and nail our efforts to break runaway spending, are now delivering daily broadsides against deficits, even as they cook up a whole host of new spending bills. Look at only a portion of their spending wish-list, and you will be staggered. Sixteen House Democratic proposals alone would raise the deficit by

almost $50 billion in fiscal year 1984 and by a whopping $192 billion over the next 5 years. It is their profligacy, not our economic recovery program, that is the source of Federal red ink.

I will not hesitate to veto their tax increases, and I must and will veto their budget-busting bills as fast as they reach my desk. And on my desk is a letter signed by 146 Congressmen, the overwhelming majority Republicans, pledging to me that they—that's the number required—will uphold my vetoes when I sign them.

Let us urge the American people to keep working at the grassroots for a constitutional amendment mandating a balanced budget. If you want to make it happen, it will happen. We'll continue the lonely battle to restrain spending. One tool I used in my California days, and which I've always been attracted to, is the line-item veto. Presidents don't have it. About 30 Governors do, and it works every time you use it.

Let's also keep our eyes on something encouraging: The deficit is coming down. The deficit is falling because of new economic growth. Even with lower tax rates, revenues are coming in strong, because those lower tax rates stimulated the economic recovery.

Economic growth is making life better for everyone, and that's the Republican blueprint for the future. The Republican message is dream the big dreams. With freedom and opportunity, there's no limit to what we can accomplish as individuals and as a nation. But let us also remember we cannot prosper unless we are secure, and we cannot be secure unless we're free. The Soviet invasion of Afghanistan, their chemical poisoning of innocent civilians, their brutal occupation and subversion of one country after another, and their recent attack against 269 innocent civilians aboard KAL flight 007 are all important reminders: We live in a dangerous world, with cruel people who reject our ideals and who disregard individual rights and the value of human life.

It is my duty as President, and all of our duties as citizens, to keep this nation's defenses second to none, so that America can remain strong—[*applause*]. Thank you. God bless you all. America is going to remain strong, free, and at peace; I know that now.

I told you a little while ago, some days are better than others. There are days, also, in which things happen. I just have to tell you this little incident. I have received some letters from the families of some of those who were on that Korean airliner. And the other day I received one from a mother whose 28-year-old daughter was on that plane. She had lost her husband the year before through a terrible illness. She had two small children. And now this mother, as grandmother, had to tell those two small children their mother was dead. And she told me how the little 6-year-old boy turned without a word and then a short time later came back and handed her a drawing he'd made of a little boy crying and said, "That's how I feel." I sometimes think if it would do any good, I'd like to send a lot of those letters to Mr. Andropov.

Peace through strength is our goal. We're undertaking the most sweeping proposals for mutual and verifiable arms reductions since nuclear weapons became a threat. In strategic nuclear forces and in measures to build confidence and trust, in intermediate-range nuclear forces and in conventional forces, we want to lessen the danger to ourselves and our children. We remain flexible in our bargaining, but as Commander in Chief, I have an obligation to protect this country, and I will not let political expediency influence these crucial negotiations.

I believe with all my heart that America is more prosperous, safe, and secure today than it was 3 years ago. One word sums up the difference between 1983 and 1980:

Hope. You can see hope being reborn. You can see confidence rising. You can feel a new spirit of optimism spreading across our land. America is surging forward again. We're meeting the challenge of improving our schools, a challenge neglected for too many years. And some day soon, we'll even welcome God back into America's classrooms. [*Applause*]

If I remember anything from my previous occupation, I should quit now. [*Laughter*]

We will explore deeper in space, cross new frontiers of high technology, make new medical breakthroughs, and we'll be doing it for the benefit of our children and our children's children. We've made a new beginning—a dramatic and far-reaching step toward a much better future.

And I urge you: Take our message to the people. Remind them where we were, what we've done, and how far together we can still go. You've always been our greatest strength. You've made the difference before; you can do it now. With your talent, your drive, your brains, and your heart, we can out-organize and out-do anyone. And if enough of you run for public office, if enough of you continue to work as you always have, American women will make history again. You'll make 1984 the year of the Republican renaissance. And all I can say to all of you is God bless you all, and God bless America.

Thank you.

Note: The President spoke at 11:45 a.m. at the Commonwealth Convention Center. He was introduced by Betty Rendel, president of the federation.

Remarks at a Fundraising Luncheon for Gubernatorial Candidate Jim Bunning in Louisville, Kentucky
October 7, 1983

I'm most pleased to be with you today to support the candidacy of an individual whose strength of character, unbounding energy, and unmatched creativity is going to make Kentucky one heck of a fine Gov-

ernor—Jim Bunning.

Kentucky hasn't had the kind of strong Republican leadership that Jim has to offer the Governor's office since the early seventies when Louie Nunn served this State. We were Governors together. I was Governor of California at the time, and I can appreciate the importance of electing Jim. He's offering exciting alternatives to government as usual. And, Jim, I'll just have to admit when I look over some of the things that you've been suggesting, it makes me want to move to Kentucky so I can vote for you. [*Laughter*]

Jim's been talking about reform that will bring business and commerce into your State. He's talking about lowering certain taxes to encourage industry to locate here. He's talking about getting rid of useless regulations that discourage economic development. He's talking about tax credits for the creation of new jobs, and about vocational training for those unprepared to meet the challenge of changing times. He's got the ideas, he knows how State government works, and he'll do the things he's talked about.

As you all know, better than me, perhaps—no, you don't know better than me because I broadcast baseball for several years—[*laughter*]—he played professional baseball for 17 years before getting into politics. He's proven his political savvy is as good as his pitching arm, and he hasn't forgotten what it means to be on a team.

I know he sincerely cares about the people he works with, and not everybody in politics is so considerate, even with the members of their own party. Some politicians are kind of like the two campers who were out hiking and spotted a grizzly bear coming over the hill, and it was headed right for them. And one of them reached into his pack as quick as he could, pulled out a pair of tennis shoes, sat down, and started putting on the tennis shoes. And the other looked at him and he said, "You don't mean you think you can outrun a grizzly?" And the fellow with the tennis shoes stood up, and he says, "I don't have to outrun the grizzly; I just have to outrun you." [*Laughter*]

Seriously, though, State government is becoming more important to the well-being of the American people. We Republicans—and I know there are a host of Democrats who agree with us about this—believe that government works best at levels close enough for people to influence the decisions that affect their lives.

Centralizing power in Washington doesn't work. It expanded the bureaucracy, it drained resources from the State and local level, but the problems remained and often got worse. When I was a young man, it's hard to believe that government in the United States only took 10 cents out of every dollar being earned. And two-thirds of that was for State and local government and one-third for the Federal Government. Today they're taking something like 44 cents out of every dollar earned, and two-thirds of that goes to the Federal Government, leaving one-third for the States and the local communities.

We're coming to the end of an era when politicians can sell the idea that the best solution to any problem is letting Washington do it because Federal money is free. Well, Washington money isn't free money, as I think most of you are well aware. It comes right out of those same pockets. Just between 1976 and 1981, the Federal tax take doubled. That deprived our economy of the resources that it needed for investment and new job creation. We fell into a pit of high inflation and economic stagnation. Some of the government programs have made little sense, except to those making a career out of administering those programs.

I remember one such program that was proposed during the war on poverty—which poverty won—[*laughter*]—when I was Governor of California. And for a time they allowed a Governor to veto, for 60 days, a Federal program, unless it was then overridden by the Federal Government. Well, this program came in and it sounded at first—it looked pretty good. They were going to take 17 of the needy, the unemployed, and they were going to put them to work helping clean up the county parks in this particular county. That sounded fine, just the kind of thing I believe in, except that as I looked closer at it, 50 percent of the budget was going to 11 administrators to make sure that the 17 got to work on time. [*Laughter*] I thought there might be an easier way to keep the parks clean than that. [*Laughter*]

But you know, it's—sometimes these government programs, it's a little bit like the story of the country preacher who called on a town about 100 miles away from his own. He went there for a revival meeting. And on the way to the church, he noticed in that town that sitting on the porch of a little country store was a man from his own hometown, a fellow that was known for his drinking. And the minister went up to him and asked what he was doing so far from home. "Preacher," he said, "beer is 5 cents a bottle cheaper here." [*Laughter*] The minister told him that didn't make much sense—the expense of traveling all that way and back, the price of lodging and all while he was there. The drinker thought for a moment and then replied, "Preacher, I'm not stupid. I just sit here and drink till I show a profit." [*Laughter*]

That was the kind of logic that fit some of the Federal programs of the last 20 years. It wasn't any better than that. But today, we know that for America to move forward and meet the challenges of tomorrow, we must have strong leadership and community involvement.

Jim Bunning is just the person to provide the kind of leadership Kentucky needs to get the people involved. There's no better example of this than the education issue of such concern to so many of us. He's taken some pretty courageous stands on that. This is a subject about which I've been deeply concerned as a parent and as a public official, and I admire him for hitting the issue head-on.

I think voters should remember that those who offer easy answers and quick fixes are doing everyone a disservice, especially our children. Jim has suggested annual testing of students and ending the automatic promotion of pupils.

Oh, Jim, I had a mother in California one day when I was Governor, a black mother who came up to me, tears in her eyes. And she said, "Don't talk to me about busing or things like that." She said, "Keep my children in the class that they're in until they learn what they're supposed to know in that class. Don't just pass them on because they came to the end of the year." And then she told me, she said, "I have a son who's a high school graduate, and he can't read the diploma they gave him."

He's proposed lengthening the school year to bring Kentucky in line with the national average, raising the compulsory age for school attendance to at least attempt to give Kentucky children a better chance to graduate from high school. Jim knows that a well-educated future generation will make Kentucky stronger economically—a view that his opponent may have missed. He's endorsed increasing the pay of your teachers, but he's also had the courage to call for merit pay and competency testing to ensure that the money is well spent.

I've looked over the things that Jim Bunning has proposed during this campaign, and I'm impressed. Since I got to Washington 3 years ago, we've tried to turn back the block grants power and authority to the States. With an individual like Jim in the Governor's office, I know that Kentuckians will benefit greatly from the new authority on block grants, the authority that it gives to the States.

Strong and effective State government is a vital part of the American system of government. Here in Kentucky, home of Henry Clay, one of the giants of American federalism, you well understand the relationship between our freedom and the balance of power between Federal and State government.

We are working on federalism at the national level. This country is as free as it is—you as individuals owe much of your freedom to this very unique thing about our country—that it was set up by the Constitution to be a federation of sovereign States, not administrative districts of a Federal Government that retained all the power itself.

It is that ability of citizens to choose where they will live that has kept government at the State levels from becoming tyrannical. It is that that preserves our precious liberty and unleashes productive forces among our citizens that produce abundance such as the world has never dreamed.

In the fall here in Kentucky, with the magnificent colors beginning to burst forth on hillside trees, you know how much God has blessed America. He has done His part. Now, I think it's up to us. With your help,

Jim Bunning will be the next Governor of Kentucky.

Thank you, and God bless you. And I can tell you in this spirit of federalism, you'd be surprised how much help it is to someone in my job if it's Republican Governors we're dealing with out there, Governors who be-lieve as we believe.

Note: The President spoke at 12:54 p.m. in the Cochran Ballroom at the Galt House Hotel. Prior to the luncheon, the President attended a reception for major donors to the Bunning campaign.

Radio Address to the Nation on the Situation in Lebanon
October 8, 1983

My fellow Americans:

I'm sure you're all aware of the debate during recent days and weeks with regard to our marines in Lebanon. Congress, on a strong bipartisan basis, has passed a resolu-tion approving their presence there for 18 months if need be. But in the debate, many questions were raised as to what they were doing there and whether their presence there was in our national interest. In the midst of all this debate, I received a letter from the father of a young marine corporal stationed in Beirut, Lebanon.

Justly proud of his son, he enclosed a clip-ping from his hometown paper. It was a letter to the editor written by his son. And here's what the young corporal had to say about the marines and whether or not there was a reason for their presence in Lebanon. His family had been sending him the home-town paper, and he'd noticed "editorials and opinions denouncing American involve-ment in the various troublespots of the world, particularly Central America and the Middle East."

He went on to say, "I've been keeping up with what's happening in Central America, and I have firsthand knowledge of what is happening in the Middle East. In the case of Central America, the general American consensus is to stay out, that we're getting into another Vietnam. Whenever American military forces go abroad, the average American believes that we should keep to ourselves and mind our own business. I'm not an advocate of war," he says, "as I've seen the ravages of war here in Lebanon. War is a very terrible thing. Yet when dip-lomatic methods fail, we must be prepared to defend and, if necessary, to die for what we believe in, for the American way of life. I do not enjoy being here in Beirut. My fellow marines and I miss the simple yet wonderful aspects of life back home that so many take for granted. Yet, we realize we'll be going home in a few months. But the people of, say, El Salvador or Lebanon are home. For them, there is no escape. It is our duty as Americans to stop the cancerous spread of Soviet influence wherever it may be, because someday we or some future generation will wake up and find the U.S.A. to be the only free state left, with commu-nism upon our doorstep. And then it will be too late."

A young marine corporal writing from Beirut, Lebanon, to his hometown paper—there's no doubt in his mind about the need for us to have a presence there. But many of us are not that sure. Many believe we are involving ourselves needlessly in someone else's quarrel and should bring our young men home and mind our own business. The corporal may not have spelled out the spe-cifics as to why it was in our best interest to be there, but he was certainly correct in his conclusion that it is our business.

Can the United States or the free world stand by and see the Middle East incorpo-rated into the Soviet bloc? What of Western Europe and Japan's dependence on Middle East oil for the energy to fuel their indus-try? Do we remember the oil embargo and the lines at our own gas stations? And didn't we assume a moral obligation to the contin-ued existence of Israel as a nation back in 1948? I've never heard anyone in this coun-try ever suggest that we should abandon

1437

that obligation.

A little over a year ago, I proposed a peace initiative for the entire Middle East. It was based on the Camp David accords and the United Nations Resolutions 242 and 338. We offered our help in bringing the Arab States and Israel together in negotiations to settle the longstanding disputes that had kept that entire area in turmoil for many years. We sought more peace treaties like the one between Egypt and Israel.

Lebanon, the site of refugee camps for a great many Palestinians, had been torn by strife for several years. There were factions, each with its own militia, fighting each other. Terrorists in Lebanon violated Israel's northern border, killing innocent civilians. Syrian forces occupied the eastern part of Lebanon. Israeli military finally invaded from the south to force the PLO attackers away from the border. There could be no implementation of our peace initiative until this situation was resolved.

With our allies—England, France, and Italy—we proposed a withdrawal of all foreign forces from Lebanon and formed a multinational force to help maintain order and stability in the Beirut area while a new Lebanese Government and army undertook to restore sovereignty throughout Lebanon.

Over the course of several months, Lebanon and Israel negotiated a friendly agreement for security of the border between the two. We stand by this as a good agreement. But Syria, which had earlier agreed to withdraw if Israel did, changed its mind, and today has some 5,000 Soviet advisers and technicians and a massive amount of new Soviet equipment in its country, including a new generation of surface-to-surface missiles—the SS–21. We have to wonder aloud about Syrian protestations of their peaceful intentions.

For a year, we've continued diplomatic negotiations leading to the present cease-fire. President Gemayel is committed to a process of national reconciliation as the means to end factional fighting. The presence of our marines as part of the multinational force demonstrates that Lebanon does not stand alone. Peace for the Middle East and a fair settlement of the Palestinian problem is truly in our national interest.

Until next week, thanks for listening, and God bless you.

Note: The President spoke at 12:06 p.m. from Camp David, Md.

Statement on the Resignation of James G. Watt as Secretary of the Interior
October 9, 1983

Today Jim Watt talked with me by telephone and delivered to me his letter of resignation. He feels that he has completed the principal objectives that he and I agreed upon when he became Secretary of the Interior. I respect his decision to leave the Government and thus have reluctantly accepted his resignation. He will continue in office until his successor is confirmed.

Jim has done an outstanding job as a member of my Cabinet and in his stewardship of the natural resources of the Nation. He has initiated a careful balance between the needs of people and the importance of protecting the environment. His dedication to public service and his accomplishments as Secretary of the Interior will long be remembered.

Nancy and I appreciate the contribution that Jim and Leilani have made to this administration, and we wish them well in their future endeavors.

Nomination of Thomas P. Shoesmith To Be United States Ambassador to Malaysia
October 11, 1983

The President announced today his intention to nominate Thomas P. Shoesmith, of Virginia, a career member of the Senior Foreign Service, Class of Career Minister, to be Ambassador to Malaysia. He would succeed Ronald D. Palmer.

Mr. Shoesmith served in the United States Army in 1943–1948 as a first lieutenant. He began his government career in 1951 as intelligence research officer in the Bureau of Intelligence and Research at the Department of State. He was consular officer in Hong Kong (1956–1958) and political officer in Seoul (1958–1960). From 1960 to 1961, he attended Japanese language training at the Foreign Service Institute and in Tokyo. He was political officer in Tokyo (1961–1963) and principal officer in Fukuo-

ka (1963–1966). In the Department he was Deputy Director (1966–1967) and Director (1967–1971) of the Office of Republic of China Affairs. In 1971–1972 he was a member of the executive seminar in national and international affairs at the Foreign Service Institute. In 1972–1977 he was Deputy Chief of Mission in Tokyo and Consul General in Hong Kong in 1977–1981. Since 1981 he has been Deputy Assistant Secretary of State for East Asian and Pacific Affairs in the Department.

Mr. Shoesmith graduated from the University of Pennsylvania (B.S., 1943) and Harvard University (M.A., 1951). His foreign language is Japanese. He was born January 25, 1922, in Palmerton, Pa.

Nomination of Helmuth A. Merklein To Be an Assistant Secretary of Energy
October 11, 1983

The President today announced his intention to nominate Helmuth A. Merklein to be an Assistant Secretary of Energy (International Affairs). He would succeed Henry E. Thomas IV.

Dr. Merklein is a professor in the department of petroleum engineering at Texas A. & M. University. Previously he was dean of the graduate school of management at the University of Dallas in 1980–1982. In 1970–1980 he was a graduate-level teacher of oil

and gas consulting. He was with Core Laboratories in reservoir engineering, reserve evaluations, and international petroleum consulting in 1965–1968.

Dr. Merklein graduated from the University of Oklahoma (B.S., 1959) and the University of Dallas (M.B.A., 1968). He received his Ph. D. from Texas A. & M. University in 1970. He is married, has two children, and resides in Irving, Tex. He was born May 26, 1935, in Sumatra, Indonesia.

Appointment of Jack L. Courtemanche as Deputy Assistant to the President for Public Liaison
October 11, 1983

The President today announced the appointment of Jack L. Courtemanche to be Deputy Assistant to the President for Public Liaison. He will succeed Jonathan Vipond III.

Since February 1, 1983, Mr. Courtemanche has been serving as Executive Director of the White House Conference on Productivity. Previously he served as president of Crown Coach Corp. in Los Angeles (1979–1983). He was vice president of Mack Trucks, Inc., in Allentown, Pa., 1974–1979.

Mr. Courtemanche is married, has six children, and resides in Washington, D.C. He was born March 9, 1935, in McMinnville, Oreg.

Announcement of the United States Delegation to the Memorial Service for Victims of the Bombing Incident in Rangoon, Burma
October 11, 1983

The President has asked Secretary of Defense Weinberger to head the official American delegation to the October 13 memorial service in Seoul for the Korean victims of the tragic incident in Burma. Other members of the delegation, representing the Government and people of the United States, will include the Deputy Secretary of State Kenneth W. Dam, Army Chief of Staff Gen. John Wickham, the American Ambassador to Korea, Richard L. Walker, the Commander of U.S. Forces Korea, Gen. Robert Sennewald, Congressman Claude Pepper of Florida, and Congressman Tony P. Hall of Ohio.

The United States deplores this vicious attack, as it does acts of terrorism whenever and wherever they occur. The President and all Americans share the grief and the deep sense of loss of the Korean people at the tragic death of these fine public servants. We admired their profound contributions to the relationship between the United States and Korea, and we knew them as friends. We mourn their loss.

Statement by Deputy Press Secretary Speakes on the Intermediate-Range Nuclear Force Negotiations
October 11, 1983

While threats to disrupt the Geneva talks have consistently been part of Soviet propaganda tactics designed to undercut support for planned U.S. INF deployments to Europe, the Soviets have not asked for a recess either in START or INF talks.

For our part the U.S. has made clear that we will stay at the negotiating table in Geneva. We will continue to work for progress, and if the deployment of Pershing and ground-launched cruise missiles has to begin because we have not reached an agreement in the INF negotiations, we will remain at the negotiating table thereafter. In that event, if an equitable agreement to reduce or eliminate U.S. and Soviet LRINF missiles can be reached, the U.S. stands ready to halt its deployments or reverse them.

I should point out that the U.S. has continued to negotiate with the Soviets despite the fact that Soviet deployment of SS–20's has continued unabated. Over 100 Soviet SS–20's with over 300 warheads have become operational since the negotiations began in November 1981.

Note: Deputy Press Secretary Larry M. Speakes read the statement during his daily press briefing for reporters, which began at 1:30 p.m. in the Briefing Room at the White House.

Statement on the Radio Broadcasting to Cuba Act
October 11, 1983

The Radio Broadcasting to Cuba Act (S. 602), which I signed on October 4, 1983, was adopted with broad bipartisan support in the Congress and responds to an important foreign policy initiative of my administration: to break Fidel Castro's monopoly on news and information within Cuba. For the first time in the 25 years of Communist domination of Cuba, the Cuban people will be able to hear the truth, and to hear it in detail, about Cuban domestic and foreign policy. The Cuban people will be in a better position to make Cuba's leaders accountable for their conduct in foreign policy, economic management, and human rights.

I would have preferred to place Radio Marti under the Board for International Broadcasting instead of the Voice of America, because the distinct nature of its mission is akin to that of Radio Free Europe and Radio Liberty. Nevertheless, I am satisfied this legislation will permit the new Cuba service to broadcast programs that promote freedom in Cuba, while maintaining the historic high standards of the Voice of America for accuracy and reliability. This kind of broadcasting is 25 years overdue.

Note: As enacted, S. 602 is Public Law 98–111, approved October 4.

Memorandum on Federal Occupational Safety and Health
October 11, 1983

Memorandum for Heads of Departments and Agencies

Subject: Federal Occupational Safety and Health

The rising number of injury and illness claims from Federal employees has meant increased human suffering, a loss of valuable services from injured employees, and increased costs for compensation payments, which are rapidly approaching a billion dollars each year.

We must make the Federal government an example in occupational safety and health. We cannot allow conditions to exist in our own workplaces which would be unacceptable in the private sector.

On December 9, 1982, I asked you to review your safety program, take every step possible to reduce injuries, and make sure that you and your staff are committed to safety.

In the interest of protecting Federal employees, I am now setting a government-wide goal of three percent per year for the reduction of workplace injuries. The goal will be in effect for five years, starting with Fiscal Year 1984, and will cover both injury and occupational health claims.

Establishing this goal gives us a standard against which to measure progress. Specific goals for agencies will be worked out with the Occupational Safety and Health Administration of the Department of Labor.

I look forward to recognizing your safety and health accomplishments at a Presidential Awards Program next year.

RONALD REAGAN

Toasts of the President and Ambassador Rinaldo Petrignani at the Italian Embassy Luncheon Commemorating Columbus Day
October 12, 1983

Ambassador Petrignani. Mr. President, your presence here today carries an extraordinary political significance and a great symbolic value. With your presence at the Italian Embassy, sir, you honor the country which gave birth to Christopher Columbus. But you also give recognition to the hundreds of thousands, the millions of other Italians who, after Columbus, came to these shores to find on the new continent a land of liberty and equality, a land where to open up wider horizons and offer renewed energy to that fascinating, unique, incomparable human venture which is the Western civilization. America can be proud of those immigrants who contributed in making her so great, so strong, so noble, so idealistic.

The strength of America and the idealism of America, the former at the service of the latter, are a guarantee to all free men, an irreplaceable guarantee for the protection and the expansion of freedom and democracy in this continent, in Europe, in the entire world.

Your gesture today, Mr. President, not only honors us, but it also reveals a generous political vision, and it embodies your personal commitment to the inspiring American concept of an open and pluralistic society. Italian Americans can be proud of what they have achieved and what they represent today in this society, shaped also by their genius and in which they have become prominent in all fields of human endeavor.

Allow me to add, Mr. President, that your presence here on the eve of the official working visit to Washington of the Italian Prime Minister, Bettino Craxi, underlines the great significance which the United States attribute to the friendship of Italy. In a world beset by uncertainties and dangers, as one of your major European partners,

Italy stands by you, bound by common commitment for the defense of peace and security and for the preservation of the precious political values of our common, historic heritage.

Never as in these days has the Atlantic alliance been such an irreplaceable bulwark for upholding the indivisible security of the West. And I would like to think that by paying tribute to Christopher Columbus we pay tribute to a forerunner of this alliance, of this bridge which spans today the two sides of the Atlantic Ocean.

Allow me in concluding, Mr. President, to read to you a message which I have received from the Italian Foreign Minister, Giulio Andreotti: "I have learned with deep appreciation that President Reagan will be present today at the Embassy of Italy in Washington on the occasion of the celebration of Columbus Day. I consider his gesture a token of friendship for the Italian people particularly significant on the eve of the visit to Washington of Prime Minister Craxi. I would like to ask you to convey to the President of the United States whom, as he might recall, I met in Rome in 1972 when he was Governor of California, the expression of my highest esteem and my best personal regards."

Ladies and gentlemen, I would like to ask you to join me in a toast to the President of the United States.

The President. Mr. Ambassador and Mrs. Petrignani and distinguished guests, it's fitting that we should be enjoying this excellent luncheon on Columbus Day in the home of Italy's Ambassador to the United States.

Italy and the United States are closely bound by ties of kinship and culture. The many millions of Americans of Italian descent—indeed, all Americans—are indebted to Italy. The historic and cultural bonds between our two peoples and nations are strengthened by the magnificent contributions Americans of Italian descent have made and are making to our country.

All Americans are aware of their many contributions in the arts, in business, in industry, and in government—accomplishments of which we, as Americans and Italians, are rightfully proud. They are tangible evidence that our brotherhood is one of common achievement, as well as one of soul and blood.

It's particularly fitting that we gather here on a day honoring Christopher Columbus, a remarkable Italian who altered the course of history by exhibiting great moral character and individual courage. Along with Galileo, da Vinci, and other great figures of the Italian Renaissance, Columbus symbolizes a quest for knowledge, a willingness and fortitude to go beyond accepted barriers to progress.

Our precious liberty, so important to Italians and Americans, depends on the quality of character that we honor on Columbus Day. Italy has long been a particularly close and important ally of the United States. In our commitment to genuine arms reductions and to the maintenance of a stable balance of power so necessary for peace, Americans and Italians are of one mind.

Within the NATO alliance, Italy is shouldering increasing responsibility through its commitment to deploy new intermediate-range missiles in Sicily if negotiations with the Soviets do not succeed in banning this category of weapons. In Lebanon, Italian troops have joined American and other forces in the difficult and dangerous task of trying to keep the peace. As constructive Italian involvement in world affairs has grown, so has our admiration and respect for your great nation.

Modern Americans are enjoying the accomplishments made possible by Columbus' initiative and courage. So, on this Columbus Day, please join me in raising our glasses to the first of the many great contributions Italians and their descendants have made to our country.

Thank you very much for having us all here. I appreciate it.

Note: The exchange of toasts began at 1:09 p.m.

Nomination of Frank J. Donatelli To Be an Assistant Administrator of the Agency for International Development
October 12, 1983

The President today announced his intention to nominate Frank J. Donatelli to be an Assistant Administrator of the Agency for International Development (Africa), U.S. International Development Cooperation Agency. He would succeed Francis Stephen Ruddy.

Since 1981 Mr. Donatelli has been an attorney with the law firm of Patton, Boggs & Blow in Washington, D.C. Previously he was with the Reagan-Bush transition in 1980–1981; regional political director for the Reagan for President Committee during the primary and general elections in 1979–1980; campaign manager for the Baker for attorney general campaign in Texas in 1978; and executive director of Young Americans for Freedom in 1973–1977.

Mr. Donatelli graduated from the University of Pittsburgh (B.A., 1971) and American University Law School (J.D., 1976). He is married, has one child, and resides in Alexandria, Va. He was born July 4, 1949, in Pittsburgh, Pa.

Statement on Signing the Multinational Force in Lebanon Resolution
October 12, 1983

I am pleased to sign into law today S.J. Res. 159, the Multinational Force in Lebanon Resolution. This resolution provides important support for the United States presence and policies in Lebanon and facilitates the pursuit of United States interests in that region on the bipartisan basis that has been the traditional hallmark of American foreign policy. In my view, the participation and support of the Congress are exceedingly important on matters of such fundamental importance to our national security interests, particularly where United States Armed Forces have been deployed in support of our policy objectives abroad. I am grateful to those of both political parties who joined in the expression of resolve reflected by the enactment of this resolution, and especially to the bipartisan leadership of Senate Majority Leader Baker, House Speaker O'Neill, House Foreign Affairs Committee Chairman Zablocki, and Senate Foreign Relations Committee Chairman Percy.

The text of this resolution states a number of congressional findings, determinations, and assertions on certain matters. It is, of course, entirely appropriate for Congress to express its views on these subjects in this manner. However, I do not necessarily join in or agree with some of these expressions. For example, with regard to the congressional determination that the requirements of section 4(a)(1) of the War Powers Resolution became operative on August 29, 1983, I would note that the initiation of isolated or infrequent acts of violence against United States Armed Forces does not necessarily constitute actual or imminent involvement in hostilities, even if casualties to those forces result. I think it reasonable to recognize the inherent risk and imprudence of setting any precise formula for making such determinations.

However, complete accord on such debatable issues is less important than the process that has taken place and the bipartisan policy goals that have been articulated.

We must not let disagreements on interpretation or issues of institutional powers prevent us from expressing our mutual goals to the citizens of our nation and the world. I therefore sign this resolution in full support of its policies, but with reservations about some of the specific congressional expressions.

There have been historic differences between the legislative and executive branches of government with respect to the wisdom and constitutionality of section 5(b) of the War Powers Resolution. That section purports to require termination of the use of United States Armed Forces in actual hostilities or situations in which imminent involvement in hostilities is clearly indicated by the circumstances unless Congress, within 60 days, enacts a specific authorization for that use or otherwise extends the 60-day period. In light of these historic differences, I would like to emphasize my view that the imposition of such arbitrary and inflexible deadlines creates unwise limitations on Presidential authority to deploy United States Forces in the interests of United States national security. For example, such deadlines can undermine foreign policy judgments, adversely affect our ability to deploy United States Armed Forces in support of these judgments, and encourage hostile elements to maximize United States casualties in connection with such deployments.

I believe it is, therefore, important for me to state, in signing this resolution, that I do not and cannot cede any of the authority vested in me under the Constitution as President and as Commander in Chief of United States Armed Forces. Nor should my signing be viewed as any acknowledgment that the President's constitutional authority can be impermissibly infringed by statute, that congressional authorization would be required if and when the period specified in section 5(b) of the War Powers Resolution might be deemed to have been triggered and the period had expired, or that section 6 of the Multinational Force in Lebanon Resolution may be interpreted to revise the President's constitutional authority to deploy United States Armed Forces. Let me underscore, however, that any differences we may have over institutional prerogatives will in no way diminish my intention to proceed in the manner outlined in my letter of September 27, 1983, to achieve the important bipartisan goals reflected in this resolution.

Indeed, I am convinced that congressional support for the continued participation of United States Forces alongside those of France, Italy, and the United Kingdom helped bring about the recent cease-fire and the start of the reconciliation process in Lebanon. The security and the stability of the Beirut area and the successful process of national reconciliation are essential to the achievement of United States policy objectives in Lebanon, as stated in the resolution. It is my fervent hope and belief that this reaffirmation of the support of the executive and legislative branches for the Government of Lebanon and for our partners in the multinational force will promote a lasting peace and hasten the return home of our Armed Forces.

Note: As enacted, S.J. Res. 159 is Public Law 98–119, approved October 12.

Statement on the 25th Anniversary of the Technical Cooperation Program
October 13, 1983

I am pleased today to congratulate Prime Minister Thatcher and the British people on the silver anniversary of the Technical Cooperation Program. It was due to the foresight of President Eisenhower and Prime Minister MacMillan that the program was established and given the high-level government support required for its initial impetus. Immediately afterwards, Canada joined, followed by Australia and New Zealand, in 1965 and 1969 respectively.

Today, we in the United States and our friends in the United Kingdom, Canada, Australia, and New Zealand lead a more secure existence as a result of this cooperative effort. The primary purpose of the program has remained as originally expressed in the Declaration of Common Purpose by President Eisenhower and Prime Minister MacMillan: that no member country possessed the resources to provide adequate defense research and development by itself and each must assist the other by sharing resources and tasks in many fields so that progress and security can be found by all.

I remain committed to the principle of cooperation in resolving all international problems. The Technical Cooperation Program is a good example of cooperation and the results that can be obtained from it.

Remarks at a White House Ceremony Marking the Beginning of the National Partnerships in Education Program
October 13, 1983

The President. Secretary Bell and Assistant Secretary Korb,[1] ladies and gentlemen, good afternoon and welcome. It's a pleasure to have you all here. I confess I get a little nervous with so many presidents and chief executive officers in the room. Who's tending the store? [*Laughter*]

May I also say hello to those who are joining us by way of closed-circuit television—the students and teachers of the Congress Heights Elementary School here in Washington. It's good to be talking to Congress Heights and to welcome all of you here for this important ceremony here at the White House. It's a home that belongs to you and to all Americans.

America's always had a love affair with learning. From polished men of letters like Thomas Jefferson to humble self-taught people like Abe Lincoln and from inventors like Thomas Edison to visionaries like Martin Luther King, Americans have put their faith in the power of education to enrich lives and to make our nation strong. We see the evidence of this in many fine schools, like Congress Heights, with thousands of dedicated superintendents, principals, and teachers. But we also face tremendous problems.

Between 1963 and 1980, Scholastic Aptitude Test scores were in a virtually unbroken decline. Too many of our States demanded too little of their students, imposing lax graduation requirements. And compared to students in other industrialized nations, many of ours performed badly. Yet even as we've recognized the challenge, our nation has begun to respond.

One of our administration's first priorities was to establish a National Commission on Excellence in Education. And we asked it to help us chart a new course that would permit us to correct the mistakes of the

---

[1] *Secretary of Education Terrel H. Bell and Lawrence J. Korb, Assistant Secretary of Defense for Manpower, Installations and Logistics.*

past. Even before the Commission released its report, grassroots America had begun to move. Since 1980 no fewer than 20 States have passed tougher certification laws so that only fully qualified teachers can enter the classroom. In about the same period, more than half the school districts in the country have raised the number of credits they require in such basics as English, science, and math. And 38 percent more school districts will upgrade their standards by 1985.

Throughout the land, parents, teachers, and school officials have begun vigorous work to improve the fundamentals—not fancy budget structures, not frills in the curriculum, but teaching and learning. To quote Secretary Bell: "What's going on now represents the greatest, most far-reaching, and most promising reform and renewal of education since the turn of the century." One aspect of this great renewal is the reason we're gathered here today.

Across the country groups of working men and women have been forming partnerships with schools—partnerships in dedication. To form a partnership, volunteers from a business, a government agency, or other organization strike an agreement with a school to develop programs that will help the school's students in a number of basic ways. The volunteers might tutor students, establish scholarship funds, donate furnishings and equipment, or teach classes.

In Dallas over a thousand businesses have formed partnerships with 175 schools, and in Chicago, 133 organizations have formed partnerships with 140 schools. San Diego's schools benefit from partnerships with groups including the Chargers and the Padres and the United States Navy. One way the Navy helps students in San Diego, incidentally, is by arranging for pen pals. And I can't imagine anything that sparks a volunteer's—or a youngster's imagination, I should say, more than a letter from a sailor describing far-off lands or islands in the South Pacific or even a sunrise at sea.

But let's remember, all those partnerships already established still involve only a few thousand American schools out of a total of some 110,000. So, today I'm issuing a challenge to America to ensure our children get the education they deserve. Let us resolve that every one of our country's public, private, and parochial schools and community colleges—all 110,000 of them—will have formed a partnership in education. The goal is lofty, but well within the reach of the Nation that can send men to the Moon.

I know that this room is filled with men and women from business and education who've helped create partnerships in education in their communities. To you, on behalf of all Americans, thank you: large companies like Xerox, IBM, Federal Express, General Motors, and CNA Insurance; organizations like the American Bar Association, the Professional Engineering Societies, and the National Association of Manufacturers; and let's not forget the smaller companies like thousands of Burger King restaurants, local Radio Shack stores, and the group and cable TV stations. There're, also, innovative programs in private schools like Philadelphia's parochial schools and Providence-St. Mel in Chicago. And to the leaders of the three TV networks who are here today, thank you for your commitment to partnerships in education.

But we all know there's much more to be done. Everyone must get involved. So, I'm directing the Federal Government to promote partnerships in education in every way that it can. Last week I signed a proclamation naming the 1983–84 school year the National Year of Partnerships in Education. My Special Assistant you met here, Jim Coyne, and his staff will work on the program throughout the year. They'll be working with State governments, industry organizations, business associations, and other groups, and working with a nationwide computer system called DATA/NET to help schools and partners get together.

I intend to sign a memorandum asking the heads of all departments and agencies of the Federal Government to follow the example of those sailors in San Diego by forming their own partnerships with local schools. Now, this won't be an expensive new government program. It'll be human

and effective with thousands of men and women whose jobs range from designing satellites to building our bridges and highways, joining those in the private sector to lend a hand to our nation's schools.

Now, I understand that the principal of Congress Heights Elementary School is here with us. Bill Dalton, would you please join me, come up here?

Mr. Dalton, all of you watching at Congress Heights, I have a surprise for you. You were told that closed-circuit TV's put in your school were there because WJLA Television here in Washington was going to form a partnership with you. Well, that wasn't quite right. With your permission, Mr. Dalton, it's the White House which would like to form a partnership with your school.

Mr. Dalton. Thank you very much.

The President. We'd like to pitch in at Congress Heights, tutoring, showing students how the White House works, helping them further develop their academic skills, and talking to them about our jobs here and the careers that we had before we came here. And by the way, if there's anybody interested in lifeguarding, sports announcing on radio, or—[*laughter*]—movie acting, I'd be happy to help, too. [*Laughter*] I didn't mention one of the better jobs that I've had, which was washing dishes in the girls dormitory. [*Laughter*]

And finally, let me just say a word to you, the students at Congress Heights. You don't have to take notes, because I promise not to give a pop quiz. You've probably heard a lot about the importance of dwindling resources. Well, I want you to know that our greatest resource is the human mind, and it isn't dwindling at all. There's no limit to the human capacity for intelligence, imagination, and wonder. And that's why giving all of you a good education is so very important.

Just a hundred years ago, in the time of our great-grandmothers and great-grandfathers, oil was nothing but so much sticky, smelly fluid. And it was the invention of the internal combustion engine that turned oil into a resource, and today oil fuels the world economy.

Just 10 years ago, around the time many

of you were born, sand was nothing but the stuff that deserts are made of. Today we use sand to make silicon chips that guide satellites through the infinite reaches of space.

So, remember, in this vast and beautiful land that God has given us, it's not what's inside the Earth that counts, but what's inside your hearts and minds, because that's the stuff that dreams are made of. And America's future is in your dreams. Make them come true.

Thank you all very much. God bless you.

Note: The President spoke at 1:49 p.m. in the East Room at the White House.

Proclamation 5116—Lupus Awareness Week, 1983
October 13, 1983

By the President of the United States of America

A Proclamation

Systemic lupus erthematosus (also known as lupus, or SLE) is a serious, potentially fatal, connective tissue disease that can affect many different organs of the body. More than 500,000 Americans are estimated to have lupus, approximately 90 percent of whom are women. The disease usually begins in adolescence or young adult life.

Scientists believe that lupus is caused by disturbances in the body's immune system; hormonal abnormalities and genetic factors also seem to be important. In its systemic form, the disease may involve the skin, joints, kidneys, heart, lungs and brain, in varying combinations.

The outlook for victims of lupus has been improving in recent years. The survival rate has increased as a result of greater awareness of the disease, improved diagnostic methods, and more effective treatments. However, new research findings and new approaches to diagnosis and improved treatment are urgently needed to eliminate lupus as a cause of human suffering. The Federal government and private voluntary organizations have developed a strong, enduring partnership committed to lupus research. I am confident that this cooperation will hasten the time when the cause and cure for the disease will be found.

In recognition of the progress being made in research, diagnostic methods and effective treatments for the cure and alleviation of lupus, and the need for greater public awareness of this disease, the Congress, by Senate Joint Resolution 102, has authorized and requested the President to proclaim the week of October 16 through October 22, 1983, as "Lupus Awareness Week."

Now, Therefore, I, Ronald Reagan, President of the United States of America, do hereby proclaim the week of October 16 through October 22, 1983, as "Lupus Awareness Week," and I call upon the people of the United States to observe this week with appropriate ceremonies and activities.

In Witness Whereof, I have hereunto set my hand this 13th. day of October, in the year of our Lord nineteen hundred and eighty-three, and of the Independence of the United States of America the two hundred and eighth.

RONALD REAGAN

[*Filed with the Office of the Federal Register, 4:29 p.m., October 13, 1983*]

Proclamation 5117—National Farm-City Week, 1983
October 13, 1983

By the President of the United States of America

A Proclamation

The Nation's farms and cities provide the framework for American economic and social life. Each serves as the economic lifeline for the other.

Farms provide the basic food, fiber, and timber for consumer needs. The rural countryside also provides watersheds, and natural environment for clear water and clean air, outdoor recreation, open spaces, and landscapes. The cities sustain industry, services, cultural centers, and house 97 percent of the population.

Each year the people of our farms and cities pause during Farm-City Week to reflect on their interdependence and the strength and vitality that each brings to our national life. It is appropriate that Farm-City Week comes near Thanksgiving, the traditional time since Colonial days for Americans to reflect on the rich bounty of the harvest. As a people we are indeed blessed to live in a land with a plentiful supply of wholesome food.

In a short period of time, the United States has developed from an agricultural economy with scattered rural outposts, clinging to life in the New World, to an efficient production system in which only three percent of the Nation's people feed and clothe the entire population. This rapid growth has been made possible through the unparalleled productivity and cooperation of farm and city people working in close harmony.

In order that farm and city people may continue to reflect on the benefits of mutual support, and to show their grateful appreciation for their combined efforts, the American people have traditionally set aside a week each year to pay tribute to farm-city people.

Now, Therefore, I, Ronald Reagan, President of the United States of America, do hereby proclaim the period November 18 through November 24, 1983, as National Farm-City Week. I call upon all Americans, in rural areas and in cities alike, to join in recognizing the accomplishments of our productive farm families and of our urban residents in working together in a spirit of cooperation and interdependence to create bounty, wealth, and strength for the Nation.

In Witness Whereof, I have hereunto set my hand this 13th day of Oct., in the year of our Lord nineteen hundred and eighty-three, and of the Independence of the United States of America the two hundred and eighth.

RONALD REAGAN

[*Filed with the Office of the Federal Register, 4:30 p.m., October 13, 1983*]

Remarks and a Question-and-Answer Session With Women Leaders of Christian Religious Organizations
October 13, 1983

The President. Thank you all very much, and good afternoon. And thank you also for honoring us by coming by here today. I'm very grateful to have this chance to speak with you. Many groups come to visit here, but I believe yours is the first leadership group of Christian women to be welcomed to the White House in a long, long time, and I'm glad to be the one that's doing the greeting. I won't speculate why this hasn't been done before. I only know that as long as I'm President, your group and others who stand up for our Judeo-Christian values will be welcome here, because you belong here.

I can't say strongly enough what a tremendous force for good you are. As lifebearers, carrying on traditions of family in the home, but also in our schools, the corporate world, in the workplace, you're teachers of cooperation, tolerance, compassion, and responsibility. No greater truth shines through than the one you live by every day: that preserving America must begin with faith in the God who has blessed our land. And we don't have the answers; He does.

Isaiah reminded us that "The Lord opens His gates and keeps in peace the nation that trusts in Him." I hope you won't mind my saying I think I know you all very well. Nelle Reagan, my mother, God rest her soul, had an unshakable faith in God's goodness. And while I may not have realized it in my youth, I know now that she planted that faith very deeply in me. She made the most difficult Christian message seem very easy. And, like you, she knew you could never repay one bad deed with another. Her way was forgiveness and goodness, and both began with love.

For some time now I believe that America has been hungering for a return to spiritual values that some of us fear we've tended to forget—things like faith, families, family values, the bedrock of our nation. Thanks to the creation of new networks of faith by so many of you and your families, we're seeing more clearly again. We're remembering that freedom carries responsibilities. And we're not set free so that we can become slaves to sin.

The Founding Fathers believed that faith in God was the key to our being a good people and America's becoming a great nation. George Washington kissed the Bible at his inauguration. And to those who would have government separate us from religion, he had these words: "Reason and experience both forbid us to expect that national morality can prevail in exclusion of religious principle." And Ben Franklin, at the time when they were struggling with what was to be the American Constitution, finally one day said to those who were working with him that, "Without God's help, we shall succeed in this political building no better than the builders of Babel." And if we ever forget that, we're lost. From that day on

they opened all of the constitutional meetings with prayer.

I pray that we won't lose that idea, and that's why I was motivated to proclaim or designate 1983 the Year of the Bible.

And I hope that we will also recognize the true meaning of the first amendment. Its words were meant to guarantee freedom of religion to everyone. But I believe the first amendment has been twisted to the point that freedom of religion is in danger of becoming freedom from religion. But keep the faith. This year the Supreme Court took two big steps toward common sense. [*Laughter*] It said that the first amendment does not prevent legislators in the Nebraska State Assembly from hiring a chaplain to open their sessions with prayer. And it said the Constitution does not prevent the State of Minnesota from giving a tax break to parents who choose private or religious schooling for their children. In both cases the Court decided in favor of what our Justice Department recommended in friend of the court briefs.

Now we're making another recommendation. We believe the city of Pawtucket, Rhode Island, and for that matter, any city in America, has the right to include the Nativity scene as part of its annual Christmas performance.

Government is not supposed to wage war against God and religion, not in the United States of America. I want to see the Congress act on our constitutional amendment permitting voluntary prayer in America's schoolrooms. And here you can be our greatest help. Tell the millions of our friends to send a message of thunder from the grassroots, fill the halls of Congress with calls, with letters and telegrams—not postcards. I understand they don't take postcards as seriously as they take letters. [*Laughter*] And tell them, "The people have waited too long; we want action."

We think it's also time for a vote on tuition tax credits. Education's the fundamental right and responsibility of every parent. And we should remember that those who pay private tuition also pay their full share of taxes to support the public school system. Tuition tax credits would only threaten public schools if you believe that more competition, greater parental choice, and stronger local control will make our schools worse, not better.

Finally, let me just say a few words about another part of freedom that is under siege: the sanctity of human life. Either the law protects human beings, or it doesn't. When we're dealing with a handicapped child—say, a mentally retarded baby girl who needs medical care to survive, is she not entitled to the protection of the law? Will she be denied her chance for love and life because someone decides she's too weak to warrant our help, or because someone has taken it upon themselves to decide the quality of her life doesn't justify keeping her alive? Is that not God's decision to make? And isn't it our duty to serve even the least of these for in so doing, we serve Him?

Our administration has tried to make sure the handicapped receive the respect of the law for the dignity of their lives. And the same holds true, I believe deeply, for the unborn. It may not help me in some polls to say this publicly, but until and unless it can be proven that the unborn child is not a living human being—and I don't think it can be proven—then we must protect the right of the unborn to life, liberty, and the pursuit of happiness.

Now, I've been talking longer than I intended, because I had a little something else to suggest here. But hardly a day goes by that I'm not told—sometimes in letters and sometimes by people that I meet and perfect strangers—and they tell me that they're praying for me. Well, thanks to Nelle Reagan, I believe in intercessionary prayer. And I know that those prayers are giving me a strength that I otherwise would not possess.

I believe in the goodness of our people. And yet, I wonder if we shouldn't be reminded of the promise in Second Chronicles: "If my people which are called by my name shall humble themselves and pray, and seek my face, and turn from their wicked ways, then I will hear from heaven and will forgive their sin and heal their land."

Well, now, I'm not going to say anything else for a little bit in the line of talking, because I just thought we might have a dialog. I know I only have a few minutes here to be with you. But sometime, some of you must have said, "If I had a chance, I would ask him—" [*Laughter*] So, why don't you ask me?

Yes?

The Supreme Court

Q. Mr. President, I was very interested—and if you had noticed, I was the first one to laugh and applaud when you mentioned the Supreme Court. I'm very concerned about the Supreme Court—nine unelected officials with no expiration date other than death, legislating morality in this country, abortion being the prime topic. Could you address that, please?

The President. Well, yes. I think we have to face the fact that there are too many times when the Court does not interpret the law, but does legislate. And I think then it is up to the people through their elected representatives to such as an amendment with regard to prayer in schools, an amendment regarding abortion, to correct that with law.

We're separated into three branches of government, and we're supposed to be blessed with checks and balances. And I don't suppose there's ever a time that one branch or the other doesn't try to seize more authority than it should have. Then it's up to those checks and balances to go to work. And I believe we've been through a period in which the Court has tended to legislate rather than interpret.

Q. The part that concerns me so much is that, you know, a lot of people say, well, we can't have prayer in schools, we can't do these things that are our God-given right, and yet, they are legislating to the other side, in other words, to the negative side——

The President. Yes.

Q. ——and to the sinful way. And they're calling—I mean, God calls abortion murder. That's what He calls it.

The President. Well, as a matter of fact, I have challenged sometimes that maybe those of us who are trying for a constitutional amendment or something, maybe we've missed an opportunity. And that is the thing that I mentioned in my remarks.

The Constitution protects life, liberty and so forth. And all we need to do, I think, is demand that someone either prove to us that the unborn is not a living being, or then recognize that it is already entitled to consitutional protection. And we have such dichotomy in the law.

Just recently there was a man arrested in Virginia. He has been tried for, believe it or not, feticide. What happened, he was robbing a public place, and a woman evidenced that—a young lady—that she perhaps recognized him, and he shot her in cold blood. He wounded her but killed the baby that she was carrying. Now, under the law, he is now arrested, not charged with wounding her, charged with killing the unborn child. Now, how can we rule that she could have killed the unborn child if she wanted to, and it was called abortion?

And I know in our own State of California that there was a case where a man beat his common law wife so severely that her unborn child was killed. And the legislature of California some years ago unanimously and almost instantaneously passed a law that anyone who maltreats a woman with child to the extent of causing the death of the unborn child shall be tried for murder. Now, if it's murder, then it's murder all the way.

Mrs. Reagan

Q. Mr. President, would you please convey to the First Lady that our prayers are with her for her continued strength, that she's a great First Lady—[*inaudible*].

The President. Thank you. I will. And may I put your mind at ease that some of those rumors that started out—yes, she has lost some weight. She—a death in her family that affected her greatly when her father died, her mother's illness, and she had lost some weight. But she caught cold. [*Laughter*] And I can assure you she was in New York yesterday to appear for 2 hours on the "Good Morning America" show with regard to drug abuse.

No, she's feeling fine, and all the rumors, I guess, when there isn't any real news, you pick rumors. [*Laughter*]

Women's Issues

Q. Mr. President, are you planning between now and election time to have a couple of televised, well-publicized televised portions on—that will show what you have done for women in the United States? We think your record is fantastic, but the grassroots voter is not hearing it because the press is only giving them the feminist view, and we want everybody to hear the truth. And I think we need to have it right directly from you.

The President. Believe me, I don't know—[*applause*]—thank you. I don't know just what procedure we're going to use to do this, but I have to tell you that I think our record with regard to what we have done for women is probably one of the best kept secrets in Washington.

They've just signaled me that—I'm getting the signal that—does that mean one more or——

Ms. Whittlesey.[1] One more.

The President. All right. Why don't we go down here and then——

Year of the Bible Proclamation

Q. Mr. President, sir, I want to thank you for proclaiming 1983 as the Year of the Bible, and I think I can speak for all Christians everywhere. But there is something in that proclamation that was a little bit unsettling, and I'd like for you to explain it to me. It said that the world is facing a tremendous challenge in the next decade. And more important than armament, than the resources of armament, more important than the resources of technology, and more important than the resources of education is resources of spirit. And I'd like to know what you mean by—that's the most important thing facing us.

The President. Well, because of what I said, I think, in my remarks here—I have believed for a long time that we got off the track and our young people got off the track. And we saw a period in the generation gap where young people were discarding all the tried-and-true values upon which civilization has been based. And the only reason for discarding them was that they were old. And I then began saying that I

———

[1] *Faith Ryan Whittlesey, Assistant to the President for Public Liaison.*

sensed that there was a hunger in America for a spiritual revival.

And I think that—yes, all the things that we may want to do—all the strength of military and so forth—all of these things are useless if we as a people are not dedicated to those values. And the basic values—and, believe me, I don't want a war and I believe that if we have the right kind of military with the right strength, they will never have to use the science they have learned. But the great values that make for civilization are the values for which people have always been willing to die. And that we must have.

I have to cut off the questions now, but do you mind just sitting for a minute while I take advantage of you and deliver a news note here, an announcement for the press that is present?

It's not often that I have a chance to be the first with some news. [*Laughter*] It usually leaks before I get around to it. But I want to share with you a decision that I've just made.

Secretary of the Interior

After examining the records of more than two dozen fine, potential nominees for the position of Secretary of the Interior, I have decided to turn once again to someone who has been a troubleshooter and a result-oriented professional. So, it is with a good deal of pleasure that I tell you that I have asked my Assistant for National Security Affairs, Judge Bill Clark, to be my nominee for this Cabinet position. He is a God-fearing westerner, fourth generation rancher, and a person I trust. And I think he will be a great Secretary of the Interior. And may I just tell you, I think he is succeeding a very fine Secretary of the Interior.

Note: The President spoke at 5:10 p.m. in Room 450 of the Old Executive Office Building.

Nomination of William P. Clark To Be Secretary of the Interior
October 13, 1983

The President today announced his intention to nominate William P. Clark to be Secretary of the Interior.

Mr. Clark has been serving as Assistant to the President for National Security Affairs since February 1982. He joined the Reagan administration in March of 1981 as Deputy Secretary of State.

From 1973 to 1981, Mr. Clark was an associate justice on the California State Supreme Court. He was appointed to the court by Governor Reagan. From 1971 to 1973 Mr. Clark was an associate justice for the California Court of Appeals. As an appellate justice, his decisions included those affecting land management and conservation issues. Previously he served as a judge for the Superior Court of California from 1969 to 1971.

From 1967 to 1969, Mr. Clark was chief of staff to Governor Reagan in Sacramento. He was responsible for the reorganization of the executive branch of State government. Mr. Clark dealt extensively with several departments of the Federal Government's executive branch as well as the congressional delegation from California.

From 1959 to 1969, he was senior partner with the law firm of Clark, Cole and Fairfield in Oxnard, Calif. Following World War II, he served in the Counter Intelligence Corps in Western Europe.

Mr. Clark attended Stanford and Santa Clara Universities and Loyola Night Law School. He is a rancher and fourth generation Californian. His father, grandfather, and great-grandfather were each ranchers. He is married to the former Joan Brauner, and they have five children. He was born October 23, 1931.

Nomination of William E. Mayer To Be an Assistant Secretary of Defense
October 14, 1983

The President today announced his intention to nominate William E. Mayer to be an Assistant Secretary of Defense (Health Affairs). He would succeed John Howard Moxley III.

Dr. Mayer is presently serving as Administrator for the Alcohol, Drug Abuse, and Mental Health Administration in Rockville, Md. Previously, he was medical director of the San Diego County Department of Health Services in 1980–1981; Chief of the U.S. Army Alcoholism Treatment Facility, Germany, in 1977–1980; associate clinical professor of psychiatry at the University of California in 1975–1977; chief deputy director of health and director, California State Department of Health, in 1973–1975; chief deputy director of mental hygiene and director, California State Department of Mental Hygiene, in 1971–1973; and director of community (county) mental health programs in Contra Costa, Humboldt, and Del Norte Counties, Calif., in 1965–1971.

He graduated from Northwestern University (B.S., 1943) and the University of Washington (B.M., 1946; M.D., 1947). He is married, has four children, and resides in Bethesda, Md. He was born September 24, 1923, in Chicago, Ill.

Message to the Congress Transmitting the Aeronautics and Space Report of the President
October 14, 1983

I am pleased to transmit this report of the Nation's progress in space and aeronautics during calendar 1982, *Aeronautics and Space Report of the President, 1982 Activities*. It is provided in accordance with Section 206 of the National Aeronautics and Space Act of 1958, as amended (42 U.S.C. 2476).

Inauguration of operational flights of the Space Transportation System in 1982 promises greatly broadened contributions from space now and for the Nation's future. Following the Shuttle's earlier test flights, which carried scientific experiments into space as well as the first Department of Defense payload, the first operational mission delivered two commercial satellites to orbit, demonstrating that the Space Shuttle provides practical, utilitarian, round-trip access to space.

Other space projects expanded vital civil and military communications, weather observation, earth resources monitoring, and studies of life sciences, the earth, the sun, and the universe—supporting the national space policy goals I enunciated in July 1982.

In outlining the space policy, I reaffirmed the United States commitment to explore and use space for the national well-being and to maintain U.S. leadership in space transportation, space science, applications, and technology.

Aeronautics projects in 1982 advanced new technology for both civil and military aircraft and supported the strong aeronautical industry essential to the Nation's security and economy. Research in basic technology continued to uphold U.S. leadership in aviation.

The Nation can be proud of these and other achievements reported for 1982.

RONALD REAGAN

The White House,
October 14, 1983.

Note: The report is entitled "Aeronautics and Space Report of the President, 1982 Activities—National Aeronautics and Space Administration" (Government Printing Office, 102 pages).

Remarks on Signing the World Food Day Proclamation
October 14, 1983

Senator Thurmond, Congressman—please, sit down—*[laughter]*—Congressman Gilman, and ladies and gentlemen:

Welcome to the White House. Today we pause to observe World Food Day, marking the anniversary of the founding of the Food and Agriculture Organization of the United Nations back in 1945. The FAO, of which the United States is a founding member, was conceived as the focal point of civilization's fight to eliminate poverty-related hunger—an admirable and worthwhile goal.

World Food Day serves to remind us that we have a long way to go to achieve what mankind set out to do. Today, more than 450 million people in the developing countries are undernourished. One child in four born in developing countries may die before the age of 5 because of malnutrition. Each year as many as 100,000 young children reportedly may go blind because of a lack of vitamin A in their daily diets. The statistics are grim; yet all Americans can be proud of our country's continuing efforts to battle world hunger.

For nearly three decades, we've carried out the largest food aid program in history. Begun under President Eisenhower, the Food for Peace program has provided over $40 billion in aid to developing countries, more food assistance than given by all the other countries combined. And in addition to funding Food for Peace at $1½ billion for this fiscal year, we're taking new steps to devote more government food stocks to the needy overseas.

So far this year, we've already given over 83,000 tons of butter, cheese, and nonfat dry milk to 14 different countries. Our food and assistance efforts are especially vital in Africa, where drought has devastated farms throughout the sub-Saharan part of the continent. We have earmarked $25 million in emergency food assistance for these drought-stricken nations and increased our economic assistance to the continent by over $80 million, bringing it to an all-time high of nearly $1 billion for this fiscal year.

Traditionally, the United States has also always been the foremost supporter of multilateral aid. We've already given well over $1 billion worth of food to the World Food Program. And just last year, this administration increased the U.S. pledge by 14 percent to a new record of $250 million.

At the same time, we make the largest single contribution to many international organizations concerned with hunger, including the Food and Agriculture Organization, the World Food Program, and the international development banks. We were there to help found these organizations, and we stand firmly with them today.

It's not just our government programs of which we can be proud. There are numerous American religious and philanthropic groups, supported by voluntary contributions, which are playing a significant role in our battle against hunger—groups like CARE, Catholic Relief Services, Lutheran World Relief, the American Jewish Distribution Committee—all represent the best of the American tradition of personal involvement.

Whether through government-sponsored programs or through the efforts of churches and private charities, America and Americans lead the way in this humanitarian endeavor. I would hope that those who criticize the United States would take time to compare our efforts with those of Communist nations, countries that so loudly proclaim their concern for the downtrodden.

Soviet efforts in the area of humanitarian relief are virtually nonexistent. I challenge the Kremlin to explain why it refuses to provide anything but weapons of destruction to the underdeveloped world. One explanation, of course, is that the Soviet system is incapable of producing enough food for its own population, much less enough to help others in need. What this points to is the undeniable relationship between free enterprise and material abundance, between freedom and caring.

Our agriculture system is made up of millions of people and a host of enterprises. It includes farmers, processors, distributors, transporters, retailers, storage operators, packagers, advertisers, and many others. It's still a system based on the profit motive and on the freedom of those involved to operate as they see fit.

It's this special *x* factor that makes our food system the most productive in the world and the gem of our economy. With less than three-tenths of 1 percent of the world's farmers and farm workers, we produce 65 percent of the world's soybeans, 48 percent of the corn, 32 percent of the sorghum, 25 percent of the oranges, 31 percent of the poultry, 26 percent of the beef, and you can go on down the line with the other products the same.

Today, wheat grown in the Midwest is eaten as pasta in Italy. Our soybeans make soy sauce used in the Orient. Our cottonseed is pressed into oil and shipped to Venezuela, and our grain is consumed in the Soviet Union.

Along with food, we have been more than willing to share our expertise in this vital area of agriculture. Over 70,000 agriculturalists have come to us for training, and we have technical assistance projects in 76 countries.

But food and technical assistance will not solve the problem in the long run. I pointed out at the Cancún Economic Summit 2 years ago that development of the private sector and the potential for trade is essential for economic progress either in industry or agriculture. We'll continue to help the hungry in every way we can. But let's remember that government repression, mismanagement, and corruption have created as much deprivation and hunger as drought and other natural disasters. Lasting progress in the battle against hunger to a large degree depends on freeing the productive forces needed to produce a better way of life.

Finally, let me add that we're committed not only to fight hunger in the world but to eliminate it anywhere it exists in our own country. Food and help are available to anyone who is hungry in America, and we intend to make sure the information on how to get it is available to all. I know there was some criticism when I announced a commission on hunger. And there was criticism that, "Well, did I mean that we weren't able to see a hungry person?" No, that commission, I've just explained what it is for. There is no need or reason for hunger anywhere in America. And what we need to find out is, is there some problem with the administration of our distribution or are there people out there who don't know where the sources are if they are in need and in hunger. And that's what we're trying to find out. Because we are providing all that is necessary to make sure that there need be no hunger in this country of ours and as little hunger in the world as we can help alleviate.

And with that said, I will now sign the proclamation.

Note: The President spoke at 1:15 p.m. in the East Room at the White House.

Proclamation 5118—World Food Day, 1983
October 14, 1983

By the President of the United States of America

A Proclamation

An adequate, wholesome food supply is essential to the physical and economic well-being of every individual and every nation. Countries throughout the world are dedicated to eliminating poverty-related hunger to the fullest extent possible. Although this objective is widely acknowledged, the resources and policies needed to achieve that object vary widely from country to country.

This Nation is richly endowed with natural resources. Through the generations, our people have developed the knowledge, the technology, the policies, and the economic system to transform our endowment into agricultural abundance. Not all nations are similarly endowed. Hunger persists throughout the world. The Food and Agriculture Organization of the United Nations estimates that as many as 500 million people suffer from poverty-related malnutrition, especially in lesser developed countries.

The United States has a long tradition of sharing its agricultural abundance with those in need. We are strongly committed to the constitution of the Food and Agriculture Organization, which calls upon member nations to "raise the levels of nutrition and standards of living of the peoples under their respective jurisdiction" and to contribute to "expanding the world economy and ensuring humanity's freedom from hunger." We have sought, and will continue to strive, to improve the economies and food production abilities of those countries where the need is greatest.

To this end, the United States has provided needy nations more than $40 billion of assistance under the Food for Peace Program since 1954. This year alone our food aid activities are assisting 70 countries. We are training an average of more than 2,000 agriculturalists per year from developing countries, and we are providing technical assistance to 50 nations in Asia, Africa, and Latin America to help develop their food research and production capabilities. In addition, we actively encourage American businesses to invest in projects that help build the agricultural economies of developing countries.

The people of the United States, as well as the people of other countries that have joined in the battle against hunger, can justifiably share a sense of accomplishment in the fact that food production per person has increased 21 percent in lesser developed countries since 1954. The concern of the international community with the problem of poverty-related malnutrition is reflected in the response to World Food Day. We particularly salute the Food and Agriculture Organization which, on World Food Day this year, celebrates 30 years of dedication to the elimination of hunger and malnutrition.

In recognition of one of the key recommendations of the 1980 report of the Presidential Commission on World Hunger, that called for efforts to be taken to increase public awareness of the world hunger problem, the Congress of the United States, by Senate Joint Resolution 81, has designated October 16, 1983, as "World Food Day" and has requested the President to issue a proclamation in observance of that day.

Now, Therefore, I, Ronald Reagan, President of the United States of America, do hereby proclaim October 16, 1983, as World Food Day and call upon the people of the United States to observe that day with appropriate activities to explore ways in which our Nation can further contribute to the elimination of hunger in the world.

In Witness Whereof, I have hereunto set my hand this fourteenth day of October, in the year of our Lord nineteen hundred and eighty-three, and of the Independence of the United States of America the two hundred and eighth.

RONALD REAGAN

[*Filed with the Office of the Federal Register, 4:38 p.m., October 14, 1983*]

Statement on Signing the Federal Anti-Tampering Act
October 14, 1983

Last year about this time, the Nation was shaken by the Tylenol tragedy in Chicago.

Seven people lost their lives as a result of that vile and reprehensible act of product tampering. The repercussions of that tragedy were felt far beyond the boundaries of Chicago, however, as every American became keenly aware of the tremendous harm that can be done by a single deranged person.

Although the FBI was heavily involved in the investigation of the Chicago tragedy, the Department of Justice quickly realized that Federal jurisdiction in such cases was questionable and that Federal law only provided misdemeanor sanctions for product tampering. During the 97th Congress, Senator Strom Thurmond steered through the Senate legislation to establish tough Federal sanctions for product tampering. Unfortunately, Senator Thurmond's bill was ultimately added to a defective House bill which I found it necessary to disapprove in January.

In this Congress I included similar legislation as part of the Comprehensive Crime Control Act, which I submitted to Congress on March 16th of this year. In addition, Senator Thurmond reintroduced separately his product tampering legislation as S. 216 in the Senate, and Representatives Bill Hughes and Hal Sawyer introduced similar legislation in the House. S. 216 was recently approved by the Congress.

S. 216 establishes Federal criminal jurisdiction over tampering with foods, drugs, cosmetics, and other consumer products. The maximum penalty for such product tampering, where it results in death, would be imprisonment for any term of years up to life plus a fine of $100,000. We believe this will put real teeth into Federal law and provide a meaningful deterrent to product tampering.

I cannot, however, let this occasion pass without noting that much more needs to be done by way of criminal justice reform. The Comprehensive Crime Control Act of 1983 proposes a broad range of anticrime measures. The Senate has moved quickly on this legislation and the Senate Committee on the Judiciary has reported virtually the entire package. We expect and urge that the full Senate will act on this legislation very soon. In light of the fact that in the 97th Congress the Senate passed a similar bill by a vote of 95–1, we are optimistic that the Senate will overwhelmingly approve this very important anticrime package.

While the Senate, both last year and again this year, has processed landmark crime legislation in the spirit of bipartisanship and compromise, the House of Representatives has taken no action whatsoever on the Comprehensive Crime Control Act. In the Senate, we have had bipartisan support led by Senators Thurmond, Laxalt, Biden, and Kennedy. In the House we have had no action, and nothing is scheduled. This is deeply troubling.

We are convinced that most Members of the House of Representatives are eager to vote on meaningful anticrime legislation. I hope the House Committee on the Judiciary and the House leadership will give the Members of the House an opportunity to vote on the Comprehensive Crime Control Act of 1983. This legislative package can make a difference. It is a reasonable and balanced package which not only strengthens criminal laws but makes those laws fairer. I urge the House of Representatives to join the Senate in taking prompt and serious action on the Comprehensive Crime Control Act.

Note: As enacted, S. 216 is Public Law 98–127, approved October 13.

Nomination of Dennis R. Patrick To Be a Member of the Federal Communications Commission
October 14, 1983

The President today announced his intention to nominate Dennis R. Patrick to be a member of the Federal Communications Commission for the unexpired term of 7 years from July 1, 1978. He would succeed Anne P. Jones.

Mr. Patrick is an attorney. Since December of 1981 he has served as Associate Director of Presidential Personnel at the White House where he has been responsible for legal and regulatory agencies. Between 1976 and 1981, Mr. Patrick practiced law with the law offices of Adams, Duque & Hazeltine in Los Angeles, Calif.

Mr. Patrick earned his undergraduate degree from Occidental College (A.B., magna cum laude, 1973). He earned his law degree from the University of California at Los Angeles School of Law (J.D., 1976). He was born on June 1, 1951, in Glendale, Calif. Mr. Patrick is married and resides in the District of Columbia.

Nomination of James L. Emery To Be Administrator of the Saint Lawrence Seaway Development Corporation
October 14, 1983

The President today announced his intention to nominate James L. Emery to be Administrator of the Saint Lawrence Seaway Development Corporation, Department of Transportation, for a term of 7 years. He would succeed David W. Oberlin.

Mr. Emery is president of Emery Corp., a management consulting firm. He was a member of the New York State Assembly for 18 years, serving as minority leader for 4 years.

He graduated from the University of Cincinnati (B.A., 1953). He is married, has three children, and resides in Geneseo, N.Y. He was born July 22, 1931, in Lakeville, N.Y.

Executive Order 12444—Continuation of Export Control Regulations
October 14, 1983

By the authority vested in me as President by the Constitution and laws of the United States of America, including section 203 of the International Emergency Economic Powers Act (50 U.S.C. 1702) (hereinafter referred to as "the Act"), and 22 U.S.C. 287c,

I, Ronald Reagan, President of the United States of America, find that the unrestricted access of foreign parties to United States commercial goods, technology, and technical data and the existence of certain boycott practices of foreign nations constitute, in light of the expiration of the Export Administration Act of 1979, an unusual and extraordinary threat to the national security, foreign policy and economy of the United States and hereby declare a national economic emergency to deal with that threat.

Accordingly, in order (a) to exercise the necessary vigilance over exports from the standpoint of their significance to the national security of the United States; (b) to further significantly the foreign policy of the United States, including its policy with respect to cooperation by United States persons with certain foreign boycott activities, and to fulfill its international responsibilities; and (c) to protect the domestic economy from the excessive drain of scarce materials and reduce the serious economic impact of foreign demand, it is hereby ordered as follows:

Section 1. Notwithstanding the expiration of the Export Administration Act of 1979, as amended (50 U.S.C. App. 2401 *et seq.*), the provisions of that Act, the provisions for administration of that Act and delegations of authority set forth in Executive Order No. 12002 of July 7, 1977 and Executive Order

No. 12214 of May 2, 1980, shall, to the extent permitted by law, be incorporated in this Order and shall continue in full force and effect.

Sec. 2. All rules and regulations issued or continued in effect by the Secretary of Commerce under the authority of the Export Administration Act of 1979, as amended, including those published in Title 15, Chapter III, Subchapter C, of the Code of Federal Regulations, Parts 368 to 399 inclusive, and all orders, regulations, licenses and other forms of administrative action issued, taken or continued in effect pursuant thereto, shall, until amended or revoked by the Secretary of Commerce, remain in full force and effect, the same as if issued or taken pursuant to this Order, except that the provisions of sections 203(b)(2) and 206 of the Act (50 U.S.C. 1702(b)(2) and 1705) shall control over any inconsistent provisions in the regulations with respect to, respectively, certain donations to relieve human suffering and civil and criminal penalties for violations subject to this Order. Nothing in this section shall affect the continued applicability of administrative sanctions provided for by the regulations described above.

Sec. 3. Provisions for the administration of section 38(e) of the Arms Export Control Act (22 U.S.C. 2778(e)) may be made and shall continue in full force and effect until amended or revoked under the authority of section 203 of the Act (50 U.S.C. 1702). To the extent permitted by law, this Order also shall constitute authority for the issuance and continuation in full force and effect of rules and regulations by the President or his delegate, and all orders, licenses, and other forms of administrative action issued, taken or continued in effect pursuant thereto, relating to the administration of section 38(e).

Sec. 4. This Order shall be effective as of midnight between October 14 and October 15, 1983, and shall remain in effect until terminated. It is my intention to terminate this Order upon the enactment into law of a bill reauthorizing the authorities contained in the Export Administration Act.

RONALD REAGAN

The White House,
October 14, 1983.

[Filed with the Office of the Federal Register, 4:37 p.m., October 14, 1983]

Message to the Congress Reporting on the Continuation of Export Control Regulations
October 14, 1983

To the Congress of the United States:

Pursuant to Section 204(b) of the International Emergency Economic Powers Act, 50 U.S.C. 1703, I hereby report to the Congress that I have today exercised the authority granted by this Act to continue in effect the system of controls, contained in 15 C.F.R. Parts 368–399, including restrictions on participation by United States persons in certain foreign boycott activities, which heretofore has been maintained under the authority of the Export Administration Act of 1979, as amended, 50 U.S.C. App. 2401 *et seq.* In addition, I have made provision for the administration of Section 38(e) of the Arms Export Control Act, 22 U.S.C. 2778(e).

1. The exercise of this authority is necessitated by the expiration of the Export Administration Act on October 14, 1983, and the resulting lapse of the system of controls maintained under that Act.

2. In the absence of controls, foreign parties would have unrestricted access to United States commercial products, technology and technical data, posing an unusual and extraordinary threat to national security, foreign policy, and economic objectives critical to the United States. In addition, United States persons would not be prohibited from complying with certain foreign boycott requests. This would seriously harm

our foreign policy interests, particularly in the Middle East. Controls established in 15 C.F.R. 368–399, and continued by this action, include the following:

National security export controls aimed at restricting the export of goods and technologies which would make a significant contribution to the military potential of any other country and which would prove detrimental to the national security of the United States;

Foreign policy controls which further the foreign policy objectives of the United States or its declared international obligations in such widely recognized areas as human rights, anti-terrorism, and regional stability;

Nuclear nonproliferation controls that are maintained for both national security and foreign policy reasons, and support the objectives of the Nuclear Nonproliferation Act;

Short supply controls that protect domestic supplies; and

Anti-boycott regulations that prohibit compliance with foreign boycotts aimed at countries friendly to the United States.

3. Consequently, I have issued an Executive Order to continue in effect all rules and regulations issued or continued in effect by the Secretary of Commerce under the authority of the Export Administration Act of 1979, as amended, and all orders, regulations, licenses, and other forms of administrative actions under that Act, except where they are inconsistent with sections 203(b) and 206 of the International Emergency Economic Powers Act.

4. The Congress and the Executive have not permitted export controls to lapse since they were enacted under the Export Control Act of 1949. Any termination of controls could permit transactions to occur that would be seriously detrimental to the national interests we have heretofore sought to protect through export controls and restrictions on compliance by United States persons with certain foreign boycotts. I believe that even a temporary lapse in this system of controls would seriously damage our national security, foreign policy and economic interests and undermine our credibility in meeting our international obligations.

5. The countries affected by this action vary depending on the objectives sought to be achieved by the system of controls instituted under the Export Administration Act. Potential adversaries are seeking to acquire sensitive United States goods and technologies. Other countries serve as conduits for the diversion of such items. Still other countries have policies that are contrary to United States foreign policy or nuclear nonproliferation objectives, or foster boycotts against friendly countries. For some goods or technologies, controls could apply even to our closest allies in order to safeguard against diversion to potential adversaries.

6. It is my intention to terminate the Executive Order upon the enactment into law of a bill reauthorizing the authorities contained in the Export Administration Act.

RONALD REAGAN

The White House,
October 14, 1983.

Letter to the Family of the Late Senator Henry M. Jackson on the Launching of the U.S.S. *Henry M. Jackson*
October 15, 1983

Dear Mrs. Jackson, Anna Marie and Peter:

The launching of a Trident Submarine is indeed a special event. But when that submarine bears the name U.S.S. *Henry M. Jackson* the event has greatly added significance. This submarine will join other strategic missile submarines named for men of great character: George Washington, Woodrow Wilson, Thomas Edison, Daniel Webster. Henry Jackson belongs among these Americans. This living vessel is a fitting monument to him. Statues and configurations of stone cannot carry on his life's work. However, the mighty ship you launch today will carry on his lifelong quest for peace for all mankind and security for our country.

Like Senator Jackson, those who built and will man the U.S.S. *Henry M. Jackson,* are content to do their job professionally and silently, foregoing greater material rewards they could claim in other fields. As with Senator Jackson, this ship's real achievement will not be in conquest but in restraint, not in waging war but in preserving peace.

The U.S.S. *Henry M. Jackson* through dec-

ades to come will be a constant reminder to the fleet and to all Americans of the virtues for which your husband and father stood: truth, peacefulness, strength and steadfastness. These were the personal traits which commanded our respect when he was alive. These are the qualities for which he will be remembered.

Nancy and I extend our every best wish,
Sincerely,

RONALD REAGAN

Note: As printed above, this item follows the text of the White House press release.

Radio Address to the Nation on the Quality of Life in America
October 15, 1983

My fellow Americans:

I know I court trouble when I dispute experts who specialize in spotting storm clouds and preaching doom and gloom. But at the risk of being the skunk that invades their garden party, I must warn them: Some very good news is sneaking up on you. The quality of American life is improving again. "Quality of life"—that's a term often used but seldom defined. Certainly our standard of living is part of it, and one good measure of that is purchasing power.

Just a few years ago, double-digit inflation was bleeding our purchasing power. Record price increases, interest rates, and taxation punished the thrifty, impoverished the needy, and discouraged entrepreneurs. When an economy goes haywire, confidence is destroyed. Well, today the tables have been turned. Double-digit inflation is gone, and confidence is coming back.

In 1980 the U.S. ranked only 10th among 20 industrial nations in per capita income. By the end of 1982, we'd climbed all the way up to third place. Our stronger dollar has increased purchasing power. Real wages are up. And inflation is down to 2.6 percent.

Sometimes when we shop we don't realize how much inflation has dropped, because prices are still going up. But they're going up much more slowly than before. If

food prices had kept rising as fast the last 2 years as the 2 years before we took office, a loaf of bread would cost 7 cents more than it does today, a half gallon of milk 18 cents more, a pound of hamburger 60 cents more, and a gallon of gas 97 cents more.

The prime interest rate has been cut nearly in half, so costs of business, mortgage, education, and car loans have dropped. The Federal income tax on a typical working family is $700 less than if our tax program had not been passed. With parents, students, entrepreneurs, workers, and consumers feeling more secure, opportunities for jobs are expanding. Our work force in September rose by nearly 400,000 to 101.9 million—the highest level in American history. And the trend will continue.

Quality of life is not just more jobs, it's also better jobs. And we're seeing better opportunities opening up for all Americans. Women, for example, filled more than half of all the new jobs in managerial, professional, and technical fields between 1980 and 1982. The number of women-owned businesses is growing five times faster than men's. The future looks brighter. To get a peek at what tomorrow's jobs and products may be, look at the venture capital industry. This is where high-powered capital is invested and much of the technological revolution is taking place.

During the first 9 months of 1983, the venture industry raised about $2½ billion— nearly three times more than in all of 1980. The General Accounting Office has already estimated that previous venture investments of some $209 million in the sample of 72 companies directly generated 130,000 jobs during the decade of the seventies. Well, if $209 million of venture capital generated 130,000 jobs in 10 years, imagine how many jobs $2½ billion will create during the next year. And like interest that compounds, growth and opportunities create more growth and more opportunities.

Capital spending by business, a key source of higher productivity and new jobs, helped propel the economy forward in the third quarter. Much of the increase in spending went for products of high technology like computers and word processors.

We're witnessing an industrial renaissance, and this is only act one. It's being nourished by incentives from lower tax rates, starting with the 1978 capital gains tax reduction, passed, incidentally, over the objections of the last administration, and followed by our own more sweeping tax cut program in 1981.

Our program to create opportunity and bring big government under control, the subsequent decline in inflation and interest rates, and prospects for robust growth have all led to another basic change: Americans' confidence in their institutions is turning up after nearly two decades of decline. A 1982 survey by the University of Michigan found people more likely to say they trusted the government to do what is right.

Looking beyond the economy, we see more evidence that the quality of life is improving. Life expectancy reached a record high last year, climbing to 74.5 years. Infant mortality declined to an all-time low with only 11.2 deaths per 1,000 live births. And the number of divorces dropped for the first time since 1962. Serious crime dropped 3 percent, the first measurable decline since 1977. Quality education, an American tradition—but one neglected for years—will be restored, thanks to leadership in Washington and vigorous action by your families at the grassroots.

Good things are happening in America. Confidence is returning. Our quality of life is improving because your voices, voices of common sense, are finally getting through. Believe me, it wasn't Washington experts who said government is too big, taxes are too high, criminals are coddled, education's basics are neglected, and values of family and faith are being undermined. That was your message; you made reforms possible.

With your help, we'll make even more progress, because I'll be the first to admit much more progress needs to be made. We're on a new road for America, a far better road, filled with hope and opportunities. Our critics may never be satisfied with anything we do, but I can only say those who created the worst economic mess in postwar history should be the last people crying wolf 1,000 days into this administration, when so many trends that were headed the wrong way are headed back in the right direction.

Thanks for listening, and God bless you.

Note: The President spoke at 12:06 p.m. from Camp David, Md.

Letter to the Chairman of the Reagan-Bush '84 Committee
October 17, 1983

Dear Paul:

I am writing this letter in response to your decision to chair Reagan-Bush '84. I deeply appreciate your action. The work of your Committee will be of great help to me at such time as I may make a formal decision to seek a second term as President.

Meanwhile, I recognize that due to the technical requirements of the Federal election laws (including the requirement for the designation of a principal campaign committee), your Committee must file with the Federal Election Commission as a committee that will be working on behalf of my re-election. This letter will serve as my consent for the purpose of allowing you to form this Committee, and I request that Angela M. Buchanan Jackson serve as the Committee's Treasurer.

Sincerely,

RONALD REAGAN

[The Honorable Paul Laxalt, United States Senate, Russell Senate Office Building, Washington, D.C. 20510]

Note: The text of the President's letter was made available by the Office of the Press Secretary.

Letter to the Chairman of the Federal Election Commission on the Reagan-Bush '84 Committee
October 17, 1983

Dear Chairman McDonald:

I have been advised that on October 17, 1983 a political committee known as Reagan-Bush '84 whose address is 440 First Street, N.W., Washington, D.C. 20001, registered with the Federal Election Commission, as my authorized campaign committee for the nomination as the Republican candidate for the office of the Presidency of the United States in 1984. Since the work of this Committee will be of great help to me at such time as I may make a formal decision to seek a second term as President, I am hereby authorizing this Committee as my principal campaign committee to allow those persons who support my candidacy to express their support in a manner that fully complies with the Federal election laws.

All correspondence directed to me with respect to this matter should be sent to my attention at the Committee's address shown above.

This statement is submitted pursuant to 11 C.F.R. § 101.1(a) in lieu of the Statement of Candidacy on FEC Form 2.

I certify that I have examined the information set forth above and to the best of my knowledge and belief it is true, correct and complete.

Sincerely,

RONALD REAGAN

[Mr. Danny Lee McDonald, Chairman, Federal Election Commission, 1325 K Street NW., Washington, D.C. 20463]

cc: Vice Chairman Lee Ann Elliott

Note: The text of the President's letter was made available by the Office of the Press Secretary.

Nomination of Lewis A. Dunn To Be an Assistant Director of the United States Arms Control and Disarmament Agency
October 17, 1983

The President today announced his intention to nominate Lewis A. Dunn to be an Assistant Director of the United States Arms Control and Disarmament Agency, Nuclear and Weapons Control Bureau. He would succeed Thomas D. Davies.

He is presently serving as Counselor to Ambassador at Large Richard T. Kennedy. Previously he was Special Assistant for Nuclear Affairs to the Under Secretary of State for Management in 1981–1982; on the professional staff of the Hudson Institute in 1974–1981, also serving as project leader in 1976–1981; and in the department of political science at Kenyon College in 1969–1974.

He graduated from Cornell University (A.B., 1965) and the University of Chicago (Ph. D., 1973). He is married and resides in Falls Church, Va. He was born January 7, 1944, in New York, N.Y.

Nomination of Francis X. Lilly To Be Solicitor of the Department of Labor
October 17, 1983

The President today announced his intention to nominate Francis X. Lilly to be Solicitor for the Department of Labor. He would succeed Timothy Ryan, Jr.

Since January 1982 Mr. Lilly has been serving as Deputy Solicitor of the U.S. Department of Labor. Previously he was Executive Assistant to the Chairman of the Board, U.S. Synthetic Fuels Corporation, in 1981; consultant to the Office of the Chief of Staff and to the Counsel's Office, the White House, in 1981; junior partner in the

law firm of Bryan, Cave, McPheeters & McRoberts in Washington, D.C., in 1979–1981; and an associate with the law firm of Arent, Fox, Kintner, Plotkin & Kahn in Washington, D.C., in 1973–1978.

Mr. Lilly graduated from Duke University (A.B., 1969) and the Catholic University of America (J.D., 1973). He is married, has four children, and resides in Bethesda, Md. He was born July 27, 1946, in Washington, D.C.

Proclamation 5119—Wright Brothers Day, 1983
October 17, 1983

By the President of the United States of America

A Proclamation

1983 marks the eightieth anniversary of the Wright Brothers' historic flight aboard a self-propelled, winged aero-vehicle. That flight, lasting but 12 seconds and spanning only 120 yards, followed 120 years of unsuccessful attempts to accomplish such a feat. Although short when measured against today's trans-meridian flights, its significance was great because it established the foundation for future successes in aviation which continue to enrich the quality of our lives today.

This year we also celebrate the bicentennial of man's first flight. Two hundred years ago, on August 27, 1783, the Montgolfier Brothers of France first launched a manned

hot air balloon into the atmosphere. Shortly thereafter, in a balloon constructed by an American lawyer, Peter Carnes, Esq., the first American ventured aloft in a tethered balloon in Baltimore.

This year also marks the twenty-fifth anniversary of the signing of the Federal Aviation Act of 1958. This legislation created the Federal Aviation Administration, which has played a central role in making civil air carriage ten times safer than it was in 1958, thus helping to advance the progress of civil aviation and to fulfill the Wright Brothers' dreams of the future role aviation would have in our world.

To commemorate the historic achievement of the Wright Brothers, the Congress, by joint resolution of December 17, 1963 (77 Stat. 402; 36 U.S.C. 169), designated the seventeenth day of December of each year as Wright Brothers Day and requested the President to issue a proclamation annually inviting the people of the United States to observe that day with appropriate ceremonies and activities.

Now, Therefore, I, Ronald Reagan, President of the United States of America, do hereby call upon the people of this Nation and their local and national governmental officials to observe Wright Brothers Day, December 17, 1983, with appropriate ceremonies and activities, both to recall the accomplishments and to stimulate the development of aviation in this country and throughout the world.

In Witness Whereof, I have hereunto set my hand this 17th day of Oct., in the year of our Lord nineteen hundred and eighty-three, and of the Independence of the United States of America the two hundred and eighth.

RONALD REAGAN

[*Filed with the Office of the Federal Register, 4:26 p.m., October 17, 1983*]

Executive Order 12445—Certification of Containers and Vehicles for Use in International Transport
October 17, 1983

By virtue of the authority vested in me as President by the Constitution and laws of the United States of America, including Section 301 of Title 3 of the United States Code, in order to transfer certain functions implementing international conventions concerning customs treatment of containers in international commerce, it is hereby ordered as follows:

Section 1. The Secretary of the Treasury is hereby delegated authority to take all actions, including the issuance of regulations, appropriate to carry out the approval and certification of containers and vehicles for international transport of goods under customs seal pursuant to the Customs Convention on the International Transport of Goods Under Cover of TIR Carnets (TIR Convention), done at Geneva on January 15, 1959 (TIAS 6633), the Customs Convention on the International Transport of Goods Under Cover of TIR Carnets (TIR Convention), done at Geneva on November 14, 1975 (TIAS), and the Customs Convention on Containers, done at Geneva on May 18, 1956 (TIAS 6634).

Sec. 2. In discharging this authority, the Secretary shall apply the procedures and technical conditions set forth in the Annexes to the Conventions set forth above, as those Conventions are modified, amended, or otherwise supplemented from time to time.

Sec. 3. The Secretary may prescribe a schedule of fees to defray the costs of the services provided under this Order.

Sec. 4. The Secretary may, to the extent permitted by law, rely upon the services of non-profit firms or associations in carrying out his duties under this Order.

Sec. 5. Regulations issued by the Secretary of Transportation under Executive Order No. 11459 shall continue in force and effect until superseded by regulations promulgated by the Secretary of the Treasury under this Order.

Sec. 6. Executive Order No. 11459 of March 7, 1969, is superseded.

RONALD REAGAN

The White House,
October 17, 1983.

[*Filed with the Office of the Federal Register, 4:27 p.m., October 17, 1983*]

Executive Order 12446—Foreign Service Retirement and Disability System
October 17, 1983

By the authority vested in me as President of the United States of America by Section 827 of the Foreign Service Act of 1980 (22 U.S.C. 4067) (hereafter referred to as "the Act"), and in order to conform further the Foreign Service Retirement and Disability System to the Civil Service Retirement and Disability System, it is hereby ordered as follows:

Section 1. Interest Rates, Deposits, Refunds, and Redeposits. (a) The second sentence of Section 805(d)(3) of the Act (22 U.S.C. 4045(d)(3)), the first sentence of Section 815 (h) (22 U.S.C. 4055(h), and the first sentence of Section 825(a) (22 U.S.C. 4065(a)), are deemed to be amended to provide that interest shall be compounded at the annual rate of 3 percent per annum through December 31, 1984, and thereafter at a rate equal to the overall average yield to the Fund during the preceding fiscal year from all obligations purchased by the Secretary of the Treasury during such fiscal year under section 819, as determined by the Secretary of the Treasury.

(b) Sections 806(a) and 816(d) of the Act (22 U.S.C. 4046(a) and 4056(d)) are deemed to be amended to exclude from the computation of creditable civilian service under section 816(a) of the Act any period of civilian service for which retirement deductions or contributions have not been made under section 805(d) of the Act unless—

(1) the participant makes a contribution for such period as provided in such section 805(d); or

(2) no contribution is required for such service as provided under section 805(f) of the Act as deemed to be amended by this Order, or under any other statute.

(c) The amendments deemed to be made by section 1 of this Order shall apply (i) to contributions for civilian service performed on or after the first day of the month following issuance of this Order, (ii) to contributions for prior refunds to participants for which application is received by the employing agency on and after such first day

of the month, and (iii) to excess contributions under section 815(h) and voluntary contributions under section 825(a) from the first day of the month following issuance of this Order.

Sec. 2. Rounding Down of Annuities. (a) Section 826(e) of the Act (22 U.S.C. 4066(e)) is deemed to be amended by striking out "fixed at the nearest" and inserting in lieu thereof "rounded to the next lowest".

(b) The amendment deemed to be made by section 2(a) of this Order shall be effective with respect to any adjustment or redetermination of any annuity made on or after the date of this Order.

Sec. 3. Later Commencement Date For Certain Annuities.

(a) Section 807(a) of the Act (22 U.S.C. 4047(a)) is deemed to be amended to read as follows:

"(a)(1) Except as otherwise provided in paragraph (2), the annuity of a participant who has met the eligibility requirements for an annuity shall commence on the first day of the month after—

"(A) separation from the Service occurs; or

"(B) pay ceases and the service and age requirements for entitlement to annuity are met.

"(2) The annuity of—

"(A) a participant who is retired and is eligible for benefits under section 609(a) or a participant who is retired under section 813 or is otherwise involuntarily separated from the Service, except by removal for cause on charges of misconduct or delinquency,

"(B) a participant retiring under section 808 due to a disability, and

"(C) a participant who serves 3 days or less in the month of retirement—
shall commence on the day after separation from the Service or the day after pay ceases and the requirements for entitlement to annuity are met.".

(b) The amendment deemed to be made by paragraph 3(a) of this Order shall become effective thirty days after the effective date of this Order.

Sec. 4. Credit For Military Service. (a) Section 805 of the Act (22 U.S.C. 4045) is deemed to be amended—

(i) by striking out subsection (e) and substituting the following subsection in lieu thereof:

"(e)(1) Each participant who has performed military or naval service before the date of separation on which the entitlement to any annuity under this chapter is based may pay to the Secretary a special contribution equal to 7 percent of the amount of the basic pay paid under section 204 of title 37 of the United States Code, to the participant for each period of military or naval service after December 1956. The amount of such payments shall be based on such evidence of basic pay for military service as the participant may provide or if the Secretary determines sufficient evidence has not been so provided to adequately determine basic pay for military or naval service, such payment shall be based upon estimates of such basic pay provided to the Department under paragraph (4).

"(2) Any deposit made under paragraph (1) of this subsection more than two years after the later of—

"(A) the effective date of this Order, or

"(B) the date on which the participant making the deposit first became a participant in a Federal staff retirement system for civilian employees,—

shall include interest on such amount computed and compounded annually beginning on the date of the expiration of the two-year period. The interest rate that is applicable in computing interest in any year under this paragraph shall be equal to the interest rate that is applicable for such year under subsection (d) of this section.

"(3) Any payment received by the Secretary under this section shall be remitted to the Fund.

"(4) The Secretary of Defense, the Secretary of Transportation, the Secretary of Commerce, or the Secretary of Health and Human Services, as appropriate, shall furnish such information to the Secretary as the Secretary may determine to be necessary for the administration of this subsection.

"(f) Contributions shall only be required to obtain credit for periods of military or naval service to the extent provided under section 805(e) and section 816(a), except that credit shall be allowed in the absence of contributions to individuals of Japanese ancestry under section 816 for periods of internment during World War II."; and—

"(ii) by redesignating subsection (f) as subsection (g).

(b) Section 816(a) of the Act (22 U.S.C. 4056(a)) is deemed to be amended by adding "(1)" after "(a)" and by adding the following new paragraphs at the end thereof:

"(2) The service of an individual who first becomes a participant on or after the date of this Order without any credit under section 816 for civilian service performed prior to October 1, 1982, shall include credit for:

"(A) each period of military or naval service performed before January 1, 1957, and

"(B) each period of military or naval service performed after December 31, 1956, and before the separation on which the entitlement to annuity under this chapter is based, only if a deposit (with interest if any is required) is made with respect to that period, as provided in section 805(e).

"(3) The service of an individual who first became a participant on or after the date of this Order with credit under section 816 for civilian service performed prior to October 1982, shall include credit for each period of military or naval service performed before the date of the separation on which the entitlement to an annuity under this chapter is based, subject, in the case of military or naval service performed after December 1956, to section 816(j), as deemed to be added by this Order.

"(4) The service of an individual who first became a participant before the date of this Order shall include credit for each period of military or naval service performed before the date of the separation on which the entitlement to an annuity under this chapter is based, subject, in the case of military or naval service performed after December 1976, to section 816(j), as deemed to be added by this Order";

(c) Section 816 of the Act (22 U.S.C. 4056) is deemed to be further amended by adding a new subsection (j) at the end thereof to read as follows:

"(1) Except as otherwise provided by statute or Executive Order, Section 8332(j) of Title 5, United States Code, relating to redetermination of credit for military and naval service, shall be applied to annuities payable under this chapter. The Secretary of State shall redetermine service, and may request and obtain information from the Secretary of Health and Human Services, as the Office of Personnel Management is directed or authorized to do in Section 8332(j).

"(2) Section 8332(j) of Title 5, United States Code, shall not apply with respect to:

(A) the service of any individual who first became a participant on or after the date of this Order without any credit under section 816 for civilian service performed prior to October 1982; or

(B) any military or naval service performed prior to 1957 by an individual who first became a participant on or after the date of this Order with credit under section 816 for civilian service performed prior to October 1982, or any period of military or naval service performed after 1956 with respect to which the participant has made a contribution (with interest if any is required) under section 805(e); or

(C) any military or naval service performed prior to 1977 by any individual who first became a participant before the date of this Order or any period of military or naval service performed after 1976 with respect to which the participant has made a contribution (with interest if any is required) under section 805(e).

(d) Section 822(a) of the Act (22 U.S.C. 4062(a)) is deemed to be amended by striking out the period at the end thereof and inserting in lieu thereof: ", less an amount determined by the Secretary of State to be appropriate to reflect the value of the deposits made to the credit of the Fund under section 805(e).".

(e) The amendments deemed to be made by Section 4 of this Order shall be effective on the date of this Order.

Sec. 5. Recomputation at Age 62 of Credit for Military Service of Current Annuitants. (a) Section 816(a) of the Act (22 U.S.C. 4056(a)) is deemed to be further amended

so that the provisions of section 8332(j) of Title 5 of the United States Code, relating to credit for military service, shall not apply with respect to any individual who is entitled to an annuity under such Act on or before the date of approval of this Order, or who is entitled to an annuity based on a separation from service occurring on or before such date.

(b) Subject to subsection (c), in any case in which an individual described in subsection (a) is also entitled to old-age or survivors insurance benefits under section 202 of the Social Security Act (or would be entitled to such benefits upon filing application therefor), the amount of the annuity to which such individual is entitled under chapter 8 of the Act (after taking into account subsection (a)) which is payable for any month shall be reduced by an amount determined by multiplying the amount of such old-age or survivors insurance benefit for the determination month by a fraction—

(1) the numerator of which is the total of the wages (within the meaning of section 209 of the Social Security Act) for service referred to in section 210(1) of such Act (relating to service in the uniformed services) and deemed additional wages (within the meaning of section 229 of such Act) of such individual credited for years after 1956 and before the calendar year in which the determination month occurs, up to the contribution and benefit base determined under section 230 of the Social Security Act (or other applicable maximum annual amount referred to in section 215(e)(1) of such Act) for each such year, and

(2) the denominator of which is the total of all wages deemed additional wages described in paragraph (1) of this subsection plus all other wages (within the meaning of section 209 of the Social Security Act) and all self-employment income (within the meaning of section 211(b) of such Act) of such individual credited for years after 1936 and before the calendar year in which the determination month occurs, up to the contribution and benefit base (or such other amount referred to in such section 215(e)(1) of such Act) for each such year.

(c) Subsection (b) shall not reduce the annuity of any individual below the amount of the annuity which would be payable under chapter 8 of the Act to the individual for the determination month if section 8332(j) of Title 5 of the United States Code applied to the individual for such month.

(d) For purposes of this section, the term "determination month" means—

(1) the first month the individual described in subsection (a) is entitled to old-age or survivors insurance benefits under section 202 of the Social Security Act (or would be entitled to such benefits upon filing application therefor); or

(2) the first day of the month following the month in which this Order is issued in the case of any individual so entitled to such benefits for such month.

(e) The preceding provisions of this section shall take effect with respect to any annuity payment payable under chapter 8 of the Act for calendar months beginning after the date of this Order.

(f) The Secretary of Health and Human Services shall furnish such information to the Secretary of State as may be necessary to carry out the preceding provisions of this section.

Sec. 6. General Limitation on Cost-of-Living Adjustment for Annuities. (a) Section 826 of the Act (22 U.S.C. 4066) is deemed to be amended to add at the end thereof the following new subsection:

"(g)(1) An annuity shall not be increased by reason of any adjustment under this section to an amount which exceeds the greater of—

"(A) the maximum pay rate payable for class FS–1 under section 403, 30 days before the effective date of the adjustment under this section; or

"(B) the final pay (or average pay, if higher) of the former participant with respect to whom the annuity is paid, increased by the overall annual average percentage adjustments (compounded) in rates of pay of the Foreign Service Schedule under such section 403 during the period—

"(i) beginning on the date the annuity commenced (or, in the case of a survivor of the retired participant, the date the participant's annuity commenced), and

"(ii) ending on the effective date of the adjustment under this section.

"(2) For the purposes of paragraph (1) of this subsection, 'pay' means the rate of salary or basic pay as payable under any provision of law, including any provision of law limiting the expenditure of appropriated funds.".

(b) The amendment made by subsection (a) of this Section shall not cause any annuity to be reduced below the rate that is payable on the date of approval of this Order, but shall apply to any adjustment occurring on or after April 1, 1983 under Section 826 of the Act to any annuity payable from the Foreign Service Retirement and Disability Fund, whether such annuity has a commencing date before, on, or after the date of this Order.

RONALD REAGAN

The White House,
October 17, 1983.

[Filed with the Office of the Federal Register, 4:28 p.m., October 17, 1983]

Nomination of John H. Riley To Be Administrator of the Federal Railroad Administration
October 17, 1983

The President today announced his intention to nominate John H. Riley to be Administrator of the Federal Railroad Administration, Department of Transportation. He would succeed Robert W. Blanchette.

Since 1979 Mr. Riley has been serving as chief counsel to Senator David Durenberger. Since 1980 he has initiated and organized the U.S. Senate Rail Caucus and American participation in the United States-Japan Rail Congress. The United States Rail Caucus is a bipartisan coalition of 36 offices focusing on rail industry issues. The United States-Japan Rail Congress is a congressional level technology exchange program between the United States Congress and the Japanese Diet.

Mr. Riley graduated from Boston College (B.A., 1968) and Cornell University Law School (J.D., 1972). He is married and resides in Falls Church, Va. He was born January 19, 1947.

Nomination of James T. Hackett To Be a Member of the Board of Directors of the Corporation for Public Broadcasting
October 17, 1983

The President today announced his intention to nominate James T. Hackett to be a member of the Board of Directors of the Corporation for Public Broadcasting. He would succeed Harry O'Connor.

Mr. Hackett is an associate with the Heritage Foundation. Previously he was Associate Director of the United States Information Agency in 1981–1983; Acting Director of the U.S. Arms Control and Disarmament Agency in 1981; Administrative Director,

U.S. Arms Control and Disarmament Agency in 1973–1981; Deputy Executive Secretary of the National Security Council in 1971–1973; and personnel officer at the Department of State in 1970–1971. He was assigned overseas as a consular and political officer at the American Embassies at Panama, Rome, and La Paz, in 1961–1969.

He is married, has two children, and resides in Sterling, Va. He was born March 26, 1931, in Boston, Mass.

Remarks Announcing the Appointment of Robert C. McFarlane as Assistant to the President for National Security Affairs
October 17, 1983

The President. Last week I took pride in announcing that one of my most trusted and valued advisers, Judge William Clark, would become Secretary of the Interior. And today I take pride again in announcing that his successor as Assistant for National Security Affairs will be another man who has won my utmost confidence and respect, Ambassador Robert McFarlane.

Bud brings a treasure of experience and talent to this new post—a decorated marine, a scholar, adviser to three Presidents, a veteran of Capitol Hill, Counselor of the Department of State, Deputy Director of the NSC staff and, most recently, my personal representative to the delicate negotiations in the Middle East. He is ideally qualified to assume these new responsibilities.

I should tell you that I was looking for more than experience in filling this post; I

also wanted someone of strong principle, someone of keen judgment, and someone who could effectively manage the affairs of the NSC. He shares my view about the need for a strong America—an effective, bipartisan foreign policy based on peace through strength. He enjoys the respect and affection of my other principal advisers in the national security community. And working closely with me, he'll provide the leadership and spirit of teamwork that we value in this administration.

And, Bud, I want to thank you for accepting this new challenge. All of us look forward to working with you in the coming months. Ambassador McFarlane will be confirmed as national security adviser.

Mr. McFarlane. Thank you, Mr. President. For someone who has devoted his life and the life of his family to government service, it's a profoundly humbling moment, one for which I'm very deeply grateful to you, Mr. President.

The opportunity to serve is, for all of us and for you, the highest gift that any of us can expect. To be given that chance for a cause and for principles in which you believe very deeply is all the more so.

I look forward to doing whatever I can to helping the completion—the fulfillment of the promise of President Reagan's goals on national security affairs. They have stemmed the tide, and they have set us on a course which I believe deeply will prove Spengler was wrong—that the West can indeed define its interests, defend them, demonstrate that freedom, democracy, free enterprise is the hope of the future.

Again, on behalf of my family, I'm deeply grateful. I look forward to working with Secretary Shultz, Cap Weinberger, Bill Casey, and further stewardship of the President's program.

Thank you.

Q. Mr. President, what about Jeane Kirkpatrick? What will happen to her now, and who will represent you in the Middle East?

The President. May I say that there was a lot of speculation and declarations that were based, again, on those faceless and nameless sources. Jeane Kirkpatrick is Ambassador to the United Nations. She continues there as Ambassador to the United Nations where she has done, I think, as magnificent a job as anyone who has ever held that post and probably more so than most. And she is invaluable in what she's doing.

Q. You're not offering her another post here in Washington?

The President. Jeane is continuing as Ambassador to the United Nations.

Q. What about the Middle East envoy's job, Mr. President?

The President. What?

Q. What about the Middle East envoy's job? Will you appoint a new envoy?

The President. This is going to be one of my hardest tasks now because of the excellence of the job that was done by Ambassador McFarlane.

Q. Did you say you will appoint someone else, sir?

The President. Well, we can't walk away as if that problem doesn't exist; it still exists.

But he has done a magnificent job there in bringing us to——

Q. Will you change the marines' order at all?

Q. Mr. President, why are we in Lebanon? And why are we letting our marines be there to get killed everyday?

The President. Because I think it is vitally important to the security of the United States and the Western World that we do everything we can to further the peace process in the Middle East.

Q. Do you think your Middle East policy needs any adjustment now? Or are you pleased that it can continue the way it is?

The President. Well, no one can be pleased until you finally get them at a negotiating table talking peace. But we made, I think, progress in a spot that is vitally important to the free world.

Q. Will you change policy now at all?

The President. No. We're going to continue. And I hope that we will continue what Ambassador McFarlane has so successfully brought, at least to this point.

Q. Do you have someone in mind, sir? Do you have someone in mind for the Mideast job? And when do you expect to make that announcement?

The President. I haven't progressed that far as yet. I will be discussing things with the new national security adviser.

Q. Will the Pershing missiles be installed on schedule unless something more is done in Geneva, sir?

The President. We have no plans to change the schedule for deployment.

Q. Mr. President, when will you announce your reelection? [*Laughter*]

The President. What?

Q. When will you announce your candidacy for reelection?

The President. Say, that's a change of subject, isn't it? [*Laughter*] I thought I would just leave that question to the Ambassador.

Q. Mr. President, are you saying that Jeane Kirkpatrick is happy in her job and all the reports are untrue that she wanted to come back to Washington?

The President. As far as I know, she's happy. And as I say, she has performed a great service there. I think that she has done so much for this country.

Q. Will she stay on through the rest of your term?

The President. Everybody tells me I have to get out of here. [*Laughter*]

Q. Will she stay on through the rest of your term?

Q. Mr. President, a Soviet general is—a Soviet general, sir, is on the record as threatening to—[*inaudible*]—U.S. starts deployment of new missiles that would put the United States on 10-minute targeting if we go ahead with INF deployment. What do you say to that, sir?

The President. [*Inaudible*]—the question.

Q. A Soviet general is quoted today, sir, as saying that if you go ahead with the INF deployment, that the Soviet Union will deploy new missiles that would put the United States under 10-minute warning—[*inaudible*].

The President. I don't exactly take a Soviet general's word as being authoritative on anything.

Q. Have you sworn off news conferences? [*Laughter*]

Q. Thank you.

Note: The President spoke at 3:30 p.m. to reporters assembled in the Briefing Room at the White House. Following the exchange, the President left the Briefing Room and Mr. McFarlane continued answering reporters' questions.

Appointment of Robert C. McFarlane as Assistant to the President for National Security Affairs
October 17, 1983

The President announced today his intention to appoint Robert C. McFarlane as Assistant to the President for National Security Affairs. He will succeed William P. Clark.

Mr. McFarlane has served as the President's Personal Representative in the Middle East since July 1983. He has also served as Deputy Assistant to the President for National Security Affairs since January 1982.

In January 1981 Mr. McFarlane was nominated as Counselor, Department of State, where he served until becoming Deputy Assistant to the President. In 1979–1981 he was a member of the professional staff of the Senate Committee on Armed Services. He was a senior research fellow at the National Defense University in Washington, D.C., in 1977–1978.

In 1976–1977 he was Special Assistant to the President for National Security Affairs. Mr. McFarlane was Executive Assistant to the Assistant to the President for National Security Affairs in 1975–1976. From 1973 to 1975, he was military assistant to Dr. Henry Kissinger at the White House. In 1971–1972 he was a White House fellow and Executive Assistant to the Counsel to the President for Legislative Affairs.

Mr. McFarlane is retired from the Marine Corps (lieutenant colonel). He is a graduate of the U.S. Naval Academy and studied international relations at the Institut des Hautes Études in Geneva, Switzerland. He is a recipient of the Distinguished Service Medal, the Nation's highest peacetime military decoration.

Mr. McFarlane and his wife Jonda have three children. They reside in Bethesda, Md. He was born July 12, 1937.

Appointment of John M. Poindexter as Deputy Assistant to the President for National Security Affairs
October 17, 1983

The President announced today his intention to appoint John M. Poindexter as the Deputy Assistant to the President for National Security Affairs. He will succeed Robert C. McFarlane.

Admiral Poindexter joined the National Security Council staff in June 1981 as Military Assistant to the Assistant to the President for National Security Affairs.

Immediately before joining the National Security Council staff, Rear Admiral Poindexter was Deputy Chief of Naval Education and Training and Chief of Staff of the Naval Education and Training Command in Pensacola, Fla. He continues in an active duty naval status in his new assignment.

In 1958 he graduated from the U.S. Naval Academy at the head of his class. He was a Burke scholar at the California Institute of Technology in Pasadena, where he earned the degree of doctor of philosophy in nuclear physics in 1964, studying under the Nobel laureate Rudolph Mossbauer.

He was on the personal staff of Secretaries of the Navy John Chafee, John Warner, and J. William Middendorf II from 1971 to 1974, and was Executive Assistant to the Chief of Naval Operations, Adm. James L. Holloway III, 1976–1978.

During his naval career, Admiral Poindexter served aboard a number of surface ships. He commanded the guided missile cruiser U.S.S. *England* (CG–22) and later commanded destroyer squadron 31. In this capacity, he was a battle group antisurface and antisubmarine warfare commander on deployments to the Western Pacific, Indian Ocean, and South Pacific.

Admiral Poindexter and his wife Linda have five children and reside in Rockville, Md. He was born in Indiana on August 12, 1936.

Remarks and a Question-and-Answer Session With Editors and Station Managers of Ethnically Oriented Publications and Radio Stations
October 18, 1983

The President. Well, ladies and gentlemen, a little over 3 years ago I kicked off my 1980 campaign at a rally held in the shadow of the Statue of Liberty and Ellis Island. And it's a memory I'll always cherish. There were many nationalities and family backgrounds represented in that rally, and yet practically all of them were Americans. One of those who hoped to be an American was the father of Lech Walesa.

All of us were or are descended from immigrants, most of whom came here looking for freedom and an opportunity to better their lot and the lot of their families. America was a land of hope for so many who suffered the pains of tyranny and deprivation. America was a magic place where anyone willing to work hard could live a decent life. And while our country had its flaws, the vision of opportunity was true enough for large numbers of immigrants to send back word of freedom and abundance.

Three years ago, it seemed like something, however, had gone terribly wrong. Stagnation and inflation were snuffing out the opportunity that had been the hallmark of our country. We were perched on the brink of an economic disaster and suffering a loss of confidence both at home and abroad. And for the first time, it was being said that America's best days were past. Well, you and I didn't believe that. And if the 1980 election carried any message, it was: Make America strong again.

The most important goal of this administration has been restoring the opportunity and the social mobility of all our citizens. This is especially significant for black and ethnic Americans, who were hit hard by economic decline. It's taken hard work and time, but we've turned this grave situation around.

The economy is—as I'm sure you've been told in the briefings already—in the first phase of sustained growth. We've brought inflation down—and I suppose somebody's already told you this, too; but anyway, I'll repeat it—from double digits to 2.6 percent for the last 12 months. And that's the lowest 12-month inflation rate in 17 years. Taxes skyrocketed in the years before we got here. We've given the people a 25-percent across-the-board reduction in their personal income tax rates. We've also, through a highly successful deregulation effort, trimmed 300 million man-hours of needless paperwork from the private sector and from State and local government.

Meanwhile, the civilian unemployment rate has dropped by 1½ percentage points since last December. The number of unemployed has dropped by 1.8 million—pardon me; 1.6 million. I guess it was just a Freudian slip. I was hoping for eight. [*Laughter*] And a healthy, growing economy has added almost 3 million of our fellow citizens to the Nation's payrolls. Blacks and teenagers made gains last month. And we look for continued improvement. They were the hardest hit in the unemployment.

Our economic recovery program made fundamental changes in Federal taxing, spending, and regulating policies. But we should never forget: It was the policies of tax, spend, and inflate that stagnated our economy, and it's been the reversal of those policies and replacing them with a positive program aimed at economic growth that has put us back on the path to a better life for all our citizens.

Along with this, we've recaptured a spirit of optimism and hope. In foreign affairs, we have reaffirmed our leadership again as an ally worthy of trust. We've begun a program to rebuild our defensive capabilities that were permitted to seriously erode during the last decade. We're firm in our belief that peace is more likely if the United States remains a strong force in the world.

In the area of nuclear weapons, we're working with our European allies to reestablish a stable balance in Europe, which was destroyed by the massive Soviet buildup in the last 10 years. We have made clear, however, that no new weapons need be deployed. We have been, and continue to be, serious in our efforts to reach arms reductions agreements with the Soviets, especially in the area of intermediate-range missiles.

Let me emphasize today—and I would urge the young people in Europe to reflect on this—it is not the United States and NATO which threaten peace. We have no intermediate, long-range missiles in Europe. And we're willing to forgo them entirely. It's the Soviet Union which has over 1,300 intermediate-range nuclear warheads threatening the countries of Europe, Asia, and elsewhere. And they continue to deploy SS–20 missiles at a rate of one a week—each missile containing three warheads. Now, these are actions of intimidation, pure and simple.

We stand ready to make any arrangement with the Soviets which will be verifiable and fair to all sides. This includes eliminating an entire class of nuclear weapons, or, if they won't go that far, at least a portion—and the more the better. But we can't negotiate forever with ourselves. If Soviet intransigence continues, we will move forward to reestablish the balance and ensure NATO's deterrent ability.

Our goal, both in the economy and in protecting our national security, is to meet the mandate of the 1980 election, to make our country the strong nation, the mighty force for good that it was meant to be.

Now, thank you all, and I know that you have some questions, maybe, and I have got a few minutes left.

Poland

Q. Heny Dende from—[*inaudible*]—Scranton, Pennsylvania. Would you consider lifting some of the sanctions against Poland in view of the recent developments that have occurred in release of prisoners?

The President. We are studying and reviewing that to make sure that this is really a change and not just cosmetic. And as you know, we have joined in many of the independent and the church-related agencies that are providing help directly to the Polish people, and we continue to do that. But before we make any real changes with regard to the Government, we feel we must know that what they have done is really a change and really a restoration of the human rights that they heretofore have denied before we make those changes and find out that they just have made a few little cosmetic gestures.

Cyprus

Q. Are you going to put any kind of pressure on the Turkish Government about giving a just solution to the Cyprus problem?

The President. To the which problem?

Q. To the Cyprus problem, to the Cyprians.

The President. Oh. I wish the Secretary of State were here. [*Laughter*] We're aware of that, but I don't know that we have involved ourselves directly and deeply in that. We have offered, as we always do, to be of help if we can. But right now I think more of our help is directed a little further east than that, on the shores of——

Q. I am speaking of 200,000 refugees in Cyprus.

The President. Yes, I know, and I hope that we can find—and help in the settlement of that.

Poland

Q. Mr. President, inasmuch as the sanctions must continue until the Polish Government actually makes some changes for the benefit of the people, do you foresee any sort of diplomatic initiative in order to get the stalemate which is currently on between the Polish Government and the United States Government—for example, the lack of exchange of ambassadors, et cetera—some sort of other initiative in order to get us from this stale point at which we've been for the last few months?

The President. Well, I think we've made it very plain to them that we're willing to move, but we're going to have to see deeds, not words, and that our interest is the welfare of the Polish people. And right now, I think the Polish people and the Polish Government are two separate entities.

Yalta Agreement

Q. Mr. President, I'll put—a difficult question. Our Vice President Bush in Vienna said a few weeks ago that American Government is considering, if I repeat it properly, to get out from the present system created in Europe by Yalta agreement. Does it mean that there is any political concept behind it, or is it just a nice expression of wishful thinking?

The President. Well, we have always felt and why we continue to have a Freedom Day for the enslaved nations of the world every year and to observe that—we think that that has to be the ultimate goal of the free world, is to bring about a time when all the people will have the very basis of democracy, which is the right of self-determination. And I don't think we should ever give that up.

I think that it underlies all of our relations with the Soviet Union. And so, I applauded when he said that in Vienna.

Afghanistan

Q. Mr. President, my name is Dr. Michael Szaz from the National Confederation of American Ethnic Groups. When are we going to break off diplomatic relations with the Soviet-imposed government in Afghanistan and extend more effective material assistance to the freedom fighters in Afghanistan?

The President. I have to say that I don't believe that breaking off diplomatic relations, even with the Soviet Union in our anger with them over this terrible deed with the Korean airliner——

Q. It's Afghanistan.

The President. What?

Q. It's Afghanistan, with the Soviet-imposed government in Kabul——

The President. Oh.

Q. ——Babrak.

The President. I see what you mean. Yes, I'm sorry. I misunderstood.

We haven't seen that as providing an advantage yet. There are some times when we think that it is very valuable to have eyes and ears on the scene of some of these places. This does not mean that we are not doing everything we can to bring about a change in that situation and get the Soviet Union out of there and restore freedom to the Afghanistan people and let those millions of refugees come home. But we don't believe that creating a wall of silence between us would be beneficial right now.

Asian Trips

Q. You canceled your visit to the Philippines. Do you still have the plan to be in South Korea? If you can, what is the main purpose to be in South Korea?

The President. What?

Q. South Korea?

The President. Yes.

Q. Mr. President, you canceled your—to visit Philippines—that you still have the plan to visit South Korea next month?

The President. We are, in fact, in a few weeks I am—we divided the trip up. We canceled part of it because I couldn't be away for the whole period of November which we had scheduled and in which the Congress, which was supposed to go on recess, was going to be here. And I'm not about to get out of town for 3 weeks and leave Congress here without me. [*Laughter*]

But we did divide, and we are going to keep the Japan and Korean part of the trip. That will take place early in November, and I will only be gone, counting the day I leave and the day I come back, that's a total of 7 days, and 3 of those are holidays. So, I'll only miss 4 days. And I figure that they can't get into too much trouble in that time. [*Laughter*]

So, I'm going to do that. But then we will reschedule the balance of the trip later, possibly in the spring.

Q. Does India fit into your schedule, sir?

The President. What?

Q. Does India fit into your schedule of the Asian trips?

The President. Not on these two trips.

Q. How about next spring?

The President. I have had the pleasure twice of having Madam Gandhi here as our guest, and she has very graciously urged me to come there. But that isn't on the schedule as yet. But I look forward to that and certainly want to do that.

Ms. Small. One more question, Mr. President.

Turkish-Armenian Conflict

Q. Mr. President, my name is Keshishian from California. I would like to know if the American Government has a stand on the Turkish genocide of the Armenians of 1915.

The President. The genocide of——

Q. The Armenians in 1915.

Ms. Small. The Turkish and Armenian genocide.

The President. Oh. I—the only official stand that I can tell you we have is one opposed to terrorism on both sides. And I can't help but believe that there's virtually no one alive today who was living in the era of that terrible trouble. And it seems to me we ought to be able to sit down now, an entirely new group of people who know only of that from reading of it, to sit down and work out our differences and bring peace at least to that segment of humanity.

Ms. Small. Thank you, Mr. President. Thank you very much.

The President. Karna tells me I have to go. Thank you all very much.

Note: The President spoke at 12:57 p.m. following a luncheon in the State Dining Room at the White House. The luncheon was part of an administration briefing session on foreign and domestic policy for the editors and station managers.

Karna Small Stringer is Deputy Assistant to the President and Director of Media Relations and Planning.

Statement on Soviet Human Rights Policies
October 18, 1983

Barely a month after attending an international conference in Madrid and joining 34 nations in a commitment to respect human rights, the Soviet Union has gone back on its word, launching a new campaign of repression against human rights activists.

Moscow has just sentenced a well-known Soviet refusenik, Iosif Begun, to 7 years imprisonment and 5 years of internal exile. The punishment of this courageous Jewish believer is the most severe measure specified in article 70 of the Soviet criminal code, dealing with dissemination of so-called anti-Soviet propaganda. Soviet persecution of religious and political dissidents is not new. In the case of Mr. Begun, the Soviet regime has refused for 13 years to honor his request to emigrate to Israel.

But Soviet policy toward Jewish emigration and dissident movements has sunk to a new low of brutality and repression. Antisemitism has escalated dramatically, as has harassment of other human rights defenders. We have received reports that Father Sigitas Tamkevicius, a Lithuanian Catholic priest active on behalf of religious freedom, is facing a similar fate as Iosif Begun.

Finally, we have received reports that Oleg Radzinskiy has also been tried. Mr. Radzinskiy, a member of the unofficial Soviet peace organization Group To Establish Trust Between the U.S. and U.S.S.R., was arrested October 28, 1982, and has been held for almost a year. The inability of Soviet authorities to tolerate any activities by those who are not members of their government-controlled, "captive" peace groups illustrates the hypocrisy of their statements. There is a night and day contrast between aggressive Soviet efforts to encourage peace demonstrations in the West and their brutal arrests and exile of peace activists in the East.

We condemn these illegal and inhumane acts. We hold the Soviet Union accountable for its violations of numerous international agreements and accords on human rights to which it is a party. We call upon the Soviets to reverse their inhumane policies and to prove to the world they will back up their words with action and start living up to their agreements.

Nomination of Terry Edward Branstad To Be a Member of the Board of Trustees of the Harry S. Truman Scholarship Foundation
October 18, 1983

The President today announced his intention to nominate Terry Edward Branstad to be a member of the Board of Trustees of the Harry S. Truman Scholarship Foundation for a term expiring December 10, 1987. He would succeed Christopher S. Bond.

He was elected Governor of Iowa in 1982. Previously he served as Lieutenant Governor of Iowa and was a member of the Iowa House of Representatives in 1972–1978. He was a senior partner in the law firm of Branstad-Schwarm in Lake Mills, Iowa.

He graduated from the University of Iowa (B.A., 1969) and Drake University (J.D., 1974). He is married, has two children, and resides in Des Moines. He was born November 17, 1946, in Leland, Iowa.

Remarks at the Presentation Ceremony for the Presidential Awards for Excellence in Science and Mathematics Teaching
October 19, 1983

Class be seated. [*Laughter*]

Well, it's wonderful to have all of you here today at the White House. We want you to enjoy our little get-together today. So, please lean back, relax, and stop worrying about what the students are doing to the substitute teachers back home. [*Laughter*]

Creativity in education: I heard the other day about a young teacher in a first grade class was having a problem informing them—they'd never had anything to do with some of the studies they would get later—informing them where their heart was and how they should put their hands over their heart when the National Anthem was played. And he finally figured it out. He said, "Put your hands on the alligator." [*Laughter*]

But, you know, the goal of these visits is to put education, the profession to which all of you have dedicated your lives, where it belongs on the national agenda, which is front and center.

Now, don't get me wrong. I've never been for politicizing this issue. In fact, it was just that tendency that I believe set us off on the wrong track a few decades ago. Too often the political side of education has been emphasized—money, regulations, bureaucracy, government intrusion, in fact, just about everything about our schools, except the two most important elements: the students, of course, and especially you, the teachers.

It's been very evident today that the American people are realizing again how important our schools are and how vital and honorable the role of the teacher is in our communities. This is especially so in the area of science and mathematics, fascinating in and of themselves as intellectual disciplines, but also vital to the success of the individual and our nation in this new era of technology.

The educational standards are going up everywhere and nowhere more sharply than in math and science. Yet with all the demands for educational reform, we mustn't forget the most important goal of all: to attract the most competent and dedicated people to teach and then to hang on to them.

In preparing for this ceremony today, we did a little calculation and discovered, using conservative estimates, of course—[*laughter*]—that each of you teachers is likely to interact with more than 5,000 students in the course of your careers. So, when I look out on this group, I not only see you master teachers, but I also see a half a million students who will have the privilege of being challenged, stimulated, and guided by you.

Is it any wonder that we place so much importance on what you do? And is it any wonder that we wanted you here today to say what sometimes just never gets said enough over the years, the simple words "Thank you"? Thank you for a job well and unselfishly done. The dedication of your lives to your students has earned the thanks of all Americans, and I take great pleasure today in expressing that gratitude for so many of them.

And at this point, I want to acknowledge the really tireless efforts of those professional organizations, especially the National Science Teachers Association and the National Council of Teachers of Mathematics, which shared their expertise and judgment with us in this round of Presidential awards.

Now, I'm sure that no one has to explain to teachers the difficulty of getting everything done in a limited period of time. My regret is that I won't have time to meet all of you individually. But with your understanding, I'd like to just call a few of you up here as representatives of all the dedicated teachers that we're honoring here today. So, will Edna Corbett, Jo Anne Rife, Tony Sedgwick, and Akehiko Takahashi, please, come up here and join me for a minute or two of embarrassment. [*Laughter*]

Edna Corbett has been an award-winning biology teacher in Portsmouth, Virginia, for nearly 20 years. I've asked her up here because she so clearly demonstrates a trait that seems so common among you successful teachers. She's just incredibly busy. In fact, I'm little surprised that you were able to squeeze in this event today. [*Laughter*] And like many of you, Mrs. Corbett is not only on the run with her school activities, like afterschool student groups, science fairs, and the inevitable faculty committees; she is fully immersed in family, professional, church, and community activities as well. I'm sure that one of the lessons she conveys to her students is how to use their time effectively.

Jo Anne Rife from Harrison, Arkansas, has taught basic science to thousands of students in smalltown school districts throughout the State. And she's done something I find reassuring. After leaving the classroom a few years ago to apply her experience as a science coordinator for a large school district, she returned, reinvigorated, to the classroom to continue serving on the frontline. Mrs. Rife has had her share of success in sending students on to careers in technical fields, including careers as science teachers. But she takes equal delight in opening the world of science to all of her students no matter what their interests are.

Tony Sedgwick from Tacoma, Washington, recognizes that mathematics is a tool that everyone needs. And he spreads his efforts generously to try to reach all kinds of students. He's as likely to be teaching "I hate math" students—[*laughter*]—at the advanced level, and his efforts have paid off. Ten years ago when he took over his high school math department, it enrolled only 21 percent out of 1,800 students and only 12 percent of its minority students. Today he has tripled those numbers.

And finally, Akehiko Takahashi is an immigrant to America and a very welcome one. He began his education in his native Japan, but finished it in Missouri, where he's been a math teacher for the past 20 years. Like Mr. Sedgwick, he teaches all levels of math, and I understand he's fiercely demanding of all his students. The students at Wentzville High know that when you get an "A" from Mr. Takahashi, you've earned an "A". Those high standards have rubbed off on his students. His math team in particular has had outstanding success and produced several superstar "mathletes." [*Laughter*]

Now, these four good sports—[*laughter*]—embody those important qualities that we found in all of you: your dedication to your profession, your breadth of experience and interests, your thorough preparation and continuing education in the subjects you teach, your insistence on hard work by your students, and your recognition that math and science are important for everyone and that everyone can be taught. So, let me at least—I'm going to shake these four hands as representative of the skills and dedications of all of you. So, just mentally figure that your hands are being shaken also. [*Laughter*]

Now that we've all shaken hands—[*laughter*]—in addition to your experiences in Washington, you, as teachers, will also have two souvenirs from your trip. One is the $5,000 grant that each of your schools will receive from the National Science Foundation for you to use in your math and science instructional programs. I know that money will be used well. The other is a handsome certificate which will be handed out by the impressive trio that are here with me—my science adviser, Jay Keyworth; Secretary of Education Ted Bell; and the Director of the National Science Foundation, Ed Knapp.

All of us remember the teacher or teachers who gave us that one extra push, that one extra bit of help just when we needed it most—the people who profoundly influenced and changed our lives. All of you here today are those selfless and dedicated professionals. So, for all your students, past and present, and students to come, for all the mothers and fathers of America, can I extend to you a heartfelt thanks, and God bless you all.

Note: The President spoke at 10:01 a.m. in the East Room at the White House.

Remarks at the 25th Anniversary Celebration of the National Aeronautics and Space Administration
October 19, 1983

Administrator Beggs, shuttle astronauts, NASA employees, ladies and gentlemen:

Thank you. I just said here a moment ago that music should have been being played first for all of them.

I had a joke about a sneak preview of "Bedtime for Bonzo," but I—[*laughter*]—I don't tell it. Mr. Beggs, I think you have a hit here.

Well, it does remind me of a story, and I have to have something to start with. It was about a—it's a true story, I understand, about a newspaper photographer out in Los Angeles. He's called in by his editor and told of a fire that was raging out there in Palos Verdes. That's a hilly area south of Los Angeles, a lovely residential area. His assignment was to rush down to a small airport, board a waiting plane, get some pictures of the fire, and be back in time for the afternoon edition.

Well, he raced down the freeway. He broke the law all the way. He got to the airport and drove his car to the end of the runway. And sure enough, there was a plane waiting with the engines all there revved up, ready to go. He got aboard, and at about 5,000 feet, he began getting his camera out of the bag, told the fellow flying the plane to get him over the fire so he could get his pictures and get back to the paper. And from the other side of the cockpit there was a deafening silence. And then he heard these words: "Aren't you the instructor?" [*Laughter*] I don't know. There must sometime have been some moments like that in what we've just seen.

Well, today we celebrate a 25th birthday. If it were the birthday of an individual, we would be marking an important milestone. At 25 a person begins to enter the most productive part of life, a time for which everything else has been just preparation for great achievements ahead. And today this is also true for the National Aeronautics and Space Administration. NASA has accomplished so much. But on its 25th birthday, we celebrate our potential as well as our accomplishments.

Being here in the Air and Space Museum is a fitting environment for this commemoration. It offers us a perspective on how far we've come and should also help us catch a glimpse of the incredible possibilities that await us in the years ahead. For 25 years NASA has been the focal point for an activity that is fundamental to the American character: blazing the trail to an exciting new frontier.

Historically, we've always been a people willing to take risks and dream great dreams. We weren't the people who stayed on the shores of the Old World. Instead we were the Italians, the Frenchmen, the Dutchmen, the men and women of every race, nationality, and religion who came here to push back the limits and in the process become Americans one and all.

A little over 200 years ago we embarked on the greatest experiment in human history with the founding of the first modern democracy. All of what we've accomplished can be traced to the energy, creativity that is unleashed when the human spirit is free. Americans have proven that there's no mountain too high, forest too thick, desert so vast, or problem so perplexing that it can serve as a barrier to the progress of free men and women.

Our forefathers and mothers spread across this continent. When they reached the western shore they didn't stop. Early in this century we built the Panama Canal and expanded the frontier of American commerce. Today that same spirit, the American spirit, is alive and well. There's no better example of it than that which is found in NASA.

It was 25 years ago when a 31-pound, cylinder-shaped satellite was launched—Explorer One, the first American satellite. And later that year, NASA was formed to oversee our space efforts: to ensure our leadership in aerospace science, to enhance cooperation with other nations in the peaceful application of space technology, to expand human knowledge of the atmosphere and space, and to pursue the practical benefits gained from these activities in order to improve the lot of mankind.

Men and women of NASA: Well done! Your accomplishments in these two and a half decades have already served your country and the people of this planet well. Today, we're reaping the returns that we've realized from our investment in space. And let me add, when the figures are put together we're not only getting our money's worth; our commitment to space has been one of the best investments we've ever made as a nation.

Communications satellites allow us cheaper and easier long-distance phone calls and live, worldwide television overseas—and coverage worldwide. The value to our country created by this leap in communications is astronomical. Similarly, weather satellites are now a part of our daily routine. Countless lives are saved and property protected when weather emergencies are charted more accurately than ever before imagined. Navigation, search and rescue, and other such activities in the air and on the sea are aided by services that you've implanted in near space.

Through satellite remote-sensing, we can find the location of new resources and better manage those we're already using. At one time, the only thing people could think of as a spinoff of our space effort was Teflon pans. [*Laughter*] In an era of high tech, all of us are now aware of what the technological advances we've made mean to our way of life. Computers and electronics are now indispensable to American economic progress and well-being.

And how does one put a dollar value on world peace? Certainly space technology has contributed enormously here as well. Our eyes-in-the-sky make us all a little safer. In the vital area of arms control, it's opened new avenues to approach the issue of verification. These are all achievements to one degree or another that can be related to our commitment to exploring and utilizing space for the benefit of mankind.

Yet, there's something which I would like to add to the list, something that can never be taken for granted in a society as free and richly diverse as ours.

We have holidays when we celebrate our freedom, but most of the time, we're on our own as independent individuals. And that is, after all, what American liberty is all about. But there are moments that bind us together, moments of sadness and happiness that make us more than a conglomeration of people living in proximity to each other. The death of President John F. Kennedy was one such moment. The sight of an American POW stepping off a plane in the Philippines after years of captivity, saluting the flag, and hearing him proclaim, "God bless America," was another. These experiences—moments of unity—build our national soul and character.

Perhaps NASA's greatest gifts have been the moments of greatness that you've allowed all of us to share. All of us—whether we were schoolteachers, actors, government employees, farmers, factory hands, secretaries, or the cop on the beat—all of us were along on those early Mercury missions. We were part of the NASA team launching probes into deep space to chart the unknown, to photograph the rings of Saturn and the surface of Mars. We were there, and our hearts were filled with such pride when Neil Armstrong, an American, the first person to set foot on the Moon, said, "One small step for a man; one giant leap for mankind." And we saluted right along with him when he planted Old Glory in the lunar soil.

NASA's done so much to galvanize our spirit as a people, to reassure us of our greatness and of our potential. In recent days the space shuttle has, as another NASA project before it—or other projects before it, captured our hearts and imaginations. Modern-day heroes like Sally Ride, Guy Bluford are emerging and inspiring new faith in our system and new hope for the future.

I was honored a year ago to be on hand to welcome the space shuttle *Columbia* when it returned from its mission and landed in the California desert on Independence Day. That was a day I and millions of other Americans will never forget.

I have to just tell you: One moment there in which with all the science and all the things that we can be told about and see, one simple sentence to me in answer to a question of mine seemed to bring all the wonder of it. How many times in the airplane you've known when you're on the approach path, and the airport is up there someplace ahead. And they hurried us up on the platform, because they said it was time to get up there, the shuttle was coming in. And they said it was on its approach. And I said, "Just where is it?" And they said, "Just over Honolulu." [*Laughter*] The whole miracle was brought home to me right then.

The space shuttle, like your many other accomplishments, didn't just happen. It's the result of hard work and a vision of the future. The shortsighted were unable to understand. In fact, some individuals who would lead America today led the fight against the space shuttle system a decade ago. What you've proven with the success of this new transportation system is that there's never a time when we can stop moving forward, when we can stop dreaming.

Right now we're putting together a national space strategy that will establish our priorities, guide and inspire our efforts in space for the next 25 years and beyond. It'll embrace all three sectors of our space program—civil, commercial, and national security. The strategy should flow from the national space policy that I announced July 4th last year.

We're not just concerned about the next logical step in space. We're planning an entire road, a "high road" if you will, that will provide us a vision of limitless hope and opportunity, that will spotlight the incredible potential waiting to be used for the betterment of humankind.

On this 25th anniversary, I would challenge you at NASA and the rest of America's space community: Let us aim for goals that will carry us well into the next century. Let us demonstrate to friends and adversaries alike that America's mission in space will be a quest for mankind's highest aspiration—opportunity for individuals, cooperation among nations, and peace on Earth.

Your imagination and your ability to project into the future will open up new horizons and push back boundaries that limit our goals on this planet. The goals you set and your success in achieving them will have much to do with our children's prosperity and safety and will determine if America remains the great nation it's intended to be. Don't be afraid to remind the rest of us that once in a while being a leader in space is a very wonderful accomplishment. It has given us the wherewithal to share with others the fruits of our adventure. The American people know this and support it. And let's continue to ensure that this program belongs to the people. Our strategy must demonstrate to them that through challenging the unknown and having the courage to aim high, their own hopes, dreams, and aspirations will be fulfilled.

There are those who preach the doctrine of limited resources. They pessimistically suggest that we're on the way to depleting all of what we have and that slowly the condition of humankind will deteriorate into a Malthusian catastrophe.

This pessimism cuts across the grain of the American character. Our history has been not of accepting what is, but striving and working with our sweat and our minds to create something better. By inventing and putting to use machines, we've improved our productivity and created enormous new wealth. By discovering medicines, we live longer. By improving our agriculture—with a big help from industry and science—our nutrition is improving.

In my lifetime, aviation has gone from those barnstorming pilots who landed their biplanes in pastures and took passengers aloft for 10 minutes at $10, to a massive industry that contributes so much to our national prosperity and way of life. By the time a young person born in the same year as NASA reaches my age, our way of life may be as much tied to space as it is today tied to aviation.

Private companies are already beginning to look to space. In this regard, the space shuttle program could well be compared to the first transcontinental railroad. And when profit motive starts into play, hold onto your hats. The world is going to see what entrepreneurial genius is all about and what it means to see America get going.

The first 25 years of NASA opened a new

era. Let us all rededicate ourselves today that NASA's next 25 years will ensure that this new chapter in history will be an American era.

I thank you for having me with you today. God bless you. And I understand that I'm to make the first slice in that cake. And if it'll just emphasize how far we've come— I remember when I was in the military as a reserve officer and we cut the cake with a cavalry saber. [*Laughter*]

Note: The President spoke at 1:16 p.m. on *the main floor of the National Air and Space Museum. He was introduced by James M. Beggs, Administrator of the National Aeronautics and Space Administration.*

Prior to his remarks, the President viewed the film "Hail Columbia" in the museum's Samuel Langley Theater. The film is an account of the first space shuttle mission.

On October 1 the President signed Proclamation 5111, proclaiming October 1 as the 25th anniversary of the National Aeronautics and Space Administration.

Nomination of William Louis Mills To Be a Member of the Council on Environmental Quality
October 19, 1983

The President today announced his intention to nominate William Louis Mills to be a member of the Council on Environmental Quality. He would succeed W. Ernst Minor.

Since 1977 Dr. Mills has been serving as associate professor of environmental and water resources engineering at Vanderbilt University in Nashville, Tenn. Previously he was associate professor of environmental health sciences and engineering at North Carolina Central University in 1973–1977; research assistant and graduate student in the department of civil engineering at the University of Kansas in 1971–1973; and an instructor in the department of biology at North Carolina Central University in 1969–1971.

He graduated from Alcorn State University (B.S., 1967), Tuskegee Institute (M.S., 1969), and the University of Kansas (Ph. D., 1973). He is married, has two children, and resides in Nashville, Tenn. He was born November 20, 1944, in Mobile, Ala.

Appointment of Bently T. Elliott as Deputy Assistant to the President and Director of Speechwriting
October 19, 1983

The President today announced his intention to appoint Bently T. Elliott to be Deputy Assistant to the President and Director of the White House Speechwriting Office. He will succeed Aram Bakshian.

Mr. Elliott joined the White House staff in April 1981. He has served in the Speechwriting Office as senior writer and recently as Acting Director.

He has a background in journalism, freelance writing, and speechwriting. Prior to his position at the White House, he joined the U.S. Chamber of Commerce in 1979 as director of executive communications. He created press operations for Representative Mickey Edwards (R-Okla.) in 1977–1978 and was speechwriter to Treasury Secretary William E. Simon in 1976. In 1970–1975 he was with CBS News as a producer of CBS Newsfilm for the domestic affiliates and foreign broadcasting clients.

Mr. Elliott graduated from Bucknell University (B.A., 1966) and received a degree in international relations at L'Institut d'Études Politiques in Paris, France. He is married to the former Adrienne Stetson of Dallas, Tex. They have three children and reside in Alexandria, Va. He was born November 6, 1944, in Bryn Mawr, Pa.

Message to the House of Representatives Returning Without Approval a Bill Conveying Certain Lands in Lane County, Oregon
October 19, 1983

To the House of Representatives:

I am returning herewith, without my approval, H.R. 1062, a bill "To authorize the Secretary of the Interior to convey, without consideration, certain lands in Lane County, Oregon."

H.R. 1062 would authorize the Secretary of the Interior to convey to any person, without consideration, the real property they claim to have been deprived of in Lane County, Oregon, as a result of a particular Bureau of Land Management (BLM) resurvey. All right, title, and interest of the United States to such property could be conveyed if an application, accompanied by such proof of title, description of land, and other information as the Secretary of the Interior may require, is received by the Secretary within five years after enactment of the bill.

The title defects affecting the beneficiaries of this legislation were caused by the reliance of the developers and subsequent purchasers of this tract on an inaccurate private survey—not by any act of the United States. To authorize the United States to convey public lands to persons who rely on erroneous private surveys is not in the public interest. Moreover, enactment of this legislation would create a clearly undesirable precedent, encouraging other persons who do not verify the validity of their title to assert claims for convey-

ance, at no charge, of the Federal lands on which they are encroaching. Without doubt, these claims would hinder effective public land management.

Moreover, administrative procedures exist under conditions set out in section 203 of the Federal Land Policy and Management Act whereby the purposes of this legislation could be accomplished through a conveyance of the property at fair market value.

H.R. 1062 is clearly inconsistent with this policy of requiring fair market value for conveyance of Federal lands. There was no error in the survey by the United States. Instead, the problem arose because of an improper private survey. There is, therefore, no justification for legislating a conveyance of this tract without payment of fair market value or for bypassing administrative procedures that already exist for the conveyance of public lands in appropriate cases.

For these reasons, I have withheld my approval of H.R. 1062.

RONALD REAGAN

The White House,
October 19, 1983.

Note: On October 25 the House of Representatives and the Senate voted to override the President's veto. As enacted, H.R. 1062 is Public Law 98–137.

The President's News Conference
October 19, 1983

Economic Recovery

The President. Good evening. I have a statement.

This week we marked an anniversary here in Washington—at least some of us did—the 1,000th day since we charted a new course for America. From the outset, we knew that a breaking with the past and beginning on the new road would be long and hard, and it has been. Coming to grips with the most serious economic crisis in postwar history has tested our mettle, our patience, and our unity. And believe me, I understand how difficult it's been to hear that America is making sure and steady progress when it's our family and friends who are suffering the ache and disappointment of hard times. But we Americans are a people of deep faith, hard work, and common sense, and we never stopped believing in ourselves. So, we're emerging with renewed confidence.

We've made great strides in these first thousand days. Inflation and interest rates are down dramatically. We've passed the first real tax cut for everyone in nearly 20 years. And now a strong recovery is sending Americans back to work. Almost 400,000 found jobs last month. We have the highest number of people working in our history— almost 102 million. Virtually every sector of the economy from construction to the auto industry to high technology is expanding, creating new hope and a more secure future.

We have the chance to build the kind of lasting economic expansion that this nation has not enjoyed since the 1960's. And I ask the Congress for cooperation in these last 4 weeks before it leaves for the year. Many key budget decisions remain, and we have a real opportunity to hold down spending and reduce deficits. And I think we should remember these deficits didn't just spring up in a thousand days. They're the product of too many years of tax and tax and spend and spend.

In these closing days of Congress, let us rededicate ourselves not to taxing people more, but to making government spend less. This is the way to keep the United States on a steady path of economic growth and opportunity for all our people.

And now, your questions. Ken—did I say Ken? Jim [James Gerstenzang, Associated Press].

Nicaragua

Q. Mr. President, regarding the recent rebel attacks on a Nicaraguan oil depot, is it proper for the CIA to be involved in planning such attacks and supplying equipment for air raids? And do the American people have a right to be informed about any CIA role?

The President. I think covert actions have been a part of government and a part of government's responsibilities for as long as there's been a government.

I'm not going to comment on what, if any, connection such activities might have had with what has been going on or with some of the specific operations down there. But I do believe in the right of a country, when it believes that its interests are best served, to practice covert activity. And then, while your people may have a right to know, you can't let your people know without letting the wrong people know, those that are in opposition to what you're doing.

Lebanon

Q. Mr. President, there's growing concern about the marines in Lebanon, and your national security affairs adviser has said that the loss of life is unacceptable and that the partition of Lebanon is unacceptable. What are you going to do about it? And I'd like to follow up.

The President. Helen [Helen Thomas, United Press International], we're going to keep on doing what we have been doing, trying to complete the plan that we launched a little more than a year ago. We know there are hazards there, and no one can feel more deeply about the loss of life and the wounding of some of our men there. We knew it was a hazardous undertaking when we joined in the multinational force. But our objective remains the same.

We have made great progress there. If you'll remember back, Beirut itself was being shelled daily in an exchange of fire that was killing literally hundreds of civilians on a daily basis, wounding others grievously, that a cease-fire followed there. A government was created. Representatives to a parliament were elected. The Israelis have withdrawn to the Awali River and have announced their intention of permanently withdrawing.

The disorders that have plagued Lebanon for some 8 years have, of course, taken over. This was one of the reasons for a multinational force, to try and have some stability while the government—and, incidentally, I left out the fact that the Lebanese Army, which has been created by this new government, and in which we've helped with training and supplies, is a fine army— not as big as it should be, for the problems it's confronted with. But the mission is to enable the Lebanese Government and its military to take over its own country with the withdrawal of all forces. Earlier in that first cease-fire there was a successful ousting of some 10,000 of the PLO militia from the country.

As long as there's a possibility of making the overall peace plan work, we're going to stay there.

Q. May I ask what plans do you contemplate? How will you broaden the peace in the Middle East and bring about a reconciliation of all the parties and the restoration of the legitimate rights of the Palestinians?

The President. Well, this—you've named exactly the goals of the plan that I proposed a year ago last September, and it began with trying to straighten up the Lebanese situation, with the border of Israel, the northern border being violated as it was by terrorist groups, innocent people there being killed. They had a responsibility to try and defend that border.

Now an agreement has been reached between the Lebanese Government and Israel. We are doing everything we can to persuade Syria to quit being a roadblock in this process. But that was the first phase, Lebanon; then, and our intention remains the same, working with the more moderate

Arab States to bring about the kind of peace with Israel that Anwar Sadat helped bring about.

Our process is following the lead that was established in the Camp David talks and the two United Nations resolutions, 242 and 338. And this is what we want to do, but, as I say, it all is kind of hinging on the resolution of Lebanon.

Yeah, Sam [Sam Donaldson, ABC News].

Martin Luther King, Jr.

Q. Mr. President, Senator Helms has been saying on the Senate floor that Martin Luther King, Jr., had Communist associations, was a Communist sympathizer. Do you agree?

The President. We'll know in about 35 years, won't we? No, I don't fault Senator Helms' sincerity with regard to wanting the records opened up. I think that he's motivated by a feeling that if we're going to have a national holiday named for any American, when it's only been named for one American in all our history up until this time, that he feels we should know everything there is to know about an individual. As I say, I don't fault his sincerity in that, but I also recognize there is no way that these records can be opened, because an agreement was reached between the family and the government with regard to those records. And we're not going to turn away from that or set a precedent of breaking agreements of that kind.

Q. Sir, what do we do then in 35 years if the records are opened and we find that Dr. King was a Communist sympathizer? Do we then try to undo the law? I mean, I'm not quite certain where the logic is there.

The President. The logic is there in that there is no way that this government should violate its word and open those records now.

I happen to—while I would have preferred a day of recognition for his accomplishments and what he meant in a stormy period in our history here, I would have preferred a day similar to, say, Lincoln's birthday, which is not technically a national holiday, but is certainly a day reverenced by a great many people in our country and has been. I would have preferred that, but since they seem bent on making it a national holiday, I believe the symbolism of that day is important enough that I'll sign that legislation when it reaches my desk.

U.S. Marines in Lebanon

Q. Mr. President, when I was in the marines the doctrine was to take the high ground and hold it and not deploy on a flat, open field like the Beirut airport. What reason is there to prevent the marines from taking some more defensible positions in pursuit of the policy for which you've sent them there?

The President. Well, Jerry [Jeremiah O'Leary, Washington Times], all of those things we're asking ourselves, and we're looking at everything that can be done to try and make their position safer. But you must remember, you were talking about when you were being trained as marines for combat. And if these marines had gone there to join in the combat on the side of whatever force we might have picked, then all of those rules would apply. But they're there as part of a multinational force to try and maintain a stability. And their sector happens to be trying to maintain that airport and open it up for traffic. So, airports just happen to be flat. And we're doing everything we can and making everything possible for them to defend themselves.

Q. Sir, does that mean that they cannot sally forth from the borders of the area to which they're assigned if they are attacked from a nearby position, whether it's high ground or not?

The President. All I can tell you is that—I can't answer that question right now, but I virtually daily tell our people that are to be in consultation with the men on the ground, the commanders there of those units or anything, that in keeping with our mission, that we can do to help ensure their safety.

Now, let me turn over in another direction. Andrea [Andrea Mitchell, NBC News]?

Martin Luther King, Jr.

Q. Mr. President, you had said in the past, a year and a half ago—following up on Sam—that you had real reservations about the expense of another national holiday. In fact, to quote you, you said, "It might be that there is no way we could afford all of those holidays that we would have with people who are also revered figures in history of many of the groups that make up our population." So, I'm wondering, why have you changed your mind now about the holiday for Dr. King? And why are you willing to sign that legislation?

The President. Because I think this has become so symbolic of what was a very real crisis in our history and a discrimination that was pretty foreign to what is normal with us and the part that he played in that—I think that the symbolism of it is worthy of this.

Q. Well, if I could follow up then, can you explain to us why you've decided to spend the coming weekend in Augusta at a golf club that is very exclusive and that we understand has no black members?

The President. I don't know anything about the membership, but I know that there is nothing in the bylaws of that club that advocates any discrimination of any kind. I saw in a recent tournament down there, a national tournament—I saw blacks playing in that tournament on that course.

I've been invited as a guest to go down and play a round of golf on the Augusta golf course. And, as I say, I think I've covered all that I know about it.

Dean [Dean Reynolds, Cable News Network]?

William P. Clark

Q. Mr. President, your recent nomination of Judge Clark as Interior Secretary shocked just about everybody but yourself and Judge Clark, I think. [*Laughter*] I wonder, sir, if you could tell us what qualifications he has for that Interior Department post?

The President. Well, I think, the qualifications of being a very able and fine administrator and manager. I have known him from the time when he was my chief of staff when I was Governor in California. I know that on the bench as a Supreme Court Justice of California he dealt with many problems of this kind. I know of his own personal interest and knowledge in this field. He's a fourth-generation rancher, as he himself has stated.

He's greatly interested in this entire subject, and I believe that he will do a fine job in carrying out the policies which I've advocated there.

Q. If I could just follow up. Did he want to leave the national security post?

The President. He expressed a very definite interest in that position, and as I say, it did not surprise me knowing of his great interest in that. And I appointed him.

Kathy [Katherine Lewis, Houston Post]?

Immigration Legislation

Q. Mr. President, after years of bipartisan work on a comprehensive immigration reform bill, it appears House Speaker O'Neill has successfully blocked action on it in the House and even suggested that you might veto it for political purposes. What, if anything, are you going to do to help House Republicans who are trying to free up that bill?

The President. I am going to try and get, and have been supportive of, some immigration legislation for a long time. This country has lost control of its own borders, and no country can sustain that kind of position.

I supported actively and worked hard for the passage twice of the Senate bill on immigration. I will admit that the House bill— I had some disagreements with some of the structure and the form of that bill, but recognized that there was a process called conference when there was differences between the two bills.

I want to sign, as quickly as possible, immigration legislation.

Now I'm going to have to shift again here. Steve [Steven Taylor, Satellite News Channel]?

1984 Presidential Campaign

Q. Thank you, Mr. President. Let's speak about reelection if we might for a moment. You have said that you want to delay the decision as long as possible to maintain your credibility with Congress, for instance. This is understandable, as I see it, as long as you run. But it's getting late, and if you don't run at this point, other Republicans who would then have an interest in it would be way behind their Democratic opponents. It would seem to hurt the party. Therefore,

practically speaking now, don't you have to run?

The President. I have to commend all of you people; you can find more different ways of asking that question. [*Laughter*]

Q. There's one way to stop us. [*Laughter*]

The President. Yes, and down the road one day, probably in the not-too-distant future, probably before my birthday— [*laughter*]—I will put your minds all at rest one way or the other.

And I don't think—in the first place, I think that campaigns are too long. And I think one of the reasons we don't have as many people voting as we should in this country is not because they haven't got an interest, but because we satiate them and we wear them out until they seem to be campaigning year in and year out and day in and day out. And if any of the Democratic candidates are listening, yes, I mean them—[*laughter*]—too with this.

So, I don't think there would be any harm done by—I know that some who've preceded me in this office have waited much longer than I'll probably wait before they've said anything about——

Q. Just to make sure, everytime we've heard it, it's been a little later. Your birthday, I think, is in February. Is that now the schedule?

The President. No, I just happened to mention that. [*Laughter*]

Q. Will we hear by Christmas?

The President. What?

Q. By Christmas, perhaps?

The President. It's possible. You know, I'm unpredictable in many ways. [*Laughter*]

Lesley [Lesley Stahl, CBS News]?

Syria

Q. Mr. President, back to the Middle East. You said that the Syrians are being a roadblock to the situation in Lebanon. But there are analysts who say that they are deliberately foot-dragging and in fact harrassing us and the marines over there in order to wear you down so that you will pull the marines out. Number one, do you agree with that assessment? Is that what the Syrians are doing? And, secondly, can you be worn down?

The President. Well, the answer to the

first part of the question is that I know the Syrians are dragging their feet, but there have been other indications as to the reason for that. Syria, for many years, has talked about a thing called Greater Syria, in which they've believed that much of Jordan and much of Lebanon truly should belong to them. And I think that they have that kind of an interest in this, and aided and abetted by about 7,000 Soviet advisers and technicians and some pretty sophisticated Soviet weaponry, I think that they are contributing to the disorder and the trouble.

Now, if they're doing it with the idea of wearing me down, they're going to be disappointed.

Q. Could you clarify that? What do you mean they'll be disappointed? What are you going to have the marines doing if they escalate, for instance?

The President. Well, the marines will always defend themselves, and we will provide that defense. But we're going to—I know that many of the Arab nations have been joining us—we're going to continue the diplomatic process that was advanced so brilliantly by Phil Habib and by Ambassador McFarlane, which brought about the present situation and the desire of the government there to now broaden its base and bring in some of the dissident groups and all. We're going to continue with that process.

But I don't think there's any way that we should stand by and just let Syria destroy what so many people want, which is peace and order there in that troubled country.

Arms Control Negotiations

Q. Mr. President, do you feel the Soviets will negotiate seriously on arms control once the Presidential election heats up? Or is it a matter of achieving an agreement in the next several months or waiting until 1985?

The President. Now, wait a minute, try that again. I think I was still thinking about some things that I would have said in addition to my other answer.

Q. Given the uncertainty that a Presidential election would create, would you feel the Soviets would still negotiate seriously on arms control once the Presidential election heats up? Or is it a matter of achieving

something between now and the time you announce, or waiting until '85?

The President. I think the Soviets are going to negotiate seriously. There is a great propaganda effort going on on their part now, because their target is—they've been encouraged by some of the demonstrations that they've helped organize throughout the world. They think maybe they could persuade our allies to turn back and not ask us for the deployment of the intermediate-range weapons. Well, we're going to deploy, and deploy on schedule. And once they see we're going to do that, and now that they know that we're determined to build our strength and not unilaterally disarm, as we so foolishly have done over recent years, I think they're going to see that the best thing for them is to negotiate with us and in good faith.

And they may do some things, they may try, as has been rumored, walk out and things of that kind. But we'll just wait at the table, and I think they'll come back.

Q. Sir, if I can follow up, do you feel confident that you will get an agreement by the end of your first term?

The President. By the end of this term?

Q. This term, yes.

The President. Well, I hope very much that we will. We've been at this. I realize the history of negotiations in the past has been long drawn out. But if you will look at some of the negotiations in the past, maybe it was long drawn out because the longer the Soviets sat there, the more we unilaterally disarmed. And they found that just by waiting they could get things that they wanted. Well, we're not doing that. We're arming.

Yes?

U.S. Marines in Lebanon

Q. Mr. President, before the United States went into Vietnam, the French suffered a devastating defeat there by putting their troops in a saucer-shaped depression with the enemy up around the sides shooting down on them. Doesn't this appear uncomfortably similar to you to the way we are deploying our troops in Lebanon on the low ground? And how soon can we expect that we're going to redeploy them to a spot that makes more sense?

The President. Well, right now, with the cease-fire, it isn't from high ground that they're being fired upon. Actually, much of this that has tragically taken lives there is literally coming from civilians, from radicals, in residential neighborhoods where we have always refrained from using artillery cover or anything of that kind. And when they were fired upon from the hills, that's when naval gunfire responded, and maybe the French at Dien Bien Phu in that terrible defeat didn't have a *New Jersey* sitting offshore as we do.

Q. But our marines are still being killed, sir.

The President. I know, and, as I say, most of this from the sniper-type fire. As a matter of fact, some of the TV news accounts have carried actual interviews with the very young men who are doing this and who are claiming their right. And yet they are not even members of some of the unofficial militia; they are just individuals that are out murdering.

And we're not sitting idly by. We're looking at every option and everything that we can do that can leave us in the position to carry out the mission for which they were sent and, at the same time, make their lives safer.

Bob [Storer Rowley, Chicago Tribune News Service]?

Iran-Iraq War

Q. Mr. President, Iran has threatened to close the Strait of Hormuz if Iraq uses its French fighters against Iranian interests. Is the U.S. prepared to use military force to stop Iran from cutting off our oil, and do you believe we would be successful?

The President. Let me just say that I don't think it would be proper for me to talk about tactics or what might be done, but I will say this: I do not believe the free world could stand by and allow anyone to close the Straits of Hormuz in the Persian Gulf to the oil traffic through those waterways.

Q. Can you say how far we'd be willing to go?

The President. No. As I say, that's for them to wonder about.

Sarah [Sarah McClendon, McClendon News Service]? I have to call on you. I talked to your boss the other day.

Q. Thank you. He enjoyed it.

Democracy Project

Sir, I want to ask you about a proposal that you are backing that's before the Senate now. I don't think they've passed it quite yet, but they're about to. It's that project for democracy. It would mean, I believe, that we would provide taxpayers money and private sector leaders to go into other countries and decide if they have a democratic government or not. And if we think they don't, then we would turn over that government and set up a government that we like. Don't you think that would get us into a lot of wars?

The President. Sarah, that's not the aim of this program. What you're talking about is the thing that I spoke to the British Parliament about when I was there at the European summit. No, what we have in mind is that the Marxist-Leninists, and the World Socialist Movement, for that matter, they've been ardent missionaries for their beliefs all over the world. And we in the democracies, where free enterprise is practiced, have just sort of thought that maybe everyone could see how well we're doing and follow our lead.

No, the proposal is for people to go and be the same kind of missionaries and see if they cannot explain democracy. One of the first meetings we had in connection with that was here in this room in which people from all over the world came, and it was a session during our election year to tell them about elections and how legitimate elections could be won; not those kind where you've only got one person to vote for and you'd better vote for him or somebody'll come and get you. And it's an education program, the idea of worldwide—and pointing out the differences—that those countries that have chosen—new countries, whether it's Taiwan, Singapore, South Korea—those countries that have chosen our idea, our way instead of statism, authoritarianism or totalitarianism. Their living standard, their prosperity, their freedom for their people is so much greater than anything the other countries have. We just want to explain to people how it works.

Gary [Gary Schuster, Detroit News]?

Outer-space Defense Program

Q. Mr. President—thank you—do you favor the 5-year program that Cap Weinberger has recommended to you for the outer-space defense of this country?

The President. Gary, nothing has actually been presented to me as yet. I'm fascinated with reading all about it, but I haven't seen it. And I can tell you that no one has suggested any such figure in the billions of dollars that have been proposed.

All of this is simply the carrying out of what I asked for quite some time ago. And that was for us to see if there is not a defensive weapon that can stop this race in offensive weapons throughout the world that can render maybe a system of horrifying weapons obsolete. And so, they're proceeding with the research on that. But I think there's a great exaggeration of the kind of money that's being talked.

Q. Well, can I follow up? Would this not create, instead of an offensive arms race, a defensive arms race between the U.S. and the Soviet Union?

The President. Well, would that be all bad?

Q. Well, that's what I'm asking you.

The President. If you've got everybody building defense, then nobody's going to start a war. And that's, maybe, part of the idea. The danger that we're in today was voiced by Dwight Eisenhower in a letter to a publisher back in 1956 in which he, a man of war, said that couldn't we see that the weapons that we're building today are making victory or defeat obsolete, that we are coming to a stage in weaponry in which there can be no victory as we've always thought of it—no winner or loser in war. There can just be the destruction of the people.

And he said, when that moment arrives—and I think it has arrived—he said, then won't we have the common sense to sit down at a negotiating table and do away with war as a means of settling our disputes.

Economic Recovery

Q. Mr. President, new figures out today show that housing starts were down pretty sharply last month, and the number of building permits went down for the second month in a row. Analysts are saying this could mean the economic recovery is going to level off, maybe kind of peter out next year. And more people are becoming concerned about high interest rates. And given the big deficits being projected by your own administration, isn't it time for some strong action by you to get interest rates down?

The President. Well, I think what we're doing is aimed at getting interest rates down. Now, I'm not sure that interest rates entirely are to blame for this. And I don't know whether the recent figures—in the first place, they're still way above what they were not too long ago, before this recovery started—running around a million seven or something. But what I want to know is, are they seasonally adjusted or not? And I have to tell you I have not seen any evidence as to whether they are. And I'm going to make an inquiry, because if they're not, then you have to say, well, is interest rate—is that the principal cause or only cause? Or is it possible because people don't start building houses back in the east and the middle west and in the snow country when autumn comes?

Now, there is a great dropoff in building. Now, if it is seasonally adjusted, then we have to look at things like the interest rates. And it wouldn't surprise me if people are waiting, because I think there's a great expectation that there's going to be further drops in the interest rates. So, anyone would be smart to wait for that drop to take place.

But what we're doing about that, and the deficit—first of all is the economic recovery program, which is working—is about half your deficit is caused by the recession. So, economic recovery can halve your estimate. Our previous estimates of the horrendous deficits have already been trimmed back by the amount of recovery that we've had so far. The other part of that is structural. It is built-in because of government spending. And I'm going to continue, as hard as I can, trying to get further reductions in government spending as a means of bringing down the deficits and getting us to the point of balanced budget, which we must reach.

I have grown up listening to the other party, year after year, in the 40-odd years in which they have controlled both Houses of the Congress, tell us that deficit spending was necessary—and a little inflation also—to maintain prosperity. Well, I used to predict out on the mashed-potato circuit that what is happening would happen—the bottom would fall out. And it did. But now that recovery—and if we can continue more spending cuts—if we had obtained the cuts we asked for in the beginning of our economic recovery program, the deficit would be $40 billion smaller than it is right now.

Ms. Thomas. Thank you, Mr. President.

Note: The President's 20th news conference began at 8:02 p.m. in the East Room at the White House. It was broadcast live on nationwide radio and television.

Remarks of the President and Prime Minister Bettino Craxi of Italy Following Their Meetings
October 20, 1983

The President. Prime Minister Craxi visits us as the leader of one of America's closest and most stalwart allies. Italy in recent years has emerged as one of the principal nations of the Western alliance. Prime Minister Craxi, by assuming leadership of the Italian people, has quickly established himself as a major figure in global politics. We're impressed by the dynamic and statesmanlike leadership provided by the new Italian Government, and we're particularly pleased by this opportunity today to deepen our consultations and broaden our cooperation with our trusted Italian friends.

Italy is playing a crucial role in the NATO effort to correct the imbalance in nuclear forces in Europe. In our discussion today Prime Minister Craxi and I reviewed the INF negotiations between the United States and the Soviet Union and reaffirmed our goal—an equitable and verifiable agreement. If Soviet intransigence continues, we're committed to NATO deployment of U.S. missiles. We remain hopeful that an understanding will be reached, and we'll continue negotiations even after initial deployments. Indeed, for 2 years the United States has negotiated in good faith while the Soviets have continued to deploy theater nuclear weapons.

The Prime Minister and I also reviewed developments in other arms control fields. The United States and Italy share a common approach to the forthcoming Conference on Disarmament in Europe, where we will be attempting to reduce the risk of surprise attack in Europe by improving observation capabilities and by providing a better understanding of military forces and activities. We're striving for reductions of conventional forces and to establish parity in ground forces in Central Europe. I expressed to the Prime Minister our deep appreciation for the positive contributions Italy is making to Mediterranean security and to the search for peace in the Middle East.

Italy was among the first nations to offer its forces for service in the Sinai to help implement the historic Camp David accords. Italian and American soldiers now are bearing the difficult burdens of peacekeeping in Lebanon. We are cooperating there not only in keeping the peace but in making peace, as well. The Prime Minister and I reviewed our common efforts to promote genuine political reconciliation within Lebanon and to work toward the restoration of Lebanese sovereignty throughout that troubled nation. I cannot overemphasize the importance of the Italian diligence in this crucial effort.

We examined the world economy, discussed our respective efforts to deal with the economic challenges we face. I expressed our understanding of the difficult economic problems Italy presently confronts and our support for the tough but essential measures the Italian Government is taking to restore balanced and noninflationary growth. I expressed the hope that our own strong recovery would help Italy lift itself out of its present recession.

I've been especially impressed by Prime Minister Craxi's commitment to attack organized crime and narcotics trafficking. We share a crucial interest in efforts to suppress the international traffic in narcotics. Accordingly the Prime Minister and I have agreed to establish a joint Italian-American working group on organized crime and narcotics trafficking.

Prime Minister Craxi comes to our shores as an especially welcome guest. In international affairs where the element of personal trust is so essential, such meetings as this are invaluable. I'm delighted to say that the Prime Minister and I have laid the basis today for continuing the open, cooperative, and mutually helpful relationship which has been traditional between our two governments and their leaders.

The Prime Minister. I am particularly grateful to President Reagan for the warm welcome accorded me during my visit to the United States. I consider this welcome primarily as a homage to the Italian nation. I also thank President Reagan for the special attention that, together with members of his government, he has dedicated to the problems and to the views which I've had the opportunity to expose to him this morning on behalf of the Italian Government.

I, myself, have conveyed to President Reagan the message of friendship from the Government of Italy and from the Italian people to the Government and to the American people, also—a friendship that belongs to the history of our democratic tradition as well as to the future of our two countries.

During our talks, which have been friendly and open and, I believe, reciprocally very useful, we have carefully examined—with mutual constructive hopes—several matters. These matters are essential to attain peace both in Europe and in the world: problems and prospects of international economy, the development of Italian-American relations, issues of common interest for industrial cooperation and for an in-depth struggle against crime and the international drug traffic connected to it.

Both the United States and Italy are firmly seeking peace, which they consider with absolute conviction the most precious gift to mankind, and are both committed to solve international problems and disputes through peaceful means. Within the framework of the Atlantic alliance, our two governments will work toward strengthening peace, aiming to maintain open prospects for negotiations in the field of disarmament and arms control so as to guarantee peace through security.

On the question of nuclear balance in Europe, which presently is the most important in East-West relations, we intend to maintain the present system of close consultation and of constructive solidarity and to develop a line of combat coherent with decisions already adopted by our countries. We have followed the path of negotiations which must remain open in any case. Should a launching of the program for the modernization of NATO missile systems occur, due to the negative negotiation policy followed by the U.S.S.R. and by the Warsaw Pact, our intention is to continue to urge Soviet willingness towards serious negotiations without preconditions, aimed at achieving a reasonable agreement, providing for some means of control and some guarantees toward an equilibrium of the agreed forces at the lowest possible level, a policy of peace, which must operate in every region of the world so as to terminate conflicts and to reduce the most dangerous frictions, in full respect of the sovereignty of nations and of the rights of peoples.

In this spirit Italy intends to assure its constructive contribution by taking upon itself direct responsibilities in humanitarian and peace missions, such as is the case for the Sinai and Lebanon, aimed at achieving unity, independence, and the reconstruction of Lebanon.

However, a policy of peace must necessarily be linked to a wider international economic cooperation. This is why we have compared our points of views on the difficult period that the world economy is experiencing. In view of fostering a stable and lasting recovery, Italy and the United States must promote a further increase in the volume of their trade and cooperation which will further strengthen the excellent political relations already existing between our two countries.

Also, in view of an ever-effective fight against organized crime which is involved in international drug traffic and which is challenging and threatening our societies, a special joint commission will be set up and the necessary steps will be taken so that it may operate in the most effective way.

In our meeting today, both President Reagan and myself have reaffirmed the feeling of friendship which binds our two countries, reaffirming the commitment of our governments for the safeguard of

peace.

Thank you.

Note: The President spoke at 1:28 p.m. to reporters assembled in the East Room at the White House. The remarks were scheduled to be given outside at the South Portico, but because of inclement weather the event was held in the East Room. Prime Minister Craxi spoke in Italian, and his remarks were translated by an interpreter.

Earlier, the President and the Prime Minister met in the Oval Office and held a working luncheon, together with U.S. and Italian officials, in the State Dining Room.

Nomination of James H. Burnley IV To Be Deputy Secretary of Transportation
October 21, 1983

The President today announced his intention to nominate James H. Burnley IV to be Deputy Secretary of Transportation. He would succeed Darrell M. Trent.

Since May 1983, Mr. Burnley has been serving as General Counsel at the Department of Transportation. Previously he was Associate Deputy Attorney General at the Department of Justice in 1982–1983; Director of VISTA in 1981–1982; partner in the law firm of Turner, Enochs, Foster, Sparrow & Burnley in Greensboro, N.C., in 1975–1981; and associate in the firm of Brooks,

Pierce, McLendon, Humphrey & Leonard in Greensboro in 1973–1975.

He served on the commercial panel of arbitrators for the American Arbitration Association and was a member of the committee on administrative law of the North Carolina Bar Association.

Mr. Burnley graduated from Yale University (B.A., 1970) and Harvard Law School (J.D., 1973). He is married, has one child, and resides in Falls Church, Va. He was born July 30, 1948, in Greensboro, N.C.

Appointment of Betty Cuevas as a Member of the Advisory Committee on Small and Minority Business Ownership
October 21, 1983

The President today announced his intention to appoint Betty Cuevas to be a member of the Advisory Committee on Small and Minority Business Ownership. She will succeed Del Green.

Mrs. Cuevas is founder, owner, and manager of Cuevas Catering Service and Cuevas Restaurant in McAllen, Tex. Previously she held various positions with a retail

food chain in San Antonio, Tex., in 1963–1971. She is a member of the Ladies LULAC Council and was president of the Mexican-American Chamber of Commerce in 1977–1978.

She is married, has three children, and resides in McAllen, Tex. She was born July 8, 1936, in San Diego, Tex.

Proclamation 5120—Metropolitan Opera Day, 1983
October 21, 1983

By the President of the United States of America

A Proclamation

Among this Nation's greatest treasures are the creative talents of our people and the opportunities available for them to develop their talents and thereby enhance the richness of our cultural life. In every artistic discipline, great American artists and institutions have established ever-rising standards of achievement to challenge and inspire successive generations.

No single institution embodies this tradition of sustained artistic achievement more fully than the Metropolitan Opera, which is celebrating 100 years of extraordinary contributions to the culture of America. Legendary performances of music theater masterpieces have filled the Metropolitan Opera House in New York, halls across the country during the Company's annual tours, and millions of American homes through live radio and television broadcasts which have become part of our national tradition. The Metropolitan Opera also reaches out to discover and encourage young American talent by auditions held throughout the country, and it nurtures and develops great singers of the future.

Through its deep involvement with artists, audiences, and patrons, and with the voluntary assistance of the members of its National Council, the Metropolitan Opera has contributed invaluably to the growth of an American opera community whose vitality and brilliance are acclaimed around the world.

In recognition of the Metropolitan Opera's extraordinary achievements and commitment to excellence, the Congress, by Senate Joint Resolution 128, has authorized and requested the President to designate October 22, 1983, the one hundredth anniversary of its first performance, as "Metropolitan Opera Day" throughout the United States.

Now, Therefore, I, Ronald Reagan, President of the United States of America, do hereby designate October 22, 1983, as Metropolitan Opera Day and call upon all Federal, State and local government agencies, interested groups and organizations, and the people of the United States to observe that day by engaging in appropriate programs and activities to show their support of America's rich heritage in music theater and one of its premier performing institutions.

In Witness Whereof, I have hereunto set my hand this twenty-first day of October, in the year of our Lord nineteen hundred and eighty-three, and of the Independence of the United States of America the two hundred and eighth.

RONALD REAGAN

[Filed with the Office of the Federal Register, 10:30 a.m., October 24, 1983]

Radio Address to the Nation on Arms Control and Reduction
October 22, 1983

My fellow Americans:

I'd like to talk to you today about the deep desire we share to reduce nuclear weapons and to make our world more safe. Just as important I want you to know why, despite all our good faith efforts, we are being frustrated in our goal to negotiate an arms reduction agreement.

No issue concerns me more and has taken up more of my time—not just in meetings with advisers but in deliberations with Members of the Congress and close and constant consultations with our allies—than this quest for a breakthrough on arms reductions. And believe me, I do so willingly, because as your President and also as a husband, father, and grandfather, I know what's at stake for everyone.

The trouble is, the obstacle to that agreement we want so dearly is not Washington, and it never has been; it's Moscow. And that's been the case in all our current arms reduction negotiations with the Soviet Union.

But today I'd like to focus on the longer range INF missile negotiations now underway in Geneva. Some have asked, "If we do want an agreement, why are we, the United States, planning to base new missiles in Europe?" Well, the question reflects some basic misunderstandings. It's been the Soviet Union who's been deploying such forces for a number of years, while the West watched and worried.

In 1977 the Soviets had in place 600 warheads on their longer range INF missiles. More significantly, they began adding the SS–20, a new, highly accurate mobile missile with three warheads, which could reach in minutes every city in Europe and many cities in the Middle East, Africa, and Asia. NATO had no comparable weapons.

In October 1979 Soviet leader Brezhnev announced a balance now exists. The Soviet Union—800 warheads; NATO—zero. Some balance. It was only at this point at the end of 1979 that the NATO alliance, not the United States alone, decided the Soviets' large and growing advantage in both nuclear and conventional forces would threaten our safety. So, the alliance made what was called the "dual-track decision." We would redress the imbalance by deploying comparable weapons, while seeking an agreement at the negotiating table that would eliminate the need for deployment.

Nothing more dramatically illustrates our sincere desire for peace than our willingness not to deploy if the Soviets would stop threatening Europe with their missiles. How did the Soviets respond? By adding one new missile every week. They now have 1,300 warheads or more, and that number is growing. NATO still has zero.

All along we've been negotiating in good faith. We asked the Soviets to consider the total elimination of these missiles. It took them less than 24 hours to answer, "Nyet."

So we proposed an interim solution, some equal but lower number, and the lower the better. With knee-jerk speed, the same answer came back again, "Nyet." And it's remained the same for all our new proposals, because the Soviets insist on a monopoly of longer range INF missiles. They offer what can only be called "a half-zero option," zero for us, hundreds of warheads for them. As I told the members of the United Nations, that's where things stand today. We will continue our efforts to make the Soviets heed the will of the world, stop stonewalling, and start negotiating in good faith.

But that wish should not become father to the thought. We must look at Soviet words and deeds with a clear head and ask some long overdue questions. Why does a regime which says it seeks peace repeatedly reject equitable proposals that would preserve peace? What are we to think of Soviet threats against NATO countries: warning Turkey it could become "a nuclear cemetery;" telling Scandinavian countries they are "a bridgehead for aggression;" and advising West Germany if new missiles are deployed, the military threat to it will grow manifold?

These are not words of a peacemaker but of a nation bent on intimidation. It is inconceivable that any Western leader would make such crude and provocative threats.

Finally, what is the credibility of a regime which exploits peace demonstrations in the West, but brutally puts down any demonstration for reduced weaponry in its own country? As President Mitterrand of France recently observed, "Pacifism is in the West, and Euro-missiles are in the East. I consider that an unequal relationship."

My fellow Americans, the values of Western civilization and the beliefs that bind free people together are being tested. The Soviets are engaged in a campaign to intimidate the West, but it will not work. At home, bipartisan support in the Congress remains strong. And the unity of our NATO alliance will not break. Just this week, Prime Minister Craxi of Italy visited the White House and assured me of Italy's continued staunch support. Earlier this year, at the Williamsburg summit, the leaders of the industrialized nations agreed the policy is correct, fair, and should go forward. The spirit of Williamsburg is as strong as ever.

There is simply no sensible alternative to the parallel goal of deterrence and arms reduction. We will remain at the negotiating table just as long as it takes to reach a breakthrough. But the Soviets must understand: NATO's mission is to defend Europe and preserve peace, which it has done for 34 years. And NATO will continue to meet its responsibilities. Our countries will remain united, strong, and we will protect the safety of our people.

Until next week, thanks for listening, and God bless you.

Note: The President's address was recorded on October 21 in the Map Room at the White House for broadcast at 12:06 p.m. on October 22.

Remarks to Reporters on the Death of American and French Military Personnel in Beirut, Lebanon
October 23, 1983

I'm not going to take any questions this morning because we're going right into meetings on the events that have taken place on this tragic weekend. But I would like to make this statement:

I know there are no words that can express our sorrow and grief over the loss of those splendid young men and the injury to so many others. I know there are no words, also, that can ease the burden of grief for the families of those young men.

Likewise, there are no words to properly express our outrage and, I think, the outrage of all Americans at the despicable act, following as it does on the one perpetrated several months ago, in the spring, that took the lives of scores of people at our Embassy in that same city, in Beirut.

But I think we should all recognize that these deeds make so evident the bestial nature of those who would assume power if they could have their way and drive us out of that area that we must be more determined than ever that they cannot take over that vital and strategic area of the Earth or, for that matter, any other part of the Earth.

Thank you.

Note: The President spoke at 8:38 a.m. at the South Portico of the White House. He was returning from a weekend stay in Augusta, Ga., after conferring for several hours with his advisers on the bombing incidents.

Proclamation 5121—Death of American and French Military Personnel in Beirut, Lebanon
October 23, 1983

By the President of the United States of America

A Proclamation

As a mark of respect for the American and French military personnel who died violently in the performance of their peacekeeping duties in the tragic bombings of October 23, 1983 in Beirut, Lebanon, I hereby order, by virtue of the authority vested in me as President of the United States of America, that the flag of the United States shall be flown at half-staff upon all public buildings and grounds, at all military posts and naval stations, and on all naval vessels of the Federal Government in the District of Columbia and throughout the United States and its Territories and possessions through Monday, October 31, 1983. I also direct that the flag shall be flown at half-staff for the same length of time at all United States embassies, legations, consular offices, and other facilities abroad, including all military facilities and naval vessels and stations.

In Witness Whereof, I have hereunto set my hand this twenty-third day of October,

in the year of our Lord nineteen hundred and eighty-three, and of the Independence of the United States of America the two hundred and eighth.

RONALD REAGAN

[*Filed with the Office of the Federal Register, 10:31 a.m., October 24, 1983*]

Statement by Deputy Press Secretary Speakes on the Death of American and French Military Personnel in Beirut, Lebanon
October 23, 1983

The President held extensive meetings today with his senior advisers to consider the United States response to the deliberate and heinous acts of international terrorism in Beirut against American and French forces. These forces are present to assist a peaceful settlement of the Lebanese crisis. This settlement is essential to regional and world peace. These attacks were clearly designed to weaken our determination and to disrupt the efforts of the Government of Lebanon to regain control and sovereignty over the country. One thing is clear: Those who sponsor these outrages believe that they can intimidate the Government of Lebanon, its people, and their friends in the international community. They are wrong. We will not yield to international terrorism, because we know that if we do the civilized world will suffer and our values will be fair game for those who seek to destroy all we stand for.

The President has directed that General P. X. Kelley, Commandant of the Marine Corps, depart for Beirut to undertake a complete review of ways to provide better protection for the marine contingent in Lebanon. We also intend to respond to this criminal act when the perpetrators are

identified. The President is consulting closely with our MNF allies and the Lebanese Government. Our actions will be resolute and consistent with stated policies and objectives.

The President is communicating with our MNF partners and the Government of Lebanon. He is stressing that we remain determined to pursue our stated objectives in Lebanon which are to ensure that Lebanon can be restored as an independent and sovereign nation, free of all foreign forces, and free to reconstitute a national consensus. We and the Government of Lebanon remain committed to the process of national reconciliation and an accommodation of the legitimate interests of all the Lebanese people. We have stressed to President Gemayel the necessity of persevering in his courageous decision to broaden the political base and composition of his government, and we will assure that he can do so without surrendering to those who reject political solutions and seek to impose their will by violent means.

Note: Deputy Press Secretary Larry M. Speakes read the statement to reporters assembled in the Briefing Room at the White House at 7:06 p.m.

Nomination of Kenneth S. George To Be Director General of the United States and Foreign Commercial Service
October 24, 1983

The President today announced his intention to nominate Kenneth S. George to be Director General of the United States and Foreign Commercial Service, Department of Commerce. This is a new position.

Mr. George is currently serving as Deputy Assistant Secretary for the Commercial Services, Department of Commerce. Previously he was Deputy to the Director General of the Foreign Commercial Services, Department of Commerce (1981–1982); president, Olix Industries (management, oil and gas exploration) in 1977–1982; and president, Tri-Merenn International (oil and gas investments) in 1976–1977. He was in real estate development with Trammell Crow Co. in 1972–1976.

Mr. George graduated from Washington and Lee University (B.A., 1970) and the University of Texas at Austin (M.B.A., 1976). He resides in Midland, Tex., and was born June 25, 1948, in Fort Worth, Tex.

Nomination of Mari Maseng To Be an Assistant Secretary of Transportation
October 24, 1983

The President today announced his intention to nominate Mari Maseng to be an Assistant Secretary of Transportation (Public Affairs). She would succeed Lee L. Verstandig.

Miss Maseng served as a speechwriter to the President at the White House in 1981–1983. Previously she was press aide to Mrs. Reagan, office of the President-elect, in 1980–1981 and special assistant to the chairman of the Reagan-Bush Committee in 1980. She was staff director for the Dole for President Committee in 1979–1980 and served as press secretary for Senator Strom Thurmond's reelection campaign in 1978. She was a reporter for the Charleston Evening Post in 1974–1978.

She received her bachelor of arts degree from the University of South Carolina in 1975. Miss Maseng was born March 15, 1954, in Chicago, Ill.

Remarks and a Question-and-Answer Session With Regional Editors and Broadcasters on the Situation in Lebanon
October 24, 1983

The President. Good afternoon. Given what has happened in Lebanon, I've put aside the remarks that I was prepared to give here today. And I'd like to read you this statement.

Yesterday's acts of terrorism in Beirut which killed so many young American and French servicemen were a horrifying reminder of the type of enemy that we face in many critical areas of the world today—vicious, cowardly, and ruthless. Words can never convey the depth of compassion that we feel for those brave men and for their loved ones.

Many Americans are wondering why we must keep our forces in Lebanon. Well, the reason they must stay there until the situation is under control is quite clear: We have vital interests in Lebanon, and our actions in Lebanon are in the cause of world peace. With our allies—England, France, and Italy—we're part of a multinational peacekeeping force seeking a withdrawal of all foreign forces from Lebanon and from the Beirut area while the new Lebanese Government undertakes to restore sovereignty throughout that country. By promoting peace in Lebanon, we strengthen the forces for peace throughout the Middle East. This is not a Republican or a Democratic goal but one that all Americans share.

Peace in Lebanon is key to the region's stability now and in the future. To the extent that the prospect for future stability is heavily influenced by the presence of our forces, it is central to our credibility on a global scale. We must not allow international criminals and thugs such as these to undermine the peace in Lebanon.

The struggle for peace is indivisible. We cannot pick and choose where we will support freedom; we can only determine how. If it's lost in one place, all of us lose. If others feel confident that they can intimidate us and our allies in Lebanon, they will become more bold elsewhere. If Lebanon ends up under the tyranny of forces hostile to the West, not only will our strategic position in the Eastern Mediterranean be threatened but also the stability of the entire Middle East, including the vast resource areas of the Arabian Peninsula.

In conjunction with our multinational force partners, we're taking measures to strengthen the capabilities of our forces to defend themselves. The United States will not be intimidated by terrorists. We have strong circumstantial evidence linking the perpetrators of this latest atrocity to others that have occurred against us in the recent past, including the bombing of our Embassy in Beirut last April. Every effort will be made to find the criminals responsible for this act of terrorism so this despicable act will not go unpunished.

And now, I know you have some questions.

Q. Mr. President, Linda Douglass from KNXT–TV in Los Angeles. What are the options? Do we increase the number of troops in Lebanon? Do we withdraw the troops in Lebanon? What do you consider the options to be?

The President. The option that we cannot consider is withdrawing while their mission still remains. And they do have a mission, contrary to what some people have intimated in the last 24 hours or so. And it is tied in with the effort that we launched more than a year ago to try and bring peace to the total area of the Middle East because of its strategic importance to the whole free world, not just the United States.

I couldn't give you a time on this. The options are—well, I have sent, as of this morning, General Kelley, the Commandant of the Marine Corps, is on his way to Lebanon to review again what we can do with regard to improving the defensive measures, the safety measures for the marines who are stationed there. And we're looking at every possible option in that regard. But the mission remains, and it remains as yet unfulfilled, although there's been tremendous success so far.

Q. Mr. President, Bill Applegate from WLS in Chicago. You discussed the diplomatic mission. What specifically is the military mission of the marines?

The President. Well, you have to go back a little bit in memory on the situation there in the Middle East. We know, of course, our country, since 1948, has been pledged to the continued existence and the security of Israel. And we've had these numerous wars between the Arab States and Israel, with a number of the Arab States, or virtually all of them, refusing to accept the existence of Israel as a nation. We have, back over the years—as witness more recently in the previous administration, the Camp David accords. So, what we submitted was the idea of us continuing to help, as we did at Camp David, in furthering that process, bringing more nations into the kind of peaceful arrangement that occurred between Egypt and Israel—producing more Egypts, if you will.

At the same time, however, and for a number of years now, Lebanon has been torn with strife. They've had factions. And from just factions and kind of rioting situations, they've developed over the years to where kind of war lords set up with their own military forces. So we recognized that before we could proceed with the peace plan—remember that when we started this, Israel had been forced across its own border, was shelling Beirut. The PLO militias inside Beirut were shelling back. The casualties were hundreds of civilians, every day, dying and being grievously wounded.

So we recognized that what we had to resolve first was this issue: to get Syria, which had crossed from the other border, to get Syria, get Israel, get the PLO organization out of Lebanon and then to have a stabilizing force while a government could be established in Lebanon and their military could then acquire the capability necessary to reinstitute their control over their own borders. And this was why the multinational force went in—to provide that stability so that when the Lebanese forces moved out, as the other forces, the Israelis and the Syrians left, there could be a maintenance of order behind them.

Now that mission remains, and it did have measures of great success. Some 5,000 of the organized PLO militias, as you'll remember, were shipped out of Lebanon. Some of those, we fear, have been infiltrated back in, mainly by way of Syria now. But that was accomplished. A government was established. We have helped very definitely with the training of the Lebanese Army, and they proved the quality of that training recently in the fighting in the hills and around Suq al Gharb. And we think that they have—they don't have the size yet to where they could take over in, let's say, the policing of that area and of the airport and still have enough manpower to go out and restore order as they're supposed to.

So that mission remains. And, as of now, they have finally agreed upon a date and a place for a meeting in which the Government of Lebanon is going to try and bring in representatives of the hostile factions within Lebanon to broaden the base of the government.

So we think that the goal is worthy, and we think that great progress has been made that would not have been made if it were not for the multinational force.

Q. Mr. President, Susan Hutchison, KIRO–TV, from Seattle. I'm a journalist, but I'm also the wife of a U.S. Marine Corps captain, and as such I am personally grieved over the loss of lives. I am wondering what message you can give to Americans who are frustrated with the loss of life in a region that historically has not known peace—and, many think, will never know peace—and yet, our men are over there as peacekeepers.

The President. I wish there were an instant answer here that would resolve all your concerns. You didn't tell me about that one when we were having lunch here.

I understand your concern. I understand all Americans' concern, and I have to say that I don't know of anything that is worse in the job I have than having to make the calls that I have made as a result of these snipings that have taken place in the past.

I wish it could be without hazard, but the alternative is to look at this region which, as I say, is vital. Our allies in Western Europe, the Japanese—it would be a disaster if a force took over the Middle East. And a force is ready to do that, as witness what has taken place in Yemen, in Ethiopia, and now the forces of some several thousand that are theirs in Syria.

The free world cannot stand by and see that happen. Yes, this has been an area torn by strife over the centuries, and yet not too many years ago, before the kind of breakup, Lebanon was a very prosperous, peaceful nation that was kind of known as the Gateway to the East. And we believe it can be again.

Probably no one—or no country was more at war with Israel than Egypt, and yet we saw Egypt and Israel come to a peace treaty and Israel give up the Sinai and so forth that it had conquered in war. We have to believe that this we must strive for, because the alternative could be disaster for all of our world.

Q. Mr. President, I'm Rollin Post from KRON in San Francisco. I want to ask you, you've addressed it now several times, the issue that we cannot get out of the Middle East. But would you address the other argument that if you're not going to get out, then let's just not put marines back in to replace those who have been killed and wounded to do exactly the same thing in the same place but, if you're going to do a job, go into Lebanon and do it with some real force, which is another argument—[*inaudible*].

The President. But you see what that entails—and that is the difficult thing—we would then be engaged in the combat. We would be the combat force. We would be fighting against Arab States, and that is not the road to peace. We're still thinking in terms of that long-range peace.

Lebanon must be resolved and resolve within itself its own problems. And incidentally, not much attention has been paid to the diplomatic process that's been going on for all of this time, and before, round-the-clock. And we now are seeking a replacement for Ambassador McFarlane, who is with us here today, who is now national security adviser—but someone to replace him. But he could tell you. And I used to sit here feeling guilty, hearing his schedule from Damascus to Beirut to Tel Aviv, back, and hours and hours of meetings. But they have all led to this present cease-fire, to this government that is now in Lebanon, and to the effort to enlarge that government. So we're keeping on with that process.

But with the present mission of the multinational force—and remember there are four nations involved there—enlarging their forces, if it would help with the mission they're performing, would be one thing. But to join into the combat and become a part of the combative force, actually all we would really be doing would be increasing the number of targets and risking, really, the start of overall conflict and world war.

No, our mission, I think, makes sense. I think it has proven itself so far. The tragedy is coming not really from the warring forces, it is coming from little bands of individuals, literally criminal minded, who now see in the disorder that's going on an opportunity to do what they want to do. And we're going to make every effort we can to minimize the risk but also to find those responsible.

Q. Lilly Flores-Vela, KIII–TV, Corpus Christi, Texas. I'd like to know what exactly is underway now, what efforts are underway to identify the casualties and those missing, and how are the relatives being notified about this?

The President. You have touched upon what is a heartbreaking part of this particular incident. That was the headquarters building. There were more than 200 men sleeping in that building when this occurred. The records, the personnel records are either destroyed or buried someplace beneath all that rubble. And because they were sleeping, many of the men were not wearing their dog tags. And the delay in notification of the families—and it must be a terrible, cruel, additional punishment for these people who wait in suspense. And we have no answers until—we're doing everything, or the marines are, that they can to identify. And when they can get actual identification, such as bodies that did have dog tags or where comrades can recognize and identify, to notify the individual families. But it's a long, tragic story because of the other, the loss of the records.

Q. Mr. President, I'm Ray Rosenblum with WBRJ in Marietta, Ohio. And I want to congratulate you on paying attention to the news media outside of Washington. And regarding the economy, I'd like to ask: If you were an investor, would you invest today in the U.S. stock market, and do you think it will continue to grow?

The President. Yes, I do, and I can't because I have a secret trust on account of I'm not supposed to know what I have anymore. [*Laughter*] So I can't buy anything like that.

But, yes, I think this recovery is solid, and I think that it is based on something that we're never had in any of the previous recessions. There have been about eight since World War II. And every one of them prior to this was treated with a quick fix, an artificial stimulant by government spending and money supply and so forth. And if you'll look back at the history of them, every one of them was followed within a matter of 2 or 3 years by another one, and each time inflation was higher and unemployment was greater than before.

But this one, we have brought inflation, as you've probably been told in briefings already, down from 2 years of double digit—and even figures as high as 17 percent—to where for the last 12 months it has been 2.6 percent, which is the lowest 12-

month average in 17 years. And I think that what we're seeing there in the stock market—it flurries a little bit, goes up, but then every once in a while there's some profit taking and it drops a few points. But I think one figure that's been ignored, and maybe all of you can treat with it—just a week or so ago it was announced that we were up now to 70—more than 78 percent of our industrial capacity is now at work. We were way down far below that to where there was just unused industrial capacity because there wasn't any demand for the product. But this is getting practically up to prosperous times to have that much of our capacity used.

Ms. Small. One more question, Mr. President.

The President. I can't ignore that look. You. [*Laughter*]

Q. [*Inaudible*]—Jean Enerson from KING-television in Seattle. You said that General Kelley is on his way—[*inaudible*]—to recommend more safety measures. If he recommends that more troops be sent in, will you do that? And what other safety measures are you considering?

The President. Well, if this were recommended on the basis that their mission, as I say, could be furthered by some difference in the size of the mission, I would certainly take seriously the recommendation of the man who's the Commandant of the entire Marine Corps.

There are a number of other things to look at, options that have been presented. We know, for example, that we have to find a new headquarters, an operational post for the headquarters, because that was totally destroyed. One of the options being consid-

ered is, could part of the support services of that kind be stationed on one of our ships that are offshore there, one of our naval vessels? More improvements in the actual defensive structure? There are any number of options, and that's why an expert is going over there to come back and tell us what can be done.

Karna has told me that I can't take anymore on account of the time was up. Karna said that that was—you did say that that was the last one, wasn't it?

Ms. Small. I said that was the last one.

The President. And I can give you the best reason in the world why I've got to leave. The President of Togo is due in my office in just about 3 minutes, and I should be there before he gets there to say hello to him.

But your remarks about treating with the regional press, believe me it is a great pleasure. And I wish—I'm going to tell them that next time they've got to schedule any luncheons like this for about a half an hour extra, or give me some free time following it so that I can run over if I want to, because you do ask questions, and I learn as much from your questions as—maybe more—than you learn from my answers. And it's been a great pleasure to have all of you here.

God bless you all, and thank you for coming.

Note: The President spoke at 1:07 p.m. at a luncheon for the editors and broadcasters in the State Dining Room at the White House.

Karna Small Stringer is Deputy Assistant to the President and Director of Media Relations and Planning.

Appointment of Two Members of the Interagency Committee on Women's Business Enterprise
October 24, 1983

The President today announced his intention to appoint the following individuals to be members of the Interagency Committee on Women's Business Enterprise. These are

new positions.

Nancy J. Risque has been serving as Special Assistant to the President for Legislative Affairs since 1981 and was appointed Deputy Director of the Office of Legislative Affairs in October 1982. Previously she was with Standard Oil Co. (Ohio) as Federal Government affairs representative in Washington, D.C. (1978–1981); energy affairs representative for the American Paper Institute in 1977–1978; and assistant to the Assistant Secretary of Commerce for Tourism, Department of Commerce, in 1975–1977. She received a bachelor of arts degree from Radford College (B.A., 1968).

Ann Wrobleski has been director of projects in the Office of the First Lady since 1981. Previ-

ously she was assistant press secretary and scheduling director for former U.S. Senator Richard Stone in 1979–1980; press secretary to U.S. Representative Lou Frey, Jr., and research assistant with the House Republican Research Committee in 1975; traveling press secretary during the 1974 Senate campaign of Jack Eckerd; and assistant press secretary to U.S. Senator Edward J. Gurney in 1973–1974. She graduated from Stephens College, Columbia, Mo., in 1972. She is married to Phil Truluck, and they reside in Washington, D.C.

Appointment of Evalu Ware Russell as a Member of the National Advisory Council on Indian Education
October 24, 1983

The President today announced his intention to appoint Evalu Ware Russell to be a member of the National Advisory Council on Indian Education for a term expiring September 29, 1986. She will succeed Gregory W. Frazier.

She is a consultant at the American Indian Institute at the University of Oklahoma. She has been a teacher of cultural studies at the Institute of American Indian Arts in Sante Fe, N. Mex., and has also lectured in public schools across Oklahoma on music, legends, customs, and other aspects of Indian culture.

She was named National Indian Educator of the Year by the National Indian Education Association in 1979–1980 and has twice received the Outstanding Indian Teacher of the Year Award from the Bureau of Indian Affairs.

She received bachelor of arts degrees in cultural studies and music at the University of Oklahoma. She is married, has three children, and resides in Yukon, Okla. She was born May 22, 1923, in Mountain View, Okla.

Remarks of the President and Prime Minister Eugenia Charles of Dominica Announcing the Deployment of United States Forces in Grenada
October 25, 1983

The President. Ladies and gentlemen, on Sunday, October 23d, the United States received an urgent, formal request from the five member nations of the Organization of Eastern Caribbean States to assist in a joint effort to restore order and democracy on the island of Grenada. We acceded to the request to become part of a multinational effort with contingents from Antigua, Barbados, Dominica, Jamaica, St. Lucia, St. Vincent, and the United States. I might add

that two of those, Barbados and Jamaica, are not members of the Organization, but were first approached, as we later were, by the OECS and asked to join in that undertaking. And then all of them joined unanimously in asking us to participate.

Early this morning, forces from six Caribbean democracies and the United States began a landing or landings on the island of Grenada in the Eastern Caribbean.

We have taken this decisive action for

three reasons. First, and of overriding importance, to protect innocent lives, including up to a thousand Americans, whose personal safety is, of course, my paramount concern. Second, to forestall further chaos. And third, to assist in the restoration of conditions of law and order and of governmental institutions to the island of Grenada, where a brutal group of leftist thugs violently seized power, killing the Prime Minister, three Cabinet members, two labor leaders, and other civilians, including children.

Let there be no misunderstanding, this collective action has been forced on us by events that have no precedent in the eastern Caribbean and no place in any civilized society.

American lives are at stake. We've been following the situation as closely as possible. Between 800 and a thousand Americans, including many medical students and senior citizens, make up the largest single group of foreign residents in Grenada.

From the start we have consciously sought to calm fears. We were determined not to make an already bad situation worse and increase the risks our citizens faced. But when I received reports that a large number of our citizens were seeking to escape the island, thereby exposing themselves to great danger, and after receiving a formal request for help, a unanimous request from our neighboring states, I concluded the United States had no choice but to act strongly and decisively.

Let me repeat, the United States objectives are clear: to protect our own citizens, to facilitate the evacuation of those who want to leave, and to help in the restoration of democratic institutions in Grenada.

I understand that several Caribbean States are asking that the Organization of American States consider the situation in Grenada. Our diplomatic efforts will be in close cooperation with the Organization of Eastern Caribbean States and the other countries participating in this multinational effort.

And now I'm very proud to present to you the Chairman of the Organization of Eastern Caribbean States and the Prime Minister of Dominica, Prime Minister Charles.

The Prime Minister. I think we were all very horrified at the events which took place recently in Grenada. We, as part of the Organization of East Caribbean States, realizing that we are, of course, one region—we belong to each other, are kith and kin; we all have members of our state living in Grenada—we're very concerned that this event should take place again.

It is true that we have managed to live with the regime since March '79. And we felt quite clearly and we had good reason to believe that the Bishop regime was seeing it our way and was on the way to have elections. And we think this is the reason why himself and his Cabinet were destroyed, because he realized that the pressure we put on him to have elections was worthwhile, was right, and he'd begun to see that the democratic institutions must be put in place in any of these small countries.

It is even more important in a small island state, poor island state, to have the democratic institutions. And this we have had for a long time, and we've continued it and we wish to continue it. Grenada was an aberration in this respect. But that these men, who had for all these years accepted the Bishop regime should then, for their own reasons—and I think the power-hungry reasons—decide to destroy the persons whom they had accepted as their leaders for so long, made us realize that this sort of assassination must not be allowed to continue in our country. It means that our people there are not safe. It means that Grenadians had never been given the chance to choose for themselves the country that they want. And, therefore, it is necessary for us to see to it that they have the opportunity to do so.

To do this, we have to isolate the persons who have committed the acts that they did last week, in killing off most of the Cabinet. And we have to ensure that, in fact, an interim government of persons of, not political greed, but persons who are good administrators and who are Grenadians who can run the country for a few months for the pure purpose of putting the country back on the democratic status, so that elections can take place as soon as possible. This is what you want to do so that Grenadians can choose for themselves the government they want and not have, every few years have governments imposed on them by persons who will otherwise——

Q. Are all the Americans safe?

Q. Mr. President, did you have information that the Soviets and the Cubans were behind this takeover of Grenada? Did the Joint Chiefs tell you that yesterday afternoon?

The Prime Minister. Want me to answer this? Yes, we do have this information. I can't give you all the details because of the safety of people concerned. But we noted with great—in the 2 weeks before the assassination took place, the movements between the Soviet Embassies and known activists and the activists returning to Grenada, obviously a conduit between some of these Russians and some of these——

Q. Mr. President, can you tell us, are all the Americans safe, sir? Can you tell us that? And how long will the American forces be on the ground there? What is their role?

The President. I could—well, we don't know how long that will be. We want to be out as quickly as possible, because our purpose in being there is only for them to enable—to take over their own affairs. As far as we know, the citizens are safe. We have been monitoring that very closely. And one of our prime objectives in the actual invasion that was almost instantly done was the securing of that St. Georges Medical College, where several hundred of the students were.

Q. What is the military situation, sir?

Q. Mr. President, as late as yesterday, your own spokesman said that Americans on Grenada were in no danger. Did you have information that things had changed?

The President. They were in no danger in the sense of that, right now, anything was being done to them. But we know that there was concern on the part of those, because already we'd been informed of several hundred who wanted to leave. But the airports were closed. There was no way of leaving. This was a case of not waiting until something actually happened to them.

But we did manage to get some intelligence out of the island, intelligence information on this. And the tenuous situation

was, as I said, the only authority that you could say of a governmental nature on that island was a 24-hour curfew with orders to shoot on sight anyone found moving in those 24 hours.

Q. What is the military situation now, sir, in Grenada? Can you tell us?

The President. I can only tell you that we've secured both the airports, and the landings have been completed. But we are yielding to the influence of General Vessey in that we don't think in these early hours of that landing that we should be on the horn asking the commanders to stop and give us detailed reports.

Q. Mr. President, do you think that the United States has the right to invade another country to change its government?

The Prime Minister. But I don't think it's an invasion—if I may answer that question.

Q. What is it?

The Prime Minister. This is a question of our asking for support. We are one region. Grenada is part and parcel of us, an organization——

Q. But you're sovereign nations, are you not?

The Prime Minister. ——and we don't have the capacity, ourselves, to see to it that Grenadians get the freedom that they're required to have to choose their own government.

Q. With what's happening in Lebanon, are we spread too thin, Mr. President?

The President. Wait one second here. No; we're not spread too thin. And let me augment what the Prime Minister just said. Once these nations, which were once British colonies, were freed, they, themselves, had a treaty. And their treaty was one of mutual support. And Grenada is one of the countries, signatories to that treaty—and observe that treaty at one time when they had a democratic government and a constitution—a constitutional government, the constitution that was left to them by the British. So, this action that is being taken is being taken under the umbrella of an existing treaty.

Q. Mr. Reagan, there are reports that a helicopter has been shot down, that a U.S. helicopter has been shot down on Grenada. Do you have any information of any U.S.

casualties on the island, sir?

Deputy Press Secretary Speakes. This is the last question, and we'll cut off after this. Last question.

Q. Do we have any information of any U.S. casualties on the island, sir?

The President. No. I have been in meetings, and we both have been busy since we arrived here. And I've only had the first report of our landings and so forth. So, I don't know whether that's true or not.

Mr. Speakes. Thank you, sir.

The President. What?

Q. What reports have you received on the success of our operation—of the U.S.-Caribbean operation?

The President. What's that?

Q. What reports have you received of the success of the operation?

The President. Of the initial operation, of landings, securing the immediate targets, taking control of the airports: completely successful.

Now, the Prime Minister and I are going to depart, but I know there are going to be a lot more technical questions of that kind and Ambassador Motley is here, and I'm going to put him before you to ask all of the technical questions you may have.

Q. What's the situation in Lebanon now?

Mr. Speakes. I'm sorry, that is the last question.

Q. Were the Soviets behind this? Were the Soviets behind the Grenada takeover?

Mr. Speakes. I'm sorry. The President said that's the last question.

Note: The President spoke at 9:07 a.m. in the Briefing Room at the White House. His remarks were broadcast live on nationwide radio and television.

White House Statement on the Commission on Civil Rights
October 25, 1983

Five months ago, the President forwarded four nominations to the Senate for positions on the Commission on Civil Rights: Morris Abram, John Bunzel, and Robert Destro to serve as Commissioners; and Linda Chavez to serve as Staff Director.

All four are Democrats with distinguished backgrounds:

Morris Abram is the former president of Brandeis University. Among his other accomplishments, Mr. Abram authored legislation outlawing Ku Klux Klan violence, fought and won the landmark one man one vote case before the Supreme Court, and served for 9 years as chairman of the United Negro College Fund.

John Bunzel, also a former university president with a long record as a thinker and activist on behalf of civil rights, was cited by the San Francisco board of supervisors for his "unswerving devotion to the highest ideals of brotherhood and service to mankind and dedicated efforts looking to the elimination of racial and religious discrimination."

Robert Destro, a professor of law, pioneered the development of legal services for a nationwide civil rights practice devoted to combating discrimination based on religion or national origin as general counsel of the Catholic League for Religious and Civil Rights.

Linda Chavez, among other professional accomplishments, has served on the staff of the House Subcommittee on Civil and Constitutional Rights and as assistant to the president of the American Federation of Teachers.

Aside from their party affiliation and high qualifications, their only common denominators are intellectual independence and lifetimes of persistence in opposing discrimination based on race, sex, national origin, or religion.

Under the Constitution and the relevant statute (42 U.S.C. 1975), members of the Commission serve at the pleasure of the President. That fact is confirmed on the certificate of appointment held by every Commissioner who has ever served—including all current members—and was acknowledged yet again last spring by the report of the House Committee on the Judiciary.

Rather than permitting the Senate to consider these nominees on their merits, some

Senators have refused to vote to move the nominations out of committee and to the Senate floor. Instead, they have claimed that the very act of nominating these distinguished individuals somehow compromises the "independence" of the Commission. That argument is not supported by history.

When controversy arose on this matter, the President directed members of his staff to meet with representatives of the Senate Judiciary Committee to see if a solution to the impasse could be reached. The President made it clear from the beginning that he was prepared to accept arrangements that permitted some or all of the current members of the Commission to remain in office. In the discussions between the White House and members of the Judiciary Committee, tentative agreements were reached on a number of occasions. Each time the President agreed to the compromise formula; each time those opposing the nominations ultimately rejected the compromise. The latest tentative agreement would have expanded the Commission to eight members now (including two of the three Presidential nominees) and then in the spring of 1984, the third Presidential nominee would replace one of the present incumbents. The President agreed to that proposal, but again it was rejected by the other side.

Because of the impasse, the legislative authorization for the Commission expired on September 30, 1983. The Judiciary Committee has before it a reauthorization bill that would specifically retain the incumbent members of the Commission, thwarting the President's ability to exercise his power of appointment.

Thus far, the President has refrained from using his authority to remove the Commissioners who would be replaced by his nominees while the Senate was considering their qualifications. But in order to break the present deadlock and allow the Commission's authority to be extended, the President has reluctantly concluded that he

has no choice but to remove the three "holdover" Commissioners. The President has therefore terminated the appointments of Mary Berry, Blandina Ramirez, and Murray Saltzman. The President has also urged the Senate to act quickly to reauthorize the Commission and to take up the pending nominations.

It should be emphasized that the issue at stake in this matter is not the removal of certain individuals or the Civil Rights Commission itself. The issue is the responsibility of the President to exercise the power given to him by law. It is that constitutional power of appointment, so long a part of the American political tradition, that is at stake here. The President is appreciative of the efforts made by a number of Senators to help reach a common solution on this matter.

The Counsellor to the President, Edwin Meese III, has sent a letter to Senators Thurmond, Dole, and Laxalt expressing that gratitude. The body of each letter reads as follows:

"On behalf of all of us at the White House, I would like to thank you for your efforts to assist in attaining a principled compromise on the confirmation of the President's appointees to the Civil Rights Commission and the reauthorization of that body.

"Throughout the past several weeks we have endeavored to arrive at a solution to the impasse in the Senate and have made several successive changes in our position, in an attempt to obtain the requisite number of votes. Your assistance in communicating our position to your colleagues and in seeking to gain support has been most helpful.

"We are naturally disappointed that, despite our numerous major concessions, the necessary number of votes for a compromise have not been forthcoming. Nevertheless, we are grateful for your support and for all you have done."

Remarks of the President and Lieutenant General Hussain Mohammad Ershad, President of the Council of Ministers of Bangladesh, Following Their Meetings
October 25, 1983

The President. Today we're honored to welcome Lieutenant General H. M. Ershad, President of the Council of Ministers of Bangladesh.

Over the past year and a half, General Ershad's government has taken steps to restore democratic institutions and economic growth to the people of Bangladesh. In our useful and cordial conversations today, the General and I have had an opportunity to discuss these admirable goals and other matters of concern to our two countries. We especially appreciate the General's dedication to the economic development of his country. The self-help reforms which his government has put in place reflect this commitment to reinvigorate development and better the lives of the Bangladesh people.

General Ershad's government understands the vital role of private enterprise. Changes taking place should attract private investment to the opportunities available in that deserving country. The United States is proud of its long association and support for the people of Bangladesh. Today we pledge our continued support. We look forward to further cooperation between our two governments as Bangladesh seeks to overcome problems of hunger, overpopulation, and poverty.

In the political realm, the General has now set in motion a process designed to build a broad base of popular support for economic and social development in his country. We endorse this goal since we believe that long-term political stability can be achieved only through representative government.

Lastly, the United States wishes to applaud Bangladesh, a member of the nonaligned movement, for its constructive approach to issues of regional and global concern. To cite only a few examples: Bangladesh clearly manifested its courage and resolve in its unswerving responses to aggression in Afghanistan and Kampuchea. It also took the lead in establishing the South Asian Regional Cooperation Organization, a body designed to build a more prosperous and stable region for the people of South Asia. Bangladesh's foreign policy has exhibited an activism, moderation, and force of moral conviction which has earned the respect of the world.

General Ershad, we hope that the remainder of your visit to this country will be pleasant, and we're happy to have had you with us.

General Ershad. Excellency, President Ronald Reagan, distinguished representatives of the United States news media, ladies and gentlemen, it is both a great privilege and pleasure for my wife and myself and for the members of my delegation to be in the United States of America.

We are grateful to President Ronald Reagan for the thoughtful and cordial invitation which he has kindly extended to visit this great country. We bring with us the warm greetings and sincere good wishes of the people of Bangladesh.

My meeting with the President was very satisfying, and I thank him for having received me despite his preoccupation at this critical moment. The comprehensive and productive exchange of views which we have just had is an unmistakable demonstration of our friendship. The object of my visit is to reinforce and consolidate the relations between the United States of America and Bangladesh, which, I'm happy to say, has been achieved.

During our meeting, the President and I covered a wide range of subjects. It gives me great pleasure to say that we have had the opportunity of reaffirming our two countries' shared perceptions and close identity of interests in strengthening the process of peace, progress, and prosperity for mankind.

I have apprised the President of the intensive level of activity which my government has undertaken to improve the quality of life of our 95 million people, a large measure of whom live in rural Bangladesh. I have explained that my government is committed to laying firm political and economic foundations for the long-term development and social benefits for our people. We have already undertaken significant measures in the fields of population control, food production, rural unemployment, and energy production. These have involved the organization and decentralization of our administration, the streamlining of our judiciary, and extensive work in reviewing colonial laws, on the one hand, and our outdated education system, on the other. We hope, sir, that these basic efforts will substantially reinforce the base we must have for the restoration and maintenance of democratic values which are integral to our society.

We are about to launch ourselves into local government elections this winter, followed by elections at progressively higher political echelons throughout 1984, leading to the elections to our Parliament in March 1985. Over 40 million people will go to the polls, not merely to elect their representative, sir, but to lay the political and economic foundation for our future, to enable our people to live freely and to live with honor and dignity by the grace of God.

The President and I have agreed to explore possible ways and means towards furthering strengthening the close bonds of friendship and cooperation between our two countries. Indeed, I am most grateful to you, sir, for the deep and abiding interest you have personally shown in the welfare and progress of our people and for the moral support and economic assistance which have been extended to us.

As members of the Organized Islamic Conference, an unaligned movement in the Commonwealth, and—[inaudible]—as chairman of the Group of 77, Bangladesh firmly believes the current international economic situation needs the closest vigilance by the whole community of nations, recognizing that interdependability is indispensable as a way of life in this day and age. The role of the United States is a crucial and critical one in this regard. It is, indeed, a matter of great satisfaction that

the President and I, in discussing these issues, fully agree that global peace and stability is closely interlinked with the need to restore confidence in the current economic climate in both developing and developed countries.

We in Bangladesh deeply appreciate the importance of the vital role of the United States in upholding the principles of maintaining peace and stability in the world, as enshrined in the charter of the United Nations. I warmly welcome your recent reassuring statement in the United Nations General Assembly in this regard.

I'd like to mention here that I have conveyed to the President our profound sorrow and anguish at the tragic loss of life in the recent days in Beirut. We share your grief, and on behalf of my government and people, I extend our heartfelt condolences to the families of the deceased.

My wife and I have been deeply touched by the warm hospitality extended to us and the members of our delegation. Our stay in the U.S. Capital, the beautiful city of Washington, though short, has been most pleasant and rewarding. I have no doubt that I speak on behalf of all of us when I say that we shall treasure these happy moments and cherish the memory of your warm friendship.

During our meeting, I extend our most cordial invitation to the President to pay a state visit to Bangladesh as early as is convenient. It is my sincere hope that you will visit our country soon and see for yourself the high esteem in which you are held and the enormous fount of good will that exists in Bangladesh for your people.

Mr. President, I wish you good health, happiness, long life, and every success. And I thank you, ladies and gentlemen of the media, for your time and patience.

Thank you.

Note: The President spoke at 1:10 p.m. to reporters assembled in the East Room at the White House.

Earlier, the President and General Ershad met in the Oval Office and held a working luncheon, together with U.S. and Bangladesh officials, in the State Dining Room.

Appointment of Three Members of the National Advisory Council on Vocational Education
October 25, 1983

The President today announced his intention to appoint the following individuals to be members of the National Advisory Council on Vocational Education:

William Edward Hardman, for a term expiring January 17, 1986. He will succeed Caroline E. Hughes. Mr. Hardman is executive vice president of National Tooling and Marketing Association in Fort Washington, Md. He is married, has four children, and resides in Bowie, Md. He was born January 15, 1919, in Orange, N.J.

Peter J. Wrenn, for a term expiring January 17,

1986. He will succeed Edward J. LaMontagne. Mr. Wrenn is president of Hudson Technology, Inc., in Chicago, Ill. He is married, has four children, and resides in Oak Park, Ill. He was born February 10, 1936, in Evanston, Ill.

Harold Robert Goldberg, for the remainder of the term expiring January 17, 1985. He will succeed James W. Griffith. Mr. Goldberg is President of the Omni Group, Inc., in Manchester, N.H. He is married, has two children, and resides in Manchester. He was born January 13, 1910, in Dover, N.H.

Letter to the Speaker of the House and the President Pro Tempore of the Senate on the Deployment of United States Forces in Grenada
October 25, 1983

Dear Mr. Speaker: (Dear Mr. President:)

On October 12, a violent series of events in Grenada was set in motion, which led to the murder of Prime Minister Maurice Bishop and a number of his Cabinet colleagues, as well as the deaths of a number of civilians. Over 40 killings were reported. There was no government ensuring the protection of life and property and restoring law and order. The only indication of authority was an announcement that a barbaric shoot-to-kill curfew was in effect. Under these circumstances, we were necessarily concerned about the safety of innocent lives on the island, including those of up to 1,000 United States citizens.

The Organization of Eastern Caribbean States (OECS) became seriously concerned by the deteriorating conditions in the member State of Grenada. The other members of the OECS are Antigua, Dominica, Montserrat, St. Kitts/Nevis, Saint Lucia, and Saint Vincent and the Grenadines. We were formally advised that the Authority of Heads of Government of Member States of the OECS, acting pursuant to the Treaty

establishing the OECS, met in emergency session on October 21. The meeting took note of the anarchic conditions and the serious violations of human rights and bloodshed that had occurred, and the consequent unprecedented threat to the peace and security of the region created by the vacuum of authority in Grenada. The OECS determined to take immediate, necessary steps to restore order in Grenada so as to protect against further loss of life, pending the restoration of effective governmental institutions. To this end, the OECS formed a collective security force comprising elements from member States to restore order in Grenada and requested the immediate cooperation of a number of friendly countries, including the governments of Barbados, Jamaica and the United States, in these efforts. In response to this call for assistance and in view of the overriding importance of protecting the lives of the United States citizens in Grenada, I have authorized the Armed Forces of the United States to participate along with these other nations in this collective security force.

In accordance with my desire that the Congress be informed on this matter, and consistent with the War Powers Resolution, I am providing this report on this deployment of the United States Armed Forces.

Today at about 5:00 AM Eastern Daylight Time, approximately 1,900 United States Army and United States Marine Corps personnel began landing in Grenada. They were supported by elements of the United States Navy and the United States Air Force. Member States of the OECS along with Jamaica and Barbados are providing approximately 300 personnel. This deployment of United States Armed Forces is being undertaken pursuant to my constitutional authority with respect to the conduct of foreign relations and as Commander-in-Chief of the United States Armed Forces. Although it is not possible at this time to predict the duration of the temporary presence of United States Armed Forces in Grenada, our objectives in providing this support are clear. They are to join the OECS collective security forces in assisting the restoration of conditions of law and order and of governmental institutions to the island of Grenada, and to facilitate the protection and evacuation of United States citizens. Our forces will remain only so long as their presence is required.

Sincerely,

RONALD REAGAN

Note: This is the text of identical letters addressed to Thomas P. O'Neill, Jr., Speaker of the House of Representatives, and Strom Thurmond, President pro tempore of the Senate.

Statement by Deputy Press Secretary Speakes on the Nuclear Planning Group of the North Atlantic Treaty Organization
October 26, 1983

The President met this morning with Secretary of Defense Weinberger in preparation for NATO's Nuclear Planning Group (NPG) ministerial meeting in Ottawa on October 27th and 28th. The Secretary of State and the national security adviser were also present. This NATO Nuclear Planning Group meeting takes on special importance because the ministers will consider a report by the NATO high-level group on the future size and composition of NATO's nuclear stockpile. The President asked for this meeting to underline his personal endorsement of the high-level group's recommendations, which the President believes are vitally important to NATO's future, and to convey his hope that the assembled NATO ministers will act favorably on them.

The NATO high-level group, chaired by Assistant Secretary of Defense Richard Perle, was formed in 1977 for the purpose of reviewing the total NATO intermediate-range and short-range nuclear force structure. The high-level group's report to defense ministers at their meeting in Canada will culminate several years work by experts from throughout the the alliance on the future size and composition of NATO's nuclear stockpile. The conclusion of this vital work will be a further step in the implementation of NATO's 1979 dual-track decision on intermediate-range nuclear force (INF) modernization and arms control. Besides addressing the modernization of NATO's longer range INF missile forces, the 1979 decision also provided for the initial net reduction of 1,000 existing NATO nuclear weapons, which has already been carried out, and committed the alliance to review further adjustments that could be made to NATO's medium and shorter range nuclear forces. The high-level group's report completes this review.

In today's meeting, the President praised the high-level group's work on this critical issue and expressed his sincere hope that NATO ministers will support the group's recommendations. Finally, the President underscored his personal opinion that, if adopted by NATO ministers, the recommendations will enhance the alliance's credibility and effectiveness in continuing to maintain peace—as it has for nearly four decades.

Proclamation 5122—National Poison Prevention Week, 1984
October 26, 1983

By the President of the United States of America

A Proclamation

Childhood poisonings continue to pose a major public health problem in the United States. Each year, more than 100,000 children are treated in hospital emergency rooms because they accidentally ingested chemical household products.

For the past 23 years, the Poison Prevention Week Council has coordinated a network of organizations which seek to raise public awareness of the importance of preventing childhood poisonings. Working together as sponsors of National Poison Prevention Week are national medical, pharmacy, nursing, dental, and hospital associations; health and safety groups; organizations representing manufacturers, packagers, and distributors of consumer products, including medicines; the media; and government agencies. Most of these groups have State and local chapters and affiliates that, along with community organizations, are the backbone of what has become a successful nationwide poison prevention program.

In recent years, the number of poisonings among children has fallen dramatically for those substances that have been required to be packaged in child-resistant closures. However, despite these successes, many childhood poisonings continue to occur. Some adults purchase regulated products in conventional rather than child-resistant packaging or, alternatively, defeat the child-resistant packaging. In addition, adults who are using potentially poisonous products sometimes are distracted for a moment by a telephone call, a doorbell, or food cooking on the stove. These seemingly innocuous distractions can have disastrous consequences if a child ingests the poisonous product. The theme of National Poison Prevention Week is "Children Act Fast . . . So Do Poisons," and this theme emphasizes how important it is that adults never leave potential poisons unattended.

To assist in encouraging the American people to learn of the dangers of accidental poisoning and to take appropriate preventive measures, the Congress, by a joint resolution approved September 26, 1961 (75 Stat. 681), requested the President to issue annually a proclamation designating the third week in March as National Poison Prevention Week.

Now, Therefore, I, Ronald Reagan, President of the United States of America, do hereby designate the week beginning March 18, 1984, as National Poison Prevention Week.

In Witness Whereof, I have hereunto set my hand this twenty-sixth day of October, in the year of our Lord nineteen hundred and eighty-three, and of the Independence of the United States of America the two hundred and eighth.

RONALD REAGAN

[*Filed with the Office of the Federal Register, 11:24 a.m., October 27, 1983*]

Nomination of Thomas F. Moakley To Be a Commissioner of the Federal Maritime Commission
October 26, 1983

The President today announced his intention to nominate Thomas F. Moakley to be a Commissioner of the Federal Maritime Commission for the term expiring June 30, 1988. This is a reappointment.

Since 1977 Mr. Moakley has been serving as a Commissioner of the Federal Maritime Commission. Previously he was port director for the Massachusetts Port Authority in 1970–1977; Postmaster for the United States Post Office in Whitman, Mass., in 1968–1970; and a computer consultant to E. Martin Heffelfinger Associates in Dedham, Mass., in 1966–1968.

Mr. Moakley graduated from Bentley College (B.A., 1940). He is married, has four children, and resides in Alexandria, Va. He was born November 3, 1921, in Boston, Mass.

Nomination of Vernon L. Grose To Be a Member of the National Transportation Safety Board
October 27, 1983

The President today announced his intention to nominate Vernon L. Grose to be a member of the National Transportation Safety Board for a term expiring December 31, 1987. He would succeed Francis H. McAdams.

Since 1982 Mr. Grose has been chairman of the Board of Omega Universal Incorp. in Woodland Hills, Calif. Previously he was vice president of Tustin Institute of Technology in Santa Barbara, Calif., in 1966–1982; director of applied technology for Northrop Ventura in 1962–1966; and director of reliability for Litton Industries in 1959–1962.

He has served on the California council on criminal justice and also in California on the Governor's Select Committee on Law Enforcement Problems.

He graduated from Whitworth College (B.S., 1950), the University of Southern California (M.S., 1967), and Southern University College (D.Sc., 1973). He is married, has six children, and resides in Canoga Park, Calif. He was born June 27, 1928.

Nomination of Edmund Stohr for the Rank of Minister While Serving as United States Representative on the Council of the International Civil Aviation Organization
October 27, 1983

The President today announced his intention to nominate Edmund Stohr, of Illinois, for the rank of Minister during the remainder of the tenure of his service as the Representative of the United States of America on the Council of the International Civil Aviation Organization.

Mr. Stohr served in the United States Air Force in 1942–1946 as a captain. He was with United Airlines in 1946–1981 in a variety of staff and management positions including European director in London, and vice president of industry affairs in Illinois. In 1981–1982 he was director of travel agency affairs at the American Automobile Association in Falls Church, Va. Since 1982 he has been the Representative of the United States of America on the Council of the International Civil Aviation Organiza-tion in Montreal.

Mr. Stohr graduated from the University of Illinois (B.S., 1941). He was born February 5, 1918, in Elgin, Ill.

Nomination of Three Commissioners of the United States Parole Commission
October 27, 1983

The President today announced his intention to nominate the following individuals to be Commissioners of the United States Parole Commission, Department of Justice, for terms of 6 years:

Vincent Fechtel, Jr., would succeed Audrey Kaslow. Mr. Fechtel is a business investor in Leesburg, Fla. He was a Florida State legislator in 1972–1980. He was the owner of various small businesses in 1963–1972. He graduated from the University of Florida (B.S., 1959). He has two children and resides in Leesburg, Fla. He was born August 10, 1936, in Leesburg.

Helen G. Corrothers would succeed Robert D. Vincent. Since 1971 she has served as superintendent of the women's unit of the Arkansas Department of Correction. Previously she was an instructor of the Arkansas Department of Correction in 1970–1971. She served in the United States Army from 1955 to 1969, discharged with the rank of captain. She graduated from Roosevelt University (B.S.) and Arkansas Baptist College (A.A.). She has one son and resides in Pine Bluff, Ark. She was born March 19, 1937, in Montrose, Ark.

Paula A. Tennant would succeed Cecil M. McCall. Since 1980 she has been serving as assistant district attorney in San Mateo, Calif. Previously she was deputy district attorney for San Mateo County in 1978–1979; a member of the U.S. Board of Parole in 1970–1976; and a member of the California Youth Authority in 1968–1970. She graduated from Lincoln University (LL.B., 1954). She was born May 23, 1913, in Kendallville, Ind., and now resides in Burlingame, Calif.

Appointment of Four Members of the National Advisory Council on Indian Education
October 27, 1983

The President today announced his intention to appoint the following individuals to be members of the National Advisory Council on Indian Education for terms expiring September 29, 1986:

Robert B. Brewington is owner of Brewington's Welding Corp. in Pembroke, N.C. He is a vocational teacher for Indian students and a member of the Indian Education Parent Committee. He is married, has four children, and resides in Pembroke. He has born January 15, 1932, in Fairmont, N.C. This is a reappointment.

Robert Keams Chiago is director, Indian teacher, and counselor of the education program at the University of Utah. Previously he was director of the native american studies program. He is married, has four children, and resides in Salt Lake City. He was born June 22, 1942, in Los Angeles, Calif. He will succeed Bobby Bighorse.

Marie Cox is the founding president of the North American Indian Women's Association. She was honored at the 1977 conference as the Outstanding Indian Woman of 1977. She is married, has one child, and resides in Midwest City, Okla. She was born January 17, 1920, in Lawton, Okla. She will succeed Nadine H. Chase.

Grace Goodeagle is an assistant in the law offices

of Fried, Frank, Harris, Shriver & Kampelman in Washington, D.C. She is a former assistant press secretary to Senator Bill Armstrong (R-Colo.). She is second vice president of the American Indian National Republican Federation. She was born June 21, 1937, in Miami, Okla., and now resides in Washington, D.C. She will succeed Danny Kevin Marshall.

Address to the Nation on Events in Lebanon and Grenada
October 27, 1983

My fellow Americans:

Some 2 months ago we were shocked by the brutal massacre of 269 men, women, and children, more than 60 of them Americans, in the shooting down of a Korean airliner. Now, in these past several days, violence has erupted again, in Lebanon and Grenada.

In Lebanon, we have some 1,600 marines, part of a multinational force that's trying to help the people of Lebanon restore order and stability to that troubled land. Our marines are assigned to the south of the city of Beirut, near the only airport operating in Lebanon. Just a mile or so to the north is the Italian contingent and not far from them, the French and a company of British soldiers.

This past Sunday, at 22 minutes after 6 Beirut time, with dawn just breaking, a truck, looking like a lot of other vehicles in the city, approached the airport on a busy, main road. There was nothing in its appearance to suggest it was any different than the trucks or cars that were normally seen on and around the airport. But this one was different. At the wheel was a young man on a suicide mission.

The truck carried some 2,000 pounds of explosives, but there was no way our marine guards could know this. Their first warning that something was wrong came when the truck crashed through a series of barriers, including a chain-link fence and barbed wire entanglements. The guards opened fire, but it was too late. The truck smashed through the doors of the headquarters building in which our marines were sleeping and instantly exploded. The four-story concrete building collapsed in a pile of rubble.

More than 200 of the sleeping men were killed in that one hideous, insane attack.

Many others suffered injury and are hospitalized here or in Europe.

This was not the end of the horror. At almost the same instant, another vehicle on a suicide and murder mission crashed into the headquarters of the French peacekeeping force, an eight-story building, destroying it and killing more than 50 French soldiers.

Prior to this day of horror, there had been several tragedies for our men in the multinational force. Attacks by snipers and mortar fire had taken their toll.

I called bereaved parents and/or widows of the victims to express on behalf of all of us our sorrow and sympathy. Sometimes there were questions. And now many of you are asking: Why should our young men be dying in Lebanon? Why is Lebanon important to us?

Well, it's true, Lebanon is a small country, more than five-and-a-half thousand miles from our shores on the edge of what we call the Middle East. But every President who has occupied this office in recent years has recognized that peace in the Middle East is of vital concern to our nation and, indeed, to our allies in Western Europe and Japan. We've been concerned because the Middle East is a powderkeg; four times in the last 30 years, the Arabs and Israelis have gone to war. And each time, the world has teetered near the edge of catastrophe.

The area is key to the economic and political life of the West. Its strategic importance, its energy resources, the Suez Canal, and the well-being of the nearly 200 million people living there—all are vital to us and to world peace. If that key should fall into the hands of a power or powers hostile to the free world, there would be a direct

1517

threat to the United States and to our allies.

We have another reason to be involved. Since 1948 our Nation has recognized and accepted a moral obligation to assure the continued existence of Israel as a nation. Israel shares our democratic values and is a formidable force an invader of the Middle East would have to reckon with.

For several years, Lebanon has been torn by internal strife. Once a prosperous, peaceful nation, its government had become ineffective in controling the militias that warred on each other. Sixteen months ago, we were watching on our TV screens the shelling and bombing of Beirut which was being used as a fortress by PLO bands. Hundreds and hundreds of civilians were being killed and wounded in the daily battles.

Syria, which makes no secret of its claim that Lebanon should be a part of a Greater Syria, was occupying a large part of Lebanon. Today, Syria has become a home for 7,000 Soviet advisers and technicians who man a massive amount of Soviet weaponry, including SS–21 ground-to-ground missiles capable of reaching vital areas of Israel.

A little over a year ago, hoping to build on the Camp David accords, which had led to peace between Israel and Egypt, I proposed a peace plan for the Middle East to end the wars between the Arab States and Israel. It was based on U.N. resolutions 242 and 338 and called for a fair and just solution to the Palestinian problem, as well as a fair and just settlement of issues between the Arab States and Israel.

Before the necessary negotiations could begin, it was essential to get all foreign forces out of Lebanon and to end the fighting there. So, why are we there? Well, the answer is straightforward: to help bring peace to Lebanon and stability to the vital Middle East. To that end, the multinational force was created to help stabilize the situation in Lebanon until a government could be established and a Lebanese army mobilized to restore Lebanese sovereignty over its own soil as the foreign forces withdrew. Israel agreed to withdraw as did Syria, but Syria then reneged on its promise. Over 10,000 Palestinians who had been bringing ruin down on Beirut, however, did leave the country.

Lebanon has formed a government under the leadership of President Gemayal, and that government, with our assistance and training, has set up its own army. In only a year's time, that army has been rebuilt. It's a good army, composed of Lebanese of all factions.

A few weeks ago, the Israeli army pulled back to the Awali River in southern Lebanon. Despite fierce resistance by Syrian-backed forces, the Lebanese army was able to hold the line and maintain the defensive perimeter around Beirut.

In the year that our marines have been there, Lebanon has made important steps toward stability and order. The physical presence of the marines lends support to both the Lebanese Government and its army. It allows the hard work of diplomacy to go forward. Indeed, without the peace-keepers from the U.S., France, Italy, and Britain, the efforts to find a peaceful solution in Lebanon would collapse.

As to that narrower question—what exactly is the operational mission of the marines—the answer is, to secure a piece of Beirut, to keep order in their sector, and to prevent the area from becoming a battlefield. Our marines are not just sitting in an airport. Part of their task is to guard that airport. Because of their presence, the airport has remained operational. In addition, they patrol the surrounding area. This is their part—a limited, but essential part—in the larger effort that I've described.

If our marines must be there, I'm asked, why can't we make them safer? Who committed this latest atrocity against them and why?

Well, we'll do everything we can to ensure that our men are as safe as possible. We ordered the battleship *New Jersey* to join our naval forces offshore. Without even firing them, the threat of its 16-inch guns silenced those who once fired down on our marines from the hills, and they're a good part of the reason we suddenly had a cease-fire. We're doing our best to make our forces less vulnerable to those who want to snipe at them or send in future suicide missions.

Secretary Shultz called me today from Europe, where he was meeting with the

Foreign Ministers of our allies in the multinational force. They remain committed to our task. And plans were made to share information as to how we can improve security for all our men.

We have strong circumstantial evidence that the attack on the marines was directed by terrorists who used the same method to destroy our Embassy in Beirut. Those who directed this atrocity must be dealt justice, and they will be. The obvious purpose behind the sniping and, now, this attack was to weaken American will and force the withdrawal of U.S. and French forces from Lebanon. The clear intent of the terrorists was to eliminate our support of the Lebanese Government and to destroy the ability of the Lebanese people to determine their own destiny.

To answer those who ask if we're serving any purpose in being there, let me answer a question with a question. Would the terrorists have launched their suicide attacks against the multinational force if it were not doing its job? The multinational force was attacked precisely because it is doing the job it was sent to do in Beirut. It is accomplishing its mission.

Now then, where do we go from here? What can we do now to help Lebanon gain greater stability so that our marines can come home? Well, I believe we can take three steps now that will make a difference.

First, we will accelerate the search for peace and stability in that region. Little attention has been paid to the fact that we've had special envoys there working, literally, around the clock to bring the warring factions together. This coming Monday in Geneva, President Gemayel of Lebanon will sit down with other factions from his country to see if national reconciliation can be achieved. He has our firm support. I will soon be announcing a replacement for Bud McFarlane, who was preceded by Phil Habib. Both worked tirelessly and must be credited for much if not most of the progress we've made.

Second, we'll work even more closely with our allies in providing support for the Government of Lebanon and for the rebuilding of a national consensus.

Third, we will ensure that the multinational peace-keeping forces, our marines, are given the greatest possible protection. Our Commandant of the Marine Corps, General Kelley, returned from Lebanon today and will be advising us on steps we can take to improve security. Vice President Bush returned just last night from Beirut and gave me a full report of his brief visit.

Beyond our progress in Lebanon, let us remember that our main goal and purpose is to achieve a broader peace in all of the Middle East. The factions and bitterness that we see in Lebanon are just a microcosm of the difficulties that are spread across much of that region. A peace initiative for the entire Middle East, consistent with the Camp David accords and U.N. resolutions 242 and 338, still offers the best hope for bringing peace to the region.

Let me ask those who say we should get out of Lebanon: If we were to leave Lebanon now, what message would that send to those who foment instability and terrorism? If America were to walk away from Lebanon, what chance would there be for a negotiated settlement, producing a unified democratic Lebanon?

If we turned our backs on Lebanon now, what would be the future of Israel? At stake is the fate of only the second Arab country to negotiate a major agreement with Israel. That's another accomplishment of this past year, the May 17th accord signed by Lebanon and Israel.

If terrorism and intimidation succeed, it'll be a devastating blow to the peace process and to Israel's search for genuine security. It won't just be Lebanon sentenced to a future of chaos. Can the United States, or the free world, for that matter, stand by and see the Middle East incorporated into the Soviet bloc? What of Western Europe and Japan's dependence on Middle East oil for the energy to fuel their industries? The Middle East is, as I've said, vital to our national security and economic well-being.

Brave young men have been taken from us. Many others have been grievously wounded. Are we to tell them their sacrifice was wasted? They gave their lives in defense of our national security every bit as much as any man who ever died fighting in a war. We must not strip every ounce of meaning and purpose from their courageous sacrifice.

We're a nation with global responsibilities. We're not somewhere else in the world protecting someone else's interests; we're there protecting our own.

I received a message from the father of a marine in Lebanon. He told me, "In a world where we speak of human rights, there is a sad lack of acceptance of responsibility. My son has chosen the acceptance of responsibility for the privilege of living in this country. Certainly in this country one does not inherently have rights unless the responsibility for these rights is accepted." Dr. Kenneth Morrison said that while he was waiting to learn if his son was one of the dead. I was thrilled for him to learn today that his son Ross is alive and well and carrying on his duties in Lebanon.

Let us meet our responsibilities. For longer than any of us can remember, the people of the Middle East have lived from war to war with no prospect for any other future. That dreadful cycle must be broken. Why are we there? Well, a Lebanese mother told one of our Ambassadors that her little girl had only attended school 2 of the last 8 years. Now, because of our presence there, she said her daughter could live a normal life.

With patience and firmness, we can help bring peace to that strifetorn region—and make our own lives more secure. Our role is to help the Lebanese put their country together, not to do it for them.

Now, I know another part of the world is very much on our minds, a place much closer to our shores: Grenada. The island is only twice the size of the District of Columbia, with a total population of about 110,000 people.

Grenada and a half dozen other Caribbean islands here were, until recently, British colonies. They're now independent states and members of the British Commonwealth. While they respect each other's independence, they also feel a kinship with each other and think of themselves as one people.

In 1979 trouble came to Grenada. Maurice Bishop, a protege of Fidel Castro, staged a military coup and overthrew the government which had been elected under the constitution left to the people by the British. He sought the help of Cuba in building an airport, which he claimed was for tourist trade, but which looked suspiciously suitable for military aircraft, including Soviet-built long-range bombers.

The six sovereign countries and one remaining colony are joined together in what they call the Organization of Eastern Caribbean States. The six became increasingly alarmed as Bishop built an army greater than all of theirs combined. Obviously, it was not purely for defense.

In this last year or so, Prime Minister Bishop gave indications that he might like better relations with the United States. He even made a trip to our country and met with senior officials of the White House and the State Department. Whether he was serious or not, we'll never know. On October 12th, a small group in his militia seized him and put him under arrest. They were, if anything, more radical and more devoted to Castro's Cuba than he had been.

Several days later, a crowd of citizens appeared before Bishop's home, freed him, and escorted him toward the headquarters of the military council. They were fired upon. A number, including some children, were killed, and Bishop was seized. He and several members of his cabinet were subsequently executed, and a 24-hour shoot-to-kill curfew was put in effect. Grenada was without a government, its only authority exercised by a self-proclaimed band of military men.

There were then about 1,000 of our citizens on Grenada, 800 of them students at St. George's University Medical School. Concerned that they'd be harmed or held as hostages, I ordered a flotilla of ships, then on its way to Lebanon with marines, part of our regular rotation program, to circle south on a course that would put them somewhere in the vicinity of Grenada in case there should be a need to evacuate our people.

Last weekend, I was awakened in the early morning hours and told that six members of the Organization of Eastern Caribbean States, joined by Jamaica and Barbados, had sent an urgent request that we join them in a military operation to restore order and democracy to Grenada. They were proposing this action under the terms of a treaty, a mutual assistance pact that existed among them.

These small, peaceful nations needed our help. Three of them don't have armies at all, and the others have very limited forces. The legitimacy of their request, plus my own concern for our citizens, dictated my decision. I believe our government has a responsibility to go to the aid of its citizens, if their right to life and liberty is threatened. The nightmare of our hostages in Iran must never be repeated.

We knew we had little time and that complete secrecy was vital to ensure both the safety of the young men who would undertake this mission and the Americans they were about to rescue. The Joint Chiefs worked around the clock to come up with a plan. They had little intelligence information about conditions on the island.

We had to assume that several hundred Cubans working on the airport could be military reserves. Well, as it turned out, the number was much larger, and they were a military force. Six hundred of them have been taken prisoner, and we have discovered a complete base with weapons and communications equipment, which makes it clear a Cuban occupation of the island had been planned.

Two hours ago we released the first photos from Grenada. They included pictures of a warehouse of military equipment—one of three we've uncovered so far. This warehouse contained weapons and ammunition stacked almost to the ceiling, enough to supply thousands of terrorists. Grenada, we were told, was a friendly island paradise for tourism. Well, it wasn't. It was a Soviet-Cuban colony, being readied as a major military bastion to export terror and undermine democracy. We got there just in time.

I can't say enough in praise of our military—Army rangers and paratroopers, Navy, Marine, and Air Force personnel—those who planned a brilliant campaign and those who carried it out. Almost instantly, our military seized the two airports, secured the campus where most of our students were, and are now in the mopping-up phase.

It should be noted that in all the planning, a top priority was to minimize risk, to avoid casualties to our own men and also the Grenadian forces as much as humanly possible. But there were casualties, and we all owe a debt to those who lost their lives or were wounded. They were few in number, but even one is a tragic price to pay.

It's our intention to get our men out as soon as possible. Prime Minister Eugenia Charles of Dominica—I called that wrong; she pronounces it Dominica—she is Chairman of OECS. She's calling for help from Commonwealth nations in giving the people their right to establish a constitutional government on Grenada. We anticipate that the Governor General, a Grenadian, will participate in setting up a provisional government in the interim.

The events in Lebanon and Grenada, though oceans apart, are closely related. Not only has Moscow assisted and encouraged the violence in both countries, but it provides direct support through a network of surrogates and terrorists. It is no coincidence that when the thugs tried to wrest control over Grenada, there were 30 Soviet advisers and hundreds of Cuban military and paramilitary forces on the island. At the moment of our landing, we communicated with the Governments of Cuba and the Soviet Union and told them we would offer shelter and security to their people on Grenada. Regrettably, Castro ordered his men to fight to the death, and some did. The others will be sent to their homelands.

You know, there was a time when our national security was based on a standing army here within our own borders and shore batteries of artillery along our coasts, and, of course, a navy to keep the sealanes open for the shipping of things necessary to our well-being. The world has changed. Today, our national security can be threatened in faraway places. It's up to all of us to be aware of the strategic importance of such places and to be able to identify them.

Sam Rayburn once said that freedom is not something a nation can work for once and win forever. He said it's like an insurance policy; its premiums must be kept up to date. In order to keep it, we have to keep working for it and sacrificing for it just as long as we live. If we do not, our children may not know the pleasure of working to keep it, for it may not be theirs to keep.

In these last few days, I've been more sure than I've ever been that we Americans of today will keep freedom and maintain peace. I've been made to feel that by the magnificent spirit of our young men and women in uniform and by something here in our Nation's Capital. In this city, where political strife is so much a part of our lives, I've seen Democratic leaders in the Congress join their Republican colleagues, send a message to the world that we're all Americans before we're anything else, and when our country is threatened, we stand shoulder to shoulder in support of our men and women in the Armed Forces.

May I share something with you I think you'd like to know? It's something that happened to the Commandant of our Marine Corps, General Paul Kelley, while he was visiting our critically injured marines in an Air Force hospital. It says more than any of us could ever hope to say about the gallantry and heroism of these young men, young men who serve so willingly so that others might have a chance at peace and freedom in their own lives and in the life of their country.

I'll let General Kelley's words describe the incident. He spoke of a "young marine with more tubes going in and out of his body than I have ever seen in one body."

"He couldn't see very well. He reached up and grabbed my four stars, just to make sure I was who I said I was. He held my hand with a firm grip. He was making signals, and we realized he wanted to tell me something. We put a pad of paper in his hand—and he wrote 'Semper Fi.' "

Well, if you've been a marine or if, like myself, you're an admirer of the marines, you know those words are a battlecry, a greeting, and a legend in the Marine Corps. They're marine shorthand for the motto of the Corps—"Semper Fidelis"—"always faithful."

General Kelley has a reputation for being a very sophisticated general and a very tough marine. But he cried when he saw those words, and who can blame him?

That marine and all those others like him, living and dead, have been faithful to their ideals. They've given willingly of themselves so that a nearly defenseless people in a region of great strategic importance to the free world will have a chance someday to live lives free of murder and mayhem and terrorism. I think that young marine and all of his comrades have given every one of us something to live up to.

They were not afraid to stand up for their country or, no matter how difficult and slow the journey might be, to give to others that last, best hope of a better future. We cannot and will not dishonor them now and the sacrifices they've made by failing to remain as faithful to the cause of freedom and the pursuit of peace as they have been.

I will not ask you to pray for the dead, because they're safe in God's loving arms and beyond need of our prayers. I would like to ask you all—wherever you may be in this blessed land—to pray for these wounded young men and to pray for the bereaved families of those who gave their lives for our freedom.

God bless you, and God bless America.

Note: The President spoke at 8 p.m. from the Oval Office at the White House. The address was broadcast live on nationwide radio and television.

Executive Order 12447—President's Private Sector Survey on Cost Control in the Federal Government
October 27, 1983

By the authority vested in me as President by the Constitution and laws of the United States of America, including the Federal Advisory Committee Act, as amended (5 U.S.C. App. I), and in order to extend the life of the President's Private Sector Survey on Cost Control in the Federal Government, it is hereby ordered that Section 4(b) of Executive Order No. 12369 of June 30, 1982, as amended, is further amended to read:

"The Committee shall terminate on December 31, 1983, unless sooner extended.".

RONALD REAGAN

The White House,
October 27, 1983.

[*Filed with the Office of the Federal Register, 11:20 a.m., October 28, 1983*]

Note: The text of the Executive order was released by the Office of the Press Secretary on October 28.

Nomination of Diego C. Asencio To Be United States Ambassador to Brazil
October 28, 1983

The President today announced his intention to nominate Diego C. Asencio, of Florida, a career member of the Senior Foreign Service, Class of Career Minister, to be Ambassador to Brazil. He would succeed Langhorne A. Motley.

Mr. Asencio was an underwriter with Prudential Insurance Co. in Newark, N.J., in 1953–1955 and served in the United States Army in 1955–1957. He entered the Foreign Service in 1957 as intelligence research analyst in the Department. He was consular officer in Mexico City (1959–1962) and political officer in Panama (1962–1964). In the Department he was Panama desk officer (1964–1965) and Special Assistant to the Assistant Secretary of State for Inter-American Affairs (1965–1967). He was political officer, then deputy chief of mission in Lisbon (1967–1972), counselor for political affairs in Brasilia (1972–1975), and Deputy Chief of Mission in Caracas (1975–1977). He was Ambassador to Colombia in 1977–1980. Since 1980 he has been Assistant Secretary of State for Consular Affairs.

Mr. Asencio received his B.S.F.S. in 1952 from Georgetown University. His foreign languages are Spanish and Portuguese. He was born July 15, 1931, in Nijar, Almeria, Spain.

Nomination of Richard D. Erb To Be United States Executive Director of the International Monetary Fund
October 28, 1983

The President today announced his intention to nominate Richard D. Erb to be United States Executive Director of the International Monetary Fund for a term of 2 years. This is a reappointment.

Since 1981 he has been serving as United States Executive Director of the International Monetary Fund. Previously he was

1523

resident fellow at the American Enterprise Institute for Public Policy Research in 1978–1981. He also served as a consultant to the Comptroller of the Currency.

In 1976–1977 he was Deputy Assistant Secretary for Developing Nations Finance, Department of the Treasury. Dr. Erb was international affairs fellow, Council on Foreign Relations, and resident economist, American Enterprise Institute for Public Policy Research in 1974–1976. In 1971–

1974 he served as Staff Assistant to the President and Director for International Monetary Affairs, Council on International Economic Policy. He was a consultant with Arthur D. Little, Inc., in 1969–1971.

He graduated from the State University of New York at Buffalo (B.A., 1963) and Stanford University (Ph. D., 1967). He is married and resides in Alexandria, Va. He was born April 15, 1941, in Wantagh, N.Y.

Nomination of Mary Kate Bush To Be Alternate United States Executive Director of the International Monetary Fund
October 28, 1983

The President today announced his intention to nominate Mary Kate Bush to be United States Alternate Executive Director of the International Monetary Fund for a term of 2 years. She would succeed Charles H. Dallara.

Since 1982 Miss Bush has been serving as Special Assistant to the Deputy Secretary of the Department of the Treasury. Previously she was at Bankers Trust Co. in New York as vice president and team leader of the World Corporate Department in 1979–1982; assistant vice president in 1977–1979; and assistant treasurer in 1976–1977. She was an account officer at Citibank in 1973–1976 and credit analyst at Chase Manhattan Bank in 1971–1973.

She graduated from Fisk University (B.A., 1969) and the University of Chicago (M.B.A., 1971). She was born April 9, 1948, in Birmingham, Ala., and now resides in Washington, D.C.

Radio Address to the Nation on Nuclear Weapons
October 29, 1983

My fellow Americans:

Before getting into today's subject, I would just like to say a heartfelt word of thanks to all of you for the thousands of wires and calls that have come in, supportive of the actions of these last few days and, particularly, supportive and grateful to those young men in uniform who are performing so magnificently.

Now today, I'd like to talk about a very important decision that was made Thursday by the Defense Ministers of the North Atlantic Treaty Organization, or NATO, as it's commonly called. This decision has great importance for us and for the NATO Alliance as a whole, because it addresses the future size and composition of our shorter range nuclear forces in Europe.

As you know, we're negotiating with the Soviets in Geneva on the longer range missiles. The current imbalance on those systems is over 350 to 0 in their favor. But with regard to the shorter range missiles, the tactical missiles, I think you'll be very pleased with today's news. But first, a little background.

The nuclear forces in Europe are fundamental to our overall strategy of deterrence and to protecting our allies and ourselves. The weapons strengthen NATO and protect the peace because they show that the alliance is committed to sharing the risks and the benefits of mutual defense. Just by being there, these weapons deter others from aggression and, thereby, serve the cause of peace. Unfortunately, we must keep them there until we can convince the Soviets and others that the best thing would be a world in which there is no further need for nuclear weapons at all.

The alliance's goal, as General Rogers, NATO's Supreme Allied Commander for Europe, has so often said, is to maintain no more military forces than are absolutely necessary for deterrence and defense.

In December of 1979 NATO reached a decision to reduce immediately the number of shorter range nuclear weapons stationed in Europe. In 1980 we carried out that decision by removing 1,000 of these weapons. The same decision also committed the alliance to a further review of the remaining systems of this category, and that brings us to our decision of Thursday.

Drawing on the recommendation put forward by a special, high-level study group, the NATO Defense Ministers decided that in addition to the 1,000 nuclear weapons which we withdrew in 1980, the overall size of the NATO nuclear stockpile could be reduced by an additional 1,400 weapons.

When these 2,400 weapons have been withdrawn, the United States will have reduced its nuclear weapons in Europe by over one-third from 1979 levels, and NATO will have the lowest number of nuclear weapons in 20 years. What this means is that the alliance will have removed at least five nuclear weapons for every new missile warhead we will deploy if the negotiations in Geneva don't lead to an agreement.

This step, taken by the alliance as a whole, stands in stark contrast to the actions of the Soviet Union. The Soviet leaders have so far refused to negotiate in good faith at the Geneva talks. Since our 1979 decision to reduce nuclear forces, the Soviet Union has added over 600 SS–20 warheads to their arsenal. Coupled with this, they offer threats and the acceleration of previous plans, which they now call countermeasures, if NATO carries through with its deployment plan intended to restore the balance.

The comparison of Soviet actions with NATO's reductions and restraint clearly illustrates once again that the so-called arms race has only one participant—the Soviet Union.

On Thursday NATO took a dramatic and far-reaching decision, a decision that puts us a giant step along the path toward increased stability in Europe and around the world. As we reduce our nuclear warheads in Europe and, of equal importance, take the necessary actions to maintain the effectiveness of the resulting force, we will continue in the future what we've accomplished so well in the past—to deter Soviet aggression. We seek peace and we seek security, and the NATO decision serves both.

Now, let me bring you up to date on the negotiations in Geneva. Progress toward an equitable, verifiable agreement on the reduction of intermediate-range nuclear missiles has been slow to come. Most recently, I proposed three initiatives which go a long way toward meeting important concerns expressed by the Soviet Union. By our actions on the talks we have ensured that all of the elements of a mutually advantageous agreement are on the table. The Soviet Union has now advanced some additional proposals of its own. We'll study these proposals, and we'll address them in the talks in Geneva.

Unfortunately, the Soviet proposals permit them to retain SS–20 missiles while not allowing NATO to deploy its own. The proposals are also coupled with an explicit threat to break off the Geneva talks. I hope that the Soviet Union is truly interested in achieving an agreement. The test will be whether the Soviets, having advanced their latest proposals, decide finally to negotiate seriously in Geneva.

For our part, we continue to seek an equitable and verifiable agreement as quickly as possible. We will stay at the negotiating table for as long as necessary to achieve such an agreement.

Thank you for listening, and God bless you.

Note: The President spoke at 12:06 p.m. from Camp David, Md.

Appointment of Robert B. Sims as Special Assistant to the President and Deputy Press Secretary for Foreign Affairs
October 31, 1983

The President today announced his intention to appoint Robert B. Sims to be Special Assistant to the President and Deputy Press Secretary for Foreign Affairs. He will succeed Leslie A. Janka.

Since June 3, 1983, he has been serving as Special Assistant to the President and Senior Director of Public Affairs on the National Security Council. A Navy public affairs specialist, Captain Sims was a senior research fellow at the National Defense University before joining the NSC staff in May 1982. He was Deputy Chief of Information for the Navy Department in 1978–1981 and Special Assistant for Public Affairs to the Secretary of the Navy in 1974–1978.

Captain Sims has worked as a daily newspaper reporter for the Jackson Sun in Jackson, Tenn., and as a weekly newspaper editor and publisher. His writings include "The Pentagon Reporters," a book to be published this year.

He has a bachelor of arts degree from Union University and masters degrees in journalism and in political science from the University of Wisconsin. He was a Rotary Foundation fellow studying international relations at the University of Sydney, Australia, and is a graduate of the National War College.

He is married, has four children, and resides in McLean, Va. He was born November 26, 1934, in Tennessee.

Appointment of David H. Welch as a Member of the Architectural and Transportation Barriers Compliance Board
October 31, 1983

The President today announced his intention to appoint David H. Welch to be a member of the Architectural and Transportation Barriers Compliance Board for a term expiring December 3, 1984. He will succeed Mason Harry Rose V.

Mr. Welch is an attorney engaged in the private practice of law in the St. Louis, Mo., area. He is director of the Missouri Association for Children with Learning Disabilities and is former vice chairman of the National Network of Learning Disabled Adults. He was a cofounder of St. Louis Young Adults with Learning Disabilities.

He graduated from Westminster College (B.A.) and the University of Tulsa, College of Law (J.D.). Mr. Welch was born August 18, 1953, in St. Louis, Mo., and now resides in St. Ann, Mo.

Remarks on Signing the National Drug Abuse Education Week Proclamation
November 1, 1983

Thank you all very much, and let me thank Senator Chiles, who sponsored National Drug Abuse Education Week in the Senate, and Congressman Bennett, who sponsored it in the House, as well as Senator Thurmond, Congressmen Gilman and Rangel. I know Congressman and Mrs. Bennett have a strong personal interest in this proclamation, and let me extend a very special welcome to Mrs. Bennett, who is with us here today.

Nancy's told me so many times that few things in her life have frightened her as much as the drug epidemic, and this is something she's living with daily by virtue of her work with those who are endangered by drugs. She's told me many personal stories of grief, but the hard statistics are there, as well.

The numbers on drug abuse are terrifying. These statistics virtually overwhelmed us for the past two decades, paralyzing our will. It was as if the problem was so large that we couldn't do anything about it. But today, as never before, America's children are getting help in the battle to keep their minds free of drugs. We're making progress against drugs, because parents and other adults finally decided to do something about it.

No longer do we think of drugs as a harmless phase of adolescence. No longer do we think of so-called hard drugs as bad and so-called soft drugs as being acceptable. Research tells us there are no such categories, that the phrase "responsible use" does not apply to drug experimentation by America's youth. And as far as the recreational use of drugs is concerned, I've never in my life heard a more self-serving euphemism by those who support drug use. There is nothing recreational about those children whose lives have been lost, whose minds have been ruined. If that's somebody's idea of recreation, it's pretty sick. Too often we've fallen into the trap of using nice, easy, pleasant, liberal language about drugs. Well, language will not sugar-coat overdoses, suicides, and ruined lives.

One of the biggest indicators that America is awakening to the harm of drugs is the wonderful outpouring of people who will launch the Chemical People Project tomorrow evening on the Public Broadcasting System. That's the project combining community action with the power of television. On the next two Wednesday evenings, special broadcasts will be seen on over 260 of the country's television stations. Simultaneously, there will be local community meetings, thousands of them all across America, in all 50 States, the District of Columbia, and Guam. There are more than 10,000 task forces out there to assist mothers and fathers who, unfortunately, have felt for too long that they were alone in the battle against drugs. Over 50,000 volunteers and 35 national organizations have dedicated themselves to making this project a success.

Last week America lost many loved ones. Well, this week we can save others.

Throwing taxpayers' money at a problem, sitting back with smug looks of self-congratulation, has been tried, and it didn't work. Business leaders recognize this and are lending a helpful hand. For example, the Keebler Company teamed up with Warner Communications last spring, and they came forth with a comic-book approach to getting the right kind of information about drugs into the hands of kids in a readable way. Other companies are coming forward, as well. The effort against drugs is coalescing with parent groups, government, business, and now, in the case of the Chemical People Project, the media is involved, as well.

Progress is being made, but it takes time to erase 20 years of lax attitudes. I'm confident we're on the right track and that education, not scare tactics, will be effective.

And now, as part of that awareness campaign, I will sign the National Drug Abuse Education proclamation.

[*At this point, the President signed the proclamation.*]

Well, thank you all again. Watch television tomorrow night. [*Laughter*]

Note: The President spoke at 1:20 p.m. in the East Room at the White House. The ceremony was attended by Members of Congress and their spouses and representatives of parents groups.

Proclamation 5123—National Drug Abuse Education Week, 1983
November 1, 1983

By the President of the United States of America

A Proclamation

Drug abuse in the United States continues to be a major threat to the future of our Nation. Millions of our citizens are risking their health and their future by abusing drugs. The effects are clearly demonstrated by the tragic reports in daily news accounts of innocent people killed by drunk drivers, death by overdose, drug-related murders, drug smuggling, and other public outrages. Less obvious, but more pervasive, are the individual tragedies which destroy a person or family and which may cause loss of a job, interruption of schooling, and a reduction in our Nation's productivity.

Federal, State, and local governments have established programs to reduce the supply of illegal drugs. Similarly, government has encouraged the establishment of facilities for providing medical treatment for those suffering from this problem and sponsored extensive research on the effects of drug use. However, government cannot hope to solve the problems of drug abuse without the help of every American.

Drug abuse is a national problem and a target of a nationwide program. All across America, our citizens, community organizations, and the private sector have recognized that they can make a difference in the battle against this serious concern. Expanded drug abuse awareness efforts, the banding together of concerned parents, and the involvement of many community groups are lowering the rate of drug abuse which prevailed during the Seventies. There has been increasing attention focused on the potential of mass communications to discourage drug abuse.

Numerous public education efforts are epitomized in the excellent Chemical People Project which will be presented on public broadcasting stations across the United States on November 2 and 9, 1983. The Chemical People Project is an example of how a grassroots approach to organizing town meetings and community efforts can break through the "wall of denial" common to alcohol and drug abuse and can stimulate constructive action where it counts—in ourselves. We must continue to encourage and support efforts to educate our citizens to the health and societal consequences of drug abuse. Such efforts are an essential foundation for a successful national program to reduce and prevent drug abuse in our country.

In order to draw attention to the seriousness of the drug abuse problem and to encourage the education of parents and children in the home, classroom, and community to the impact of illegal drug abuse, the Congress, by Senate Joint Resolution 57, has designated the week of November 2 through November 9, 1983, as National Drug Abuse Education Week.

Now, Therefore, I, Ronald Reagan, President of the United States of America, do hereby proclaim the week of November 2 through November 9, 1983, as National Drug Abuse Education Week. I call on all Americans to join the battle against drug abuse to protect our children so that we ensure a healthy and productive generation of Americans as our contribution to the future.

In Witness Whereof, I have hereunto set my hand this first day of November, in the year of our Lord nineteen hundred and eighty-three, and of the Independence of the United States of America the two hundred and eighth.

RONALD REAGAN

[*Filed with the Office of the Federal Register, 10:34 a.m., November 2, 1983*]

Nomination of Robert McVey To Be a Commissioner of the United States Section of the International North Pacific Fisheries Commission
November 1, 1983

The President today announced his intention to nominate Robert McVey to be a Commissioner of the United States Section of the International North Pacific Fisheries Commission for a term expiring June 4, 1987. This is a reappointment.

Since 1982 Mr. McVey has been a Commissioner of the United States Section of the International North Pacific Fisheries

Commission. He also serves as director of the Alaska region for the National Marine Fisheries Service in Juneau, Alaska. Previously he served as deputy director in Alaska for 10 years.

Mr. McVey is married, has two children, and resides in Juneau, Alaska. He was born February 19, 1932, in Stockton, Kans.

Remarks on Signing the Bill Making the Birthday of Martin Luther King, Jr., a National Holiday
November 2, 1983

The President. Mrs. King, members of the King family, distinguished Members of the Congress, ladies and gentlemen, honored guests, I'm very pleased to welcome you to the White House, the home that belongs to all of us, the American people.

When I was thinking of the contributions to our country of the man that we're honoring today, a passage attributed to the American poet John Greenleaf Whittier comes to mind. "Each crisis brings its word and deed." In America, in the fifties and sixties, one of the important crises we faced was racial discrimination. The man whose words and deeds in that crisis stirred our nation to the very depths of its soul was Dr. Martin Luther King, Jr.

Martin Luther King was born in 1929 in an America where, because of the color of their skin, nearly 1 in 10 lived lives that were separate and unequal. Most black Americans were taught in segregated schools. Across the country, too many could find only poor jobs, toiling for low wages. They were refused entry into hotels and restaurants, made to use separate facilities. In a nation that proclaimed liberty and justice for all, too many black Americans were living with neither.

In one city, a rule required all blacks to sit in the rear of public buses. But in 1955, when a brave woman named Rosa Parks was told to move to the back of the bus, she said, "No." A young minister in a local Baptist church, Martin Luther King, then organized a boycott of the bus company—a boycott that stunned the country. Within 6 months the courts had ruled the segregation of public transportation unconstitutional.

Dr. King had awakened something strong and true, a sense that true justice must be colorblind, and that among white and black Americans, as he put it, "Their destiny is tied up with our destiny, and their freedom is inextricably bound to our freedom; we cannot walk alone."

In the years after the bus boycott, Dr. King made equality of rights his life's work. Across the country, he organized boycotts, rallies, and marches. Often he was beaten, imprisoned, but he never stopped teaching nonviolence. "Work with the faith", he told his followers, "that unearned suffering is redemptive." In 1964 Dr. King became the youngest man in history to win the Nobel Peace Prize.

Dr. King's work brought him to this city

often. And in one sweltering August day in 1963, he addressed a quarter of a million people at the Lincoln Memorial. If American history grows from two centuries to twenty, his words that day will never be forgotten. "I have a dream that one day on the red hills of Georgia, the sons of former slaves and the sons of former slave owners will be able to sit down together at the table of brotherhood."

In 1968 Martin Luther King was gunned down by a brutal assassin, his life cut short at the age of 39. But those 39 short years had changed America forever. The Civil Rights Act of 1964 had guaranteed all Americans equal use of public accommodations, equal access to programs financed by Federal funds, and the right to compete for employment on the sole basis of individual merit. The Voting Rights Act of 1965 had made certain that from then on black Americans would get to vote. But most important, there was not just a change of law; there was a change of heart. The conscience of America had been touched. Across the land, people had begun to treat each other not as blacks and whites, but as fellow Americans.

And since Dr. King's death, his father, the Reverend Martin Luther King, Sr., and his wife, Coretta King, have eloquently and forcefully carried on his work. Also his family have joined in that cause.

Now our nation has decided to honor Dr. Martin Luther King, Jr., by setting aside a day each year to remember him and the just cause he stood for. We've made historic strides since Rosa Parks refused to go to the back of the bus. As a democratic people, we can take pride in the knowledge that we Americans recognized a grave injustice and took action to correct it. And we should remember that in far too many countries, people like Dr. King never have the opportunity to speak out at all.

But traces of bigotry still mar America. So, each year on Martin Luther King Day, let us not only recall Dr. King, but rededicate ourselves to the Commandments he believed in and sought to live every day: Thou shall love thy God with all thy heart, and thou shall love thy neighbor as thyself.

And I just have to believe that all of us—if all of us, young and old, Republicans and Democrats, do all we can to live up to those Commandments, then we will see the day when Dr. King's dream comes true, and in his words, "All of God's children will be able to sing with new meaning, '. . . land where my fathers died, land of the pilgrim's pride, from every mountainside, let freedom ring.' "

Thank you, God bless you, and I will sign it.

Mrs. King. Thank you, Mr. President, Vice President Bush, Majority Leader Baker and the distinguished congressional and senatorial delegations, and other representatives who've gathered here, and friends.

All right-thinking people, all right-thinking Americans are joined in spirit with us this day as the highest recognition which this nation gives is bestowed upon Martin Luther King, Jr., one who also was the recipient of the highest recognition which the world bestows, the Nobel Peace Prize.

In his own life's example, he symbolized what was right about America, what was noblest and best, what human beings have pursued since the beginning of history. He loved unconditionally. He was in constant pursuit of truth, and when he discovered it, he embraced it. His nonviolent campaigns brought about redemption, reconciliation, and justice. He taught us that only peaceful means can bring about peaceful ends, that our goal was to create the love community.

America is a more democratic nation, a more just nation, a more peaceful nation because Martin Luther King, Jr., became her preeminent nonviolent commander.

Martin Luther King, Jr., and his spirit live within all of us. Thank God for the blessing of his life and his leadership and his commitment. What manner of man was this? May we make ourselves worthy to carry on his dream and create the love community.

Thank you.

Note: The President spoke at 11:06 a.m. in the Rose Garden at the White House.

As enacted, H.R. 3706 is Public Law 98–144, approved November 2.

Nomination of A. C. Arterbery To Be a Member of the Board of Directors of the African Development Foundation
November 2, 1983

The President today announced his intention to nominate A. C. Arterbery to be a member of the Board of Directors of the African Development Foundation for a term of 6 years. This is a new position.

He has been with TRW Systems and Energy for 22 years and presently serves as manager of information resources. Previously he was project manager of a fiber optics technology project. In recent years he helped establish and is now a board member of the International Technical Assistance Corp.

He graduated from California State University at Los Angeles and attended Missouri University Law School and the University of Southern California Graduate School of Business. He is married, has one child, and resides in Los Angeles, Calif. He was born August 4, 1930, in Bristow, Okla.

Appointment of Eight Members of the President's Advisory Committee on Women's Business Ownership
November 2, 1983

The President today announced his intention to appoint the following individuals to be members of the President's Advisory Committee on Women's Business Ownership. These are new positions:

Evelyn Echols is president of International Travel Training Courses, Inc., in Chicago, Ill. She is married, has two children, and resides in Chicago. She was born April 5, 1915, in La Salle, Ill.

Robert R. McMillan is vice president of public affairs for Avon Products, Inc., in New York, N.Y. He is married, has three children, and resides in Garden City, N.Y. He was born May 21, 1932, in New York City.

Patricia S. Nettleship is president of Northern Pacific Construction Co. in Santa Monica, Calif. She has six children and resides in Santa Monica. She was born September 18, 1940, in Ventura, Calif.

Beth Davis Rogers is president of Davis Pacific Corp. in Santa Monica, Calif. She is married, has three children, and resides in Los Angeles, Calif. She was born January 11, 1945, in Los Angeles.

Susan B. Sarvis is president of LTS, Inc., in Manchester, N.H. She is married, has two children, and resides in Manchester. She was born August 5, 1945, in Cleveland, Ohio.

Helen Sanchez-Usitalo is a financial consultant with Sanchez-Usitalo Associates in Dallas, Tex. She is married, has one child, and resides in Dallas. She was born November 26, 1942, in Houston, Tex.

Maeley L. Tom is deputy administrative officer of the California State Assembly in Sacramento, Calif. She is married, has one child, and resides in Sacramento. She was born December 10, 1941, in San Francisco, Calif.

Ruth M. Trotter is president of the Stork Shop, Inc., in Memphis Tenn. She has two children and resides in Memphis. She was born June 24, 1920, in Trenton, Tenn.

Appointment of Two Members of the President's Advisory Council on Private Sector Initiatives
November 2, 1983

The President today announced his intention to appoint the following individuals to be members of the President's Advisory Council on Private Sector Initiatives. These are new positions:

Lupe Anguiano is founder, president, and chief executive officer of the National Women's Employment and Education, Inc. She was the southwest regional director of the southwest regional office for the Spanish Speaking National Council of Catholic Bishops in 1973–1977. Previously she was with the United States Department of Health, Education and Welfare serving in Social and Rehabilitation Services (1973), in the Office for Civil Rights, Higher Education (1972), and in the Office of the Secretary for the Women's Action Program in 1970–1971. She graduated from Antioch University (M.A., 1978). She was born March 12, 1929, in LaJunta, Colo., and now resides in San Antonio, Tex.

Thomas Vail is president, publisher, and editor of the Plain Dealing Publishing Co. in Cleveland, Ohio. He has served as publisher and editor of The Plain Dealer since 1963. He has been a member of the President's Health Manpower Commission and the U.S. Advisory Commission on Information. He was a National Brotherhood Week chairman of the National Conference of Christians and Jews in 1969. He graduated from Princeton University (1948). He is married, has three children, and resides in Hunting Valley, Ohio. He was born June 23, 1926, in Cleveland, Ohio.

Statement by Deputy Press Secretary Speakes on United States Sanctions Against Poland
November 2, 1983

In the past months, we and our allies have been engaged in extensive dialog on the situation in Poland. Very serious problems still remain. The Polish Government continues to defy the wishes of the majority of the Polish people; a number of political prisoners are still incarcerated and indictments have been brought against certain of these prisoners; free labor unions have not been restored; no genuine economic reforms have been implemented and stringent censorship still exists.

For these reasons, our sanctions presently remain in place. These include the suspension of Polish civil aviation privileges in the United States; the freeze on Export-Import Bank's line of export credit insurance for Poland; the implementation of a no-exceptions policy which restricts export licensing of high technology items to Poland; opposition to the extension of any new credits and Poland's entry into the IMF [International Monetary Fund]; suspension of Poland's MFN [most-favored-nation] status; curtailment of the shipment of nonhumanitarian agricultural commodities for distribution by the Polish Government; suspension of joint travel under the Maria Sklodowska Curie Fund which finances joint scientific research projects; and curtailment of Polish fishing in U.S. waters.

In the hope of inducing the Polish Government to begin pursuing a path of national reconciliation and restore free trade unions, the President has endorsed two limited steps. Specifically, the United States jointly with its allies has agreed to enter into discussions on the Polish debt to official creditors. We seek repayment of U.S. loans to Poland. In this regard, the United States is not extending Poland new credits nor supporting Poland's entry into the IMF. As a bilateral step, we have agreed to permit Polish officials to engage in discussions with private fishing companies about potential fishing arrangements. Our ban on Polish fishing in U.S. waters still remains in place.

Moreover, even though discussions have been authorized no actual allocation of fish will be provided at this time. Rather, any future allocation of fish at the end of the discussions will be contingent on the Polish Government's actions on human rights.

These steps taken represent a limited response to very modest improvement in the human rights situation in Poland. The United States has taken note of the successful June visit of His Holiness John Paul II to his homeland, and of the release of the majority of political prisoners in Poland. We are waiting for the Polish Government to take definitive action to restore the human rights of the Polish people—rights which belong to them from birth and which are not government's to take away.

Remarks Announcing the Appointment of Donald Rumsfeld as the President's Personal Representative in the Middle East
November 3, 1983

The President. Before this morning's announcement, I'd like to share some information with you that I received on the phone last night.

Secretary of Defense Cap Weinberger called to inform me that hostilities in Grenada have ended and that he has instructed our military commanders to begin withdrawing their forces within a few days.

What this means is that the situation is stable; no sniper fire or other form of military resistance is evident on the island. Our objectives have been achieved, and as soon as the logistics permit, American personnel will be leaving.

I'd like to add that the members of the Armed Forces have conducted themselves in the finest tradition of the military. We can be proud of the courage and professionalism that we've seen from the people down there. The American students called them rescuers. The citizens of Grenada have hailed them as liberators. I think the whole lot of them deserve the respect and admiration of our country.

The operation was not without cost. Those who were killed, wounded, or injured in this operation, I believe, are heroes of freedom. They not only rescued our own citizens, but they saved the people of Grenada from repression and laid aside a potential threat to all the people of the Caribbean. After viewing the massive horde of Soviet weapons found on that island, who knows what evil the liberation of Grenada achieved for us, or averted in the years ahead.

And now, on to the business at hand. I'm pleased to announce today the appointment of Donald Rumsfeld as my special representative for the Middle East. I can't think of a better individual in whom to entrust the coordination of our role in the Middle East peace process and in the Lebanon negotiations.

Don Rumsfeld has had a distinguished career in public service. He's had experience in wide areas of government and public policy—including military service as a naval aviator; in the legislative branch, as a Member of the United States Congress; and in the executive branch, where his many appointments included Chief of Staff of the White House, member of the Cabinet, and U.S. Secretary of Defense. I am grateful that he's agreed to take on this special assignment and that G. D. Searle & Company, where he serves as president and chief executive officer, has made it possible for him to lend his talents to his country for a while.

He'll be joining the team immediately, and in view of the serious job that he's undertaking, we're happy to have an individual of his stature on board so quickly.

Ambassador Richard Fairbanks, who is now in Geneva, has told me that he will continue his critical involvement in these issues, and I am grateful for his dedication. We intend to work and use the talents of our best minds to achieve a just and lasting peace in the Middle East.

I announced in September 1982 a realistic set of principles which we consider the best chance for a resolution of the Arab-Israeli conflict. No one's come up with a better proposal since. I'm confident that progress in Lebanon will add momentum to the serious efforts that are going on to establish this broader peace.

We hope that the leaders of Lebanon who are now meeting in Geneva will put the problems of the past aside. They have it within their ability to move toward a national consensus. Progress in their talks could lead to the withdrawal of all foreign forces from Lebanon and the establishment of a truly representative government.

We're proud as Americans of the part we're playing to bring peace to this troubled region, and now Don Rumsfeld will be our point man in that effort. I've known Don over the years, and I recognize the talent and vigor that he can bring to bear on these weighty problems. I hope all those who share our sincere desire for peace in the Middle East will work with our new representative.

So, Don, good luck, and our hearts are with you.

Q. Mr. President, Nicaragua says you intend to invade that country. Do you, sir?

The President. Who says?

Q. Nicaraguan leaders, sir.

The President. I haven't believed anything they've been saying since they got in charge, and you shouldn't either.

Q. Mr. President, does the success of Grenada, as you view it, that operation mean that you might be able to apply the military in similar situations elsewhere?

The President. No, I can't foresee any situation that has exactly the same things that this one had. It had exactly what we announced in the beginning: the need to protect the lives and the safety and freedom of about a thousand Americans, most of them students down there in a medical school, and in answer to a request on the part of the other nations bound by treaty together in the east Caribbean, that we lend our support to them in freeing this up because they lacked the strength and capability of doing it.

Q. Well, if somebody else asks, would you be willing to do it again?

The President. As I say, if all the conditions were the same, I don't see why our reason would be any different. But I don't foresee any similar situation on the horizon.

Q. Mr. President, why did 100 nations in the United Nations not agree with you that this was a worthwhile venture?

The President. Helen [Helen Thomas, United Press International], 100 nations in the United Nations have not agreed with us on just about everything that's come before them where we're involved. And, you know, it didn't upset my breakfast at all.

Q. Mr. President, some people say that the U.S. has now lost the moral high ground, that there's no difference between what we did in Grenada and what the Soviets did in Afghanistan. What's your response to that?

The President. Oh for heaven sakes. Anyone who would link Afghanistan to this operation—and incidentally, I know your frequent use of the word "invasion"—this was a rescue mission. But in Afghanistan, if you will recall, when the Soviets installed their choice of head of state for Afghanistan and in the process in changing the forces there, an American Ambassador was murdered in Afghanistan. And then, against all the opposition of the Afghanistan people, they have used every vicious form of warfare, including chemical warfare, the killing of women and children—that has caused even some of their own men to desert because they will not carry out the orders to kill women and children. And they're still there after a long period of time, longer than I've been in this office. As compared to what we did in answer, actually, to an appeal that first came from the Governor General of the island, who was in house arrest, to his fellow states there in the Caribbean—or appealing for rescue, and we helped in the rescue.

Granted that we contributed the bulk of the power, but only because the others were limited in their ability to do that. And this was a rescue mission. It was a successful rescue mission, and the people that have been rescued, and the Grenadians that have been liberated, are down there delighted with and giving every evidence of appreciation and gratitude to our men down there.

Q. Mr. President, are you concerned about our allies? Are you concerned——

Deputy Press Secretary Speakes. Thank you. We'll turn it over to the Ambassador.

The President. Well, now, listen, you're departing from the reason for the gathering here.

Q. A question on the Mideast, sir?

The President. Don, take over.

Mr. Speakes. We'll let the Ambassador handle it, Sam [Sam Donaldson, ABC News].

Q. Is the cancellation of the Israeli withdrawal pact with Lebanon something that you think would serve any interest now? Syria seems to want it, sir.

The President. No, I don't think that that should happen.

Q. How about freezing it? Freezing it?

The President. In that climate? [*Laughter*]

Mr. Speakes. Thank you.

Ambassador Rumsfeld. Thank you, Mr. President, sir.

I will be very brief. The President has indicated the assignment. The President, as he indicated, has set forth the policy of this country with respect to the Middle East. And Secretary Shultz, as recently as last month before the House Foreign Affairs Committee, elaborated further. They have asked me if I could arrange myself to be helpful with respect to this, or try to be helpful. Certainly, it is an important part of the world, a troubled and dangerous part of the world, and I have accepted.

I'd be happy to repond to questions.

Q. Mr. Rumsfeld, some people say this is a no-win job and that in fact, some people before you had been asked to take it and had turned it down. Why did you take it, and is it a no-win job?

Ambassador Rumsfeld. Well, I guess time will tell. It seems to me that it is such an important part of the world to our country, and that it is not surprising that successive Presidents have asked individuals to attempt to work on it for periods of time, and that that is in our interest to try to do.

The fact that the problems there are intractable and difficult and have persisted over long periods doesn't mean that the United States should ignore them. Rather, I think it suggests that it's worth our best efforts, and that's what's intended.

Q. There are stories that you consider this a steppingstone to higher office. Is that why you took the job?

Ambassador Rumsfeld. No.

Q. Are those stories made out of whole cloth, sir? May I just ask if those stories are true?

Ambassador Rumsfeld. I just said no.

Q. In light of the explosion which killed 230 marines, have you or the Secretary of State or the President given any thought to changing the mission of the marines or the scope of the area they control, to make their positions more defensible than they clearly are now?

Ambassador Rumsfeld. I'm the wrong person to ask. I've been in the process of trying to arrange myself to spend time on this, and I have——

Q. How much time are you going to spend on it?

Q. When are you going to get involved?

Q. Have you set a limit?

Ambassador Rumsfeld. I'm going to be getting involved almost immediately, and I will be spending full time for what would probably be a rather extended period of time.

Q. Years?

Ambassador Rumsfeld. No, I am not severing my relationship with Searle. I will be obviously away for prolonged periods, and we have arranged ourselves that that's workable from our standpoint.

Q. Is there any conflict of interest built into that then?

Ambassador Rumsfeld. I am not a lawyer, but the lawyers have looked at it, and they tell me there isn't anything approximating a conflict.

Q. Will you remain president of Searle?

Ambassador Rumsfeld. The statutes of the United States apparently envisioned these kinds of arrangements. They've been used before, and there's nothing unusual about it.

Q. When will you leave for the Middle East?

Ambassador Rumsfeld. I don't know. I want to spend some time here and get briefed up and visit with people who've been involved previously. Then I'll make that kind of a judgment.

Q. Will you spend some time at the Geneva peace talks?

Ambassador Rumsfeld. I don't have any timetable at the moment. This has all happened very promptly.

Mr. Speakes. Last question, here. David [David Hoffman, Washington Post]?

Q. Do you expect to have a deputy in this job or help from Mr. Atherton, the former Ambassador, the departing Ambassador?

Ambassador Rumsfeld. I have made no plans with regard to any personnel questions——

Q. Are you thinking of this in terms of——

Ambassador Rumsfeld. ——really. I'm just starting, and we'll be addressing those kinds of questions along with the others.

Q. What makes you think you can succeed——

Q. Are you thinking of this in terms of years, as a long-term commitment?

Mr. Speakes. Ann [Ann Compton, ABC News] is asking the question, and that's the last question. Last question—Ann.

Q. Are you thinking of this in terms of years and a long-term commitment? And what do you think you can do to bring about some accommodation from the Syrians?

Ambassador Rumsfeld. The answer is, I don't know what can be done. I don't think anyone does. And the answer to the first part of the question is that the assignment is indefinite. And what I intend to do is to immerse myself in it and hope that I can be helpful.

Thank you very much.

Note: The President spoke at 9:55 a.m. to reporters assembled in the Briefing Room at the White House.

Appointment of Donald Rumsfeld as the President's Personal Representative in the Middle East
November 3, 1983

The President today announced his intention to appoint Donald Rumsfeld as his Personal Representative in the Middle East with the personal rank of Ambassador. He will succeed Robert C. McFarlane.

Mr. Rumsfeld has served as president and chief executive officer of G. D. Searle & Company since 1977. Previously Mr. Rumsfeld served as Secretary of Defense in 1975–1977; Chief of Staff, the White House, in 1974–1975; U.S. Ambassador to the North Atlantic Treaty Organization located in Belgium in 1973–1974; Counsellor to the President and Director of the Economic Stabilization Program in 1970–1972; and Director of the Office of Economic Opportunity and Assistant to the President in 1969–1970. He was elected to the U.S. Congress from Illinois in 1962 and reelected in 1964, 1966, and 1968.

In 1977 Mr. Rumsfeld was awarded the Nation's highest civilian award, the Presidential Medal of Freedom. Mr. Rumsfeld presently serves as a member of the boards of directors of Sears, Roebuck and Co. and of Eastern Air Lines and as chairman of the board of the Rand Corp. He also serves on the President's U.S. General Advisory Committee on Arms Control and on the U.S. Presidential Commission on the Conduct of U.S.-Japan Relations.

He graduated from Princeton University (1954). He is a married, has three children, and resides in Winnetka, Ill. He was born July 9, 1932.

Nomination of Joseph A. Cannon To Be an Assistant Administrator of the Environmental Protection Agency
November 3, 1983

The President today announced his intention to nominate Joseph A. Cannon to be an Assistant Administrator of the Environmental Protection Agency (Air, Noise and Radiation). He would succeed Kathleen M. Bennett.

Since 1981 he has been serving as Associate Administrator for Policy and Resources Management at the Environmental Protection Agency. Previously he was an associate with the law firm of Andrews, Kurth, Campbell & Jones in 1979–1981; associate with the firm of Morgan, Lewis & Bockius in 1978–1979; and law clerk to Judge Aldon J. Anderson, U.S. District Court for the District of Utah in 1977–1978.

Mr. Cannon graduated from Brigham Young University (B.A., 1974; J.D., 1977). He is married, has four children, and resides in Annandale, Va. He was born July 31, 1949, in Salt Lake City, Utah.

Proclamation 5124—National Diabetes Month, 1983
November 3, 1983

By the President of the United States of America

A Proclamation

Diabetes mellitus is a chronic disease that now threatens the lives of approximately 11 million Americans. Although careful treatment can control many of the short-term metabolic effects of diabetes, the disease is also associated with serious long-term complications that affect the eyes, kidneys, nerves, and blood vessels of the heart, brain, and extremities. In addition to its devastating toll in terms of human suffering, the cost of medical care for diabetic patients and associated losses due to disability and premature mortality now exceed $10 billion annually in the United States alone.

Fortunately, the outlook for clinical advances related to the diagnosis, treatment, cure, and, ultimately, the prevention of diabetes and its complications has never been as promising as it is today. Recent research advances have included the synthetic production of purified human insulin to ensure adequate supplies of this essential hormone, the development of improved methods for insulin administration, new technologies for monitoring critical blood sugar levels, new therapies for the treatment of diabetes-related kidney, eye, and cardiovascular diseases, and improved clinical capabilities for reducing the increased perinatal morbidity and mortality associated with diabetic pregnancies.

In addition, remarkable advances have also been made in developing procedures that permit the successful transplantation of insulin-producing cells into diabetic animals without the need for chronic suppression of the immune system. As these and related studies are extended to humans, they may lead directly to the development of a cure for some of the most serious types of diabetes and to a means to prevent, arrest, or reverse the long-term complications of this disease.

Recent advances in basic biomedical research are providing new insights into the multiple causes of diabetes. We anticipate that these studies will help to identify individuals at risk for developing diabetes so that we may ultimately develop approaches that will prevent the disease and its complications altogether. Basic and clinical research advances have significantly reduced diabetes-related morbidity and mortality and have measurably improved the quality of life for people with diabetes. Nevertheless, much remains to be done before the cure and prevention of diabetes and its complications become a reality. Toward this goal, the Federal government, in cooperation with the private sector, will continue in the same determined spirit to lead the way toward eliminating diabetes as a major public health problem both for current and future generations.

Now, Therefore, I, Ronald Reagan, President of the United States of America, in accordance with Senate Joint Resolution 121, do hereby proclaim the month of November, 1983, as National Diabetes Month,

and I call upon all government agencies and the people of the United States to observe this month with appropriate programs, ceremonies, and activities.

In Witness Whereof, I have hereunto set my hand this 3rd day of November, in the year of our Lord nineteen hundred and eighty-three, and of the Independence of the United States of America the two hundred and eighth.

RONALD REAGAN

[*Filed with the Office of the Federal Register, 12:31 p.m., November 4, 1983*]

Remarks at the Reagan-Bush Campaign Reunion
November 3, 1983

Thank you. And for all of us up here, thank you very much for a very warm welcome. It always makes you suspect there's a Republican or two in the crowd. [*Laughter*] But I'm pleased to be here and to see so many old friends. And a special greeting—I know someone is here—my Press Secretary, Jim Brady, and his lovely wife, Sarah.

Well, I want to thank all of you for giving so much of your time and labor to make this administration possible. In the end, it's not glitter and gloss but the grit and determination from an army of supporters that makes victory possible—and will make it so again in '84.

You know, back in 1980 our administration inherited a mess: an economy with raging inflation and soaring interest rates, a dangerously weakened national defense, a foreign policy that had allowed American influence—a force for freedom and peace in the world—to shrink. What the Democrats had done to our country reminds me of a story. [*Laughter*] A little girl said to her mother, she said, "You know that beautiful jug you told me had been handed down to us in our family from generation to generation?" And her mother said, "Yes, what about it?" She said, "Well, this generation just dropped it." [*Laughter*]

With your help, our administration was elected to put the pieces back together

again. We cut the growth of Federal spending. We pruned needless regulations. And George Bush was in charge of the team that was doing that, and it has saved hundreds of millions of man-hours of work in filling out needless government papers. We reduced personal income tax rates, and we passed an historic reform called tax indexing.

Now, today, just 2 years after we set our policies in place, our nation has one big program to help every American man, woman, and child. It's called economic recovery. And you can tell it's working because, as I've said several times already, they don't call it Reaganomics anymore. [*Laughter*]

You know, I've said something else before, but it needs saying again: We didn't come to Washington to raise the people's taxes; we came here to restore opportunity and to get this economy moving again. We don't face large deficits because Americans aren't taxed enough; we face those deficits because the Congress still spends too much. And I am still opposed to those who suggest that now we should raise taxes on individuals and businesses, and I'm prepared to veto tax increases if they send them to my desk, no matter how they arrive.

Let them keep their hands off the recovery and start doing what they were elected to do, which is to get spending under control once and for all.

Now just as we're turning the economy around, we've strengthened our national defense and have given a new sense of purpose to American foreign policy. In the military, the number of combat-ready units has increased a third since 1980, and morale has shot up high. We're attracting better recruits, and we're keeping them longer, because we're finally giving them better pay, better equipment, and the respect they deserve.

In foreign policy, we've let the world know once again that America stands for the political, religious, and economic freedom of mankind. And something else: Under this administration, our nation is through wringing its hands and apologizing. Americans don't put up walls to keep people in. We don't have armies of secret police to keep them quiet. And we don't put political and religious dissidents in jail, and we would never coldbloodedly shoot a defenseless airliner out of the sky.

In two places last week—Beirut and Grenada—Americans lost their lives and were wounded while protecting lives, defending freedom, and fostering peace. In Beirut, we won't be intimidated by terrorists. We will redouble our efforts to help the people of Lebanon find peace.

In Grenada, the thugs who seized power in a bloody coup have already been replaced by administrators of good will who will prepare the country for democratic elections. We've had broad and bipartisan support for our actions in Grenada. Yes, there were some critics, but I'd like to suggest that those critics take a moment to listen to interviews with Grenadians rejoicing at their new freedom, or to meditate on the photo of an American medical student rescued by U.S. Rangers, kissing the good earth of South Carolina after he got off the plane at Charleston Air Force Base.

You know, as of last night, those in charge of that marvelous operation—which they put together in 48 hours and kept it a secret until they could land there—they,

last night, declared hostilities at an end. And today, the engineers of the 82d Airborne are repairing roads and bridges and damaged buildings and homes down there. And the Medical Corps, now that our wounded have been evacuated, are taking care of the people on Grenada, vaccinating children, doing those things that are associated with public health chores. In other words, we're doing what America has always done, and I don't know that we've ever had any better missionaries for our country abroad than GI's in uniform.

We all grieve over the lives of those splendid young men that were lost in Beirut and Grenada. But I just have to believe we can honor their memory best by not withdrawing from our role in the world, but by remaining the force for freedom and peace that makes America the brightest star of hope in the world today.

In 1980 our nation faced a crucial choice: We could continue to decline or we could work, instead, to make a new beginning. The American people chose the path of courage, and our administration was elected to make that new beginning. Everyone here, whether you stuffed envelopes or planned campaign strategy, helped to change the course of American history.

In 1984 we'll have another great political battle to wage. Republican candidates across the country will once again need your support, your time, your skill, and your sweat. For the good of our country, let's wage this battle with all the determination and dedication that we have in us. I believe all of us share a dream. It's a dream of an America that offers opportunity to all her citizens. It's a dream of America as a mighty force for good will among the nations. And with faith in our God and confidence in our cause, we're making that great dream come true.

So, from all of us, thank you, and God bless you.

Note: The President spoke at 7:09 p.m. in the International Ballroom at the Washington Hilton Hotel.

Letter to the Senate Majority Leader on the Commission on Civil Rights
November 3, 1983

Dear Howard:

In April of this year, I transmitted to Congress the Civil Rights Reauthorization Act of 1983. The leading features of my proposal—a twenty-year extension of the Commission's life (the longest in history) and staggered, fixed terms for the members—were fully consonant with the recommendations made by a unanimous Civil Rights Commission.

On August 4, the House rejected the idea of a lengthy extension and voted instead for a five-year authorization. It also rejected a proposal for specified terms, while adopting a provision which stated that commissioners could in the future be removed only for cause.

Although I continue to believe in the merits of my original proposal, I believe that we should all come together behind a reauthorization bill that will pass quickly, in the interest of saving the United States Civil Rights Commission from extinction at the end of this month. Accordingly, I very strongly urge you and your colleagues to adopt the House-passed bill, which is now being held at the Senate desk. That is the quickest and least controversial way of ensuring that the Commission's life will be extended.

There are, no doubt, those who would like to see the Commission expire. I am not one of them. The Commission's work is not done. It still has an important contribution to make to the Nation and to the cause of civil rights. I hope that the Senate will join me in the effort to guarantee the Commission's future life.

Sincerely,

/S/ RONALD REAGAN

Note: The letter was addressed to Senate Majority Leader Howard H. Baker, Jr.

As printed above, this item follows the text of the letter released by the Office of the Press Secretary on November 4.

Remarks to Military Personnel at Cherry Point, North Carolina, on the United States Casualties in Lebanon and Grenada
November 4, 1983

Officers and men and women of the corps, ladies and gentlemen, I came here today to pay homage to the heroes of Lebanon and Grenada. We grieve along with the families of these brave, proud Americans who have given their lives for their country and for the preservation of peace.

I have just met with the families of many of those who were killed. I think all Americans would cradle them in our arms if we could. We share their sorrow. I want all of you who lost loved ones and friends to know that the thoughts and prayers of this nation are with you.

If this country is to remain a force for good in the world, we'll face times like these, times of sadness and loss. Your fellow citizens know and appreciate that marines and their families are carrying a heavy burden.

America seeks no new territory, nor do we wish to dominate others. We commit our resources and risk the lives of those in our Armed Forces to rescue others from bloodshed and turmoil and to prevent humankind from drowning in a sea of tyranny.

In Lebanon, along with our allies, we're working hard to help bring peace to that war-torn country and stability to the vital Middle East. In seeking to stabilize the situation in Lebanon, you marines and sailors—and our French, Italian, and English companions—are peacekeepers in the truest sense of the word.

The world looks to America for leadership. And America looks to the men in its Armed Forces—to the Corps of Marines, to the Navy, the Army.

Freedom is being tested throughout the world. In Burma, that government has announced conclusive evidence of North Korean responsibility for the atrocity taking the lives of many members of the Korean Government. We stand with South Korea, and I will be going there next week to carry our message to them, a message of revulsion of this atrocity, determination to stand with our friends in support of freedom.

In the Middle East this morning, we have learned of yet another terrorist assault similar to the attack against our marines, this time against an Israeli site in Tyre, Lebanon.

In spite of the complexity and special hardships of the Lebanese crisis, we have stood firm. As ever, leathernecks are willing to accept their mission and do their duty. This honest patriotism and dedication to duty overwhelms the rest of us.

In Grenada, our military forces moved quickly and professionally to protect American lives and respond to an urgent request from the Organization of Eastern Caribbean States. We joined in an effort to restore order and democracy to that strife-torn island. Only days before our actions, Prime Minister Maurice Bishop had been brutally murdered, along with several members of his Cabinet and unarmed civilians. With a thousand Americans, including some 800 students, on that island, we weren't about to wait for the Iran crisis to repeat itself, only this time, in our own neighborhood—the Caribbean.

In a free society there's bound to be disagreement about any decisive course of action. Some of those so quick to criticize our operation in Grenada, I invite them to read the letters I've received from those students and their families. They know this was no invasion; they know it was a rescue mission. Marines have a saying—"We take care of our own." Well, America, with the help of marines, will take care of our own.

And our brave marines, soldiers, and special forces—including the truly gallant Navy Seals—were not just coming to the aid of our students. I hope every American will be able to hear the stories of the political prisoners who have been freed. The citizens of Grenada, who watched helplessly as their country was being stolen from them and turned into a staging area for totalitarian aggression—these same Grenadians are hailing us as liberators, and they're doing everything they can now to help. Every American can be proud of the professional and gallant job that our Armed Forces have done. And all of us can rejoice that they're coming home.

I came here today to honor so many who did their duty and gave that last, full measure of their devotion. They kept faith with us and our way of life. We wouldn't be free long, but for the dedication of such individuals. They were heroes. We're grateful to have had them with us.

The motto of the United States Marine Corps: "Semper Fidelis"—always faithful. Well, the rest of us must remain always faithful to those ideals which so many have given their lives to protect. Our heritage of liberty must be preserved and passed on. Let no terrorist question our will or no tyrant doubt our resolve. Americans have courage and determination, and we must not and will not be intimidated by anyone, anywhere.

Since 1775, marines, just like many of you, have shaped the strength and resolve of the United States. Your role is as important today as at any time in our history.

Our hearts go out to the families of the brave men that we honor today. Let us close ranks with them in tribute to our fallen heroes, their loved ones, who gave more than can ever be repaid. They're now part of the soul of this great country and will live as long as our liberty shines as a beacon of hope to all those who long for freedom and a better world.

One of the men in the early days of our nation, John Stuart Mill, said, "War is an ugly thing, but not the ugliest of things. The ugliest is that man who thinks nothing is worth fighting or dying for and lets men better and braver than himself protect him." You are doing that for all of us.

God bless you, and thank you for what you're doing.

Note: The President spoke at 12:06 p.m. at Cherry Point Marine Corps Air Station.

Earlier, following his arrival at the air station, the President went to Camp Lejeune, where he attended a memorial service for those killed in Lebanon and Grenada and in honor of those wounded or missing. After the service, he went to the Second Marine Divison Headquarters Building, where he met with families of the honored dead.

Following his remarks, the President returned to Washington, D.C.

Nomination of Samuel W. Speck, Jr., To Be an Associate Director of the Federal Emergency Management Agency
November 4, 1983

The President today announced his intention to nominate Samuel W. Speck, Jr., to be an Associate Director of the Federal Emergency Management Agency (State and Local Programs and Support). He would succeed Lee M. Thomas.

Since 1977 Mr. Speck has served as State senator for the 20th district of Ohio and serves as Republican whip of the Ohio Senate. He is a member of the Finance and Education and Retirement Committees and is former chairman of the Energy, Natural Resources and Environment Committee. He is also an associate professor of political science at Muskingum College and serves as a member of the American Political Science Association and as a fellow of the African Studies Association.

He graduated from Muskingum College (1959) and Harvard University (M.A., 1963; Ph. D., 1968). He is married, has two sons, and resides in New Concord, Ohio. He was born January 31, 1937, in Canton, Ohio.

Appointment of Jean Hails as a Member of the President's Advisory Committee on Women's Business Ownership
November 4, 1983

The President today announced his intention to appoint Jean Hails to be a member of the President's Advisory Committee on Women's Business Ownership. This is a new position.

Since 1981 she has been owner, chief executive officer, and treasurer of The Hails Companies, Inc., in Roswell, Ga. She was vice president, treasurer, and comptroller in 1970–1981. She was founding and charter member of the Georgia Chapter of the Associated Builders & Contractors, Inc.

She is married, has six children, and resides in Roswell, Ga. She was born April 23, 1940, in Princeton, Ala.

Nomination of William E. Seale To Be a Commissioner of the Commodity Futures Trading Commission
November 4, 1983

The President today announced his intention to nominate William E. Seale to be a Commissioner of the Commodity Futures Trading Commission for a term expiring April 13, 1988. He would succeed James M. Stone.

Mr. Seale was vice president of government relations for Commodity Exchange, Inc., in New York City, in 1979–1983. Previously he was legislative assistant to U.S. Senator Walter D. Huddleston in 1975–1979 and in the Department of Agricultural Economics at the University of Kentucky in 1970–1975.

He is the author of several publications on agriculture. He graduated from the University of Kentucky (A.B., 1963; M.S., 1969; Ph. D., 1975). He is married, has three children, and resides in McLean, Va. He was born February 10, 1941, in Lynchburg, Va.

Notice of the Continuation of the Iran Emergency
November 4, 1983

On November 14, 1979, by Executive Order No. 12170, the President declared a national emergency to deal with the threat to the national security, foreign policy and economy of the United States constituted by the situation in Iran. Notices of the continuation of the national emergency were transmitted by the President to the Congress and the *Federal Register* on November 12, 1980, November 12, 1981, and November 8, 1982. Because our relations with Iran have not yet been normalized and the process of implementing the January 19, 1981 agreements with Iran is still underway, the national emergency declared November 14, 1979 must continue in effect beyond November 14, 1983. Therefore, pursuant to section 202(d) of the National Emergencies Act (50 U.S.C. 1622(d)), I am so continuing the national emergency with respect to Iran declared on November 14, 1979. This notice shall be published in the *Federal Register* and transmitted to the Congress.

RONALD REAGAN

The White House,
November 4, 1983.

[*Filed with the Office of the Federal Register, 3:13 p.m., November 4, 1983*]

Message to the Congress Concerning the Continuation of the Iran Emergency
November 4, 1983

To the Congress of the United States:

Section 202(d) of the National Emergencies Act (50 U.S.C. 1622(d)) provides for the automatic termination on the anniversary date of a declaration of emergency, unless prior to the anniversary date the President publishes in the *Federal Register* and transmits to Congress a notice stating that the emergency is to continue in effect beyond the anniversary date. I have sent to the *Federal Register* for publication the enclosed notice stating that the Iran emergency is to continue in effect beyond the November 14, 1983 anniversary date. Similar notices were sent to the Congress and the *Federal Register* on November 12, 1980, November 12, 1981, and November 8, 1982.

The crisis between the United States and Iran which began in 1979 has eased, but it has not been fully resolved. The internal situation in Iran remains uncertain; the war between Iran and Iraq continues. The international arbitral tribunal established for the adjudication of claims of U.S. nationals against Iran and by Iranian nationals against the United States continues to function; however, full normalization of commercial and diplomatic relations between the U.S. and Iran will require more time. In these circumstances, I have determined that it is necessary to maintain in force the broad authorities that may be needed to respond to the process of implementation of the January 1981 agreements with Iran and the eventual normalization of relations.

RONALD REAGAN

The White House,
November 4, 1983.

Message to the Congress Reporting on Developments Concerning the Declaration of a National Emergency With Respect to Iran
November 4, 1983

To the Congress of the United States:

Pursuant to Section 204(c) of the International Emergency Economic Powers Act (IEEPA), 50 U.S.C. Section 1703(c), I hereby report to the Congress with respect to developments between my last report of May 2, 1983, and mid-October 1983, concerning the national emergency with respect to Iran that was declared in Executive Order No. 12170 of November 14, 1979.

1. The Iran-United States Claims Tribunal, established at The Hague pursuant to the Claims Settlement Agreement of January 19, 1981, continues to make progress in arbitrating the claims of U.S. nationals against Iran. Since my last report, the Tribunal has rendered 42 more decisions for a total of 82 final decisions. Sixty-two of these decisions have been in favor of American claimants. Forty-two were awards on agreed terms, authorizing and approving payment of settlements negotiated by the parties and 20 were adjudicated. Total payments to successful American claimants from the Security Account stood at just under $88 million, as of October 1. Of the remaining 20 decisions, 12 dismissed claims for lack of jurisdiction, seven dismissed claims on the merits and one approved withdrawal of a claim. As of October 1, the Tribunal had held 111 prehearing conferences and 68 hearings on the merits and scheduled another eight prehearings and nine hearings through mid-November. In addition, two full Tribunal sessions of five days each were scheduled for October and early November.

2. The Department of State continues to coordinate the efforts of the concerned government agencies in presenting U.S. claims against Iran, as well as U.S. responses to claims brought by Iran. The Department has devoted a great deal of time to responding to cases brought by Iran under Articles II(3) and VI(4) of the Claims Settlement Agreement, which establish Tribunal jurisdiction over questions of interpretation and implementation of the Algiers Accords. In the last six months, the United States has replied to all of the allegations raised by Iran in a major interpretive dispute concerning the United States' implementation of the Algiers Accords. The Tribunal has scheduled eight prehearing conferences or hearings on these issues. In addition, Iran has filed three more interpretive disputes, requesting clarification of: the Tribunal's jurisdiction over dual national claims; its authority to grant interest on awards; and the criteria for determining corporate nationality. Each of these questions had previously been decided by the Tribunal or a chamber

thereof. The United States has filed replies in these three cases.

3. Since my last report, there has been further activity in resolving the government-to-government claims based on contracts for the provision of goods or services. Of the 64 claims filed by Iran against the United States, nine have been withdrawn or terminated and one has resulted in an award on agreed terms. The Tribunal has received pleadings from both sides in the remaining cases and in almost all of the 18 claims which the United States filed against Iran. Since, in many instances, the tribunal has announced its intention to decide the official claims on the pleadings, only one prehearing conference and one hearing have been scheduled.

4. Since my last report, the Tribunal has rendered a number of significant decisions. In at least six instances, Iran has filed suit in Iranian courts against claimants at the Tribunal on issues similar to those before the Tribunal. In each case, the Tribunal has requested Iran to stay the Iranian court proceedings in Iran until the Tribunal has had a chance to determine its jurisdiction over the claims. Iran, however, has yet to comply with any of these requests. On other matters, the Tribunal has found a contract to exist between a United States claimant and Iran in the absence of a formal written document, and it continues to award successful claimants interest on their awards. The Tribunal has begun to enforce more vigorously its filing deadlines, rejecting a number of Iranian counterclaims on the grounds that they were filed too late and refusing to consider pleadings filed after the established deadline.

5. In the last six months, the United States has proposed to the Tribunal that it adopt a test case approach in arbitrating the 2,742 remaining claims for less than $250,000 each. The United States has categorized all these claims according to the type of loss involved. Under this approach, the Tribunal would select a few cases in each category for a full hearing. Based on the decisions in each category, claims experts would then arbitrate the remaining cases in each category, subject to tribunal ratification of their decisions.

6. In the period since my last report,

there have been several changes in the Tribunal's composition. The resignation of Judge Pierre Bellet, one of the three third-party arbitrators, became effective on August 1. Because the six party-appointed arbitrators were not able to agree on a successor, the Appointing Authority, previously designated by the Secretary General of the Permanent Court of Arbitration in The Hague, appointed Professor Willem Riphagen of the Netherlands to replace Judge Bellet. Professor Riphagen, a former legal adviser to the Netherlands Ministry of Foreign Affairs, was a professor of international law at the University of Rotterdam. He has served as an *ad hoc* judge on the International Court of Justice, has presided over an arbitration between the United States and France, and has acted as Special Rapporteur for the International Law Commission.

7. On September 5, the Tribunal accepted the resignation of M. Jahangir Sani, one of the Iranian-appointed arbitrators, effective upon the availability of a successor. On September 14, Iran announced that it was appointing Parviz Ansari Moin to replace Mr. Sani. Mr. Ansari has worked in the Iranian Ministry of Justice for approximately ten years.

8. The Algiers Accords also provided for direct negotiations between U.S. banks and Bank Markazi Iran concerning the payment of nonsyndicated debt claims of U.S. banks against Iran from the escrow account established at the Bank of England in January 1981 with the deposit of $1.418 billion. Significant progress has been made in the past six months in settling these claims. As of mid-October, 24 settlements, totaling approximately $919 million, had been reached. From the $919 million paid to U.S. banks, the banks paid $327 million to Iran in settlement of Iran's claims against them, primarily for interest on domestic deposits. The Export-Import Bank received $419 million. About 25 bank claims remain outstanding.

9. During the past six months, the Department of State has begun to renovate and prepare for rental diplomatic and consular properties of Iran in the United States. In the absence of diplomatic relations between the United States and Iran, these

properties have remained vacant and in many instances have deteriorated. To preserve them and to generate income for their upkeep, the Department of State, pursuant to a license granted in September by the Department of the Treasury, will sell moveable property left in or around Iranian premises following the break in diplomatic relations with Iran on April 7, 1980.

10. The Treasury Department's Office of Foreign Assets Control has established procedures authorizing the sale of blocked Iranian property in the United States and the eventual disposition of the proceeds of such sales. Much of this property is tangible property, including property which has not been authorized to be exported from the United States because of its potential military applications. In the six-month period preceding this report, three sales of such tangible property have been licensed. No sales had taken place as of mid-October. Several direct settlements of disputes between holders of such tangible property and Iran have occurred recently.

11. Despite the progress made by the Tribunal in the past six months, significant American interests remain unresolved. Iran has challenged five of the Tribunal's awards in the District Court of The Hague, seeking to invalidate them. Thus, financial and diplomatic aspects of the relationship with Iran continue to present an unusual challenge to the national security and foreign policy of the United States. By separate action of this date, I am extending the emergency with respect to Iran beyond the November 14, 1983 anniversary. I shall continue to exercise the powers at my disposal to deal with these problems and will continue to report periodically to the Congress on significant developments.

RONALD REAGAN

The White House,
November 4, 1983.

Proclamation 5125—National Reye's Syndrome Week, 1983
November 4, 1983

By the President of the United States of America

A Proclamation

Reye's Syndrome is a serious illness that may attack the brain and liver of a child recovering from influenza, chicken pox, or some other viral infection. The cause of this disease—which affects an estimated 600 to 1,200 children in the United States each year—is unknown.

The first signs of Reye's Syndrome in a child are repeated vomiting, fatigue, and general irritation. The disease may progress to a life-threatening stage. If early symptoms are recognized and treated promptly, however, it is less likely that the disease will cause dangerous brain swelling, coma, or death.

New treatments are being developed to help victims of Reye's Syndrome recover. This improved outlook is a direct result of scientific research carried out by public and private investigators and physicians, many of whom are supported by the American Reye's Syndrome Associations, the National Reye's Syndrome Foundation (Ohio), the National Reye's Syndrome Foundation (Michigan), and the United States Public Health Service. Within the Public Health Service, the Centers for Disease Control, the Food and Drug Administration and the National Institutes of Health are carrying out research projects and constant surveillance of cases.

Much still remains to be learned about Reye's Syndrome. Coordinated research is needed to find better ways to treat this disorder and ultimately to prevent it. Public education is also essential, because parents and physicians can help to protect the Nation's children from its lethal effects if they learn to recognize this disease in its earliest stages.

To enhance the public's awareness of the gravity of Reye's Syndrome, the Congress, by Senate Joint Resolution 34, has designated the week of November 7 through November 13, 1983, as "National Reye's Syndrome Week" and has authorized and requested the President to issue a proclamation in observance of that week.

Now, Therefore, I, Ronald Reagan, President of the United States of America, do hereby proclaim the week beginning November 7, 1983, as National Reye's Syndrome Week, and I call upon the people of the United States to observe that week with appropriate ceremonies and activities.

In Witness Whereof, I have hereunto set my hand this fourth day of November, in the year of our Lord nineteen hundred and eighty-three, and of the Independence of the United States of America the two hundred and eighth.

RONALD REAGAN

[*Filed with the Office of the Federal Register, 11:01 a.m., November 7, 1983*]

Nomination of Robert Francis Kane To Be United States Ambassador to Ireland
November 4, 1983

The President today announced his intention to appoint Robert Francis Kane, of California, to be United States Ambassador to Ireland. He would succeed Peter H. Dailey, who is resigning to return to private business.

The President also announced that Ambassador Peter Dailey, who helped organize the administration's public diplomacy effort on European arms control and security issues earlier this year, will continue to advise the administration on these issues.

Mr. Kane has been in the private practice of law as a senior director in the firm of Ropers, Majeski, Kohn, Bentley, Wagner, and Kane in Redwood City, Calif., since 1979. On October 7, 1983, President Reagan nominated Mr. Kane to be a member of the Board of Directors of the Legal Services Corporation. From 1971 until 1979, he served as a Justice on the California Court of Appeal, to which he was appointed on April 2, 1971, by Governor Reagan and thereafter elected in 1974.

Governor Reagan appointed Mr. Kane to be a Superior Court Judge, San Mateo County, on November 27, 1968, and he was elected for a 6-year term in June of 1970. From 1952 until 1969, Mr. Kane was an attorney in private practice in San Francisco (1952–1955) and Redwood City (1955–1969). In 1978 Mr. Kane was the recipient of the St. Thomas More Award and in 1979 of the Principal Award for Public Address Category by the Freedom Foundation at Valley Forge. He is a fellow of the American College of Trial Lawyers and the International Society of Barristers and a member of the American Board of Trial Advocates.

Mr. Kane received his A.A. degree from San Mateo Junior College in 1948 and attended the University of Southern California. In 1952 he earned his J.D. from the University of San Francisco. From 1944 to 1946, he served in the U.S. Navy. He is married to the former Mary Catherine Galligan, and they have five children and reside in San Mateo. Mr. Kane was born March 15, 1926, in Denver, Colo.

Proclamation 5126—National Family Week, 1983
November 4, 1983

By the President of the United States of America

A Proclamation

The family and family life are central to our American heritage. Family bonds give us an anchor in the past, as well as hope for the future. It is within the family that tradition is created, individuals grow, and faith is nurtured. Through family living, we discover who we are, how to interact with our fellowman, and the values that make a free society possible.

Families perform the daily tasks that sustain and renew us, including raising children and caring for the elderly. Families not only provide better health but also serve the special needs of the handicapped. In particular, those who have opened their homes through adoption and foster care deserve special thanks for offering the gift of family life to our Nation's less fortunate children.

Today, amid new pressures and needs, America is relearning the importance of its families. For instance, success in the national fight against drug and alcohol abuse must begin with a strong and united family. We are newly aware that the family cannot be taken for granted, and that the support of a family can never truly be replicated.

In recognition of the importance of the family as an essential unit of our free and orderly society, the Congress, by Senate Joint Resolution 45, has authorized and requested the President to designate the week beginning on November 20, 1983, as "National Family Week."

Now, Therefore, I, Ronald Reagan, President of the United States of America, do hereby proclaim the week of November 20 through November 26, 1983, as National Family Week. I applaud the men and women who uphold our families in many ways, as parents, grandparents, as the daughters and sons of older Americans.

I invite the Governors of the several States, the chief officials of local governments and all our citizens to observe this week with appropriate ceremonies and activities. During a week in which we will also observe Thanksgiving Day, I especially invite all Americans to give thanks for the family relationships with which we have been blessed.

In Witness Whereof, I have hereunto set my hand this 4th day of November, in the year of our Lord nineteen hundred and eighty-three, and of the Independence of the United States of America the two hundred and eighth.

RONALD REAGAN

[*Filed with the Office of the Federal Register, 11:30 a.m., November 7, 1983*]

Executive Order 12448—Regulations Related to Voiding or Rescission of Contracts
November 4, 1983

Exercise of Authority Under Section 218 of Title 18, United States Code

By the authority vested in me as President by the Constitution and statutes of the United States of America, including section 218 of title 18 of the United States Code, and in order to provide federal agencies with the authority to promulgate regulations for voiding or rescinding contracts or other benefits obtained through bribery, graft or conflict of interest, it is hereby ordered as follows:

Section 1. The head of each Executive department, Military department and Executive agency is hereby delegated the authority vested in the President to declare void and rescind the transactions set forth in section 218 of title 18 of the United States Code in relation to which there has been a final conviction for any violation of chapter 11 of title 18.

Sec. 2. The head of each Executive department and agency described in section 1 may exercise the authority hereby delegated by promulgating implementing regulations; provided that the Secretary of Defense, the Administrator of General Services and the Administrator of the National Aeronautics and Space Administration jointly shall issue government-wide implementing regulations related to voiding or rescission of contracts.

Sec. 3. Implementing regulations adopted pursuant to this Order shall, at a minimum, provide the following procedural protections:

(a) Written notice of the proposed action shall be given in each case to the person or entity affected;

(b) The person or entity affected shall be afforded an opportunity to submit pertinent information on its behalf before a final decision is made;

(c) Upon the request of the person or entity affected, a hearing shall be held at which it shall have the opportunity to call witnesses on its behalf and confront any witness the agency may present; and

(d) The head of the agency or his designee shall issue a final written decision specifying the amount of restitution or any other remedy authorized by section 218, provided that such remedy shall take into consideration the fair value of any tangible benefits received and retained by the agency.

RONALD REAGAN

The White House,
November 4, 1983.

[*Filed with the Office of the Federal Register, 11:02 a.m., November 7, 1983*]

Radio Address to the Nation on America's Veterans
November 5, 1983

My fellow Americans:

Next Friday, November 11th, we'll celebrate Veterans Day—the day America sets aside to honor millions of our finest heroes. They are the men and women who defend our country and preserve our peace and freedom. This Veterans Day offers more reason than ever to think about what these special people mean to America.

Our most recent heroes—those still serving and those who have just come back from Beirut and Grenada—carried on with the same dedication and valor as their colleagues before them. If we remember that their dedicated service is in defense of our freedom and if we understand that they put their lives on the line so we might enjoy justice and liberty, then their sacrifices will not be in vain. This is our obligation. And this has been the spirit of Veterans Day from the beginning.

Veterans Day was originally called Armistice Day. It was first celebrated in 1919, the year we commemorated the armistice ending a war that was to have ended all wars. Two years later, a solemn ceremony was held in Châlons-sur-Marne, a town in northeastern France. The ceremony would have deep meaning for America. The remains of four unknown American soldiers had been brought to the town square from four American military cemeteries in France. An American sergeant, Edward F. Younger, placed a bouquet of white roses on one of the caskets. The American Unknown Soldier of World War I had been designated. After transport across the Atlantic aboard Admiral Dewey's flagship, the cruiser *Olympia*, our nation laid this hero to rest in Arlington National Cemetery on Armistice Day, November 11, 1921.

Sixty-two years have now passed. Millions of people from every corner of the world have come to the Tomb of the Unknown

Soldier to pay their respects to America's fallen heroes. The First World War did not end all wars. The assault on freedom and human dignity did not end. Our nation had laid to rest too many other heroes. From Guadalcanal and Omaha Beach to Mig Alley and Pork Chop Hill, from Khe Sanh and the A Shau Valley to Beirut, America's best continue to give of themselves for us and for freedom-loving people everywhere. Yes, veterans have given their best for all of us, and we must continue to do our best by them.

Today, I reaffirm my determination to obtain the fullest possible accounting for our Americans missing in Southeast Asia. The sacrifices they made and may still be making and the uncertainty their families still endure deeply trouble us all. We must not rest until we know their fate.

Our hearts turn also to our disabled veterans. Their sacrifices and hardship endure every day of the year. A compassionate government will show them that we do remember and honor them. We will meet their special needs. In particular, there is no substitute for caring, quality health care, and that care will be provided.

Yesterday, I had the opportunity to visit Camp Lejeune, North Carolina. I went there to pay tribute to the many who gave their last full measure of their devotion. They kept faith with us and, indeed, they were heroes. Where do we get such brave young Americans? And where do we get those that came to their aid—the marines in Beirut who witnessed an unspeakable tragedy and returned to their posts with the same dedication and even greater resolve; the air crews working around the clock; the Army doctors performing medical miracles; and the sailors helping in countless ways? Such men and women can only come from a nation that remains true to the ideals of our Founding Fathers.

I also met with families and friends of those who lost their lives. I share their sorrow, and they have my prayers, as I know they have yours. These brave men protected our heritage of liberty. We must carry on. I believe we can and will. The spirit and patriotism that made America great is alive and well.

There was a brief ceremony in a hospital ward of Fort Bragg, North Carolina, last week that showed what I'm talking about. News photographers were taking pictures of soldiers who had just been awarded Purple Hearts and other decorations for valor. One wounded soldier, Private First Class Timothy Romick of the First Battalion, 75th Rangers, wearing a Purple Heart and a Combat Infantry Badge on his pajamas, interrupted the photographers. He said, "Wait a minute." And he pulled out a small American flag. This young Army ranger put the flag above his decorations. And then he said, "Okay. You can take your pictures now, because this is what I'm proudest of."

Each time our nation has called upon our citizens to serve, the best have come forward. Words cannot express our gratitude and admiration. But we can and should take the opportunity on this Veterans Day to remember their gift to us. When you see one of our young men and women in uniform on the street or someplace, how about a smiling "hello" and, maybe, a "thank you."

Veterans know better than anyone else the price of freedom, for they've suffered the scars of war. We can offer them no better tribute than to protect what they have won for us. That is our duty. They have never let America down. We will not let them down.

Until next week, thanks for listening, and God bless you.

Note: The President spoke at 12:06 p.m. from Camp David, Md.

Remarks at a White House Ceremony for Medical Students and United States Military Personnel From Grenada
November 7, 1983

The President. Secretary Weinberger, General Vessey,[1] and all of you students and all of the men and women who are here in uniform:

I'm so glad to meet you and to be able to say it officially—welcome home. I can't tell you when I've been so happy and, I might add, relieved to have such guests here on the South Lawn. So a very warm and grateful welcome to you all, and welcome to the Ambassadors and other special guests who are here.

Let me tell you how this little get-together came about. I'm actually playing matchmaker today. You students sent me so many moving telegrams of appreciation about the military fellows who rescued you, I thought it might be nice if you had the chance to tell them yourselves. So, here in this more peaceful setting are representatives of all the four units that participated and were there with you on Grenada.

In letter after letter, you spoke of your deep respect for those who risked their lives and in some circumstances gave their lives so that you'd be safe. A great many of you said you believed you'd be dead or held hostage today if it weren't for the courageous men whose business it is to be courageous—our soldiers, sailors, marines, and airmen. I wish I could give every military person who participated in the Grenada rescue copies of your telegrams and letters.

Some of you also wrote of your anger that certain people belittled the danger that you were in. And I must say this angered me a little, too. It's very easy for some smug know-it-all in a plush, protected quarter to say that you were in no danger. I have wondered how many of them would have changed places with you. [*Laughter*]

Some of our fellows didn't make it back. Ted and Jan Stathos wrote me a letter, as so many of you did, and I'd like to read just

---

[1] *Secretary of Defense Caspar W. Weinberger and Gen. John W. Vessey, Jr., Chairman of the Joint Chiefs of Staff.*

one small passage because it says so much.

"While we waited for the rangers to evacuate our campus at"—and I hope I'm pronouncing this right—"at Grand Anse, we experienced many chilling and sad moments. The most upsetting of these was the sight of an American helicopter being shot down by enemy fire. There were tears in everyone's eyes as we scanned the ocean water for the sight of any survivors. We knew then how much our lives meant to the brave men fighting for our safety."

I wish I could tell you all the acts of heroism that I've been hearing. Sergeant Steven Trujillo, a Ranger, is one example. His unit was engaged in an air assault on the Calivigny Compound which was held by Cuban forces. Sergeant Trujillo was in the first of four helicopters to go into the compound under intense enemy fire. Upon landing, Sergeant Trujillo saw the three other helicopters lose control and crash into one another. Immediately, and with complete disregard for his own personal safety, he ran across open terrain to the downed aircraft, exposing himself to enemy fire, flying shrapnel, and possible explosion of the burning helicopters. With only the lives of his fallen comrades in mind and while still in the open and exposed to intense automatic and small arms fire, Sergeant Trujillo began administering first aid to the critically wounded. Upon arrival of the battalion's physician's assistant, Sergeant Trujillo returned to the crashed aircraft several times, removing the wounded soldiers, carrying them across terrain to a safer location, and administering medical aid. During the entire time he came under automatic and small arms fire. His unselfish actions were instrumental in saving the lives of a platoon leader and several other seriously wounded soldiers. And the inspiring thing is that Sergeant Trujillo would have risked his life for each of you, as well.

From your letters to me, I know how deep your gratitude—even affection—is for these men. Some of you have asked how you can express that respect and affection. Well, you've been doing a marvelous job already. Nothing could make those men prouder than the statements you've made to America about their bravery and devotion to a cause larger than themselves.

A few years ago it seemed that America forgot what an admirable and essential need there is for a nation to have men and women who would give their lives to protect their fellow citizens. What you saw 10 days ago was called patriotism. What those men did for you they would do for any American in trouble. And the way you can best honor those who died in Grenada is to speak out about their courage and commitment as they risked their lives for yours and as so many of you have been doing already.

Unbelievably, the other day a reporter asked me what was the difference between our invading Grenada and the Soviets invading Afghanistan? And the question sort of touched my temperature control. [*Laughter*] I answered. And among the things I said was that there was no comparison between the savage invasion of Afghanistan with its slaughter of innocent men, women, and children—civilians—and the heroic rescue mission of our young Americans. Our troops are already leaving Grenada, but don't hold your breath waiting for the Soviets to leave Afghanistan.

The Afghanistan people aren't meeting the soldiers with friendly waves and gifts of flowers and fruit over there. A CBS news poll shows that an overwhelming majority of the Grenadians—91 percent—are glad the United States came to Grenada. I think that tells a lot about the differences between democracy and totalitarianism.

Now, I'm not going to take up all the time here. But it's good to have both students and servicemen together under more peaceful circumstances. And would you do me a favor? When you all leave today, would you try not to be as dramatic as it was on your last leavetaking? [*Laughter*]

But thank you for coming. God bless all of you. And now, I believe that Jean Joel and Jeff Geller want to say a few words.

Mr. Geller. President and Mrs. Reagan, distinguished members of the military, fellow students:

It is indeed a great honor to speak to you today. When I first spoke to the press and said that I wanted to thank President Reagan and the military, I never dreamed that I'd have a chance to do it personally.

I am here today to say a few words on behalf of the student body of St. George's University School of Medicine. I think that I can speak not only on behalf of the students but also on behalf of all the families of the students in expressing our gratitude to both you, Mr. President, and every member of the military that took part in our evacuation. We owe each and every one of you a debt that we can never repay.

I can recall the joy and pride that I felt as the rangers first emerged over the hill behind my dormitory. I looked out from my dormitory window and, upon hearing that they were Americans, I shouted for joy and thought to myself, "They haven't forgotten us, because we're Americans."

I think that we are often so caught up in criticizing our government and our military that we lose sight of the admirable qualities that they possess. Two weeks ago, I saw those qualities in action. For the American military, I have only praise. They acted in a manner that all Americans can be proud of.

Prior to this experience, I had held liberal political views which were not always sympathetic with the position of the American military. I think a lot of us who don't have a firsthand view are often skeptical when we hear that our military is involved in a faraway place. We don't always understand why our soldiers are fighting abroad. Well, let me say that I have learned a lot from this experience. It's one thing to view an American military operation from afar and quite another to be rescued by one.

We are a group of young men and women dedicated to study medicine so that we can save lives. Let us also remember that many lives were lost in saving ours. Let us honor those American men who gave their lives so that someday we can save others.

To you, President Reagan, I must add a special thank you. On behalf of my parents and of all the students' parents, thank you for bringing us back to the United States. There is truly no place like home.

Ms. Joel. I'm very proud and honored to

be here today, and I believe I represent not only my own class but all of St. George's University School of Medicine when I say that I am grateful to the U.S. military for their actions. I never had so much faith or pride in my country than during the 24 hours I spent under war conditions in Grenada.

Probably the most poignant moment for me, personally, was Tuesday night, in the library that we converted into a makeshift medical unit. I thought about the fact that just 24 hours earlier I had been studying here and how abrupt the change was from academics to reality. They brought in a soldier with three bullet wounds in his right arm and chest, and the man was in excruciating pain. While I attempted to assist the extremely self-sufficient thoracic surgeon as he inserted a chest catheter for drainage, I thought about this man on the table. I mean, a total stranger to me, and yet, an American who was willing to jeopardize his life not only for my personal safety but for the causes of our country.

These professional men, with their unspoken dedication to the United States and to our standards of freedom and democracy, have my great respect. My experience in Grenada, especially in the library medical unit, has reaffirmed my personal dedication to medicine and my commitment to complete my education. But it has also reaffirmed my faith and respect in the citizens of our country, especially those citizens in the military. As a representative of St. George's University School of Medicine, I would like to thank President Reagan and the military for their concern for our personal safety and to say that among such company, I am proud to be an American.

Roxana Mehran. President Reagan, the honorable military, and the student body:

On behalf of the students of St. George's University School of Medicine, I would like to present you with this small token of our appreciation for saving our lives. To the United States military and you, President Reagan, in appreciation for your prompt action that guaranteed our safe return from Grenada, from the students of St. George's University School of Medicine.

The President. I proudly accept that, only as the acceptor, in the realization that it goes to the men and women in uniform in our armed services.

Jay More. President Reagan, on behalf of the students, the very grateful students, of St. George's University School of Medicine who appreciate both your rescue mission in Grenada and your continued support for all citizens pursuing their American dream, we give you a plaque in the shape of the United States for bringing us home to America. We thank you.

The President. Thank you. Thank you very much.

Note: The President spoke at 10:45 a.m. on the South Lawn of the White House.

Prior to the ceremony, the President met in the Oval Office with student representatives from St. George's University School of Medicine.

Interview With Nobutaka Shikanai of Fuji Television of Japan on the President's Trip to Japan
November 7, 1983

Mr. Shikanai. The bonds of friendship between Japan and the United States are among the strongest in the world. As President of the United States, do you have any special message for the Japanese people?

The President. Well, yes, I do. Number one, we're looking forward very much to our trip, which will begin tomorrow. And this will be the third time that we have had the opportunity of visiting Japan, so we are looking forward to this return.

But I think the message that I would have is that the close friendship that we do have and the relationship, overall, imposes on Japan and the United States a responsibility to the world to foster peace and prosperity. Between us, Japan and the United States are responsible for one-third of all the gross national product of the world. We are the two greatest trading partners—our relationship between each other that way. But we can make such a contribution to easing the tensions in the world and bringing the prosperity and the peace that I think the people of all the world want. Some governments may not want that, but the people want it. And between us, as I say, we have a great duty.

Mr. Shikanai. You are now having the most difficult and egregious time as President. What are the real, major objectives of your trip to Japan?

The President. Well, I think that we have a number of things that we need to talk about, because we are such close friends and allies. I think, for one thing, we have some differences with regard to trade. And as we discussed when Prime Minister Nakasone was here for the Williamsburg summit, we discussed the need for all the world to get away from the idea of protectionism in trade, trying to maintain an advantage over someone else.

The great growth and prosperity of Japan in trade and industry is due to the idea of democracy and free trade. And so free trade must also be fair trade. And I am concerned that here in our own country some of the restraints on our exports to your country have led some to a feeling of protectionism and that they must do something in retaliation. I feel that as we loosen the restraints between us in trade, that is the answer to those who could give us political problems in both our countries—to the Prime Minister, to myself, here. So, we will be discussing all those ways in which we can restore that trade.

We have between us the biggest trade between any two countries in the world. And there is a dangerous imbalance now in that trade. So, those will be some of the things that I hope to be discussing.

Mr. Shikanai. While some Japanese feel our country should be unarmed and neutral, Prime Minister Nakasone considers cooperation between Japan and the United States absolutely necessary to Asian peace and security. I would appreciate your comment on this.

The President. Well, I agree with Prime Minister Nakasone very much. The Pacific Basin is the area of the future, and Japan—I recognize you have some constitutional problems with this—but a strong Japan, a Japan able to manage more of its own defense, will be a great factor for stability in that whole area. And while we're talking peace, there are some who seem to suggest that if you're talking military strength, you're talking against peace. Well, I don't know of anyone that ever got into a war because they were too strong.

What we need is to be able to deter others who are destabilizing—the forces, such as from the Soviet Union with their attempts at expansionism. What we need is to have the military strength to deter aggression at the same time that we try to convince the aggressors that they, too, will be better off in a peaceful world.

So yes, we appreciate very much what Japan has done in increasing their own defense. I know that a goal, and one I hope they'll achieve soon, is to be able to protect for 1,000 miles around your trade lines and your supply lines. And we want to continue the relationship we have in that regard.

Mr. Shikanai. Trade friction between Japan and the United States is serious. Do you sometimes worry that it may influence bilateral relations between our two countries?

The President. Well, I'm afraid I almost answered that question in advance to your earlier question there. Yes, those restrictions which I mentioned a moment ago. We must find where, fairly, we can reconcile the differences between our currencies. We must remove restrictions that impair trade back and forth, and we must—just as we're friends and allies in everything else—we must have that same kind of approach to our trade with each other, our opening of our capital markets to each other for investment.

Mr. Shikanai. American relations with the People's Republic of China and the Soviet Union influence our own relations with them. Could you discuss current American policy toward these two countries?

The President. Well, with regard to the

Republic of China, we are working very hard to establish a stronger relationship, one that has always in the past characterized the relationship between our country and China. I think we've been making great progress. Prime Minister Zhao Ziyang will be visiting here this winter, and next spring I expect to visit the People's Republic of China myself.

With the Soviet Union, we have to recognize there that there is where we must have the strength to deter aggression. They seem bent on worldwide expansionism. They have 50 divisions on the Chinese border. They have about 120 SS–20 nuclear missiles on that border. They have the largest fleet, the largest of their fleets is in the Pacific, in the area of both Japan and the People's Republic of China. So, there we must have the patience to convince them that peace would be to their advantage, also. And in the meantime, the only way to protect the peace is to have the strength to deter.

But we are very pleased with the progress we've made with the People's Republic of China in establishing friendship there.

Mr. Shikanai. You and I happen to be the same age. I, too, was born in 1911. You and I also share a deep commitment to democracy and freedom, and we long for peace around the world. It seems, however, that the forces of violence and hate are growing. What are the prospects for peace in the world, despite recent tragedies in Beirut, Rangoon, and KAL 007?

The President. Those tragic events recently, the terrorist acts, what has happened to our men in Beirut, are all evidences of how necessary it is for those of us who can, for countries like Japan and the United States, to erase the causes of such hatred and to work ceaselessly for peace.

Yes, you and I were born in the same year. I like to think it was a good vintage year. But we've had an opportunity to see war and peace throughout these years, to see how foolishly sometimes war came upon us, and at the same time to see the spread of democracy and what it has brought. When you look at your own country, when

you look at South Korea, when you look at Hong Kong, Taiwan, Singapore and see where the principles of free commerce and trade, the principles of democracy are at work, how much better off they are than those countries that have followed the totalitarian path of communism and statism.

So, I think that while things can look dark and threatening, I think the very fact that there is awareness now on the part of many of us who have seen the other, that yes, we can bring peace. We can prove the need for it. And I think there's more awareness in the world today that in order to have peace we must have strength. So, I am not discouraged by what is going on.

Mr. Shikanai. Many people, both here and in the rest of the world, now refer to Japan as an economic superpower. Within the overall context of U.S.-Japan relations, what are your principal expectations for this new, more powerful Japan?

The President. Well—and I think this is a classic example for the world—there is one superpower in the world today that is recognized as such simply because of its military strength and not because of any achievements that it has made in commerce and industry or the living standard of its people. In fact, to maintain their military strength, that power has denied the comforts of living to its people.

On the other hand, you are the second industrial and commercial power in the world. So in that sense you have become a superpower in the peaceful pursuits of commerce and trade and good living for your people. And that is well deserved. That's why we are allies.

Mr. Shikanai. Thank you very much.

The President. Well, thank you for the opportunity.

Mr. Shikanai. Have a nice trip to Japan.

The President. We are looking forward to it. Thank you.

Mr. Shikanai. See you in Tokyo.

The President. I look forward to it. Thank you very much.

Note: The interview began at 11:35 a.m. in the Library at the White House. It was taped for later broadcast in Japan.

Interview With Jung-suk Lee of the Korean Broadcasting System on the President's Trip to the Republic of Korea
November 7, 1983

Mr. Jung. This is my once in a lifetime opportunity. Thank you very much.

Mr. President, it seems to me that the timing of your visit to Korea couldn't be more timely and more appropriate to witness the anger and sorrow of the Korean people. What significance do you give to your forthcoming visit to Korea, sir?

The President. Well, hopefully, to talk over any problems we may have, although they would be very few because of the strong relationship that we have there. Certainly, my visit was not planned with these tragedies in mind that have taken place. But the very fact that they have and the two great tragedies that have befallen your own country—the airplane massacre and then the terrible deeds in Rangoon—make it even more imperative that we continue to strengthen the bonds between our two countries.

So, I'm looking forward to this trip. President Chun visited us here, and I'm happy to have the opportunity to make a return visit over there to—well, I guess it could be summed up in that I think it's important that people talk to each other instead of about each other.

Mr. Jung. Last week, the Burmese Government announced officially that the North Koreans were fully responsible for the recent murder of 17 Korean Government officials and journalists. Yet the Government of Korea was very restrained in its response to this senseless provocation in Burma. America also has had a similar experience, terrorist acts, most recently in Beirut. How, Mr. President, can we prevent such uncivilized acts in the future?

The President. Well, let me say first of all that I admire your government's restraint under this extreme provocation. It's very easy and I know it's only human to want to strike out in retaliation. I had those same feelings about the tragedy in Beirut. But getting the people directly responsible and doing something to indicate that terrorism does have its punishment is a little different than just blindly striking out, and that's why, as I say, I admire the restraint that your government has shown.

The main thing that we must do about terrorism, though, is show the terrorists that it doesn't work. We know that the terrorist act against our own people in Beirut was designed to make us retreat, to make us say, "Well, we'll take our men out of there. We'll abandon the mission that they were sent to perform." Well, we're going to prove to them that terrorist acts are not going to drive us away.

And in the meantime, I think that all of us must recognize the savagery of those who are responsible for these things and thus make sure that we've taken every step we can for the protection of our people and our personnel. And beyond that, we just have to, as we have an expression, "stay the course."

Mr. Jung. The next question is about the Pacific Basin community evolution. A close cooperation among Pacific Basin nations is necessary to take a full advantage of the region's potential. In this context, President Chun of Korea has proposed a summit conference to discuss a closer cooperation. My question is, what future role the U.S. are playing in the Pacific region?

The President. I think a very close role because the United States is a Pacific nation, also. I was Governor of California for 8 years, and I came to realize, with our 1,100-mile frontage on the Pacific Ocean, that we are a nation of the Pacific Basin. So, I foresee much greater and closer cooperation and relationship between the United States and the nations of East Asia and look forward to it because I think that is the new frontier in the world.

Mr. Jung. Korea is among America's top 10—to be exact, 9th—trading partners in terms of trade volume. However, complaints of protectionism have been heard by both sides. Mr. President, how can we best ensure that our trading relationship grows and prospers without any friction?

The President. Well, I think, again, that this is one of the things to be talked about, because we know from history and experience that protectionism might have a short-term advantage. But in the long range, it destroys prosperity, it doesn't create it. And since we are such close trading partners—in fact, we import more from Korea than any other country in the world. And I think that where there are friction points with regard to trade restrictions, tariffs or whatever, we must study every one of those and make sure that we do not drift into protectionism but have the ultimate in free trade between us.

Mr. Jung. Prior to your taking office, the withdrawal of American troops from Korea was proposed by a previous administration. I understand you have no plan either to reduce or withdraw American troops from Korea. My question is, do you think, however, that one division of combat troops is enough in size to deter a North Korean attack?

The President. Right now, yes, I believe that it is, and with the knowledge of other forces that we have within range. And part of that is because of the great development of the Republic of Korea's own military forces and the great progress that has been made there. At the same time, we continue to watch this. When it was advocated that we withdraw those troops, before I was President, just as a citizen and a candidate, I objected and disapproved of that suggestion. So, I think it is imperative that while we see no need now for a change that we continue to observe closely, and if ever we feel the tensions have reached a point where that would be necessary that we augment those troops, that we do so.

We are allied with South Korea. We have been now—as a matter of fact, we're observing the 100th year of a relationship with your country. So I feel that what is there is adequate, mainly because of the strength of the Korean forces themselves. Adequate now, but we'll do whatever is necessary.

Mr. Jung. The Republic of Korea and the PRC, that's China, currently have no diplomatic relations. While the PRC continues to support North Korea, their attitude towards Korea considerably seems to have softened since the normalization of the diplomatic relation with the United States. My question is, what do you feel are the prospects for normal relations between the PRC and the Republic of Korea?

The President. I would think that it would be stabilizing to the entire area and that, while care be exercised, that both countries should seriously look at the possibilities and the prospects for a better relationship.

Mr. Jung. You have visited when you were Governor of California. What impression did you have about Korea and its people, sir?

The President. Well, from all that I had known of an earlier Korea and what I saw there on that visit made me think I was living in the presence of a miracle. The great development of Korea, the modernization that had taken place—it was a thriving, energetic, industrial, and very productive society that I saw, and I came away greatly impressed.

Mr. Jung. In recent weeks, U.S. economy has shown a good sign of upturn after a long recession. What is, Mr. President, your assessment for the outlook of the world economy in coming months, sir?

The President. Well, I'm convinced that we are, here in our country, on a road to a solid recovery. We have brought inflation down to a fraction of what it was. We've cut our interest rates in half—we have much further to go in that. And our unemployment is dropping rapidly. As a matter of fact, just last month our unemployment reached a point that in our most optimistic predictions we had thought we wouldn't reach for another year or more. And I believe that the United States recovering that much can have an effect worldwide in the other countries where recession has prevailed, so that I'm optimistic that we are on our way to a solid recovery and it will be worldwide.

Mr. Jung. Thank you, Mr. President, and please have a nice trip.

The President. Thank you very much. I'm looking forward to it.

Note: The interview began at 11:50 a.m. in the Library at the White House. It was taped for later broadcast in the Republic of Korea.

Letter to the Speaker of the House and the Chairman of the Senate Foreign Relations Committee Reporting on the Cyprus Conflict
November 7, 1983

Dear Mr. Speaker: *(Dear Mr. Chairman:)*

In accordance with Public Law 95–384, I am herewith submitting a bimonthly report on progress toward a negotiated settlement of the Cyprus problem.

Since my last report (August 18, 1983), the Greek Cypriots and the Turkish Cypriots have responded privately to an initiative undertaken by UN Secretary General Perez de Cuellar in early August to promote the resumption of the intercommunal talks which have been suspended since May of this year. At the same time, Turkish Cypriot leader Denktash proposed a meeting between himself and President Kyprianou with the Secretary General. The Secretary General is examining the responses and proposals with a view toward bringing both sides back to the conference table.

The Administration's policy throughout the period under review has been one of continued active support for the Secretary General's role, including his August initiative. We have assured the Secretary General and the two Cypriot communities that we support the early resumption of the talks to focus on the substantive issues separating the two communities.

Our activities over the period have included high-level meetings between senior State Department officials and leaders of both the Government of Cyprus and the Turkish Cypriot community. In addition, we have reiterated to both the Government of Greece and Government of Turkey our strong desire to see substantive progress in the intercommunal negotiating process.

During the period since my last report, Secretary Shultz's Special Cyprus Coordinator, Christian A. Chapman, retired from the Foreign Service. Richard Haass was appointed by the Secretary to replace Mr. Chapman. Assistant Secretary Burt and Mr. Haass will appear before the House Foreign Affairs Committee soon to outline the present situation on the island and to describe the Administration's Cyprus policy.

Sincerely,

RONALD REAGAN

Note: This is the text of identical letters addressed to Thomas P. O'Neill, Jr., Speaker of the House of Representatives, and Charles H. Percy, chairman of the Senate Foreign Relations Committee.

Message to the Senate Transmitting the United States-Sweden Convention on Taxation and Fiscal Evasion
November 7, 1983

To the Senate of the United States:

I transmit herewith, for Senate advice and consent to ratification, the Convention between the Government of the United States of America and the Government of Sweden for the Avoidance of Double Taxation and the Prevention of Fiscal Evasion with Respect to Taxes on Estates, Inheritances, and Gifts, signed at Stockholm on June 13, 1983. I also transmit the report of the Department of State on the Convention.

The Convention is the first of its kind to be negotiated between the United States and Sweden. It will apply, in the United States, to the Federal estate tax, the Federal gift tax, and the Federal tax on generation-skipping transfers and, in Sweden, to the inheritance tax and the gift tax.

A principal feature of the Convention is that the country of the transferor's domicile may tax transfers of estates and gifts and generation-skipping transfers on a worldwide basis, but must credit tax paid to the other State on the basis of location or *situs* of specified types of property.

I recommend that the Senate give early and favorable consideration to the Convention and give its advice and consent to ratification.

RONALD REAGAN

The White House,
November 7, 1983.

Nomination of Donna F. Tuttle To Be an Under Secretary of Commerce
November 7, 1983

The President today announced his intention to nominate Donna F. Tuttle as Under Secretary of Commerce for Travel and Tourism. She will succeed Peter McCoy.

Since November 1979 Mrs. Tuttle has been active in political campaign management, serving as chairman or finance director in a number of State, local, and national campaigns. Between 1975 and 1979, Mrs. Tuttle founded and operated a real estate investment, renovation, and interior design business in southern California. Prior to that, Mrs. Tuttle taught history at the secondary level in the Los Angeles County city school system.

Mrs. Tuttle has long been active in civic, cultural, and charitable organizations. Among other things, she has served on the board of trustees of the Coro Foundation, the Natural History Museum, the Junior League of Los Angeles, and was appointed by the President to the John F. Kennedy Center Board of Trustees.

She earned her undergraduate degree in history at the University of Southern California (B.A., 1969) and her graduate degree in education from the University of California at Los Angeles (1970). She is married, has two children, and resides in Washington, D.C. She was born April 21, 1947.

Nomination of Richard M. Scaife To Be a Member of the United States Advisory Commission on Public Diplomacy
November 7, 1983

The President today announced his intention to nominate Richard M. Scaife to be a member of the United States Advisory Commission on Public Diplomacy for a term expiring July 1, 1985. He would succeed Mae Sue Talley.

He is publisher of the Tribune Review Publishing Co. in Pittsburgh, Pa. He has served as chairman and publisher of the Sierra Publishing Co. in Sacramento, Calif.; publisher of Lebanon News Publishing Co. in Lebanon, Pa.; director of First Boston, Inc., in New York, N.Y.; and chairman of Calvary, Inc., in Pittsburgh, Pa.

Mr. Scaife graduated from the University of Pittsburgh (B.A., 1957). He is married, has two children, and resides in Pittsburgh, Pa. He was born July 3, 1932, in Pittsburgh.

Letter Accepting the Resignation of Dennis LeBlanc as Associate Administrator of the National Telecommunications and Information Administration
November 7, 1983

Dear Dennis:

It is with great regret that I accept your resignation as Associate Administrator of the National Telecommunications and Information Administration, effective October 28, 1983. During the many years we have known you, Nancy and I have come to regard you as almost a member of the family. We have relied on your expertise and your foresight to handle so many of the daily problems in communications and other areas that it is going to be very hard to imagine things flowing smoothly in your absence.

We want you to know, however, that we are delighted at the opportunity that has opened up for you in the private sector. You can be sure that Nancy and I send you our very best wishes for every future success and happiness, even as we remember with great pleasure the many years you have been with us.

Sincerely,

RONALD REAGAN

November 3, 1983

Mr. President:

This is to inform you that I have submitted my resignation to Secretary Baldrige. As you know, I resigned to accept a position with The Pacific Telephone and Telegraph Company. It has been an honor and a privilege to serve in your administration, and I will always treasure the memories of that service.

DENNIS LeBLANC

Note: As printed above, this item follows the text of the letters released by the Office of the Press Secretary.

Remarks on Departure for Japan and the Republic of Korea
November 8, 1983

Well, we thank you very much. Goodness, who's tending store? [*Laughter*]

Well, in a few moments, as you know, Nancy and I will be aboard Marine One to begin the first leg of our trip to Japan and Korea. We've looked forward for a long time to visting both countries and, I can say, visiting them again. We make this journey as ambassadors for peace and prosperity between the citizens of our two lands— or three lands.

We'll travel a great distance, but I know we'll meet with many good friends and people who feel close to America and to our people. Our country is a Pacific nation—and I mean "Pacific" in the terms of an ocean, not just peaceful—and this trip will spotlight the great importance that we place on our ties with Northeast Asia and the Pacific Basin.

Our three countries share treasures of a rich and varied past. As freedom-loving people, we also share a great dream. Japan, Korea, and America are the nations of the future. We're builders of tomorrow and working as partners to make tomorrow better and more secure. We can do this because Korea, for one, ranks among our top 10 partners in trade worldwide. Japan, of course, is our top partner, economically.

Our Pacific trade has exceeded our trade with Europe during the eighties. This dynamic growth points to the importance of our economic relations, particularly in trade and financial matters with both countries. Four out of five new manufacturing jobs created in the last 5 years were in export-related industries. We still work hard, and will, to foster a new era of equality and economic cooperation in our bilateral relations.

The Soviet shooting down of KAL 007, their continued military buildup in Asia, including the development of the SS–20 missiles there, are grim reminders to us that we live in a dangerous world. I will reaffirm America's commitment to remain a reliable partner for peace and stability in the region and in the world.

Now, in both Tokyo and Seoul, we will look for ways to make the region even more stable and secure. Like all good things, partnerships require a willingness to listen and to work hard and to compromise. And that's the spirit of our trip. I'm confident that our bonds of friendship will be strengthened in the next few days.

As we reach out to each other, we'll also be reaching out to the rest of the world. Closer relations in the Pacific make for more prosperous conditions worldwide. And the increasing global responsibilities being undertaken by both Japan and Korea are very positive developments for those who cherish peace and seek economic progress and human freedom. I believe we'll grow closer and grow together if we keep our eyes fixed on our community of interests and shared values.

Faith, freedom, and equality of opportunity will inspire us. Economic growth will reward us, and free and fair trade will enhance us. And through peace—or peace through strength will sustain us.

Again, we welcome this opportunity to get to show the good people of Japan and Korea that we want to know them better. And we're most thankful that we'll be able to spend some time on our trip also with our service men and women over there.

Now, I thank you all very much for coming to see Nancy and me off. And because some of you have suggested that you're doing this, thank you for your prayers, and you'll be in our thoughts and very close to our hearts. And now there isn't anything left to say but goodby, and God bless you.

Note: The President spoke at 7:30 a.m. in the East Room at the White House to administration officials and members of the White House staff.

Nomination of Frank Henry Habicht II To Be an Assistant Attorney General
November 8, 1983

The President today announced his intention to nominate Frank Henry Habicht II to be an Assistant Attorney General, Land and Natural Resources Division, Department of Justice. He would succeed Carol E. Dinkins.

Mr. Habicht is currently Deputy Assistant Attorney General (Land and Natural Resources Division). Previously he was Special Assistant to the Attorney General of the United States (1981–1982); a member of the Presidential transition team for the U.S. Department of Justice (1980); and was with the law firm of Kirkland & Ellis (1978–1981).

Mr. Habicht graduated from Princeton University (A.B., 1975) and the University of Virginia Law School (J.D., 1978). He is married, has one child, and resides in Washington, D.C. He was born April 10, 1953, in Oak Park, Ill.

Proclamation 5127—National Christmas Seal Month, 1983
November 8, 1983

By the President of the United States of America

A Proclamation

Chronic diseases of the lung afflict well over 17 million Americans, cause more than 200,000 deaths annually, and cost the Nation more than $29.4 billion in lost wages and medical expenses plus untold dollars in lost productivity.

Chronic obstructive pulmonary diseases have been among the fastest rising causes of death. Almost seven million Americans, including over two million children, suffer from asthma. Two and one-half million Americans have emphysema, while almost eight million suffer from chronic bronchitis. Furthermore, it is expected that deaths from lung cancer will surpass breast cancer as the leading cause of cancer deaths among American women during this decade.

Leading the fight in the voluntary sector to prevent illness, disability, and death from lung disease is the American Lung Association—the Christmas Seal people—a non-profit public health organization supported by individual contributions to Christmas Seals and other donations.

The Nation's first national voluntary public health organization, the Association was founded in 1904 to combat tuberculosis. Since 1907, Christmas Seals have been used to raise funds through private contributions to help educate Americans about this disease. In its early years, the National Tuberculosis Association pioneered school programs aimed at motivating young people to establish healthful living patterns. That tradition remains strong, as the American Lung Association continues to give high priority to its health education activities in the schools.

In addition, the American Lung Association, through its community lung Associations, helps educate the public, patients and their families about lung diseases; sponsors community action programs for good lung health; underwrites medical research; supports education for physicians and other health care workers; and wages vigorous campaigns against cigarette smoking and air pollution. The primary source of funding for more than 70 years has been Christmas Seals. This year, Christmas Seals will be in 60 million homes.

In recognition of the American Lung Association's continuing efforts to eliminate all chronic diseases of the lung, the Congress, by Senate Joint Resolution 188, has designated the month of November 1983 as "National Christmas Seal Month" and has requested the President to issue a proclamation in observance of that month.

Now, Therefore, I, Ronald Reagan, President of the United States of America, do hereby proclaim November 1983 as National Christmas Seal Month, and I call upon all Government agencies and the people of the United States to observe this month with appropriate activities and by supporting the Christmas Seal program.

In Witness Whereof, I have hereunto set my hand this eighth day of November, in the year of our Lord nineteen hundred and eighty-three, and of the Independence of the United States of America the two hundred and eighth.

RONALD REAGAN

[*Filed with the Office of the Federal Register, 2:55 p.m., November 8, 1983*]

Remarks at Elmendorf Air Force Base, Alaska, En Route to Japan and the Republic of Korea
November 8, 1983

Governor, Senator Murkowski, Congressman Young, General, distinguished guests here, and all of you ladies and gentlemen:

It's been a while since Nancy and I were in Alaska. Now, that line would make it sound as if we're not tenderfeet still. We've been here once. We came in the dark, and we left in the dark. [*Laughter*] And we still are looking forward to a time when we can be here with more time, certainly, than we have today, when we can see some of the beauty of this wonderful land.

You know, I know that you are kind to a tenderfoot up here. I remember the story of one who arrived, and an old fellow up here was showing him the routine with the sledge dogs. And he said, "Look, you can walk among them. You can pat them on the head. You can feed them. Don't fall down." [*Laughter*] And you know, that's good advice in Washington. [*Laughter*] I was going to even almost try to fool you. I could prove that I know a little about Alaska. I was going to recite "The Shooting of Dan McGrew." But I won't.

But I want you to know I've always had an admiration for the spirit of this State. And I won't deny that I have a special kinship with your delegation. And, Governor, you'll forgive me, but I don't know of any other States where the entire congressional delegation is Republican.

But Alaska does represent something very special to most Americans. You are the conquerors of the last frontier. Many of your values and ways are reminiscent of those that built our great country. Your love of nature and the land, your individualistic pride, your spirit of enterprise, all these things have contributed to a well-deserved Alaskan mystique. My only request to you is keep doing what you do best.

One thing your State is known for is its outside activities, of course, especially hunting and fishing. And that reminds me of a story. [*Laughter*] It's a story about down there in the other 48, a young fellow that was making quite a killing fishing and selling the fish to the local restaurant in this small town. And the game warden began to get a little suspicious about the catch that he was bringing in every day. So, knowing the sheriff was an uncle of this young fellow, he asked him why he didn't go fishing with his nephew and find out where he was catching and how he was catching all those fish. So, the sheriff asked, and the nephew said, "Sure."

Elmer and the sheriff rode out into the middle of the lake, and the sheriff started to get ready to put his line in. And Elmer reached in the tackle box, came out with a stick of dynamite, lit the fuse, threw it in, the explosion, and the fish came belly-up. And he started to gather them in, and the sheriff says, "Elmer, you have just committed a felony." Elmer reached in the tackle box, came up with another stick of dynamite, lit the fuse, handed it to the sheriff, and said, "Did you come here to fish or talk?" [*Laughter*]

Well, you may not catch them with dynamite, but your State is responsible for two-fifths, 40 percent of America's fish harvest. Your State is a treasure trove of resources vital to our economy and to the well-being of every American. One-eighth of our gold comes from Alaska. And just how vulnerable would we be had we followed the advice of those who opposed the Alaskan oil pipeline?

Today we should all say, "Thank you, Alaska," because Alaskan oil accounts for one-fifth of our total domestic production. And all of this concerns more than economic growth, as important as that is. Alaska possesses 10 of the 16 vital materials needed for our nation's security. In short, you add tremendously to our economic well-being and to our security. And you do it with only 443,000 people, and that's pretty impressive.

In the future Alaska will play an even greater role. Here in Anchorage we're as close to Tokyo, Japan's capital, as we are to our own capital in Washington. Your State bridges the Western Hemisphere and the Far East. Like California, you're part of an economic community on the Pacific rim which will be ever more important to our way of life in the years ahead.

My visit to Japan and Korea will, I hope, underline the significance that we place on our ties with Northeast Asia and the countries of the Pacific. In the 21st century we can foresee vastly expanding economic, political, and cultural bonds with these countries. I believe we'll witness a wave of productive and creative endeavors improving the quality of life on both sides of the Pacific.

The peoples of the Pacific understand hard work. They're not afraid of technology and innovation. They have the Yankee spirit that we once called our own. We're in the midst of restoring that spirit. Here in Alaska you never lost it. Alaska, with its vast resources, strategic location, and enterprising people, will play an increasingly important role as the potential of the Pacific unfolds.

Our progress depends on a strong United States. We've come a long way in strengthening our economy in the last few years. We've brought inflation down dramatically, and we've put our economy back on the road to robust growth after years of stagnation. And as I've said, you Alaskans contributed far beyond your numbers in these endeavors.

Peace is essential if we're to realize our economic potential. And to maintain peace we must maintain a strong defense. Alaska has much of which to be proud on this account—[*applause*]—you have much to be proud of in this account as well. You are a first line of defense. This is becoming evermore apparent in the wake of the Soviets' brutal downing of a civilian airliner.

May I take this opportunity to thank all of our service personnel who are stationed here. Now, many of you are far from home; sometimes you're lonely. Sometimes, until you get used to it, I suppose the elements are tough. But each one of you contributes to our security in a very real way. I just want you all to know your families and friends appreciate you, and so do 230 million other Americans.

I'd also like to thank your congressional

delegation, Senators Stevens and Murkowski and Congressman Young, for their unswerving support for a strong national defense. Your representatives to Washington are showing that Alaskans are willing to do what is necessary to protect our freedom and preserve the peace.

Now, Ted Stevens was unable to join us today because he's continuing his outstanding work in managing the Department of Defense's appropriation bill on the floor of the Senate. And just before we landed, I was told that it was worthwhile his staying there, because George Bush, as Vice President, cast the tie-breaking vote to pass the military appropriations bill.

You know, but I'm grateful that Senator Murkowski and Congressman Young could be here. And leaving Ted there, you know, that's a little bit like that story of the Texas Ranger, that they sent him to a town where there was a riot, and the mayor met him, and the mayor looked over his shoulder and said, "Well, where are the rest?" And he says, "Well, you've only got one riot." [*Laughter*] Well, it only took one Alaskan there on the floor of the Senate to get the job done today.

Back in June, I signed into law a bill that was declaring what you were just told a few minutes ago, that January 3d would be Alaskan Statehood Day, marks that great milestone, your 25th anniversary as a member of the United States. And I'm certain that Alaska's next 25 years will be enriching and rewarding years for you, the residents of this mighty State and for the rest of your fellow citizens down below.

Alaska only cost us $7 million. You know, that was quite a real estate deal. I don't think anyone would try to buy it for even a couple of million dollars profit on that today.

Well, I thank you for having us with you in this brief stopover that we have here before we continue on our way. And certainly we thank you very much for coming out here to see us. Mainly thank you for being Americans and for making us so proud. And God bless you all.

Note: The President spoke at 11:54 a.m. to military personnel and their families in

Hangar 2 on the Air Force base. Following his remarks, the President traveled to Tokyo, Japan.

In his opening remarks, the President re- *ferred to Governor William Sheffield of Alaska and Brig. Gen. Gerald Bethke, Commander, United States Armed Forces, Alaska.*

Toasts of the President and Prime Minister Yasuhiro Nakasone of Japan at a Luncheon in Tokyo
November 10, 1983

The Prime Minister. Mr. President, Mrs. Reagan, distinguished guests, please allow me to say a few words on behalf of the Government and people of Japan and on my own behalf. Welcome to the President of the United States of America and Mrs. Reagan.

I wish to express anew my gratitude to the President and Mrs. Reagan and the American people of all walks of life for the most heartwarming welcome accorded to me during my visits to Washington in January and May.

In particular, I will never forget the wonderful birthday surprise the President and Mrs. Reagan arranged for me at the White House in May. Today I am deeply pleased to be able to reciprocate your thoughtfulness in my humble way.

Mr. President, you may recall that in our meeting in May, we promised to cooperate with each other, you as a pitcher and I as a catcher. We have been living up to our promise since then, not only as a formidable battery over the Pacific but also as excellent teammates of the free world.

While in the world of baseball both the World Series and the Japan Series are over, the World Series in the world of politics in which the President and I are together taking part still has quite a few innings left. [*Laughter*] I am convinced that we will achieve brilliant results in this World Series by putting our efforts together. [*Laughter*]

In closing, I wish to propose a toast to the continued health of the President and Mrs. Reagan, as well as the members of his suite, and to the prosperity of the United States of America.

The President. Mr. Prime Minister, Mrs. Nakasone, members of the Diet, distin- guished guests, and ladies and gentlemen, just before this delightful luncheon we finished the second of two long, productive talks. I don't know who was pitching and who was catching—[*laughter*]—but those talks demonstrated that despite the 5,000 miles of ocean between us and the difference in our geography, history, and culture, Japan and America share the same deeply held values.

Both our nations are democracies founded on the sacredness of the individual. We both believe that every person deserves to be listened to, so we give all of our citizens a voice in government. And we both hold that every man and woman has certain inalienable rights, so we enshrine these rights in law.

As the American educator Robert Hutchins wrote, "Democracy is the only form of government that is founded on the dignity of man—not the dignity of some men, or rich men, or educated men . . . but on all men." Democratic freedoms, we both know, make a nation not only noble but dynamic. Individuals in democracies can give full scope to their energies and talents, conducting experiments, exchanging knowledge, and making breakthrough after breakthrough.

In just the past few decades, men and women acting in freedom have markedly improved the health and living standards of the whole human race. Innovations in fertilizers, farm machinery, land use made in democracies have increased agricultural output across the world.

Medical advances made in democracies, from the discovery of penicillin to the identification of vitamins, means that people everywhere on Earth live longer than ever before. And electronics breakthroughs made in democracies have produced a telecommunications network that links nations around the globe. Of course Japan has been leading the way in one of those—electronics. And, Mr. Prime Minister, I can't resist telling you that we Americans who have traditionally prided ourselves in being the first with the most have now met our competition. [*Laughter*] I understand that in a single Tokyo store, one can find 205 varieties of stereo headphones and 100 different television models.

Today it's the democracies—especially Japan and America—that are leading a high-tech revolution that promises to change life on Earth even more profoundly than did the industrial revolution of a century ago. This revolution ranges from electron microscopes that can inspect molecules to satellites that are probing the dark infinities of space. It's a revolution that's making industries vastly more efficient, putting the world's great literature, film, and music at families' fingertips, and producing medical breakthroughs that are helping many of the blind see and many of the handicapped to walk.

State-controlled economies, by contrast, just haven't been able to keep up. Before Korea was divided, its industrial center was in the north. Today the Republic of Korea outproduces North Korea by 3 to 1. In Europe the per capita income of West Germany is more than twice that of East Germany. As we both know, Mr. Prime Minister, the true division in the world today is not between east and west, but between progress and stagnation, between freedom and oppression, between hope and despair.

Looking back on his long career, one of Japan's foremost leaders, Yukio Ozaki, said, "For the happiness of one nation we should endeavor toward the enhancement of the happiness of the entire world." Both Japan and America share this view, and we both know that the happiness of the world depends on liberty.

Mr. Prime Minister, as a man who has worked tirelessly to defend and promote human freedom, you have led a career of long and varied service to your country. You first won a seat in the Diet in 1947; since 1959 you've held five Cabinet posts; and today you lead your nation. With gratitude for your efforts, on behalf of the American people, I salute you.

And, ladies and gentlemen, also please join me in a toast to His Imperial Majesty, the Emperor of Japan.

Note: Prime Minister Nakasone spoke at 2:13 p.m. at the luncheon he and Mrs. Nakasone hosted for the President and Mrs. Reagan in the Banquet Hall of the Prime Minister's official residence. The Prime Minister spoke in Japanese, and his remarks were translated by an interpreter.

Earlier in the day, the President and the Prime Minister held an hour-long meeting in the second floor lounge of the residence. At the conclusion of the meeting, they were joined by Mrs. Reagan and Mrs. Nakasone and attended a reception which preceded the luncheon.

Remarks of the President and Prime Minister Yasuhiro Nakasone of Japan Following Their Meetings in Tokyo
November 10, 1983

The Prime Minister. For the people and Government of Japan, as well as for my wife and myself, it is indeed a great pleasure to welcome the President of the United States of America and Mrs. Reagan as state guests.

Yesterday and today, the President and I had very productive meetings covering a wide range of subjects. Through these meetings, we reconfirmed the importance for Japan and the United States, two countries sharing the common ideas and values of freedom and democracy of promoting further cooperation towards peace and prosperity of the world.

The President has a clear recognition of the importance of the Asian and the Pacific region. His present visit to Japan and the Republic of Korea and his planned visit to China next year amply testify this fact, together with his visit to the countries in Southeast Asia, which I am sure will be rescheduled in the future. The economic dynamism in the Asian and the Pacific region is one of the central elements in the expansion of the world economy. Thus, the President and I are in full agreement that we should continue to make efforts for the further development of the Asian and the Pacific region.

Mr. President, I issued on November 1st the Tokyo Statement jointly with Chancellor Kohl of the Federal Republic of Germany, in line with the spirit of the political statement adopted at the Williamsburg summit in May this year declaring that we should maintain the unity and solidarity among the Western countries in our joint endeavor in pursuit of freedom, peace, and stability of the prosperity of the world economy, and of the development in the Third World.

As I know the recent events of increasing tension in the East-West relations, as well as frequent occurrences of regional disputes and violence in various parts of the world, I am worried that the peace in the world could be gravely threatened if such trends continue and amplify themselves. Under such circumstances, I firmly believe that the countries of the world should renew their resolve for the maintenance of freedom, peace, and stability, for the revitalization of the world economy, and for the prosperity of the peoples of the world.

I further believe that the rational dialogs and negotiations should be conducted to solve such international conflicts and disputes, and that the parties concerned should spare no effort in taking step-by-step measures or gradual approach in pursuit of ultimate goals, and should carry on steady and realistic endeavors. This I consider is particularly pertinent to the arms control negotiations.

The Western countries should stand firmly in unity and solidarity for freedom and peace and should not hesitate to bear any hardships in upholding this cause. All these points are included in the Tokyo Statement. It is, indeed, truly significant, Mr. President, that you have fully endorsed this statement in our meeting.

The President and I had exchanges of views on East-West relations with emphasis on the question of arms control and on the situation in such areas as Asia, the Middle East, and Central America.

With regard to the INF negotiations in particular, it was reconfirmed that the negotiations should not be conducted at the sacrifice of the Asian region, but should be conducted on a global basis, taking the Asian security into consideration.

With respect to the recent bombing in Burma, the very act of terrorism, we agreed that it should be strongly condemned as an inexcusable conduct in challenge of world peace and order and that continued efforts must be made to bring about lasting peace and stability on the Korean peninsula.

On the Middle East, I expressed my deep appreciation for the role played by the multinational forces for stabilizing the situation in Lebanon.

The Japan-U.S. security arrangements are the foundation of the peace and security of Japan and the Far East. I wish to express that Japan will continue her efforts towards further strengthening the credibility of the Japan-U.S. security arrangements. With respect to the improvement of our defense capability, I wish to continue to make further efforts along the lines of the joint communique of May 1981.

As to the international economy, the President and I reconfirmed—in line with the declaration of the Williamsburg summit—the importance of obtaining sustained, noninflationary growth of the world economy, of rolling back protectionism, and of lowering the prevailing high interest rates. We consider them important, together with extending financial cooperation, in order to alleviate the plight of the developing countries, which are suffering from accumulated debts.

With regard to bilateral economic issues, we acknowledge the achievements made thus far and agree to continue our efforts for the solution of the remaining issues. In this context, I highly appreciated the pledge by the President to combat protectionism in the United States.

The President and I are in full agreement on the importance of the yen-dollar issue. We have agreed on establishing consultative fora on exchange rate issues and investment. In this connection, I asked for continued U.S. efforts to lower U.S. interest rates.

The President and I have also underscored the importance of greater two-way investment flows between our two countries, and I expressed my concern that the unitary method of taxation is becoming a serious impediment to the Japanese investment in the United States. I stressed the importance of promoting the preparations of a new round of multilateral trade negotiations in order to consolidate the free trading system and to inject renewed confidence in the world economy. I am very glad that the President has strongly supported my view. We intend to call on other countries to join in our efforts.

Mr. President, in the present international situation, you are shouldering enormous global responsibilities. I will, on my part, make as much contribution as possible to the peace and prosperity of the world.

Thank you very much.

The President. Well, on behalf of the American people and our government, I would like to thank His Imperial Majesty the Emperor, Prime Minister Nakasone, and the Government and people of Japan for the generous and warm reception that you have extended to my wife, Nancy, myself, and my staff during our trip to your country.

Prime Minister Nakasone, as you've been told, have just completed 2 days of very productive discussions on a wide range of bilateral issues and global affairs. As leaders of two great Pacific nations, we're guardians of a strong, rich, and diverse relationship. Japan and America are bound by shared values of freedom, democracy, and peace. We're committed to greater future cooperation across a broad spectrum of political, economic, security, educational, culture, and scientific affairs.

I have come as a friend of Japan seeking to strengthen our partnership for peace, prosperity, and progress. I will leave Japan confident that our partnership is stronger than before and confident that we're giving birth to a new era in Japanese-American relations. We have agreed to move forward with an agenda for progress by drawing upon the great well of talent, drive, determination, and creativity of our free peoples. We welcome Japan's more assertive role as a fellow trustee of peace and progress in international economic and political affairs.

We have discussed global issues, and we hold many similar views on opportunities for cooperation. The principles that Prime Minister Nakasone has enunciated as the Tokyo Statement are principles that I fully endorse. Together we have no greater responsibility than to make our world a safer place.

There are serious threats to peace on the Korean peninsula, in the Middle East, in the Caribbean, and over the Northwestern Pacific. Also, the attitude on the part of our adversary at the negotiating table on arms talks is at odds with the will of the world to reduce the weapons of war and build a more stable peace.

I conveyed to the Prime Minister my satisfaction that our mutual security relationship is proceeding smoothly. Japan is host to 45,000 American troops, and our bases in Japan, made possible by the Treaty of Mutual Cooperation and Security, are essential not only to the defense of Japan but also contribute to peace and prosperity in the Far East. As for Japan's defense efforts, the United States remains convinced that the most important contribution Japan can make toward the peace and security in Asia is for Japan to provide for its own defense and share more of the burden of our mutual defense effort.

During our discussions on arms control, I assured Prime Minister Nakasone that we seek global reductions in the Soviet's intermediate-range SS–20's to the lowest level possible. The United States will take no action in the intermediate nuclear forces negotiations that adversely affects the security of Asia. We agreed on the urgency of achieving consensus on comprehensive international safeguards to prevent the spread of nuclear weaponry.

Prime Minister Nakasone and I discussed

Japan and America's compelling international economic responsibilities as spelled out at the Williamsburg summit. Together we must press for continuing liberalization of the international trade and financial system, fight protectionism, promote economic development without inflation by encouraging the growth of free enterprise throughout the world, and share the obligation of assisting developing countries, including those facing severe debt problems. We also agreed to enhance coordination in foreign assistance.

Trade issues figure prominently in the Japan-U.S. relationship. There's no simple, overnight solution to our trade problems, but we have agreed to exert our best and continued efforts to solve these issues. We welcome recent actions by your government to reduce trade barriers, and I've emphasized the importance of further measures to open the Japanese market to trade and investment.

I didn't come to negotiate specific trade issues, but I did indicate certain issues of immediate importance to us. Because of both their trade and consumer significance, for example, we're seeking reductions in Japan's tariffs on certain products in which the U.S. is highly competitive. Japanese quotas on agricultural products are a cause for concern. In return, the United States must combat protectionism in our country, and I have given the Prime Minister my pledge to do so.

Progress in Japan-U.S. trade issues can foster greater trade liberalization efforts worldwide, such as the Prime Minister's call for a new round of multilateral trade negotiations, which I heartily endorse.

I expressed confidence that the United States can be a reliable long-term supplier of energy, particularly coal, to Japan. And I was pleased that Prime Minister Nakasone shared this view. Expanded energy trade will mean more jobs for Americans and greater security for both our countries.

With the approval of Prime Minister Nakasone and myself, a joint press statement is being released today by Finance Minister Takeshita and Treasury Secretary Reagan—Regan—[*laughter*]—I tried to get him to pronounce it the other way—on the yen-dollar issue and other financial and economic issues of mutual interest. We agree that the commitments and steps outlined in that statement will further strengthen economic relations between the United States and Japan.

We have noted the importance of the yen-dollar exchange rate, of free and open capital markets in each country. We stress the need for closer economic consultations between the two governments. A ministerial-level working group is being set up to monitor each side's progress in carrying out the agreed-upon actions to improve the yen-dollar exchange rate.

Our mutual commitment toward specific steps to achieve open capital markets will allow the yen to reflect more fully Japan's underlying political stability and economic strength as the second largest economy in the free world. In addition, we've agreed to instruct our economic sub-Cabinet members to form a committee to promote mutual investments.

Progress must come one step at a time, but Japan and America have begun taking those steps together. I've been heartened that beginning with our first meeting last January, continuing with the Williamsburg summit, and now again during our visit this week, Prime Minister Nakasone and I have agreed that our two great democracies share special responsibilities to each other and to the world. Let us continue to go forward, building on our progress step by step. We must set milestones to monitor the success of our agenda for progress and to assure the followthrough that is essential. And I will be discussing this matter in more detail with the Prime Minister tomorrow.

This visit has strengthened the bonds of friendship between our two great nations. We are now better prepared to work together as partners to build a more peaceful and prosperous future at home and throughout the world. We know what needs to be done; we know how it must be done. Let us have the faith to believe in each other, the courage to get on with the job, and the determination to see it through.

Thank you very much.

Note: Prime Minister Nakasone spoke at 2:35 p.m. to reporters assembled in the au-

ditorium of the Prime Minister's official residence. The Prime Minister spoke in Japanese, and his remarks were translated by an interpreter.

Following the President's remarks, he and Mrs. Reagan returned to Akasaka Palace, where they stayed during their visit.

Nomination of Milton Russell To Be an Assistant Administrator of the Environmental Protection Agency
November 10, 1983

The President today announced his intention to nominate Milton Russell to be an Assistant Administrator of the Environmental Protection Agency (Policy and Evaluation). He would succeed Lee L. Verstandig.

Mr. Russell is currently senior fellow and director, Center for Energy Policy Research, Resources for the Future, in Washington, D.C. Previously he was senior staff economist, Council of Economic Advisers, the White House (1974–1976); assistant professor, economics department, Southern Illinois University (1964–1974); and visiting professor, department of economics, University of Edinburgh (1970–1971).

Mr. Russell graduated from Texas College of Arts and Industries (B.A., 1955) and the University of Oklahoma (M.A., 1957; Ph. D., 1963). He is married, has three children, and resides in Washington, D.C. He was born October 28, 1933, in Corpus Christi, Tex.

Nomination of John Arthur Moore To Be an Assistant Administrator of the Environmental Protection Agency
November 10, 1983

The President today announced his intention to nominate John Arthur Moore to be Assistant Administrator for Toxic Substances of the Environmental Protection Agency. He would succeed John A. Todhunter.

Mr. Moore is currently director, Toxicology Research & Testing Program, National Institute of Environmental Health Sciences (NIEHS), National Institutes of Health (NIH), and Deputy Director, National Toxicology Programs, NIH. Previously he was Associate Director, Research Resources Program, NIEHS, NIH (1976–1979); adjunct professor, department of pathology, Duke University (1975–1982); and Chief, Environmental Biology Branch, NIH (1973–1981).

He graduated from Michigan State University (B.S., 1961; D.V.M., 1963; M.S., 1967). He is married, has three children, and resides in Raleigh, N.C. He was born February 9, 1939, in Salem, Mass.

Nomination of Bernard D. Goldstein To Be an Assistant Administrator of the Environmental Protection Agency
November 10, 1983

The President today announced his intention to nominate Bernard D. Goldstein to be an Assistant Administrator of the Environmental Protection Agency (Research and

Development). He would succeed Stephen John Gage.

Dr. Goldstein is currently professor and chairman of the department of environmental and community medicine and professor, department of medicine, at Rutgers Medical School. Previously he was associate professor and assistant professor, departments of environmental medicine and medicine, New York University School of Medicine (1968–1980).

Dr. Goldstein graduated from the University of Wisconsin (B.S., 1958) and New York University School of Medicine (M.D., 1962). He is married, has two children, and resides in Westfield, N.J. He was born February 28, 1939, in New York, N.Y.

Statement by Deputy Press Secretary Speakes on the Situation in Lebanon
November 10, 1983

We're revolted that once again the people of Lebanon have been subjected to terror and injury, this time around Tripoli, by the radical and brutal behavior of Palestinian factions and their supporters. It is tragic that once again the civilian population of Lebanon is victim to hostilities not of their making and over which they are unable to exercise influence and control.

We urge the governments in the area to bring their influence to bear constructively to end the fighting. We suggest that all governments be open to any suggestions from appropriate international organizations for humanitarian and relief efforts to relieve the suffering. As a first specific step to assist, the United States is in the process of contributing $1 million to the International Red Cross to be used for relief activities in Lebanon.

Note: Deputy Press Secretary Larry M. Speakes read the statement to reporters during his afternoon briefing in the Akebono Room at the Okura Hotel in Tokyo.

Remarks at a Reception for American and Japanese Businessmen in Tokyo, Japan
November 10, 1983

Chairman Inayama, Vice President Fukushima, Ambassador Mansfield, and honored members of the America-Japan Society, the Keidanren, and the American Chamber of Commerce in Japan:

I don't usually go around in these clothes, but I'm dining with His Imperial Majesty tonight. [*Laughter*] But I'm delighted to have this chance to meet with such a distinguished group of Japanese and American leaders.

Before I go any further, may I extend my early birthday greeting to someone who couldn't be here, my good friend and your distinguished former Prime Minister, Mr. Nobazuki Kishi, who in just 3 days turns 88.

This gathering marks the way that we Americans and Japanese rely on each other for our prosperity. Japan and America are separated by thousands of miles of ocean, different languages, and different cultures, yet in our robust trade—everything from food to computers—we've found a way to help each other create abundance.

In 1967, my first year as Governor of California, trade between our two countries amounted to $5.7 billion, and I remember how much importance even then my fellow Governors and I placed on trade with Japan. By 1974, my last year as Governor, the figure had shot up to $23 billion. And this year it's expected that Japan will account for a tenth of all of America's exports, more than any other nation overseas; that America will buy a quarter of all Japanese exports; and that total trade between our two nations will surpass $60 billion.

Our vigorous trade has given us a chance to learn from one another, and it is in large part because of that trade that today our nations are leading a technological revolution that promises to change life even more profoundly than did the Industrial Revolution of a century ago.

All of us want to keep Japanese-American business healthy and expanding. And that means we must continue to promote not just trade but free trade. To the Japanese here tonight, let me say, "Congratulations." Many in this room played a key role over the past three-and-a-half decades in making Japan an economic miracle. Your imagination, energy, and determination have made this nation one of the most prosperous on Earth and focused economic growth throughout the Pacific Basin.

And now that Japan has become a giant in the world economy, your nation shares the responsibility for keeping that economy strong. In recent years, Japan has begun to open its markets to more goods and services from abroad. Prime Minister Nakasone has continued these positive actions, and we appreciate all your efforts.

America does have trade problems with Japan, and we seek the cooperation of your government so we can solve them together. We must work for lower barriers on both sides of the Pacific. And we hope to see your capital markets open to more foreign participation. This will help establish a greater international role for the yen and would contribute to an improvement in the imbalance between our two currencies.

As leaders of Japanese business, you can help make certain that Japan leads in the drive for greater free trade to strengthen the international economy. The well-being of both our nations will depend, to a large extent, on your efforts.

I've heard—well, as leaders of Japanese business, you can make certain that Japan leads in the drive for greater free trade to strengthen the international economy. The well-being of both our nations will depend, to a large extent, on your efforts. I've heard about the private efforts of Japanese businessmen to establish a permanent home for the America-Japan Society of Tokyo and other organizations dedicated to expanding cultural exchanges and good will between our two countries. And I hope these efforts succeed.

To the Americans here tonight, let me say simply, "Keep up the good work." You're pioneers, showing that although doing business here is hard work, the rewards are worth it. More and more, Japan is proving a fruitful market for American goods and services. Your fine example will encourage other American businesses to follow you here and expand Japanese-American trade still further.

And in January, you'll be pleased to hear the Department of Commerce is sending a high-level delegation of American business people, led by Richard McElheny, Assistant Commerce Secretary for Trade Development, and Jim Jenkins, my Deputy Counsellor at the White House, on a special trade mission to Japan.

And I want you to know that as Americans doing business in Japan, you have this administration's full support. We're working as hard in Washington as you are here to make certain your opportunities in Japan keep growing. The Tsukuba Exposition will provide an excellent opportunity for America to demonstrate the latest in technology. I hope many of your companies will be able to participate and cooperate in this exposition with Jim Needham, who's directing the U.S. Pavilion.

The message I want to leave with everyone here tonight is simple. It's a lesson history has taught us again and again. Protectionism hurts everyone, but free trade benefits all.

I understand that it's a tradition in Japan for businessmen to make contracts final simply by giving their word or shaking hands. That kind of transaction, of course, requires deep mutual trust and respect. Neither of our nations can open its markets completely in an afternoon. But working step by step and without delay, we can build that kind of mutual trust and respect.

Again, thank you for your very warm and gracious welcome.

Note: The President spoke at 6:56 p.m. in the Hagoromo-No-Ma Room at the Akasaka Palace.

Toast at the Imperial Banquet in Tokyo, Japan
November 10, 1983

Your Imperial Majesty, Mr. Prime Minister and Mrs. Nakasone, distinguished ladies and gentlemen:

You have honored us with a magnificent and unforgettable occasion this evening, and we express our sincere thanks to you.

One hundred and thirty-one years ago our ancestors began gradually laying the foundation for one of the most significant relationships between two countries anywhere in the world. When our people first met on shores not too far from here, we had difficulty understanding each other. Few cultures and histories could have been more different than our two were in the 1850's.

And today, the language of our two countries is still different, but we understand and appreciate each other as never before. We, in fact, depend on each other and benefit beyond calculation from our relationship. We're not only major trading partners; we're also cooperating in a host of international and political endeavors to strengthen peace and increase prosperity beyond our own borders.

Basic to all our efforts are the close and cooperative ties that we've built between our people, from young students who study in each other's schools and universities, to the daily interaction of our businessmen, politicians, scientists, creative artists, and athletes. The multitude of personal and professional relationships is like millions of threads binding us together with a strength and resilience that will not be broken.

The ties between our people are based on common ideals and values. But beyond this, our people like and admire each other. Americans appreciate the energy and hard work of the Japanese. And while in the arena of business we're indeed competitors, we are friendly competitors, and we respect one another.

If friendship has meaning, it can be found in the genuine feelings and commitment between our two peoples. As the American philosopher Emerson wrote, "The only way to have a friend is to be one." The American people admire Japan, its great progress, its people's fortitude and dedication, its splendid and delicate culture, its increasingly vital role in world affairs.

We admire you, Your Majesty, because you symbolize this nation's history and traditions and represent the dramatic transformation of these beautiful islands and stalwart people. Your love of country and for Japan's democratic institutions, your devotion to science, to the search for truth, your deep attachment to nature around you— these and many other aspects of your life and that of your splendid family, give your people strength and unite them in their beliefs and ideals.

Your Majesty, every spring from all over the United States Americans come to their capital in Washington, D.C., to view the beauty of cherry blossoms. This beauty is a gift from Japan. The cherry trees were presented to us by the city of Tokyo in 1912.

Last year the Flower Association of Japan presented 1 million flowering cherry tree seeds to the people of the United States so this beauty could be spread throughout our country. In January of this year, our National Arboretum presented flowering dogwood seeds to your country. These flowers can serve to remind us of the beauty of our friendship. Unlike these trees which blossom only once a year, let the flower of our friendship be never ending.

Our two countries, beginning their relationship in confusion and uncertainty, now are the closest of friends and partners. My visit to your country has reaffirmed my confidence in the future of our relations. May they ever be as close as they are today.

And, ladies and gentlemen, I ask you to join me in a toast to Their Imperial Majesties, the Emperor and Empress of Japan.

Note: The President spoke at 9:13 p.m. in the Banquet Hall at the Imperial Palace in response to a toast by Emperor Hirohito. Following the dinner, the President and Mrs. Reagan returned to Akasaka Palace, where they stayed during their visit.

Address Before the Japanese Diet in Tokyo
November 11, 1983

Mr. Speaker, Mr. President, Mr. Prime Minister, distinguished Members of the Diet:

It is with great honor and respect that I come before you today, the first American President ever to address the Japanese Diet.

I have been in your country only 2 days. But speaking for my wife, Nancy, and myself, may I say you have more than made us feel at home. The warmth of your welcome has touched our hearts. In welcoming us, you pay tribute to the more than 230 million Americans whom I have the privilege to represent. From all of us—all of them to you we reach out to say: The bonds of friendship which unite us are even greater than the ocean which divides us. *Nichibei no yuho wa eien desu.* [Japanese-American friendship is forever.]

It was a dozen years ago on an autumn day like this one that I first visited Japan, and today, as then, I feel energy, initiative, and industry surging through your country in a mighty current for progress. And just as before, I am struck by a unique gift of the Japanese people: You do not build your future at the expense of the grace and beauty of your past.

Harmony is a treasured hallmark of Japanese civilization, and this has always been pleasing to Americans. Harmony requires differences to be joined in pursuit of higher ideals, many of which we share. When former President Ulysses S. Grant visited here in 1878, he discovered Japan is a land of enchantment.

During his stay, he met with the Emperor, and their discussion turned to democracy, the pressing issue of the day. President Grant observed that governments are always more stable and nations more prosperous when they truly represent their people.

I am proud to help carry forward the century-old tradition, meeting first with your Emperor on my arrival and now meeting with you a great milestone in your history: the 100th session of the Diet under the modern Japanese Constitution. In 6 years you will celebrate your 100th anniversary of representative government in Japan, just as we will celebrate the birth of our own Congress. I bring you the best wishes and heartfelt greetings from your American counterparts, the Congress of the United States.

One cannot stand in this chamber without feeling a part of your proud history of nationhood and democracy, and the spirit of hope carrying the dreams of your free people. Of all the strengths we possess, of all the ties that bind us, I believe the greatest is our dedication to freedom. Japan and America stand at the forefront of the free nations and free economies in the world.

Yes, we are 5,000 miles apart; yes, we are distinctly different in customs, language, and tradition; and yes, we are often competitors in the world markets. But I believe the people represented by this proud parliament and by my own United States Congress are of one heart in their devotion to the principles of our free societies.

I'm talking about principles that begin with the sacred worth of human life; the cherished place of the family; the responsibility of parents and schools to be teachers of truth, tolerance, hard work, cooperation, and love; and the role of our major institutions—government, industry, and labor—to provide the opportunities and security—opportunities and security free people need to build and leave behind a better world for their children and their children's children.

America and Japan are situated far apart, but we are united in our belief that freedom means dedication to the dignity, rights, and equality of man. Yukichi Fukuzawa, the great Meiji-era educator, said it for you: "Heaven has made no man higher or no man lower than any other man."

Our great American hero Abraham Lincoln put it in political perspective for us: "No man is good enough to govern another man without that other's consent." We both value the right to have a government of our own choosing. We expect government to serve the people; we do not expect the people to serve government.

America and Japan speak with different tongues, but both converse, worship, and work with the language of freedom. We defend the right to voice our views, to speak words of dissent without being afraid, and to seek inner peace through communion with our God.

We believe in rewarding initiative, savings, and risk-taking. And we encourage those who set their sights on the farthest stars and chart new paths to progress through the winds and waters of commerce. Others censor and stifle their citizens. We trust in freedom to nurture the diversity and creativity that enriches us all. I like what your poet Basho said: "Many kinds of plants and each one triumphant in its special blossoms."

Finally, our freedom inspires no fear because it poses no threat. We intimidate no one, and we will not be intimidated by anyone. The United States and Japan do not build walls to keep our people in. We do not have armies of secret police to keep them quiet. We do not throw dissidents into so-called mental hospitals. And we would never coldbloodedly shoot a defenseless airliner out of the sky. We share your grief for that tragic and needless loss of innocent lives.

Our two countries are far from perfect. But in this imperfect and dangerous world, the United States and Japan represent the deepest aspirations of men and women ev-

erywhere—to be free, to live in peace, and to create and renew the wealth of abundance and spiritual fulfillment.

I have come to Japan because we have an historic opportunity, indeed, an historic responsibility. We can become a powerful partnership for good, not just in our own countries, not just in the Pacific region but throughout the world. Distinguished ladies and gentlemen, my question is: Do we have the determination to meet the challenge of partnership and make it happen? My answer is without hesitation: Yes we do, and yes we will.

For much of our histories, our countries looked inward. Well, those times have passed. With our combined economies accounting for half the output of the free world, we cannot escape our global responsibilities. Our industries depend on the importation of energy and minerals from distant lands. Our prosperity requires a sound international financial system and free and open trading markets. And our security is inseparable from the security of our friends and neighbors.

The simple hope for world peace and prosperity will not be enough. Our two great nations, working with others, must preserve the values and freedoms our societies have struggled so hard to achieve. Nor should our partnership for peace, prosperity, and freedom be considered a quest for competing goals. We cannot prosper unless we are secure, and we cannot be secure unless we are free. And we will not succeed in any of these endeavors unless Japan and America work in harmony.

I have come to your country carrying the heartfelt desires of America for peace. I know our desires are shared by Prime Minister Nakasone and all of Japan. We are people of peace. We understand the terrible trauma of human suffering. I have lived through four wars in my lifetime. So, I speak not just as President of the United States, but also as a husband, a father, and as a grandfather. I believe there can be only one policy for preserving our precious civilization in this modern age. A nuclear war can never be won and must never be fought.

The only value in possessing nuclear

weapons is to make sure they can't be used ever. I know I speak for people everywhere when I say our dream is to see the day when nuclear weapons will be banished from the face of the Earth.

Arms control must mean arms reductions. America is doing its part. As I pledged to the United Nations less than 2 months ago, the United States will accept any equitable, verifiable agreement that stabilizes forces at lower levels than currently exist. We want significant reductions, and we're willing to compromise.

In the strategic arms reduction talks, American negotiators continue to press the Soviet Union for any formula that will achieve these objectives. In the longer range INF talks, we are pursuing the same course, even offering to eliminate an entire category of weapons. I'm very conscious of our negotiating responsibility on issues that concern the safety and well-being of the Japanese people. And let me make one thing very plain. We must not and we will not accept any agreement that transfers the threat of longer range nuclear missiles from Europe to Asia.

Our great frustration has been the other side's unwillingness to negotiate in good faith. We wanted to cut deep into nuclear arsenals, and still do. But they're blocking the dramatic reductions the world wants. In our good-faith effort to move the negotiations forward, we have offered new initiatives, provided for substantial reductions to equal levels, and the lower the level the better. But we shall wait. We still wait for the first positive response.

Despite this bleak picture, I will not be deterred in my search for a breakthrough. The United States will never walk away from the negotiating table. Peace is too important. Common sense demands that we persevere, and we will persevere.

We live in uncertain times. There are trials and tests for freedom wherever freedom stands. It is as stark as the tragedy over the Sea of Japan, when 269 innocent people were killed for the so-called cause of sacred airspace. It is as real as the terrorist attacks last month on the Republic of Korea's leadership in Rangoon and against American and French members of the international peacekeeping force in Beirut.

And yes, it is as telling as the stonewalling of our adversaries at the negotiating table, and as their crude attempts to intimidate freedom-loving people everywhere.

These threats to peace and freedom underscore the importance of closer cooperation among all nations. You have an old proverb that says, "A single arrow is easily broken, but not three in a bunch." The stronger the dedication of Japan, the United States, and our allies to peace through strength, the greater our contributions to building a more secure future will be. The U.S.-Japan Treaty of Mutual Cooperation and Security must continue to serve us as the bedrock of our security relationship. Japan will not have to bear the burden of defending freedom alone. America is your partner. We will bear that burden together.

The defense of freedom should be a shared burden. We can afford to defend freedom; we cannot afford to lose it. The blessings of your economic miracle, created with the genius of a talented, determined, and dynamic people, can only be protected in the safe harbor of freedom.

In his book, "In Quest of Peace and Freedom," former Prime Minister Sato wrote: "In the hundred years since the Meiji Restoration, Japan has constantly endeavored to catch up and eventually overtake the more advanced countries of the world." Well, I don't think I'll be making headlines when I say, you've not only caught up; in some cases, you've pulled ahead. [*Laughter*] Here again, our partnership is crucial. But this time, you can be teachers.

To all those who lack faith in the human spirit, I have just three words of advice: Come to Japan. Come to a country whose economic production will soon surpass the Soviet Union's, making Japan's economy the second largest in the entire world. Come to learn from a culture that instills in its people a strong spirit of cooperation, discipline, and striving for excellence; and yes, learn from government policies which helped create this economic miracle—not so much by central planning, as by stimulating competition, encouraging initiative, and rewarding savings and risk-taking.

Our country has made great strides in this direction during the last 3 years. We're correcting past mistakes. Hope is being reborn. Confidence is returning. America's future looks bright again. We have turned the corner from overtaxing, overspending, record interest rates, high inflation, and low growth. The United States is beginning the first stage of a new industrial renaissance, and we're helping pull other nations forward to worldwide recovery.

But some in my country still flinch from the need to restrain spending. Under the guise of lowering deficits, they would turn back to policies of higher taxes. They would ignore the lesson of Japan. A look at Japan's postwar history yields two stunning conclusions. Among the major industrialized countries, your tax burden has remained the lowest and your growth and saving rates the highest. Savers in Japan can exempt very large amounts of interest income from taxation. Your taxes on so-called unearned income—[laughter]—are low. You have no capital gains tax on securities for investors. And the overwhelming majority of your working people face tax rates dramatically lower than in the other industrial countries, including my own. And incentives for everyone—that's the secret of strong growth for a shining future filled with hope, and opportunities and incentives for growth, not tax increases, is our policy for America. Sometimes I wonder if we shouldn't further our friendship by my sending our Congress here and you coming over and occupying our Capitol Building for a while.

Partnership must be a two-way street grounded in mutual trust. Let us always be willing to learn from each other and cooperate together. We have every reason to do so. Our combined economies account for almost 35 percent of the world's entire economic output. We are the world's two largest overseas trading partners. Last year Japan took about 10 percent of our total exports, and we bought some 25 percent of yours. Our two-way trade will exceed $60 billion in 1983, more than double the level of just 7 years ago.

At the Williamsburg summit last May, the leaders of our industrial democracies pledged to cooperate in rolling back protectionism. My personal commitment to that goal is based on economic principles, old-fashioned common sense, and experience. I am old enough to remember what eventually happened the last time countries protected their markets from competition: It was a nightmare called the Great Depression. And it was worldwide. World trade fell at that time by 60 percent. And everyone—workers, farmers, and manufacturers were hurt.

Let us have the wisdom never to repeat that policy. We're in the same boat with our trading partners around the globe. And if one partner in the boat shoots a hole in the boat, it doesn't make much sense for the other partner to shoot another hole in the boat. Some say, yes, and call that getting tough. Well, forgive me, but I call it getting wet all over. Rather than shoot holes, let us work together to plug them up so our boat of free markets and free trade and fair trade can lead us all to greater economic growth and international stability.

I have vigorously opposed quick fixes of protectionism in America. Anticompetitive legislation like the local content rule, which would force our domestic manufacturers of cars to use a rising share of U.S. labor and parts—now, this would be a cruel hoax. It would be raising prices without protecting jobs. We would buy less from you. You would buy less from us. The world's economic pie would shrink. Retaliation and recrimination would increase.

It is not easy for elected officials to balance the concerns of constituents with the greater interests of the Nation, but that's what our jobs are all about. And we need your help in demonstrating free trade to address concerns of my own people. Americans believe your markets are less open than ours. We need your support to lower further the barriers that still make it difficult for some American products to enter your markets easily. Your government's recent series of actions to reduce trade barriers are positive steps in this direction. We very much hope this process will continue and accelerate. In turn, I pledge my support to combat protectionist measures in my own country.

If we each give a little, we can all gain a lot. As two great and mature democracies, let us have the faith to believe in each other, to draw on our long and good friendship, and to make our partnership grow. We are leaders in the world economy. We and the other industrialized countries share a responsibility to open up capital and trading markets, promote greater investment in each other's country, assist developing nations, and stop the leakage of military technology to an adversary bent on aggression and domination.

We believe that the currency of the world's second largest free-market economy should reflect the economic strength and political stability that you enjoy. We look forward to the yen playing a greater role in international financial and economic affairs. We welcome the recent trend toward a stronger yen. And we would welcome Japan's increasingly active role in global affairs. Your leadership in aid to refugees and in economic assistance to various countries has been most important in helping to promote greater stability in key regions of the world. Your counsel on arms reduction initiatives is highly valued by us.

We may have periodic disputes, but the real quarrel is not between us. It is with those who would impose regimentation over freedom, drudgery over dynamic initiative, a future of despair over the certainty of betterment, and the forced feeding of a military goliath over a personal stake in the products and progress of tomorrow.

You and your neighbors are shining examples for all who seek rapid development. The Pacific Basin represents the most exciting region of economic growth in the world today. Your people stretch your abilities to the limit, and when an entire nation does this, miracles occur. Being a Californian I have seen many miracles hardworking Japanese have brought to our shores.

In 1865 a young Samurai student, Kanaye Nagasawa, left Japan to learn what made the West economically strong and technologically advanced. Ten years later he founded a small winery at Santa Rosa, California, called the Fountaingrove Round Barn and Winery. Soon he became known as the grape king of California. Nagasawa came to California to learn and stayed to enrich our lives. Both our countries owe much to this Japanese warrior-turned-businessman.

As the years pass, our contacts continue to increase at an astounding rate. Today some 13,000 of your best college and graduate students are studying in America, and increasing numbers of U.S. citizens are coming here to learn everything they can about Japan. Companies like Nissan, Kyocera, Sony, and Toshiba have brought thousands of jobs to America's shores. The State of California is planning to build a rapid speed train that is adapted from your highly successful bullet train. In 1985 the United States will join Japan in a major exhibition of science and technology at Tsukuba, another symbol of our cooperation.

For my part, I welcome this new Pacific tide. Let it roll peacefully on, carrying a two-way flow of people and ideas that can break from barriers of suspicion and mistrust and build up bonds of cooperation and shared optimism.

Our two nations may spring from separate pasts; we may live at opposite sides of the Earth; but we have been brought together by our indomitable spirit of determination, our love of liberty, and devotion to progress. We are like climbers who begin their ascent from opposite ends of the mountain. The harder we try, the higher we climb and the closer we come together—until that moment we reach the peak and we are as one.

It happened just last month. One American and two Japanese groups began climbing Mt. Everest—the Japanese from the side of Nepal and the Americans from the side of Tibet. The conditions were so difficult and dangerous that before it ended two Japanese climbers tragically lost their lives. But before that tragedy, those brave climbers all met and shook hands just under the summit. And then, together, they climbed to the top to share that magnificent moment of triumph.

Good and dear friends of Japan, if those mountaineers could join hands at the top of the world, imagine how high our combined 350 million citizens can climb, if all of us work together as powerful partners for the cause of good. Together there is nothing that Japan and America cannot do.

Thank you very much. God bless you.

Note: The President spoke at 9:35 a.m. in

the Assembly Hall of the House of Representatives at the National Diet Building. At the conclusion of the session, the President and Mrs. Reagan attended a reception with the leadership of the Diet and other Japanese officials in the Speaker's Drawing Room. Following the reception, the President and Mrs. Reagan returned to Akasaka Palace, where they stayed during their visit to Japan.

Joint Statement on Japan-United States Energy Cooperation
November 11, 1983

Prime Minister Nakasone and President Reagan share the view that further progress be made in energy trade and cooperation in oil, natural gas and coal between Japan and the United States as outlined in the following Joint Policy Statement recommended by the Japan-United States Energy Working Group:

Taking account of the energy prospects for the entire Pacific basin, the two countries agree that the sound expansion of U.S.-Japan energy trade will contribute to the further development of the close economic and energy security relationship which exists between the two countries.

They will continue to discuss and find ways of developing this trade for the mutual benefit of both countries, noting the importance of long-term cooperation, the central role of the private sector, and the need for a balance between economic cost and energy security.

Both countries consider Alaska to be a particularly promising area for joint development of energy resources. Both governments will encourage private sector discussions regarding the possibilities for such development.

With regard to trade in oil, gas and coal, we have agreed on the following next steps:

A. The U.S. and Japan recognize that if legislative barriers can be removed, the U.S. has the potential to ship substantial quantities of crude oil to Japan, thereby increasing economic incentives for U.S. oil production and helping to diversify Japan's energy sources. The U.S. will continue to keep under review the removal of restrictions on exports of domestic crude oil.

B. The U.S. and Japan will encourage private industry in both countries to undertake now the pre-feasibility or feasibility studies necessary to determine the extent to which Alaskan natural gas can be jointly developed by U.S. and Japanese interests.

C. The U.S. and Japan will encourage private industry in both countries to discuss the possibility of concluding long-term coal contracts and jointly developing mines and transportation systems to make American coal more competitive in the Japanese market.

D. In this regard, the two countries welcome the examinations underway of the technical and economic aspects of several steam coal projects by private companies concerned on both sides. As economic recovery proceeds, Japan will encourage its industries to consider purchase of more competitively priced U.S. steam coal to meet future demands not already covered by existing contracts. In addition, Japan will invite the private sector concerned to explore the possibility of further increasing substitution of coal for oil in electrical generation.

E. With regard to metallurgical coal, both sides noted that the depressed state of world steel manufacturing had reduced demand for traded coal. However, in view of the fact that the U.S. has been a major supplier to the Japanese market, both sides will endeavor to maintain the level of Japanese imports of U.S. coal. Japan expects that imports of competitively priced U.S. metallurgical coal will not continue to decline, and will encourage its steel industry to increase U.S. coal imports when conditions in the industry permit.

F. As a first step toward developing U.S.-Japan coal trade, from a mid- to long-term prospective, a mission composed of representatives of major Japanese coal users and other appropriate interests will visit the U.S. to meet with major coal mining and transportation interests. The purpose of this mission will be to explore the possibility of expanding coal trade between the U.S. and Japan, and the possibility of conducting a major study of the opportunities for reducing the delivered price in Japan of U.S. coal.

Interview With Representatives of NHK Television in Tokyo, Japan
November 11, 1983

Q. Good evening, Mr. President. On behalf of all my colleagues present here and of the truly nationwide audience, I would like to thank you, first of all, for having agreed to do this interview.

I understand that you have prepared a statement for the Japanese people that perhaps you would like to make right now. Please, Mr. President.

The President. Well, thank you very much. And may I say how delighted Nancy and I are to be back in Japan. The last time we visited Japan was 1978 at the invitation of one of your Diet Members, Shintaro Ishihara. I was also here in 1971, when I had the pleasure of seeing Kyoto, your beautiful, ancient capital city.

There is so much in Japan's history and culture that impresses us. Americans are full of admiration for the Japanese people, the warmth of your ways, your spirit of initiative and teamwork, and your strong traditions of devotion to family, education, and progress.

You have brought great development and prosperity to your country. We know that the struggle for better living was often difficult in earlier days. But endurance, tenacity, and sheer hard work—qualities which I understand are beautifully portrayed in your popular TV drama, "Oshin"—have brought your nation great economic success.

Recently I received a letter from Masayasu Okumura, principal of the Nishisawa School in Akita Prefecture, which I understand is very far from Tokyo. Mr. Okumura invited Nancy and me to visit his country school and his 27 students. Mr. Okumura, I wanted to drop in on your school and talk with your students, but our stay in Japan this week has been too short. We wish we had time to meet more people and see more of your beautiful country, including such places as Kyoto, Hokkaido, Hiroshima, Nara, and Nagasaki.

But we depart tomorrow, confident that our relations are strong and good. As I have said to the Diet today, we may live thousands of miles apart, but we're neighbors, friends, and partners, bound by a community of interests and shared values. Michitaro Matsusaki, one of Japan's earlier diplomats, said to Commodore Perry in 1854 what millions of us feel today: Japan and America, all the same heart.

Our countries enjoy great prosperity. We live in free and open societies. But much of the world lives in poverty, dominated by dictators unwilling to let people live in peace and freedom. That's why our relationship is so important. Japan and America shoulder global responsibilities, but with every responsibility comes opportunity.

We can share with the world our secrets of economic growth and human progress. We can offer the sunlight of democracy to people everywhere who dream of escaping the darkness of tyranny to decide their own destinies.

Japan and America are nations of the future, builders of tomorrow, and together we can build a brighter tomorrow. We can make this world a much safer, more secure, and prosperous place. I know with all my heart that if we have faith to believe in each other, to trust in the talent and goodness of the hard-working people in our great cities and small towns, then, yes, we will make our partnership grow, and together there is nothing Japan and America cannot do.

And now, I'd be delighted to answer some questions that you may have for me.

The President's Hobbies

Q. Thank you very much, Mr. President.

Q. Mr. President, listening to your statement, like many other people I find that you are indeed a great communicator. I say this not because you said very kind words about our famous city of drama, but because I think that your personal style on television is more relaxed and informal than that of many other politicians. That is why, with your approval, Mr. President, I would like to conduct this interview in a very informal way so that the Japanese people can get a clearer view of your personality.

Since your arrival, Mr. President, Japanese people have been following very closely your visit. And yesterday we saw that you enjoyed a lot about our demonstration of Yabusame at Meiji Shrine. What did you think of that typical traditional Japanese sport? And if I may ask, apart from horse riding, what are your personal hobbies, Mr. President?

The President. Well, horseback riding is certainly one, and all the things that go with having a ranch. I do a lot of the work whenever I have the opportunity to get there that has to be done around a ranch. As a matter of fact, just this summer we had a number of days at the ranch, and I managed to build, with the help of two friends, build about 400 more feet of fence that we built out of telephone poles. [*Laughter*] And it can get a little back breaking, but I enjoy that.

Someone once asked me when I was ever going to have the ranch finished, and I said I hope never, because I enjoy that. But there are other things, of course. I enjoy reading. I enjoy athletics of other kinds. And now, thanks to the generosity of your Prime Minister since his last visit there—while I don't get to play golf very often, I will now be playing it with a brand new set of golf clubs which he presented to me.

Views on Visit to Japan

Q. Well, you have now completed almost all the events of your very full schedule for Japan. Yesterday you gave us your official view of the visit, but I wonder if you could give us now a more personal view of this visit?

The President. Well, yes, I'm very pleased with what has taken place here. First of all the warmth of the reception from all your people, and I mean not just the people of diplomacy and government that I had dealings with, but your people there on the streets and their showing of hospitality and friendship has been very heartwarming. But I have always believed that we only get in trouble when we're talking about each other instead of to each other. And since we've had an opportunity here to not only speak with your Diet but then to meet with your Prime Minister and others—and, of course, I have been greatly honored to have been received by His Imperial Majesty, your Emperor—I think that we have established a human kind of bond, not just one that is framed in diplomacy, but an understanding of each other as people. And I think that the world needs more of this.

Q. Mr. President, I would like you to know, in the first place, that many of my compatriots will be surprised and very happily so at the inclusion of Hiroshima and Nagasaki on the list of the places that you'd like to visit or you wish you could visit. And to this end, of course, you'll have to be a young—[*inaudible*]—sagacious man so that you'll be able to fulfill your and our common desire in this regard. Now, are you going to be one? Are you going to be a sagacious man?

The President. Well, I'm certainly going to try. This is too dangerous a world to just be careless with words or deeds. And if ever there was a need for the world to work toward peace and to work out of the dangerous situation that we're in, that time is now.

East-West Relations

Q. On a more, a little more serious note, Mr. President, my question is exactly related to this point. And that is, because of the experience that we in Japan went through, we are very genuine in hoping even for a very minimum, limited progress in the arms control talks which are currently underway. And just as it took another Republican President with very conservative credentials to effect a rapprochement very successfully with China, there are Japanese who hope that, perhaps, your hard-line policy may lead to the relaxation of East-West tensions. And in light of these hopes and expectations, Mr. President, could you comment on these talks? And, also, I would appreciate it a great deal if you would give us your assessment of the current state of and, perhaps, future prospects for U.S.-Soviet relations, particularly in the arms control area.

The President. Well, now, if all of your question—you prefaced it with remarks about the People's Republic of China. Yes, we're working very hard to improve relations there and establish trust and friendship. And I think we've made great progress. I know there is a question that is raised sometimes with regard to our friends on Taiwan—the Republic of China. And I have to say, there, that I have repeatedly said to the leaders of the People's Republic of China that they must understand that we will not throw over one friend in order to make another. And I would think that that would be reassuring to them, that they, then, might not be thrown over at some time in the future.

U.S.-Soviet Relations

But with regard to the Soviet Union—and you mentioned my hard line. And that is—I know I'm described that way a great deal. [*Laughter*] What is being called a hard line, I think, is realism. I had some experience with Communists—not of the Soviet kind, but domestic, in our own country, some years ago when I was president of a labor union there.

And I feel that we have to be realistic with the Soviet Union. It is not good for us, as some in the past have, to think, well, they're just like us and surely we can appeal to, say, their kindliness or their better nature. No. I think they're very materialistic. They're very realistic. They have some aggressive and expansionist aims in the world. And I believe that, yes, you can negotiate with them; yes, you can talk to them. But it must be on the basis of recognizing them as the way they are and then presenting the proposals in such a way that they can see that it is to their advantage to be less hostile in the world and to try and get along with the rest of the nations of the world. And if this is hard-line, then I'm hard-line.

But it is important because of, also, your opening remarks with reference to the great nuclear forces in the world. We are going to stay at that negotiating table. We won't walk away from it. We're going to stay there trying, not as we have in the past to set some limits or ceilings on how many more missiles would be built, how much more growth they could take in those weapons, we want a reduction in the numbers. But really and practically, when we start down that road, and if we can get cooperation from them in reducing them, we should then continue down that road to their total elimination.

Many years ago, after he became President, Dwight Eisenhower, as President, wrote a letter to a noted publisher in our country. And he said in that letter that we had to face the fact that weapons were being developed in which we could no longer see a war that would end in victory or defeat as we had always known it. But the weapons were such that it would end in the destruction of human kind. And, as he said, when we reach that moment, then let us have the intelligence to sit down at a table and negotiate our problems before we destroy the world.

I see it also in another way that he didn't mention. Once upon a time, we had rules of warfare. War is an ugly thing, but we had rules in which we made sure that soldiers fought soldiers, but they did not victimize civilians. That was civilized. Today we've lost something of civilization in that the very weapons we're talking about are designed to destroy civilians by the millions. And let us at least get back to where we once were—that if we talk war at all, we talk it in a way in which there could be victory or defeat and in which civilians have some measure of protection.

Q. Thank you very much, Mr. President.

Arms Control and Reduction

Q. Mr. President, you referred to the current situation as being very dangerous. And in recent months we have witnessed one act of violence after another—the assassination of Mr. Aquino in the Philippines, and the shooting down of the Korean Airlines passenger jet, the terrorist bombing in Rangoon, and again in the bombing in Lebanon, Beirut, and the regional conflicts that persist at many different parts of the world, including the Middle East and the Caribbean. I think we certainly live in a very dangerous world, and your administration has advocated very strongly for building more effective defense capabilities of the United States and of its allies.

Now my question is, Mr. President, my question is that the kind of danger that the world faces today would be minimized if the United States and its partners, including Japan, become stronger militarily?

The President. Yes, and this is part of that realism that I meant. I once did a lot of negotiating across a table as a labor leader on behalf of a union, and I think I know and understand the give and take of negotiations. But for a number of years now, recently, we have sat at the table in meetings with the Soviet leaders who have engaged in the biggest military buildup in the history of mankind. And they sat on their side of the table looking at us and knowing that unilaterally we were disarming without getting anything in return. They didn't have to give up anything. They saw themselves get stronger in relation to all of us as we, ourselves, made ourselves weaker.

I think realistically to negotiate arms reductions they have to see that there is a choice. Either they join in those arms reductions, or they then have to face the fact that we are going to turn our industrial might to building the strength that would be needed to deter them from ever starting a war.

Wars don't start because a nation is—they don't start them when they are weak; they start them when they think they're stronger than someone else. And it is very dangerous to let them see that they have a great margin of superiority over the rest of us. There's nothing to prevent them from then becoming aggressive and starting a war.

Now, if they know that they cannot match us—and when I say us, I mean our allies and Japan and the United States—they cannot match us if we are determined to build up our defenses. So they then face the fact that as we build them up, they might then find themselves weaker than we are.

It was all summed up in a cartoon in one of our papers. This was before the death of Leonid Brezhnev. Brezhnev was portrayed talking to a Russian general, and he was saying to the general, "I liked the arms race better when we were the only ones in it." *[Laughter]*

Q. Let me just follow up my question. Some of the dangers that I refer to do not take place only in the context of the confrontation between the United States and the Soviet Union. I think some of the regional conflicts have indigenous roots for that. And I just wonder if we are not having the kind of crises and dangers that don't lend themselves to the military solutions, which might call for some other approach to solving these problems and thereby reducing the tension in the world as a whole.

The President. Well, if I understand your question correctly, what we're talking about is—you mentioned the Middle East. Once upon a time, nations like our own with oceans around us, we could have a defensive army on our own land, we could have coastal artillery batteries, and we knew that if a war came to us, it would come to our shores and we would defend our shores. Today there are strategic points in various places in the world. The Middle East is one. Could the allies, Western Europe, could Japan stand by and see the Middle East come into the hands of someone who would deny the oil of the Middle East to the industrialized world? Could we see that energy supply shut off without knowing that it would bring absolute ruin to our countries?

There are other areas. More than half of the minerals that the United States needs for its own industries comes from spots all over the world. Well, an aggressor nation, a nation that maybe has designs on other nations, recognizes that also. We have to look and see where are those strategic spots which we cannot afford to let fall.

With the problem of Cuba in the Mediterranean—in the Caribbean, we have to recognize that more than half of all of our shipping of those necessities we must have come through the Caribbean. It wasn't an accident that back in the First World War that the German submarine packs took up their places there. We know that the strategic waterways of the world—the Soviet Union has now built up the greatest navy in the world, and the biggest part of that navy is here in the Pacific, in the vicinity of your own country. But they know, as anyone must know in world strategy, that there are a limited number of choke points, sea passages that are essential to your livelihood and to ours. You can start with the Panama Canal and the Suez Canal, but then the Straits of Gibraltar, but then right here in the passages that lead to your own island, the Malacca and the Makassar Straits. There are a total of no more than 16 in the whole world. And a nation that could dominate those narrow passages and shut them off to our shipping could secure victory without firing a shot at any of us.

The American Economy

Q. Let us turn to an economic issue.

Q. Mr. President, the American economy has been rapidly improving, we hear, yet unemployment is still high. Could you tell us what you believe will happen to the American domestic economy in the coming year and whether the improvement of the American economy, domestic economy will help to resolve remaining trade problems between the United States and Japan?

The President. Well, the American economy is improving. This recession that we've just been going through is the eighth that we've known in the last 40 or so years. And each time in the past our government has resorted to what I call a quick fix. It has artificially stimulated the money supply; it has stimulated government spending, increased taxes on the people which reduced their incentive to produce. And yes, there would be seeming recovery from the recession which would last about 2 or 3 years because it was artificial, and then we would be into another recession. And each time

the recession was deeper and worse than the one before.

Well, we embarked on an economic program that was based on reducing government spending to leave a greater share of the earnings of the people in the hands of the people. We not only reduced the spending, we reduced taxes. And it was set out to be a lasting and real recovery.

When we started in 1981 our recession was about—roughly 12½ percent. People were saying that it couldn't be eliminated in less than 10 years. Our interest rates were more than double what they are now. Our program, once put into effect, and as the tax cuts did have the effect we hoped they would have on the ability of people to purchase but also the incentive of their being allowed to keep more of the money they earned—the inflation for the last year has been running at about 2½ percent or so, down from the 12.4. The interest rates, as I said, have been halved. We have a long way to go. The last thing to recover will be unemployment. But even there, last month our unemployment dropped to a rate that in our own optimistic predictions we had said would not happen until the end of 1984. And here it is in 1983, down to what we'd predicted that far ahead.

We've come down from a very high unemployment rate to 8.7 percent. And I think that we're on the road to a solid recovery. I'll tell you, when our political opponents were claiming that our plan wouldn't work, they named it Reaganomics. [*Laughter*] And lately, they haven't been calling it Reaganomics anymore. I assume, because it's working. [*Laughter*]

But what it will do for the rest of the world and our own relationship, I think that our country—I think your country, largely—certainly between the two of us, we do affect the world's economy. The world has been in recession. And I think that the United States and Japan and, certainly, with us together, we can help bring back and bring out of recession the rest of the industrial world.

Trade With Japan

Q. Mr. President, you said that—in the National Diet this morning—that you have vigorously opposed the quick fix of protectionism in America. But there remains the danger of protectionist legislation to restrict Japanese imports to the United States. Do you believe such anticompetitive legislation will be passed? And in regard to this, what do you think of the steps which Japan has been taking to further open up its own markets?

The President. We heartily approve. And one of the things that we've been discussing are some of the points of difference that still remain between our two marketplaces. And I have pointed to the danger of those in our Congress who, because of the unemployment, think the answer could be protectionism. Well, I think that protectionism destroys everything we want. I believe in free trade and fair trade. And yet, the pressure on them as legislators to adopt these bills, these measures—I am opposed to them—and yet, as I say, I know they're under that pressure. And they're tempted. And they're talking of this. There probably have been 40 bills that have been brought up and proposed, all of which would have some elements in them of protectionism.

But as I described it in the speech to the Diet this morning, protectionism is—that's the case of one fellow shooting a hole in the bottom of the boat, and then the other fellow answers by shooting another hole in the boat. Well, you don't get well; you get wet. And I don't want us to start shooting holes in the bottom of the boat.

U.S.-Japan Cultural Exchanges

Q. Well, Mr. President, unfortunately time is running out. And that will be our last question.

I understand you have a strong interest in increasing personal contacts between the Japanese and the Americans.

The President. Yes.

Q. Do you have any idea, specific idea how this could be accomplished?

The President. Well, yes. I think we can increase our student exchange. Almost 14,000 of your fine young people are in our country now. We would like to see more of ours coming here. There is talk now of the Association of Japanese and American Businessmen in using private funds, having an American House in Tokyo as we have a Japanese House in New York, both designed for more cultural exchange, more things such as student exchange and all. And I believe, again, that's another example of people talking to each other instead of about each other.

Q. Well, Mr. President, I'm awfully sorry, but that's all the time we had. And I thank you very much on behalf of all these participants.

The President. Well, thank all of you for the opportunity. I'm sorry the time went by so fast. Maybe my answers were too long. [*Laughter*]

Note: The interview began at 6:22 p.m. in the Shairan-No-Ma Room at the Akasaka Palace.

Remarks on Arrival at Kimpo Airport, Seoul, Republic of Korea
November 12, 1983

I bring to you, Mr. President, to the people of Korea the warmest expressions of friendship from the American people. The friendship between our two peoples is a long and a close one. It has endured more than a century. It has been molded in struggle, hardened through danger, and strengthened by victory.

Since those days three decades ago when young Koreans and Americans fought together in the cause of human freedom, the world has undergone swift and sometimes violent change. Yet the peace, economic progress, and freedom from foreign domination that have characterized modern Korea are testimony to their vigilance and their sacrifice.

We are resolved never to forget the dangers they so bravely resisted, nor abandon the struggle they so willingly joined. Today, in a tense time of peace, we stand together as we once did in time of war. Our purpose is the same, our resolve unshaken. We renew today our commitment to each other and to the cause of Korean and American freedom.

As we begin a second century of friendship between our peoples, Nancy and I are particularly happy to return to this beautiful country. We look forward to seeing old friends and making new ones. But our hope most of all is that our visit will bring the people of Korea and the United States even closer together, and that our mutual efforts in pursuit of peace will bear fruit, not just for the Korean and the American people but for all the peoples of the Earth.

We're grateful to the Korean people and the Government of Korea for this invitation. Let me assure you we bring with us the fondest hopes of the American people for continued peace and prosperity in this scenic "Land of the Morning Calm."

Thank you.

Note: The President spoke at 10:41 a.m. in the International Terminal at the airport in response to welcoming remarks by President Chun Doo Hwan of the Republic of Korea. Following the arrival ceremony, President and Mrs. Chun accompanied the President and Mrs. Reagan to the residence of Richard L. Walker, U.S. Ambassador to the Republic of Korea, where the Reagans stayed during their visit.

Address Before the Korean National Assembly in Seoul
November 12, 1983

Speaker Chae, Vice Speaker Yun, Vice Speaker Koh, distinguished Members of the National Assembly, and honored guests:

I'm privileged to be among such friends. I stand in your Assembly as Presidents Eisenhower and Johnson have stood before me. And I reaffirm, as they did, America's support and friendship for the Republic of Korea and its people.

Not long after the war on this peninsula, your President paid a visit to Washington. In his remarks at the state dinner, President Eisenhower spoke of the Korean people's courage, stamina, and self-sacrifice. He spoke of America's pride in joining with the Korean people to prevent their enslavement by the North. In response, your first President expressed his country's deep, deep appreciation for what America had done. He concluded by saying, "I tell you, my friends, if I live hundreds of years, we will never be able to do enough to pay our debt of gratitude to you."

Well, I have come today to tell the people of this great nation: Your debt has long been repaid. Your loyalty, your friendship, your progress, your determination to build something better for your people has proven many times over the depth of your gratitude. In these days of turmoil and testing, the American people are very thankful for such a constant and devoted ally. Today, America is grateful to you.

And we have long been friends. Over a hundred years ago when American ships first approached Korea, our people knew almost nothing of each other. Yet, the first words from the kingdom of Chosun to the emissaries from America were words of welcome and hope. I would like to read part of that greeting to the Americans, because it tells much of the Korean people's character.

"Of what country are you? . . . are you well after your journey of 10,000 *le* through winds and waves? Is it your plan to barter merchandise . . . or do you rather wish to pass by to other places and to return to your native land? All under heaven are of one original nature, clothes and hats are very different and language is not the same, yet they can treat each other with mutual friendship. What your wish is, please make it known. . . ."

The journey from America is now swift. The winds and waves no longer endanger our way. But the rules of conduct which assist travelers are the same today as they were over a century ago, or even in ancient times. The weary are restored, the sick healed, the lost sheltered and returned safely to their way. This is so on all continents among civilized nations.

Our world is sadder today, because these ancient and honorable practices could not protect the lives of some recent travelers. Instead of offering assistance to a lost civilian airliner, the Soviet Union attacked. Instead of offering condolences, it issued denials. Instead of offering reassurances, it repeated its threats. Even in the search for our dead, the Soviet Union barred the way. This behavior chilled the entire world. The people of Korea and the United States shared a special grief and anger.

My nation's prayers went out to the Korean families who lost loved ones even as we prayed for our own. May I ask you today to pause for a moment of silence for those who perished. Please join me in this tribute in which the spirit of our two peoples will be as one.

[*The moment of silence was observed.*]

Amen.

In recent weeks, our grief deepened. The despicable North Korean attack in Rangoon deprived us of trusted advisers and friends. So many of those who died had won admirers in America as they studied with us or guided us with their counsel. I personally recall the wisdom and composure of Foreign Minister Lee, with whom I met in Washington just a few short months ago. To the families and countrymen of all those who were lost, America expresses its deep sorrow.

We also pledge to work with your government and others in the international community to censure North Korea for its uncivilized behavior. Let every aggressor hear our words, because Americans and Koreans speak with one voice. People who are free will not be slaves, and freedom will not be lost in the Republic of Korea.

We in the United States have suffered a similar savage act of terrorism in recent weeks. Our marines in Lebanon were murdered by madmen who cannot comprehend words like "reason" or "decency." They seek to destroy not only peace but those

who search for peace. We bear the pain of our loses just as you bear the pain of yours. As we share friendship, we also share grief.

I know citizens of both our countries as well as those of other nations do not understand the meaning of such tragedies. They wonder why there must be such hate. Of course, regrettably there is no easy answer. We can place greater value on our true friends and allies. We can stand more firmly by those principles that give us strength and guide us, and we can remember that some attack us because we symbolize what they do not: hope, promise, the future. Nothing exemplifies this better than the progress of Korea. Korea is proof that people's lives can be better. And I want my presence today to draw attention to a great contrast. I'm talking about the contrast between your economic miracle in the South and their economic failure in the North.

In the early years following World War II, the future of Korea and of all Asia was very much in doubt. Against the hopes of Korea and other new nations for prosperity and freedom stood the legacies of war, poverty, and colonial rule. In the background of this struggle, the great ideological issues of our era were heard: Would the future of the region be democratic or totalitarian? Communism, at that time, seemed to offer rapid industrialization. The notion that the people of the region should govern their own lives seemed to some an impractical and undue luxury. But Americans and the people of Korea shared a different vision of the future.

Then North Korea burst across the border, intent on destroying this country. We were a world weary of war, but we did not hesitate. The United States, as well as other nations of the world came to your aid against the aggression, and tens of thousands of Americans gave their lives in defense of freedom.

As heavy as this price was, the Korean people paid an even heavier one. Civilian deaths mounted to the hundreds of thousands. President Johnson said before this very Assembly, "Who will ever know how many children starved? How many refugees lie in unmarked graves along the roads south? There is hardly a Korean family which did not lose a loved one in the assault from the North."

In 1951, in the midst of the war, General Douglas MacArthur addressed a Joint Session of our Congress. He spoke of you, saying, "The magnificence of the courage and fortitude of the Korean people defies description." As he spoke those words, our Congress interrupted him with applause for you and your people.

After the war, Koreans displayed that same fortitude. Korea faced every conceivable difficulty. Cities were in ruins; millions were homeless and without jobs; factories were idle or destroyed; hunger was widespread; the transportation system was dismembered; and the economy was devastated as a result of all these plagues. And what did the Korean people do? You rebuilt your lives, your families, your homes, your towns, your businesses, your country. And today the world speaks of the Korean economic miracle.

The progress of the Korean economy is virtually without precedent. With few natural resources other than the intelligence and energy of your people, in one generation you have transformed this country from the devastation of war to the threshold of full development.

Per capita income has risen from about $80 in 1961 to more than 20 times—$1,700 today. Korea has become an industrial power, a major trading nation, and an economic model for developing nations throughout the world. And you have earned the growing respect of the international community. This is recognized in your expanding role as host to numerous international events, including the 1986 Asian games and the 1988 Olympics.

Now as the years have passed, we know our vision was the proper one. North Korea is one of the most repressive societies on Earth. It does not prosper; it arms. The rapid progress of your economy and the stagnation of the North has demonstrated perhaps more clearly here than anywhere else the value of a free economic system. Let the world look long and hard at both sides of the 38th parallel and then ask: "Which side enjoys a better life?"

The other side claims to be the wave of the future. Well, if that's true, why do they need barriers, troops, and bullets to keep their people in? The tide of history is a freedom tide, and communism cannot and will not hold it back.

The United States knows what you've accomplished here. In the 25 years following the war, America provided almost $5½ billion in economic aid. Today that amounts to less than 6 months' trade between us. That trade is virtually in balance. We are at once Korea's largest market and largest source of supplies. We're a leading source of the investment and technology needed to fuel further development. Korea is our ninth largest trading partner, and our trade is growing.

Korea's rapid development benefited greatly from the free flow of trade which characterized the 1960's and 1970's. Today, in many countries, the call for protectionism is raised. I ask Korea to join with the United States in rejecting those protectionist pressures to ensure that the growth you've enjoyed is not endangered by a maze of restrictive practices.

And just as we work together toward prosperity, we work toward security. Let me make one thing very plain. You are not alone, people of Korea. America is your friend, and we are with you.

This year marks the 30th anniversary of the mutual defense treaty between the United States and the Republic of Korea. The preamble to that treaty affirms the determination of our two countries to oppose aggression and to strengthen peace in the Pacific. We remain firmly committed to that treaty. We seek peace on the peninsula. And that is why United States soldiers serve side by side with Korean soldiers along your demilitarized zone. They symbolize the United States commitment to your security and the security of the region. The United States will stand resolutely by you, just as we stand with our allies in Europe and around the world.

In Korea, especially, we have learned the painful consequences of weakness. I am fully aware of the threats you face only a few miles from here. North Korea is waging a campaign of intimidation. Their country is on a war footing, with some 50 divisions and brigades and 750 combat aircraft. The

North has dug tunnels under the demilitarized zone in their preparations for war. They are perched and primed for conflict. They attacked you in Rangoon, and yet, in spite of such constant threats from the North, you have progressed.

Our most heartfelt wish is that one day the vigil will no longer be needed. America shares your belief that confrontation between North and South is not inevitable. Even as we stand with you to resist aggression from the North, we will work with you to strengthen the peace on the peninsula.

Korea today remains the most firmly divided of the states whose division stemmed from World War II. Austrian unity was reestablished peacefully 10 years after the war. Germany remains divided, but some of the pain of that division has been eased by the inner-German agreement of a decade ago. I know the Korean people also long for reconciliation. We believe that it must be for the people of this peninsula to work toward that reconciliation, and we applaud the efforts you've made to begin a dialog. For our part, we would, as we've often stressed, be willing to participate in discussions with North Korea in any forum in which the Republic of Korea was equally represented. The essential way forward is through direct discussions between South and North.

Americans have watched with a mixture of sadness and joy your campaign to reunite families separated by war. We have followed the stories of sisters torn apart at the moment of their parents' deaths; of small children swept away in the tides of war; of people who have grown old not knowing whether their families live or have perished.

I've heard about the program that uses television to reunite families that have been torn apart. Today, I urge North Korea: It is time to participate in this TV reunification program and to allow your people to appear. I would say to them, whatever your political differences with the South, what harm can be done by letting the innocent families from North and South know of their loved ones' health and welfare? Full reunification of families and peoples is a most basic human right.

Until that day arrives, the United States, like the Republic of Korea, accepts the existing reality of two Korean States and supports steps leading to improved relations among those states and their allies.

We have also joined with you over the past 2 years in proposing measures which, if accepted, would reduce the risk of miscalculation and the likelihood of violence on the peninsula. The proposals we have made, such as mutual notification and observation of military exercises, are similar to ones negotiated in Europe and observed by NATO and the Warsaw Pact. These proposals are not intended to address fundamental political issues, but simply to make this heavily armed peninsula a safer place. For we must not forget that on the peninsula today there are several times more men under arms and vastly more firepower than in June of 1950. We will continue to support efforts to reduce tensions and the risks of war.

I have spoken of the need for vigilance and strength to deter aggression and preserve peace and economic progress, but there is another source of strength, and it is well represented in this Assembly. The development of democratic political institutions is the surest means to build the national consensus that is the foundation of true security.

The United States realizes how difficult political development is when, even as we speak, a shell from the North could destroy this Assembly. My nation realizes the complexities of keeping a peace so that the economic miracle can continue to increase the standard of living of your people. The United States welcomes the goals that you have set for political development and increased respect for human rights for democratic practices. We welcome President Chun's farsighted plans for a constitutional transfer of power in 1988. Other measures for further development of Korean political life will be equally important and will have our warm support.

Now, this will not be a simple process because of the ever-present threat from the North. But I wish to assure you once again of America's unwavering support and the high regard of democratic peoples everywhere as you take the bold and necessary steps toward political development.

Over 100 years ago you asked earlier

American travelers to make their wishes known. Well, I come today to you with our answer: Our wish is for peace and prosperity and freedom for an old and valued ally.

In Washington several weeks ago, a memorial service was held for those who had perished on Flight 007. During that service, a prayer was read. I would like to read you that prayer, because it is a prayer for all mankind.

"O God . . .

Look with compassion on the whole human family;

Take away the arrogance and hatred which infect our hearts;

Break down the walls that separate us;

Unite us in bonds of love;

And work through our struggle and confusion to accomplish your purposes on earth;

That, in your good time, all the nations and races may serve you in harmony . . . ."

That, too, is our wish and prayer. *Anyonghi keshipshiyo.* [Stay in peace.]

Thank you, and God bless you.

Note: President Reagan spoke at 12:30 p.m. in the Assembly Chamber at the National Assembly Building. He was introduced by Chae MunShich, Speaker of the National Assembly.

Prior to the Assembly session, the President and Mrs. Reagan attended a tea in the Speaker's Reception Room. Following the President's address, he and Mrs. Reagan attended a reception with National Assembly leaders in the Assembly Lobby.

Remarks at a Reception for Korean Community Leaders in Seoul
November 12, 1983

Ladies and gentlemen, good evening. Nancy and I are honored to be so warmly greeted by your distinguished group.

We've come to Korea to demonstrate the deep and affectionate concern that the American people have for your country. Our hearts went out to you in the wake of the two murderous attacks on your citizens, and we came today to say that we'll continue to steadfastly stand by you. We hope our presence in your country will show the world our firm support for Korea.

Probably the most important contribution we can make here is to continue helping protect your national security. Our shared commitment to your defense is symbolized by the presence of American soldiers standing with Koreans along the demilitarized zone. This is the shield that enables you to pursue your bold economic and political objectives.

We also support your development of a democratic political system. As you know, the United States pays close attention to political developments in Korea, particularly those that are affecting democratic rights—a matter very important to Americans. We do this not because we believe our security commitment gives us a right to intervene in your internal affairs, but simply because such issues are at the center of our own political ideology and, we feel, are reflected, then, in our foreign policy.

But in approaching such internal matters, I believe it's important to adhere to the discipline of diplomacy, rather than indulging in public posturing. This has been the policy of our administration throughout the world. Where we feel strongly about a particular situation, we make our views known, often quite candidly, to the appropriate level of the government concerned.

I have faith in the Korean people's ability to find a political system meeting their democratic aspirations, even in the face of the heavy security challenge presented by the North. You have accomplished so much already in the face of that threat. Who would have predicted a mere 20 years ago that an impoverished Korea would become one of the world's legendary economic success legends?

This was a Korean accomplishment. Your friends offered help and guidance as these were needed, but they didn't seek to dictate your course. Political development may, in some respects, be a more difficult process, but it, too, is one in which you alone must control.

I respect and strongly support President Chun's pledge to turn over power constitutionally in 1988. This will be an invaluable political legacy to the Korean people. And I believe in the will and ability of the Korean people to develop the foundations required for viable democratic institutions. The shared democratic aspirations of our two peoples are important to our relationship, and continued progress toward the broadening of democracy in Korea strengthens the ties between our two countries. As you continue along this path of political evolution, you do so with our deep support, our affection, and our prayers.

And, again, we thank you from the bottom of our hearts for your warm and very gracious welcome from the first moment that we arrived here today. We are deeply grateful. God bless you.

Note: The President spoke at 6:45 p.m. at the U.S. Embassy.

Toast at the State Dinner in Seoul, Republic of Korea
November 12, 1983

Mr. President, Nancy and I both want to thank you and Madame Chun for your gracious hospitality and your warm words of welcome to us. We're delighted and honored to return here to visit your dynamic country.

Much has been written concerning the Korean economic miracle of the past decades. The startling industry and progress of the Korean people are gaining increasing international recognition and respect. Only recently the Interparliamentary Union met in Seoul, and a new series of international events will culminate here in the 1988 Summer Olympics. This will be a proud moment for Korea. You and the Korean people have every right to feel joy in your hearts.

Mr. President, as Korea grows in international stature, you will hear increasing calls for assistance from allies and friends, calls to defend and promote the values—political, economic, and humanitarian—that both our peoples seek to live by.

Our mutual belief in economic freedom, for example, Mr. President, must not only be defended but spread as far as possible throughout the world. The 66 years that have followed the Russian Revolution and its attempt to turn Communist theory into practice have been marked by tragic failure. Innumerable variations of the Marxist economic system have brought stagnation, waste, and hardship to many countries and many peoples. We must never tire of reminding the world of this. We must never tire of explaining and promoting the free market system and its benefits.

And so, too, Mr. President, we must resist internal threats to our economic freedom, the calls to choke off international trade, to somehow protect jobs by denying our consumers the benefits of freedom of choice. The $12 billion in trade between our two countries has provided innumerable jobs to both our nations, and we must redouble our efforts to expand rather than constrict that trade.

Our political values also face unremitting challenges. Democracy and freedom of opinion are virtues the free world must cherish and defend. They distinguish us from totalitarian states. They are the source of our strength as nations, the very reason for our existence.

And finally, the most basic human values—our concern for the rights of the individual, our belief in the sacredness of human life—there also, these go to the heart of our existence. The murder of 269 innocent people in a defenseless airliner, the very absence here tonight of some of your nation's finest public servants—these events have written in blood the stark contrast between those nations that respect human life and those that trample it. The vicious attack in Rangoon dramatizes the threat your people face. We must stand together to confront this dangerous challenge and to preserve the peace. And this we will do.

The increasing strength of the United States, our allies, and the progress of nations like Korea—as contrasted with the continuing failure and moral decline of the Communist nations—only serve to strengthen my conviction: The tide of history is a freedom tide, and communism cannot and will not hold it back.

Our first hundred years of friendship are history; we are now beginning to write the history of our second hundred years. May the new era of Korean-American partnership be even more fruitful than the last. And may it bring to both our peoples a stronger prosperity, a renewed friendship and confidence, and the genuine peace and security which we so fervently seek.

Will you all join me in a toast to the Korean people, our staunch allies and good friends, and to the President of the Republic of Korea and Madame Chun.

Note: President Reagan spoke at 8:54 p.m. in the State Dining Room at the Blue House in response to a toast by President Chun Doo Hwan. After the Korean folk entertainment which followed the dinner, the President and Mrs. Reagan returned to the residence of Richard L. Walker, U.S. Ambassador to the Republic of Korea, where they stayed during their visit.

Radio Address to the Nation on the President's Trip to Japan and the Republic of Korea
November 12, 1983

My fellow Americans:

I'm sure you've heard Nancy and I have been traveling far from home this week. We're visiting two of America's most valued friends in the Pacific, Japan and the Republic of Korea.

The great energy and vitality of these free people is most impressive, and we're enchanted by the treasures of their past. We visited the revered and lovely Meiji Shrine in Tokyo. While there, we watched an exhibition of Yabusame, a spectacular equestrian sport dating hundreds of years, where riders gallop at full gait shooting arrows at three separate targets. On Friday I had the honor of being the first American President to address the Japanese Diet, their national parliament.

Today we're in South Korea, a staunch ally recently struck by great tragedy—the downing of Korean Air Lines Flight 007, followed by the assassination of key members of the Korean Cabinet. This has brought grief and bitterness to this part of the world, but it has also brought new determination. Free people, no matter where they live, must stand together against terrorism. We stand united with the people of Japan and Korea.

I will underline our commitment on Sunday when I visit our GI's along the demilitarized zone at the 38th parallel. Our soldiers are serving with our Korean allies to deter aggression from the Communist North. Working with our partners to make tomorrow more prosperous and more secure is what our trip is all about.

America is a Pacific nation with good reason to strengthen our ties in this region. Mike Mansfield, our Ambassador to Japan, likes to say, "The next century will be the century of the Pacific." The citizens of our lands may live 5,000 miles apart, we may be different in customs, language, and traditions, and yes, we are often competitors in the world's markets. But what unites us is more important—our love of freedom and our optimism for the future.

Japan, Korea, the United States, and our many other friends in the Pacific region are building a better tomorrow. Individual opportunity coupled with hard work and reward produces astonishing results. When an entire society pursues these goals, miracles occur. Japan and Korea are classic examples of nations rising from the ashes of war to set standards of economic prosperity that dazzle the world.

There's much talk in the Congress of protecting American jobs, but protectionism is defensive and dangerous. Erecting barriers always invites retaliation, and retaliation is a threat to the one out of every eight American jobs dependent on our exports. At the end of this vicious cycle are higher costs for consumers and lost American jobs, the exact opposite of what we all want.

Let's recognize Japanese and Korean efficiency for what it is. If their products are better made and less expensive, then Americans who buy them benefit by receiving quality and value. And that's what the magic of the marketplace is all about.

The best course for us to take is to take the offensive and create new jobs through trade, lasting jobs tied to the products and technology of tomorrow. I'm confident American products can compete in world markets if they can enter foreign markets as easily as foreign products can enter ours. Currently they can't. Restrictions and tariffs limit U.S. imports into Japan and Korea. In our meetings I've insisted that reciprocity and open markets are vital to our mutual prosperity.

Prime Minister Nakasone and I have agreed on an agenda for progress to reduce and gradually eliminate these barriers. My goal is to help our farmers bring Japanese consumers lower prices for beef, citrus, and other agricultural goods, help our mining, coal, and gas industries export energy resources to a resource-poor Japan, and help our communications industries find new markets for their satellites and other products.

I also encouraged the Prime Minister to open his capital markets to more foreign investment. This will increase demand for Japanese yen, helping its price rise in relation to the dollar, thereby making it easier for the Japanese to buy our products and making our products better able to compete in other markets.

Economic issues are important, but as I noted, freedom and peace exist in an uneasy climate here. We need to remember that Japan and Korea are key allies. They know what living in the shadow of communism is like. It was a Japanese communications center that tracked the cold, calculating words of that Soviet pilot who gunned down the Korean airliner and 269 innocent victims.

Japan contributes about $20,000 for every U.S. soldier stationed here. Both Korea and Japan are committed to help us defend peace, and both are carrying an important share of the military burden. They and we share the same hopes and dreams for our loved ones. We're civilized nations believing in the same virtues of freedom and democracy.

The Williamsburg summit this summer brought together representatives of the Atlantic alliance and Japan in a common strategy for economic growth and military security. It demonstrated that our free world, spread across oceans, can join together to protect peace and freedom.

On this trip, we and our Pacific friends are taking another important step forward together. We've made our partnership stronger, and that means tomorrow can be better for us, our children, and people everywhere.

Until next week, thanks for listening, and God bless you.

Note: The President's address was recorded on November 11 while in Tokyo, Japan, for broadcast at 12:06 p.m. on November 12 in the United States.

Remarks to American Troops at Camp Liberty Bell, Republic of Korea
November 13, 1983

It's an honor for me to be with you. And as you see, this morning, the first thing when I got here, somebody made sure that I would be dressed in what the well-dressed man, American, is wearing, and I'm very proud to have that.

Somebody asked me if I'd be safe up here so close to North Korean troops, and I said, "I'll be with the 2d Infantry Division."

You know, this prompts a story, and I can't help but tell it. Back in World War II days a young draftee was complaining about some of the methods of the Army and the way the Army did things and was asking an old Regular Army sergeant about this. And the Regular Army sergeant said, "Son, look, if you were in charge of a brand new country and you were creating your army for that brand new country and you finally got a division created, what would you call it?" And the kid said, "Well, I guess I'd call it the 1st Division." He said, "Well, in the United States they called the first one the 2d Division and," he said, "when you understand that, you'll understand everything there is to know about the Army."

This has been an experience that I will always remember. There's no better proof of the relationship between strength and freedom than right here on the DMZ in Korea. You are in the frontlines of freedom, and I want each of you to know that I bring you warm greetings from your family and your friends back in the States. And I bring something else, too—the gratitude of 230 million Americans who told me to tell you, "We love you, 2d Infantry Division."

You stand between the free world and the armed forces of a system that is hostile to everything we believe in as Americans. The Communist system to the North is based on hatred and oppression. It brutally attacks every form of human liberty and declares those who worship God to be enemies of the people. Its attack against the leaders of the South Korean Government in Rangoon made clear what kind of enemy you face across the DMZ.

In so many ways the Korean peninsula is symbolic of the larger world. In the South, energy and creativity abound. The positive mood of the people, their enthusiasm and work are propelling this part of Korea into the 21st century and a new era of opportunity and prosperity. To the North, the Communist regime's heavy hand stagnates the economy, suppresses the spirit of the people. Like most Communist regimes, the only thing it can produce well is repression and military might. The only thing deterring the use of that military might is a commitment by the Korean people here in the South and the dedication of brave men and women like yourselves.

You in the 2d Infantry Division and in the other branches of the Armed Forces are our shield against the tyranny and the deprivation that engulfs so much of the world.

After speaking to many Koreans, both in and out of government, I know that they, like our own citizens, are profoundly grateful to you. We fully understand the hardship of your task. We know about the cold, windswept nights that leave you aching from head to foot, I'm sure. We know about having to stay awake and alert on guard duty when you'd rather be at a movie or doing something more pleasant back home. We know about the birthdays and the holidays that you can't spend with your loved ones. And we know about the danger. You're facing a heavily armed, unpredictable enemy with no record—or regard, I should say, for human life.

Let's always remember August 18th, 1976, the day that two Army officers, Major Arthur Bonifas and First Lieutenant Mark Barrett, were murdered across the road from here by ax-wielding North Korean troops. Let me state for the record—and I know you feel this way—nothing like that better happen again.

The self-doubts of the 1970's are giving way in America to a new era of confidence and a sense of purpose. Communism is not the wave of the future and it never was—

freedom is. And it's good to see people beginning to wake up to that fact.

Yes, we, too, have our faults. But we've got a heck of a lot more to be proud of, and we're not afraid to say so. In Lebanon, for example, our marines are peacekeepers in the truest sense of the word. We're there to give some chance to people of that troubled land, a region whose destiny is crucial to our security. More than 230 of our marines—actually, I understand the final count now is—the final identification is 239 of our marines and soldiers gave the last, full measure of devotion in that honorable endeavor. And each of us is indebted to every one of them.

Recently, as you know, we sent our forces to the island of Grenada. Some critics compared that operation with the Soviet invasion of Afghanistan. Well, let me just say there's something seriously wrong with anyone who can't see the difference between 100,000 Soviets trying to force a dictatorship down the throats of the Afghan people and America and eight Caribbean democracies joining to stop Cubans and local Communists from doing the same thing in Grenada.

And let me ask a question of my own. Why are the Soviets being attacked by the people of Afghanistan, while our U.S. and Caribbean forces have been greeted as liberators by the people in Grenada? The answer is: No people in history have ever chosen to be slaves.

We have held interviews with some of the Soviet soldiers who have deserted in Afghanistan. And a significant thing is, in different areas, without their having a chance to communicate with each other or even knowing about each other, one of the prime reasons they have given us—young Russians, men like yourselves, only from Russia—for deserting is they were ordered to kill women and children. And some of them proved that there is still some hope there among the people if the people can ever get a chance to speak.

People everywhere want to be free. That's the difference between Afghanistan and Grenada, and between North Korea and South Korea. Let me just repeat to you what I said to the American people. My paramount concern in Grenada was protecting the lives of our citizens living there. And anyone who questions whether their lives were in jeopardy should read the letters I've received from those students. And on television we saw them dropping down when they stepped off the planes in Carolina, kissing the ground as they arrived on American soil. And just the day before I left on this trip, we had some 400 of them on the South Lawn of the White House to meet some of the men who had come back after freeing them. And that's all you needed was to see their gratitude to your comrades in uniform, and hear their statements of what they felt their plight was, and how they had truly been saved.

And only 10 years ago, youngsters of that age in too many places in our country were throwing rocks at men in uniform. Well, there's a different attitude now. And when you're rotated and you're back home, I think you're going to find out how proud the American people are of you. To call what we did in Grenada an invasion, as many have, is a slur and a misstatement of fact. It was a rescue mission, plain and simple.

We Americans bear a heavy burden. Others must do their part. The people of Korea, the Republic of Korea, are certainly doing their share. Yet, if freedom is to survive, if peace is to be maintained, it will depend on us. Our commitment in Korea exemplifies this heavy responsibility. We've stood shoulder to shoulder with the Korean people for 30 years now. It reflects well on the character of our country that we've been willing to do this in a land so far away from home. And in the end, it is this strength of character that will make the difference between slavery and freedom—but more important, between peace and war.

Thirty-three years ago, Americans gallantly fought and died on the gulleys, in the hills of the Korean peninsula here. One of them was Master Sergeant Stanley Adams and another was Captain Lewis Millet. They both led bayonet charges against vastly superior forces. Another hero was Master Sergeant Ernest Kouma, who exposed himself to enemy fire by manning his machinegun from the back of his tank and in so doing saved his comrades from an onslaught that could have devastated their ranks. A fourth was Lieutenant Colonel John Page, one of the heroes of the Chosin Reservoir, whose ingenuity and bravery saved so many.

And all of these were Congressional Medal of Honor recipients. Yet, we know that all who fought here were heroes and deserve our respect. They did their duty, and by doing so they protected not only Korea but a whole generation of Americans.

By the way, one of the children of a Medal of Honor recipient I just mentioned, Captain Lewis Millet, sent me a telegram a few days ago in support of the Grenada rescue mission.

Well, today you carry on an honorable tradition of those who went before you. And I know that you're keeping faith with them and with their families and friends. Americans are now standing tall and firm. No terrorist should question our resolve, and no tyrant should doubt our courage. Your division motto is "Fit to fight, second to none." Well, you've lived up to that motto, and we're proud of you for it. And with your courage and dedication as an example, we're going to make as certain as we can that the United States remains second to none.

I have never been as proud as I am right

now and from what I've seen here. And I know that in spite of what I said about our people back home, I'm not sure that very many of them realize that you aren't just sitting here doing some kind of garrison duty. And I'm going to do everything I can to make sure that the folks back home know what you really are doing.

So, soldiers of the 2d Infantry Division, God bless you, and God bless America. Thank you.

Note: The President spoke at 12:14 p.m. in the mortar bunker area of the camp, which is located near the DMZ (demilitarized zone) dividing the Republic of Korea and the Democratic People's Republic of Korea.

Earlier in the day, the President attended a worship service at the camp. He then went to Guard Post Collier in the DMZ for a tour and a briefing.

Following his remarks at the camp, the President joined troops of the 2d Infantry Division for lunch in the Mess Hall. He then went by helicopter to the Republic of Korea Army 1st Corps headquarters. After viewing a parade and tae kwon do drill, the President returned to the residence of Richard L. Walker, U.S. Ambassador to the Republic of Korea, where he stayed during his visit. The Ambassador's residence is located is Seoul.

Joint Statement Following Meetings With President Chun Doo Hwan of the Republic of Korea
November 14, 1983

1. At the invitation of President Chun Doo Hwan, the President of the United States and Mrs. Ronald W. Reagan paid a state visit to the Republic of Korea from November 12 to 14, 1983. The two Presidents met at the Blue House on November 12 and again on November 13 for discussions of both bilateral and world affairs. The talks were held in a most cordial and open atmosphere.

President Reagan addressed the National Assembly, visited field installations of both the Korean and the United States Armed

Forces, and also met with senior Korean officials, other Korean citizens, and a group of American businessmen.

2. President Chun expressed his appreciation to President Reagan for America's steadfast support in the wake of the tragedies which the people of Korea have endured so recently: the September 1 Soviet attack on a Korean civil airliner, and the October 9 North Korean terrorist attack in Burma which tragically claimed the lives of 17 innocent Koreans, among them many of the nation's most important leaders in eco-

nomics, diplomacy, and politics.

Both Presidents noted the thorough and conclusive investigation by the Government of Burma of the Rangoon bomb atrocity, which has produced unequivocal evidence that the North Korean regime perpetrated this deliberate act of state terrorism. They agreed that such acts cannot be tolerated, and called for effective international sanctions against North Korea. President Reagan affirmed his admiration for the resolution and courage of the Korean people and their leaders in the face of these barbaric acts.

President Chun expressed his condolences to President Reagan and the American people on the tragic loss of life caused by the October 23 attack on the United States Marine Barracks in Beirut. President Chun and President Reagan joined in declaring the unswerving opposition of the Korean and American peoples to such acts of terrorism, and pledged continued efforts to remove the scourge of terrorism from the earth.

3. The two Heads of State exchanged views on a variety of international issues of mutual concern. President Reagan outlined United States determination to strengthen the defenses of the United States and its allies around the world, to bring about a reduction of tensions in volatile regions such as the Middle East, and to reach an agreement with the Soviet Union to reduce the global deployment of strategic weapons.

President Chun explained in detail the overall security situation on the Korean peninsula with particular reference to the continuing threat from North Korea, reflected in its military buildup and aggravated by its domestic problems.

Both Presidents reaffirmed the importance of maintaining deterrence and stability on the Korean peninsula, thereby ensuring peace there and in Northeast Asia, a region of critical strategic significance.

President Reagan stated that the United States would continue to fulfill its role and responsibilities as a Pacific power, dedicated to maintaining peace and stability in the region. President Chun avowed his full support for these efforts.

4. In particular, President Reagan, noting that the security of the Republic of Korea is pivotal to the peace and stability of North-

east Asia and in turn, vital to the security of the United States, reaffirmed the continuing strong commitment of the United States to the security of the Republic of Korea. The two Presidents pledged to uphold the obligations embodied in the Republic of Korea-United States Mutual Defense Treaty signed in 1953, noting the success of that alliance in deterring aggression for more than thirty years.

President Reagan stressed that the United States would continue to maintain United States forces in Korea and to strengthen their capabilities. President Chun reaffirmed his support for the presence in Korea of American military forces as part of the United Nations and Combined Forces Commands.

President Reagan noted that Korea spends six percent of its GNP on defense and further noted the efforts of the Republic of Korea to modernize and upgrade its defense capabilities. The two Presidents concurred that this program is essential if peace is to be maintained. President Reagan reconfirmed that the United States will continue to make available the weapons systems and technology necessary to enhance the strength of Korea's armed forces.

5. President Chun explained the Korean government's continuing efforts for the resumption of dialogue between South and North Korea and its policy for peaceful reunification with a view to easing tensions on the Korean peninsula, and achieving the Korean people's long-cherished aspiration for peaceful reunification. Expressing support of the United States for the sincere and patient efforts of the Republic of Korea, President Reagan especially noted President Chun's comprehensive Proposal for Democratic Reunification through National Reconciliation put forth on January 22, 1982.

President Reagan reconfirmed that the United States would not undertake talks with North Korea without full and equal participation of the Republic of Korea. The two Presidents reaffirmed that any unilateral steps toward North Korea which are not reciprocated toward the Republic of Korea by North Korea's principal allies would not be conducive to promoting stability or peace in the area.

6. President Reagan expressed his admiration and support for the expanding and increasingly active international diplomacy of the Republic of Korea, and took note of the determination of the Republic of Korea to pursue an open door policy of dialogue with all nations.

The two Presidents noted the significance of their respective nation's role as the hosts to important global gatherings and events, including the Los Angeles Olympics of 1984 and the Seoul Olympics of 1988. Both countries will abide by their commitments to admit representatives of all nations to participate in these international events.

7. Recognizing the growing importance of the Asia-Pacific region and also the growing sense of community among the Pacific rim countries, the two Presidents agreed that frequent exchanges at all levels among the nations of the Pacific are necessary to enhance regional cohesion. They also agreed that multilateral relations among the countries in the region should be further strengthened in the fields of trade, finance, science, technology, culture, and tourism.

8. The two Presidents expressed their belief that the Republic of Korea should be accepted in the United Nations pursuant to the principle of universality of the U.N. and that the entry of the Republic of Korea to the U.N. would contribute both to the reduction of tensions on the Korean peninsula and the maintenance of international peace. President Reagan promised continuing support for the entry of the Republic of Korea into the U.N.

9. The two Presidents affirmed the importance of defending and strengthening freedom and the institutions that serve freedom, openness, and political stability.

10. President Chun and President Reagan exchanged views on a range of economic issues. They noted the importance of ensuring that global economic recovery not be hindered by reversion to protectionism. In particular, President Reagan welcomed the trade liberalization measures being undertaken and planned by the Korean government, despite its continuing deficit in foreign trade and the global trend of protectionism. Both Presidents agreed that such steps are an example of the positive actions all trading nations must take to defend the world trade system against protectionist attacks and recognized an urgent need for concerted international efforts in this direction.

Both Presidents noted with satisfaction the continued expansion of bilateral trade, which totaled over $11 billion in 1982, making the Republic of Korea one of the United States' most important trading partners and fifth largest market for United States agricultural products, and the United States the Republic of Korea's largest trading partner in exports as well as imports. They agreed that this continued growth of bilateral trade attests to the vitality of U.S.-Korean economic relations.

President Chun also expressed his appreciation for President Reagan's strong commitment to free trade and hoped that the Republic of Korea's major export commodities will be given greater access to the United States market with the continuation of the Republic of Korea's eligibility for GSP benefits on a non-discriminatory basis. President Reagan took note of President Chun's views on these issues. In this regard, both Presidents recognized the necessity of coordinated actions by their respective governments to reduce various tariff and non-tariff barriers.

11. President Chun explained the recent efforts by the Korean government to create a more favorable environment for foreign investment in the Republic of Korea and invited the United States to take advantage of such improved opportunities. Both Presidents noted that a hospitable climate for foreign investors in both countries will continue to contribute to the flow of technology and to an expansion of employment opportunities in the Republic of Korea and the United States. Both Presidents also noted that the continued participation of American firms in the Republic of Korea's major development projects by providing competitively-priced and high-quality goods and services is another indication of the strong and cooperative economic ties that link the Republic of Korea and the United States.

12. President Chun and President Reagan discussed prospects for further broadening

cooperation in the fields of technology and energy. They agreed to further promote programs for scientific and technological cooperation.

President Reagan assured President Chun that the United States will remain a reliable supplier of energy resources and energy technology, and in particular, that the United States will seek to assist the Republic of Korea to obtain stable energy supplies in the event of a security emergency. In this regard, President Reagan noted positively the Korean government's efforts to build up energy reserves for economic emergencies. President Chun expressed his appreciation for the United States' pledge, and the Republic of Korea's interest in the purchase and development of energy resources in the United States.

13. President Chun and President Reagan took note of the strong and myriad bonds of friendship and cooperation that have linked the United States and the Republic of Korea in the post-war era, and judged those ties to be in excellent condition. As one reflection of the expanding scope and importance of those relationships, President Reagan informed President Chun of the intention of the United States to establish in the near future a consulate in Pusan, Korea's second greatest city and a focal point of the U.S.-Korean economic intercourse. President Chun welcomed that decision.

President Chun and President Reagan pledged to carry forward the full range of security, political, economic, scientific and cultural meetings and consultations on our joint agenda, in order to maintain and deepen our already excellent relations in those diverse fields.

14. The two Presidents underscored the necessity for the promotion of mutual understanding and exchanges between the Korean and American peoples, and agreed to work toward expanded cultural and educational exchanges. The two Presidents expressed their satisfaction with the promotion of American studies in the Republic of Korea as well as of Korean studies in the United States.

15. President and Mrs. Reagan expressed their deep appreciation to President and Mrs. Chun for the warm welcome they received in the Republic of Korea, and their heartfelt thanks to the people of the Republic of Korea for the hospitality, graciousness and good will they had been shown.

The two Presidents agreed that exchanges of visits between the two Presidents have contributed to the further development of the existing friendly relations between the two countries. In that context, President Reagan asked President Chun to visit Washington again at a mutually convenient time, and President Chun accepted that invitation with appreciation.

Remarks Upon Returning From the Trip to Japan and the Republic of Korea
November 14, 1983

Thank you all for coming out to greet us, and thank you for minding the store while we were away. I know I speak for Nancy and for everyone of our party when I say it's great to be home.

We won't keep you long, but I just want to tell you how proud I am of everyone who helped make this trip a great success. We traveled nearly 16,000 miles to visit two countries that are vital to us and to our future. Japan and Korea have very different roots from our own, but each of us is a Pacific nation, and we're bound together by a great treasure of shared values—our love of freedom and democracy, the drive, determination, and skill of our people, and our optimism for the future.

Mike Mansfield, our very wise Ambassador in Tokyo, likes to say, "The next century will be the century of the Pacific." And he's right. The East Asian and Pacific region is growing faster than any other region in the world. Japan has become our largest overseas trading partner, and Korea ranks among our top 10 worldwide. We're building a future together. This means we shoulder great responsibilities, but we also have tremendous opportunities. And working as partners to make tomorrow better and more secure is what this trip is all about.

Well, I'm pleased to report some good news. America's partnerships are stronger, and prospects for a more secure peace and prosperity are better today than a week ago.

In Japan we established an agenda for progress so we can solve problems and create jobs, security, and safety for our families and for theirs. That agenda ranges from efforts to lower trade barriers to assisting recovery of the U.S. auto industry, to expanding our energy trade, promoting greater investment in capital markets, cooperating in defense technology, encouraging exports and imports of high technology, coordinating our foreign assistance efforts, and expanding our cultural programs.

We also agreed on an approach to correct the imbalance between the Japanese yen and the American dollar. Our currencies should reflect the political stability and economic strength that our two countries enjoy. In Japan's case this will mean a stronger yen, which means that American products will compete more effectively in world markets.

Because of the breadth and complexity of these issues, I intend to establish a management group, under the leadership of the Vice President, to assure essential followup action. If each side is willing to give a little, then all of us will gain a lot.

Diplomacy is important. Strengthening the spirit of friendship is the best way to solve problems and create lasting partnerships. And I can't tell you how proud I was to have the historic opportunity to address the Japanese Diet and all the people of Japan. I told them what we Americans feel in our hearts—that we, like they, are people of peace, that we deeply desire a nuclear arms reduction agreement, and that we will never walk away from the negotiating table.

Those who disagree with the United States get plenty of publicity. But one thing becomes more plain to me each time I travel: Across the globe, America is looked to as a friend and as a leader in preserving peace and freedom. This was certainly true in Japan and Korea.

I was at one of the meetings in Korea, and I just assumed that Nancy was out sightseeing or probably even shopping for souvenirs. And knowing Nancy as well as I do, I wasn't surprised when I came home and found that she had two little Korean friends, Lee Kil Woo and Ahn Ji Sook. They have come over to the States where they're going to be treated at St. Francis Hospital in Roslyn, New York. And Nancy met them by way of a very remarkable woman, Harriet Hodges, who has succeeded in bringing some 600 children like this, who needed medical attention that could only be given here in this country, to bring them to the United States.

So, they've had their first Air Force ride—or airplane ride, and they've had their first helicopter ride, and they've been very active for some 16 or 17 hours. [*Laughter*]

I wish you could have been with us in Korea—a country scarred by the recent bombing in Rangoon and the Korean airliner tragedy. The South Koreans live under the shadow of Communist aggression. They understand the value of freedom, and they're paying the price to defend it. You know, sometimes you hear events are more symbolism than substance. Well, there's more than symbolism when over a million Koreans line the streets to wave and cheer Americans and to thank America for helping keep them free.

There's more than symbolism in the threat to the people of Seoul, who live within range of North Korean artillery just some 30 kilometers away. And there's more than symbolism in the danger to our American soldiers helping to guard the border of the DMZ, often in weather that leaves them freezing from their heads to their toes.

I have just been looking forward to telling the American people we've had such a wrong impression. I think most of us just sort of pictured our forces over there as kind of garrison troops, just waiting on hand that anything should happen. That's not true. They are combat ready, and they are the farthest advanced toward a potential enemy of any American forces in the world.

I reaffirmed to the Korean people America's commitment to their peace and freedom and encouraged them to develop further their democracy. And I must tell you that one of the most unforgettable experiences of my life was the time I spent Sunday afternoon and morning with our brave troops at the DMZ.

If you could have been with me, you would have been at the worship service Sunday morning that we had with our soldiers in an open field, less than a mile from one of the most tyrannical regimes on Earth. And there, singing, was a choir of little girls, not much bigger than this one, all orphans from an orphanage that is maintained and supported by our GI's. And they have done this with several others there. The young men and women of the 2d Infantry Division maintain those institutions.

And to hear these children closing the service, singing "America, the Beautiful" in our language, was a spiritual experience. And you would have heard, if you'd been at that service, their chaplain telling us that we were standing on the edge of freedom. Being there teaches us that freedom is never free, nor can it be purchased in one installment. We can only struggle to keep it, pass it on to the next generation, and hope they'll preserve it for their children and their children's children.

And that's the risk that our soldiers have accepted day in and day out for more than 30 years. As that chaplain reminded us, "Greater love hath no man than to lay down his life for his friends." And this they have done at the DMZ. I was honored to meet our men, and I promised them that I would tell the American people how crucial their jobs are, not just to the people of Korea but to people everywhere who love freedom. So much of what we take for granted each day we owe to these heroes and others like them around the world. They make us so proud to be Americans.

Coming home from Korea and Japan, all of us bring with us renewed energy and renewed commitment to our fundamental goals, building a new era of peace and prosperity—just as soon as we readjust our clocks. [*Laughter*]

God bless you, and God bless this wonderful country. Thank you.

Note: The President spoke at 12:02 p.m. on the South Lawn of the White House to administration officials and members of the White House staff.

Nomination of Deane Roesch Hinton To Be United States Ambassador to Pakistan
November 14, 1983

The President today announced his intention to nominate Deane Roesch Hinton, of Illinois, a career member of the Senior Foreign Service, Class of Career Minister, to be Ambassador to the Islamic Republic of Pakistan. He would succeed Ronald I. Spiers.

Mr. Hinton entered the Foreign Service in 1946 as political officer in Damascus. From 1949 to 1951, he was principal officer in Mombasa. He attended economic studies at Fletcher School of Law and Diplomacy and Harvard University from 1951 to 1952. In 1955–1958 he was financial officer in Paris. In the Department he was intelligence research officer in the Bureau of Intelligence and Research from 1955 to 1958. In 1958–1961 he was chief of the overseas development and finance section in Brussels/USEC. He attended the National War College in 1961–1962. In the Department he was chief of the commodity programming division in the Bureau of Economic Affairs (1962–1963) and Director of the Office of Atlantic Political-Economic Affairs in the Bureau of European Affairs (1963–1967). In 1967–1969 he was Director of the

USAID Mission and counselor for economic affairs in Guatemala, and in Santiago in 1969–1971. He served at the White House as Assistant Executive Director, then Deputy Executive Director, of the Council on International Economic Policy in 1971–1974. He was Ambassador to the Republic of Zaire (1974–1975) and senior adviser to the Under Secretary of State for Economic Affairs in the Department (1975–1976). In 1976–1979 he was United States Representative to the European Communities with rank and status of Ambassador, Brussels, and Assistant Secretary of State for Economic and Business Affairs in the Department in 1979–1981. In 1981–1983 he was Ambassador to El Salvador.

Mr. Hinton graduated from the University of Chicago (A.B., 1943). He served in the United States Army in 1943–1945 as second lieutenant. His foreign languages are French and Spanish. He was born March 12, 1923, in Ft. Missoula, Mont.

Nomination of Harold K. Phillips To Be a Member of the Board of Directors of the Inter-American Foundation, and Designation as Vice Chairman
November 14, 1983

The President today announced his intention to nominate Harold K. Phillips to be a member of the Board of Directors of the Inter-American Foundation for a term expiring September 20, 1988. He would succeed Alberto Ibargüen. Upon Mr. Phillips' confirmation, the President intends to designate him Vice Chairman.

Mr. Phillips is currently chairman of the board of Joe Phillips Dodge and president of Hal Phillips Pontiac. He also is an instructor at the Pepperdine University School of Business.

Mr. Phillips graduated from the University of Redlands (B.S., 1963) and Harvard University School of Business Administration (M.B.A., 1967). He resides in Burbank, Calif., and was born September 1, 1940, in Glendale, Calif.

Nomination of William Evans To Be a Member of the Marine Mammal Commission, and Designation as Chairman
November 15, 1983

The President today announced his intention to nominate William Evans to be a member of the Marine Mammal Commission for a term expiring May 13, 1985. He would succeed James C. Nofziger. The President also intends to designate him Chairman.

Mr. Evans is currently a biologist and executive director at Hubbs/Sea World Research Institute in San Diego, Calif. Previously he was head of the bioanalysis group, underseas sciences department, at the Naval Ocean Systems Center. Mr. Evans is the author of more than 60 published technical papers and has coauthored several books. He holds three patents for marine systems, including a device for tagging and tracking marine animals.

Mr. Evans graduated from Ohio State (M.S., 1954) and UCLA (Ph. D., 1975). He is married, has two children, and resides in Escondido, Calif. He was born October 11, 1930, in Elkhart, Ind.

Nomination of Francis Carter Coleman To Be a Member of the Board of Regents of the Uniformed Services University of the Health Sciences
November 15, 1983

The President today announced his intention to nominate Francis Carter Coleman to be a member of the Board of Regents of the Uniformed Services University of the Health Sciences, Department of Defense, for the term expiring May 1, 1989. This is a reappointment.

Dr. Coleman is currently a consultant in pathology and laboratory management in Tampa, Fla. Previously he was vice president and medical director of Town and Country Hospital (1980).

Dr. Coleman graduated from Mississippi College (B.A., 1935) and Tulane University School of Medicine (M.D., 1941). He is married, has four children, and resides in Tampa. He was born May 14, 1915, in Jackson, Miss.

Accordance of the Personal Rank of Ambassador to Otto J. Reich While Serving as Coordinator for Public Diplomacy for Latin America and the Caribbean
November 15, 1983

The President has accorded the personal rank of Ambassador to Otto J. Reich, of Virginia, while serving as Coordinator for Public Diplomacy for Latin America and the Caribbean.

Mr. Reich served in the United States Army in 1966–1969 as first lieutenant. In 1970–1971 he was staff assistant to Congressman W. R. Hull, Jr., of the United States House of Representatives. He was research fellow at the Center for Strategic and International Studies in 1971–1972, and vice president for international development at Cormorant Enterprises in Miami, Fla., in 1972–1973. He was international representative at the Florida Department of Commerce in Coral Gables, Fla. (1973– 1975), and community development coordinator of the city of Miami (1975–1976). In 1976–1981 he was director of Washington operations at the Council of the Americas in Washington, D.C. He was Assistant Administrator for Latin America and the Caribbean at the Agency for International Development in 1982–1983. Since 1983 he has been Coordinator for Public Diplomacy for Latin America and the Caribbean, Department of State.

Mr. Reich graduated from the University of North Carolina (B.A., 1966) and Georgetown University (M.A., 1973). His foreign language is Spanish. He was born October 16, 1945, in Havana, Cuba, and became a naturalized United States citizen in 1966.

Letter Accepting the Resignation of Kenneth M. Duberstein as Assistant to the President for Legislative Affairs
November 15, 1983

Dear Ken:

It is with great reluctance and regret that I accept your resignation as Assistant to the President for Legislative Affairs, effective December 15, 1983.

Since the transition period, you have guided our relations, first with the House of Representatives and then during the past two years with the Senate as well. Your service to our country and to me has consistently been at an uncommon level of excellence.

When we came into office in January 1981, many said the promises made during the campaign could not be achieved, the Congress would not go along, the votes would not be there. You led the way toward building the coalition in the House which resulted in our initial victories on Gramm-Latta I and II and the 1981 tax cut bill. These significant victories signaled to all the fundamental change in direction we had promised would not be forestalled.

Your leadership in the management of relations with the Congress has enabled us to continue on the path to sustained economic growth and a renewed national security. The votes on the Hill have become more difficult since the honeymoon days but we have persevered to victory upon victory. In large measure, these successes have been due to your understanding of the Hill, your personal associations with so many Senators, Members, and staff, your ability at developing legislative strategy, and your tireless devotion to ensuring sound public policy. In every sense, you are a real pro.

Within the White House and the Administration, we have all benefited from your wise counsel, cheerful teamwork and commitment to achieving the results we seek. Your way with people is a rare and precious resource.

The fundamental importance you have placed on a sound working relationship with the Congress has become a hallmark of our Administration. As a result, we have been able to build broad bipartisan coalitions in the House and Senate to enact the Social Security Reform Act, the MX-Peacekeeper, the Caribbean Basin Initiative, the Tax Equity and Fairness Reform Act and the War Powers in Lebanon Resolution.

As you prepare to return to private life, Ken, I want to salute you for a job exceedingly well done. You and your lovely bride, Sydney, have sacrificed greatly in loyal service to our country and to me. I know there will be many times when I will ask for your counsel and assistance.

Nancy and I send our best wishes for every future happiness and success.

Sincerely,

RON

[The Honorable Kenneth M. Duberstein, Assistant to the President for Legislative Affairs, The White House, Washington, D.C. 20500]

Dear Mr. President:

After considerable thought, I have decided to resign my position and return to the private sector shortly after the end of this session of the 98th Congress. It has been an honor and a privilege to serve as Assistant to the President for Legislative Affairs during the past two years and, prior to that, as Deputy Assistant to the President in charge of the House of Representatives. But it is time to renew the family life I have forgone and repair the financial security that has been sacrificed.

Not too many years ago, political scientists, pols, pundits and other serious students of the Washington scene were observing that our American system of government didn't seem to be working. There appeared to be gridlock, inertia, an inability to address, let alone solve, the major problems confronting our nation. Some believed our institutions of government were outdated, producing deadlock not decision in this modern, complex era. They are not saying this anymore.

In three short years, you have demonstrated that our system of government does work and that the fundamental change in direction you promised in the 1980 campaign could be set in motion. Working in harmony with the Congress, you have led the way to economic recovery and a restored national security. I am proud to have been part of that effort.

Beginning with the transition period after your election, you have built a sound, strong and superb working relationship with the Congress. The dividends from the priority you have placed each day on that relationship are not just the scores of legislative victories you have achieved. They are the results you promised: lower interest rates, declining inflation, more employment, less excessive and unnecessary regulation, reduced tax rates for individuals and businesses, a slower rate of growth of federal spending, a stronger national defense here at home and a renewed respect for our nation abroad.

From the early legislative successes of Gramm-Latta I and II and the 1981 tax cut bill to this year's Social Security Reform Act, the Caribbean Basin Initiative, the MX-Peacekeeper votes and the War Powers in Lebanon Resolution, you have benefitted greatly from outstanding teamwork in the Senate under the leadership of Majority Leader Howard Baker and in the House under Republican Leader Bob Michel. Their uncommon loyalty, effectiveness, leadership and willingness to go the extra mile on your behalf made the crucial difference on so many legislative initiatives. Your good relationship with Speaker O'Neill—even before 6:00 p.m.—has enabled you to reach out and work for the common good with all Members during critical times.

Much remains to be done. I am hopeful you will seek re-election and am confident you will be re-elected with a renewed mandate, continued Republican control of the Senate and increased support in the House.

Thank you for the confidence you have placed in me and for the opportunity to serve you and the country during the past three years. I look forward to working vigorously for your re-election and hope you will call on me for other assignments.

With every good wish to you and Nancy.
Sincerely,

KEN

[The President, The White House, Washington, D.C. 20500]

Appointment of M. B. Oglesby, Jr., as Assistant to the President for Legislative Affairs
November 15, 1983

The President today announced his intention to appoint M. B. Oglesby, Jr., to be Assistant to the President for Legislative Affairs, effective December 15, 1983. He would succeed Kenneth M. Duberstein.

Mr. Oglesby is currently serving as Deputy Assistant to the President for Legislative Affairs. In his new position, he will serve as the President's chief liaison with the United States Congress.

Previously he served as minority staff associate for the House Energy and Commerce Committee, dealing principally with railroad, environmental, and commerce-related legislation. Mr. Oglesby also served as deputy and acting director of the State of Illinois Washington office and as executive assistant to Congressman Edward Madigan (R-Ill.). Prior to coming to Washington, he served in Illinois State government as an assistant to Gov. Richard Ogilvie and as executive assistant to the speaker of the house. Mr. Oglesby also spent 3½ years in management positions with Illinois Bell Telephone Co.

He attended the University of Illinois in Champaign. He is married, resides in Bethesda, Md., and was born October 1, 1942, in Flora, Ill.

Nomination of Mary A. Grigsby To Be a Member of the Federal Home Loan Bank Board
November 15, 1983

The President today announced his intention to nominate Mary A. Grigsby to be a member of the Federal Home Loan Bank Board for the remainder of the term expiring June 30, 1986. She would succeed James Jay Jackson.

Since June of this year, Mrs. Grigsby has been serving as vice chairman of United Savings of Texas. Previously she was with Houston First American Savings as director and president in 1971–1980; administrative vice president and executive vice president in 1967–1971; secretary in 1963–1967; loan department officer in 1958–1963; in the legal department in 1946–1958 and the accounting department in 1941–1946.

She graduated from the University of Texas (M.B.A.). She is married, has one child, and resides in Houston, Tex. She was born July 25, 1916, in Elyria, Ohio.

Remarks by Telephone to the Annual Conference of the Republican Governors Association in Chicago, Illinois
November 15, 1983

The President. Hello.

Governor Atiyeh. Good morning, Mr. President.

The President. Hi, Vic, how are you?

Governor Atiyeh. I'm not too shoddy at all.

The President. Well, listen, I appreciate this opportunity to talk at least a minute or two with all of you during the Republican Governors Association annual conference there. And I'd like to thank Bob Orr on the fine job that he's done as chairman for the past year and, Vic, to congratulate you as the incoming chairman. I look forward to continuing a close, productive working relationship that I've enjoyed with the Republican Governors.

I understand that the theme for this year's conference is "Creative Solutions to State Problems." Well, having been one of you, I can honestly say that I have firsthand knowledge of the difficult problems you face as Governors, and, working together, I know that we can find the solutions.

Governor Atiyeh. Mr. President, we appreciate that, and we have full knowledge of, of course, your Governorship and especially so as chairman, in 1968, of this association. It's kind of nice to know that you're in the company with someone as illustrious as you are.

We've passed some resolutions that you may have some interest in—as a matter of fact, I know you will—resolutions that relate to economic recovery. We applauded your efforts in foreign policy and appreciate very much the clear strength that you've shown in the variety of instances occurring around the Nation, and we certainly are appreciative of that.

You'll be glad to know—at least, I'm sure you will—that we reaffirmed the concept of a line-item veto power for the President of the United States.

The President. Well, bless you.

Governor Atiyeh. You're welcome. We thought it was kind of nice ourselves as Governors. Picking up on the theme of your interest in education, here again we recognize, as Governors, how important that is within our own States as well as nationally, and some sense the frustration that Congress hasn't acted on your crime control package, and we urge them to move forward on that issue.

The President. Well, I appreciate that more than I can say. We really need that. And that's a——

Governor Atiyeh. It's really a matter of

you picking those elements, Mr. President, that are important to us as Americans. And we as Governors feel very much the same, that it is important that those items move forward.

I want you to know that we had a great meeting today. I want to thank you for the good work of Frank Fahrenkopf as our national chairman, doing an outstanding job, and we're very, very thankful for the fact that he's there in Washington guiding the national party.

Ed Rollins spoke to us in the morning breakfast, and there were many questions asked, which I indicated today—indicated a very keen, very keen interest on the part of the Governors here to make sure that your reelection took place. And you can be assured of my personal support and, as well as I know of, my fellow Governors.

The President. Well, I am most grateful to all of you, and, regarding the resolutions you've passed, keeping this recovery strong, of course, is going to take control of Federal spending. And I'm very pleased to hear about that resolution. I hope you'll make sure your State delegations in Congress know about it.

On the line-item veto, I can't agree more strongly. I believe that the President of the United States should have line-item authority just as most Governors in this country do. I know what it did for me when I was a Governor. And we stop to think that in 1974 back here the Congress passed what they thought was a program to straighten out and get control of the budgeting proc-

ess. And from 1974 until the beginning of 1982, the result of that has been $560 billion in additional national debt.

I'm particularly pleased also with your resolution on education. The initiative for raising standards and improving education generally has got to come from you and from the State level and the local communities, and I applaud your leadership.

You might be interested to know that I'm meeting with Members of Congress today on tuition tax credits. Getting that passed is an important step that we can take at the Federal level to improve education policy for the Nation.

Well, I know you've got a lot of work to do, and I don't think I should take up any more of your time. So, again, I just want to thank you for all you're doing. I look forward to working with you in the days ahead, and I'll say goodby now, and God bless all of you.

Governor Atiyeh. Mr. President, let me just finally end with one other thought, because I know you have a great helpmate. I want you to know that I personally thank First Lady Nancy for her efforts in that program on drug and alcohol abuse, called "Chemical People." You make a great team, and we're proud of you. And we thank you very much for calling us.

The President. Well, thank you. I'll tell her, and she'll be very proud and happy to hear that. Thank you. Goodby.

Note: The President spoke at 12:45 p.m. from the Oval Office at the White House.

Remarks to Reporters During a Meeting With Republican Senators on Tuition Tax Credit Legislation
November 15, 1983

The President. These gentlemen and I have been meeting here on the subject of tuition tax credit, which, I believe, comes before you tomorrow in the Senate. And the opposition to it that has presented a case of somehow that this threatens public education in any way—it does not.

It does not in any way take away from

the financial support of public education, but it recognizes the equity in making a provision for people who do not use the public school system, who send their children to parochial or independent schools for whatever reason, and support fully, as fully as anyone else, the public school system financially, through their taxes and, at the same time, pay a tuition for their children going to these independent schools. And this proposal is merely one that up to a certain amount allows a tax credit for a portion of their tuition to in some way balance the fact that they are supporting the two school systems.

We believe, in addition to this, the independent, the parochial schools in this country, have offered a choice for the American people, and at the same time, they have helped, through their very presence, keep up the quality of education in the schools through simple competition.

And we think it's a most important issue and has been too long in the doing. And it's time that this break was given to those parents, a simple tax equity.

Q. Will it pass?

The President. What?

Q. You have hopes that it will pass?

Senator Dole. We're going to do our best.

Deputy Press Secretary Speakes. Thank you.

The President. We're going to do our best.

Note: The President spoke at 2:42 p.m. in the Cabinet Room at the White House.

Letter to the Presidium of the Supreme Soviet of the U.S.S.R. on the 50th Anniversary of Diplomatic Relations Between the United States and the Soviet Union
November 16, 1983

To: The Presidium of the USSR Supreme Soviet

Fifty years have passed since diplomatic relations were established between our countries. As we note this anniversary, I hope that we can recommit ourselves to working constructively on the problems before us.

The United States has no higher aim nor more urgent goal than achieving and preserving world peace and security.

Let us seek ways, despite the differences in our governments, philosophies and values, to cooperate in reducing international tensions and creating a safer world.

If we can work together to this end, we shall be fulfilling the promise of November 16, 1933, when formal ties between our countries began.

/S/ RONALD REAGAN

Mr. President:

November 16th will mark 50 years from the moment of the establishment of diplomatic relations between the Union of Soviet Socialist Republics and the United States of America. This is a major landmark in relations between our two states.

In establishing diplomatic relations, both sides proceeded from a recognition of the fundamental difference in their socio-economic systems, but at the same time from a recognition that this difference is not an obstacle to normal interstate relations.

This principle is of lasting significance. The Soviet state, unfailingly devoted to the cause of peace among peoples and to the development of equitable, mutually advantageous relations, is to this day firmly guided by this principle in its relations with the USA.

We assume that there is a basis in our countries for proper appreciation of the significance of such a date as the 50th anniversary of the establishment of diplomatic relations.

PRESIDIUM OF THE SUPREME
SOVIET OF THE USSR

Moscow

Note: As printed above, this item follows the text of the letters released by the Office of the Press Secretary.

Nomination of Stephanie Lee-Miller To Be an Assistant Secretary of Health and Human Services
November 16, 1983

The President today announced his intention to nominate Stephanie Lee-Miller to be an Assistant Secretary of Health and Human Services (Public Affairs). She would succeed Pamela Needham Bailey.

Since 1981 she has been serving as Special Assistant for Public Affairs at the Department of Commerce. Previously she was owner and partner of Contact California, a public relations company; administrative director of the NAACP Legal Defense and Educational Fund; and public affairs community programs director for the Coro Foundation in 1971–1977.

She graduated from California State University (B.A., 1971) and Occidental College (M.A., 1975). She was born March 7, 1950.

Nomination of Maurice Lee Barksdale To Be an Assistant Secretary of Housing and Urban Development
November 16, 1983

The President today announced his intention to nominate Maurice Lee Barksdale to be an Assistant Secretary of Housing and Urban Development (Housing—Federal Housing Commissioner). He would succeed Philip Abrams.

Since 1982 Mr. Barksdale has been Deputy Assistant Secretary of Multifamily Housing Programs at the Department of Housing and Urban Development. Previously he was president of HMB Management Co. in 1975–1982; regional vice president of Essex and Union Mortgage Co.; vice president, Citizens Trust Bank, in 1974–1975; and senior vice president for urban affairs and member, Sey and Co., Inc., in 1971–1974.

He graduated from the University of Texas (B.A.) and is a candidate for a M.L.A. at Texas Christian University. He is married, has three children, and resides in Washington, D.C. He was born January 7, 1939.

Nomination of John G. Keane To Be Director of the Bureau of the Census
November 16, 1983

The President today announced his intention to nominate John G. Keane to be Director of the Census, Department of Commerce. He would succeed Bruce Chapman.

Since 1972 Mr. Keane has been president of Managing Change, Inc., in Barrington, Ill. Previously he was vice president of resource and planning of J. Walter Thompson in Chicago, Ill., in 1968–1972; and vice president, account supervisor, and director of research services of North Advertising, Inc., in Chicago, Ill., in 1966–1968.

He graduated from Syracuse University (A.B., 1952), the University of Notre Dame (B.S.C., 1955), Indiana University (M.B.A., 1956), and the University of Pittsburgh (Ph. D., 1965). He is married, has three children, and resides in Barrington, Ill. He was born July 3, 1930, in Fort Wayne, Ind.

Nomination of James G. Stearns To Be a Director of the Securities Investor Protection Corporation, and Designation as Chairman
November 16, 1983

The President today announced his intention to nominate James G. Stearns to be a Director of the Securities Investor Protection Corporation for a term expiring December 31, 1985. This is a reappointment. The President also intends to redesignate him Chairman.

He has been serving as Chairman of the Securities Investor Protection Corporation since 1982. Previously he was Director of the Office of Alcohol Fuels, Department of Energy, in 1981; a self-employed rancher in 1975–1981; secretary of agriculture and services for the State of California in 1972–1975; and director of conservation for the State of California in 1967–1972.

Mr. Stearns attended Oregon State College. He is married, has three children, and resides in Arlington, Va. He was born January 29, 1922, in Lapine, Oreg.

Message to the Senate Transmitting the United States-Denmark Convention on Taxation and Fiscal Evasion
November 16, 1983

To the Senate of the United States:

I transmit herewith for Senate advice and consent to ratification, the Protocol amending the Convention between the Government of the United States of America and the Government of the Kingdom of Denmark for the Avoidance of Double Taxation and the Prevention of Fiscal Evasion with respect to Taxes on Income, signed at Washington on June 17, 1980. The Protocol was signed at Washington on August 23, 1983, together with an exchange of letters. I also transmit the report of the Department of State on the Protocol.

The Senate Committee on Foreign Relations deferred consideration of the Convention pending the negotiation of amendments to certain of its provisions. The Protocol takes into account recent changes in Danish tax laws. It also takes into account positions expressed by the Senate in its recent consideration of other United States income tax treaties.

I recommend that the Senate give early and favorable consideration to the Protocol and give its advice and consent to ratification.

RONALD REAGAN

The White House,
November 16, 1983.

Message to the Congress Reporting a Budget Rescission and Deferrals
November 17, 1983

To the Congress of the United States:

In accordance with the Impoundment Control Act of 1974, I herewith propose one rescission of $30,000,000 in contract authority for the Department of the Interior and two new deferrals of budget authority totaling $72,164,000 for the Department of Energy.

The details of the proposed rescission and

the deferrals are contained in the attached reports.

RONALD REAGAN

The White House,
November 17, 1983.

Note: The attachments detailing the proposed rescission and deferrals are printed in the Federal Register *of November 23, 1983.*

Nomination of Leslie Lenkowsky To Be Deputy Director of the United States Information Agency
November 17, 1983

The President today announced his intention to nominate Leslie Lenkowsky to be Deputy Director of the United States Information Agency. He would succeed Gilbert A. Robinson.

Mr. Lenkowsky is presently serving as director of research for the Smith Richardson Foundation, Inc., in New York, N.Y. Previously he was special consultant to Senator Daniel P. Moynihan in 1977–1980; visiting instructor, government department, Franklin & Marshall College in 1976; staff assistant to the secretary, Pennsylvania Department of Public Welfare, Harrisburg, in 1975–1976; teaching assistant at Harvard University and program assistant for the Office of Economic Opportunity in Washington, D.C. (1971–1973).

He graduated from Franklin & Marshall College (A.B., 1968) and is working toward his Ph. D. at Harvard University. He is married, has one child, and resides in New York, N.Y. He was born March 30, 1946, in New York City.

Remarks at the Swearing-in Ceremony for Susan M. Phillips as Chairman of the Commodity Futures Trading Commission
November 17, 1983

Secretary Block. Mr. President, Senator Jepsen, ladies and gentlemen, it's a privilege and an honor for me to have the opportunity to swear in the Chairman of the Commodity Futures Trading Commission. Susan Phillips was born in Virginia, but spent more time in Iowa, I guess, than anyplace else—out in the "tall corn State." It's second to Illinois, Roger, but it's a good corn State. The responsibility that she assumes—she's been managing that as Acting Chairman since last May. And it's a very important responsibility, especially from the standpoint of agriculture.

Farmers use the commodity markets for hedging commodities and hedging grains, to lock in prices. The grain companies and the industry use it very effectively. And it's vitally important. Very early on, we spent a lot of time in Illinois—the Illinois Farm Bureau—working with the Commodity Futures Trading Commission to ensure that those who were on the Commission had a very firm grasp of agriculture and how it related to the responsibilities of the Commission.

So, we're just delighted to have her here. And I'm delighted to have the opportunity to manage this swearing in.

So, if you'd come forward and—with her mother, Mrs. Phillips—please.

[At this point, the Secretary of Agriculture administered the oath of office.]

Congratulations.

The President. Well, I'm very pleased to have all of you here in this home that belongs to all Americans. And I'm delighted to see Dr. Susan M. Phillips sworn in as Chairman of the Commodity Futures Trading

Commission.

Susan's career represents a long record of high achievement. In 1967 she graduated Phi Beta Kappa from Agnes Scott College in Georgia. And in 1971 Susan earned her master's in finance and economics from Louisiana State, and in 1973 she received her doctorate in finance from the same university. Susan then went on to the University of Iowa, where she served as an associate professor and then as vice president of finance. In the course of her career, Susan has done important research, published many articles, contributed to four books, and been a Brookings Institution economic policy fellow at the Securities and Exchange Commission.

Two years ago I promoted her to—or nominated her, I should say—to become the first woman Commissioner of the CFTC. She's discharged her duties in that post with distinction. And, in a few moments—well, as a matter of fact, when I wrote that note down there I thought that I was going to go on first. [*Laughter*] So, I'll back up and start over again. [*Laughter*] So, as of a few moments ago, Susan became the first woman Chairman of a Federal financial regulatory agency in American history.

And, Susan, as you take your new place in the public eye, I just have to say I can't think of anyone who could better reflect the skill and experience of the women in our administration. From Ambassador Jeane Kirkpatrick to Secretary of Health and Human Services Margaret Heckler, from Secretary of Transportation Elizabeth Dole to Susan and others, more than a thousand women in this administration hold policy-making positions. And they hold those positions because of their superb qualifications and not because of some quota.

You know, that brings me to a story— almost everything does. [*Laughter*] Maybe I've told this story to you before, but then you'll just have to hear it again, because life not only begins at 40 but so does lumbago and the tendency to tell the same story over and over again. [*Laughter*]

But it was an accident scene. An injured individual lying there on the pavement, a crowd had begun to gather, a woman was bending down over him. And a man rushed up, shoved her aside, and said, "Let me at him, I've studied first aid." And she meekly stepped back, and he went down and went to work with his first aid knowledge. And at one point she finally tapped him on the shoulder and she says, "When you come to that part about calling the doctor, I'm right here." [*Laughter*]

So, today Susan becomes head doctor at the Commodity Futures Trading Commission. This Commission is one of my favorites, because it proves that government can do a good job without soaking up taxpayers' money or overregulating the marketplace. In a town where so many agencies have billion-dollar budgets, the CFTC budget is only about $26 million. You see, you don't have to be here long to start saying "only" $26 million. [*Laughter*] Yet, the Commission successfully oversees a vast and crucial sector of our economy. And by working in partnership with the industry's own regulatory organizations, the Commission does its job without hindering industry growth and innovation.

And, Susan, I know that you'll give the same intelligence and energy to this new job that you've given to all your endeavors. And I'm confident you'll keep the Commodity Futures Trading Commission efficient, ensure the integrity of our futures markets, promote industry growth, and protect the public good.

And now, good luck, God bless you, and get to work. [*Laughter*]

Dr. Phillips. Mr. President, Secretary Block, Senator Jepsen, friends and colleagues, thank you for sharing with me one of the most thrilling moments of my life.

Mr. President, in late 1981 when you lured me away from the sheltered life at the University of Iowa—and away from Big Ten Football, also might I add——

Secretary Block. Just in time. [*Laughter*]

Dr. Phillips. ——you gave me the privilege of participating in the exciting and important field of futures trading as a Commissioner at the CFTC. I will always be grateful to you for that opportunity.

During my years of teaching and financial research, then working at the Securities and Exchange Commission on options, deregulatory and market structure issues, I was even then fascinated with the potential for pricing and risk management offered by futures trading. In the trading pits of New York, Chicago, and the Midwest, agricultural products, energy supplies, financial instruments, and other materials essential to the world economy are bought and sold in open, competitive bidding. These markets exemplify the American concept of free and open trade. They set the pricing standards for commodities throughout the world.

Even representatives from countries with more tightly controlled economies than ours have expressed to me the importance of the integrity of U.S. futures markets. Nothing should ever be allowed to harm these markets or interfere in the vital services they offer.

For the opportunity you've now given me to chair the CFTC, I can only say a simple thank you. Out of my gratitude for this opportunity flows a sense of responsibility to you, to the Congress, and to the American people, who are influenced by what happens in these markets.

Under my Chairmanship, I hope the CFTC will continue its commitment to efficient oversight and enforcement, the encouragement of industry self-regulation. Ours is a small agency, staffed with expert and enthusiastic people who have a big job to do and who, I believe, do it well. I look forward to my continued association with them.

I'm especially happy that my mother is able to be here today. When I was growing up, she tried to teach me not to swear. But now she's come to Washington twice to hear me swear. [*Laughter*] But I don't think she minds.

Mr. President, once again, thank you for your confidence in me. I will do my best to justify that confidence.

Note: The ceremony began at 1:48 p.m. in the Roosevelt Room at the White House.

Statement on the Establishment of the Baltic States Service of Radio Liberty
November 18, 1983

Today, November 18, 1983, as Americans of Latvian heritage commemorate the 65th anniversary of the declaration of independence of the Baltic Republic of Latvia, the new Baltic States Service of Radio Liberty will begin its inaugural broadcast to the people of Estonia, Latvia, and Lithuania. The Baltic States Service unites the formerly separate Estonian, Latvian, and Lithuanian services of Radio Liberty.

Latvian Independence Day is a timely and fitting occasion to begin the operations of the new Baltic States Service division. Latvia, along with her neighbors Estonia and Lithuania, were invaded by Soviet forces in 1940 and still remain under the yoke of Soviet oppression. One of the most insidious forms of oppression continues to be the denial of freedom of speech and access to information.

The people of the three Baltic Republics look to the United States international broadcasting services as their informational lifeline. Radio Liberty, an integral part of the international broadcast network, serves as a surrogate press, providing current information on events which the Government of the Soviet Union has censored and prohibited for use by the media.

The establishment of the Baltic radio division reaffirms United States policy of not recognizing the forcible and unlawful incorporation of Estonia, Latvia, and Lithuania into the Soviet Union. The new call signal, "the Baltic States Service of Radio Liberty," will reinforce the distinct identities of the Baltic States and separate them from the rest of the Soviet Union.

By uniting the three Baltic services of Radio Liberty, we have enhanced their administrative operations and increased the political and psychological impact of the broadcasts on its listeners. We will continue seeking methods to improve our broadcasts to ensure that the right to know for the Baltic peoples is not blocked by Communist oppressors.

As we note Latvian Independence Day and the establishment of the Baltic States Service, this administration reaffirms its resolve to maintain our commitments to the people of Estonia, Latvia, and Lithuania in their struggle to regain freedom and self-determination.

Note: On the same day, the White House announced that Radio Liberty would broadcast the President's statement from Munich, Federal Republic of Germany, to the Baltic States and the Soviet Union on November 18.

Nomination of John A. Bohn, Jr., To Be First Vice President of the Export-Import Bank of the United States
November 18, 1983

The President today announced his intention to nominate John A. Bohn, Jr., to be First Vice President of the Export-Import Bank of the United States. He would succeed Charles Edwin Lord.

Since 1981 he has been serving as U.S. Director of the Asian Development Bank. Previously he was vice president, correspondent banking division, and manager, international personal banking department, of the Wells Fargo International Banking Group in 1980–1981; manager, administration and development, international banking group, Wells Fargo, 1979–1980; division manager, North American division, Wells Fargo, in 1974–1979; and manager of the international group for Wells Fargo in 1972–1974.

He graduated from Stanford University (A.B., 1960) and Harvard Law School (L.L.B., 1963). He attended the London School of Economics and the Graduate School of Credit and Financial Management at Stanford University. He is married, has four children, and resides in Belvedere, Calif. He was born October 31, 1937, in Oakland, Calif.

Nomination of Simeon Miller Bright To Be a Commissioner of the Postal Rate Commission
November 18, 1983

The President today announced his intention to nominate Simeon Miller Bright to be a Commissioner of the Postal Rate Commission for the term expiring November 22, 1988. This is a reappointment.

Since July 1977 he has been serving as Commissioner of the Postal Rate Commission. Previously he was owner of Sim Bright Real Estate & Investments in 1974–1977; coordinator of the cooperative education program at Potomac State College, West Virginia University, in 1973–1976; manager of J. Dorsey Real Estate Co. in 1971–1974; lecturer at the University of Maryland in 1969–1970; and special assistant to the Assistant Postmaster General, Bureau of Personnel, in 1965–1969.

Mr. Bright graduated from West Virginia University (B.A., 1949; M.A., 1950). He is married, has three children, and resides in Alexandria, Va. He was born September 11, 1925, in Keyser, W. Va.

Nomination of Priscilla L. Buckley To Be a Member of the United States Advisory Commission on Public Diplomacy
November 18, 1983

The President today announced his intention to nominate Priscilla L. Buckley to be a member of the United States Advisory Commission on Public Diplomacy for a term expiring July 1, 1986. She would succeed Leonard Silverstein.

Since 1959 Ms. Buckley has been managing editor of National Review magazine. She served as contributing editor and in-house reporter for the magazine in 1956–1959. She was elected to the board of directors of National Review in 1980. In 1953–1956 she was a correspondent for United Press International in Paris, France.

She graduated from Smith College (B.A., 1943). Ms. Buckley was born October 17, 1921, in New York City and now resides in Sharon, Conn.

Statement on Signing the Bill Authorizing a Congressional Gold Medal Honoring the Late Representative Leo J. Ryan
November 18, 1983

I am pleased today to affix my signature to the bill H.R. 3348, honoring the late Congressman Leo J. Ryan by authorizing a special Congressional Gold Medal of appropriate design to be struck and presented to his family.

Today marks the fifth anniversary of the day Leo Ryan was tragically struck down by an assassin's bullet on a faraway airport runway in Guyana. As his colleagues have noted in their tribute to him, it was typical of Leo Ryan's concern for his constituents that he would investigate personally the rumors of mistreatment in Jonestown that reportedly affected so many from his district.

Leo Ryan is the 88th recipient of a Congressional Gold Medal and only the 4th Member of Congress to receive this high honor from his colleagues.

Note: As enacted, H.R. 3348 is Public Law 98–159, approved November 18.

Nomination of Ruth O. Peters To Be a Governor of the United States Postal Service
November 18, 1983

The President today announced his intention to nominate Ruth O. Peters to be a Governor of the United States Postal Service for the remainder of the term expiring December 8, 1987. She would succeed Paula D. Hughes.

Ms. Peters was Director of the Office of Postmasters (1976–1980); General Manager, Employment and Placement Division, U.S. Postal Headquarters (1971–1976), and Chief, Research and Examination Branch, U.S. Postal Headquarters (1957–1971).

Ms. Peters graduated from the University of Southwest Louisiana (B.A., 1948) and American University (M.A., 1958). She resides in Arlington, Va., and was born April 19, 1925, in Oakdale, La.

Statement on Senate Confirmation of the Nomination of William P. Clark as Secretary of the Interior
November 18, 1983

I am deeply grateful to the Members of the United States Senate for their prompt action on the nomination of William P. Clark to be Secretary of the Interior.

Bill Clark brings to that post all of the qualities necessary to be an outstanding public servant—integrity, dedication, common sense, and a willingness to work hard on behalf of his fellow countrymen. I know he will be a great asset to our government.

He shares with me an abiding respect for our natural resources and for the splendid beauty which is uniquely American. Throughout his stewardship at Interior, Bill will be looking for ways to meet the legitimate interests of all segments of our society.

I welcome Bill Clark—a talented and conscientious man—to the Cabinet.

Note: Mr. Clark was sworn in as Secretary of the Interior at a ceremony in the Oval Office at the White House on November 21.

Nomination of Four Members of the National Council on the Handicapped
November 18, 1983

The President today announced his intention to nominate the following individuals to be members of the National Council on the Handicapped for terms expiring September 17, 1986. These are reappointments.

H. Latham Breunig is past president of the Alexander Graham Bell Association for the Deaf. He was with Eli Lilly and Company for over 40 years. He resides in Arlington, Va., and was born November 19, 1910.

Michael Marge is currently a professor of communicative disorders and child and family studies at Syracuse University. He resides in Fayetteville, N.Y., and was born October 26, 1928.

Alvis Kent Waldrep, Jr., is founder and chief executive officer of the Kent Waldrep International Spinal Cord Research Foundation, Inc. He resides in Grand Prairie, Tex., and was born March 2, 1954.

Sandra Swift Parrino is currently director of the Office of the Disabled in Ossining, N.Y. She resides in Briarcliff Manor, N.Y., and was born June 22, 1934.

Executive Order 12449—National Bipartisan Commission on Central America
November 18, 1983

By the authority vested in me as President by the Constitution and laws of the United States of America, including the Federal Advisory Committee Act, as amended (5 U.S.C. App. I), it is hereby ordered that Section 2(b) of Executive Order No. 12433, establishing the National Bipartisan Commission on Central America, is amended to provide as follows:

"(b) The Commission shall report to the President by February 1, 1984.".

RONALD REAGAN

The White House,
November 18, 1983.

[Filed with the Office of the Federal Register, 11:45 a.m., November 18, 1983]

Radio Address to the Nation on the First Session of the 98th Congress
November 19, 1983

My fellow Americans:

Like many of you coming home for Thanksgiving, the Members of Congress adjourned yesterday to return to their districts. They can take some satisfaction from a change in the public's attitude about their performance. According to a Harris survey, confidence in the Congress—as well as in other major American institutions—has increased over the past year. There are some good reasons for that, and one of the most important can be summed up in two words: economic growth. Even the most committed pessimists are reluctantly concluding America is enjoying one humdinger of an economic recovery.

Pretty soon people will stop talking about economic recovery and begin discussing a new phenomenon we haven't seen since the 1960's—a powerful, long-lasting economic expansion. Because whether we're looking at industrial production—which has registered the biggest 12-month increase in 7 years—or factory use—now at a 2-year high—or the drop in unemployment—which has been faster than in the past six recoveries—or inflation—which remains below 3 percent, the best performance since 1967—we're looking at an economy whose engines are humming with open track ahead.

From autos to housing and from construction to high technology, growth is strong, confidence is building, and progress is being made. The Congress deserves its share of the credit both for helping us pass some key reforms and for bravely resisting attempts by some to return us to the old days of tax and tax and spend and spend.

As most of you know, our bipartisan commission on social security recommended, and the Congress adopted, a landmark bill setting the social security system on a sound financial footing. At the same time, the Congress granted our request for the first major overhaul of the medicare program which provides health insurance protection for retired and disabled Americans.

Before our returns [reforms], the medicare laws required that we pay hospitals on a cost-plus basis, footing the bill for whatever cost they wound up incurring in treating medicare patients. So, hospitals had little incentive to hold down costs. Under our new reforms, hospitals will be paid a fixed price to care for each illness. If they control costs, they'll retain sufficient funds to upgrade the quality of their care. We estimate these reforms will save taxpayers over $20 billion in the next 5 years, and the savings can be realized without taking benefits away from anyone.

The Congress helped ensure a responsible continuation of revenue sharing, which supports vital economic activities in local communities. I was also pleased to sign into law several key appropriations bills. The spending levels were not as low as we requested, but they were lower than liberal Members wanted, and that would have meant higher deficits.

Perhaps the greatest contribution of the Congress was not what it did for us, but what it didn't do to us. The big spenders are still alive and well. And these people spared no effort to take away the third year of your tax cut, to delay indexing—the historic reform that'll protect you from being pushed by inflation into higher tax brackets—and to hit you with huge new tax increases. Well, with the help of responsible Republicans and Democrats, we fought them back and won. And with your help, we'll keep fighting and winning.

The record on the domestic side, however, was not all roses. The single, greatest failure of the Congress continues to be its inability to pass a responsible budget to help bring down deficits. By "responsible," I don't mean a budget that raises taxes to accommodate higher spending; I mean a budget that reduces spending to match revenues. You, the people, should not be forced to subsidize their extravagance. They should force themselves to spend within your means. Handcuffing big spenders and stopping them from taxing more of your earnings will be our first order of business come January.

I was also distressed that the Senate voted down—and the House refused to consider—our bill to provide tuition tax credits to deserving families. It was charged that this bill would have favored the rich. Well, that's a false charge. Those in high tax brackets were not eligible for the tax credits. The bill would have benefited those low- and middle-income people who bear the burden of tuition to send their children to parochial or independent schools and, at the same time, pay their full share of taxes to support the public school system. There would be no loss of revenue to public education, but there would be healthy competition among schools, which would improve the quality of education in both systems. Tuition tax credits and other unfinished business Americans want and need, like prayer in school and enterprise zones, will be pushed again by us as soon as the Congress returns.

I believe we're seeing another positive change that's making us feel more confident about our country—a return to bipartisanship in foreign policy. Our administration's highest goal is to help build a safer, more secure and peaceful world. That mission rests upon the twin pillars of deterrence and dialog, upon a military balance together with serious negotiations to resolve differences peacefully. Thanks to bipartisan support, we're doing both. We're restoring America's military strength, and we're pursuing large reductions in nuclear weapons through genuine arms control. Last week I told the Diet, the Japanese legislature, our goal must be the eventual elimination of all such weapons.

We've had bipartisan support for our rescue mission in Grenada and for our continued peacekeeping role in Lebanon. And this same spirit of putting country before party helped pass the Caribbean Basin Initiative to stimulate trade, cooperation, and progress with our Caribbean neighbors and a bill to start up Radio Marti, the voice of truth to the imprisoned people of Cuba. I've said it before and I'll say it again, I don't believe for one minute America's best days are behind her. And judging by their confidence, neither do the American people.

Until next week, thanks for listening, and God bless you.

Note: The President spoke at 12:06 p.m. from the Oval Office at the White House.

Remarks of President Reagan and President Gaafar Mohamed Nimeiri of the Sudan Following Their Meetings
November 21, 1983

President Reagan. It's been an honor and a pleasure to welcome President Nimeiri to Washington once again. President Nimeiri is a friend. Few can match his courage and foresight as a peacemaker in Africa and in the Middle East. I place great value on his insights and wise counsel and appreciate this opportunity to speak with him directly.

In our discussions, we found ourselves in basic agreement on critical issues in the Middle East and the Horn of Africa. President Nimeiri and I reviewed efforts to find a solution to the conflict in Chad. We're agreed that the first step necessary to achieve that end is the withdrawal of Libyan forces from Chad. Likewise, we're of one mind on the need to support African countries threatened by Libyan-supported aggression.

We also discussed the urgent need to

reach a just and comprehensive peace for the Middle East. A key to this is a settlement that would permit all states in the region to live in peace with secure borders, while at the same time protecting the legitimate rights of the Palestinian people. I thanked President Nimeiri for his continued support of our current peace initiative.

On bilateral issues, I reaffirmed our willingness to help the Sudan meet the economic and military challenges that it faces. We applaud the Sudan's efforts to reinvigorate its private sector and reform governmental policies that hinder economic progress. Economic development is of utmost importance to the people of the Sudan. And in this endeavor, the United States is happy to lend a hand to a friend.

President Nimeiri's visit underlines the significant role that Sudan is playing in Africa and the Middle East. The people of America are proud to stand with the people of the Sudan as friends and partners for peace and progress.

President Nimeiri. I would like to thank President Reagan for his invitation to me to come to visit once again the United States. And I would like to say to him that we are very pleased by our friendship to the people of the United States.

President Reagan and myself have discussed bilateral relations between our two countries and reviewed ways and means to further strengthen them. We are hoping that the important role played by the United States towards refugees will continue and expand at a time where we in the Sudan face and cater to ever-increasing numbers from our neighboring countries, especially Ethiopia.

In Africa, we have been—and still are—very concerned about the destabilization policies represented by Libya and its intervention in the internal affairs of others. Libya is undermining the unity of Chad by invading and occupying its territory and plotting against the unity and stability of the Sudan. Ethiopia and Libya are both playing a very dangerous role and executing policies serving the interests of a superior power.

In the Middle East, the Sudan is fully committed to a just solution to the Palestinian problem. In this context, the Sudan stands firm behind the Fez resolution. And it also supported the Reagan initiative as a step towards a more comprehensive solution. We deplore and regret the continued bloodshed in Lebanon and call on all parties to save Lebanon and its independence. We also condemn all policies and practices aimed at liquidating the PLO and deplore the shedding of Arab blood by Arab hands.

Israel remains the cause of the problem in the Middle East. We call on President Reagan to exert his utmost to stop the Israeli expansion policy and play the role becoming a great power that has such a great interest in the Arab world. And we call, also, on the Soviet Union to assist in peace progress in the Middle East.

Thank you.

Note: The President spoke at 1:21 p.m. to reporters assembled at the South Portico of the White House.

Earlier, the two Presidents met in the Oval Office and then held a working luncheon, together with U.S. and Sudanese officials, in the State Dining Room.

Statement on Signing the Veterans' Health Care Amendments of 1983
November 21, 1983

I am signing today H.R. 2920, the Veterans' Health Care Amendments of 1983, a bill which expands the health benefits available to our nation's 29 million veterans.

I am especially pleased with those provi-

sions of H.R. 2920 that are designed to help meet the needs of aging veterans. For example, this bill will allow the Veterans Administration (VA) to provide older veterans with health care services in VA and community day health care centers. This will permit veterans to receive needed services without becoming inpatients in VA facilities. The bill expressly authorizes VA to assist veterans, usually older veterans, in obtaining residential care in community facilities following VA care. H.R. 2920 also provides an increase in per diem rates to States to help defray the costs of veterans' care in State homes as an incentive to States to continue building and expanding these facilities for veterans.

H.R. 2920 contains other health-care related provisions, such as an extension of the community-based Vet Centers program which provides Vietnam veterans with psychological readjustment counseling services. In addition, it requires the Administrator of Veterans Affairs to establish an advisory committee on women veterans and to assure that VA health care facilities can meet the gender-specific health care needs of women veterans.

There are, however, provisions in this bill which greatly concern me—provisions which would give the VA special personnel authorities and property disposal procedures not available to other agencies. These provisions are unnecessary and costly and continue a recent, disturbing trend of giving the VA special treatment and exempting it from generally applicable executive branch rules.

Despite my reservations about the bill's compensation and property management provisions, I am approving this measure because of my strong commitment to the welfare of America's veterans.

Note: As enacted, H.R. 2920 is Public Law 98–160, approved November 21.

Statement by Deputy Press Secretary Speakes on the President's Meeting With President Spyros Kyprianou of Cyprus
November 21, 1983

In his meeting with the President, President Spyros Kyprianou of the Republic of Cyprus deplored the unilateral declaration of a separate political entity in northern Cyprus and urged U.S. support for a Cyprus settlement which included a reversal of this unilateral act.

The President noted our deep distress at the unilateral action by the Turkish Cypriots and that we had supported a British resolution at the United Nations deploring the Turkish Cypriot action and urging cooperation with U.N. efforts to promote a peaceful settlement. The President said that the United States stands foursquare behind the U.N. Secretary-General's good offices effort and emphasized the importance of reestablishing a dialog between the two communities on Cyprus.

The President also noted that he had personally spoken with the U.N. Secretary-General on Friday about his difficult task and offered to help in any way possible. In recognizing that the situation is complex, the President asked that the Government of Cyprus not let this ill-advised unilateral act preclude consideration of any opportunities that may emerge for progress towards a settlement.

Statement on Signing a Bill To Commemorate the Centennial of the Birth of Eleanor Roosevelt
November 21, 1983

I have signed today S.J. Res. 139, a joint resolution which is designed to commemorate the centennial of the birth of Eleanor Roosevelt.

This centennial offers an opportunity to honor one of the great First Ladies of this country whose contributions to humanity were not limited to her stay in the White House but continued thereafter on a worldwide basis.

I have been advised by the Attorney General that in view of the requirements of the appointments and the incompatibility clauses of the Constitution, a majority of the members of the Commission, and therefore the Commission itself, may perform only ceremonial and advisory functions.

Note: As enacted, S.J. Res. 139 is Public Law 98–162, approved November 21.

Statement on the 20th Anniversary of the Death of President John F. Kennedy
November 22, 1983

On November 22, 1983, we mark the 20th anniversary of the death of President John F. Kennedy. This young and vibrant man was struck down by an assassin's bullet in one of the most tragic episodes in our nation's history.

The events of that day in Dallas ushered in a wave of universal mourning that led people of all races and religions to fill their churches, temples, and mosques to pray for the fate of this one man. Never before in the history of the world had the thoughts of 4 billion people been focused in such a singular way.

Later, leaders from around the world would come to walk and stand shoulder to shoulder to pay tribute to this leader of the free world and eloquent spokesman for America.

People not yet born or too young to remember have learned of the deep trauma and grief his death brought to our country. We all remember the bright smile and wit he added to public life. He was dedicated to a strong America and the pursuit of the best for all our citizens. His leadership reflected one of his favorite quotes from Aristotle that defined the state of happiness as the exercise of all a man's "vital powers along the lines of excellence."

Across the Potomac River from the White House burns the Eternal Flame in Arlington Cemetery that marks J. F. K.'s final resting place. It is a flame that will always bring his spirit to our hearts and those of generations to come.

Question-and-Answer Session With Reporters on the Intermediate-Range Nuclear Force Negotiations
November 23, 1983

The President. Good morning. Any significance to the fact that you're now on the left of me instead of the right? [*Laughter*]

Q. That's what we want to know. What do you think of the Soviet walkout, and does this increase the possibility of a nuclear confrontation in the world?

The President. No, I still don't believe there's danger of a nuclear conflict as long as we have the deterrent power that we have. I don't think that I'm surprised by what they did this morning, but I am disappointed. And I can't believe that it's going to be permanent. We'll be ready to continue negotiations at any time that they want to come back.

Let me just point out the two superpowers are the only force that can preserve the peace and maintain peace. And we have, for 2 years, and we were the ones who initiated these discussions about eliminating, if possible, the intermediate-range weapons in Europe at a time when NATO had none. And during these 2 years or so of negotiations and talks, they have continued to add a hundred of their triple-warhead SS–20 missiles to the stock they already had. At the same time, they are proclaiming that we are the aggressors in wanting to accede to NATO's demand and put any missiles at all in Europe, where there are none.

Now, we, at present, have plans and are going to continue with withdrawing tactical and theater weapons, 1,400 more than we've already withdrawn. So, I think the evidence is very plain as to which country of the two is sincerely and honestly working toward a reduction of armaments.

Q. What do you think motivated them, and will they put missiles in Eastern Europe?

The President. What's that?

Q. What do you think motivated the Russians, and will they put missiles, their missiles, now directly in Eastern Europe?

The President. Well, they have announced that this is their intention, but I understand that there's also some unhappiness and dissatisfaction on the part of some of the Eastern European countries about their doing that.

Q. Mr. President, do you think they will come back, and how soon?

The President. I don't know how soon. I can't put a time on it. I think they'll come back, because I think they must be aware, as much as we are, that there cannot and must not be a nuclear confrontation in the world by the only two nations that truly have the great destructive capability, nuclear capability. So, I have to believe they'll come back. And I can tell you that we're not going to sit here with false pride. We will do everything that we can to bring them back.

Q. Like what, Mr. President?

The President. What?

Q. Like what? What will you do to bring them back?

The President. Continuing to persuade them that it's to their advantage as well as anyone else's.

Q. Are you investigating your own staff?

The President. I don't comment on any security violations or any investigation of the same.

Okay. Well, happy Thanksgiving.

Note: The exchange began at 9 a.m. at the South Portico of the White House. Following the exchange, the President left for Rancho del Cielo, his ranch near Santa Barbara, Calif., where he spent the Thanksgiving holiday.

Proclamation 5128—National Disabled Veterans Week, 1983
November 23, 1983

By the President of the United States of America

A Proclamation

All too often, we take for granted the freedoms that we enjoy. We must be ever mindful, however, of the sacrifices made by those men and women who have served in our Nation's armed forces in defense of those freedoms. We especially owe a debt of gratitude to those veterans who became disabled in the service of our country, for they truly know the price of freedom. Daily, these selfless men and women must endure hardship and lost opportunities because of the sacrifices they have made. We must accord them the respect and honor that they deserve.

We must also recognize the significant contributions these special men and women have made. Both in military service and in civilian life, they have been a source of inspiration and admiration, overcoming adversity with pride and dignity.

It is most fitting, therefore, that the Congress, by House Joint Resolution 283, has designated the week beginning November 6, 1983, as "National Disabled Veterans Week."

Now, Therefore, I, Ronald Reagan, President of the United States of America, do hereby proclaim the week beginning November 6, 1983, as National Disabled Veterans Week.

In Witness Whereof, I have hereunto set my hand this twenty-third day of November, in the year of our Lord nineteen hundred and eighty-three, and of the Independence of the United States of America the two hundred and eighth.

RONALD REAGAN

[*Filed with the Office of the Federal Register, 11:49 a.m., November 23, 1983*]

Proclamation 5129—Florence Crittenton Mission Week, 1983
November 23, 1983

By the President of the United States of America

A Proclamation

This year marks one hundred years of outstanding public service to young women by the Florence Crittenton Mission organization. In 1883, Charles Nelson Crittenton of New York opened his first mission which, in the words of its original Congressional charter, was to assist troubled young women to "seek reformation of character . . . (and) to reach positions of honorable self-support" and thereby make a new start in life.

The Florence Crittenton Mission today has grown to a network of 39 agencies in 26 States. It has achieved distinction in providing a wide range of services to young women, from residential care to career counseling.

The Congress, by House Joint Resolution 383, has designated the week beginning November 6, 1983 as "Florence Crittenton Mission Week" and has authorized and requested the President to issue a proclamation in observance of that week.

Now, Therefore, I, Ronald Reagan, President of the United States of America, do hereby proclaim the week beginning November 6, 1983, as Florence Crittenton Mission Week.

In Witness Whereof, I have hereunto set my hand this twenty-third day of November, in the year of our Lord nineteen hundred and eighty-three, and of the Independence of the United States of America the two hundred and eighth.

RONALD REAGAN

[*Filed with the Office of the Federal Register, 11:50 a.m., November 23, 1983*]

Proclamation 5130—Anti-Defamation League Day, 1983
November 23, 1983

By the President of the United States of America

A Proclamation

Since its inception, the Anti-Defamation League has worked to strengthen the democratic underpinnings of American society and to establish a harmonious unity of friendship and understanding amidst this Nation's religious, racial, and ethnic diversity. The Anti-Defamation League has combatted, counteracted, and worked to educate the public against anti-Semitism, racism, and the extremists of totalitarianism. The Anti-Defamation League also has articulated the special concerns and interests of the American Jewish community in upholding human rights and civil liberties in this country and throughout the world and served as an effective advocate for friendship with Israel.

The Anti-Defamation League and its leaders and supporters set an example of leadership and participation in events and programs to affect the well-being and future of all people. In purpose and program, the Anti-Defamation League espouses and fulfills the highest ideals and aspiration of Americans of all faiths, races, and cultural origins.

The Congress, by House Joint Resolution 408, has designated November 12, 1983, as "Anti-Defamation League Day" and has authorized and requested the President to issue a proclamation in observance of that day.

Now, Therefore, I, Ronald Reagan, President of the United States of America, do hereby proclaim November 12, 1983, as Anti-Defamation League Day.

In Witness Whereof, I have hereunto set my hand this twenty-third day of November, in the year of our Lord nineteen hundred and eighty-three, and of the Independence of the United States of America the two hundred and eighth.

RONALD REAGAN

[*Filed with the Office of the Federal Register, 11:51 a.m., November 23, 1983*]

Statement on Soviet Union Withdrawal From the Intermediate-Range Nuclear Force Negotiations
November 23, 1983

I deeply regret that the Soviet Union has chosen to discontinue the present round of Intermediate-range Nuclear Forces negotiations in Geneva. While their decision did not come as a surprise, it is a terrible disappointment. The search for an agreement to reduce nuclear weapons is so important to people everywhere that the effort cannot be abandoned.

Common sense demands that we continue. We have negotiated for 2 years while the Soviets have continued to deploy their SS–20 missiles. There is no justification for their breaking off negotiations just as NATO is beginning to restore the balance. The United States will never walk away from the negotiating table. Peace is too important.

We are prepared to resume the talks at once. The initiatives we have placed on the negotiating table have only one objective: to reach a fair agreement that reduces the level of nuclear arms. The United States and its NATO allies are united in our commitment to succeed.

We have no higher priority than the reduction of nuclear weapons. Arms reductions are the only sound course to a safer future. We seek sound and verifiable agreements that meet the legitimate security interests of both sides.

We are continuing other negotiations with the Soviet Union—on strategic arms reductions, on the reduction of conventional forces in Europe, on a chemical weapons ban and, soon, on confidence-building measures aimed at preventing military surprises in Europe.

The people of the world deserve and want our negotiations to succeed. We look forward to the day when the Soviet Union hears their call and returns to the INF negotiating table. Our negotiations have been on the right course. We must persevere if we are to serve the cause of peace.

Statement on the Soviet Response to the United States Reaction to the Discontinuance of Intermediate-Range Nuclear Force Negotiations
November 24, 1983

We can only be dismayed at this Soviet statement. It is at sharp variance with the stated wish of the Soviet Union that an agreement be negotiated.

While we are dismayed, we are determined to renew our efforts to entirely do away with the land-based, intermediate-range nuclear missile systems. We continue to seek negotiations in good faith.

Note: The President's statement was made in response to a statement by Soviet President Yuriy V. Andropov.

Radio Address to the Nation on the Resignation of Secretary of the Interior James G. Watt
November 26, 1983

My fellow Americans:

There's a change of management over at the Department of Interior. James Watt has resigned, and Judge William Clark has taken his place.

When Jim became Secretary of Interior he told me of the things that needed doing, the things that had to be set straight. He also told me that if and when he did them, he'd probably have to resign in 18 months. Sometimes the one who straightens out a situation uses up so many brownie points he or she is no longer the best one to carry out the duties of day-to-day management. Jim understood this. But he also realized what had to be done, and he did it for more than 30 months, not 18.

Now, with the change in management, it's time to take inventory. The Federal Government owns some 730 million acres—about one-third of the total land area of the United States. The Department of Interior has jurisdiction over most of that, including our national parks, wildlife refuges, wilderness lands, wetlands, and coastal barriers. Not included in those 730 million acres are our offshore coastal waters, the Outer Continental Shelf, which is also Interior's responsibility. And I've asked Bill Clark to review policy, personnel, and process at the Department of the Interior.

Our national parks are the envy of the world, but in 1981 they were a little frayed at the edges. Since 1978 funds for upkeep and restoration had been cut in half. Jim Watt directed a billion-dollar improvement and restoration program. This 5-year effort is the largest commitment to restoration and improvement of the park system that has ever been made.

You, of course, are aware of the economic crunch we've been facing. Yet, even so,

Secretary Watt set out to increase protection for fragile and important conservation lands. In 1982 he proposed that 188 areas along our gulf and Atlantic coasts be designated as undeveloped coastal areas. And that proposal became the basis for the historic Coastal Barrier Resources Act. This act covers dunes, marshes, and other coastal formations from Maine to Texas—lands that provide irreplaceable feeding and nesting grounds for hundreds of species of waterfowl and fish. And, under Secretary Watt, we've added substantial acreage to our parks and wildlife refuges and some 15,000 acres to our wilderness areas.

Interior is also in charge of preserving historic sites and structures. In the economic recovery program we launched in 1981 we gave a 25-percent tax credit for private sector restoration of historic structures. The result has been private investment in historic preservation five times as great as in the preceding 4 years. Secretary Watt has explored other ways to involve the private sector in historic preservation. And one of the efforts we're all proudest of is the campaign to restore Ellis Island and that grand lady in New York Harbor, the Statue of Liberty. This campaign is being led by Lee Iacocca, the chairman of Chrysler, and is being financed almost entirely by private contributions.

Preservation of endangered species is also a responsibility of the Department, and the approval and review of plans to bring about recovery of endangered plant and animal species has nearly tripled in the 30 months of Secretary Jim Watt. From the very first, Jim pledged to the Governors of our 50 States that the Department would be a good neighbor, that they would be included in land planning, and that small tracts of isolated Federal lands would be made available to communities needing land for hospitals, schools, parks, or housing. He also stated that isolated small tracts would be sold to farmers and ranchers.

An example of what I'm talking about is a strip of land 1 mile long and only 2 to 20 feet wide that was recently sold. I think you can imagine how these efforts must have erased some problems private landowners had with clouded title to their property.

Of course, all this was distorted and led to protests that he was selling national parks and wilderness. What he actually did was sell, in 1982, 55 tracts that totaled only 1,300 acres, and this year, 228 tracts totaling a little over 10,000 acres. The largest parcel was 640 acres; that's 1 square mile. None of it was park, wildlife refuge, wilderness, or Indian trust lands. They are not for sale. And not one acre of national parkland was leased for oil drilling or mining, contrary to what you may have read or heard.

When territories were becoming States, they were promised title to Federal lands within their borders, some lands to be used for public education. But as more and more Western States joined the Union, there began to be a delay; in fact, a permanent delay in turning over these lands. Jim Watt promised the Governors that if they'd identify lands they had a right to claim under their statehood acts, we'd make the Federal Government honest. The Governors responded, and as a result, by the end of this year more land will have been delivered to the States to support their school systems than at any time since 1969.

Changes have been made in the management of forest lands which are eligible for multiple use. Those lands will provide lumber on a sustained-yield basis. This will benefit Americans who cherish the dream of owning their own home.

We've made giant strides in implementing a national water policy which recognizes State primacy in managing water resources. People must be a part of our planning, and people need a reliable, safe drinking water supply, water for generating power, and water for irrigation.

Since I've mentioned energy, let me touch on that for a minute. It's estimated that 85 percent of the fuel we need to keep the wheels of industry turning is on Federal-owned property, including the Outer Continental Shelf. Efforts to increase the supply of energy have been carried out in full compliance with environmental stipulations. We can and will have an increased energy supply with an enhanced environment.

James G. Watt has served this nation well. And I'm sure William Clark will do the same.

Till next week, thanks for listening, and

God bless you.

Note: The President spoke at 9:06 a.m. from Rancho del Cielo, his ranch near Santa Barbara, Calif.

Statement on Signing a Fiscal Year 1984 Appropriations Bill
November 28, 1983

I am today signing H.R. 3222. I am doing so, however, with strong reservations about the constitutional implications of section 510 of this bill. Section 510 purports to prohibit the expenditure of appropriated funds on "any activity, the purpose of which is to overturn or alter the per se prohibition on resale price maintenance in effect under Federal antitrust laws. . . ." I do not understand Congress to have intended by this provision to limit or direct prosecutorial discretion, or otherwise to restrict the government's ability to enforce the antitrust laws within the framework of existing case law. Thus, despite the breadth of its language, pursuant to the advice of the Attorney General, I interpret section 510 narrowly to apply only to attempts to seek a reversal of the holdings of a certain line of previously decided cases. Even as narrowly construed, however, the provision potentially imposes an unconstitutional burden on executive officials charged with enforcing the Federal antitrust laws. Therefore, I believe it is my constitutional responsibility to apply section 510 in any particular situation consistently with the President's power and duty to take care that the laws be faithfully executed.

Another provision of concern is the section which purports to mandate continued funding for current grantees of the Legal Services Corporation at essentially the same level of funding as in fiscal year 1983 unless action is taken prior to January 1, 1984, by directors of the Corporation who have been confirmed by the Senate. To the extent that this provision may be intended to disable persons appointed under the Constitution's provision governing Presidential appointments during congressional recesses from performing functions that directors who have been confirmed by the Senate are authorized to perform, it raises troubling constitutional issues with respect to my recess appointments power. The Attorney General has been looking into this matter at my request and will advise me on how to interpret this potentially restrictive condition.

Note: The President signed the bill into law in a ceremony in the Roosevelt Room at the White House.

As enacted, H.R. 3222 is Public Law 98–166, approved November 28.

Remarks on Signing the National Decade of Disabled Persons Proclamation
November 28, 1983

The Vice President and I are very happy to welcome all of you here to the White House.

Just a few minutes ago, I had the pleasure of meeting the men and women who are sharing the platform with us this morning. And this fine group has recently been named the Outstanding Handicapped Federal Employees of the Year. And we're proud that they're part of the Federal Government's team.

I also want to thank those Members of Congress who are here today, some of whom returned from their districts because of the importance of this ceremony.

All of you in this room know that courage, patience, and hard work go a long way, and no one knows it better than my Press Secretary, Jim Brady. Jim has inspired people everywhere and continues to do so. And, Jim, we're delighted that you could take part in today's ceremony.

In a few minutes, I'll sign a proclamation designating 1983 through 1982 [1992] the National Decade of Disabled Persons. Proclamations can summon good people to action and light the path of hope. And this proclamation, we think, will do both.

The 1981 International Year of Disabled Persons and the 1982 National Year of Disabled Persons stimulated new activity to improve the lives of our disabled Americans. Consciousness was raised, new partnerships formed, barriers reduced, and opportunities increased. Our own efforts in the White House, for example, have helped generate a number of private projects involving transportation, elementary school tutoring, eye diagnosis, and surgery. But we can't rest on past success. The task before us is to maintain our momentum and to do more.

Today I'm establishing a clear national goal. Let us increase the economic independence of every disabled American and let us begin today.

The disabled want what all of us want: the opportunity to contribute to our communities, to use our creativity, and to go as far as our God-given talents will take us. We see remarkable achievements in medicine, technology, education, rehabilitation, and in preventive medicine. Voluntary efforts by the private sector help in a thousand ways. America is a caring society, but too often, Federal programs discourage full participation by society. Outmoded attitudes and practices that foster dependence are still with us. They are unjust, unwanted, and nonproductive. Paternalism is the wrong answer.

The maze of Federal programs complicates matters even more. Thirty-two Federal agencies fund handicapped research. There are at least 42 separate Federal programs specifically targeted toward the handicapped population with an annual budget in excess of $36 billion. More than a hundred other programs provide handicapped services and support. Now, many good things are being done, and Federal programs help in countless ways. But the patchwork quilt of existing policies and programs can be as much of a hindrance as a help. Programs overlap, they work at cross purposes, and worst of all, they don't always point toward independence and jobs. So, we have a lot of work to do, and this work will be done.

Since last April, a White House working group on handicapped policy has been looking at ways to better translate our goals of economic independence into an agenda for action. And that agenda is now underway. The administration's review of the regulations implementing Public Law 94–142, the Education of All Handicapped Children's Act, has been completed. The regulations are fine the way they are. No changes will be made, and the program will be protected in its present form.

Now, today, I'm also announcing three new initiatives. We believe that each will result in far better coordination and consistency among Federal programs.

The Department of Health and Human Services will direct a program to strengthen private sector job opportunities. And this initiative will feature a new job cataloging service and a national campaign to coordinate and stimulate employment possibilities for the severely disabled.

Help is also needed to assist in the transition from special education to community integration and job placement. The Departments of Education and Health and Human Services have established a program to assist special education students during this transition.

And finally we're putting together a national information and referral system. The handicapped, their families, and physicians need to be able to cut through the maze of public and private services and gain timely access to information and programs. This new network, managed by the private sector, will provide this badly needed service.

Now, I know these programs are only a beginning, but we believe equal opportunity, equal access, and greater economic independence must be more than slogans. Whenever government puts welfare and charity before the opportunity for jobs, it misses the mark. By returning to our traditional values of self-reliance, human dignity, and independence, we can find the solution together. We can help replace chaos with order in Federal programs, and we can promote opportunity and offer the promise of sharing the joys and responsibilities of community life.

I believe we can make this dream come true. You may face limitations, but not one of you here today lacks the courage, the will, or the heart to do what others say cannot be done.

There's a young lady with us today who's demonstrated that so well. Jennifer Boatman has spinal bifida, a serious malformation of the spine. Well, Jennifer's handicap didn't stop her from saving the life of a 5-year-old boy. When Jennifer saw young Joshua Mikesell tumbling through a whitewater stretch of the North Umpqua River in southwestern Oregon, she didn't hesitate one second. She jumped into the swift mountain stream, swam to the boy, and pulled him to the river bank. Joshua's father called it a miracle.

It's also the story of the courage and capability of America's disabled. And for all of us it's the ultimate expression of love. Greater love hath no man than to lay down his life for a friend.

You know, someone has said that a hero is no braver than any other person. He or she is just braver 5 minutes longer. [*Laughter*] Well, Jennifer, that's you, and it makes us all proud and thankful. Your courage, your compassion, and your commitment to America's disabled opened the way to a life of quality for all people.

Let us rededicate ourselves to the tasks ahead. Let the spirit of the National Decade of Disabled Persons capture our imagination. In partnership between the public and private sector, among national, State, and local organizations, and between the disabled and the abled we can win the battle for dignity, equality, and increased economic opportunity for all Americans.

And now I shall go sign the proclamation. And God bless all of you; thank all of you.

Note: The President spoke at 11:55 a.m. in the East Room at the White House.

Proclamation 5131—National Decade of Disabled Persons
November 28, 1983

By the President of the United States of America

A Proclamation

During the 1981 International Year and the 1982 National Year of Disabled Persons, we learned about the many accomplishments of disabled persons, both young and old. We also gained vast new insights into the significant impact that access to education, rehabilitation, and employment have on their lives.

The progress we have made is a tribute to the courage and determination of our disabled people, to innovative research and development both in technology and training techniques to assist the disabled, and to those—whether in the private or public sectors—who have given so generously of their time and energies to help enrich the lives of disabled persons.

We must encourage the provision of rehabilitation and other comprehensive services oriented toward independence within the context of family and community. For only through opportunities to use the full range of their potential will our disabled citizens attain the independence and dignity that are their due.

In furtherance of the initiatives encouraged by observance of the International Year of Disabled Persons, the United Nations General Assembly has proclaimed the years 1983 through 1992 as the United Nations Decade of Disabled Persons. The Congress of the United States, by House Concurrent Resolution 39, has requested the President to take all steps within his authority to implement, within the United States, the objectives of the United Nations Decade of Disabled Persons as proclaimed by the United Nations General Assembly on December 3, 1982.

Now, Therefore, I, Ronald Reagan, President of the United States of America, do hereby proclaim the years 1983 through 1992 as the National Decade of Disabled Persons. I call upon all Americans in both the private and public sectors to join our continuing efforts to assist disabled people and to continue the progress made over the past two years.

In Witness Whereof, I have hereunto set my hand this twenty-eighth day of November, in the year of our Lord nineteen hundred and eighty-three, and of the Independence of the United States of America the two hundred and eighth.

RONALD REAGAN

[*Filed with the Office of the Federal Register, 10:48 a.m., November 29, 1983*]

Appointment of W. Dennis Thomas as Deputy Assistant to the President for Legislative Affairs (House)
November 28, 1983

The President today announced his intention to appoint W. Dennis Thomas to be Deputy Assistant to the President for Legislative Affairs (House). He will succeed M. B. Oglesby, who will become Assistant to the President for Legislative Affairs on December 15, 1983.

Mr. Thomas was confirmed on March 11, 1981, as Assistant Secretary of the Treasury for Legislative Affairs. Previously he served as administrative assistant to Senator William Roth with responsibilities including work on the Finance Committee, Governmental Affairs Committee, and the Joint Economic Committee. He was on the staff of Senator J. Glenn Beall, Jr., serving as administrative assistant in 1974–1976 and executive assistant in 1971–1974. In 1969–1970 he was special assistant to then Congressman Beall.

Mr. Thomas graduated from Frostburg State College (B.A., 1965) and the University of Maryland (M.A., 1967). He is married, has one son, and resides in Westminster, Md. He was born December 8, 1943.

Proclamation 5132—National Home Care Week, 1983
November 28, 1983

By the President of the United States of America

A Proclamation

Health care in the home is as old as medical treatment itself. Today it presents Americans with important new opportunities. As an integrated part of our health care system, the home setting can offer the comfort of familiar surroundings and the flexibility of personalized treatment. It can preserve the dignity and independence of individuals and prevent or postpone institutionalization for millions of patients each year. In a significant number of cases, home care can even reduce the cost of medical treatment.

America's home health care system has been growing rapidly in recent years with more than 4,000 certified agencies now providing home care. As our elderly population grows, home health care promises to become even more important in the future. There is still much to be learned about home health care, including when it can be most beneficial, how it can make our health care system more efficient, and how it can reinforce the efforts of millions of American families who provide care for their own members. The Federal government, the States, and the private sector are vigorously pursuing the knowledge that will let us make the best use of this promising resource.

In recognition of the benefits to be derived from home health care services through home health agencies providing skilled nursing services, physical therapy, speech therapy, social services, occupational therapy, and home health aide services, and the many private and charitable organizations which also provide these services, the Congress, by Senate Joint Resolution 122, has designated the week of November 27, 1983, through December 3, 1983, as "Na-

tional Home Care Week" and has authorized and requested the President to issue a proclamation in observance of that week.

Now, Therefore, I, Ronald Reagan, President of the United States of America, do hereby proclaim the week beginning November 27, 1983, as "National Home Care Week." I call upon the people of the United States to observe that week with appropriate ceremonies and activities.

In Witness Whereof, I have hereunto set my hand this 28th day of November, in the year of our Lord nineteen hundred and eighty-three, and of the Independence of the United States of America the two hundred and eighth.

RONALD REAGAN

[*Filed with the Office of the Federal Register, 10:49 a.m., November 29, 1983*]

Appointment of Douglas A. Riggs as Special Assistant to the President for Public Liaison
November 29, 1983

The President today announced the appointment of Douglas A. Riggs to be Special Assistant to the President for Public Liaison.

Mr. Riggs joined the Office of Public Liaison in July 1983 as an Associate Director with responsibility for establishing a liaison with organized labor.

Mr. Riggs is a lawyer and most recently practiced with the Seattle firm of Bogle and Gates in the Anchorage, Alaska, office, where he resided for the past 17 years. Previously he served as special counsel and ad-

ministrative assistant to the Governor of Alaska, and director of the Alaska State Housing Authority.

He received his undergraduate degree from Brigham Young University, a masters degree in labor relations from West Virginia University, and a law degree from Cornell University.

Mr. Riggs is married and resides in Washington, D.C. He was born August 20, 1944, in Rigby, Idaho.

Remarks of the President and Prime Minister Yitzhak Shamir of Israel Following Their Meetings
November 29, 1983

The President. We have held 2 days of intensive talks with Prime Minister Shamir and his colleagues, covering a broad range of subjects including political, military coop-

eration, Lebanon, Israel's economic situation, and the pursuit of the Middle East peace process. And these discussions, as could be expected between close friends and allies, have been very productive. We reconfirmed the longstanding bonds of the friendship and cooperation between our two countries and expressed our determination to strengthen and develop them in the cause of our mutual interests.

We have agreed on the need to increase our cooperation in areas where our interests coincide, particularly in the political and military area. And I am pleased to announce that we have agreed to establish a joint political-military group to examine ways in which we can enhance U.S.-Israeli cooperation. This group will give priority attention to the threat to our mutual interest posed by increased Soviet involvement in the Middle East. Among the specific areas to be considered are combined planning, joint exercises, and requirements for prepositioning of U.S. equipment in Israel.

We've agreed to take a number of other concrete steps aimed at bolstering Israel's economy and security. These include asking Congress for improved terms for our security assistance to Israel; using military assistance for development of the Lavi aircraft in the United States and for offshore procurement of Lavi components manufactured in Israel; permitting U.S. contractors to enter into contracts with the Government of Israel consistent with U.S. law, which would allow Israeli industry to participate in the production of U.S. weapons systems procured with foreign military sales credits; offering to negotiate a free trade area with Israel.

A main focus of our meetings was the agony of Lebanon and the threats there to our common interests. We examined, together, Soviet activities in the Middle East and found a common concern with the Soviet presence and arms buildup in Syria. We reaffirmed our commonly held goals of a sovereign, independent Lebanon free of all foreign forces, and of security for Israel's northern border.

We agreed that every effort must be made to expedite implementation of the May 17th agreement between Israel and Lebanon. Adequate security arrangements for Israel's northern border must be assigned the highest priority. We're hopeful that such arrangements can be concluded soon.

We, of course, discussed the broader goal of peace between Israel and its Arab neighbors. The Egyptian-Israeli peace treaty remains the cornerstone of the peace process. I reaffirmed my commitment to the September 1 initiative as the best way to realize the promise of Camp David and the U.N.S.C. Resolutions 242 and 338 upon which it was built.

As you can see, our 2 days together have revealed substantial areas of agreement and resulted in a number of specific concrete steps that we'll take to strengthen our ties. We have also discussed some issues on which we do not see eye to eye. But disagreements between good friends do not alter the unique and sturdy foundation of our relationship.

I know that Prime Minister Shamir shares with me the renewed conviction that the warm friendship between the United States and Israel will endure and strengthen.

The Prime Minister. I am grateful for the invitation extended to me by President Reagan to come here to Washington for these discussions. The Minister of Defense and I have had the opportunity to conduct very thorough discussions with the President, the Secretary of State, the Secretary of Defense, and their senior colleagues and advisers. These discussions have been carried out in the spirit of the traditional friendship and the common bonds of mutual understanding that bind our two countries.

We reaffirmed our determination to ensure the withdrawal of all foreign forces from Lebanon. The only basis for a settlement of the Lebanese problem is the full implementation of the May 17, 1983, agreement in all its parts. We have discussed with the President and the Secretaries the necessary steps that could facilitate the carrying out of this agreement. Syria constitutes today a major threat to the peace in our area by occupying more than 60 percent of Lebanon and by its massive concentration of Soviet arms and personnel on Syrian territory.

Israel is ready to renew the peace process and discuss the final status of Judea and Samaria, following the autonomy period in the framework of the sole agreed basis for negotiations, namely the Camp David accords. We discussed during our visit here the major threat that terrorism constitutes to the peace, and we shall pursue our fight against it in close cooperation with the United States.

Due to the need to ensure our security, a large part of our budget is spent on defense. We hope that the American administration will increase their assistance program, taking into account the great sacrifices made by Israel in the peace treaty, by relinquishing the oil wells and building new installations as a result of the withdrawal from Sinai. New measures designed to encourage the development of our economy by establishing a free trade area, by sharing new technology will enhance Israel's strength and enable us to pursue our economic program so vital to the well-being of our society.

In order to advance the search for peace and to strengthen the ties between our two countries, we decided to establish the mechanism necessary to determine the details of the nature and scope of our cooperation inter alia in the fields of prepositioning of equipment for military readiness, joint exercises, and other relevant fields. We have agreed to establish a joint political-military committee to work on the details of these agreed matters. The aim of this cooperation is to strengthen Israel and deter threats to the region. The group will hold periodic meetings, starting the first

week of January 1984.

I wish to once again thank the President and the people of the United States for their strong support of Israel and for the warm feelings conveyed to the Minister of Defense and myself by the President, the Vice President, the Secretary of State, and the Secretary of Defense. We will proceed on the road to peace with increased vigor. I return to Jerusalem strengthened in my conviction that with the aid of the United States of America and fortified by the friendship of its people and government, a strong Israel can indeed achieve peace.

Thank you.

Note: The President spoke at 1:24 p.m. to reporters assembled at the South Portico of the White House.

Earlier, the President and the Prime Minister, together with the Vice President and Israeli Defense Minister Moshe Arens, met in the Oval Office. They then met with U.S. and Israeli advisers in the Cabinet Room and attended a luncheon in the State Dining Room.

On November 28 the President and the Prime Minister met in the Oval Office. They were accompanied by the Vice President, Secretary of State George P. Shultz, Secretary of Defense Caspar W. Weinberger, Ambassador Donald Rumsfeld, the President's Personal Representative in the Middle East, and Israeli Defense Minister Arens.

Remarks on Signing the Local Government Fiscal Assistance Amendments of 1983
November 30, 1983

Good afternoon. I learned in public speaking once that you were never supposed to open any remarks with an apology, but I also found out in this job, 9 times out of 10 you have to apologize for being late. So, I apologize for keeping you all waiting.

I'm delighted to see Members of Congress, the mayors, and the other local officials who are here in the White House this afternoon. It's good to have you in the

house that belongs to all of us—from every city, county, and town.

Like millions of Americans, I grew up in a small town. Back in Dixon, Illinois, government officials and the citizens they were serving knew each other. They were part of the same community, lived next door to each other, and went to the same high school football games, and bumped into each other at the grocery. Dixon officials knew what the people of Dixon needed, and they were able to meet those needs with efficiency and imagination.

Local government meeting local needs—that's a fundamental principle of good government. Many government workers here in Washington are diligent and dedicated; I've found that out. And yet they can't know the American people as well as you or Congressmen or mayors, county and local officials.

If those at the grassroots are to get their jobs done and get them done right, we must give them the resources they need. This bill will send $4.6 billion from Washington back to our cities, counties, and towns. The money will not be spent as Washington dictates, but as local officials choose. It will support police and fire protection, libraries, street maintenance, and other basic local services. And since less than 1 percent of the total will be used for administration, the general revenue sharing program will set a superb example of government efficiency for other Federal programs.

It took a lot of doing to hammer this bill together. But funding a program at this level will enable us to continue our partnership with local governments without fueling deficits.

My heartfelt thanks to all who helped build the wide and bipartisan support that this bill enjoyed. For my part, signing this bill represents a great personal pleasure. I pledged my support for revenue sharing to the United States Conference of Mayors back in 1980, and since then, I've repeated my—or restated my support before the National League of Cities, the National Association of Counties, the National Association of Towns and Townships, and many others.

The Federal Government never spent money more wisely than by devoting it to general revenue sharing. Today I'm delighted to reaffirm my support with a pen—two pens. Pens only write one word—government pens do. [*Laughter*]

So, I thank you all, and God bless you. I will now get my name on that piece of paper.

Note: The President spoke at 3:14 p.m. in the State Dining Room at the White House.

As enacted, H.R. 2780 is Public Law 98–185, approved November 30.

Statement on Signing the United States Commission on Civil Rights Act of 1983
November 30, 1983

I have signed today H.R. 2230, establishing a new Commission on Civil Rights. I believe that the birth of this Commission can serve as another milestone in our long struggle as a nation to assure that individuals are judged on the basis of their abilities, irrespective of race, sex, color, national origin, or handicap.

I take this opportunity to reaffirm this administration's commitment to these ideals, which the civil rights laws of the United States were designed to implement and which it will be the central mission of this Commission to articulate and defend.

The bill I have signed today is, of course, a product of negotiation and compromise. While, as noted, I am pleased that the Com-mission has been re-created so that it may continue the missions assigned to it, the Department of Justice has raised concerns as to the constitutional implications of certain provisions of this legislation. I have appended a recitation of these reservations.

During the preceding 6 months there has been considerable debate on the past and the future of the Commission on Civil Rights, but all seem to agree that the Commission's best and most productive years were its earlier ones. I believe that it is no coincidence that those years were characterized by open debate and a devotion to the principle of equal treatment under the law. With the bill I have signed today and the quality of appointments that can be made to the Commission, there is cause for confidence that the Commission's best years are yet to come.

Statement by the Department of Justice

Under the terms of H.R. 2230, four members of the Commission will be appointed by the President, two members by the President pro tempore of the Senate, and two members by the Speaker of the House of Representatives. The Commission itself is not placed clearly within any of the three branches of government created by the United States Constitution, and restrictions have been placed upon the power of the President to remove members of the Commission.

Agencies which are inconsistent with the tripartite system of government established by the Framers of our Constitution should not be created. Equally unacceptable are proposals which impermissibly dilute the powers of the President to appoint and remove officers of the United States. The Civil Rights Commission is, however, unique in form and function and should therefore not become a precedent for the creation of similar agencies in the future.

The new appointment procedure created by the Congress has effectively imposed constitutional limitations on the duties that the Commission may perform. The basic purpose of the old Commission on Civil Rights—to investigate, study, appraise, and report on discrimination—would be maintained, and most of its current authorities would remain intact. However, because half of the members of the Commission will be appointed by the Congress, the Constitution does not permit the Commission to exercise responsibilities that may be performed only by "Officers of the United States" who are appointed in accordance with the Appointments Clause of the United States Constitution (Article II, Section 2, clause 2). Therefore, it should be clear that although the Commission will continue to perform investigative and informative functions, it may not exercise enforcement, regulatory, or other executive responsibilities that may be performed only by officers of the United States.

Note: On the same day, the White House announced that the President appointed Clarence M. Pendleton, Jr., of California, to be a member of the U.S. Commission on Civil Rights for a term of 6 years and designated him as Chairman. The President also appointed Linda Chavez Gersten, of the District of Columbia, as Staff Director of the Commission.

As enacted, H.R. 2230 is Public Law 98–183, approved November 30.

Statement on Signing the Supplemental Appropriations Act, 1984
November 30, 1983

In signing this appropriation legislation, which includes funding for the Multilateral Development Banks, I would like to clarify one point. While I firmly believe that we must continue the valuable and productive unofficial relations with the people of Taiwan, and I strongly support efforts to ensure their continued participation in the Asian Development Bank, certain terminology used in the amendment to the bill concerning this issue is not consistent with United States Government policy, which recognizes the People's Republic of China as the sole, legal Government of China. I want to make clear that my signing of this bill does not reflect any change in the position of four successive Presidents with respect to China, nor should it be interpreted as any shift in the United States Government's recognition policy.

Note: As enacted, H.R. 3959 is Public Law 98–181, approved November 30.

Statement by Deputy Press Secretary Speakes on the President's Action Withholding Approval of Legislation Concerning El Salvador
November 30, 1983

The President today withheld approval of H.R. 4042, an enrolled bill that would require two Presidential certifications regarding El Salvador in 1984 or until the enactment of new legislation imposing conditions on U.S. military assistance for that country.

This administration is firmly committed to the protection of human rights, economic and political reforms, the holding of elections, and progress in prosecuting the cases of murdered American citizens in El Salvador. However, the process of certification as called for in H.R. 4042 would not serve to support these endeavors.

His decision to oppose this certification legislation reflects the administration's policy that such requirements distort our efforts to improve human rights, democracy, and recovery in El Salvador. The key certification provisions of the present bill are already addressed in this year's continuing resolution which requires a separate certification on progress in the area of land reform and withholds 30 percent of military assistance funds until the Government of El Salvador has completed the investigation and trial in the churchwomen's case.

At the same time, the President wishes to emphasize that the administration remains fully committed to the support of democracy, reform, and human rights in El Salvador. Those very concerns are a central component of our policy. They were clearly articulated by our Ambassador, Tom Picker-

ing, as recently as last Friday. The withholding of approval from H.R. 4042 in no way reflects a lessening of our interests in these critical areas. The President has also instructed the Department of State to continue to provide the Congress with periodic public reports—the next on January 16, 1984—on the political, economic, and military situation in El Salvador.

Working with the leadership of the Government of El Salvador, we will reconfirm our joint resolve to take whatever action is necessary to help the Government of El Salvador to end the reprehensible activities of the violent right as well as the violent left. The United States will also work to preserve and expand the progress that has been achieved in the area of land reform and to maintain the momentum toward holding open and democratic elections next year in accordance with the provision of the new constitution being prepared in El Salvador's Constituent Assembly.

There must exist a genuine awareness, both in the U.S. as well as in El Salvador, that our countries' strong and productive relationship can only be based on shared values in justice and democracy and on concerted and sustained efforts to achieve these goals. We know that President Alvaro Magaña of El Salvador shares these views, and we will remain in touch on developing enhanced efforts that will strengthen human rights ties.

Letter to the Speaker of the House and the President of the Senate on the Designation of 11 Countries as Caribbean Basin Economic Recovery Act Beneficiaries
November 30, 1983

Dear Mr. Speaker: (Dear Mr. President:)

Pursuant to Section 212 of the Caribbean Basin Economic Recovery Act (CBERA), I wish to inform you of my intent to desig-

nate the following eleven Caribbean Basin countries and entities as beneficiaries of the trade-liberalizing measures provided for in this Act: Barbados, Costa Rica, Dominica,

Dominican Republic, Jamaica, Panama, Netherlands Antilles, Saint Lucia, Saint Vincent and the Grenadines, Trinidad and Tobago, and Saint Christopher-Nevis. Designation will entitle the products of said countries, except for products excluded statutorily, to duty-free treatment for a period beginning on January 1, 1984 and ending on September 30, 1995. As beneficiaries, these eleven also have the opportunity to become eligible for the convention expense tax deduction under Section 274(h) of the Internal Revenue Code of 1954, by entering into an exchange of information agreement with the United States on tax matters.

Designation is an important step for these countries in their battle to revitalize and rebuild their weakened economies. Designation is also significant because it is further tangible evidence of the constructive cooperation between the United States and the peoples and governments of the Caribbean Basin.

My decision to designate the group of eleven flows out of discussions held between this Administration and potential beneficiary countries and entities regarding the designation criteria set forth in Section 212 of the CBERA. Our discussions with the eleven began rapidly and were concluded last month. However, active and constructive discussions are underway with other potential beneficiaries, and I hope to designate a number of additional countries in the near future.

The eleven countries have demonstrated to my satisfaction that their laws, practices and policies are in conformity with the designation criteria of the CBERA. The governments of these countries and entities have communicated on these matters by letter with Secretary of State Shultz and Ambassador Brock and in so doing have indicated their desire to be designated as beneficiaries (copies of the letters are attached). On the basis of the statements and assurances in these letters, and taking into account information developed by United States Embassies and through other sources, I have concluded that the objectives of the Administration and the Congress with respect to the statutory designation criteria of the CBERA have been met.

I am mindful that under Section 213(B)(2) of the CBERA, I retain the authority to suspend or withdraw CBERA benefits from any designated beneficiary country if a beneficiary's laws, policies or practices are no longer in conformity with the designation criteria. The United States will keep abreast of developments in the beneficiary countries and entities which are pertinent to the designation criteria.

This Administration looks forward to working closely with its fellow governments in the Caribbean Basin and with the private sectors of the United States and the Basin countries to ensure that the wide-ranging opportunities opened by the CBERA are fully utilized.

Sincerely,

RONALD REAGAN

Note: This is the text of identical letters addressed to Thomas P. O'Neill, Jr., Speaker of the House of Representatives, and George Bush, President of the Senate.

Proclamation 5133—Implementation of the Caribbean Basin Economic Recovery Act
November 30, 1983

By the President of the United States of America

A Proclamation

1. Sections 211 and 218 of the Caribbean Basin Economic Recovery Act (the CBERA) (19 U.S.C. 2701, 2706) confer authority upon the President to proclaim duty-free treatment for all eligible articles from any country which has been designated a "beneficiary country" in accordance with the provisions of section 212 of the CBERA. I

am designating the countries and territories or successor political entities set forth in the Annex as "beneficiary countries" under section 212 of the CBERA. I have previously notified the House of Representatives and the Senate of my intention to make such designation, together with the considerations entering into my decision, pursuant to subsection 212(a)(1)(A) of the CBERA.

2. In order to implement the duty-free treatment provided in accordance with the provisions of the CBERA, it is necessary to modify the Tariff Schedules of the United States (TSUS) (19 U.S.C. 1202), thus incorporating the substance of relevant provisions of the CBERA, and of actions taken thereunder, into the TSUS, pursuant to section 604 of the Trade Act of 1974 (the Trade Act) (19 U.S.C. 2483).

Now, Therefore, I, Ronald Reagan, President of the United States of America, acting under the authority vested in me by the Constitution and the statutes of the United States, including but not limited to sections 211 and 218 of the CBERA and section 604 of the Trade Act, do proclaim that:

(1) The countries set forth in general headnote 3(g)(i) of the TSUS, as added by paragraph (2) of this Proclamation, are designated as beneficiary countries.

(2) A new general headnote 3(g) of the TSUS is hereby added as set forth in the Annex, and present general headnote 3(g) is redesignated as general headnote 3(h).

(3) A new headnote 4 to subpart A of part 10 of schedule 1 of the TSUS is hereby added as set forth in the Annex.

(4) The provisions of this Proclamation shall be effective with respect to all articles that are entered, or withdrawn from warehouse for consumption, on or after the effective date of this Proclamation and on or before September 30, 1995.

(5) This Proclamation shall be effective on January 1, 1984.

In Witness Whereof, I have hereunto set my hand this 30th day of Nov., in the year of our Lord nineteen hundred and eighty-three, and of the Independence of the United States of America the two hundred and eighth.

RONALD REAGAN

[*Filed with the Office of the Federal Register, 3:06 p.m., December 1, 1983*]

Note: The annex to the proclamation is printed in the Federal Register *of December 5, 1983.*

The text of the proclamation was released by the Office of the Press Secretary on December 1.

Statement by Deputy Press Secretary Speakes on Implementation of the Caribbean Basin Economic Recovery Act
December 1, 1983

Late yesterday the President designated eleven countries (Barbados, Costa Rica, Dominica, Dominican Republic, Jamaica, the Netherlands Antilles, Panama, Saint Christopher and Nevis, Saint Lucia, Saint Vincent and the Grenadines, and the Government of Trinidad and Tobago) as the beneficiaries of the rights and privileges accorded under the Caribbean Basin Economic Recovery Act. The governments of these countries have, on behalf of all the citizens living under their jurisdiction, demonstrated to the United States Government a determination to accelerate economic progress in this hemisphere and to see the rewards of that progress bring a better life for all in this hemisphere.

These eleven countries will begin enjoying the benefits of the act on January 1, 1984. After that date these governments will have unencumbered duty-free access to the U.S. market on terms that recognize our important goal of increasing commercial exchange between our countries and within the hemisphere generally. The United States is also now prepared to extend to these nations special tax advantages which can benefit tourism and other sectors of their economy.

The President has been particularly gratified by the bipartisan support which the Caribbean Basin Initiative has received in the United States. Through the democratic process our people have been able to express their sympathy for the needs and aspirations of their neighbors in the Caribbean. The President shares with all Americans a deep feeling of pride in the continuation and, in its way, a new beginning of our friendship with the peoples of the Caribbean Basin.

Note: Deputy Press Secretary Larry M. Speakes read the statement during his daily briefing for reporters, which began at 12:30 p.m. in the Briefing Room at the White House.

Remarks of President Reagan and President Amin Gemayel of Lebanon Following Their Meetings
December 1, 1983

President Reagan. It's been my great pleasure to once again welcome our friend, President Gemayel, to Washington. President Gemayel symbolizes Lebanon's hopes for unity, peace, and stability—goals for which all of us are working so hard and for which many Americans and many more Lebanese have sacrificed their lives.

We admire President Gemayel's personal courage. We applaud his determination to free his country of all foreign forces and to reunite the Lebanese people. Lebanon once shined like a jewel in the sun, and America will do what it can to support Lebanon's efforts to restore her tranquility and independence.

To this end, we stand by the May 17th agreement as the best and most viable basis for the withdrawal of Israeli forces from Lebanon. And once again, I appeal to the other external forces to leave Lebanon.

I was particularly impressed by the initiative that President Gemayel took in calling for national dialog. Today he and I have discussed his programs for national unity. And, Mr. President, your efforts to broaden the base of your government, bringing in Lebanon's many communities, will do much to rebuild a stable and prosperous Lebanon. It will do much to restore confidence in the future. It will do much to stop the loss of so many innocent lives.

President Gemayel has already achieved a measure of success through the effective leadership that he demonstrated during the first round of reconciliation talks in Geneva. Yet, there is still a long way to go, and Lebanon can count on our help.

Our marines, along with our allies in the multinational force, are in Beirut to demonstrate the strength of our commitment to peace in the Middle East. And I know you agree with me, Mr. President, that the American people can be proud of the job that our marines are doing. Their presence is making it possible for reason to triumph over the forces of violence, hatred, and intimidation.

My special representative for the Middle East, Don Rumsfeld, returned recently from his first round of meetings in the region. He'll be returning to the area soon and will be working directly with President Gemayel to arrange foreign troop withdrawals and to pursue Lebanese national reconciliation.

We're delighted to have you with us today, Mr. President, and we wish you Godspeed on your return home.

President Gemayel. Mr. President, I want to thank you and the American people to whom we in Lebanon owe so much.

This is my third visit to Washington and probably the most important because of the intensity of the crisis in Lebanon and the region. Yet, I'm confident that actions, properly conceived and executed at this time, can result in dramatic movement toward stability, security, and peace.

Today we explored, as partners, the best

ways and means not to merely implement agreement but going beyond the letter of the law to set up the most appropriate mechanism and conditions for the achievement of our common interests and policy objectives. We found ourselves in full agreement on the necessity of withdrawal of all external forces from Lebanon and the full restoration of the Lebanese sovereignty and exclusive authority over all of Lebanon's territory within its internationally recognized borders. This, and this alone, will put an end to the continuing tragedy which is now engulfing not only Lebanese but Americans in Lebanon as well. Hence, it is imperative for us all to break the cycle of violence which has been preventing the people of Lebanon for the past decade from exercising their divine and natural right of self-determination and the shaping of a free, modern society in full social and economic partnership.

I found in Washington full comprehension of the fact that leading Lebanon out of the present impasse is not only a question of justice and right but also a matter of common interest both for its neighbors and the U.S.

I view our discussions today with a sense of pride and accomplishment, and I'm gratified by President Reagan's commitment, and the support of the American people. I look forward, with hope, that actions taken as a result of our discussions, fortified by the courage and vision of the American and Lebanese people, will result in peace in Lebanon and the entire region.

Note: President Reagan spoke at 1:25 p.m. to reporters assembled at the South Portico of the White House.

Earlier, the two Presidents and officials, including the Vice President, Secretary of State George P. Shultz, and Ambassador Donald Rumsfeld, the President's Personal Representative in the Middle East, met in the Oval Office. They then met, together with U.S. and Lebanese officials, in the Cabinet Room and attended a luncheon in the State Dining Room.

Statement on Signing the Office of Federal Procurement Policy Act Amendments of 1983
December 1, 1983

I have today signed H.R. 2293, a bill that authorizes appropriations for the Office of Federal Procurement Policy through the end of fiscal year 1987, while clarifying and enhancing the authorities and responsibilities of that office.

This legislation is an important component of my administration's far-ranging efforts to reform the wasteful and inefficient procurement practices of the Federal Government.

The Office of Federal Procurement Policy—part of the Office of Management and Budget—is responsible for providing overall governmentwide leadership and direction of Federal procurement policy. It is also responsible for overseeing the Federal procurement reforms that I initiated through issuance of Executive Order No. 12352 in March 1982, which are an essential element of this administration's ongoing Reform 88 program.

This legislation will help to strengthen the fundamental characteristics of wise and economical procurement—including the increased use of full and open competition—in the marketplace.

I congratulate those Members of Congress who were responsible for the development and sponsorship of H.R. 2293, especially Senators Cohen and Chiles and Congressmen Brooks and Horton.

Note: As enacted, H.R. 2293 is Public Law 98–191, approved December 1.

Proclamation 5134—Carrier Alert Week, 1983
December 2, 1983

By the President of the United States of America

A Proclamation

A major problem faced by our Nation's elderly and homebound is isolation. For many, friends and spouses have died, and families have moved away. When no one is left to check in on these individuals on a regular basis, illness or injury may go undetected until more serious consequences—even death—may result.

The United States Postal Service and the National Association of Letter Carriers are doing something to alleviate this problem. In growing numbers of towns and cities all across America, they are involved in a program called "Carrier Alert" in which mail carriers monitor the mailboxes of participating residents for unusual accumulations of mail which may signal distress. When such an accumulation occurs, the Postal Service notifies a local sponsoring social service agency which investigates and provides any necessary assistance.

Because mail carriers are in a unique position to be able to spot this kind of trouble quickly, the "Carrier Alert" program provides an effective and valuable service to the community. Participation in the program is entirely voluntary and costs nothing to postal customers. Since the inception of the "Carrier Alert" program in 1982, numerous press accounts around the country have documented instances in which the

program has saved the lives or eased the sufferings of elderly or disabled people who would have been left to languish alone in their pain but for a carrier's concern.

To encourage the American people to become more aware of the "Carrier Alert" program, to participate more broadly in it, and to recognize the efforts of the United States Postal Service and the National Association of Letter Carriers in providing this public-spirited assistance, the Congress, by Senate Joint Resolution 141, has designated the week of December 4, 1983, through December 10, 1983, as "Carrier Alert Week" and has authorized and requested the President to issue a proclamation in observance of that week.

Now, Therefore, I, Ronald Reagan, President of the United States of America, do hereby proclaim the week beginning December 4, 1983 as "Carrier Alert Week." I call upon the American people to observe that week with appropriate ceremonies and activities.

In Witness Whereof, I have hereunto set my hand this second day of December, in the year of our Lord nineteen hundred and eighty-three, and of the Independence of the United States of America the two hundred and eighth.

RONALD REAGAN

[*Filed with the Office of the Federal Register, 11:59 a.m., December 2, 1983*]

Appointment of A. C. Lyles as a Member of the President's Advisory Council on Private Sector Initiatives
December 2, 1983

The President today announced his intention to appoint A. C. Lyles to be a member of the President's Advisory Council on Private Sector Initiatives. This is a new position.

Mr. Lyles is president and chief executive

officer of A. C. Lyles Films in Hollywood, Calif. He was affiliated with Paramount Pictures for 44 years, serving 30 years as a producer-writer-partner in numerous theatrical features and television shows. He is currently an independent producer and packager of motion pictures and network television programs.

Mr. Lyles is married and resides in Los Angeles, Calif. He was born May 17, 1918, in Jacksonville, Fla.

Question-and-Answer Session With High School Students on Domestic and Foreign Policy Issues
December 2, 1983

Unemployment Rate

The President. Well, hello again. And it's good to see all of you here. And before I start taking the questions, could I just give you a little news? If you've been too busy here to hear it, this morning they released the unemployment figures for the Nation for the month of November. And it's down to 8.2 percent—370,000 more people went to work last month. And the significance of that figure to us, though, is about how fast that makes the recovery, because 8.2 percent was what we had predicted would be true at the end of 1985. So, we're a little ahead of schedule on the recovery.

But now I understand that someone has been designated as the first questioner.

Grenada

Q. Mr. President, my name is Silvia Vilato from Our Lady of Lourdes Academy in Miami, Florida. First of all, I would like to commend you and your staff on the handling of the situation in Grenada. I feel that this event brought about a national spirit which was greatly needed in these times of crisis. And my question is: The Grenada affair saw the most direct confrontation with the Castro regime in recent years. Would you envision any further confrontation in the future, or do you feel that Fidel Castro got the message? *[Laughter]*

The President. Well, thank you, first of all, very much. I think possibly not only he but a number of others got the message all right, that the United States—we're not warlike, we want peace; but we know that we can't buy peace at any price. And when our national security is concerned the world better know that we're going to do whatever is necessary for the safety and protection of our freedoms and the people of this country.

So, we don't plan any confrontations. That'll be up to them. And under the same circumstances and with the same request made by our neighbors that was made by six of the countries down there, I think we would probably react in the same way.

Youth

Q. Mr. President, my question to you today concerns us—the Nation's youth. As far as I know, we, the youth, have no form of representation in the Government. What has been done to ensure that we have the representation that we should have?

The President. Well, I wouldn't say that you don't have representation in government. You know, we have a number of programs, and this, while it is not exactly connected with the Government, it certainly gives you access to government. But we try to represent all of the people in the country. And I think that the things that we do through education and through all of those who deal with you is comparable to an actual representation by youth.

Student Aid

Q. Mr. President, I'm Diane Lipman from North Miami Beach Senior High School, Miami, Florida. My question is, will more money be set aside for financial aid for students who wish to attend college but can't afford it on their own?

The President. We think that an adequate amount is set aside. Today, 40 percent of all the students going to college in this country are eligible for some form of financial aid from the Government. This has gone up, has multiplied several times over what it was just not too many years ago. In addition to that, of course, then the idea there are student loan funds out in the private sector—foundations that do that sort of thing. But the government alone is providing help of some kind for 40 percent of the students. And let me just say, I know that problem intimately, because I worked my own way through college. And one of the better jobs that I had was—at that time, I was washing dishes in the girls' dormitory. [*Laughter*]

Programs for the Needy

Q. Mr. President, my name is Jo Lynn Anderson from Center High School, and I live in Center, Texas. How do you react to the fairness issue being raised, suggesting that your budget cuts in social services have hurt the poor and those less able to afford, you know, the aid like welfare and day care and like that?

The President. Well, this whole charge of fairness, I think, is political demagoguery and is done for political purposes. Having been a Governor for 8 years and thus participated in administering many of the Federal programs, I was aware of what a high percentage of the money for those programs went to the bureaucracy, was spent in administrative overhead.

I give you an example of a program that was supposed to—Federal program supposed to put 17 unemployed people in one of our counties in California into some jobs helping out in the maintenance of parks. Now it sounds pretty logical, except that half of the budget was going to go to 11 administrators—to make sure that the 17 got to work on time, I guess. But it seemed to me it was out of balance.

What we've been doing is redirecting the aid actually to the truly needy. You would be surprised at how—under the management of those programs—how the ceiling had gone up on earnings to where people who really were self-sustaining were getting government grants and government aid at the expense of their neighbors. And those neighbors weren't making as much money as they were.

We have redirected this. And this is also true in the previous question of aid to the students. We found that people who should normally be expected to be able to send their children to college were getting this

help, financial help.

So, we have redirected more of these programs to the people who truly need it. And we're actually—this government is providing 95 million meals a day. We are subsidizing housing for more than 10 million families in the country today. There has been no real cutback or decline in aid to the people who through no fault of their own must depend on the rest of us for help. We've just tried to make government a little bit more efficient.

Now some of these who are squealing the loudest are some of the bureaucrats that were proven unnecessary and also some of the people who never should have been on the programs in the first place.

For example, I had a message the other day from a man in a small town down in Mississippi. And he was writing to me about food stamps in his area, because there's a 31-percent unemployment rate in that particular town. And he was telling of some of the things, of people getting $2,400 a month and receiving food stamps. Well, for them to do that means that someone else who really has need for them is being cheated and is not being able to get the help that they should have.

So I think we are being fair, and I think we're being fair, also, to the working men and women in this country who are sharing their earnings to help those who are unable to take care of themselves.

Views on the Presidency

Q. Mr. President, I am Vicki Kessler from Manzano High School in Albuquerque, New Mexico. What do you feel are the necessary qualities for someone to run for a public office, especially the Presidency?

The President. What is the necessary quality? Well, I'll tell you, I would put it this way. I don't think that any public office should be viewed by someone as just a good job that they might like to have for their own personal career. I think you really have to believe in something and think that you can bring about an improvement by serving in public office in order to bring about this reform or to do this good that you think the government should be doing.

Now, I don't know whether that answers

your question about me, but I do know that for about 25 years, before I ever dreamed that I would seek public office—never wanted to, was very happy in my previous line of work—but some way, back from being a sports announcer, I guess, I got on the mashed-potato circuit, as I call it. [*Laughter*] And since I didn't sing or dance, I usually wound up being an after dinner speaker at somebody's banquet. And I always did my own speeches. And I, over the years, was talking more and more about the things that I saw wrong in government that should be corrected. And, then, when through a set of circumstances some people prevailed upon me to run for Governor, I think what finally—and it came about through those speeches—why I saw it as an opportunity to, instead of just talking about these problems, to do something about them. And that's it.

Communication With the Soviet Union

Q. Mr. President, my name is Stephen Carter. I'm from the Law Magnet High School in Dallas, Texas. With Soviet Premier Andropov sick, and with the recent death of Brezhnev a couple years ago, do you see any real, foreseeable problems for the United States in dealing with another Soviet premier should he die?

The President. Well, it's true that there's difficulty, and there has been in this period and before his illness. When a new man is just taking over and getting his government organized, there's a period in there in which he's not ready to get out and start talking with someone else about international affairs. So, there would be that period again, if there is a change of leadership.

I will say this, on the other hand, though, that we are in communication at a number of levels with people in the Soviet Union. We're not just incommunicado. We have people that have channels and through the State Department and all, that we're in contact. I have even communicated with personal, handwritten letters, myself.

And we feel that the two superpowers, in the position we're in in the world today, with all the tensions and with all the possibility for a tragic error, that we can't discontinue our conversation and our meetings with them. But because you don't see an

awful lot about this in the public media, it is going on.

I happen to be a believer in what I've called quiet diplomacy. For example, if you make a demand on the other government and you say, "You've got to do this; we don't like what you're doing," and it's on the front page of the papers and on the TV news, in the world of politics you've put that person in a position where he can hardly give in, because then in the eyes of their own people they would be accepting orders from another government. So on many of the touchiest points, you deal quietly in the background with an individual there. And you say, "Look, we're not going to go out making speeches about this, but this is a problem. And it's a problem that affects our relations with each other. And if you were doing, could see your way to doing this—whatever that particular thing is—believe me, our relations would be much better." And we've been doing this. And I have to tell you, it works.

Now, I think I've got to go back there. There are too many hands.

Immigration and Refugee Policy

Q. Hello, Mr. President. My name is Annette Lauredo, and I go to Saint Brendan's High School in Miami, Florida. My question is, does your administration plan to develop some kind of concrete immigration policy to help alleviate the problems caused by the thousands of refugees coming to the shores in South Florida and also in other States, year after year?

The President. Well, yes, there is a policy in this country. First of all, the policy on immigration is that, as you know, there are quotas. We know we can't take everyone. So people are on waiting lists from various countries, depending on how much of their quota has been used for direct immigration.

As for refugees, that's a different problem. Our country historically has always offered itself as a shelter for those who are persecuted and those who have fled persecution and are refugees, such as the boat people from Vietnam. Now we do have an overall figure on that.

We have legislation, however, in the Congress right now, that we've been trying to get passed—and we've had trouble getting it passed—having to do with this entire problem and with immigration and trying to close our borders, or control our borders, I should say, against those who are neither immigrants or refugees and who just come into the country and suddenly disappear into the whole population. But we have to a certain extent lost control of our borders. There are a great many illegal migrants coming into our country, and we're trying with this legislation to restore it to legal immigration and at the same time keep the door open for those refugees.

El Salvador

Q. Mr. President, my name is Kirk Kiester. I attend Fort Lauderdale Christian School in Fort Lauderdale, Florida. This week you vetoed a bill passed by Congress which linked military aid in El Salvador with human rights. Why did you veto this bill, and how can we justify supporting governments, be they leftwing or rightwing, which violate human rights?

The President. Well, we're not supporting leftwing or rightwing governments who violate human rights. The situation in El Salvador, and this was the reason for the veto, the situation is that for 400 years El Salvador has been dominated by dictators of one kind or another. It's from a heritage that goes back to the very beginning of their country.

Then, a few years ago, and for the first time, a government came into power in El Salvador—wasn't elected, overthrew one of those dictatorships. But it truly was aimed at being democratic. And the result was they had an election more than a year ago. And they elected a democratic form of government. Eighty-three percent of their people went to the polls to vote. The leftist guerrillas that are fighting the Government had a slogan at the time of that election. They said to the people, "Vote today and die tonight," meaning they would kill the people if they went to vote. And the people defied them. I've told repeatedly of a story of one woman that some of our Congressmen, who were there as observers, saw in the line waiting to vote who had been wounded by the guerrillas, shot with a rifle. And she refused to leave the line for medi-

cal attention until she could vote. Now that's the government of El Salvador.

Now, yes, there are holdovers. There are people left who aren't part of those leftist guerrillas, but who want the form of dictatorship and the totalitarianism—the privileged class concept that they had before this democratic government. And they are the so-called murder squads and doing the things they're doing to violate human rights.

The democratic government, beset by thousands of guerrillas on the left, would have a lot better chance of apprehending these death squads and handling the extreme rightists if they were not beset by the guerrillas. And the Congress, by holding down the help that we can give to this El Salvador government, is simply leaving them in a position of—well, they can keep on fighting, but they don't have the means to actually win yet. They're just dragging on. And at the same time, they can't handle these two things at once.

But the other thing we noticed was that if we have this thing of having to certify every few months to the Congress in order to get this aid, there are people, both on the left and right, who know that if they step up the violation of human rights—the murders and so forth, so that we can't certify, they—from whichever side—are helping to win their battle against the democratic government.

So, I vetoed the bill. What I want is for Congress to give us the help that should be provided. And 3 dollars out of every 4 that we're spending down there is being spent on social reforms and economic help, not on the military. Only a fourth of the help is helping them militarily, but we need to help them more.

We're doing everything we can, not only to help that Government deal with these rightwing squads, but I'm going to voice a suspicion now that I've never said aloud before. I wonder if all of this is rightwing, or if those guerrilla forces have not realized that by infiltrating into the city of San Salvador and places like that, that they can get away with these violent acts, helping to try and bring down the Government, and the rightwing will be blamed for it.

1645

Now, I'm not absolving the rightwing. We know there are rightwing assassins and murder squads and so forth, but we're doing everything we can to control that. I didn't think this bill would help.

Central America

Q. Mr. President, my name is Robert Pupo, from Belen Jesuit Preparatory School in Miami, Florida. First of all, I would like to commend you for giving America a strong and efficient administration for almost 3 years now.

The President. Thank you.

Q. My question is, if the situation in Central America worsens, would you consider sending American troops into this area?

The President. Is it worsened by sending American troops into the area? Was that your question?

Q. If the situation in Central America worsens and becomes a threat to American security, will you consider sending troops—American troops—into Central America?

The President. Well, it would have to be very evident that it was a direct threat to the United States. The truth of the matter is, dating back to some days when the big colossus of the North, the United States, did lean on and practice what was called gunboat diplomacy—our own friends and neighbors down there don't want us to send that kind of military help. They don't want our troops down there, and we respect them for that. President Magaña of El Salvador has said, "Yes, we need some help; we need weapons, ammunition; we need training." And we're providing that for them. But he said, "We will provide the manpower. We don't want yours." So, yours was a kind of a hypothetical question and mine is a hypothetical answer. It would have to be something that we saw as actually a threat to our security and our safety, and then we would be defending ourselves, not someone else.

China and Taiwan

Q. Mr. President, my name is Samantha Gamboa. I attend the High School for Law Enforcement and Criminal Justice in Houston, Texas. For what reasons are you going to China in April, and what do you plan on accomplishing?

The President. Well, President Nixon some years ago opened the door to what was Communist China—still professes to be Communist, although it has undergone many reforms and liberalizations of that kind of rule. But here are around a billion people in the world—capable, energetic people. And it didn't seem right, as he felt at that time, that we should shut the doors, not communicate at all.

He opened the doors, and the two Presidents between him and me have continued that. We have bettered the relations, I think, vastly. We've opened up trade both ways between the two countries. Their head man is coming to our country to visit in January, I believe, and we accepted his invitation to go there.

But I think it comes down to this: that you only get in trouble when people are talking about each other instead of to each other. And so we get better understanding each time that we have these meetings. Our Secretary of State, our Secretary of Defense have both made visits there. The Vice President has visited. And they exchange and visit here. And we deal with trade problems, we deal with further opening of—such as cultural relations of people back and forth to become more familiar with each other. And I think it is a worthwhile thing to do.

But in saying that, let me add one thing. We have a very delicate problem with them, and that is the situation with Taiwan, because both governments claim to be the government of China. That is their problem. But we have made it plain, it is a problem that must be settled peacefully between them. And we have made it plain, also, that in continuing and trying to build this friendship, relationship with the People's Republic of China on the mainland, we in no way retreat from our alliance with and our friendship with the Chinese on Taiwan. They have been allies of ours going all the way back to World War II. We are friends, and repeatedly we have said to the government of mainland China that they should appreciate the fact that we're not going to throw aside one friend in order to make another. And then they ought to feel more comfortable that we can be friends with them, too.

The Caribbean

Q. Good afternoon, Mr. President. My name is Cadet Douglas Hewitt, from Valley Forge Military Academy in Wayne, Pennsylvania.

The President. I visited there.

Q. In 1962 President Kennedy intervened in a Soviet action to attempt to stop the placement of Soviet medium-range ballistic missiles in Cuba. Recently Soviet—[*inaudible*]—Mig–23's have been placed in Cuba and Nicaragua. As I see it, there is no U.S. advance fighter aircraft stationed in the Caribbean Basin. Do you think that we should station possibly F–16's in Guantanamo Bay Naval Base or Howard Air Force Base in Panama to stop the threat of a strike anywhere in the Caribbean Basin or possibly the southern United States or possibly the Panama Canal?

The President. Well, we're aware of those planes that are in those areas. And I'd call to your attention that we have carrier squadrons that are on duty in the Caribbean and over on the Pacific side, off that side of Central America. And we think that we have sufficient force and sufficient warning for our own bases that we can handle that.

When the Cuban missile crisis came along, the situation was far different. And I don't mean to take anything away from President Kennedy. But at that time the United States had about an 8 to 1 nuclear superiority over the Soviet Union. So when we stood up and looked them in the eye, they blinked.

Yes. I'm sorry, there are a lot of hands that I didn't get to.

Q. Excuse me, Mr. President. My name is John Lopez, from Albuquerque, New Mexico. And on behalf of the Close-Up Foundation, we would like to thank you for this great opportunity.

The President. Well, that was a good, easy question. Thank you very much.

Note: The President spoke at 1:34 p.m. in Room 450 of the Old Executive Office Building. The question-and-answer session was taped for later broadcast on the Cable Satellite Public Affairs Network.

The participants were part of the Close-Up Foundation program, a nonpartisan educational foundation providing secondary school students opportunities to study the American political system.

Radio Address to the Nation on the American Family
December 3, 1983

My fellow Americans:

This is a very special time of year for us, a time for family reunions and for celebrating together the blessings of God and the promises He has given us. From Thanksgiving to Hanukkah, which our Jewish community is now celebrating, to Christmas in 3 weeks' time, this is a season of hope and of love.

Certainly one of the greatest blessings for people everywhere is the family itself. The American Family Institute recently dedicated its book of essays, "The Family in the Modern World," to Maria Victoria Walesa, daughter of Danuta and Lech Walesa, to whose christening came 7,000 Poles expressing their belief that the family remains the foundation of freedom. And, of course,

they're right. It's in the family where we learn to think for ourselves, care for others, and acquire the values of self-reliance, integrity, responsibility, and compassion.

Families stand at the center of society, so building our future must begin by preserving family values. Tragically, too many in Washington have been asking us to swallow a whopper: namely, that bigger government is the greatest force for fairness and progress. But this so-called solution has given most of us a bad case of financial indigestion. How can families survive when big government's powers to tax, inflate, and regulate absorb their wealth, usurp their rights, and crush their spirit? Was there compassion for a working family in 21½-

percent interest rates, 12½-percent inflation, and taxes soaring out of sight? Consider the cost of childrearing. It now takes $85,000 to raise a child to age 18, and family incomes haven't kept up. During the 1970's real wages actually declined over 2 percent. Consider taxes. In 1948 the tax on the average two-child family was just $9. Today it is $2,900.

As economic and social pressures have increased, the bonds that bind families together have come under strain. For example, three times as many families are headed by single parents today as in 1960. Many single parents make heroic sacrifices and deserve all our support. But there is no question that many well-intentioned Great Society-type programs contributed to family breakups, welfare dependency, and a large increase in births out of wedlock. In the 1970's the number of single mothers rose from 8 to 13 percent among whites and from 31 to a tragic 47 percent among blacks. Too often their children grow up poor, malnourished, and lacking in motivation. It's a path to social and health problems, low school performance, unemployment, and delinquency.

If we strengthen families, we'll help reduce poverty and the whole range of other social problems.

We can begin by reducing the economic burdens of inflation and taxes, and we're doing this. Since 1980 inflation has been chopped by three-fourths. Taxes have been cut for every family that earns a living, and we've increased the tax credit for child care. Yesterday we learned that our growing economy reduced unemployment to 8.2 percent last month. The payroll employment figure went up by 370,000 jobs.

At the same time, new policies are helping our neediest families move from dependence to independence. Our new job training law will train over a million needy and unemployed Americans each year for productive jobs. I should add that our enterprise zones proposal would stimulate new businesses, bringing jobs and hope to some of the most destitute areas of the country. The Senate has adopted this proposal. But after 2 years of delay, the House Democratic leadership only recently agreed to hold its first hearing on the legislation. This is a jobs bill America needs. And come January, we expect action.

We're moving forward on many other fronts. We've made prevention of drug abuse among youth a top priority. We'll soon announce a national missing children's center to help find and rescue children who've been abducted and exploited. We're working with States and local communities to increase the adoption of special-needs children. More children with permanent homes mean fewer children with permanent problems.

We're also stiffening the enforcement of child support from absent parents. And we're trying hard to improve education through more discipline, a return to the basics, and through reforms like tuition tax credits to help hard-working parents.

In coming months, we'll propose new ways to help families stay together, remain independent, and cope with the pressures of modern life. A cornerstone of our efforts must be assisting families to support themselves. As Franklin Roosevelt said almost 50 years ago, "Self-help and self-control are the essence of the American tradition."

In Washington everyone looks out for special interest groups. Well, I think families are pretty special. And with your help, we'll continue looking out for their interests.

Till next week, thanks for listening, and God bless you.

Note: The President spoke at 12:06 p.m. from Camp David, Md.

Statement on the Death of Representative Clement J. Zablocki
December 3, 1983

Nancy and I were deeply saddened today to learn of the death of Congressman Clement Zablocki. Clement Zablocki served his constituency and his country with dedication and integrity. He was a strong and effective advocate for the causes in which he so deeply believed. But above all else, he was an American of great patriotism who could always be counted upon to put country ahead of politics. I will miss his wise counsel. We send our deepest sympathy to his family.

Remarks and a Question-and-Answer Session With Reporters on the United States Airstrike in Lebanon
December 4, 1983

The President. Good afternoon.

For some time now, we have been flying regular and routine reconnaissance flights with unarmed planes in Lebanon as a part of the protection and defense of our forces there. We notified the Syrians of this some time ago, assuring them that the planes were unarmed, that this was purely for reconnaissance. There have been some instances of firing at those planes now and then from unknown sources. But early yesterday, two such reconnaissance missions were fired upon by literally hundreds of antiaircraft and a combination of surface-to-air missiles, which were coordinated from several sites by the Syrians. Early today, we responded to this unprovoked attack by striking back at those sites from whence had come the attack.

We don't seek hostilities there. Our mission remains what it was: to help stabilize the situation in Beirut until all the foreign forces can be withdrawn and until the Government of Lebanon can take over the authority of its own territory. But we are going to defend our forces there. And this was the reason—or the purpose of the mission earlier today.

Q. Are you going to negotiate to get the pilots back? Aren't there two lost or unaccounted for?

The President. Yes. We've had this report that two of the pilots, or the crew of one plane—two planes were shot down of ours. The pilot, as you know, was rescued that landed outside of that area. Two inside. I don't have any further word except that we are attempting to negotiate their release.

There have been rumors or reports of some kind of the loss of one, but we have no substantiation of that.

Q. What do the Syrians say?

Q. Is there a danger of——

Q. What do the Syrians say about it? Have they said anything?

The President. I am going to find all that out, because we're just—our Embassy has been notified, and they're making contact.

Q. Mr. President, are they escalating the war, sir?

Q. Mr. President, if they shoot at us again, will we shoot back?

Q. Are we at war with Syria?

The President. Wait a minute. What?

Q. Do you fear a military confrontation with Syria at this point?

The President. Do we fear a military confrontation with Syria? Well, I think that's the wrong word. I think the question is wrong. We don't want such a thing; we don't desire it. But—and I think this'll answer your question over here at the same time about if it happens again, will we fire back—we haven't fired at anyone unless it has been to return fire against attacks made upon our forces.

Yes, if our forces are attacked, we will respond. We're going to defend our personnel that is there.

Q. Is this coordinated with the Israelis,

Mr. President?

The President. What's that?

Q. Is this coordinated with the Israelis, sir?

The President. No. I heard some rumors to that effect. And I suppose the situation of President Gemayel and Prime Minister Shamir both being here and the fact that they have responded with fire to some areas led people to suppose that. No, we knew nothing of their operations, and there was no contact with them regarding ours. And the Prime Minister has responded to that question and said that they were only aware of it after it happened.

Q. Do we think President Assad is still running Syria? Do we think President Assad is in good shape to run Syria?

The President. Well, that's—your guess is as good as mine. We don't know. The conflicting stories that are coming out of there, the attempt now to portray him as being active and on the scene—we really have no assurance one way or the other.

Q. Do we think that's had an effect on this firing at our aircraft?

The President. I wouldn't know. All I know is that this was coordinated by the Syrians.

Q. Are the two pilots POW's now?

Q. Does this complicate American efforts to negotiate the Syrians out of Lebanon?

The President. What?

Q. How seriously does this retaliatory attack complicate hopes to negotiate a Syrian exit from Lebanon?

The President. Well, I hope that it doesn't make it any more difficult. I hope that the reaction would be the other way. But we're going to continue with the mission that we embarked upon some time ago, and that is to bring peace to that area.

So, now, that's about all. Thank you.

Note: The President spoke at 1:39 p.m. at the South Portico of the White House. He was returning to the White House from Camp David, Md.

Remarks at the Jewish Community Center of Greater Washington During the Observance of Hanukkah
December 4, 1983

Well, thank you all very much, and may I just say what an honor and a joy it is to be with you this afternoon for this Hanukkah celebration.

The family activities that you've planned here, so many children, teenagers, and parents, is of great importance to the meaning of America, the wealth of our culture, and the strength of our values. Preserving the strength of families and family values is the key to America's future.

We've just seen the beautiful symbolic lighting of the Hanukkah menorah. At sundown you and your families will light your own menorahs. As we heard, when God kept the oil in the eternal flame burning for 8 days, he gave us the miracle of Hanukkah, a holiday of hope and rededication for every Jewish family.

We're reminded of Jewish unity and diversity by the eight separate branches of

the menorah coming together as one. And as the menorah's light grows stronger, with one candle being lit each day, we can feel the flame of freedom burning in your hearts. And that flame should inspire people everywhere.

Hanukkah is symbolic of the Jewish struggle to resist submission to tyranny and to sustain its spiritual heritage. No people have fought longer, struggled harder, or sacrificed more to survive, to grow, and to live in freedom than the people of Israel.

Whether we be Americans or Israelis, we are all children of Abraham, children of the same God. The bonds between our two peoples are growing stronger, and they must not and will never be broken.

Israel's quest for peace and security is in constant peril from those driven by hatred and violence. But as I told Prime Minister Shamir last week, Israel has a friend in

America, and good friends stand together.

We're also making sure that Israel is not hurt in the United Nations. Ambassador Kirkpatrick is our watchdog on this, and let me assure you, one thing about Jeane, she is a very determined woman. But just so no one gets any ideas, let me be blunt: If Israel is ever forced to leave the U.N., the United States and Israel will leave together.

I think it's wonderful that the American Jewish community is using Hanukkah to assist Jews in the Soviet Union. And how good it is to know that, at this very moment, Jews who have fled oppression are here with us taking their first steps toward becoming American citizens. On behalf of more than 230 million Americans, may I say to you, welcome to your new family.

We know that the emigration of Jews from the Soviet Union is practically stopped. They're constantly ridiculed, harassed, beaten, and arrested by Soviet authorities. It's no exaggeration to say their entire Jewish population feels it is under siege. Today, Soviet Jews are fighting for their future and their freedom, as the Maccabees once did. But their fight is a peaceful one. Some are struggling to emigrate from the Soviet Union. Many others are trying to assert their rights to practice their religion and preserve their heritage. In their struggle, we must not forsake them. We will not remain silent.

Our hearts go out to heroes like Anatoly Shcharanskiy and Iosif Begun, imprisoned for their love of God and freedom. And there are so many more.

We will not remain silent when Avi Goldstein, a 10-year-old boy being harassed by the KGB, asked visiting Samantha Smith to convey his family's appeal for emigration. We will not remain silent when Lev Furman, one of Moscow's leading Hebrew teachers, has been persecuted, seen his house vandalized, and been robbed of his teaching materials.

To every religious dissident trapped in this cold, cruel existence, we Americans send our love and support. We appeal to people everywhere to open their hearts and to raise their voices in support of our brothers and sisters. Together, let us pray that the warm lights of Hanukkah will spread the spirit of freedom and reach, comfort, and sustain every person who is suffering tonight.

Happy Hanukkah, and God bless you all.

Note: The President spoke at 3:24 p.m. in the auditorium of the community center, which is located in Rockville, Md.

Remarks at a White House Reception for Kennedy Center Honorees
December 4, 1983

Good evening again. I'm very pleased to welcome you all to the White House, the home that belongs to all of us.

President Kennedy once said that he looked forward to an America "not afraid of grace and beauty, an America respected throughout the world not only for its strength but for its civilization as well." Well, today we join the John F. Kennedy Center for the Performing Arts in honoring five Americans who have taught us a great deal about grace and beauty, five who've helped build a distinctive American civilization.

Even as a little girl, Katherine Dunham loved to dance. When only 8, she created a neighborhood controversy by staging a cabaret to raise money for her church. [*Laughter*] At the University of Chicago, she founded her own dance troupe and discovered anthropology, a discipline that enabled her to study the dance of many cultures.

In the decades since, Miss Dunham has become a noted anthropologist, an author, a great choreographer, and a role model for an entire generation of dancers. Her studies have taken her to Brazil, the Caribbean, and Africa. I understand that in one Caribbean city her startled host began to worry when she disappeared into the bush to study voodoo. But they calmed down when she gave them a concert and danced to the music of Debussy.

In professional dance, Miss Dunham became known for presenting black dances in their original context. She's renowned for the work with her company of dancers, singers, and musicians, for her schools in New York, which have trained hundreds, and for her choreography of shows and films such as "The Emperor Jones," "Cabin in the Sky," and "Stormy Weather."

Today, thanks in large measure to you, Miss Dunham, we not only have dance in America, we have American dance. And all the world loves you for it.

Virgil Thomson grew up in Kansas City but left America for Paris, where he lived until World War II. He decided that if he was going to starve as a composer, then, in his words, he "preferred to starve where the food is good." [*Laughter*]

He's composed symphonies; operas; motion picture scores; church music; over a hundred musical portraits; incidental music for theatrical productions; concertos; piano sonatas; songs with English, French, Spanish, and Latin texts; and much more. His music reflects his love of European culture, but again and again it's unmistakably American.

He wrote "The Seine at Night" in tribute to Paris, but he also wrote "Wheatfield at Noon" in tribute to Missouri. Music critic for the New York Herald Tribune during the forties and early fifties, Mr. Thomson has written eight books on music and has received the Pulitzer Prize. His latest book, "A Virgil Thomson Reader," won the National Book Critics' Circle Award for 1982.

No one has labored longer, with greater integrity and determination, or with more success to promote the cause of American music than this gentleman, Virgil Thomson.

Elia Kazan left Turkey for America with his family when he was 4. He went to Williams College, majored in English, and said his only ambition was "to stay out of my father's business." Well, Elia, you succeeded. In your senior year you turned to drama, and in the more than half century since, you've made millions of us mighty

grateful that you did.

Elia has directed "Death of a Salesman," "JB," and "Cat on a Hot Tin Roof." He cofounded the Actors Studio that trained Marlon Brando, Paul Newman, James Dean, and hundreds of others, and served as co-director of the repertory theater of Lincoln Center. And he's pushed forward cinematic technique with the freely moving style of "Panic on the Streets," the focus on brilliant individual performances in "Streetcar Named Desire," and the realism of "On the Waterfront." More recently, he's adapted two of his own novels for the screen: "America, America" and "The Arrangement."

Elia, with your boundless energy, your great talent and love of life, you have lifted American drama to a peak of excellence that inspires us all. And we thank you from the bottom of our hearts.

Now, the last two artists that we're honoring tonight are special friends of Nancy's and mine, Frank Sinatra and Jimmy Stewart.

Francis Albert Sinatra was born in Hoboken, New Jersey, and started to like music when his uncle gave him a ukulele. And one day in 1936, he went to a Jersey City vaudeville house to see Bing Crosby. After the show, Frank suddenly announced that he was becoming a singer.

In 1937 his group, the Hoboken Four, won first prize on Major Bowes' Original Amateur Hour. [*Laughter*] And for the next year and a half, he sang at the Rusty Cabin, a north Jersey roadhouse, for $15 a week. Let me repeat that. For a year and a half— [*laughter*]—Frank Sinatra worked for $15 a week. But it paid off. He got a $10-a-week raise. [*Laughter*]

After working with Harry James, Frank joined the Tommy Dorsey Band and started to develop a distinctive song style—long phrases and glissando—that's technical talk for crooning. [*Laughter*] Today, Frank Sinatra has recorded more hits than just about anybody else, hits like "Night and Day," "That Old Black Magic," "Strangers in the Night," "New York, New York," and so many more.

Through the years, Frank's been in a movie or two: "It Happened in Brooklyn,"

"On the Town," his Oscar-winning role in "From Here to Eternity." And Frank got a chance to sing with his old hero, Bing Crosby, in one of the most enjoyable movies ever made, "High Society."

You know, Frank, if they'd only given me roles like that, I never would have left Hollywood. [*Laughter*] Except for the musical numbers, they'd have had to get you to dub the voice in. [*Laughter*]

Well, all along, your style has been relaxed and full of life. You're given millions of us fond memories, immeasurable joy. And one other thing, Frank, you did it your way.

Now, James Stewart grew up in a town called Indiana, Pennsylvania. At Princeton he acted in musicals and, after graduation, got a part in a summer production of "Good-bye Again" in Falmouth, Massachusetts. He played the chauffeur, spent 3 minutes on stage, and spoke exactly two lines. But he packed those lines with so much humor that he was noticed by visiting New York critics.

In 1932 he went to New York, stayed for 2½ years and appeared in eight plays. Jimmy was a fine stage actor, but there was a medium on the west coast he wanted to try. So, in 1935 he took a train to Hollywood.

During his first 5 years there, Jimmy made 24 movies. They included a classic of American film, "The Philadelphia Story," and a movie about an idealistic Senator that I wish everyone in this town would study, "Mr. Smith Goes to Washington."

During World War II, Jimmy interrupted his career. After winning his wings in the Army Air Corps, he spent a year instructing cadets and then went to Europe, where he flew 25 missions over enemy territory. And if he looks like a patriot on the screen, that's because he is: Brigadier General Jimmy Stewart of the Air Force Reserve.

And the war over, Jimmy plunged back into his work. And his credits now include more than 80 pictures. He's worked with all the greats—directors like Capra and Hitchcock, and actresses like Hepburn, and actors like Henry Fonda and Clark Gable and Cary Grant. He's fought rawhide outlaws in the "Far Country," led pioneers in "Bend of the River," flown the Atlantic in the "The Spirit of St. Louis," and held long conversations with an invisible, giant rabbit as the unforgettable Elwood P. Dowd in "Harvey." [*Laughter*]

We think of the Stewart character as open, kind, and honest—just like the boy next door. Well, Nancy and I and his friends can tell you that that's not just some screen character; that's the real Jimmy Stewart.

You know, there's a story I have to tell. When Jack Warner, head of Warner Brothers, first heard that I was running for Governor of California, he said, "No, no. Jimmy Stewart for Governor; Reagan for best friend." [*Laughter*]

But, Jimmy, you once said, "The great thing about the movies is you're giving people little, tiny pieces of time that they never forget." Well, no one has given our nation more of those cherished moments than you have, my friend.

Henry James, the American novelist, once wrote, "Art is the shadow of humanity." These five people have spent their lives casting those magnificent and powerful shadows. In dance, drama, and music, they've taught us what it means to be human. And by drawing on and adding to the openness, verve, and color of life in our country, they've taught us what it means to be American.

Katherine Dunham, Virgil Thomson, Elia Kazan, Frank Sinatra, and Jimmy Stewart, on behalf of every American, thank you, and God bless you all.

Note: The President spoke at 6:18 p.m. in the East Room at the White House.

Following the reception, the President went to the John F. Kennedy Center for the Performing Arts for a gala performance honoring the award recipients.

Remarks During a Conference Call With Chancellor Helmut Kohl of the Federal Republic of Germany and Crewmembers of the Space Shuttle *Columbia*
December 5, 1983

The President. Greetings from Washington. Chancellor Kohl is with us all the way from Athens, Greece; along with you astronauts hovering in space, with me here in Washington, and the whole world listening, this is one heck of a conference call.

Seriously though, this space shuttle mission represents the enormous potential available to mankind. The Spacelab, in which the experiments are being carried out, was designed and built by the European Space Agency. The Federal Republic of Germany and other European contributors can be especially proud of this achievement.

It is fitting that on this the German-American tricentennial a German astronaut is part of the shuttle team. The shuttle is demonstrating that technology can be used to bring people together in a new spirit of enterprise and cooperation to better their lives, ensure the peace of mankind.

I know Chancellor Kohl agrees with me that this shuttle mission, with its German and American crew, represents the highest aspirations of our two peoples. Chancellor Kohl, this is a great day. Perhaps you could give us your thoughts on this marvelous occasion.

The Chancellor. Thank you very much, Mr. President. It is a terrific experience for us to be able to talk together this way and to talk to the crew as well. Above all, I would like to send my best wishes to my countryman. Dear Herr Merbold, I would like to take this opportunity to assure you and your colleagues, your team members, that I and all countrymen in Germany have, with great excitement and pride, been following your flight for days now.

We are proud, indeed, that your participation in this highly successful experiment is, at this time, demonstrating in such an impressive way the close ties between Europe and the United States and that it shows, once again, that we Europeans are in fact able to hold our own in terms of technology of the future. This U.S.-European shuttle mission is, indeed, a convincing proof of the closeness between Europe and the United States.

President Reagan has already pointed out that it is an exceedingly happy circumstance of which, of course, we are very much aware that it is possible at this time to have a German scientist, a European astronaut as a member of the crew at this particular time—at the time of the tricentennial celebrations of German-American relations, remembering the time when the first Germans came to the United States.

I am especially happy that our countryman Ulf Merbold is aboard the shuttle at this time. We hope that this joint enterprise will indeed lead to further successful cooperation between the United States and the Europeans in the area of space research, and I would like to tell you, Mr. Merbold, and you crewmembers that I hope you will have a healthy and happy return to your families.

Commander Young. Mr. President and Mr. Chancellor, we're delighted that you could visit with us today in the space shuttle *Columbia* and visit with us in the Spacelab. We're standing—or rather, floating in the Spacelab right now, and I'd be very pleased to introduce my fine crew. They performed in a totally outstanding manner throughout this mission, and I expect big things, scientifically and technically, to come from the results.

The pilot is Major Brewster Shaw. He's up on the mid-deck right now, along with mission specialists Dr. Robert Parker and Dr. Owen Garriott. Back here in Spacelab with me is Byron Lichtenberg—Dr. Byron Lichtenberg and Dr. Ulf Merbold. Byron will now give you a short tour around the Spacelab.

Dr. Merbold. Guten tag, Herr Bundeskanzler.

Dr. Lichtenberg. Good morning, Mr.

President.

The Chancellor. Hello, Mr. Merbold.

The President. Good morning.

Dr. Lichtenberg. We'd like to take a little bit of time to tell you a little bit about the science that we've been doing here on board Spacelab. I'll give you a brief tour from this end of the Spacelab module.

We've been doing several experiments in many different disciplines. Some of those use equipment that is mounted in a pallet outside the back of the Spacelab, and we control these through control panels here in the Spacelab. Other experiments are done inside the module, using equipment here.

And on my right, we have a rack of dedicated life-sciences experiments in which we do experiments in plant growth and a variety of experiments in the adaptation of the human being to weightlessness. We are particularly interested in looking at the vestibular system, the inner ear, and how a person adapts to the weightless environment of space life.

Other experiments we do utilize a scientific airlock here in front of me, and we have several experiments from Europe that we have put into this airlock and deployed into space.

The first one is an experiment to investigate the Earth's magnetic field lines and what happens when we inject a beam of electrons into the Earth's atmosphere to create artificial northern lights, or aurora borealis. There's another experiment, called the very wide field camera, which comes from a French aerospace laboratory, to take ultraviolet pictures of the stars. Both of these experiments have performed extremely well, and we have been able to deploy them into space repeatedly to take measurements.

I'd like to turn it over now to Ulf, and he'll continue the tour of the Spacelab. Thank you, sir.

Commander Young. I'd like to say to Ulf that German-American relations have never been better aboard Spacelab. They're great.

Dr. Merbold. Good morning, Mr. President. *Grüss Gott, Herr Bundeskanzler.* I might quickly move over to one of the facilities here which we have on board to process all sorts of materials, particularly crystals, new alloys, and I think that is par-

ticularly important for application.

We might be able to create new semiconductors for the electronic industry. We have one experiment here to create new materials for turbine blades, such that airplane engines could run at higher temperatures, which would save a lot of fuel. And so, we are trying to do a lot of things to make life in the future easier and better.

Commander Young. And if you gentlemen have any questions, we'd be certainly glad to answer them, either here or on the mid-deck.

The President. I don't know whether the Chancellor has any questions.

The Chancellor. Thank you very much, Herr Merbold, for this brief introduction which, of course, has been most impressive for someone like me who is not an expert.

My most important question is to you. How do you feel? How do you manage?

Dr. Merbold. [*Answers in German*][1]

The Chancellor. Millions of your countrymen, Mr. Merbold, are thinking of you and wish you and your crewmembers all the best.

Dr. Merbold. Thank you.

The President. I have one question, if I could. What do you see as the greatest potential for the use of space?

Commander Young. Mr. President, I see it as a place where humanity can live and work and make things better for people on Earth.

The President. Well, I'd like to take this opportunity to congratulate the entire crew. You're doing a fantastic job, and we're proud of you. Your energy, creativity, and your courage are an inspiration to us all.

It's hard to believe, when looking at the highly sophisticated project we've just witnessed, that it was just over 25 years ago that the United States launched its first satellite, a 31-pound, cylinder-shaped projectile named Explorer I. Shortly after that, NASA, the National Aeronautics and Space Administration, was created to make sure mankind got every benefit possible from the exploration of space.

---

[1] *The remarks were not translated by the interpreter.*

Our investment in space has been an exceptional bargain. Byproducts now touch our lives in so many ways. This hookup, as well as the calls every day of millions of people around the world, are made via communications satellites. Weather and navigation satellites guide us and help us protect our lives and property. The high-tech spinoffs of our space effort are too numerous to list. The experiments on this shuttle mission will add to the treasury of human knowledge and be put to practical use improving our lives right here on Earth.

This mission is also a shining example of international cooperation at its best. The Spacelab we've just toured was a gift to the United States from our European friends. Building on that good will, this is the first time a citizen from another country has joined one of our space missions as a member of the crew. It is an exciting first. It must be particularly exciting for our German friends.

Chancellor Kohl, I just want to tell you that it's such an honor for us to be together in demonstrating to the world that when people are free and work together, there's nothing that can't be accomplished. Together the free people of the world with the use of technology are building a world of prosperity and peace never imaginable a few decades ago.

Chancellor Kohl, perhaps you have some parting thoughts.

The Chancellor. Mr. President, I would like to thank you very much for your kind words. I thank you primarily for the fact that you have done us the honor to select our countryman to participate in this team. That was a great honor for the Germans and the Europeans, as well.

I would like to congratulate the entire crew on their mission and on the excellent scientific results which they have been able to achieve. This is, in fact, an effort which furthers peace. It has been made possible by the cooperation between Europe and the United States. And we do hope that our future will be similar, that it will be characterized by cooperation between the two sides of the Atlantic.

Herr Merbold, to you and your crewmembers, our best wishes for a happy return. I would like to also tell you that we hope that your scientific results will be impressive. And I hope, for the sake of all of us, that what you will bring back from this mission will indeed contribute to further development of science and technology in the interest and the service of peace and mankind.

And finally—and I think that's probably the most important—I'd like to express my best wishes for all your families. And I hope that Frau Merbold and her children and the wives and children of your team are—our best wishes are with them as well.

The President. Thank you. And Commander Young—John Young, do you have anything you would like to say?

Commander Young. We certainly appreciate your taking the time to come and visit with us. We've certainly enjoyed talking to you about what we're going to do in space. And we think it'll be of great benefit and great significance. And we're delighted that you and the Chancellor have shown so much interest in the space program.

The President. Well, I thank Chancellor Kohl and you. And thank you, all of our astronauts. God bless you, and Godspeed on your journey home.

Note: The President spoke at 9:47 a.m. from the Oval Office at the White House. The Chancellor spoke in German, and his remarks were translated by an interpreter.

For a statement on the conclusion of the space shuttle mission, see page 1672.

Remarks to Members of the National Conference of United States Attorneys
December 5, 1983

I thought of all the jokes I knew about lawyers and everything and decided—[*laughter*]—I wouldn't tell any of them.

I know there's one thing—I'm quite sure that when you go to social gatherings or cocktail parties, something of that kind, that when you're introduced and your profession is given, someone doesn't immediately start asking for free advice, as they do with doctors. [*Laughter*] In the business that I used to be in there was a very noted playwright, Moss Hart, and Moss just was addicted that if he met someone, anyone with the title of "Doctor," he immediately started finding a low back pain or something else he could talk about. [*Laughter*] And one night at a cocktail party he was introduced to a Dr. Jones, and he immediately started in. And the friend who'd introduced them, embarrassed, said, "Moss, Dr. Jones is a doctor of economics." And Moss was only stopped for about 10 seconds. He said, "I bought some stock the other day"—[*laughter*]——

But we're awfully glad to have you here today. You are, as the Attorney General said, among the highest officials this administration has, as they say in Washington, "in the field." Now, what that means is that you're out in the real world. You're on the frontlines. You're one of our closest, most direct contacts with the people. And perhaps more than just about anyone in government, what you do each day affects the lives and fortunes of thousands, sometimes millions of your fellow Americans. And what an impact you're having. I know the Attorney General's very proud of your work, and when I heard about your conference, I wanted to take a few minutes to express our pride and gratitude for the job that you're doing.

I know many of you made considerable sacrifices in accepting the U.S. attorney appointment. I also know the monetary rewards you derive from it are not large. That's why we appreciate the enormous contribution you've been making for the past couple of years and the accomplishments your hard work has made possible.

What a relief to be able to say, thanks to our law enforcement community at the Federal, State, and local levels, crime statistics in America are finally coming down, and they'll stay down. But I know that a few people, who note that we have less people in the crime-prone age, now want to attribute the encouraging downward trend in crime to this statistical correlation. Well, a coincidence isn't a correlation. The truth is that crime has sometimes risen with population growth and sometimes not. There's nothing historically inevitable about it. The really key factor has always been the will of a society to punish those who prey on the innocent and the willingness of the leaders of that society, especially those in the judiciary and the law enforcement system, to enforce that will.

Whether it's this administration's crackdown on drug traffickers and organized crime or the tougher sentencing laws being passed in so many States, the evidence abounds that Americans want to reassert basic values—values that say right and wrong do matter, that the individual is responsible for his actions, and that society must protect itself from career criminals who prey on the innocent and undermine the respect for law vital to freedom and prosperity.

Crime is starting to come down because for the first time in many years at the Federal, State, and local levels we are putting career criminals in jail in greater numbers and for longer periods of time. This itself is a reflection of the return to common sense and moral values that I've mentioned. The statistics bear this out. Just take the case of major drug prosecutions. In fiscal 1983 Federal law enforcement took out of circulation 2¾ million pounds of illicit drugs and 20 million doses of dangerous prescription drugs.

And the numbers of arrests and indictments are dramatically up. Organized crime convictions are up from 515 in fiscal

1981 to 1,331 in 1983. And I know that you've been especially active in pressing for collection of civil and criminal fines in government debt and fraud cases. In fact, the amount collected by the Justice Department this year is double what it was last year. So, all of you've played a major role in bringing about enormous changes in a very short period of time.

And yet, I feel the full weight of your contribution is still to be felt. As you know, we've had to spend much of our time in setting the stage for change. We had to get you the tools that you need to do your job. And we're getting results. After years of decline in our investigative forces, more than a thousand new investigators and 200 new prosecutors are joining the fight against crime this year.

We've improved State and local cooperation through your own local law enforcement coordinating committees and the Justice Department's Governors Project. We've added prison space and improved training opportunities for local and State police. With your help and leadership, our 12 new regional drug task forces are beginning to bring in the big cases against drug traffickers.

And, as I'm sure many of you know, our organized crime commission held some widely publicized hearings last week here in Washington. The commission will be the first indepth look at this problem since the Kefauver hearings. It will put the menace of organized crime front and center on the American agenda, and I'm certain that its work will make your job easier.

When I announced a year ago many of these steps, including the drug task forces and organized crime commission, I said that our goal was a frontal assault on criminal syndicates in America, and I stand by those words today. I know some people like to say that we shouldn't aim too high in our goals against the syndicates. They say the mob has been around for a long time and government will never eliminate the human impulses that lead to this kind of criminal activity. Well, I've always believed that government can break up the networks, the tightly organized regional and national syndicates that make up organized crime.

So, I repeat, we're in this thing to win.

There will be no negotiated settlements, no détente with the mob. It's war to the end where they're concerned. Our goal is simple: We mean to cripple their organization, dry up their profits, and put their members behind bars where they belong. They've had a free run for too long a time in this country. But while—*[applause]*——

Now I'm sure we'll do it. [*Laughter*]

But while drug trafficking and, certainly, organized crime remain our major concerns, I did want to say a few words about the importance of your work in the area of fraud against the government. I've referred to this before as an unrelenting national scandal. I want to urge you today to redouble your efforts to end this scandal. I hope that when these cases come to your attention, you'll remember that those who defraud the government are not just stealing from an institution; they're stealing from the Brooklyn cab driver, the Detroit autoworker, the Texas dirt farmer, and all the millions of honest working people in this county who pay their taxes and abide by the law.

One final note: A great many Americans, like myself, have become concerned at the widespread distribution of extreme forms of obscene materials, materials that degrade human beings—women, children, and men alike. There are Federal laws that restrict obscenity, and I think it's time to see that those laws, as interpreted by the Supreme Court, don't need tighter enforcement in your districts.

You have an impressive record that will grow even more impressive with the years ahead. But there's one important piece of unfinished business I must bring to your attention and that of the public: If we're going to ask law enforcement officials like yourselves to wage war on crime, we've got to give you the tools you need. We now have a number of crime initiatives on the Hill. You know many of the provisions—determinate sentencing, bail reform, increased protection for witnesses and victims, enhanced drug penalties, reinstitution of the death penalty, moderation of the exclusionary rule, and many similar measures that the American people have been demanding at the State and local level for many years.

As you know, the legislation also has provisions which are important to the State and local law enforcement agencies—surplus property, justice assistance, and certain forfeiture provisions. These items are consistent with the increased cooperation you facilitate with these agencies through your respective law enforcement coordinating committees.

The American public is overwhelmingly in favor of this kind of tough anticrime legislation. I think that's one reason why the Senate passed most of those provisions last year by a vote of 95 to 1. Now, it's important for the entire Congress to act, especially the House of Representatives, where this legislation has been tied up in committee far too long. You need this legislation. The American people want it. And now is the time for Congress to pass it.

Important changes have come to America in the last 2½ years. Our economy's growing. Our national security is improved. And crime is starting to come down. We're on the upward road again. And this is due, in no small part, to the work of each of you.

You know, if there's been one thing about this current job that bothers me, it is that there never seems to be enough time to say thank you to all the people like yourselves who are making the difference. Today, I wanted to take that time and thank you not just for myself but for the American people whose lives and futures are safer and more assured because of your unselfish efforts. And I just wanted to come over and say thank you, and God bless you all.

Note: The President spoke at 1:31 p.m. in the State Dining Room at the White House.

Announcement of the Cultural Agreement Between the United States and India
December 5, 1983

The President today announced a special cultural exchange agreement between the United States and India for 1984 through 1986. The agreement, first discussed during the official visit of the Indian Prime Minister, Indira Gandhi, to the United States in July 1982, puts emphasis on the United States in India for 1984 and on India in the United States in 1985.

The President also announced that Mrs. Reagan will serve together with Mrs. Gandhi as Honorary Chairpersons for the respective National Committees organizing the program for the Festival of India in the United States in 1985.

Dillon Ripley, Secretary of the Smithsonian Institution, will chair the U.S. National Committee, and the India National Committee will be chaired by Smt. Pupul Jaya-kar. The Indo-U.S. Subcommission on Education and Culture will assist in the programing for the Festival.

From the spring of 1985 until the spring of 1986, the Festival of India will offer a comprehensive view of the highlights of social and cultural life in India from ancient times to the present day. It will depict the variety, character, and quality of modern India by presenting the continuity of traditional skills in folk and classical arts simultaneously with India's industrial and technological advances.

The Festival will consist of a series of exhibitions and programs of music, dance, drama, and films, as well as seminars, workshops, and lectures on various aspects of Indian literature, arts, and social sciences. Major U.S. art institutions will participate in the Festival.

Appointment of Three Members of the Commission on Civil Rights
December 6, 1983

The President today appointed the following individuals to be members of the U.S. Commission on Civil Rights:

Morris B. Abram is currently a partner with the law offices of Paul, Weiss, Rifkind, Wharton and Garrison in New York, N.Y. Between 1968 and 1970 Mr. Abram served as president of Brandeis University. Mr. Abram has long devoted himself to the cause of securing civil rights for all Americans. In 1946 he was a member of the American prosecutorial staff at the International Military Tribunal in Nuremberg, Germany. Between 1962 and 1964, he served as a member of the U.N. Subcommittee on the Prevention of Discrimination and Protection of Minorities by appointment of President Kennedy. Between 1963 and 1968 he served as president of the American Jewish Committee. Between 1965 and 1968 he served as U.S. Representative to the United Nations Commission on Human Rights. Between 1970 and 1979, Mr. Abram served as chairman of the United Negro College Fund. Since 1961 he has served as a member of the Executive Committee of the Lawyers' Committee for Civil Rights Under Law. Mr. Abram earned his undergraduate degree from the University of Georgia (B.A., summa cum laude, 1938), and his doctor of jurisprudence from the University of Chicago (J.D., 1940). Thereafter, he attended Oxford University as a Rhodes Scholar (B.A., 1948; M.A., 1953). Mr. Abram was born June 19, 1918, in Fitzgerald, Ga., and resides in New York, N.Y. He is a Democrat and will serve for a term of 6 years.

Esther Gonzalez-Arroyo Buckley is currently a secondary school teacher at Cigarroa High School, Laredo, Tex., teaching mathematics and science. She has a Texas State teaching certificate in mathematics, biology, and Spanish. She serves as chairperson of the science department, Accreditation Committee, and the Superintendent's Advisory Committee of the Laredo Independent School District, a predominantly Hispanic district. She previously served by appointment of the Governor of Texas on the Teacher Professional Practices and Ethics Commission. Between 1974 and 1977 she served as a teacher with the Migrant Compensatory Education Project and later the Migrant Youth Corps. She taught English as a second language for adults at Laredo Junior College between 1972 and 1976. She is the chairman of the Webb County (Texas) Republican Party. Ms. Buckley earned her undergraduate degree from the University of Texas (B.A., magna cum laude, 1967) and her graduate degree in education and Spanish from Laredo State (M.S., with honors, 1975). She is a charter member of the Laredo chapter of Kappa Delta Pi, an honors fraternity in education, and Phi Delta Kappa, a professional fraternity in education. Ms. Buckley was born March 29, 1948, in Laredo, Tex., and resides there. She is a Republican and will serve for a term of 3 years.

John H. Bunzel, formerly president of San Jose State University in San Jose, Calif., is currently serving as a senior research fellow at the Hoover Institution at Stanford University, Stanford, Calif. A longtime supporter of civil rights, Mr. Bunzel was honored in 1974 by the Board of Supervisors of the city and county of San Francisco when he was awarded a Certificate of Merit for "unswerving devotion to the highest ideals of brotherhood and service to mankind and dedicated efforts looking to the elimination of racial and religious bigotry and discrimination." Mr. Bunzel earned his undergraduate degree from Princeton University (A.B., magna cum laude, 1948), his master's degree from Columbia University (M.A., 1949), and his doctorate in political science from the University of California at Berkeley (Ph. D., 1954). Mr. Bunzel was born April 15, 1924, in New York, N.Y., and resides in Belmont, Calif. He is a Democrat and will serve for a term of 3 years.

The President previously announced the appointment of:

Clarence M. Pendleton, Jr., to be a member of the U.S. Commission on Civil Rights and designated Mr. Pendleton to be Chairman. Mr. Pendleton served as a member and Chairman of the previous Civil Rights Commission between March 19, 1982, and November 30, 1983. Since 1975 Mr. Pendleton has been president of the Urban League of San Diego, Calif. He is also president of the San Diego County Local Development Corp., a nonprofit subsidiary of San Diego Urban League, Inc., and president of Building for Equal Opportunity (B.F.E.O.), a profitmaking subsidiary of the San Diego Urban League. He was director of the Model Cities Department, city of San Diego, in 1972–1975; director, Urban Affairs, National Recreation and Park Association, in 1970–1972; recreation coordinator, Model Cities Agency, city of

Baltimore, Md., in 1968–1970; and instructor in physical education and recreation, Howard University, Washington, D.C., in 1958–1968. He has served on the Community Education Advisory Council, U.S. Office of Education, since 1979 and the Governor's Task Force on Affordable Housing, State of California, since 1978. Mr. Pendleton graduated from Howard University (B.S., 1954; M.A., 1962). Mr. Pendleton was born November 10, 1930, in Louisville, Ky., and resides in La Jolla, Calif. He is a Republican and will serve for a term of 6 years.

The President also previously announced the appointment of:

Linda Chavez, to be Staff Director for the U.S. Commission on Civil Rights. Ms. Chavez served as Staff Director of the previous Civil Rights Commission between August 16, 1983, and November 30, 1983. Ms. Chavez served as assistant to the president of the American Federation of Teachers, AFL–CIO, Washington, D.C., from 1982 to 1983. She served as an editor for the American Federation of Teachers from 1977 to 1982. As such she was responsible for editing several publications, including American Teacher, American Educator, and Healthwire. During 1981, she acted as a consultant to ACTION in Washington, D.C. Previously she served as a member of the professional staff of the Civil and Constitutional Rights Subcommittee of the House Judiciary Committee. Ms. Chavez graduated from the University of Colorado (B.A., 1970). She has done graduate work and taught at the University of California at Los Angeles. Ms. Chavez was born June 17, 1947, in Albuquerque, N. Mex. She is a Democrat.

Remarks at a Dinner Honoring General Jimmy Doolittle
December 6, 1983

I haven't had as much trouble getting on since I did a picture with Errol Flynn. [*Laughter*]

I thank you, and I just wanted to say that I'm honored to accept the Jimmy Doolittle Fellowship award, who helped so many students receive technical and vocational training.

Now, ladies and gentlemen, I know that all of you feel as I do tonight, that it is an honor and a privilege to salute an authentic hero and an American legend. In this country whose history is so rich with wartime valor and genius, only a few events have held a special place in the memory of the American people: Washington's ride across the Delaware, Stonewall Jackson's ride around the Union right and then up the Shenandoah Valley, Douglas MacArthur's brilliant invasion of Inch'ŏn, and of course the courageous and daring raid in 1942 by a handful of Americans led by Jimmy Doolittle.

And, General, if you'll forgive me, I do have a question I've been wanting to ask you for the last several weeks. How did you get away with not taking any newsmen along? [*Laughter*]

But seriously, General, it is for each one of us here tonight a privilege to be with you, to salute you not only for the heroism of your 30 seconds over Tokyo but for your service and devotion to our country over a great many years.

Many of us have a personal recollection of the hope that you and your men gave the American people in the darkest days of World War II. And if you don't mind me saying so, I also remember serving with you in another of your public-spirited exploits back in 1964 when we worked together for a man who was also an Air Force general known to many of you in this room and who is here tonight, Barry Goldwater.

I like to think that many of the dreams of a strong America that we had then are coming true today. This is only one more reason why the name of Jimmy Doolittle remains an inspiration to me and to the American people. The name's very mention reminds us that no matter how difficult the odds or how great the potential sacrifice, a dare for the sake of freedom and our fellow men is a dare well worth taking.

So, ladies and gentlemen, will you join me in a toast to a magnificent American, a man whose name will be remembered as long as the virtues of valor and patriotism last, Jimmy Doolittle.

Note: The President spoke at 10 p.m. in the National Air and Space Museum. Prior to his remarks, Senator Barry Goldwater of Arizona made him a fellow in the Jimmy Doolittle Educational Fellowship Program, which is a program of the Aerospace Education Foundation. The Air Force Association and its Aerospace Education Foundation sponsor the dinner annually.

Remarks at the Welcoming Ceremony for King Birendra Bir Bikram Shah Dev of Nepal
December 7, 1983

The President. Nancy and I welcome you to the White House and the United States of America.

It's a particular pleasure to have King Birendra back in our country for the first time since his student days. We hope that you will again feel at home and among friends here, not only at the White House, which you visited as Crown Prince, but throughout our country. And, Queen Aishwarya, this is your first visit to the United States, and we hope that our good will and hospitality will encourage you to return again.

The United States and Nepal are on opposite sides of the globe. We face different challenges, and our cultures symbolize the diversity with which mankind views the world. Yet our ties have grown stronger since our countries established relations in 1947. The vast distance which separates us is bridged with a miracle of modern communications and transportation. Our distinct cultures are linked in our peoples' common commitment to peace and human progress.

In Nepal, Your Majesty, you've set forth to win the battle against illiteracy, disease, hunger, and poverty. The challenges you face on the frontier of modernization are formidable. The very topography which makes Nepal one of Earth's most beautiful sites makes your task more difficult by limiting the amount of arable land and complicating communications. Although improved health and nutrition in your country has saved lives, it has also increased the pressures on finite resources. Education and information have expanded the horizons of your citizens, but have also raised their expectations.

Your development program, which began some 30 years ago, exemplifies the wise and progressive leadership provided by your family. From your grandfather's decision to seek modernization down to the present day, your people have been blessed by something money cannot buy: wise leadership. This, coupled with your country's hard-working people, tremendous hydroelectric potential, and access to substantial technical and financial support from the international community, all represent opportunities for dramatic progress.

America is proud that for a third of a century we've played a part in your development efforts. The record reflects the close partnership of our governments and peoples. We plan to continue American investment in Nepal's economic development during the next 5 years, including the funding of new agricultural research and training projects, areas which Your Majesty has identified as vital to improving the well-being of your people.

The Peace Corps will also continue its important work in Nepal. More than 2,000 volunteers have served in your country, one of our largest Peace Corps posts. The 180 volunteers presently there are carrying on their fine tradition of competence and compassion.

Your Majesty, you, your father, and your grandfather before you have been the architects of Nepal's efforts to build a better future. In the political arena your reforms are enlisting public participation in identifying national goals, thus guaranteeing that your people have a stake in their future.

The United States respects these and other initiatives Your Majesty is making to develop popular institutions consistent with the spirit of the Nepalese people. There is every reason to be confident that your goals of economic progress, political stability, and national security will be reached. America is happy to offer encouragement and support in these noble efforts.

Your Majesty's moral leadership in condemning the Soviet invasion of Afghanistan is much appreciated here. We should not forget the heroism of the Afghan people in their fight for the freedom and independence of their country.

We're also grateful for the courage your nation has shown in the cause of peace. Nepal has been willing to do more than just cast a ballot at the United Nations. It has volunteered its military personnel to serve in some of the world's most troubled areas, giving depth and meaning to Nepal's commitment to peace. The world needs more nations like Nepal which are willing to help shoulder the burden of preserving peace as well as advocating it in world forums.

Once again, Your Majesties, welcome to America. We look forward to getting to know you better as a means of enriching the deep friendship which has always characterized our relations.

The King. Mr. President, Mrs. Reagan, ladies and gentlemen, I'd like to thank you, Mr. President and Mrs. Reagan, for this welcome ceremony and for the warmth with which my wife and I, along with the members of my entourage, have been received here. I also wish to convey to you—and through you, to the Government and people of the United States—greetings and good wishes of the Government and people of Nepal.

For me it is also a nostalgic moment. I recall with fondness the time I had stood by my august father, late King Mahendra, on a similar occasion, in a similar setting here in 1967.

I do not feel a complete stranger to this land. Indeed, I come to you in the spirit of a friend who has had the benefit of studying in one of your leading institutions of learning. Inspired as Nepal and the United States are by the common goals of striving for freedom and dignity of man, it is also a fulfilling experience for me to be back here again.

Mr. President, few things in the history of man have been as eventful as the discovery of this new-found land. It gave birth to a republic known not only for its inspiring ideals but also for the most epoch-making feats of scientific endeavor. Viewed from this angle, America stands on the very forefront of modern history. Indeed, what the United States represents is a harmonious amalgam of high human and material achievements rarely surpassed elsewhere in the world. As a nation that has brought about such profound changes, it is only natural to look up to this country in joining hands with the rest of the world to herald a new age of peace, understanding, friendship, and prosperity for all.

Committed as we are in Nepal to these ideals, we hold you, Mr. President, in high esteem and wish to see the United States as a bulwark of peace and stability, cherishing the belief that all nations of the world— whether big or small, rich or poor, developed or developing—must have a place under the Sun.

It is in this spirit that I look forward to exchange views with you, Mr. President, on matters of mutual interest. I also hope to meet other leaders and seek the opportunity to renew my acquaintances with friends that I have known. I'm confident that our visit to this country will be fruitful as well as memorable.

Thank you.

Note: The President spoke at 10:10 a.m. on the South Lawn of the White House, where King Birendra was accorded a formal welcome with full military honors.

Following the ceremony, the President and the King met in the Oval Office. They were then joined by U.S. and Nepalese officials for further discussions.

Statement on Western Economic Sanctions Against Poland
December 7, 1983

We have great respect and admiration for Lech Walesa, the courageous leader of Poland's free trade union movement. We shall give immediate and serious consideration to the issues he has raised and will consult closely with our allies on this matter.

Note: The statement was issued in response to Mr. Walesa's urging that the United States and other Western nations end the sanctions against the Polish Government.

Toasts of the President and King Birendra Bir Bikram Shah Dev of Nepal at the State Dinner
December 7, 1983

The President. You got mighty quiet all of a sudden. [*Laughter*]

Well, Your Majesties, honored guests, ladies and gentlemen, today King Birendra and I had the opportunity to review our bilateral relations and to discuss our international concerns. We also had the chance to get to know one another as individuals. I'm pleased to inform you tonight that not only are relations between Nepal and the United States good, but King Birendra and I have each discovered a new friend.

Our discussion of bilateral relations revealed a refreshing lack of difficulties. Notwithstanding the great distance that separates our two nations, Nepal and the United States through the years have enjoyed a particularly amicable relationship. We prefer to think of you, Your Majesties, as neighbors on the other side of the world. We're so pleased that you've made this neighborly visit. It will serve to expand the good will between our peoples when more Americans, as I did today, get the chance to meet you personally.

Americans respect individuals of courage and conviction. And to give you some idea of how this applies to King Birendra, one of His Majesty's many talents is parachuting. We have a great deal in common—[*laughter*]—but let me hasten to say we found our common ground in another of his interests—horseback riding. [*Laughter*]

Your Majesty, the highest mountain on our planet, Mount Everest, is in Nepal. So are 8 of the world's 10 highest peaks. And the character of your people, the sincerity of your convictions stand as tall and strong as your mountains.

Any American who's visited Nepal returns home in awe, not only of the majestic beauty of your land but also of the religious strength of your people. There are countless religious shrines in Nepal—outward symbols of your country's greatest strength. And, Your Majesty, this spiritual side which is so important to your nation speaks well of you and your countrymen.

Today we had the opportunity to discuss a proposal of which you and your people can be rightfully proud. Through the Nepal Zone of Peace concept, you're seeking to ensure that your country's future will not be held back by using scarce resources for military purposes. We Americans support the objectives of Your Majesty's Zone of Peace proposal, and we endorse it. We would only hope that one day the world in its entirety will be a zone of peace.

In the meantime, we encourage you to continue to work closely with your neighbors to make Nepal's Zone of Peace a reality. Your innovative approach to peace and development could be a foundation for progress throughout the region. We wish you success.

It is an honor to have you with us, Your Majesties. Now, would all of you please join me in a toast to His Majesty, King Birendra, to Her Majesty, Queen Aishwarya, and to the people of Nepal.

The King. Mr. President, Mrs. Reagan, distinguished ladies and gentlemen, I'm touched by your cordial welcome and the warm words with which you and Mrs. Reagan have received us here in Washington. We're equally honored by the generous remarks you, Mr. President, have just made about my country and people.

Seen from Washington, Nepal is almost on the other side of the globe, and yet, as this friendly gathering here tonight shows, distance notwithstanding, friendship and cordiality based on shared ideals can exist between countries that are geographically far apart. In 1947, as soon as Nepal broke her age-old isolation by seeking friendship beyond her borders, it was with the United States of America that Nepal sought to establish her diplomatic relations.

Since 1951, the year when my grandfather, late King Tribhuvan, led the Nepalese people to democracy, we have looked to the United States as a land of freedom and fulfillment. The enduring ideals of the Founding Fathers of America, who spoke to men of liberty and independence, have inspired men throughout the world, including those of us living in the mountain fastness of Nepal.

In our part of the world, if America is looked upon as a land of gold, grain, and computers, a country of skyscrapers and space shuttle, she is also regarded as a nation committed to respect man and his dignity. A land of discovery, America has distinguished herself in being inventive, in breaking new grounds, and opening newer horizons of knowledge for the betterment of man.

With a country such as the United States, one wonders if Nepal has anything in common. On the surface, there may seem very little. Yet, as men living in the same planet, we have common stakes in the global peace, prosperity, and, indeed, the survival of man in dignity and freedom.

We're happy to see, Mr. President, your efforts to maintain peace and stability around the world. The Nepalese people join me in appreciating the understanding with which on behalf of the people and the Government of the United States you have extended support to the concept of Nepal as a Zone of Peace. This recognition, I assure you, will go down not only as an important landmark in the history of our relations but also as a testimony of your personal commitment to the cause of peace, stability, and freedom.

Nepal rejoices in the achievements of the American people in different fields of human endeavors. The initiative and enterprise of your people are exemplary. Yet, what happens in this part of the world sends its ripples even to the roadless villages of Nepal. We receive their fallout. When America suffers a temporary drought, millions around the world get affected.

Indeed, if I may seek your indulgence, I would like to mention something that on the surface may sound trivial, but sometimes it is the small thing that can bring about profound changes. The corn maize in Nepal was introduced from this part of America, as were the potatoes from the Andes nearly 300 years ago. These new crops not only altered our hill economy but even the mode of life, by making settlements possible in the mountain terraces of Nepal.

Evidently, we do not live in islands, but in a world bound in a nexus of interdependence. What happens in America ceases, therefore, to be a local event. The United States as such has shown a consistent understanding towards this and has assisted Nepal in stretching her hand of friendship and cooperation in many fields, including the building of infrastructures.

May I take this opportunity, therefore, to thank you, and through you, to the people and Government of the United States for the support we have received in meeting the challenges of development in Nepal.

Mr. President, in recent years, America has brought glory to humanity by landing man on the Moon. It is indeed thrilling to reflect that one can soar into space to explore the unknown and scan the stars. Yet these adventures into outer space would carry still deeper meaning if the part of humanity living in Nepal could also rid themselves of their continuing poverty. Herself, a least developed, land-locked country, Nepal has always sought understanding and cooperation from our friends and neighbors. In fact, since the time I assumed responsibilities, I have sought that the minimum of basic needs must not be denied to people anywhere in the world. In this regard, I take comfort in the reassurance that the United States will continue to extend cooperation on a long-term basis into the future.

Modern technology, Mr. President, has reduced distance and joined us all into a family of nations. This situation demands that we create an enduring relationship based on a sense of purpose and meaning. With Nepal and countries in her region willing to join hands with the United States and other international agencies in a creative effort for prosperity by putting into use a fragment of their human and capital resources to harness the water potentials of Nepal, it would not only enable them to walk over a long road to progress for our region, as a whole, but would also continue to build bridges of understanding between a most advanced and a least developed nation of the world. It would also mean eliminating the perils of hunger on the one hand, and the danger of instability and extremism on the other.

I have no doubt that Nepal and the United States can cooperate in many fields of creative endeavors. As countries that have shown respect to the uniqueness of the individual, we believe in the conservation of the natural as well as the spiritual heritage of man. But most important of all, we both honor the freedom of man and the independence of nations. In this regard, we appreciate the support the United States has shown consistently to our identity as a nation.

Mr. President, I cherish the fruitful exchange of views we have had recently with each other. You have been very reassuring, and I wish to thank you and Mrs. Reagan for the warmth of hospitality shown to me, my wife, and members of my entourage.

Excellencies, ladies and gentlemen, may I now request you to join me in proposing a toast to the health and happiness of President Ronald Reagan of the United States of America, and the First Lady, Mrs. Nancy Reagan, to the peace and prosperity of the American people, and to the further development of friendship between Nepal and the United States.

Thank you.

Note: The President spoke at 9:54 p.m. in the State Dining Room at the White House.

Remarks and a Question-and-Answer Session With Reporters on Strategic Arms Reduction Talks
December 8, 1983

The President. I've been waiting for the sound to get a little less. I just wanted to say something, and then I'm not going to take any more questions, or anything. I've got to get aboard to go to Indianapolis.

But I just wanted to say something about this supposed breakoff of negotiations in START and call to your attention that the Soviet Union—this was a regular adjournment; it was scheduled to take place—and the Soviet Union, in departing, simply said that they were not prepared at this time to set a date for resumption of meetings.

But I thought also that it might be a pretty good time to state our own position

on this and why we're going to continue attempting these negotiations. It was just 30 years ago today, on December 8th, 1953, that President Dwight Eisenhower made a speech on this very subject of nuclear weapons. And in that speech, he said, "To the making of these fateful decisions, the United States pledges before you . . . its determination to help solve the fearful atomic dilemma—to devote its entire heart and mind to find the way by which the miraculous inventiveness of man shall not be dedicated to his death, but consecrated to his life." And this administration endorses this view completely, and this is what we are dedicated to.

Q. So, you're not concerned about the breakoff at this time? I know it was the end of the talks but——

The President. Yes.

Q. ——it also sounds very tough and final.

The President. Well, other than in this one, I think—they're pretty careful about their choice of words. And all they said in this one was that they were not prepared at this time to set a date for when they would come back.

Q. So, you're convinced they will?

The President. I am very hopeful they will. I think this is more encouraging than a walkout and simply saying they won't be back.

Q. Will Shultz meet Gromyko in——

Q. Mr. President, do you think it may be time for a summit meeting?

Q. Do you think Secretary Shultz will meet Gromyko in Sweden?

The President. He's taking that up with the ministers right there now, and I would support such a thing. I think that it would be—and that would sort of answer your question, too. I think there's some prepara-

tion. There's been no indication from them of any desire for such a meeting. But Secretary Shultz meets Gromyko in Stockholm at that meeting. And we have not been out of touch. We have kept in communications in a number of levels.

Deputy Press Secretary Speakes. Mr. President, we'd better get underway.

Q. Mr. President, is there any thought being given to moving the marines away from the airport in Beirut?

The President. There has been some talk for a long time about a change in assignment there, and that still goes on.

Q. Are you likely to approve that—changing their position?

The President. Well—[*inaudible*]—it as a move that dovetailed in with the Lebanese military force, and I don't know what the military problems are or what they might be resolving right now.

Q. Is Mr. Baker going to be a baseball commissioner?

The President. I'll leave that to him.

Note: The President spoke at 1:37 p.m. at the South Portico of the White House as he was leaving for a trip to Indianapolis, Ind.

Remarks at the National Forum on Excellence in Education in Indianapolis, Indiana
December 8, 1983

Thank you, Secretary Bell, Governor Orr, the other Governors here, Mr. Mayor, other mayors, and the Members of Congress, the guests here on the dais, and you ladies and gentlemen. And a special greeting to the students who are with us here today from six Indiana junior and senior high schools.

Three days—I have an uncomfortable feeling that the spot I now occupy could result in just being an echo of what has probably been said several times already. But it's great to be back in Indianapolis, and great to be back with Hoosiers.

Just, oh, 10 minutes or so coming in here, east of here, the clouds broke, and suddenly down below you could see the fertile soil of your wonderful State and those orderly

farms. And it was somewhat different from an old story about a farmer here in Indiana who took over a parcel of creekbottom land that had never been cleared. It was covered with rocks and brush, but he went to work. He cleared the brush, he hauled the rocks away, he cultivated, he fertilized, he planted, created a garden spot. And then one Sunday, proud of what he'd accomplished, he asked the reverend at the church if he wouldn't drop by after the service and see what he had done.

Well, the reverend came out, and he was impressed. He said, "That's the tallest corn I've ever seen. The Lord certainly has blessed this land." And he said, "Those melons, I've never seen anything big as that. Praise the Lord." And he went on that way about every crop; but he saw tomatoes, squash, beans, everything, praising the Lord for all that the Lord had done for that land. And the old farmer was getting pretty edgy and finally couldn't take it any longer. And he said, "Reverend, I wish you could have seen this place when the Lord was doing it by himself." [*Laughter*]

Well, maybe it's a little like that with education. God gives us sons and daughters with bright, eager minds, but it's up to us to cultivate and plant their seeds of knowledge.

For more than a century and a half, American schools did that job and did it well. Nearly 200 years ago, Massachusetts enacted the first comprehensive State school law in the new republic, and other States enacted similar laws. And soon America boasted the first public school system on Earth.

In the decades that followed, our rich network of public, church, and private schools performed a miracle. With the tide after tide of immigrants thronging to our shores, our schools taught the children of those new Americans skills to earn their livings, a new language, and a new way of life—democracy.

The motto of the United States is "E Pluribus Unum," from many, one. Well, more than any other institution, our schools built that one from the many.

And today our children need good schools more than ever. We stand on the verge of a new age, a computer age when medical breakthroughs will add years to our lives. Information retrieval systems will bring all the world's great literature, music, and drama into the family home. And advances in space travel will make the space shuttle *Columbia* look as old-fashioned as Lindbergh's plane, *The Spirit of St. Louis*. But if our children are to take their places as tomorrow's leaders we must teach them the skills they need.

If America is to offer greater economic opportunity to her citizens, if she's to defend our freedom, democracy, and keep the peace, then our children will need wisdom, courage, and strength—virtues beyond their reach without education. In the words of Thomas Jefferson: "If a nation expects to be ignorant and free . . . it expects what never was and never will be."

And yet, today, some of our schools aren't doing the job they should. Of course, there are many fine schools and thousands of dedicated superintendents, principals, and teachers. But from 1963 to 1980, Scholastic Aptitude Test scores showed a virtually unbroken decline. Science achievement scores of 17-year-olds have shown a steady fall. And, most shocking, today more than one-tenth of our 17-year-olds are functionally illiterate.

Now, some insist there's only one answer: more money. But that's been tried. Total expenditures in our nation's schools this year, according to the National Center for Education Statistics, will total $230 billion. Now, that's up almost 7 percent from last year, about double the rate of inflation—more than double the rate of inflation and more than double what we spent on education just 10 years ago. So, if money alone were the answer, the problem would have been shrinking, not growing.

American schools don't need vast new sums of money as much as they need a few fundamental reforms. I believe there are six that can and will turn our schools around.

First, we need to restore good old-fashioned discipline. In too many schools across the land, teachers can't teach because they lack the authority to make students take tests and hand in homework. Some don't even have the authority to quiet down their class. In some schools, teachers suffer verbal and physical abuse. I can't say it too forcefully: This must stop.

We need to write stricter discipline codes, then support our teachers when they enforce those codes. Back at the turn of the century, one education handbook told teachers that enforcing discipline—and I quote—"You have the law back of you. You have intelligent public sentiment back of you." We must make both those statements true once again.

Second, we must end the drug and alcohol abuse that plagues hundreds of thousands of our children. Chemical abuse by young people not only damages the lives of individual users; it can create a drug culture at school. We need to teach our sons and daughters the dangers of drug and alcohol abuse, enforce the law, and rehabilitate the users. Whatever it takes, we must make certain that America's schools are temples of learning, and not drug dens.

Third, we must raise academic standards. Today, 35 States require only 1 year of math for a high school diploma; 36 require only 1 year of science. Many exchange students from foreign countries—Japan, West Germany, and others—are quick to point out that our academic standards are not as tough as theirs.

They used to visit the capitol in Sacramento every once in—well, every year. And I would have the exchange students in. And as Governor, I had one question I would always ask them. And I would flinch a little, because I knew the answer. I would ask them how our schools compared to theirs. And it would always be the same. There'd be kind of some sly exchanges of smiles, and then they'd begin to giggle, and then they would inform me how hard school was back where they came from and what a vacation this had been being here.

Our sons and daughters need to do more work, to do better work, and to spend more time in school. Now, that's not a prescription for gloomy students. Instead, educators have found again and again that when students know their parents and teachers believe them capable of a great deal and expect them to perform accordingly, students gain self-confidence, enjoy their work, and live up to those high expectations.

Fourth, we must encourage good teaching. Teachers should be paid and promoted on the basis of their competence and merit. Hard-earned tax dollars should encourage the best. They have no business rewarding mediocrity.

Fifth, we must restore parents and State and local governments to their rightful place in the educational process. Decisions about discipline, curriculum, and academic standards, the factors that make a school good or bad, shouldn't be made by people in Washington. They should be made at the grassroots, by parents, teachers, and administrators in their communities.

And sixth and last, we must teach the basics. Too many of our students are allowed to abandon vocational and college prep courses for general ones. So, when they graduate from high school they're prepared for neither work nor higher education. And compared to other industrialized countries, we're slipping far behind in such basic areas as in the sciences and math. In Japan, specialized study in mathematics, biology, and physics starts in sixth grade. In the Soviet Union, students learn the basic concepts of algebra and geometry in elementary school. So, Japan, with a population only about half the size of ours, graduates from college more engineers than we do, while the Soviet Union graduates from college almost five times more engineering specialists than we do.

But it isn't just basic subjects that need to be taught; it's also basic values. I believe that unless we educate our children all that we are—the great devotions, the crucial writings, and the technical knowledge that have permitted millions to live in abundance and freedom—then all these successes are in jeopardy. If we fail to instruct our children in justice, religion, and liberty, we will be condemning them to a world without virtue. They'll live in a twilight of civilization where great truths were forgotten.

In schools across the country, students are being taught the dangers of nuclear weapons and the burdens of national defense. Well, let's make certain they understand not only the price of defending America but the price of failing to. As students from St. George's University School of Medicine learned in Grenada, freedom is not free. It can be easily lost, but is worth sticking up for.

One other idea at the core of our basic values. I just have to believe that the loving God who has blessed this land should never have been expelled from America's classrooms. When we open ourselves to Him, we gain not only moral courage but intellectual strength. If the Members of Congress can start each day with a moment for prayer and meditation, so can our children in their schools.

Now, the Federal Government can support these reforms and do so without recycling still more tax dollars or imposing still more regulations. And our administration is doing just that. We've taken 29 narrow categorical education programs and replaced them with a block grant to give State and local education officials greater freedom. We've instituted major regulatory reforms to dig educators out from under mountains of redtape. And because parents should have the right to choose the schools they know are best for their children, we have proposed education vouchers and tuition tax credits, concepts that the polls show the American people support overwhelmingly. And we're going to keep pressing until they're passed.

In October I signed a proclamation that named this school year the National Year of Partnerships in Education. The proclamation urged businesses, labor unions, and other groups of working people to form partnerships with schools in their communities. Here in Indianapolis, for example, a program managed by the Chamber of Commerce has brought 13 companies together with 9 schools at all grade levels. The companies are helping out with everything from teaching practical job skills to providing tutors in math and science.

I've asked government workers to join the Partnerships in Education effort, and we at the White House have formed a partnership with Congress Heights Elementary School in Washington, in probably the poorest district of that city.

I've directed the Departments of Justice and Education to find ways that we can help teachers and administrators enforce discipline. And this afternoon, I'm delighted to announce a new program to recognize outstanding students, the President's Academic Fitness Awards. These awards will be modeled on the Presidential Physical Fitness Awards begun under President Johnson. I'll be appointing a Commission on Academic Fitness to work out the details of the program with our nation's educators, and I look forward to presenting the first awards at the White House.

But despite these Federal efforts, the main responsibility for education rests with our States, and they're moving forward. Since our administration placed education at the top of the national agenda, we've been seeing a grassroots revolution that promises to strengthen every school in the country. From Maine to California, parents,

teachers, school officials, and State and local officeholders have begun vigorous work to improve the fundamentals—not fancy budget structures, not frills in the curriculum, but teaching and learning. In the words of Secretary Bell, "There is currently in progress the greatest, most far-reaching, the most promising reform and renewal of education we have seen since the turn of the century."

Since 1980 more than half of our 16,000 school districts have increased the number of credits they require in such basic subjects as English, science, and math. Almost 40 percent are set to raise their standards by 1985. Today, all 50 States have task forces on education; 44 are increasing graduation requirements; 42 are studying improvements in teacher certification; and 13 are establishing master teacher programs.

State by State, success stories are mounting. In Mississippi last December, the legislature passed a bill to improve teachers' pay and, for the first time since the fifties, implement compulsory school attendance. In Iowa, where only 1,560 high school students took calculus last year, the State is putting together a program of incentives for students who take upper-level math and science courses. In Tennessee, Governor Lamar Alexander has proposed a Better Schools Program that would beef up teaching in math and science and provide pay incentives for excellent teachers.

In New Jersey, Governor Tom Kean has a proposal that deserves wide support. Under his plan, the New Jersey board of education would allow successful mathematicians, scientists, linguists, and journalists to pass a competency test in their subjects and then go into classrooms as paid teaching interns. If they performed well, they would be issued permanent teaching certificates at the end of a year. And right here in Indiana, under the superb leadership of Governor Robert Orr, you've initiated Project Prime Time, a basic skills program for early grades. And you've increased high school graduation requirements for the first time in half a century.

The 50 States taking action to solve problems with efficiency and imagination—this is federalism in action. You—our Nation's

Governors, legislators, school board members, school administrators, and teachers—are meeting America's educational needs with common sense, vigor, and prudent use of taxpayers' dollars that Washington could never match. On behalf of the American people, I thank you.

I wish I could tell you all the success stories that I've heard about individual schools—the 152 that received Secondary School Recognition Awards, so many others. Lincoln Park High, for example, used to be one of the worst schools in the city of Chicago. And then, District Superintendent Margaret Harrigan came along and turned it into one of the best schools in the State of Illinois. Today, Lincoln Park High boasts a school of science that offers a college-level course in biochemistry, a school of languages that offers French, German, Italian, and Spanish, and a tough 2-year international baccalaureate program that last year had 200 applicants for 30 places.

In my home State of California, El Camino High, in Sacramento, used to suffer from all the ills that plague so many schools—drug and alcohol abuse, poor attendance, declining enrollment, low achievement. And then, El Camino principal, Dr. Joe Petterle, and the board of education put together a program designed to stress the fundamentals.

One measure required applicants and their parents to sign a form stating in part, "(We) understand that El Camino High School will stress the basics, require homework, not have a smoking area, be a closed campus, require reasonable standards of dress, and have well-defined and enforced discipline and attendance policies." Today, achievement at El Camino is climbing. The daily student absence rate has dropped from 14 percent to under 4 percent, and the school has its maximum enrollment of 1,700 students and a waiting list of almost 400.

A few moments ago, I spoke about the superb education American schools gave to

immigrants in decades past. Well, I would like to close by reading an essay by a modern-day immigrant, a student who went to El Camino High. His name: Trong Bui.

And he wrote: "As a Vietnamese refugee, I immigrated to America . . . with my family in search of freedom . . . . During this difficult stage of adjustments in my life, faculty members and students at El Camino . . . were especially important to me for without their invaluable help, I could not have progressed. . . . When I first came to El Camino, the only English word that I knew was 'hello,' and I needed an interpreter to communicate with my counselor. But . . . this year I will graduate from El Camino High School with honors . . . . I have also been admitted to the California State University of Sacramento with honors.

"With the invaluable knowledge that I obtained from going to El Camino High School, I will be able to face the world with great confidence, knowing that I am well prepared to meet any challenge in my future and that I will not die the way I was born, nameless."

An education that trains the mind and fills the heart with hope—that's the treasure American schools used to give their students. And if all of us—officeholders, school officials, teachers, and parents—provide our schools with the support they need, I'm confident that in coming years American schools will give our sons and daughters richer treasure than ever before.

I thank all of you for the part that you're playing in rebuilding America's schools. I thank you for inviting me back to this great State, and God bless you all.

Note: The President spoke at 3:47 p.m. in Hall B of the Indianapolis Convention Center. He was introduced by Secretary of Education Terrel H. Bell.

Following his remarks, the President met at the convention center with Indiana Republican leaders and then returned to Washington, D.C.

Statement on the Conclusion of the Space Shuttle *Columbia* Mission
December 8, 1983

The whole world is delighted to see *Columbia* and Spacelab back on the ground, safe and sound after a truly successful 10-day adventure.

Our congratulations to the entire shuttle team—the astronauts as well as the thousands on the ground who made this mission possible. In particular, I want to thank the dean of American astronauts, Commander John Young, our German friend, Ulf Merbold, the European Space Agency, and all the folks at NASA. Well done!

Your great success is a shining example of what free people working together can do.

This cooperative effort between Americans and Europeans will add to our treasure of human knowledge and be put to practical use, improving our lives on Earth.

New horizons have been discovered and old boundaries pushed back. It proves that there's never a time when we should stop dreaming. We will continue to challenge our imagination and aim high. The ultimate frontier of space will be a quest for mankind's highest aspirations—the opportunity for individuals, cooperation among nations, and peace on Earth.

Remarks to Members of the American Enterprise Institute for Public Policy Research
December 8, 1983

Bill Baroody, thank you.

Ladies and gentlemen, as you've just been told, I'm not dressed for the occasion, because I came by way of Indianapolis. [*Laughter*] And I'm delighted to be able to stop by here, however. And I thank you for that warm reception. It's an honor to be back with members of the AEI family.

On the way in, I did a little Christmas shopping. I'm giving Tip O'Neill a copy of Bill Simon's book on tax reform. [*Laughter*]

In 1980 I had the privilege of joining you at this dinner when all of us mourned the death of Bill Baroody, Sr. Tonight it's a great pleasure to return here on a happier occasion—to give a salute to Bill, Jr., and to all the rest of you who have carried on so nobly and so well. As President Ford—if he hadn't been here on his way someplace else—would have borne witness, you richly deserve this 40th birthday celebration.

In the 40 years since its founding, the American Enterprise Institute has prospered by combining careful analysis with straightforward talk. You've demonstrated the crucial importance of limited government, a strong defense, and private initia-

tive. Your driving concern has been the everyday citizen. And you've done everything that you could to help American families earn their livings and raise their children in prosperity and peace.

All along, distinguished AEI economists, such as the late Dr. William Fellner, argued that overtaxing, spending, and regulating would lead us to ruin. And by 1980 it nearly had. Inflation and interest rates had reached record levels, and investment had started to decline. As one economist wrote, "When we looked at the American economy, we saw an enormous, vigorous, and innovative giant being entangled in a net, and gradually nibbled away by minnows."

Well, today, thanks in large measure to your efforts and to that of others, America has cut the growth of Federal spending, pruned needless regulations, reduced personal income tax rates, passed tax indexing, and begun to rebuild her defenses.

I know tonight is called a public policy dinner. I can't help thinking it's more like Thanksgiving. Despite AEI's good work over all these years, a few in this town still haven't gotten the message. They have a knee-jerk solution to every problem from A to Z: spend more and raise taxes. Well, forgive me, but I disagree. Let me follow the AEI example and present a few facts.

Given the rate of inflation in the midseventies, the effective tax rate on real capital gains, in many cases, amounted to over 100 percent. Investment money dried up. Even one of the most brilliant minds in computers, Gene Amdahl—one of the leading inventors of the IBM–360—had to go to Japan for capital when he decided to start his own company.

Then, in 1978, we had a capital gains tax reduction, over the strong objections of the last administration. And in June—or in 1981, I should say, we passed our own tax reduction package, which reduced capital gains tax rates even more.

Today investment money, so crucial to driving the whole economy and creating more jobs, is becoming available again. During the first 9 months of 1983 the venture capital industry raised some $2½ billion, nearly three times as much as in all of 1980. Together with our personal income tax cuts these capital gains tax cuts helped rescue the economy and start the recovery. And economic recovery not only helps the American people; it helps bring down government deficits.

So, let me repeat something I've said before. We don't face large deficits because Americans aren't taxed enough; we face large deficits because government spends too much. And I welcome the help of the Congress to restrain spending, not to raise taxes.

I can't overstate the debt of this administration to you at AEI. You did so much of the intellectual groundwork for our policies. And to help put those policies in place you've given us over two dozen outstanding men and women to work in this administration—our Ambassador to the United Nations, Jeane Kirkpatrick, our Ambassador to West Germany, Arthur Burns, our Chairman for the Federal Trade Commission, Jim Miller, my Assistant for Management and

Administration at the White House, John Rogers, and many, many more.

Tonight I should tell you that with great reluctance I have accepted the resignation of one of your alumni, my Assistant for Communications, David Gergen. For 3 years he has served me with exceptional creativity, loyalty, and dedication. President Ford would have shaken his head yes in agreement, because he would have known from his own days at the White House, Dave is devoted to honest, open, and decent government. And we shall miss him. Happily I can also tell you that he's leaving to rejoin the AEI family and to join the Institute of Politics at Harvard.

The—in the years ahead—[*applause*]. Thank you. I really wasn't waiting for that, I just paused. [*Laughter*] But in the years ahead, the vigorous research into public policy that AEI stands for must go on. As your theme states, competition of ideas is fundamental to a free society. I'm confident that AEI will carry on this vital work another four decades and beyond. You, the members of the AEI family, are true intellectuals, men and women thoroughly dedicated to the life of the mind. But you're also true patriots, completely dedicated to the life of this country. And on behalf of the American people, may I thank you. And God bless you all.

Thank you.

Note: The President spoke at 8:15 p.m. in the International Ballroom at the Washington Hilton Hotel. He was introduced by William J. Baroody, Jr., president of the institute.

On December 9 the White House announced that Mr. Gergen's resignation would become effective in January 1984 and that the functions of his office would be assumed by both Michael K. Deaver, Deputy Chief of Staff and Assistant to the President, and Richard G. Darman, Assistant to the President and Deputy to the Chief of Staff.

Letter to the Speaker of the House and the President Pro Tempore of the Senate on United States Armed Forces in Grenada
December 8, 1983

Dear Mr. Speaker: (Dear Mr. President:)

In accordance with my desire that you be kept informed concerning the situation in Grenada, about which I reported to you on October 25, I am providing this further report on the presence of United States Armed Forces in Grenada.

Since then, the circumstances which occasioned the introduction of United States Armed Forces into Grenada have substantially changed. On November 2, the armed conflict in Grenada came to an end, and our task now, together with neighboring countries, is to assist the Grenadians in their effort to restore and revitalize their political institutions in a stable security environment.

Although it is still not possible to predict the precise duration of the temporary presence of United States Armed Forces in Grenada, our forces are continuing to work closely with other components of the collective security force in assisting the Grenadian authorities in the maintenance of conditions of law and order and the restoration of functioning governmental institutions to the island of Grenada.

All elements of the U.S. Marines and U.S. Army Rangers have now been withdrawn from Grenada; at this time, less than 2,700

U.S. Armed Forces personnel remain on the island. U.S. Armed Forces will continue to withdraw from the island as a part of a process whereby a peacekeeping force, composed of units contributed by friendly countries, takes over these responsibilities. I anticipate that this will be accomplished in the near future and that any members of the U.S. Armed Forces remaining in Grenada thereafter will have normal peacetime assignments, such as training, local security and the furnishing of technical services.

I am satisfied that the objectives of our operation in Grenada, including the protection of U.S. citizens, are being met successfully because of the valor and effectiveness of our forces. I ask for your continuing support as we strive to assist the people of Grenada in their efforts to restore peace, order, and human rights to their island.

Sincerely,

RONALD REAGAN

Note: This is the text of identical letters addressed to Thomas P. O'Neill, Jr., Speaker of the House of Representatives, and Strom Thurmond, President pro tempore of the Senate.

The text of the letters was released by the Office of the Press Secretary on December 9.

Remarks on Signing the Bill of Rights Day and Human Rights Day and Week Proclamation
December 9, 1983

I thank you all for being here today to underscore our national recognition of human rights.

The degree of freedom in our country is something of which Americans are rightfully proud. Unlike many other countries which find their cohesion in cultural and social traditions, the citizens of our country

find their unity and their heritage in the liberty that is shared by people with diverse cultural backgrounds.

When Americans think about the nature of human rights, we begin with what Abraham Lincoln called "the definition and axioms of free society contained in the Declaration of Independence." Well, that testament of liberty declares that all men are created equal and are endowed by their Creator with inalienable rights. To secure these rights, it states "governments are instituted among men deriving their just powers from the consent of the governed." Well, those words reveal the meaning of human rights and our philosophy of liberty that is the essence of America.

Sometimes we in free countries forget the richness of that precious possession. Our human rights are respected, so our freedom is almost indivisible—invisible, I should say. There are no walls, no troops or guns to prevent us from traveling. There are no guards at our churches or spies in our congregations. And there are no censors at the newspapers or universities.

People who live in tyranny, however, can see freedom much more clearly. It shines like a candle in the midst of darkness, and America's freedom shines through a world of stormy seas, giving hope to tens of millions of people for a better way of life.

As Americans, it's our responsibility to speak out against blatant affronts to human rights. Yes, we must and we will speak out against the incarceration of Soviet dissidents in psychiatric wards, against the barbaric persecution of the members of the Bahai faith in Iran, against the racial injustice of the apartheid system in South Africa, and against the persecution of the Catholic Church and the Solidarity labor movement in Poland.

Just a personal note of regret: It's particularly unfortunate that Solidarity leader Lech Walesa, who has been awarded the Nobel Peace Prize for his valiant efforts to achieve peaceful reconciliation within Poland, feels that he cannot leave his own country to accept that prize out of concern that he would not be permitted to return.

We cannot believe in human rights and ignore the activities of death squads in some Central American countries, the persecution of the churches and to the Miskito Indians in Nicaragua, and the resurgence of repression against national and religious groups in the Soviet Union, including Jews, Baptists, Lithuanian Catholics, Central Asian Moslems, and even members of the Russian Orthodox clergy.

We will, of course, maintain a strong defense, but an equally potent weapon against tyranny is to proclaim the truth. I think one of our great failings has been permitting leftist dictatorships to seize the initiative in the international debate. The adversaries of freedom allocate enormous resources to promote their brutal systems and propagate blatant lies. But we in the democracies, in comparison, have spent far too little to offer the world our message of democracy, human rights, and truth.

To turn this situation around, I've made supportive democracy a central goal of American foreign policy. And, specifically, to correct these communication gaps, we are significantly expanding the international broadcasting capabilities of the United States. We are strengthening operations of the Voice of America, Radio Free Europe, Radio Liberty, and we're establishing Radio Marti to communicate directly with the Cuban people.

Saint John told us, "Ye shall know the truth and the truth shall make you free." Well, in many countries people aren't even allowed to read the Bible. It is up to us to make sure the message of hope and salvation gets through.

You know—I should have brought it with me, although maybe some of you have seen it—but I have a little book, about that big, and about that thick, that contains a verse or two, printed in small type in that little thing, from the Bible. It was smuggled out of Russia and was finally delivered to me as an example of what they do just to try and cling to their faith and belief, that when someone has a Bible, they then take just a verse so that everyone can have at least some words—a few words of the Scripture—and in something that can be easily hidden. And that, when we think of our own freedom, makes it very evident.

I've done something else—I have to interject here, although this is not an occasion for humor. But I've had a kind of a hobby lately of collecting by way of dissidents stories that are told behind some of those iron curtains and those iron walls by the people themselves, showing their own cynicism about the system under which they're forced to live. And one recently that I heard had to do with three dogs that were having a conversation: an American dog, a Polish dog, and a Russian dog. And the American dog was telling them about how, well, he barks and that in our country his master gives him some meat. And the Polish dog says, "What's meat?" [*Laughter*] And the Russian dog says, "What's bark?" [*Laughter*]

But seriously, all of us who live in freedom are linked in spirit with those brave men and women being persecuted for demanding their rights or struggling to establish democracy.

With us today in the front rows and on stage are a number of courageous individuals who've suffered for their belief in human rights and democracy. They come from countries which differ markedly from each other, and yet they're all heroes of the same cause. Their devotion to political and religious liberties unites them as it unites all of us who are committed to the freedom of mankind.

I note with sadness and concern that one hero not with us today, Dr. Andrei Sakharov, is reported to be seriously ill. This good and courageous man has struggled for years on behalf of human rights, and he's now banished to the city of Gorki—supposedly free; he just can't leave Gorki. It's my hope that in the name of humanity the Soviet authorities will permit this noble individual to live his life in freedom and dignity.

In honoring these heroes today, we proclaim our confidence that good and decent people will triumph over evil. Dictatorships can pass away. On the right, we've seen it happen in recent years, in Spain, in Portugal, in Greece, in Argentina. On the left, totalitarian ideologies that brutalize human

beings to rebuild mankind into that which it is not are destined to fail. Totalitarianism on the left, just like nazism before it, will be disgarded by a disgusted humanity. Much depends on us, but we can be confident that the tide of history is indeed running on the side of freedom.

This month marks the anniversary of two milestones in mankind's journey to freedom. December 15th is the 192d anniversary of our Bill of Rights. And 35 years ago, recoiling from the horror and the destruction of World War II, on December 10th the United Nations adopted the Universal Declaration of Human Rights. Those of us who went through that terrible conflict saw the Declaration as an important international standard, something that could help build a better world. Well, today we reaffirm our commitment to the ideals expressed in the Declaration.

To commemorate these advances in freedom, I am declaring December 10th, Human Rights Day, the week beginning December 10th as Human Rights Week, and December 15th, Bill of Rights Day. Let this be a call to action for all Americans. We must rededicate ourselves to respect at home for those fundamental human rights which form the basis of our self-definition as a people and a nation. We must also assure those brave men and women struggling for democracy around the world that we will be true to ourselves by supporting our common cause.

I thank you very much. God bless all of you, and with that said, I will sign the declaration.

Note: The President spoke at 11:06 a.m. in Room 450 of the Old Executive Office Building.

Proclamation 5135—Bill of Rights Day and Human Rights Day and Week, 1983
December 9, 1983

By the President of the United States of America

A Proclamation

On December 15, 1791, our Founding Fathers rejoiced in the ratification of the first 10 amendments to the Constitution of the United States—a Bill of Rights which has helped guarantee all Americans the liberty we so cherish.

One hundred and fifty-seven years later, on December 10, 1948, the United Nations adopted the Universal Declaration of Human Rights, an effort aimed at securing basic human rights for the peoples of all nations.

Americans have long honored the gift of liberty. So it is with glad hearts and thankful minds that on Bill of Rights Day we recognize the special benefits of freedom bequeathed to posterity by the Founding Fathers. They had a high regard for the liberty of all humanity as reflected by Thomas Jefferson when he wrote in 1787, "A bill of rights is what the people are entitled to against every government on earth." In this century alone thousands of Americans have laid down their lives on distant battlefields in Europe, Asia, Africa, and in our Western Hemisphere itself in defense of the basic human rights.

When the Universal Declaration of Human Rights was adopted by the United Nations General Assembly in 1948, Americans hoped that the Jeffersonian vision was about to be realized at last. The Universal Declaration, it was believed, would embody the consensus of the international community in favor of human rights and individual liberty. And the United Nations, it was further thought, would serve as the instrument through which the observance of human rights by governments would be enforced by the international community.

Thirty-five years after the adoption of the Universal Declaration, it is clear that these hopes have been fulfilled only in part. Nevertheless, the Universal Declaration remains an international standard against which the human rights practices of all governments can be measured. Its principles have become the basis of a number of binding international covenants and conventions. At the United Nations, it has served to strengthen the arguments of those governments which are genuinely interested in promoting human rights.

Still, the fact remains that even as we celebrate Bill of Rights Day and Human Rights Day, human rights are frequently violated in many nations. In the Soviet Union, for example, brave men and women seeking to promote respect for human rights are often declared mentally ill by their government and incarcerated in psychiatric institutions. In Poland, the free trade-union movement Solidarity has been brutally suppressed by the regime. Throughout Eastern Europe and the Baltic States, the rights of workers and other basic human rights as the freedom of speech, assembly, and religion and the right of self-determination are denied. This same tragic situation also occurs just 90 miles off our southern coast. In South Africa the apartheid system institutionalizes racial injustice, and in Iran the Bahai people are being persecuted because of their religion. And, in Afghanistan and Southeast Asia, toxic weapons, the use of which is outlawed by international conventions, are being utilized by foreign occupation forces against brave peoples fighting for their freedom and independence.

As Americans recall these and other human rights violations, we should reflect on both the similarities and the differences between the Bill of Rights and the Universal Declaration of Human Rights. Both great human rights documents were adopted in the aftermath of a bitter war. Both envision a society where rulers and ruled are bound by the laws of the land and where government rests on the consent of the governed, is limited in its powers, and has as its principal purpose the protection of individual liberty.

Yet while the Bill of Rights was adopted by a Nation in which free institutions already flourished, many of the countries which adopted the Universal Declaration of Human Rights lacked free institutions. Since human rights are the product of such institutions as a free press, free elections, free trade unions, and an independent judiciary, it is not surprising that formal adherence to the Universal Declaration by governments which suppress these institutions has resulted in no real human rights gains.

By posing as champions of human rights, many governments hope to disguise their own human rights abuse. It was with special pleasure that I noted the recognition offered by the Nobel Peace Prize to Lech Walesa for his real efforts on behalf of human rights in a country where the government speaks only of the illusion of human rights.

Human rights can only be secured when government empowers its people, rather than itself, through the operation of free institutions. Because our Founding Fathers understood this, we are blessed with a system of government which protects our human rights. Today, let us rededicate ourselves to respect these rights at home and to strive to make the words of the Universal Declaration a living reality for all mankind.

Now, Therefore, I, Ronald Reagan, President of the United States of America, do hereby proclaim December 10, 1983 as Human Rights Day and December 15, 1983, as Bill of Rights Day, and call upon all Americans to observe the week beginning December 10, 1983 as Human Rights Week. During this period, let each of us give special thought to the blessings we enjoy as a free people and renew our efforts to make the promise of our Bill of Rights a living reality for all Americans and, whenever possible, for all mankind.

In Witness Whereof, I have hereunto set my hand this 9th day of December, in the year of our Lord nineteen hundred and eighty-three, and of the Independence of the United States of America the two hundred and eighth.

RONALD REAGAN

[*Filed with the Office of the Federal Register, 4:56 p.m., December 9, 1983*]

Executive Order 12450—Interagency Committee on Handicapped Employees
December 9, 1983

By the authority vested in me as President by section 501(a) of the Rehabilitation Act of 1973 (Public Law 93–112), it is hereby ordered that Section 1 of Executive Order No. 11830 of January 9, 1975, as amended, is further amended by revising subsection (3) to provide "Secretary of Education, Co-Chairman"; by redesignating subsection (9) as subsection (10); and by inserting a new subsection (9) to provide "Secretary of Health and Human Services.".

RONALD REAGAN

The White House,
December 9, 1983.

[*Filed with the Office of the Federal Register, 4:57 p.m., December 9, 1983*]

Radio Address to the Nation on the Situation in Lebanon
December 10, 1983

My fellow Americans:

I'd like to talk to you today about the deep desire we all share to bring peace to Lebanon.

These past several weeks have brought bitter tragedy and sorrow to all of us. The loss of even one of our splendid young Americans is an enormous price to pay. The number of dead and wounded is a terrible burden of grief for all Americans. It's unimaginably more so for the families who have lost a father, husband, a son, or a brother. Their deaths are testimony to the savage hatreds and greedy ambitions which have claimed so many innocent Lebanese lives.

The human toll in Lebanon is staggering. Lebanon's losses since 1975 would be comparable to the United States losing 10 million of its citizens. What conceivable reason can there be for this wanton death and destruction?

Lebanon's suffering began long before a single marine arrived. In the early 1970's many thousands of Palestinians entered Lebanon. Lebanon's fragile political consensus collapsed, and a savage civil war broke out.

The Palestinians also had a military, the armed PLO. Trained in terrorist tactics by Soviet-bloc nations and Libya, the PLO joined the civil war and attacked Israeli targets, villages and schools across the border between Lebanon and Israel.

In the midst of all this, Syria was asked to intervene and stop the civil war. In the process, it occupied a large part of Lebanon. However, Syria did nothing to control terrorism against Israel's northern border. Israel decided to neutralize the PLO and, in June 1982, mounted a full-scale invasion across the border. This resulted in another major round of fighting between Syria, the PLO, and Israel. Shelling and bombing pounded Beirut. Thousands more died.

We negotiated a cease-fire and then joined the multinational force at the request of the Lebanese Government to make possible the peaceful separation of the forces. This is the second time in 25 years that we have come to support the Lebanese Government in restoring peace.

In 1958 President Eisenhower used a bipartisan congressional resolution to send 8,000 American soldiers and marines to Lebanon. When order was restored, our military came home. But in 1958 there were no occupying foreign armies, and there was no Soviet presence in Syria. Today, there are more than 7,000 Soviet military advisers and technicians.

In September 1982 I offered a plan to bring peace to the region. It called for a just solution to the Palestinian problem as well as a reasonable settlement of issues between the Arab States and Israel.

Success in Lebanon is central to sustaining the broader peace process. We have vital interests in the Middle East which depend on peace and stability in that region. Indeed, the entire world has vital interests there. The region is central to the economic vitality of the Western World. If we fail in Lebanon, what happens to the prospects for peace, not just in Lebanon but between Israel and her neighbors and in the entire Middle East?

Once internal stability is established and withdrawal of all foreign forces is assured, the marines will leave. But because we care about human values for ourselves, so must we be concerned when freedom, justice, and liberty are abused elsewhere. That's the moral basis which brought our marines to Lebanon.

We have acted with great restraint despite repeated provocations and murderous attacks. Our reconnaissance flights have only one purpose, and the Syrians know it: to give the greatest possible protection to our troops. We will continue to do whatever is needed to ensure the safety of our forces and our reconnaissance flights.

The peace process is slow and painful, but there is progress which would not have been possible without the multinational force. Last May with our help the Governments of Lebanon and Israel negotiated an agreement providing for the withdrawal of Israeli forces. In September when the Israelis pulled back their forces from the Shuf Mountains near Beirut, Lebanese attempts to extend their authority into this area were met by violent opposition from forces supported by Syria. We will redouble our diplomatic efforts to promote reconciliation and achieve withdrawal of all foreign forces.

At a recent meeting in Geneva all the Lebanese parties agreed to recognize the present government as the legitimate representative of the Lebanese people. Talks have begun to broaden the base of the government and to satisfy the legitimate grievances of all the people.

My special envoy, Ambassador Don Rumsfeld, has returned to the region and will continue trying to move the peace process forward on all fronts. Lebanon's agony must end.

Today is the 35th anniversary of the United Nations Universal Declaration of Human Rights. The Lebanese people are struggling for their human rights. We call upon everyone involved to give that birthright back to the Lebanese.

Until next week, thanks for listening, and God bless you.

Note: The President spoke at 12:06 p.m. from Camp David, Md.

Interview With Bruce Drake of the New York Daily News
December 12, 1983

The Middle East

Mr. Drake. I wonder if we could start right off on the Mideast, Mr. President. A Congressman said last week, after those hearings that they had on the Hill, that it seemed to him the marine force had become more of a lightning rod for attack than a peacekeeping force. And I was wondering whether you feel that the marines, in that particular position that they're in now, continue to serve a useful purpose, and whether you're likely to redeploy them.

The President. Well, I believe this, that while we had hoped in this whole plan and in sending, at Lebanon's request, this multinational force, that casualties could be avoided. But I have to believe that what is happening is an indication of the determination of some others to prevent Lebanon from having either peace or its sovereignty as a nation. And if there is a lightning-rod effect to the multinational force—because this is happening to other forces there other than our own—it is that their chances of destroying the peace in Lebanon would be enhanced if they could get us to go home.

Mr. Drake. "They" meaning?

The President. Meaning the forces. First of all, there are forces in Lebanon that are

fighting not just with the new government of Lebanon but are fighting with each other. They have been for years. That's what caused the breakdown of Lebanon several years ago. But they're aided and abetted by others who have other ideas. The Syrians, for example, have made it plain that they believe that Lebanon is really intended to be a part of a greater Syria.

Mr. Drake. I think what I was getting at—you said in your speech after the terrorist bombing on the marines that their operational role at the airport was to prevent the area from becoming a battleground. It would seem that it has become a battleground.

The President. Yes. But remember—remember that when this whole thing was conceived, Lebanon, itself, was a battlefield, with thousands of innocent men, women, and children being slaughtered because of armed forces that were fighting in that congested city, using it as a battlefield. And remember that elsewhere, there was no stable Government of Lebanon. There were these other factions fighting each other.

The proposal was that, when finally the PLO—which was one of the battling factions—was ousted and left, that a multinational force would go in—the idea that the two nations, Syria and Israel, would leave. Both had agreed to—said that when the other left, they would leave Lebanon.

The multinational force was to be a sort of "keeping order force" while the Lebanese Government reinstated itself, developed an armed force that could then take over in these war-torn areas as those two nations left. Remember that originally, there was no quarrel on the part of Lebanon of Syria invading, because it was invading against the PLO. So, Lebanon actually invited Syria to come in and help because of this kind of trouble.

Now, the multinational force went in. I think there were a great many accomplishments. The fighting stopped. There was some withdrawal, and then Syria reneged on its agreement and has refused to leave. There is an agreement now between Lebanon and Israel, which Israel has agreed that it will leave. But it can't leave as long as it's threatened by the Syrian forces there.

But the Lebanese Government has created an army, and we have trained that army. We have provided materiel and weapons in great amounts. And so, the purpose is still there.

Mr. Drake. Is the purpose served by keeping them at the airport in specific?

The President. Actually the airport is probably not as hazardous as it might be to be where some of the other forces are that are out actually patrolling the streets, threatened by snipers and so forth everyday. But the importance is that's the only airport in Lebanon. If they're to have any communication with the outside world, if they're to have traffic back and forth—including our own people, our own diplomats who are trying to help in this process—that airport must be kept open. And they were there to keep the airport open.

Mr. Drake. So, your inclination is to keep them there?

The President. No. My function is only that the multinational force—that includes the leaders of those other three countries—that we must have a visible showing of our multinational force in Lebanon to perform their function. But as the actual tactics and locale, that I leave to the military.

Mr. Drake. Let me ask you a broader

question about it. We've, so far, lost 250 lives, and many Americans seem to feel that Lebanon is a place where another disaster could happen at any time. We've had a direct military exchange with the Syrians. Are you worried that fears of war, of escalation will cause public and congressional support of your policies to erode? And what can you say to assure Americans that we are not about to be drawn into the kind of quagmire that it has been for so many other countries?

The President. We're not about to be drawn in. Let me call to your attention there's going to be no firing by the marines unless they are fired upon and they defend themselves. That's far different than going in as an aggressive force that is now going to advance and conquer territory. There's no intention on the part of the multinational force to do that.

So, no, there's not going to be a war involving us.

Mr. Drake. What about congressional support? You must have read the papers over the last days. There are all sorts of reports that the congressional mood is turning again. Are you concerned about that?

The President. Certainly, I'm concerned. But I wish that some of those who are weakening in their resolve would recognize they're weakening precisely because that's what those who are committing the assaults on our forces—why they have committed them. They feel that, if they can make enough trouble, that we will withdraw.

Mr. Drake. Let me ask you this to sort of interject. You know there was another terrorist attack on one of our Embassies this morning in Kuwait. You were reported last week to have made mention of a thousand terrorists massing, I think it was, in Lebanon. Is that an accurate report? And do you think that the attack today in Kuwait signals some sort of intensive campaign of terrorism that we're going to face in the next few months?

The President. Well, even you in the press have had some information that led you to print stories that worldwide terrorism, some of these—[inaudible]—on the increase and that the threats extend far and wide. You mentioned before about the casualties, the bulk of the casualties, the tragedies that we sustained in Beirut were from just one such suicide mission.

Mr. Drake. Right.

The President. But now to indicate that that doesn't only happen in Beirut is this thing in Kuwait. And apparently the same people are claiming credit who claimed credit for the assault on us, on the French, on our Embassy, which proceeded any attack on our military forces.

This is a tactic that is being used by the kind of people that we're trying to prevent from taking over in yet another country—Lebanon.

Mr. Drake. Do you believe it's connected to this group of terrorists that you reportedly spoke of to the—Lew Lehrman's group last week?

The President. Do I what?

Mr. Drake. It was reported that when you met with the Citizens for America last week, you made reference to this large group of terrorists that had massed, I think, in Lebanon, you said. Do you or your officials connect the attack today to that?

The President. Let me just say that there was sufficient evidence for me to feel safe in making that statement.

Mr. Drake. Mr. President, in Syria—excuse me—some reports from Lebanon say that the Syrians' success in downing our two bombers had shaken the confidence of some Lebanese in us as a protector. Do you feel that's the case? And I also wanted to ask you whether you had any second thoughts about older aircraft being used for that mission when, as you've often said, we have the *New Jersey* offshore with its 16-inch guns.

The President. Let me set the record straight on that. All that I did—I don't give tactical orders to the military when there is a mission that has been approved to be carried out. All I said was that I hoped that they would consider that and see if that was a viable alternative, because it wouldn't present more of a safety factor. And the decision, for a number of actual tactical reasons, was that the airstrike—for one thing, the forces that we were going after are mobile. And there would be no way just in an artillery attack to know whether we're still shooting at them or not, or whether

they've gone someplace else.

I don't believe—the beginning of your question—I don't believe that there's been any lessening on the part of the Lebanese in their trust in the multinational force or their belief that it is essential.

Mr. Drake. You don't think that the shooting down of the planes had a propaganda effect to help the Syrians in that region?

The President. Well, the Syrians immediately jumped onto the bandwagon of propaganda. But they haven't reported anything about the success of that mission. We knocked out a number of very important installations, including blowing up an ammunition dump.

So, yes, there were casualties. Yes, one of them was a complete tragedy. There were some things that—the planning of that couldn't have been foreseen. The weather lowered in; they had to go in at a lower altitude. But, as I say, I think the mission accomplished its purpose.

Mr. Drake. What about the pact that we made with the Israelis? As Secretary Shultz is finding out, in the Mideast a lot of moderate and other Arabs are asking how can we say this doesn't undermine our credibility as a peacemaker, as an honest broker, in Lebanon and the Mideast as a whole, if we have now entered into this military pact with the Israelis.

The President. Well, I think that we have an answer to that and have been giving the answer to them on this. This relationship with the Israelis is something that we've had since 1948. And a restatement of it or a dealing with some specifics with the new government now in Israel is a natural thing to do.

But the net point is that at the same time we're doing that, we are working with the moderate states. For example, one thing that was mentioned was the possibility of joint maneuvers. Well, we've had joint maneuvers with some of the other Arab States. We have, regularly, joint maneuvers with Egypt. We have forces in other places there.

Mr. Drake. But that's as we see it, Mr. President. Isn't there—don't you concede that there's a factor that they see it a different way since there's been this longstanding enmity with Israel?

The President. Yes, but there seems to be a change when they find out that at the same time, we informed Israel of what we were going to continue to do with regard to the moderate Arab States.

Mr. Drake. Well, did we get any concessions that the moderate Arab States had hoped we would get from Israel, such as some more conciliatory statements on the settlement policy?

The President. No, there's a difference of opinion on that, and it has existed since Camp David, on the settlements. But we made our position plain that we still believe that that should stop—that is one of the subjects for negotiation in a peace process. But we did tell them what we were going to do with regard to other Arab States who also require some of the same kind of cooperation that we're giving Israel, and we're going to do that.

Mr. Drake. You've often—as recently as your radio address on Saturday—mentioned the large Soviet presence in Syria. But you haven't said what it is you think their immediate design is. Is it just Soviet troublemaking? Are they prepared, do you think, for a confrontation in the region? What do you think the Soviets are up to?

The President. I don't know that there's any sign that they want a confrontation, particularly with us. But there's no question about their interest in the Middle East, and there's no question but that where there is trouble of any kind, they don't mind stirring the pot.

Now, just take a look at Ethiopia, South Yemen, and you can see that the Soviets have eyed the Middle East. It is a place of strategic importance to, particularly, the Western World—Europe and Japan. Where would they turn to, what would they do if suddenly a force should shut off the energy supply that comes from the Middle East?

Now, the Soviet Union does not need the Middle East for that purpose. The Soviet Union has the greatest supply of oil reserves in the world. It is the greatest producer of energy.

Mr. Drake. Well, is there anything that you're expecting as far as what they intend in the region? Do we—you do not expect

that the Soviets are trying to shift confrontation to that region? Do you think that they're just filling contractual obligations to an ally?

The President. Well, I think very much they want to be involved and have a stake in the Middle East. And you can't ignore the things that, as I say, that they've done in Yemen and Ethiopia, there in the horn of Africa. You can't ignore Afghanistan. You can't ignore the divisions that they have at the border of Iran.

As a matter of fact, the Russian desire to move in that direction toward warm water precedes even the Soviets.

Mr. Drake. On a completely different aspect of the Middle East, I've listened to you for many years, and you always spoke with emotion about the PLO. What are your thoughts on the fate of Arafat—you know, where he stands today, and also on the specific issue of whether Israel, us, or the U.N. should provide guarantees for him to leave the country?

The President. Well, I think our own view is here that his absence from Lebanon would be a step forward.

Mr. Drake. Do you think the Israelis are going to permit it, or do you——

The President. I don't know. We haven't communicated directly—or I haven't—with them on this point and their now sudden statement about this. But I have to say that we had evidence that Arafat—remember, he is one of those who has, as some Arab States have, declared that Israel has no right to exist as a nation, that it was war to the death with them. But then he modified that position in his discussions with King Hussein of Jordan, with regard to negotiations for peace, and then was overruled by his own people, which must have been the growing prominence of that radical force in the PLO that has been fighting him.

Now, it's a case of will the real Mr. Arafat stand up. I don't know whether he has lost any leadership in the PLO. I don't know whether that modification still exists or whether he is willing to go further with that. I think that he would find great support among the PLO. I think the PLO people, the Palestinians on the West Bank are more moderate and don't want war.

They want a peaceful solution to their problems.

Mr. Drake. Are we going to ask—are we going to press the Israelis diplomatically to let him leave?

The President. I have to tell you, with our people, the Secretary of State abroad and all—had a meeting on that.

Mr. Drake. Let me ask—there's one thing I have to ask——

Deputy Press Secretary Speakes. That's got to be the last one.

Hunger in America

Mr. Drake. There's one thing I have to ask which is on the question of Ed Meese's comments the other day. I'm sure you've read it. I'm sure you read the controversy, all the reaction from the Democrats. I wonder if you could tell me your feelings about that and in specific whether you agree with his assertion that there's considerable information that some people who can afford to do otherwise are going to soup kitchens for free food?

The President. I'm delighted to set the record straight on that.

Let me preface it by saying one thing: As long as there is one person in this country who is hungry, then that's one person too many, and something must be done about it. And I happen to know that Ed Meese agrees with that.

Reading the entire script of the interview, I have to say that the reaction ignored much of what was in that interview and distorted the meaning of what he had said.

Now, we ourselves are the ones who have encouraged this getting into the picture of private groups, church groups, others in providing meals and the food centers. I've visited some of them myself around the country. We have contributed surplus foods to these people and to these food centers to help in what they're doing.

It isn't a case that this is to fight off starvation. What we envisioned with this is that the government does all that it can to try and see that there is no hunger. But others can make life also a little easier, maybe a lot easier, for these people in going beyond just the absolute necessities and, by these efforts, making sure that families can have a little more than bare necessities, which makes life worth living——

Mr. Drake. Well, could I——

The President. Now, let me just say this——

Mr. Drake. Sorry.

The President. We have found—first of all, we are spending more on nutrition in this country than has ever been spent before in the history of the country. More people are getting food stamps than have ever gotten them before. I rejoice in these private groups, because there are more of those helping than have ever helped before.

But what he probably was trying to point out is that any time you've got a program of this kind—how do we find cheaters on welfare, people that are getting welfare and being supported by their fellow citizens who don't really have a need and who should not be there. Well, isn't it logical to suggest that people of the same train of mind are going to take advantage of those who are privately trying to help? Now, the situation is that those private groups have no way of checking on the credentials of someone who comes there. They have opened their doors to invite those in—the hungry in.

Now, this leads to why we have a commission—and that, too, has been distorted, I'm afraid, in the accounting or the recounting of the—the press and others have, every once in a while on an annual basis, have brought up finding an individual or people or a family that is doing without and that is hungry. I want to know why, because I know what we're doing; I know what the private sector's doing. And this commission was sent out not to find out if there's hunger in America; it was sent to find out how widespread is this. How many people are there who are suffering this? And is it because of some bungling in our distribution system? Is it because of people who don't know the way to find these programs? It could be some of both. And if so, we want to find out how do we communicate better and say to someone who is hungry, "Look, here is how you find out the answer to your problem. Go here and there; appeal to the right people."

Mr. Drake. Could I ask one more question?

Mr. Speakes. We're right on the ground.

Terrorism

Mr. Drake. I just want to ask quickly, what are your feelings with this security business? Is the White House becoming sort of a fortress? There's now this report that Secret Service are going to be armed with ground-to-air missiles in case there's an attack from a plane. Does this——

The President. I haven't heard anything about that—such a thing. I have to say that I don't inquire too much. I have a great faith in our security forces and I—like the military, I leave them to do what they believe in their own best judgment.

Mr. Drake. It sounds like you might be safer somewhere else. [*Laughter*]

The President. Well, in Kuwait, for example? [*Laughter*] This is the problem with worldwide terrorism. We do have some information on what they have threatened, their activities worldwide, and there are precautions that have to be taken.

Mr. Drake. Should make campaigning difficult.

The President. Well, yes. I have my own idea of one of the things about this terrorism. It's almost an impossible thing to detect and confine, but I believe that the countries and the groups in whose name the terrorists are operating have a responsibility.

For example, in this in Kuwait, if this is an Iranian group—claims that this is part of a holy war and this is being done in the interest of the Government of Iran, then I think Iran has a responsibility to curb and curtail these things being done in their name, just as I would feel that if somebody went out doing these things and said they were doing them in the interest of the United States, I would feel that I had a responsibility to corral them and stop them.

Mr. Drake. Thank you, Mr. President.

Note: The interview began at 10:37 a.m. on board Air Force One as the President was traveling to New York, New York.

Remarks at the Annual Convention of the Congressional Medal of Honor Society in New York City
December 12, 1983

Arnold and Zack Fisher, Mrs. MacArthur, Ron Ray, Tex McCrary, distinguished Congressional Medal of Honor recipients, Members of the Congress, and ladies and gentlemen:

I thank you for such a very warm welcome.

I have to tell you that back in Hollywood I was warned that I should never share the spotlight with small children or animals. They would upstage you and steal the scene every time. But there was never a word of warning about sharing the stage with a presentation such as we've just seen. And first of all, I have to get the lump out of my throat.

May I just say when Americans see this, they're going to feel a deep pride in themselves, in their country, and a sense of humble gratitude for their fellow citizens whose deeds were memorialized in this production. My congratulations and thanks to everyone who made this film possible.

It's a great privilege today and a very great honor to participate in this event. Your efforts to serve remind us of America's heritage and its purpose.

An America that is militarily and economically strong is not enough. The world must see an America that is morally strong with a creed and a vision. We are such people. This is what has led us to dare and to achieve. For us values count. They are the wellspring of our American way of life, the real meaning of the Hall of Honor—service to country, patriotism, honor, and sacrifice.

Those words in the film so stir the soul:

"Not to be heroes, but to serve. Not to die, but to live. Not because we wanted to, but because there was a need."

Last week in Beirut, there was a need. Six marines heard that four of their buddies were in trouble. They went to help. Fifteen minutes later, eight fine, young Americans had added their names to the long list of those who have given their lives for their country. There was a need. Greater love hath no man than this, that he lay down his life for his friends.

God bless all of you here today. And, yes, God bless those who never lived to know that what they had done was heroic.

The price of freedom is high, but never more costly than the loss of freedom. And freedom, we must always remember, is never more than one generation away from extinction. Each generation must do whatever is necessary to preserve it and pass it on to the next, or it will be lost forever.

We must deal with the world as it is and not the way we would like it to be. If we turn a blind eye and a deaf ear when totalitarian regimes brutalize the hopes and dreams of people, we demean the valor of every person who struggles for human dignity and freedom. And we also demean all those who have given that last full measure of devotion.

The quest for freedom continues to build. There is a revolution going on in this world, a revolution for freedom and democratic ideals. It may not capture the headlines, but it is there, and it's growing. That is the real message of our time, and it may just be the reason why those who don't like to hear the truth are so worried.

History doesn't offer many crystal clear lessons for those who manage our nation's affairs, but there are a few. And one of them surely is a lesson that weakness on the part of those who cherish freedom inevitably brings a threat to that freedom. Tyrants are tempted. With the best intentions, we have tried turning our swords into plowshares, hoping that others will follow. Well, our days of weakness are over. Our military forces are back on their feet and standing tall.

Modern equipment is being delivered to troops, and more is on the way. The mobility and firepower of our ground forces are being strengthened with up-to-date equipment. And no longer is the American military being asked to defend freedom with equipment from wars past. I'm also pleased to report that training and readiness rates have really soared. Too often, we forget that the bulk of our defense dollars are spent to keep the troops well-trained, equipment in working order, spare parts and ammunition on hand.

And we do none of this because we seek war. Indeed, we hope we will preserve the peace. But when our citizens are threatened, it is government's responsibility to go to their aid, as we did in Grenada.

Our forces had what they needed to get the job done. And now the world knows that when it comes to our national security, the United States will do whatever it takes to protect the safety and freedom of the American people.

May I just say that, as of this morning, 950 of the 82d Airborne are enplaned on their way back to this country—the last of the combat troops in Grenada. What are known as military service force—engineers, Seabees, medical personnel, and military police—will stay there in a detachment to help that country get back on its feet, and to replace and rebuild things that need replacing and rebuilding.

On wonderful thing is that today when you see a young man or woman in uniform, they chose to wear that uniform. And they wear it with honor. And they serve their country because they're proud to do so. And I know that our service men and women feel that it is an honor. And I hope this makes you as proud as it does me. From Grenada to Lebanon to the Demilitarized Zone of Korea to the NATO line in Europe, young Americans are carrying on in the finest tradition of those before them. They care; they understand; and they continue to give willingly of themselves.

There was a recent article in a Newsweek magazine that made the point very well. A 40-year-old father with five sons noted that he grew up in a generation where the military service was to be avoided. The recruiting stations were places to stage protests. Now his eldest son, in college, wants to be all that he can be, one of the select few.

Each trip to the recruiting office generates enthusiasm among his younger brothers, who are proud of their older brother.

The father wrote in that article, "My children somehow have settled on a place where it is their assumption that this country is right and just unless they are shown otherwise." Well, his children believe the basic values that made America great, God bless them.

And here today, with all of you who believe those values so much that you went beyond the call of duty in defending them—many like you are no longer with us. They will be honored and remembered not just because you and they heeded the call of duty but because you and they performed above and beyond that call.

That's the meaning of this greatest recognition our country can give. Wear it proudly, because it is so much a part of what makes America unique in all the world. Yes, heroism in combat is recognized in every nation. But there is something in this particular recognition that is peculiar to our way of life. Maybe you'll let me illustrate it with a story.

World War II, I was in the Horse Cavalry Reserve, so it was only natural that when I was called up to active duty, I found myself an adjutant in an Air Corps post. [*Laughter*] The post happened to come directly under Air Corps Intelligence, so the general orders and all the citations from every branch of the service came over my desk. And I used to delay their arrival at the commanding officer's desk while I slipped them under my blotter so that I could read them in the leisure of the evening—read those wonderful statements, those unbelievable statements of what individuals, all over the world in our Armed Forces had done, particularly those who were being cited for the Congressional Medal of Honor.

And some years after the war was over, I read where a man in Moscow had been awarded their highest honor, their gold medal, but apparently they don't give citations as we do to tell what the medal was awarded for. This man was a Spaniard, had lived in Moscow for 4 years. He'd been a refugee from the Spanish Civil War. He was an interpreter. There wasn't anything in that to warrant his getting the medal. I dis-

covered that 8 years before that he had been in Castro's Cuba, but apparently nothing there. But a journalist, who had the ability to research further than I did, came up with the total story. Before the 8 years in Cuba, he had spent 23 years in Mexico, in prison. He was the man who buried that ice axe mountaineers, mountain climbers carry in the head of Leon Trotsky.

And I found my memory going back to those things that I had read during the war, any one of them a thrilling story of heroism above and beyond the call of duty. But one in particular seemed appropriate at that time. A B–17 coming back across the channel from a raid over Europe, badly shot up by antiaircraft, the ball turret that hung underneath the belly of the plane had taken a hit. The young ball-turret gunner was wounded, and they couldn't get him out of the turret there while flying.

But over the channel, the plane began to lose altitude, and the commander had to order bail out. And as the men started to leave the plane, the last one to leave—the boy, understandably, knowing he was left behind to go down with the plane, cried out in terror—the last man to leave the plane saw the commander sit down on the floor. He took the boy's hand and said, "Never mind, son, we'll ride it down together." Congressional Medal of Honor, posthumously awarded.

They in another society give their highest honor to a political assassin. We gave ours to a man who would sacrifice his life simply to bring comfort to a boy who had to die. I think that explains the great difference between our societies and the great significance of this particular award.

The bedrock of our strength is America's moral and spiritual character. Peace with freedom is the highest aspiration of the American people. We negotiate for peace. We sacrifice for it. We will never surrender for it.

Our commitment to arms reduction is unshakable. We'll not give up our search for peaceful solutions in the Middle East or Central America or elsewhere. But let us hope and pray that a tomorrow will come in which we will never have to call upon the courage of men and women in the field of battle. General Douglas MacArthur expressed this hope when he said: "Could I have but one line a century hence, crediting me with a contribution to the advancement of peace, I would yield every honor which have been accorded me by war."

God bless all of you, and may God continue to bless this land. Thank you. [*Applause*]

Thank you very much. I'm not doing an encore. I just have to—before I—please, sit down.

I've been given a very pleasant chore, and I hope that it is a surprise for Zach Fisher. I hope it's a surprise. I've learned in Washington, that that's the only place where sound travels faster than light. [*Laughter*]

The Intrepid Sea-Air-Space Museum is Zachary Fisher, its founder and chairman. And there is a plaque being held here. They said that he would hold it because it weighs 40 pounds. [*Laughter*] I can lift 40 pounds, but I'll let you. Zachary Fisher, we're presenting you this plaque. It's given with the heartfelt thanks of millions of Americans.

The inscription reads: "Due to the tireless and dedicated work of many Americans, the *Intrepid* will serve as an inspiration to both young and old for years to come. One man deserves special tribute—Zachary Fisher—a patriotic American who never forgot and who cares so much."

[*At this point, the President presented the plaque to Mr. Fisher, chairman of the board of directors of the Intrepid Sea-Air-Space Museum Foundation. Following remarks by Mr. Fisher, Col. Ron Ray, president of the Congressional Medal of Honor Society, presented the Society's Patriots Award to the President, who responded as follows.*]

Thank you all very much.

There are no words to express how honored I feel because, particularly, of all of you and what you mean who made this possible. My feelings are also compounded by a little guilt. It's a medal for patriotism. But it's so easy to love America that I don't know whether you're entitled to a medal for doing that. But I do. And I must say, thank you very much.

I just have to say one thing so that you all won't be in suspense. Ron is going to be able to tell his mother now the picture was "The Outlaw" and the girl was Larraine Day. [*Laughter*]

Note: The President spoke at 1:27 p.m. in the Imperial Ballroom at the Sheraton Centre Hotel. He was introduced by Arnold Fisher, a member of the board of trustees of the Intrepid Sea-Air-Space Museum's Hall of Honor.

Following his appearance at the luncheon, the President met with New York ethnic leaders at the hotel and then returned to Washington, D.C.

Nomination of David C. Jordan To Be United States Ambassador to Peru
December 12, 1983

The President today announced his intention to nominate David C. Jordan, of Virginia, as Ambassador to Peru. He would succeed Frank V. Ortiz, Jr., who was recently appointed to be Ambassador to Argentina.

Mr. Jordan was a teaching assistant at the University of Pennsylvania in 1961–1962 and an assistant professor at Pennsylvania State University in 1964–1965. Since 1965 he has been with the University of Virginia in Charlottesville, Va., serving as assistant

professor (1965–1968); associate professor (1968–1972); and professor (since 1972). He also served as chairman of the department of government and foreign relations in 1969–1977. He was an instructor at San Marcos University (Peru) in 1961; at the University of La Plata (Argentina) in 1975; at the University of Salvador (Argentina) in 1975; and served as visiting professor at the University of Chile in 1982.

Mr. Jordan graduated from Harvard University (A.B., 1957), the University of Virginia (LL.B., 1960), and the University of Pennsylvania (Ph. D., 1964). His foreign language is fluent Spanish. He was born April 30, 1935, in Chicago, Ill.

Appointment of Three United States Commissioners of the International Pacific Halibut Commission
December 12, 1983

The President today announced his intention to appoint the following individuals to be United States Commissioners of the International Pacific Halibut Commission. These are new positions:

Richard I. Eliason, for a term of 2 years. Mr. Eliason is a State senator in Alaska. Previously he was a member of the Alaska State House of Representatives (1969–1970; 1973–1980) and served as mayor of the city of Sitka in 1967–1978. He has served as an advisory member or commissioner of the Pacific Marine Fisheries Commission since 1966. He was born October 14, 1925, in Seattle, Wash., and now resides in Sitka, Alaska.

Robert W. McVey, for a term of 1 year. Since 1980 Mr. McVey has been Director of the Alaska Region for the National Marine Fisheries Service (NMFS). Previously he was Deputy Director of Alaska Region for the NMFS in 1970–1980. He graduated from the University of Missouri (B.A., M.A.). He was born February 19, 1932, in Stocktin, Kans., and now resides in Juneau, Alaska.

George A. Wade, for a term of 2 years. He is chairman and chief executive officer of the VWH Co., Ltd., in Seattle, Wash. Dr. Wade is chairman of the Historic Seattle Preservation and Development Authority and a member of the Washington Export Council. He graduated from Yale University (B.S.) and the University of Washington (M.B.A., Ph. D.). He was born May 14, 1929, in Seattle, Wash., where he now resides.

Nomination of Herbert Schmertz To Be a Member of the United States Advisory Commission on Public Diplomacy
December 13, 1983

The President today announced his intention to nominate Herbert Schmertz to be a member of the United States Advisory Commission on Public Diplomacy for a term expiring April 6, 1985. He would succeed Olin C. Robison.

Mr. Schmertz is a director of Mobil Corp. and a director and vice president of Mobil Oil Corp. He joined Mobil in 1966 as manager of the corporate labor relations department and became manager of corporate planning coordination in October 1968. He became vice president for public affairs in July 1969 and became president of Mobil Shipping and Transportation Co. in 1973. He returned to the public affairs position in 1974, was elected to the board of directors of Mobil Oil Corp. in 1976, and to the board of Mobil Corp. in 1969.

He is a member of the President's Commission on Broadcasting to Cuba. He graduated from Union College (A.B., 1952) and Columbia University (LL.B., 1955). He is married, has four children and resides in New York, N.Y. He was born March 22, 1930, in Yonkers, N.Y.

Appointment of Robert Youngdeer as a Member of the National Advisory Council on Indian Education
December 13, 1983

The President today announced his intention to appoint Robert Youngdeer to be a member of the National Advisory Council on Indian Education for the term expiring September 29, 1985. He will succeed Noah Woods.

Mr. Youngdeer is chief of the Eastern Band of Cherokee Indians in Cherokee, N.C. He is married and has two children. He was born April 13, 1922, in Cherokee, N.C., where he now resides.

Remarks on Signing the National Drunk and Drugged Driving Awareness Week Proclamation
December 13, 1983

Well, John—Governor Volpe, I thank you very much for this report. I thank all of you, too. I'm delighted that so many were able to join us for this important event. Secretary Dole, distinguished Members of Congress, members of our Commission, concerned parents and all who've worked so hard to prevent drunk and drugged driving—and, of course, the surprise, Elizabeth, that you had here, I'm most grateful for that. And I'm going to take it back to the office, and I'm going to read all those names that are on that long sheet of paper, I assure you.

Well, you've seen the beautiful Christmas decorations that are already up here in Washington. One of my favorites is the banner down near the National Christmas Tree. It says, "Peace on earth to men of good will." A little change in the usual expression there, but I think it's pretty suitable. We as Americans across the country, as we begin to gather with family and friends, today we're helping to make this holiday season what it ought to be—a time of peace and not of tragedy.

Drunk or drugged driving accounts for annual costs of over $20 billion in medical and rehabilitation costs, insurance payments, and lost production. There was a higher figure on the air last night given on some of the news, much higher, several times higher than that for the total cost if you added in a number of other elements,

all of them which could be associated with alcohol and the abuse of it.

Each year drunk or drugged drivers cause half of all the highway fatalities, injure some 700,000 men and women and children. For those between the ages of 16 and 24, alcohol-related crashes represent the leading cause of death. I know the members of the committee have found out all of these statistics.

A drunk or drugged person behind the wheel of an automobile isn't a driver; he or she is a machine for destruction. The American people have paid the bills, seen the damage, and felt the heartache, and I think they're saying, "Enough."

Last year, when we observed National Drunk and Drugged Driving Awareness Week, I said that if we worked hard enough we'd make progress, and as John just told us, we have. Twenty-two States and the District of Columbia have enacted tougher drunk-driving laws. And in part, because of those actions last year the highway death toll in America did drop, and the total drop was 10 percent.

Reports so far this year show that the annual death toll is still dropping, and again John gave us the figures on that. And the credit for this great achievement goes to you here today and to thousands of others throughout our country—have so diligently pursued community and legal action to end drunk driving.

Your most important contribution has been a change in public attitude. Today, drunk driving isn't a bad habit to be excused; it's a crime to be stopped.

On behalf of the American people, I thank you. Let me also say a word of thanks to the members of our Commission on Drunk Driving. You've done an outstanding job, both in heightening public awareness of the problem and in developing recommendations for dealing with it.

And a special thanks to John Volpe. John, you've had a long career of distinguished public service. I could call you, as I did, Governor, because that's a title you get for life. Mr. Secretary or Mr. Ambassador, that's another title you get for life. But today, you're Mr. Chairman. And in recognition of the leadership that you've given to this Commission, and of your faithful service to our country, I am proud to present you with this Presidential Citizens Medal. Congratulations, my friend.

In proclaiming National Drunk and Drugged Driving Awareness Week, let's all do so with a renewed sense of commitment. Every accident that we prevent will keep fellow Americans from suffering and give our nation a merry, *merrier* Christmas.

So, I thank you all, and God bless you.

And now I'll get over there and write with those pens that can write one word at a time. [*Laughter*]

Note: The President spoke at 1:47 p.m. in Room 450 of the Old Executive Office Building. Prior to his remarks, he received the final report of the Presidential Commission on Drunk Driving from Governor John Volpe. The report is entitled "Presidential Commission on Drunk Driving—Final Report, November 1983" (Government Printing Office, 39 pages).

The text of the citation accompanying the Presidential Citizens Medal presented to Governor Volpe read as follows:

Governor John A. Volpe has served the people of the State and this Nation with great distinction for three decades as Governor of Massachusetts, Secretary of Transportation, Ambassador to Italy, and Chairman of the Presidential Commission on Drunk Driving. His acknowledged success in each of these public service roles reflects his distinguished leadership qualities and high sense of personal commitment. His outstanding work with the Commission in its campaign against drunk driving is part of an outstanding career dedicated to preserving the lives and enhancing the welfare of all Americans.

Proclamation 5136—National Drunk and Drugged Driving Awareness Week, 1983
December 13, 1983

By the President of the United States of America

A Proclamation

The most serious problem on our Nation's highways is drunk driving. Drunken drivers kill and injure more people on the roads than any other cause. The cost of this slaughter is staggering, as much as $25 billion each year.

The drunk driving problem has stirred outrage among citizen groups, which have succeeded in arousing national interest in the problem. In response to these concerns,

many States have set up task forces to examine their drunk driving laws. Several States have already enacted amendments to strengthen their laws. To encourage these efforts, I established the Presidential Commission on Drunk Driving in April 1982. That Commission successfully completed its work and has prepared a landmark report of its findings.

There is also a generally unrecognized menace in a category akin to the drunken driver: the drugged driver. The drugged driver is also a public hazard, perhaps less recognized because the cause of the individual's behavior may be less apparent. The driver who operates a motor vehicle while under the influence of mind-altering drugs also presents a significant danger on the roads. The problem of the drugged driver is growing, and the American people must become more aware of this added threat.

In recognition of the threat that drunken and drugged drivers pose to the safety of our citizens, to heighten public awareness of the societal costs of such drivers, and to encourage and support efforts to decrease traffic fatalities caused by drunken and drugged drivers, the Congress, by Senate Joint Resolution 119 (Public Law 98–103), has designated the week of December 11, 1983, through December 17, 1983, as "National Drunk and Drugged Driving Awareness Week" and has requested the President to issue a proclamation in observance of that week.

Now, Therefore, I, Ronald Reagan, President of the United States of America, do hereby proclaim the week beginning December 11, 1983, as National Drunk and Drugged Driving Awareness Week. I call upon the people of the United States to observe this week with appropriate activities in their homes, offices, schools, and communities. I ask all of us to be mindful of the dangers of driving while drunk or drugged and to use this observance to intensify our efforts to prevent sadness and tragedy from intruding on our joyful holiday season.

In Witness Whereof, I have hereunto set my hand this thirteenth day of December, in the year of our Lord nineteen hundred and eighty-three, and of the Independence of the United States of America the two hundred and eighth.

RONALD REAGAN

[*Filed with the Office of the Federal Register, 11:16 a.m., December 14, 1983*]

Appointment of William L. Roper as Special Assistant to the President for Health Policy
December 13, 1983

The President today announced his intention to appoint William L. Roper to be Special Assistant to the President for Health Policy. He will assume duties on December 15, 1983.

Dr. Roper is health officer and director of the Jefferson County, Alabama, Department of Health, in Birmingham. He previously served in this position from 1977 to 1982. He teaches health policy and public health administration at the University of Alabama in Birmingham School of Public Health. In 1981–1982 he was assistant state health officer in Alabama and legislative liaison for the Alabama Department of Public Health. Dr. Roper was a White House fellow in the White House Office of Policy Development from 1982 to 1983, with responsibility for health policy issues.

Dr. Roper received his B.S. degree from the University of Alabama, where he was elected to Phi Beta Kappa and was named the distinguished undergraduate scholar of the College of Arts and Sciences for 1970. He received his M.D. degree from the University of Alabama School of Medicine, where he was elected to Alpha Omega Alpha, the honor medical society, and president of his class in each of the 4 years. He received his M.P.H. degree from the University of Alabama in Birmingham School of Public Health. He was intern and then resident in pediatrics at the University of Colorado Medical Center in 1974–1977. He is board-certified in the medical specialties of pediatrics and preventive medicine. He has served on many professional and community boards and is the author of several articles.

He was born on July 6, 1948, in Birmingham, Ala. He is married to Maryann Jedziniak Roper, and they reside in Birmingham.

Question-and-Answer Session With Reporters on Domestic and Foreign Policy Issues
December 14, 1983

The President. Good morning. I don't have any opening statement. But I just figured that it might be a good idea to come in here and get your questions now, and then I won't have to tonight at the press party at the White House.

Sam [Sam Donaldson, ABC News]?

The Middle East

Q. Mr. President, your Secretary of Defense has said that Syria sponsored and directed the attack against the U.S. marines in October. And many officials in your administration have said privately that Iran has been behind attacks in Kuwait and in Lebanon. My question, sir, is: Are we going to retaliate against the Governments of Syria or Iran?

The President. No. We have taken a position—and it is our policy that if this continues—we're not there to shoot first or to enter into combat. But I'm never going to send our men anyplace where they wouldn't be allowed to defend themselves. And it's been our policy that if they are attacked, they will defend.

Now, we've seen these instances of being attacked. And we have retaliated as nearly as we can against those who have actually done the attacking. And we want no conflict with Syria. Certainly, we're not there to enter into a war. And we continue to try and communicate and negotiate with them to let them know that, if they'll stop shooting at us there won't be any problems between us.

Q. But, sir, if I may, how—if Iran is—the Government of Iran, the Ayatollah Khomeini is behind some of this, how do we convince Iran to stop it?

The President. No. The best evidence that we have—you couldn't go into court and say that Khomeini ordered this—but what we do know is that a group that has been taking credit for these attacks and has claimed that they're responsible for many of them is a group that seems to be of some size, that is definitely with an Iranian con-nection. Now, whether that's with the government or that they just are Iranians, and they seem to be—well, they voice things that would indicate that they're interested in a kind of a holy war. They are a sect in the Islamic world.

Q. Mr. President, you said last Saturday in your radio address that you would keep the marines in Lebanon until that country had internal stability. Sir, that country—respectfully—has never had internal stability. Isn't that the kind of open-ended commitment that will mean many more marines dying and years and years of an American involvement there?

The President. No, I think we're making more progress than appears on the surface. And the original goal was the withdrawal of the foreign forces and then the reinstitution of the Government of Lebanon and helping them, as we have, to train and raise a force in which they can assume control over their own territory. The multinational force, they felt, was absolutely necessary. And they still feel that way, to be able to do some maintaining of order as they would then have to move out toward their borders once the foreign forces have gone. Now, this is still the goal, still the thing that we're trying to do.

In Geneva there was progress made where even those who are opposing each other within the country, the opposing factions, recognized the Gemayel government and agreed upon that government. Now, the thing of the multinational force, what I'm trying to say is, there are two ways in which they could be withdrawn. One of them would be if we achieve our goal. The second would, of course, would be if there was such a collapse of order that it was absolutely certain that there was no solution to the problem. There would be no reason for them to stay there.

Q. Are you saying, then, that you would consider withdrawing the marines if it appeared that the Gemayel government could not extend its authority beyond Beirut and could not create some kind of coalition?

The President. Well, we're getting into hypotheticals now of what the situation—I'm simply saying that if there was a complete collapse and there was no possibility of restoring order, there would be no purpose in the multinational force.

But let me call to your attention that it's not just us, that all of the nations of the multinational force, within a matter of days recently, have reaffirmed their determination that the mission is sound and that we're all going to stay there.

Well, Helen [Helen Thomas, United Press International].

Q. Mr. President, isn't there growing political pressure for you to pull out fairly soon, and aren't we—have we lost our role as peacemaker and into—a role of peacekeeper into a role of escalating violence? My question is, there are reports that you will pull the troops out before the political conventions this summer.

The President. I've seen those reports quoting unnamed sources again. Well, here's a named source, and I will tell you now, no decision that I'm going to make on anything of this kind is related to the election or the conventions or anything political. As a matter of fact, on all major issues I have reiterated more than once to our Cabinet that I don't want to hear the political ramifications of any major issue.

And on this one, there is no harder job or part of this job——

Q. But do you think——

The President. ——than putting our forces—let me say—someplace where these young men and women could be endangered. And, certainly, what we do in that regard is not based on any political consideration.

Q. Will it weigh in when you run for reelection?

The President. You meant, of course, *if* I run for reelection.

Q. Haven't you decided?

The President. You'll know January 29th, won't you?

Helen, no, there's just no way that political—the politics could be considered in an issue of this kind where the lives of our young people in uniform are involved.

Q. Mr. President?

The President. Yes, Bill [Bill Plante, CBS News], and then I'd better move back there.

Fiscal Year 1985 Budget

Q. We thought you were supposed to be in a budget meeting this morning, sir, although we're certainly delighted you came to see us instead. Does that mean that you've already decided the basics of next year's budget? Will there be a contingency tax as Secretary Regan suggested the other day? He seemed pretty solid on it.

The President. Well, the canceling of the budget meeting this morning was just for another reason. No, we're not close to any decision. These are meetings in which we take up various segments of the budget, preliminary estimates and so forth. So, they can be handled anytime within the next few days.

But with regard to a contingency tax, first of all, I can tell you there won't be any tax in 1984. The thing is that's always been back of the contingency tax—and I think this is what Don Regan was saying—was that such a tax would only be considered on the basis of getting the spending reductions that we must have.

This whole matter of looking only at the deficits out there—and I don't minimize them; I've been preaching too long, for a quarter of a century now, against deficit spending and having these deficits—but the deficit is a symptom of the problem, a result of the problem. The problem is the Federal Government is taking too big a percentage from the private sector of the gross national product. And the answer to getting rid of deficits and not running up more deficits comes with reducing that percentage that the Federal Government is taking.

Now, if you get to the absolute point in which government cannot be any further reduced in size and cost and then it is still out of line with revenues, you would have to make an adjustment on that side. But if you would look at it actually, when a government is taking too much money, then it's got to match that with one of two ways: It's got to do a tax, or it's got to reduce government cost, one or the other—or it's got to borrow, I should say. Now, either way you're taking more money from the private sector, whether you borrow it or whether you tax it.

And the real answer is to cure the disease, which is to get government down to a percentage figure that is consistent with having a sound economy.

Q. Well, sir, a number of economists, including Mr. Feldstein, have said that it's because of your military spending and your tax cuts that we have these deficits, and that taxes, some kind of taxes, are going to be the only answer.

The President. I think that's been a little out of context also. I reviewed the whole situation where Mr. Feldstein spoke on that, and he made an answer that I think any one of us could have made. The answer was said that, "Well, yes, if the defense budget were reduced, and if you hadn't tried this tax thing, reduced revenues for taxes, yes, the budget would be—or the deficit would be smaller." He did not say that it would be right to do those things, either to increase the tax or to reduce the defense spending.

Now, let me point out that some 20 years ago, during the Kennedy administration, defense spending was 47.8 percent of our budget. We are under 29 percent with regard to defense spending. We're spending about double on social reforms and social programs as to a percentage of the budget as was spent in those Kennedy years.

So, just to count the number of dollars, you have to look at defense and say, "What is necessary for our national security?" And then if there's anything unnecessary, yes, eliminate it, but if everything there is necessary from sound thinking for our national security, then you can't reduce beyond that point.

I've got to go back to the back of the room here.

Deputy Press Secretary Speakes. This is the last question.

Nuclear Arms Reduction Negotiations

Q. Mr. President, on arms control, do you expect to do anything, take any positive measure to bring the Soviets back to the negotiating table?

The President. Yes, we are trying to stay in communication with them. And I have to believe that they will come back, because it

is to their advantage to come back. They stand to gain as much or more than anyone in coming back to those talks. So, we're still determined on the reduction, particularly of nuclear weapons, and I am determined that once you start down that path, we must come to the realization that those weapons should be outlawed worldwide forever.

Q. Sir, would 1984 be a year for a summit, perhaps?

The President. Are you trying to ask whether I'm going to be busy in 1984 or not? When the time is right, you don't go by what is a time period that is right for it. When there is an opportunity and evidence that we can achieve something, that there is an agenda that can go on the table in which some gains can be made for both sides, then you have a summit. You don't have one just to say that you've had a summit, because too many people get disappointed.

Hunger in America

Now, he says that I've taken the last question. Could I just volunteer some information, though? I'm sorry that none of you— maybe one of you that I didn't call on would have asked about Mr. Meese and hunger.

Q. Yes, we were going to ask.

The President. You were? [*Laughter*] Well, let me just say—I'll volunteer, instead of an opening statement, a closing statement on that.

I believe the manner in which that's been treated by a great many of you is totally out of context with the entire interview which he gave. The policy, and my own feeling in this administration, is that if there is one person in this country hungry, that is one too many, and we're going to do what we can to alleviate that situation. And I happen to know that he feels the same way.

Now, one journalist the other night on one of the weekend talk programs said that we should be out on the front steps of the White House cheering those private agencies that are providing meals and providing evening dinners and lunches and so forth to the needy. Well, I may not be out on the front steps shouting, but you bet I'm cheering them. As a matter of fact, this is part of our private initiative program.

We've done everything we can to encourage this. Wherever possible, we have supplied surplus foods to them, because even—whatever we've done, we're doing more to feed the hungry in this country today than has ever been done by any administration. More money is being spent; more people are getting food stamps. All of these things we're doing. But this private sector aid is essential also, because where government can justify providing the necessities, there is a need also, as there's always been, to help provide some of those things over and above bare necessity that make life worth living, and the private sector is doing that and doing it splendidly—not only with the meals being served but with food distribution centers, and we're helping there also.

But, that—and it all ties into the commission that some have said, "Well, why? Don't we know that people are hungry?" That wasn't the purpose of the commission, and I'm waiting now for the January report.

We get anecdotes that some of you have reported on, individual cases or something, of people that are hungry. What we want to find out is why. Is it a lack of or a fault in our distribution system at the government level? Or is it that there are people out there who don't know what's available to them or how to find their way to a government program? Or is there—well, I think I've covered most of what it could be that they don't know how to find this, or that we somehow are bungling, bureaucratic-wise, in making—at a distribution. This is what we want to find out. Is there something we can resolve so that there won't be anyone, either through their own ignorance of what's available, or through falling between the cracks in a bureaucratic process, that we can resolve that and see that there is no one overlooked who's hungry.

Q. You don't think, sir, that those people were cheating who—you don't—the statement was that people might be going to a soup kitchen because they wanted to do it. You don't think that's happening?

The President. What I think was distorted in the reporting of that—and that I'll only take because it was part of my statement; then I'm going to run before you ask any more questions—that I think this is where there was something out of context. For example, we know that there are people who are not deserving of welfare who have been getting welfare. And one of our jobs has been—and not too well understood—to weed out, because every time someone who has the means and yet is subsisting on the help of their fellow citizens is doing that, they are reducing our ability to care for the truly needy. So, we try to clean up there.

Well, if that's true there, I'm sure that it must be true in these private groups. The difference is that these very worthwhile charitable efforts on the part of churches and community groups, unions, and others that are doing this, they have no way to establish eligibility. They can't set a rule and say, we're going to quiz you and determine whether—they have to accept that people that come and ask for help must be needful. But on the other hand, if there are people who will cheat with regard in getting welfare, I think it's possible that some might be cheating in this other. But that doesn't mean that you close down the private groups, because I'm quite sure that the vast majority of the people who seek aid there, it is of benefit to them and their families.

Q. But his answer was pretty all-inclusive.

The President. What?

Q. His answer was pretty all-inclusive—that they were going there, they had the money, they didn't want to pay.

The President. All we know is we had some anecdotal incidents, too, that we knew about.

Q. Don't forget to file in Illinois and New Hampshire, Mr. President. [*Laughter*]

Note: The President spoke at 11:31 a.m. in the Briefing Room at the White House. The session was broadcast live on nationwide radio and television.

Proclamation 5137—American Heart Month, 1984
December 14, 1983

By the President of the United States of America

A Proclamation

Diseases of the heart and blood vessels are among the Nation's most important health problems. This year one and one-half million Americans will suffer a heart attack, and nearly one million people will die from diseases of the heart. The economic drain on our resources in the form of direct medical costs and lost wages and production will exceed $60 billion.

Since 1948, the United States Public Health Service and a private voluntary organization, the American Heart Association, have joined in a concerted effort to combat cardiovascular diseases. These organizations have channeled their efforts and resources to reduce heart disease through such measures as prevention, diagnosis, and treatment; training of new research workers and clinicians; support for community service programs; and public education.

It is gratifying to note that mortality rates for heart disease and stroke are declining. Deaths from coronary heart disease have declined by more than 25 percent since 1972, while those from stroke have decreased by more than 40 percent. In large part, this favorable trend is the result of more Americans being aware of the personal risk factors for heart disease and adopting healthier life styles by changing their habits in such critical areas as smoking, cholesterol intake, exercise, and in controlling high blood pressure.

At the same time, science and medicine have made great strides in the past few years in technology to diagnose and treat diseases of the heart and blood vessels. The dedicated scientists and clinicians who labor to uncover the hidden causes of heart disease also deserve recognition. Lifesaving technology now in the hands of physicians has brought about more certain diagnoses of these diseases as well as the means to treat heart conditions that in the near past were considered beyond effective treatment.

Recognizing the need for all Americans to help in the continuing battle against cardiovascular disease, the Congress, by joint resolution approved December 30, 1963 (77 Stat. 843; 36 U.S.C. 169b), has requested the President to issue annually a proclamation designating February as American Heart Month.

Now, Therefore, I, Ronald Reagan, President of the United States of America, do hereby proclaim the month of February, 1984, as American Heart Month. I invite the Governors of the States, the appropriate officials of all other areas subject to the jurisdiction of the United States and the American people to join with me in reaffirming our commitment to the search for new ways to prevent, detect, and control cardiovascular disease in all of its forms.

In Witness Whereof, I have hereunto set my hand this 14th day of Dec., in the year of our Lord nineteen hundred and eighty-three, and of the Independence of the United States of America the two hundred and eighth.

RONALD REAGAN

[*Filed with the Office of the Federal Register, 9:59 a.m., December 15, 1983*]

Proclamation 5138—National Day of Prayer, 1984
December 14, 1983

By the President of the United States of America

A Proclamation

In 1787, a then-elderly Benjamin Franklin said to George Washington as he presided over the Constitutional Convention, "I have lived, sir, a long time, and the longer I live the more convincing proofs I see of this truth, that God governs in the affairs of men. And if a sparrow cannot fall to the ground without his notice, is it probable that an empire can rise without his aid?"

With these words, Mr. Franklin called upon the Convention to open each day with prayer, and from the birth of our Republic, prayer has been vital to the whole fabric of American life.

As we crossed and settled a continent, built a Nation in freedom, and endured war and critical struggles to become the leader of the Free World and a sentinel of liberty, we repeatedly turned to our Maker for strength and guidance in achieving the awesome tasks before us.

From the poignancy of General Washington's legendary prayer in the snow at Valley Forge to the dangerous times in which we live today, our leaders and the people of this Nation have called upon Divine Providence and trusted in God's wisdom to guide us through the challenges we have faced as a people and a Nation.

Whether at the landing of our forebears in New England and Virginia, the ordeal of the Revolutionary War, the stormy days of binding the thirteen colonies into one country, the Civil War, or other moments of trial over the years, we have turned to God for His help. As we are told in II Chronicles 7:14: "If my people, who are called by my name, will humble themselves and pray and seek my face and turn from their wicked ways, then I will hear from heaven and will forgive their sin, and will heal their land."

By Joint Resolution of the Congress approved April 17, 1952, the recognition of a particular day set aside each year as a National Day of Prayer has become part of our unification as a great Nation. This is a day on which the people of the United States are invited to turn to God in prayer and meditation in places of worship, in groups, and as individuals. Since 1952, each President has proclaimed annually a National Day of Prayer, resuming the tradition started by the Continental Congress.

Now, Therefore, I, Ronald Reagan, President of the United States of America, do hereby proclaim Thursday, May 3, 1984, as National Day of Prayer. I call upon the citizens of this great Nation to gather together on that day in homes and places of worship to pray, each after his or her own manner, for unity of the hearts of all mankind.

In Witness Whereof, I have hereunto set my hand this 14th day of Dec., in the year of our Lord nineteen hundred and eighty-three, and of the Independence of the United States of America the two hundred and eighth.

RONALD REAGAN

[*Filed with the Office of the Federal Register, 10 a.m., December 15, 1983*]

Letter to the Speaker of the House and the President Pro Tempore of the Senate Reporting on United States Participation in the Multinational Force in Lebanon
December 14, 1983

Dear Mr. Speaker: (Dear Mr. President:)

I am providing herewith a further report with respect to the situation in Lebanon and the participation of the United States Armed Forces in the Multinational Force. This report, prepared by the Secretaries of State and Defense, is consistent with Section 4 of the Multinational Force in Lebanon Resolution. This report also includes the information called for by the House version of the Resolution and is submitted in accordance with its more restrictive time limits.

I remain convinced that Congressional support for our continued participation in the Multinational Force is critical to peace, national reconciliation, and the withdrawal of all foreign forces from Lebanon. We will, of course, keep you informed as to further developments with respect to this situation.

Sincerely,

RONALD REAGAN

Note: This is the text of identical letters addressed to Thomas P. O'Neill, Jr., Speaker of the House of Representatives, and Strom Thurmond, President pro tempore of the Senate.

Message to the Congress Reporting Budget Deferrals
December 14, 1983

To the Congress of the United States:

In accordance with the Impoundment Control Act of 1974, I herewith report five new deferrals of budget authority totaling $354,427,600 and five supplementary deferrals of budget authority totaling $511,079,613.

The deferrals affect programs in Funds Appropriated to the President; the Departments of Defense (Military), Energy, Health and Human Services, Justice and Treasury; and the Railroad Retirement Board.

The details of the deferrals are contained in the attached reports.

RONALD REAGAN

The White House,
December 14, 1983.

Note: The attachments detailing the deferrals are printed in the Federal Register *of December 22, 1983.*

Remarks and a Question-and-Answer Session With Editors of Gannett Newspapers on Domestic and Foreign Policy Issues
December 14, 1983

The President. Well, it's a pleasure for me to speak directly to you—the editors, publishers, and news directors in 35 cities from Utica to Tucson. Gannett represents one of the most creative forces in American journalism today. And under your able leadership, Al Neuharth, Gannett has 85 daily newspapers, 13 radio stations, 6 TV stations, and a successful new venture that's reshaping the print media, your nationwide newspaper, called U.S.A. Today.

Now, I am going to take your questions, but I can't let an opportunity like this go by to say a few words about our economy and foreign policy with the hope that you'll share a few of those words with your listeners, viewers, and readers.

We've reduced the growth of government spending. We've pruned needless regulations and reduced personal income tax rates. We passed an historic tax reform called tax indexing that means that government can never again profit by creating inflation. And today, just over 2 years since these policies were put in place, we're seeing a vigorous recovery.

The prime rate is only a little bit more than half what it was when we took office.

Inflation has plummeted to 2.9 percent during the past year. Factory orders, retail sales, and productivity are all up from a year ago. And during the past 16 months, the stock market has risen sharply, boosting investment in productive sectors of the economy and raising the value of pension funds that so many millions of our people depend on.

Unemployment is still too high, but last month it showed how fast it was dropping when it went down by nearly half a percentage point. Federal deficits pose a challenge, and some in the Congress are saying the answer is a tax increase. But it was tax cuts that gave birth to the recovery, and this recovery's boosting government revenues. Deficits are caused by government spending too large a percentage of the gross national product. The solution is for government spending to be reduced to a point that it neither causes a deficit nor interferes with the ability of the economy to grow.

So, I hope the Congress will help us reduce deficits by cutting spending, not by putting a bigger burden on the backs of the American taxpayers.

Just as we're turning the economy around, I think we're bringing a new sense of purpose and direction to foreign policy. In Grenada we set a nation free. In Central America we're giving firm support to democratic leadership. And I believe that, thanks in large measure to the American example of what a free people can do, there's a rising freedom tide in the world today from Poland to Argentina and Venezuela.

In Lebanon the peace process is arduous and painful, but there has been some progress in spite of the continued horror tales that we are subjected to. Talks have begun to broaden the government's base and to satisfy legitimate grievances. And the goal must be internal stability and the withdrawal of all foreign forces.

In Europe the NATO alliance has held firm, despite months of Soviet bluster. Sooner or later, the Soviets are going to realize that arms reductions are in their best interest. When they do, we'll be at the table waiting for them, ready to go on negotiating from strength and in good faith.

As we pray for peace on Earth in this holiday season, the American people should know that, because we've strengthened our defenses and shown the world our willingness to negotiate, the prospects for peace are better than they've been in many years. I'm convinced that historians will look back on this as the time that we started down a new and far better road for America.

And, Al, could I just say, again, one other thing? I sure do like a press policy that is based on hope, legitimate hope, and not just undue optimism. I think the things that we've seen throughout the depths of this recession prove the quality of the American people—that in the very depths of it, more money was given to charity and to worthy causes than has ever been given before in our nation's history.

Today the partnerships with schools—we call attention at the national level to the problem in education, and suddenly business groups, communities, organizations are forming partnerships with schools throughout the country to help in whatever way they can. Name it, and the people, themselves, are finding an answer for it.

And I think you're right, that I think when you look at a TV news program sometime and the national news—and they have to announce that unemployment went down by hundreds of thousands of people in just the 1-month period. And then they immediately switch to showing some derelicts sleeping on heating grates, and so forth, to take the taste out of our mouth of that good news that they'd just given is the only excuse I can find for doing that. But you must have some questions.

I think he defers to you. [*Laughter*]

1984 Presidential Campaign

Q. Mr. President, this—I'm Al Neuharth with Gannett. This group met this morning with George Steinbrenner, the owner of the New York Yankees, and he disappointed us by refusing to discuss his career plans for Billy Martin in 1984. Would you wipe out some of that disappointment by talking with us about your 1984 career plans? [*Laughter*]

The President. Well, I'll tell you, I'll be a little late with the answer. On January 29th you shall know all. I will make a statement regarding my plans. And I don't know, maybe what Mr. Steinbrenner is going by is the old baseball superstition that, you know, if you're pitching a no-hitter, don't say anything about it. That was one of the hardest jobs for me as a baseball announcer, when I was a sports announcer. The pitcher— you're going into the seventh inning, and he hasn't allowed a hit. And I wouldn't say it; I wouldn't mention it because it's supposed to jinx him.

Mr. Steinbrenner. I'm waiting for your decision the 29th because if you're not going to stay here, I want you. [*Laughter*]

The President. Thank you very much. It's nice to have an ace in the hole. [*Laughter*]

Reporters in Grenada

Q. Mr. President, I'm John Quinn of U.S.A. Today. Mr. Secretary just said he went around the barn on this question.[1] I'd like to ask you, sir, your own views after the fact on the decision not to have pool press at the Grenada action, and if that happened again, do you think that would be the policy to follow again?

The President. Not to have what?

Q. A pool press representative.

The President. Well, I don't know how far George went around the barn, but there was no conscious decision by anyone in his department over there or in the White House that said, "Now, we must zero in and not let the press go." We only had 48 hours to plan that operation. We knew the Cubans were a lot closer than we were. The primary concern, as voiced by the Chiefs of Staff, was: minimize casualties.

So, in that limited time, they planned what turned out to be a most successful and brilliant operation aimed at immediately getting to the locale of the some 800 students that were there and offering them protection, and so forth. And I was responsible for only one part of that. I said that this is going to be a military operation in which civilians are not going to sit back here in the White House or in the Government and look over the shoulders of the field commanders who were there on the scene, and

---

[1] *Prior to the President's arrival, Secretary of State George P. Shultz addressed the editors and answered questions.*

they were going to run the operation. Now, it was only when some of you started squealing that I discovered that part of one of their decisions had been that they would go in without press.

I have to ask your understanding of this. The preparations that would have been needed, the word that would have had to go out, just offered too much of a possibility of a leak. I have found out that the White House—I don't know how it holds the rain out. [*Laughter*] Sometimes I read memos in the paper that I haven't gotten yet. [*Laughter*] But we felt that it was absolutely imperative that we have the ultimate in security. We knew that a half dozen other governments knew because they had requested us.

I am going around the barn now, George. I have to tell you this, that even there while we had to have some contact with them, we did not actually even declare to them that we were going in, that we were going to do it or what our plans were. And it worked.

Now, I won't do—in any operation of the same kind, I won't do what someone suggested, and that is that, yes, sir, we guarantee the press go along, and we put them right in the front row of the landing barges, so they'll be the first off. [*Laughter*] I won't do that.

Yes?

Federal Budget

Q. Mr. President, I am Charles Overby from Jackson, Mississippi. And I've covered your campaign since 1968, and I've heard you give some stemwinder speeches on tax deficits—budget deficits. What you said to us just a while ago, does that mean you're rejecting Secretary Regan's contingency tax increase? And do you have in your own mind how much of a budget deficit might be too much?

The President. I think any deficit is too much. I've been preaching for the last quarter of a century or more that government— well, we should have had the rule that Jefferson advocated back in his day when he said that the one thing lacking in the Constitution was a rule that the Federal Government could not borrow a penny. Now, you might have an emergency like war where you'd do that.

But deficits, deficits are the result of a disease. And to look alway and focus on the deficit and ignore what brought them about—when you have deficits, the government is spending, taking too big a share from the private sector. And when it does that and over and above its revenues, you can go one of two ways: You can either borrow, or you can raise taxes. But in either case, you are taking more money out of the private sector when that's already what the trouble is.

So, I think that the answer to deficits must be control of government spending and getting this government back to a certain percentage. I can't tell you what that exact percentage is, but I know that we're taking too much now.

There ought to be a point that we can figure out is the optimum point at which if you go beyond that percentage point in government taking from the private sector, you are interfering with prosperity and with a sound economy. And once decided on that point, we do that. So, whichever way, borrowing or raising taxes, is just further going to harm the economy.

We need to zero in—we've only gotten about 40 percent of what we asked for from 1981 on in spending cuts. If we had gotten all that we asked for, the deficit today would be $50 billion less than it is.

So, this is—now, on taxes, yes, it could possibly be that in our organization—it's hard to tell with a recession whether the tax structure that we have in place is sufficient to match what we think should be the spending outlay. Once, as recovery comes on and we're sure that it is definite and we can do some measuring, we can look and see, did we overdo? Is there room there for some tax increases?

So, what Don Regan was talking about was a contingency tax that says to the Congress, "If you will make the cuts that are necessary and the cuts that we're going to ask for, and then that isn't enough, yes, we will have in mind, as a contingency, a tax increase, then, to flesh this out and go after the rest of the deficit." So, I feel that way.

I will make one promise. I would resist and would veto any attempt at a tax cut

that is passed for 1984. As a matter of fact, I believe the economy's got a better chance to continue recovering if there isn't one in '85. The original contingency tax we suggested would be one that would go into effect in '86 if the Congress had done what we said and had made all the cuts that needed to be made.

Q. You said "tax cut." Did you mean "tax increase?"

The President. Or tax increase. I'm sorry. Tax increase.

Incidentally, let me just warn you about something that most people have forgotten. 1977, under the previous administration, they passed some social security reforms, and those called for years of increases in the social security tax, and those go all the way through the rest of this decade. Those increases alone are going to match the tax cuts that we have made already. All we did was head off further tax increases as to what they're taking out of your pockets.

By the end of the decade, the tax rate is going up for social security to 7.65 percent from the employee and the employer. So, that's more than 15 percent. And at the same time, every year virtually, they're increasing the amount of income against which that tax is assessed. So, you're going to be having some tax increases, and they're not saying anything about those. I think what they want is, with people's tendency to forget, they want, are looking forward to the day when they can say, they're my tax increases. I didn't pass them, and I don't want them.

Minimum Wage; Unemployment

Q. Christy Bulkeley, editor and publisher of Danville, Illinois. The first Federal pay grade is about 25 percent higher than the minimum wage. Have you looked at that and considered reestablishing the minimum wage as the least pay level for jobs just as we have to live with it?

The President. The minimum wage—I take it, if I understand correctly, the minimum wage is——

Q. The lowest Federal pay grade is 25 percent higher than the minimum wage is. We all have to live with the minimum wage as our lowest pay grade for the least jobs.

I've wondered if you've considered reducing that pay grade to the same level we live with, the minimum wage, as the lowest point?

The President. No, I can't recall anyone has proposed any such thing or that we've even discussed that, but I would have to tell you that I believe a lot of our ills are due to the minimum wage. I think we have priced a number of people and jobs out of existence by making the price for them too high. And if you go back, figures will bear out that every time the minimum wage increases, there is an increase, particularly in young people who have no job skill to bring to the market.

The very least that we should do—and we haven't been able to get any response from Congress to this—the least that we should do is have two stages and have a lower minimum wage today for young people who are entering the job market for the first time and have no skill to bring to—they're the ones that are sitting on the sidelines because no one can afford to hire them.

Q. That's precisely my point. Your lowest paying job in the Federal Government pays even 25 percent——

The President. Yeah.

Q. ——more than the minimum wage. And I guess I'm not sure that the least job in government is worth 25 percent more than the minimum wage.

The President. Oh. [*Laughter*] Well, you'd get a lot of bureaucratic answer to that. But no, I think the minimum wage was really designed for the most menial of jobs, the jobs requiring no particular job skill, the entry jobs and so forth. And I think it's been overdone. And, as I say, it's caused some of our problems.

Incidentally, when you hear the—oops, well, just let me say just one more thing. And then I'll—she's going to tell me, "One more question," aren't you?

Ms. Small.[2] Yes.

_____

[2] *Karna Small Stringer, Deputy Assistant to the President and Director of Media Relations and Planning.*

The President. All right. [*Laughter*]

Let me say that the biggest percentage of unemployment that's keeping our percentage level so high is for teenagers, young people. And I sometimes think that this isn't a fair measurement of unemployment, because would it interest you to know that almost 48 percent of those who are listed as unemployed teenagers are presently going to school? They're looking for after-school jobs or weekend jobs. We all did. I did when I was in school myself. But to tie that, as a measure of the Nation's unemployment and—is, kind of, taking our attention away from the real problem, which is the wage-earner with a family to support, the person that is out there with a job skill and no job to which he can apply it.

But I think we should ask some questions about unemployment. I asked one question of the Labor Department, and we've got a new answer already. I found out that they weren't counting our military as employed. [*Laughter*] And, now that they do, the unemployment rate is lower. [*Laughter*]

Yes, sir.

Defense Spending

Q. Mr. President, I'm Bob Brenner from Olympia, Washington. Do you, currently, have any contingency plans that might include reducing military spending as a way to decrease the deficit?

The President. On military spending—I ran on the idea that we had been starving our military for so long that there really was a window of vulnerability. I think we've closed, largely, that window of vulnerability. We haven't closed it completely. We haven't caught totally up. But we've made a great difference.

Now, with malice aforethought, I asked Cap Weinberger to take that job. He was my finance director, for a time, when I was Governor, and he didn't earn the name "Cap the Knife" for nothing. [*Laughter*] But what everyone, particularly in the Congress, seems unwilling to admit is that they have been, themselves—over there, under his direction, reducing the budgets as they find ways to save and ways to improve.

All these horror stories recently about the high price of spare parts—those are our figures. We're the ones who found those high prices, and we're the ones who are doing something about it. And we've already had a number of indictments; we have had refunds; we've had dismissals of personnel—we're getting at that. We sent some inspectors out that were mean as junkyard dogs, and they found that this was going on.

But the way I feel that we have to look at defense is this: You look at defense not as how much do we want to spend. What is necessary to assure our national security? What weapon systems? What numbers of personnel and all? And once you've decided on that, then you figure out—and figuring just as sharply as you can with a sharp pencil—what does it cost to provide that kind of national security? And if you've gotten it down to where all the waste is out—and we've taken advantage of our reduction of inflation below what our anticipation was. I can tell that right now the defense budget that is presently being talked about has been cut by the Secretary of Defense $16 billion, before he came in with it.

Now, to go to the Congress with this and then have them say, "Oh, no, we only want to spend x number of dollars," then you have to say to the Congress, "All right, then what is it that you want to do without? What weapon system do you want to do away with? Or do you want to cut the pay for the military?"

I can tell you that when I started here, everyone said that we would have to reinstitute the draft, that the volunteer military would never work. Would you be interested to know that it not only has worked—I get a lump in my throat when I see those young people out there, those young men and young women in uniform; their esprit de corps, their pride—and would it interest you to know that we have the highest percentage of high school graduates in the military that we have ever had in our history, even back in wartime when we were drafting so many millions.

We have the highest percentage above average—the average intelligence level in the military. We have a waiting line of people who want to enlist in the service. We have the highest retention now of noncommissioned officers. When we came here

the first year, if we had gone to a draft, we didn't have enough noncommissioned officers to train the draftees, and that's all changed.

And I tell you, when I get a letter from a hundred marines stationed over in Europe, and those marines write me, as they did about a year ago in the budget talk, and say, "If giving us a pay cut will help our country, cut our pay." I wouldn't cut their pay if I bled to death. The response from them, all of them, is just so remarkable.

Their pride, their—I've made a lot of telephone calls lately, tragic calls to families of those who've lost their lives. And I hang up the phone in worse shape than they were on the phone. I've never heard such pride; I've never heard such willingness to accept that this was necessary. And I've learned that the hardest thing that a President will ever have to do, as far as I'm concerned, is issue an order that some of our uniformed personnel have to go into an area where there is a possibility of harm to them. That's the one—that's the only problem that ever causes me to lose sleep.

But now I think that the military budget, the defense budget—incidentally, when we set out over a 5-year period, we had expected to increase over the Carter projections for the next 5 years, that $116 billion. We have already, ourselves, cut $79 billion out of that $116 billion increase, and still we have a military that is further up to readiness—well, you saw the result in Grenada.

And I wish you could all have been on the South Lawn when about 400 of those students from Grenada came there at our invitation, and we had 40 of the military back from Grenada from all four branches. And to see them, all the same age, roughly, the medical students and the military, and to see those students—they couldn't keep their hands off those young men in uniform. Everyone wanted to tell them personally that they had saved their lives.

I had some come up to me and tell me that when they were escorted to the helicopters and there'd been gunfire all around, that our men in uniform placed themselves in a position that if there was firing on them, they would be hit, not the students. They shielded the students with their bodies. And it was a wonderful thing to see.

I've got a great deal of hope and optimism about the future of this country now, having weathered all the riots on the campus when I was a Governor, to now see the quality of these young people and their dedication.

I didn't mean to make a speech, but I can't help it. I'm all wound up on that particular subject.

Ms. Small. Thank you, Mr. President.

The President. Thank you all very much.

Q. Are you going to propose a minimum wage this year?

The President. We've tried in Congress several times. We can't get any interest on the—this is on the minimum wage. Yes, I'm going to keep trying. You bet.

Note: The President spoke at 1:05 p.m. in Room 450 of the Old Executive Office Building.

Remarks of the President and Prime Minister Pierre Elliott Trudeau of Canada Following Their Meeting
December 15, 1983

The President. The Prime Minister and I have just concluded a very useful and a wide-ranging discussion of some of the most crucial issues that are facing the people of Canada and the United States and, indeed, facing people everywhere.

Prime Minister Trudeau briefed me on his recent discussions with leaders in Europe and Asia, on his concerns for world peace and disarmament and improving the East-West dialog. We fully share the concerns for peace which the Prime Minister has expressed. We appreciate his strong statements supporting the joint efforts of the Western allies to negotiate meaningful arms reductions and to promote dialog with other nations.

And I thank you, Mr. Prime Minister, for coming here, sharing your ideas with us. And we wish you Godspeed in your efforts to help build a durable peace.

The Prime Minister. Well, as you have just heard, the President supported what is being known as my peace initiative. But I think he did more than support it. I think he has been showing through his administration and the past months, at least, that as far as we are concerned on the NATO side, we want to change the trend line. We want to make it clear that not only the alliance is strong, that it will defend itself, that it will not be intimidated but that it is also pursuing peace.

And if I were to tell you, for instance,

that the President agrees that we shouldn't seek military superiority in NATO, we should seek a balance; that we do not think that a nuclear war can be won; that we think that the ideal would be to see an end to all nuclear arms; it might come as news at least to some of the press in Canada, because we haven't been hearing that. But this is what the President said at the Diet in Japan, and this is what our Foreign Ministers have said just a few days ago in Brussels, that we respect each other's legitimate security interests.

Whether this is news or not, I don't know, but this, at least in perception, is a complete change of a trend line which I saw when I embarked in my initiative several months ago, as one which was going downwards rather than upwards, which was—to use Carrington's phrase—which was characterized by "megaphone diplomacy." In Brussels last week, there was no megaphone diplomacy. There was a call for dialog repeated two or three times in the message and in the communique.

So, I'm grateful—not that I've said anything new this morning—but I'm grateful that I was able to hear from the President of the United States, the leader of the alliance, that these are not just words, that these correspond to the intention of the alliance, and that the other side can know, the Warsaw Pact can know that we're not trying to be superior, we're not trying to not recognize their legitimate security interests. We just want them to realize we want to be at least equal in balance and that they should recognize ours. And I think this is a great step forward.

I'll say nothing though—maybe I will say something about the decision of NATO to send Foreign Ministers to Stockholm. This is really stating that the politicians are taking hold of the peace issue. It is no longer for the nuclear accountants, it is for the political leaders, themselves.

Thank you.

Note: The President spoke at 12:09 p.m. to reporters assembled on the South Grounds of the White House. The Prime Minister spoke in both English and French. His remarks in French were not translated for the American press or included in the White House press release.

Earlier, the President and the Prime Minister, together with U.S. and Canadian officials including the Vice President, Secretary of State George P. Shultz, Secretary of Defense Caspar W. Weinberger, and Canadian Secretary of State for External Affairs Allan J. MacEachen, met in the Oval Office.

Appointment of Marshall Jordan Breger as Special Assistant to the President for Public Liaison
December 15, 1983

The President today announced the appointment of Marshall Jordan Breger to be Special Assistant to the President for Public Liaison. Mr. Breger will serve as the liaison with the American Jewish community and the academic community.

Prior to his appointment, Mr. Breger was associated with the Heritage Foundation as a visiting fellow in legal policy and is on leave from the New York School of Law, where he was an associate professor of law.

Additionally, he was an associate professor of law at the State University of New York at Buffalo Law School and the University of Texas Law School.

He graduated from the University of Pennsylvania (B.A., M.A., 1967; J.D., 1973) and received a B. Phil (Oxon) degree from the Oriel College, Oxford University. Mr. Breger is married and resides in Washington, D.C. He was born August 14, 1946.

Appointment of Jean Lawson Stone as a Member of the National Voluntary Service Advisory Council
December 15, 1983

The President today announced his intention to appoint Jean Lawson Stone to be a member of the National Voluntary Service Advisory Council. This is a new position.

Mrs. Stone is former mayor of the village of Scarsdale, N.Y. She now serves as a trustee of Rollins College. She served as a member of the board of trustees for the village and town board in 1978–1981 and as

police commissioner in 1980. She has served as chairman of the zoning and planning, public safety, and personnel committees for the village of Scarsdale.

Mrs. Stone graduated from the University of Texas (B.F.A., 1945). She is married, has four children, and resides in Scarsdale, N.Y. She was born February 23, 1924, in Del Rio, Tex.

Remarks on Lighting the National Community Christmas Tree
December 15, 1983

My fellow Americans:

In just a moment we'll be lighting our National Christmas Tree, continuing a wonderful tradition that was started by President Coolidge 60 years ago.

I know there's a special feeling that we share when we push the button lighting up that tree. It's as if each one of those twinkling lights sends a new spirit of love, hope, and joy through the heart of America.` And, of course, the brightest light of all is the Star of Peace, expressing our hopes and prayers for peace for our families, our communities, our nation, and the world.

On behalf of our fellow citizens, Nancy and I would like to thank all of you on the Ellipse who have given America such a beautiful Christmas present, the 1983 Pageant for Peace.

Christmas is a time for giving, and as we reach out to family and friends, I hope we'll also open our hearts to those who are lonely and in need, citizens less fortunate than ourselves, brave soldiers working to preserve peace from the tip of Alaska to the shores of Lebanon, to the DMZ in Korea, families maintaining a constant vigil for their missing in action, and millions forbidden the freedom to worship a God who so loved the world that He gave us the birth of the Christ Child so that we might learn to love each other. I know they would welcome your expressions of love and support.

Many stories have been written about Christmas. Charles Dickens' "Carol" is probably the most famous. Well, I'd like to read some lines from a favorite of mine called, "One Solitary Life," which describes for me the meaning of Christmas. It's the story of a man born of Jewish parents who grew up in an obscure village working in a carpenter shop until he was 30 and then for 3 years as a preacher. And, as the story says, he never wrote a book, he never held an office, he never had a family, he never went to college, he never traveled 200 miles from the place where he was born. He never did one of the things that usually accompany greatness.

While still a young man, the tide of popular opinion turned against him. His friends ran away. One of them denied him. He was turned over to his enemies. He went through the mockery of a trial. He was nailed upon a cross between two thieves. While he was dying, his executioners gambled for the only piece of property that he had on Earth. When he was dead he was taken down and laid in a borrowed grave.

Nineteen wide centuries have come and gone. And today he is the centerpiece of much of the human race. All the armies that ever marched, all the navies that were ever built, and all the parliaments that ever sat, and all the kings that ever reigned, put together, have not affected the life of man upon Earth as powerfully as this one solitary life.

I have always believed that the message of Jesus is one of hope and joy. I know there are those who recognize Christmas Day as the birthday of a great and good man, a wise teacher who gave us principles to live by. And then there are others of us who believe that he was the Son of God, that he was divine. If we live our lives for truth, for love, and for God, we never need be afraid. God will be with us, and He will be part of something much larger, much more powerful and enduring than any force here on Earth.

Now, tonight I have a very special person here with me to spread our Christmas joy. Her name is Amy Benham, and she comes all the way from Westport, Washington. Amy recently wrote the leaders of a public-spirited project named "Make A Wish" and said, "The Christmas tree that lights up for our country must be seen all the way to heaven. I would wish so much to help the President turn on those Christmas lights."

Well, Amy, the nicest Christmas present I could receive is helping you make your dream come true. When you press the button over here—we're going over there— the whole world will know that Amy Benham lit up the skies, sending America's love, hope, and joy all the way to heaven and making the angels sing.

And now, you and I will walk over so you can light the tree. And then after that's done we'll all join in singing one of our favorite Christmas carols, "Joy to the World." So, let's go over here.

Note: The President spoke at 5:47 p.m. at the South Portico of the White House during the annual Christmas Pageant of Peace.

Remarks at a White House Ceremony Inaugurating the National Endowment for Democracy
December 16, 1983

Good morning and welcome. It's good to have you all here to help celebrate the launching of a program with a vision and a noble purpose.

The National Endowment for Democracy is, just as we've been told, more than bipartisan; it's a genuine partnership of Republicans and Democrats, of labor and business, conservatives and liberals, and of the executive and legislative branches of government.

It's such a worthwhile, important initiative that I'm tempted to ask: Why hasn't it been done before? Well, we're doing it now, and it's largely because of the hard work of good people. Chuck Manatt, Frank Fahrenkopf, Dante Fascell, Bill Brock, Lane Kirkland, Mike Samuels, you have my heartfelt thanks and warmest congratulations. And a special thank you to our Vice President, who has been carrying this message for quite some time now on missions here and there throughout the world.

The establishment of the National Endowment goes right to the heart of America's faith in democratic ideals and institutions. It offers hope to people everywhere.

Last year in London I spoke of the need and obligation to assist democratic development. My hope then was that America would make clear to those who cherish democracy throughout the world that we mean what we say.

What had been preying on my mind that prompted me to say that in that speech to the Parliament was that in my lifetime, my adult lifetime, the world has been beset by "-isms". And we remember one of those -isms that plunged us into a war. And it

suddenly dawned on me that we, with this system that so apparently works and is successful, have just assumed that the people would look at it and see that it was the way to go. And then I realized, but all those -isms, they also are missionaries for their cause, and they're out worldwide trying to sell it. And I just decided that this nation, with its heritage of Yankee traders, we ought to do a little selling of the principles of democracy.

Speaking out for human rights and individual liberty and for the rule of law and the peaceful reconciliation of differences, for democratic values and principles, is good and right. But it's not just good enough. We must work hard for democracy and freedom, and that means putting our resources—organizations, sweat, and dollars—behind a long-term program.

Well, the hope is now a reality. The National Endowment for Democracy, a private, nonprofit corporation funded by the Congress, will be the centerpiece of this effort. All Americans can be proud of this initiative and the congressional action which made it possible.

By engaging the energies of our major political parties, of labor, business, and other groups, such as the academic community, the forces of democracy will be strengthened wherever they may be. They'll have a caring group of Americans to go to, to get assistance from, advice, and cooperation.

This program will not be hidden in shadows. It'll stand proudly in the spotlight, and that's where it belongs. We can and should be proud of our message of democracy. Democracies respect individual liberties and human rights. They respect freedom of expression, political participation, and peaceful cooperation. Governments which serve their citizens encourage spiritual and economic vitality. And we will not be shy in offering this message of hope.

Through the National Endowment, the private sector will promote exchanges between the American people and democratic groups abroad. It'll stimulate participation in democratic training programs and institution building overseas. The Endowment will work closely with those abroad who seek to chart a democratic course, and all this work will be sensitive to the needs of individual groups and institutions. And, of course, it will be consistent with our own national interests.

The National Endowment will let the people at the grassroots, who make our democracy work, help build it elsewhere. And the organizations that are now being formed by the Republican and Democratic parties and by labor and business will be the key to success. There'll also be expressions of what's best and most valuable in American public life.

Now, we're not naive. We're not trying to create imitations of the American system around the world. There's no simple cookbook recipe for political development that is right for all people, and there's no timetable. While democratic principles and basic institutions are universal, democratic development must take into account historic, cultural, and social conditions.

Each nation, each movement will find its own route. And, in the process, we'll learn much of value for ourselves. Patience and respect for different political and cultural traditions will be the hallmark of our effort. But the combination of our ideas is healthy. And it's in this spirit that the National Endowment reaches out to people everywhere—and will reach out to those who can

make a difference now and to those who will guide the destiny of their people in the future.

Much depends on us. But we can be confident that the tide of history is a freedom tide. That's the real message of our time. And it may be just the reason why those who don't like to hear the truth are so worried.

The nine countries which joined the United Nations since 1978 are democracies. In Africa, important states like Nigeria and Senegal have entered fully into the community of democratic states. In our hemisphere, 27 out of 35 countries are democracies now, or in transition. And just last week, Argentina completed its dramatic return, with the inauguration of President Alfonsin.

Yes, beyond the world's troublespots lies a deeper, more positive, and hopeful trend. The march of democracy and the National Endowment will be a part of it. Of course, any undertaking will ultimately be judged by the challenges it accepts and those that it overcomes. All of you in this room have good reason to be proud. You've accepted a worthy challenge.

The National Endowment for Democracy can make lasting and important contributions. It's up to all of us to make it happen, to harness the resources, experience, and wisdom of both the public and the private sectors. It's up to us to broaden our efforts, make them grow. And with the people in this room, I know we can, and I know we will.

So, again, thank you, good luck, and God bless all of you.

Note: The President spoke at 11:39 a.m. in Room 450 of the Old Executive Office Building. Among those present in the audience were the members of the board of directors of the Endowment.

Radio Address to the Nation on Drunk Driving
December 17, 1983

My fellow Americans:

This is the season when we appreciate our families and friends and spend time looking for just the right gifts for them. We arrange our homes with decorations and make an effort to prepare for special moments. Yet, during these holiday festivities our loved ones are in danger. That's why I want to ask you today for your help.

Unless all of us unite to take action, thousands of our citizens, perhaps a member of your own family, will suffer terrible deaths. I wish I were overstating the case, but I'm not. And there are tens of thousands of parents who have lost children. Their heartaches and tears are testament to the magnitude of the threat that hangs over us.

If I were alerting you about a foreign power brutally murdering tens of thousands of our fellow citizens, a cry for bold action would sweep our country. Well, I'm not referring to a foreign enemy; I'm talking about drunk drivers.

Due to the irresponsible use of alcohol, 25,000 Americans—men, women, and children—are killed each year. The statistics are overwhelming. We've lost more than a quarter of a million of our countrymen to drunk drivers in the last 10 years. That's 500 every week, 70 every day, one every 20 minutes.

Every year, nearly 700,000 people are injured in alcohol-related crashes. Every one of these casualties is someone's son or daughter, husband or wife, mother, father, or friend. The personal tragedies behind the statistics are enough to break your heart.

A few days ago, Mr. and Mrs. Gerald Price of Johnson City, Tennessee, joined me at the White House to proclaim this week National Drunk and Drugged Driving Awareness Week. It was fitting they be here. About 2½ years ago, their son Timothy was killed by a drunk driver. Then, just a year ago, their daughter Elizabeth was killed when a drunk driver veered onto her side of the road.

All of us can share the grief of these parents who lost two of their children in separate incidents. But now is not just the time for sympathy; now is the time to act. The Prices were at the White House when I officially received the report of our Commission on Drunk Driving.

Commission Chairman John Volpe and the other members took their jobs seriously, and they've made some suggestions you ought to know about. Right off the bat, we should understand there are no magic solutions. It'll take a long-term commitment, coming at the problem from different directions.

The first step, according to the Commission, is making sure that our friends and neighbors—as well as the people in the city halls and in the State legislatures—fully comprehend what we're facing.

Secretary of Transportation Elizabeth Dole has been speaking tirelessly around the country on this issue. Just this week, the Licensed Beverage Information Council, the Outdoor Advertising Association of America, and Secretary Dole joined in unveiling this year's Friends Don't Let Friends Drive Drunk campaign to enlist all of us to protect our friends from themselves. This is an excellent example of the private sector and government working together to attack a serious problem.

We must change the lax attitude about driving when there's even a question about sobriety. We'll need to be stern at times, but putting our foot down can save someone's life.

The Commission found out that some of our laws and law enforcement are lax, as well. Some drunks have been arrested more than once, but they're still out there on the highways. What greater travesty could there be than knowing your loved one was killed by an individual already convicted of drunk driving?

We must make it harder on the first-timers. And we must make sure that repeat offenders are taken off the road. The Commission made numerous, specific recommendations, and we're moving forward on them. But in a free society such as ours, with the separation of powers between Federal, State, and local governments, it will take all of us working together.

Much of the credit for focusing public attention goes to the grassroots campaign of organizations like MADD, Mothers Against Drunk Drivers, and RID, Remove Intoxicated Drivers. The activists in these organizations, many of whom have lost loved ones to drunk drivers, have helped strengthen laws and law enforcement at the State and local level. And in those States that have toughened their laws and their enforcement, lives have been saved.

The automobile has always been close to the hearts of Americans. We've valued our mobility as a precious freedom, and individual ownership of a car has provided greater mobility to more people than ever before. If there's one lesson we've learned in the last 200 years, it is that with freedom must come responsibility.

Some of our citizens have been acting irresponsibly. Drinking and driving has caused the death of many innocent people. It is up to us to put a stop to it, not in a spirit of vengeance but in the spirit of love.

I pray that each of you will have a safe and happy holiday. Until next week, thanks for listening, and God bless you.

Note: The President spoke at 12:06 p.m. from the Oval Office at the White House.

Interview With Garry Clifford and Patricia Ryan of People Magazine
December 6, 1983

Q. Thank you very much for having us back. It's a great honor for us to be here.

The President. Well, it's a pleasure.

Views on the Presidency

Q. One of the things I wanted to ask you was I think that most Americans thought the job of being President was impossible when you took office, and I think things have changed, and they feel that you thrive on it. And I sort of wanted to ask you how you discipline yourself and how you plan your activities so that it won't overwhelm you?

The President. Well, maybe the 8 years as Governor gave me some advance training for this, because I do remember that when I first became Governor there was a period that I went through in which I thought the world had fallen on my head. And I guess I learned there.

Q. But isn't this more difficult? I mean——

The President. Oh, yes.

Q. ——isn't there more people and more paper, and more—[*inaudible*]?

The President. Yes. And yet, I have to say that I think that the Presidency—the near-est thing to it in the country is a governorship. You don't have a foreign policy, which does add some problems, but it is the same thing. And it used to be—if you'll look back at earlier days, in which our Presidents were mainly found among the Governors. And I think that is a better training place than, for instance, serving in the legislature or something.

Q. You'd still recommend it?

The President. Yes. But the other thing— I've never felt better in my life, physically.

Q. You certainly look it, Mr. President.

The President. I have a little gym upstairs that I get to every afternoon before the day is over.

Q. Tell me, would you recommend the job to a friend?

The President. Yes. He might not be a friend afterwards—[*laughter*]—but, no, I have to say that for someone who really wants to do some things that he believes strongly in, this is the most fulfilling experience I've ever had in my life.

Q. Mr. President, we were curious. Many times in the last 6 weeks you've been awakened from a deep sleep with a world crisis. How do you get the news? Who brings it to you? Do you have to have coffee? Do you stay up all night? Does Mrs. Reagan get up with you?

The President. No, I try to slip out without her, although—it's usually the phone.

Q. Is it a special phone?

The President. No, usually, just the bedside phone, that then—well, when we were—when it has happened—it happened at Atlanta, Georgia, when we were on that weekend there. Well, there were two such calls and two such issues. And one of them was the phone, and, simply, it was Bud McFarlane asking could I come up in the livingroom and meet the Secretary of State there. So, I whispered that I was just going out in the livingroom for a little bit, hoping that she'd go back to sleep, and I put on a robe and went out there. Then the second incident down there, one of the stewards, he just slipped in, tiptoed in and touched me on the shoulder and whispered to me, and I slid out and did the same thing again. But then you stay there and do what has to be done.

Q. Well, are you alert immediately? Do you need coffee or anything?

The President. No, I wake up easy. And then, more recently at Camp David, it was phone calls, not in the middle of the night in this case. I wasn't up yet, but it was——

Q. Do you get to dislike having the phone ring because you think there's a problem when it rings?

The President. Yes. I can't say that I pick it up with dread, because many times it's just a correction or some information on something or other. But it has to be faced.

Q. It's usually a problem, often a problem.

The President. Usually, yes.

Commitment of U.S. Armed Forces; Lebanon

Q. I wanted to ask you, do you think the American people are behind the commitment of troops for military action, and do you think—this is a more serious question—do you think that the number of casualties influences how they feel about something?

The President. Oh, it has to. This has to be the hardest thing in all of this job, and certainly in my life, and that is committing these splendid young men and women to

tasks where you know there is that threat. I've never been so proud of anything as I am of the people in our Armed Forces.

A few years ago there was an entirely different situation. Everyone said the volunteer military wouldn't work. Well, it is working, and there is an esprit de corps, there's a pride out there among them. And this puts a lump in my throat. And then to—even one of them, to have a horrible accident or incident such as the one in Lebanon, there just is no way to make that easy.

But the thing is to try and—well, first of all, I think many people jump to events—not People—[*inaudible*]—such thing as the grassroots. But press and political figures that—on the Grenada rescue mission—that immediately jumped to the conclusion that this was some kind of a warlike thing that everyone would be angry at. It was kind of interesting to see so many of them have to try to crawl back in off the end of the limb when they found out that the American people understood very well what we were doing and supported it.

Now it's harder for them to understand Lebanon, because in Lebanon, they were not sent there to fight; that, hopefully, there would be no combat. We knew there was a risk because of the kind of violence that had been taking place in the streets over there for a long time. But the whole idea of the multinational force was in connection with our own peace proposal for the Middle East.

Lebanon was stalling that, if you remember. You had Israel and Syria both in. Israel had crossed the border because PLO terrorist units were attacking villages across their northern border from Lebanon. The Lebanon Government, as of several years ago, was virtually powerless in the face of what can only be termed warlords in their own country, of several factions, each with its own militia, fighting each other and fighting the Government. And you couldn't proceed with the peace mission until we resolved this problem.

So, we sent a force in with the idea that—well, first of all, they'd gotten some 10,000 PLO out; now the idea was that both Israel and Syria get out, then a stabilizing force there while the Lebanese Government reformed and created a military force in which it could then take over jurisdiction of its own territory.

Well, the first blow was that the Syrians, after saying, yes, they would get out, said, no, they wouldn't. The Israelis were prepared to get out. Both sides wanted—the idea was they would go out simultaneously. And so our force there is there for that purpose. And there wouldn't have been a shot fired by a marine or by our Navy or Air Force if they had not been shot at. And when that happened, I said wherever we send them, they're going to have the right to defend themselves and fire back.

Lebanon

Q. Mr. President, I'm curious. Your political godfather, or grandfather, if you will, Barry Goldwater, Senator Goldwater, is even calling for the boys to come back from Beirut. And I'm wondering, how far are you willing to commit troops, or how far are you willing to escalate?

The President. It isn't a case of whether we will escalate. That is up to the Syrians and to some of those rebel groups that are fighting the Lebanese military. But we have only fired back when we have been attacked. And I am hopeful that after this last exchange that the Syrians will decide that they don't want to go on on that path.

Q. But, Mr. President, if they remain recalcitrant, if they remain—the Israelis have been bombing them and strafing them and haven't really budged them. If they remain the same and they remain shooting at our reconnaissance flights and downing more fliers, what is the next step?

The President. Well, we're taking the next step right now. Don Rumsfeld[1] is on his way back there, and we still are going to try for a political solution. We're going to try to negotiate with the Syrians and make them understand.

Q. But if they don't want to negotiate, if they find it in their best interests to be a thorn in your side, what do you do then?

The President. Well, that becomes a kind

_____

[1]*President's Personal Representative in the Middle East.*

of a hypothetical question in which I almost have to wait and see what the circumstances are. Actually, the Lebanese military—which we have helped to train and have equipped and which is a very good military force—is supposed to be resolving the situation for themselves as we try to maintain a little stability in Beirut while they can go forward and do this.

Syria's Role in the Middle East

Q. Do you see a day, either in your own—in your next term, for instance, or in the very near future, where President Assad could be as, sort of, the dominant—the present day dominant force in the Arab world; where he could become something like what Anwar Sadat became to us? I mean, do you ever see that kind of relationship ever being able to develop?

The President. I don't see any reason why not. We've made great progress with the other Arab States, the more moderate states. I think that they are very ready for a negotiated settlement, continuing on with the Camp David accords and the U.N. resolutions. Syria is the big kid and the bad kid on the block, and the other Arab States have been trying, themselves, to persuade Syria to join in this effort and to withdraw. And now a new element has been introduced by Syria. They hadn't mentioned this before when earlier they said, oh, yes, they would get out, too. They now are not pretending that there is any assault on them or that they're in any danger and that's why they are staying there; they are now claiming that Lebanon properly is a part of a greater Syria. This is outright armed aggression now on their part, hoping to expand their territory at the expense of Lebanon and—they've even indicated—at the expense of Jordan.

The Film "The Day After"

Q. Mr. President, moving off of that People Magazine question, how did you assess the film "The Day After?" And do you think movies have a way of forming political opinion?

The President. Well, any motion picture or any drama or play is based on one thing: It isn't successful unless it has or evokes an emotional response. If the audience does not have an emotional experience, whether it's one of hating something or crying or having a lot of laughter, then you've got a failure out there.

Well, certainly there was an emotional response to this type of horror film. But apparently it has not had a lasting impact; I haven't seen very much reference to it any more. And maybe one of the reasons was because it was—[*inaudible*]—it was a horror film, showing you what I'm sure all of us all knew, that a nuclear war is unthinkable, it is sheer horror, it must not happen. But it left you with no idea or solution, no suggestion as to what to do about it.

And I think that my own reaction to it was, look, if anything, if this can add to what we can say about the fact that there must not be a nuclear war, then maybe the people will understand why we're trying so desperately to get a reduction in those weapons worldwide. And I hope that if we start down the reduction road that the other side will see the common sense in eliminating them totally. Not since 1946 has there been such a suggestion, and that was made by this country. And even then, when we were the only ones, really, with a stock of such weapons, the Soviet Union refused.

Q. Let me ask you this question: If Yuriy Andropov had been in the room with you watching the film that night, would you have said that very same thing to him?

The President. Yes.

Q. And anything else?

The President. Yes, I would have told him that the only way there could be war is if they start it; we're not going to start a war.

U.S.-Soviet Relations

Q. Let me ask you this: Do you have any second thoughts about calling the Soviet Union an evil empire? I think you called the Soviet Union that once. Do you have second thoughts about that? Do you wish you hadn't done it?

The President. No. I think that it was high time that we got some realism and got people thinking that for too long we have kind of viewed them as just a mirror image of ourselves, and that maybe we could appeal to their good nature. And we've gone through the experience in a number

of years past of saying, well, if we cancel weapons systems, if we unilaterally disarm, maybe they'll see that we're nice people, too, and they'll disarm. Well, they didn't. They just kept on increasing.

Q. So you see them as really a source of evil?

The President. Yes, because you have to look at the impact on what we were just talking about, with Lebanon. There they are with thousands of military advisers and technicians and so forth in Syria, have provided Syria with weapons that are not purely defense weapons—ground-to-ground missiles that can cover virtually every target from Syria in Israel. And they are the ones that seek, whether it's out of paranoia on their part—and, believe me, everyone's an enemy, and so they have to be aggressive—or whether it is the Marxist-Leninist theory, more than a theory—commitment—that was handed them, and that was that they must support uprisings wherever they take place in the world to bring about a one-world Communist state.

Now, no Russian leader has ever refuted that. As a matter of fact, he hasn't had time yet, but every Russian leader up to Andropov, at some time or other, has publicly restated his commitment to world conquest—world communizing.

Prophecies of Armageddon

Q. Let me ask you a question out of that. In the Jerusalem Post you were quoted—and I don't know if the quote was accurate—as saying that this generation might see Armageddon, that a lot of the Biblical prophecies are sort of being played out today, or could be—[*inaudible*].

The President. Where was that?

Q. In the Jerusalem Post. And I was going to say, is this really true? Do you believe that?

The President. I've never done that publicly. I have talked here, and then I wrote people, because some theologians quite some time ago were telling me, calling attention to the fact that theologians have been studying the ancient prophecies—What would portend the coming of Armageddon? —and have said that never, in the time between the prophecies up until now has there ever been a time in which so many of the prophecies are coming together. There have been times in the past when people thought the end of the world was coming, and so forth, but never anything like this.

And one of them, the first one who ever broached this to me—and I won't use his name; I don't have permission to. He probably would give it, but I'm not going to ask—had held a meeting with the then head of the German Government, years ago when the war was over, and did not know that his hobby was theology. And he asked this theologian what did he think was the next great news event, worldwide. And the theologian, very wisely, said, "Well, I think that you're asking that question in a case that you've had a thought along that line." And he did. It was about the prophecies and so forth.

So, no. I've talked conversationally about that.

Q. You've mused on it. You've considered it.

The President. [*Laughing*] Not to the extent of throwing up my hands and saying, "Well, it's all over." No. I think whichever generation and at whatever time, when the time comes, the generation that is there, I think will have to go on doing what they believe is right.

Q. Even if it comes?

The President. Yes.

Presidential Security

Q. To ask you a serious question which comes out of this, I see around—since my last visit here—many more signs that the government is worried about terrorism, that it's—[*inaudible*]. Do you, yourself, think about dying, think about the fear of the position you're in?

The President. Well, you can't help but be conscious, because the security measures are all so evident to you. But if you mean do I go around fearful and looking over my shoulder, no. I have confidence in the security people. I had one taste of——

Q. Yes, and a touch of another.

The President. And I never second guess the security people. When they tell me they're going to do something or change some way of doing things that we're doing,

I accept that that's——

Q. Is this something that you talk about, for instance, to Mrs. Reagan or your children?

The President. No.

Q. Or is it something you just—it's better left unsaid?

The President. Yes, very much so, because I think it was harder for them when it did happen than it was for me, and much more difficult for her, especially to get over.

It's a lot easier to worry about someone else than it is to worry about yourself, and so I know what must go through her mind when I set out on some expedition or some public appearance or something. And I wish it didn't have to be.

Q. Does your bullet-proof shirt or jacket or coat or whatever hang in the family quarters? Or do they keep it someplace else?

The President. No, no. They keep it. And they come, having it in hand, and they kind of come in flinching, because they know that I—[*laughing*].

Q. What do you say?

The President. I do not accept it with good grace.

Q. What do you say, though, when they put it on you?

The President. Oh, even an occasional unprintable word. [*Laughter*]

But I also know that they would not be bringing it in unless they felt there was a reason for it. But it isn't a pleasant—it's uncomfortable. [*Laughter*] That's the main——

Q. Is it bulky, or is it heavy, or what?

The President. Well, it's bulky. And I work so hard in that gym up there. And they say everybody out there in the audience will think I'm getting fat. [*Laughter*]

Lie Detector Tests

Q. Mr. President, away from Armageddon and all this talk of dying, and back to 1984. Did you cringe when you had to sign the order to have your own aides take a lie detector test? And I'm curious: Have you ever taken one? And how did you feel?

The President. No, I never have. But I didn't sign an order for them to take it. This has been misconstrued, and I bless you for giving me a chance to explain it.

We had a meeting that came up on national security—rules and regulations of the security of the information there. And there was a leak. And it was a leak which could have cost some Americans their lives. And this is a criminal act when there's a violation of national security. And I called the Justice Department on this—I thought it was serious enough—and I said I want an investigation of how this happened, to guard against it in the future.

Now, such an investigation, without my designating it as such—if it is a violation of national security, it is a criminal investigation. If it is a criminal investigation, the FBI has the right to ask for lie detector tests. But, being a criminal investigation, the individual has the right to refuse them, and that's all. But that's been distorted—that I suddenly——

Q. Well, have you ever taken one?

The President. No.

Q. No. Okay. Did your aides—[*inaudible*]? I mean did they take them——

The President. I don't know. I don't even know whether the FBI even asked for them or not. They determine that, and that is within the law. And then if somebody says no, they report that also in their investigating report that they asked and it was refused. But I don't know whether any had been given or any had been asked for.

Democratic Presidential Opponents

Q. Mr. President, who do you think the easiest Democrat would be to beat in 1984?

The President. If I answered that question I might be helping them to choose out of that octet they've got out there, and I'm not going to help them in their choice.

Q. But there's not one you'd rather—you're relishing running against?

The President. [*Laughing*] Oh, there may be, but I haven't said yet that I'm running.

Mrs. Reagan

Q. I have two questions that I would—not till Christmas. I'd like to ask two questions. What I was thinking, in this year of living dangerously, I wondered how in the world can you maintain the very obvious romance you have with Mrs. Reagan? I mean romance takes time, and it takes mood, and it takes not being harried. And what sort of special things do you do to maintain this togetherness in these tough times?

The President. Well, I don't know. We've always been very close, and there developed, as there would in 30-odd years, little things that kind of—traditional, or that have a meaning to us from times back.

Q. Can you cite any of them that—I mean, I think especially in your article in Parade, you showed how much you loved her and how much the romance continues and whatever. I just wondered if there's sort of small things you do to keep this touchingness together?

The President. Well, there are certain occasions when we leave notes for each other and things of that kind that we still do.

Q. Is there a special place you leave them, or——

The President. Oh, no, it just depends on where—well, things like on the breakfast tray and, on certain occasions, cards—I always remember.

Q. Could I ask one more question for my mother, who you gave a story to last year, and we kept hearing from our readers about the peg-legged pig. Do you remember the story you told about the pig with the wooden leg?

The President. Oh——

Q. We thought that this has become a tradition for the magazine, and we wondered, do you have a good story to tell the readers and, indeed, my mother, who is now 84 this year—a very good story?

The President. Well, I can't repeat that because I've done that story. Yes, I have one that I've told in a couple of speeches lately that I kind of enjoy, and that is a young fellow from a small town, and he would make a very good living selling fish to the local restaurants. But the Fish and Game people got a little curious as to where he was coming up with all these fish. And his uncle happened to be the sheriff, so he said, "Why don't you ask your nephew if you can go fishing with him some day, and I'd like to know where he's getting these fish?" So the uncle did. And they were out in the middle of the lake, and the uncle started to put his line in the water. The nephew reached in the tackle box, pulled out a stick of dynamite, lit it, threw it in— the explosion, and belly up came all the fish. And he started pulling them in. And his uncle said, "Nephew Elmer," he says, "do you realize you've just created a felony?" Elmer reached in the tackle box and came up with another stick of dynamite and lit the fuse and handed it to the sheriff and says, "Did you come out here to fish or to talk?" [*Laughter*]

Q. Very good, Mr. President.

Q. Mr. President, thank you very, very much, once again. I hope you and the First Lady have a merry Christmas.

The President. Well, thank you. The same to you.

Q. We certainly appreciate it.

Note: The interview was conducted in the Oval Office at the White House.

The transcript of the interview was released by the Office of the Press Secretary on December 19.

Interview With Marvin Stone and Joseph Fromm of U.S. News & World Report
December 15, 1983

U.S.-Soviet Arms Negotiations

Q. Mr. President, as we look ahead into 1984, we would ask that you address six of the most critical foreign policy issues that concern Americans.

First, in the year ahead, how do you propose to rebuild a working relationship with the Soviet Union and revive meaningful arms control negotiations?

The President. We can do it, because those negotiations are as much value to the Soviet Union as they are to anyone else. Even more important.

I have to point out that, with all this talk about the supposed strain in relations, there is an inference that somehow it is our fault. But we didn't kill Russian citizens by shooting down a civilian airplane. We didn't attempt to conquer an adjacent country to ours. We didn't walk out on negotiations and refuse to give a date for when we would resume. If there is a strain, it has not been caused by us.

Q. Do you believe the extended absence of Andropov from the picture—where under certain circumstances you might have been able to have a meaningful exchange with him—is affecting this relationship with the Soviets?

The President. I still think we can continue to deal with them and resolve problems between us. The biggest problem we all face is achieving genuine peace in the world. I don't think they want a confrontation any more than we do.

We'll be at that negotiating table when the Soviets decide to come back ready to negotiate in good faith. We have never broken off communications. We have at several levels continued to meet with the Soviets—and we are ready. I know, on the other hand, that the absence of Andropov must have had some influence on their side on exactly what could be done.

I believe that the Soviet Union has more to gain than we, or anyone else, in taking a look at changing the situation and, in effect, them joining the family of nations the way the rest of us have who are concerned with peace.

Middle East

Q. Issue number two deals with the Middle East. A main concern is Lebanon. Do you believe that in 1984 it is going to be possible to withdraw our marines? And will it be feasible to do that only if and when a stable government is able to unify Lebanon?

The President. Yes, it will be possible to withdraw the marines in 1984. And that applies as well to the whole multinational force. Let me remind you why we sent the marines to Lebanon as part of the multinational force.

Our whole idea all along has been to

1717

bring peace to the Middle East area generally and to act as a kind of go-between to bring these warring nations together. But Lebanon stood in the way. You will remember that in the summer of 1982 Beirut was being shelled in every direction, and in 1976 the authorities there had asked the Syrians to come in and help keep order, because the Government of Lebanon was virtually nonexistent and powerless to do anything about it.

The multinational force moved in and created conditions that led to the partial withdrawal of the Israelis. Now there has been a change in Syria's position. Even after a request from the Lebanese Government to withdraw, the Syrians have refused, and they are still there.

We believe that the purpose of the multinational force would be accomplished with the withdrawal of the other foreign powers and the establishment of a stable Lebanese Government, supported by a rebuilt Lebanese Army. We have done a fine job of training and equipping the Lebanese Army. It needs to be some bigger than it is. But it is a good and a well-trained force. And it has performed well.

The idea was that as the foreign forces left and as the Lebanese forces moved out toward their borders to reinstitute control and stop the internecine fight, the multinational force would maintain order—for example, in areas like Beirut—because the Lebanese military couldn't do both. This is still the goal.

Q. Is that still a realistic goal?

The President. I think that, with all that's happening, we're overlooking the progress that's been made. At recent discussions in Geneva, all of those involved—even those who are presently hostile—agreed to recognize the Gemayel government as the legitimate Government of Lebanon.

Another sign of progress is the fact, as I mentioned, that the Lebanese Army has been brought up to a capability it did not have before.

But now further progress hinges particularly on Syria, which is the stopping block in its refusal to withdraw—even though it had once agreed to leave and said that if Israel left, it would leave.

I don't say that the multinational force has to stay until all those foreign forces are out. I think that even if they gave an assurance that they're going to go and start the process maybe we could then leave.

Terrorism

Q. Subject three: With the prospect of continuing widespread terrorist attacks, how can the United States retaliate, especially when such attacks are inspired or sponsored by governments?

The President. One of the hardest things, of course, is to prove that the terrorist attacks are sponsored by a government. For example, these groups that are taking credit for the recent suicide attacks are believed to have an Iranian connection. There is a faction of Iranians that believe in a holy war. We do have the evidence that Khomeini has spoken a number of times about advocating a holy war in the Moslem world to promote his type of fundamentalism. So, it's hard not to believe that he must, in some way, instigate or at least egg on those that are doing these things.

But the important thing about terrorism is not to be turned back by it. It is a worldwide threat, as we know. The threat is right here in our own country. It's everyplace in the world.

Q. What can be done to counter the terrorist threat?

The President. I believe that if terrorists are claiming triumphs when they do these terrible deeds, acknowledging what their goal is and that they have a connection with some country—then I think it's up to the government of that country to try to curb and control such groups. If some of our own terrorist groups commit these outrages—such as the group that just bombed a naval recruiting station in New York—it's our responsibility to corral them, find out who and what they are, and bring them to justice. But the same is true for all the other countries.

But the one thing we can't do is what so many people, even here in our own country, are advocating in the face of the terrorist attacks against our forces in Lebanon. That is to bring home the marines from Lebanon. If terrorism can succeed in its goal, then the world is going to find itself under the control of the terrorists. You have to stand against that and not let it succeed.

Q. What do you do if a government is actually responsible, as you say, for instigating terrorism? Can you really ask that kind of a government to assume responsibility for controlling these terrorists?

The President. In those cases, I think that the civilized world has to get together and see what action can be taken. This does not necessarily mean warlike action, but pressures that can be put on a government—pressures such as saying to that government, "You start taking some steps to control this, or you'll be outlawed in the rest of the world."

Q. Another issue; you're going to China in the spring. What, in your view, is going to be necessary to develop closer relations with that country, particularly in the strategic field? And do U.S. ties with Taiwan inhibit the process of improving relations with China?

U.S.-China Relations

The President. I don't think they do. I know that the People's Republic of China is uncomfortable with our position on Taiwan. But we have reiterated time and time again to them that the people of Taiwan are long-time friends and, in fact, once were allies of ours. We have recognized that there is one China and that its capital is Peking. But we believe that the differences between Peking and Taiwan should be settled by peaceful negotiations.

We can't cast aside one friend in order to make another. We have argued to representatives of the People's Republic that they themselves should take some comfort from that because it's assurance to them that we wouldn't throw them aside to make friends with someone else.

I think we've made great progress. I know that sometimes the Government of the People's Republic has to speak out about this issue, but our trade relations and cooperation in the area of high technology, all of these things represent milestones and successive steps in improving our relations.

Now, the head of their government is coming here, and I am going there in the spring. We're going to find other areas where we can improve and increase our

relationship—cultural exchanges, things of that kind. All of this, I think, is on a good track. We've made some gains.

Central America

Q. Fifth: What strategy does the administration intend to pursue in Central America? Is it to underwrite the Government of El Salvador indefinitely? And in Nicaragua, is it to settle for nothing less than the overthrow of the Sandinistas?

The President. Our policy in Central America is regional. This is very much what the Contadora process is. We're supporting the efforts of the Contadora group—Mexico, Venezuela, Panama, and Colombia—to assure that democratic elections are used to settle the internal political conflicts and that verified agreements assure peace among the countries.

Now, as for the El Salvador Government: There has been important progress in recent years achieving democratic ideals, practices, and policy. They're beset by Cuban- and Soviet-backed insurgents who don't want that kind of government. They want the old-fashioned idea that we've seen for the last few hundred years—the idea that if you have a revolution, it is only to exchange one set of rules for another set of rulers. For once, we've got a government there that says: "No. This is to be revolution to change that process."

At the same time that the Government in El Salvador is fighting against this potent enemy on the left, they're being harassed from behind by small violent rightwing groups who want to go back to the old concept of government over the people, not by the people. So, we shouldn't be blaming the present Government of El Salvador for not being able to deal effectively with these rightists when it is beset by this other force on the left.

I think that the thing that is dragging this out are the limitations placed on our aid by the Congress. It's almost as if they're saying, "Well, we'll give you just enough to let them bleed to death slowly." What we really need—and remember that three-fourths of our aid is for economic and social reforms, and the other 25 cents out of each dollar is for military aid—is the kind of aid that will let them accomplish the job and eliminate this leftwing guerrilla force that is doing the attacking.

At the same time, wherever we can, we should help them find out these behind-the-scenes moves by the violent right that we will not accept. And where the government needs help in dealing with this, we should help. That was one of the missions that Vice President Bush performed when he was in El Salvador recently. I think some progress has been made in that regard. But we shouldn't let the violent right keep us from doing what is necessary to end the war that's going on.

Q. And Nicaragua—is overthrow of the Sandinistas the U.S. policy?

The President. No. We are not demanding the overthrow of that government. All they have to do is go back to the 1979 democratic commitments they made to the OAS as part of the political agreement leading to the end of the Somoza regime. Remember, the U.S. gave them immediate diplomatic recognition and significant financial aid until we found out that one faction of the revolutionaries was exiling or imprisoning their more democratic partners in the revolution, who discovered the Sandinistas intended to have a totalitarian form of government.

Now, the Sandinistas' promises of human rights, of democratic principles, of free elections, union rights, and so forth—all of those promises were made in writing to the Organization of American States when they persuaded the OAS, during the revolution, to persuade Somoza to resign, which he did. They have not kept that contract.

Some of the leaders of the *contras* were fighting alongside of them in the revolution and then were ousted, just as Castro ousted the same kind of people and imprisoned some of his best lieutenants because they wouldn't go along with him to a Communist, totalitarian form of government.

Nicaragua could solve its problem right now. If this Nicaraguan Government wants to go back to the promises of the revolution, we'll step in and help.

And what is the sixth issue?

U.S. Military Power

Q. It deals with the use of power. The other day you spoke of "the end of the days of weakness" with the rebuilding of American military power. How do you envision the use of military power in pursuit of this country's foreign policy?

Q. Mainly, what we're talking about is deterrence. I have always believed—in fact, the Chinese had this idea thousands of years ago—that your army is really doing its job if it never has to fight. I view it from that standpoint.

The President. After years and years of unilateral disarming on our side, with this country canceling weapons systems and so forth for domestic political reasons, the Soviets didn't have to give anything up. I think it was all explained in my favorite cartoon. It was the cartoon that portrayed Brezhnev when he was still alive, and it had him talking to a Russian general. Brezhnev said, "I liked the arms race better when we were the only ones in it."

Now, the Soviets have found out they are facing a belated U.S. modernization program which will assure the effectiveness of our deterrent. I think that is the only reason they came to the table to discuss arms reductions. They have come to realize that we'll do whatever is necessary to make it evident that hostile moves on their part would result in equal or greater punishment to them. That's the purpose of our military buildup, and it certainly worked in Geneva.

Note: The interview was conducted in the Oval Office at the White House.

As printed above, this item follows the text of the White House press release, which was released on December 19.

Remarks on Presenting the Presidential Rank Awards to Members of the Senior Executive Service
December 19, 1983

I assume that you've all been in here long enough to get warm. [*Laughter*] Just walking across the street if my voice quavers, it isn't emotion. [*Laughter*] I'm cold.

But good morning, and welcome. It's always a pleasure to meet with the people who are responsible for making our government work. The ability of this or any other administration to succeed is—in no small measure depends on the energy, the dedication, and the spirit of our Federal employees. And government service is a partnership—in other words, a relationship between political leaders, who do most of the talking, and career employees, who do most of the work.

When we speak of government, we may think of an impersonal bureaucracy with lots of regulations and paperwork, but just as this is a government of the people, it's also a government run by people—people like you, who've committed your lives and your careers to jobs that are vital to our nation. Your work is government, and without you it would come quickly to a halt.

Even if there were no awards like those for today, most of our Federal employees would still do their best, working to give our citizens honest government. People don't choose government service for prestige, glamour, or recognition. They're not trying to get rich. They're just trying to make a difference, and that's important.

In this centennial year anniversary of the Civil Service, we should remember that government is only as good as the people who make it work one day at a time. Government must limit what it does, but it still must perform its responsibilities with care and professionalism. You can't have good programs without good people. Well, you're the good people. And the Presidential Rank Awards provide the opportunity to recognize your great services to our nation. And it gives us a chance to show our appreciation for your contributions, your imagination, and your hard work.

These awards also provide an incentive for all Federal employees to help us improve the effectiveness of government. There's always room for improvement. You haven't earned your awards by luck. It's because of exceptional performance.

The nearly 7,000 members of the Senior Executive Service are among the finest group of executives anywhere. To be singled out and selected for the prestigious Presidential Rank Award is an honor. You have good reason to be proud, and America is fortunate to have you on our team.

You've searched for ways to reduce the growth of the budget, and you succeeded. You've looked for more efficient ways to run programs, and you've found them. You've tried to better serve our citizens, and you're doing it. From the Johnson Space Center to the Fish and Wildlife Service in Anchorage, Alaska, and from the Department of State to the VA Medical Center in Gainesville, Florida, you are on the frontlines, day in and day out, setting high standards for us all.

And, ladies and gentlemen, you're what is best about government: the commitment and determination of individual citizens in service to our nation. Through your efforts, we can make today's Federal Government a model for the generation that'll follow us. And I'm counting on you, and so are the American people.

So, God bless you, and thank you all very much for all that you are doing.

Note: The President spoke at 11:50 a.m. at the presentation ceremony in Room 450 of the Old Executive Office Building. Following his remarks, Donald J. Devine, Director of the Office of Personnel Management, introduced the 38 award winners to the President.

Proclamation 5139—National Care and Share Day
December 19, 1983

By the President of the United States of America

A Proclamation

Voluntarism is a uniquely American tradition. The concept is as old as our Nation itself. It was individuals working towards dreams, visions, and hopes that created this country. Today, that vitality still exists, as manifested in the large number of private initiative and volunteer efforts in which Americans strive to improve the lives of their fellow citizens. People from all walks of life; of all ages, races, and income levels; members of business and labor; and community organizations of all types are contributing their share in partnerships with neighbors and friends to help others.

In this holiday season and time of giving, I call upon all Americans to reflect this spirit of generosity and private initiative by providing additional food to those in need. I enlist the aid of each American who is able to donate an item of food for the needy. In addition, I strongly urge those in the food industry to donate and distribute extra food to food banks, so that this effort may complement the government programs which are providing unprecedented levels of total food assistance to low-income Americans.

Now, Therefore, I, Ronald Reagan, President of the United States of America, do hereby proclaim December 19, 1983, as National Care and Share Day and call upon the people of the United States to pay tribute to acts of charitable voluntarism and to promote community involvement in caring for the needs of our neighbors.

In Witness Whereof, I have hereunto set my hand this 19th day of December, in the year of our Lord nineteen hundred and eighty-three, and of the Independence of the United States of America the two hundred and eighth.

RONALD REAGAN

[*Filed with the Office of the Federal Register, 2:57 p.m., December 19, 1983*]

Appointment of 10 Members of the Cultural Property Advisory Committee
December 19, 1983

The President today announced his intention to appoint the following individuals to be members of the Cultural Property Advisory Committee for a term of 2 years:

James William Alsdorf is chairman of the board and director of Alsdorf International, Ltd., in Chicago, Ill. He was born August 16, 1913, in Chicago, Ill., and now resides in Winnetka.

Patricia Rieff Anawalt is consulting curator for the Museum of Cultural History at the University of California at Los Angeles. She was born March 10, 1924, in Ripon, Calif., and now resides in Los Angeles.

Clemency Chase Coggins is an associate in pre-Columbian art for the Peabody Museum of Archaeology and Ethnology at Harvard University. She was born June 12, 1934, in New York City and now resides in Auburndale, Mass.

James G. Crowley III is a private art dealer in Spartanburg, S.C. He was born August 28, 1949, in Spartanburg, where he now resides.

Arthur A. Houghton III is associate curator of antiquities at the J. Paul Getty Museum in Santa Monica, Calif. He was born May 6, 1940, in New York City and now resides in Pacific Palisades, Calif.

Michael Kelly is chairman of the board and chief executive officer of Kelco Industries, Inc., in Woodstock, Ill., where he resides. He was born July 9, 1925, in Flint, Mich.

John J. Slocum is a trustee and member of the executive committee of the Archaeological Institute of America in Kenmore Station, Borton, R.I. He was born March 1, 1914, in Lakewood, N.J.

Alfred E. Stendahl is director of Stendahl Art Galleries in Los Angeles, Calif. He was born December 4, 1915, in Los Angeles and now resides in North Hollywood, Calif.

Denver Fred Wendorf, Jr., is distinguished professor at Southern Methodist University in Dallas, Tex., and is former chairman of the Depart-

ment of Anthropology there. He was born July 31, 1924, in Terrell, Tex., and now resides in Lancaster, Tex.

Leslie Elizabeth Wildesen is adjunct professor for the Department of History at Portland State University in Portland, Oreg., where she resides. She was born December 5, 1944, in Phoenix, Ariz.

Memorandum on Nonrubber Footwear Exports From Taiwan
December 19, 1983

Memorandum for the United States Trade Representative

Subject: Memorandum of Determination under Section 301 of the Trade Act of 1974

Pursuant to section 301(a)(2) of the Trade Act of 1974 (19 U.S.C. 2411(a)(2)), I have determined that there are no unreasonable or discriminatory acts, policies or practices as alleged in Investigation 301–38. To help eliminate the difficulties United States footwear producers have experienced in attempting to gain access to the footwear market in Taiwan, however, I direct that offers received regarding marketing assistance for exporters of United States produced footwear, and of other measures that might provide greater market access for United States footwear exporters, be pursued.

This determination, together with the Statement of Reasons, shall be published in the *Federal Register.*

RONALD REAGAN

Statement of Reasons

Background

On December 9, 1982, the United States Trade Representative initiated an investigation under section 302(b)(2) of the Trade Act of 1974 based upon a petition filed by the Footwear Industries of America, the Amalgamated Clothing and Textile Workers Union, AFL–CIO, and the United Food and Commercial Workers International, AFL–CIO. The petition alleged that trade restricting practices of Brazil, Japan, Korea and Taiwan denied market access to United

States exports of non-rubber footwear. The investigations of the practices of Brazil, Japan and Korea are being conducted under the dispute settlement procedures of the General Agreement on Tariffs and Trade.

The investigation of Taiwanese practices centered on the import licensing procedure that allegedly restricted imports of non-rubber footwear and on tariff and customs charges. The American Institute in Taiwan (AIT) and the Coordinating Council for North American Affairs (CCNAA) consulted regarding these matters on January 17 and September 21 of this year.

Basis for Determination

Section 301(a)(2) authorizes the President to take all appropriate and feasible action in response to any act, policy or practice of a foreign country or instrumentality that is inconsistent with the provisions of, or otherwise denies benefits to the United States under, any trade agreement, or that is unjustifiable, unreasonable, or discriminatory and burdens or restricts United States commerce. The investigation revealed that imports of non-rubber footwear into Taiwan have been exempt from import licensing requirements, or have been subject to automatic approval by foreign exchange banks, since 1973. Evidence, therefore, does not indicate that import licensing procedures constitute a barrier to United States exports of non-rubber footwear. Beginning in September of 1982, a series of temporary tariff reductions on non-rubber footwear were implemented. These temporary tariff reductions have been extended administratively until mid-1984. Legislative approval for permanent tariff reductions for these items is being sought.

The tariff reductions are as follows:

Item No. and Description	In percent	
	Old rate	New rate
6400 Footwear with outer soles of leather or composition leather. Footwear (other than footwear falling within heading #6401) with outer soles of rubber or artificial plastic material:		
.01 With leather uppers	65	50
.02 With vegetable uppers......	60	45
.03 With synthetic or regenerated or glass fiber uppers..................................	60	45
.04 With animal fiber or furskin uppers	85	60
.05 Safety shoes with steel toe protection for laborers' use....................................	25	20
.06 Other....................................	60	50

No further tariff reductions for footwear are planned in the immediate future. The CCNAA indicated that, in principle, requests for further tariff reductions in specific footwear products might be received sympathetically if there were some evidence that United States suppliers would benefit significantly. The United States has maintained that the existence of high tariffs dissuades United States exporters from exploring the Taiwan market.

The CCNAA has advised AIT of the willingness of the Taiwan Footwear Manufacturers Association (TFMA) to assist the United States footwear industry in marketing and promoting United States produced footwear products in Taiwan. The AIT has offered to include non-rubber footwear in AIT's Market Research Program on Taiwan during fiscal years 1984 and 1985.

The information gathered during the investigation of this case does not indicate that any restrictive trade practices are acting as a barrier to United States exports of non-rubber footwear. In light of the offer of marketing assistance and indications that proposals regarding specific tariff reductions would be received sympathetically, discussions directed toward assisting exporters of United States manufactured footwear to enter the Taiwan market should be continued.

[Filed with the Office of the Federal Register, 1:13 p.m., December 20, 1983]

Proclamation 5140—Proclamation of Trade Agreements With Japan and Spain Providing Compensatory Concessions
December 19, 1983

By the President of the United States of America

A Proclamation

1. Pursuant to section 350 of the Tariff Act of 1930 (19 U.S.C. 1351), the President, on October 30, 1947, entered into the General Agreement on Tariffs and Trade (hereinafter referred to as "the GATT"), and by Proclamation 2761A of December 16, 1947 (61 Stat. (pt. 2) 1103), made the obligations of the GATT effective provisionally for the United States on January 1, 1948. The GATT includes a schedule of United States concessions, designated as Schedule XX, annexed thereto (61 Stat. (pt. 5) A1157). The GATT, Schedule XX, and Proclamation 2761A have been supplemented by subsequent agreements, schedules, and proclamations.

2. By Proclamation No. 4713 of January 16, 1980 (45 F.R. 3561), the President proclaimed temporary increased rates of duty, pursuant to sections 203(a)(1) and 203(e)(1) of the Trade Act of 1974 (the Trade Act) (19 U.S.C. 2253(a)(1) and 2253(e)(1)) and in

accordance with Articles I and XIX of the GATT, on certain nonelectric cooking ware of steel, enameled or glazed with vitreous glasses, effective through January 16, 1984. These rates were in addition to the duties and staged reductions thereof previously agreed to in concessions by the United States.

3. The Governments of Japan and Spain had benefited from the concessions previously granted by the United States. As a result of the increased duties, the benefits contemplated to accrue to Japan and Spain were substantially reduced.

4. The restoration of the contemplated benefits of the tariff concessions to Japan and to Spain would promote the trade of the United States and those countries. Pursuant to section 123(a) of the Trade Act (19 U.S.C. 2133(a)), I have determined that, as a result of the action taken pursuant to section 203 of the Trade Act (19 U.S.C. 2253), the United States should enter into trade agreements with Japan and Spain. Having complied with the provisions of the Trade Act, I have further determined that, in order to maintain the general level of reciprocal and mutually advantageous concessions, certain existing duties of the United States should be modified to carry out such agreements.

5. Following consultations between the Government of the United States and the Governments of Japan and Spain, the United States concluded a Memorandum of Understanding with Respect to Action by the United States on Porcelain-on-Steel Cookware Pursuant to GATT Article XIX with Spain on July 29, 1983, and a similar Memorandum with Japan on September 6, 1983. These agreements, negotiated by my duly empowered representative, set forth temporary reductions in or suspensions of the duties applicable to specified articles which the United States has agreed to implement to restore the balance of tariff concessions.

Now, Therefore, I, Ronald Reagan, President of the United States of America, by the authority vested in me by the Constitution and the statutes of the United States of America, including sections 123 and 604 of the Trade Act (19 U.S.C. 2133 and 2483), do hereby proclaim:

(1) The Tariff Schedules of the United States (TSUS) (19 U.S.C. 1202) are modified as provided in the Annex to this proclamation.

(2) Part 1 of Schedule XX to the GATT is modified to take into account the modification set forth in the Annex to this proclamation.

(3) This proclamation shall be effective with respect to articles entered, or withdrawn from warehouse for consumption, on or after January 1, 1984, and before the close of December 31, 1987, unless the period of its effectiveness is earlier expressly suspended, modified, or terminated.

(4) The Commissioner of Customs shall take such action as the United States Trade Representative shall direct in the implementation and administration of this proclamation.

In Witness Whereof, I have hereunto set my hand this 19th day of December, in the year of our Lord nineteen hundred and eighty-three, and of the Independence of the United States of America the two hundred and eighth.

RONALD REAGAN

[*Filed with the Office of the Federal Register, 10:57 a.m., December 20, 1983*]

Note: The annex to the proclamation is printed in the Federal Register *of December 22, 1983.*

Christmas Message
December 20, 1983

It is a very special pleasure for Nancy and me to extend warmest greetings and best wishes to all of you during this most joyous of holiday seasons.

This festive occasion is celebrated in many different ways. We exchange gifts, attend church services, decorate our homes and Christmas trees, and enjoy a family dinner. But perhaps the tradition that most warms the heart is the sound of Christmas music.

Of all the songs ever sung at Christmastime, the most wonderful of all was the song of exaltation heard by the shepherds while tending their flocks on the night of Christ's birth. An angel of the Lord appeared to them and said: "Fear not: for, behold, I bring you good tidings of great joy, which shall be to all people. For unto you is born this day in the city of David a Savior, which is Christ the Lord." Suddenly there was with the angel a multitude of voices praising the Heavenly Father and singing: "Glory to God in the highest, and on earth peace, good will toward men."

Sometimes, in the hustle and bustle of holiday preparations we forget that the true meaning of Christmas was given to us by the angelic host that holy night long ago. Christmas is the commemoration of the birth of the Prince of Peace, Jesus Christ, whose message would truly be one of good tidings and great joy, peace and good will. During this glorious festival let us renew our determination to follow His example.

Won't all of you join with Nancy and me in a prayer for peace and good will. May a feeling of love and cheer fill the hearts of everyone throughout this holiday season and in the coming year.

We hope this Christmas will be especially wonderful and that it will usher in a new year of peace and prosperity.

RONALD REAGAN

Executive Order 12451—Continuation of Export Control Regulations
December 20, 1983

By the authority vested in me as President by the Constitution and laws of the United States of America, including section 203 of the International Emergency Economic Powers Act (50 U.S.C. 1702) (hereinafter referred to as "IEEPA"), 22 U.S.C. 287c, and the Export Administration Act of 1979, as amended (50 U.S.C. App. 2401 *et seq.*) (hereinafter referred to as "the Act"), it is hereby ordered as follows:

Section 1. In view of the extension by Public Law 98–207 (December 5, 1983), of the authorities contained in the Act, Executive Order No. 12444 of October 14, 1983, which continued in effect export control regulations under IEEPA, is revoked, and the declaration of economic emergency is rescinded.

Sec. 2. The revocation of Executive Order No. 12444 shall not affect any violation of any rules, regulations, orders, licenses and other forms of administrative action under that Order which occurred during the period that Order was in effect. All rules and regulations issued or continued in effect under the authority of the IEEPA and that Order, including those published in Title 15, Chapter III, Subchapter C, of the Code of Federal Regulations, Parts 368 to 399 inclusive, and all orders, regulations, licenses and other forms of administrative action issued, taken or continued in effect pursuant thereto, shall remain in full force and effect, as if issued, taken or continued in effect pursuant to the Act until amended or revoked by the proper authority. Nothing in this Order shall affect the continued applicability of the provision for the administration of the Act and delegations of authority set forth in Executive Order No. 12002 of July 7, 1977 and Executive Order No. 12214 of May 2, 1980.

Sec. 3. All orders, licenses, and other forms of administrative action issued, taken or continued in effect pursuant to the authority of the IEEPA and Executive Order No. 12444 relating to the administration of section 38(e) of the Arms Export Control Act (22 U.S.C. 2778(e)) shall remain in full force and effect until amended or revoked under proper authority.

Sec. 4. This Order shall take effect immediately.

RONALD REAGAN

The White House,
December 20, 1983.

[*Filed with the Office of the Federal Register, 10:22 a.m., December 21, 1983*]

The President's News Conference
December 20, 1983

The Nation's Economy

The President. Good evening. I have a few remarks here before taking your questions.

With the holiday season upon us, I'm delighted to see Americans giving each other the best Christmas present possible: a strong economy that will ensure more jobs and opportunities in the months ahead. Confidence is in the air and with good reason. Today's encouraging news on the strength of housing starts and personal income, recent reports on prices, retail sales, employment, and factory use, all confirm a welcome fact: 1983 has been a banner year for the American economy with the United States economy enjoying a strong recovery and its lowest rate of inflation since the 1960's.

Wholesale prices last month actually fell. Consumers are flocking into stores during the holiday season. Our factories are operating at nearly 80 percent of capacity, up more than 10 percentage points from a year ago. Unemployment is still too high, but there are more people working in this country today than ever before, and every month we're creating over 300,000 new jobs.

In the last few weeks I've been involved in a number of meetings about next year's budget, and it's clear that here in Washington all of us, both in the Congress and in the executive branch, still have our work cut out for us. If the Congress will help me to restrain government spending, we can justify the people's confidence and keep America moving forward. We can make 1984 a year of strong and steady progress for America: continuing economic growth, unemployment coming down, and inflation staying under control.

And now, before we begin the questions, I'd like to wish the members of the White House Press Corps a very happy holiday season.

Helen [Helen Thomas, United Press International]?

Lebanon

Q. Mr. President, last week you said that if there's a complete collapse, you'll pull the troops out of Lebanon. Did you mean that if Gemayel fails to put together a broad, viable government that you'd pull out, or can you clarify? And I'd like to follow up.

The President. Yes, I can clarify, Helen. Actually I was asked a hypothetical question about whether there were any other circumstances other than achieving our goal by which the marines might leave or the whole multinational force, and I tried—I guess I tried to give a hypothetical answer to that and maybe a bad choice of words.

I simply meant that the only thing I—and I don't foresee this—but the only thing I could think of, other than achieving our goal, would be if perhaps that government and the forces that he's dealing with in trying to broaden the government, if there should be a complete change of course to the place that we were no longer asked to be there, that they were going in a different direction than the one that brought us in in the first place at their request, then I suppose that would be a reason for bringing them out. But I wasn't trying to send anyone a message or anything. I was just trying to say, well, yes, you can't say there isn't *any* other way by which they wouldn't come out.

Israel

Q. Mr. President, do you think that you've put the U.S.—the peacekeeper role in jeopardy by making a military pact at this time with a country that's invaded, annexed, and occupied Arab land?

The President. Helen, we didn't make any pact or anything that was different than what has been our relationship all along. There was a reaffirmation of this. In talking to Prime Minister Shamir we also emphasized to him that we were going to go forward with our relations with the moderate Arab States as part of our hope for being a catalyst—or trying to be—in bringing them all together and ending once and for all these hostilities that have so disturbed that area and caused such tragedy for so long.

It really—there was no signed agreement or anything else. We were really reaffirming the relationship that we've had since 1948, but at the same time, as I say, telling them that if we're to have any chance of bringing them together or continuing a process that started at Camp David, where Egypt and Israel wound up with a peace treaty—if we're to have a chance of bringing that kind of a peace, we've got to befriend all those countries. And they've got to be able to trust us that we can be fair to all of them.

El Salvador

Q. Mr. President, the death squad activity is continuing in El Salvador. I was wondering, are you satisfied now with the progress the government there is making in halting it, and if not, how long can you continue supporting a nation where this takes place?

The President. Well, I feel that we have

to continue supporting them just as long as we would supporting them against the leftist guerrillas that are trying to take over the government. We have a situation here of a 400-year history of mainly military dictatorships. And now, for the first time, virtually, in all that country's history, we have a government that has made it plain that they are trying to establish democratic principles and policies.

They're being assailed from the left by the Cuban- and Soviet-backed guerrilla forces. But at the same time they're being sniped at from the rear by—they're called the death squads and the so-called rightists, who, by the same token, don't want democracy. They want to go back to what they've had in this 400-year history. And the El Salvador Government has made great progress in establishing democracy. They're hindered in their fight against the guerrillas by this action behind their backs. But you have to look at punishing that government for trying to be democratic when it is being assailed from radicals from both sides—I think our obligation is to try and help democracy triumph there, and this is why we've offered some help.

And I must say, when the Vice President went down there recently and told them about how essential it is to get a handle on this force from the rear as well as the one on their front that they're fighting, he was very well received, and there was no disagreement with what he said. And there has been a stepped-up effort, and they want technical help from us in that regard that we are willing and can provide.

Q. Was the Vice President carrying a direct message from you on the death squads?

The President. Yes, yes. And he had his own words, also, about it, and I'm in complete agreement with those, too.

Chris [Chris Wallace, NBC News]?

Bombing in Beirut

Q. Mr. President, the House subcommittee investigating the bombing in Beirut has found—and I quote—"very serious errors in judgment were made both by officers on the ground and up the military command." Do you feel that disciplinary action should be taken against officers found responsible by Congress or the Pentagon?

The President. Well, Chris, there are two reports. There's a very voluminous report and a complete one that has been brought in by the military team that's been investigating this, as well as the congressional group. Both of those have just arrived at the Defense Department, and Secretary Weinberger is having a complete study made of them and then will submit a report to me on his findings, probably within the next several days. But, as I say, they are voluminous, and it's going to take a little while. So, I can't comment now until I see what those findings have been in both reports.

The Secretary also has said that, other than things that must remain classified for security reasons, he also intends to make public the findings in those reports as quickly as possible.

Q. Well, if I may follow up, sir, 2 days after the bombing, the Marine Commandant, P. X. Kelley, was in Beirut and said that he was completely satisfied with the security there. Was he being straight with the American people, and do you still have confidence in him?

The President. Yes, I do, very much. And I think he was, on the basis of what he saw, what was there—I think the main issue, then, that he was addressing himself to was, could anyone prepare themselves for this unusual attack that took such a tragic toll? And the moving of the men in such numbers into that building was done because that was the safest building from the standpoint of the weapons that had been used against them up until that point—mortar fire, small-arms fire—and it was a steel-reinforced concrete building. So, I—no, I don't think he was attempting to cover up for anyone.

Lesley [Lesley Stahl, CBS News]?

Terrorism

Q. Mr. President, there have been in the past few weeks dumptrucks surrounding the White House. When you traveled to Indianapolis, there were buses blocking intersections to protect you. There are reports that there are gound-to-air missiles now near the White House. Could you tell the

American people what the nature of the threat is and how this all makes you feel as President to have this going on around you?

The President. I just feel such popularity must be deserved. [*Laughter*]

No, let me just say on that, I—frankly, I had not noticed the blocked intersections. I hadn't paid any attention to it, and I was waving to the people along the street in that appearance. The only thing I regret is the inconvenience—when necessary moves have to be made—the inconvenience that I can cause to many other people in this.

There are no specific or definite threats that any of us know of here. We only know that worldwide there has been a call in a number of these terrorist groups for stepped-up violence. The term "United States" has been used as a potential target.

Actually, there has been a decline. Last year, there were 52 terrorist incidents in the United States. This year, so far—and the year's practically over—there've only been 31. And there has been no call for special measures or legislation or tactics of any kind.

But I think it is simply a case of having seen what has happened in the stepped-up violence in the Middle East, mainly. It would be—it's far easier to explain taking precautions than it is to have something happen and then have to explain why you didn't do something about it.

Q. But are you concerned that by building these barriers that you may give the impression that you might be giving in to threats and terrorists?

The President. Well, I don't think it's giving in to set up a barricade to keep somebody from doing this. You know, there have been attempts to ram the gates at the White House during these 3 years that we've been here. There've been some people that have gone over the fence.

So, I think that these are just normal security precautions in a climate that has shown us that this sort of thing can happen. And, as far as I'm concerned, I haven't let it interfere with my sleep or my work in the office.

John [John Aubuchon, Independent Network News]?

Situation in Lebanon

Q. Mr. President, a question and follow-up, sir. It seems evident from the polls that the American people do not support the U.S. Marine presence in Lebanon right now. Respectfully, sir, whether the policy is right or wrong, do you believe the public will put up with continuing American deaths there?

The President. Well, I can understand the public opinion, because they're hearing great attacks from a number of sources on our presence there; some of them, I think, politically motivated. But I have to say this about the mission, the purpose in being there. And let me just take a moment, if I can, on this. They do have a purpose and a mission there. And there has been a result from this and progress made.

If you will recall, it's been several years, of course, since Lebanon, kind of, came unglued and the government was helpless to stop some of the troubles in its own land. But we had the factor of more than a million refugees, Palestinian refugees in Lebanon. They've been there for decades. And over this period of time, they created their own militia, the PLO, a military and terrorist group. Well, this group was not only causing trouble within Lebanon; it was crossing the northern border of Israel. It was preying on civilians, citizens there. And, finally, Israel crossed the border into Lebanon.

The first goal was to simply push them back some 25 miles so they'd be beyond rocket or artillery range. But the others just repeated and then kept on attacking them. So, they went all the way to the edge of Beirut. And then we had a war taking place right within the city of Beirut in which thousands of civilians have been killed and wounded by this kind of combat.

In the meantime, during all of this, the Lebanese asked the Syrians—asked them to come in and help preserve order, because in Lebanon we had, and have, groups—various, sometimes religious groups, but other groups that kind of, like warlords with their own militias. And they're fighting each other and, at times, fighting against the forces of the Lebanese Government.

We were then asked to come in with the multinational force. And we went in, once the government had been formed there and once the PLO, when they were rejected, as they were—granted they came back later by way of Syria, but the goal and the idea was for the two foreign forces that were then left in there after the PLO left, for them to get out. But the Lebanese Government needed time to build its strength to where it could then go in with these internecine groups that were fighting there—go in and establish order over its own territory.

Israel, having completed its mission, announced its willingness and intention to get out. Syria did, too. And then for some reason Syria reneged on that promise and has refused to get out, even though they have now been officially asked to get out by the government that asked them to come in.

During the occupation by both Syria and the Israelis, they managed to keep some hold on those fighting groups in there, some order. The mission of the multinational force is what it was then. We have helped train the Lebanese Army, and it is a capable force. We have armed it. And when the other forces—the foreign forces get out and the Lebanese military advances to try and establish order in their land, the multinational force is supposed to, behind them, try to achieve some stability and maintain order, because Lebanon doesn't have the forces to do both. Well, this is the mission.

And, as I say, progress has been made. The warring forces meeting in Geneva have acknowledged that the Gemayel government is the legitimate government of Lebanon. There is an agreement that has been reached and signed between Lebanon and Israel in which Israel has agreed in writing that they will withdraw. Indeed, I think they're anxious to. Now, the stumbling block still seems to be Syria.

But at the same time, the Gemayel government is trying to bring these other forces in Lebanon, and if they will remember that they're Lebanese also and they want a Lebanon for the Lebanese people, they will come in at his request and join the government. And he's trying to broaden the base of the government to give them representation and end that kind of fighting there.

Now, I think, as I say, that progress has been made toward the goal when you think back to where we were when airplanes and artillery were destroying the civilian sections of Beirut.

Q. But, sir, respectfully, each week the U.S. seems to be using greater and greater firepower there. We had returning hostile fire, then artillery, then airstrikes, and now the 16-inch guns of the *New Jersey.* You said last week that you don't want escalation or a war. Can you avoid it without Syrian cooperation?

The President. You can avoid war. But I will say this, and I'll reiterate it: I will not okay a mission or ask or order our Armed Forces to go someplace where there is danger and tell them that they have not the right to defend themselves. So, when the sniping began and there was no retaliation, I made it plain by way of the channels in the Pentagon, as far as I was concerned, when an American military man is shot at, he can shoot back. And I think that there's been some indication that rather than stepped-up activity that there has been some pause for thought on those that were deciding that the multinational forces were fair game.

I don't say that they won't try these terrorist activities again; I'm sure they will. But are we, and where would we be in the world—are we to let the terrorists win? Are we to say that, well, if terrorists are going to be active, we'll give in to them; we'll back away?

Sam [Sam Donaldson, ABC News]?

The News Media

Q. Mr. President, on the press, Secretary Shultz said the other day that in World War II, reporters went along because on the whole they were on our side. And then he observed that these days it always seems that the reporters are always against us, and they're trying to report things to screw things up. Is that your view of the press also?

The President. Now, you're not going to get me into the middle of that, are you? I'm simply going to say that I do believe, Sam, that sometimes, beginning with the Korean

conflict and certainly in the Vietnam conflict, there was more criticizing of our own forces and what we were trying to do to the point that it didn't seem that there was much criticism being leveled on the enemy. And sometimes I just wish that we could get together on what is of importance to our national security in a situation of that kind, what is endangering our forces, and what is helping them in their mission.

Q. Well, sir, is one of the problems a definition of the word "us"? When Secretary Shultz uses it, or if you say "our forces," do you think he was using it in terms of an administration, the Reagan administration——

The President. No.

Q. ——or let's say the Carter administration? In other words, is "us" the administration in power, or is there a higher duty that the press has?

The President. I thought that the "us" he was talking about was our side militarily. In other words, all of America.

Yes. No—Alfreda [Alfreda Madison, Black Media, Inc.].

Civil Rights

Q. Thank you, Mr. President. It appears, Mr. President, that you are going to run for reelection——

The President. It does? [*Laughter*]

Q. Well, you said you were going to announce something on the 29th. You have completely alienated blacks by your assault on the gains for justice and equality made by them in the past. You're ignoring the needs and wishes of the Hispanics. You have cut programs that benefit the poor, and you're against equal rights for women. So, do you think you'll have enough white males to win, and aren't your actions really hurting Republican national and State candidates?

The President. Alfreda, I know that this has been widely heralded that all these things are true. They aren't true.

We haven't, in our social reforms, picked on anyone, and, indeed, what we have done when we came here was my belief—and we operated on this basis—that it wasn't that we were feeding too many of the needy; we were taking care of too many of the nonneedy. And where we have trimmed rolls, we've trimmed them up at the upper level. Today, any family with an income at a level of 130 percent of poverty, the poverty level, or lower, is eligible for these government programs, and, indeed, we are taking care of more people than we've ever taken care of before.

And there has been nothing in our programs or anything else that can be taken as prejudice against any sector of our society. Indeed, with regard to the civil rights movement and racial prejudice in this country, I'm old enough to have been on the right side of that long before the term "civil rights" was ever used.

And with regard to women, I think the record shows that the laws we've changed, the regulations we're changing all the time, the number of appointments, there's no prejudice there.

But I do know that a perception has been created and right today with these employment figures that I gave, with the drop in unemployment, blacks and women are getting a higher proportion of those new jobs than is anyone else.

Q. [*Inaudible*]—follow up on that because there are 17 and 5 percent—five-tenths percent of the blacks are still unemployed. And discrimination plays a part in it. And you seem to be against those methods that have been put into place for eradicating discrimination.

The President. No.

Q. And you said to me in——

The President. Not at all.

Q. ——a telephone conversation that one of the causes was the seniority system. And I asked you what you would do about it, and you said, "We have speeded the process." But you didn't explain that process. I wish you would explain to me that process.

The President. What process is this?

Q. That's what I'm asking you.

The President. Well, no, I mean—what I—I lost something there.

Q. Okay. I asked you—I said to you, you were against the Boston and Detroit cases, and you said, "Well, that was because of the seniority system." You wouldn't—and I asked you what you would do about that, because blacks would still be the last hired and the first fired. You said, "We'll have to

speed up the process." I asked you, what did you mean by "the process," and I didn't get an answer. I wish you would explain that.

The President. Well, I think you're—I think that you've given an example there that is a very difficult one because of fairness to all people involved where you pick a situation in which seniority and service is the basis for employment. And you also picked at a level of government in which the Federal Government has no business interfering. There isn't anything that we can do unless there's an outright violation of some individual's civil rights.

But I just think that there can be commonsense programs worked out to where you won't have to wait until someone has accumulated a great many years of seniority before he becomes eligible; that there might be some fair way in which you can recognize the rights of seniority, but also recognize the fact that others don't have seniority because, for a long time, they were discriminated against.

Yeah.

U.S. Marines in Lebanon

Q. Mr. President, you said earlier tonight that you would not send American soldiers or marines into a situation where they could not fight back. Haven't we sent them into a role in Beirut, a political, a diplomatic role as peacekeepers where they do not have adequate safeguards against terrorism?

The President. No, I don't know what you call adequate safeguards against terrorists or what we would call it. You know anytime that you—and particularly in a place like that, where even innocent civilians in the street are mowed down simply because snipers want to shoot someone—it's been that kind of a scene. It's that kind of a thing that we're trying to resolve in behalf of the innocent people there who want to live in peace like the rest of us.

Sometime I'm going to impose on you and read some of the letters that I get from people in Lebanon who tell us what life would be like if the multinational force wasn't there, and what it has meant in their lives as individuals living in the midst of that kind of brutality and bloodshed. And I was under no illusion—and I have to tell you that I have discovered for myself that the hardest thing you'll ever have to do in this job is give an order that put some of those wonderful young men and women in our military uniforms in places like that. But in the interest of our own national security and in the interest of overall peace, some of these things have to be done.

The Middle East is a tinderbox. It is the one place that could start a war that no one wanted because of its importance, particularly to the free world and to our allies. And we can't just turn away and say if we don't look, it'll go away. And this all started because of our determination to try and bring about peace between those factions that have been for so long warring with each other. The moderate Arab States again and the progress that we've made—there was a refusal on their part to even acknowledge the right of Israel to exist as a nation. So, therefore, there could be no negotiation.

Anwar Sadat, God rest his soul, broke out of that mold, and we have peace between two countries. And the territory of the Sinai has been returned to Egypt by Israel, and they're at peace with each other. Our goal was to see if we couldn't find more leaders and more governments that would become Egypts, in a sense, in settling their disputes and having peace.

And today the very fact that there's an indication that they are willing and prepared to negotiate differences indicates that they no longer are holding that position of refusing to let Israel exist.

Q. Sir, to follow up, though.

The President. What?

Q. Can I just ask—does it give you some pause when conservative thinkers like William F. Buckley, Jr., and Richard Viguerie suggest that you should be taking the marines home?

The President. Well, I take my friend Bill more seriously. I read that column, too, and I'll have to have a talk with him shortly.

Q. Mr. Reagan, the subcommittee report that was mentioned earlier tonight also concluded that continued deployment of the marines will almost certainly lead to further casualties. I know you don't want to discuss what the security arrangements were before the attack, but what about now? Are you confident that as of tonight the marines in Beirut are as protected as they can be, given where they are?

The President. I won't be able to answer that again until I too see the reports, particularly the report that is coming in that's very voluminous and must go into great detail. It's about that thick, and it has been made by military experts. So, I just can't comment until I know.

Q. Well, if I could just ask you, sir, then, are you saying that you aren't sure at this point whether tonight the marines are as adequately protected as they can be?

The President. I think they are to the extent that those on the field and the officers that are involved there are doing everything they can to ensure that. And I just have to assume that. And I think that I'm justified in assuming it.

Lt. Robert Goodman

Q. Mr. President, within days of your inauguration in 1981, you vowed that Americans would not be held hostage again. Well, the Syrians are holding airman Lieutenant Robert Goodman and say they won't release him until the marines leave Lebanon. Do you consider Lieutenant Goodman a hostage? And what efforts are underway to secure his release?

The President. Well, we have believed for a long time that the settlement there must be—in this whole area—must be political. I should have said this earlier, in my answer before about the history of this Lebanese situation. But we've had Ambassadors there from Phil Habib to Ambassador McFarlane, and now, Don Rumsfeld, because we're determined that there is a possibility. And it is the only way. You cannot—this can't be settled by force. And it is going to be settled that way.

And Ambassador Rumsfeld has been in Damascus. He has met with the Syrians. Certainly, that is very high on the agenda. The Syrians claim that he's a prisoner of war. Well, I don't know how you have a prisoner of war when there is no declared war between nations. I don't think that makes you eligible for the Geneva accords.

But, yes, we want that young man back. And, as I say, we're not missing anything, any possibility in trying to bring to terms these various factions so that we can achieve the goal of restoring order, a broader based government in Lebanon acceptable to more of the people, those that are presently hostile to this government, and the foreign forces back to their own borders.

Q. But, sir, is Lieutenant Goodman, in your opinion, a hostage? And do you think the Syrians will use him as a bargaining chip?

The President. I doubt that very much. I really do. In the sense of holding it up for trading something or other, no, I don't believe so. But I'm sorry that he is there. And I'm glad he is alive. But we're going to make every effort to get him back as quickly as possible.

Ms. Thomas. Thank you, Mr. President, and Merry Christmas.

The President. All of you had two questions tonight. [*Laughter*]

Q. What are you buying your wife for Christmas?

Q. Do you agree with Larry Speakes[1] on the press?

Q. What do you want for Christmas?

The President. What?

Q. What do you want for Christmas?

The President. What do I want for Christmas? You know what I'm going to say.

Q. What?

The President. Peace.

Q. Well, what do you want in a box? [*Laughter*]

The President. If you could get it in a box, I'll take it in a box. [*Laughter*]

Q. How do you package it—is that the problem?

The President. No, I'll tell you, I'm very happy. And I would just like to feel that all of you have a very happy holiday and a Merry Christmas and for all of the people in America, I hope that they all have hope now and can see the progress being made.

Q. Has it been a good year for you, sir?

The President. Yes, except for a lot of phone calls that I've had to make and some letters.

---

[1] *Deputy Press Secretary to the President.*

Q. How could it be better next year?

The President. Not making those phone calls, writing those letters, and the continuation of the recovery; and I'm sure it will continue——

Q. Do you agree with Larry Speakes on his statement on the press, Mr. President? [*Laughter*]

Q. Mr. President, when will the marines come home?

The President. I don't know which statement you're talking about.

Q. He said that the press are all patriots and all great Americans and never try to screw anything up. Do you agree with that, Mr. President?

Mr. Speakes. He agrees with everything. [*Laughter*] That's a good one to quit on.

The President. I agreed with him when he said I was all through. [*Laughter*]

Q. When will the marines come home?

Q. How did he mean that?

Q. When will the marines come home, do you think?

The President. The marines will come home as quickly as it is possible to bring them home in accomplishing our mission. And I'm glad you asked that. I'm glad I did stay just for that, because I want to say one thing. There have been some suggestions——

Q. Sir, could you say it where we could hear you? [*Laughter*]

The President. There have been some suggestions made with regard to bringing them home that some of my considerations might be based on the fact that in an election year—and politics are coming up—I will tell you this: No decision regarding the lives and the safety of our servicemen will ever be made by me for a political reason.

Q. But you did say in an interview that they'd come home this year. [*Inaudible*]—next year? Didn't you——

Q. Presidente, *Feliz Navidad y Próspero Año Nuevo.* [Merry Christmas and a Happy New Year.]

Q. ——in 1984?

Q. Does that mean you're running?

The President. What?

Q. Does that mean you're running?

The President. I told you you'd find out before my birthday, and I'm keeping my word.

Note: The President's 21st news conference began at 8:02 p.m. in Room 450 of the Old Executive Office Building. It was broadcast live on nationwide radio and television.

Message to the Congress Reporting a Budget Rescission and Deferral
December 21, 1984

To the Congress of the United States:

In accordance with the Impoundment Control Act of 1974, I herewith report one proposed rescission of budget authority totaling $1,700,000 and one revised deferral of budget authority totaling $21,061,187.

The actions affect programs in the Departments of Health and Human Services and Labor.

The details of the proposed rescission and deferral are contained in the attached reports.

RONALD REAGAN

The White House,
December 21, 1983.

Note: The attachments detailing the proposed rescission and deferral are printed in the Federal Register *of December 27, 1983.*

Appointment of Three Assistants to the President for National Security Affairs
December 21, 1983

The President today announced the appointments of Robert M. Kimmitt and Donald R. Fortier as Deputy Assistants to the President for National Security Affairs, and William F. Martin as Special Assistant to the President for National Security Affairs and Deputy Executive Secretary of the National Security Council.

Mr. Kimmitt, Executive Secretary and General Counsel of the NSC, has served since May 1983 as Special Assistant to the President for National Securitry Affairs. Prior to that time he was NSC Director of Legislative Affairs and Security Assistance. He is a graduate of the U.S. Military Academy at West Point and Georgetown University Law Center.

Mr. Fortier, NSC Senior Director for Policy Development, has served since May 1983 as NSC Senior Director of Political-Military Affairs and Special Assistant to the President for National Security Affairs, and prior to that as NSC Director of Western European and NATO Affairs. He had previously served as Deputy Director of the State Department Policy Planning Staff, on the House Foreign Affairs Committee staff, and the Rand Corp. He is a graduate of Miami University and the University of Chicago.

Mr. Martin previously served as NSC Director of International Economic Affairs. He has also held posts at the State Department, the International Energy Agency of the Organization for Economic Cooperation and Development in Paris, and the Massachusetts Institute of Technology. He holds degrees from the Wharton School of the University of Pennsylvania and MIT.

Assistant to the President for National Security Affairs Robert C. McFarlane announced today the designation of Capt. Thomas C. Shull, U.S. Army, as his military assistant. Captain Shull has served since June 1983 as NSC Deputy Executive Secretary. He previously served as a White House fellow. He is a graduate of the U.S. Military Academy at West Point and the Harvard Business School.

Statement on Central America Following a Meeting With Ambassador Richard B. Stone
December 22, 1983

Last April 27, before the Joint Session of the Congress, I signaled our deep concern with the need for advancing peaceful and democratic solutions in troubled Central America. In that speech I indicated my intention to name a special envoy for Central American negotiations. Ambassador Richard B. Stone, our special envoy, has performed extraordinary service in communicating with the countries of Central America and the Contadora group to help bring democratization and an end of fighting to all the countries of the region.

Ambassador Stone has just informed me of the current status of the various efforts at achieving a peaceful settlement in Central America. I want to reiterate my support and commitment to his delicate but crucial mission. As my personal representative, he speaks for me in our efforts to advance peace and democracy in this nearby area. He plans to return to the area shortly after the first of the year, and I join with all in wishing him the greatest success in his mission.

Note: The President's meeting with Ambassador Stone was held in the morning in the Oval Office at the White House. Other participants in the meeting included the Vice President, Secretary of State George P. Shultz, Assistant to the President for National Security Affairs Robert C. McFarlane, and Assistant Secretary of State for Inter-American Affairs Langhorne A. Motley.

Executive Order 12452—Revised List of Quarantinable Communicable Diseases
December 22, 1983

By the authority vested in me as President by the Constitution and laws of the United States of America, including Section 264(b) of Title 42 of the United States Code, it is hereby ordered as follows:

Section 1. Based upon the recommendation of the National Advisory Health Council and the Assistant Secretary for Health of the Department of Health and Human Services, and for the purposes of specifying certain communicable diseases for regulations providing for the apprehension, detention, or conditional release of individuals to prevent the introduction, transmission, or spread of communicable diseases, the following named communicable diseases are hereby specified pursuant to Section 264(b) of Title 42 of the United States Code: Cholera or suspected Cholera, Diphtheria, infectious Tuberculosis, Plague, suspected Smallpox, Yellow Fever, and suspected Viral Hemorrhagic Fevers (Lassa, Marburg, Ebola, Congo-Crimean, and others not yet isolated or named).

Sec. 2. Executive Order No. 9708 of March 26, 1946, Executive Order No. 10532 of May 28, 1954, and Executive Order No. 11070 of December 12, 1962, are hereby revoked.

RONALD REAGAN

The White House,
December 22, 1983.

[Filed with the Office of the Federal Register, 3:53 p.m., December 22, 1983]

Nomination of Pringle P. Hillier To Be an Assistant Secretary of the Army
December 22, 1983

The President today announced his intention to nominate Pringle P. Hillier to be an Assistant Secretary of the Army (Financial Management). He would succeed Joel E. Bonner, Jr.

Mr. Hillier is currently Acting Assistant Secretary of the Army for Installations, Logistics and Financial Management. Previously he was Principal Deputy Assistant Secretary of the Army for Installations, Logistics and Financial Management (1980–1983); Principal Analyst, Ground Forces, Congressional Budget Office (1978–1980);

and Ground Forces Program Analyst, Office of the Secretary of Defense, Planning, Analysis and Evaluation (1974–1978).

Mr. Hillier graduated from the United States Military Academy (B.S., 1961), Arizona State University (MSE, 1969), Army Command and General Staff College (1971), and Harvard University Executive Program, National and International Security (1979). He is married, has three children, and resides in Fairfax, Va. He was born May 20, 1939, in Fort Worth, Tex.

Proclamation 5141—Imports of Petroleum and Petroleum Products
December 22, 1983

By the President of the United States of America

A Proclamation

The Secretary of Energy has advised me that no purpose is currently served by the existing system of licensing of imports of petroleum and petroleum products. The Secretary of Energy also recommends that I retain the current prohibition on imports of Libyan crude oil into the United States, its territories and possessions, which was adopted in Proclamation No. 4907, on the ground that such imports would be inimical to the United States national security. The Secretary further recommends that he continue to monitor imports of petroleum and petroleum products in order to be able to advise me as to the need for further action, as appropriate, under Section 232 of the Trade Expansion Act of 1962, as amended.

I agree with the recommendations of the Secretary of Energy.

Now, Therefore, I, Ronald Reagan, President of the United States of America, by the authority vested in me by the Constitution and laws of the United States, including Section 232 of the Trade Expansion Act of 1962, as amended (19 U.S.C. 1862), do hereby proclaim that:

Section 1. Proclamation No. 3279, as amended, is revoked.

Sec. 2. The Secretary of Energy shall continue to monitor imports of petroleum and petroleum products and shall, from time to time, in consultation with the Secretary of State, the Secretary of Commerce, and such other federal agencies as he deems appropriate, review the status of such imports with respect to the national security. The Secretary shall inform the President of any circumstances which in his opinion might indicate the need for further action by the President under Section 232 of the Trade Expansion Act.

Sec. 3. (a) No crude oil produced in Libya may be imported into the United States, its territories or possessions.

(b) The Secretary of the Treasury may issue such regulations and interpretations as he deems necessary to implement this section.

Sec. 4. The Secretary of Energy may continue to consider requests for refund of fees paid under Proclamation No. 3279, as amended, if such requests were filed with the Secretary prior to the effective date of this Proclamation. Any such requests shall be considered in accordance with the previously applicable provisions of Proclamation No. 3279, as amended, and implementing regulations thereunder.

Sec. 5. The revocation of Proclamation No. 3279, as amended, shall not affect the authority of any federal department or agency to institute and conduct any administrative, civil or criminal audit, investigation or proceeding based on any act committed or liability incurred while the Proclamation was in effect.

Sec. 6. The revocation of Proclamation No. 3279, as amended, shall not affect the presently applicable tariff rates for imports of petroleum and petroleum products, as reflected in the Tariff Schedules of the United States, Schedule 4, part 10.

Sec. 7. This Proclamation shall be effective immediately.

In Witness Whereof, I have hereunto set my hand this 22nd day of December, in the year of our Lord nineteen hundred and eighty-three, and of the Independence of the United States of America the two hundred and eighth.

RONALD REAGAN

[*Filed with the Office of the Federal Register, 10:20 a.m., December 23, 1983*]

Executive Order 12453—Reports With Respect to Loans and Credits Extended to Poland
December 23, 1983

Delegation to the Secretary of State

By the authority vested in me as President of the United States of America by Section 301 of Title 3 of the United States Code, in order to assign certain functions to the Secretary of State, it is hereby ordered as follows:

Section 1. The functions vested in the President by Section 620 of the Agriculture, Rural Development and Related Agencies Appropriations Act, 1984 (H.R. 3223) ("the Act"), as enacted into law by Section 101(d) of the Joint Resolution "Making further continuing appropriations for the fiscal year 1984" (Public Law 98–151), and any function, which may be vested in the President by any other legislation, requiring the submission of periodic reports to Congress as a condition for the payment of United States funds in satisfaction of guarantees or assurances given by the United States with respect to loans made and credits extended to the Polish People's Republic, are delegated to the Secretary of State.

Sec. 2. Before making the determination and providing the written reports referred to in Section 620 of the Act, as enacted into law by Section 101(d) of Public Law 98–151, or in any other legislation which contains a reporting requirement referred to in Section 1 above, the Secretary of State shall confer with the Secretary of the Treasury and, as appropriate, with the Secretary of Agriculture and the heads of other interested Executive departments and agencies.

RONALD REAGAN

The White House,
December 23, 1983.

[*Filed with the Office of the Federal Register, 3:53 p.m., December 23, 1983*]

Letter Accepting the Resignation of J. Lynn Helms as Administrator of the Federal Aviation Administration
December 23, 1983

Dear Lynn:

It is with regret that I accept your resignation as Administrator of the Federal Aviation Administration, effective January 31, 1984.

You have served as Administrator of the FAA during one of its most eventful and productive periods. Although the firm stand you took during the air traffic controllers' strike is your best known accomplishment, the follow-up to that story is less well known. You have taken seriously the mandate I gave you to modernize our nation's air transportation system and make it the safest and most efficient in the world. The actions you have taken to accomplish this goal will be remembered for many years to come, and I want to thank you personally for a job well done.

Nancy and I send you our best wishes for every future success and happiness.

Sincerely,

RONALD REAGAN

[The Honorable J. Lynn Helms, Administrator, Federal Aviation Administration, 800 Independence Avenue S.W., Washington, D.C. 20591]

Dear Mr. President:

With great appreciation for the privilege of serving you for nearly three years as Administrator of the Federal Aviation Administration, I am now tendering my resignation.

As you know, the past three years have been dramatic ones for the nation's air transportation system and for the FAA. When you took office, there were many challenges facing the FAA. The air traffic controllers' strike was imminent. The nation's airspace was in need of a systematic modernization program. The national system of airports was in need of an integrated plan to ensure availability and balanced access to all user segments. There were numerous other pressing needs. All had to be acccomplished in a period of great budgetary restraint, without sacrificing safety and convenience.

We have met these challenges, and I believe my job is now largely done. With your firm support, we kept the nation's airplanes flying during the controllers' strike, bringing the air traffic control system capacity back to pre-strike levels rapidly on a schedule I outlined at the start of the strike. We have developed and implemented several new systems and programs to make our airspace safer and our regulatory process more effective.

Most important, we laid out a master strategic plan for the FAA to the end of this century, consisting of five major elements:

- a systems design of a modernized and safer air traffic control system
- development of a methodology to improve the safety and efficiency of the nation's airspace
- a long-range National Integrated Airport System plan
- a detailed plan to automate the diverse information resource management needs of the FAA in a cost-effective manner, and
- a three-phase plan to improve the work environment and human relations culture at the FAA, which is now entering its third phase.

Much of this strategic plan has already been put into place. I am absolutely confident that the superb professional career management team at the FAA fully accepts and believes in the course we have established. My successor will reap a legacy of detailed programs, plans, and funding of which I am proud.

You have given me the opportunity to preside over perhaps the most fertile and dynamic period in the history of aviation development and safety. It has been a very demanding task. The commitment of time and energy required to run the FAA is enormous, leaving little time for anything else. The outstanding quality of the career

FAA staff, and its willingness to work virtually around-the-clock with me to handle these demands, has earned my greatest respect and appreciation.

Early last summer, with our objectives accomplished or on the way, I decided to leave government service no later than February 1984. Because of the importance of preserving the progress we have made, I felt obligated to remain through the FY 1985 budget formulation period. That process is now completed, and the time is at hand to implement my decision to return to the private sector in order to resume an active role in strategic consulting and business planning.

To allow time for the new Administrator to prepare for Congressional hearings and for orderly transfer of functions, I will plan to remain as Administrator through January 31, 1984. I have so advised the Secretary of Transportation.

I am extremely proud to have been a part of this Administration. It has been an honor to serve under you and your two great Secretaries of Transportation, Drew Lewis and Elizabeth Dole. You have established a progressive record in aviation safety and modernization that sets a new standard for Presidential action in the aviation field. It has been an honor to participate in that process.

Very truly yours,

LYNN

J. Lynn Helms

Statement on Humanitarian Assistance for Central America
December 23, 1983

As we celebrate the many blessings of our great nation and share the spirit of Christmas, we should take the time to consider the plight of those not far from our shores in Central America. The turmoil there is taking an incredible human toll. There are more than 850,000 refugees and displaced persons in Costa Rica, Honduras, El Salvador, Guatemala, and Mexico. In El Salvador alone, more than 400,000 men, women, and children have been forced to flee their homes by guerrillas seeking control of the country through violence. Tens of thousands more have fled the brutal revolution of broken promises in Nicaragua.

Meeting the desperate needs of the victims of aggression and oppression is a key part of what we are seeking to achieve in the region. Through our government programs, we have relieved some of the human suffering in the region. Much more can be done, and much more needs to be done. Help from individual American citizens is very important. Government funding encourages the help of private voluntary organizations, but your personal support is essential to keep them going. The greatest need is to improve the delivery of aid to the needy and involve more of our own private voluntary organizations in this delivery effort.

You can make a difference, and I encourage you to contact voluntary agencies working in Central America in which you have confidence. They need your financial support and your technical and medical skills. If you would like to contribute or offer your services and don't know of a volunteer organization, please write the American Committee for Voluntary Agencies, 200 Park Avenue South, New York, N.Y. 10003. I can't think of a better way to share the spirit of Christmas and work for peace on Earth and good will toward mankind.

Interview With Reporters on Domestic and Foreign Policy Issues
December 23, 1983

Administration's Accomplishments in 1983

Q. Looking back over the past year, what do you think you did wrong, and what would you have done differently?

The President. Well, I think there are always things that you'll think you did wrong. But I think, basically, we have continued on the path that we set in 1981. The progress that we've made economically is apparent. It is the first time in many years that we've had a recovery from a recession in which not only is industrial—well, let's say just productivity—increasing, personal earnings increasing, inflation and unemployment both going down—all of these things happening at the same time. This hasn't happened in a recovery for many, many years, which makes me believe we are on a firm footing and have laid a foundation for a solid recovery. That part is won.

There are things—if you say what should we have done differently?—well, there are things. In trying to negotiate bipartisan agreements on some of these, you look back and think, well, maybe if we'd worked harder in one direction or another we might have gotten more cooperation in our need to reduce government spending.

On the international scene, I think that our continued buildup of our strength has changed international relations a great deal. I don't think without that we would have had the beginning negotiations that we've had with regard to reduction of nuclear weapons, both the INF and the START talks. I think it is due to that.

I think we've got a finer relationship than we've had for a long time with our own friends and allies. This is particularly true in the efforts that we've made in Asia, as well as our longtime friends in Europe.

So, all in all, I think that there has been progress. But it is a foundation laid for more progress.

Q. If I could just—but surely—was there anything you went back at the end of the day and said, "Oh, darn, I really"—you know—"that didn't work right, we should

have done it." Is there any one thing that you can pick out?

The President. Oh, well, I probably could get incensed about—but this was before 1983, earlier than that—going for the tax bill on the assumption that we'd been promised about $3 in reductions in spending for every dollar of tax revenue, and we have never seen the $3 in reduced spending.

The Middle East

Q. Mr. President, do you think the new rapprochement between Arafat and Mubarak now opens the way as a breakthrough for the possibility of your peace plan getting moving and Hussein taking part?

The President. Well, Helen, I'm always a little leery about saying a breakthrough, but I do think this: We are optimistic about this because if you look at the relationship there and the two countries—or the two peoples that were involved, Mubarak is the head of state of the one country in the Arab world that has gone forward and has a peace treaty with Israel. We're hopeful that the peace process will bring about more Arab nations making their peace with Israel.

Obviously, a part of that process depends on a fair and just settlement of the Palestinian question. And Arafat has, in the past, has been one who has refused to recognize Israel's right to exist as a nation. But the fact that earlier, and before this split in the PLO ranks, he had begun to discuss with King Hussein negotiations and participating in those negotiations on behalf of the Palestinians—then that broke down with the split in the Palestinian movement.

Now I think that what President Mubarak is doing is talking to him about returning to where he was earlier, making contact with King Hussein, and getting those peace negotiations, our peace proposal, underway again.

Q. Do you think there's a good chance?

The President. Yes, I do. I really do, because we had believed that a settlement in Lebanon had to precede going further with that. I don't think that's necessarily true now. I think enough progress has been made there that we can go forward with the peace movement.

Q. May I follow up, Mr. President? Israel has denounced the talks between Arafat and President Mubarak, saying it was a pure violation of the Camp David agreements. Would you respond to that?

The President. Well, I don't think it was a violation. I can understand their feelings in view of the recent tragedy in Jerusalem, and the group taking credit for that claimed to be a PLO group and all. But at the same time, I think as they look at this a little more clearly, they will see that Mubarak, based on the experience of Egypt and its willingness to go forward for peace, is simply trying to persuade others to change their thinking.

There was one point not too long before the peace treaty with Egypt, in which Egypt was as violent in its hostility as perhaps today the elements of the PLO are. So, who is better able to try and bring in another person into the peace process than someone who has made the change that Egypt has made?

Q. Do you think Mr. Arafat is still a popular leader among the Palestinians themselves?

The President. Well, this is what we need to find out. I can't believe that that radical group that, under the influence of the Syrians, created all this tragedy around Tripoli and the innocent people that were killed because of the violence of that battle—I can't believe that the millions of Palestinians are going to choose that leadership.

The Soviet Union and Arms Negotiations

Q. Mr. President, on a slightly different subject, you mentioned that due to our arms buildup, that brought the Soviets to the negotiating table. And now we've had a breakdown in the arms talks, and there seems to be an increased level of tension. Do you think we are at a confrontation state with the Soviets?

The President. No.

Q. And what do you see as the chance of an arms accord in 1984?

The President. Well, we're going to keep on with that. And, actually, the Soviets have not said no. They said they wouldn't set a date yet for the resumption of these talks.

Q. On INF they just walked out.

The President. What?

Q. On the INF talks they just walked out.

The President. Yes, but since then there have been statements to the fact that they just are not ready and that they're unwilling at this point to set a date. I believe they will be back, and I believe we're further from a confrontation possibility because of the deterrent capability of the United States and our allies at this point. I think there was a far more unstable condition when we had let our own strength deteriorate to the point that there was a window of vulnerability.

And I would like to call your attention to one thing. There have been 19—prior to this, to our talks—there have been 19 efforts since World War II to engage the Soviet Union in talks about arms reduction. There has never been any progress made in those. The SALT talks, actually, were not arms reductions; they were supposed to be setting a ceiling on how many more weapons would be built. And that has not been ratified, the SALT II treaty.

But in these negotiations, even though the Soviets were not as forthcoming as we would like to have had them be, they still did make a couple of offers to reduce the number of their weapons. Now, that is the first time they have ever done that in any negotiations, in all these previous 19 attempts. And I think that now that they see that we are determined to maintain our own ability to defend ourselves, and our allies with us are included in that, I think that they have to see that these negotiations are in their interest as well as ours.

Q. Do you have any signals that they are actually planning to come back? Or are you just looking at it from your—what you see as common sense?

The President. No. I think the things that we have heard. I think that this is, you might say, almost a part of the negotiating process. Their whole principal move over this last year or so has been an effort to stop the deployment of the intermediate-range weapons that were asked for by NATO. And the fact that we're going ahead, this, maybe, could be tied to that as still, you might say, an element of negotiating. But we are going to proceed with the installation of those weapons.

Q. And you don't think it's 3 minutes to 12, the doomsday clock? The scientists seem to think so.

The President. Well——

Q. And they think it's a more dangerous world now.

The President. Well, maybe the scientists know more about science. And from the standpoint of the power of the weapons, yes, they are more powerful; they are more destructive on both sides than they were before. And maybe looking at it from a scientist's viewpoint, that moves up their doomsday clock. But they're not involved in the diplomatic and political end of this as we are.

Q. But, sir, you only have 3—really, 3 minutes now to make a decision on war and peace according to the nuclear scientists. There would be 3 minutes on each side.

The President. Well, now, Helen, in the Bible weren't we told that a long period of time was only a moment or even a second to God? I don't know what their 3 minutes refers to. I know it doesn't refer to 3 minutes——

Q. You think it would be a lot longer for you to decide?

The President. Well, I'm wondering. On their doomsday clock, each minute on that clock—is that weeks? Is that months? Is that years? They've never said what it is. But, no, I believe that actually—and I can understand their feeling—all that they hear and, forgive me, but a lot of the editorial content is that, "Oh, there are great tensions." There has been, let's say, more heat in rhetoric. There has not been more heat in the actual relationship. At the time that the rhetoric was being used from both sides, our negotiators were sitting there at the table negotiating.

Q. Mr. President, can I come back on the prospects of these talks, these arms talks? There's a lot of concern, especially in Europe, that with the lack of dialog between West and the East, especially as the U.S. is entering an election year—if you run for reelection—that the Soviets are not likely to help you. How do you see the prospects for some kind of an agreement before the elections?

The President. Well, I would hope that the Soviet Union would remember their failure in trying to influence the German election and decide not to go down that road again. But as far as I am concerned, whoever our candidate may be, I don't think any decisions on a subject of this kind should be made on our part, on our side, on the basis of—as I said the other night—political considerations.

We are going to continue to do everything we can to resume and achieve arms reductions, as sizable as we can make them, and ultimately I would hope total elimination of nuclear weapons. They have no real place in a civilized world. The goal is peace. And I've been a little disturbed by the tendency of so many in this country who seem to feel that somehow we're at fault, when they are the ones who left the table without setting a date for return.

Q. So, you're not going to make any proposal before——

The President. Oh, we're in communication. We haven't broken off communications. We're not, as we've been portrayed, that the two superpowers are here separated with no contact at all. No, we're in communication with them. And we want to continue these policies that would lead toward reduction of arms and that would lead toward peace.

I am prepared to say if the Soviet Government wants peace, there will be no war, because I know for a fact that no other country wants war with the Soviet Union. The ball is really in their court. If they want peace, they can have it.

Q. And isn't that, though, what's kept the peace, this mutual terror?

The President. I think the deterrent capability, yes. See, we have a weapon here in the world today, the nuclear weapon, that for the first time in the history of all man's weapons has never resulted in a defensive weapon being created against it. The only thing we have is deterrence. The only thing we have is the knowledge that on both sides the punishment would be more than any nation could afford. If they started it, they would have to be prepared to accept virtually as much punishment as they were administering. And this has kept the peace.

I've had some meetings with young people who brought this very subject up, and they're greatly concerned. And I've asked them a question, and I must say they come up with a pretty sound answer. I've said, "We're the only ones that have ever used a nuclear weapon—in Japan in World War II. Would we have used that weapon if we knew they also had that weapon and could use it back against us?" And without fail, every group I've ever said this to has decided that, no, we would never have used the weapon.

Q. So, that's the real deterrent to war.

The President. Yes, yes.

Central America

Q. Mr. President, in Central America recently there have been some apparently conciliatory gestures from Nicaragua. Do you think these are sincere moves, or are they propaganda ploys, and do you intend any response to them?

The President. I think that there is more they can do than they've done. I think the situation with them right now is covered by the words of Demosthenes in the Athenian marketplace 2,000 years ago when he said, "What man would let another man's words, rather then his deeds, tell him who is at peace and who is at war with him?"

Q. So, you don't think too much of these gestures then?

The President. No, we've made it plain. There, again, there's been contact. And Ambassador Stone has made it plain to them that all they have to do is reinstitute the principles of their own revolution—the things that they promised the people they were going to bring about if their revolution succeeded. And they have not done that. They betrayed their own revolution and created a totalitarian state.

Q. Well, if you turn Demosthenes around, might the people in Managua not say, "We want to see some deeds from the United States."

The President. Well, what hostile deeds have they seen?

Q. Well, they think of Grenada, for one. Maybe we think—maybe you think it was a very benign——

The President. Well, I think——

Q. Rebel forces preparing to invade——

The President. But those rebel forces are part of their own original revolution—the people that, once they succeeded, were ousted because they wanted to institute the democratic policies.

Q. But they're being armed by us.

The President. Well, we set out after the revolution succeeded—and prior to my administration, the previous administration immediately started to come to the financial aid, economic aid, to the Sandinista government until it found out that the Sandinista government was not keeping the promise of its revolution. And the aid was withdrawn.

Now, to invoke Grenada, here again I think the words of the Grenadian people themselves, the Governor General, the people of Grenada, our own people who were there and were rescued have revealed this was not an invasion. This was something in the nature of a commando operation, and it was a rescue mission. And the people of Grenada have made it very plain that they feel they, too, were rescued. And the fact that we have withdrawn our combat troops so precipitously, that some of the Grenadians are a little alarmed—that they don't think we should have left yet.

Pentagon Report on U.S. Marines' Security in Lebanon

Q. Mr. President, have you seen the Pentagon report yet, or do you know anything about it? It's so critical of——

The President. It has finally been delivered over here. It hasn't reached me as yet.

Q. Right. You have not been briefed——

The President. No.

Q. ——at all on it?

The President. No.

Q. It sounds devastating.

The President. Well, I'm not going to comment until I see it.

Q. Do you have any—you don't really have any idea what's in it?

The President. No more than I read in the papers.

Q. Do you think that a lot of people are going to suffer from it?

The President. I just—Helen, I just can't

comment until I see it.

Q. We've all heard that it in some way criticizes everyone in the chain of command. Do you philosophically, or in any way, feel that that chain of command is—you're at the top of it in this case—and you bear some of that responsibility?

The President. Well, there's no way to discount responsibility. As Commander in Chief, the operation could not have gone forward without my approval. And so, in that sense, I think the investigation was being very thorough. Yes, there would have been no mission without my decision to go forward with it.

The Middle East

Q. Mr. President, in Lebanon, President Pertini of Italy today called for a withdrawal of the Italian contingent of the multinational force. Apparently there have been 15 countries who were asked to join that force and who have refused. Are you not concerned that the United States, by siding with Israel, is going to end up alone in Lebanon?

The President. No. I think that there was a not completely thorough statement of our meeting with Prime Minister Shamir. It was portrayed, and many people saw it, as somehow arriving at some new coalition with them, and even the word "conspiracy" was used by some in there. But, no, there was a reaffirmation by us of what our relationship with Israel has been since 1948. And we discussed this not from any standpoint of Israel and its relationship with Arab countries, in the sense of taking their part in anything of that kind. We're dedicated to the idea of trying, if we can, to act as a friend to both the Arab States and Israel in settling those longtime disputes and bringing about the kind of peace that we find between Egypt and Israel now.

Q. Do you think a U.N. force would be better in there?

The President. I would have wished from the very first for a U.N. force. But what has prevented it? The Soviet Union veto. If you look at the UNIFIL [United Nations Interim Force in Lebanon] force that is presently in the south of Lebanon, it is so bound by restrictions that were imposed in order to get the Soviet Union vote that it literally is

helpless to do anything. It isn't that these people are ineffective or that they aren't capable, they are restricted.

Q. So then they couldn't possibly be replaced?

The President. Well, I could still hope that the Soviet Union now would recognize the value of having a U.N. force in there. And as I say, we would have preferred this from the very first, but it was something that couldn't be obtained.

Where was I on——

Q. I was asking, aren't you concerned of the growing reluctance of your allies to assume part of the burden in Lebanon?

The President. Well, we have been in communication. And I think that they understand better now, because we were just as forthright in talking to Prime Minister Shamir about our intentions in our dealings with the Arab States and the things that we were going to do in linkage with them. All of this aimed at being able—if a mediator can be of use in that peace process that we proposed—to ensure a fair solution to the problems. We have no plan that we're going to impose. That would be wrong of us to go in and say, "Here is the peace plan." It must be negotiated out. On one side there is territory, on the other side there could be assurances of security. And someplace there has to be a balance in there in which one is traded for the other.

But that is up to them to negotiate. And I think our meeting with the Foreign Minister of Egypt, my own personal communication with President Mubarak, other communications that we have made straightening out what the situation was and what our relationship with Israel is and what we want in a relationship with them. And I don't think—I think there was some discomfort at first; I don't think so any more.

Mr. Gergen.[1] Excuse me. You have a 3 o'clock meeting. Make this the last question.

Q. But is there any concern that 15 other allied nations are asked to join this force and have backed out, or——

The President. Ah, but you're going back. Remember when—I think this was back

---

[1] *David R. Gergen, Assistant to the President for Communications.*

when we were putting it together, we were trying to get forces that would join in it. Well, now, there could be a number of reasons why a nation wouldn't. There could be the very fact of cost to some nations. And remember, this recession has been worldwide.

So, whatever their reasons were—but this was back when we were trying to put the multinational force together. And I think the very fact that the United Kingdom, that Italy, France, and the United States were able to provide what we thought was an adequate force for the purpose we had in mind——

Ambassador Jeane J. Kirkpatrick

Q. We've got four true-and-false questions. Is Jeane Kirkpatrick leaving? [*Laughter*] Yes or no?

The President. No. Jeane came in as she has every year.

Possibility of U.S.-Soviet Summit

Q. Will you go for a summit?

The President. What?

Q. Will you go for a summit if the Soviets propose it?

The President. Well, I've always been willing to go if there is a possibility of accomplishing something.

Goals for 1984

Q. And what do you want to happen next year?

The President. I want the recovery to continue. I want us to achieve more control over spending. And therefore, I would hope that the press would reveal to the people of this country how valuable line-item——

Q. Veto. [*Laughter*]

The President. ——line-item veto could be in the helping to get control over extravagance.

Q. We'll tell them.

The President. And——

Q. It will be in your budget proposal then?

The President. And I would hope that we would be far more advanced toward peace and toward a reduction of nuclear weapons.

Q. And a new tax?

The President. What?

Q. A new tax?

The President. I would hope that that wouldn't be necessary.

Q. Thank you.

Note: The interview began at 2:37 p.m. in the Oval Office at the White House. It was conducted by Helen Thomas, United Press International; James R. Gerstenzang, Associated Press; Michael Gelb, Reuters; and Pierre Rousselin, Agence France-Presse.

The transcript of the interview was released by the Office of the Press Secretary on December 24.

Radio Address to the Nation on Christmas
December 24, 1983

My fellow Americans:

Like so many of your homes, the White House is brimming with greens, colorful decorations, and a tree trimmed and ready for Christmas day. And when Nancy and I look out from our upstairs windows, we can see the National Christmas Tree standing in majestic beauty. Its lights fill the air with a spirit of love, hope, and joy from the heart of America.

I shared that spirit recently when a young girl named Amy Benham helped me light our national tree. Amy had said that the tree that lights up our country must be seen all the way to heaven. And she said that her wish was to help me turn on its lights. Well, Amy's wish came true. But the greatest gift was mine, because I saw her eyes light up with hope and joy just as brightly as the lights on our national tree. And I'm sure they were both seen all the way to heaven, and they made the angels sing.

Christmas is a time for children, and rightly so. We celebrate the birthday of the Prince of Peace who came as a babe in a manger. Some celebrate Christmas as the birthday of a great teacher and philosopher. But to other millions of us, Jesus is much more. He is divine, living assurance that God so loved the world He gave us His only begotten Son so that by believing in Him and learning to love each other we could one day be together in paradise.

It's been said that all the kings who ever reigned, that all the parliaments that ever sat have not done as much to advance the cause of peace on Earth and good will to men as the man from Galilee, Jesus of Nazareth.

Christmas is also a time to remember the treasures of our own history. We remember one Christmas in particular, 1776, our first year as a nation. The Revolutionary War had been going badly. But George Washington's faith, courage, and leadership would turn the tide of history our way. On Christmas night he led a band of ragged soldiers across the Delaware River through driving snow to a victory that saved the cause of independence. It's said that their route of march was stained by bloody footprints, but their spirit never faltered and their will could not be crushed.

The image of George Washington kneeling in prayer in the snow is one of the most famous in American history. He personified a people who knew it was not enough to depend on their own courage and goodness; they must also seek help from God, their Father and Preserver.

In a few hours, families and friends across America will join together in caroling parties and Christmas Eve services. Together, we'll renew that spirit of faith, peace, and giving which has always marked the character of our people. In our moments of quiet reflection I know we will remember our fellow citizens who may be lonely and in need tonight.

"Is the Christmas spirit still alive?" some ask. Well, you bet it is. Being Americans, we open our hearts to neighbors less fortunate. We try to protect them from hunger and cold. And we reach out in so many ways—from toys-for-tots drives across the country, to good will by the Salvation Army, to American Red Cross efforts which provide food, shelter, and Christmas cheer from Atlanta to Seattle.

Churches are so generous it's impossible to keep track. One example: Reverend Bill Singles' Presbyterian Meeting House in nearby Alexandria, Virginia, is simultaneously sponsoring hot meals on wheels programs, making and delivering hundreds of sandwiches and box loads of clothes, while visiting local hospitals and sending postcards to shut-ins and religious dissidents abroad.

Let us remember the families who maintain a watch for their missing in action. And, yes, let us remember all those who are persecuted inside the Soviet bloc—not because they commit a crime, but because they love God in their hearts and want the freedom to celebrate Hanukkah or worship the Christ Child.

And because faith for us is not an empty word, we invoke the power of prayer to spread the spirit of peace. We ask protection for our soldiers who are guarding peace tonight—from frigid outposts in Alaska and the Korean demilitarized zone to the shores of Lebanon. One Lebanese mother told us that her little girl had only attended school 2 of the last 8 years. Now, she said, because of our presence there her daughter can live a normal life.

With patience and firmness we can help bring peace to that strife-torn region and make our own lives more secure. The Christmas spirit of peace, hope, and love is the spirit Americans carry with them all year round, everywhere we go. As long as we do, we need never be afraid, because trusting in God is the one sure answer to all the problems we face.

Till next week, thanks for listening, God bless you, and Merry Christmas.

Note: The President spoke at 12:06 p.m. from the Oval Office at the White House.

Remarks and a Question-and-Answer Session With Reporters on the Pentagon Report on the Security of United States Marines in Lebanon
December 27, 1983

The President. Good morning.

I received the report of the Long commission last Friday and have reviewed it thoroughly. The report draws a conclusion that the United States and its military institutions are by tradition and training inadequately equipped to deal with the fundamentally new phenomenon of state-supported terrorism. I wholeheartedly agree.

The thrust of the history of this country is that we've recognized a clear distinction between being at peace with other states and being at war. We have never before faced a situation in which others routinely sponsor and facilitate acts of violence against us while hiding behind proxies and surrogates which claim—they claim they do not fully control.

Now, this problem is not unique to Lebanon. We've seen the ugly manifestation in Kuwait, the terrorist bombing in Rangoon, the senseless murder of Turkish diplomats, the attack on the Pope, the bombing of our own Capitol, and on the streets of London.

In the days ahead we need to systematically redevelop our approach to this problem, recognizing that the worst outcome of all is one in which terrorists succeed in transforming an open democracy into a closed fortress. Now, one fact, though, is already obvious: The problem of terrorism will not disappear if we run from it. This is not to say that we're not working as urgently as possible to create political conditions in Lebanon that will make it possible for us to remove our forces. But we must not delude ourselves into believing that terrorism will vanish on the happy day that our forces come home.

For terrorists to be curbed, civilized countries must begin a new effort to work together, to share intelligence, to improve our training and security and our forces, to deny havens or legal protection for terrorist groups and, most important of all, to hold increasingly accountable those countries which sponsor terrorism and terrorist activity around the world.

The United States intends to be in the forefront of this effort. For the near term, corrective action is being urgently taken to ensure the maximum possible security of our forces. Nearly all the measures that were identified by the distinguished members of the Commission have already implemented—or have already been implemented, I should say—and those that have not will be very quickly.

The Commission report also notes that the mission of the marines is extremely difficult, and with this, too, there can be no dispute. We recognized the fact at the beginning, and we're painfully mindful of it today. But the point is that our forces have already contributed to achievements that lay the foundation for a future peace, the restoration of a central government, and the establishment of an effective national Lebanese Army. We do not expect utopia, but I believe that we're on the verge of new progress toward national reconciliation and the withdrawal of foreign forces.

And let me finally say that I have soberly considered the Commission's word about accountability and responsibility of authorities up and down the chain of command. And everywhere more should be done to anticipate and prepare for dramatic terrorist assaults. We have to come to grips with the fact that today's terrorists are better armed and financed, they are more sophisticated, they are possessed by a fanatical intensity that individuals of a democratic society can only barely comprehend.

I do not believe, therefore, that the local commanders on the ground, men who have already suffered quite enough, should be punished for not fully comprehending the nature of today's terrorist threat. If there is to be blame, it properly rests here in this Office and with this President. And I accept responsibility for the bad as well as the good.

In this holiday season, our minds are drawn more than ever to the Middle East. And while the violence of this region has been the cause of much of our anguish— certainly over the recent years—it is also worth recalling that the three great religions of the modern world have their roots in this ancient and austere soil.

From this paradox, we can take hope. And I intend to bend every effort to ensure that those who died in this tragedy can claim as their ultimate legacy the mantle of peacemaker over this troubled and vital land.

Q. Mr. President, there have been—it's understood that you've been very concerned that these two reports might indicate that these men did die in vain. Do you have that fear or concern?

The President. No. I've been concerned that sometimes, in some of the debate and some of the political discussion about this, that an effort will be made to create this. And I think it would be tragic for the families who have lost a loved one if this comes about, because it hasn't been in vain. The cause was worthwhile, or four major nations would not have engaged in trying to find a solution.

Q. And so you intend to stay in Lebanon to see this through?

The President. We are reviewing all the facets of this—the locale, everything else— and going to intensively look at all the alternatives there might be. But I do believe that, yes, that while there's hope for peace we have to remain.

Q. Mr. President, you suggest in your statement that some sort of international commission be established to combat terrorism on an international front. Is that what you're saying here?

The President. No. I was talking about nations, themselves, recognizing that this terrorism isn't just some fanatical individual who gets an idea and goes out on his own. There is evidence enough—even if you couldn't go into court with it—that it has at least a kind of tacit encouragement from various political groups, and even from some states.

We have to recognize that. And then I believe rather than an international commission, I think that a much better exchange of intelligence information, everything of that kind that we can get.

The terrorist activities have multiplied, as the report shows, to three or four times as many incidents around the world as there were in 1968. And, incidentally, 53 percent of those have been aimed at American—at United States' targets.

Q. Sir, if I may ask just one followup. You say in your statement we should expect more terrorism. And the impression that I get—and, perhaps, the American people may get—is that government knows a lot more than it's saying about what we could expect. I mean is there, again, any definite plan that you've discovered which may lead to, perhaps, more terrorism in this country?

The President. Well, we just know that these various groups have threatened. Well, and many times you, yourselves, in the press, have carried these threats where they've made them public, that they are going to continue these activities and step them up.

Q. Mr. President, if there's no change in the situation, is there a time when you would want to bring the troops home?

Deputy Press Secretary Speakes. Let's make this the last question, please.

The President. Well, he also had his hand up.

Mr. Speakes. Oh, all right——

Q. Right.

Mr. Speakes. ——and then the last one.

The President. I was caught there between two.

Let me just say that I got into trouble a little while ago from trying to answer a hypothetical question with a hypothetical answer. And various interpretations were placed on it.

We are making every effort, and stepping up our diplomatic efforts, to bring about what I think must be the answer—not a military, but a political solution there. And we're going to, as I say, step those up and continue doing everything we can to bring that about.

There is reason to believe that the presence of the multinational force has made some progress. We have, now, an agreement between Lebanon and Israel which has Israel's agreement to withdraw. I don't believe that it's impossible to have a similar kind of agreement with Syria, which would recognize some of Syria's interests. And we know that at Geneva there was a kind of tacit recognition that the present government of Lebanon was the government of Lebanon.

Q. Mr. President, do you welcome Jesse Jackson's trip to Syria to try and win the release of Lieutenant Goodman?

The President. Well, I would like to have some better understanding of what is contemplated there, because sometimes efforts of this kind can be counterproductive.

We are doing everything we can, and working as completely as we can, diplomatically, to bring about his release. And it's possible that, sometimes, someone with the best of intentions could change the balance unfavorably.

Q. He's going to call you. Are you going to take his call?

The President. Why, certainly. I wouldn't have any reason not to.

Mr. Speakes. Thank you, Mr. President.

Q. Thank you.

The President. All right.

Well, I hope you all had a merry Christmas. And Happy New Year.

Note: The President spoke at 9:16 a.m. in the Briefing Room at the White House. The report was prepared by a commission headed by retired Adm. Robert L. J. Long.

Statement on the Fourth Anniversary of the Soviet Invasion of Afghanistan
December 27, 1983

While Americans are thankful for the blessing of peace at home this holiday season, we do not forget that the tragic war in Afghanistan continues. For 4 long years the Soviet Union has occupied that unhappy land. But for 4 long years the brave Afghan people have held the might of a Soviet occupation force at bay. These Islamic fighters in a faraway land have given new meaning to the words "courage," "determination," and "strength." They have set the standard for those who value freedom and independence everywhere in the world.

Afghanistan's freedom fighters—the resistance or *mujahidin*—represent an indigenous movement that swept through their mountainous land to challenge a foreign military power threatening their religion and their very way of life. With little in the way of arms or organization, the vast majority of the Afghan people have demonstrated that they will not be dominated and that they are prepared to give their lives for independence and freedom. The price they have so willingly paid is incalculable.

While we will continue to do our part to maintain and improve the U.S.-Soviet dialog, we cannot remain silent on the tragedy of Afghanistan. There should be no misunderstanding that the Soviet occupation of Afghanistan has created serious international tensions. It is not only the Afghan themselves who oppose the Soviet occupation of their country but virtually the entire world community. This has been demonstrated time and again in five consecutive votes of the United Nations General Assembly, when resounding majorities of the world's nations called upon the Soviet Union to end its occupation and restore the independence and nonaligned status of Afghanistan. In fact the most recent U.N. resolution was adopted on November 23 by the largest vote yet: 116 to 20.

Early this year, I had the privilege of receiving in my office a group of six Afghan freedom fighters. I was moved by their simple dignity and pride and their determination to continue their struggle for independence. These brave individuals have returned to the fight.

The struggle for a free Afghanistan continues. This is not because of any outside manipulation, but because of the Afghan people's own desire to be free. And their struggle will continue until a negotiated political settlement can be found to allow the Afghan people to determine their own destiny.

Our goal is to do everything we can to help bring about a peaceful solution which removes the Soviet forces from Afghanistan, ends the agony and destruction of the Afghan nation, and restores that country's independence and nonalignment. Clearly, a neutral and nonaligned Afghanistan would not be a threat to its huge Soviet neighbor.

Thus, we mark the fourth anniversary of the Soviet invasion with sadness and continued indignation. But we are convinced that a settlement is possible, and we are glad that consultations in the U.N. process of indirect talks will go on. We call upon the Soviet Union to reach a settlement of the crisis which restores the freedom, independence, and nonalignment of Afghanistan.

Let all of us who live in lands of freedom, along with those who dream of doing so, take inspiration from the spirit and courage of the Afghan patriots. Let us resolve that their quest for freedom will prevail, and that Afghanistan will become, once again, an independent member of the family of nations.

Nomination of Reese H. Taylor, Jr., To Be a Member of the Interstate Commerce Commission, and Designation as Chairman
December 27, 1983

The President today announced his intention to nominate Reese H. Taylor, Jr., to be a member of the Interstate Commerce Commission for a term expiring December 31, 1985. This is a reappointment. The President also intends to redesignate him Chairman upon appointment.

Mr. Taylor has been a member and Chairman of the Interstate Commerce Commission since 1981. In 1971 Mr. Taylor became a partner in the law firm of Laxalt, Berry & Allison of Carson City, Nev. In 1978 the firm was reorganized and incorporated as Allison, Brunetti, MacKenzie & Taylor, Ltd. His work with the firm consisted primarily of an administrative law practice, with particular emphasis on regulatory matters pertaining to public utilities and transportation companies.

In 1967–1971 he was chairman of the Public Service Commission of Nevada and in 1967–1969 was also vice chairman of the Nevada Tax Commission. In 1967–1971 he was also a member of the Governor's cabinet and his Civil Defense Advisory Council. Previously he was associated with law firms in Las Vegas, Nev., and Los Angeles, Calif.

Mr. Taylor graduated from Stanford University (1949) and Cornell Law School (1952). He is married and has three children. He was born in Los Angeles, Calif., on May 6, 1928.

Memorandum on Drunk and Drugged Driving
December 28, 1983

Memorandum for All Federal Employees

Subject: Drunk and Drugged Driving

As we bring this year to a close in holiday celebration, I want to call to your attention the serious problem of drunk and drugged driving. It is one of the leading causes of violent death in our Nation.

Each year we lose over 25,000 lives, injure over 700,000 Americans and suffer billions of dollars in economic costs due to this problem. Five hundred Americans die each week—71 each day—that's one American death every 20 minutes. Every one of these casualties is someone's son or daughter, husband or wife, mother, father, or friend.

Communities nationwide have responded to this menace by organizing such groups as Mothers Against Drunk Driving (MADD) and Remove Intoxicated Drivers (RID). Task forces in many cities and States are working to solve this problem. Private sector programs alerting employees to the drunk and drugged driving problem are multiplying. Legislators, spurred by concerned citizens, are making changes in laws to reduce the loss of life and injury caused by drunk and drugged driving.

We as Federal employees have an impor-

tant role to play in removing the drunk and drugged drivers from our roads. Your heightened awareness, coupled with your continued commitment to halt this needless death and destruction, can make a difference, particularly during the holiday season.

I hope your resolutions for the New Year will include not mixing alcohol or drugs with driving, driving defensively at all times, and wearing your safety belts regularly—your best defense against the drunk and drugged driver.

Together we can make this holiday season a truly joyous one and the coming year the safest one yet on our roadways.

RONALD REAGAN

Letter to the Speaker of the House and the President of the Senate on the Designation of Certain Countries as Caribbean Basin Economic Recovery Act Beneficiaries
December 29, 1983

Dear Mr. Speaker: (Dear Mr. President:)

Pursuant to Section 212 of the Caribbean Basin Economic Recovery Act (CBERA), I wish to inform you of my intent to designate the following nine Caribbean Basin countries and entities as beneficiaries of the trade-liberalizing measures provided for in this Act: Antigua and Barbuda, Belize, the British Virgin Islands, El Salvador, Grenada, Guatemala, Haiti, Honduras, and Montserrat. Designation will entitle the products of said countries, except for products excluded statutorily, to duty-free treatment for a period beginning on January 1, 1984 and ending on September 30, 1995. As beneficiaries, these nine also have the opportunity to become eligible for the convention expense tax deduction under Section 274(h) of the Internal Revenue Code of 1954, by entering into an exchange of information agreement with the United States on tax matters.

Designation is an important step for these countries in their battle to revitalize and rebuild their weakened economies. Designation is also significant because it is further tangible evidence of the constructive coop-

eration between the United States and the peoples and governments of the Caribbean Basin.

My decision to designate the group of nine flows out of discussions held between this Administration and potential beneficiary countries and entities regarding the designation criteria set forth in Section 212 of the CBERA. Our discussions with the nine were concluded this month subsequent to the designation of eleven countries and entities on November 30. Discussions are still underway with other potential beneficiaries, and I will designate additional countries as this becomes appropriate.

The nine countries have demonstrated to my satisfaction that their laws, practices and policies are in conformity with the designation criteria of the CBERA. The governments of these countries and entities have communicated on these matters by letter with Secretary of State Shultz and Ambassador Brock and in so doing have indicated their desire to be designated as beneficiaries (copies of the letters are attached). On the basis of the statements and assurances in these letters, and taking into account information developed by United States Embassies and through other sources, I have concluded that the objectives of the Administration and the Congress with respect to the statutory designation criteria of the CBERA have been met.

I am mindful that under Section 213(B)(2) of the CBERA, I retain the authority to suspend or withdraw CBERA benefits from any designated beneficiary country if a beneficiary's laws, policies or practices are no longer in conformity with the designation criteria. The United States will keep abreast of developments in the beneficiary countries and entities which are pertinent to the designation criteria.

This Administration looks forward to working closely with its fellow governments in the Caribbean Basin and with the private sectors of the United States and the Basin countries to ensure that the wide-ranging opportunities opened by the CBERA are fully utilized.

Sincerely,

RONALD REAGAN

Note: This is the text of identical letters addressed to Thomas P. O'Neill, Jr., Speaker of the House of Representatives, and George Bush, President of the Senate.

The text of the letters was released by the Office of the Press Secretary on December 30.

Proclamation 5142—To Amend Proclamation 5133 Implementing the Caribbean Basin Economic Recovery Act
December 29, 1983

By the President of the United States of America

A Proclamation

1. Section 212 of the Caribbean Basin Economic Recovery Act (the Act) (19 U.S.C. 2702) authorizes the President to designate certain countries and territories or successor political entities as "beneficiary countries" under the Act. In Proclamation 5133 of November 30, 1983, I designated several countries and territories as "beneficiary countries". I am now adding Antigua and Barbuda, Belize, El Salvador, Grenada, Guatemala, Haiti, Honduras, Montserrat, and the British Virgin Islands to the list of "beneficiary countries". I have notified the House of Representatives and the Senate of my intentions to designate these countries and given the considerations entering into my decision.

2. In order to add these countries to the list of beneficiary countries, I am amending the Annex to Proclamation 5133. I am also making certain technical corrections to the Annex to that proclamation.

Now, Therefore, I, Ronald Reagan, President of the United States of America, acting under the authority vested in me by the Constitution and the statutes of the United States, including but not limited to Section 212 of the Act, do proclaim that:

(1) The list of countries in the Annex to Proclamation 5133 of November 30, 1983, is hereby amended by adding, in alphabetical order, "Antigua and Barbuda", "Belize", "El Salvador", "Grenada", "Guatemala", "Haiti", "Honduras", "Montserrat", and "Virgin Islands, British".

(2) The references to "the United States Committee for the Implementation of Textile Agreements" in the Annex to Proclamation 5133 of November 30, 1983, are corrected to read "the United States".

(3) The reference to TSUS items "748.45–478.50" in the Annex to Proclamation 5133 of November 30, 1983, is corrected to read "748.45–748.50".

In Witness Whereof, I have hereunto set my hand this twenty-ninth day of December, in the year of our Lord nineteen hundred and eighty-three, and of the Independence of the United States of America the two hundred and eighth.

RONALD REAGAN

[*Filed with the Office of the Federal Register, 11:23 a.m., January 3, 1984*]

Note: The text of the proclamation was released by the Office of the Press Secretary on December 30.

Executive Order 12454—President's National Security Telecommunications Advisory Committee
December 29, 1983

By the authority vested in me as President by the Constitution and statutes of the United States of America, and in accordance with the provisions of the Federal Advisory Committee Act, as amended (5 U.S.C. App. I), it is hereby ordered that the President's National Security Telecommunications Advisory Committee, established by Executive Order No. 12382, is continued until September 30, 1985.

RONALD REAGAN

The White House,
December 29, 1983.

[*Filed with the Office of the Federal Register, 11:24 a.m., January 3, 1984*]

Note: The text of the Executive order was released by the Office of the Press Secretary on December 30.

Executive Order 12455—President's Private Sector Survey on Cost Control in the Federal Government
December 29, 1983

By the authority vested in me as President by the Constitution and laws of the United States of America, including the Federal Advisory Committee Act, as amended (5 U.S.C. App. I), and in order to extend the life of the President's Private Sector Survey on Cost Control in the Federal Government, it is hereby ordered that Section 4(b) of Executive Order No. 12369 of June 30, 1982, as amended, is further amended to read: "The Committee shall terminate on January 31, 1984, unless sooner extended.".

RONALD REAGAN

The White House,
December 29, 1983.

[*Filed with the Office of the Federal Register, 11:25 a.m., January 3, 1984*]

Note: The text of the Executive order was released by the Office of the Press Secretary on December 30.

Executive Order 12456—Adjustments of Certain Rates of Pay and Allowances
December 30, 1983

By the authority vested in me as President by the Constitution and laws of the United States of America, it is hereby ordered as follows:

Section 1. Statutory Pay Systems. Pursuant to the provisions of subchapter I of chapter 53 of title 5 of the United States Code, the rates of basic pay and salaries are adjusted, as set forth at the schedules attached hereto and made a part hereof, for the following statutory pay systems:

(a) The General Schedule (5 U.S.C. 5332(a) at Schedule 1;

(b) The Foreign Service Schedule (22 U.S.C. 3963) at Schedule 2; and

(c) The schedules for the Department of Medicine and Surgery, Veterans Administration (38 U.S.C. 4107) at Schedule 3.

Sec. 2. Senior Executive Service. Pursuant to the provisions of section 5382 of title 5 of the United States Code, the rates of basic pay are adjusted, as set forth at Schedule 4 attached hereto and made a part hereof, for members of the Senior Executive Service.

Sec. 3. Pay and Allowances for Members of the Uniformed Services. Pursuant to the provisions of Section 901 of Public Law 98–94 (97 Stat. 634), the rates of monthly basic pay (37 U.S.C. 203(a)), the rates of basic allowances for subsistence (37 U.S.C. 402), and the rates of basic allowances for quarters (37 U.S.C. 403(a)) are adjusted, as set forth at Schedule 5 attached hereto and made a part hereof, for members of the uniformed services.

Sec. 4. Executive Salaries. The Executive Salary Cost-of-Living Adjustment Act (Public Law 94–82, 89 Stat. 419) provides for adjustments in rates of pay and salaries as set forth at the schedules attached hereto and made a part hereof, for the following:

(a) The Vice President (3 U.S.C. 104) and the Executive Schedule (5 U.S.C. 5312–5316) at Schedule 6;

(b) Congressional Salaries (2 U.S.C. 31) at Schedule 7; and

(c) Judicial Salaries (28 U.S.C. 5, 44(d), 135, 172(b), 252, and 11 U.S.C. 68(a), and Sections 401(a), 404(a), 404(b), and 404(d) of Public Law 95–598) at Schedule 8.

Sec. 5. Effective Date. The adjustments in rates of monthly basic pay and allowances for subsistence and quarters for members of the uniformed services, and all other adjustments of salary or pay, shall be effective on the first day of the first applicable pay period beginning on or after January 1, 1984.

Sec. 6. Executive Order No. 12387 of October 8, 1982, is superseded.

RONALD REAGAN

The White House,
December 30, 1983.

[*Filed with the Office of the Federal Register, 11:26 a.m., January 3, 1984*]

Note: The schedules are printed in the Federal Register *of January 4, 1984.*

Radio Address to the Nation on New Year's Eve
December 31, 1983

My fellow Americans:

New Year's Eve is a time for looking back on the year past, and in a moment, I want to talk about all that 1983 meant to America. But first I want to mention the topic of my radio talk 2 weeks ago—drunk driving.

A drunk or drugged person at the wheel of a car isn't a driver, that person is a machine of destruction. So, let's enjoy all the wonderful celebrations that go with New Year's Eve, but, please, when we drive, let's drive sober.

Nineteen eighty-three was the 207th year for our Grand Old Republic. Though the year had its measure of hardship and even tragedy, it was a time when we Americans acted with courage, self-confidence, and vigor.

We had reason to feel glad. America was on the mend. And as our economy regained strength, we watched the progress of a sparkling recovery—one of the strongest recoveries in 20 years. I said from the beginning it would take time for our economic program to work. You can't cure 25 years of failed economic policies overnight. And, yes, we had some hard months at first. But 1983 saw our patience pay off as our program took hold.

On this New Year's Eve, the prime interest rate is 11 percent, about half of what it was when we took office. Inflation for 1983 is running at only 3.2 percent, about a quarter of what it was just 3 years ago. Housing starts are running 60 percent higher than on this day last year.

Nineteen eighty-three saw the stock market reach new highs as it pumped vast new funds into the economy and raised the value of pension funds where millions of working Americans have their savings. During 1982, American manufacturers sold 5.8 million new cars. This year, they've sold 6.7 million.

As our basic industries and agriculture gain new strength, American ingenuity and enterprise are creating whole new industries—industries like robotics and bioengineering. Just a few years ago, home computers were unheard of. By the end of 1982, American companies had sold some 2½ million home computers. This year, the figure is expected to climb to 7½ million.

This is one of the seasons when we Americans fly the most, to visit family and friends, because there's nothing like being home for the holidays. Well, the deregulation of the airline industry has increased competition and helped push fares down. And deregulation of banking is helping millions.

In 1983, for the first time, everyday savers and small businesses received marked interest rates, earning 3½ billion dollars in additional income. The best news of all: On New Year's Eve 1982, 100.8 million Americans had jobs. But today, the figure has climbed by 3.6 million, an all-time high for our nation.

All this means that in 1983 it was easier to pay bills, put children through college, buy homes, or borrow the money to start a new business than it had been in many years. Once again, the American economy has begun to reward fresh ideas and good, hard work.

Just as 1983 saw our economy recovering, it saw a new sense of purpose in our Armed Forces and foreign policy. In the military, morale has soared. Some pundits used to claim we could only attract recruits when our economy was weak. But now, even with a strong economy and growing opportunities in civilian life, our Armed Forces are attracting more and better qualified recruits than ever. There's one statistic that shows just how dramatic the turnaround has been. If 1979 Air Force retention rates had continued, three out of four pilots would have left the service after their first tours. In 1983, better than three out of four stayed in.

Morale has improved partly because we've given our men and women in uniform better pay and better equipment. But I just have to believe the courage of our soldiers and marines in Lebanon and Grenada has a lot to do with it. And, as we celebrate the New Year, I wonder whether you would all join Nancy and me in setting aside a moment to remember those who, in 1983, gave their lives in the cause of freedom and to pray for those brave young men spending this day so far from home.

In foreign policy, this year we've given firm support to democratic leadership in Central America. In Grenada we set a nation free. In Asia, our trip to Japan and Korea further strengthened our partnership with those nations. In Europe, 1983 saw the NATO alliance pass through harsh trials, but the alliance has emerged more firmly united than ever—more ardent in the cause of freedom and peace, more dedicated to the paths of deterrence and dialog.

In Lebanon, the road to peace has proven long and hard, but there has been progress that would have been impossible without our marines and the other troops in the multinational peacekeeping force. Representatives of all Lebanese factions agreed in Geneva to recognize the government of President Amin Gemayel. And talks have begun that will broaden the government's base. It isn't easy. Progress is painfully slow, but progress is being made.

Nineteen eighty-three was a good year for America. If all of us keep pulling together, we can make 1984 even better. Happy New Year and, until next week, thanks for listening, and God bless you all.

Note: The President's remarks were recorded on December 28 at the Century Plaza Hotel in Los Angeles, Calif., for broadcast on December 31.

Appendix A—Digest of Other White House Announcements

The following list includes the President's public schedule and other items of general interest announced by the Office of the Press Secretary and not included elsewhere in this book.

July 2

The White House announced that Secretary of State George P. Shultz called the President in the morning to report on and discuss his current talks in South Asia, as well as the status of matters in the Middle East. Based upon these talks, the President directed Secretary Shultz to make an effort to stop in the Middle East before returning to the United States.

July 6

The President met at the White House with members of the White House staff.

July 7

The President met at the White House with:
—members of the White House staff;
—Ambassador Richard B. Stone, Special Representative of the President to Central America, prior to departure for a visit to that region;
—a group of former special agents in charge of the White House Secret Service detail;
—the Cabinet Council on Human Resources, to discuss a report on urban conditions;
—Lewis Glaser, who prepares quill pens for the U.S. Supreme Court;
—Mrs. Delores Ballachino, a pen pal of the President's since 1941, and her family.

The President presented the Paul Boucher Award to Lawrence Cresce, Assistant Inspector General of Investigations, Department of Transportation. The award was created by the President's Council on Integrity and Efficiency in memory of the Inspector General of the Small Business Administration. The ceremony took place in the Roosevelt Room at the White House.

The President transmitted to the Congress the 18th annual report on the status of the National Wilderness Preservation System.

The White House announced that the President telephoned the Vice President upon his return from his trip to Europe. The Vice President was at his residence in Kennebunkport, Maine, at the time of the conversation. The President expressed "the deep appreciation of the Nation for a job well done" and told the Vice President he looked forward to meeting with him

to be briefed on the results of his trip early next week. "You carried our banner well and made us all proud," the President said.

July 8

The President met at the White House with:
—members of the White House staff;
—the National Security Council;
—the President's Commission on Strategic Forces, to discuss progress made in implementing recommendations in the Commission's report;
—Secretary of State George P. Shultz and members of the White House staff, to discuss the Secretary's recent trip to South Asia and the Middle East.

The President spoke by telephone with Annette Baily Gossett, whose 10-month-old daughter, Ashley, was awaiting a liver transplant in Minneapolis, Minn.

The President spoke by telephone from Camp David, Md., to a fundraising dinner for Senator Bob Kasten in Milwaukee, Wis., and a job-a-thon held by KGAN–TV in Cedar Rapids, Iowa.

July 10

The President returned to the White House from Camp David.

July 11

The President met at the White House with:
—members of the White House staff;
—A. W. Clausen, Chairman of the International Bank for Reconstruction and Development (World Bank), to discuss financial matters, including the International Development Association and the International Monetary Fund;
—Foreign Minister Hans-Dietrich Genscher of the Federal Republic of Germany, who reported on German Chancellor Helmut Kohl's meeting in the Soviet Union with President Yuriy V. Andropov.

The President met in the afternoon with Richard G. Darman, Assistant to the President and Deputy to the Chief of Staff, and Fred F. Fielding, Counsel to the President. The President reviewed a letter from Mr. Fielding to Donald J. Albosta, chairman of the congressional subcommittee that is investigating the possible unauthorized acquisition of Carter White House or campaign materials by the Reagan campaign. Mr. Fielding prepared the letter at the President's request, in response to Chairman Albosta's letter to the President dated June 29. In the meeting, the President instructed that procedures be worked out between the Department of Justice and the subcommittee to provide the subcommittee with access to materials to assist in its investigation, while ensuring the integrity of the Justice Department's investigation.

In the evening, the President went to the John F. Kennedy Center for the Performing Arts for a concert in observance of the 180th anniversary of the Marine Band.

July 12

The President met at the White House with:
—members of the White House staff;
—the Republican congressional leadership, to discuss the Middle East, Central America, and arms control;
—the National Security Council;
—Alejandro Orfila, Secretary General of the Organization of American States;
—the Cabinet Council on Commerce and Trade, to discuss an independent study of the 700 Government-owned laboratories and how the Federal Government can more efficiently utilize research from these laboratories;
—a group of religious leaders who support a constitutional amendment for school prayer;
—Representative Guy V. Molinari of New York, to discuss the National Children's Liver Disease Awareness Week proclamation;
—Representative Carroll A. Campbell, Jr., of South Carolina, and the poster child for the Allergy and Asthma Foundation of America;
—Senator Richard G. Lugar of Indiana and John T. Roberts, the new president of Kiwanis International;
—Senator Jeremiah Denton of Alabama and America's Junior Miss for 1983.

In an Oval Office ceremony, the President received diplomatic credentials from Ambassadors Gerhard Herder of the German Democratic Republic, Meir Rosenne of Israel, Celso Pastor de la Torre of Peru, Giovinella Gonthier of the Seychelles, and Paul Peters of Luxembourg.

The White House announced that the President will include visits to the Philippines and Thailand in his November trip to East Asia, at the invitation of those Governments. In Manila, the President will meet with President Ferdinand E. Marcos. In Bangkok, he will be the guest of the King and Queen and will meet with Prime Minister Prem Tinsulanonda. As announced on June 27, the President also will visit Indonesia, Japan, and the Republic of Korea. Mrs. Reagan will accompany the President on the trip.

July 13

The President met at the White House with:
—members of the White House staff;
—Lee Iacocca, chairman of the Chrysler Corp.;
—Representatives Robert H. Michel of Illinois, Trent Lott of Mississippi, and Phil Gramm of Texas, who presented the President with a letter, signed by 146 Members of Congress, stating their support of Presidential vetoes of certain appropriations and authorization bills that materially exceed the administration's 1984 budget;
—Secretary of State George P. Shultz and Ambassador Max Kampelman, to discuss the Conference on Security and Cooperation in Europe, prior to Ambassador Kampelman's return to Madrid for the continuation of the talks.

The President requested the Congress to provide an additional appropriation of $118 million in fiscal year 1983 for the Department of Agriculture for child nutrition programs. This increase reflects a higher level of participation in the program. The President also requested 1983 appropriation language for the Veterans Administration to increase the limitation of travel expenses in the medical care program and appropriations in 1984 to repay debts to the Treasury for the Federal Railroad Administration. Included in the transmittal is a request for $1.2 million for the office of the Architect of the Capitol in the legislative branch.

July 14

The President met at the White House with:
—members of the White House staff;
—a group of Republican Members of the House of Representatives, to discuss the International Monetary Fund;
—the Vice President;
—the Cabinet;
—a group of Republican Members of the House of Representatives, to discuss the International Monetary Fund;
—Sir Geoffrey Howe, Foreign Secretary of the United Kingdom;
—representatives of the National Radio Broadcasters Association, who presented the President with an award;

In the evening, the President hosted a dinner in the Residence for members of the President's Commission on Strategic Forces and their spouses.

July 15

The President met at the White House with:
—members of the White House staff;
—a group of his foreign policy advisers;
—members of the Business Roundtable.

In the afternoon, the President left the White House for a weekend stay at Camp David, Md.

The White House announced that the President accepted the resignation of Lilla Tower as Director of the Institute of Museum Services, National Foundation on the Arts and the Humanities, effective July 19.

July 17

The President returned to the White House from Camp David, Md.

The President spoke by telephone with former Secretary of State Henry A. Kissinger to discuss the Chairmanship of the National Bipartisan Commission on Central America.

July 18

The President met at the White House with:
—members of the White House staff;
—former Deputy Secretary of State Walter J. Stoessel, Jr., to discuss human rights.

July 19

The President met at the White House with:
—members of the White House staff;
—representatives of education organizations.

The President spoke by telephone to the National Association of Counties meeting in Milwaukee, Wis.

The White House announced that the President has invited President Abdou Diouf of Senegal to make an official working visit to the White House. President Diouf has accepted the invitation and will meet with President Reagan at the White House on August 10.

The President requested the Congress to provide an additional appropriation of $484,000 in fiscal year 1983 and $2.2 million in fiscal year 1984 for the Department of the Interior to pursue the collection of assessed penalties and alternative enforcement actions against violators of the Surface Mining Control and Reclamation Act. The President also requested $57.4 million in fiscal year 1984 for the Veterans Administration to provide funds to conduct the Agent Orange epidemiological study.

July 20

The President met at the White House with:
—members of the White House staff;
—representatives of private sector and Jewish organizations, to discuss Central America;
—the President's Economic Policy Advisory Board.

The White House announced that the President has invited President António dos Santos Ramalho Eanes of Portugal to make a state visit to the United States. President Eanes has accepted the invitation and will meet with President Reagan at the White House on September 15.

July 21

The President met at the White House with:
—members of the White House staff;
—the Vice President, for lunch;
—Dr. DeWayne Piehl and Mrs. Jackie Middleton, Multiple Sclerosis Mother and Father of the Year;
—Ambassador Paul H. Nitze, U.S. Representative to the Intermediate-range Nuclear Force negotiations, and Assistant to the President for National Security Affairs William P. Clark;
—the Cabinet Council on Natural Resources and the Environment, to discuss timber defaults in the northeast United States;
—the Cabinet Council on Food and Agriculture, to discuss the agricultural payment-in-kind program.

July 22

The President met at the White House with members of the White House staff.

July 23

The President and Mrs. Reagan attended funeral services at St. Matthew's Cathedral and burial services at Arlington National Cemetery for Frank Reynolds, broadcast journalist, who died on July 20.

Following the services, the President and Mrs. Reagan went to Camp David, Md., for the remainder of the weekend.

July 24

The President returned to the White House from Camp David.

July 25

The President met at the White House with:
—members of the White House staff;
—Dr. Henry A. Kissinger, Chairman of the National Bipartisan Commission on Central America, Secretary of State George P. Shultz, Assistant to the President for National Security Affairs William P. Clark, and U.S. Representative to the United Nations Jeane J. Kirkpatrick;
—Representatives Thomas S. Foley of Washington and Richard Cheney of Wyoming, to discuss their recent trip to the Soviet Union;
—Senator Howard H. Baker, Jr., of Tennessee and Representative Robert H. Michel of Illinois, for an update on the current legislative agenda.

The President transmitted to Congress the 1982 annual report of the Saint Lawrence Seaway Development Corporation and the 14th annual report of the National Corporation for Housing Partnerships and the National Housing Partnership.

The White House announced that the President has invited President Mobutu Sese Seko of Zaire to make an official working visit to the White House. President Mobutu has accepted the invitation and will meet with President Reagan at the White House on August 4.

July 26
The President met at the White House with:
—members of the White House staff;
—Valéry Giscard d'Estaing, former President of France.
The President announced that Secretary of Defense Caspar W. Weinberger will visit China September 25–29. During the visit, Secretary Weinberger will meet with Zhang Aiping, Minister of National Defense of China, and other Chinese leaders on matters of mutual interest. Secretary Weinberger's trip is in response to an invitation by the Defense Minister.

July 27
The President met at the White House with:
—members of the White House staff;
—Harry N. Walters, Administrator of the Veterans Administration, and James Currieo, commander, and Cooper Holt, executive director, Veterans of Foreign Wars, to discuss Central America;
—Republican Members of the House of Representatives, to discuss the International Monetary Fund.

July 28
The President met at the White House with:
—members of the White House staff;
—the Vice President, for lunch;
—Minister of Foreign Affairs Yitzhak Shamir and Minister of Defense Moshe Arens of Israel, Secretary of State George P. Shultz, Secretary of Defense Caspar W. Weinberger, Assistant to the President for National Security Affairs William P. Clark, and Ambassador Robert C. McFarlane, the President's Personal Representative in the Middle East;
—the Cabinet Council on Commerce and Trade, to discuss the U.S. steel and textile industries;
—Nhanny Heil and her mother, Evelyn Warren Heil;
—Myles Robert René Frechette, U.S. Ambassador to Cameroon, Arthur Winston Lewis, U.S. Ambassador to Sierra Leone, and Peter Jon de Vos, U.S. Ambassador to Mozambique, prior to their departure for their overseas posts.
The President spoke by telephone with Mr. and Mrs. Stuart Thomas at Children's Hospital in Pittsburgh, Pa. He called to inquire about the condition of their daughter, Candice, who had

undergone liver transplant surgery earlier that day.
The White House announced that the President has invited President Mauno Koivisto of Finland to make an official working visit to Washington. President Koivisto has accepted the invitation and will meet with President Reagan at the White House on September 26.

July 29
The President met at the White House with:
—members of the White House staff;
—Secretary of State George P. Shultz, Ambassador Robert C. McFarlane, the President's Personal Representative in the Middle East, and Ambassador Richard Fairbanks, Special Adviser to the Secretary of State.
The President left the White House for a weekend stay at Camp David, Md.

July 31
The President returned to the White House from Camp David.

August 1
The President met at the White House with Secretary of Housing and Urban Development Samuel R. Pierce, Jr.
The President declared a major disaster for the State of Arkansas as a result of severe storms and flooding, beginning on July 2, which caused extensive damage.

August 2
The President met at the White House with:
—members of the White House staff;
—Republican congressional leaders and Secretary of State George P. Shultz, to discuss Central America;
—the Joint Chiefs of Staff;
—the Cabinet Council on Legal Policy, to discuss regulatory reform and crime issues;
—the Cabinet Council on Food and Agriculture, to discuss meat imports;
—Members of Congress, who introduced constituents or presented items from their home States;
—the Senate Steering Committee, to discuss the legislative agenda for the remainder of the congressional session.
The White House announced that the President sent a letter on August 1 through the U.S. Embassy in Tegucigalpa to President Roberto Suazo Córdova of Honduras, who had earlier been hospitalized. The letter expressed President Reagan's hopes for President Suazo's quick recovery.
The President transmitted to Congress the eighth annual report of the Nuclear Regulatory Commission.

August 3
The President met at the White House with:
—members of the White House staff;
—members of Citizens for America, a volunteer organization interested in conservative issues;
—representatives of the space industry, for a working luncheon to discuss commercial space enterprises;
—Ambassador Richard B. Stone, Special Representative of the President to Central America, to discuss the Ambassador's recent trip to that area.

August 4
The President met at the White House with:
—members of the White House staff;
—the Vice President, for lunch;
—executive committee members of the Senate and House of Representatives Steel Caucuses;
—John Young, Chairman of the President's Commission on Industrial Competitiveness;
—Jason Hardman, 13, who founded a library in Elsinore, Utah, members of his family, Eleanor Hashim, Chairman of the National Commission on Libraries and Information Science, and members of the Utah congressional delegation;
—Robert S. Bowen, recipient of the 7 millionth President's Council on Physical Fitness Award;
—18 recipients of scholarships from the Ronald W. Reagan Scholarship program at Eureka College, Eureka, Ill.

August 5
The President met at the White House with:
—members of the White House staff;
—Ambassador Edward L. Rowny, Special Representative for Negotiations, U.S. Arms Control and Disarmament Agency, to discuss round four of the strategic arms reduction talks recently concluded in Geneva, Switzerland.
The President left the White House for a weekend stay at Camp David, Md.

August 7
The President returned to the White House from Camp David.

August 8
The President met at the White House with:
—members of the White House staff;
—Thomas R. Pickering, U.S. Ambassador to El Salvador, and Secretary of State George P. Shultz.
The President announced his intention to appoint Becky Norton Dunlop, Deputy Assistant to the President and Deputy Director of Presidential Personnel, to be Chairperson of the Interagency Committee on Women's Business Enterprise. She will succeed Angela M. Buchanan.

August 9
The President met at the White House with:
—members of the White House staff;
—the National Security Council;
—a group of Hispanic leaders, to discuss issues of concern to the Hispanic community, including economic development and education;
—the Cabinet, to receive a report by the Southwest Border States Working Group on the economic conditions of the counties that line the Mexican border in California, Arizona, and Texas, particularly with respect to the peso devaluation;
—a group of White House fellows, who will be leaving the program later this month.

August 10
The President met at the White House with members of the White House staff.

August 11
The President met at the White House with:
—members of the White House staff;
—a group of Hispanic appointees of the administration, to discuss issues of concern to the Hispanic community.
The White House announced that on behalf of the District of Columbia government, the President has transmitted to Congress requests for supplemental appropriations for fiscal year 1983 for the District of Columbia in the amount of $1.2 million.

August 12
The President met at the White House with members of the White House staff.
The President requested that Congress provide an additional $60 million in fiscal year 1984 for construction and operating funds for the Waste Isolation Pilot Plan to test and demonstrate technologies for the safe disposal of defense-related nuclear waste. In addition, the President requested funds in fiscal year 1984 to renovate visitor facilities located in national parks. The renovation work would be done by the National Park Foundation, and the Foundation would also accept contributions from the private sector for this project. The $5.8 million in Federal funds requested for this project would be fully offset by reductions in the program that had previously done this work. The President also requested appropriation·language that would transfer the aid to land-grant college programs from the Department of Education to the Department of Agriculture in compliance with recently enacted legisla-

tion, and $3.1 million in fiscal year 1984 for the U.S. International Trade Commission to provide for the expenses of relocating the Commission staff.

The President left the White House for an extended trip, including visits to Tampa, Fla.; El Paso, Tex.; La Paz, Baja California, Mexico; and New Orleans, La. Following these visits, the President will go to Rancho del Cielo, his ranch near Santa Barbara, Calif., and will return to Washington, D.C., on September 5.

August 15

Following his appearance at the annual national convention of the Veterans of Foreign Wars in New Orleans, La., the President traveled to Rancho del Cielo, his ranch near Santa Barbara, Calif.

August 16

The White House announced that the President has invited Lt. Gen. Hussain Mohammad Ershad, President of the Council of Ministers of Bangladesh, to make an official working visit to the White House. General Ershad has accepted the invitation and will meet with the President on October 25.

The White House announced that the President has recess appointed Linda Chavez Gersten to be Staff Director of the Commission on Civil Rights.

The White House announced that the President has accorded the personal rank of Ambassador to Millicent Fenwick, of New Jersey, in her capacity as United States Representative to the Food and Agriculture Organization of the United Nations in Rome.

August 19

The President declared a major disaster for the State of Texas as a result of Hurricane Alicia, beginning on or about August 18, which caused extensive property damage.

August 21

The President and Mrs. Reagan left Rancho del Cielo, their ranch near Santa Barbara, Calif., and went to Los Angeles, where they stayed at the Century Plaza Hotel.

August 22

In the morning, the President met at the Century Plaza Hotel in Los Angeles, Calif., with Senator Pete Wilson of California.

The White House announced that the President was informed of the death of Mrs. John C. Stennis, wife of the Senator from Mississippi. The President expressed his condolences and those of Mrs. Reagan in a private communication with Senator Stennis.

August 23

The President went to Seattle, Wash., to address the annual convention of the American Legion. He then returned to the Century Plaza Hotel in Los Angeles, Calif.

August 25

While in Los Angeles, Calif., the President addressed the Hispanic Economic Outlook Preview luncheon at the Biltmore Hotel. He remained overnight at the Century Plaza Hotel.

August 26

The President left Los Angeles and went to San Diego, Calif., where he addressed the Republican Women's Leadership Forum at the Bahia Hotel. He then attended a fundraising reception for Representative Robert Lagomarsino of California. Late in the afternoon, the President and Mrs. Reagan arrived at Rancho del Cielo, their ranch near Santa Barbara, where they planned to remain until Labor Day.

August 28

The President spoke by telephone with members of the White House staff from Rancho del Cielo, his ranch near Santa Barbara, Calif. They discussed the announcement of Israeli Prime Minister Menachem Begin's decision to resign and the trip to the Middle East and Europe of Ambassador Robert C. McFarlane, the President's Personal Representative in the Middle East.

August 29

The President designated Senator John W. Warner of Virginia as the Personal Representative of the President to the bicentennial celebration of the Treaty of Paris. The 200th anniversary of the signing of the Treaty of Paris, which ended the War of Independence between the United States and Great Britain, will be celebrated in Paris from August 30 to September 3.

August 30

The President spoke by telephone with members of the White House staff to discuss the situation in Lebanon.

The President spoke by telephone to a gathering in Marietta, Ga., where the 1983 Little League World Series champions were being saluted by their hometown.

August 31

The President spoke by telephone with the Vice President, who reported on the current situation in Lebanon as determined by the special situation group he had chaired.

The President spoke by telephone with members of the White House staff to discuss the Soviet attack on Korean Air Lines Flight 007.

September 1

The President spoke by telephone with members of the White House staff and Secretary of State George P. Shultz to discuss the Soviet attack on the Korean Air Lines Flight 007.

The President telephoned Mrs. Larry McDonald from Rancho del Cielo, his ranch near Santa Barbara, Calif. Mrs. McDonald is the widow of Representative Larry McDonald of Georgia, who was killed in the Soviet attack on Korean Air Lines Flight 007.

The White House announced that the President has invited Prime Minister Robert Mugabe of the Republic of Zimbabwe to make an official working visit to the United States. Prime Minister Mugabe has accepted the invitation and will meet with the President at the White House on September 13.

The White House announced that the President has invited Prime Minister Margaret Thatcher of the United Kingdom to make an official working visit to the United States. Prime Minister Thatcher has accepted the invitation and will meet with the President at the White House on September 29.

September 2

The President left Rancho del Cielo, his ranch near Santa Barbara, Calif., and returned to the White House. En route to Washington, he telephoned Mrs. Henry M. Jackson from Air Force One. Mrs. Jackson is the widow of Senator Jackson of Washington, who died on September 1.

Upon his return to the White House, the President met with his national security and foreign policy advisers and other administration officials to discuss the Soviet attack on Korean Air Lines Flight 007.

September 3

In the morning, the President met at the White House with his national security and foreign policy advisers and other administration officials to discuss the situation in the Middle East. Ambassador Robert C. McFarlane, the President's Personal Representative in the Middle East, presented a status report on the current situation in Lebanon.

The President had lunch at the White House with Secretary of State George P. Shultz.

September 4

The President held a roundtable discussion at the White House with the bipartisan congressional leadership and administration officials on the Soviet attack on Korean Air Lines Flight 007, the situation in the Middle East, and U.S. objectives for Lebanon.

September 6

The President met at the White House with:

—members of the White House staff;
—Secretary of State George P. Shultz, prior to departure for Madrid, Spain, for the session of the Conference on Security and Cooperation in Europe and a meeting with Foreign Minister Andrey A. Gromyko of the Soviet Union;
—the National Security Council;
—Sherman Swenson, chairman and chief executive officer of B. Dalton Booksellers, which made a $3 million commitment toward eliminating illiteracy through its national literacy initiative program;
—the Cabinet, for an update on the economy, the fiscal year 1985 budget process, the situation in the Middle East, and the Soviet attack on Korean Air Lines Flight 007;
—leaders of the United Jewish Appeal.

The White House announced that Kenneth M. Duberstein, Assistant to the President for Legislative Affairs, will represent the President at memorial services in Washington, D.C., for Senator Henry M. Jackson of Washington. The Vice President will represent the President at funeral services for Senator Jackson in Washington State on September 7.

September 7

The President met at the White House with members of the White House staff.

September 8

The President met at the White House with:

—members of the White House staff;
—Ambassador Jeane J. Kirkpatrick, U.S. Representative to the United Nations, to discuss current events at the United Nations with regard to the Soviet attack on Korean Air Lines Flight 007;
—the Vice President, who will be leaving September 11 for visits to Morocco, Algeria, Tunisia, Yugoslavia, Romania, Hungary, and Austria;
—the Cabinet Council on Legal Policy, to review the third quarterly report of the Attorney General concerning gender-based distinctions in Federal statutes.

The President transmitted to the Congress the third annual report on activities undertaken by the U.S. Synthetic Fuels Corporation and the Department of Energy to implement the development of synthetic fuels under the Defense Production Act of 1950, as amended.

September 9

The President met at the White House with members of the White House staff.

The President went to the National Cathedral for a memorial service for victims of the Soviet attack on Korean Air Lines Flight 007. Following the service, the President met and spoke briefly to families and friends of the passengers.

The White House announced that the President will deliver the U.S. speech to the General Debate of the United Nations General Assembly on September 26. The President also will use the occasion to call on the Secretary-General of the United Nations and to meet with selected world leaders.

The President spoke by long-distance teleconference to the Republican Western Regional Conference, which was held in Scottsdale, Ariz.

The President designated Senator Richard G. Lugar of Indiana as the Personal Representative of the President to the German-American Tricentennial Celebration, to be held September 9 in Hambach, Germany.

September 10

The President met at the White House with:
—Secretary of State George P. Shultz;
—the National Security Council.

September 12

The President met at the White House with:
—members of the White House staff;
—members of the President's Commission on Industrial Competitiveness;
—the Cabinet Council on Economic Affairs, for an economic update;
—Governors Scott M. Matheson of Utah, James R. Thompson of Illinois, and John Carlin of Kansas, who reported on the summer meeting of the National Governors' Association.

Late in the afternoon, the President hosted a reception at the White House for contributors to the Republican Party from Michigan and Ohio.

September 13

The President met at the White House with:
—members of the White House staff;
—former Governor Daniel J. Evans of Washington, who has been appointed by Governor John Spellman as U.S. Senator following the death of Senator Henry M. Jackson;
—the Cabinet, for an update on foreign policy matters given by Secretary of State George P. Shultz and a report on drought conditions by Secretary of Agriculture John R. Block;
—a group of Hispanic educators, to discuss the administration's education policies and programs affecting the Hispanic community.

Late in the afternoon, the President hosted a reception at the White House for the Eagles, major Republican Party contributors.

September 14

The President met at the White House with:
—members of the White House staff;

—Secretary of State George P. Shultz, for a luncheon meeting to discuss foreign policy matters.

The President met in the Oval Office with Secretary of Transportation Elizabeth H. Dole, J. Lynn Helms, Administrator, and Donald R. Segner, Associate Administrator for Policy and International Aviation, Federal Aviation Administration (FAA), to discuss the September 15 meeting in Montreal, Canada, of the International Civil Aviation Organization on the Soviet attack on Korean Air Lines Flight 007. Mr. Helms will head the U.S. delegation to the meeting. Edmund Stohr from the State Department also is an official delegate to the meeting. Advisers to the delegation are Mr. Segner, Irene Howie from FAA's General Counsel's office, Gordon L. Streeb, Deputy Assistant Secretary of State for International Economic and Social Affairs, and Clark Norton, from the State Department's Bureau of International Organization Affairs.

The President participated in a teleconference call with Senators Howard H. Baker, Jr., of Tennessee and Robert Dole of Kansas to discuss tuition tax credits.

September 15

The President met at the White House with:
—members of the White House staff;
—the Cabinet Council on Natural Resources and the Environment, for a report on acid rain by William D. Ruckelshaus, Administrator of the Environmental Protection Agency;
—members of the executive committee of the International Rescue Committee, an organization that provides assistance to refugees;
—representatives of the National Association of Home Builders.

The White House announced that the visit of President Mauno Koivisto of Finland to the United States, originally scheduled for September 26, has been rescheduled for September 27.

The President requested that the Congress provide the following:
—$106 million in fiscal year 1983 supplemental appropriations for the Veterans Administration for compensation and pensions and readjustment benefits to cover shortfalls in these programs.
—amendments reducing the fiscal year 1984 appropriations request for the Department of Defense by nearly $4.9 billion, which primarily reflects reduced inflation and fuel costs and the MX missile deployment decision.
—a reduction of $317.3 million in the fiscal year 1984 request for appropriations for payment to the Social Security Trust Fund, which reflects the enactment of the Social

Security Amendments of 1983. This legislation eliminated the requirement for an annual appropriation for benefits resulting from past military service by eligible recipients.

—$22.2 million in additional 1984 appropriations for the National Institutes of Health and the Centers for Disease Control, thereby enabling further research and surveillance on Acquired Immune Deficiency Syndrome. This increase will be offset by fiscal year 1984 reductions in other Department of Health and Human Services programs.

—a reduction of $20 million to the fiscal year 1984 request for appropriations for contributions to the Inter-American Development Bank, resulting from the slower than anticipated pace of multilateral negotiations to establish the institution. The initial contribution by the United States will not be needed until 1985.

—$10 million in additional fiscal year 1984 appropriations for the Department of Commerce, thereby enabling the National Oceanic and Atmospheric Administration to continue development of a new weather radar system.

—also included in this request are appropriations proposals for the Departments of Agriculture, Health and Human Services, and Interior, the General Services Administration, and the Veterans Administration.

—a proposal to fund increased benefit costs in the supplemental security income program. Part of the increase is for a $20-a-month benefit increase enacted in the Social Security Amendments of 1983. The $318 million will be provided by transfer of funds from the medicaid program.

September 16

The President met at the White House with:
—members of the White House staff;
—Secretary of State George P. Shultz and Ambassador Richard B. Stone, Special Representative of the President to Central America;
—a group of education and religious leaders, to discuss tuition tax credits;
—Prince Philippe of Belgium;
—Republican National Committee members, for a luncheon meeting to discuss administration programs and policies.

The President announced his intention to designate Maria Lucia Johnson as Vice Chairman of the Merit Systems Protection Board. Ms. Johnson has been serving as a member of the Board since May 10.

The President designated the following individuals to be members of the United States Delega-

tion to attend the independence ceremonies of St. Christopher-Nevis, which are to be held in Basseterre, St. Christopher-Nevis, from September 16-20:

Personal Representative of the President, with the rank of Special Ambassador, to head the Delegation:

Milan D. Bish, American Ambassador to Barbados

Personal Representative of the President, with the rank of Special Ambassador:

Carol B. Hallett, western director for Citizens for America, Sacramento, Calif.

Representatives of the President, with the rank of Special Ambassador:

Rear Adm. Richard T. Hedger, Commander, United States Forces in the Caribbean, Key West, Fla.;

Rear Adm. Donald C. Thompson, Commander, Seventh Coast Guard District, Miami, Fla.;

Howard Jenkins, Jr., former member, National Labor Relations Board, Kensington, Md.;

St. George I. B. Crosse, special adviser for minority programs, Department of Housing and Urban Development, Randallstown, Md.;

Samuel F. Segnar, president and chief executive officer, INTERNORTH, Inc., Omaha, Nebr.;

Alberto R. Cardenas, Chairman of the Presidential Advisory Committee on Small and Minority Business Ownership, Coral Gables, Fla.

In the afternoon, the President left the White House for a weekend stay at Camp David, Md.

September 18

The President returned to the White House from Camp David.

The President and Mrs. Reagan attended a performance in the East Room, where Leontyne Price and James Levine presented young members of the Metropolitan Opera. As part of the series "In Performance at the White House," the event was videotaped for later broadcast by the Public Broadcasting Service.

September 19

In the morning, the President telephoned George Allen, Chairman of the President's Council on Physical Fitness and Sports. Coach Allen was in Indianapolis, Ind., for the groundbreaking for the United States Fitness Academy.

The President met at the White House with members of the White House staff.

September 20

The President met at the White House with members of the White House staff and held a National Security Council meeting before departing for South Carolina.

While in Columbia, S.C., the President telephoned John Ayer at the Baptist Hospital of

Miami, Fla., to commend him on his successful efforts to rescue a young woman from an angry crowd.

September 21

The President met at the White House with:
—members of the White House staff;
—President Roberto Suazo Córdova of Honduras.

In an Oval Office ceremony, the President met with representatives of the Boys Clubs of America and the five regional finalists in the 37th annual National Youth of the Year competition, which is sponsored by the Boys Clubs and Reader's Digest. The President announced the selection of Mark Perry, 18, of North Little Rock, Ark., as the 1983 winner and presented him with an engraved plaque.

September 22

The President met at the White House with:
—members of the White House staff;
—Kenneth L. Brown, U.S. Ambassador to the Congo, Robert E. Fritts, U.S. Ambassador to Ghana, and Robert H. Miller, U.S. Ambassador to Ivory Coast, prior to their departure for their overseas posts;
—Greg Gross, 12, of Baton Rouge, La., the good will ambassador for the International Summer Special Olympics;
—Jeremiah Dellas, 7, of St. Louis, Mo., the 1983 National Epilepsy Poster Child;
—the incoming White House fellows.

The President attended a reception in the Indian Treaty Room of the Old Executive Office Building for American Women in Radio and Television.

The President attended a reception in the East Room for national board members of the Smithsonian Institution.

The President declared a major disaster for the State of California as a result of severe storms and flash flooding beginning on August 15, which caused extensive property damage.

September 23

The President met at the White House with:
—members of the White House staff;
—the National Security Council.

The President had lunch in the Oval Office with Associate Justice Sandra Day O'Connor and her husband, John, in recognition of Justice O'Connor's appointment to the Supreme Court. She was sworn in to office on September 25, 1981.

Late in the afternoon, the President attended a reception in the State Dining Room for members of the National Aquarium Society.

The White House announced that the President has invited President Hosni Mubarak of Egypt to make an official working visit to the United States. President Mubarak has accepted the invitation and will meet with President Reagan at the White House on September 30.

September 26

The White House announced that the President has designated John A. Svahn, Assistant to the President for Policy Development, as Chairman of the Property Review Board. He will succeed Edwin L. Harper.

September 27

The President met at the White House with members of the White House staff.

September 28

The President met at the White House with:
—members of the White House staff;
—Republican congressional leaders, to review the current legislative agenda;
—Republican Members of the House of Representatives, to discuss the War Powers Resolution;
—the Cabinet Council on Management and Administration, to discuss management efficiency.

The President met in the Oval Office with Secretary of Agriculture John R. Block and several Members of Congress to discuss the situation in drought-affected areas of the country. The President instructed Secretary Block to reduce emergency loan interest rates by 3 percent, from 8 to 5 percent, for all farmers operating in counties designated eligible in the natural disaster emergency loan program for the 1983 crop season.

The White House announced that Zhao Ziyang, Premier of the State Council of the People's Republic of China, will visit the United States in January of 1984. The visit has been under discussion for some time and will continue the dialog between the two countries on a wide range of bilateral and international topics. Specific dates are now being worked out. In addition, President Reagan has accepted the invitation of Premier Zhao to visit China in April of 1984, and specific dates are under discussion. Premier Zhao's visit will be the first such visit by a Chinese Premier to the United States. President Reagan's visit to China will be the first by a U.S. President since United States-China relations were normalized 5 years ago.

September 29

The President met at the White House with:
—members of the White House staff;
—the National Security Council.

The President met in the Oval Office with Prince Bandar of Saudi Arabia. The Prince, who is the Saudi Ambassador-designate to the United

States, represented King Fahd in the discussions leading to the cease-fire in Lebanon and played an instrumental role in the negotiations.

September 30
The President met at the White House with members of the White House staff.

October 1
The President and Mrs. Reagan hosted a private dinner for Princess Margaret of the United Kingdom in the Residence.

October 3
The President met at the White House with:
—members of the White House staff;
—President Aristides Pereira of Cape Verde;
—Government officials, to mark the kick-off of the 1983 Combined Federal Campaign;
—members of the President's Commission on Strategic Forces and Ambassador Edward L. Rowny, Special Representative for Negotiations, U.S. Arms Control and Disarmament Agency, to discuss the strategic arms reduction talks;
—Senators Charles H. Percy of Illinois, Sam Nunn of Georgia, and William S. Cohen of Maine, and Representatives Norman D. Dicks of Washington, Les Aspin of Wisconsin, and Albert Gore, Jr., of Tennessee, to discuss the strategic arms reduction talks.

The President hosted a reception in the Residence for Justices of the Supreme Court to mark the beginning of the court's new term. Also attending the reception were Attorney General William French Smith, Deputy Attorney General Edward C. Schmults, and Solicitor General Rex E. Lee.

The White House announced that at the request of the President, the Vice President, accompanied by Mrs. Bush, has accepted the invitation of Prime Minister Edward Philip George Seaga to visit Jamaica between October 16 and 18. Following his visit to Jamaica, the Vice President and Mrs. Bush will visit Puerto Rico to address a meeting of mayors from leading Latin American cities. The Vice President's meeting with the Prime Minister and other members of the Jamaican Government further highlight our close ties with Jamaica and our interest in the country's continued economic development in other areas of mutual concern. The Vice President's visit to Puerto Rico will continue the close relationships with Latin American leaders at the local level on a range of problems of concern in our hemisphere.

The President announced his intention to appoint Daniel Oliver, who has been nominated to be General Counsel of the Department of Education, as a member of the Council of the Administrative Conference of the United States for a term of 3 years. He would succeed T. Timothy Ryan, Jr.

The President requested that the Congress provide an additional appropriation of $150 million in fiscal year 1984 for the Veterans Administration for the veterans job training program. This program, which is authorized by the Emergency Veterans' Job Training Act of 1983, would provide funds to reimburse employers for one-half of the wages of eligible unemployed Korean war and Vietnam-era veterans participating in an approved job-training program. This request included $25 million to extend the eligibility of veterans enrolled in education programs authorized by chapter 34, title 38 of the United States Code.

October 4
The President met at the White House with:
—members of the White House staff;
—a bipartisan group of Members of Congress, to discuss the strategic arms reduction talks;
—representatives of the American Business Conference;
—Secretary of Energy Donald P. Hodel, to discuss the 1983 national energy policy plan;
—the Cabinet Council on Commerce and Trade, to discuss the Federal Communications Commission's decision and pending legislation on telephone access charges.

The White House announced that the President has invited Prime Minister Bettino Craxi of Italy to make an official working visit to the United States. The Prime Minister has accepted the invitation and will meet with the President at the White House on October 20.

The President, on the recommendation of Senate Minority Leader Robert C. Byrd, designated Senator Daniel Inouye of Hawaii as a senior counselor to the National Bipartisan Commission on Central America. He is succeeding Senator Henry M. Jackson of Washington.

October 5
The President met at the White House with:
—members of the White House staff;
—the Republican congressional leadership, to discuss arms control and reduction and the legislative agenda;
—Patrolman D. C. Russell from Oklahoma City, Okla., who was injured in an accident involving the motorcade which transported the President during his visit to the city;
—members of the board of directors of the Associated Press.

The President declared a major disaster for the State of Arizona as a result of severe storms and flooding beginning on or about September 23, which caused extensive property damage.

October 6

The President met at the White House with:
—members of the White House staff;
—the Vice President, for lunch;
—Brig. Gen. Hazel W. Johnson-Brown, USA, and Rear Adm. Frances Shea, USN, recent retirees from the nurse corps.

The President spoke by telephone with representatives of the Association of Southeast Asian Nations who were meeting with Secretary of State George P. Shultz in New York City. He expressed his regret at having to postpone his visits to the Philippines, Thailand, and Indonesia.

In an Oval Office ceremony, the President awarded the National Security Medal to Clarence L. "Kelly" Johnson, an aeronautical engineer responsible for several advances in the design of a number of this country's most famous aircraft.

The President transmitted to the Congress the 1982 annual reports prepared by the Departments of Labor and Health and Human Services on activities of their departments under the Occupational Safety and Health Act of 1970.

In the evening, the President hosted a barbecue on the South Grounds of the White House for Members of Congress.

October 7

Following his visit to Louisville, Ky., the President went to Camp David, Md., for the weekend.

The White House announced that the President has designated William J. Casey, Director of Central Intelligence, to be the President's Personal Representative to the funeral of Terence Cardinal Cooke on October 10. He will be accompanied by:

Raymond J. Donovan, Secretary of Labor
Margaret M. Heckler, Secretary of Health and Human Services
Michael K. Deaver, Deputy Chief of Staff and Assistant to the President
William P. Clark, Assistant to the President for National Security Affairs
Edward V. Hickey, Jr., Assistant to the President and Director of Special Support Services
Adm. J. D. Watkins, Chief of Naval Operations
William A. Wilson, President's Personal Representative to the Holy See
Clare Boothe Luce, member, President's Foreign Intelligence Advisory Board

October 10

The President returned to the White House following a weekend stay at Camp David, Md.

October 11

The President met at the White House with:
—members of the White House staff;

—William A. Wilson, the President's Personal Representative to the Holy See;
—Secretary of Defense Caspar W. Weinberger, who will head the U.S. delegation to the memorial service in Seoul for Korean victims of the bombing in Rangoon, Burma;
—Wu Xueqian, Minister of Foreign Affairs of the People's Republic of China;
—members of the White House staff, to discuss the selection of a successor to James G. Watt as Secretary of the Interior.

In the evening, the President went to Memorial Stadium in Baltimore, Md., for the first game of the 1983 World Series between the Baltimore Orioles and the Philadelphia Phillies.

The White House announced that on October 9, the President sent a letter of condolence to President Chun Doo Hwan of the Republic of Korea on the deaths of the Korean officials in the bombing in Rangoon, Burma.

The White House announced that on October 10, the President sent a letter of congratulations to Yitzak Shamir, the new Prime Minister of Israel. The letter underscored the President's determination to maintain the friendly and warm relationship with the Israeli Government and to maintain our historic ties with that nation.

October 12

The President met at the White House with members of the White House staff.

October 13

The President met at the White House with:
—members of the White House staff;
—Ambassador Jeane J. Kirkpatrick, U.S. Representative to the United Nations;
—a group of his advisers, for a budget overview meeting;
—Senator Paul Laxalt of Nevada, to discuss the Senator's plans for the filing of a committee to support the President's reelection effort.

In an Oval Office ceremony, the President received diplomatic credentials from Ambassadors Ibrahim Izziddin of Jordan, Ratu Jone Filipe Radrodro of Fiji, Stanislav Suja of Czechoslovakia, Venceo Hazi of Hungary, Sergio Correa Affonso da Costa of Brazil, and Ellom-Kodjo Schuppius of Togo.

In an Oval Office ceremony, actor Hugh O'Brian presented the President with the Albert Schweitzer Award, which is presented to individuals who have distinguished themselves through service to mankind and, in particular, motivation and education of youth. The President is one of four recipients of the award, which is presented by the Hugh O'Brian Youth Fellowship.

October 14

The President met at the White House with:

—members of the White House staff;
—Wadia Haddad, foreign policy adviser to President Amin Gemayel of Lebanon;
—Secretary of State George P. Shultz and Ambassador Robert C. McFarlane, the President's Personal Representative in the Middle East, who reported on the situation in the Middle East;
—Secretary of State George P. Shultz, for lunch.

The President participated in a meeting of the White House Management Conference for Non-Career Executives in Room 450 of the Old Executive Office Building.

The White House announced that the President has invited Prime Minister Robert D. Muldoon of New Zealand to make an official working visit to the United States. The Prime Minister has accepted the invitation and will meet with the President at the White House on February 24, 1984.

Late in the afternoon, the President left the White House for a weekend stay at Camp David, Md.

October 16
The President returned to the White House from Camp David.

October 17
The President met at the White House with:
—members of the White House staff;
—the Cabinet, to discuss drug policy;
—the current Miss America, Vanessa Williams.

During a meeting with Senator Paul Laxalt of Nevada, the President signed two letters in connection with the formation of the Reagan-Bush '84 Committee. One letter acknowledged Senator Laxalt's chairmanship of the committee and requested that Angela M. Buchanan serve as the campaign committee's treasurer. The other letter informed Danny Lee McDonald, Chairman of the Federal Election Commission, of the President's authorization of the committee. Also attending the Oval Office meeting were Frank J. Fahrenkopf, Jr., chairman of the Republican National Committee, former Secretary of Transportation Drew L. Lewis, Ms. Buchanan, campaign director Edward J. Rollins, and members of the White House staff.

The President requested that the Congress provide additional appropriations of $20.4 million for the Department of Commerce in fiscal year 1984 for the launch of the LANDSAT D Prime "earth sensing" satellite. This launch is necessary at this time to replace the LANDSAT 4 satellite that is now orbiting. LANDSAT 4 has experienced system malfunctions and needs replacement.

October 18
The President met at the White House with:
—members of the White House staff;
—the National Security Council.

October 19
The President met at the White House with:
—members of the White House staff;
—members of the U.S. Savings Bond Volunteer Committee.

The White House announced that the President will visit Japan and the Republic of Korea November 9–14 at the invitation of the Governments of Japan and the Republic of Korea. The President will be accompanied by Mrs. Reagan. The President and Mrs. Reagan will visit Japan November 9–12 and Korea November 12–14. The President will depart Washington on November 8, with a brief stopover at Elmendorf Air Force Base, Alaska, and will return to Washington on November 14, with another brief stopover at Elmendorf Air Force Base.

October 20
The President met at the White House with:
—members of the White House staff;
—the Cabinet Council on Commerce and Trade, to receive information on financial interests and syndication in the broadcast industry;
—former Director of Central Intelligence Richard Helms, to present Mr. Helms with the National Security Medal.

The President attended a reception in the Indian Treaty Room at the Old Executive Office Building for the U.S. Olympic Ski Team.

October 21
The President met at the White House with:
—members of the White House staff;
—administration officials and members of the White House staff, to discuss the fiscal year 1985 Federal budget;
—business leaders, to discuss natural gas decontrol legislation;
—members of the National Bipartisan Commission on Central America, to discuss their recent visit to the region.

The President spoke by telephone with Mrs. Martin Luther King, Jr.

The President announced his intention to nominate Harry O'Connor to be a member of the Board of Directors of the Corporation for Public Broadcasting for the remainder of the term expiring March 26, 1986. He would succeed Diana Lady Dougan.

The President left the White House for a weekend stay at the Augusta National Golf Club in Augusta, Ga. He was accompanied by Secretary of State George P. Shultz and Secretary of the Treasury Donald T. Regan.

October 23

The President met at the White House with his senior advisers and held two separate meetings with his national security and foreign policy advisers to discuss the situation in Lebanon. Those attending the meetings included the Vice President, Secretary of State George P. Shultz, Secretary of Defense Caspar W. Weinberger, Gen. John W. Vessey, Jr., Chairman of the Joint Chiefs of Staff, Gen. P. X. Kelley, Commandant of the Marine Corps, Deputy Director of Central Intelligence John N. McMahon, Counsellor to the President Edwin Meese III, Chief of Staff and Assistant to the President James A. Baker III, Deputy Chief of Staff and Assistant to the President Michael K. Deaver, and Assistant to the President for National Security Affairs Robert C. McFarlane.

In the afternoon, the President received a telephone call from President Amin Gemayel of Lebanon.

October 24

The President met at the White House with:
—members of the White House staff;
—Arthur A. Hartman, U.S. Ambassador to the Soviet Union;
—President Gnassingbé Eyadéma of Togo;
—the Joint Chiefs of Staff;
—several Members of Congress in a series of separate photo sessions with their constituents;
—a group of Republican Members of Congress, to discuss issues concerning women.

The President spoke by telephone with Speaker of the House Thomas P. O'Neill, Jr., and Senate Majority Leader Howard H. Baker, Jr., to discuss the situation in Lebanon.

In an Oval Office ceremony, the President received diplomatic credentials from Ambassador George Papoulias of Greece and Prince Bandar bin Sultan bin Abd al-Aziz Al Saud, Ambassador from Saudi Arabia.

The President declared a major disaster for the State of New Mexico as a result of severe storms and flooding beginning on September 18, which caused extensive property damage.

In the evening, the President met in the Residence with the congressional leadership and administration officials to discuss the situation in Grenada. Those attending the meeting included Speaker of the House Thomas P. O'Neill, Senate Majority Leader Howard H. Baker, Jr., House Majority Leader James C. Wright, Jr., House Republican Leader Robert H. Michel, Senate Minority Leader Robert C. Byrd, Secretary of State George P. Shultz, Secretary of Defense Caspar

W. Weinberger, Gen. John W. Vessey, Jr., Chairman of the Joint Chiefs of Staff, Counsellor to the President Edwin Meese III, Chief of Staff and Assistant to the President James A. Baker III, Deputy Chief of Staff and Assistant to the President Michael K. Deaver, Assistant to the President for National Security Affairs Robert C. McFarlane, Assistant to the President and Deputy to the Chief of Staff Richard G. Darman, and Assistant to the President for Legislative Affairs Kenneth M. Duberstein.

October 25

The President met at the White House with:
—Prime Minister Eugenia Charles of Dominica, to discuss the situation in Grenada;
—Secretary of State George P. Shultz and Secretary of Defense Caspar W. Weinberger, to discuss the situation in Grenada;
—the bipartisan congressional leadership, to dicuss the situation in Grenada;
—the Cabinet, to discuss the situation in Grenada;
—the National Security Council.

October 26

The President met at the White House with:
—members of the White House staff;
—Fred Lebow, director of the New York City Marathon, and the three winners of the October 23 race: Rod Dixon, winner, Grete Waitz, winner of the women's division, and John Paul Cruz, the first person to complete the race with only one leg who did not use an artificial limb.

The President met in the Old Executive Office Building with members of the Republican Jewish Coalition.

The President declared a major disaster for the State of Oklahoma as a result of severe storms and flooding beginning on October 19, which caused extensive property damage.

The President met with the Vice President in the evening following the Vice President's return from Lebanon. At the request of the President, the Vice President had visited with wounded marines and sailors and had met with President Amin Gemayel while in Lebanon.

October 27

The President met at the White House with:
—members of the White House staff;
—Governor Robert D. Orr of Indiana, to discuss the upcoming annual meeting of the Republican Governors Association;
—Prime Minister John Compton of St. Lucia.

The President transmitted to the Congress the 1982 annual report of the National Advisory Council on Adult Education.

October 28

Throughout the day, the President met at the White House with members of the White House staff. In the afternoon, he left the White House for a weekend stay at Camp David, Md.

October 30

The President returned to the White House from Camp David.

October 31

The President met at the White House with:
—members of the White House staff;
—representatives of the U.S. steel industry, to discuss the industry's recovery and steel marketing issues.

The President spoke by telephone with former President Jimmy Carter to express his condolences on the death of Mrs. Lillian Carter, President Carter's mother.

At a ceremony in the Roosevelt Room, the President signed the Departments of Labor, Health and Human Services, and Education, and Related Agencies Appropriation Act, 1984. Among those attending the ceremony were the Vice President, Secretary of Labor Raymond J. Donovan, Secretary of Health and Human Services Margaret M. Heckler, Secretary of Education Terrel H. Bell, and Members of Congress.

The President attended a reception in the Roosevelt Room for members of the board of directors of United Press International.

November 1

The President met at the White House with:
—members of the White House staff;
—Secretary of State George P. Shultz, Secretary of Defense Caspar W. Weinberger, Gen. John W. Vessey, Jr., Chairman of the Joint Chiefs of Staff, and Republican congressional leaders, to discuss Grenada, Lebanon, and legislative priorities for the remaining congressional session;
—the Cabinet, to discuss the fiscal year 1985 Federal budget;
—United States Ambassador to Bahrain Donald C. Leidel, prior to departure for his overseas post.

November 2

The President met at the White House with:
—members of the White House staff;
—former President Gerald R. Ford.
The President requested that the Congress provide the following:
—$3 million in fiscal year 1984 for the African Development Foundation, which promotes nongovernmental small-scale development projects in Africa to complement other U.S. development assistance efforts.

—$55 million in fiscal year 1984 for the construction of a joint facility at Ras Banas, Egypt.

This transmittal also included items for the legislative branch and the National Foundation on the Arts and the Humanities.

November 3

The President met at the White House with:
—members of the White House staff;
—the Vice President, for lunch;
—Republican Members of the Senate, to discuss Federal debt ceiling legislation.

The President transmitted to the Congress the 13th annual report on hazardous materials transportation, which covers calendar year 1982.

November 4

Prior to their departure for North Carolina, the President and Mrs. Reagan met in the Diplomatic Reception Room with the family of Marine Cpl. Thomas Perron, who was killed in Lebanon.

The President transmitted to the Congress the fifth annual report of the Department of Energy.

The White House announced that the President has designated Ambassador at Large Vernon A. Walters as his personal representative, with the rank of Special Ambassador, to attend inauguration ceremonies in Male on November 11 for Maumoon Abdul Gayoom, recently reelected as President of the Republic of Maldives.

The President left the White House for a weekend stay at Camp David, Md.

November 6

Following a weekend stay at Camp David, the President returned to the White House and met with Prime Minister Edward Philip George Seaga of Jamaica.

November 7

The President met at the White House with:
—members of the White House staff;
—participants in the Philadelphia Urban Education Partnership, a public-private partnership between the Federal Government, Provident Mutual Insurance Co. of Philadelphia, and Lincoln University and Cheyney State College, two historically black colleges.

The White House announced that the President has invited President Gaafar Mohamed Nimeiri of the Sudan to make a working visit to the United States. President Nimeiri has accepted the invitation and will meet with President Reagan at the White House on November 21.

The White House announced that the state visit of Their Majesties the King and Queen of Nepal, which was announced on March 2, has been scheduled for December 7.

November 9

The President and Mrs. Reagan were met at Haneda Airport in Japan by U.S. Ambassador to Japan Mike Mansfield and Mrs. Mansfield, the Japanese Ambassador to the United States and Mrs. Okawara, members of the Suite of Honor, and senior U.S. Embassy personnel. The President and Mrs. Reagan then went to Akasaka Palace, where they stayed during their visit to Japan.

Later in the day, the President and Mrs. Reagan participated in a formal arrival ceremony at the palace with Emperor Hirohito. The President and the Emperor then went to the Imperial Palace, where they were joined by Mrs. Reagan for a visit in the Audience Room. Following their visit with Emperor Hirohito, the President and Mrs. Reagan returned to Akasaka Palace, where they stayed during their visit to Japan.

The President met late in the afternoon with Prime Minister Yasuhiro Nakasone at Akasaka Palace. Secretary of State George P. Shultz and Japanese Foreign Minister Shintaro Abe also attended the meeting, which was followed by an expanded session with U.S. and Japanese officials.

November 10

In the morning, the President and Mrs. Reagan visited the Meiji Shrine and attended a horseback archery event at Yabusame Field.

Early in the evening, the President hosted a reception at Akasaka Palace for supporters of the Ronald W. Reagan Scholarship Program of Eureka College. Those attending the reception included the president of Eureka College, Dr. Dan Gilbert, former Japanese Prime Minister Takeo Fukuda, honorary chairman of the scholarship's steering committee, and John Amos, chairman of the scholarship's steering committee.

The White House announced that President Reagan will meet with President Chaim Herzog of Israel on November 22 at the White House.

November 11

Upon his return to Akasaka Palace after addressing the Diet, the President attended a reception in the Hagoromo-No-Ma Room for members of the press. The reception was hosted by Ambassador Mike Mansfield, U.S. Ambassador to Japan.

Later in the morning, the President and Mrs. Reagan went to Hinode-Cho School, where they were met by Prime Minister Yasuhiro Nakasone and Mrs. Nakasone. After greeting Hirai High School students, they went to the Nakasone's country residence for a private luncheon. The President met with Prime Minister Nakasone in the study at the residence before departing with Mrs. Reagan for Akasaka Palace.

In the afternoon, Emperor Hirohito visited with the President and Mrs. Reagan at Akasaka Palace. A farewell ceremony followed the visit.

In the evening, the President and Mrs. Reagan attended a reception in the Asahi-No-Ma Room at Akasaka Palace honoring the U.S. Marine Corps birthday.

November 12

Prior to departing Tokyo for the trip to the Republic of Korea, the President and Mrs. Reagan had a farewell visit with Prime Minister Yasuhiro Nakasone and Mrs. Nakasone in the Asahi-No-Ma Room at Akasaka Palace.

Following the session at the National Assembly in Seoul, the President and Mrs. Reagan went to the Blue House where they attended a luncheon with President Chun Doo Hwan and Mrs. Chun. The President met privately with President Chun before and after the luncheon. They were joined by their advisers in an expanded session following their post-luncheon meeting in the Study of the Blue House. After the meetings, the President and Mrs. Reagan returned to the residence of Ambassador Richard L. Walker, U.S. Ambassador to Korea, where they stayed during their visit to the Republic of Korea.

November 13

In the evening, the President went to the Blue House for a bilateral meeting with Korean President Chun Doo Hwan and U.S. and Japanese officials. President Reagan and President Chun then had a private meeting in the Study. Following the meetings, President Reagan returned to the residence of Ambassador Richard L. Walker, U.S. Ambassador to Korea, where he stayed during his visit to the Republic of Korea.

November 14

In the morning, the President attended a breakfast reception at the residence of Ambassador Richard L. Walker, U.S. Ambassador to Korea, for members of the Chamber of Commerce of the United States.

The President and Mrs. Reagan then went to the Blue House, where they were greeted by Korean President Chun Doo Hwan and Mrs. Chun, who accompanied them to Kimpo Airport. After a farewell ceremony at the airport, the President and Mrs. Reagan boarded Air Force One for the flight to the United States.

November 15

The President met at the White House with:
—members of the White House staff;
—Republican congressional leaders, to discuss his trip to Japan and the Republic of Korea and the legislative agenda.

The White House announced that the President has invited King Juan Carlos and Queen Sofia of Spain to visit Washington during the course of their private visit to the United States. The King and Queen have accepted the invitation and will meet with the President and Mrs. Reagan at the White House on December 8.

The President requested that the Congress provide a $30-million supplemental appropriation to construct a fueling pier in Keflavik, Iceland.

November 16

The President met at the White House with:
—members of the White House staff;
—the Cabinet Council on Commerce and Trade, to discuss the commercialization of space flight missions;
—local State officials, to discuss the enterprise zones legislation.

The President attended a reception in the Roosevelt Room for former Secretary of the Interior James G. Watt.

The President transmitted to the Congress the second annual report on Alaska's mineral resources.

November 17

The President met at the White House with:
—members of the White House staff;
—the Vice President, for lunch;
—Bishop James W. Malone, president, and Monsignor Daniel F. Hoye, general secretary, National Conference of Catholic Bishops;
—the Cabinet Council on Human Resources, to discuss social programs which affect the American family;
—Heather Ross, a 9-year-old from Hamler, Ohio, who had written a letter to the President.

The President transmitted to the Congress the following annual reports:
—the 15th annual report of the Department of Transportation;
—the 19th annual report on the status of the National Wilderness Preservation System;
—the 18th annual report of the Department of Housing and Urban Development.

The White House announced that the President has invited Prime Minister Yitzhak Shamir of Israel to make an official working visit to the United States. The Prime Minister has accepted the invitation and will meet with the President at the White House on November 29. The Prime Minister will be accompanied by Defense Minister Moshe Arens.

November 18

The President met at the White House with:
—members of the White House staff;

—leaders of the National Association of Attorneys General.

The President designated Sandra Swift Parrino as Chairman of the National Council on the Handicapped.

The President telephoned Mrs. Brooke Knapp to congratulate her on being the first person to complete an around-the-world, pole-to-pole flight in a corporate jet and for setting 40 new records on the way. Mrs. Knapp was in Los Angeles, Calif., at the time of the call.

The President declared a major disaster for the State of Idaho as a result of an earthquake occurring on October 28, which caused extensive property damage.

November 21

The President met at the White House with members of the White House staff.

The President attended the swearing-in ceremony in the Oval Office for William P. Clark as Secretary of the Interior.

In a Rose Garden ceremony, the President received the 36th annual Thanksgiving turkey from representatives of the National Turkey Federation. The turkey will be donated in the President's name to the Children's Farm in Reston, Va.

In an Oval Office ceremony, the President received diplomatic credentials from Ambassadors Peter Helemisi Mtetwa of Swaziland, Peter Douglas Laurie of Barbados, Henry Edney Conrad Cain of Belize, Mahamat Ali Adoum of Chad, and Leon Maxime Rajaobelina of Madagascar.

The White House announced that the President has recess appointed Ronald B. Frankum, of California, to be a member of the Board of Directors of the Legal Services Corporation, effective November 19. He will succeed Daniel M. Rathbun.

November 22

The President met at the White House with:
—members of the White House staff;
—Foreign Minister Ilter Turkmen of Turkey;
—President Chaim Herzog of Israel;
—Agostino Cardinal Casaroli, Secretary of State of the Vatican City State.

In the morning, the President went to a memorial service for President John F. Kennedy at Holy Trinity Church.

In an Oval Office ceremony, the President presented the Federal Aviation Administration's Award for Extraordinary Service to Mrs. Brooke Knapp. Mrs. Knapp recently became the first person to complete an around-the-world, pole-to-pole flight in a corporate jet. The award was presented in recognition of Mrs. Knapp's record-setting flights.

In an Oval Office ceremony, the President met with representatives of the American Lung Association to officially launch the association's annual Christmas Seal drive. Attending the meeting were Andy Williams, 1983 Christmas Seal chairman, and 12-year-old Maureen Barnes, National Superstuff Youth representative.

The President met in the Oval Office with Charlie Sampson, the 1982 world champion bullrider who was severely injured while participating in the Professional Rodeo Cowboy Association's rodeo at the Capital Centre in Landover, Md., on September 24. Secretary of Commerce Malcolm Baldrige, who had attended the rodeo with the President, and WRC-TV sports director George Michael also attended the meeting.

Early in the evening, the President attended a reception in the Residence for the Senatorial Trust.

The White House announced that at the request of the President, the Vice President, accompanied by Mrs. Bush, will lead the U.S. delegation to the inauguration of Raul Alfonsin as President of Argentina on December 10. Other members of the delegation will be designated by the President at a later date.

November 23

The President left the White House and went to Rancho del Cielo, his ranch near Santa Barbara, Calif., for the Thanksgiving holiday weekend.

November 27

The President returned to the White House from Rancho del Cielo, his ranch near Santa Barbara.

November 28

The President met at the White House with members of the White House staff.

The White House announced that the aggregate report on personnel, prepared pursuant to title 3, section 113, of the United States Code, for fiscal year 1983, was transmitted to the Speaker of the House and the President of the Senate.

November 29

The President met at the White House with:
—members of the White House staff;
—a bipartisan group of Members of Congress, to discuss the Dairy and Tobacco Adjustment Act of 1983.

November 30

The President met at the White House with:
—members of the White House staff;

—Prince Bandar bin Sultan, Saudi Arabian Ambassador to the United States, who delivered a letter from King Fahd;
—the National Security Council;
—the Vice President, Secretary of the Treasury Donald T. Regan, David A. Stockman, Director of the Office of Management and Budget, Martin S. Feldstein, Chairman of the Council of Economic Advisers, and members of the White House staff, to discuss the fiscal year 1985 Federal budget;
—the Cabinet Council on Economic Affairs, to discuss the budget.

The President recess appointed Dennis R. Patrick, of the District of Columbia, as a member of the Federal Communications Commission for the unexpired term of 7 years from July 1, 1978. He would succeed Anne P. Jones.

December 1

The President met at the White House with:
—members of the White House staff;
—Minister of Foreign Affairs Lee Won Kyung of the Republic of Korea;
—the Cabinet Council on Commerce and Trade, to discuss the proposed permanent orbital space station.

The President attended a gospel music performance at Shiloh Baptist Church in Washington, D.C. As part of the series "In Performance at the White House," the event was taped for later broadcast by the Public Broadcasting Service.

December 2

The President met at the White House with:
—members of the White House staff;
—the National Security Council.

In an Oval Office ceremony, the President signed a bill designating the Federal building to be constructed in Savannah, Ga., as the Juliette Gordon Low Federal Building. The ceremony was attended by Members of Congress from Georgia and Virginia.

The White House announced that the President has invited President Rudolph Kirchschläger of Austria to make a state visit to the United States. President Kirchschläger has accepted the invitation and will meet with President Reagan at the White House on February 28, 1984.

The President recess appointed Ruth O. Peters, of Virginia, as a Governor of the United States Postal Service for the remainder of the term expiring December 8, 1987. She would succeed Paula D. Hughes.

The President left the White House for a weekend stay at Camp David, Md.

December 4

The President returned to the White House from Camp David.

December 5

The President met at the White House with:

—members of the White House staff;

—Clayton E. McManaway, Jr., U.S. Ambassador to Haiti, Daniel A. O'Donohue, U.S. Ambassador to Burma, Diego C. Asencio, U.S. Ambassador to Brazil, and William H. Luers, U.S. Ambassador to Czechoslovakia, prior to departure for their overseas posts.

The President made the following recess appointments:

—Harold K. Phillips, of California, as a member of the Board of Directors of the Inter-American Foundation for a term expiring September 20, 1988. He would succeed Alberto Ibargüen.

—Vernon L. Grose, of California, as a member of the National Transportation Safety Board for the term expiring December 31, 1987. He would succeed Francis H. McAdams.

December 6

The President met at the White House with:

—members of the White House staff;

—Prime Minister Kennedy Alphonse Simmonds of St. Christopher-Nevis;

—Governor George Deukmejian of California.

The President sent a congratulatory message to President-elect Jaime Lusinchi of Venezuela.

The President made the following recess appointments:

—Stephanie Lee-Miller, of the District of Columbia, as an Assistant Secretary of Health and Human Services (Public Affairs). She would succeed Pamela Needham Bailey.

—Maurice Lee Barksdale, of Texas, as an Assistant Secretary of Housing and Urban Development (Housing—Federal Housing Commissioner). He would succeed Philip Abrams.

—Louis Roman DiSabato, of Texas, as a member of the National Museum Services Board for a term expiring December 6, 1987. He would succeed Lloyd Hezekiah.

—Leslie Lenkowsky, of New York, as Deputy Director of the United States Information Agency. He would succeed Gilbert A. Robinson.

—Helga Lieselotte Pennewell, of Maryland, as a member of the Presidential Commission for the German-American Tricentennial.

The President announced the following individuals to be members of the U.S. delegation to the celebration of Kenya's 20th year of independence. Secretary of Housing and Urban Development Samuel R. Pierce, Jr., will serve as chairman of the delegation, which will leave on December 9 and return on December 11.

Secretary Pierce

Gerald Thomas, U.S. Ambassador to Kenya

William Pickard, chairman of the board of directors, African Development Foundation, Detroit, Mich.

Anne Burford, attorney, Denver, Colo.

Rita Di Martino, U.S. Representative to UNICEF, New York, N.Y.

Hector Barreto, president of the United States Hispanic Chamber of Commerce, Kansas City, Mo.

Willie Davis, businessman, Los Angeles, Calif.

John Fonteno, businessman and assistant professor, Texas Southern University, Houston, Tex.

Henry Lucas, chairman, New Coalition for Economic and Social Change, San Francisco, Calif.

Tony Salinas, rancher, Hebronville, Tex.

Leonard Spearman, president, Texas Southern University, Houston, Tex.

The White House announced that the Vice President will lead the delegation attending the inauguration of Raul Alfonsin as President of Argentina. Accompanying the Vice President and Mrs. Bush in the official delegation will be:

Frank V. Ortiz, Jr., U.S. Ambassador to Argentina

Assistant Secretary of State for Inter-American Affairs Langhorne A. Motley

Gen. Paul Gorman

Representative Robert J. Lagomarsino of California

Deputy Secretary of the Treasury R. T. McNamar

Ambassador Richard Stone, the President's Personal Representative to Central America

Ambassador J. William Middendorf II, Permanent U.S. Representative to the Organization of American States

December 7

The President met at the White House with:

—members of the White House staff;

—regional directors of Citizens for America;

—members of the Tuition Tax Credit Coalition.

The President recess appointed Simeon Miller Bright, of West Virginia, as a Commissioner of the Postal Rate Commission for the term expiring November 22, 1988. This is a reappointment.

The White House announced that because of the news of the recent air tragedy in Madrid, King Juan Carlos I of Spain has cut short his private visit to the United States, including his December 8 meeting with the President, which was previously announced, and is returning to Spain.

December 8

The President met at the White House with:

—members of the White House staff;

—the President's Export Council;

—the Vice President, for lunch.

The President recess appointed Donna F. Tuttle, of California, as Under Secretary of Commerce for Travel and Tourism. She will succeed Peter McCoy.

December 9

The President met at the White House with members of the White House staff.

The President left the White House for a weekend stay at Camp David, Md.

December 11

The President returned to the White House from Camp David.

The President and Mrs. Reagan participated in the taping of the NBC television program "Christmas in Washington" at the National Building Museum.

December 12

The President met at the White House with members of the White House staff.

December 13

The President met at the White House with:

—members of the White House staff;

—Members of Congress from North Carolina and South Carolina, to discuss textile imports.

The President announced his intention to appoint Gale W. McGee as a member of the Presidential Commission for the German-American Tricentennial. This is a new position. This appointment was recommended by the President pro tempore of the Senate.

The President recess appointed Mary Kate Bush as United States Alternate Executive Director of the International Monetary Fund for a term of 2 years.

The President declared a major disaster for the State of Alabama as a result of severe storms, tornadoes, and flooding, beginning on December 2, which caused extensive property damage.

The President and Mrs. Reagan hosted a Christmas party on the State Floor for Members of Congress.

December 14

The President met at the White House with members of the White House staff.

The President and Mrs. Reagan hosted a Christmas party on the State Floor for members of the press.

December 15

The President met at the White House with:

—members of the White House staff;

—the Vice President, for lunch;

—Senator John Danforth of Missouri, to discuss the Senator's upcoming trip to Africa;

—Fred Waring, to present him with the Congressional Gold Medal;

—Capt. Grace Hopper, a 77-year-old computer pioneer for the U.S. Navy, who is being pro-

moted to Commodore on the Navy retired list;

—editors of the Ladies Home Journal, who presented the President with a bound edition of the 100th anniversary issue of the magazine, which contains an article written by the President entitled, "In Praise of American Women."

The White House announced that the President has invited Premier Zhao Ziyang of the People's Republic of China to make a state visit to the United States. Premier Zhao has accepted the invitation and will meet with the President at the White House on January 10, 1984.

The President requested that the Congress provide $1.8 billion in fiscal year 1984 supplemental appropriations to cover the cost of the January 1984 military and civilian pay raise for the Department of Defense-Military.

The President and Mrs. Reagan hosted a Christmas party on the State Floor for members of the press.

December 16

The President met at the White House with:

—members of the White House staff;

—the Cabinet Council on Commerce and Trade, to discuss textile imports.

The President announced his intention to appoint Alfred Hugh Kingon as Assistant Secretary of Commerce to be an Executive Branch Commissioner-Observer on the Commission on Security and Cooperation in Europe. He will succeed William H. Morris, Jr.

December 19

The President met at the White House with:

—members of the White House staff;

—Nicolas M. Salgo, U.S. Ambassador to Hungary.

December 20

The President met at the White House with:

—members of the White House staff;

—members of the American Security Council, for a luncheon meeting.

The President designated Morris B. Abram as Vice Chairman of the Commission on Civil Rights.

December 21

The President met at the White House with:

—members of the White House staff;

—Deputy Prime Minister Kamal Hassan Ali of Egypt;

—the Vice President and Secretary of State George P. Shultz, for lunch.

The President declared an emergency for the State of Mississippi as a result of flash flooding on

December 3 and 4, which caused extensive property damage.

December 22

The President met at the White House with:
—members of the White House staff;
—Ambassador Donald H. Rumsfeld, the President's Personal Representative in the Middle East, the Vice President, Secretary of State George P. Shultz, Assistant to the President for National Security Affairs Robert C. McFarlane, and Assistant Secretary of State for Near Eastern and South Asian Affairs Richard W. Murphy;
—pollster Richard Wirthlin;
—Ambassador Jeane J. Kirkpatrick, U.S. Representative to the United Nations.

The White House announced that the President has invited President François Mitterrand of France to make a state visit to the United States. President Mitterrand has accepted the invitation and will meet with President Reagan at the White House on March 22, 1984.

The White House announced that the President has invited Prime Minister Mahathir bin Mohamad of Malaysia to make an official working visit to the United States. The Prime Minister has accepted the invitation and will meet with the President at the White House on January 18, 1984.

December 23

Throughout the day, the President met at the White House with members of the White House staff.

The President requested that the Congress provide a $50 million fiscal year 1984 supplemental appropriation for grants to State and local agencies for the cost of storing and distributing surplus food donated by the Commodity Credit Corporation.

The President redesignated Clinton Dan McKinnon as Chairman and designated Barbara E. McConnell as Vice Chairman of the Civil Aeronautics Board for the period ending December 31, 1984, effective January 1, 1984.

December 25

The President and Mrs. Reagan spent Christmas at the White House with members of their family and friends.

December 27

The President and Mrs. Reagan left the White House for a trip to Los Angeles, Calif., where they stayed at the Century Plaza Hotel.

December 29

The President and Mrs. Reagan left Los Angeles, Calif., and traveled to the home of Walter and Leonore Annenberg in Palm Springs, Calif., where they stayed through New Year's Day.

Appendix B—Nominations Submitted to the Senate

The following list does not include promotions of members of the Uniformed Services, nominations to the Service Academies, or nominations of Foreign Service officers.

Submitted July 8

Paul A. Volcker,
of New Jersey, to be Chairman of the Board of Governors of the Federal Reserve System for a term of 4 years (reappointment).

Submitted July 11

Charles C. Cox,
of Texas, to be a member of the Securities and Exchange Commission for the term expiring June 5, 1988, vice John R. Evans, term expired.

Submitted July 13

Kenneth W. Starr,
of Virginia, to be United States Circuit Judge for the District of Columbia Circuit, vice George E. MacKinnon, retired.

Submitted July 14

Peter Jon de Vos,
of Florida, a career member of the Senior Foreign Service, Class of Counselor, to be Ambassador Extraordinary and Plenipotentiary of the United States of America to the People's Republic of Mozambique.

Helen M. Witt,
of Pennsylvania, to be a member of the National Mediation Board for the term expiring July 1, 1985, vice Robert Joseph Brown, resigned.

Thomas Ostrom Enders,
of Connecticut, a career member of the Senior Foreign Service, Class of Career Minister, to be Ambassador Extraordinary and Plenipotentiary of the United States of America to Spain.

Thomas R. Pickering,
of New Jersey, a career member of the Senior Foreign Service, Class of Career Minister, to be Ambassador Extraordinary and Plenipotentiary of the United States of America to El Salvador.

Submitted July 18

David John Markey,
of the District of Columbia, to be Assistant Secretary of Commerce for Communications and Information, vice Bernard J. Wunder, Jr., resigned.

A. Wayne Roberts,
of Massachusetts, to be Deputy Under Secretary for Intergovernmental and Interagency Affairs, Department of Education, vice John H. Rodriguez, resigned.

Charles G. Wells,
of Illinois, to be a member of the Board of Directors of the African Development Foundation for a term of 4 years (new position).

Albert Lee Smith, Jr.,
of Alabama, to be a member of the Federal Council on the Aging for a term expiring December 19, 1985, vice Jacob Clayman, term expired.

Submitted July 21

Morton R. Galane,
of Nevada, to be United States District Judge for the District of Nevada, vice Roger D. Foley, retired.

John F. Keenan,
of New York, to be United States District Judge for the Southern District of New York, vice Lloyd F. MacMahon, retired.

James B. Roche III,
of Massachusetts, to be United States Marshal for the District of Massachusetts for the term of 4 years, vice James I. Hartigan, retired.

Thomas C. Rapone,
of Pennsylvania, to be United States Marshal for the Eastern District of Pennsylvania for the term of 4 years, vice Edward D. Schaeffer, term expired.

Submitted July 25

Edmund DeJarnette,
of Virginia, a career member of the Senior Foreign Service, Class of Minister-Counselor, to be Ambassador Extraordinary and Plenipotentiary of the United States of America to the Central African Republic.

Submitted July 25—Continued

Alvin L. Alm,
of Massachusetts, to be Deputy Administrator of the Environmental Protection Agency, vice John Whitlock Hernandez, Jr., resigned.

Henry F. Schickling,
of Pennsylvania, to be a member of the Board of Directors of the Overseas Private Investment Corporation for a term expiring December 17, 1985 (new position).

Submitted July 26

Frederick M. Bernthal,
of Tennessee, to be a member of the Nuclear Regulatory Commission for the term of 5 years expiring June 30, 1988, vice John Francis Ahearne, term expired.

Submitted August 1

Charles Franklin Dunbar,
of Maine, a career member of the Senior Foreign Service, Class of Counselor, to be Ambassador Extraordinary and Plenipotentiary of the United States of America to the State of Qatar.

Danny J. Boggs,
of Virginia, to be Deputy Secretary of Energy, vice W. Kenneth Davis, resigned.

Thomas J. Healey,
of New Jersey, to be an Assistant Secretary of the Treasury, vice Roger William Mehle, Jr., resigned.

Richard L. McElheny,
of Arizona, to be an Assistant Secretary of Commerce, vice William H. Morris, Jr., resigned.

The following-named persons to be members of the Board of Directors of the National Institute of Building Sciences for terms expiring September 7, 1984:

MacDonald G. Becket, of California, vice Warner Howe, term expired.

Kyle Clayton Boone, of North Carolina, vice Blanca G. Cedeño, term expired.

Submitted August 4

Robert Hopkins Miller,
of Washington, a career member of the Senior Foreign Service, Class of Career Minister, to be Ambassador Extraordinary and Plenipotentiary of the United States of America to the Republic of Ivory Coast.

Submitted August 15

Matthew V. Scocozza,
of Tennessee, to be an Assistant Secretary of Transportation, vice Judith T. Connor, resigned.

Submitted August 18

Donald Charles Leidel,
of the District of Columbia, a career member of the Senior Foreign Service, Class of Minister-Counselor, to be Ambassador Extraordinary and Plenipotentiary of the United States of America to the State of Bahrain.

John C. McGraw,
of Pennsylvania, to be Assayer of the Mint of the United States at Philadelphia, Pennsylvania, vice Jack Herbert Keller, resigned.

Gwyneth Gayman,
of California, to be a member of the National Council on Educational Research for a term expiring September 30, 1984, vice Bernard C. Watson, term expired.

Robert Oberndoerfer Harris,
of the District of Columbia, to be a member of the National Mediation Board for the term expiring July 1, 1986 (reappointment).

Submitted August 22

Alan Lee Keyes,
of California, to be the Representative of the United States of America on the Economic and Social Council of the United Nations, with the rank of Ambassador.

George E. Moose,
of Maryland, a Foreign Service officer of class one, to be Ambassador Extraordinary and Plenipotentiary of the United States of America to the People's Republic of Benin.

Philip Abrams,
of Massachusetts, to be Under Secretary of Housing and Urban Development, vice Donald I. Hovde, resigned.

Brig. Gen. Jerome Bernard Hilmes,
330–28–3943, United States Army, to be a member of the Mississippi River Commission, under the provisions of Section 2 of an Act of Congress, approved 28 June 1879 (21 Stat. 37) (33 U.S.C. 642).

Submitted August 31

George Roberts Andrews,
of Maryland, a career member of the Senior Foreign Service, class of Minister-Counselor, to be

Submitted August 31—Continued
Ambassador Extraordinary and Plenipotentiary of the United States of America to Mauritius.

Richard H. Francis,
of Virginia, to be President of the Solar Energy and Energy Conservation Bank, vice Joseph S. Bracewell.

Barbara E. McConnell,
of the District of Columbia, to be a member of the Civil Aeronautics Board for the remainder of the term expiring December 31, 1983, vice Elizabeth E. Bailey, resigned.

Barbara E. McConnell,
of the District of Columbia, to be a member of the Civil Aeronautics Board for the term of 6 years expiring December 31, 1989 (reappointment).

Saundra Brown Armstrong,
of California, to be a Commissioner of the Consumer Product Safety Commission for a term of 7 years from October 27, 1983, vice Edith Barksdale Sloan, term expiring.

Submitted September 7

Henry F. Cooper, Jr.,
of Virginia, to be an Assistant Director of the United States Arms Control and Disarmament Agency, vice David Marion Clinard, resigned.

James B. Roche III,
of Massachusetts, to be United States Marshal for the District of Massachusetts for the term of 4 years, vice James I. Hartigan, retired.

Thomas C. Rapone,
of Pennsylvania, to be United States Marshal for the Eastern District of Pennsylvania for the term of 4 years, vice Edward D. Schaeffer, term expired.

Submitted September 8

Clayton E. McManaway, Jr.,
of the District of Columbia, a career member of the Senior Foreign Service, Class of Minister-Counselor, to be Ambassador Extraordinary and Plenipotentiary of the United States of America to Haiti.

The following-named persons to be members of the Board for International Broadcasting for the terms indicated:

For a term expiring April 28, 1986:

Ben J. Wattenberg, of the District of Columbia (reappointment).

Submitted September 8—Continued
For a term expiring May 20, 1986:

Frank Shakespeare, of Connecticut (reappointment).

Submitted September 9

Edmund DeJarnette,
of Virginia, a career member of the Senior Foreign Service, Class of Minister-Counselor, to be Ambassador Extraordinary and Plenipotentiary of the United States of America to the Central African Republic.

Peter Jon de Vos,
of Florida, a career member of the Senior Foreign Service, Class of Counselor, to be Ambassador Extraordinary and Plenipotentiary of the United States of America to the People's Republic of Mozambique.

Robert Hopkins Miller,
of Washington, a career member of the Senior Foreign Service, Class of Career Minister, to be Ambassador Extraordinary and Plenipotentiary of the United States of America to the Republic of Ivory Coast.

Charles Franklin Dunbar,
of Maine, a career member of the Senior Foreign Service, Class of Counselor, to be Ambassador Extraordinary and Plenipotentiary of the United States of America to the State of Qatar.

Millicent Fenwick,
of New Jersey, for the rank of Ambassador during the tenure of her service as United States Representative to the Food and Agriculture Organization in Rome.

C. Roger Vinson,
of Florida, to be United States District Judge for the Northern District of Florida, vice Lynn C. Higby, resigned.

Martin L. C. Feldman,
of Louisiana, to be United States District Judge for the Eastern District of Louisiana, vice Jack M. Gordon, deceased.

Francis M. Mullen, Jr.,
of Virginia, to be Administrator of Drug Enforcement, vice Peter B. Bensinger, resigned.

Danny J. Boggs,
of Virginia, to be Deputy Secretary of Energy, vice W. Kenneth Davis, resigned.

Richard L. McElheny,
of Arizona, to be an Assistant Secretary of Commerce, vice William H. Morris, Jr., resigned.

Submitted September 9—Continued
William Perry Pendley,
of Wyoming, to be an Assistant Secretary of the
Interior, vice Daniel N. Miller, Jr., resigned.

Joan M. Gubbins,
of Indiana, to be a member of the National Council on Educational Research for a term expiring
September 30, 1985, vice Alice Coig McDonald.

David J. Armor,
of California, to be a member of the National
Council on Educational Research for a term expiring September 30, 1986, vice Robert E. Nederlander.

The following-named persons to be members of
the Board of Directors of the African Development Foundation for the terms indicated:

For terms of 2 years:

Chester A. Crocker, an Assistant Secretary of
State (new position).
Francis Stephen Ruddy, an Assistant Administrator of the Agency for International Development (new position).

For terms of 4 years:

Patsy Baker Blackshear, of Maryland (new position).
Charles G. Wells, of Illinois (new position).

For a term of 6 years:
William F. Pickard, of Michigan (new position).

The following-named persons to be members of
the Board for International Broadcasting for the
terms indicated:

For terms expiring April 28, 1984:

Joseph Lane Kirkland, of the District of Columbia (new position).
Arch L. Madsen, of Utah (new position).
James Albert Michener, of Pennsylvania (new
position).

For terms expiring April 28, 1985:

Clair W. Burgener, of California (new position).
Michael Novak, of the District of Columbia,
vice Thomas H. Quinn, term expired.

For a term expiring April 28, 1986:

Malcolm Forbes, Jr., of New Jersey, vice Mark
Goode, term expired.

The following-named persons to be members of
the Commission on Civil Rights:
Morris B. Abram, of New York, vice Mary
Frances Berry.
John H. Bunzel, of California, vice Blandina
Cárdenas Ramirez.
Robert A. Destro, of Wisconsin, vice Murray
Saltzman.

Submitted September 9—Continued
Albert Lee Smith, Jr.,
of Alabama, to be a member of the Federal
Council on the Aging for a term expiring December 19, 1985, vice Jacob Clayman, term expired.

The following-named persons to be members of
the Interstate Commerce Commission for the
terms indicated:

*For the remainder of the term expiring December
31, 1984:*

Paul H. Lamboley, of Nevada, vice Darius W.
Gaskins, Jr., resigned.

For a term expiring December 31, 1985:

Jane E. M. Holt, of the District of Columbia,
vice Reginald E. Gilliam, Jr., resigned.

The following-named persons to be members of
the Board of Directors of the National Institute of
Building Sciences for terms expiring September
7, 1984:

MacDonald G. Becket, of California, vice
Warner Howe, term expired.
Kyle Clayton Boone, of North Carolina, vice
Blanca G. Cedeño, term expired.

Helen M. Witt,
of Pennsylvania, to be a member of the National
Mediation Board for the term expiring July 1,
1985, vice Robert Joseph Brown, resigned.

Elliot Ross Buckley,
of Virginia, to be a member of the Occupational
Safety and Health Review Commission for the
term expiring April 27, 1989, vice Bertram R.
Cottine, term expired.

Henry F. Schickling,
of Pennsylvania, to be a member of the Board of
Directors of the Overseas Private Investment
Corporation for a term expiring December 17,
1985 (new position).

Charles C. Cox,
of Texas, to be a member of the Securities and
Exchange Commission for the term expiring June
5, 1988, vice John R. Evans, term expired.

Susan Wittenberg Liebeler,
of California, to be a member of the United
States International Trade Commission for the remainder of the term expiring December 16,
1988, vice Michael J. Calhoun, resigned.

Submitted September 12

Jack E. Ravan,
of Georgia, to be an Assistant Administrator of
the Environmental Protection Agency, vice Frederic A. Eidsness, Jr., resigned.

Submitted September 12—Continued

Daniel Anthony O'Donohue,
of Virginia, a career member of the Senior Foreign Service, Class of Minister-Counselor, to be Ambassador Extraordinary and Plenipotentiary of the United States of America to the Socialist Republic of the Union of Burma.

Susan E. Phillips,
of Virginia, to be Director of the Institute for Museum Services, vice Lilla Burt Cummings Tower, resigned.

Submitted September 13

Kenneth W. Starr,
of Virginia, to be United States Circuit Judge for the District of Columbia Circuit, vice George E. MacKinnon, retired.

Sherman E. Unger,
of Ohio, to be United States Circuit Judge for the Federal Circuit, vice Robert L. Kunzig, deceased.

John P. Vukasin, Jr.,
of California, to be United States District Judge for the Northern District of California, vice Stanley A. Weigel, retired.

Morton R. Galane,
of Nevada, to be United States District Judge for the District of Nevada, vice Roger D. Foley, retired.

John F. Keenan,
of New York, to be United States District Judge for the Southern District of New York, vice Lloyd F. MacMahon, retired.

Bruce D. Beaudin,
of the District of Columbia, to be an Associate Judge of the Superior Court of the District of Columbia for a term of 15 years, vice John D. Fauntleroy, retired.

Submitted September 14

Maryanne Trump Barry,
of New Jersey, to be United States District Judge for the District of New Jersey, vice H. Curtis Meanor, resigned.

Terry Calvani,
of Tennessee, to be a Federal Trade Commissioner for the term of 7 years from September 26, 1983, vice David A. Clanton, term expiring.

William Lee Hanley, Jr.,
of Connecticut, to be a member of the Board of Directors of the Corporation for Public Broadcasting for a term expiring March 1, 1984, vice Gillian Martin Sorensen, term expired, to which

Submitted September 14—Continued

position he was appointed during the last recess of the Senate.

Katherine D. Ortega,
of New Mexico, to be Treasurer of the United States, vice Angela M. Buchanan, resigned.

Submitted September 15

Linda Chavez Gersten,
of the District of Columbia, to be Staff Director for the Commission on Civil Rights, vice Louis Nunez, resigned, to which position she was appointed during the last recess of the Senate.

Submitted September 19

Nan R. Huhn,
of the District of Columbia, to be an Associate Judge of the Superior Court of the District of Columbia for a term of 15 years, vice David Luke Norman, retired.

Submitted September 20

Terence A. Todman,
of the Virgin Islands, a career member of the Senior Foreign Service, Class of Career Minister, to be Ambassador Extraordinary and Plenipotentiary of the United States of America to Denmark.

Thomas J. Curran,
of Wisconsin, to be United States District Judge for the Eastern District of Wisconsin, vice Myron L. Gordon, retired.

Diane K. Steed,
of the District of Columbia, to be Administrator of the National Highway Traffic Safety Administration, vice Raymond A. Peck, Jr., resigned.

A. James Barnes,
of the District of Columbia, to be an Assistant Administrator of the Environmental Protection Agency (new position—P.L. 98–80 of August 23, 1983).

Josephine S. Cooper,
of Virginia, to be an Assistant Administrator of the Environmental Protection Agency (new position—P.L. 98–80 of August 23, 1983).

John C. Martin,
of Virginia, to be Inspector General, Environmental Protection Agency, vice Matthew Norman Novick, resigned.

Louis Roman DiSabato,
of Texas, to be a member of the National Museum Services Board for a term expiring De-

Submitted September 20—Continued
cember 6, 1987, vice Lloyd Hezekiah, term expired.

Submitted September 26

Reginald Bartholomew,
of Virginia, a career member of the Senior Foreign Service, Class of Minister-Counselor, to be Ambassador Extraordinary and Plenipotentiary of the United States of America to the Republic of Lebanon.

Nicolas M. Salgo,
of Florida, to be Ambassador Extraordinary and Plenipotentiary of the United States of America to Hungary.

Gerald Eustis Thomas,
of California to be Ambassador Extraordinary and Plenipotentiary of the United States of America to the Republic of Kenya.

Clarence J. Brown,
of Ohio, to be Deputy Secretary of Commerce, vice Guy W. Fiske, resigned.

Courtney M. Price,
of the District of Columbia, to be an Assistant Administrator of the Environmental Protection Agency (new position—P.L. 98–80 of August 23, 1983).

Submitted September 27

Nicholas A. Veliotes,
of California, a career member of the Senior Foreign Service, Class of Career Minister, to be Ambassador Extraordinary and Plenipotentiary of the United States of America to the Arab Republic of Egypt.

Submitted September 29

Ronald I. Spiers,
of Vermont, a career member of the Senior Foreign Service, Class of Career Minister, to be Under Secretary of State for Management, vice Jerome W. Van Gorkom.

The following-named persons to be Representatives and Alternate Representatives of the United States of America to the Thirty-eighth Session of the General Assembly of the United Nations:

Representatives:

Jeane J. Kirkpatrick, of Maryland
John Langeloth Loeb, Jr., of New York
Joel Pritchard, United States Representative from the State of Washington
Stephen J. Solarz, United States Representative from the State of New York

Submitted September 29—Continued
Jose S. Sorzano, of Virginia

Alternate Representatives:

Constantine Nicholas Dombalis, of Virginia
Alan Lee Keyes, of California
Charles M. Lichenstein, of the District of Columbia
Lyn P. Meyerhoff, of Maryland
William Courtney Sherman, of Virginia

Hugh W. Foster,
of California, to be United States Alternate Executive Director of the International Bank for Reconstruction and Development for a term of 2 years, vice George R. Hoguet, resigned.

Submitted October 3

Raymond J. O'Connor,
of New York, to be a member of the Federal Energy Regulatory Commission for a term expiring October 20, 1987, vice Charles M. Butler III, term expiring.

Robert H. Morris,
of Maryland, to be Deputy Director of the Federal Emergency Management Agency (new position).

Neal B. Freeman,
of Virginia, to be a member of the Board of Directors of the Communications Satellite Corporation until the date of the annual meeting of the Corporation in 1985, vice Justin Dart, resigned.

Earl Oliver,
of Illinois, to be a member of the Railroad Retirement Board for the term of 5 years from August 29, 1983 (reappointment).

Submitted October 5

Richard W. Murphy,
of Maryland, a career member of the Senior Foreign Service, Class of Career Minister, to be an Assistant Secretary of State, vice Nicholas A. Veliotes, resigned.

Submitted October 6

The following-named persons to be the Representative and Alternate Representatives of the United States of America to the Twenty-seventh Session of the General Conference of the International Atomic Energy Agency:

Representative:

Donald P. Hodel, of Oregon

Submitted October 6—Continued

Alternate Representatives:

Richard T. Kennedy, of the District of Columbia

Nunzio J. Palladino, of Pennsylvania

Richard Salisbury Williamson, of Virginia

Submitted October 7

The following-named persons to be members of the Board of Directors of the Legal Services Corporation for the terms indicated:

For the remainder of the terms expiring July 13, 1984:

Leaanne Bernstein, of Maryland, vice David B. Satterfield III.

Claude Galbreath Swafford, of Tennessee, vice Howard H. Dana, Jr.

Robert A. Valois, of North Carolina, vice William F. Harvey.

For terms expiring July 13, 1986:

William Clark Durant III, of Michigan, vice Frank J. Donatelli, resigned.

Robert Francis Kane, of California, vice Milton M. Masson, Jr., term expired.

Michael B. Wallace, of Mississippi, vice Donald Eugene Santarelli, term expired.

Submitted October 11

Robert E. Lamb,
of Georgia, a career member of the Senior Foreign Service, Class of Minister-Counselor, to be an Assistant Secretary of State, vice Thomas M. Tracy, resigned.

William H. Luers,
of Illinois, a career member of the Senior Foreign Service, Class of Career Minister, to be Ambassador Extraordinary and Plenipotentiary of the United States of America to the Czechoslovak Socialist Republic.

Frank V. Ortiz, Jr.,
of New Mexico, a career member of the Senior Foreign Service, Class of Minister-Counselor, to be Ambassador Extraordinary and Plenipotentiary of the United States of America to Argentina.

T. M. Alexander, Sr.,
of Georgia, to be a member of the Board of Directors of the African Development Foundation for a term of 6 years (new position).

David A. Zegeer,
of Kentucky, to be Assistant Secretary of Labor for Mine Safety and Health, vice Ford Barney Ford.

Ralph Leslie Stanley,
of Virginia, to be Urban Mass Transportation Administrator, vice Arthur E. Teele, Jr., resigned.

Submitted October 11—Continued

Susan Meredith Phillips,
of Iowa, to be Chairman of the Commodity Futures Trading Commission, vice Philip F. Johnson, resigned.

Robert Michael Isaac,
of Colorado, to be a member of the Board of Trustees of the Harry S. Truman Scholarship Foundation for a term expiring December 10, 1987, vice Richard A. King, term expired.

Submitted October 14

Daniel J. Horgan,
of Florida, to be United States Marshal for the Southern District of Florida for the term of 4 years, vice Carlos C. Cruz.

Submitted October 18

Thomas P. Shoesmith,
of Virginia, a career member of the Senior Foreign Service, Class of Career Minister, to be Ambassador Extraordinary and Plenipotentiary of the United States of America to Malaysia.

The following-named persons to be members of the Board of Directors of the Inter-American Foundation for the terms indicated, to which positions they were appointed during the recess of the Senate from August 4, 1983, until September 12, 1983:

For the remainder of the term expiring September 20, 1984:

Langhorne A. Motley, of Alaska, vice Thomas O. Enders, resigned.

For a term expiring September 20, 1988:

J. William Middendorf II, of Virginia, vice Marc E. Leland, term expired.

Lewis A. Dunn,
of Virginia, to be an Assistant Director of the United States Arms Control and Disarmament Agency, vice Thomas D. Davies, resigned.

William E. Mayer,
of California, to be an Assistant Secretary of Defense, vice John Howard Moxley III, resigned.

Helmuth A. Merklein,
of Texas, to be an Assistant Secretary of Energy (International Affairs), vice Henry E. Thomas IV, resigned.

John H. Riley,
of Virginia, to be Administrator of the Federal Railroad Administration, vice Robert W. Blanchette, resigned.

Submitted October 18—Continued
Frank J. Donatelli,
of Virginia, to be an Assistant Administrator of the Agency for International Development, vice Francis Stephen Ruddy.

James T. Hackett,
of Virginia, to be a member of the Board of Directors of the Corporation for Public Broadcasting for the remainder of the term expiring March 1, 1984, vice Harry O'Connor, resigned.

Dennis R. Patrick,
of the District of Columbia, to be a member of the Federal Communications Commission for the unexpired term of 7 years from July 1, 1978, vice Anne P. Jones, resigned.

Terry Edward Branstad,
of Iowa, to be a member of the Board of Trustees of the Harry S. Truman Scholarship Foundation for a term expiring December 10, 1987, vice Christopher S. Bond, resigned.

Withdrawn October 18

Morton R. Galane,
of Nevada, to be United States District Judge for the District of Nevada, vice Roger D. Foley, retired, which was sent to the Senate on September 13, 1983.

Submitted October 19

William P. Clark,
of California, to be Secretary of the Interior.

Submitted October 21

James L. Emery,
of New York, to be Administrator of the St. Lawrence Seaway Development Corporation for a term of 7 years, vice David W. Oberlin, term expired.

Submitted October 24

W. Tapley Bennett, Jr.,
of Georgia, a career member of the Senior Foreign Service, Class of Career Minister, to be an Assistant Secretary of State, vice Powell Allen Moore, resigned.

Thomas G. Hull,
of Tennessee, to be United States District Judge for the Eastern District of Tennessee, vice Frank W. Wilson, deceased.

Submitted October 25

James H. Burnley IV,
of North Carolina, to be Deputy Secretary of Transportation, vice Darrell M. Trent, resigned.

Submitted October 25—Continued
Daniel Oliver,
of Connecticut, to be General Counsel of the Department of Agriculture, vice A. James Barnes.

William Louis Mills,
of Tennessee, to be a member of the Council on Environmental Quality, vice W. Ernst Minor, resigned.

Harry O'Connor,
of California, to be a member of the Board of Directors of the Corporation for Public Broadcasting for the remainder of the term expiring March 26, 1986, vice Diana Lady Dougan, resigned.

Submitted October 27

Charles H. Price II,
of Missouri, to be Ambassador Extraordinary and Plenipotentiary of the United States of America to the United Kingdom of Great Britain and Northern Ireland.

Submitted October 31

Diego C. Asencio,
of Florida, a career member of the Senior Foreign Service, Class of Career Minister, to be Ambassador Extraordinary and Plenipotentiary of the United States of America to Brazil.

Edmund Stohr,
of Illinois, for the rank of Minister during the remainder of his service as the Representative of the United States of America on the Council of the International Civil Aviation Organization.

Lenore Carrero Nesbitt,
of Florida, to be United States District Judge for the Southern District of Florida, vice C. Clyde Atkins, retired.

Mari Maseng,
of South Carolina, to be an Assistant Secretary of Transportation, vice Lee L. Verstandig, resigned.

Kenneth S. George,
of Texas, to be Director General of the United States and Foreign Commercial Services (new position—Public Law 97–377 of December 21, 1982).

Thomas F. Moakley,
of Virginia, to be a Federal Maritime Commissioner for the term expiring June 30, 1988 (reappointment).

The following-named persons to be Commissioners of the United States Parole Commission for

Submitted October 31—Continued

terms of 6 years:

Helen G. Corrothers, of Arkansas, vice Robert D. Vincent, resigned.

Vincent Fechtel, Jr., of Florida, vice Audrey A. Kaslow, term expiring.

Paula A. Tennant, of California, vice Cecil M. McCall, term expiring.

Submitted November 1

W. Eugene Davis,
of Louisiana, to be United States Circuit Judge for the Fifth Circuit, vice Robert A. Ainsworth, deceased.

Stanley S. Harris,
of Maryland, to be United States District Judge for the District of Columbia, vice John Lewis Smith, Jr., retired.

G. Kendall Sharp,
of Florida, to be United States District Judge for the Middle District of Florida, vice Ben Krentzman, retired.

George E. Woods,
of Michigan, to be United States District Judge for the Eastern District of Michigan, vice Patricia J. Boyle, resigned.

Joseph E. diGenova,
of the District of Columbia, to be United States Attorney for the District of Columbia for the term of 4 years, vice Stanley S. Harris.

Submitted November 3

Jane A. Restani,
of Virginia, to be a Judge of the United States Court of International Trade, vice Herbert N. Maletz, retired.

Submitted November 4

Joan M. Clark,
of New York, a career member of the Senior Foreign Service, Class of Career Minister, to be Assistant Secretary of State for Consular Affairs, vice Diego C. Asencio.

James E. Goodby,
of New Hampshire, a career member of the Senior Foreign Service, Class of Minister-Counselor, for the rank of Ambassador during the tenure of his service as United States Representative to the Conference on Confidence on Security Building Measures and Disarmament in Europe.

Sol Polansky,
of the District of Columbia, a career member of the Senior Foreign Service, Class of Minister-

Submitted November 4—Continued

Counselor, for the rank of Ambassador during his tenure of service as Vice Chairman of the United States Delegation to the Strategic Arms Reductions Talks (START) and Department of State Representative.

A. C. Arterbery,
of California, to be a member of the Board of Directors of the African Development Foundation for a term of 6 years (new position).

Joseph A. Cannon,
of Virginia, to be an Assistant Administrator of the Environmental Protection Agency, vice Kathleen M. Bennett, resigned.

William E. Seale,
of Virginia, to be a Commissioner of the Commodity Futures Trading Commission for the term expiring April 13, 1988, vice James M. Stone, term expired.

Samuel W. Speck, Jr.,
of Ohio, to be an Associate Director of the Federal Emergency Management Agency, vice Lee M. Thomas.

Mary Kate Bush,
of New York, to be United States Alternate Executive Director of the International Monetary Fund for a term of 2 years, vice Charles H. Dallara, resigned.

Francis X. Lilly,
of Maryland, to be Solicitor for the Department of Labor, vice T. Timothy Ryan, Jr., resigned.

Submitted November 7

Alfred L. Atherton, Jr.,
of Florida, a career member of the Senior Foreign Service, with the personal rank of Career Ambassador, to be Director General of the Foreign Service, vice Joan M. Clark, resigned.

Donna F. Tuttle,
of California, to be Under Secretary of Commerce for Travel and Tourism, vice Peter McCoy, resigned.

Richard M. Scaife,
of Pennsylvania, to be a member of the United States Advisory Commission on Public Diplomacy for a term expiring July 1, 1985, vice Mae Sue Talley, term expired.

Submitted November 8

Geoffrey Swaebe,
of California, to be Ambassador Extraordinary and Plenipotentiary of the United States of America to Belgium.

Frank Henry Habicht II,
of the District of Columbia, to be an Assistant Attorney General, vice Carol E. Dinkins, resigned.

Elizabeth V. Hallanan,
of West Virginia, to be United States District Judge for the Southern District of West Virginia, vice Dennis R. Knapp, retired.

Vernon L. Grose,
of California, to be a member of the National Transportation Safety Board for the term expiring December 31, 1987, vice Francis H. McAdams, term expired.

William Caldwell Harrop,
of New Jersey, a career member of the Senior Foreign Service, Class of Career Minister, to be Inspector General of the Department of State and the Foreign Service, vice Robert L. Brown, resigned.

The following-named persons to be members of the Board of Directors of the Legal Services Corporation for the terms indicated:

For the remainder of the term expiring July 13, 1984:

Paul B. Eaglin, of North Carolina, vice Robert Sherwood Stubbs II.

For a term expiring July 13, 1986:

Pepe J. Mendez, of Colorado, vice Robert E. McCarthy, term expired.

Submitted November 10

James Harvie Wilkinson III,
of Virginia, to be United States Circuit Judge for the Fourth Circuit, vice John D. Butzner, Jr., retired.

John R. Hargrove,
of Maryland, to be United States District Judge for the District of Maryland, vice Shirley B. Jones, resigned.

Submitted November 14

Bernard D. Goldstein,
of New Jersey, to be an Assistant Administrator of the Environmental Protection Agency, vice Stephen John Gage.

Submitted November 14—Continued
John Arthur Moore,
of North Carolina, to be Assistant Administrator for Toxic Substances of the Environmental Protection Agency, vice John A. Todhunter, resigned.

Milton Russell,
of the District of Columbia, to be an Assistant Administrator of the Environmental Protection Agency, vice Lee L. Verstandig.

Submitted November 15

Deane Roesch Hinton,
of Illinois, a career member of the Senior Foreign Service, Class of Career Minister, to be Ambassador Extraordinary and Plenipotentiary of the United States of America to the Islamic Republic of Pakistan.

Harold K. Phillips,
of California, to be a member of the Board of Directors of the Inter-American Foundation for a term expiring September 20, 1988, vice Alberto Ibarguen, term expired.

Submitted November 16

Michael Ira Burch,
of Florida, to be an Assistant Secretary of Defense, vice Henry E. Catto, Jr., resigned.

Stephanie Lee-Miller,
of the District of Columbia, to be an Assistant Secretary of Health and Human Services, vice Pamela Needham Bailey.

John G. Keane,
of Illinois, to be Director of the Census, vice Bruce Chapman.

James G. Stearns,
of Nevada, to be a Director of the Securities Investor Protection Corporation for a term expiring December 31, 1985 (reappointment).

Richard D. Erb,
of Virginia, to be United States Executive Director of the International Monetary Fund for a term of 2 years (reappointment).

Francis Carter Coleman,
of Florida, to be a member of the Board of Regents of the Uniformed Services University of the Health Sciences for the term expiring May 1, 1989 (reappointment).

Mary A. Grigsby,
of Texas, to be a member of the Federal Home Loan Bank Board for the remainder of the term

expiring June 30, 1986, vice James Jay Jackson, resigned.

Maurice Lee Barksdale,
of Texas, to be an Assistant Secretary of Housing and Urban Development, vice Philip Abrams.

Submitted November 17

William Evans,
of California, to be a member of the Marine Mammal Commission for the term expiring May 13, 1985, vice James C. Nofziger, term expired.

Richard Thomas Montoya,
of Texas, to be an Assistant Secretary of the Interior, vice Pedro A. Sanjuan, resigned.

Leslie Lenkowsky,
of New York, to be Deputy Director of the United States Information Agency, vice Gilbert A. Robinson, resigned.

Submitted November 18

The following-named persons to be Representatives and Alternate Representatives of the United States of America to the Twenty-second Session of the General Conference of the United Nations Educational, Scientific, and Cultural Organization:

Representatives:

Jean Broward Shevlin Gerard, of New York
Tirso Del Junco, of California
Helen Marie Taylor, of Virginia
Charles Z. Wick, of California

Submitted November 18—Continued
Alternate Representatives:

Elliott Abrams, of the District of Columbia
Frederick W. M. Guardabassi, of Florida
Joseph Carlton Petrone, of Iowa

The following-named persons to be members of the National Council on the Handicapped for terms expiring September 17, 1986:

H. Latham Breunig, of New York (reappointment).
Michael Marge, of New York (reappointment).
Sandra Swift Parrino, of New York (reappointment).
Alvis Kent Waldrep, Jr., of Texas (reappointment).

John A. Bohn, Jr.,
of California, to be First Vice President of the Export-Import Bank of the United States, vice Charles Edwin Lord, resigned.

Simeon Miller Bright,
of West Virginia, to be a Commissioner of the Postal Rate Commission for the term expiring November 22, 1988 (reappointment).

Priscilla L. Buckley,
of Connecticut, to be a member of the United States Advisory Commission on Public Diplomacy for a term expiring July 1, 1986, vice Leonard Silverstein, term expired.

Ruth O. Peters,
of Virginia, to be a Governor of the United States Postal Service for the remainder of the term expiring December 8, 1987, vice Paula D. Hughes,

Appendix C—Checklist of White House Press Releases

The following list contains releases of the Office of the Press Secretary which are not included in this book.

Released July 5

Advance text:
Remarks at the annual convention of the American Federation of Teachers in Los Angeles, Calif.

Statement:
The President's decision to grant import relief to the U.S. specialty steel industry—by Deputy Press Secretary Larry M. Speakes

Transcript:
Press briefing on the import relief program for the specialty steel industry—by Ambassador William E. Brock, United States Trade Representative

Released July 12

Fact sheet:
Proposed fair housing legislation

Transcript:
Press briefing on the proposed fair housing legislation—by William Bradford Reynolds, Assistant Attorney General, Civil Rights Division of the Department of Justice, and John J. Knapp, General Counsel of the Department of Housing and Urban Development

Announcement:
Nomination of Kenneth W. Starr to be United States Circuit Judge for the District of Columbia Circuit

Released July 14

Fact sheet:
Executive Order 12432, minority business enterprise development

Released July 18

Advance text:
Remarks at the 47th quadrennial convention of the International Longshoremen's Association in Hollywood, Fla.

Released July 19

Announcement:
Nomination of Thomas C. Rapone to be United States Marshal for the Eastern District of Pennsylvania and James B. Roche III to be United States Marshal for the District of Massachusetts

Released July 20

Announcement:
Nomination of Morton R. Galane to be United States District Judge for the District of Nevada and John F. Keenan to be United States District Judge for the Southern District of New York

Released July 21

Transcript:
Press briefing on his meeting with the President to discuss the Intermediate-range Nuclear Force negotiations in Geneva, Switzerland—by Ambassador Paul H. Nitze, U.S. Representative to the negotiations

Released July 22

Transcript:
Press briefing on his appointment as the President's Personal Representative in the Middle East—by Robert C. McFarlane, Deputy Assistant to the President for National Security Affairs

Released July 28

Advance text:
Remarks on signing Executive Order 12435, establishing the President's Commission on Organized Crime

Fact sheet:
President's Commission on Organized Crime

Transcript:
Press briefing on the President's Commission on Organized Crime—by Attorney General William French Smith, William H. Webster, Director of the Federal Bureau of Investigation, and Judge Irving R. Kaufman, Chairman-designate of the Commission

Transcript:
Press briefing on a United States-Soviet Union long-term grain sales agreement—by Ambassador

Released July 28—Continued
William E. Brock, United States Trade Representative, and Secretary of Agriculture John R. Block

Advance text:
Remarks at a White House reception for members of the National Council of Negro Women

Released July 29

Transcript:
Press briefing on Labor Department release of figures on business sector output, productivity, and average labor cost of production—by Martin S. Feldstein, Chairman of the Council of Economic Advisers

Released August 1

Advance text:
Remarks at the annual meeting of the American Bar Association in Atlanta, Ga.

Released August 2

Fact sheet:
Proposed management improvement initiatives

Released August 5

Statement:
Round four of the strategic arms reduction talks (as read by Ambassador Edward L. Rowny, Special Representative for Negotiations, U.S. Arms Control and Disarmament Agency, at his press briefing)

Transcript:
Press briefing on his meeting with the President to discuss round four of the strategic arms reduction talks—by Ambassador Edward L. Rowny, Special Representative for Negotiations, U.S. Arms Control and Disarmament Agency

Released August 12

Advance text:
Remarks at the annual convention of the United States Hispanic Chamber of Commerce in Tampa, Fla.

Released August 13

Advance text:
Remarks at the 35th annual convention of the American G.I. Forum in El Paso, Tex.

Transcript:
Press briefing on the establishment of an interagency action group to implement recommendations of the Southwestern Border States Working Group—by Assistant to the President for Cabinet Affairs Craig L. Fuller

Released August 13—Continued
Fact sheet:
Federal initiatives in the Southwest border region

Released August 14

Transcript:
Press briefing on the meeting between President Reagan and President Miguel de la Madrid Hurtado of Mexico—by Secretary of State George P. Shultz and Mexican Secretary of Foreign Relations Bernardo Sepúlveda Amor

Released August 15

Advance text:
Remarks at the 84th annual convention of the Veterans of Foreign Wars in New Orleans, La.

Released August 23

Excerpts:
Text of remarks at the 65th annual national convention of the American Legion in Seattle, Wash.

Advance text:
Remarks at the 65th annual national convention of the American Legion in Seattle, Wash.

Released August 25

Excerpts:
Text of remarks at the Hispanic Economic Outlook Preview luncheon in Los Angeles, Calif.

Advance text:
Remarks at the Hispanic Economic Outlook Preview luncheon in Los Angeles, Calif.

Released August 26

Excerpts:
Text of remarks at the Republican Women's Leadership Forum in San Diego, Calif.

Advance text:
Remarks at the Republican Women's Leadership Forum in San Diego, Calif.

Released August 31

Fact sheet:
Federal employee pay increase

Released September 3

Transcript:
Press briefing following his meeting with the President—by Ambassador Paul H. Nitze, U.S. Representative to the Intermediate-range Nuclear Force negotiations in Geneva, Switzerland

Released September 3—Continued
Statement:
On the Intermediate-range Nuclear Force negotiations—by Ambassador Paul H. Nitze, U.S. Representative to the negotiations in Geneva, Switzerland

Released September 5

Advance text:
Address to the Nation on the Soviet attack on Korean Air Lines Flight 007

Fact sheet:
Address to the Nation on the Soviet attack on Korean Air Lines Flight 007

Fact sheet:
U.S.-U.S.S.R. agreement on cooperation in the field of transportation

Excerpts:
Radio transmissions of two Soviet pilots who participated in the attack on Korean Air Lines Flight 007

Released September 7

Fact sheet:
Proposed adult literacy initiative

Released September 8

Statement:
The President's meeting with the Cabinet Council on Legal Policy to review the third quarterly report of the Attorney General prepared pursuant to Executive Order 12336 of December 21, 1981, concerning gender-based distinction in Federal statutes

Transcript:
Press briefing on the President's meeting with the Cabinet Council on Legal Policy to review the third quarterly report of the Attorney General concerning gender-based distinction in Federal statutes—by Deputy Press Secretary Larry M. Speakes and William B. Reynolds, Assistant Secretary of Justice for Civil Rights

Released September 9

Announcement:
Nomination of Martin L. C. Feldman to be United States District Judge for the Eastern District of Louisiana and C. Roger Vinson to be United States District Judge for the Northern District of Florida

Released September 12

Advance text:
Remarks to the National Association of Towns and Townships

Fact sheet:
Proposed national productivity and innovation legislation

Released September 13

Fact sheet:
Presidential Awards for Excellence in Science and Mathematics Teaching

Released September 14

Announcement:
Nomination of Maryanne Trump Barry to be United States District Judge for the District of New Jersey

Transcript:
Press briefing on the meeting of the International Civil Aviation Organization to be held in Montreal, Canada, on September 15, concerning the Soviet attack on Korean Air Lines Flight 007—by Secretary of Transportation Elizabeth H. Dole, J. Lynn Helms, Administrator, and Donald R. Segner, Associate Administrator for Policy and International Aviation, Federal Aviation Administration

Advance text:
Remarks at the Republican National Hispanic Assembly fundraising dinner

Released September 19

Announcement:
Nomination of Nan R. Huhn to be an Associate Judge of the Superior Court of the District of Columbia

Released September 20

Advance text:
Remarks to the students and faculty of the University of South Carolina in Columbia

Advance text:
Remarks at a fundraising dinner for Senator Strom Thurmond of South Carolina in Columbia

Announcement:
Nomination of Thomas J. Curran to be United States District Judge for the Eastern District of Wisconsin

Released September 22

Advance text:
Remarks at the White House Conference on Productivity

Released September 25

Transcript:
Press briefing on the President's meetings throughout the day with foreign leaders and on the cease-fire in Lebanon—by Secretary of State George P. Shultz

Released September 26

Transcript:
Press briefing on the cease-fire in Lebanon—by Secretary of State George P. Shultz

Advance text:
Address to the 38th Session of the United Nations General Assembly in New York, N.Y.

Fact sheet:
Address to the 38th Session of the United Nations General Assembly in New York, N.Y.

Transcript:
Press briefing on foreign policy issues and the President's meetings with foreign leaders throughout the day—by Secretary of State George P. Shultz

Fact sheet:
Challenge Grant Amendments of 1983

Released September 27

Advance text:
Remarks at the annual meetings of the Board of Governors of the World Bank and the International Monetary Fund

Released September 28

Transcript:
Press briefing on the President's decision to reduce interest rates on natural disaster emergency loans for eligible farmers in drought-stricken areas of the country—by Secretary of Agriculture John R. Block

Released September 29

Transcript:
Press briefing on the proposed pension equity legislation—by Nancy J. Risque, Special Assistant to the President for Legislative Affairs and Deputy Director of Legislative Affairs, and Daniel Benjamin, Acting Assistant Secretary for Policy, Department of Labor

Released September 29—Continued
Fact sheet:
Proposed pension equity legislation

Released October 3

Advance text:
Remarks at a dinner marking the 10th anniversary of the Heritage Foundation

Released October 4

Advance text:
Remarks announcing new U.S. initiatives in the strategic arms reduction talks

Fact sheet:
New U.S. initiatives in the strategic arms reduction talks

Transcript:
Press briefing on the 1983 National Energy Policy Plan—by Secretary of Energy Donald Paul Hodel

Released October 5

Advance text:
Remarks at a ceremony marking the beginning of the job training partnership program

Released October 6

Transcript:
Remarks at the barbecue on the South Grounds of the White House for Members of Congress

Released October 7

Advance text:
Remarks at the 22d biennial convention of the National Federation of Republican Women

Released October 13

Statement:
On the increase in retail sales—by Deputy Press Secretary Larry M. Speakes

Statement:
On his nomination to be Secretary of the Interior—by Assistant to the President for National Security Affairs William P. Clark

Released October 14

Statement:
On the increase in industrial production—by Deputy Press Secretary Larry M. Speakes

Released October 14—Continued

Announcement:
Nomination of Daniel J. Horgan to be United States Marshal for the Southern District of Florida

Released October 18

Statement:
Deployment of Soviet short- and medium-range missiles—by Deputy Press Secretary Larry M. Speakes

Statement:
Research and development in ballistic missile defense—by Deputy Press Secretary Larry M. Speakes

Released October 19

Advance text:
Remarks at a celebration marking the 25th anniversary of the National Aeronautics and Space Administration

Released October 20

Statement:
Gross national product figures for the third quarter—by the Deputy Press Secretary Larry M. Speakes

Statement:
Meeting of the Cabinet Council on Commerce and Trade to discuss broadcast syndication rules—by Deputy Press Secretary Larry M. Speakes

Released October 24

Announcement:
Nomination of Thomas G. Hull to be United States District Judge for the Eastern District of Tennessee

Transcript:
Press briefing following their meeting with the President to discuss issues of concern to women—by Representatives Bobbi Fiedler of California, Olympia J. Snowe of Maine, Barber B. Conable, Jr., of New York, and Lynn Martin of Illinois

Fact sheet:
Tax equity for women

Released October 25

Statement:
Consumer Price Index figures for September—by Deputy Press Secretary Larry M. Speakes

Released October 27

Text:
Telex received by the President supporting U.S. action in Grenada from students of St. George's University School of Medicine at Kingston Medical College, St. Vincent

Advance text:
Address to the Nation on events in Lebanon and Grenada

Released October 28

Statement:
Index of leading economic indicators for September—by Deputy Press Secretary Larry M. Speakes

Announcement:
Nomination of Lenore Carrero Nesbitt to be United States District Judge for the Southern District of Florida

Released October 29

Advance text:
Radio address to the Nation on nuclear weapons

Released October 31

Announcement:
Nomination of W. Eugene Davis to be United States Circuit Judge for the Fifth Circuit

Announcement:
Nomination of Stanley S. Harris to be United States District Judge for the District of Columbia, G. Kendall Sharp to be United States District Judge for the Middle District of Florida, and George E. Woods to be United States District Judge for the Eastern District of Michigan

Released November 1

Announcement:
Nomination of Joseph E. diGenova to be United States Attorney for the District of Columbia

Released November 2

Announcement:
Nomination of Jane A. Restani to be a Judge of the United States Court of International Trade

Released November 3

Statement:
United Nations General Assembly resolution on U.S. action in Grenada—by Deputy Press Secretary Larry M. Speakes

Released November 3—Continued

Transcript:
Press briefing on the President's trip to Japan and the Republic of Korea—by Secretary of State George P. Shultz

Advance text:
Remarks at the Reagan-Bush campaign reunion

Released November 4

Excerpts:
Remarks to military personnel at Cherry Point, N.C., on the U.S. casualties in Lebanon and Grenada

Advance text:
Remarks to military personnel at Cherry Point, N.C., on the U.S. casualties in Lebanon and Grenada

Released November 8

Advance text:
Remarks on departure for the trip to Japan and the Republic of Korea

Announcement:
Nomination of Elizabeth V. Hallanan to be United States District Judge for the Southern District of West Virginia

Released November 10

Advance text:
Toast at a luncheon hosted by Prime Minister Yasuhiro Nakasone of Japan in Tokyo

Transcript:
Press briefing on the joint U.S.-Japanese statement on the yen-dollar exchange rate—by Deputy Secretary of the Treasury R. T. McNamar

Advance text:
Remarks at a reception for American and Japanese businessmen in Tokyo

Advance text:
Toast at the imperial banquet hosted by Emperor Hirohito of Japan in Tokyo

Statement:
Producer Price Index figures for October—by Deputy Press Secretary Larry M. Speakes

Released November 11

Advance text:
Address before the Japanese Diet in Tokyo

Transcript:
Press briefing on the President's visit to Japan—by Secretary of State George P. Shultz

Released November 11—Continued

Announcement:
Nomination of John R. Hargrove to be United States District Judge for the District of Maryland

Announcement:
Nomination of James Harvie Wilkinson III to be United States Circuit Judge for the Fourth Circuit

Released November 12

Advance text:
Remarks on arrival in Seoul, Republic of Korea

Advance text:
Address before the Korean National Assembly in Seoul

Advance text:
Remarks at a reception for Korean community leaders in Seoul

Advance text:
Toast at the state dinner hosted by President Chun Doo Hwan of Korea in Seoul

Released November 13

Advance text:
Remarks to U.S. troops at Camp Liberty Bell, Republic of Korea

Transcript:
Press briefing on the President's visit to the Republic of Korea—by Secretary of State George P. Shultz

Released November 14

Statement:
The President's trip to Japan and the Republic of Korea (as read by the President on returning to the White House)

Released November 16

Transcript:
Press briefing on their meeting with the President to discuss enterprise zones legislation—by Mayors George Voinovich of Cleveland, Ohio; John Smith of Prichard, Ala.; and Vincent Schoemehl of St. Louis, Mo.; and Councilman Michael Lyons of Norwalk, Conn.

Released November 23

Announcement:
Information on the heart surgery performed on Ahn Ji Sook, the 7-year-old Korean girl who accompanied the President on his return from the Republic of Korea

Released December 5

Transcript:
Press briefing on the mission of the space shuttle *Columbia* and the Spacelab—by James M. Beggs, Administrator of the National Aeronautics and Space Administration, and Erik Quistgaard, director general of the European Space Agency

Released December 6

Transcript:
Press briefing on his meeting with the President—by Prime Minister Kennedy Alphonse Simmonds of St. Christopher-Nevis

Released December 7

Transcript:
Remarks to reporters concerning the 20th anniversary of Connie Gerrard Romero as a member of the White House Press Office staff—by Deputy Press Secretary Larry M. Speakes

Released December 8

Advance text:
Remarks at the National Forum on Excellence in Education in Indianapolis, Ind.

Released December 8—Continued
Advance text:
Remarks at a reception sponsored by the American Enterprise Institute for Public Policy Research

Released December 12

Advance text:
Remarks at the annual convention of the Congressional Medal of Honor Society in New York, N.Y.

Released December 14

Transcript:
Remarks and a question-and-answer session on foreign policy issues ,with editors of Gannett newspapers—by Secretary of State George P. Shultz

Released December 16

Statement:
U.S. textile trade policy and procedures—by Deputy Press Secretary Larry M. Speakes

Appendix D—Acts Approved by the President

Approved June 27

S. 639 / Public Law 98–43
Lebanon Emergency Assistance Act of 1983.

Approved July 12

S. 925 / Public Law 98–44
An act to make certain technical corrections in the Atlantic Salmon Convention Act of 1982.

H.R. 3133 / Public Law 98–45
Department of Housing and Urban Development-Independent Agencies Appropriation Act, 1984.

S. 680 / Public Law 98–46
An act entitled the "Gladys Noon Spellman Dedication".

Approved July 13

S. 273 / Public Law 98–47
An act to amend section 8(a) of the Small Business Act.

H.R. 1746 / Public Law 98–48
An act to authorize appropriations for the Navajo and Hopi Indian Relocation Commission.

H.R. 2713 / Public Law 98–49
An act to amend the Public Health Service Act to authorize appropriations to be made available to the Secretary of Health and Human Services for research for the cause, treatment, and prevention of public health emergencies.

Approved July 14

H.R. 3132 / Public Law 98–50
Energy and Water Development Appropriation Act, 1984.

H.R. 3135 / Public Law 98–51
An act making appropriations for the Legislative Branch for the fiscal year ending September 30, 1984, and for other purposes.

Approved July 15

H.R. 2065 / Public Law 98–52
National Aeronautics and Space Administration Authorization Act, 1984.

Approved July 15—Continued
H.R. 1271 / Public Law 98–53
An act with regard to Presidential certifications on conditions in El Salvador.

S.J. Res. 68 / Public Law 98–54
A joint resolution to authorize and request the President to designate July 16, 1983, as "National Atomic Veterans' Day".

Approved July 19

S.J. Res. 18 / Public Law 98–55
A joint resolution designating September 22, 1983, as "American Business Women's Day".

S.J. Res. 34 / Public Law 98–56
A joint resolution designating "National Reye's Syndrome Week".

Approved July 22

S. 929 / Public Law 98–57
An act to amend the Act of July 2, 1940, as amended, pertaining to appropriations for the Canal Zone Biological Area.

Approved July 25

S.J. Res. 96 / Public Law 98–58
A joint resolution to designate August 1, 1983, as "Helsinki Human Rights Day".

H.R. 3392 / Public Law 98–59
An act to amend the Agricultural Act of 1949.

Approved July 27

S.J. Res. 77 / Public Law 98–60
A joint resolution designating "National Animal Agriculture Week".

Approved July 28

S. 459 / Public Law 98–61
An act to authorize and direct the Secretary of the Interior to convey, by quitclaim deed, all right, title, and interest of the United States in and to certain lands that were withdrawn or acquired for the purpose of relocating a portion of the city of American Falls out of the area flooded by the American Falls Reservoir.

Appendix D

Approved July 29

H.J. Res. 258 / Public Law 98–62
A joint resolution designating August 3, 1983, as "National Paralyzed Veterans Recognition Day".

Approved July 30

H.R. 3069 / Public Law 98–63
Supplemental Appropriations Act, 1983.

Approved August 2

S. 419 / Public Law 98–64
An act to provide that per capita payments to Indians may be made by tribal governments, and for other purposes.

H.R. 2637 / Public Law 98–65
An act to amend the District of Columbia Self-Government and Governmental Reorganization Act to increase the amount authorized to be appropriated as the annual Federal payment to the District of Columbia.

Approved August 4

H.R. 1935 / Public Law 98–66
An act to ratify an exchange agreement concerning National Wildlife Refuge System lands located on Matagorda Island in Texas.

Approved August 5

H.R. 2973 / Public Law 98–67
An act to promote economic revitalization and facilitate expansion of economic opportunities in the Caribbean Basin region, to provide for backup withholding of tax from interest and dividends, and for other purposes.

S.J. Res. 56 / Public Law 98–68
A joint resolution to designate the month of August 1983 as "National Child Support Enforcement Month".

Approved August 8

S.J. Res. 67 / Public Law 98–69
A joint resolution to designate the week of September 25, 1983, through October 1, 1983, as "National Respiratory Therapy Week".

S. 143 / Public Law 98–70
An act to authorize the Twenty-nine Palms Band of Luiseno Mission Indians and the Confederated Salish and Kootenai Tribes of the Flathead Reservation to lease for ninety-nine years certain lands held in trust.

Approved August 11

H.J. Res. 139 / Public Law 98–71
A joint resolution to designate the week beginning June 24, 1984, as "Federal Credit Union Week".

S. 272 / Public Law 98–72
An act to improve small business access to Federal procurement information.

S. 930 / Public Law 98–73
An act to authorize the Smithsonian Institution to purchase land in Santa Cruz County, Arizona.

S. 727 / Public Law 98–74
An act to authorize the Secretary of the Interior to set aside certain judgment funds of the Three Affiliated Tribes of Fort Berthold Reservation in North Dakota, and for other purposes.

H.J. Res. 321 / Public Law 98–75
A joint resolution to proclaim a day of national celebration of the two hundredth anniversary of the signing of the Treaty of Paris.

Approved August 12

H.R. 1646 / Public Law 98–76
Railroad Retirement Solvency Act of 1983.

Approved August 15

H.R. 2355 / Public Law 98–77
Emergency Veterans' Job Training Act of 1983.

H.R. 3329 / Public Law 98–78
Department of Transportation and Related Agencies Appropriations Act, 1984.

H.R. 3394 / Public Law 98–79
Student Loan Consolidation and Technical Amendments Act of 1983.

Approved August 23

S. 1696 / Public Law 98–80
An act authorizing three additional Assistant Administrators of the Environmental Protection Agency.

S. 1797 / Public Law 98–81
An act to name the United States Post Office Building to be constructed in Fort Worth, Texas, as the "Jack D. Watson Post Office Building".

S.J. Res. 85 / Public Law 98–82
A joint resolution to designate September 26, 1983, as "National Historically Black Colleges Day".

Approved August 23—Continued

S.J. Res. 98 / Public Law 98–83
A joint resolution to designate October 2 through October 9, 1983, as "National Housing Week".

S.J. Res. 116 / Public Law 98–84
A joint resolution to designate the week of September 4, 1983, through September 10, 1983, as "Youth of America Week".

Approved August 26

H.R. 2895 / Public Law 98–85
An act to designate the Federal Building and United States Courthouse at 450 Golden Gate Avenue, San Francisco, California, as the Phillip Burton Federal Building and United States Courthouse.

H.R. 3232 / Public Law 98–86
An act to amend title 28 of the United States Code to authorize payment of travel and transportation expenses of newly appointed special agents of the Department of Justice.

H.J. Res. 297 / Public Law 98–87
A joint resolution providing for appointment of Jeannine Smith Clark as a citizen regent of the Board of Regents of the Smithsonian Institution.

H.R. 3190 / Public Law 98–88
Extra Long Staple Cotton Act of 1983.

S. 46 / Public Law 98–89
An act to revise, consolidate, and enact certain laws related to vessels and seamen as subtitle II of title 46, United States Code, "Shipping".

H.R. 1372 / Private Law 98–1
An act to provide for the operation of certain foreign-built vessels in the coastwise trade of Alaska.

Approved August 29

H.R. 3677 / Public Law 98–90
An act to amend title XVIII of the Social Security Act to increase the cap amount allowable for reimbursement of hospices under the medicare program.

Approved August 30

H.R. 3549 / Public Law 98–91
An act to amend the Bankruptcy Rules with respect to providing notice.

Approved September 2

H.R. 3409 / Public Law 98–92
An act to amend the Federal Supplemental Compensation Act of 1982 with respect to the number of weeks of benefits paid in any State.

Approved September 20

S.J. Res. 131 / Public Law 98–93
A joint resolution designating "National Cystic Fibrosis Week".

Approved September 24

S. 675 / Public Law 98–94
Department of Defense Authorization Act, 1984.

Approved September 26

S. 1872 / Public Law 98–95
Challenge Grant Amendments of 1983.

Approved September 27

H.J. Res. 132 / Public Law 98–96
A joint resolution designating the week beginning September 25, 1983, as "National Adult Day Care Center Week".

H.J. Res. 218 / Public Law 98–97
A joint resolution to designate the month of September of 1983 as "National Sewing Month".

Approved September 28

H.J. Res. 353 / Public Law 98–98
A joint resolution condemning the Soviet criminal destruction of the Korean civilian airliner.

H.J. Res. 229 / Public Law 98–99
A joint resolution to authorize and request the President to issue a proclamation designating April 22 through April 28, 1984, as "National Organ Donation Awareness Week".

Approved September 29

H.R. 3914 / Public Law 98–100
An act to require the Secretary of Agriculture to make an earlier announcement of the 1984 crop feed grain program and of the 1985 crop wheat and feed grain programs.

S. 118 / Public Law 98–101
An act to provide for the establishment of a Commission on the Bicentennial of the Constitution.

Approved September 30

S.J. Res. 82 / Public Law 98–102
A joint resolution designating November 1983 as "National Alzheimer's Disease Month".

S.J. Res. 119 / Public Law 98–103
A joint resolution to designate the week of December 11, 1983, through December 17, 1983, as "National Drunk and Drugged Driving Awareness Week".

Approved September 30—Continued
S. 1625 / Public Law 98–104
An act to amend the District of Columbia Retirement Reform Act.

S. 1850 / Public Law 98–105
An act to amend title 38, United States Code, to extend for one year the authority of the Veterans' Administration to provide certain contract medical services in Puerto Rico and the Virgin Islands.

Approved October 1

H.J. Res. 284 / Public Law 98–106
A joint resolution commemorating the Twenty-fifth Anniversary of the National Aeronautics and Space Administration.

H.J. Res. 368 / Public Law 98–107
A joint resolution making continuing appropriations for the fiscal year 1984, and for other purposes.

H.R. 3962 / Public Law 98–108
An act to extend the authorities under the Export Administration Act of 1979 until October 14, 1983.

H.J Res. 366 / Public Law 98–109
A joint resolution to provide for the temporary extension of certain insurance programs relating to housing and community development, and for other purposes.

Approved October 3

S.J. Res. 81 / Public Law 98–110
A joint resolution to authorize and request the President to designate October 16, 1983, as "World Food Day".

Approved October 4

S. 602 / Public Law 98–111
Radio Broadcasting to Cuba Act.

S.J. Res. 142 / Public Law 98–112
A joint resolution designating the week of October 3 through October 9, 1983, as "National Productivity Improvement Week".

Approved October 5

S.J. Res. 140 / Public Law 98–113
A joint resolution to provide for the designation of the week of October 2 through October 8, 1983, as "Myasthenia Gravis Awareness Week".

Approved October 7

H.J. Res. 137 / Public Law 98–114
A joint resolution authorizing and requesting the President to issue a proclamation designating the period from October 2, 1983, through October 8, 1983, as "National Schoolbus Safety Week of 1983".

Approved October 11

H.R. 2972 / Public Law 98–115
Military Construction Authorization Act, 1984.

H.R. 3263 / Public Law 98–116
Military Construction Appropriations Act, 1984.

H.R. 3871 / Public Law 98–117
An act to amend the Omnibus Budget Reconciliation Act of 1982 to provide that the figure used in determining hourly rates of pay for Federal employees not be changed before the comparability adjustment in the rates of pay for such employees has been made for fiscal year 1984.

H.R. 4101 / Public Law 98–118
An act to extend the Federal Supplemental Compensation Act of 1982, and for other purposes.

Approved October 12

S.J. Res. 159 / Public Law 98–119
Multinational Force in Lebanon Resolution.

H.R. 3813 / Public Law 98–120
An act to amend the International Coffee Agreement Act of 1980.

S. 1465 / Public Law 98–121
An act to designate the Federal Building at Fourth and Ferry Streets, Lafayette, Indiana, as the "Charles A. Halleck Federal Building".

S. 1724 / Public Law 98–122
An act to designate the Federal Building in Las Cruces, New Mexico, as the "Harold E. Runnels Federal Building".

Approved October 13

S. 884 / Public Law 98–123
An act to provide for the use and distribution of funds awarded the Red Lake Band of Chippewa Indians in docket numbered 15–72 of the United States Court of Claims.

S. 1148 / Public Law 98–124
An act to provide for the use and distribution of funds awarded the Assiniboine Tribe of the Fort Belknap Indian Community, Montana, and the Assiniboine Tribe of the Fort Peck Indian Reservation, Montana, in docket numbered 10–81L by

Approved October 13—Continued
the United States Court of Claims, and for other purposes.

H.R. 3415 / Public Law 98–125
District of Columbia Appropriation Act, 1984.

S.J. Res. 102 / Public Law 98–126
A joint resolution to designate the week of October 16, 1983, through October 22, 1983, as "Lupus Awareness Week".

S. 216 / Public Law 98–127
Federal Anti-Tampering Act.

Approved October 14

H.R. 3379 / Public Law 98–128
An act to name a United States Post Office Building in the vicinity of Lancaster, Pennsylvania, the "Edwin D. Eshleman Post Office Building".

H.R. 2840 / Public Law 98–129
Fur Seal Act Amendments of 1983.

S.J. Res. 128 / Public Law 98–130
A joint resolution to designate the day of October 22, 1983 as "Metropolitan Opera Day".

Approved October 17

H.R. 3835 / Public Law 98–131
An act to designate the United States Post Office Building in Oshkosh, Wisconsin, as the "William A. Steiger Post Office Building".

S. 1894 / Public Law 98–132
An act to designate the Foundation for the Advancement of Military Medicine as the "Henry M. Jackson Foundation for the Advancement of Military Medicine", and for other purposes.

Approved October 18

H.R. 1556 / Public Law 98–133
An act to authorize the conveyance of the Liberty ship John W. Brown.

S. 1499 / Public Law 98–134
Mashantucket Pequot Indian Claims Settlement Act.

Approved October 24

H.R. 3929 / Public Law 98–135
Federal Supplemental Compensation Amendments of 1983.

H.R. 3321 / Public Law 98–136
An act to provide for the striking of medals to commemorate the Louisiana World Exposition.

Approved October 25

Note: The following bill became law over the President's veto of October 19. (See page 1485 of this book.)

H.R. 1062 / Public Law 98–137
An act to authorize the Secretary of the Interior to convey, without consideration, certain lands in Lane County, Oregon.

Approved October 28

H.R. 3044 / Public Law 98–138
An act to grant the consent of the Congress to an interstate agreement or compact relating to the restoration of Atlantic Salmon in the Connecticut River Basin, and to allow the Secretary of Commerce and the Secretary of the Interior to participate as members in a Connecticut River Atlantic Salmon Commission.

Approved October 31

H.R. 3913 / Public Law 98–139
Departments of Labor, Health and Human Services, and Education, and Related Agencies Appropriation Act, 1984.

S. 96 / Public Law 98–140
Lee Metcalf Wilderness and Management Act of 1983.

H.R. 1213 / Public Law 98–141
Public Lands and National Parks Act of 1983.

Approved November 1

S.J. Res. 57 / Public Law 98–142
A joint resolution to designate the week of November 2, 1983 through November 9, 1983, as "National Drug Abuse Education Week".

S.J. Res. 189 / Public Law 98–143
A joint resolution extending the expiration date of the Export-Import Bank Act of 1945.

Approved November 2

H.R. 3706 / Public Law 98–144
An act to amend title 5, United States Code, to make the birthday of Martin Luther King, Jr., a legal public holiday.

H.R. 730 / Private Law 98–2
An act for the relief of Ronald Goldstock and Augustus M. Statham.

H.R. 732 / Private Law 98–3
An act for the relief of Gregory B. Dymond, Samuel K. Gibbons, Jack C. Kean, James D. Nichols, and Roy A. Redmond.

Approved November 2—Continued
H.R. 745 / Private Law 98–4
An act for the relief of Stephen C. Ruks.

Approved November 3

S.J. Res. 121 / Public Law 98–145
A joint resolution to designate November 1983 as National Diabetes Month.

Approved November 4

H.R. 3363 / Public Law 98–146
An act making appropriations for the Department of the Interior and related agencies for the fiscal year ending September 30, 1984, and for other purposes.

S.J. Res. 45 / Public Law 98–147
A joint resolution designating the week of November 20, 1983, through November 26, 1983, as "National Family Week".

Approved November 7

S. 552 / Public Law 98–148
An act to designate the Federal Building in Fort Myers, Florida, as the "George W. Whitehurst Federal Building and United States Courthouse".

S. 1944 / Public Law 98–149
An act to allow the obsolete submarine United States ship Albacore to be transferred to the Portsmouth Submarine Memorial Association, Incorporated, before the expiration of the otherwise applicable sixty-day congressional review period.

Approved November 11

S. 461 / Public Law 98–150
An act to amend the Ethics in Government Act of 1978 to make certain changes in the authority of the Office of Government Ethics, and for other purposes.

Approved November 14

H.J. Res. 413 / Public Law 98–151
A joint resolution making further continuing appropriations for the fiscal year 1984.

Approved November 15

H.J. Res. 283 / Public Law 98–152
A joint resolution designating the week beginning November 6, 1983, as "National Disabled Veterans Week".

S.J. Res. 122 / Public Law 98–153
A joint resolution to designate the week of November 27, 1983, through December 3, 1983, as "National Home Care Week".

Approved November 16

S.J. Res. 188 / Public Law 98–154
A joint resolution to designate the month of November 1983 as "National Christmas Seal Month".

H.J. Res. 408 / Public Law 98–155
A joint resolution designating November 12, 1983, as "Anti-Defamation League Day" in honor of the league's seventieth anniversary.

Approved November 17

H.J. Res. 383 / Public Law 98–156
A joint resolution to designate the week beginning November 6, 1983, as "Florence Crittenton Mission Week".

S. 448 / Public Law 98–157
An act to authorize rehabilitation of the Belle Fourche irrigation project, and for other purposes.

S.J. Res. 92 / Public Law 98–158
A joint resolution designating the week beginning May 13, 1984, as "Municipal Clerk's Week".

Approved November 18

H.R. 3348 / Public Law 98–159
An act to honor Congressman Leo J. Ryan and to award a special congressional gold medal to the family of the late Honorable Leo J. Ryan.

Approved November 21

H.R. 2920 / Public Law 98–160
Veterans' Health Care Amendments of 1983.

H.J. Res. 308 / Public Law 98–161
A joint resolution increasing the statutory limit on the public debt.

S.J. Res. 139 / Public Law 98–162
A joint resolution to commemorate the centennial of Eleanor Roosevelt's birth.

Approved November 22

H.R. 2910 / Public Law 98–163
An act to amend the Act of November 2, 1966, regarding leases and contracts affecting land within the Salt River Pima-Maricopa Indian Reservation.

H.R. 2915 / Public Law 98–164
An act to authorize appropriations for fiscal years 1984 and 1985 for the Department of State, the United States Information Agency, the Board for International Broadcasting, the Inter-American Foundation, and the Asia Foundation, to establish

Approved November 22—Continued
the National Endowment for Democracy, and for other purposes.

H.R. 3885 / Public Law 98–165
Grand Ronde Restoration Act.

Approved November 28

H.R. 3222 / Public Law 98–166
Departments of Commerce, Justice, and State, the Judiciary, and Related Agencies Appropriations Act, 1984.

Approved November 29

S. 376 / Public Law 98–167
An act to amend the Debt Collection Act of 1982 to eliminate the requirement that contracts for collection services to recover indebtedness owed the United States be effective only to the extent and in the amount provided in advance appropriation Acts.

H.R. 2077 / Public Law 98–168
An act to amend title 5, United States Code, to extend the Federal Physicians Comparability Allowance Act of 1978, and for other purposes.

H.R. 2592 / Public Law 98–169
An act to transfer from the Director of the Office of Management and Budget to the Administrator of General Services the responsibility for publication of the catalog of Federal domestic assistance programs, and for other purposes.

S. 807 / Public Law 98–170
An act to amend the boundaries of the Cumberland Island National Seashore.

H.R. 2590 / Public Law 98–171
An act to amend the Agricultural Adjustment Act to authorize marketing research and promotion projects, including paid advertising, for filberts, and to amend the Potato Research and Promotion Act.

H.J. Res. 93 / Public Law 98–172
A joint resolution to provide for the awarding of a special gold medal to Danny Thomas in recognition of his humanitarian efforts and outstanding work as an American.

S. 1168 / Public Law 98–173
An act to declare that the United States holds certain lands in trust for the Kaw Tribe of Oklahoma.

S. 1837 / Public Law 98–174
An act to designate the Federal Building in Seattle, Washington, as the "Henry M. Jackson Federal Building".

Approved November 29—Continued
H.R. 24 / Public Law 98–175
An act to make certain land owned by the United States in the State of New York part of the Green Mountain National Forest.

H.R. 594 / Public Law 98–176
An act to amend section 1 of the Act of June 5, 1920, as amended, to authorize the Secretary of Commerce to settle claims for damages of less than $2,500 arising by reason of acts for which the National Oceanic and Atmospheric Administration is responsible.

H.R. 4013 / Public Law 98–177
An act to extend the Small Business Development Center program administered by the Small Business Administration until January 1, 1985.

H.J. Res. 168 / Public Law 98–178
A joint resolution to designate the week beginning May 27, 1984, as "National Tourism Week".

H.J. Res. 421 / Public Law 98–179
A joint resolution providing for the convening of the second session of the Ninety-eighth Congress, and for other purposes.

H.R 3385 / Public Law 98–180
Dairy and Tobacco Adjustment Act of 1983.

H.R. 726 / Private Law 98–5
An act for the relief of James A. Ferguson.

Approved November 30

H.R. 3959 / Public Law 98–181
Supplemental Appropriations Act, 1984.

S.J. Res. 44 / Public Law 98–182
A joint resolution to authorize the President to issue a proclamation designating the week beginning on March 11, 1984, as "National Surveyors Week".

H.R. 2230 / Public Law 98–183
United States Commission on Civil Rights Act of 1983.

H.R. 2479 / Public Law 98–184
An act to amend the Act of March 3, 1869, incorporating the Masonic Relief Association of the District of Columbia, now known as Acacia Mutual Life Insurance Company.

H.R. 2780 / Public Law 98–185
Local Government Fiscal Assistance Amendments of 1983.

S. 450 / Public Law 98–186
Mail Order Consumer Protection Amendments of 1983.

Approved November 30—Continued
S.J. Res. 141 / Public Law 98–187
A joint resolution to designate the week of December 4, 1983, through December 10, 1983, as "Carrier Alert Week".

H.J. Res. 324 / Public Law 98–188
A joint resolution to designate the week beginning January 15, 1984, as "National Fetal Alcohol Syndrome Awareness Week".

H.R. 2196 / Public Law 98–189
An act to extend the authorization of appropriations of the National Historical Publications and Records Commission for five years.

H.R. 4294 / Public Law 98–190
An act to name the Veterans' Administration Medical Center in Altoona, Pennsylvania, the "James E. Van Zandt Veterans' Administration Medical Center", and to name the Veterans' Administration Medical Center in Dublin, Georgia, the "Carl Vinson Veterans' Administration Medical Center".

H.R. 724 / Private Law 98–6
An act for the relief of Carlos Mebrano Gatson.

Approved December 1

H.R. 2293 / Public Law 98–191
Office of Federal Procurement Policy Act Amendments of 1983.

S. 726 / Public Law 98–192
An act to amend and extend the Tribally Controlled Community College Assistance Act of 1978, and for other purposes.

S. 1046 / Public Law 98–193
An act to clarify the applicability of a provision of law regarding risk retention.

S. 2129 / Public Law 98–194
Rural Health Clinics Act of 1983.

S. 1503 / Public Law 98–195
An act to direct the Secretary of Agriculture to release on behalf of the United States a reversionary interest in certain land in the State of Delaware.

S. 577 / Public Law 98–196
An act to provide for the conveyance of certain Federal lands adjacent to Orchard and Lake Shore Drives, Lake Lowell, Boise project, Idaho.

H.J. Res. 405 / Public Law 98–197
A joint resolution to extend the term of the Presidential Commission for the German-American Tricentennial, and for other purposes.

Approved December 1—Continued
S.J. Res. 111 / Public Law 98–198
A joint resolution expressing the sense of the Congress with respect to international efforts to further a revolution in child health.

Approved December 2

S. 1341 / Public Law 98–199
Education of the Handicapped Act Amendments of 1983.

H.R. 2395 / Public Law 98–200
An act to extend the Wetlands Loan Act.

H.R. 2785 / Public Law 98–201
An act to amend the provisions of the Federal Insecticide, Fungicide, and Rodenticide Act relating to the scientific advisory panel and to extend the authorization for appropriations for such Act.

H.R. 2906 / Public Law 98–202
An act to amend the Arms Control and Disarmament Act in order to extend the authorization for appropriations.

H.R. 3765 / Public Law 98–203
An act to declare that the United States holds certain lands in trust for the Las Vegas Paiute Tribe.

H.R. 4252 / Public Law 98–204
An act to suspend the noncash benefit requirement for the Puerto Rico nutrition assistance program, to provide States with greater flexibility in the administration of the food stamp program, and for other purposes.

S. 505 / Public Law 98–205
An act to designate the Federal building to be constructed in Savannah, Georgia, as the "Juliette Gordon Low Federal Building".

H.J. Res. 311 / Public Law 98–206
A joint resolution to proclaim March 20, 1984, as "National Agriculture Day".

Approved December 5

H.R. 4476 / Public Law 98–207
An act to extend the authorities under the Export Administration Act of 1979, and for other purposes.

H.J. Res. 381 / Public Law 98–208
A joint resolution to provide for appointment of Samuel Curtis Johnson as a citizen regent of the Board of Regents of the Smithsonian Institution.

Approved December 6

S. 974 / Public Law 98–209
Military Justice Act of 1983.

S. 1099 / Public Law 98–210
National Oceanic and Atmospheric Administration Marine Fisheries Program Authorization Act.

Approved December 8

H.R. 1035 / Public Law 98–211
An act to make certain technical amendments to improve implementation of the Education Consolidation and Improvement Act of 1981, and for other purposes.

Approved December 8—Continued
H.R. 4185 / Public Law 98–212
Department of Defense Appropriation Act, 1984.

S. 589 / Public Law 98–213
An act to authorize $15,500,000 for capital improvement projects on Guam, and for other purposes.

H.R. 2755 / Public Law 98–214
Federal Communications Commission Authorization Act of 1983.

Approved December 9

H.R. 2968 / Public Law 98–215
Intelligence Authorization Act for Fiscal Year 1984.

Subject Index

ABM. *See* Arms and munitions

AFDC. *See* Aid to Families with Dependent Children

AFL–CIO. *See* American Federation of Labor & Congress of Industrial Organizations

AID. *See* Development Cooperation Agency, U.S. International

ANZUS alliance—268

ASEAN. *See* South East Asian Nations, Association for

AWACS. *See* Arms and munitions

Abby Aldrich Rockefeller Folk Art Center—799

Abortion—95, 153, 167, 254, 361, 876, 880, 1313, 1451

Abraham Lincoln, U.S.S.—1142

Academic Fitness Awards, President's—1670

Acid rain. *See* Environment

ACTION—33, 436, 533, 921, 922, 1391

Administration. *See other part of subject*

Adoption. *See* Children and youth

Adult Day Care Center Week, National—1371

Adult Education, National Advisory Council on—835

Adult literacy. *See* Education

Advertising Council, National—1236

Advisory boards, committees, councils, etc. *See other part of subject*

Aeroflot—1229, 1240, 1295, 1343

Aeronautics and Space Administration, National—712, 713, 887, 916, 1395, 1454, 1481, 1549, 1655, 1672

Aerospace Education Foundation—1662

Afghanistan
Ambassador, U.S.—1534
Soviet occupation—24, 271, 430, 675, 774, 1433, 1476, 1534, 1552, 1595, 1663, 1683, 1750

Afghanistan Day—429, 430

Africa
See also specific country
Administration policies—124, 201, 476, 675, 766, 1193, 1392
Food assistance. *See* Food assistance
Italian role—777
Northern region, Libyan role—242, 1132, 1144, 1145, 1618
Southern region—271, 675, 1268, 1282, 1285, 1313
Soviet role—1193, 1683
Vice President's visit. *See* Vice President

African Development Bank—201, 203, 204

African Development Foundation—395, 542, 575, 1037, 1403, 1531

African Unity, Organization of—476, 766, 1139

Afro-American (Black) History Month, National—177

Afro-American Life and History, Association for the Study of—177

Aged
See also Health and medical care; Social security system
Administration policies—107, 657
Commodity distribution. *See* Food assistance
Nursing home residents—644

Agence France-Presse—1746

Agency. *See other part of subject*

Aging, Federal Council on the—1036

Agriculture
See also Food stamps
Administration policies—28, 89, 107, 147, 212, 427, 428, 448
Corn—1098
Dairy products—30, 428, 448, 1194
Developing countries, U.S. assistance—1104, 1456
Drought, U.S.—1275, 1312
Export policies, U.S.—31, 89, 333, 426, 575, 1025
Farmworkers—47
Food banks—33
Grain—29, 428, 575, 725, 771, 776, 1098, 1135, 1155, 1296, 1390
Latin America, U.S. assistance—1154
Molasses—1340
Payment-in-kind program. *See* Agriculture, Department of
Productivity, U.S.—89, 426, 1104, 1456
Sirups—936, 938, 1340
Soybeans—1098
Sugars—685, 740, 936, 938, 1340
Tobacco—880, 1312
Wheat—272, 1025, 1098, 1155, 1390

Agriculture, Department of
Agriculture Day ceremonies—425
Arboretum, National—1573
Assistant Secretaries—218, 1297
Budget—12, 168, 169, 1402
Commodity Credit Corporation—333, 1195
Disaster assistance, role—1181, 1275
Employment practices—241
Farmers, assistance—107
Farmers Home Administration—29, 299, 428
Feed grain programs—1390
General Counsel—1400
Milk price support program—1194
Payment-in-kind program—30, 147, 425, 427, 1275

El Salvador—Continued
  Medical assistance, U.S.—811, 812, 1276
  Military adviser, U.S., death—775
  Military and economic assistance, U.S.—87,
    337, 374–377, 388, 390, 454, 602, 603, 606,
    641, 664, 775, 788, 811, 812, 933, 1084, 1086,
    1275, 1636, 1645, 1719
  PLO role—570
  President—345, 376, 377, 882, 933, 1157, 1636
  Regional conflict. *See* Latin America
  Sugar exports to U.S. *See* Agriculture
  Trade with U.S.—1752, 1753
  Vice President's visit. *See* Vice President
Elderly. *See* Aged
Election Commission, Federal—854, 1464
Elections
  Campaign appearances. *See specific State*
  Campaign ethics—931
  Congressional elections, President's views—
    1372, 1430
  Electorate, President's views—1405
  Foreign policy, role—1743
  Presidential campaign materials, 1980—929,
    931, 934, 1020, 1089
  Presidential campaign supporters, 1980, meet-
    ings with President—1538
  Reelection, President's—15, 194, 212, 273, 301,
    337, 484, 590, 625, 648, 729, 842, 1274, 1339,
    1357, 1359, 1463, 1472, 1489, 1538, 1539,
    1694, 1700, 1716, 1730
  Voter support for President—1359
  Voting rights. *See* Civil rights
Electrical Workers, International Brotherhood
  of—494
Electronics Association, American. *See* American
  Electronics Association
Elementary School Principals, National Associa-
  tion of—1105
Emergency Management Agency, Federal—209,
  632, 719, 1181, 1542
Emergency Veterans' Job Training Act—1173,
  1178
Employ the Handicapped Week, National—1379
Employment Policy, National Commission for—
  878, 1401
Employment and Training Administration. *See*
  Labor, Department of
Employment and unemployment
  Administration policies—16, 17, 19, 59, 73, 91,
    106, 112, 133, 135, 137, 145, 149, 156, 164,
    170, 184, 185, 196, 206, 214, 225, 227, 238,
    239, 296, 303, 338, 346, 349, 381, 387, 407,
    413, 433, 447, 453, 502, 505, 568, 647, 652,
    678, 754, 941, 945, 1043, 1064, 1069, 1100,
    1133, 1330, 1336, 1394, 1420, 1648, 1702,
    1705, 1732
  Blacks. *See* Blacks
  Cyclical unemployment—338, 343, 381, 504
  Enterprise zones. *See* Enterprise zones
  Gasoline tax, effect—20, 304
  Handicapped. *See* Handicapped

Employment and unemployment—Continued
  Health care for unemployed. *See* Health and
    medical care
  Job-a-thons—58, 541, 566, 1064, 1069
  Monthly statistics—1020, 1022, 1222, 1642
  Recovery program, relationship. *See* Economic
    recovery program
  Report—459
  Structural unemployment—17, 58, 67, 112,
    133, 185, 206, 238, 338, 343, 356, 381, 382,
    453, 500, 501, 504, 619, 647, 678, 754, 865,
    1133, 1394
  Williamsburg Economic Summit policy—798
  Women. *See* Women
  Youth. *See* Children and youth
Encyclopaedia Britannica, Inc.—1029
Endangered species. *See* Conservation
Endowment. *See other part of subject*
Energy
  Administration policies—147, 783, 1413, 1626
  Budget—737, 1019, 1096
  Coal—147, 674, 1569, 1579
  Conservation—873
  Emergency response procedures—6
  Indian resources. *See* Indians, American
  Japan-U.S. cooperation—65, 1569, 1579, 1593,
    1600
  Korea-U.S. cooperation—1599
  Natural gas—45, 204, 280, 308, 311, 469, 470,
    674, 726, 1413, 1579
  Nuclear energy—21, 91, 350, 579, 580, 873
  Oil—6, 14, 20, 45, 148, 166, 186, 196, 206, 212,
    214, 280, 290, 300, 304, 308, 311, 332, 427,
    449, 469, 527, 705, 1413, 1519, 1563, 1579,
    1737
  Powerplant fuel use—1147
  Williamsburg Economic Summit policy—797
Energy, Department of
  Assistant Secretary—1439
  Budget—169, 369, 564, 1402, 1610, 1699
  Defense nuclear waste disposal—21, 873
  Deputy Secretary—1097
  Energy Regulatory Commission, Federal—
    1382, 1427
  Energy Research, Office of—581
  General Counsel—431
  Natural gas estimates—309
  Secretary—21, 580, 581, 1413, 1426, 1737
  Under Secretary—894
Energy Agency, International—674, 772
Energy Regulatory Commission, Federal. *See*
  Energy, Department of
Energy Research, Office of. *See* Energy, Depart-
  ment of
Energy resources commission. *See* Fiscal Ac-
  countability of the Nation's Energy Resources,
  Commission on
Engineers, Corps of. *See* Army, Department of
  the

Public Broadcasting Service—1527
Public Diplomacy, U.S. Advisory Commission on—1559, 1615, 1689
Public Employees' Appreciation Day—26, 27
Public Health Service. *See* Health and Human Services, Department of
Pulaski memorial day. *See* General Pulaski Memorial Day

Qatar, U.S. Ambassador—1090

Radiation Control for Health and Safety Act of 1968—607
Radio Broadcasting to Cuba Act—1441
Radio Corporation of America—887
Radio Free Europe/Radio Liberty—255, 1054, 1250, 1251, 1441, 1613, 1675
Radio Marti. *See* Information Agency, U.S.
Railroad Administration, Federal. *See* Transportation, Department of
Railroad industry
    Labor disputes—232–233, 494, 495, 499
    Retirement system—923, 1149, 1150
Railroad Passenger Corporation, National—169
Railroad Retirement Board—11, 169, 737, 923, 1149, 1150, 1182, 1368, 1403, 1699
Railroad Retirement Solvency Act—1149, 1150
Railroad Women, American Council of. *See* American Council of Railroad Women
Railroad Yardmasters of America—494
Railway and Airline Clerks, Brotherhood of—494
Railway Association, U.S.—169, 1403
Railway Carmen of the United States and Canada, Brotherhood of—494
Reagan Administration Executive Forum—79
Reagan-Bush '84 Committee. *See* Elections
Reconstruction and Development, International Bank for—772, 1248, 1362, 1368
Red Cross, American National. *See* American National Red Cross
Red Cross, International—1571
Red Cross Month—83, 155, 325
Reform 88. *See* Government agencies and employees, management reform
Refugees. *See* Immigration and naturalization
Regional Commerce and Growth Association—161
Regional councils, Federal—272
Regulatory reform
    Administration policies—106, 139, 140, 149, 150, 162, 170, 172, 290, 292, 298, 308, 311, 340, 410–412, 502, 683, 707, 708, 729, 907, 919, 941, 1152, 1262, 1329, 1538
    Enterprise zones. *See* Enterprise zones
    Maritime affairs. *See* Maritime affairs
    Paperwork reduction—836, 839, 899, 959, 1109, 1255, 1330, 1405, 1431, 1475, 1538
    Regulatory Relief, Presidential Task Force on—150, 298, 410, 683, 1202, 1405, 1538
Religion
    See also specific religious group and observance
    Prayer in schools. *See* Education

Religion—Continued
    President's views—151, 178, 359, 1450–1452
Religious Broadcasters, National—151
Remove Intoxicated Drivers—1711, 1752
Republic. *See other part of subject*
Republican Congressional Committee, National—700
Republican Governors Association—1606
Republican Majority Fund—1372
Republican National Committee—126, 1208
Republican National Hispanic Assembly—1277
Republican Northeast Regional Leadership Conference—1335
Republican Party
    See also Elections
    State party organizations, fundraisers, etc. *See specific State*
    Women, role. *See* Women
Republican Senatorial Committee, National—621, 700
Republican Women, National Federation of—1429
Republican Women's Leadership Forum—820, 1203
Reserve System, Federal—170, 171, 173, 190, 282, 283, 290, 591, 593, 597, 648, 725, 841, 887, 1066, 1330
Respiratory Therapy Week, National—1289
Retired Executives, Service Corps of. *See* Service Corps of Retired Executives
Reuters—1746
Revenue sharing, Federal. *See* State and local governments
Revolutionary War. *See* American Revolution
Rexnord and Tenneco, Inc.—1391
Reye's Syndrome Week, National—1546
Rhode Island, mayor of Cranston—1338
Rifle Association, National—659
Rockefeller Folk Art Center. *See* Abby Aldrich Rockefeller Folk Art Center
Rodeo Cowboy Association, Professional—1344, 1345
Romania
    Emigration—817, 818
    Trade with U.S.—329, 817, 818
    Vice President's visit. *See* Vice President, European visits
Ruiz Food Products, Inc.—690

SALT. *See* Strategic Arms Limitation Talks
SCORE. *See* Service Corps of Retired Executives
START. *See* Strategic Arms Reduction Talks
Sabine River Compact Administration—317
Safe Boating Week, National—768
St. Christopher-Nevis
    Grenada, role. *See* Grenada
    Trade with U.S.—1637, 1638
St. George's University School of Medicine—1553, 1669
Saint Lawrence Seaway Development Corporation. *See* Transportation, Department of
St. Louis Post-Dispatch—156

Name Index